T0337439

Handbook of
THE ECONOMICS OF INTERNATIONAL MIGRATION

Volume 1A The Immigrants

INTRODUCTION TO THE SERIES

The aim of the Handbooks in Economics series is to produce Handbooks for various branches of economics, each of which is a definitive source, reference, and teaching supplement for use by professional researchers and advanced graduate students. Each Handbook provides self-contained surveys of the current state of a branch of economics in the form of chapters prepared by leading specialists on various aspects of this branch of economics. These surveys summarize not only received results but also newer developments, from recent journal articles and discussion papers. Some original material is also included, but the main goal is to provide comprehensive and accessible surveys. The Handbooks are intended to provide not only useful reference volumes for professional collections but also possible supplementary readings for advanced courses for graduate students in economics.

Kenneth J. Arrow and Michael D. Intriligator

Handbook of
THE ECONOMICS OF INTERNATIONAL MIGRATION

Volume 1A The Immigrants

Edited by

BARRY R. CHISWICK
George Washington University
and
IZA—Institute for the Study of Labor

PAUL W. MILLER
Curtin University

Amsterdam • Boston • Heidelberg • London • New York • Oxford
Paris • San Diego • San Francisco • Singapore • Sydney • Tokyo
North-Holland is an imprint of Elsevier

ELSEVIER

North-Holland is an imprint of Elsevier

The Boulevard, Langford Lane, Kidlington, Oxford OX5 1GB, UK
Radarweg 29, PO Box 211, 1000 AE Amsterdam, The Netherlands

Notice
No responsibility is assumed by the publisher for any injury and/or damage to persons or property as a matter of products liability, negligence or otherwise, or from any use or operation of any methods, products, instructions or ideas contained in the material herein. Because of rapid advances in the medical sciences, in particular, independent verification of diagnoses and drug dosages should be made

British Library Cataloguing in Publication Data
A catalogue record for this book is available from the British Library

Library of Congress Cataloging-in-Publication Data
A catalog record for this book is available from the Library of Congress

ISBN–13: 978-0-444-53764-5

For information on all North-Holland publications
visit our website at http://store.elsevier.com/

CONTENTS

Dedication   *vii*

Reviewers   *ix*

Preface   *xi*

Introduction   *xiii*

In memoriam: Paul W. Miller (1955–2013)   *xvii*

Volume 1A: The Immigrants

Part I. The Determinants of International Migration

1. Migration Theory   3

Örn B. Bodvarsson, California State University
Nicole B. Simpson, Colgate University
Chad Sparber, Colgate University

2. Two Centuries of International Migration   53

Joseph P. Ferrie, Northwestern University
Timothy J. Hatton, Australian National University

Cameo 1. World Migration in Historical Perspective: Four Big Issues   89

Jeffrey G. Williamson, Harvard University

Part II. The Adjustment of Immigrants

3. The Adjustment of Immigrants in the Labor Market   105

Harriet Orcutt Duleep, College of William and Mary

4. The Human Capital (Schooling) of Immigrants in America   183

James P. Smith, RAND Corporation

5. International Migration and the Economics of Language   211

Barry R. Chiswick, George Washington University
Paul W. Miller, Curtin University

6. Immigrants and Immigrant Health   **271**

Heather Antecol, Claremont McKenna College
Kelly Bedard, University of California, Santa Barbara

7. Immigrants and Demography: Marriage, Divorce, and Fertility   **315**

Alícia Adserà, Princeton University
Ana Ferrer, University of Waterloo

Cameo 2. Immigrants and Religion   **375**

Carmel U. Chiswick, George Washington University

8. Immigrants' Access to Financial Services and Asset Accumulation   **387**

Nour Abdul-Razzak, University of Chicago
Una Okonkwo Osili, Indiana University-Purdue University at Indianapolis
Anna L. Paulson, Federal Reserve Bank of Chicago

9. From Aliens to Citizens: The Political Incorporation of Immigrants   **443**

Pieter Bevelander, Malmö University
Mikael Spång, Malmö University

10. Selective Out-Migration and the Estimation of Immigrants' Earnings Profiles   **489**

Christian Dustmann, University College London
Joseph-Simon Görlach, University College London

Part III. Types of Immigrants

11. High-Skilled Immigration in a Globalized Labor Market   **537**

James Ted McDonald, University of New Brunswick
Christopher Worswick, Carleton University

12. The Refugee/Asylum Seeker   **585**

Aimee Chin, University of Houston
Kalena E. Cortes, Texas A&M University

13. Undocumented Immigration and Human Trafficking   **659**

Pia Orrenius, Federal Reserve Bank of Dallas
Madeline Zavodny, Agnes Scott College

14. Guest or Temporary Foreign Worker Programs   **717**

Philip Martin, University of California, Davis

Index   *775*

DEDICATION

To the Memory of Paul W. Miller: Husband, Father, and Economist.

REVIEWERS

Alicia Adserà
Princeton University

Catalina Amuedo-Dorantes
San Diego State University

Heather Antecol
Claremont McKenna College

Susan L. Averett
Lafayette College

Thomas Bauer
University of Bochum

Michael Beenstock
Hebrew University

Harry Bloch
Curtin University

Barry R. Chiswick
George Washington University

Carmel U. Chiswick
George Washington University

Sara de la Rica
University of the Basque Country

Christian Dustmann
University College London

Gil Epstein
Bar-Ilan University

Delia Furtado
University of Connecticut

Ira Gang
Rutgers University

Marina Gindelsky
George Washington University

Ted H. Gindling
University of Maryland, Baltimore County

Victor Ginsburgh
Free University of Brussels

Gilles Grenier
University of Ottawa

Timothy Hatton
Australian National University

Lawrence M. Kahn
Cornell University

Sherrie Kossoudji
University of Michigan

Evelyn Lehrer
University of Illinois at Chicago

B. Lindsay Lowell
Georgetown University

Philip Martin
University of California, Davis

James Ted McDonald
University of New Brunswick

Paul W. Miller
Curtin University

Pia Orrenius
Federal Reserve Bank of Dallas

Dan-Olof Rooth
Linnaeus University

Mathias Sinning
Australian National University

Chad Sparber
Colgate University

Mehmet Serkan Tosun
University of Nevada, Reno

Derby Voon
Curtin University

Eskil Wadensjö
Stockholm University

Anthony Yezer
George Washington University

Madeline Zavodny
Agnes Scott College

PREFACE

When I started my research on international migration in the mid-1970s, there had been very little research by economists on this issue. Over the years, I have been gratified to witness the enormous growth in interest among economists in international migration. The interest became broad, including such topics as immigrant adjustment and impact on the labor market, on investment in skills (in particular, education and language), immigrant impacts on demographic issues (e.g., marriage, fertility, and health status), and the enforcement of immigration law, as well as impacts on the macro-economy, fiscal matters, trade and finance, economic growth, and a host of other topics for the origin and destination countries. Then, over time, the literature became deep, not just an article or two here and there on particular immigration topics, but a deep body of research that is ever building on itself. The time is now right for a Handbook on immigration in the distinguished Elsevier series.

Paul W. Miller and I drafted a proposal for a *Handbook of the Economics of International Migration*. Elsevier approved our proposal, and then the real work began. We identified a list of about 30 topics that would cover most of the relevant issues regarding international migration. We then identified economists who were outstanding scholars on these topics and who we felt would provide first-rate chapters. We wanted serious academic and policy analyses, devoid of the political rhetoric that all too often dominates public policy discussions of immigration issues.

Although we contacted only one author per chapter, given the massive effort that each chapter would require, we encouraged the designated author to take on co-authors and most of them did so. While we gave the authors the general topic for their chapters, we left the specifics up to them. We appreciate the scholarly commitment shown by each of the authors.

We also approached a few senior scholars to write "Cameos". These are shorter big think papers. We interacted with the cameo writers to identify their themes, but overall their instructions were to let their creative juices flow on a topic or issue of their choice. We very much value their contributions as well.

As the first drafts of the chapters and cameos were submitted, we sent each out to one or two reviewers, other specialists on the topic of the particular chapter. The review process was single-blinded, the authors not knowing who their specific reviewers were. We are maintaining the anonymity of the particular reviewers for each chapter, but a list of the reviewers and their affiliations is included preceding this Preface. Paul and I also served as reviewers, sharing our thoughts with the authors on the draft chapters and the reviewers' comments. The chapters benefited from the review process.

The authors and reviewers are an international group having their affiliations in twelve and nine different countries respectively. We thank each of them for their invaluable contributions. As a result of these efforts, nearly 90 economists were involved in this project.

This project could not have been completed without the outstanding administrative support of our research assistants, Marina Gindelsky of George Washington University and Derby Voon of Curtin University. We appreciate the financial support for their activities provided by George Washington University and the Australian Research Council.

We are indebted to Michael Intriligator and Kenneth Arrow, the editors of the Elsevier Handbook in Economics series, for encouraging the project. We also appreciate the support we received from the Elsevier editorial staff, Scott Bentley and Joslyn Chaiprasert-Paguio.

The joy that would otherwise accompany the completion of this project is marred by Paul Miller's battle with a long and difficult illness that resulted in his death in November 2013. This was a major loss to the immigration research community and the economics profession.

Barry R. Chiswick
Washington, DC
March 2014

INTRODUCTION

Barry R. Chiswick
George Washington University
and
IZA—Institute for the Study of Labor

Migration appears to have been a human characteristic from time immemorial to this day. Modern humans may have developed in Africa, but they spread across the globe in prehistoric times. Hunter/gatherers engaged in both seasonal migration following the migration of herds and the ripening of fruits and nuts, and long-term migration in response to climate change, population pressures, war, violence, and other factors. The first book of the Hebrew bible, Genesis, is replete with stories of migration in response to economic forces (e.g, as when the Israelites went to Egypt due to a famine in Canaan), and family migration (e.g., as when Rebecca left her father's home to join Isaac, who was to be her husband). And of course there is the refugee migration related in the book of Exodus, as the Israelites fled slavery in Egypt for the Promised Land.

This *Handbook of the Economics of International Migration* focuses on contemporary migration, migrants, and public policy toward migration. The focus is on people who cross national boundaries, referred to as immigrants, rather than internal migrants. The theory and the basic principles would be equally applicable to internal migration, although the institutional environment would differ. Governments have always been interested in who leaves and who wishes to enter their domain. It was just over a century ago that national governments instituted major restrictions on the conditions, number, and characteristics of who might enter their countries. Although today we view governments as having the right to limit who enters, but not the right to bar exit, this was not always the case. Serfdom and slavery had the effect of barring exit; in modern times so, too, did the Berlin Wall to prevent people from fleeing East Germany and the bar of Jewish emigration from the Soviet Union.

While historians and sociologists devoted more attention to the flow of people across national boundaries, economists were slower to recognize the importance of international migration. Over the first seven decades of the twentieth century, there were few studies of immigration, or immigrants, by economists—isolated studies that did not stimulate broader interest. Since the late 1970s, however, research on international migration by economists, using the methodology and tools of modern economics, has increased rapidly. This Handbook is the product of this development. The chapters are divided into two volumes: Volume 1A, "The Immigrants," focusing on the international migrants as individuals, and Volume 1B, "The Impact and Regional Studies," focuses on the consequences for nations of international migration.

Volume 1A, Part I is on the "Determinants of International Migration," with two chapters and a cameo. The first chapter sets out the theory behind international migration, while the second is an economic history of international migration over the past two centuries. Part I ends with a Cameo paper that has a broader perspective—four big issues for international migration.

Part II, "The Adjustment of Immigrants," is concerned with the manner and extent to which immigrants adjust to the destination. The general pattern is that as immigrants alter their behavior and make investments in their human capital in response to the new set of economic and other incentives and opportunities in the destination, with the passage of time they more closely resemble the people in the host country. This Part includes nine separate chapters on a range of topics, including the labor market, schooling, language proficiency, health, the capital market, demographic behavior (including marriage, divorce and fertility), as well as citizenship (and civic participation) and a Cameo on religion. Religious behavior changes in response to the new set of incentives provided by migration and so, too, do religious institutions. Not all immigrants stay in the destination, and the last chapter in Part II is on the out-migration or return migration of international migrants.

Immigrants differ in their motives for migrating, the jobs they take, their legal status, and their actual or intended destination. Part III, "Types of Immigrants," has chapters on four different themes. The first is on high-skilled immigrants that are increasingly being sought by the immigrant-receiving countries. High-skilled workers are developing internationally transferable skills that increase their mobility across country borders. They will be the new mobile labor force. This is followed by a chapter on refugees and asylum seekers. These are individuals whose migration is motivated primarily by personal safety and freedom, as distinct from conventional economic incentives.

Undocumented or illegal migrants, the subject of a third chapter, face different experiences than legal economic migrants, as do participants in the most pernicious migration of all, the illegal trafficking in people. The fourth chapter studies those who by choice, or by restriction, will be in the destination temporarily as seasonal or short-term workers, known as guest or temporary workers.

The first section in Volume 1B, Part IV, "The Impact of Immigration," includes seven chapters on the impact of international migration, primarily on the destination, but with some insights on the origin. These include the impact on the distribution of income, a topic that has acquired considerable attention in recent years. Another topic is the fiscal impact on government—that is, the taxes raised and benefits expended due to immigration. This is followed by chapters on immigrants as entrepreneurs, on international trade, and on capital formation. These studies have implications for the impact of immigration on economic growth, the subject of a separate chapter. The next two chapters focus on what immigrants do with their income and wealth. To what extent do they send remittances to their family members and others left behind in the origin? And finally, to what extent are investments made in the human capital of their descendants born in their destination?

The final part, Part V, "Regional Studies," is a series of regional or country-specific analyses. The first is on the United States, in absolute numbers the largest recipient of international migrants, even though the legal entrants are far fewer than those wanting to immigrate. Although much of the emphasis on Latin America and the Caribbean is on their being source countries, they also constitute important destinations, which is the subject of the second chapter.

Europe had been primarily a region of out-migration to the Americas and Oceania for the past 500 years, but in the past 60 years has become a major region of in-migration. In addition to international migration within Europe (mainly from the south and east to northwestern Europe), there have been major migrations from Africa, the Middle East and Asia, some as permanent economic migrants, some as temporary workers who stayed, and others as refugees.

The rest of the volume focuses on regions outside of the usual areas studied, the Americas and Europe. Israel is a small country whose Jewish population has grown rapidly, although episodically, over the past century. Most of these immigrants are refugees from Europe, North Africa, and other Middle Eastern countries.

This is followed by a Cameo on Australia. Australia has also seen a relatively large increase in its population in recent decades due to immigration. The cameo explores the effects of the dramatic changes in immigration policies in recent years. Does its experience provide insights for the reform of immigration policy in other countries?

Africa is the subject of the next chapter. Africa is experiencing substantial migration (short term and long term) across the various country borders, both economic migrants seeking higher earnings and refugees fleeing war and terror. Various African countries are also experiencing substantial emigration from the continent, particularly to Europe.

The final chapter in the Handbook is on the Gulf Cooperation Council (GCC) countries in the Persian Gulf. These countries had been less developed. They are now rich in oil wealth, but are generally labor scarce. They do not want permanent immigrants and rely on guest worker programs to fill (on a rotating basis) low-skilled construction and domestic service jobs and high-skilled professional jobs. The consequences are explored for their economies of bringing in relatively large numbers of foreign workers on temporary guest-worker visas.

Each chapter or cameo in this Handbook can stand on its own, providing the reader with new data, new analyses, and new insights regarding international migration, particularly in recent decades. Taken together, however, they provide an extraordinary amount of information and analysis from a historical and global perspective. They will stand the test of time and will be invaluable for students and researchers of international migration, as well as for those merely curious about this increasingly important facet of the economy and society.

Geographic mobility has been a theme of human existence since time immemorial, and will continue to be so for millennia to come.

IN MEMORIAM: PAUL W. MILLER (1955–2013)*

Paul W. Miller, a leading scholar in labor economics, lost his long and heroic battle with cancer on Wednesday, November 27, 2013 in Perth, Australia. Paul was a prolific scholar who expanded and deepened the boundaries in labor economics, particularly in the fields of labor markets and the economics of immigration, of language, and of human capital. He published extensively on three continents and received numerous awards for his research.

Paul W. Miller was born on December 30, 1955 in Dunedoo, New South Wales, Australia. He earned his Bachelor's degree with Honors from Australia's University of New England and went on to receive his Master's degree (1978) and his Ph.D. (1982) in Economics from the Australian National University in Canberra. Paul's academic career was based in Australian universities, although in the first decade after receiving his Ph.D. he accepted several visiting appointments in Canada, the UK, and the US. For much of his career (1987–2010) he was at the University of Western Australia in Perth. During this period he demonstrated his keen administrative skills as Head of the Department of Economics (1994–2001) and Inaugural Head of the School of Economics and Commerce (2003–2005). He left university administration because his passion was academic research. In his last five years at UWA he was Australian Professorial Fellow of the Australian Research Council. In 2010 he became Professor of Economics at Curtin University in Perth, a position he held until his death.

Paul was best known for his research on the economics of immigration, labor markets, the economics of language, and the economics of education. His forte was in developing new models or adapting pre-existing models to new circumstances, developing testable hypotheses and skillfully testing them. Paul had a deep respect for data, and was very

* Reprinted with permission from the Newsletter of the Royal Economic Society, January 2014.

concerned about the quality of the data he analyzed. His empirical work was thoughtful, and he was careful not to draw inferences and conclusions beyond what his model and data analysis could support. He believed in the importance of testing for the robustness of findings, sometimes by applying alternative statistical techniques to a given dataset, sometimes using alternative datasets, often from different countries, for the same test, and sometimes both. He also believed in the importance of clear exposition, avoiding formalism unless it advanced the analysis. His interest was in using economics and econometrics to enhance our understanding of skill formation and its labor market consequences.

Paul's greatest impact was through his scholarly publications. His published work included more than 170 articles in refereed journals, 32 papers as chapters in books, and numerous shorter pieces and book reviews. He published ten books and monographs and at the time of his death was co-editing this Handbook. His papers were published in the leading general economic journals on three continents (*American Economic Review*, *Economic Journal*, *Economic Record*), as well as the major journals in several fields, including labor economics, immigration, economics of education, and population economics. The impact of this research was both demonstrated and enhanced by the numerous reprinting of his papers. His Institute for the Study of Labor (IZA) Discussion Papers were downloaded often enough to place him in the top 1% of IZA DP authors.

Paul was highly effective as a sole author, but he also seemed to enjoy collaborative relationships. Among his refereed journal articles he had 31 different co-authors, some involving only one paper but with others there were multiple papers published over a span of many years. His co-authors included students (or former students), research assistants, colleagues, and others, myself included. He was an easy person to have as a co-author—original, smart, and generous, he listened, responded, and shared. He was gracious and modest, confident but not self-important.

I benefitted both professionally and personally from my collaborative relationship with Paul. I was invited to serve as an external reader of his ANU Ph.D. dissertation on immigrant earnings in Australia and was immediately impressed by the quality of his analysis and his ability to extract insights from the limited data available for Australia at that time. We met shortly thereafter during his first visiting appointment in North America and began our research collaboration that spanned three decades, producing over 60 journal articles and chapters in books and several edited volumes. It was a pleasure to watch Paul mature as a scholar. Initially his shy nature discouraged him from giving papers at academic conferences, but as his confidence grew so too did his conference presentations, and they were always outstanding. Two aspects that never changed, however, were his willingness and ability to work hard on his research and his commitment to producing research of the highest quality.

Paul's impressive research contributions were acknowledged formally as well as informally. He received several "best paper" awards, was Elected Fellow, Academy of the Social Sciences in Australia, was inducted into the ANU Distinguished Alumni Hall of Fame, and received the Honorary Fellow Award of the Economic Society of Australia. He was an IZA Research Fellow (since 2004). He is included in *Who's Who in Economics* based on the high frequency of citations to his research.

Paul W. Miller's death is a great loss to the economics profession. He will be missed.

Barry R. Chiswick
Professor and Department Chair
Department of Economics
George Washington University
Washington, DC
December 2013, revised January 2014

The Determinants of International Migration

CHAPTER 1

Migration Theory*

Örn B. Bodvarsson**, Nicole B. Simpson†, Chad Sparber†

**California State University, Department of Economics, TAH 328, 6000 J Street, Sacramento, CA 95819, USA
†Colgate University, Department of Economics, 13 Oak Dr., Hamilton, NY 13346, USA

Contents

1. Overview	4
2. From Adam Smith to the New Millennium	4
2.1 Pre-1960 literature	5
2.2 Forming the core of migration theory: migration as human capital investment	8
2.3 Early extensions of the Sjaastad model	15
2.3.1 The migrant as a consumer	15
2.3.2 The influence of kinship and migrant networks	17
2.3.3 Migration decisions in a life-cycle context	18
2.3.4 The effects of uncertainty on migration	19
2.3.5 What happens when the family is the decision-making unit?	22
2.3.6 Migration as a response to relative deprivation	24
2.3.7 The influence of age on the migration decision	25
3. Recent Theoretical Analyses of Why People Migrate	26
3.1 A static human capital model with endogenous migration	27
3.1.1 Adding migration costs	28
3.1.2 Incorporating immigration policy	29
3.1.3 Incorporating self-selection	30
3.1.4 Blending self-selection and migration costs	31
3.1.5 Accounting for income inequality	32
3.1.6 Introducing credit and poverty constraints	32
3.1.7 Accounting for unemployment	33
3.1.8 Incorporating taxes and social insurance	34
3.1.9 Accounting for political institutions	35
3.2 A static human capital model with endogenous migration and endogenous wages	35
3.2.1 Accounting for network effects	37
3.2.2 Distinguishing between individual and household migration decisions	37
3.2.3 The relationship between trade and migration	37
3.3 Dynamic models with endogenous migration and physical capital accumulation	38
3.3.1 Immigration policy in a dynamic framework	40
3.3.2 Accounting for remittance behavior	40
3.3.3 Dynamic models with human capital accumulation	41

* The authors would like to thank Pia Orrenius, Barry Chiswick, and participants at the 2012 Southern Economic Association Meetings in New Orleans for detailed comments. All errors are our own.

       3.3.4 *Accounting for temporary, return, and circular migration*   42

       3.3.5 *Dynamic models with human capital accumulation, circular migration, and brain drain*   43

4. Conclusions and Implications for Further Research   44

References   46

1. OVERVIEW

This chapter provides a comprehensive expository survey and synthesis of the theoretical literature on the determinants of migration. There are four themes to the chapter: (1) Most importantly, migration is an act of human capital investment, thus the core of migration theory is based upon the human capital investment model. People migrate if the returns to doing so outweigh the costs. (2) There is no theoretical distinction between internal (domestic) and external (international) migration, though the types and magnitudes of entry barriers vary across the two forms of migration. (3) While most of the theoretical literature focuses on migration as a static decision, more recent models have incorporated dynamic features of migration. (4) Much remains to be done to further refine the theory of international migration.

The chapter is divided into three sections. Section 2 provides a narrative highlighting the migration theory literature starting with Adam Smith (1776) and ending roughly in 2000. The section is especially important for readers wanting a historical perspective into economists' understanding of migration. It establishes the broad themes that continue to influence immigration models today, including the recognition of human capital investment as the key motive for migration. Section 3 discusses much more recent literature. Though it covers a relatively short period in the development of economic thought, this literature is quite large. The papers surveyed in this section delve more deeply into the themes identified by their predecessors by introducing more formal analytical rigor and new insights to the existing immigration framework. Two important innovations are the inclusion of endogenous and dynamic elements into the decision-making process.[1] In the concluding section, we suggest further refinements of the theory.

2. FROM ADAM SMITH TO THE NEW MILLENNIUM

In this section, we survey literature beginning with Adam Smith and continuing through roughly the year 2000. The narrative is divided into three subsections. The first details pre-1960 literature on the determinants of migration. While this literature is small, it laid important groundwork for later analysis. It was not until the advent of the human capital

---

[1] In both Sections 2 and 3 of this chapter, most of the literature that we discuss highlights US immigration, but it is not our intention to focus on the US case only. In fact, any of the models discussed can be easily applied to any source–destination pair.

model in the early 1960s and the pioneering work on migration by Sjaastad (1962) that the theoretical literature on the determinants of migration really began to form. Our second subsection surveys this literature, highlighting what became the core of migration theory—that migration is an act of human capital investment and that migrants respond to spatial differences in labor market opportunities net of costs. Finally, the third subsection discusses alternative motives for migration that economic researchers identified fairly early in the literature's development.

2.1 Pre-1960 literature

Adam Smith (1776) was the first economist to write on migration. In his *An Inquiry into the Nature and Causes of the Wealth of Nations*, Smith wrote:

> . . . the wages of labour vary more from place to place than the price of provisions. The prices of bread and butcher's meat are generally the same or very nearly the same through the greater part of the United Kingdom. These and most other things which are sold by retail, the way in which the labouring poor buy all things, are generally fully as cheap or cheaper in great towns than in the remoter parts of the country . . . But the wages of labour in a great town and its neighbourhood are frequently a fourth or a fifth part, twenty or five-and-twenty per cent higher than at a few miles distance. Eighteen pence a day may be reckoned the common price of labour in London and its neighbourhood. At a few miles distance it falls to eight pence, the usual price of common labour through the greater part of the low country of Scotland, where it varies a good deal less than in England. Such a difference of prices, which it seems is not always sufficient to transport a man from one parish to another, would necessarily occasion so great a transportation of the most bulky commodities, not only from one parish to another, but from one end of the kingdom, almost from one end of the world to the other, as would soon reduce them more nearly to a level. After all that has been said of the levity and inconstancy of human nature, it appears evidently from experience that a man is of all sorts of luggage the most difficult to be transported.

This quote foreshadows research in the migration field that was to take place two centuries later. Smith observed that the rural/urban wage differential substantially exceeded the differential for commodity prices. Regional differences in commodity or factor prices provide opportunities for arbitrage. Intercity movements of goods (trade) arbitrages away commodity price differentials, whereas intercity movements of people (migration) arbitrages away wage differentials. Smith thus suggested that migration is a response to spatial disequilibrium in labor markets and that a key determinant of migration is spatial differences in the returns to labor supply. Hicks (1932, p. 76) made the same point one and a half centuries later when he stated that ". . . differences in net economic advantages, chiefly *differences in wages*, are the main causes of migration" (our italics).

Smith's example would seem to imply that if regional differences in wages exceed regional differences in prices, migration would be plentiful and trade would be modest. Yet Smith found trade to be more intense than migration. The reason is that migration is hampered by certain barriers that trade is not. This is apparent when he states "man is of all sorts of luggage the most difficult to be transported." Smith did not identify these migration barriers but they would surely include both direct and indirect costs such as relocation expenses, the abandonment of firm-specific assets, the sacrifice of pension rights, and the psychological costs of leaving family and friends behind. Smith astutely observed a regularity still present today—that migration flows are often small despite very substantial international wage differences. The reason is simple: international migration costs are simply too high relative to the gains. By the same reasoning, the large and persistent spatial dispersion of wages Smith saw in the UK likely resulted from low levels of migration.[2]

Ravenstein (1889) provided perhaps the first important analysis after Smith (1776) that significantly contributed to understanding the determinants of migration and helped lay the groundwork for much research that was to follow. He used British census data on nationality and residence along with vital statistics and immigration records to establish seven "laws" of migration. Greenwood (1997) summarizes the laws as the following: (1) most migrants move only a short distance and usually to large cities; (2) cities that grow rapidly tend to be populated by migrants from proximate rural areas and gaps arising in the rural population generate migration from more distant areas; (3) out-migration is inversely related to in-migration; (4) a major migration wave will generate a compensating counter-wave; (5) those migrating a long distance tend to move to large cities; (6) rural persons are more likely to migrate than urban persons; and (7) women are more likely to migrate than men.

Zipf (1946) hypothesized that the volume of migration between two places will be in direct proportion to the product of the populations of the two locations, and inversely proportional to distance. This "$P(1)P(2)/D$" hypothesis—where $P(1)$ is origin population, $P(2)$ is destination population, and D is distance between origin and destination—came to be known as the *gravity model* of migration.[3]

---

[2] Shields and Shields (1989) suggested that Smith's observation can be captured by the expression for wage convergence below. Labor moves from place i to place j if the wage is higher in j than i, with the amount of migration related to the wage difference as follows: $M_{ij} = \beta_{ij}(W_j - W_i)$, where W is the wage, M is the number of migrants, and β reflects impediments to migration (e.g., distance, imperfect information, and any artificial restrictions that have the effect of blocking the adjustment of wages to migration). The greater is β the lower are the impediments to migration.

[3] The gravity model of migration is an application of Newton's law of gravity, which is used to predict the level of interaction between two bodies. Newton's law states that "Any two bodies attract one another with a force that is proportional to the product of their masses and inversely proportional to the square of the distance between them." In applying Newton's law, Ravenstein's (1889) insight was to treat "mass" as the population of a place and "distance" as referring to miles between two places. The intuition behind the gravity model of migration is that since larger places attract people, ideas, and goods more than smaller places, and more proximate places have a greater attraction, there should be more migration between two places that are more populated and/or are more proximate. The gravity model has also been widely used to describe international trade flows. See Tinbergen (1962), Linneman (1966), Anderson (1979), and Deardorff (1998) for important developments.

The gravity model has very important economic implications. First, by proposing that the volume of migration will be inversely related to the distance between origin and destination locations, the model allows for distance to serve as a proxy for the costs of migration. This is intuitively appealing since longer distances traveled usually imply greater explicit and implicit migration costs, and hence act as a deterrent to migration. Second, it predicts that the volume of migration will be higher for origin and destination communities with large populations. This too has intuitive appeal. At any point in time, some fraction of people in the origin will face opportunities in alternative locations that exceed their opportunities at home, net of migration costs, and those persons will migrate. Assuming that this fraction is constant, then the number of people choosing to emigrate will increase with home population size. Similarly, as the population of the destination community rises, the number of employment opportunities will rise, which will induce more immigration.[4]

Upon reflection on the writings of Smith (1776), Hicks (1932), Ravenstein (1889), and Zipf (1946), one can see the emergence of the core of migration theory that would develop more formally beginning in the 1960s: migration is primarily driven by a desire to maximize one's return to human capital investment. People respond to spatial differences in labor market opportunities by migrating if those opportunities dominate the costs of relocation. Opportunities to migrate are proportional to population size, while migration costs are related to distance. Though these insights laid the foundation for the core of formal theoretical models to follow, it is important to note that empirical studies in this period began to identify more specific determinants of migration that theorists would later incorporate into their models as well. Two papers, discussed below, are particularly noteworthy.

First, Jerome's (1926) empirical analysis linked American business cycle fluctuations in employment with fluctuations in net migration from Europe.[5] Though his paper focused on the business cycle and did not include any theoretical model of migration, his findings provided clear motivation for important work in the migration field that came years later. In particular, he found that: (i) Immigration appeared to respond to changes in domestic employment conditions. That is, his results support the prediction of the traditional economic model of migration—which came four decades later—

---

[4] There is an additional implication: since Zipf's (1946) original formulation includes the product of the origin and destination populations, this implies that the marginal effect of a change in the origin population on migration will depend on the size of the destination population and vice versa.

[5] We should also mention an important study by Douglas (1919) on the skill distribution of immigrants between 1871 and 1909. Foreshadowing work decades later on the determinants of the composition of migration flows, Douglas used basic statistical analysis to dispute a widely held assertion at the time that more recent migration flows (coming primarily from Southeastern Europe) had on average lower skill levels than less recent flows (coming primarily from Northwestern Europe). Douglas showed that the newer flows comprised proportionately 50% more skilled worker than the older flows.

that the most important determinant of relative migration flows is the spatial differences in real earnings.[6] (ii) Immigration was more sensitive to labor market conditions in the destination region than in the source region. Thus, he was the first to argue for asymmetric effects between "demand pull" and "supply push" factors, finding that destination region conditions are more important in pulling immigrants into a region than origin region conditions are in pushing emigrants out. (iii) There is a two-way causality between immigration and domestic employment. This finding foreshadowed the huge literature on the labor market impact of immigration that began to develop real momentum in the 1990s.

Second, Kuznets and Rubin (1954) analyzed the role of policy and macroeconomic conditions in affecting the costs and benefits of immigration. In particular, they assessed how war and restrictive immigration policies dampened population growth in the USA between 1870 and 1940. Among many important results, Kuznets and Rubin established that the revolutionary change in immigration policy following World War I, coupled with the Great Depression, were likely responsible for a 29.3% reduction in the number of foreign-born persons in the USA during the 1930s, a decade when total population grew by nearly 9 million. In contrast, immigration contributed about one-seventh of the total growth in population, and about 20% of the growth in the labor force between 1870 and 1910. Confirming some of the findings of Jerome (1926), Kuznets and Rubin found that long-term swings in immigration tended to follow long-term swings in GDP per worker. Furthermore, they presented evidence indicating that cyclical changes in in- and out-migration helped to moderate the business cycle, or at least the cycle's effect on native unemployment.

The studies discussed above were collectively important in recognizing early that migration decisions are driven by potential costs and benefits. It was not until the development of the human capital investment model in the 1960s, however, that theoretical models of the determinants of migration were formalized.

2.2 Forming the core of migration theory: migration as human capital investment

The notion of migration as human capital investment is a unifying theme that serves as the most fundamental idea underlying most current economic theories of migration. Unfortunately, it is easy to lose sight of this theme since language in the literature has tended to treat internal (within-country) and external (international) migration as distinct phenomena. Various oft-cited expository surveys (e.g., Massey et al., 1993; Greenwood, 1997;

---

[6] We also want to highlight Hansen's (1940) comprehensive analysis of flows of American- and Canadian-born persons in each other's countries. His study traced flows as early as the seventeenth century and found that Americans and Canadians frequently "intermingled," moving to places where there were the highest returns to land, labor or capital, and regardless of whether these places were south or north of the border between the two countries.

Lucas, 1997) may have reinforced this tendency, while much of the literature through the mid-1980s—which focused on understanding internal migration flows—may have inadvertently created the misleading perception that internal and international migration are theoretically distinct.

We contend that there is a single theory of migration derived from an application of the traditional human capital model that does not depend on whether migration is internal or international. Migration across "regions" or "countries" can be viewed more or less synonymously, though it is clear that institutional aspects may differ across internal and external migration decisions due to regulations and legal restrictions, language, culture, and other institutional factors. That potential international migrants face different entry barriers than people considering domestic moves is important for understanding an individual's decision set, but it does not change the underlying motive to move— the possibility of realizing better opportunities far from home. In fact, the severity of such barriers has varied across time and space. International barriers are relatively recent in world history, whereas internal migration restrictions have long existed, including prohibitions on serfs from freely moving to cities in medieval Europe, the substantial legal barriers to internal migration in Czarist Russia and the USSR, and China's internal passport system ("Hukou") today. We imagine the modern United States as a country without restrictions on interstate mobility, yet state-specific occupational licensing laws act as barriers to internal migration much in the same way as immigrant quotas are barriers to external migration. One does not need different models to account for these phenomena. Rather, one needs a single model that accounts for different costs.

The human capital model implies that the migrant's goal is to maximize utility by choosing the location that offers the highest net return to human capital, hence labor supply.[7] Accordingly, we will call this view the "labor supply" view of migration. Sjaastad (1962), who pioneered the application of human capital theory to understanding migration, argued that migration is the act of locating one's skills in that market that offers the highest return. While migration can be skill-augmenting,[8] the important point

---

[7] Most economists presume that the primary reason for migrating is to maximize one's income, specifically income earned in the labor market. Hence, it is taken for granted that utility maximization is achieved through the maximization of income. However, people can migrate for reasons other than income maximization, e.g., family reunification, seeking refuge or political asylum, etc. Those reasons are compatible with utility maximization, but not necessarily with income maximization. We will assume for now that when the migrant seeks out the location that provides the highest utility, he is simultaneously seeking the market that provides him with the highest possible income.

[8] Migration can *indirectly* lead to augmentation of one's skills, however. For example, migration could result in a person locating to an employer that makes more efficient use of her skills and thus allows her human capital to grow faster through on-the-job training than would be the case in the origin. As another example, while we usually think of migration as a phenomenon among people already out of school and working, we can think of migration as the act of moving to an educational institution (e.g. a foreign graduate program) that adds the most to one's human capital. Migration as an educational investment has received much less attention in the literature.

is that by relocating, a person avails herself of the market that provides the highest return to her skills. In fact, if we think of migration as the act of moving to that market which maximizes one's income, then migration need not always be a significant change in geographic location. For example, a person can "migrate" by changing occupations (e.g. he may switch from being a schoolteacher to a real estate agent, but stay in the same general area).[9] By rationalizing migration to be a form of human capital investment, Sjaastad's model added a dynamic element, time, to the migration problem.

While Sjaastad did not provide a formal mathematical model, he asserted that the prospective migrant calculates the value of the opportunity available in the market at each alternative destination relative to the value of the opportunity available in the market at the point of origin, subtracts away the costs of moving (assumed to be proportional to migration distance), and chooses the destination that maximizes the present value of lifetime earnings. Nearly all modern neoclassical economic analyses of the migration decision proceed from this basic framework.[10] Within this framework, migration is treated generally as a once-and-for-all decision involving a change in the location of one's employment, and is no more than an inter-temporal version of the labor market model applied to the case of migration. The model can easily be used to show that prospective migrants respond to differences in real earnings differences across labor markets in different geographic locations.

Non-monetary gains enjoyed from moving (e.g., amenities such as better climate and recreational opportunities, a desirable social, political or religious environment, or more desirable quantities of public goods available at the destination) are not counted among migration returns in the classical Sjaastad model. This does not mean that the influences of amenities and consumption goods are irrelevant. Sjaastad reasoned that spatial differences in such influences on migration will already be accounted for by geographic differences in living costs (his model includes spatial differences in real pecuniary returns to migration). For example, a more pleasant climate in California versus Minnesota should already be reflected in higher prices for California real estate.[11]

---

[9] Polachek and Horvath (1977) pointed out that "Migration is defined as the flow of people from one given point or set of points in space to another point or set over some finite time interval. Often a minimum distance criterion, that need not be uniform for all inhabitants, is implicitly assumed ... Yet under less restrictive definitions that, for example, may include occupational changes, such a person would be classified as a migrant" (p. 105). Their study did not deal explicitly with occupational changes, though.

[10] We refer the reader here to expository surveys by Greenwood (1975, 1985, 1997), Molho (1986), Shields and Shields (1989), Bauer and Zimmermann (1995), Ghatak et al. (1996), and Gorter et al. (1998).

[11] Shields and Shields (1989) suggest an interesting implication of this. If differences in real estate prices are the primary source of differences in the costs of living between origin and destination, then the returns to human capital investment forthcoming from migration would be reflected in *nominal* income differences. Consequently, we would argue that if one adjusts nominal income differences for differences in the costs of living, one would be mixing together the investment and consumption returns to migration, a strategy that would likely be at odds with Sjaastad's suggestions for modeling migration as human capital investment.

Costs of migration might include losses from selling one's home, car or appliances prior to the move, or additional expenses incurred to replace certain assets left behind at the destination. Also, a move will sometimes necessitate a loss of job seniority, employer contributions to pension plans, and other types of employment benefits. Importantly, however, Sjaastad's framework includes features of a gravity model by viewing distance as a proxy for migration costs. The greater the distance traveled, the greater are the monetary costs of migration such as transportation expenses, food and lodging costs for oneself and one's family during the move, and interruptions in income while between jobs. The cost of acquiring information about job vacancies will rise with distance, whether the information is acquired formally (advertisements in publications and employment agencies) or informally (provided by friends and relatives, for example). Distance can also raise psychological costs of migration since it leads to uncertainty about the new community and its quality of life, displeasure from breaking ties with family and friends, and other stresses of relocation. Furthermore, potential migrants might consider negative spillover effects on friends and family left behind.[12]

Altogether, Sjaastad's model accounts for four aspects of the migration investment decision: (i) the imperfect synchronization of migration's benefits and costs over time; (ii) earnings differences between origin and destination locales; (iii) cost of living differences between the origin and destination; and (iv) the migrant's rate of time preference. Suppose that there are geographic differences in earnings and that a person will retire in T periods. Let W_t^A represent earnings per period in the origin, W_t^B earnings per period available in the destination, CL_t^A an index measuring the cost of living in the origin, CL_t^B an index measuring the cost of living at the destination, i the discount rate, and C the cost of migration. In discrete time, the present value of the net gain to migration π is

$$\pi - \sum_{t=1}^{T} \frac{\left(W_t^B - W_t^A\right)}{(1+i)^t} - \sum_{t=1}^{T} \frac{\left(CL_t^B - CL_t^A\right)}{(1+i)^t} - C(D, X) \tag{1.1}$$

where D is distance between origin and destination locales and X is a vector of any other determinants of migration costs.[13] In continuous time, the present value is

---

[12] Schwartz (1973) suggested that psychological costs will indeed vary with distance, arguing that migrants often make visits and phone calls to their previous locations to reduce the psychological displeasures of moving, and these costs typically rise with distance. See also Lundborg (1991) for further development of this concept.

[13] Some costs are unlikely to be related to distance. For example, the costs of occupational licensure vary across states, as do vehicle registration costs. In the case of international migration, the costs of obtaining visas will vary according to the country of entry.

$$\pi = \int\limits_{t=0}^{T} \left[W_t^B - W_t^A - CL_t^B + CL_t^A \right] e^{-rt} \mathrm{d}t - C(D, X) \qquad (1.2)$$

In both the discrete- and continuous-time versions of the model[14] the decision-maker moves only if $\pi > 0$. If multiple destinations are possible, then equations (1.1) and (1.2) are computed for all alternatives and the individual chooses the option yielding the highest value of π. All theoretical applications of the human capital model to migration behavior use some permutation of equations (1.1) or (1.2).

Sjaastad's work has substantially influenced most modern studies of migration. However, it is a very simplified framework and it is important to emphasize its limitations. We emphasize these limitations not necessarily to criticize the framework offered by Sjaastad, but rather to stress that researchers' interests in overcoming these limitations served as the impetus for much of the subsequent literature. These limitations include:

1. *It is a single period model.* The model does not explain why some people migrate on multiple occasions during their lifetimes and it provides no implications relating the likelihood of migration to a person's position in her life-cycle. Some researchers have argued that migration is a life-cycle decision problem, meaning that it is a decision that depends upon the person's age, what point he is at in his career, and how much he values income relative to leisure. For example, it is well known that many older persons tend to have a lower likelihood of migration than younger persons. Overcoming this limitation would require a dynamic model examining the migration decision in the context of a person's life-cycle.

2. *The unit of analysis is the individual.* Some researchers have argued that the preferences and goals of a potential migrant's friends and family members must be taken into account when analyzing the migration decision. For example, if a husband and wife both work, then the husband's decision to migrate is likely to depend upon his wife's career prospects at the destination and vice versa. Overcoming this limitation would require a model in which the decision-making unit is the family, not just one person in isolation.

3. *"Push" or "pull" effects are assumed to be symmetrical.* Migration can be induced by enhanced income opportunities in the destination (the most common "pull" factor) or deteriorating income opportunities in the origin (a common "push" factor). It is well known in the empirical migration literature that pull factors tend to be stronger than push factors, but the Sjaastad model does not offer a clear rationale for such

---

[14] Sjaastad did not specify an equation for the net present value of migration gains. Therefore, equations (1.1) and (1.2) should be viewed as general formulations of the investment problem verbalized by Sjaastad. Note also that all theoretical and empirical studies involving the human capital investment approach to the study of migration flows utilize some behavioral model that is equivalent to, or is some permutation of, equations (1.1) or (1.2).

differential effects. Overcoming this limitation would require more complex versions of Sjaastad's framework.[15]

4. *Migrants are assumed to be perfectly informed.* It is very likely that a prospective migrant will be uncertain about the size and path of his lifetime earnings stream at the destination. This uncertainty is expected to be particularly acute for those contemplating international migration involving very long distances and changes in language and customs. Migration uncertainty may be less important for someone who must choose between long-term contracts with known compensation both at home and away (e.g., a tenured college professor who is contemplating a move to another university). It can be significant, though, for persons in piece pay occupations (salespeople, agriculture, self-employed persons, etc.), those in occupations where there is significant risk of disruptions in employment, or for those who are contemplating an occupational change. The greater is the degree of uncertainty, the greater will be both informational and psychological costs. If there is uncertainty, the individual's attitudes toward risk will influence his choice to migrate. If a person is sufficiently risk averse and the perceived level of risk at the destination is sufficiently high, he may choose not to migrate. The Sjaastad model does not address how migrants can cope with uncertainty, nor does it ask whether the degree of uncertainty is dependent on the amount of past migration. For example, one would expect that if there are greater ties between the origin and destination due, say, to greater past migration, then there will be lower information costs. Uncertainty could be endogenous to the amount of past migration and is likely to be connected with the amount of psychological costs. Sjaastad did not consider past migration and assumed constant psychological costs. However, psychological costs could depend upon the size of the migrant community and are likely to increase with distance migrated. Overcoming this limitation would require accounting for uncertainty in the decision-making process.

5. *Remittances are ignored.* Many international migrants remit some of their destination country earnings back home. If a prospective migrant plans to do this, then the benefits to migration will include the benefits of remitting. Assume that the benefits

---

[15] A more sophisticated analysis was later provided by Chiswick (1999), who portrays the migrant as calculating the net rate of return to migration. In Chiswick's model, there are two fundamental components—the (gross) rate of return from migration and the interest cost of funds to finance it. Suppose the spatial income difference rises. Because of the wealth effect, the effect on the prospective migrant's behavior depends upon whether the greater income difference resulted from a higher destination wage or a lower origin wage. A higher destination wage means the migrant's wealth would be higher than before if he moved, whereas a lower origin wage means that the dollar wealth gain from migrating would not be any different. Thus, a higher destination wage tends to enhance migration's lure more than a lower origin wage. Furthermore, Chiswick's analysis suggests that for the same rate of return, the interest cost of funds depends upon whether wages increase in the destination or decrease in the origin. If wages increase in the destination, interest costs tend to be relatively lower compared to the case where wages in the origin fall.

of migration rise with an increase in the home country value of remittances received. Then, the benefits of migrating will be positively related to the real exchange rate between the destination and source countries. For example, if the price of the destination country's currency in the source country rises, adjusted for inflation, remittances received by family and friends back home will be more valuable. The appreciation of the destination country's currency will thus boost the benefits of migration. Furthermore, the returns to migration will be augmented the lower are the costs of remitting earnings back home. For example, the recent growth in the international money transfer industry is due mostly to the growth of both legal and illegal migration. Technological advances in that industry, combined with greater competition, should result in lower costs for transferring funds, which should boost the amount of migration. Overcoming this limitation would require incorporating remittances, exchange rates, and financial sector innovations into the model.

Though we credit Sjaastad for his contributions conceptualizing migration as human capital investment, he was not the only economist in the 1960s to do so. Gary Becker's first writings on human capital theory, which came only a few years after Sjaastad published his pioneering work, provide another important example. In his book, which builds upon the work of Schultz (1961) and was the impetus for what is now the very extensive literature on human capital theory, Becker (1964, p. 7) states "The many forms of such [human capital] investments include schooling, on-the-job training, medical care, *migration*, and searching for information about prices and income" (our italics). Echoing Sjaastad, Becker argues that the decision to relocate is, first and foremost, an investment decision because it involves the incurring of direct and indirect costs up-front in order to realize an (uncertain) payoff in the future.[16]

The pioneering work of Sjaastad and Becker is enormously helpful in understanding the international migration decision. An international migrant incurs transportation, visa, opportunity, and non-monetary costs now in hopes of a payoff in the destination in the future. The expected payoff could be a superior return to one's human capital in the destination region (the case of labor market migration), but there could be other payoffs such

---

[16] Becker makes repeated references to the causes, as well as consequences, of migration throughout his book. In a discussion of specific training, he mentions the likelihood of imperfect transferability of human capital, especially in high-skill areas, across borders (pp. 27–28). He observes that there is often relatively little worker mobility across borders despite huge real international earnings differences (p. 28). He observes that immigrants, when doing international job searches, often have to pay their own way to the destination country (pp. 32–33). He observes that younger persons are more likely to migrate than older persons, all other things being equal (p. 50). He predicts that temporary migrants to urban areas will have less incentive to invest in urban skills than permanent residents (p. 51), and he observes that abler persons have a higher proclivity to migrate (p. 63). All of these observations and predictions are, in one way or another, implications of a model based on the view that migration is a form of human capital investment.

as greater political freedom, reduced risk of loss and limb in the destination country (the case of refugee migration), or the emotional/psychological benefits of being with relatives in the destination (the case of family migration). Or the expected payoff could be the acquisition of skills in the destination region through study at educational institutions, training opportunities, or unique employment opportunities only available in the destination.

There are clearly a wide variety of motives for international migration. While the primary interest in the literature has been economic migration, one cannot discount the importance of other motives. In recent decades, US immigration has been substantially driven by the desire for family reunification. Many countries have absorbed large numbers of refugee migrants. Migration is frequently driven as much by consumption motives (e.g., retirees' search for warmer climates) as by work interests. It is not unusual to see families move because they seek a higher quality of life elsewhere, not necessarily higher income. Nevertheless, *all* forms of voluntary migration, including those that may seem to be motivated by non-economic factors, are in the main determined or influenced by conventional economic (human capital) forces.

2.3 Early extensions of the Sjaastad model

It is convenient to think of the Sjaastad model as taking a "labor supply view" of migration in which an individual's principal motivation for migration is to improve the rate of return to his/her human capital, net of migration costs. Most alternative models of migration are simply extensions of this model, adding, for example, additional motives for migration and/or explicit sources of migration costs. In this subsection, we survey the early literature extending Sjaastad's model.

2.3.1 The migrant as a consumer

Sjaastad's human capital investment model of migration does not account for amenities in the utility function, but rather counts them as geographic differences in the costs of living. By focusing on income differences as the lone motivation for migration, however, the human capital model implicitly assumes that all goods are tradable, thereby effectively treating utility and income synonymously. In contrast, many regional economists emphasize that migration is primarily a *consumption* decision.[17] That is, the "consumer model" of migration offers a richer specification of the human capital hypothesis that separates tradable and non-tradable goods (i.e., amenities) in the utility function directly. By placing greater weight on amenities, the model can generate stable

---

[17] This literature was partly motivated by disappointing results from tests of the Sjaastad model. By the 1980s, these tests frequently failed to confirm spatial differences in earnings as a determinant of migration. For a sampling of important early papers emphasizing the consumer model of migration, see Rosen (1974), Graves (1979, 1983), Greenwood (1997), Glaeser and Shapiro (2003), and Green et al. (2006).

equilibria with equal utility across regions and unequal levels of income even in the absence of migration costs.[18]

Typical models based on the consumption view proceed from the assumption that households and firms are always in equilibrium at their different locations. Regional income disparities do not necessarily mean that there will be utility gains from migrating. If gains are available, they will be arbitraged away quickly because mobility is high, information costs are low, and markets are generally quite efficient. Consequently, persistent regional differences in wages, rents, and prices represent a compensating differential for regional differences in amenities. Some areas have features that are more attractive than other areas. Thus, there will be a spatial equilibrium that reflects differences in amenities across localities.

According to the consumer model of migration, migration flows are triggered by changes in life-cycle factors such as the onset of retirement or changes in real incomes that will alter the demand for amenities. For example, long-term technological advances will raise peoples' real incomes and, assuming that amenities are normal goods, boost the demand for those amenities. Because amenities tend to be distributed unevenly, migration will occur. Consequently, amenity-rich areas will experience in-migration, driving down wages and driving up land prices, whereas in amenity-poor areas, wages will rise and rents will fall. Technological advances could have the same effects on producer demand for amenities. An important point made by practitioners of the consumption view is that migration cannot spatially equilibrate wages. People will only migrate if the value they attach to amenities exceeds the lower purchasing power that results from decreased wages and increased rents.

The notion that people migrate in response to spatial differences in amenities also extends to public goods. Long before regional economists were constructing models relating spatial equilibrium to amenities, Tiebout (1956) argued that an important factor explaining why people move from one locality to another is differences in the quality of public goods such as police and fire protection, education, hospitals, courts, beaches, parks, roads, and parking facilities. According to the Tiebout hypothesis, consumers "vote with their feet," picking communities that best satisfy their preferences for public goods. Hence, location decisions of households will depend on the local fiscal policies of various localities. Furthermore, the greater the number of localities and the more diffuse is the distribution of the quality of public goods among them, the closer the consumer/voter will come to satisfying his preference pattern.

---

[18] A related, but alternative, methodology comes from Shields and Shields (1989). Motivated by the *new household economics* literature of Becker (1965), Lancaster (1966), and Willis (1973), they model migration as a household decision contingent upon household production costs that are influenced by locational amenities.

Country differences in amenities may help explain international migration flows to some extent. For example, a country's political system, the risk of persecution, the likelihood of cultural acceptance, how permissive the environment is to creative expression, the crime rate, and weather are all potentially strong determinants of migration. Furthermore, international migrants could be searching for higher levels of public goods such as quality health care, educational systems, and judicial systems. However, the consumption view cannot deny that relative migration flows and destination choice are still going to be influenced by conventional economic (human capital) forces. Moreover, the costs of international migration may be prohibitively high. Thus, while the consumer model of migration adds insight into the migration decision, it is not unreasonable to prefer the more simplified human capital models to explain interregional migration flows.

2.3.2 The influence of kinship and migrant networks

In Sjaastad's model, pecuniary migration costs depend only on distance traveled, nonpecuniary psychological costs are constant, and there are zero information costs. Later work has argued that psychological and information costs are likely to fall when there is greater access to family, friends, and other previous migrants in the destination. In the sociology-based migration literature, the community of family and friends at the destination is often referred to as a *kinship network* and the community of earlier migrants is referred to as a *migrant network*. Access to these networks can greatly improve the efficiency of migration. For example, Yap (1977) has suggested that migration to an area will be enhanced if migrants have relatives and friends already there, languages in the origin and destination are similar, or if a relatively large stock of migrants from the origin previously migrated to the destination earlier in time. A similar point has been made by Hugo (1981), Taylor (1986), and Massey and Garcia Espana (1987). If a person is moving to an area where there is a network of migrants already there, that could result in lower employment search costs, lower costs of securing housing and child care, and more protection from crime. Having family and friends already at the destination could reduce the stress associated with an interregional move and significantly reduce language barriers in the destination.

If kinship and migrant networks are effective in reducing information and psychological costs, then migration costs will be endogenous to the volume of past migration. Specifically, moving costs should decrease with the number of migrants already settled in the destination. Carrington et al. (1996) tested a discrete-time model of internal migration based on the assumption of endogenous mobility costs. They hypothesize that with endogenous mobility costs, migration builds over time and the volume of migration may increase even as destination–origin wage differentials narrow. Furthermore, their model demonstrates that migration tends to follow specific geographic channels, with the first cohort of migrants being those with the lowest migration costs.

The incorporation of kinship and migrant networks into the migrant's objective function is straightforward. For example, rather than just assuming some general migration cost function with no underlying determinants, the model could relate migration costs to a risk variable such as the probability of earnings losses during some initial period at the destination, but this risk variable will be lower the greater is the size of kinship and/or migrant networks. This was done by Taylor (1986),[19] who developed a model of household[20] labor allocation that incorporates the influence of kinship networks at the destination in reducing the risks of migrating. He argues that kinship networks influence household labor decisions by serving as "migration insurance," i.e. insurance against income loss at the destination. The benefits component of the migrant's objective function could also include the assumption that kinship and migrant networks augment utility because of the psychological gain that comes from having familiar faces and contacts in a new place.

Though the examples above identify the lessened psychological costs of migration associated with larger migrant networks at the destination, a less-cited literature highlights the increased costs associated with kinship networks. That is, individuals with well-established kinship networks at home will experience deep psychological costs from leaving behind family and friends should they decide to migrate. Various researchers have suggested that these costs are likely to increase with distance traveled (see Beals et al., 1967; and Schwartz, 1973).

Ultimately, the desire to increase one's income remains the primary motivating force behind the migration decision in both the classical human capital investment model and models emphasizing kinship networks. The only fundamental difference between the two is that the latter provides a richer explanation for non-pecuniary migration costs. Such costs are no longer constant, and are reduced by the presence of extensive kinship and migrant networks in the destination. Networks can therefore stimulate migration. In Section 3.2.1, we provide a longer discussion of more recent work in this area.

2.3.3 Migration decisions in a life-cycle context

The Sjaastad model treats migration as a single-period problem. It does not explicitly address return migration (the decision to return to the home region) or circular migration (the decision to frequently cross a border). Instead, the Sjaastad model implicitly assumes that such actions arise only when the particular costs and benefits of migration change to alter the migration decision. Empirically, many people have a high periodicity of migration, whereas others have a low periodicity. The Sjaastad model is silent on the causes of this heterogeneity other than to assume that repeat migrants are those whose migration

---

[19] See also Goodman (1981).

[20] The decision-making unit in Taylor's model is the family, but his model is easily applicable to the individual.

costs and benefits change more frequently than others. That is, explanations for repeat and return migration are not predictions formally implied by the Sjaastad model, but instead are simply assumptions.

Polachek and Horvath (1977) argue that if migration is viewed as an investment process undertaken at each stage of the life-cycle, then refutable explanations emerge for the periodicity of migration. They proceed from the assumption that what matters to people are locational characteristics, and that relocation involves choosing the set of characteristics that maximizes utility. Locations can be thought of as composites of various locational characteristics such as unemployment rates, prices, industrial composition, occupational opportunities, or per-capita governmental expenditures on education. As a person moves through his/her life-cycle, his/her demand for locational characteristics changes.

A second essential point in the Polachek and Horvath (1977) model is their recognition of and emphasis on the costs of acquiring information about alternative locations. Such costs entail a joint investment with mobility. Mobility is a response to changing demand for locational attributes, but location choice can only be facilitated by the acquisition of information that reveals where one can find desirable attributes.[21] Mobility is thus the outcome of changes in individual demand for known locational characteristics.

Because there are multiple stages to the life-cycle, it is very likely that there will be multiple episodes of mobility during a person's life. Migrants with high periodicities are those whose preferences, benefits, and costs change more rapidly than others. Furthermore, older persons will migrate less frequently than younger persons. These and other implications are derived formally using an optimal control theory framework that treats the choice of locational attributes, information, goods, and human capital acquisition as simultaneously determined.

Importantly, Polachek and Horvath (1977) also demonstrate that without information search and the acquisition of human capital, their model reduces to the simple Sjaastad model of dichotomous choice. It simply treats migration as a continual process of revising one's demand for locational attributes over the life cycle, concurrent with human capital acquisition. More recently, dynamic macroeconomic models have been used to better understand circular migration. We discuss those developments in Section 3.3.3.

2.3.4 The effects of uncertainty on migration
The Sjaastad model assumes that a migrant can be certain to secure employment in the destination. If migrants find work at the destination instantly upon arrival and migration

---

[21] The problem, as Polachek and Horvath (1977) point out, is that mobility causes information to depreciate, resulting in losses. The losses in information value must be weighed against the gains that come from moving to a place with more desirable attributes.

costs are non-existent, a pure disequilibrium model would thus imply complete wage convergence between origin and destination locales. This assumption is clearly problematic. A number of development economists, beginning with Todaro (1969, 1976) and Harris and Todaro (1970), have argued that this assumption is very unrealistic for cases involving rural-to-urban migration in developing countries.[22] They point out that when rural migrants come to the city, there can be a long waiting period before a job is secured in the urban "modern" sector. When the migrant arrives in the urban area, he typically joins a large pool of unemployed and underemployed workers, all spending time in the urban "traditional" sector, where they are either fully or partly unemployed and often performing menial tasks for low pay. Todaro's work may be viewed as a modification of the Sjaastad model, where expected income at the destination is substituted for actual income:

$$\pi = \int_{t=0}^{T} \left[p(t) W_t^B - W_t^A - CL_t^B + CL_t^A \right] e^{-rt} dt - C(D, X) \tag{1.3}$$

where $p(t)$ is the probability a migrant will be employed in the modern urban sector in period t, B is the destination (i.e., the urban sector), and A is the origin (i.e., the rural sector). Recall that D is distance between the origin and destination, and X is a vector of any other determinants of migration costs. In this context, rural-to-urban migration will continue as long as the expected wage in the urban sector, net of migration costs, equals the wage in the rural sector (where the probability of finding employment is assumed to be 100%). This basic model was subsequently extended by a number of researchers to take into account other important and unique features of developing countries.[23] Unemployment risk has also been captured in modern models of international migration, which we discuss in Section 3.1.7.

Wage uncertainty in the destination can also be modeled as a sequential search process in which the migrant maximizes expected net income and faces a stationary probability

---

[22] For a very thorough review of the literature on internal migration in LDCs, see Lucas (1997). For a very recent and thorough review specifically of the literature on rural to urban internal migration in LDCs, see Lall et al. (2006).

[23] Harris and Todaro (1970) extended the Todaro (1969) model to the case where there is a wage subsidy policy in the urban sector and restrictions on rural-to-urban migration. They demonstrated that: (a) under certain conditions, either policy can lead to welfare improvement; and (b) maximum welfare improvement will result from implementing the policies concurrently. Bhagwati and Srinivasan (1974) demonstrate, however, that once the migrant's utility function is explicitly considered, either policy can be shown to be welfare-maximizing. Corden and Findlay (1975) extended the Harris and Todaro model to allow for capital mobility, whereas Fields (1979) extended it to allow for job search by migrants, preferential hiring by educational level, and labor turnover. Calvo (1978) extended the Harris and Todaro model to include a trade union in the urban sector, whose objective is to maximize the difference between its members' incomes and what they would earn in the rural sector.

distribution of wages at the destination (Pickles and Rogerson, 1984; McCall and McCall, 1987). In each period, an observation from that distribution is revealed in the form of a wage offer and an individual compares the offer with his reservation wage (e.g., the wage at the origin). When a wage draw exceeds the reservation wage net of migration costs, the individual migrates. This process also affects the length of time before a move is made, if a move is made at all. One important implication of the model is that the more (less) favorable labor market conditions are at the origin, the longer (shorter) it will take for a sufficiently attractive wage offer to arrive at the destination, hence the longer (shorter) it will take on average for an individual to decide to migrate. This may help explain a key stylized fact that regional and international migration are "slow bleed" phenomena in which migration responds only sluggishly to real income differences.[24]

Burda (1993, 1995) offered a somewhat different explanation for how labor market uncertainty in the destination can lead to this slow bleed nature of migration. He argues that it often pays to delay making a relocation decision until more information is received. In Burda's models, the migrant has to choose between two strategies: (i) migrate immediately and take the risk that migration will be more profitable than staying at home; or (ii) wait until he knows for sure whether migration is profitable or not. Procrastination has value—it will be more profitable to delay a migration decision if the benefits of waiting for information exceed the costs. In equilibrium the probability of receiving good news about the destination's labor market is equivalent to the probability of migrating. Thus, the expected net gain of deferring the decision to migrate is the net gain of migrating when the destination's labor market is favorable, weighted by the probability that market conditions will be favorable. This gain can be higher than what would be enjoyed if migration took place immediately; hence postponement of the migration decision to the second period can make this person even better off. This is what Burda (1993, 1995) called the *option value of waiting* to migrate and it represents gains to procrastination.[25] An important caveat to Burda's analysis, however, is that there are also costs of waiting. For example, superior job opportunities in the destination are options with expiration dates as well. Waiting can sometimes result in the better job offers disappearing, and this risk must also be accounted for in the waiting decision.

---

[24] For example, Burda (1995) found that following a large spike immediately after reunification of West and East Germany, migration from the East to the West was surprisingly sluggish despite very large real wage differences. This type of pattern, where migration is sluggish, despite significant real income differentials between countries, has been found for other prominent cases of migration as well.

[25] Burda developed a formal theoretical model, deriving an expression for the option value of waiting, which is the excess of the value of a waiting strategy over the value of a strategy in which migration is undertaken immediately. He demonstrated that the value of the migration option is inversely related to the current wage gap, positively related to migration costs, has an ambiguous relationship with the discount rate, is inversely related to the wage gap when destination conditions are unfavorable, is positively related to the probability of unfavorable market conditions, and independent of the wage gap when conditions are favorable.

2.3.5 What happens when the family is the decision-making unit?

The earliest models of migration do not distinguish between personal and family decisions. Sjaastad's (1962) focus is on the individual and there is no analysis of how his migration may affect other persons close to him. The implicit assumption in early research on the migration decision is that if the migrant is part of a family, then the welfare of the rest of the family is unaffected by that person's decision to relocate. For a large proportion of internal and international moves, however, migration is indeed a family decision and everyone in the family is affected by it. Extensions of the Sjaastad (1962) model to include family ties date back to the mid-1970s. These extensions were designed to address two questions: (1) When the whole family migrates, how is the decision to migrate made when family members have conflicting interests? (2) Why would part of the family migrate while the other part stays at home? We discuss each of these questions below.

Work modeling family migration decisions began with Sandell (1977), Polachek and Horvath (1977), and Mincer (1978). These models assume that family members might have conflicting interests. If the entire family migrates, then relocation may enhance the well-being of some family members, but may reduce it for others. Even though the household head's income and job satisfaction may improve with relocation, other family members may suffer income losses, as well as psychological costs that result from leaving family and friends behind, adjusting to a new language and culture, etc. All other things being equal, family ties have a greater tendency to discourage migration than to encourage it.

Mincer's (1978) model of the family migration decision can be easily described. Suppose for simplicity that the household includes just two persons, a husband and a wife. Allow ΔI_H to be the change in the present value of the husband's income stream were he to relocate to another region or country, and let ΔI_W be the change in the present value of the wife's income stream were she to move with him. Note that ΔI_H is equivalent to the husband's "private" gains to migration, the gains he would enjoy if he were single and were deciding on his own to migrate. Similarly, ΔI_W measures the wife's private gains to migration; if she were not married, she would move if the private gains were positive.

Let us assume that this two-person family has two alternatives to choose from: (i) both migrate together; or (ii) both stay at the origin.[26] How then does the family decide whether or not to migrate? Mincer argues that the requirement for migration to take place is not that both persons have positive gains to migration (both ΔI_H and $\Delta I_W > 0$), but rather that the net sum of the family's gains is positive:

$$\Delta I_W + \Delta I_H > 0 \qquad (1.4)$$

---

[26] We rule out the possibility that one person migrates, while the other stays behind, as is the case with many "commuting couples," i.e. couples where each spouse has a separate home connected with his/her workplace, but the two spend time together at one or both of those homes periodically.

The insight here is that the family may migrate even if the two persons have conflicting interests. What matters is not what migration does to each person's private gains, but to the joint gains of this multi-person decision-making unit. If the private gains to migration for each person are positively correlated, then each family member agrees whether or not to migrate and the decision is individually efficient. If the private gains to migration for each person are negatively correlated, however, then it will be privately inefficient for one of the family members to migrate, although it may be efficient for the family unit to do so. This may arise, for example, if the husband is in a different occupation than his wife and their labor markets are very different in both the origin and destination. In the event that the husband experiences a gain from migration, the wife a loss, but the joint gains are still positive, then the wife is a *tied mover*—she follows her husband even though her employment outlook is better at home. Suppose, in contrast, that the wife's loss from migration dominates the husband's gain. Then, he is a *tied stayer*, which means that he sacrifices superior employment opportunities available elsewhere because his wife is much better off in their current place of residence.

The Mincer model can quite easily be expanded to analyze other economic phenomena. For example, it has interesting and important implications for such factors as marital formation, marital stability, and the labor supply decision of the "tied" party. Of particular note for immigration economists, it can be used to describe the emergence of commuting couples as an alternative to the migration decision—that is, couples in which one partner chooses to commute great lengths instead of moving the entire family to a new destination. Moreover, expansions of the Mincer model that endogenize the tied partner's labor supply decision will deliver a richer set of migration and labor supply implications that depend upon both partners' opportunities. That is, such models can better describe whether one or both partners move, commute, leave the labor market, settle for an inferior job, find improved labor market opportunities, or remain at home in their current occupation of employment.

Another strand of literature emphasizing the role of the family in the migration decision emerged in the 1980s. This literature, beginning with Stark and Levhari (1982), Stark (1984, 1991), and Katz and Stark (1986), focuses mostly on explaining migration from developing to developed countries and emphasizes the role of migrant remittances. The premise of this literature is that the household chooses whether or not to send a family member away to work. The decision to send a family member overseas, for example, is essentially a "family portfolio diversification decision"—a decision to try to hedge against risk and to ease liquidity constraints. These researchers have suggested that migration: (i) is a response to various market failures experienced by families and households in developing countries; and (ii) provides an alternative source of capital for families and ensures stability in consumption.

The core feature of this collective decision-making model is that the family or household, unlike the individual, can control risk through diversification of household resources. Some members of the family, for example, can be assigned to work in the local economy, while others may be sent to work in foreign labor markets where conditions are negatively correlated with local labor markets. If there is a downturn in the local labor market and the household faces a liquidity constraint, then having a family member working overseas in a strong labor market eases the constraint because the migrant can remit his income home. According to this literature, the decision to have family members migrate is a response to a lack of risk-hedging mechanisms such as crop insurance markets, futures markets, unemployment insurance, and capital markets. In fact, modern models of immigration exploit the insurance role of immigration as a household-level decision (as discussed in Section 3.2.2).

2.3.6 Migration as a response to relative deprivation

Stark (1984, 1991), Katz and Stark (1986), Stark and Taylor (1989, 1991), and Stark and Yitzhaki (1988) suggest that migrants are motivated to relocate by a desire to improve their income relative to members of their reference group. "Relative deprivation" models[27] argue that utility is influenced from knowing how one's income ranks relative to his peers.[28] In the context of migration, the reference group is assumed to be other income-earning people at the origin. A person's feelings of relative deprivation will be greater, all other things being equal, the lower his income ranks in the distribution. Furthermore, his utility will rise if his ranking in the income distribution rises, even if his absolute income stays the same.[29] If migration leads to higher absolute income elsewhere (adjusted for cost of living differences), then a person's utility rises because (i) consumption opportunities have improved and (ii) feelings of relative deprivation have been assuaged.

To illustrate these concepts more precisely, define $F(Y)$ as the cumulative income distribution in a person's reference group and $b[1 - F(Y)]$ as the disutility felt from not having an income that is higher than Y^*. The relative deprivation $RD(Y^*)$ experienced with absolute income Y^* is

$$RD(Y^*) = \int_{Y^*}^{Y'} b[1 - F(z)]dz \qquad (1.5)$$

---

[27] The concept of relative deprivation is due originally to the social psychologist W.C. Runciman (1996).

[28] Stark's (1984) example was that, "In a well-defined reference group—an army regiment or a university faculty—we are promoted from time to time on par with our peers. We are always aware of opportunities elsewhere, but decide not to pursue them. Assume that one fine day, arriving in a cheerful mood at the officers' or faculty club, we find out that everyone else has been promoted or tenured, but that we were not. In the army one would be likely to put in for an immediate transfer; in academic life—actively seek to offer elsewhere; one becomes *relatively deprived* (Stark's italics), resents it, and decides to 'migrate'" (pp. 210–211).

[29] It follows logically that feelings of relative deprivation will fall if the incomes of one's peers fall, but one's own income stays the same.

where Y' is the highest income earned by someone in the reference group. The individual's feelings of relative deprivation will fall (rise) if income rises above (falls below) Y^*. If migration results in a higher income of Y', then relative deprivation falls by an amount equal to the following:

$$RD(Y^*) - RD(Y') = \int_{Y^*}^{Y'} b[1 - F(z)] \mathrm{d}z - \int_{Y''}^{Y'} b[1 - F(z)] \mathrm{d}z \qquad (1.6)$$

While the notion that relative deprivation motivates migration is very easy to understand and may be appealing, it is easily subject to criticism. First, the behavior predicted by relative deprivation models is often not consistent with what we tend to observe in migration behavior. According to relative deprivation models, the benefit of migration depends upon a person's position in the income distribution. This means that, for example, a person's relative deprivation improves if he/she moves from being in the 50th percentile of the income distribution in a high-income country to being in the 95th percentile of the income distribution in a low-income country. The model implies that if the gain in utility from the reduction in relative deprivation is high enough, the person would move from a high-income country to a low-income country. However, this is rarely observed. Indeed, most domestic and international migrants receive higher absolute real incomes in the destination, but on lower rungs of the income distribution compared to the origin. Second, relative deprivation is an explanation rooted in the migrant's tastes, which are impossible to measure. Third, many would argue that relative deprivation is a concept that cannot be extended to cases other than rural-to-urban migration in relatively poor countries.

Nonetheless, there are some potentially important testable implications of the relative deprivation hypothesis. First, it implies that characteristics of the income distribution of the migrant's source country will influence the decision to migrate. For example, if absolute income stays the same, but the variance of the distribution or the degree of positive skewness rise, this will alter utility and raise a person's incentive to migrate. Second, the relative deprivation hypothesis is capable of contradicting the traditional hypothesis that expected income differentials across two regions or countries must be positive in order to induce migration. Altogether, however, though feelings of relative deprivation are indeed a motive very different from the others discussed, they do not necessarily replace or contradict the human capital investment motive for migration. Concerns about relative deprivation may be best viewed as an additional motive for migration within a larger human capital investment model.

2.3.7 The influence of age on the migration decision

It is well known that international migrants tend to be young. The theoretical literature on the relationship between age and migration decisions is surprisingly thin, though some early literature provides insights. Becker (1964) argued that the propensity to migrate will tend to decrease with age because the expected net present value of benefits from relocation will, due to greater duration of stay in the destination, be higher for younger persons. This implies that migration rates for persons from the lower (higher) end of the source region's age distribution will be higher (lower).[30]

Gallaway (1969), in contrast, suggested an ambiguous relationship between age and the probability of migration. On the one hand, older workers face higher costs of relocation because (i) they face a greater expected cost of not being able to fully transfer pension rights accumulated in retirement programs; (ii) the expected costs of liquidating physical investments in the origin are often higher; and (iii) they face greater psychic costs from uprooting themselves from long-held jobs and dwellings. On the other hand, migration will tend to be more affordable for older workers because they often earn more money and have more assets than young workers.

David (1974) suggested that seniority rights (which provide protection from the risk of layoffs) will be lost following a move. Schwartz (1976) emphasized the importance of psychic costs, arguing that as persons get older, they will invest more in relationships with family members and friends and the emotional costs of severing those relationships will be higher. Building upon Schwartz's work, Lundborg (1991) suggested that the demand for return visits will depend on the length of time spent at the destination, age at the time of migration, and the stock of prior migrants from the origin residing in the destination. An increasingly important form of internal and international migration is undertaken by the aged. This has important implications for the destination labor market—such as greater demand by the aged for caregiving services—as well as direct implications for the demographic distribution of the population.[31]

3. RECENT THEORETICAL ANALYSES OF WHY PEOPLE MIGRATE

The previous section provided a narrative survey and assessment of the theoretical literature on the determinants of migration through roughly 2000. In this section, we survey mostly post-2000 literature, but with a greater focus on the mathematical mechanics behind the models. Common between both sections, however, is recognition that human capital investment forms the center of migration models. The most recent models of the determinants of migration are characterized by their emphasis on the endogeneity

---

[30] Schlottmann and Herzog (1984) described this as "age selectivity of migration." They focused on how career and geographic mobility interact in influencing this age selectivity. Using data on interstate migration for 1965–70, they concluded that failure to account for this interaction will tend to overstate the negative influence of age on the probability of migration. It should be noted that Schlottmann and Herzog focused on this particular empirical issue and did not provide a theoretical model with any novel implications regarding the relationship between age and proclivity to migrate.

[31] Bodvarsson and Hou (2010) re-examined these theoretical issues using a model of the migration decision that captures all the above effects of age on the migration decision, in addition to other influences not discussed in the literature. They demonstrated that age will have an ambiguous effect on the proclivity to migrate; in some cases, the returns to migration can rise with age.

of the migration decision and of wages. Simple models treat migration as a static decision determined by exogenous wages that vary across different levels of human capital. More rigorous models treat migration as a dynamic decision with endogenous wage determination and human capital accumulation.

This section is divided into three subsections. In the first, we discuss somewhat less complex static models with endogenous migration, whereas the second discusses more complex models that add the feature of endogenous wages. The third subsection then explores dynamic models of migration.

3.1 A static human capital model with endogenous migration

As a framework for understanding recent theoretical developments on the determinants of international migration, we begin by describing a simple model where the migration decision is endogenous. The basic two-country framework will deliver an equation that pinpoints the migration rate between the two countries. We then add various components to the model, in line with recent work, to isolate the importance of various factors in affecting migration rates. For simplicity, we abstract from return and circular migration such that the model will produce migration rates from one region to another.[32]

Let us begin by assuming that the world economy consists of two regions (or countries), A and B. There is a continuum of agents in each region. Agents are heterogeneous with respect to skill level: they are either unskilled (u) or skilled (s). The precise definition of this dichotomy is not crucial for understanding the fundamental nature of theoretical models, but most researchers define skilled workers as those with at least some college education. The measure of agents with skill i is defined as Ω_i for $i = \{u, s\}$.

Agents maximize their utility over consumption and leisure. Each is endowed with one unit of time, which can be allocated to leisure activities or supplied to the firm. Agents choose a region in which to reside by comparing the expected value of living in each. For simplicity, assume that the expected value of living in region j depends on the after-tax wage rates, w_j^i, faced by an agent with skill level i. Thus, the level of human capital of an agent determines his/her wage rate at home and abroad. An agent of skill i solves the following maximization problem:

$$\max \left\{ \lambda^i E\left[u\left(c_A^i, l_A^i\right)\right] + \left(1 - \lambda^i\right) E\left[u\left(c_B^i, l_B^i\right)\right] \right\} \tag{1.7}$$

subject to the budget constraints:

$$c_A^i = w_A^i\left(1 - l_A^i\right) \text{ and } c_B^i = w_B^i\left(1 - l_B^i\right)$$

The agent chooses how much to consume, c_A^i, the amount of time to devote to leisure activities, l_A^i, and the probability of remaining in region A, λ^i for $\lambda^i \in [0,1]$. The after-tax wage rate, w_j^i, is taken as given.

---

[32] Later in the chapter, we will discuss how these important aspects of migration have been incorporated in models.

Expected utility depends on the migration decision, and hence the expected value of living in each region. Following Rogerson (1988), agents randomize over migration. The allocation of consumption and leisure will depend upon their region of residence. λ^i is defined as the probability that the allocation $\{\dot{c}_A^i, \dot{l}_A^i\}$ is realized (i.e., that the agent lives in region A), whereas $1 - \lambda^i$ is the probability that the allocation $\{\dot{c}_B^i, \dot{l}_B^i\}$ is realized (that the agent lives in region B). Since there is a continuum of agents in each region, the representative agent of type i in each region determines the equilibrium fraction of type i agents living in region A. Similarly, the probability of living in region B for a specific type of agent is equivalent to the fraction of that type living in region B.

In equilibrium interior solutions (i.e., cases in which migration occurs at a rate less than 100%), an agent of skill i must be indifferent between living in region A and living in region B. Thus, it must be that $E[u(\dot{c}_A^i, \dot{l}_A^i)] = E[u(\dot{c}_B^i, \dot{l}_B^i)]$ for all i. In corner solutions, $\lambda^i = 0$ implies that the agent strictly prefers to live in region B; if $\lambda^i = 1$, the agent strictly prefers to live in region A.

3.1.1 Adding migration costs

The model represented in equation (1.7) abstracts from migration costs and policy, two factors that play important roles in affecting the flow of migrants between two regions. One puzzle, as discussed earlier, is that observed international migrant flows are small given the huge real income differentials across countries. This implies that significant migration costs must be present so that net benefits of migration are small once moving costs are taken into consideration. Following Chiswick (1999), migration costs may be explicit travel or admissions costs, or they may be implicit costs associated with time spent looking for a job, language and cultural assimilation, distance from family, a preference for home, or psychological costs (see Urrutia, 1998; Chiquiar and Hanson, 2005; Hunt, 2006; Clark et al., 2007; Hatton and Williamson, 2011; and Grogger and Hanson, 2011).[33] Migration costs may depend on the specific pair of origin and destination countries. For example, travel costs may depend on the distance between the two countries. Other types of migration costs, such as home preference, might only depend on the origin country. We will allow for the most general case in the model, which allows costs to depend on both the source and destination countries.

Costs can be explicitly modeled as an exogenous loss of utility associated with migration that depends on the region of origin and the destination.[34] If the costs are measured in utils, then the maximization problem for an agent of skill i migrating to region j becomes:

---

[33] Refer to Section 2.2 for a more thorough discussion of the various types of migration costs.

[34] Alternatively, costs can be measured in consumption goods, and hence put directly into the budget constraint, which becomes: $\dot{c}_j^i = w_j^i(1 - \dot{l}_j^i) - \gamma_{A,B}^i$. Theoretically, it makes no difference.

$$\max\left\{\lambda^i E\left[u\left(c_A^i l_A^i\right)\right] + \left(1-\lambda^i\right)E\left[u\left(c_B^i l_B^i\right)\right] - \gamma_{A,B}^i\right\} \tag{1.8}$$

where $\gamma_{A,B}^i$ represents the costs of an agent of skill i from region A migrating to region B. Notice that migration costs depends on skill level, indicating that human capital is once again playing a role in the migration decision. Abstracting from endogenous labor supply for the moment by fixing $l_j^i = 0 \, \forall \, i, j$, the probability that individual i will migrate from region B to region A is:

$$\lambda^i = \text{Prob}\left[\left(E\left[u\left(c_A^i\right)\right] - E\left[u\left(c_B^i\right)\right] - \gamma_{A,B}^i\right) > 0\right] \tag{1.9}$$

Often, utility is assumed to be linear (Ortega and Peri, 2009; Beine et al., 2011; Grogger and Hanson, 2011; Simpson and Sparber, 2013), such that $\lambda^i = \text{Prob}[E[c_A^i - c_B^i - \gamma_{A,B}^i] > 0]$ or $\lambda^i = \text{Prob}[E[w_A^i - w_B^i - \gamma_{A,B}^i] > 0]$. Given distributional assumptions on w_j^i, the emigration rate can be estimated using equation (1.9). If wages are exogenous and observable, λ^i can be defined as the ratio of the number of immigrants from origin region B in destination A ($M_{A,B}$) over the native population of the source region B (M_B). That is, $\lambda^i = M_{A,B}/M_B$ is the migration rate from region B to A, and it depends explicitly on the after-tax wage (or income) differential between the source and destination region net of migration costs. Assuming wages are known for certainty (an assumption to be relaxed later), the baseline model of endogenous migration yields the following specification:

$$\text{Migration rate}_{A,B}^i = w_A^i - w_B^i - \gamma_{A,B}^i \tag{1.10}$$

Equation (1.10) reinforces the point that the migration decision depends critically on human capital via wages and migration costs. Also notice that equation (1.10) can be expressed in terms of migrant flows since the migration rate is the ratio of the flow of immigrants from region B to A over the size of the population of region B. Equation (1.10) can be rearranged so that migrant flows are on the left-hand side of the equation and population size is on the right-hand side. This is often the specification used in recent gravity models of immigration, including Karemera et al. (2000), Lewer and Van den Berg (2008), Ortega and Peri (2009), Mayda (2010), and Beine et al. (2011).[35]

3.1.2 Incorporating immigration policy

Laws usually restrict the flow of migrants across countries, and sometimes restrict movements across regions within a country as well. Immigration policy can be modeled directly in migration costs, whereby costs for certain types of immigrants (identified by skill level and/or region of origin) are higher for those who face tighter immigration restrictions. As immigration policy tightens for an individual from region i with skill j, γ_j^i in equation (1.10) would rise, implying that the migration rate would fall for that group of

---

[35] Depending on the distributional assumptions of wages, equation (1.10) may also be written in log form as in Borjas (1987) and Ortega and Peri (2009), for example.

individuals. This is in line with Clark et al. (2007), for example, which specifies immigration costs that vary with immigration policy and skill level. Various other mechanisms could be imbedded into the model to incorporate immigration policy, such as including a measure that represents the probability that an immigrant from region B will be allowed to stay in region A (as in Mayda, 2010). In this case, there is an immigration quota in the destination region, and once the quota is reached, new immigrants are not allowed to enter and those in the destination region may be sent home.

Migration costs are the most straightforward and common way of accounting for immigration policy in theoretical models. However, immigration policy can also be modeled in other ways. For example, suppose border enforcement restricts the movement of people across borders and adds to the costs of migration by increasing the time spent moving. The time spent migrating results in lost wages in the source and destination. Thus, border enforcement can be modeled as a tax on migrant wages (see Guzman et al., 2008). Alternatively, immigration policy can take the form of interior enforcement schemes such as employer sanctions (such as in Ethier, 1986), whereby employers in the destination face increased hiring costs, especially in the case of illegal immigrants. In this way, immigration policy is raising the input costs for firms that hire immigrants. If these costs are passed along to workers in the form of lower wages, they reduce the incentive to migrate. If instead employers absorb the costs, output prices could rise.

3.1.3 Incorporating self-selection

The simple model in equation (1.10) allows wage differentials and migration costs to vary across skill type, so immigration rates depend critically on the (exogenous) level of human capital. However, variation in migration rates can also arise due to the unobservable characteristics and skills that potential migrants possess. This is the key insight of Borjas's (1987) self-selection model. Unobservable characteristics imply that migration rates will vary not only by human capital, but will also depend upon the *distribution* of the returns to human capital (wages) in the origin and destination regions.[36]

In this framework, the migration decision is driven by both the average relative wage gain from immigrating and whether the immigrants' skills would be rewarded by moving abroad (that is, by where the potential immigrant stands in the wage distribution). Notice that the returns to immigration are not only captured by wages, but other factors such as wage inequality, the progressivity of income taxes, and redistribution via social insurance. Importantly, the variance of earnings and the transferability of skills across regions are important components in the immigration decision. Equation (1.10) can be rewritten as

---

[36] Also see Borjas and Bratsberg (1996), which examined selection consequences in a model that allows people of different exogenous skill levels to decide both whether to migrate and whether to return.

$$\text{Migration rate}^i_{A,B} = \frac{\ln\left(w^i_A\right) - \ln\left(w^i_B\right) - \gamma^i_{A,B}/w^i_A}{\sigma} \tag{1.11}$$

where σ represents the standard deviation of the error terms in destination and origin region wages, which depends on each region's earnings variance, the degree of skill transferability across regions, and the interaction of the origin and destination earnings variances.[37] Note that the migration rate depends on relative wage differences and migration costs ($\gamma^i_{A,B}$) relative to the destination wage rate (w^i_A).

The main finding of the Borjas model is that immigration occurs when the destination offers higher relative returns to the individual's skill set (i.e., human capital), assuming mean wages are higher. Consequently, differences in income inequality and the transferability of skills are important determinants of immigration. In Borjas (1991), earnings variance is driven in part by observable characteristics (such as education and experience) such that the migration decision varies by the mean education level in each region, for example. This extension allows the model to predict that migration rates rise (fall) with the mean (variance) education level of the origin region. This has important implications for what types of individuals—skilled or unskilled—have an incentive to migrate.

3.1.4 Blending self-selection and migration costs

Migrant selectivity can arise due to distributional assumptions on observed or unobserved wage components, as discussed above. However, selectivity can also arise under alternative specifications for migration costs. For example, different from Borjas (1987), Chiswick (1999) assumes that skills are observable and that wages in the origin and destination do not depend on labor market experience. Instead, migration costs that do not depend on the wage or skill level play an important role in determining which types of migrants have an incentive to migrate. The baseline model in this case is similar to equation (1.10) but with more elaborate explicit and implicit migration costs (that do not depend on skill level i).[38] Specifically, higher explicit migration costs yield a positive selection bias for those who earn the highest wages in the destination since their gains are large enough to offset the high costs.

Alternatively, Chiquiar and Hanson (2005) extend the Borjas model to incorporate migration costs that decrease in education with self-selection in observable levels of education. In this environment, high-skill migrants face relatively low migration costs. This, combined with the selectivity of skills, can explain why Mexican immigrants in the US are more educated than their counterparts in Mexico, but less educated than the average US citizen.

---

[37] We have simplified notation for ease of exposition. A complete description of the Borjas (1987) model can be found in Bodvarsson and Van den Berg (2009).

[38] Once again, we refer the interested reader to Bodvarsson and Van den Berg (2009), who offer a comprehensive description of the Chiswick (1999) model.

In recent work, Grogger and Hanson (2011) developed a model where absolute differences in earnings and fixed migration costs are the primary determinants of migration, rather than relative earnings and costs (as in Borjas, 1987, 1991). In fact, our simple model outlined in equation (1.10) is very close to the specification of Grogger and Hanson (2011), but they include an unobserved idiosyncratic component in utility. They also decompose the migration costs into fixed monetary costs (specific to the origin–destination pair) and a component that varies by skill. The model of Grogger and Hanson (2011) suggests that increases in the absolute differences in earnings between high- and low-skilled workers in destination regions lead to more migration, and the mix of migrants is more skilled.

3.1.5 Accounting for income inequality
In equation (1.10), after-tax wages are the relevant measure of income since the model represents an individual's migration decision. This is consistent with microeconomic models of migration that use wages as a measure of income (such as Borjas, 1987, 1991; Chiquiar and Hanson, 2005; Orrenius and Zavodny, 2005; and Hunt, 2006). However, the model can be generalized to the macro-level by incorporating aggregate measures of income (such as GDP). In fact, some measure of income in the origin and/or destination country is included in almost every model explaining international migration. Recently, Clark et al. (2007), Lewer and Van den Berg (2008), Lewer et al. (2009), Ortega and Peri (2009), and Mayda (2010) all incorporate per-capita GDP (in the origin and/or destination country) as a key determinant of cross-country immigrant flows.

In addition to average income, the individual's relative income position within a society forms part of the decision to migrate, as discussed in Section 2.3.6 above. This provides a theoretical foundation for the empirical observation that migration rates in the poorest regions are not necessarily the highest, and that migration rates increase with income inequality. Borjas (1987) shows that, conditional on mean wages, high-skill immigrants from low inequality locations prefer to move to relatively high inequality locations, while the low skilled will prefer relatively low inequality locations (although Chiswick (1999) points out that this finding emerges due to the lack of fixed migration costs in the model). Stark (1991) also discusses income inequality as a determinant of immigration. According to Rotte and Vogler (1998, p. 5), "There is a higher incentive to migrate if one is poor among rich than if one is poor among poor." Rotte and Vogler (2000), Brücker and Defoort (2006), Brücker and Schröder (2006), Clark et al. (2007), Ortega and Peri (2009), and Mayda (2010) are among others to present theoretical models incorporating income inequality as a determinant of bilateral migration flows.

3.1.6 Introducing credit and poverty constraints
An important literature has emerged on the role of credit constraints in migration. There are often significant costs to migration, but if perfect credit markets exist, migrants could

borrow to finance these costs. However, credit markets are imperfect, and more so in developing countries. In addition, future income streams are uncertain with migration, making financial contracts difficult to impose. Such constraints provide an explanation for a phenomenon regularly found in the empirical literature and discussed earlier—that pull effects are stronger determinants of migration than push effects (see Hunt, 2006; Pedersen et al., 2008; Warin and Svaton, 2008; Zaiceva and Zimmermann, 2008; and Mayda, 2010). That is, poverty constraints and imperfect capital markets might prevent source region income from affecting migration decisions since worsening conditions simultaneously increase the incentive to leave while decreasing the ability to do so.

Orrenius and Zavodny (2005) built on the Borjas (1987) selection model to incorporate features involving access to credit markets. In their model, migrants must save to cover migration costs. Since access to formal and informal credit markets varies with income, Orrenius and Zavodny (2005) assume that savings and hence the migration decision depends on the level of human capital. By imposing a cash-in-advance constraint, their model argues that tight credit constraints and insufficient savings to cover up-front migration costs have worked to limit unskilled Mexican migration to the US below levels that would otherwise occur.

Belot and Hatton (2008) and Hatton and Williamson (2011) also include poverty constraints as a determinant of emigration. The premise is that potential migrants from developing countries who live near the subsistence level will not be able to provide collateral for future earnings since the earnings will be acquired abroad, making it difficult for the lender to recoup loan payments. However, migrant networks may mitigate the poverty constraint via remittances (which will be discussed more below) and financial support upon arrival. For individuals with high migration costs and low levels of skills, the poverty constraint will more likely be binding. For individuals with access to larger migrant networks, the poverty constraint will less likely be binding.[39]

3.1.7 Accounting for unemployment

In the simple model above, expected wages depend upon both wages of employees and the probability of being employed in each period. Thus, unemployment could be incorporated directly into the model via expected wages and can affect migrant selectivity (Karemera et al., 2000; Pedersen et al., 2008). Migrants are predicted to move to high wage and low unemployment regions (Hunt, 2006). In addition, unemployment rates are higher among illegal migrants (than legal ones) since it is more difficult to obtain employment and employers often face sanctions for hiring undocumented migrants. Thus, the flow of illegal immigrants is likely to be more responsive to unemployment rates than would be the flow of legal immigrants. In addition, attitudes toward

---

[39] Shen et al. (2010) also included credit constraints to analyze the effect of migration and remittances on inequality.

immigration tend to move with business cycles. As the macroeconomy worsens, so does the pressure to hire native workers, making it more difficult for legal and illegal immigrants to find work.

3.1.8 Incorporating taxes and social insurance

The model in equation (1.10) consists of wages net of taxes and government transfers. Both components can be treated as independent factors that affect the migration decision, such that equation (1.10) can be expressed explicitly in terms of taxes and transfers, as in

$$\text{Migration rate}^i_{A,B} = \left[w^i_A \left(1 - \tau^i_A \right) + T^i_A \right] - \left[w^i_B \left(1 - \tau^i_B \right) + T^i_B \right] - \gamma^i_{A,B} \qquad (1.12)$$

where τ^i_j, T^i_j are the tax rate and government transfers respectively in region j for a worker of skill i. Once again, the migration rate depends critically on human capital via taxes and government transfers, in addition to wages and migration costs. Notice that the migration rate falls with the tax rate and rises with government transfers at the destination region B, and vice versa with respect to the origin region A, *ceteris paribus*.

Government transfers in the destination (as a form of social insurance) may act as a magnet for immigrants. Welfare payments can be viewed as a substitute for earnings during the time spent searching for a job, mitigating unemployment risk. The theoretical model of Borjas (1999), for example, suggests that given high migration costs, immigrants will geographically sort themselves into US states that offer generous welfare benefits, and more so than natives. Borjas and Trejo (1993) found that origin country characteristics explain a significant share of welfare participation rates in the United States. However, several studies have found no such effect, including Zavodny (1997), Urrutia (1998), and Pedersen et al.(2008).

Retirement or pension plans that expropriate wage income early in life and provide subsidies later in life have the potential to affect the migration decision at various stages of the life-cycle. For example, the degree of portability of pension plans may influence the migration decision. In addition, the generosity of public pension plans may act as an additional magnet for immigrants, or the high taxes needed to finance these generous systems may deter immigration. While there is literature that examines the role that immigration may play in financing pension plans (Storesletten, 2000; Krieger, 2005), little work exists that considers how pension plans (private or public) influence the migration decision.

Notice that in equation (1.12), if the government budget is assumed to balance in each region, the transfers T^i_j would drop out of the migration rate, such that only the tax rate matters in the migration decision. High tax rates among destination regions may detract immigrants by reducing the relative return to labor, but tax rates are typically highly (positively) correlated with public social expenditure, which may attract immigrants (according to the welfare magnet theory). Thus, it is not clear in equation (1.12) how taxation in both the origin and destination regions affects migration. In practical terms, tax rates are relevant only for relatively rich origin and destination countries in which income taxes are collected, and for high-skilled individuals who face non-trivial income tax rates. However, little work has been done that isolates the effect of taxation on international migration. One exception is Andersen (2005), who analyzes the role that taxes play in reducing the incentive for skilled workers to emigrate.

3.1.9 Accounting for political institutions

Recent work has explored the role of political institutions in influencing immigrant flows. Following Mayda (2010), one way to embed political institutions into a theoretical migration model is to assume that pairs of destination and origin countries with similar institutions should have lower migration costs. Empirical work often proxies this by identifying countries with common colonial ties (Mayda, 2010) or measures of political freedom (Rotte and Vogler, 2000). Alternatively, Hatton and Williamson (2011) consider the role of political events in the origin country on immigration, including civil wars, upheavals, and abuse of human and civil rights. In their model, political rights are captured by potential immigrants having non-economic preferences for their origin country. Equation (1.10) can be rewritten as:

$$\text{Migration rate}^i_{A,B} = w^i_A - w^i_B - \gamma^i_{A,B} - z^i_{A,B} \tag{1.13}$$

where $z^i_{A,B}$ represents the compensating differential of an individual's non-economic preference to immigrate from region A to region B. For example, if the political situation in the origin is bad relative to the situation in the destination, $z^i_{A,B}$ could be negative, increasing the benefits of migration and hence the migration rate.

In addition, political rights, individual freedom, and political instability may affect the migration decision, as empirically documented in Karemera et al. (2000). These ideas stem from Borjas (1989), who discusses how political conditions may affect the non-random sorting of immigrants, especially for refugees. Migration might also affect corruption in the destination country. For example, Mariani (2007) developed a model of migration in which high-skilled workers moving abroad choose between rent-seeking behavior (i.e., corruptive activities) and productive activities. Mariani (2007) found that with endogenous migration, "There is even less room for a positive role of skilled labor mobility in the perspective of reducing rent-seeking (in the destination country)" (p. 627).

3.2 A static human capital model with endogenous migration and endogenous wages

Wages are exogenous in the models presented in the previous subsection as there is no general equilibrium adjustment when labor moves across countries (or regions). We now relax this assumption and allow the stock of unskilled labor in each region to depend upon three things: (i) the measure of unskilled agents in the world (Ω_u); (ii) the fraction of unskilled agents who migrate to that region (λ^u to region A and $1 - \lambda^u$ to region B); and (iii) the amount of labor supplied by unskilled agents, ($1 - l^u$). Note that labor supply is now elastic (above it was assumed to be inelastic). The quantities of unskilled labor in regions A and B are $U_A = \Omega_u \lambda^u (1 - l^u)$ and $U_B = \Omega_u (1 - \lambda^u)(1 - l^u)$. Similarly, the amount of skilled labor in each region depends on the measure of skilled agents (Ω_s), the fraction of skilled agents who migrate to that country (λ^s in country A and $1 - \lambda^s$ in country B), and the amount of labor supplied by skilled agents $(1 - l^u)$ so that $S_A = \Omega_s \lambda^s (1 - l^s)$ and $S_B = \Omega_s (1 - \lambda^s)(1 - l^s)$.

In this framework, profit maximization of the representative firm delivers first-order conditions that determine wages. Depending on the specification of the production function $F_j(Z_j, U_j, S_j)$ in each region j where Z_j represents total factor productivity (TFP), unskilled and skilled labor could be complements or substitutes in production. Either way, diminishing marginal returns imply that an increased number of unskilled (skilled) workers in a region will reduce the unskilled (skilled) wage rate. Hence, unskilled wages in region j are now: $w_j^u = \partial F_j(Z_j, U_j, S_j)/\partial U_j$ and skilled wages are $w_j^s = \partial F_j(Z_j, U_j, S_j)/\partial S_j$. Migration will change the relative returns to skills that each region offers. For example, a large inflow of unskilled immigrants into a region will lower the unskilled wage rate, reducing the incentive for more immigration. In addition, TFP in each region will have important effects on the relative wage in each region. In equilibrium, individuals must still be indifferent to living in the origin and destination region, once migration costs are considered.

With endogenous wages, the model yields the following specification:

$$\text{Migration rate}_{A,B}^i = M\left(Z_A, U_A, S_A, Z_B, U_B, S_B, \gamma_{A,B}^i\right) \tag{1.14}$$

where $M(\ )$ is a function that depends on the production function specification $F(\ )$. Different from equation (1.10), the migration rate depends on the stock of unskilled and skilled labor in each region (which includes both domestic and foreign workers) and TFP differentials, but it does not depend on exogenous wage differentials.

This specification is consistent with the literature that considers schooling levels, demographics, and income levels as important determinants of immigration. For example, Hatton and Williamson (2011) focused on the supply side of immigration by considering how origin country demographics and education affect emigration from developing countries. In their specification, income depends on human capital levels in each country and an idiosyncratic component that may vary across countries. In addition, migration rates depend positively on the proportion of young adults in the population and on network effects (as discussed in Section 2.3.7). For example, Hunt (2006) claimed that younger people are more likely to migrate since they have (i) a longer time horizon to recoup migration costs; (ii) more time to benefit from good economic conditions abroad; (iii) less firm- and location-specific human capital than older people, lowering their costs of migration; and (iv) less on-the-job training and hence a lower opportunity cost of time, thus lowering their cost of human capital investment.

3.2.1 Accounting for network effects

Notice that with endogenous wages, the migration model suggests that the stock of workers (of each skill type) affects the return to migration. The stock of workers in the destination region is comprised of natives and previous migrants, and given the assumptions about the complementarities in production between workers of various skill levels and regions of origin, it is plausible that new immigrants benefit both directly and indirectly from having a network of migrants in the destination (as discussed in Section 2.3.2). This could be modeled explicitly, as a stock of workers from the same origin region, or via migration costs—migrants with a larger network may experience lower migration costs, increasing the net gain of migration (Carrington et al., 1996; Munshi, 2003; Pedersen et al., 2008; McKenzie and Rapoport, 2010). In fact, the pattern of migrant selectivity can heavily rely on the existence and use of networks. As a result, much of the immigration literature incorporates the stock of previous migrants from the origin country residing in the destination country as an important determinant in international migration, including work by Bartel (1989), Bauer and Zimmermann (1995), Zavodny (1997), Orrenius and Zavodny (2005), Clark et al. (2007), Mayda (2010), Hatton and Williamson (2011), Grogger and Hanson (2011), and Simpson and Sparber (2013).

3.2.2 Distinguishing between individual and household migration decisions

As noted in Section 2.3.5, most migration models focus on the individual's decision even though migration is often a family decision. If the family unit as a whole decides whether it will migrate or if it sends a member of the household abroad, then the model must incorporate the consumption, income, and migration costs of the entire family. Immigration is a form of insurance against household and macro-level shocks in the origin country. Remittances (which are discussed in more detail below) are the primary insurance mechanism for migrants and allow family members who migrate abroad the opportunity to send a portion of their income back home. In addition, families often help to relax the tight borrowing constraints that potential migrants face, especially to help finance the move. Recent work on migration as a family decision (Anam et al., 2008; Shen et al., 2010) indicates that real option theory can pinpoint the optimal migration time and length when households desire to diversify the location of family members in order to reduce income risk, for example.

3.2.3 The relationship between trade and migration

Iranzo and Peri (2009) provided a theoretical connection between trade and migration by expanding the Heckscher–Ohlin two-country trade model. Individuals are differentiated by skill, and countries possess different levels of technology. Firms in each country are monopolistically competitive, and gains from trade arise from increased product variety.

Technology complements skills, thereby implying that skilled agents from low-technology countries have the greatest incentive to migrate.

In the absence of trade and with low migration costs, Iranzo and Peri (2009) found that workers at the tails of the skill distribution have the incentive to migrate, consistent with the self-selection model. The presence of trade has small effects on the migration decision. Though this implies that the model offers predictions similar to more typical models of the determinants of migration, the implication sharply contrasts with the Heckscher–Ohlin model since differences in technology allow for factor price differences to persist, providing workers with a continued incentive to migrate across borders.

3.3 Dynamic models with endogenous migration and physical capital accumulation

In most of the discussion so far, migration has been treated as an event that occurs once, such that the benefits and costs of migration are experienced instantaneously (or at least are modeled as such). Developments in dynamic stochastic general equilibrium modeling have allowed researchers to model the migration decision within a more realistic setting. In this section, we highlight how the theory on international migration has evolved in recent years to incorporate the dynamics of the migration decision and show, once again, that human capital is a central component to this decision.

A few studies have endogenized migration in a dynamic general equilibrium framework. Examples include Galor (1986), Djajic (1989), Glomm (1992), Wong (1997), Urrutia (1998), Klein and Ventura (2009), and Mandelman and Zlate (2012). The standard dynamic model of endogenous migration extends the baseline model in equation (1.10) to incorporate physical capital accumulation. If physical capital is assumed to be mobile, then a fixed factor of production (such as land) with diminishing returns must be introduced to guarantee equilibrium in which labor and capital are moving across the two regions without moving costs (Wildasin, 1994; Simpson, 2001; Klein and Ventura, 2009). A life-cycle model of migration assumes that agents live for T periods, accumulate assets that are used as income streams in future periods, and make a migration decision at some point during their lifetimes that may be reversed in future periods to allow for return migration.

The utility an agent receives would then depend on her capital accumulation and migration decisions. For now, we assume that there are no borrowing/lending restrictions in the model and that there is no return migration. Also, human capital is exogenous (which we will relax below), such that agents are either unskilled or skilled. Agents compare the present value of lifetime income among four alternatives: (1) remain unskilled and stay in the home region; (2) remain unskilled and migrate; (3) invest in education and stay in the source region; or (4) invest in education and migrate. The value function for an agent represents the best choice of these four options. In this setting, agents face migration costs (which are once again specific to skill level within the region of origin).

With perfect capital mobility, the return to physical capital is equal across regions. In interior solution equilibria, an agent from region j must be indifferent to the four alternatives. Hence, the migration decision depends on the relative returns to skills in each region (net of taxes and government transfers), migration costs, the stock of unskilled and skilled workers in each region, the stock of physical capital in each region (K_A, K_B), the stock of land in each region (L_A, L_B), and the relationship between the production inputs (assuming endogenous factor prices). That is, the migration rate for individuals of skill i and age a would depend on:

$$\text{Migration rate}_{A,B}^{i,a} = M\left(Z_A, U_A, S_A, Z_B, U_B, S_B, \gamma_{A,B}^i, \tau_A^i, \tau_B^i, K_A, K_B, L_A, L_B\right) \quad (1.15)$$

where all variables are defined as before, i denotes skill level, A is the origin region and B is the destination, and assuming a government budget constraint holds in each region (the time subscripts are dropped for ease of exposition). If factor prices are exogenous, equation (1.15) would not depend on the inputs to production (Z_j, U_j, S_j, K_j, L_j) in region j but instead depends on exogenous factor prices (w_j, R, q_j), where R is the world interest rate (net of depreciation) and q_j is the return on land in each region. An important innovation in the dynamic setting from Klein and Ventura (2009) is that migration rates are heterogeneous with respect to age and hence can vary over the life-cycle. Note, however, that given the interrelatedness of the endogenous and exogenous variables over time, the researcher cannot obtain closed-form solutions for equation (1.15) under reasonable assumptions for utility, production, and human capital accumulation functions. Most often, the researcher must resort to computational methods to obtain solutions, following Urrutia (1998), Klein and Ventura (2009), and Mandelman and Zlate (2012).

Urrutia (1998) uses a dynastic overlapping generations model to analyze the effect of migration costs on the self-selection of immigrants, building on the work of Borjas (1987) and Chiswick (1999) in which human capital is exogenous. Migration costs, which include fixed costs and loss of ability (as in Chiswick, 1999), dictate the selectivity of migrants in a dynamic model of endogenous migration. When the fixed cost is relatively low, immigrants are selected from the bottom of the ability distribution. The opposite occurs if the fixed migration cost is relatively high.

The dynamic model of Klein and Ventura (2009) considered the role of TFP differentials across countries when barriers to entry exist. Barriers to entry include skill loss associated with migration and paying a fixed resource cost. In their framework, they find that modest productivity differentials lead to large increases in the migration rate. As a result, output differentials increase as capital chases labor into the country with the productivity advantage. They find that capital accumulation and mobility can accentuate the welfare losses of barriers to entry, consistent with the findings of Michael (2003). In fact, in their analysis of the transitional dynamics, Klein and Ventura (2009) found that the removal of barriers to entry has large and immediate effects on migration rates, but the effects dampen over time. The welfare gains associated with removing barriers to entry are significant, and are much larger than the losses experienced by natives of the destination country.

3.3.1 Immigration policy in a dynamic framework

In a dynamic framework, the effects of immigration policy on migration decisions are more complicated. Guzman et al. (2008) developed an overlapping generations model of migration in which technological progress in the smuggling industry has important effects on migration and savings decisions. For example, when smugglers are more efficient, migrants spend less time evading border patrol and more time working and saving in the destination country. Higher savings results in higher wages abroad but lower returns to savings. The net effect on migration depends on which of these two effects is larger. Similarly, Guzman et al. (2008) showed how tighter immigration policy via more border enforcement (which is financed by higher lump sum taxes) has ambiguous effects on migration rates because it lowers the capital–labor ratio in the destination country. In their framework, the key mechanism is how smuggling and border enforcement affects savings, and how the effects on savings translate into important effects for the migration decision. Importantly, the model assumes that migrants can contribute to the destination country's capital stock, following Benhabib (1996).

3.3.2 Accounting for remittance behavior

In equation (1.15), the migration rate depends on the level of capital stock in each region. Migrants save throughout their lifetimes, and those savings can be used to finance consumption during retirement. However, migrants' savings are being increasingly used to finance contemporaneous consumption of the individual's family left back home (in the origin country). Worldwide, remittances represent a significant component of GDP for countries that are large suppliers of immigrants. In the model, remittances can be thought of as part of the savings decision, with that portion of the capital stock going back to the origin country. That is, the location of the capital stock matters, and must be accounted for in the model. The migration decision will depend on the expected remittance behavior of a potential migrant, as often dictated by other family members (requiring the model to be representative of a household rather than an individual). Or one can assume that remittances alleviate credit constraints of the migrant, lowering the costs of migration (as discussed below).

A recent paper by Shen et al. (2010) developed a dynamic model of the household's migration decision where households face liquidity constraints, bequests are used to smooth intergenerational income, and remittances equalize income within a household (of both migrants and non-migrants). The focus of the paper is to analyze how migration and remittance behavior affects income inequality in the origin country, but the framework allows for endogenous migration and remittance decisions.[40]

---

[40] A related paper by Rapoport and Docquier (2006) provided a review of the determinants of remittances.

Taking a different approach, Mandelman and Zlate (2012) quantified the extent to which immigration and remittances respond to business cycles in the origin and destination countries. Using a calibrated quantitative macroeconomic model, they found that immigration and remittance flows are procyclical such that in good times immigrant flows increase to the destination but in bad times they retreat. When the sunk costs of migration are lowered (which represent border enforcement), migrant flows are more responsive to business cycles. Important innovations in their paper consist of having both endogenous migration and remittance decisions, and assuming complex relationships between the inputs to production. For example, domestic and foreign labor are substitutes in production, whereas the capital of skilled and unskilled labor is imperfectly substitutable.

3.3.3 Dynamic models with human capital accumulation

Human capital is exogenous in the dynamic migration model described in equation (1.15). However, the model can be adjusted so that one may analyze the interaction between endogenous human capital accumulation and migration. In this environment, agents are endowed with an initial level of human capital, h_0^i (i.e. inherent ability), and benefit from the existing stock of human capital, H_t, in region j. Human capital evolves depending on the individual time investment (s_t^i, if labor supply is endogenous), explicit costs of financing education such as tuition fees (e_j), the migration decision (λ_t^i), and human capital depreciation via skill loss as a result of imperfect transferability of skills (δ_j^i). A human capital accumulation function could be specified as:

$$h_{t+1}^i = H\left(H_t^j, h_0^i, s_t^i, \lambda_t^i, e_j, \delta_j^i\right) \tag{1.16}$$

where H is a function that dictates the relationship between the various inputs of human capital over time. The standard assumptions regarding H are that human capital exhibits diminishing returns and that the inputs to production are complementary in the production of new human capital (Dustmann and Glitz, 2011). In this case, the migration rate would depend on education costs in each region (e_j) and migration costs, in addition to all of the other factors of production. The timing of the human capital decision is also important, since human capital accumulation could occur either simultaneously with or preceding the migration decision.

Chiswick and Miller (2011) considered the role of human capital investment for migration between two countries with similar income levels and a high degree of skill transferability. In the typical setting with imperfect skill transferability across countries, immigrants have the incentive to invest in their human capital following migration as a way to increase their earnings abroad and to catch up to natives. However, when skills are perfectly transferable across countries (i.e., two rich countries with similar culture and language), there is no incentive for human capital accumulation following migration. In this setting, migration is a "two-way street." The earnings of immigrants, which are initially higher than natives, decline towards those of natives, allowing for the possibility of negative assimilation.

Dustmann and Glitz (2011) developed a comprehensive dynamic model with endogenous migration and human capital accumulation (but with exogenous wages and no savings decision). Their model allows for different types of migration patterns: the individual can migrate temporarily or permanently, and human capital can be acquired both at home and abroad. Hence, they incorporate migration decisions regarding the initial migration and the length of the migration. In this framework, migration decisions depend on the relative returns to skill in both the origin and destination, in addition to the length of migration (which, among other factors, affects the degree of skill transferability across countries). Similar to our dynamic framework (in equation (1.15)), the migration decision depends on the initial level of ability and the age of the migrant. Those with high ability and who migrate earlier in life experience steeper wage profiles and higher wage growth.

The Dustmann and Glitz (2011) model also can be used to analyze the flow of international students. For example, migrants who obtain skills abroad may be induced to return home to take advantage of the higher returns to skill. Earlier work by Rosenzweig (2006) developed a theoretical model of international student flows, where the transferability of skills across countries varies for individuals. For individuals who obtain schooling abroad, their skills are more easily transferable, leading to a higher return for skills and a higher likelihood of obtaining employment in the destination country.

3.3.4 Accounting for temporary, return, and circular migration

Most theories of migration treat it as an event that occurs only once. That is, individuals (or households) make the migration decision, and if they migrate, they remain in the destination country.[41] The dynamic model of equation (1.15) similarly ignores the possibility of multiple migration decisions. However, dynamic theoretical models of migration exist in which the initial migration is exogenous but the migrant living abroad can choose to move back home at some point in time. Galor and Stark (1990) provided a canonical two-period model, and found that the level of savings explicitly depends on the likelihood of returning home. Both Hill (1987) and Djajic and Milbourne (1988) developed life-cycle models of migration in which agents have a preference for location. Agents can choose total time allocated to working in the home and foreign country, in addition to the number of trips. Djajic and Milbourne (1988) focused on guest-worker migration and considered the interaction between savings and the length of stay in the foreign country. Recently, Dustmann and Mestres (2011) investigated the interaction between savings (physical capital accumulation) and return migration. The amount saved may affect when the agent finds it optimal to return home, and vice versa.

---

[41] Borjas and Bratsberg (1996) and Polachek and Horvath (1977) are early exceptions.

Several papers by Dustmann and co-authors have recently incorporated decisions regarding migration duration that aid in analyzing temporary migration (see Dustmann, 1997, 2003; Dustmann and Kirchkamp, 2002; Dustmann et al., 2011; Dustmann and Glitz, 2011; and Dustmann and Mestres, 2011). For example, Dustmann (2003) developed a dynamic model of return migration to determine how wage differentials between the origin and destination country affect the optimal migration duration. The stock of labor in each country depends not only on the migration decision and the net flow of migrants, but also on the duration of migration. Migration decisions are endogenous. As the stock of labor in each country adjusts, so do wages, which changes the migration decision. Durations decrease in response to increasing wage differentials.

Dustmann et al. (2011) allowed for the possibility that individuals obtain their human capital abroad and return home to capitalize on the relative high domestic returns to skill. That is, the location of human capital accumulation depends on the relative costs of skill acquisition and the rate at which skills are augmented in each country. They employ a dynamic Roy model where skills are two-dimensional such that skills evolve as migrants learn abroad (i.e. a "self-productive" strategy). As such, the selectivity of migrants depends on the returns to skill in each country and the composition of those who initially emigrate. The approach in Dustmann et al. (2011) is novel in that they obtained tractable solutions in a dynamic migration model and discussed how differences in skill transferability across countries can generate different migration outcomes, both in terms of emigration and return migration rates. This is quite promising for future work.

3.3.5 Dynamic models with human capital accumulation, circular migration, and brain drain

Dynamic models of migration and human capital formation are intimately tied to an important consequence of immigration feared by many policymakers—the potential exodus of high-skilled labor or what is often called "brain drain." In the dynamic migration model of Beine et al. (2008), individuals invest in education during their youth and choose to migrate in adulthood. Similar to the model above, human capital investment is costly and depends on ability and personal investment. In addition, individuals may face important credit constraints in acquiring education. To simplify the model, the authors assume that only skilled workers can migrate. Interestingly, the model predicts that losses from brain drain will be small as long as the skilled emigration rate does not get too high. Skilled migration raises the return on human capital in the source country, incentivizing non-migrants to invest in human capital. This "brain gain" helps offset the brain drain usually associated with skilled migration.[42]

[42] See Mountford (1997), Vidal (1998), and Beine et al. (2001, 2003) for further work indicating that the outflow of skills associated with brain drain may entice those at home to accumulate more skills. Fan and Yakita (2011) developed a two-period model of human capital to isolate the conditions when brain gain and brain drain occur.

Beine et al. (2008) are not alone in finding that brain drain fears may be overstated. Mayr and Peri (2009) combined the insights of Borjas and Bratsberg's (1996) model of return-migrant selection with those from the dynamic human capital acquisition literature in order to analyze joint education, migration, and return migration decisions under different policy environments. They found that both return migration and the education incentives of the sort envisioned by Beine et al. (2008) help to increase human capital levels in the source region. Furthermore, they demonstrated that the selection of return migrants depends upon both the initial selection of emigrants and whether wage premiums for having lived abroad vary across education level. Altogether, the evidence suggests that a richly specified model incorporating endogenous educational attainment and circular migration is necessary for a full understanding not only of the consequences of migration flows, but of their causes as well.

4. CONCLUSIONS AND IMPLICATIONS FOR FURTHER RESEARCH

In this chapter, we have surveyed theories of the economic determinants of migration. The chapter began by outlining the primary forces driving migration. Though some theories might stress the role of consumption, family decision-making, or various non-economic factors, the fundamental premise of most migration theories is that migration is driven by spatial differences in the net returns to factor supply and is a response to labor market disequilibrium. A big step in the development of migration theory was taken by Sjaastad (1962), who articulated a theory of migration as a form of human capital investment—people relocate because it adds to lifetime earnings.

In general, migration models are adept at describing both internal and international migration. That is, the human capital model is suitable for explaining both forms of labor flows. Nonetheless, authors have added specific features to the human capital model to focus on one form of migration over another. For example, Borjas (1987) applied Sjaastad's (1962) model to develop a theory of international migration, arguing that migration is not only influenced by net earnings differences between countries, but also by factors such as international differences in income inequality and the degree of skills transferability. Recently, Clark et al. (2007) extended this model to include the effects of immigration policy. Other authors have suggested that people move to assuage feelings of relative deprivation, as a solution to a household portfolio diversification problem, or to exploit migrant network effects flowing from the destination country.

The large literature examining the impact of international migration on destination and/or origin regions typically assumes that migration is exogenous (i.e., the flow of migrants across regions is fixed). However, many recent models have taken an important step in incorporating endogenous migration into theoretical models in order to fully account for both the determinants and consequences of migration. Such models might incorporate decisions regarding whether or not to migrate, the duration of residence away from home, and whether to migrate again. Factors influencing these decisions include the role of migration costs, immigration policy, income and income inequality, networks, family ties, political institutions, and trade. This is certainly not a comprehensive list, but it instead represents a starting point for researchers interested in considering other possible factors.

In an open-economy model (with two or more regions), the migration decision can be paired with other decisions, such as savings and schooling decisions, to allow for more complex and realistic depictions of the various pressures associated with migration. As we have documented, advances in recent years have allowed for these possibilities by using dynamic models of endogenous migration. The migration decision has long-lasting effects not only for migrants and their families, but also for residents of the origin and recipient regions. It is important to sort out how these effects feed into the individual migration decision and the consequent impact on aggregate migrant flows. For example, the general equilibrium effects that occur as large quantities of skilled and unskilled workers move across countries can be significant, and can change depending on how the capital stock evolves.

Despite the robust literature on the theoretical determinants of migration, we believe that plenty of work remains to be done. For example, a model that incorporates relocation and income remittance as joint decisions has yet to be fully explored. If remitting is the reason behind migration, then the migration decision has to be made with that in mind. Factors that affect remittances, such as the macroeconomic conditions in both the origin and destination countries, can be isolated so that policymakers can better understand how migrant flows respond to them. In fact, the extent to which business cycles in both the origin and destination affect the magnitude and composition of migrant flows is still not fully understood. Mandelman and Zlate (2012) represent an excellent starting point for this work. Also, work by Ben-Gad (2008) suggests that the degree of capital–skill complementarity in the production technology has important welfare implications for natives due to immigration. These production complementarities may be important to the immigration decision, as they change how skill-specific wages respond to the flow of unskilled and skilled labor and physical capital across countries. Determining the extent to which assumptions regarding the production technology change the size and composition of migrant flows is an avenue that is worth pursuing in the future.

Certainly, immigration policy is dynamic in that it responds to political and economic pressures over time. Currently, there is no dynamic political economy model that considers how immigration policy evolves over time and how it affects the composition and magnitude of migrant flows. Immigrant flows clearly respond to changes in policy, so understanding these linkages should be crucial in developing immigration policy.

We conclude by submitting that international migration flows are probably best explained by a unified theory that combines the current model of international migration as human capital investment with roles for household portfolio diversification, consumption interests, and migrant network effects. Theoretical issues that remain unaddressed or unresolved include:

1. The effects of migrant age on the propensity to migrate. Young migrants sacrifice less home-specific human capital and face a longer stream of potential earnings in destination regions. Nonetheless, older migrants might have greater propensities to migrate if, for example, they have larger assets to finance the migration decision or have larger general human capital endowments that can command high returns in the destination. More generally, there has been no thorough theoretical examination into how the source region's age distribution influences emigration rates.
2. The effects of exchange rates. Since many international migrants remit a portion of destination country earnings back to their home countries, exchange rates will influence the returns to migration. Exchange rates have not, however, appeared in theoretical models of migration.
3. The joint migration and remittance decision. The decision to migrate may occur at the same time as the remittance choice. How these joint decisions are made and their implications are not well understood.
4. Distinct determinants of illegal immigration. Very little theory has attempted to address whether the decision to be an illegal immigrant differs structurally from the decision to migrate legally.

The above list is not intended to be exhaustive, but includes topics that may be particularly fruitful at this time. While the lack of a unified theory might seem daunting, it is also very exciting, for it means that much innovative research lies ahead.

REFERENCES

Anam, M., Chiang, S., Hua, L., 2008. Uncertainty and international migration: An option cum portfolio model. J. Labor Res. 29 (3), 236–250.

Andersen, T.M., 2005. Migration, taxation and educational incentives. Econ. Lett. 87 (3), 399–405.

Anderson, J., 1979. A theoretical foundation for the gravity equation. Am. Econ. Rev. 69, 106–116.

Bartel, A.P., 1989. Where do the new United States immigrants live? J. Labor Econ. 7 (4), 371–391.

Bauer, T., Zimmermann, K.F., 1995. Integrating the East: The Labour Market Effects of Immigration, CEPR (Centre for Economic Policy Research) Discussion Paper No. 1235.

Beals, R., Levy, M., Moses, L., 1967. Rationality and migration in Ghana. Rev. Econ. Stat. 49, 480–486.

Becker, G., 1964. Human Capital: A Theoretical and Empirical Analysis, with Special Reference to Education. National Bureau of Economic Research, New York.

Becker, G., 1965. A theory of the allocation of time. Econ. J. 75, 493–517.

Beine, M., Docquier, F., Rapoport, H., 2001. Brain drain and economic growth: Theory and evidence. J. Dev. Econ. 64, 275–289, Elsevier.

Beine, M., Docquier, F., Rapoport, H., 2003. Brain Drain and LDCs' Growth: Winners and Losers, IZA (Institute for the Study of Labor) Discussion Paper No. 819.

Beine, M., Docquier, F., Rapoport, H., 2008. Brain drain and human capital formation in developing countries: Winners and losers. Econ. J. 118 (528), 631–652, Royal Economic Society.

Beine, M., Docquier, F., Oden-Defoort, C., 2011. A panel data analysis of the brain gain. World Dev. 39 (4), 523–532.

Belot, M.V.K., Hatton, T.J., 2008. Immigrant Selection in the OECD. CEPR (Centre for Economic Policy Research) Discussion Paper No. 571.

Ben-Gad, M., 2008. Capital-skill complementarities and the immigration surplus. Rev. Econ. Dynam. 11, 335–365.

Benhabib, J., 1996. On the political economy of immigration. Eur. Econ. Rev. 40 (9), 1737–1743.

Bhagwati, J., Srinivasan, T., 1974. On reanalyzing the Harris-Todaro model: Policy rankings in the case of sector-specific sticky wages. Am. Econ. Rev. 64, 1063–1093.

Bodvarsson, Ö., Hou, J.W., 2010. The Effects of Aging on Migration in a Transition Economy: The Case of China. IZA Discussion Paper 5070, http://www.iza.org.

Bodvarsson, Ö., Van den Berg, H.F., 2009. The Economics of Immigration: Theory and Policy. Springer, Heidelberg, Germany.

Borjas, G.J., 1987. Self-selection and the earnings of immigrants. Am. Econ. Rev. 77 (4), 531–553.

Borjas, G.J., 1989. Economic theory and international migration. Intern. Mig. Rev 23 (3), 457–485.

Borjas, G.J., 1991. Immigration and self-selection. In: Abowd, J.M., Freeman, R.B. (Eds.), Immigration, Trade and the Labor Market. University of Chicago Press, pp. 29–76.

Borjas, G.J., 1999. Immigration and welfare markets. J. Lab. Econ. 17 (4), 607–637.

Borjas, G.J., Bratsberg, B., 1996. Who leaves? The outmigration of the foreign-born. Rev. Econ. Stat. 78 (1), 165–176.

Borjas, G., Trejo, S.J., 1993. National origin and immigrant welfare recipiency. J. Publ. Econ. 50 (3), 325–344, Elsevier.

Brücker, H., Defoort, D., 2006. Inequality and the (self-)selection of international migrants: theory and novel evidence, IZA Discussion Paper 2052.

Brücker, H., Schröder, P.J.H., 2006. International Migration with Heterogeneous Agents: Theory and Evidence, IZA (Institute for the Study of Labor) Discussion Paper No. 2049.

Burda, M., 1993. The determinants of East-West German migration. Eur. Econ. Rev. 37, 452–461.

Burda, M., 1995. Migration and the option value of waiting. Econ. Soc. Rev. 27, 1–19.

Calvo, G., 1978. Urban unemployment and wage determination in LDCs: Trade unions in the Harris-Todaro model. Int. Econ. Rev. 19, 65–81.

Carrington, W.J., Detragiache, E., Vishwanath, T., 1996. Migration with endogenous moving costs. Am. Econ. Rev. 86 (4), 909–930.

Chiquiar, D., Hanson, G.H., 2005. International migration, self-selection, and the distribution of wages: Evidence from Mexico and the United States. J. Polit. Econ. 113 (2), 239–281.

Chiswick, B., 1999. Are immigrants favorably self-selected? Am. Econ. Rev. 89 (2), 181–185.

Chiswick, B.R., Miller, P.W., 2011. The "negative" assimilation of immigrants: A special case. Ind. Labor Relat. Rev. 64 (3), 502–525.

Clark, X., Hatton, T.J., Williamson, J.G., 2007. Explaining U.S. immigration, 1971–1998. Rev. Econ. Stat. 89 (2), 359–373.

Corden, W., Findlay, R., 1975. Urban unemployment, intersectoral capital mobility and development policy. Economica 42, 59–78.

David, P., 1974. Fortune, risk, and the micro-economics of migration. In: David, P., Reder, M. (Eds.), Nations and Households in Economic Growth. Academic Press, New York.

Deardorff, A., 1998. Determinants of bilateral trade: Does gravity work in a classical World? In: Frankel, J. (Ed.), Regionalization of the World Economy. University of Chicago Press, Chicago.

Djajic, S., 1989. Skills and the pattern of migration: The role of qualitative and quantitative restrictions on international labour mobility. Int. Econ. Rev. 30, 795–809.

Djajic, S., Milbourne, R., 1988. A general equilibrium model of guest-worker migration: A source-country perspective. J. Int. Econ. 25, 335–351.

Douglas, P., 1919. Is the new immigration more unskilled than the old? Reprinted in: Zimmermann, K., Bauer, T., 2002. The Economics of Migration. vol. 3. Elgar, Northampton, MA.

Dustmann, C., 1997. Return migration, uncertainty and precautionary savings. J. Dev. Econ. 52, 295–316.

Dustmann, C., 2003. Return migration, wage differentials, and the optimal migration duration. Eur. Econ. Rev. 47 (2), 353–369.

Dustmann, C., Glitz, A., 2011. Migration and education. In: Hanushek, E., Machin, S., Woessman, L. (Eds.), Handbook for the Economics of Education. vol. 4. North Holland, Amsterdam, The Netherlands, pp. 327–439.

Dustmann, C., Kirchkamp, O., 2002. The optimal migration duration and activity choice after re-migration. J. Dev. Econ. 67, 351–372.

Dustmann, C., Mestres, J., 2011. Savings, Asset Holdings, and Temporary Migration. IZA (Institute for the Study of Labor) Discussion Paper No. 5498.

Dustmann, C., Fadlon, I., Weiss, Y., 2011. Return migration, human capital accumulation and the brain drain. J. Dev. Econ. 95 (1), 58–67.

Ethier, W.J., 1986. Illegal immigration. Am. Econ. Rev. 76 (2), 258–262.

Fan, X., Yakita, A., 2011. Brain drain and technological relationship between skilled and unskilled labor: Brain gain or brain loss? J. Popul. Econ. 24 (4), 1359–1368, Springer.

Fields, G., 1979. Place-to-place migration: Some new evidence. Rev. Econ. Stat. 56, 21–32.

Gallaway, L., 1969. Age and labor mobility patterns. South. Econ. J. 36, 171–180.

Galor, O., 1986. Time preference and international labor migration. J. Econ. Theor. 38, 1–20.

Galor, O., Stark, O., 1990. Migrants' savings, the probability of return migration and migrants' performance. Int. Econ. Rev. 31 (2), 463–467.

Ghatak, S., Levine, P., Price, S., 1996. Migration theories and evidence: An assessment. J. Econ. Lit. 10, 159–198.

Glaeser, E., Shapiro, J., 2003. Urban growth in the 1990s: Is city living back? J. Reg. Sci. 43, 139–165.

Glomm, G., 1992. A model of growth and migration. Canadian Journal of Economics 24 (4), 901–922.

Goodman, J., 1981. Information, uncertainty, and the microeconomic model of migration decision making. In: De Jong, G., Gardner, R. (Eds.), Migration Decision Making: Multidisciplinary Approaches to Micro-Level Studies in Developed and Developing Countries. Pergamon Press, New York.

Gorter, C., Nijkamp, P., Poot, J., 1998. Regional and urban perspectives on international migration: An overview. In: Gorter, C., Nijkamp, P., Poot, J. (Eds.), Crossing Borders: Regional and Urban Perspectives on International Migration. Brookfield Ashgate, UK.

Graves, P., 1979. A life-cycle empirical analysis of migration and climate, by race. J. Urban Econ. 6, 135–147.

Graves, P., 1983. Migration with a composite amenity: The role of rents. J. Reg. Sci. 23, 541–546.

Green, G., Deller, S., Marcouiller, D., 2006. Amenities and Rural Development Theory, Methods, and Public Policy. Elgar, Northampton, MA.

Greenwood, M., 1975. Research on internal migration in the United States: A survey. J. Econ. Lit. 13, 397–433.

Greenwood, M., 1985. Human migration: theory, models and empirical studies. J. Reg. Sci. 25, 521–544.

Greenwood, M., 1997. Internal migration in developed countries. In: Rosenzweig, M., Stark, O. (Eds.), Handbook of Population and Family Economics. Elsevier, Amsterdam.

Grogger, J., Hanson, G.H., 2011. Income maximization and the selection and sorting of international migrants. J. Dev. Econ. 95 (1), 42–57, Elsevier.

Guzman, M.G., Haslag, J.H., Orrenius, P.M., 2008. On the determinants of optimal border enforcement. Econ. Theor. 34 (2), 261–296.

Hansen, M., 1940. The Mingling of the Canadian and American Peoples. Russel & Russel, New York.

Harris, J., Todaro, M., 1970. Migration, unemployment and development: A two-sector analysis. Am. Econ. Rev. 60, 126–142.

Hatton, T.J., Williamson, J.G., 2011. Are Third World emigration forces abating? World Dev. 39 (1), 20–32.

Hicks, J., 1932. The Theory of Wages. Macmillan, London.

Hill, J.K., 1987. Immigrant decisions concerning duration of stay and migratory frequency. J. Dev. Econ. 25 (1), 221–234.

Hugo, G., 1981. Village-community ties, village norms, and ethnic and social networks: A review of evidence from the third World. In: Dejong, J., Gardner, R. (Eds.), Migration Decision Making: Multidisciplinary Approaches to Micro-Level Studies in Developed and Developing Countries. Pergamon Press, New York.

Hunt, J., 2006. Staunching emigration from East Germany: Age and the determinants of migration. J. Eur. Econ. Assoc. 4 (5), 1014–1037.

Iranzo, S., Peri, G., 2009. Migration and trade: Theory with an application to the Eastern-Western European integration. J. Int. Econ. 79 (1), 1–19.

Jerome, H., 1926. Migration and Business Cycles. National Bureau of Economic Research, New York.

Karemera, D., Oguledo, V.I., Davis, B., 2000. A gravity model analysis of international migration to North America. Appl. Econ. 32 (13), 1745–1755.

Katz, E., Stark, O., 1986. Labor migration and risk aversion in less developed countries. J. Labor Econ. 4 (1), 134–149.

Klein, P., Ventura, G., 2009. Productivity differences and the dynamic effects of labor movements. J. Monetary Econ. 56, 1059–1073.

Krieger, T., 2005. Public Pensions and Immigration: A Public Choice Approach. Elgar, Northampton, MA.

Kuznets, S., Rubin, R., 1954. National Bureau of Economic Research Occasional Paper 46. Immigration and the Foreign Born. National Bureau of Economic Research, New York.

Lall, S., Selod, H., Shalizi, Z., 2006. Rural–Urban Migration in Developing Countries: A Survey of Theoretical Predictions and Empirical Findings, World Bank Policy Research Working Paper 3915.

Lancaster, K., 1966. A new approach to consumer theory. J. Polit. Econ. 74, 132–157.

Lewer, J.J., Van den Berg, H., 2008. A gravity model of immigration. Econ. Lett. 99 (1), 164–167.

Lewer, J.J., Pacheco, G., Rossouw, S., 2009. Do Non-Economic Quality of Life Factors Drive Immigration. IZA Discussion Paper No. 4385.

Linneman, H., 1966. An Econometric Study of International Trade Flows. North-Holland, Amsterdam.

Lucas, R., 1997. Internal migration in developing countries. In: Rosenzweig, M., Stark, O. (Eds.), Handbook of Population and Family Economics. Elsevier, Amsterdam.

Lundborg, P., 1991. An interpretation of the effects of age on migration: Nordic migrants' choice of settlement in Sweden. South. Econ. J. 58, 392–405.

Mandelman, F., Zlate, A., 2012. Immigration, remittances and business cycles. J. Monetary Econ. 59 (2), 196–213, Elsevier.

Mariani, F., 2007. Migration as an antidote to rent-seeking. J. Dev. Econ. 84 (2), 609–630.

Massey, D., Garcia Espana, F., 1987. The social process of international migration. Science 237, 733–738.

Massey, D., Arango, J., Graeme, H., Kouaouchi, A., Pellegrino, A., Taylor, J., 1993. Theories of international migration: A review and appraisal. Popul. Dev. Rev. 19, 431–466.

Mayda, A.M., 2010. International migration: A panel data analysis of the determinants of bilateral flows. J. Popul. Econ. 23 (4), 1249–1274.

Mayr, K., Peri, G., 2009. Brain drain and brain return: Theory and application to Eastern–Western Europe. B. E. J. Econ. Anal. Pol. 9 (1), Article 49.

McCall, B., McCall, J., 1987. A sequential study of migration and job search. J. Labor Econ. 5, 452–476.

McKenzie, D., Rapoport, H., 2010. Self-selection patterns in Mexico U.S. migration: The role of migration networks. Rev. Econ. Stat. 92 (4), 811–821.

Michael, M.S., 2003. International migration, income taxes and transfers: A welfare analysis. J. Dev. Econ. 72, 401–411, Elsevier.

Mincer, J., 1978. Family migration decisions. J. Polit. Econ. 86 (5), 749–773.

Molho, I., 1986. Theories of migration: A review. Scot. J. Polit. Econ. 33, 396–401.

Mountford, A., 1997. Can a brain drain be good for growth in the source economy. J. Dev. Econ. 53 (2), 287–303.

Munshi, K., 2003. Networks in the modern economy: Mexican migrants in the U.S. labor market. Q. J. Econ. 118 (2), 549–599.

Orrenius, P.M., Zavodny, M., 2005. Self-selection among undocumented immigrants from Mexico. J. Dev. Econ. 78, 215–224, Elsevier.

Ortega, F., Peri, G., 2009. The Causes and Effects of International Migration: Evidence from OECD Countries 1980–2005. NBER. Working Paper No. 14833.

Pedersen, P.J., Pytlikova, M., Smith, N., 2008. Selection and network effects: Migration flows into OECD countries 1990–2000. Eur. Econ. Rev. 52, 1160–1186.

Pickles, A., Rogerson, P., 1984. Wage distribution and spatial preferences in competitive job search and migration. Reg. Sci. 18, 131–142.

Polachek, S., Horvath, F., 1977. A life cycle approach to migration: Analysis of the perspicacious peregrinator. In: Ehrenberg, R. (Ed.), Research in Labor Economics. JAI Press, Greenwich, CT.

Rapoport, H., Docquier, F., 2006. The economics of migrants' remittances. Handbook on the Economics of Giving, Reciprocity and Altruism. Elsevier.

Ravenstein, E., 1889. The laws of migration. J. Roy. Stat. Soc. 52, 241–305.

Rogerson, R., 1988. Indivisible labor, lotteries and equilibrium. Journal of Monetary Theory and Policy 21 (1), 3–16.

Rosen, S., 1974. Hedonic prices and implicit markets: Product differentiation in pure competition. J. Polit. Econ. 82, 34–55.

Rosenzweig, M., 2006. Global wage differences and international student flows. In: Collins, S., Graham, C. (Eds.), Brookings Trade Forum 2006: Global Labor Markets? Brookings Institution Press, Washington, DC.

Rotte, R., Vogler, M., 1998. Determinants of International Migration: Empirical Evidence for Migration from Developing Countries to Germany. IZA (Institute for the Study of Labor) Discussion Paper No. 12.

Rotte, R., Vogler, M., 2000. The effects of development on migration: Theoretical issues and new empirical evidence. J. Popul. Econ. 13 (3), 485–508, Springer.

Runciman, W., 1996. Relative Deprivation and Social Justice. Routledge and Kegan Paul, London.

Sandell, S., 1977. Women and the economics of family migration. Rev. Econ. Stat. 59, 406–414.

Schlottmann, A., Herzog, H., 1984. Career and geographic mobility interactions: Implications for the age selectivity of migration. J. Hum. Resour. 19, 72–86.

Schultz, T., 1961. Investment in human capital. Am. Econ. Rev. 51, 1–17.

Schwartz, A., 1973. Interpreting the effects of distance on migration. J. Polit. Econ. 81, 1153–1169.

Schwartz, A., 1976. Migration, age, and education. J. Polit. Econ. 84, 701–719.

Shen, I., Docquier, F., Rapoport, H., 2010. Remittances and inequality: A dynamic migration model. Journal of Economic Inequality 8 (2), 197–220, Springer.

Shields, G., Shields, M., 1989. The emergence of migration theory and a suggested new direction. J. Econ. Surv. 3, 277–304.

Simpson, N., 2001. Redistributive Policies and Migration. Ph.D. Dissertation, University of Iowa.

Simpson, N., Sparber, C., 2013. The short- and long-run determinants of unskilled immigration into U.S. states. South. Econ. J. 80 (2), 414–438.

Sjaastad, L., 1962. The costs and returns of human migration. J. Polit. Econ. 70, 80–93.

Smith, A., 1776. An Inquiry into the Nature and Causes of the Wealth of Nations, 1937 edition. Modern Library, New York.

Stark, O., 1984. Rural-to-urban migration in LDCs: A relative deprivation approach. Econ. Dev. Cult. Change 32, 475–486.

Stark, O., 1991. The Migration of Labor. Basil Blackwell, Oxford.

Stark, O., Levhari, D., 1982. On migration and risk in LDCs. Economic Development and Culture Change 31 (1), 191–196.

Stark, O., Taylor, J., 1989. Relative deprivation and international migration. Demography 26, 1–14.

Stark, O., Taylor, J., 1991. Migration incentives, migration types: The role of relative deprivation. Econ. J. 101, 1163–1178.

Stark, O., Yitzhaki, S., 1988. Labor migration as a response to relative deprivation. J. Popul. Econ. 1, 57–70.

Storesletten, K., 2000. Sustaining fiscal policy through immigration. J. Polit. Econ. 108 (2), 300–324.

Taylor, J., 1986. Differential migration, networks, information and risk. In: Stark, O. (Ed.), Research in Human Capital and Development. In: vol. 4. JAI Press, Greenwich, CT.

Tiebout, C., 1956. A pure theory of local expenditures. J. Polit. Econ. 64, 416–425.

Tinbergen, J., 1962. Shaping the World Economy. Twentieth Century Fund, New York.

Todaro, M., 1969. A model of labour migration and urban unemployment in less developed countries. Am. Econ. Rev. 59, 138–148.

Todaro, M., 1976. Internal Migration in Developing Countries. International Labour Organization, Geneva.

Urrutia, C., 1998. On the Self-Selection of Immigrants. Universiad Carlos III de Madrid, Mimeo.

Vidal, J.P., 1998. The effect of emigration on human capital formation. J. Popul. Econ. 11 (4), 589–600.

Warin, T., Svaton, P., 2008. European migration: Welfare migration or economic migration? Global Econ. Q. 8 (3), 1–30.

Wildasin, E.D., 1994. Income redistribution and migration. Canadian Journal of Economics 27, 637–656.

Willis, R., 1973. A new approach to the economic theory of fertility behavior. J. Polit. Econ. 81 (supplement), 514–565.

Wong, K., 1997. Endogenous growth and international labor migration: the case of a small open economy. In: Jensen, B., Wong, K. (Eds.), Dynamics, Economic Growth, and International Trade. University of Michigan Press, Ann Arbor, pp. 289–336.

Yap, L., 1977. The attraction of cities: A review of the migration literature. J. Dev. Econ. 4, 239–264.

Zaiceva, A., Zimmermann, K.F., 2008. Scale, diversity, and determinants of labour migration in Europe. Oxf. Rev. Econ. Pol. 24 (3), 427–451.

Zavodny, M., 1997. Welfare and the locational choices of new immigrants. Economic Review – Federal Reserve Bank of Dallas 1997, 2–10, Second Quarter 1997.

Zipf, G., 1946. The [P(1)P(2)/D] hypothesis; On the intercity movement of persons. Am. Sociol. Rev. 11, 677–686.

CHAPTER 2

Two Centuries of International Migration

Joseph P. Ferrie*, Timothy J. Hatton**
*Department of Economics, Northwestern University, Evanston, IL 60208-2600, USA
**University of Essex, Colchester CO4 3SQ, UK; and Australian National University

Contents

1. Migration and Globalization to 1950	53
1.1 Evolving migration systems	53
1.2 The rise of mass migration from Europe	56
1.3 Immigrant selection and assimilation in the New World	58
1.4 The effects of migration at home and abroad	60
1.5 Migration in Asia	62
1.6 The policy backlash and de-globalization	64
2. International Migration Since 1950	66
2.1 Long-run trends	66
2.2 What drove postwar migration?	69
2.3 Immigrant selection and assimilation in the developed world	70
2.4 Immigrant selection and the brain drain	73
2.5 The labor market effects of immigration	74
2.6 Trends in immigration policy	76
2.7 Public attitudes and immigration policy	79
3. International Migration and Policy in the Future	80
3.1 How many migrants?	80
3.2 Can policy rise to the challenge?	82
References	83

1. MIGRATION AND GLOBALIZATION TO 1950

1.1 Evolving migration systems

Long-distance migration is not new. For thousands of years humans have moved around the globe in search of food, in flight from enemies, or in pursuit of riches, spreading their cultures, languages, diseases, and genes. Human settlement spread through Europe, Africa, and Asia but the process was very slow. In the Middle Ages, short-distance migration was curtailed by European feudalism but, even after its demise, many workers were tied to the land and urban dwellers jealously guarded their privileges. Legal impediments (such as England's Statute of Artificers of 1563) constrained migration even into the eighteenth century. But among those with the freedom and the resources to move, the scope for long-distance migration expanded as the means of transport improved. Most significant for Europeans was the "discovery" of the New World—the vast lands of North and South America and Australasia. Yet for 300 years intercontinental migration was largely confined to military and other adventurers, merchants, and seamen. Except at time of war, for most Europeans, migration beyond the kingdom or principality was rarely contemplated, and much the same was true in Asia and Africa.

The opening of the New World brought unprecedented opportunity, not just for treasure but also for production and trade. Labor shortages were acute but costs were high. Until the nineteenth century the dominant forms of intercontinental migration were coercion and contract. The most important development was the North Atlantic triangular trade, which brought slaves to the Caribbean islands and the eastern seaboard of the American continent. As Table 2.1 shows, between 1492 and 1820 slaves accounted for more than three-quarters of the 11.3 million migrants to the Americas, while Europeans accounted for less than a quarter. The surge of immigration from Europe in the 60 years to 1880 saw these proportions dramatically reversed. Yet it was not until 1880 that the cumulative flow of Europeans to North America exceeded that of Africans.

In all, about 12 million slaves were transported to the Americas, under horrendous conditions and with very high mortality rates. The volume of the slave trade was greatest in South America and the Caribbean; by 1850, 4.5 million slaves had been forcibly transported to Brazil alone (Lovejoy, 1982). For much of the colonial period South America's economies were based on large extractive or agricultural enterprises, making it difficult to attract settlers. Although the indigenous population provided a local source of labor, African slaves made up a much larger share of the total labor force in South America than in the north. But by the eighteenth century the system was in decline. In 1807 the slave trade was banned in the British Empire and in 1808 the United States stopped slave imports. This movement spread rapidly in Europe, with abolition in Denmark, Portugal, Sweden, France, and the Netherlands in the first two decades of the nineteenth century. In parts of South America and the Caribbean the slave trade lingered a little longer.

Up to 1820 about 2.6 million Europeans migrated to the Americas, mainly from Britain, Portugal, and Spain. About a quarter of these went under contracts of indenture or as convicts. The indenture system began in 1607 when the Virginia Company recruited laborers from England to work in its Jamestown colony (see Galenson, 1984, pp. 2–6). Workers agreed to serve for a fixed term, after which they were free. In exchange for their service, servants received the costs of their passage and subsistence during their term. Gradually a market in indentures arose, with agents recruiting workers at English ports, placing them under contract, and selling the contracts to ship's captains, who in turn sold them to planters on arrival in the colonies.[1] This system solved the

---

[1] Under these contracts the length of service varied inversely with the worker's predicted productivity, such that the value was equal to a uniform seven pounds, which reflected the cost of passage.

Table 2.1 Migration to the Americas, 1492–1880

	1492–1580	1530–1640	1640–1700	1700–1760	1760–1820	1492–1760	1492–1820	1820–1880
Panel A: Slave and non-slave migrants								
All migrants	265	998	1358	3593	5098	6214	11,312	15,998
African slaves (000s)	68	607	829	2846	4325	4350	8675	2296
(% of all migrants)	(25.7)	(60.8)	(61.0)	(79.2)	(84.8)	(70.0)	(76.7)	(14.4)
Europeans (000s)	197	391	529	747	773	1864	2673	13,702
(% of all migrants)	(74.3)	(39.2)	(39.0)	(20.8)	(15.2)	(30.0)	(23.3)	(85.6)
Panel B: Composition of non-slave migrants								
Servants (000s)	0	49	236	128	89	413	502	651
(% of non-slaves)		(12.4)	(44.4)	(17.3)	(11.5)	(22.1)	(19.0)	(4.7)
Convicts (000s)	3	8	23	61	34	95	129	20
(% of non-slaves)	(1.5)	(2.0)	(4.3)	(8.2)	(4.4)	(5.1)	(4.9)	(0.1)
Free (000s)	194	359	273	552	650	1358	2008	13,051
(% of non-slaves)	(98.5)	(85.6)	(51.3)	(74.5)	(84.1)	(72.8)	(76.1)	(95.1)

Some of those included in the lower panel are not Europeans.
Source: Eltis (2002, pp. 62, 67).

problem of capital market failure. The demand for plantation labor was strong, and English workers provided a willing supply, but most were too poor to finance the journey and could not provide the collateral for a loan.

Between the 1630s and the American Revolution, half to two-thirds of British migrants to North America traveled as indentured servants. But the system soon came under pressure, particularly in the sugar colonies, where servants faced harsh working conditions and planters exploited a growing supply of slaves (Galenson, 1984, p. 11). Although they were not perfect substitutes, by the late seventeenth century, slaves were displacing indentured servants as the main source of labor in the southern mainland colonies. But the main reason that the supply of indentured servants from Europe dried up was that increasing numbers were able to finance the journey without having to sell themselves into bondage (Galenson, 1984; Grubb, 1994). The demise of the slave trade brought some revival of contract labor. But this time it was laborers from China and India going chiefly to sugar-producing and other tropical plantation economies.

1.2 The rise of mass migration from Europe

The period from 1820 to the First World War saw the rise of mass migration; over this hundred-year period 55 million Europeans emigrated to North America (71%), South America (21%), and Australasia (7%). Several features are worth noting. First, the number of migrants increased. Before mid-century it was just a trickle compared with what followed. It averaged around 300,000 per annum up to the 1870s, rising steeply to a peak of 1.4 million in the years before the First World War (Figure 2.1). Second, the source-country composition changed. In the middle decades of the nineteenth century emigrants came chiefly from Britain and Ireland, Germany, and the Scandinavian countries. But as Figure 2.1 shows, the great surge in emigration from the 1870s was dominated by the countries of southern and eastern Europe, notably Italy, Spain, Austria-Hungary, and Russia. Such statistics hide enormous variations in emigration rates. The highest was Ireland with a gross emigration rate of 13 per thousand per annum between 1850 and 1913. Countries such as Sweden and Norway had rates approaching five per thousand in 1870–1913, while the rates for Germany and Belgium were less than two per thousand and that for France was very small.

Different perspectives have been invoked to explain variations in emigration across time and place (Lowell, 1987, Ch. 2; Massey et al., 1998, Ch. 2). One feature that such theories must explain is that, during the transition to modern economic growth, national emigration rates often increased gradually, accelerated to a peak, and then went into decline—a pattern sometimes called the mobility transition (Zelinsky, 1971). Wages in Europe were barely half those in the New World (much less for some source countries) and this provided strong economic incentives. But real wage gaps alone cannot explain why poor countries often had low emigration rates and why emigration often increased as

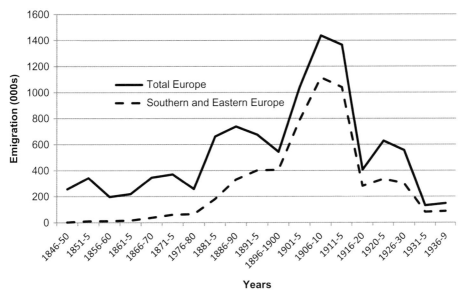

Figure 2.1 *Intercontinental emigration from Europe, 1846–1939.* Source: *Kirk (1946, p. 297).*

development took place. One factor is the demographic transition, which produced large cohorts of young adults for whom opportunities to inherit smallholdings or enter into skilled occupations or small business was limited. Analysis of cross-country trends in emigration shows that demographic effects were important and that urbanization also played a role (Hatton and Williamson, 1998, p. 43).

Much of the literature has focused on migrant networks as a key element in European migration. Once established, migration streams cumulated as previous emigrants provided new migrants with pre-paid tickets for the passage, food and shelter on arrival, and established immigrant networks to help gain access to job opportunities. Up to 90% of arrivals in the US were meeting a friend or relative. This reduced the costs and uncertainties of long-distance migration and it also eased the poverty constraint. This helps to explain differences in emigration patterns from countries at similar levels of development. In Ireland the Great Famine effectively ejected a million migrants, mostly to the US. Thus, after mid-century even the poorest Irish migrant would have benefited from the assistance of previous emigrants, and so emigration depended less on the migrant's own resources and more on the potential gains (Hatton and Williamson, 2005, p. 65). As a result, Irish emigration declined as economic conditions at home improved. By contrast in Italy, which had few emigrants before 1870, the poverty constraint was more important and hence emigration increased as the economy developed (Gomellini and Ó Gráda, 2011).

The "friends and relatives effect" also helps to explain why emigration was often concentrated on specific localities of origin and destination. But choice among destination countries involved additional factors such as cultural and linguistic affinity with the country of origin. Thus, emigrants from Italy, Spain, and Portugal revealed much stronger preferences for South American countries such as Argentina and Brazil than did other European emigrants. Given these affinities and the pulling power of previous migrants, these streams persisted in spite of the growing relative attraction of the US. However, when new streams of emigration arose, such as that from southern Italy from the 1890s, economic advantage carried more weight. Thus, migrants from the urban north of Italy continued to favor South America over North America while the rural southern Italians migrated in increasing numbers to the urban United States. But there is little evidence for substitution between New World destinations; instead the alternatives seem to have been for migration within and between countries in Europe.

Although most migrants were permanent settlers an increasing proportion returned. The conventional estimate is that by the end of the nineteenth century about a third of European migrants to the US were returning, usually within a few years. However, a recent study puts the return rate at around twice this level in the 1900s (Bandiera et al., 2013). Falling transport costs and voyage times relative to the wage gains contributed to the trend. But the upward trend in return migration owes most to the changing country composition of emigration, particularly the growing share from southern Europe. Many of these emigrants intended to return home and use their savings to start families and sometimes to establish farms or businesses and thus the outflow was dominated by males (Hatton and Williamson, 2005, p. 80). There was also a growing trend toward seasonal migration, most notably as the so-called *golondrinas*, who moved with the harvest seasons between Italy and the River Plate.

1.3 Immigrant selection and assimilation in the New World

Emigrant streams of the early nineteenth century were often led by farmers and artisans from rural areas, traveling in family groups, many of whom were intending to acquire land and settle permanently at the New World's expanding frontier (Erickson, 1994). By the 1830s these "pioneer migrants" were giving way to those that were somewhat more representative of the populations from which they were drawn (Cohn, 2009, Ch. 5). In the Hesse-Cassel region of Germany between 1832 and 1857, emigration rates were highest from villages where land was scarce, where wages were higher, and where there was some history of emigration. The highest emigration rates were among artisans—those with transferrable skills and enough resources to emigrate. Those with resources such as land were not constrained by poverty but they had less incentive to move; on the other hand, unskilled laborers were often more constrained (Wegge, 2002). Network effects seem to have been strong, as reflected by the fact that those that could be identified as networked carried less cash with them (Wegge, 1998).

On arrival in the New World most migrants gravitated to communities of immigrants from the same origin. Evidence for individual immigrants in the US indicates that there was some downward occupational mobility on arrival, but this was followed by steep upward mobility, especially for young and literate immigrants from Britain and Germany (Ferrie, 1999, Ch. 5). There was also a strong link between the occupational and geographical mobility of immigrants. More than two-thirds of immigrants arriving in the 1840s moved county in the following decade. Relative to non-movers, laborers who moved location increased their wealth—the more so the further they moved (Ferrie, 1999, Ch. 6). In Brazil those that arrived on *colonato* contracts from the 1880s often succeeded in acquiring land, and by 1940 the foreign-born owned a third of all farms and factories (Klein, 1995, pp. 211–212). In Argentina, Italian immigrants ascended from initial smallholding to become the major business class.

As successive European countries entered into transatlantic migration, pioneer migrants gave way to mass migrants. The later arrivals may have been less energetic and enterprising, but were they still positively selected on labor market characteristics? In the decades after 1870 half of the Danish emigrants and nearly two-thirds of the Irish emigrants were aged between 15 and 29, as compared with less than a third of the home populations (Hatton and Williamson, 2005, p. 78). They also carried low dependency burdens to the New World, which maximized the lifetime gains and minimized the costs of migration. But how did they compare with their peers who stayed behind? In a recent study, Abramitsky et al. (2012) compared Norwegian emigrants to the US from the 1870s with those that stayed behind. They found that the emigrants were negatively selected in the sense that they had lower occupational attainment by 1900 than non-migrants with similar characteristics. By following a sample of young men from the British 1851 census to the US 1880 census and the British 1881 census, Long and Ferrie (2013) found that British emigrants were negatively selected as well.

These recent findings are consistent with an older view of the "huddled masses" but not with subsequent revisionism. Examining cross-sectional data on earnings, Hatton (1997) found that newly arrived immigrants in the US around the turn of the century suffered a substantial earnings disadvantage but that their wages subsequently converged on those of the native-born. Second-generation immigrants often outperformed those with native-born parents, suggesting that they inherited some degree of positive selection but avoided the first-generation disadvantage. Recently, Abramitsky et al. (2014) examined occupational scores for immigrants in 1900, 1910, and 1920. Panel data estimates indicate that those who remained in the sample suffered no initial disadvantage and therefore no advance in occupational attainment as compared with the native-born. They conclude that much of the apparent convergence observed in other studies can be accounted for by two factors: (1) negatively selected return migration and (2) declining quality of arrival of successive immigrant cohorts. It seems likely, however, that these effects would be weaker in the nineteenth century when transport costs were higher and return migration lower.

Economic outcomes differed across country of origin, and this sparked growing concern in the US, where the Immigration Commission devoted four years (1907–1910) to examining every aspect of the economic and social life of immigrants. The Commission drew a sharp distinction between the "old immigrants" from the countries of northwestern Europe and the "new immigrants" from southern and eastern Europe. They took a dim view of the latter as "largely a movement of unskilled laboring men, who have come, in large part temporarily, from the less progressive and advanced countries of Europe," characterizing them as "far less intelligent" and "actuated by different ideals" than the old immigrants (quoted in Hatton and Williamson, 1998, p. 124). Re-examination of this issue, even with the Commission's own data, largely debunked this sharp distinction (Chiswick, 1992; Minns, 2000). Nevertheless there were differences between nationalities, largely associated with source-country language, culture, and education. One study suggests that the shifting composition of immigration between 1873 and 1913 accounted for a reduction of around 5% in the average earnings of immigrants (Hatton, 2000). As noted further below, these effects are small as compared with those that occurred after the Second World War and they might be smaller still if return migration were taken into account.

1.4 The effects of migration at home and abroad

The economic effects of immigration have been a source of debate in the past as in the present, not least because of the link to policy. It is worth illustrating the issues with a textbook diagram (Figure 2.2), where there are two countries R (receiving) and

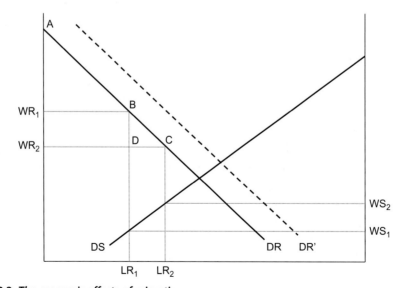

Figure 2.2 The economic effects of migration.

S (sending) with combined labor force measured as the width of the box. The respective real wage rates are measured on the vertical axes. DR is the migrant-receiving country's downward sloping labor demand curve while that of the sending country, DS, slopes down from right to left. Before migration, the receiving country has labor supply LR_1, and its wage, WR_1, exceeds that of the sending country, WS_1. Migration from S to R increases the labor force in the receiving country to LR_2, so that the wage falls to WR_2. In the sending country the labor force shrinks and the wage increases to WS_2. Note also the distributional effects: the income of other (fixed) factors of production in country R as measured by the area of the triangle A–B–WR_1 increases after migration to A–C–WR_2. In the context of the greater Atlantic economy, three questions follow from this. First, did immigration depress wages in the New World and increase them in the Old, and did it contribute to transatlantic wage convergence? Second, did other globalization forces shift labor demand curves such that they offset or reinforced the partial equilibrium effects illustrated in Figure 2.2? And third, how did migration alter the distribution of income in sending and receiving countries?

Several different approaches have been used to assess the impact of mass migration on real wage rates. One of these is to correlate wage changes with immigration across localities within a country. Using this approach, Ljungberg (1997) found that emigration from Sweden explains about half of the rise in Swedish wages across Swedish counties between 1870 and 1910. Goldin (1994) found a negative relationship between wage growth and immigration across US cities between 1890 and 1923. However, as noted further below, local effects of immigration may not be a good guide to national effects if there is significant internal mobility in response to immigration flows. Taylor and Williamson (1997) instead estimated the labor demand elasticity for a panel of 15 countries and then applied this to the change in the country labor force induced by post-1870 migration. They calculated that, in the absence of immigration, the real wage in 1910 would have been higher by 27% in Argentina, by 17% in Australia, and by 9% in the US. Conversely, absent emigration, real wages would have been lower by 24% in Ireland, by 22% in Italy, but by only 5% in Britain and 2% in Germany. Overall the real wage ratio between the New World and the Old World fell by 11%, whereas under the no-migration counterfactual it would have increased by 11% (Taylor and Williamson, 1997, p. 41).

Assessment of the wage effects using computable general equilibrium models produces wage effects that are broadly similar to those from applying labor demand elasticities. But they also allow some assessment of other aspects of nineteenth century globalization, such as international capital mobility. It seems likely that much of the capital that flowed from the Old World to the New World was, in effect, chasing the higher returns brought about by immigration-induced labor force growth. In the New World international capital inflows meant that capital to labor ratios, labor productivity, and real wages grew more rapidly than otherwise. Indeed, capital mobility attenuated the real wage effects of migration on both sides of the greater Atlantic economy. One estimate suggests that, in the absence of migration, the real wage in 1910 would have been higher by 34% in the US and lower by 12% in Britain. But if capital had also retreated to Europe then the US wage would have been only 9% higher while the British wage would have been 7% lower (O'Rourke et al., 1994, p. 209).

Even though capital market arbitrage attenuated the transatlantic convergence of real wages, there were other country-specific factors, such as land. As land scarcity increased relative to labor in the New World, land prices and rents increased relative to wage rates, while the opposite occurred in the Old World. As the average landowner was richer than the average worker these developments contributed to increasing inequality in the New World and decreasing inequality in the Old World. For the former, these effects are illustrated in Figure 2.2, where the fixed factor is now interpreted as land. Wage–rental ratios converged in the greater Atlantic economy between 1870 and 1913, but with considerable diversity. In Australia and Canada, where wage–rental ratios were falling, the trends differed across colonies and provinces (Emery et al., 2007; Shanahan and Wilson, 2007). Both within and between countries, these trends were influenced by the scale of emigration, the structure of the economy, and the reaction to globalization. In Europe, the rise in the wage–rental ratio was more muted in countries that resorted to agricultural protection (France, Germany, and Spain) than in those that maintained free trade (O'Rourke and Williamson, 1999; see also Bohlin and Larsson, 2007, on Sweden).

These trends are reflected in transatlantic convergence of the ratios of average income (GDP per capita) to unskilled wages (Hatton and Williamson, 2005, p. 120). The effects of migration may also be reflected in the wage distribution. If skilled and unskilled workers were imperfect substitutes then unskilled immigration should increase wage inequality. Up to 1914 immigration increased the share of unskilled labor in the US and Canada, where the skill premium increased, and reduced it in Britain, where the skill premium narrowed (Anderson, 2001). Betrán and Pons (2004) tested the relationship between net migration and the skill premium on a wider set of countries. They found that net immigration increased the wage premium in the US but that net emigration narrowed it in France, Italy, Spain, and the UK. But such effects can only be observed in the presence of other influences such as skill-biased technical change, capital intensity, and structural change, as well as differences in labor market institutions.

1.5 Migration in Asia

Most of the historical focus has been on what is sometimes called the greater Atlantic economy. Yet this accounts for only a third to 40% of long-distance international migration in the era up to 1940 (McKeown, 2004, p. 156). Among the more notable streams was the 50 million or more migrants from India and South China to labor-scarce regions such as Burma, Ceylon, parts of Southeast Asia, and the Pacific islands, as well as more distant locations on the coast of Africa, South America, and the Caribbean. These migrations gathered pace in the mid-nineteenth century and were driven largely by the global trade boom in primary commodities. Even more neglected is the 50 million or so moving from Northeastern Asia and Russia to Manchuria, Siberia, Central Asia, and Japan. The Russian and Chinese migrations to Siberia and Manchuria took off from the 1890s, partly driven by improved access to abundant land and partly by rivalry between the Russian and Chinese governments (McKeown, 2004, p. 158).

Migrations in southern and eastern Asia seem to have been driven by much the same forces that were observed in transatlantic migration, notably wage gaps and the stock of previous migrants (Huff and Caggiano, 2007). Just as in Europe, the regional origins of migrants were very unevenly distributed, with notably high rates of emigration from Calcutta and Madras in India and Guangdong and Fukien in China, and from coastal regions generally. Much of this was temporary migration and the migrants were often recruited by agents (the *kangani* system) and transported in gangs to the plantations. Of the 15 million immigrants to Burma, Thailand, and Malaya between 1881 and 1939 about four-fifths returned, typically after a stay of 3–5 years (Huff and Caggiano, 2007, pp. 38–39).

Smaller numbers traveled to the plantation enclaves of the Caribbean, Africa, and the Pacific islands. They were largely shut out of the richest New World countries by the costs of migration and, from the 1880s, by anti-Asian immigration policies. For these migrants, the ratios of the costs of passage to source-country incomes were about 10 times those facing Europeans emigrating to the New World. Not surprisingly a large proportion traveled under contracts of indenture (mainly Indians) or under the credit-ticket system (mainly Chinese). As with the earlier European migration, the key element of indentured servitude was the length of the contract (Northrup, 1995, pp. 115–116). The greater the distance, the longer it took to recover the costs of passage and recruitment, and hence the longer was the contract. However, the rewards were higher too. Wage ratios between origin and destination in the range of five to nine were two to three times those for migration to Southeast Asia, or for indentured Europeans in an earlier era (Hatton and Williamson, 2005, p. 137). In contrast to the Europeans, these migrations were intended to be temporary and the contracts included the return trip. Nevertheless they did plant permanent populations such as the Indians in Mauritius, British Guyana, Natal, Trinidad, Reunion, and Fiji.

We know much less about the labor market impact of migrations within Asia. Given the vast populations of India and China, some observers have followed W.A. Lewis in characterizing the migrant labor supply to Southeast Asian destinations as highly elastic. If so, then wages at the destinations should be pinned down by wages at the source plus the costs of passage. Huff and Caggiano (2007, 2008) found that the wages of Indian migrants in Burma and Malaya and the wages of Chinese in Thailand and Malaya were cointegrated with wages in the respective source countries, with little trend in the wage gap and little evidence of reverse causality. Thus, the long-run supply of labor to these booming Asian economies seems to have been more elastic than was the supply of European labor to the New World.

1.6 The policy backlash and de-globalization

As transatlantic migration rose to ever greater heights in the decades before 1914, the pressures to restrict immigration mounted. And especially so in the US, where the Immigration Act of 1917 imposed a literacy test, which was followed in 1921 by the introduction of the first numerical quota. It has been suggested that mass immigration sowed the seeds of its own destruction in the form of a policy backlash. This policy response can be better understood by asking two questions (Foreman-Peck, 1992, p. 360). First, who gains and who loses from immigration? And second, who is in a position to do something about it? The first relates to the demand for immigration restriction and the second to the supply.

From 1850 to 1880, when the *rate* of immigration to the US was actually greater than in the early twentieth century, the only political backlash was the rise in the 1850s of the "Know Nothing" party in local and national elections, though their agenda was never focused on explicit immigrant restriction and instead focused on limiting the political power of the most recently arrived immigrants (Higham, 2002, Ch. 1). Their support was strongest among urban artisans, the group that suffered most from immigrant wage competition before the Civil War (Ferrie, 1999, p. 173). From the 1880s immigrants were becoming less skilled and more ethnically diverse. Opinion hardened and the open door policy began to change, notably with the Chinese Exclusion Act of 1882 and the restrictive 1907 "Gentleman's agreement" with Japan. One study of attitudes to immigration among Kansas workmen in the 1890s suggests that negative attitudes were driven more by the scale of immigration than by its ethnic composition (Richardson, 2005). In the years preceding the 1917 Immigration Act, Goldin (1994) found that a member of the House of Representatives was more likely to vote for restriction the slower the growth of wage rates in his district in the preceding years and the faster the growth of the foreign-born population.

Restrictive policies came later in other immigration countries, in some cases because of the concentration of political power. As the franchise widened it typically percolated down the hierarchy of class and income, diluting the political weight of landowners and capitalists. At the turn of the twentieth century voting rates were about one-third for adults in the US but less than 10% in Latin America, where the *latifundia* retained its grip on power (Engerman and Sokoloff, 2005). Consequently, immigration restrictions came later in Latin America. In Argentina, electoral reform in 1912 and labor unrest paved the way (Sánchez-Alonso, 2013). It also came somewhat later in the British Dominions, which were relatively democratic. One reason is the imperial connection, as a result of which there was much less diversification in the sources of immigration and less change in the skill composition.

Nevertheless there was a similar trend towards restriction and exclusion, such as the White Australia policy of 1901 and the dictation tests introduced in Cape Colony and Natal in 1897, New Zealand in 1899, and British Columbia in 1907. Other policies included the introduction of head taxes on immigrants and tighter shipping regulations, as well as the progressive withdrawal of subsidized passages such as in Australia after 1913 and Brazil between 1917 and 1927. Using a policy index for five New World countries from 1870 to 1930, Timmer and Williamson (1998) found that the hardening of immigration policies was underpinned by slow real wage growth and increasing inequality, as well as by the scale of immigration itself. In Argentina growing inequality and the falling relative education of immigrants were key influences (Sánchez-Alonso, 2013). But the timing of restriction was often associated with big shocks: war and depression.

The globalization boom in the half-century before 1914 was brought to an abrupt end by war and economic turmoil. As Figure 2.1 shows, after a brief revival in the 1920s gross emigration from Europe fell to a level below that of the mid-nineteenth century. In the US the pressure for restriction mounted over two decades before political interest groups coalesced to pass the 1917 Immigration Act and the emergency quota that followed in 1921 was introduced just as the unemployment rate rose to 11.7%, from 5.2% in 1920. In other settler countries pressures for restriction brought incremental reforms until the Great Depression triggered a more radical retreat from open door immigration policies.[2] Two questions emerge. First, how much of the decline in migration was driven by policy and how much by other factors? And second, did the decline in mass migration reverse some of the trends that were associated with its rise?

As compared with the pre-war decade, interwar immigration fell more steeply in the US than in other settler countries. The quotas set in 1921 and 1924 were massively skewed towards immigrants from Britain, Ireland, and Germany.[3] In the 1920s these numerical limitations were largely binding, particularly for southern and eastern Europeans, but by the 1930s even these quotas were not being filled (Gemery, 1994, p. 181). In Canada and Australia immigration recovered more strongly in the 1920s

---

[2] This took different forms in different countries. In Australia, policy was tightened in 1924 and 1928, and then in 1930 a £50 immigration fee was introduced (equivalent to about four months' earnings for a British worker). In Canada the mildly restrictive Immigration Acts of 1906, 1910, and 1923 (Chinese exclusion) were followed by tougher regulation in 1930 and 1931 when Orders in Council banned all new immigration except for British and Americans with sufficient capital or assured employment. In New Zealand an act with similar effect was passed in 1931 (and the Department of Immigration was closed in 1932). In unifying South Africa, the immigration laws of 1902 and 1906 (framed along similar lines to those of Australia) were followed in 1930 by a national origins quota based on the American model (see Daniels, 1995). In 1932 Argentina introduced the requirement for immigration of a prior contract or financial means. In 1934 Brazil introduced an American-style quota system as part of a wider nativist backlash.

[3] The 1921 Act introduced an overall quota of 356,000 on immigrants from the Eastern Hemisphere, with country quotas restricted to 3% of the foreign-born population at the 1910 census. The 1924 (Johnson–Reed) Act reduced the overall quota to 165,000, with country quotas (now based on the ancestry of the US population) restricted to 2% of the foreign-born population in 1890.

but the 1930s collapse was equally severe. Long-run trends also played a part: those European countries for which the door remained open were on the downswing of their emigration cycles. Migration chains had been broken by war and displacement and emigration became more difficult (Kirk, 1946, p. 88). But above all, the Great Depression was more severe in the New World than in the Old. Thus, immigration restrictions introduced in the 1930s had some effects on immigrant numbers, but more important was the legacy of immigration control that they left for the future.

In New World countries labor force growth slowed, the rise in inequality was reversed, and skill premia fell faster than in the Old World (Hatton and Williamson, 2005, pp. 124, 191–197). It remains unclear to what degree these trends were due to migration or to other de-globalization forces. Such trends might have eased pressure for restriction once the depression passed, but other forces were at work. One was the drying up of international capital flows. As noted earlier, international capital flows cushioned the negative impact of immigration on wages in the New World. International capital flows underwent a modest revival in the 1920s but came to an abrupt halt in 1930. Thus, capital market disintegration reinforced the more immediate influences on policy. Nowhere was this more marked than in Latin America, where the depression triggered inward-looking economic policies that included tough immigration controls.

The pattern in Asia was somewhat different. Migration under indentured servitude faced increasing political pressure from the middle of the nineteenth century. On the fringes of the Atlantic economy, where there was potential competition with workers of European origin, it was fiercely opposed and severely restricted. But it survived longer in island economies like those of the West Indies, Mauritius, Reunion, and Fiji. Indian contract labor was finally abolished by Britain in 1916 (and in India a few years later) but by that time it had been in decline for more than two decades, mainly because of diminishing demand for migrant labor (Hatton and Williamson, 2005, p. 150).

In Southeast Asia as a whole immigration peaked in the 1920s but the 1930s saw a turn to restriction as export markets collapsed. Thus, Thailand introduced a literacy test and costly residence permits while Malaya embarked on a policy of large-scale subsidized repatriation (Huff, 2001). In regions that were less dependent on exports and foreign capital the reaction was less severe. And in Northeast Asia, which was little affected by the Great Depression, migration continued unabated until the 1940s.

2. INTERNATIONAL MIGRATION SINCE 1950

2.1 Long-run trends

The decline in international migration of the interwar years was reversed in the postwar era as economic conditions improved but the revival was constrained by immigration policies that were established in the previous era. For the world as a whole there has been an upward trend since the 1960s but the globalization of labor has been much more

Table 2.2 World migrant stock

	Year						
	1965	*1975*	*1985*	*1990a*	*1990b*	*2000*	*2010*
Migrant stock (millions)							
World	75.2	84.5	105.2	119.8	155.5	178.5	213.9
Africa	8.0	11.2	12.5	15.6	16.0	17.1	19.3
Asia	31.4	29.7	38.7	43.0	50.9	51.9	61.3
Latin Am. and Carib.	5.9	5.9	6.4	7.5	7.1	6.5	7.5
North America	12.7	15.0	20.5	23.9	27.8	40.4	50.0
Europe	14.7	19.5	23.0	25.1	49.4	57.6	69.8
Oceania	2.5	3.3	4.1	4.6	4.4	5.0	6.0
Percentage of world migrant stock							
World	100.0	100.0	100.0	100.0	100	100	100
Africa	10.6	13.2	11.9	13.1	10.3	9.6	9.0
Asia	41.8	35.1	36.8	35.9	32.7	29.1	28.7
Latin Am. and Carib.	7.9	6.8	6.1	6.2	4.6	3.6	3.5
North America	16.9	17.8	19.5	20.0	17.9	22.6	23.4
Europe	19.6	23.1	21.8	20.9	31.8	32.3	32.6
Oceania	3.3	3.9	3.9	3.9	2.8	2.8	2.8
Migrant stock as a percentage of population							
World	2.3	2.1	2.2	2.3	2.9	2.9	3.1
Africa	2.5	2.7	2.3	2.5	2.5	2.1	1.9
Asia	1.7	1.3	1.4	1.4	1.6	1.4	1.5
Latin Am. and Carib.	2.4	1.8	1.6	1.7	1.6	1.2	1.3
North America	6.0	6.3	7.8	8.6	9.8	12.7	14.2
Europe	2.2	2.7	3.0	3.2	6.9	7.9	9.5
Oceania	14.4	15.6	16.9	17.8	16.2	16.1	16.8

There are differences of definition in the figures for 1965–90a and 1990b–2010. The most important is due to the break-up of the Soviet Union, which is included with Europe for the earlier years. Reclassification into individual republics added about 27 million to the world international migrant stock in 2000.
Sources: 1965–1990a from Zlotnick (1998, p. 431); 1990b and 2000 from United Nations online database at: <http://esa.un.org/migration/index.asp>.

limited than that of international trade and finance. As shown in Table 2.2, the total number of international migrants increased by a factor of almost 3 between 1965 and 2010. But as a proportion of the world's population, the growth in the migrant stock is more modest, increasing from a low of just over 2% in the 1970s to nearly 3%. Equally important, the trends have differed widely by region as some pre-existing trends revived, others reversed, and new migration streams emerged.

In the traditional settler countries, the US, Canada, Australia, and New Zealand, immigration rates recovered but not to the pre-World War I level. Thus, in the US the annual immigration rate fell from 11.6 per thousand in the 1900s to 0.4 per thousand in the 1940s before rising to 4.0 per thousand in the 1990s. In Canada and Australia the early postwar revival was stronger and the subsequent increase somewhat slower. For all four countries together gross immigration increased from around half a million per annum in the early 1950s to a million in the 1990s. But the most striking feature is the shift in the sources of immigrants. This can be seen most clearly for the US, where the share of new immigrants from Europe fell from 56.2% in the 1950s to just 13.1% in the 2000s. Western Europe, once the principal source of migrants to the New World, evolved from a region of emigration into a region of immigration. Migration to and within Europe also grew rapidly in the early postwar years, notably in (West) Germany, where the foreign labor force share rose from 0.4% in 1955 to 10.5% in 1972 (Bauer et al., 2005, p. 207). Britain and Scandinavia, followed later by Ireland, Italy, and Spain, experienced a gradual transition from net emigration to net immigration.

The reverse transition occurred in Latin America. Having once been a magnet for European immigrants, its failure to match the economic growth of Europe, and especially the US, accelerated a pre-existing trend towards net emigration. In Latin America and the Caribbean, the number born outside the region fell from 3.7 million to 3.0 million between 1960 and 1980, while the number of expatriates increased from 1.9 million to 4.8 million. The most striking case is that of the Mexican-born in the US, which increased from under a million in 1970 to more than 9 million in 2000. More recent is the revival of emigration from Eastern Europe and the former Soviet States. The mass displacements after World War II involved westward migration of 12 million ethnic Germans from Poland, Czechoslovakia, and the Soviet Union, but that movement was sharply curtailed from 1950 as communist regimes imposed strict controls on emigration from which only a trickle of refugees escaped. Following the fall of the Berlin Wall in 1989 and the dissolution of the Soviet Union in 1991, there was a sharp increase in emigration to a peak of 1.2 million, mostly to the EU-15, the US, and Israel. There was also a surge of migration to Russia that peaked in 1992–5, notably of ethnic Russians from newly independent republics (Mansoor and Quillin, 2006, pp. 24–30).

A largely new development in the postwar period was substantial migration to North America and Western Europe from Asia, notably from China, Japan, and Korea, as well as from the Indian subcontinent. From some countries such as the Philippines they came through recruitment schemes; in others such as Vietnam and Cambodia, a surge of refugees established streams that persisted largely through family reunification. There was also a substantial stream of migrants to the Middle East. Israel attracted 3 million Jewish settlers, mainly from Europe, in the four decades after its founding in 1948. Very different was Asian migration to the Persian Gulf. The oil-producing Gulf States (Bahrain, Kuwait, Oman, Qatar, Saudi Arabia, and the United Arab Emirates) attracted migrants, first from other Arab states and then from the 1970s from across Asia, initially from India and Pakistan, and subsequently from Bangladesh, Sri Lanka, and Southeast Asia. By 1990 the foreign-born exceeded one-third of the population of the six Gulf states. In contrast to the permanent settlers to Israel, these guest workers from Asia came under strictly enforced short-term contracts and without the prospect of permanent residence, integration, and family reunification (Fargues, 2011).

2.2 What drove postwar migration?

What determined the volume and direction of postwar migration? And how much does this differ from the age of mass migration before the First World War? In the presence of binding immigration restrictions one might expect that the characteristics of migration would simply reflect the rationing imposed by policy and not the underlying incentive to migrate. Yet for the largest destination country, the US, income gaps, inequality, source-country demographics, and the migrant stock all influenced the flow of immigrants from different source countries (Clark et al., 2007). The fact that such forces remained influential reflects partly the competition for visas between immigrants from different source countries, and partly the fact that many immigrants (such as those moving through family reunification) were not subject to numerical limits. Immigration policies served both to attenuate the effects of economic and demographic variables and to affect the numbers directly. For rich destination countries the average tightening of entry laws reduced immigration by about 6% (Ortega and Peri, 2012).

The short-run responsiveness of migration to economic conditions depends on policy and also on proximity. Migration for employment was responsive to demand conditions under European guest worker policies up to the early 1970s, when immigrants were drawn first from Italy, Greece, Spain and Portugal, and then from North Africa, Turkey and what was then Yugoslavia (Karras and Chiswick, 1999). Similarly, migration from the Indian subcontinent to the Gulf States responded closely to demand. Nevertheless supply conditions also mattered, as with Philippine migrants to the US under the overseas employment program set up in 1974 (McKenzie et al., 2012). Proximity and policy also underpinned the ebb and flow of migration from Mexico to the US, where temporary migration under the Bracero Program of 1942 to 1964 gave way to waves of undocumented migration. High mobility across porous borders is also a feature of migration within sub-Saharan Africa (Hatton and Williamson, 2003).

In the long run, a number of other fundamentals have shaped the scale and persistence of migration between pairs of source and destination countries (Pedersen et al., 2008; Mayda, 2010; Adsera and Pytlikova, 2012; Belot and Ederveen, 2012). The first is geographic distance, which is often interpreted as reflecting the costs of migration and can be seen in the geographic clustering of migration streams, and especially in settlement patterns of contiguous countries. The second key element is cultural affinities, most obviously sharing a common language (and to a lesser degree also cognate languages) and common religion. Other links such as colonial legacies and links through trade and politics have gradually faded in importance. But the most dominant factor is the stock of previous immigrants from a given source country at a particular destination, which builds in strong persistence. In the nineteenth century the so-called friends and relatives effect represented a very strong "pull factor." And it remains strong in recent times, reinforced by immigration policies that emphasize family reunification as the main entry route (Beine et al., 2011b).

One of the key features of international migration from the nineteenth century to the present is that the poorest countries often have relatively low emigration rates. A number of studies have found it easier to detect the pull effect of host country income than the push effect of living standards in source countries (e.g., Mayda, 2010). As in the nineteenth century, while an increase in home income reduces the *incentive* to emigrate, it also increases the *ability* to emigrate for liquidity-constrained potential emigrants. Thus, the higher is the poverty rate, the lower is the emigration rate. But as in the past, assistance from previous emigrants helps to ease the poverty constraint and so network effects are stronger the poorer is the source country. This helps to explain why immigration to the US diversified so quickly towards Asia and Latin America in the wake of the 1965 immigration policy reform. Immigration from Asia grew rapidly up to the 1990s as the friends and relatives effect took hold and then subsequently eased as the incentive to migrate declined. By contrast, migration from Africa was constrained by high poverty rates and an initially low migrant stock, but is now rising fast (Hatton and Williamson, 2011).

2.3 Immigrant selection and assimilation in the developed world

The performance of immigrants in host country labor markets shaped attitudes to immigration and influenced immigration policy. In his pioneering analysis of immigrants and natives in the 1970 US census, Chiswick (1978) found that, soon after arrival, male immigrants had earnings 10% lower than comparable native-born workers. But after 13 years they had caught up and after 20 years their earnings exceeded those of the native-born by 6%. A succession of studies have confirmed that immigrants do catch up in earnings in the decade after arrival by around 1% per year (for example, Lalonde and Topel, 1991, p. 89; Antecol et al., 2003, p. 24). Tracking immigrant cohorts between two successive censuses, Borjas (1995) found that the catch-up rates were somewhat lower but that the initial immigrant disadvantage had increased. While the immigrants of the 1950s and 1960s had relatively high initial earnings and sometimes overtook the native-born, more recent cohorts have suffered a much larger initial disadvantage and have failed to assimilate rapidly enough to catch up. Table 2.3 shows that while immigrant males in the US earned 4.1% more than native-born males in 1960, by 1990 they were earning 16% less. For recent immigrants the difference is even greater.

Part, but not all, of this trend can be accounted for by a decline in immigrant educational attainment relative to the native-born. As shown in the lower panel of Table 2.3, there was a particularly large increase in the relative share of immigrants with less than

Table 2.3 Relative wage and relative education of immigrants in the United States, 1960–1990

	1960	1970	1980	1990
Percentage earnings differential relative to the native-born				
All immigrants				
Earnings unadjusted	4.1	−0.1	−9.7	−16.3
Earnings adjusted	1.3	−1.7	−7.1	−10.0
Recent immigrants				
Wage unadjusted	−13.9	−18.8	−32.8	−38.0
Wage adjusted	−16.2	−19.8	−24.1	−26.9
Percentage point difference in educational attainment relative to native-born				
All immigrants				
Education >16 years		3.5	2.4	0.0
Education <12 years		3.2	14.3	22.1
Recent immigrants				
Education >16 years		12.9	7.5	4.9
Education <12 years		5.6	13.1	20.4

Recent immigrants are those who arrived in the five years preceding the census date. Adjusted wages are obtained after controlling for age, educational attainment and region.
Sources: Borjas (1999, p. 1724); Borjas (1995, p. 208).

12 years of education. But immigrant performance deteriorated even after controlling for education and the most important source of that decline is the shift in the source-country composition of immigrants. The immigrant-weighted average source country income per capita was 49% of US income per capita in the 1950s and this fell to 22% in the 1990s. Over the same period this ratio fell from 65% to 31% for Canada, from 73% to 49% for Australia, and from 96% to 45% for Germany (Hatton and Williamson, 2007, p. 223). These trends bear an uncanny resemblance to the increase in the share of immigrants from lower income countries in the age of mass migration before 1914. Although both experiences invoked similar concerns it is worth stressing that the earnings gaps between "new" and "old" immigrants have been much greater in the postwar period that in the earlier era (Hatton, 2000, p. 525).

Differences in socio-economic status between immigrants and natives can be accounted for in four ways. The first is individual characteristics. Clearly education and skills are important to labor market success, but those that are acquired in the origin country may be worth little in the host country labor market. Chiswick and Miller (2008, 2009) observed that immigrants are often found in occupations lower than their education levels would predict, and especially so for immigrants from less developed countries. And as human capital is more important now than it was a century ago, this could account for some of the difference between now and then. Equally important to labor market success is proficiency in the host country language. Chiswick and Miller (1995, 2010) found that speaking the language enhances earnings by 8–16%. These two things are related.

Second, it is widely believed that immigrant networks are an important key to assimilation, at least in the years shortly after arrival (Munshi, 2003). Immigrant communities help new immigrants become established by helping them gain access to employment. But these communities may also become ghettos or ethnic enclaves, which by insulating immigrants can slow down the assimilation process. Over the longer term assimilation also takes place at the community level and in part it reflects the evolution of attitudes in the host society. The longer the immigrant community has been established, the better adjusted it becomes, and the more the host society comes to accept that ethnic group. Evidence for the US indicates that the presence of a large number of immigrants from the same origin tends to depress relative earnings of new immigrants while a long history of immigration from that source raises relative earnings (Hatton and Leigh, 2011). Thus, the pre-1914 new immigrants eased the path for postwar cohorts from the same countries.

Third, assimilation patterns also differ across host countries depending on the structure of the labor market and the welfare state. Antecol et al. (2003) found that the increasing probability of employment accounted for almost all of the growth in immigrant incomes over the first 20 years in Australia compared with about half in the US. Australia's more egalitarian wage structure and greater regulation restricted immigrants' access to good jobs but delivered higher initial wage rates and slower wage growth for those who gained employment (Gregory et al., 1992; Miller and Neo, 2003). Such findings are also common in Europe, where participation rates of immigrants are lower than those of natives and unemployment rates are typically twice as high. This is the culmination of a steady deterioration. In Sweden the employment rate for male immigrants fell from 65% in 1970–79 to 38% in 1993–98 while the unemployment rate increased from 8% to 26%. Over the same period rates of earnings assimilation were low and relative earnings for immigrants declined (Bengtsson et al., 2005, p. 31).

Lastly it matters not just where immigrants came from but under what circumstances. The evidence suggests that patterns of assimilation differ by visa category and thus policy has an important role. For immigrants who arrived in Canada between 1980 and 2000, DeVoretz et al. (2005) found that, seven years after arrival, those who came as family migrants or refugees had incomes that were 40% lower than those who migrated through the employment stream. Refugees were much more likely to depend on welfare benefits than other classes of immigrants. Other studies for Canada and Australia confirm that employment stream immigrants are the most successful in the labor market followed by family migrants and then refugees (Cobb-Clark, 2006; Aydemir, 2011). These differences are even more marked in Europe, where larger welfare states and higher unemployment interacts with immigration policies that have increasingly emphasized family and humanitarian immigration.

2.4 Immigrant selection and the brain drain

Migration is non-random because the incentive to migrate differs between individuals and across source and destination countries. Against the background of trends in the labor market performance of immigrants, destination countries have become increasingly concerned with selecting highly skilled and educated migrants. The standard model of immigrant selection (the Roy model) predicts that if the rate of return to skills is higher in the destination than in the source country, then immigrants will be positively selected, and vice versa (Borjas, 1987). But immigrant selection also depends on the costs of migration, on selective immigration policies, and on the other variables that drive migration decisions.

For the rich OECD countries the share of high educated among immigrants is similar to that of the native-born (notwithstanding that the former often receive lower earnings given their skills). The English-speaking countries have the highest immigrant skills relative to natives while for most countries of continental Europe immigrant skills are substantially below those of natives. This reflects the sorting of high educated migrants towards destinations with the higher return to skills (Grogger and Hanson, 2011). Skill-selective migration policies might also be expected to be important, but only where they apply to a significant share of the flow. For the US the lack of skill selectivity has been offset by the incentive effects of the high return to skills. By contrast, countries in Europe that have less unequal income distributions and larger proportions of refugees have larger shares of low-skilled immigrants.

Across source countries, there is a positive correlation between the share of high educated emigrants relative to non-emigrants and the source-country return to skills (Belot and Hatton, 2012). This is the opposite of what the Roy model suggests. One reason is that low-skilled potential emigrants from poor and unequal countries are constrained by poverty. Once this is taken into account, the negative relationship between the source-country return to human capital and the relative share of skilled emigrants is revealed (Belot and Hatton, 2012). Survey evidence from poor countries on intentions to emigrate tells much the same story (Liebig and Sousa-Poza, 2004). The evidence also suggests that the larger is the existing diaspora of previous emigrants, the less positively selected is the current flow (Beine et al., 2011a). Thus, over the long run, immigrant selection has been influenced by two key forces. The first is that economic growth in the developing world has gradually eased the poverty constraint and expanded the potential for migration from the poorest countries. The other is that following the establishment of an initial flow, the friends and relatives effect, by easing the poverty constraint, expanded the migration possibilities for less skilled immigrants.

Nevertheless, the selection of high-skilled immigrants from the developing world, partly the result of policy, has led to concerns about the brain drain. Such concerns were raised in the 1960s and 1970s with the first surge of emigration from third world countries. The brain drain is particularly severe for countries that are small, middle income, and close to rich destinations. Thus, for Guyana, Jamaica, and Haiti, more than 80% of the high educated have emigrated, and the rates also exceed 50% for a number of countries in sub-Saharan Africa (Docquier and Rapoport, 2012). Of even greater concern are the high rates of emigration in certain key professions such as doctors and nurses from Africa and engineers and IT specialists from India. However, while the absolute size of the brain drain has increased, the rates relative to source-country populations have not (Docquier and Rapoport, 2012, pp. 688–689). This is partly because of the general rise in education in less developed countries, and partly because network effects and falling migration costs have widened the possibilities for the less skilled.

While the scale of the brain drain has become clear, its effects on the origin countries have been debated, specifically whether or not skilled emigration leads to a compensating brain gain in the source country. One mechanism is where the widening possibility of emigration acts as a broad stimulus to schooling, while only some of those with additional education actually emigrate (Mountford, 1997). The evidence strongly suggests that there is some educational response to emigration, the net effect of which varies across source countries. Countries like China, India, Indonesia, and Brazil all experienced modest net educational gains while smaller countries in Central America, the Caribbean, and sub-Saharan Africa experienced significant net losses (Beine et al., 2008, p. 644). Such compensating effects may be due in part to the use of remittances for education in poverty-constrained households in origin countries. There is also some evidence of brain gain where return migrants promote knowledge transfer and diffusion, for example among IT specialists returning to India (Kapur, 2010, Ch. 4). They may also promote trade and foreign direct investment. More indirectly, a highly educated diaspora may positively influence economic and political institutions in origin countries (Docquier and Rapoport, 2012, p. 712).

2.5 The labor market effects of immigration

Immigration policies in the developed world have been influenced by the actual or perceived effects of policy. As before, Figure 2.2 provides a useful starting point. For the receiving country, R, the immigration surplus (area B–C–D) may be small and is likely to be dominated by the distributive effects. With full enfranchisement, those with most to lose have power over policy. Workers lose (WR_1–B–D–WR_2) and they have the most votes; capitalists gain (WR_1–B–C–WR_2) but have few votes; immigrants have the most to gain (as their wage increases from WS_1 to WR_2) and they have no votes at all *ex ante*. This political calculus would be altered either if some workers gain at the expense of others or if the labor demand curve shifts to the right, from DR to DR′, offsetting the wage effects. In the absence of such a demand shift, if wages are sticky downwards, then immigration creates unemployment.

As in the nineteenth century, the effects of immigration are hard to discern, but recent history offers some useful natural experiments. The first is the inflow into metropolitan France following the latter's independence in 1962. About 900,000 mainly French-born expatriates or *pieds-noirs* flowed into France, adding 1.9% to the population and 1.6% to the labor force. Hunt (1992) found that the overall effect was to reduce the real wage by 1.3%, and to increase the unemployment rate by 0.3 percentage points. Thus, the Algerian immigration shock was sufficiently large to have a clear effect on the French labor market. Larger still was the influx to Portugal when independence struggles in Angola and Mozambique reached a climax in 1974–76. The 600,000 *retornados* added 7% to the population in these few years. Carrington and di Lima (1996, p. 244) found that the influx of *retornados* reduced the Portuguese wage by around 3–6% while the aggregate unemployment rate increased by around 2 percentage points. These effects can also be clearly seen when comparing real wage and employment trends in Portugal with those of its nearest neighbors, France and Spain (Hatton and Williamson, 2005, p. 304). These examples suggest distinct wage and employment effects despite sometimes being interpreted to the contrary.

Another "natural experiment" is provided by the influx of Russian Jews to Israel when the Soviet Union lifted its restrictions on emigration late in 1989. This immigration shock added 610,000, or about 7%, to the population in the first two years and topped a million by the mid-1990s. As a result the working-age population increased by 8% up to 1992 and 12% up to 1997. Non-immigrant employment fell by about 5 percentage points in the first few years and then total employment grew as the immigrants were absorbed into employment and the labor market adjusted. Real wages plunged in the early 1990s and then hovered at about 10% below the preceding trend for the rest of the decade (Hatton and Williamson, 2005, p. 300). However, the wage effect was mitigated by inward capital flows (Cohen and Hsieh, 2000) that eventually raised labor productivity, shifting the labor demand curve as illustrated in Figure 2.2. These examples suggest that immigration leaves an imprint but that it fades over time.

The effects of immigration vary widely between different segments of the labor market. In his study of the US labor market, Borjas (2003) analyzed these effects at the national level across groups by education and experience. Between 1980 and 2000 the immigration-induced decline in average male earnings was 3.2% but for those with less than high school education the decline was 8.9%. If immigrants are less than perfect substitutes with natives then the true effects may be much smaller and more of the impact would fall on previous immigrants (Ottaviano and Peri, 2012). But immigrants are often found to be further down in the distribution of earnings and occupations than their skills would suggest (Chiswick et al., 2008; Dustmann et al., 2012). For this reason as well, the negative impacts are felt most among less skilled natives, not just in earnings but also in employment. Across OECD countries the evidence suggests that a 1 percentage point increase in the immigrant share increases native unemployment by 0.3 percentage points.

But this effect is larger and more persistent in countries where there is greater labor market regulation (Jean and Jimenez, 2007).

These differences are also reflected in the fiscal effects of immigration. Estimates of the net fiscal contribution of immigration depend on two interacting factors. First, those with more than high school education generally make a net contribution (Smith and Edmonston, 1997, p. 334; Storesletten, 2000). One recent general equilibrium estimate suggests that the decline in the relative skills of US immigrants since the 1965 policy reform substantially reduced the fiscal (and overall) gains from immigration (Chojnicki et al., 2011). Second, the more generous is the welfare state and the less flexible is the labor market the greater the net burden imposed by low-skilled immigrants (Storesletten, 2003; Boeri, 2010). For some European countries the fiscal costs increased as welfare states expanded and as the labor market status of immigrants deteriorated—as, for example, in Sweden between 1970 and the mid-1990s (Ekberg, 1999, p. 423). In countries where welfare states are smaller and immigrants have limited access to benefits and welfare services, fiscal burdens are much less of a concern.

2.6 Trends in immigration policy

The early postwar years saw a gradual loosening of immigration policy in the developed world. As noted earlier, that includes the traditional immigration countries, Western Europe and new growth areas such as the Gulf States and countries as diverse as South Africa, Korea, Japan, and Thailand. Until the 1970s the economic climate was more benign than it had been during the interwar period and thus immigrants were more easily absorbed. But several other factors were important. In contrast to the interwar period, capital flowed more freely and international trade barriers fell, so that less of the adjustment to immigration fell on wages (Hatton and Williamson, 2008). Added to this, the shift away from resource-based industries (or the expansion of the resource base) and rapid productivity growth shifted the labor demand curve to the right (DR to DR' in Figure 2.2).

But other factors were working against the expansionary policies of the 1950s and 1960s. One was the growing concerns in several countries about the deterioration of the labor market conditions for low-skilled immigrants. A classic case is the sudden termination of the European guest-worker programs when economic conditions in Germany and elsewhere in Europe suddenly worsened in the early 1970s. Dramatic policy tightening, for which the oil shock was the trigger, followed mounting disquiet about immigration. In Britain and France the growth of immigration from poorer parts of the world (partly a consequence of de-colonialization) led to a tightening of policies in the late 1960s and early 1970s (Verbunt, 1985, pp. 136–147; Hatton and Wheatley Price, 2005, pp. 122–130). Such policies were often supported by reference to labor market conditions and welfare state burdens, although there were often deeper, more xenophobic reasons. In Canada (1967), Australia (1979), and New Zealand (1991), where immigration had been restricted to Europeans, points systems were introduced to select immigrants for skills. One exception is the US, which did not turn to restriction or selection, although there were strong pressures to do so in the 1990s.

Perhaps the backlash is best observed in the response to the surge of asylum seekers from the mid-1980s mainly in the EU-15 (Hatton, 2011, Ch. 6). Although all EU countries are signatories of the 1951 Refugee Convention, its provisions left room for a considerable tightening of policy. This involved three dimensions. The first was the tightening of border controls and visa requirements. The second was in the procedures for granting refugee status; the proportion of applicants to EU-15 countries who were granted some form of status fell from a half in 1985 to 30% a decade later. And third there was a progressive toughening in the restrictions placed on asylum seekers and reductions in their living standards during the processing of their applications. After some decline in the mid-1990s asylum applications surged again at the turn of the century and this triggered another round of tightening, especially in the wake of the attacks of September 11th 2001.

Overall immigration policies seem to have become more restrictive up to the 1990s. The United Nations periodic survey of government views and policies indicates that among developed countries the proportion of governments believing that immigration was too high peaked at one-third in the mid-1990s, when three-fifths of them were aiming to reduce it (Table 2.4). Since then both indices have declined in the developed world, a trend that is much less marked for less developed countries. For the developed countries, a gradual easing of policy can also be seen in policy indices relating both to the entry of immigrants and to the conditions under which they can stay (Ortega and Peri, 2012). This trend continued to the early 2000s but has probably since been reversed.

The overall effect of policies since the late 1960s was to squeeze out labor migrants while increasing the selectivity of those who still arrived through the employment

Table 2.4 Government Immigration policies, 1976–2005

	1976	1986	1996	2001	2005
Percentage reporting immigration too high					
All countries	7	20	21	23	17
More developed countries	18	24	33	29	8
Less developed countries	3	19	17	21	20
Percentage aiming to restrict immigration					
All countries	7	20	40	40	22
More developed countries	18	38	60	44	12
Less developed countries	3	15	34	39	25

Sources: United Nations (2002, p. 18); United Nations (2009, pp. 74–76).

channel. For the US the share of family migration is nearly three-quarters. But even for countries like Australia and Canada that are famous for their selective immigration policies based on points systems, the share of immigration accounted for by family reunification is more than half. For most European countries the largest component is free migration within the EU or the common travel area. Excluding these, among 14 European countries in 2008, the share arriving through the employment stream averaged little more than a quarter, with nearly 60% coming through family reunification and a further 15% as refugees. Recent initiatives in EU countries have sought to increase selectivity in the employment stream while constraining family reunification and clamping down ever more severely on asylum seekers and illegal immigrants.

In Asia and Africa policy has evolved through several stages. In the immediate post-colonial era most countries lacked coherent immigration policies and border controls, especially with contiguous countries. Work permit systems were developed in the 1980s and 1990s in regional hubs such as Korea, Singapore, and South Africa. These became increasingly formalized and, in some, the temporary worker programs developed into bilateral agreements that resembled the earlier European guest-worker programs. By 2003 Malaysia had bilateral agreements with eight countries, including the Philippines, Sri Lanka, Thailand, and Indonesia. They were sometimes subject to temporary stops, restrictions, and repatriations as economic conditions deteriorated, as in Nigeria in the early 1980s, South Africa in 1988, and Malaysia in 1997–98. But for many countries, including those in South America such as Argentina and Brazil, limited policy effectiveness meant mounting numbers of illegal immigrants. Although policy focused principally on low-skilled temporary employment, recent developments include some easing of restrictions on family reunification and, more importantly, a shift towards skilled worker programs, such as those in Japan, Taiwan, Korea, and India.

By far the greatest challenge for some of the world's poorer countries has been the influx of refugees, as conflict flared in neighboring countries. In 2010 four-fifths of the world's 10 million refugees were located in developing countries, with Pakistan, Iran, and Syria each hosting more than a million and Chad, Jordan, and Kenya hosting around 400,000 (UNHCR, 2011, pp. 62–64). Fragile host countries in African conflict zones became increasingly unwilling or unable to provide for refugees as the numbers increased in the 1980s. Refugees were sometimes pushed back or encouraged to return, even though the host countries were signatories to the UN Refugee Convention or regional conventions. In Africa and in some Asian countries they have been quarantined in camps without access to civil status or employment in the host country. In Middle Eastern countries they have more often been absorbed in urban areas with few rights and protections and with limited opportunity for assimilation. However, some of these pressures have eased as returns and resettlements have outpaced the rate of new displacements and the total stock of refugees has declined by almost half since the peak of 1992.

2.7 Public attitudes and immigration policy

In the era of globalization before World War I, most Western countries had a franchise that was heavily weighted towards the property-owning upper and middle classes. This picture changed dramatically during the first half of the twentieth century as the right to vote percolated down the socio-economic scale (Hatton and Williamson, 2007, p. 228). The logic of Figure 2.2 provides good reason why immigration policies should have been much more restrictive since 1950 as compared with the nineteenth century. Even if skilled workers benefit from immigration, the widening franchise still swung the pendulum against immigration. Surveys of public opinion indicate that attitudes to immigration are typically negative, but not overwhelmingly so. On a five-point scale between increasing immigration a lot (1) and reducing it a lot (5) the average over 26 countries in the ISSP survey of 2003 was 3.8. Responses to questions on whether immigrants take jobs and whether immigration is good for the economy are somewhat less negative at 3.1 and 3.2.

The strongest finding in the analysis of attitudes is that negative sentiment towards immigration is strongest among those with low education. This can be interpreted in two ways. The first is that the less educated are concerned about the potential labor market competition from low-skilled immigrants (Scheve and Slaughter, 2001; Mayda, 2006; O'Rourke and Sinnott, 2006). The other is that the more educated have greater tolerance towards minorities and are more positive about ethnic and cultural diversity (Dustmann and Preston, 2007; Hainmueller and Hiscox, 2007). Studies of immigration opinion have also found that concerns about the fiscal costs weigh heavily with some citizens (Facchini and Mayda, 2009; Boeri, 2010). This helps to explain why attitudes are often somewhat negative even among those higher up the scale of class, education, and income. Not surprisingly, as a reference point, the current scale of immigration matters too (Lahav, 2004; Sides and Citrin, 2007).

There is very little evidence on how public sentiment has changed over the long run. One exception is the US, where the proportion wishing immigration to be reduced increased mildly to peak in the early 1980s and again in the mid 1990s and then declined (Simon, 2004, p. 21). The rise in the early 1980s reflects the effects of recession while that of the mid-1990s was associated with a surge of immigration and mass legalizations. Given the importance of education in shaping individual attitudes, the growth in average education over the last half-century should have produced more liberal sentiment. But other factors have worked in the opposite direction, particularly the number and the types of immigrants, welfare state expansion, and skill-biased technical change. In most OECD countries attitudes towards asylum seekers, illegal immigrants, and boat people deteriorated steeply in the 1980s and 1990s as the numbers increased. In Australia the proportion wanting the government to "turn back the boats" increased from a quarter in the late 1970s to more than a half in the early 2000s (Betts, 2001, p. 44). In Europe, negative sentiment towards immigrants and asylum seekers has also been associated with the growing influence of far-right political parties.

Given that the median voter favors reducing immigration, it is perhaps surprising that immigration policies have remained as liberal as they have. In an important paper, Freeman (1995) argued that in liberal democracies, immigration politics is characterized by an expansionary bias:

> Popular opinion is typically restrictionist, but not well articulated. Organized opinion, reflecting the distribution of the costs and benefits of immigration, is more favorable. Organized opinion has more impact on policy because vote-maximizing politicians find it in their electoral interest to cater to it. The normal clientelistic politics of immigration nonetheless tend to evolve into a more open interest-group politics within particular immigration cycles.
>
> *(Freeman, 1995, pp. 886–887)*

Anti-immigration sentiment is diffuse while pro-immigration sentiment is concentrated, and this shapes policy in both social and economic dimensions. Some see immigration politics as a social and cultural issue and therefore distinct from trade, on which the debate is more narrowly economic (Greenaway and Nelson, 2006). Here the pro-immigration pressure groups range from ethnic minority interests to those concerned with civil rights and humanitarian issues; in some countries these are counterbalanced by nativist and nationalist lobbies. The other dimension is employer lobby groups, which according to Figure 2.2 are pro-immigration, and which are concentrated, organized, and well resourced. In the US, business groups have invested substantial resources in lobbying for sector-specific visa allocations in temporary worker programs. The evidence suggests that this activity is successful although it is often opposed by organized labor (Facchini et al., 2011). The strength of industry lobbies and the weakness of unions is one reason why immigration policies have remained more open in the US than in other countries.

3. INTERNATIONAL MIGRATION AND POLICY IN THE FUTURE

3.1 How many migrants?

Will international migration increase or decrease? Some observers think that the potential for migration is vast and that pressure will continue to build. Thus, Pritchett (2006, p. 138) writes that "there are five irresistible forces in the global economy creating growing pressures for greater movement of labor ... from poorer to richer countries." These include divergences in demographic trends and differences in economic growth across world regions. The most obvious indicator of these pressures is the vast income gaps that exist around the world. Allowing for differences in skill, immigrants to the US from low- and middle-income countries earn on average five times the wage at home; for those from the poorest countries it would be ten times. Even allowing for differences in selection, potential emigrants from the Philippines could increase their incomes by a factor of 3.5, those from Haiti by 7.8 (Clemens et al., 2009). These gaps are much greater than the ratios of around 2 that drove the great transatlantic migrations before 1914. And the widening gap between rich and poor countries probably added to migration pressure—at least up until the early 1990s.

Survey evidence suggests that potential emigration is enormous. Among adults in poor and middle-income countries more than a quarter say they would like to emigrate, a proportion that exceeds half in some African countries (Torres and Pelham, 2008). In the late 1990s the proportion expressing an intention to emigrate was 41% in Ghana, 20% in Morocco, 38% in Senegal, and 12% in Egypt, and these were mostly for economic reasons (Van Dalen et al., 2005, p. 752). Yet only a fraction of those expressing the intention actually migrate, because of poverty, policy, or family ties. Another symptom of migration pressure is the volume of illegal migration. In the US the stock of illegal immigrants, about three-fifths of whom are from Mexico, increased from around 3 million in the early 1980s to exceed 10 million by the 2000s (Passell, 2007, p. 12). However, there is some evidence that the pressure has eased, with a decline in the annual flow from half a million to 150,000 (Passell and Cohn, 2010). In Europe, similarly porous borders to the south and east, combined with tougher policies towards asylum, saw the stock of illegals rise to around 3–5 million in 2002, since when it has declined (European Commission, 2009, p. 12).

While the absolute level of migration pressure is hard to measure, some insight can be gained from examining trends in the forces that determine observed migration. Looking at immigration to the US, Canada, and Germany there is some evidence that the forces driving immigration from Asia, the Middle East and North Africa, as well as Latin America and the Caribbean, increased until the early 1990s and then eased. The inverted U shape of the emigration cycle is reminiscent of the trends in European emigration in the nineteenth century and has often been noted in postwar emigration histories (Massey et al., 1998, Ch. 4; Durand, 2009). The most important forces in the slowdown are the demographic transition and the educational revolution, and these trends are likely to continue into the future (Hatton and Williamson, 2011). The exception is sub-Saharan Africa, where modest economic growth, by easing the poverty constraint, is likely to increase migration pressure.

These scenarios are predicated on existing immigration policies, which undoubtedly hold back a very large amount of potential emigration. Estimates of the worldwide gains to completely eliminating such barriers range from around one-half to one-and-a-half times global GDP (Clemens, 2011, p. 86). Such estimates are based upon full equalization of wages and (as Figure 2.2 suggests) most of the gains go to the migrants themselves. But such counterfactuals are not remotely feasible: upwards of half the population of non-OECD countries would need to emigrate. Nevertheless substantial gains would result from a far more modest loosening. One estimate suggests that immigration from poor countries equivalent to 3% of the OECD labor force would increase the income of the emigrants by a total of $170 billion (0.6% of world income) and bring a total gain of about the same amount (Winters et al., 2003). Even this exceeds by a considerable margin the estimated gains from the elimination of all remaining barriers to international trade.

3.2 Can policy rise to the challenge?

Those who recognize that the gains to liberalizing migration far exceed that from other liberalizations have often argued for open border policies. But it is far from clear what combination of economic incentive and political initiative could make this happen on a global scale. As the logic of Figure 2.2 makes clear, for an immigration country, as long as the potential losers (actual or perceived) outnumber the potential gainers, national policies will remain restrictive. Equally important, those with the most to gain are the potential immigrants and they do not have a vote *ex ante* on the immigration policies of the countries they would like to enter.

One possible solution that has sometimes been suggested is a multilateral agreement that would lower the barriers to migration in the same way as the GATT/WTO has done for international trade. But there is a good reason for the contrasting histories of trade and migration (Hatton, 2007). Despite the fact that freer trade is normally in each country's individual interest, negotiations at the WTO are based on the exchange of "concessions" for market access. Thus, one of the key principles is reciprocity. But while trade flows are balanced, migration flows are not. It is difficult to imagine that access to the labor markets of poor countries would be a sufficiently attractive concession to induce rich countries to open their labor markets. Added to that, those countries that send migrants do not, on the whole, place any value on seeing more of their citizens emigrate. According to the UN's periodic survey, only 5% of developing country governments in 2005 thought that the level of emigration from their country was too low, while 27% thought that it was too high (United Nations, 2009, p. 74).

One possibility would be to link migration to trade negotiations in the WTO, or to other issues such as the environment. But the WTO's GATS Mode 4 (providing mobility for the supply of services) has been little used, and adding further dimensions to already deadlocked negotiations is unlikely to work. An alternative is to build upon existing regional cooperation in trade and other dimensions, the most advanced example being the European Union. Others include the ECOWAS in West Africa, COMESA in Eastern and Southern Africa, and MERCOSUR and the Andean Community in South America. These have agreements in principle to facilitate cross-border movement, but they have not been implemented. Where development gaps between the countries are small by world standards, migration is driven more by comparative advantage, making two-way flows a more realistic prospect and offering some potential for building agreements based on reciprocity. However, the gains would be correspondingly modest. Where the gaps are large, such as between Mexico and the US within NAFTA, open borders are much less likely to emerge. But the recent expansion of the EU to embrace poorer countries of Eastern Europe suggests that deepening and extending existing agreements is a long-term possibility.

What about agreements between rich and poor countries, potentially on opposite sides of the globe? For highly skilled and educated workers there is little need for formal agreements as such migrants are increasingly seen as a benefit to the destination. But such programs as the US H–1B visa or the EU's blue card could be expanded without being seen as a threat through the labor market or the national budget. A somewhat greater challenge is the admission of low-skilled immigrants, something that faces greater resistance despite the relative scarcity of low-skilled labor in developed economies. Here the most feasible development would be bilateral agreements for temporary migration, which could be adjusted to labor market conditions and would generate time-limited welfare state entitlements. Such agreements went out of fashion in OECD countries because they were seen as leading either to permanent settlement or to illegal migration. However, it has been suggested that such side-effects can be avoided if the right incentives are provided and if there is adequate enforcement (Boeri et al., 2002, Ch. 6; Schiff, 2004). These incentives include the employer posting a bond that is returnable when the migrant leaves at the end of the contract and deferring some of the migrant's pay until he or she returns to the source country. Existing agreements often include one of these but not both and it is argued that, in addition, source-country cooperation is needed in order to avoid generating new waves of illegal immigration. Some observers see scope for agreements in which the central focus is expanding guest-worker programs in exchange for cooperation in controlling illegal immigration, although it is not clear how effective such schemes would be.

REFERENCES

Abramitsky, R., Platt-Boustan, L., Eriksson, K., 2012. Europe's tired, poor, huddled masses: Self-selection and economic outcomes in the age of mass migration. Am. Econ. Rev. 102, 1832–1856.

Abramitsky, R., Platt-Boustan, L., Eriksson, K., 2014. A nation of immigrants: Assimilation and economic outcomes in the age of mass migration. J. Polit. Econ. 122, 467–506.

Adsera, A., Pytlikova, M., 2012. The Role of Language in Shaping International Migration, IZA Discussion Paper 6333, Bonn.

Anderson, E., 2001. Globalisation and wage inequalities, 1870–1970. Eur. Rev. Econ. Hist. 5, 91–118.

Antecol, H., Cobb-Clark, D.A., Trejo, S.K., 2003. Immigration policy and the skills of immigrants to Australia, Canada and the United States. J. Hum. Resour. 38, 192–218.

Aydemir, A., 2011. Immigrant selection and short-term labor market outcomes by visa category. J. Popul. Econ. 24, 451–475.

Bandiera, O., Viarengo, M., Rasul, I., 2013. The making of modern America: Migratory flows in the age of mass migration. J. Dev. Econ. 102, 23–47.

Bauer, T., Dietz, B., Zimmermann, K.F., Zwintz, E., 2005. German migration, assimilation and labour market effects. In: Zimmermann, K.F. (Ed.), European Migration: What Do We Know? Oxford University Press, Oxford.

Beine, M., Docquier, F., Rapoport, H., 2008. Brain drain and human capital formation: Winners and losers. Econ. J. 118, 631–652.

Beine, M., Docquier, F., Özden, C., 2011a. Diasporas. J. Dev. Econ. 95, 30–41.

Beine, M., Docquier, F., Özden, C., 2011b. Dissecting Network Externalities in International Migration, INRES Discussion Paper 2011-22, Louvain.

Belot, M.V., Ederveen, S., 2012. Cultural barriers in migration between countries. J. Popul. Econ. 25, 1077–1105.

Belot, M.V., Hatton, T.J., 2012. Immigrant selection in the OECD. Scand. J. Econ. 114, 1105–1128.

Bengtsson, T., Lundh, C., Scott, K., 2005. From boom to bust: The economic integration of immigrants in postwar Sweden. In: Zimmermann, K.F. (Ed.), European Migration: What Do We Know? Oxford University Press, Oxford.

Betrán, C., Pons, M.A., 2004. Skilled and unskilled wage differentials and economic integration, 1870–1930. Eur. Rev. Econ. Hist. 8, 29–60.

Betts, K., 2001. Boatpeople and public opinion in Australia. People Place 9, 34–38.

Boeri, T., 2010. Immigration to the land of redistribution. Economica 77, 651–687.

Boeri, T., Hanson, G.H., McCormick, B., 2002. Immigration Policy and the Welfare System. Oxford University Press, Oxford.

Bohlin, J., Larsson, S., 2007. The Swedish wage-rental ratio and its determinants, 1877–1926. Aust. Econ. Hist. Rev. 47, 49–72.

Borjas, G.J., 1987. Self selection and the earnings of immigrants. Am. Econ. Rev. 77, 531–553.

Borjas, G.J., 1995. Assimilation and changes in cohort quality revisited: What happened to immigrant earnings in the 1980s? J. Labor. Econ. 13, 201–245.

Borjas, G.J., 1999. The economic analysis of immigration. In: Ashenfelter, O., Card, D. (Eds.), Handbook of Labor Economics, vol. 3A. North Holland, New York, pp. 1697–1760.

Borjas, G.J., 2003. The labor demand curve *is* downward sloping: Reexamining the impact of immigration on the labor market. Q. J. Econ. 118, 1335–1374.

Carrington, W.J., di Lima, P.J.F., 1996. The impact of 1970s repatriates from Africa on the Portuguese labor market. Ind. Labor Relat. Rev. 49, 330–347.

Chiswick, B.R., 1978. The effect of Americanization on the earnings of foreign-born men. J. Polit. Econ. 86, 897–921.

Chiswick, B.R., 1992. Jewish immigrant skill wages in America in 1909: An analysis of the Dillingham Commission data. Explor. Econ. Hist. 29, 274–289.

Chiswick, B.R., Miller, P.W., 1995. The endogeneity between language and earnings: International analyses. J. Labor. Econ. 13, 246–288.

Chiswick, B.R., Miller, P.W., 2008. Why is the payoff to schooling smaller for immigrants? Lab Econ 15, 1317–1340.

Chiswick, B.R., Miller, P.W., 2009. The international transferability of immigrants' human capital skills. Econ. Educ. Rev. 28, 162–169.

Chiswick, B.R., Miller, P.W., 2010. Occupational language requirements and the value of English in the US labor market. J. Popul. Econ. 23, 353–372.

Chiswick, B.R., Le, A.T., Miller, P.W., 2008. How immigrants fare across the earnings distribution in Australia and the United States. Ind. Labor Relat. Rev. 61, 353–373.

Chojnicki, X., Docquier, F., Ragot, L., 2011. Should the US have locked heaven's door? Reassessing the benefits of postwar immigration. J. Popul. Econ. 24, 317–359.

Clark, X., Hatton, T.J., Williamson, J.G., 2007. Explaining U.S. immigration, 1971–1998. Rev. Econ. Stat. 89, 359–373.

Clemens, M.A., 2011. Economics and emigration: Trillion-dollar bills on the sidewalk? J. Econ. Perspect. 25, 83–106.

Clemens, M.A., Montenegro, A.C., Pritchett, L., 2009. The Place Premium: Wage Differences for Identical Workers across the U.S. Border, Center for Global Development Working Paper 148, Washington.

Cobb-Clark, D.A., 2006. Selection policy and the labour market outcomes of new immigrants. In: Cobb-Clark, D.A., Khoo, S. (Eds.), Public Policy and Immigrant Settlement. Edward Elgar, Cheltenham.

Cohen, S., Hsieh, C.-T., 2000. Macroeconomic and Labor Market Impact of Russian Immigration in Israel. Unpublished paper, Bar Ilan University.

Cohn, R.L., 2009. Mass Migration under Sail: European Antebellum Immigration to the United States. Cambridge University Press, New York.

Daniels, R., 1995. The growth of restrictive immigration policy in the colonies of settlement. In: Cohen, R. (Ed.), The Cambridge Survey of World Migration. Cambridge University Press, Cambridge.

DeVoretz, D.J., Beiser, M., Pivnenko, S., 2005. The economic experiences of refugees in Canada. In: Waxman, P., Colic-Peisker, V. (Eds.), Homeland Wanted: Interdisciplinary Perspectives on Refugee Settlement in the West. Nova Science, New York.

Docquier, F., Rapoport, H., 2012. Globalization, Brain Drain, and Development. J. Econ. Lit. 50, 681–730.

Durand, J., 2009. Processes of Migration in Latin America and the Caribbean (1950–2008), UNDP Research Paper 2009/24, New York.

Dustmann, C., Preston, I.P., 2007. Racial and economic factors in attitudes to immigration. Berkeley Electronic Journal of Economic Analysis and Policy, Advances 7, Article 62.

Dustmann, C., Frattini, T., Preston, I.P., 2012. The effect of immigration along the distribution of wages. Rev. Econ. Stud. 80, 145–173.

Ekberg, J., 1999. Immigration and the public sector: Income effects for the native population in Sweden. J. Popul. Econ. 12, 278–297.

Eltis, D., 2002. Free and coerced migrations from the Old World to the New. In: Eltis, D. (Ed.), Coerced and Free Migration: Global Perspectives. Stanford University Press, Stanford, CA.

Emery, J.C.H., Inwood, K., Thille, H., 2007. Heckscher-Ohlin in Canada: New estimates of regional wages and land prices. Aust. Econ. Hist. Rev. 47, 22–48.

Engerman, S.L., Sokoloff, K.L., 2005. The evolution of suffrage institutions in the New World. J. Econ. Hist. 65, 891–921.

Erickson, C., 1994. Leaving England: Essays on British Emigration in the Nineteenth Century. Cornell University Press, Ithaca, NY.

European Commission, 2009. Clandestino: Final Report. www epim info/wp. . ./clandestino final-report-november-2009.pdf.

Facchini, G., Mayda, A.M., 2009. Does the welfare state affect individual attitudes toward immigrants? Rev. Econ. Stat. 91, 295–314.

Facchini, G., Mayda, A.M., Mishra, P., 2011. Do interest groups affect US immigration policy? J. Int. Econ. 85, 114–128.

Fargues, P., 2011. Immigration without inclusion: Non-nationals in nation-building in the Gulf states. Asian Pac. Migrat. J. 20, 273–292.

Ferrie, J.P., 1999. Yankeys Now: Immigrants in the Antebellum United States. Oxford University Press, New York.

Foreman-Peck, J., 1992. A political economy of international migration, 1815–1914. Manchester School 60, 359–376.

Freeman, G.P., 1995. Modes of immigration politics in liberal democratic states. Int. Migrat. Rev. 29, 881–902.

Galenson, D.W., 1984. The rise and fall of indentured servitude in the Americas: An economic analysis. J. Econ. Hist. 44, 1–26.

Gemery, H.A., 1994. Immigrants and emigrants: International migration and the US labor market in the Great Depression. In: Hatton, T.J., Williamson, J.G. (Eds.), Migration and the International Labor Market. Routledge, London, pp. 1850–1939.

Goldin, C.D., 1994. The political economy of immigration restriction in the United States. In: Goldin, C., Libecap, G. (Eds.), The Regulated Economy: A Historical Approach to Political Economy. University of Chicago Press, Chicago.

Gomellini, M., Ó Gráda, C., 2011. Outward and Inward Migrations in Italy: A Historical Perspective. Banca d'Italia. Economic History Working Paper No. 8.

Greenaway, D., Nelson, D., 2006. The distinct political economies of trade and migration policy: Through the window of endogenous policy models. In: Fodors, F., Langhammer, R. (Eds.), Labor Mobility and the World Economy. Springer, Berlin, pp. 295–327.

Gregory, R.G., Anstie, R., Klug, E., 1992. Why are low skilled immigrants in the United States poorly paid relative to their Australian counterparts? In: Abowd, J.M., Freeman, R.B. (Eds.), Immigration. Trade and the Labor Market. University of Chicago Press, Chicago, pp. 385–406.

Grogger, J., Hanson, G., 2011. Income maximization and the selection and sorting of international migrants. J. Dev. Econ. 95, 42–57.

Grubb, F., 1994. The end of European immigrant servitude in the United States: An economic analysis of market collapse, 1772–1835. J. Econ. Hist. 54, 794–824.

Hainmueller, J., Hiscox, M.J., 2007. Educated preferences: Explaining individual attitudes toward immigration in Europe. Int. Organ. 61, 399–442.

Hatton, T.J., 1997. The immigrant assimilation puzzle in late nineteenth century America. J. Econ. Hist. 57, 34–62.

Hatton, T.J., 2000. How much did immigrant "quality" decline in late nineteenth century America? J. Popul. Econ. 13, 509–525.

Hatton, T.J., 2007. Should we have a WTO for international migration? Econ. Pol. 22, 339–383.

Hatton, T.J., 2011. Seeking Asylum: Trends and Policies in the OECD. Centre for Economic Policy Research, London.

Hatton, T.J., Leigh, A., 2011. Immigrants assimilate as communities, not just as individuals. J. Popul. Econ. 24, 389–419.

Hatton, T.J., Wheatley Price, S., 2005. Migration, migrants and policy in the United Kingdom. In: Zimmermann, K.F. (Ed.), European Migration: What Do We Know? Oxford University Press, Oxford.

Hatton, T.J., Williamson, J.G., 1998. The Age of Mass Migration: Causes and Economic Impact. Oxford University Press, New York.

Hatton, T.J., Williamson, J.G., 2003. Demographic and economic pressure on migration out of Africa. Scand. J. Econ. 105, 465–486.

Hatton, T.J., Williamson, J.G., 2005. Global Migration and the World Economy: Two Centuries of Policy and Performance. MIT Press, Cambridge, MA.

Hatton, T.J., Williamson, J.G., 2007. A dual policy paradox: Why have trade and immigration policies always differed in labor-scarce economies? In: Hatton, T.J., O'Rourke, K.H., Taylor, A.M. (Eds.), The New Comparative Economic History. MIT Press, Cambridge MA.

Hatton, T.J., Williamson, J.G., 2008. The impact of immigration: Comparing two global eras. World Dev. 36, 345–361.

Hatton, T.J., Williamson, J.G., 2011. Are Third World emigration forces abating? World Dev. 39, 20–32.

Higham, J., 2002. Strangers in the Land: Patterns of American Nativism, 1860–1925, second ed. Rutgers University Press, New Jersey.

Huff, G., Caggiano, G., 2007. Globalization, immigration and Lewisian elastic labor in pre-World War II Southeast Asia. J. Econ. Hist. 67, 33–68.

Huff, G., Caggiano, G., 2008. Globalization and labor market integration in late nineteenth- and early twentieth-century Asia. Res. Econ. Hist. 25, 285–347.

Huff, W.G., 2001. Entitlements, destitution and emigration in the 1930s Singapore Great Depression. Econ. Hist. Rev. 54, 290–323.

Hunt, J., 1992. The impact of the 1962 repatriates from Algeria on the French labor market. Ind. Labor Relat. Rev. 45, 556–572.

Jean, S., Jimenez, M., 2007. The Unemployment Impact of Immigration in OECD Countries, OECD Economics Department Working Paper 563, Paris.

Kapur, D., 2010. Diaspora, Development, and Democracy: The Domestic Impact of International Migration from India. Princeton University Press, Princeton, NJ.

Karras, G., Chiswick, C.U., 1999. Macroeconomic determinants of migration: The case of Germany 1964–1988. Int. Migrat. 37, 657–677.

Kirk, D., 1946. Europe's Population in the Interwar Years. Princeton University Press, Princeton, NJ.

Klein, H.S., 1995. European and Asian migration to Brazil. In: Cohen, R. (Ed.), The Cambridge Survey of World Migration. Cambridge University Press, Cambridge.

Lahav, G., 2004. Public opinion toward immigration in the European Union: Does it matter? Comp. Polit. Stud. 37, 1151–1183.

Lalonde, R.J., Topel, R.H., 1991. Labor market adjustments to increased immigration. In: Abowd, J.M., Freeman, R.B. (Eds.), Immigration. Trade and the Labor Market. University of Chicago Press, Chicago, pp. 167–199.

Liebig, T., Sousa-Poza, A., 2004. Migration, self-selection and income inequality: An international perspective. Kyklos 57, 125–146.

Ljungberg, J., 1997. The impact of the great emigration on the Swedish economy. Scand. Econ. Hist. Rev. 44, 159–189.

Long, J., Ferrie, J.P., 2013. British, American, and British-American Social Mobility: Intergenerational Occupational Change among Migrants and Non-Migrants in the Late 19th Century. Unpublished paper, Northwestern University.

Lovejoy, P.E., 1982. The volume of the Atlantic slave trade: A synthesis. J. Afr. Hist 23, 473–501.

Lowell, B.L., 1987. Scandinavian Exodus: Demography and Social Development of 19th Century Rural Communities. Westview Press, Colorado.

Mansoor, A., Quillin, B., 2006. Migration and Remittances: Eastern Europe and the Former Soviet Union. World Bank, Washington, DC.

Massey, D.S., Arango, J., Hugo, G., Kouaouci, A., Pellegrino, A., Taylor, J.E., 1998. Worlds in Motion: Understanding International Migration at the End of the Millennium. Oxford University Press, New York.

Mayda, A.M., 2006. Who is against immigration? A cross-country investigation of attitudes towards immigrants. Rev. Econ. Stat. 88, 510–530.

Mayda, A.M., 2010. International migration: A panel data analysis of the determinants of bilateral flows. J. Popul. Econ. 23, 1249–1274.

McKenzie, D., Theoharides, C., Yang, D., 2012. Distortions in the international migrant labor market: Evidence from Filipino migration and wage responses to destination country economic shocks, World Bank Policy Research Working Paper 6041, Washington, DC.

McKeown, A., 2004. Global migration, 1846–1940. J. World Hist. 15, 155–189.

Miller, P.W., Neo, L.M., 2003. Labour market flexibility and immigrant adjustment. Econ. Rec. 79, 336–356.

Minns, C., 2000. Income, cohort effects and occupational mobility: A new look at immigration to the United States at the turn of the 20th century. Explor. Econ. Hist. 37, 326–350.

Mountford, A., 1997. Can a brain drain be good for growth in the source economy? J. Dev. Econ 53, 287–303.

Munshi, K., 2003. Networks in the modern economy: Mexican migrants in the U.S. labor market. Q. J. Econ. 118, 549–599.

Northrup, D., 1995. Indentured Labor in the Age of Imperialism, 1834–1922. Cambridge University Press, Cambridge.

O'Rourke, K.H., Sinnott, R., 2006. The determinants of individual attitudes towards immigration. Eur. J. Polit. Econ 22, 838–861.

O'Rourke, K.H., Williamson, J.G., 1999. Globalization and History: The Evolution of the Nineteenth Century Atlantic Economy. MIT Press, Cambridge, MA.

O'Rourke, K.H., Williamson, J.G., Hatton, T.J., 1994. Mass migration, commodity market integration and real wage convergence. In: Hatton, T.J., Williamson, J.G. (Eds.), Migration and the International Labor Market. Routledge, London, pp. 1850–1939.

Ortega, F., Peri, G., 2012. The Effect of Income and Immigration Policies on International Migration, NBER Working Paper 18322, Boston.

Ottaviano, G.I.P., Peri, G., 2012. Rethinking the effects of immigration on wages. J. Eur. Econ. Assoc. 10, 152–197.

Passell, J.S., 2007. Unauthorized Migrants in the United States: Estimates, Methods, and Characteristics, OECD Social, Employment and Migration Working Paper 57, Paris.

Passell, J.S., Cohn, D., 2010. U.S. Unauthorized Immigration Flows are Down Sharply since Mid-Decade. Pew Research Center Report, Washington, DC.

Pedersen, P.J., Pytlikova, M., Smith, N., 2008. Selection and network effects-Migration flows into OECD countries 1990–2000. Eur. Econ. Rev. 52, 1160–1186.

Pritchett, L., 2006. Let their People Come: Breaking the Deadlock on Global Labor Mobility. Brookings Institution, Washington, DC.

Richardson, G., 2005. The origins of anti-immigrant sentiments: Evidence from the heartland in the age of mass migration. B.E. Press, Topics in Economic Analysis & Policy 5, Article 11.

Sánchez-Alonso, B., 2013. Making sense of immigration policy: Argentina, 1870–1930. Econ. Hist. Rev. 66, 601–627.

Scheve, K.F., Slaughter, M.J., 2001. Labor market competition and individual preferences over immigration policy. Rev. Econ. Stat. 83, 133–145.

Schiff, M., 2004. When Migrants Overstay their Legal Welcome: A Proposed Solution to the Guest-Worker Program, IZA Discussion Paper 1401, Bonn.

Shanahan, M.P., Wilson, J.K., 2007. Measuring inequality trends in colonial Australia using factor price ratios: The importance of boundaries. Aust. Econ. Hist. Rev. 47, 6–21.

Sides, J., Citrin, J., 2007. European opinion about immigration: The role of identities, interests and information. Br. J. Polit. Sci. 37, 477–504.

Simon, R., 2004. Immigration and Crime across Seven Nations. Unpublished paper, IZA, Bonn.

Smith, J.P., Edmonston, B., 1997. The New Americans: Economic, Demographic, and Fiscal Effects of Immigration. National Academies Press, Washington, DC.

Storesletten, K., 2000. Sustaining fiscal policy through immigration. J. Polit. Econ. 108, 300–324.

Storesletten, K., 2003. Fiscal implications of immigration – a net present value calculation. Scand. J. Econ. 105, 487–506.

Taylor, A.M., Williamson, J.G., 1997. Convergence in the age of mass migration. Eur. Rev. Econ. Hist. 1, 27–63.

Timmer, A.S., Williamson, J.G., 1998. Immigration policy prior to the 1930s: Labor markets, policy interactions, and globalization backlash. Popul. Dev. Rev. 24, 739–771.

Torres, G., Pelham, B., 2008. One-Quarter of World's Population May Wish to Migrate. http://www.gallup.com/poll/108325/onequarter-worlds-population-may-wish-migrate.aspx UNHCR, 2011. Statistical Yearbook, 2010. United Nations High Commissioner for Refugees, Geneva.

United Nations, 2002. International Migration Report 2002. UN Population Division, New York.

United Nations, 2009. International Migration Report 2006: A Global Assessment. UN Population Division, New York.

Van Dalen, H.P., Groenewold, G., Schoorl, J.J., 2005. Out of Africa: What drives the pressure to emigrate? J. Popul. Econ. 18, 741–778.

Verbunt, G., 1985. France. In: Hammar, T. (Ed.), European Immigration Policy: A Comparative Study. Cambridge University Press, Cambridge, pp. 127–164.

Wegge, S.A., 1998. Chain migration and information networks: Evidence from nineteenth-century Hesse-Cassel. J. Econ. Hist. 58, 957–986.

Wegge, S.A., 2002. Occupational self-selection of European emigrants: Evidence from nineteenth century Hesse-Cassel. Eur. Rev. Econ. Hist. 6, 365–394.

Winters, L.A., Walmsley, T.L., Wang, Z.K., Grynberg, R., 2003. Liberalising temporary movement of natural persons: An agenda for the development round. World Econ. 26, 1137–1161.

Zelinsky, W., 1971. The hypothesis of the mobility transition. Geogr. Rev. 61, 219–249.

Zlotnick, H., 1998. International migration 1965–1996: An overview. Popul. Dev. Rev. 24, 429–468.

CAMEO 1

World Migration in Historical Perspective: Four Big Issues

Jeffrey G. Williamson
Harvard University and the University of Wisconsin

Contents

1. Emigration Life Cycles, Industrial Revolutions, and Demographic Transitions   89
2. Brain Drain, Brain Gain, Skill Premia, and Endogenous Schooling Responses   91
3. Migration, Remittances, Financial Development, and Convergence   94
4. Migration Timing, the Ten Percent Rule, and Political Backlash   98
Acknowledgments   100
References   100

1. EMIGRATION LIFE CYCLES, INDUSTRIAL REVOLUTIONS, AND DEMOGRAPHIC TRANSITIONS

While I prefer the phrase emigration life cycle, some call it the migration hump and Wilbur Zelinsky (1971) called it the mobility transition: Stretching over perhaps a half-century, sending countries typically trace out a rise from low to high emigration rates, reach a peak, and then fall, with circular migration tacked on at the end. Zelinsky associated the increase in mobility with modernization, industrialization, and urbanization, as well as with the demographic transition. As far as I know, this life-cycle framework was first used to explain nineteenth century European emigration (Akerman, 1976, p. 25). Perhaps more importantly, economic historians have decomposed these emigration life cycles to identify the transitional forces at work, in particular industrial revolutions and demographic transitions (Hatton and Williamson, 1998, pp. 48–49; 2005, Ch. 4).

Although we now live in a world where host countries restrict immigration, the same life cycles have appeared over the past half-century. Indeed, they have been even steeper on the upside and downside, and shorter in length (Martin and Taylor, 1996; Hatton and Williamson, 2005), than they were a century ago when immigration was almost completely "free". The explanations are clear: both industrial revolutions and demographic transitions have been far more dramatic in the current global century than they were in the first global century.

How should we use this stylized historical fact? A common prediction made by observers of the modern scene is that there will be increasing immigration pressure in the future of high-wage countries (Pritchett, 2006), but such predictions depend very

Handbook of the Economics of International Migration, Volume 1A
ISSN 2212-0092, http://dx.doi.org/10.1016/B978-0-444-53764-5.09983-7

much on where today's developing countries are in their emigration life cycles. If most are on the steeply rising part then the common prediction might be correct, but if most are at their peak or on the downside of the life cycle then migration pressure will recede rather than increase. Thus, one group argues that economic development in poor countries will stem the emigrant tide, while another argues that it will increase the tide (Nyberg-Sørensen et al., 2002; de Haas, 2007). Empirical work by Timothy Hatton and myself (Hatton and Williamson, 2011) favors the first: most of Asia, Latin America, and the European periphery have finished their emigration life cycles; only sub-Saharan Africa lags behind, although that may be a big "only".

What accounts for the emigration life cycle? It helps to break this problem down into two parts. First, what determines how many potential emigrants are at risk, since bigger numbers drive up the emigration rate. Second, what determines whether potential emigrants will actually move? Modern research tends to stress microanalysis and thus the second often ignores the macrodimensions of the first. Economic historians have not ignored the former, and history shows that it has mattered.

Now, let's repeat the question: What accounts for the emigration life cycle? Since standard migration theory predicts that rising relative income at home produced by growth miracles and income catch up should reduce emigration, those declining incentives to emigrate must have been overturned by other forces working in the opposite direction. One key offset in the past was the rising birth rate and the falling child mortality rate, which 20 years later created large shares of young, mobile adults in the sending country population. Thus, the demographic transition put an increasing share of the sending country population at risk. The second key offset was the gradual reduction in poverty at home, an event caused by industrial revolutions and catching up at home, a force that increased the ability of potential emigrants to invest in the move. While the income gap between sending and receiving countries fell during catch-up, there still was a gap for migrants to exploit and, more to the point, there were an increasing number of potential emigrants who could finance the move. A third offset was carried by the fall in transport costs associated with surging internal transport improvements up to World War I, and the scale economies achieved on overseas migration routes. Historical evidence suggests, however, that this offset was far bigger in the late nineteenth century than it has been since the 1970s. A fourth offset was sending country educational catch-up, serving to better equip potential emigrants with host country skills, an issue that will come up again below. An additional offset on the upside was the powerful network effects embedded in rising stocks of previous emigrants resident abroad, sending remittances and offering help with job search (today including help navigating illegal entrance).

As the demographic transition played itself out, as sending country growth miracles subsided to modern steady states, and as educational catch-up slowed down, the rise in emigration rates on the upside faded, the rates themselves peaked and then started to fall on the downside. The downside of the life cycle has always obeyed standard economic theory, but it was and is often extended by the migrant-stock and network effect (Hatton and Williamson, 1998, Ch.2; 2005, Ch. 4).

To complicate matters a little, industrial revolutions and demographic transitions in sending countries have always been correlated with sometimes violent political transitions. A huge literature debates causality, an issue that I will duck here. The point is this: State formation, or more often reformation, creates transitions during which institutions are uprooted, which in turn creates some losers who exit (Zolberg, 1983). The most obvious modern cases are the transitions in Eastern Europe and the former Soviet Union, events that generated mass outflow in the early 1990s, aided by better opportunities to escape. Transitions have also taken the form of lengthy civil wars, generating bursts of emigration, which often persist through network effects. Such political upheavals can create migration humps such as in Central America during the 1970s and 1980s, when emigration induced by conflicts subsequently ebbed. In the late twentieth century, the effects of civil war and terror can be most clearly seen in the number of asylum applications in the developed world. These peaked in 1992 and have since declined, following the life-cycle pattern of Third World emigration (Hatton and Williamson, 2006). Much of the post-1992 decline in asylum applications can be attributed to abating violence and civil war, but also to tougher asylum policies (Hatton, 2009). But even in an environment of ethnic cleansing, economics and demographics matter, and the best historical example of this is that of the Jews fleeing Eastern Europe up to World War I (Boustan, 2007).

This brief survey raises an important question that deserves more attention: Does an understanding of the fundamentals driving past emigration help provide some guide to future trends in Third World emigration? As I pointed out above, Timothy Hatton and I (2011) certainly think so. Our work suggests that emigration pressure in the Third World—determined by source country growth miracles, demographic transitions, education revolutions, poverty reduction, and migrant stock dynamics—has been abating. Projections into the future—even assuming host countries resume the growth they had before the Great Recession—suggest that emigration pressure will decline, and that its composition will be much more African (in the midst of its life cycle) and much less Asian and Hispanic (at the end of their life cycles). It seems clear that history matters.

2. BRAIN DRAIN, BRAIN GAIN, SKILL PREMIA, AND ENDOGENOUS SCHOOLING RESPONSES

Like today's emigrants, European emigrants prior to the 1920s had higher levels of schooling than those who stayed behind. They were also taller, healthier, and probably less risk averse. Furthermore, they came from the middle of the income and wealth distribution: the poor at the bottom were trapped, and thus stayed home; the rich at the top had a good thing going, and thus had no reason to move. All of this implies a human capital outflow or, in standard rhetoric, brain drain. But what about the huge numbers that returned: for example, at least 80% of the Italians who left for northern Europe and the New World returned home between 1880 and 1930. Didn't they return with valuable skills learned abroad, skills they would not have accumulated at home? Didn't at least some strive to improve the quality of institutions, government, and the way markets worked at home? I wish I could say that economic historians have the evidence that speaks to these questions, but they do not. Like modern emigrants from the Third World, it is very difficult to identify who, how many, and whether return migrants were negatively or positively selected. Thus, a recent World Bank paper explored the impact of emigration on institutions, but said nothing about return migration (Docquier et al., 2011). However, economic historians know quite a bit about schooling responses.

The emigration of young adults raises the expected return to education of younger stayers who remain in school a little longer, hoping to use the added schooling in labor markets abroad. This is true of the Third World today, and the same was probably true of the poor parts of Europe before 1939, and between 1950 and 1975. Not only did European emigration raise the demand for primary schooling for the next younger cohort, but it also seems to have helped provoke a schooling supply response from European governments. However, we are not sure how much (but see Giffoni and Gomelinni, 2012).

The US 1917 Immigration Act imposed a literacy test, something that had been debated by Congress for 22 years. The literacy test was expected to create a barrier to poor European immigrants, and Congress thought it would raise US immigrant quality and reduce their numbers. The Act failed since a revolution in the provision of free and public elementary education had by then spread east and south to backward Europe. For example, between 1881 and 1931, Italian literacy rates soared: from 20% to 60% in southern Italy, Sicily, and Sardinia; from 35% to 80% in central Italy; from 40% to 85% in Venice and Emilia; and from 60% to 95% in the northern triangle (Kirk, 1946). The story was similar in other poor parts of Europe that lagged behind the industrial leaders. Thus, the US literacy test failed to keep out poor European immigrants since a primary school and literacy revolution back home made it possible for them to hurdle the barrier.

Was the European literacy revolution exogenous? I doubt it: Opportunities abroad raised the demand for schooling at home. True, an exogenous schooling revolution would have equipped young Europeans to function better in foreign labor markets. Causation probably went both ways, and economic historians need to join development economists to establish the causation.

What about host countries? During the mass migrations between 1870 and 1913, rich labor-scarce countries with big immigration rates underwent rising inequality and poor labor-abundant countries with big emigration rates underwent falling inequality. During the anti-global and immigrant-restricted interwar years, 1921–38, the correlation disappeared. Indeed, some previously emigrating countries like Italy underwent rising inequality, while some previously immigrating countries like Australia, Canada, and the US underwent falling inequality. This is only a correlation, of course: Immigration policy may have been correlated with some omitted variables and the omitted variables may have been doing all the work. Still, at least the correlation keeps the immigration-breeds-inequality hypothesis on the table.

Now consider what happens when 150 years of US labor force growth is correlated with earnings inequality. Rapid rates of labor force growth coincided with rising earnings in equality and skill premia, while slow rates of labor force growth took place during episodes when earnings inequality was decreasing and the skill premia was falling. Furthermore, 1909–29 and 1929–48 were two periods when the skill premia was falling especially quickly and the growth rates of the (unskilled) labor force were especially slow (Williamson, 2007). There was a great egalitarian leveling in American incomes between the first and second thirds of the century. The ratio of wages of the top to the bottom 10% in manufacturing fell by almost a third between 1890 and 1940. Pay ratios of skilled to unskilled fell by two-thirds between 1907 and 1952. Weekly wage dispersion among white men fell by more than a quarter between 1940 and 1965, as did the share of the top 10% of income earners.

Some favor the view that an exogenous and revolutionary change in the supply of secondary and tertiary schooling must have overwhelmed the skill-using bias that characterized twentieth century economic progress (Goldin and Katz, 2001, 2008). Such exogenous schooling forces would, of course, have helped erase the skill premium, compress the wage structure, and level incomes. But what about exogenous and revolutionary changes in unskilled labor supplies associated in large part with the demise of mass migration? These policy-induced immigration forces would have reinforced the policy-induced schooling forces, and a number of recent studies offer considerable support for the thesis (Martin and Viarengo, 2008; Hunt, 2012; Lafortune et al., 2013).

If mass migration before the Great War contributed to high and rising inequality and skill scarcity in New World host countries, while its absence after the quotas contributed to the decline in skill scarcity and less inequality there, then we should see opposite trends in the European sending countries. While both sides of the Atlantic may have shared the same technological events, the boom and bust in mass migration must have left different inequality and schooling marks on either side of the Atlantic. Much more work remains to be done on this issue, but what evidence we have at hand seems to be consistent with the hypothesis. The mass migration boom and bust appears to be a good candidate to help explain the asymmetric inequality trends between Europe and the New World. A good illustration of how policy-induced immigration forces created greater unskilled labor scarcity, declining skill premia, and lower earnings inequality is not hard to find for the US: The quota-induced absence of European immigrants crowded in southern blacks to good northern jobs that offered much better earnings and living standards than did share cropping in the south. Since the Great Black Migration—which took place in the absence of European immigrants (Collins, 1997)—greatly improved the relative income position of blacks between 1910 and 1950, it helps account for the great leveling of incomes in the middle third of the twentieth century, and offers one important channel through which exogenous changes in European mass migration contributed to the leveling.

What about US schooling? Consistent with the evidence of the great leveling in the middle third of the twentieth century, the returns to US schooling declined from World War I to the 1960s (Goldin, 1999, Tables 6 and 7). For young men, the return to a high school degree fell from 11–12% in 1914 to 7% in 1959, while the return to a college degree fell from about 15% to 9% over the same period (Goldin and Katz, 2001, Table 2.4). How much of this was due to a policy-induced scarcity of unskilled and poorly schooled immigrants that lowered the rate of return to schooling by raising the opportunity costs of staying in school? How much of it was due instead to an exogenous schooling glut that lowered those rates?

It is important to stress that the immigrant scarcity and the schooling glut hypotheses are not competing: instead, they are mutually supporting. The exogenous and endogenous schooling hypotheses also need not be competing, since both forces might have been operating. Still, we would like to know which was doing most of the work.

There is no doubt about the fact that US secondary school enrollment soared from 1910 to 1940, rising from about 14% to 71% (Goldin, 1998; Goldin and Katz, 2001, pp. 59–60, Figure 2.5), and an increasing number of the graduates took white-collar office and factory jobs. But why did the US high school movement begin around 1900 or 1910? Why not later, as was true of Europe? Surely some part of the schooling boom could have been an endogenous response to the large skill premium, schooling scarcity, and a high return to education in the late nineteenth century when mass migration reached its crescendo. The issue has not yet been resolved. The payoff to future research on the schooling-endogeneity hypothesis will be great since it speaks to modern brain drain debates and whether and how human capital formation responds to mass migration in host and source country.

3. MIGRATION, REMITTANCES, FINANCIAL DEVELOPMENT, AND CONVERGENCE

The late nineteenth century Atlantic economy exhibited two key features. First, it was one of mass migration in unprecedented quantities. Second, it underwent an impressive convergence in living standards. Poor countries around the European periphery tended to grow faster than the rich industrial leaders at the European center, and often even faster than the labor-scarce countries overseas. True, those catching up on the European leaders were not in Asia, Africa, the Middle East, or Eastern Europe. Still, there *was* convergence in the Atlantic economy. Convergence of what? Although GDP per worker-hour estimates are the most popular measure used in the convergence literature, real wage rates are the better measure if our interest is the impact of global migration on sending and receiving labor markets.

The Atlantic economy was perturbed by two profound shocks during the first half of the nineteenth century: early industrialization in Britain, which then spread to a few countries on the European continent; and resource "discovery" in the New World, triggered by sharply declining international transport costs. Tariff barriers were high prior to mid-century even in Britain (the Corn Laws were repealed only in 1846); international trade was still modest; international migration was not yet "mass" (the famine-induced Irish flood of migrants was not released until the late 1840s); and global capital markets were as yet underdeveloped. The result of these two perturbations was therefore to produce a steep real wage divergence in the Atlantic economy during the first half of the nineteenth century. Economists are taught that really important shocks to any market are followed, with a lag, by transitions to a new equilibrium. The Latin Americans call this transition from 1870 to 1913 the *belle époque*, North Americans refer to it as their *gilded age*, and revealingly the English dub it their *Victorian* and *Edwardian failures*. The most extensive living standard convergence the Atlantic economy has ever seen occurred during the transition from the mid-century to World War I (Williamson, 1995). True, the speed per decade wasn't quite as fast as that recorded during the post-World War II growth miracle (Crafts and Toniolo, 1996), but it was close.

How much of the convergence in the pre-World War I Atlantic economy was due to mass migration? How much was due to capital accumulation and productivity catch-up?

The literature has assessed the labor force impact of these migrations (Taylor and Williamson, 1997; Hatton and Williamson, 2005, Table 6.2). The impact varied greatly: Argentina's labor force was augmented most by immigration (86%), Brazil's the least (4%), and the US in between (24%), the latter below the New World average of 40%; Ireland's labor force was diminished most by emigration (45%), France and the Netherlands the least (1% and 3%), and Britain in between (11%), the latter just a little below the Old World average of 13%. These, then, are the Atlantic economy mass migrations whose labor market impact we wish to assess.

The standard way of dealing with this question in the classroom is illustrated in Figure C1.1 (Hatton and Williamson, 2005, Figure 6.3), where we simplify things by looking only at the wage gap between New World and Old World. New World wages and labor's marginal product are on the left-hand side and Old World wages and labor's marginal product are on the right-hand side. The world labor supply is measured along the horizontal axis. An equilibrium distribution of labor occurs at the intersection of the two derived labor demand schedules (O and N). Instead, we start at l^1, where labor is scarce in the New World, and thus where the wage gap between the two regions is very large, $w_n^1 - w_o^1$. If mass migrations redistribute labor towards the New World, say to l^2, the wage gap collapses to $w_n^2 - w_o^2$, and all the observed wage convergence would be attributable to migration. However, the same kind of convergence could have been achieved

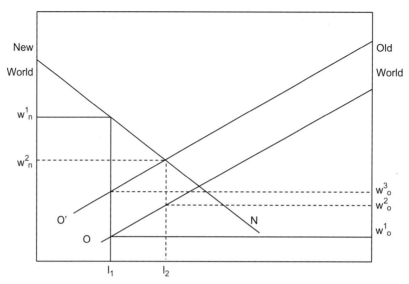

Figure C1.1 *Allocating labor supplies between New and Old World.*

by a relative labor demand shift: a shift in O to O′, an event driven perhaps by faster accumulation and productivity advance in the Old World. The no-migration counterfactual invokes the standard *ceteris paribus* assumption: We adjust population and labor force according to the net migration (and labor participation) rates observed during the period, and assume that technology, capital stocks, prices, and all else remain constant. No doubt the assumption imparts a bias on the measured impact of mass migration, but let's see whether the magnitudes for the Atlantic economy are large enough to warrant further debate over bias.

Migration affects long-run equilibrium wages to the extent that it influences aggregate labor supply. The labor demand elasticities have been estimated econometrically, and the results have been used to assess the impact on real wages in 1910 had there been zero net migration after 1870 in all countries (Taylor and Williamson, 1997, Table 4). The experiment suggests that the mass migrations lowered wages and labor productivity a lot in the New World and raised them a lot in the Old World. Not surprisingly, the biggest impact is reported for those countries that experienced the biggest migrations: emigration raised Irish wages by 32%, Italian by 28%, and Norwegian by 10%; and immigration lowered Argentine wages by 21%, Australian by 15%, Canadian by 16%, and American by 8%.

This partial equilibrium assessment is bigger than it would be in general equilibrium; for example, it ignores global capital market responses, although this latter shortcoming will be repaired in a moment. Whether an overstatement or not, the experiment suggests that in the absence of the mass migrations, real wage dispersion would have *increased* by 7%, rather than having decreased by 28% as it did in fact. Wage gaps between New and Old World in fact declined from 108% to 85%, but in the absence of the mass migrations they would have *risen* from 108% to 128% in 1910. The counterfactual suggests that more than all (125%) of the real wage convergence in 1870–1910 (log measure of dispersion) was attributable to migration, something of an overkill.

So, it appears that migration over-explains late nineteenth century convergence. Or does it? Remember that there were *other* powerful forces at work too. We know that capital accumulation was more rapid in the New World, so much so that the rate of capital deepening was faster in the US than in any of her competitors (Wright, 1990). Thus, the mass migrations may have been at least partially offset by capital accumulation, and a large part of it was being financed by international capital flows, which reached magnitudes unsurpassed before or since (Obsfelt and Taylor, 2004). The evidence that capital chased after labor is extensive (Clemens and Williamson, 2004), so Taylor and Williamson (1997) made exactly this kind of adjustment to the overkill result just reported. They added the assumption that international capital flows were sufficient to equalize rates of return between sending and receiving countries. The capital-chasing-labor offsets are very large. Whereas mass migration over-explained the observed real wage convergence using the model without capital chasing labor, it explains about 70% using the model with capital chasing labor, leaving approximately 30% to other forces. The convergence power of free migration, when it is tolerated, can be substantial. Convergence explanations based on technological or accumulation catch-up in closed-economy models miss this point. The millions on the move in the late nineteenth century did not.

Could the mass migration also have had a dynamic impact on catch-up and convergence? Recall Figure C1.1, where we noted that convergence could also have been achieved by a relative demand shift: a shift in O to O′, an event driven perhaps by faster accumulation and productivity advance in the Old World. How might emigration have produced that effect at home? One way is through remittances.

Since the nineteenth century unrestricted migrations (as a labor force share) were often bigger than the restricted ones today, it's not surprising that the remittance flows (as a share in GDP) were often bigger as well (Magee and Thompson, 2006; Esteves and Khoudour-Castéras, 2009). Although, like migration itself, remittances underwent great volatility, their share in GDP reached as high as 5–7% in Greece, Italy and Portugal, and 2.5–3.2% in Finland, Norway and Spain, compared with an average of 3.5% in 2006 (Esteves and Khoudour-Castéras, 2011, p. 451). There is a very extensive literature which documents that financial deepening fosters growth by augmenting accumulation rates and investment productivity. There is a more recent literature that documents that remittances to the developing world augment financial deepening (Martinez Peria et al., 2007; Giuliano and Ruiz-Arranz, 2009). Not only were the same forces operative in the nineteennth century, but it appears that their effects were even bigger (Esteves and Khoudour-Castéras, 2011, p. 456).

4. MIGRATION TIMING, THE TEN PERCENT RULE, AND POLITICAL BACKLASH

The Great Recession has cast a harsher light on immigration and immigration policy. Sagging host-country labor markets have led to calls for even tougher restrictions on potential competition from immigrant workers and ballooning fiscal deficits have heightened fears about the (alleged) added welfare burden of immigrants. How has immigration responded to slumps? Has it induced policy backlash? The past 150 years offer some answers.

International migration has always been sensitive to the business cycle. While long-run trends in migration are influenced by economic and demographic fundamentals, short-run movements are driven by the state of labor markets in both host and sending countries. During the great nineteenth century European migrations, the flows were very volatile, *much* more so than economic conditions in either host or sending country to which the migrants responded.

Not surprisingly, historical research has shown that emigration is negatively related to unemployment at the destination and positively related to unemployment at the source. But what happens when economic conditions deteriorate (unemployment rises) at *both* source *and* destination, as has been true during every global economic crisis since the 1870s? History yields an unambiguous answer: host country conditions *always* dominate.

The rise in unemployment abroad had nearly three times the effect on UK emigration between 1870 and 1913 compared with a rise in UK unemployment. During the slump of the 1890s, migration to the US and Australia did not fall, like output, just by something like 5% or 10%, it evaporated entirely. During the Great Depression in the 1930s, net immigration to the US, Canada, Australia, and Argentina turned *negative* as new immigration virtually ceased and as previous immigrants headed home. For countries of emigration, the result was just the opposite—as the global depressions deepened, their labor markets became even more glutted as fewer left and more returned.

Thus, migration's response to global recessions tends to soften labor market slumps in host countries and intensify them in source countries. I don't think modern analysts have taken enough notice of this fact. Economic historians have. During the big 1890s US depression, net migrant exits shaved off about 1.6 percentage points from the unemployment rate. That is, the unemployment rate would have risen by 6.7 percentage points without the fall in immigration between 1892 and 1896 instead of recording the actual 5.1 percentage point rise. History tells us that for every 100 jobs lost in high-wage host countries, 10 fewer immigrants arrived. This 10% rule applied to the 1890s and the Great

Depression, but does it apply today? On the one hand, legal migration should be less responsive to business-cycle conditions with tough immigration policies in place. On the other hand, those moving under family reunification policies (half of US immigration) are much less restricted, and most recent migrants have the option to return home. Of course, there are no quotas facing illegals, a group that is especially sensitive to employment conditions.

So what's the answer? The relationship between unemployment and the net immigration rate per thousand of the population (including illegals) between 1990 and 2004 was inverse (Hatton and Williamson, 2009, Figure 1). When the relationship is estimated the 10% rule appears: for every 100 jobs lost, 10 fewer immigrants arrive on net.

Immigration has always been a safety valve that mitigates labor market effects of host-country recessions. It should therefore mute anti-immigrant sentiment but, paradoxically, it does just the opposite. Protracted recessions appear to lead to cumulative negative reactions to the immigrant *stock*, as opposed to the flow, thus providing an opportunity for anti-immigrant forces to gather strength. And so it is that anti-immigrant sentiment rose in every US recession since the mid-nineteenth century, despite sharply falling immigration. It happened in the 1840s with the rise of the US Know-Nothing political movement, and it happened again in the 1890s when the US Congress began to debate the immigration restrictions that were imposed in 1917 and the 1920s.

Public opinion across the OECD favored tighter restrictions on immigration even before the Great Recession arrived. Will the Great Recession and its aftermath provide just the political impetus needed to convert this latent anti-immigrant sentiment into much more restrictive immigration laws? Perhaps. But there are reasons to think that the backlash will not be anywhere near as dramatic today as past history might suggest. After all, since the 1970s anti-immigrant sentiment has not risen as sharply as the much bigger rise in immigration. Also, the median voter is much less threatened by direct labor market competition than would have been true 30 or even 130 years ago. More important still, and as I argued above, the long-run demographic and economic forces that ratcheted up world migration for most of the late twentieth century are now in decline.

Having said all of this about host countries, where are all the studies that assess the impact of unrequited immigration in sending countries in the wake of the most recent severe global crisis? For example, we are told that net (legal and illegal) Mexican immigration to the US dropped from a flood to a drought. What has been the resulting impact on Mexican labor markets? Or on Philippine labor markets? Or on Maghreb labor markets? Or on Polish labor markets? Here economic historians must share the blame: Sad to say, I can cite no serious historical study assessing the impact of global crises on sending European labor markets between the 1870s and the 1930s.

ACKNOWLEDGMENTS

I gratefully acknowledge previous comments and suggestions from Timothy Hatton; this work draws heavily on our book *Global Migration and the World Economy* (2005).

REFERENCES

Akerman, S., 1976. Theories and methods of migration research. In: Rundblom, H., Norman, H. (Eds.), From Sweden to America: A History of the Migration. University of Minnesota Press, Minneapolis.

Boustan, L.P., 2007. Were Jews political refugees or economic migrants? Assessing the persecution theory of Jewish emigration, 1881–1914. In: Hatton, T.J., O'Rourke, K.H., Taylor, A.M. (Eds.), The New Comparative Economic History: Essays in Honor of Jeffrey G. Williamson. MIT Press, Cambridge, MA, pp. 267–290.

Clemens, M., Williamson, J.G., 2004. Wealth bias in the first global capital market boom 1870–1913. Econ. J. 114, 311–344 (April).

Collins, W.J., 1997. When the tide turned: Immigration and the delay of the great migration. J. Econ. Hist. 57, 607–632 (September).

Crafts, N.F.R., Toniolo, G., 1996. Economic Growth in Europe Since 1945. Cambridge University Press, Cambridge.

De Haas, H., 2007. Turning the tide? Why development will not stop migration. Dev. Change 38 (5), 819–841.

Docquier, F., Lodigiani, E., Rapoport, H., Schiff, M., 2011. Emigration and Democracy. Centro Studi Luca D'Agliano Development Studies, Turin, Italy, Working Papers 307 (May).

Esteves, R., Khoudour-Castéras, D., 2009. A fantastic rain of gold: European migrants' remittances and balance of payments adjustment during the gold standard period. J. Econ. Hist. 69 (4), 951–985.

Esteves, R., Khoudour-Castéras, D., 2011. Remittances, capital flows, and financial development during the mass migration period, 1870–1913. Eur. Rev. Econ. Hist. 15, 443–474 (December).

Giffoni, F., Gomelinni, M., 2012. Endogenous Schooling in the Age of Mass Migration, Unpublished (November).

Goldin, C., 1998. America's graduation from high school: The evolution and spread of secondary schooling in the twentieth century. J. Econ. Hist. 58, 345–374 (June).

Goldin, C., 1999. The Returns to Skill in the United States Across the Twentieth Century. NBER Working Paper 7126, National Bureau of Economic Research, Cambridge, MA (May).

Goldin, C., Katz, L.F., 2001. Decreasing (and then increasing) inequality in America: A tale of two half-centuries. In: Welch, F. (Ed.), Increasing Income Inequality in America. University of Chicago Press, Chicago, pp. 37–82.

Goldin, C., Katz, L.F., 2008. The Race between Education and Technology. Harvard University Press, Cambridge, MA.

Guiliano, P., Ruiz-Arranz, M., 2009. Remittances, financial development, and growth. J. Dev. Econ. 90 (1), 144–152.

Hatton, T.J., 2009. The rise and fall of asylum: What happened and why. Econ. J. 119 (535), F183–F213.

Hatton, T.J., Williamson, J.G., 1998. The Age of Mass Migration: An Economic Analysis. Oxford University Press, New York.

Hatton, T.J., Williamson, J.G., 2005. Global Migration and the World Economy: Two Centuries of Policy and Performance. MIT Press, Cambridge, MA.

Hatton, T.J., Williamson, J.G., 2006. Refugees, asylum seekers and policy in Europe. In: Foders, F., Langhammer, R.J. (Eds.), Labor Mobility and the World Economy. Springer, Heidelberg, Germany.

Hatton, T.J., Williamson, J.G., 2009. Global Economic Slumps and Migration. CEPR Vox. Centre for Economic Policy Research, London (29 April).

Hatton, T.J., Williamson, J.G., 2011. Are Third World emigration forces abating? World Dev. 39, 20–32 (January).

Hunt, J., 2012. The Impact of Immigration on the Educational Attainment of Natives, IZA Discussion Paper 6904 (October).

Kirk, D., 1946. Europe's Population in the Interwar Years. Princeton University Press for the League of Nations, Princeton, NJ.

Lafortune, J., Tessada, J., Gazmuri, A., 2013. Lured In and Crowded Out? Estimating the Impact of Immigration on Natives' Education using Early XXth Century US Immigration. Unpublished, PUC, Santiago (August).

Magee, G., Thompson, A., 2006. The global and local: Explaining migrant remittances flows in the English-speaking world, 1880–1914. J. Econ. Hist. 66 (1), 177–202.

Martin, F., Viarengo, M., 2008. American Education in the Age of Mass Migration. Kennedy School of Government, unpublished (October).

Martin, P.L., Taylor, J.E., 1996. The anatomy of a migration hump. In: Taylor, J.E. (Ed.), Development Strategy, Employment and Migration: Insights from Models. OECD, Paris.

Martinez Peria, M.S., Mascaro, Y., Moizeszowicz, F., 2007. Do remittances effect recipient countries' financial development? In: Fajnzylber, P., Lopez, H. (Eds.), Remittances and Development: Lessons from Latin America. World Bank, Washington, DC, pp. 171–215.

Nyberg-Sørensen, N., Van Hear, N., Engberg-Pedersen, P., 2002. The migration–development nexus, evidence and policy options, state-of-the-art overview. Int. Migrat. 40 (2), 3–47.

Obsfelt, M., Taylor, A.M., 2004. Global Capital Markets: Integration, Crisis, and Growth. Cambridge University Press, Cambridge.

Pritchett, L., 2006. Let Their People Come: Breaking the Gridlock on Global Labor Mobility. Center for Global Development, Washington, DC.

Taylor, A.M., Williamson, J.G., 1997. Convergence in the age of mass migration. Eur. Rev. Econ. Hist. 1, 27–63 (April).

Williamson, J.G., 1995. The evolution of global labor markets since 1830: Background evidence and hypotheses. Explor. Econ. Hist. 32, 141–196 (April).

Williamson, J.G., 2007. Inequality and schooling responses to globalization forces: Lessons from history. In: Migration, Trade and Development. Dallas Federal Reserve Bank, Dallas, TX.

Wright, G., 1990. The origins of American industrial success, 1879–1940. Am. Econ. Rev. 80, 651–668 (September).

Zelinsky, W., 1971. The hypothesis of the mobility transition. Geogr. Rev. 61 (2), 219–249.

Zolberg, A., 1983. The formation of new states as a refugee-generating process. Am. Acad. Soc. Sci. 467 (1), 24–38.

PART II

The Adjustment of Immigrants

CHAPTER 3

The Adjustment of Immigrants in the Labor Market

Harriet Orcutt Duleep

Thomas Jefferson Program in Public Policy, College of William and Mary, Williamsburg, VA 23187-8795, USA; and IZA

Contents

1. Immigrant Labor Market Outcomes—Theoretical and Methodological Considerations	108
1.1 International skill transferability and investment in host-country-specific skills	108
1.2 An occupational mobility model	110
1.3 Testing the IAM's predictions about immigrant earnings and cross-sectional bias	111
1.4 A decline in immigrant entry earnings	112
1.5 Expanding on Chiswick's Theoretical Model and Borjas's discovery of an unexplained decline in immigrant entry earnings	114
1.5.1 Theoretical extensions of Chiswick's IAM	114
1.5.2 Empirical extensions	116
1.6 Methodological points	118
1.6.1 Other issues with following cohorts	121
1.6.2 Excluding zero earners and the self-employed	123
2. Individual Attributes and Motives for Migrating	124
2.1 Level of schooling	125
2.1.1 Skill transferability and where immigrants receive their schooling	126
2.1.2 How skill transferability interacts with level of schooling	127
2.1.3 Controlling for education in immigrant adjustment models	127
2.2 Ability	128
2.3 Constraints	130
2.4 The importance of being permanent	131
2.5 Country of origin	134
2.6 Admission status	138
2.6.1 Admission on the basis of kinship versus skills	138
2.6.2 Kinship admissions and other types of labor market adjustment	138
2.6.3 Refugees	139
2.6.4 The undocumented	141
3. Beyond the Individual—Economic and Social Contexts Affecting Labor Market Outcomes	142
3.1 The structure of the labor market	143
3.2 Enclaves	143
3.3 The permanence of the community	146
3.4 The state of the labor market	146
3.4.1 Other effects of the state of the labor market on immigrant adjustment	148
3.5 Structural changes over time in the host economy	149

Handbook of the Economics of International Migration, Volume 1A
ISSN 2212-0092, http://dx.doi.org/10.1016/B978-0-444-53764-5.00003-7

4. Labor Market Outcomes for Immigrant Women   150
   4.1 The Family Investment Hypothesis: theoretical underpinnings   151
   4.2 The Family Investment Hypothesis: empirical support   152
   4.3 Ramifications of immigrant women joining the labor market   153
   4.4 Family-based models of immigrant labor market adjustment and fertility   154
   4.5 Following cohorts: another look at the Family Investment
       Hypothesis   155
   4.6 Two mysteries about testing for the Family Investment Hypothesis   156
5. Immigrant Economic Adjustment: Evidence from Countries Other than the United States 157
   5.1 Country of origin, structural changes, and declines in immigrant initial earnings 158
   5.2 Evidence of convergence   158
   5.3 The importance of being permanent   159
   5.4 The flexibility of a country's labor market and society   160
6. Summary and Directions for Further Research   162
   6.1 The Occupational Mobility Model   163
   6.2 The Immigrant Human Capital Investment Model   163
   6.3 Empirical offspring of the IAM   164
   6.4 Immigrant ability and the relative flexibility of societies   165
   6.5 Skill acquisition   166
   6.6 Beyond the individual   168
   6.7 Immigrant women   169
   6.8 Permanence   170
   6.9 A concluding caveat   171
Acknowledgments   171
References   171

The adjustment of immigrants to their host country's labor market provides insight on numerous immigration-related research and policy issues. Do skills transfer across national labor markets? Do low-earning migrants have the incentive or ability to engage in human capital investment? Do immigrants assimilate, or is it just that those who start from poor positions who return home? More generally, our growing understanding of migrant behavior indicates the inter-relatedness of all major decisions made by migrants including the decision to migrate, social and economic assimilation, and emigration. The decision to work, whether one is employed, how long one stays, earnings, and occupation—reflecting both aspects of labor market opportunity and human capital investment decisions—are central to each of these.

Learning how immigrants fare in the labor market requires discerning from the available data the earnings growth of immigrants as they live in their host country. In the US, the first studies to use nationwide data on individuals generally measured immigrant earnings growth with a single year of decennial census data comparing the earnings of immigrants who were recently arrived with the earnings of immigrants who had been in the US multiple years (Chiswick, 1978a, 1979). Later studies used two censuses. Doing so provided information on the earnings growth of year-of-entry immigrant cohorts that are identified in both censuses (Borjas, 1985). Then, three censuses were used permitting analysis of how changes in the initial earnings of immigrant cohorts relate to changes in subsequent earnings growth; dividing the sample of immigrants into high- and low-emigration countries, these studies also pioneered testing the sensitivity of earnings growth estimates to selection bias from emigration (Duleep and Regets, 1994a, 2002).[1]

In recent years, the use of longitudinal data that trace the earnings of the same individuals has flourished. In the United States, efforts to study immigrant adjustment with individual longitudinal data have used Social Security administrative records matched to survey data (Hu, 2000; Duleep and Dowhan, 2002a, b; Lubotsky, 2007, 2011); the New Immigrant Survey—a panel survey of new legal immigrants (Jasso et al., 2000; Akresh, 2006, 2007, 2008); matched Current Population Survey data (Duleep and Regets, 1997a; Demombynes, 2002); and longitudinal data in the Survey of Income and Program Participation (Hall and Farkas, 2008).[2] With longitudinal data on individuals, selective emigration can be removed as a spurious contributor to earnings growth estimates by following the same individuals over time (Duleep and Regets, 1997a; Duleep and Dowhan, 2002a, b).

The use of panel survey data and administrative longitudinal records to study the adjustment of immigrants has thrived in other countries as well. Forays into immigrant adjustment with longitudinal data include Italy's Quarterly Labour Force Survey ISTAT (e.g., Venturini and Villosio, 2002), the German Socio-Economic Panel GSEOP (e.g., Constant and Massey, 2003; Constant and Zimmermann, 2004), Danish register-based panel data (e.g., Husted et al., 2001; Nielsen et al., 2004), the Swedish panel datasets LINDA (e.g., Hansen and Lofstrom, 2009) and LOUISE (e.g., Rashid, 2004), the Australian Longitudinal Survey of Immigrants LSI (e.g., Chiswick et al., 2005b) and the Australian Household, Income and Labour Dynamics HILDA (e.g., Cobb-Clark et al., 2012a, b); the UK Quarterly Labour Force Survey QLFS (e.g., Frijters et al., 2005), and Canada's administrative record data (e.g., DeSilva, 1996).

Examining these efforts over time and across countries unfolds an interesting interplay of how researchers perceive changes in immigration, the methods they use to measure immigrant earning growth, and the assumptions behind those methods.

How immigrants fare in the labor market has taken on greater urgency in recent years due to a well-documented decline in the initial earnings of immigrant men in the US and other host countries, a decline that persists controlling for inter-cohort changes in immigrant schooling levels and ages. The importance of this decline depends on whether the initial disadvantage experienced by recent immigrants (relative to natives and relative to earlier immigrant cohorts) persists throughout immigrants' working lives. One line of

---

[1] Also refer to Chiswick (1980), discussed in Section 1.6.1.
[2] The earliest use of US longitudinal data on individual earnings was Chiswick (1980), discussed later.

inquiry suggests that underlying the decline in initial earnings is a decline in immigrant ability, imparting an important and permanent disadvantage to the long-term labor market adjustment of recent US immigrants (Borjas, 1985, 1987, 1992a–c, 1994). Another stream of research suggests that the entry earnings decline stems from a decline in source-country to host-country skill transferability and is accompanied by increased earnings growth (Duleep and Regets, 1994a, 1996c, 1997b, c, 1999, 2002). Since the lower entry earnings are associated with increased human capital investment, the initial earnings disadvantage experienced by recent immigrants decreases over immigrants' working lives and is associated with benefits to the US economy (Duleep and Regets, 2002; Duleep, 2007).

Section 1 begins with methodological and theoretical considerations central to the analysis of immigrant earnings trajectories. Theoretical considerations include the transfer of immigrant skills to the host country's labor market, the transfer of immigrant skills to the production of new human capital, and the concept of immigrant quality. Method-ological considerations include the repercussions of controlling for cohort effects by including cohort-specific dummy variables, potential biases due to immigrant emigra-tion, and why cross-sectional estimates of earnings growth often approximate estimates from assumption-free analyses that follow individuals or cohorts of individuals.

Section 2 introduces individual attributes and motives that shape the concepts dis-cussed in Section 1. Section 3 follows with social and economic contexts that affect immigrant labor market outcomes. The labor market behavior of immigrant women is the subject of Section 4 and brings to the fore a family perspective. Section 5 offers a framework for examining whether consistent findings on immigrant adjustment occur across the labor markets of major economically developed immigrant-host countries. The chapter ends with key points and directions for future research.

1. IMMIGRANT LABOR MARKET OUTCOMES—THEORETICAL AND METHODOLOGICAL CONSIDERATIONS

1.1 International skill transferability and investment in host-country-specific skills

The intensity with which social scientists study immigrant adjustment trails the ebbs and flows of immigration. As the great wave of US immigration in the late nineteenth and early twentieth centuries came to a close, the University of Chicago's sociology depart-ment spawned a model of immigrant assimilation. Most closely associated with the works of Robert E. Park, this model portrayed immigrants' trajectories in the host country as a single process that applied to all immigrants, culminating in their cultural and economic assimilation (e.g. Park et al., 1921).[3] In contrast to developments in sociological research

---

[3] Also refer to Park's collected works published posthumously (Park, 1950).

that were to appear decades later, Park's assimilation model focused on the individual and ignored contextual variables such as the structure of the labor market and group-specific mechanisms of economic adjustment.

With the adoption of a restrictive immigration policy in the 1920s, and near immigration shut-down till 1965, immigrant adjustment lost its luster as an interesting research topic, only to reappear with the resurgence of immigration in the 1960s. Accompanying its re-emergence was the birth of a new labor economics focused on human capital investment. Led by economists such as T.W. Schultz, Becker, and Mincer, this new field pursued the idea that individuals make decisions about how much and what type of schooling and training to pursue in much the same way that decisions are made about physical capital, with benefit/cost comparisons guided by estimates of net present value or internal rate of return. With newly minted public-use microdatasets from the decennial censuses, scholars began to estimate models of individual earnings as a function of human capital, measured by years of schooling and age.

A key concept in the new labor economics was that the cost of human capital investment includes opportunity costs, such as the earnings lost by pursuing further schooling or taking jobs that offer more training but less pay. Opportunity costs could also include psychic costs, such as the emotional despair of leaving family and friends when deciding to migrate.[4] Another principle guiding the new labor economics was that human capital may be specific to particular jobs, or readily transferable from job to job. Within the new labor economics, Chiswick (1978a, b, 1979, 1980) pioneered the study of immigration.

Echoing Park's thesis of assimilation and focus on the individual, Chiswick developed a model of immigrant labor market adjustment. He theorized that when immigrants enter the US, or other host country, they lack (in varying degrees) the skills specific to that country that would enable their human capital to be fully valued in the labor market of their new home. Immigrants initially earn less than similarly qualified natives because the specific skills and knowledge associated with their years of schooling and experience are not valued as much by employers as are the skills of individuals who were raised and schooled in the host country. Assimilation in this context is acquiring specific skills that enable immigrants to earn on a par with host-country natives of comparable experience and education.

To increase the labor market value of their source-country human capital, immigrants engage in various forms of human capital investment such as learning English, pursuing informal and formal schooling and training, and becoming knowledgeable about the destination country's institutions, production methods, and technical terms. The specific "skills" needed to increase the labor market value of source-country human capital could

---

[4] Though long part and parcel of theoretical migration models (Sjaastad, 1962), psychic costs of migration are rarely explored empirically. An exception is Barrett and Mosca (2013).

also include credentials such as a diploma or training certificate that is recognized by the destination country's employers or needed to perform particular kinds of work in the host country. As English and other host-country-specific skills or credentials are gained, the value of the immigrant's source-country human capital—expressed both in terms of the individual's earnings and occupation—approaches that of a comparably educated and experienced native: the aerospace engineer, who could not get a job in aerospace, much less engineering, now lands a job in his field and earns accordingly.

The following theoretical prediction emerges from Chiswick's conceptualization. Immigrants who lack highly transferable skills would experience greater initial unemployment, start at lower earnings—the less transferable the skills, the lower their earnings—but also experience higher earnings growth than natives of the host country or immigrants with highly transferable skills with similar levels of education and experience. The higher earnings growth results from the acquisition of destination-specific skills bringing to life the source-country human capital.

Chiswick's Immigrant Assimilation Model specifies that immigrants acquire destination-relevant human capital at a decreasing rate with duration in the destination: human capital investments would be embarked on in terms of their respective earnings gains; the payoff time for such investments would be greatest the earlier they were done. The largest earnings gains would be during immigrants' initial years, tapering off with time in the host country.

Once the specific skills that restore the value of an immigrant's source-country skills are learned, immigrants would proceed on a similar human capital investment path as their host-country equivalents, but at a lower level of earnings. During the time they were learning skills to restore the labor market value of the human capital they came with, the earnings of natives (and immigrants with highly transferable skills) were continuing to grow. There is no reason embedded in this model for why the earnings of immigrants who initially lacked host-country skills would completely catch up to their native-born counterparts.

1.2 An occupational mobility model

Though rarely considered as longitudinal data, US census data contain longitudinal aspects; the 1970 Census asked individuals about their current occupation and their occupation five years ago.[5] Chiswick used this information to study the occupational trajectories of immigrants before and after they migrated to the US. For immigrants who had migrated within the last five years, the 1965 and 1970 occupations illuminate the last job before migration and the first job after migration. For immigrants who had been in the US more than five years, the 1965 and 1970 occupation data reveal the occupational mobility of immigrants with time in the US. Chiswick appropriately entitled his study "A Longitudinal Analysis of Occupational Mobility of Immigrants."

---

[5] Unfortunately, this question was discontinued in censuses following the 1970 census.

Starting with the Immigrant Assimilation Model, Chiswick developed an occupational mobility model that further emphasized the idea that immigrants invest in host-country-specific skills to restore source-country human capital (Chiswick, 1978b). Chiswick postulated that immigrants' occupational mobility follows a U-shaped pattern—an initial downgrading from the immigrant's last job before migration and a subsequent upgrading as host-country-specific skills are acquired. The depth of the "U" would depend on several factors: *The immigrant's original occupation*—the skills associated with some occupations transfer from one country to another more easily than for other occupations. *The immigrant's source country*—the more linguistically, institutionally, and culturally distinct, the greater the initial downgrading and the greater the subsequent steepness of the recovery. *The immigrants' level of skill*—immigrants with low levels of skills, such as day laborers, would experience little or no occupational downgrading, hence little or no investment in US-specific skills to recover the original occupation; their occupational trajectories would trace a shallow "U". These hypotheses find support in Chiswick's original analysis with the 1970 Census data and in subsequent explorations with longitudinal data (e.g., Jasso and Rosenzweig, 1995; Chiswick et al., 2005a; Akresh, 2006; Chiswick and Miller, 2008, 2009; Zorlu, 2013).

1.3 Testing the IAM's predictions about immigrant earnings and cross-sectional bias

Chiswick (1978a, 1979) and others found empirical support for the Immigrant Assimilation Model's predictions about immigrant earnings trajectories using a single cross-section of data; Chiswick's seminal research was based on 1970 census data. Using cross-sectional data, analysts measure immigrant earnings growth by comparing the earnings of recently arrived immigrants with the earnings of immigrants with similar demographic characteristics and education who have been in the host country longer.

The census, and other surveys that ask when immigrants came to the US to stay, make it possible to identify "year-of-entry" immigrant cohorts. For instance, with the 1970 census one can identify immigrants who came to the US in the years 1965–70, 1960–64, 1955–59, 1950–54, and before 1950. The 1969 earnings (reported on the 1970 census) of immigrants who entered the US in 1965–70 provide an estimate of immigrants' initial earnings. The 1969 earnings of immigrants who entered the US in 1955–60 are an estimate of the earnings that immigrants achieve after living 10–15 years in the US. The difference in earnings between the recent entrants and the longer-term residents is a "cross-sectional" estimate of immigrant earnings growth.

Studies that have used the cross-sectional methodology estimate high earnings growth for immigrants, substantially exceeding that of US natives. With time in the US, the earnings of most immigrants approach and even equal (or surpass) those of their US-born statistical twins. In accord with the notion of immigrants restoring their source-country human capital, immigrants coming from non-English-speaking countries experienced more unemployment and lower earnings initially than their English-speaking counter-parts, but higher earnings growth (Chiswick, 1979). The discovery that immigrant earn-ings ultimately equal or surpass natives' earnings was attributed to immigrants being positively selected on unmeasured attributes such as motivation.

The cross-sectional approach generally estimates immigrant earnings growth with an earnings regression, using cross-sectional variation to statistically measure the relationship between "years since migration" and immigrant earnings while controlling for other var-iables such as age and years of schooling. It assumes that once observable characteristics are controlled for, the initial earnings and earnings growth of entering immigrants mimics the earnings paths of earlier immigrants.

Chiswick (1980) questioned this assumption and proposed that findings of high immigrant earnings growth based on a single cross-section might reflect cross-sectional bias: inter-cohort changes in unmeasured variables that affect immigrant earnings could affect estimates of immigrant earnings growth. Chiswick (1980) devised the following test. In what appears to be the first use of US longitudinal individual data to study immi-grant earnings, Chiswick measured actual earnings growth with the National Longitu-dinal Survey of Adult Males by following over time the earnings of immigrants who had entered the US in various years. He then compared this wage growth with that pro-jected by a cross-sectional estimation on the same data. If cross-sectional bias were present and important, the two estimates should differ. If cross-sectional bias was unimportant, the two estimates should be similar. The two estimates of earnings growth were similar and Chiswick concluded that cross-sectional bias was not a problem.

What Chiswick did not consider was the possibility that immigrants' initial earnings, con-trolling for education and experience, might have declined over time. If immigrant earnings growth increased as immigrant entry earnings decreased then estimates of earnings growth from cross-sectional and longitudinal data would be similar, even though a decline in the adjusted entry earnings of immigrants defies a key assumption of cross-sectional estimation.

1.4 A decline in immigrant entry earnings

Using multiple censuses, Borjas (1985, 1987, 1992a–c) discovered a dramatic decline in the entry earnings of immigrant men, a decline that persisted within age and education categories. The decline was particularly apparent since the 1960s, when US immigration policy changed from a national origins system, favoring Western European immigration, to a family-based policy that greatly altered the source-country composition of US immigration. This unexplained decline in immigrant entry earnings invalidated a key precept of the cross-sectional methodology that the initial earnings of immigrant cohorts, adjusting for levels of human capital, do not change over time.

Borjas then proceeded to measure immigrant earnings growth, pooling two censuses. The information that informs the estimation of the relationship between earnings and years since migration comes from the 10-year earnings growth of the year-of-entry cohorts that are identified in both censuses. By using the 1970 and 1980 censuses, for instance, it is possible to follow over 10 years the earnings of immigrants who immigrated in 1965–70, 1960–64, 1955–59, 1950–54, and before 1950, since these year-of-entry cohorts are identified in both censuses.

Had Borjas's empirical methodology followed Chiswick's human-capital-investment perspective, the discovery of a decline in immigrant adjusted entry earnings might have inspired a methodology that would permit both entry earnings and earnings growth to vary. Instead, Borjas proposed that the decline in immigrant adjusted entry earnings stemmed from a decline in immigrant ability. Conceivably, changes in immigrant ability could affect entry earnings without affecting earnings growth.

Borjas's estimating equation resembled Chiswick's: Immigrant earnings growth is estimated in an earnings regression by statistically measuring the relationship between years since migration and immigrant earnings, controlling for age and years of schooling. It introduced, however, a categorical (zero–one) variable for each year of entry, to capture earnings differences across year-of-entry cohorts. The categorical variables permit the entry earnings of immigrant cohorts to change, thus permitting the estimated relationship between years since migration and earnings to begin at different earnings levels. The earnings growth rates of year-of-entry immigrant cohorts are assumed to be constant once observable variables, such as age and education, are accounted for.

Thus, Borjas's methodology abandoned one assumption of the cross-sectional methodology—inter-cohort constancy in the adjusted entry earnings of immigrants—but retained another: inter-cohort constancy in earnings growth. Decomposing the cross-sectional earnings growth into within- and across-cohort changes in immigrant earnings measured at the same stage in the assimilation process—and assuming no coincident change in earnings growth—Borjas concluded that much of the estimated cross-sectional earnings growth was due to an over-time decline in the quality of immigrants:

Instead of the rapid growth found by cross-section studies, the cohort analysis predicts relatively slow rates of earnings growth for most immigrant groups.

(Borjas, 1985)

Pairing slow rates of earnings growth with dramatically lower entry earnings painted a bleak picture of the economic adjustment of recent US immigrants with the large initial earnings disadvantage persisting unabated throughout the working lives of immigrants.

Borjas correctly showed that in a situation as in the US and other economically developed countries where immigrant initial earnings were falling over time, pairing the initial earnings of more recent immigrants with the earnings achieved by earlier immigrants after 10–15 years in the US overstates the earnings growth of the *earlier* immigrants. It does not follow, however, that the earnings growth of earlier cohorts is a good predictor of the earnings growth of more recent cohorts.

1.5 Expanding on Chiswick's Theoretical Model and Borjas's discovery of an unexplained decline in immigrant entry earnings

1.5.1 Theoretical extensions of Chiswick's IAM

Building on Chiswick's Immigrant Assimilation Model (IAM) and concept of skill transferability, Duleep and Regets (1999, 2002) developed an Immigrant Human Capital Investment (IHCI) model that formalized Chiswick's concept of skill transferability to the labor market with the parameter τ_M and highlighted the implications of two previously ignored aspects of skill transferability.[6]

One, immigrants whose source-country skills do not fully transfer to the US labor market will, by virtue of their lower wages, have a lower opportunity cost of human capital investment than natives or immigrants with high-skill transferability.[7] Two, the undervalued source-country human capital in the US labor market is useful for learning new skills. Persons who have learned one set of skills—even if those skills are not valued in the destination-country labor market—have advantages in learning new skills: they have learned how to learn. Moreover, common elements between old and new skills aid learning.[8] With the parameter τ_P, Duleep and Regets (2002) incorporated in their model the transfer of source-country skills to the production of host-country human capital.

Combining the lower opportunity cost of human capital investment for immigrants lacking immediately transferable skills to the host-country labor market with the role of untransferred human capital in the production of destination-country human capital creates a greater incentive for low-skill-transferability immigrants to invest in human capital than will be true of either high-skill-transferability immigrants or natives with similar levels of education and experience (Duleep and Regets, 1994a, 1999, 2002). These two concepts, when combined with a higher return to investment stemming from the complementarity of foreign and US human capital (Chiswick, 1978a, 1979), add ballast to the prediction that immigrants whose skills do not immediately transfer to the host country will have a greater incentive to learn than earn. It follows that they will have lower initial earnings and higher earnings growth.

Because immigrants will invest more in US human capital than natives, and low-skill-transferability immigrants will invest more than high-skill-transferability immigrants (holding initial human capital levels constant), immigrants will experience higher earnings growth than natives and, among immigrants, there will be an inverse relationship between entry earnings and earnings growth. Across groups, the lower the entry earnings,

---

[6] Studies that have used the IHCI model as a base include Akresh (2007) and Van Tubergen and Van de Werfhorst (2007).

[7] The time they spend learning new skills, instead of applying their current skills to earning, is less costly than it is for natives or for high-skill-transferability immigrants, who earn more with the same level of schooling and experience.

[8] For more discussion on this point, refer to Duleep and Regets (1999, 2002).

the higher the earnings growth and over time, as entry earnings fall (rise), earnings growth increases (decreases). The theoretical concepts added by Duleep and Regets intensify Chiswick's prediction that, controlling for education and age, there will be an inverse relationship between immigrant entry earnings and earnings growth.

With its emphasis on the low opportunity cost of human capital investment for immigrants lacking transferable skills paired with the value of source-country human capital for learning new skills, a distinguishing prediction of the IHCI model is that the higher incentive to invest in human capital pertains not only to host-country-specific human capital that restores the value of specific source-country human capital (the foreign-born aeronautical engineer who learns English so that he can pursue aeronautical engineering again), but to new human capital investment in general. When demand shifts, requiring new skills to be learned, immigrants who initially lacked host-country-specific skills will be more likely to pursue new opportunities than will natives or immigrants with highly transferable skills.

A native-born aerospace engineer well launched into his career or an immigrant with highly transferable skills allowing him to immediately pursue a job in his field would be reluctant to undertake computer training or an MBA. This would be true even if the training facilitated an ultimately better paid line of work because of the lost wages that such training incurs. The low opportunity cost for a similarly educated immigrant who could not initially transfer his source-country human capital paired with the value of his human capital in producing new human capital might make pursuing further training an attractive option.

High rates of human capital investment that are not tied to restoring immigrants' specific source-country skills would give immigrants greater ability to adapt to changing skill needs in the economy, potentially adding significant flexibility to the host-country economy. Green (1999) found a greater propensity of immigrants to change occupations than natives beyond what can be explained by an assimilation effect; the timing of the changes across year-of-entry cohorts suggests that they are in response to an evolving demand for different types of labor market skills.

The IHCI model is easily extended to accommodate several concerns. Most importantly, the model is altered to reflect ρ, the probability of staying, as well as $\mathbf{w_s}$, the return on human capital in the source country, and τ_s, the proportion of destination-country human capital usable in the source country. The most important insight that this framework provides for immigrant earnings patterns is that a more (less) permanent immigrant will have more (less) incentive to invest in destination-country-specific skills,[9] thereby increasing (reducing) earnings growth (Duleep and Regets, 1999).[10]

---

[9] As an emigrating immigrant has no need of host-country skills to increase τ_2, there is less reason to invest even when $\tau_s = 1$.

[10] Also see Dustmann (2000) on this point.

1.5.2 Empirical extensions

Using decennial census data, Duleep and Regets (1994a, 2002) replicated Borjas's finding that immigrant entry earnings, within education and age categories, had declined. Their methodological approach for measuring immigrant earnings growth was informed by Chiswick's theoretical model and their extensions of that model: as the adjusted entry earnings of immigrants declined, there should be a corresponding increase in earnings growth.

To test for an inverse relationship between immigrant entry earnings and earnings growth, Duleep and Regets used the data judiciously so as to avoid making assumptions. Rather than pooling the various year-of-immigration cohorts, they only followed from one census to the next the earnings of entry cohorts. This reduces the information that is used, but assures that the findings are not the result of an assumed relationship: In the presence of a systematic relationship between entry earnings and earnings growth, following year-of-immigration cohorts other than the entry cohorts requires assuming a relationship between immigrant entry earnings and earnings growth.[11]

Without imposing any restrictions on either entry earnings or earnings growth, Duleep and Regets (1992, 1994a, b, 1997b, 2002) followed country-of-origin/age/education cohorts of immigrants across the 1960–80 and 1970–90 decennial censuses.[12] For instance, using the 1980 census, they measured the 1979 earnings of immigrants, ages 25–54, who entered the US between 1975 and April 1980. Using the 1990 census, they measured the 1989 earnings of the same cohort of immigrants—those who entered the US in 1975–80 and were 35–64 years old in 1990. Similarly, using the 1970 and 1980 censuses, they measured the entry earnings and earnings after 10–14 years of US residence of immigrants who entered the country in 1965–70. They also measured the earnings of comparably aged US natives to provide estimates of relative immigrant earnings growth. Their analyses show that as immigrants' entry earnings decreased, earnings growth increased.

Duleep and Regets also examined the relationship between immigrant entry earnings and earnings growth across groups, again finding that within age–education groups, the lower the entry earnings, the higher the earnings growth. Dividing countries of origin according to level of economic development, they found that immigrants coming from less economically developed regions of the world have lower entry earnings but higher earnings growth than immigrants of similar age and education coming from economically

---

[11] Note that this approach avoids confounding effects of age and assimilation and the choice of an appropriate reference group (Kossoudji, 1989; Friedberg 1992, 1993; LaLonde and Topel, 1992).

[12] In describing their methodology, Duleep and Regets (2002) wrote "Median earnings were measured within education and age subsets for 24 countries or regions of origin. (Median rather than mean earnings were used since the median is a much less volatile measure of central tendency in small samples.) Entry earnings were measured by the earnings reported in 1980 by the 1975–80 entry cohort. The earnings growth rate of each of the country/age/education groups was then measured by the difference between their 1980 earnings and their respective earnings ten years later, as measured by the 1990 census, dividing the difference by their 1980 earnings. An alternative approach would be to first estimate a parametric model and then, using the predicted values, estimate the correlation between the predicted entry earnings and predicted earnings growth."

developed countries. To isolate the inverse relationship from coincidental country-of-origin effects, Duleep and Regets used the 1970, 1980, and 1990 censuses to relate *changes* in entry earnings to *changes* in earnings growth *for the same country*. A strong inverse relationship between entry earnings and earnings growth emerged.[13]

The Duleep/Regets findings, based on numerous country/age/education cohorts, agree with the LaLonde and Topel (1991, 1997) comparison of 1970 earnings and 1970–80 earnings growth for five ethnic groups, and with the Schoeni (1997) finding of low initial wages but fast wage growth for East Asian immigrants and high initial wages but slow wage growth for European immigrants.[14] Other confirmatory evidence, with novel applications and insights, includes analyses of several matched CPS files (Demombynes, 2002), of specific groups in the US (Lin, 2013), and of Canadian data (Aydemir and Skuterud, 2005; Green and Worswick, 2012).

To circumvent potential problems with changing cohort composition in the Duleep/Regets census-based analyses, Duleep and Dowhan (2002a, b) used longitudinal Social Security Administration earnings data matched to the 1994 March Current Population Survey (CPS) to follow for 10 years the annual earnings of the same working-age foreign- and native-born men, from multiple year-of-immigration cohorts. They found that foreign-born men who immigrated in 1960–64 initially earned on a par with US natives, those who immigrated in 1965–69 initially earned 17% less than their US-born statistical twins, and those who immigrated after 1969 initially earned 28–46% below their US-born counterparts, with an unadjusted foreign-born deficit ranging from 38% to 51%. However, at the 10-year mark, substantial earnings convergence occurs.

The convergence occurs because as the relative entry earnings of immigrants fell, their relative earnings growth increased. The earnings growth rates of the early immigrant cohorts closely approximated those of US-born men. Then, starting with the 1970–74 cohort, immigrant earnings growth rates exceeded those of the US born. The longitudinal analyses, unadjusted and adjusted for foreign-born/native-born differences in education and age, underscore two key points: post-1969 immigrants tend to have faster earnings growth than natives; and as the entry earnings of immigrants decreased, their earnings growth, relative to natives, increased.

---

[13] Their finding of a strong inverse relationship persists even when several methodological concerns are taken into account. Duleep and Regets (1994a, b, 2002) introduced a simple method to circumvent regression-to-the-mean bias in cohort analyses of entry earnings and earnings growth and a method for testing the sensitivity of the estimated inverse relationship to the effects of emigration.

[14] They also confirm the Schoeni finding of low initial earnings and slow earnings growth for Mexican immigrants during the 1980s. This finding does not hold, however, for all of Latin America or for Mexican immigrants of earlier periods. The 3 million legalizations in the 1980s under the 1986 Immigration Reform and Control Act might have made this a uniquely difficult period in the labor market for Mexican immigrants due to increased competition. Equally plausible is a sample selection bias (Ahmed and Robinson, 1994): Mexican immigrants illegal at the time of the 1980 census might have been more likely to be counted in 1990, after legalization.

In summary, the theoretical prediction of an inverse relationship between immigrant entry earnings and earnings growth that flows from Chiswick's IAM and is further buttressed by the IHCI model is supported by empirical analyses that circumvent potential cross-sectional bias by following individual or cohort earnings, using assumption-free methodologies to control for potential biases from emigration and sampling error (Duleep and Regets 1994a, b, 1996c, 1997a, b). Holding age and years of schooling constant, a persistent pattern emerges regardless of whether immigrant earnings patterns are analyzed over time, across groups, or both: There is a strong inverse relationship between immigrant entry earnings and earnings growth.

1.6 Methodological points

Recent empirical efforts to measure immigrant earnings growth generally pool evidence from multiple year-of-entry immigrant cohorts, either in pooled cross-sections or in longitudinal data. Cohort differences are "captured" with the inclusion of categorical (0–1) variables, as opposed to describing each cohort separately. This methodology, pioneered by Borjas and first estimated with data from two decennial censuses, continues to be used with other sources of data, including longitudinal data on individuals. It is the model of immigrant earnings shown in labor economics textbooks.

Although variously referred to as the pooled cross-sectional approach or the cohort fixed effects model, it might also be called the "stationary earnings growth" model because it assumes that the earnings growth rate of year-of-entry immigrant cohorts is constant once observable variables, such as age and education, are accounted for. This approach obfuscates important over-time changes in the earnings paths of immigrants. It also fails to fix cross-sectional bias.

Figure 3.1 illustrates some key concepts. The left-hand side displays the cross-sectional methodology for estimating immigrant earnings growth. It shows the earnings that we would observe in a single cross-section from census year t. We see the entry earnings of the most recent cohort (Point A) and the earnings that the earlier cohort (cohort $t-10$) achieves after 10 years in the US (Point D). Unobserved, at time t, are the earnings that the earlier cohort of immigrants first earned when they came to the US 10 years ago (Point C). By pairing the initial earnings of the recent cohort (cohort t) with the earnings at the 10-year point of the earlier cohort (cohort $t-10$), the cross-sectional method overestimates the earnings growth of the earlier cohort. The line A–D will accurately represent the earnings trajectory of the more recent cohort only if the earnings growth of the more recent cohort exceeds that of the earlier cohort to such an extent that the recent cohort's earnings catch up in 10 years to the earlier cohort's earnings at the 10-year mark.

The right-hand side of Figure 3.1 displays the fixed-cohort-effect methodology for estimating immigrant earnings growth. It shows the earnings that we would observe by pooling data from two decennial censuses, one from census year t, the other from census year $t-10$. With the addition of the earlier data, we now observe the initial earnings of

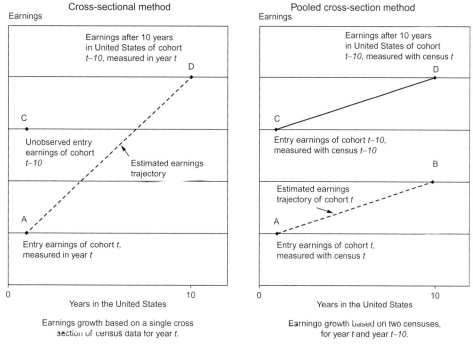

Figure 3.1 *Estimates of immigrant earnings growth based on two methods.*

cohort $t-10$ (Point C). The line C–D is the actual earnings trajectory of this earlier cohort. The line A–B is the projected earnings trajectory of the more recent cohort (cohort t). It will accurately predict the more recent cohort's earnings trajectory if and only if there has been no inter-cohort change in immigrant earnings growth. If there is a systematic relationship between immigrant entry earnings and earnings growth, then estimates of earnings growth based on this method can be seriously flawed. Ironically, with an inverse relationship between immigrant entry earnings and earnings growth, cross-sectional estimates of earnings growth will more accurately predict immigrant earnings growth than the method developed to overcome cross-sectional bias!

The top and bottom panels of Figure 3.2 show with solid lines the actual earnings trajectories based on Social Security administrative longitudinal individual data for various cohorts of immigrant men relative to US natives, weighted to have the same age and education distributions as the foreign-born men. The broken lines show the estimated earnings trajectories. The top panel estimations use the cross-sectional method: the initial earnings of each cohort are linked with the earnings, after 10–15 years, of the previous cohort. The estimated earnings trajectories in the bottom panel are based on the fixed cohort effect method: each estimated trajectory is constructed using an average of the earnings growth rates of the preceding cohorts. The fact that the cross-sectional method provides more accurate estimates for recent immigrant cohorts reflects the fact that as

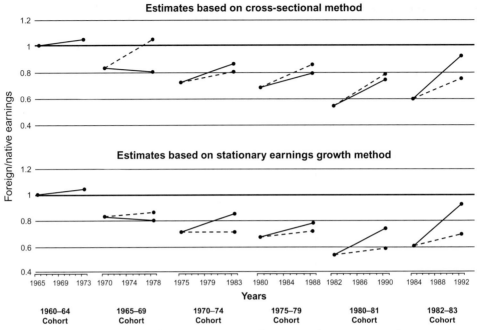

Figure 3.2 *Earnings trajectories of foreign-born men relative to US-born men: actual versus estimated based on two methodologies.*

immigrant entry earnings have fallen, earnings growth has increased to such an extent that the adjusted earnings of recent immigrants, after 10–15 years in the US, closely approximate the earnings, at the 10- to 15-year mark, of earlier immigrants.

Following cohorts with census data, Duleep and Regets (1994a, 2002) found that despite a 23.4% drop in immigrant initial earnings relative to US natives between the 1965–70 and the 1975–80 entry cohorts, there is very little difference between the cohorts in their relative earnings after 10–14 years in the US—85.4% for the 1965–70 cohort and 83.9% for the 1975–80 cohort (Table 3.1). This is because the more recent immigrant cohort, with lower relative entry earnings, had a much higher earnings growth rate. The effect is even more dramatic when separating into age and education groups. In each case, the more recent cohort, with lower relative entry earnings, surpasses the initially higher-earning earlier immigrant cohort in relative earnings (Table 3.1).[15] A similar

---

[15] Although these results suggest that the earnings of recent immigrants approach those of natives, they do not imply that the earnings of recent immigrants will, on average, exceed those of natives. In research following immigrants for 20 years, Duleep and Regets (2002) found that although the inverse relationship continues beyond the initial 10-year period (the earnings growth increase associated with lower initial earnings continues beyond the initial 10-year period), it is about one-third of the 10-year effect. The decrease in the ratio of immigrant to native earnings growth rates is also apparent in the Duleep/Dowhan longitudinal data analyses.

Table 3.1 Median earnings of immigrant men relative to natives during the first five years in the United States and ten years later: 1965–70 and 1975–80 immigrant entry cohorts

	1965–70 cohort		1975–80 cohort	
	1969 ratio to natives (measured with 1970 census data)	1979 ratio to natives (measured with 1980 census data)	1979 ratio to natives (measured with 1980 census data)	1989 ratio to natives (measured with 1990 census data)
Ages 25–54, all education levels	0.653	0.854	0.500	0.839
25–39 years old, 1–12 years of school	0.631	0.706	0.486	0.750
25–39 years old, more than 12 years of school	0.577	0.864	0.463	0.886
40–54 years old, 1–12 years of school	0.594	0.769	0.417	0.867
40–54 years old, more than 12 years of school	0.522	0.720	0.479	0.788

Estimates based on the 1970 Census of Population 1% Public Use Sample, the 1980 Census of Population 5% "A" Public Use Sample, and a 6% microdata sample created by combining and reweighting the 1990 Census of Population 5% and 1% Public Use samples.

picture emerges with the longitudinal data. Despite varying start points, immigrant earnings for each cohort are converging to the same earnings level at 10 years (Figure 3.3).

In summary, the inverse relationship invalidates the popular approach of controlling for cohort effects by including a zero–one variable for each cohort in analyses that pool more than one cross-section to measure immigrant earnings growth or in analyses that pool cohorts in longitudinal data. Since cohorts that vary in their entry-level earnings systematically vary in their earnings growth, each cohort must either be separately examined (Duleep and Regets, 1994a, 2002) or the inverse relationship incorporated into the analysis (Duleep and Regets, 1992, 1996a, b). The inverse relationship between immigrant entry earnings and earnings growth also explains the seeming enigma as to why recent immigrant studies using longitudinal data have found high earnings growth that resembles the earnings growth estimated in cross-sectional studies.

1.6.1 Other issues with following cohorts

Following cohorts using multiple decennial censuses (or other data sources), as in the Duleep/Regets studies, avoids cross-sectional bias, but still raises several concerns about whether the data on a particular cohort, measured at two distinct points in time, represent the same individuals. Earnings growth estimates may be affected by changes in census

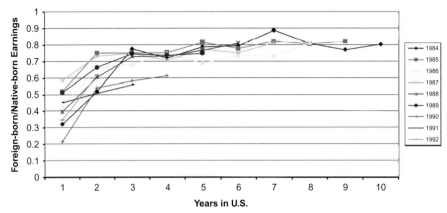

Figure 3.3 *Ratio of foreign-born to native-born median earnings of men by years in US of recent immigrant cohorts (adjusted).* Source: *Earnings estimates based on longitudinal Social Security Administration earnings data matched to the 1994 March Current Population Survey.*

coverage; how successfully the census "captures" individuals in various groups varies markedly between censuses (Passel and Luther, 1990; Ahmed and Robinson, 1994). For instance, Duleep and Regets (2002) confirm Schoeni's (1997) finding of low initial earnings and slow earnings growth for Mexican immigrants during the 1980s. Yet this result may reflect sample selection bias—Mexican immigrants who were undocumented at the time of the 1980 census might have been more likely to be counted in 1990 after the IRCA legalization.[16] To an unknown degree, immigrant emigration also affects these earnings growth estimates.[17]

How selection bias caused by emigration affects measures of earnings growth is not a well-settled issue. Some evidence suggests that it is the less successful who are most likely to emigrate (e.g., Lubotsky, 2007).[18] If true then earnings growth estimates based on

---

[16] An analysis of 1980 and 1990 census data consistent with a sample selection explanation for the Mexican results is contained in Ahmed and Robinson (1994).

[17] Relevant studies on emigration include Keely and Kraly (1978), Warren and Peck (1980), Chiswick (1980), Warren and Kraly (1985), and Warren and Passel (1987). For a review and other theoretical and empirical results, refer to Duleep (1994) and Ahmed and Robinson (1994). A sensitivity test of cohort results to emigration is in Duleep and Regets (1994a, b, 2002).

[18] The idea that the less successful are most likely to emigrate first originated in studies of internal migration. Yezer and Thurston (1976) proposed this theory in a study of US migration. Vanderkamp (1972, p. 465) provided indirect evidence that return migrants may "have experienced a negative return on their mobility investment." Further insights came from DaVanzo and Morrison (1981) and DaVanzo (1976, 1983), who introduced the idea that whether it is the unsuccessful who return depends on the timing of the migration: "Only those migrants who return promptly ... conform to the 'failure' stereotype ..." (DaVanzo, 1983, p. 558). In analyses of international emigration, Duleep (1994) and Constant and Massey (2003) model the timing of emigration.

following immigrant cohorts are biased upwards, since lower earning individuals would not be in the sample for later censuses.

Other studies suggest the reverse. Comparing wage regressions for Mexican immigrants estimated on samples including and excluding emigrants, Lindstrom and Massey (1994) conclude that the strong positive relationship between immigrant experience and wages is not an artifact of selective emigration. Chiswick (1980) failed to find evidence that, controlling for education, the unsuccessful are more likely to emigrate: "If anything, re-emigration rates are higher the greater the transferability of skills and if the original migration is economic in nature" (Chiswick, 1980, p. 4A-17). Consistent with the notion that emigration is highest for those with the most transferable skills, Jasso and Rosenzweig (1990) estimated higher emigration rates for European immigrants than for immigrants from Asia and the Western Hemisphere; Duleep et al. (1999) found that investment in US human capital positively correlates with lower emigration.

How emigration is measured may affect what researchers find. Matching data from the 1983 and 1995 Censuses of Israel, Beenstock et al. (2010) discovered that exits from the labor force due to death, absence from the labor force, and inability to match—*but not emigration*—are associated with lower earnings in 1983.

Context may also matter. Borjas and Bratsberg (1996) found that immigrants from countries with relatively unequal income distributions have relatively low earnings; within those groups, the probability of emigrating rises with earnings ability. Immigrants from countries with relatively equal income distributions have relatively high earnings; within those groups, the probability of emigration rises the lower the immigrant earnings ability. Constant and Massey's (2003) study also suggests the importance of context: the likelihood of return migration is strongly affected by the range and nature of social attachments immigrants have in Germany and in their countries of origin.

Given the variety of findings, the best course, when following synthetic cohorts, is to empirically test the sensitivity of one's results to emigration (including any other type of exits from the labor force). This can be done by dividing the sample of immigrants into high- and low-emigration (or other departure) countries. For instance, using 10-year emigration calculated using the number of observations for each cohort on subsequent censuses (adjusted to sampling proportion), Duleep and Regets (1994a,b, 2002) categorize country-of-origin cohorts as having high or low attrition rates, and examine how their key results are affected once emigration variation is reduced.

1.6.2 Excluding zero earners and the self-employed

Many researchers are aware of emigration as a potential problem when following cohorts. Yet emigration is not as serious as other common exclusions that stem from adopting Mincer-style earnings functions.

The Mincer-style earnings functions commonly used by labor economists were designed to measure returns to human capital, primarily measured by experience and education. For this purpose, it makes sense to minimize measurement error and bias by eliminating from the sample the self-employed (whose earnings include a return to physical capital) and those not employed (whose potential return to human capital is not observed) and to try to control for the sample selection biases introduced by these exclusions. In following cohorts across censuses, however, these standard sample exclusions introduce a different form of problem—classes of individuals out of the sample in one census and in the other.

Immigrant regression models that pool entry cohorts from two or more censuses typically limit the sample to employed individuals. Yet individuals unemployed or out of the labor force during the first census, perhaps because of low employability or time spent in school, might be fully employed, and hence in the sample, during the second. This issue applies to any cohort followed between censuses, but it is particularly important for a study of immigrants since immigrants have high occupational mobility and high in-school rates. Immigrants may also move from wage and salary jobs (thereby included in one census) to self-employment (thereby generally excluded).

Researchers following cohorts should consider measuring entry earnings and earnings growth rates for all individuals, including zero earners; excluding these classes of individuals in the first census measurement, but not the second, likely understates immigrant earnings growth for many immigrant groups. In analyses of 1980 and 1990 census data, Lofstrom (2000, 2002) found that including the self-employed reduces the immigrant-native earnings gap by 14%.

Duleep and Regets's model theoretically predicts an inverse relationship only when source-country human capital is held constant. Yet they find faster earnings growth for low-entry-earning immigrants even when age and education are not controlled. Using the Duleep/Regets methodology, Borjas replicated their finding controlling for education and age, but was unable to replicate their result not controlling for education and age. This may be because his analysis excluded zero earners and the self-employed.

2. INDIVIDUAL ATTRIBUTES AND MOTIVES FOR MIGRATING

Individual attributes such as ability and human capital relevant to the earnings of natives are also relevant to immigrant labor market adjustment. Additionally, the degree to which human capital transfers to the host-country labor market affects immigrant earnings. If source-country human capital transfers easily, immigrant earnings profiles resemble those of similarly schooled and experienced natives; the less transferable source-country skills are, the lower immigrants' initial earnings, relative to natives, but the higher their earnings growth, reflecting a higher propensity to invest in human capital.

Beyond the amount and portability of immigrant human capital, why someone moves affects labor force outcomes. People move to achieve short-term goals, such as earning money to send back home, and long-term goals, such as gaining better opportunities for themselves or for their children. People also move to leave situations: to flee a war, to fly away from the family nest, and to escape constraints on their dreams.

Why people move affects migration outcomes because it determines whether migrants have skills that easily transfer to the new labor market, the type of context that will surround them in their new location, whether their move is planned or abrupt, and—most importantly—whether it is permanent or temporary. Section 2 examines how the attributes of individuals—schooling, ability, intent to stay, country of origin, and admission status—interact with the concepts discussed in Section 1.

2.1 Level of schooling

Relative to natives, the entry earnings of immigrants with a high school education or less are lower for those who enter the US at older working ages compared with those who enter at younger working ages. This relationship holds for each entry cohort (Table 3.2) and across regions of origin (Table 3.3). For adult immigrants younger than 40, education's beneficial earnings' effect grows with time (Table 3.4). Examining the more recent cohort, the initial earnings of the more educated exceed the earnings of the less educated

Table 3.2 Median entry earnings of immigrant men relative to the US-born over time

	Ratio of 1969 earnings of the 1965–70 immigrant cohort to US natives (measured with 1970 census data)	Ratio of 1979 earnings of the 1975–80 immigrant cohort to US natives (measured with 1980 census data)	Ratio of 1989 earnings of the 1985–90 immigrant cohort to US natives (measured with 1990 census data)
Ages 25–54, all education levels	0.653	0.500	0.406
25–39 years old, 1–12 years of school	0.631	0.486	0.529
25–39 years old, more than 12 years of school	0.577	0.463	0.485
40–54 years old, 1–12 years of school	0.594	0.417	0.381
40–54 years old, more than 12 years of school	0.522	0.479	0.500

Estimates based on the 1970 Census of Population 1% Public Use Sample, the 1980 Census of Population 5% "A" Public Use Sample, and a 6% microdata sample created by combining and reweighting the 1990 Census of Population 5% and 1% Public Use samples.

Immigrant cohorts are defined by the year they reported to the Census as the year they came to the US to stay. Because no labor force status restrictions are placed on the census cohorts, median earnings are computed on samples that include zeros.

Table 3.3 Median entry earnings in 1989 of immigrant men, aged 25–54, who entered the United States between 1985 and 1990 relative to the US-born, by immigrant region of origin: ratio of 1989 earnings of the 1985–90 immigrant cohort to US natives

	All	25–39 years old; 1–12 years of school	25–39 years old; more than 12 years of school	40–54 years old; 1–12 years of school	40–54 years old; more than 12 years of school
All immigrants	0.406	0.529	0.485	0.381	0.500
By region of origin					
Asia	0.443	0.589	0.434	0.316	0.439
Central/South America	0.364	0.506	0.447	0.376	0.401
Western Europe	1.010	1.147	0.931	0.845	1.372

Estimates based on a 6% microdata sample created by combining and reweighting the 1990 Census of Population 5% and 1% Public Use samples.

Table 3.4 Earnings ratio of high-education immigrants to low-education immigrants at entry and ten years later, immigrants 25–39 years old

	1965–70 cohort		1975–80 cohort	
All	1.26	1.83	1.30	2.05
Central/South America*	1.29	1.53	1.17	1.75
Asia	1.25	2.18	1.27	1.68
Europe	1.29	1.67	1.50	1.61

Estimates based on the 1970 Census of Population 1% State Public Use Sample based on the 5% questionnaire, the 1980 Census of Population 5% "A" Public Use Sample, and a 6% microdata sample created by combining and reweighting the 1990 Census of Population Public Use 5% and 1% Public Use samples.
*Mexico is included in Central America.
The annual 1969 earnings, as measured by the 1970 Census, of immigrant men who entered the US between 1965 and 1970.
The annual 1979 earnings, as measured by the 1980 Census, of immigrant men who entered the US between 1965 and 1970.
The annual 1979 earnings, as measured by the 1980 Census, of immigrant men who entered the US between 1975 and 1980.
The annual 1989 earnings, as measured by the 1990 Census, of immigrant men who entered the US between 1975 and 1980.
Source: The ratios in this table are based on earnings estimates presented in Duleep and Regets (2002).

by 30%; 10 years later, their earnings are double those of the less educated. The growing differential harks back to an earlier point: the entry earnings of immigrants are a poor predictor of immigrant economic success.

2.1.1 Skill transferability and where immigrants receive their schooling

Following Chiswick's skill transferability thesis, the extent to which immigrants receive their schooling in the host versus source country should affect their earnings trajectories;

source-country schooling should be of more value to immigrant's new labor market when combined with that country's schooling. Friedberg (1993, 2000), Schoeni (1997), Bratsberg and Ragan (2002), and Akresh (2006, 2007) found that immigrants receive lower returns to their education than do natives, particularly when host-country education does not supplement source-country schooling.

Absent direct measures of pre- and post-migration schooling, researchers use total years of schooling and year of immigration to divide schooling into its source- and host-country parts. Doing so introduces measurement error, which reduces the size of the model's estimated coefficients and creates a systematic bias, which may explain why studies with information on actual schooling find higher educational investment with higher levels of schooling (e.g., Chiswick and Miller, 1994; Van Tubergen and Van de Werfhorst, 2007) whereas studies lacking direct measures do not.

2.1.2 How skill transferability interacts with level of schooling

In most human capital models, prior education exerts an ambiguous effect upon investment decisions: An increase in an individual's education increases both the opportunity cost of time spent in human capital investment and the productivity of that time.

In the IHCI model (Duleep and Regets, 2002), source-country human capital that is not valued in the destination-country's labor market is useful for gaining new skills. Since it is not valued in the host-country's labor market, it does not increase the opportunity cost of time spent in human capital investment. The greater propensity to invest in human capital by low-skill-transferability versus high-skill-transferability immigrants (and by immigrants versus natives) should increase with education.

Empirical findings support this prediction. Duleep and Regets (2002) found that the earnings growth of the more educated versus the less educated is higher for immigrants from economically developing countries than it is for immigrants from economically developed countries. Interacting education with admission status (a possible indicator of skill transferability), Duleep and Regets (1996a) found that the higher earnings growth of kinship versus employment-based immigrants increases with education.

2.1.3 Controlling for education in immigrant adjustment models

In accordance with their model, Duleep and Regets (2002) found that, at every age above 21, recent immigrants report higher school attendance than their native counterparts. When they follow various forms of human capital investment by cohorts across censuses, Duleep et al. (1999) found higher school attendance rates for immigrant groups with low initial earnings (relative to natives of similar levels of schooling and age) than for groups with relatively high initial earnings.

The greater propensity to invest in schooling by those with low initial skill transferability persists with time in the US. For instance, large numbers of the 1975–80 cohort of Indochinese immigrant men attended school in 1990 at ages 35 and older, 10–15 years after entering the US. Indeed, all of the Indochinese ethnic groups—particularly the Hmong, with a fifth of the 1975–80 cohort in school in 1990—have higher in-school rates 10–15 years after entry than the non-refugee Asian immigrant groups, whose own school attendance is more than double that of the West European immigrants (Duleep et al., 1999).

Education is commonly held constant in immigrant earnings regressions. Yet the formal education of immigrants 25 years old and older is far from fixed, particularly for those with low skill transferability. Since immigrants are more likely to attend school than natives, studies that control for educational achievement hide immigrant relative earnings growth; the lower the initial adjusted earnings of immigrants, the more that earnings growth via educational investment is hidden.

2.2 Ability

Although immigrants have historically been viewed as a select group of highly motivated individuals, the precipitous fall in their adjusted earnings spurred speculation that the labor market "quality" of immigrants had fallen.

Building on Roy's theory of self-selection,[19] Borjas proposed that a decline in immigrant ability—measured by a decline in immigrant adjusted entry earnings—stemmed from an increase in the income inequality of the countries contributing to US immigration (Borjas 1987, 1992a–c). When countries have relatively egalitarian income distributions:

> ... the source country in effect 'taxes' able workers and 'insures' the least productive against poor labor market outcomes. This situation obviously generates incentives for the most able to migrate to the US and the immigrant flow is positively selected ... Conversely, if the source country offers relatively high rates of return to skills (which is typically true in countries with substantial income inequality ...), the United States now taxes the most able and subsidizes the least productive. Economic conditions in the US relative to those in the country of origin become a magnet for individuals with relatively low earnings capacities, and the immigrant flow is negatively selected.
> **(Borjas, 1992b, p. 429)**

Borjas (1987, p. 537) observed that prior to the 1965 Immigration and Nationality Act, the national origins quota system, based on the late nineteenth and twentieth century US ethnic composition, "encouraged immigration from (some) Western European countries and discouraged immigration from all other countries." Measuring the income accruing to the top 10% of households versus the bottom 20%, Borjas (1992a) determined that the

---

[19] The cornerstone of Borjas's model is Roy's theory of self-selection on outcomes articulated in "Thoughts on the Distribution of Earnings" (Roy, 1951). Roy's framework for analyzing comparative advantage— why an individual chooses one path versus another—undergirds the development of controlling for selection bias in labor economics (Heckman, 1979).

amount of dispersion in the average immigrant's source country doubled in the postwar period, with most of that increase occurring after 1960.

> *The new flow of migrants originates in countries that are much more likely to have greater income inequality than the United States. It would not be surprising, therefore, if the quality of immigrants declined as a result of the 1965 Amendments.*
>
> **(Borjas, 1987, p. 537)**

Relating the extent of inequality in immigrant-source countries to the relative quality of US immigrants (measured by the wage differential between entering immigrants and natives of the same age and education), Borjas concluded that income inequality strongly and negatively correlates with immigrant ability.

But the lower entry earnings of immigrants that Borjas related to source-country income inequality were accompanied by increases in earnings growth (Section 1.3). Though it is theoretically ambiguous whether lower labor market ability lowers initial earnings,[20] under any human capital model, a decline in immigrant labor market ability would not increase earnings growth. What then explains the empirical validation of Borjas's income–distribution–ability thesis?

One reason is his use of aggregate data on region-of-origin variables. Source-country variables offer the tantalizing prospect of achieving a more holistic understanding of economic and societal assimilation; they are used in studies ranging from immigrant earnings to immigrant fertility. Nevertheless, their use opens a Pandora's Box of facile conclusions. Assigning all sample individuals from a given country the same average value makes it difficult to parse out, for instance, the effects of immigrants coming from less economically developed countries versus countries with less equal income distributions.[21]

Average values of country-of-origin characteristics may also misrepresent the immigrants whose behavior we seek to explain. In an analysis that focuses on immigrant earnings controlling for education, the relevant distribution to test the income distribution–immigrant ability thesis is the earnings distribution individuals of a given level of education face, not the income distribution of the entire country. A country with a large proportion of illiterates and a large proportion of Ph.D.s would have an extremely unequal income distribution relative to the US. Yet the earnings distribution of Ph.D.s might be narrower in that country than the earnings distribution of American Ph.D.s. In such a case, it would be the higher quality Ph.D.s that would have the most to gain by migrating to the US.

---

[20] *Ceteris paribus*, higher ability individuals would theoretically be expected to invest in more human capital than lower ability individuals, which would lower the initial earnings of the higher ability group.

[21] Though Borjas focused on an increase in the inequality of US immigrant source countries, post-1965 immigrants are also more likely to come from countries that are less economically developed relative to the US than was true of earlier cohorts (Reimers, 1996). Cross-sectionally, less economically developed countries are more likely to have less equal income distributions.

Another measurement issue concerns how immigrant quality is gauged. Entry earnings poorly predict immigrant success (Section 1.3). What would happen in Borjas's analysis had earnings growth been used as the measure of immigrant quality?

Finally, note that concerns about declining immigrant quality, as measured by a decline in immigrant entry earnings, are nurtured by a rather unusual comparison—a comparison of recent immigrants with immigrants who entered the US during and immediately following a very restrictive period of US immigration history.[22,23]

2.3 Constraints

Constraints in the origin country may make *any* measure of immigrant ability suspect. Though Borjas used initial earnings, other scholars have used educational attainment as a measure of immigrant ability. Jensen et al. (2006) argue:

> *Because educational supply constraints are more likely to bind in rural areas [of developing countries], all else constant, levels of education attainment in rural areas will be lower. If this is the case, interpreting education differences across the population of migrants from developing countries as reflective of broader quality differentials clearly is problematic, since high-ability individuals from educationally supply-constrained rural areas may have low levels of education attainment.*
>
> *(Jensen et al., 2006)*

Using a measure of an individual's education, relative to the source-country community the individual lives in, they found that the propensity to migrate to the US rises with "relative" education:

> *. . . if, as appears to be the case in much of Mexico, educational attainment is supply constrained, completed years of education is flawed as a measure both of the entry-level stock of human capital and the possible trajectory of human capital over time . . . To the extent that Mexican migrants possess low human capital, the explanation within our model is that they are high-ability individuals who have been constrained in obtaining education.*
>
> *(Jensen et al., 2006)*

The notion of constraints could be more broadly applied. To what extent is the decision to migrate to another country motivated by educational, social, cultural, legal, and

---

[22] The Immigration Act of 1924, following a series of restrictive laws, imposed the country's first permanent immigration limit and established a national-origin quota system that governed US immigrant admissions for decades. The annual quotas prescribed for each nationality reflected the US population in 1920, favoring migrants from northern and western Europe while sharply reducing total immigrant inflow.

[23] Beyond problems with the empirical test for changes in immigrant quality, other theoretical perspectives lead to different predictions about immigrant ability. Common to many models of domestic and international migration (Sjaastad, 1962; Polachek and Horvath, 1977; Chiswick, 1978a) is the notion that migration is an investment that involves both direct and opportunity costs; individuals or families will migrate only when the returns to migration exceed these costs. Other relevant studies on the relationship between the propensity to migrate and earnings ability include O'Neill (1970), Schultz (1975), Schwartz (1976), and Yezer and Thurston (1976).

historical constraints that hinder the mobility of individuals in their origin country and how does that affect the evolution of immigrant skills and earnings with time in their new country?

In a paper challenging Chiswick's skill transferability explanation for initial occupations in the host country,[24] Piracha et al. (2012) found with the Australian Longitudinal Survey of Immigrants that occupation–education mismatches in the source country predict occupation–education mismatches in the host country. They argue that the mismatch in the source country indicates lower ability, as opposed to skills-transferability issues of those who migrate.

Alternatively, individuals who choose to migrate may face constraints in their home country that they wish to escape by moving to less restrictive societies and starting again. To test this perspective requires examining what happens over time to the earnings and human capital investment of the mismatched immigrants in their new country.

2.4 The importance of being permanent

The degree to which the host country is viewed as a permanent home affects the balance immigrants seek between learning and earning.[25] Indeed, it is difficult to think of a single dimension of immigrant behavior that would not be affected by whether immigrants intend to stay. Starting a business, pursuing jobs with on-the-job training, attending classes, and learning English take time and money and may initially lower earnings. These investments would only be undertaken if the benefits for making them could be reaped. Immigrants who do not intend to stay are likely persons who can work in their host country without investing, such as employees of foreign-owned firms who primarily interact with other employees and persons who come to work in US jobs requiring minimal US-specific skills.

How long immigrants intend to stay will affect the types of jobs they pursue. We would expect the careers of those who intend to stay permanently to be characterized by greater human-capital investment than the careers of temporary immigrants.[26] Based on studies of guest workers in Europe, US undocumented workers from Mexico and the Caribbean, and the migration of Southern and Eastern European peasants to the US in the late nineteenth and early twentieth centuries, Piore (1979) noted that the transience of certain immigrant groups was essential to their willingness to take secondary-sector jobs that would otherwise be viewed as undesirable.[27]

---

[24] Refer to the discussion on Chiswick's occupational mobility model in Section 1.2.

[25] The potential importance of permanence as a factor affecting immigrant behavior has been discussed and explored in a variety of contexts (e.g., Piore, 1979; Portes and Bach, 1985; Duleep, 1988; Waldinger, 1989; Duleep and Sanders, 1993; Chiswick and Miller, 1998; Duleep and Regets, 1999; Duleep et al., 1999; Dustmann, 2000; Cortes, 2004a).

[26] Also relevant is how transferable the human capital is back to the source country.

[27] A similar argument is voiced in interviews with employers in the hotel industry as to why natives do not apply for jobs held by immigrants (Waldinger, 1996).

With different investment patterns, the earnings profiles of permanent versus transient immigrants should differ. Adjusting for levels of human capital, the earnings of immigrants who anticipate staying would be lower at first, rise more sharply, and eventually surpass those of less permanent immigrants as the benefits of initial investments accrued. Of course, immigrants who initially intended to stay may leave and those who initially intended to leave may stay. Nevertheless, intent to stay, whenever it occurs, likely exerts a powerful force on the propensity to invest in human capital with corresponding effects on immigrant earnings profiles.

To illuminate how intentions to stay affect earnings growth, Duleep and Dowhan (2002a, b) exploited two definitions of year of immigration in matched CPS–Social Security data. The CPS year-of-immigration question "When did you come to the US to stay?" suggests permanence in the US. The Social Security earnings data identify the year individuals first earned in the US. With these two pieces of information, immigrants can be divided into two groups—those whose first US earnings coincide with an intent to stay permanently, and those who earned in the US for several years before deciding to stay permanently. A clear difference emerges: Immigrants whose first earnings coincide with intent to stay have higher earnings growth. The results suggest that intent to stay affects immigrant investment in a host country's human capital.

Permanence is important even for those with minimal levels of schooling, as vividly illustrated comparing two groups of poorly educated, mostly illegal, immigrants.

Traditional sources of information on immigrants, such as the census, shed little light on the experiences of illegal aliens. To illuminate the experiences of this elusive group, Douglas Massey launched a novel information-gathering strategy—the Mexican Migration Project (MMP). By the very way the data are collected, the MMP picks up information on migrants who are—at least initially—relatively transient: interviews are conducted in the winter months, when many migrants return home to join their families. Out-migrant samples are also taken, matching communities with migrants residing in the US.[28] Studies of these data reveal a population that mostly lacks legal status in the US, who transit back and forth between the US and Mexico, and generally experience low US earnings growth.

To learn about the US economic adjustment of illegal immigrants from China, Zai Liang applied Massey's strategy and created the China International Project. Chunyu (2011) used these data to trace the work trajectories of immigrants from China's Fujian province, the source of the largest wave of Chinese emigration in the 1990s.

---

[28] See Massey and Zenteno (1999) for further information. The collected data, compiled in a comprehensive database, has formed the foundation of numerous studies such as Massey (1987), White et al. (1990), Massey and Singer (1995), Singer and Massey (1998), Phillips and Massey (1999), and Donato et al. (1992), and Orrenius and Zavodny (2005).

Like their Mexican counterparts, these immigrants are mostly illegal and poorly educated: 41% possess an elementary-school education or less. Yet, in stark contrast to the Mexican undocumented immigrants, Fujianese immigrants plan to stay permanently in the US; few return to China. As a result of being part of a permanent US community, Fujianese immigrants often work for co-ethnics, and they experience substantial earnings' growth.

A window on the effect of permanence within the more generally transient Mexican undocumented population is opened by examining those individuals who applied for legal status under the 1986 Immigration and Reform and Control Act (IRCA). Under IRCA, 1.7 million persons were legalized by 1990, 1.3 million of whom were Mexican. Individuals could become legal if they could show "long-term" residence in the US.[29] Those who were both willing and able to apply for legalization form a relatively permanent subset of the undocumented population.

From IRCA's processing system, the Legalized Population Survey (LPS) file was formed, with data on the jobs and earnings of these individuals when they first entered the US, when they sought legal permanent residence, and several years later. Using the 1989 LPS, Powers and Seltzer (1998) found that despite relatively stagnant US wage growth between 1979 and 1987, median earnings grew 21% in real terms for undocumented immigrant men between their initial job in the US and when they applied for legalization. Using a status score that reflects detailed occupations, Powers and Seltzer also found meaningful upward mobility for the LPS population in the period before they were legalized.[30] Their results suggest that within a population generally characterized by impermanence and low earnings mobility, meaningful mobility exists for those who are permanent.

The role of permanence is further probed using the Mexican Migration Project to look within the more transient population of Mexican migrants. Massey (1986) found that as migrants gain US experience, they form social and economic ties that increase the chances of settling permanently in the US; over time, migrants bring family over. With the greater permanence, more stable, better-paying jobs are secured.

If the decision to invest in host-country-specific human capital and the decision to stay permanently are jointly determined then the expected return to investment in US human capital that immigrants initially face should positively correlate with the degree to which they subsequently stay. Measuring the expected return by the difference between a cohort's initial and subsequent earnings, Duleep et al. (1999) find a direct correspondence.

---

[29] For Specialized Agricultural Workers, the requirements for legalization were much more lenient (only 90 days of continuous agricultural employment in the past year), thereby providing a potential natural experiment to elucidate the effect of permanence.

[30] The initial scores of this population place the undocumented in the lower fifth of all occupations in the US. By the time of application for legalization, the immigrants were in the second lowest quintile.

Permanence varies by legal status (North and Houston, 1976), country of origin (Portes and Mozo, 1985; Jasso and Rosenzweig, 1990; Duleep and Sanders, 1993; Duleep, 1994; Ahmed and Robinson, 1994; Duleep et al., 1999), and level of economic development (Duleep and Dowhan, 2008). Groups that vary in the extent to which they are permanent will vary in their earnings and occupational trajectories. Changes in permanence should also cause changes in earnings trajectories. With data from various southern California surveys, Cornelius and Marcelli (2000) found that recent Mexican migrants are more likely to settle permanently. Massey (2011) found that with recent efforts to constrain illegal immigration, the undocumented are less likely to return to Mexico. With these changes, the adjusted entry earnings of Mexican immigrants should decrease and their earnings growth increase.

2.5 Country of origin

In their study aptly titled, "What's in a Name? Country-of-Origin Influences on the Earnings of Immigrants in the United States," Jasso and Rosenzweig (1986, p. 75) comment:

> Studies that have described immigrant cohorts, assessed the progress of immigrants in the United States, and examined the role of ethnicity in labor market behavior have assigned to country of origin a prominent part.

The role of country of origin has been explored in many contexts that relate in one way or another to immigrant labor market adjustment, including its effect on English proficiency (e.g., Chiswick and Miller, 1992; Rivera-Batiz, 1992), immigrant unemployment and union membership (DeFreitas, 1991, 1993), immigrant networks and businesses (Bailey, 1987; Waldinger, 1986), native/immigrant and recent/earlier immigrant labor market competition (e.g., Rivera-Batiz and Sechzer, 1991; Gang and Rivera-Batiz, 1994a), natives' attitudes towards immigrants (Gang and Rivera-Batiz, 1994b), remittances (Simon, 1989), and the role of women (e.g., Blau, 1980; Chiswick, 1980; Reimers, 1985; MacPherson and Stewart, 1989; Duleep and Sanders, 1993).

As the first economist to theoretically model how country of origin might affect immigrant adjustment, Chiswick (1978a, b, 1979) proposed several hypotheses relating country-specific factors, such as English speaking, to the degree to which source-country skills transfer to the host-country labor market. Jasso and Rosenzweig (1986) identified source-country attractiveness, economic conditions, and costs of migration as critical factors in country-of-origin's effect on immigrant earnings.

Interest in the effect of country of origin on immigrant earnings intensified with changes in the national-origin composition of immigrants to the US and other economically developed countries. Prior to the 1960s, US immigration was predominantly European; most recent immigrants come from Asian and Hispanic countries. As noted earlier, the country-of-origin shift was accompanied by a steep decline in immigrant entry earnings.

Census-based analyses reveal that the initial US earnings of immigrants vary enormously depending on their country of origin (Figure 3.4).[31] The entry earnings of immigrants from the source regions that dominate recent US immigration (Asia and Central and South America) are about half or less of the earnings of US natives, whereas the entry earnings of Western European immigrants resemble those of the US born. These differences persist within age and education categories (Table 3.3).

A key factor underlying the variation in immigrants' initial US earnings appears to be the source country's level of economic development. Immigrants from regions with levels of economic development similar to the US, such as Western Europe and Japan, have initial earnings approaching or exceeding those of comparably educated and experienced US natives. Those hailing from economically developing countries have low

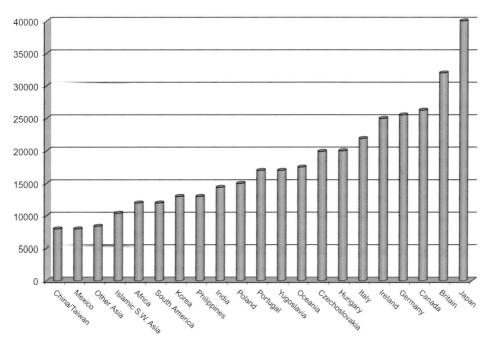

Figure 3.4 *Median 1989 US earnings of men aged 25–54, who immigrated in the years 1985–90, by country of origin.*

[31] Figure 3.4 shows by country of origin the 1989 median initial earnings of working-age immigrant men who entered the US between 1985 and 1990. The 1989 median earnings estimates for the 1985–90 cohort are based on a 6% microdata sample created by combining and reweighting the 1990 Census of Population 5% and 1% Public Use samples.

initial earnings relative to their US-born counterparts. Plotting the median 1989 US earnings of immigrant men who entered the US in 1985–90 against the 1987 per adult GDP of each source country[32] reveals a positive relationship between immigrant entry earnings and level of economic development (Figure 3.5).[33]

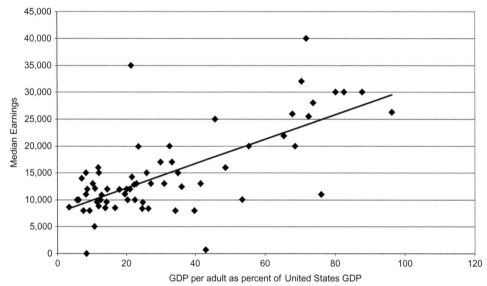

Figure 3.5 *The relationship between gross domestic product (GDP) per adult and US median initial earnings of immigrant men, by country of origin.*

[32] The 1987 per adult GDP of each source country is as a percentage of the US per adult GDP. The observations in Figure 3.5 on US median earnings for immigrant men and GDP per adult as a percentage of US GDP per adult are for the following countries: Argentina, Australia, Bangladesh, Bolivia, Brazil, Canada, Chile, China, Colombia, Costa Rica, Czechoslovakia, Dominican Republic, Ecuador, Egypt, El Salvador, Fiji, France, West Germany, Greece, Guatemala, Guyana, Haiti, Honduras, Hong Kong, Hungary, India, Indonesia, Iran, Ireland, Israel, Italy, Jamaica, Japan, Jordan, The Republic of Korea, Laos, Malaysia, Mexico, Morocco, Myanmar, Netherlands, New Zealand, Nicaragua, Nigeria, Pakistan, Panama, Peru, Philippines, Poland, Portugal, Romania, South Africa, Spain, Sri Lanka, Sweden, Switzerland, Syria, Taiwan, Thailand, Trinidad and Tobago, Turkey, USSR, United Kingdom, Venezuela, and Yugoslavia. All countries for which we had information on the GDP per adult were included. Median earnings for immigrant men in the 1985–90 cohort from the aforementioned 65 countries were estimated using a 6% microdata sample created by combining and reweighting the 1990 Census of Population 5% and 1% Public Use samples. The statistics on GDP per adult as a percentage of US GDP per adult are from Heston and Summers (1991).

[33] When the median 1989 entry earnings of immigrant men in the 1985–90 cohort are regressed on source-country GDP, the estimated coefficient indicates that the initial earnings of immigrant men increase 2280 dollars for each 10-percentage-point change in the country-of-origin GDP measure. The R^2 is 0.48.

One hypothesis for this relationship suggests that source-country variations in immigrants' initial earnings stem from variations in the skills learned by growing up and working in different source countries: The skills of immigrants from economically developed countries transfer more easily to the US (or other economically developed countries) because the source and host countries share similar educational systems, industrial structures, and labor market reward structures (Chiswick 1978a, b, 1979; Mincer and Ofek, 1982).

Rather than the skills learned in less developed countries being less applicable to the US, Duleep and Regets (1997b) suggest that limited opportunities in less-developed countries make it worthwhile for individuals to migrate even when immigration entails substantial post-migration investments in new skills and credentials such as learning English, undertaking a US degree program, or starting a business. The incentive for migration to the US will be particularly great if aspects of the non-transferable human capital aid in the creation of US human capital.

An implication of the opportunities explanation for less transferable skills is that it may not always be that the skills of individuals in less-developed countries are less applicable to the US, but that constraints in those countries make it worthwhile for persons to migrate even when they lack a particular set of skills that are immediately transferable; their equivalents in countries with opportunities similar to those of the US would not find it worthwhile to immigrate. This explanation accommodates findings that the quality of schooling in several less economically developed countries exceeds that of the US (Rivera-Batiz, 1996). It also accommodates otherwise inexplicable intergroup patterns of English proficiency and entry earnings. Duleep and Regets (1992) found the education and age-adjusted entry earnings of Korean, Indian, Filipino, and Chinese immigrants to be similar despite enormous variation in their English proficiency. The similarity is not surprising, however, if intergroup differences in skill transferability stem from variations in immigrant selection based on inter-country differences in opportunities; the common link these countries share is less opportunity vis-à-vis the US.[34]

Regardless of whether variations in skill transferability arise from variations in the skills learned in immigrants' origin countries or from an opportunity-driven selection mechanism or both, Chiswick's Immigrant Assimilation Model (Section 1.1) and the Duleep and Regets IHCI model (Section 1.3) predict that the initial divergence in immigrant earnings by country of origin will diminish with duration in the US. Chiswick (1978a, 1979) found country-of-origin earnings convergence in estimations with microdata from the 1970 Census. Following entry cohorts of immigrants across pairs of decennial census data, Duleep et al. (2013) found that earnings-related characteristics other than country of origin become better predictors of immigrant earnings with time in the US and that the earnings of demographically comparable immigrants, regardless of origin, converge.

---

[34] Cobb-Clark (2004) also found "anomalous" results between English language proficiency and labor market employment experience among recent Australian immigrants.

2.6 Admission status

2.6.1 Admission on the basis of kinship versus skills

The US Immigration Act of 1965 eliminated country-specific quotas and created a system favoring applicants with family members in the US. Under this law, in effect until 1990, spouses, minor children, and parents of US citizens were admitted without regard to numerical limitations. Of the numerically restricted visas, 80% were reserved for the adult children and siblings of US citizens and for the spouses and children of legal permanent resident aliens. Twenty percent of the numerically restricted visas were allocated to an occupational-skills category that rewarded applicants in occupations for which labor is deemed scarce (skilled and unskilled) and professionals with advanced degrees or persons of exceptional ability.[35]

By the very nature of their admission, employment-based immigrants have specific skills that immediately transfer to the US. As they enter to fill specific jobs—and are paid accordingly—employment-based immigrants would have no more incentive than US natives to invest in new human capital. Kinship-based immigrants, because they lack specific skills that are immediately valued by the US labor market, will have relatively low initial earnings and a higher propensity to invest in new human capital than either US natives or employment-based immigrants with comparable levels of schooling. With time, the earnings of family and occupation-based immigrants converge (Duleep and Regets, 1992, 1996a, b; Jasso and Rosenzweig, 1995; and, in Canada, DeSilva, 1996).[36]

2.6.2 Kinship admissions and other types of labor market adjustment

Beyond earning trajectories, family admissions may affect other aspects of labor market adjustment (Lowell, 1996).[37] Case-study evidence suggests that extended family and community networks promote human capital investment among immigrants with low initial levels of US-specific skills.[38] A survey of various immigrant groups in Australia

---

[35] The taxonomy presented here is approximate.

[36] Compared with Canada and Australia, the US has placed greater emphasis on family reunification versus productivity characteristics in determining who shall enter. Yet Duleep and Regets (1992) and Antecol et al. (2003) found that immigrant earnings assimilation differs little among these countries once the shared US border with Mexico is taken into account. An interesting area for further research is what explains the apparent disconnect between these findings suggesting that admission policies do not have much effect, and the research of Jasso and Rosenzweig, DeSilva, and Duleep and Regets that suggests that type of admission affects immigrant earnings trajectories? One possibility is that immigrants from economically developing countries will strive to enter under any admission criteria.

[37] Information on sponsorship rates and family patterns of the foreign born may be found in Boyd (1989), Jasso and Rosenzweig (1989), Woodrow-Lafield (1994), and Schulte and Wolf (1994).

[38] Examples include Bailey (1987), Bonacich and Modell (1980), Gallo and Bailey (1996), Jiobu (1996), Light (1972), Waldinger (1986, 1989), and Kim and Hurh (1996).

concludes that family and informal networks provide the most important and frequently utilized services for most immigrants (Morrissey et al., 1991).

Kinship-based communities may facilitate immigrant business formation by providing a supply of trusted employees with a low variance in employee performance (Duleep and Wunnava, 1996; Jiobu, 1996). Case-study evidence suggests that extended families foster the high self-employment rates of certain immigrant groups: Kim and Hurh (1996) documented the important role relatives play in the entrepreneurial ventures of Koreans; Khandewal (1996) cites examples within the US-Indian immigrant community. Examining the likelihood that an Asian or Hispanic immigrant starts a business, Duleep and Regets (1996b) found that the most important predictor, dwarfing all other variables, is whether an immigrant has siblings in the US.

2.6.3 Refugees

Chiswick suggested two ways in which refugees would differ from economic migrants. One, they would be less selected on innate ability and motivation:

> . . . if greater labor market ability and motivation raise earnings relatively more than they raise the cost of migration, the rate of return from migration is greater for the more able and motivated, and they will have a higher propensity to migrate.
>
> *(Chiswick, 1978a, pp. 900–901)*

> Although economic migrants tend to be favorably self-selected on the basis of high innate ability and economic motivation, this self-selection is less intense for refugees with similar demographic characteristics, whose migration is primarily influenced by the political and social environment.
>
> *(Chiswick, 1979)*

Two, because of the abruptness of their migration, they would have fewer transferable skills than economic migrants:

> Since the earning power of one's skills plays a primary role in economic migration and a secondary role in refugee migration, a cohort of the latter is likely to include a larger proportion of workers with skills that have little international transferability. Refugee migration generally arises from a sudden or unexpected change in political conditions . . . As a result, refugees are less likely than economic migrants to have acquired readily transferable skills and are more likely to have made investment specific to their country of origin.
>
> *(Chiswick, 1979, p. 365)*

Combining insights from Chiswick's Immigrant Assimilation Model and Duleep and Regets' IHIC model, low skill transferability is linked to high human capital investment and earnings growth because:

- There is a lower opportunity cost of human-capital investments when initial host-country earnings opportunities are low.
- Skills not immediately valued in the host-country labor market are still useful in the production of host-country human capital.

- Host-country skills may often complement source-country skills and make them more usable in the host-country labor market.

In an analysis that follows the earnings growth and human capital investments of immigrants entering the US in 1975–80, Duleep et al. (1999) found that within age/education groups, men from economically developed countries, such as Japan and Western Europe, had high initial earnings but relatively low earnings growth. Men from the developing countries in Asia generally had low initial earnings and high earnings growth.

Among the more educated, however, the 1975–80 cohort of Vietnamese refugees began their US lives with higher earnings than did immigrants from the non-refugee developing-country Asian countries. This suggests that their skill transferability exceeded that of their developing-country, non-refugee counterparts. (Perhaps the first to leave Vietnam had contacts that assured them jobs in the US.) In keeping with the skill-transferability thesis, the earnings growth of the 1975–80 cohort of highly educated Vietnamese was low relative to their non-refugee Asian counterparts.

Among the poorly educated, entry earnings were lower for all of the Indochinese refugee groups than for the non-refugee Asian developing-country groups. This suggests that skill transferability was lower for these Indochinese than for their non-refugee Asian counterparts. In line with the skill-transferability thesis, their earnings growth and investment in schooling and English proficiency exceeded that of their non-refugee counterparts.

In a similar analysis following the 1975–80 cohort of immigrants, Cortes (2004a) compared refugees with economic migrants and concluded that the refugees' implied greater permanence explains their higher human-capital investment and earnings growth. Yet the Indochinese refugee groups were no more permanent than Asian immigrants from economically developing countries, who were highly permanent (Duleep et al., 1999).[39] What distinguishes the Indochinese refugees from their Asian non-refugee counterparts is the nature of their permanence, not its degree. The permanence of the non-refugee Asian immigrants was voluntary; for refugees, it was forced.

These intergroup comparisons suggest the following generalizations meriting further exploration. Low-skill-transferability immigrants, who are permanent, will have relatively high propensities to invest in host-country human capital regardless of whether their permanence is voluntary or forced. Refugees whose skills are highly transferable will have relatively low propensities to invest in host-country human capital, despite their permanence. That the patterns of skill transferability, human capital investment, and earnings are similar for immigrants and refugees from economically developing countries

---

[39] Within age groups, the attrition rates were lower for immigrants from Asian economically developing countries than for the Indochinese refugees. Since intercensal attrition rates may be affected by changes other than emigration, the lower attrition rates for immigrants from economically developing Asian countries do not prove that they were more permanently attached to the US than the Indochinese refugees. It does suggest that the immigrants from economically developing Asian countries and the Indochinese refugees are similar in terms of their permanence.

suggests that the theoretically predicted ability difference between refugees and economic immigrants may not be important.

2.6.4 The undocumented

Does legal status, per se, affect the labor market adjustment of immigrants?

Legal and illegal immigrants differ in many ways other than their legal status: US illegal immigrants from Mexico have less schooling and English proficiency than their legal counterparts (e.g., Rivera-Batiz, 1999). Yet, controlling for such differences, their earnings and job trajectories should still differ because of lower permanence among much of the illegal population.[40]

Massey (1987) used MMP data to explore the effect of legal status and found that employer-specific human capital critically affects wage levels. Legal immigrants have more employer-specific human capital because they are at jobs four times longer than illegal immigrants. Perhaps then legal status contributes to the higher wages of the documented by lengthening job tenure? Yet, even among the undocumented, permanent immigrants experience greater earnings growth than non-permanent immigrants and pursue jobs with greater stability (Section 2.4). The legal-status effect in Massey's analysis may reflect greater permanence rather than legal status per se.

Since those who strive to be legal are more permanent, separating the effects of permanence from the effects of legal status is challenging. One way would be to see whether—among the permanent—there is a change relevant to earnings and occupational mobility that can be clearly attributed to gaining legal status.

As noted in Section 2.4, those who applied for legalization under IRCA form a relatively permanent subset of the undocumented. Using the 1989 and 1992 Legalized Population Surveys, Powers et al. (1998) compared the occupations of legalized immigrant men and women with the occupations they held when they were legalized. A positive picture of occupational mobility emerges. Men move into more skilled jobs (food service, skilled janitorial work) from less skilled jobs (out of farm work and other unskilled laboring).[41] Though it is tempting to ascribe the occupational mobility to legalization, Powers et al. also found occupational mobility prior to legalization (Section 2.4).

In another effort to tease out a legalization effect, Rivera-Batiz (1999) compared the wages, before and after legalization, of Mexican illegal-alien men and women, represented in the 1989 and 1992 LPS, with the wages of Mexican (presumably legal) immigrants in the 1990 Census. His analysis hints at direct and indirect legalization

---

[40] Passel (1999) estimated that 75% of any given cohort of undocumented immigrants emigrate before 10 years. Note the exception of illegal immigrants from China discussed in Section 2.3.

[41] Much less mobility was evident among women. The concentration decreased somewhat, with 50% of women concentrated in only eight occupations at the time of US entry to 50% of women being concentrated in 10 occupations. Private household cleaners and textile machine operators remained the number one and two jobs for legalized women in 1992.

effects. Indirectly, a post-legalization wage gain among the previously undocumented immigrants stems from a relative growth in educational attainment and English proficiency. Rivera-Batiz argued that this growth in human capital might not have occurred had the immigrants remained unauthorized. Concomitantly, a large growth in the relative wages of the formerly undocumented occurred that cannot be explained by the growth in their human capital.

Perhaps most persuasive are the before-after legalization analyses with the 1989 and 1992 LPS of Cobb-Clark and Kossoudji.[42] They injected an illuminating twist into their analyses of occupational mobility by highlighting a job characteristic that should be important *if* legalization, per se, had an effect—occupations for which the penalty of being unauthorized was relatively high. Prior to legalization, unauthorized occupational mobility consisted of "occupational churning" within a limited set of jobs. With legalization, the formerly undocumented move into occupations that were previously off limits because of the high probability of being caught. Although other factors such as English proficiency strongly correlate with occupational mobility, legal status, once introduced into the regression, swamps all other characteristics in contributing to occupational mobility.

3. BEYOND THE INDIVIDUAL—ECONOMIC AND SOCIAL CONTEXTS AFFECTING LABOR MARKET OUTCOMES

Although much sociological research has emphasized the importance of individual human capital, in line with the preponderance of economic research (see, for instance, Jasso and Rosenzweig, 1990; McAllister, 1995; Farley, 1996; Kahn and Whittington, 1996; Livingston and Kahn, 2002), sociologists have also explored how predictors of immigrant economic assimilation are affected by contexts that cannot necessarily be measured by individual traits (Portes, 1995a; Portes and Rumbaut, 1996).[43] These include the impact of immigrant enclaves and the importance of local labor market structures (Light, 1984; Sanders and Nee, 1996; Reitz, 2001).

The various contextual variables that have been considered in sociological research and how they may affect immigrant economic adjustment are reviewed in Portes (1995a, b), Brettell and Hollifield (2000), Bean and Stevens (2003), and Hirschman et al. (1999). With the study of context, the model of assimilation proffered by Park in the 1920s has grown to embrace a wide range of labor market outcomes exemplified in the concept of "segmented assimilation."[44]

---

[42] Relevant references include Cobb-Clark and Kossoudji (1999) and Kossoudji and Cobb-Clark (2000, 2002). Also refer to Cobb-Clark et al. (1995).

[43] For instance, sociologists introduced to the study of immigrant labor market adjustment the potentially powerful roles of cultural and historic contexts (Bean and Stevens, 2003).

[44] Segmented assimilation was first introduced in Portes and Zhou (1993). Also see Zhou (1997).

Whereas Sections 1 and 2 focused on individual attributes that affect immigrant labor market adjustment, Section 3 adds to the model social and economic contexts, a research agenda fueled by a symbiotic relationship between economists and sociologists.

3.1 The structure of the labor market

A context that affects immigrant earnings trajectories is the structure of the host-country's labor market. One conceptualization is based in human capital theory. Another, introduced by the economists Averitt (1968) and Doeringer and Piore (1971), postulates that two types of demand determine the characteristics of jobs in the economy. Jobs in the primary sector (responding to the stable component of demand) are "good jobs" characterized by security, responsibility, and career lines; jobs in the secondary sector (responding to demand that is highly variable) are dead-end jobs. The dual labor market theory contends that it is not so much the human capital of individuals that determines their earnings trajectories, but the characteristics of the job a person is in. Jobs are, to some extent, "parceled out" with some groups benefiting from the employment fruits of the primary sector while others, primarily poorly educated minorities and immigrants, are shunted off to the secondary sector.

Dual labor market theory—the subject of a continuing and spirited debate among economists (see, for instance, Dickens and Lang, 1985, 1988; Heckman and Hotz, 1986; and Launov, 2004)—comprises one pillar underlying the sociological concept of segmented assimilation, that different groups of immigrants, with the same level of schooling and experience, may nonetheless occupy very different worlds (for a review and updated description of labor market segmentation research, refer to Hudson, 2007).

3.2 Enclaves

In segmented assimilation, one world that immigrants may occupy, in addition to the primary and secondary sectors, is the "enclave economy" (see, for instance, Xie and Greenman, 2011).

How is an enclave economy defined? Jiobu (1996, p. 104) comments:

Although details vary from author to author, in general enclave theorists postulate that some racial-ethnic groups have come to dominate economic niches within the broader economy. These niches, frequently called enclaves, are economic arenas staked out by a particular group. Thus ethnic entrepreneurs create business establishments, hire co-ethnic workers, and market goods or services to co-ethnic consumers and, sometimes, to majority consumers as well. Ethnic entrepreneurs tend to specialize in certain lines of business and they typically deal with other co-ethnic entrepreneurs when it comes to purchasing materials for production or resale. Quite often these enterprises are physically located in a specific area of a city, although physical contiguity is not a necessary feature of an ethnic economy.

Discussions of large differences in the economic success of various ethnic groups often revolve around the role of the ethnic enclave. Jiobu (1996) provided case-study evidence of early twentieth-century Japanese immigrants who, despite intense discriminatory obstacles and modest origins, eventually reached parity with non-Hispanic whites (Duleep, 1988). More generally, case studies by other scholars (e.g., Light 1972, 1984; Portes and Bach, 1985; Gallo and Bailey, 1996; Waldinger, 1986, 1989; Bailey, 1987; Bailey and Waldinger, 1991) suggest that enclaves help immigrants lacking access to primary sector jobs bypass the confines of the secondary sector.[45]

In contrast to Portes and others who advance the "enclave-economy hypothesis"—that immigrants in an enclave-labor market receive earning returns to human capital equal to the earnings returns of immigrants in the primary labor market—several studies, by economists and sociologists, estimated detrimental enclave effects on immigrant labor market adjustment. Chiswick and Miller (1992) found that living in a language enclave area negatively affects acquisition of the host-country language, an effect that is especially large for poorly educated immigrants. Using 1990 Census PUMS data, Chiswick and Miller (2002) found that the greater the linguistic concentration of immigrants' origin language where immigrants live, the lower their earnings, independent of the negative effects on language acquisition. From a survey of Colombian and Dominican immigrants in New York City, Gilbertson and Gurak (1993) concluded that the enclave confers few, if any, advantages to its members. In a paper intriguingly entitled "A Warm Embrace or the Cold Shoulder: Wage and Employment Outcomes in Ethnic Enclaves," Pedace and Rohn (2008) used the non-public use, one-in-six sample of the 2000 US Census to estimate an ethnic concentration effect. They generally found that enclaves adversely affect wages and, to a lesser but still statistically significant degree, employment as well. Using New Immigrant Survey data to compare the economic outcomes of immigrants working in ethnic enclaves versus the mainstream economy, Xie and Gough (2011) estimated negative enclave effects for several immigrant groups.

If enclaves are harmful, why do immigrants—particularly poorly educated immigrants—favor them? Scholars also estimate various effects for networks even though it seems implausible that using networks could ever lower wages.[46] Comparing immigrants in San Diego with immigrants in Hamamatsu, Japan, Cornelius et al. (2003) found that using social networks in job search negatively affected immigrant wages in San Diego but positively affected immigrant wages in Hamamatsu. They attributed the difference to the role of context. An alternative explanation is that "use of networks" identifies different types of immigrants in the two cities.

To what extent are the estimated detrimental enclave effects a reflection of the options of the individuals who choose to join enclaves? With the 1980 Census of Population, McManus (1990) found that large enclaves provide better jobs for persons who are not proficient in English. Bauer et al. (2005), using MMP data on Mexican–US

---

[45] Other references on enclaves include: Wilson and Portes (1980), Light et al. (1994), Kaplan (1997), Logan et al. (2002).

[46] Refer to Kanas et al. (2012) for a study of the effects of various types of networks.

migration, found that Mexican migrants with poor English skills migrate to locations with a large enclave; those with good English skills choose locations with a small enclave.

Of course, immigrants may choose to work in enclaves because of non-pecuniary benefits such as the enjoyment of being with others who share the same background. Nevertheless, the case studies of Portes and Bach (1985), Bailey (1987), Waldinger (1989), and Gallo and Bailey (1996) suggest economic reasons that motivate poorly educated immigrants to choose enclaves, even with significant initial wage penalties. They document an immigrant sector in various industries characterized by mutually beneficial arrangements in which recent immigrants working as unskilled laborers at low wages (or even no wages) in immigrant-run businesses receive training and other forms of support that eventually lead to more skilled positions or self-employment.

Sanders and Nee (1987) found that Cuban and Chinese immigrants working in enclave economies gain lower returns to human capital than their wage-and-salary primary-sector counterparts whereas the earnings returns of the self-employed match those of US natives. Using 1980 and 1990 census data to study the highly skilled, Lofstrom (2000) estimated a positive enclave effect on self-employment, with the adjusted earnings of self-employed immigrants exceeding the earnings of wage-and-salary immigrants and natives, as well as the earnings of self-employed natives (also refer to Lofstrom, 2011).

The case of Korean immigrants is particularly intriguing with respect to why immigrants choose an enclave route. The exceedingly high prevalence of self-employment among Korean immigrants is matched by their exceedingly low English proficiency (Duleep et al., 1999). Kim and Hurh (1986) found that despite high levels of education, 72% of self-employed Korean immigrants had worked in the US as blue-collar workers, service workers, or as employees of Korean stores. They conclude:

> *The current engagement in self-employed small businesses appears to be a result of their socio-economic adaptation to the limited occupational opportunity available to them in the United States as evidenced by the nature of the jobs they held prior to their business entry. In this sense, the immigrants' current business operation may be considered an emergent phenomenon which grew out of the opportunity structure open to Korean immigrants in the United States and the immigrants' utilization of their ethnic resources in response to such an opportunity structure.*

An alternative explanation is that the immigrants' self-employment grew out of the opportunity structure in Korea relative to the US that, combined with their ethnic resources, made it worthwhile to migrate to the US despite very limited English. Detailed surveys at place-of-origin communities of the type that Massey pursued to study Mexican–US immigration could elucidate this process.

Immigrants who work in ethnic enclaves and immigrants who work in the mainstream economy likely differ in ways that may be difficult to measure or adjust for. Moreover, snapshots in time can be misleading in studies that compare enclave and mainstream immigrants if the shapes of their earnings trajectories differ. Another approach for analyzing the enclave effect would be to compare the long-term earnings trajectories of poorly educated immigrants in groups with and without an enclave economy. Over their working lives, do poorly educated immigrants in groups with enclaves do better or worse than poorly educated immigrants in groups without enclaves?

3.3 The permanence of the community

The permanence of an immigrant's group or community is another context that likely affects immigrant labor market adjustment. Differences in permanence can shape rates of acculturation, determine the extent to which immigrant communities emerge, and mold the larger society's impressions of the immigrant population. Beyond affecting individual decisions such as learning English, permanence affects group characteristics that in turn influence the social and economic prospects of individuals. The permanence of the immigrant community determines whether there are enclaves for immigrants to join. Absent a cadre of permanently attached members, there may be no good alternatives to secondary-sector employment for some immigrant groups.

Chunyu (2011) found that Fujianese immigrants in the US, who experience substantial earnings' growth (Section 2.4), often work for co-ethnics as a result of being part of a permanent, albeit undocumented, community in the US. In comparing the economic assimilation of two refugee groups in Miami, Cubans and Haitians, Stepick (1996) asks what accounts for the much lower economic success of Haitians, even when compared with the less advantaged Mariel Cuban refugees? (Also see Portes and Stepick, 1985; and Portes and Truelove, 1987.) Stepick primarily attributes their lower progress to lower levels of social capital:

> *The Cuban community is characterized by an extraordinary solidarity . . . between its elite of entre-preneurs and professionals and the broad working class . . . This solidarity combined with the Cubans' political and economic capital creates the Cuban enclave, an economic, social, and political construction that has eased the entry of newly-arrived refugees and boosted the economic advancement of earlier-arriving ones.*

Stepick noted that a key element undermining social cohesion in the Haitian community is the lack of an early established permanent community in the US:

> *As some remained in Haiti and others fled to northern cities [in the United States], the elite Haitians neither abandoned their homeland totally nor established a beachhead for subsequent refugees, as had Cubans in Miami.*

Lacking an enclave option, Haitians find secondary-sector employment or remain unemployed (Portes and Stepick, 1985).

3.4 The state of the labor market

The state of the labor market is another context that affects immigrant labor market adjustment. Social scientists frequently use the identifying assumption that "period effects," often driven by the impact of macroeconomic conditions on labor-market outcomes, are identical between immigrants and natives. Under this assumption, differences in labor-market outcomes between immigrants and natives will be insensitive to the point of the business cycle in which the data were collected. If, however, period effects differ between immigrants and natives, then immigrant/native differences will fluctuate with the macroeconomic conditions prevailing at the time the data are collected.

Comparing estimates of earnings assimilation based on pairs of individual years from 1981 to 1992 of the Survey of Consumer Finances (SCF)[47] with those based on Canadian census data, McDonald and Worswick (1998) discovered that their SCF–Census comparisons were greatly affected by which SCF years they chose to use. They further discovered that immigrant earnings assimilation was higher in expansionary periods and lower in recessionary periods (refer also to McDonald and Worswick, 1999a, b). Differences in unemployment rates between recently arrived immigrant men and Canadian-born men were also found to be larger in recessions than in expansions (McDonald and Worswick, 1997).

An analysis based on data collected in a recessionary period would indicate high unemployment rates for recent immigrants compared to natives; an equivalent analysis based on data collected during an expansion would imply small differences in immigrant-native unemployment rates. Under the usual assumption that period effects analogously affect immigrants and natives, the two analyses based on data taken from two different macroeconomic contexts would suggest very different interpretations of the overall unemployment performance of immigrants.[48]

Beyond the effect of current macroeconomic conditions on current labor market outcomes, past macroeconomic conditions may affect future labor market outcomes. Immigrants who arrive in the host country in periods of high unemployment may suffer permanent "scarring" that negatively impacts later labor market outcomes. Nakamura and Nakamura (1992b) found a scarring effect; Chiswick et al. (1997) did not. Longitudinal data on multiple cohorts, with quantitatively important inter-cohort variations in labor market conditions at entry, could help settle the issue.

How macroeconomic conditions affect immigrants versus natives likely varies with immigrant attributes. Immigrants working in demand-sensitive secondary jobs should be most affected by the business cycle (including leaving the country). Following the last-hired, first-fired scenario, immigrants as relative newcomers in primary-sector jobs should be more affected by economic downturns than natives. On the other hand, immigrants lacking immediately transferable skills have a greater incentive to invest in new

---

[47] The Canadian SCF is very similar to the US March Current Population Survey.

[48] Crossley et al. (2001) found that estimates from cohort fixed effects models of immigrant receipt of unemployment benefits and social assistance vary with the choice of survey years. Sensitivity of benefit receipt to macroeconomic conditions likely underlies the cohort-specific dynamics in benefit receipt.

skills; their greater flexibility to make employment switches (a function of the flexibility of their host country's economy) may make them less affected than natives to economic downturns. Finally, immigrants, including the poorly educated, may enter niches or enclaves that are less affected by general economic conditions.

Hall and Farkas (2008) used longitudinal Survey of Income and Program Participation (SIPP) monthly data to explore individual-level determinants of earnings trajectories for immigrants and natives with a high school diploma or less. They estimated their model for two periods, 1996–99, a period of strong labor market demand, and 2001–03, a period of weak labor market demand:

> During the earlier period (of relatively strong national labor market demand), the earnings of low-skill native workers increased at a rate of 0.3% per month, while those of immigrants grew slightly faster. During the later period (of relatively weak labor market demand), the earnings of natives did not grow significantly, but those of immigrants increased at a (statistically significant) rate of 0.3% per month.
>
> **(Hall and Farkas, 2008, p. 635)**

3.4.1 Other effects of the state of the labor market on immigrant adjustment

A leitmotif of this chapter is that immigrants balance learning and earning. Labor market conditions may affect immigrant decisions whether to earn or learn, decisions that then shape immigrant earnings profiles. Van Tubergen and Van de Werfhorst (2007) found that educational investments are stronger among immigrants who arrived in the Netherlands during periods of high unemployment.[49]

The state of the labor market may also affect the type of employment immigrants pursue. With 19 waves of the German Socio-Economic Panel, Constant and Zimmermann (2004) probed transitions between wage-and-salary employment, unemployment, and self-employment. Their results suggest that the business cycle crucially affects these transitions: immigrants use self-employment both to avert unemployment and as a conduit back to regular employment.

Finally, changes in the state of the labor market can influence the shape of immigrant earnings trajectories. A tenet of Chiswick's Immigrant Assimilation Model is that as immigrants live and work in their host countries, they acquire destination-relevant human capital at a decreasing rate: the largest earnings gains are in the initial years; with time, the rate of earnings growth tapers off. Yet changes in the state of the labor market, that are not accounted for, can hide this picture. Beenstock et al. (2010) hypothesize and present evidence that the mass immigration to Israel from 1989 to 1995 raised the return to Israeli-specific human capital among long-duration immigrants to such an extent as to hide the underlying assimilation model of decreasing earnings growth with duration.

---

[49] Note that they may not have discovered this had they not used a model that permits differentiating between starting schooling versus continuing schooling.

3.5 Structural changes over time in the host economy

Beyond the ups and downs of the business cycle, enduring shifts in the economy may affect immigrant labor market outcomes. A well-documented feature of the recent economy is an increasing wage gap between the highly educated and poorly educated. Many scholars believe that industrial changes in the US and other economically developed countries have narrowed job opportunities for the poorly educated. Some argue (e.g., Bound and Johnson, 1992) that skill-biased technological change is largely responsible for the increased inequality and that the earnings potential of low-skill individuals, relative to those with higher skills, is substantially less than in the immediate post-World War II period.

Chiswick (1991) and LaLonde and Topel (1992) argued that the 1970–80 decline in immigrant entry earnings (adjusted for measured characteristics) is partially due to a general decline in the relative wages of low-skilled workers. Lubotsky (2011), using matched survey–Social Security administrative data, concluded that the rising returns to skill have placed immigrants at a relative disadvantage during the last 20 years. Rumbaut (1994) examined the effects of the changing structure of the economy on immigrants and concluded:

> Adapting to the United States is not what it used to be. The general trend at the turn of the century was to find a blue collar job . . . Today, the society is far more differentiated than it was at the turn of the century. You have increasingly an hour-glass economy with a lot of minimally paying low-level jobs and a lot of well-paying professional jobs.

Yet others cite the immigrant experience to question the skills-mismatch hypothesis. Peterson and Vroman (1992, p. 12) note:

> If employers are looking for better educated workers, and the lack of jobs in the manufacturing sector explains the [downward] pressure on black employment, what accounts for the strong demand for immigrant Hispanic workers, who on average have less schooling and fewer skills?

Duleep and Dowhan (2002a, b) found high earnings growth for immigrants, relative to natives, at percentiles below the median; except for the recession at the beginning of the 1980s, immigrant earnings trajectories (relative to natives) remained remarkably stable from the early 1970s through the 1990s, at all percentiles. Powers and Seltzer (1998) found that the median inflation-adjusted weekly earnings of poorly educated immigrant men increased 21% during a period in which the average earnings of native men declined (Section 2.4). Using a multivariate analysis that models intercepts and slopes separately, Hall and Farkas (2008) found significant wage growth for poorly educated immigrants:

> These results cast doubt on the strong version of segmented labor market theory, in which low-skill immigrants are permanently consigned to dead-end jobs with no wage appreciation.
>
> **(Hall and Farkas, p. 619)**

These findings do not refute the idea of a structural change in the labor market that disproportionately afflicts the poorly educated. It does suggest that poorly educated immigrants are not more disadvantaged than their native-born counterparts, and may be less so. If so, why?

Case-study evidence provides tantalizing hints that immigrants, including the poorly educated, successfully occupy and/or create economic niches, leading to a more promising prognosis of their economic mobility in the new economy. Even without enclave economies (in which immigrant entrepreneurs hire immigrant workers), case-study research suggests that employment opportunities for the poorly educated are dominated by groups with well-developed networks and, in this regard, immigrants have an advantage (Waldinger, 1996). Finally, if immigrants self-select in the host country, wouldn't those who are most able to adjust to the new structural conditions be the ones to migrate? Some evidence of this phenomenon may be seen in the immigrant presence in personal care services, for which demand remains high.

4. LABOR MARKET OUTCOMES FOR IMMIGRANT WOMEN

An individual's decision to migrate is often part of a family decision over where the family should live and work and where children are to be educated. A complete analysis of immigrant labor market adjustment would follow the labor force decisions, earnings, school enrollment, and fertility outcomes of families through time. Moreover, men's labor market outcomes, typically the focus of earlier economic studies, may not be fully understood without considering the activities of their wives (Morrison and Lichter, 1988; Jensen, 1991).

How the family copes with immigration is particularly important given the low initial earnings of men in several immigrant groups.[50] If intergroup variations in immigrant men's initial earnings reflect the selection of more or less able individuals, and persons of similar ability marry, then the relative economic position of immigrant groups with low initial earnings for men should worsen with wives' earnings included. To the extent that husbands and wives have similar levels of host-country-specific skills when they first immigrate, a skills-transferability hypothesis predicts that a family perspective worsens the initial but not necessarily subsequent relative economic position of immigrant groups with low initial earnings for men. A third conceptual framework—the Family Investment Hypothesis—predicts that a family perspective improves the initial but not necessarily subsequent relative economic position of immigrant groups with low initial earnings for men. Understanding the labor force behavior of immigrant women is key to understanding which, if any, of these scenarios prevails.

[50] The studies of Morokvasic (1984), Reimers (1985), Gurak and Kritz (1992), Donato (1993), Kahn and Whittington (1996), and Foner (1997, 1998) highlight the role of women and the family in facilitating economic assimilation; Jensen (1991) found that the ameliorative input of secondary earners is greater for some immigrant groups than it is for natives.

Factors that affect the labor force behavior of native-born women also affect immigrant women. Children and expected labor market productivity, for instance, affect whether immigrant women join the labor force (e.g., Stier, 1991). Paralleling the earnings and employment assimilation of immigrant men, the decision of immigrant women to work and their earnings positively correlate with years since migration, reflecting the learning of skills relevant to the host-country labor market (Chiswick, 1980). Nevertheless, the labor force behavior of immigrant women differs from that of men, and women's labor force behavior varies across immigrant groups.[51] To understand these differences, researchers have pursued a family perspective.

4.1 The Family Investment Hypothesis: theoretical underpinnings

The term "Family Investment Hypothesis" (FIH) was coined in a paper by Duleep and Sanders (1993) that sought to explain large differences that persisted across immigrant groups in the propensity of married immigrant women to work, after traditional variables that affect female labor force participation, and variables that measure skill transferability, such as years since migration and English proficiency, were included.

The traditional model of female labor force participation posits that a woman works if her market wage (W_M), the wage she can receive if she works, which is a function of factors such as education, exceeds her reservation wage (W_R), the wage she must receive in order to work, which is a function of factors such as whether a baby is at home and the husband's income. A woman works if $W_M > W_R$ at zero hours of work. To this model, the FIH adds the following concept: Family members can increase a family's future labor income either directly, pursuing activities that increase their own skill levels, or indirectly, by engaging in activities that finance, or otherwise support, the investment activities of other family members. In a FIH focused on women as secondary earners, a woman works if $W_M + E(q) > W_R$, where q is the change in the net present value of family income that results from the increased investment in the husband's host-country-specific human capital, financed by the wife working.

Specifically, let γ_I be the husband's earnings stream from investment financed by the wife working and let γ_{NI} be the husband's earnings stream that would exist if the wife did not work; r is the market interest rate and p_t is the probability that the family is in the host country in time period t (the probability that they have not emigrated). The expected

---

[51] Powers and Seltzer (1998) looked at occupational status and mobility of immigrants who were legalized under the Immigration Reform and Control Act, and found that earnings, status and mobility of men exceed those of women. Bean and Tienda (1987) showed that, among Hispanics, labor force participation effects of education and English proficiency are stronger for women than men. Boyd (1984), in an analysis of Canadian immigrants, uncovered considerable stratification among groups of immigrant women in the extent to which their occupational status is below that of natives. Several studies found that female immigrants have lower rates of labor force participation than men, but also note marked differences across ethnic groups (Bean et al., 1985; Portes and Bach, 1985; Perez, 1986; Stier and Tienda, 1992).

family investment return to the wife working is $E(q) = \Sigma\ 1/(1 + r)^{t-1}(\gamma_{I,t} - \gamma_{NI,t})p_t$. It depends on the net effect of the investment on the husband's earnings, and how long the family stays in the host country. The price of the wife's non-market activity includes her market wage, as in the traditional model of a woman's decision to work, and the return to work in terms of the investment it finances.

Controlling for factors that affect a woman's market and reservation wages, the higher the return to financing her husband's investment in host-country-specific skills, the more likely she will work. Thus, women who are similar in every other respect—child status, schooling, English proficiency, time in the US, husband's income—could dramatically differ in their labor force participation rates. Across immigrant groups, the greater the average return to investment in host-country-specific human capital for immigrant men, the greater the propensity for women in these groups to work.

Conceptually, the Family Investment Hypothesis has its roots in the study of domestic migration. Mincer (1978, pp. 750–751) hypothesized that "... net family gain rather than net personal gain motivates [the] migration of households." If the net individual returns to migration are of opposite sign for the husband and wife, but the net family gain is positive, then "... one spouse moves along with the other even though his (or her) 'private' calculus dictates staying."

Similarly, the Family Investment Hypothesis (FIH) proposes that net family gain rather than personal gain motivates immigrant family decisions about work. In the initial years following immigration, immigrant women married to men who initially lack host-country-specific skills will be more likely to work but less likely to undertake human capital investment, with jobs that pay more during the period in which the husband's investment in host-country skills is most intense. Their initial earnings will be higher than would otherwise be the case, their earnings profile by foregoing investment flatter, and their propensity to work and hours of work will decline as the husband's host-country-specific human capital grows.

4.2 The Family Investment Hypothesis: empirical support

One approach to test the FIH compares the work patterns of immigrant married women (relative to native-born women) with the work patterns of immigrant married men (relative to native-born men). Using 1970 US census data, Long found that the earnings of married immigrant women, which were initially greater than those of native-born women, decreased with years in the US. This led him to speculate that:

> ... wives in immigrant families that have recently entered the US ... work to help finance their husbands' initial investments in schooling or job skills required in U.S. labor markets. Later, as earnings of their spouses rise with time in the US, foreign-born wives reallocate their time from market to nonmarket activities and their earnings are reduced.
>
> *(Long, 1980, p. 628)*

With Canadian data, Beach and Worswick (1993) found the initially higher hours worked of recently arrived immigrant women decreased with years since migration; immigrant married women also had flatter wage profiles than Canadian-born married women.[52]

Another test for the FIH uses variation across immigrant groups in the likely extent to which immigrant husbands invest in host-country human capital, holding constant a woman's own level of host-country skills measured, for instance by her years since migration and level of host-country language proficiency. Duleep and Sanders (1993), with 1980 census data, and Duleep et al. (1999), with 1980 and 1990 census data, found that groups with the largest expected growth in immigrant men's earnings have the highest labor force participation of married immigrant women. Adding permanence to their analysis, a striking, nearly linear, relationship emerges between the propensity of married immigrant women to work and the return to investment in US-specific human capital by husbands. With Canadian data, Baker and Benjamin (1997) compared the hours and wage trajectories of immigrant women married to foreign-born men versus immigrant women married to Canadian natives. The former work more upon arrival, have flatter wage profiles, and a lower propensity to invest in schooling than immigrant women married to native-born men.

Long (1980) did not explicitly test the FIH by linking a woman's labor force participation to her husband's time in the US. The wife's labor force participation should decrease as the husband works in the host country since the return to investment declines with years in the host country (Chiswick, 1978a, 1979). Duleep and Sanders (1993) and Baker and Benjamin (1997) found an inverse relationship between a husband's years since migration and the wife's labor force participation, controlling for her own years since migration and other relevant variables. In their analysis of school enrollment behavior in Australia, Cobb-Clark et al. (2005) found evidence of the FIH for immigrant families that have problems transferring source-country human capital, such as immigrants without pre-arranged employment.

4.3 Ramifications of immigrant women joining the labor market

Sociological research focused on the role that immigrant women play within the household finds that households become less patriarchal and more egalitarian as women gain access to social and economic resources previously beyond their reach.[53] As women work, the long-term strategies of couples may diverge (see, for instance, Grasmuck

[52] Also refer to Stier (1991), and Ngo (1994). For instance, Ngo (1994) used census data on Hong Kong to examine the extent to which immigrant wives' employment is conditioned on the assimilation strategy adopted by their families.

[53] See, for instance, Pessar (1987), Grasmuck and Pessar (1991), Hondagneu-Sotelo (1994), and Espiritu (1997). Yet immigrant women in the labor force still have family duties and can carry the double burden of work and household work (Pesquera, 1993).

and Pessar, 1991; Hondagneu-Sotelo, 1992, 1994; Gilbertson and Gurak, 1993; and Landsdale and Ogena, 1995); women may avoid returning to their home countries, realizing that a return entails their retirement from work (Grasmuck and Pessar, 1991).

Prevalent in this research is the idea that the experience of working changes the attitudes of immigrant women towards work and increases their attachment to the labor force. This idea resonates with a key labor economics finding—the importance of persistence: Regardless of the reason a woman begins to work, once she has started to work, she is likely to continue to do so (see in particular Nakamura and Nakamura, 1985, 1992a, b; Shapiro and Mott, 1994; and Shaw, 1994).

To determine the influence of persistence on immigrant women's work decisions, Duleep and Sanders (1994) exploited longitudinal features of census microdata that permit following work behavior: A woman is defined as currently working (working in time t) if, in the 1980 census, she reports working in the 1980 census week; as working last year (time $t-1$) if she reports working in 1979; and as working in time $t-5$ if she reports working in 1975. Analysis of the three-prong panel reveals that once an immigrant woman starts to work—even if she was not working in her country of origin—she continues to work.[54]

4.4 Family-based models of immigrant labor market adjustment and fertility

There also has been some investigation of the potentially complex relationships between husbands' and wives' labor supply and human capital investment behavior in conjunction with household fertility decisions. Studies of immigrant fertility, alone and linked to women's labor force participation, are key to this endeavor (examples include Bloom and Killingsworth, 1985; Kahn, 1988, 1994; Swicegood et al., 1988; Ford, 1990; Blau, 1992; Duleep and Sanders, 1994; Bean et al., 2000; Carter, 2000).

The immigration "disruption" on fertility found by Blau (1992) coupled with the large effects of having a baby on labor supply rates found by Duleep and Sanders (1994) suggest that fertility may be an important dimension in family-based models of immigrant labor market adjustment. Of particular interest is whether shortly after arrival in the host country immigrant women's fertility declines. This would support Blau's "immigration fertility disruption" thesis and also resonate with the FIH. Under the FIH, secondary earners will work to increase the family's current income so as to maintain household consumption while the primary earner pursues investment activities expected to lead to higher long-run earnings for the family. The FIH would predict relatively low fertility during the initial years in the host country so as to divert time to income-generating activities.

---

[54] Using the $t-5$ definition and limiting their sample to women who migrated to the US in the five-year period immediately prior to the census, Duleep and Sanders (1993) found that country-of-origin labor force participation did not explain intergroup variations in US labor force participation.

4.5 Following cohorts: another look at the Family Investment Hypothesis

Most empirical findings in support of the FIH are based on cross-sectional data. While recent studies confirm a positive correlation across groups between variations in the unexplained propensity of immigrant women to work and the expected return to human capital investment by immigrant men, analyses that follow cohorts over time have not found hours and wage assimilation profiles conforming to FIH predictions.

Using the 1981 and 1991 Canadian Censuses to compare immigrant and native women, Worswick (1996) found only weak evidence for the FIH from wage and labor supply estimations. Following entry cohorts with the 1980 and 1990 US censuses, Duleep (1998) and Duleep et al. (1999) did not find that adjusted intergroup differences in the propensity to work and hours worked decrease with time in the US. Moreover, they found steeper not flatter wage profiles of immigrant women in groups where the return to investment in host-country skills is highest for immigrant men. Indeed, the earnings profiles of immigrant women mimic those for immigrant men. Blau et al. (2003) and Cortes (2004a) found similar results with the 1980 and 1990 censuses.

Using longitudinal individual data, Duleep and Dowhan (2002b) found that recent cohorts of immigrant women, like recent cohorts of immigrant men, have high earnings growth (for immigrant men, see Duleep and Dowhan, 2002a). Further rebuttals of the FIH come from a comparison of married and single immigrants in Israel (Cohen-Goldner et al., 2009) and a study of Swedish immigrants (Rashid, 2004) that used both longitudinal and across-group evidence, thereby jointly exploiting two strategies to test the Family Investment Hypothesis.[55]

To explain the juxtaposition of their labor force participation results (supporting the FIH) with their over-time hours worked and wage results (countering the FIH), Duleep et al. (1999) added persistence to the FIH model (also see Duleep, 1998; Duleep and Dowhan, 2002a, b). If women who start to work in response to the husband's human capital investment continue to work, then intergroup differences that initially arose because of differences in the expected investment return would persist

The problem with the Duleep et al. model is that one could just as easily relate a woman's decision to work to her own expected return to human capital investment: Evidence from the cohort and longitudinal analyses shows that groups with high earnings growth for women are also the groups where women are more likely to work. In fact, if we think of work itself facilitating human capital investment—women who face a high investment return are more likely to work—the labor force participation results for women fit the human capital investment models of Chiswick and Duleep and Regets. This goes against the "learn versus earn" paradigm in discussions about the role of

---

[55] Both the Cohen-Goldner et al. (2009) and Rashid (2004) studies used intriguing methods to overcome potential selection bias.

opportunity cost in immigrant human capital investment (Section 1.3). Perhaps, however, learn versus earn is not the right paradigm—perhaps it is learn and earn.

Akresh (2007) used the New Immigrant Survey to examine different types of human capital investment by immigrants. Not surprisingly, individuals work fewer hours while they are enrolled in school. Of note, however, is Akresh's finding that:

> ... even while enrolled, most individuals continue to work full time or close to full time and do not dramatically decrease their labor supply to make the investment.

(Akresh, 1997, p. 873)

4.6 Two mysteries about testing for the Family Investment Hypothesis

To end Section 4, let us try to resolve two mysteries about testing for the FIH that bring us back to methodological points discussed in Section 1.4. First, why did people find results from the cross-sectional analyses that supported the FIH predictions? And, since Baker and Benjamin (1997) used cohort data from pooling two Canadian censuses, why did their results support the FIH when all other cohort-based studies did not, including the study by Blau et al. (2003) that closely replicates (with US data) the Baker/Benjamin methodology?

The first mystery is illuminated by the two panels based on longitudinal Social Security earnings data in Figure 3.6. The first panel shows the earnings profiles of immigrant men, for six year-of-entry cohorts, relative to US-born men; the second shows the earnings profiles of immigrant women, for the same six year-of-entry cohorts, relative to US-born women. Two realities are revealed, neither of which supports the FIH. For the early cohorts, immigrant women have relatively flat earnings growth *when immigrant*

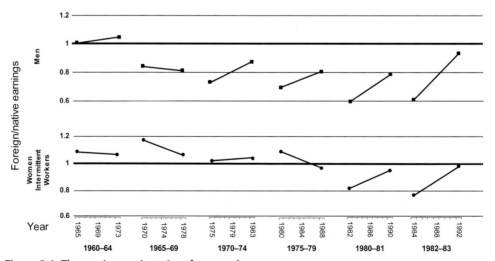

Figure 3.6 *The earnings trajectories of men and women.*

men also have relatively flat earnings growth. For the recent cohorts, immigrant women have relatively high earnings growth *when immigrant men also have relatively high earnings growth*.

The transition from flat to high earnings growth occurs earlier for men than for women. There is thus a period when low initial earnings/high earnings growth profiles of immigrant men are paired with high initial earnings/low earnings growth profiles of immigrant women, in apparent congruence with the FIH.

Baker and Benjamin (1997) found support for the FIH in a comparison of the educational investment and earnings profiles of immigrant women married to immigrant men, versus immigrant women married to Canadian-born men. According to the FIH women married to immigrant men should invest less in human capital and have relatively flatter earnings profiles than women married to Canadian natives. One piece of proof is that immigrant women married to Canadian natives show relatively high educational investment. Yet, rather than reflecting a greater tendency for immigrant women married to natives to invest in human capital, it may simply reflect that, in Canada, attending college is the most likely route by which immigrant women and Canadian natives marry.

The second support for the FIH in Baker and Benjamin comes from a comparison of earnings profiles estimated using the pooled cohort methodology, in which cohort effects are controlled for with the inclusion of dummy variables for each cohort.

In their rebuttal of the Baker and Benjamin work, Blau et al. (2003, p. 430) stated:

> *While Baker and Benjamin cite studies ... for the United States that obtain results ... consistent with their Canadian findings, these studies are based on a single cross-section of data. As Borjas (1985) showed, if the unmeasured characteristics of cohorts of immigrants are changing over time, as appears to be the case in the United States, such studies may produce biased estimates of immigrant assimilation effects. This problem may be mitigated by employing more than one nationally representative cross-section as we do here and as Baker and Benjamin did in their analysis of Canada.*

As discussed in Section 1, the pooled cohort methodology that Blau et al. and Baker and Benjamin use assumes that changes in unmeasured characteristics of cohorts affect intercepts but not slopes. With changing growth rates, this method averages the cohort-specific growth rates hiding transformations in wage and hours profiles that occur. Figure 3.6 illustrates that it does not make sense to attribute meaning to an intergroup comparison of the average earnings growth for the various groups because the results are sensitive to intergroup differences in the timing of transitions in earnings' growth.

5. IMMIGRANT ECONOMIC ADJUSTMENT: EVIDENCE FROM COUNTRIES OTHER THAN THE UNITED STATES

Two questions motivate this penultimate section. Are there consistent findings about immigrant adjustment across economically developed countries? If not, why not?

5.1 Country of origin, structural changes, and declines in immigrant initial earnings

The well-documented decline in the initial earnings of immigrants has been a concern to US researchers and policymakers alike. Underlying the decline has been a dramatic change in the source-country composition of US immigration, with post-1960s immigrants more likely to come from economically developing countries in contrast to the US immigration that followed the imposition in the 1920s of national origins admission restrictions. The earnings profiles of today's immigrants from economically developed countries resemble the earnings profiles of US natives whereas immigrants from economically developing countries—except those who enter via occupational skills—tend to have low initial earnings, relative to their US-born statistical twins, but high earnings growth.

Similar findings emerge from other economically developed, immigrant-host countries. Using data from the 1981 and 1996 New Zealand Censuses, Winkelmann (2005) documented a decline in the incomes of recent immigrants that is explained by changes in the source-country composition of New Zealand immigrants; immigrants with English backgrounds fare better than those with non-English backgrounds. Straubhaar and Golder (2005) showed that Northern European immigrants fare better in Switzerland than their southern European and non-European counterparts. In a multi-European country comparison, Dustmann and Frattini (2011) concluded that immigrants from the less economically developed non-European Union countries are particularly disadvantaged, even when compared with European natives with similar levels of schooling. With changes in the national-origin mix of immigrants in Ireland, Barrett and Duffy (2008) found an over-time decline in immigrants' initial occupational status; immigrants from the less economically developed New Member States of the European Union have the lowest occupational attainment.

In tandem with concerns about falling entry earnings and changes in the national-origin mix of recent US immigrants are concerns that structural changes in the US economy have made immigrant integration more difficult (Section 3.4). This theme is also echoed in other countries. In *The Times They are A-Changin'*, Rosholm et al. (2006) used panel data from 1985 to 1995 to study the labor market integration of various immigrant groups in Sweden and Denmark. Despite differing labor market conditions between the two countries during this time, similar declines in the employment prospects of immigrants occurred. The authors concluded that shared structural changes have put more recent immigrants at a disadvantage.

5.2 Evidence of convergence

A key finding in the US is that there is an inverse relationship between entry earnings and earnings growth. Immigrants from economically developing countries start at low initial earnings, compared with US natives of similar measurable skill levels, but experience higher earnings growth than do immigrants coming from economically developed countries.

The international literature generally supports the US finding that immigrant earnings start out lower than natives' earnings, but increase over time. In a review of British immigration studies, Hatton and Price (2005) concluded that labor market conditions improve for immigrants the longer they live in the UK; Winkelmann (2005) showed that New Zealand immigrants have lower incomes initially, but reach parity with natives after 20–30 years. With the 1984–95 Danish panel data, Husted et al. (2001) showed that immigrants—particularly non-refugee immigrants—partially assimilate to natives in 10 years. Eckstein and Weiss (2004) found that the average wages of former Soviet Union immigrants approach, but do not converge to, the wages of comparable Israeli natives.

Convergence also appears in occupational studies. Chiswick et al. (2005a, b) found occupational mobility for recent immigrants with the Australian Longitudinal Survey of Immigrants. Using Labor Force Surveys 2004 and 2005 from Statistics Netherlands, Zorlu (2013) showed that immigrant occupational achievement significantly improves with time in the Netherlands with initial beginning points and subsequent improvement varying according to source-country to host-country skill transferability.

5.3 The importance of being permanent

In contrast to the above findings that, with time, immigrants' earnings converge to those of natives, a different picture emerges when migrants have guest-worker origins.

Examining a series of cross-sections, and controlling for occupational and industrial categories, as well as schooling levels, Bauer et al. (2002) found that, in most years, Portuguese migrants to Germany, the majority of whom entered as guest workers, earn more than their German counterparts. Using data from the German Socio-Economic Panel, Constant and Massey (2005) also found higher wages for German guest workers *holding occupational status constant.*[56] Not controlling for occupational status, however, Constant and Massey found little job mobility over time for the guest workers and a resultant widening gap between them and Germans.

This comparison harks back to the discussion of the importance of permanence in Section 2.4. Shorter time horizons by immigrants will affect their human capital investment decisions. Though guest workers may out-earn their native-born counterparts in the same job—perhaps due to their longer experience in that particular occupation/industry category—their long-term earnings trajectories will be flatter than their non-guest-worker immigrant counterparts.

---

[56] Note that, in contrast to the Bauer et al. study, guest workers in the Constant/Massey study included persons from Italy, Greece, Spain, Yugoslavia, and Turkey.

There are also intergenerational implications of permanence. Historically, groups that were permanently attached to the US showed greater intergenerational progress in educational attainment than groups who were less permanent, and changes in permanence have been accompanied by changes in educational attainment. A likely reason for this is that educational expectations are tied to the place that a family is attached to. If a significant part of the community is tangentially attached to the host country, as would be the case in communities where a large percentage are going back and forth, then expectations for their children's education will be influenced by the country of origin. In his article "Return Migration, Investment in Children, and Intergenerational Mobility: Comparing Sons of Foreign and Native Born Fathers," Dustmann (2008) found that the greater the permanence of the father, the greater the educational investments in the son.

5.4 The flexibility of a country's labor market and society

One would expect similarities in immigrant adjustment across host countries that are economically developed with market economies. Once we delete from the picture guest-worker programs, and control for differences in immigrant skill levels, will immigrants from the same source country but in various host countries exhibit similar patterns of labor market adjustment?

Not necessarily. The flexibility of a country's labor market should affect the labor market adjustment of immigrants. Rigid structures governing wages and employment would make finding employment a major challenge for immigrants who initially lacked transferable skills. With less labor market rigidity, immigrants from economically developing countries would have shorter initial periods of unemployment, lower initial wages, and higher earnings growth.

One would expect to find more investment in human capital by immigrants in countries with flexible labor markets: A supple labor market structure would make it easier for immigrants to receive training and to switch into new occupations in response to demand changes. One would expect a positive association between the degree of a country's labor market flexibility and the strength of the predicted inverse relationship between immigrant entry earnings and earnings growth.

Beyond rigid or supple labor market structures, countries may differ in terms of how much they facilitate education and career changes—with some countries having fairly rigid tracks, starting at young ages, and others facilitating educational and career changes throughout life.[57] Whether societies promote or dissuade adult education and career shifts would also affect the human capital investment of immigrants and mold their earnings trajectories.

---

[57] Note that, in addition to cultural and historical differences, labor market rigidity may also affect the extent to which a society embraces educational and occupational changes throughout life.

The "Overall Strictness of Employment Protection" index (Figure 3.7), published by the Organization for Economic Cooperation and Development, is a gauge for the rigidity of labor markets in various countries. The US is the least rigid.

Casual comparisons of the US immigrant experience with that of countries higher up the rigidity scale lends circumstantial support to the labor-market-flexibility/immigrant experience hypotheses discussed above.[58] For instance, from their study of immigrant unemployment in the US, Chiswick and Hurst (2000) conclude: "Unemployment problems associated with immigrants appear to be short-term transitional adjustments." In contrast, Frijters et al. (2005), in their study of UK immigrants, found immigrants generally have less successful job searches and longer periods of unemployment than natives. Hansen and Lofstrom (2009) found that immigrants in Sweden between 1990 and 1996 were more likely to be unemployed in consecutive years than were natives. The Rosholm et al. (2006) study of Swedish and Danish immigrants reveals that between

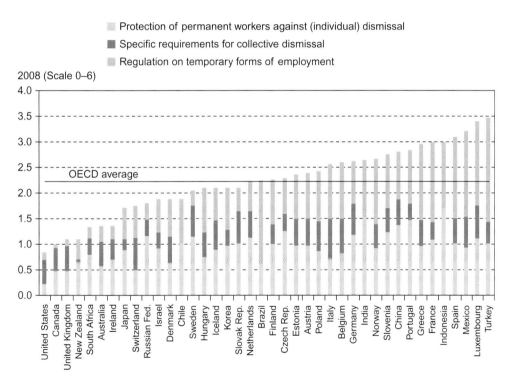

Figure 3.7 Employment protection in 2008 in OECD and selected non-OECD countries. Scale from 0 (least stringent) to 6 (most restrictive).

---

[58] For an analysis of the effects of minimum wages within the US, see Cortes (2004b). Using CPS data and looking at low-income workers, Cortes found that immigrants earn less than natives, but with an increase in the minimum wage, she found no significant difference between immigrants' and natives' wages.

1984 and 1995 immigrants had fewer employment opportunities than did natives. Husted et al. (2001) comment:

> Part of the explanation behind the large differences in the unemployment rates for Danish born and immigrants may be the compressed Danish wage structure . . . for Denmark and other countries with high minimum wages, a large part of the assimilation mechanism lies in simply getting a job.

Analyzing immigrant–native wage gaps in their paper "Qualifications, Discrimination, or Assimilation?," Nielsen et al. (2004) concluded that "a large fraction of [the wage] gap would disappear if only immigrants could find employment and thus accumulate work experience."

With data from an employee survey in Ireland, Barrett et al. (2013) broached a much less researched topic—whether immigrants are as likely to receive employer-provided training as comparable natives. They found that immigrants, and in particular immigrants from the less economically developed New Member States of the EU, are less likely to receive training. The cause is twofold: immigrants are less likely than natives to be employed by training-oriented firms, and within the less training-oriented firms they are less likely to receive training.

In what appears to be the first thorough exploration of the nexus between immigrant economic adjustment and the labor market flexibility of the host country, Miller and Neo (2003)[59] found that the entry earnings of US immigrants relative to US natives of similar characteristics are lower than the entry earnings of Australian immigrants, relative to Australian natives. Concomitantly, Australian immigrants experience much higher unemployment rates than their US counterparts during their first years in the host country. Examining over-time earnings trajectories reveals that the rate of immigrant adjustment is greater in the US than in Australia and, at each measured point, the unemployment rate experienced by Australian immigrants, relative to Australian natives, exceeds that of the US immigrants.

6. SUMMARY AND DIRECTIONS FOR FURTHER RESEARCH

The Immigrant Assimilation Model (IAM) developed by Chiswick was the first labor economics model of immigrant labor market adjustment. Chiswick (1978a, 1979) observed that migrants often lack skills specific to their destination country that would permit their source-country human capital to be fully valued—"transferred"—to the host-country labor market. As English and other US-specific skills or credentials are gained, the value of the immigrant's source-country human capital is restored.

Starting with the concept of skill transferability, the Immigrant Assimilation Model predicts that immigrants with low skill transferability will have low initial (adjusted) earnings but high earnings growth as they pursue a course of investment in human capital that

---

[59] Efforts to compare immigrants across countries along other related dimensions than the Miller/Neo effort include Büchel and Frick (2004), Antecol et al. (2006), Chiswick et al. (2008), and Dustmann et al. (2010).

increases the transferability of their source-country skills to the host-country's labor market. The IAM ushered in a labor-economics field of immigration; its productive life continues as evidenced by its theoretical, methodological, and empirical offspring.

6.1 The Occupational Mobility Model

IAM's first theoretical offspring was Chiswick's Occupational Mobility Model, in which he hypothesized that immigrant occupational mobility follows a U-shaped pattern (Chiswick, 1978b). This model—and its associated hypotheses concerning the depth of the "U"—continue to be confirmed in several time periods and countries. For instance, the model's hypotheses hold up in a recent analysis of Australian longitudinal data that includes information on the pre-immigration occupation, the "first" occupation in Australia, and the occupation after three and a half years in Australia (Chiswick et al., 2005a, b). Another confirmation comes from the US New Immigrant Survey:

> *An immigrant's motivation to ascend the occupational ladder quickly can be particularly high if his or her initial labor market experience involved occupational downgrading, which is a phenomenon found to be as high as 50% … especially for immigrants from regions that differ culturally and linguistically from the host country …*
>
> **(Akresh, 2007; also refer to Akresh, 2008)**

And, in a paper examining immigrant occupational mobility in the Netherlands:

> *… immigrants start with jobs at the lower levels of skill distribution. Their occupational achievement improves significantly with the duration of residence. The extent of this initial disadvantage and the rate of adjustment vary across immigrant groups according to the transferability of skills associated with their cultural and linguistic distance from Dutch society. Turks and Moroccans face the greatest initial dip and achieve the highest rate of adjustment while the opposite holds for Caribbean and Western immigrants.*
>
> **(Zorlu, 2013)**

6.2 The Immigrant Human Capital Investment Model

Another theoretical offspring of IAM is the IHCI model developed by Duleep and Regets (2002). Building on the IAM's concepts, the IHCI model brought to life two overlooked aspects of immigrant skill transferability. One, immigrants whose source-country skills do not transfer fully to the new labor market will have a lower opportunity cost of human capital investment than otherwise similar natives or immigrants with high skill transferability. Two, initially undervalued source-country skills in the host-country labor market are useful for learning new skills.[60]

---

[60] Although the IHCI model was developed to understand immigrant economic assimilation, its two additional concepts could be more broadly applied, for instance to women returning to the labor market after home duty or individuals returning to work after periods of unemployment.

With its emphasis on the low opportunity cost of human capital investment for immigrants lacking transferable skills, paired with the value of source-country human capital for learning new skills, a distinguishing implication of the IHCI model is that the higher incentive to invest in human capital pertains not only to host-country-specific human capital that restores the value of specific source-country human capital, but to new human capital in general. A topic for further research, along the lines pursued by David Green (1999), is what are the effects on a nation's economic productivity of the skill acquisition of immigrants that accompanies their high earnings growth?

6.3 Empirical offspring of the IAM

If one reads Chiswick's "The Effect of Americanization on the Earnings of Foreign-Born Men" alongside Borjas's "Assimilation, Changes in Cohort Quality, and the Earnings of Immigrants," it is immediately apparent that if the theory of the former is correct, the methodology of the latter is incorrect (refer to Chiswick, 1978a; and Borjas, 1985): If skill transferability is positively related to entry earnings (the lower the skill transferability, the lower the initial earnings) and negatively related to earnings growth (the lower the skill transferability, the higher the earnings growth) then it does not make sense to allow entry earnings to vary via a fixed cohort effects model while assuming stationary earnings growth across immigrant cohorts. More generally, when intercept and slope are jointly determined then holding slopes constant, while allowing intercepts to vary, is as nonsensical as holding intercepts constant, while allowing slopes to vary.

Following individuals over time, versus cohorts, solves many problems including cross-sectional bias. Nevertheless, the cohort fixed-effect methodology dominates the field even when researchers use longitudinal data on individuals (important exceptions include Hall and Farkas, 2008; Green and Worswick, 2012; and Lin, 2013). Following entry cohorts of immigrants, Duleep and Regets (2002) conclusively showed that changes in immigrant (adjusted) entry earnings are inversely related to changes in immigrant earnings growth, a relationship that persists controlling for immigrant emigration and regression to the mean (also see Duleep and Regets, 1996c, 1997a, b; Duleep and Dowhan, 2002a).

Measured and unmeasured factors that affect initial earnings likely affect earnings growth. Immigrants balance learning and earning. As a consequence, initial conditions, whether initial earnings or education, may be poor predictors of subsequent conditions.

The inverse relationship between immigrant-adjusted entry earnings and earnings growth, and the fact that immigrant groups pursue varying strategies in their labor market adjustment, make intergroup and immigrant–native comparisons challenging. Groups are commonly compared using their average earnings, at a given age. Such comparisons may be misleading, however, if groups vary in the extent to which they invest in human capital with attendant effects on the shapes of their earnings profiles. Intergroup comparisons of returns to schooling and experience may also be deceptive if assimilation strategies, and accompanying earnings patterns, vary by education level within groups.[61] A more transparent methodological approach is to compare the earnings trajectories of immigrants versus natives and across immigrant groups, by education level and age, rather than controlling for education and age in a regression. If sample size is a constraint, then variables can be controlled for across groups in a non-parametric fashion via weighting, an approach used by sociologists more than a half century ago but now embraced by some economists.[62]

Beyond making immigrant/native and across-immigrant-group comparisons challenging, the high earnings growth of post-1970 US immigrants, coupled with their low initial earnings, brings to mind a broader question. To what extent have immigrant earnings played a significant role in the over-time growth in US earnings inequality? If significant, then it is important to consider this in conjunction with immigrants' relatively high earnings growth.

6.4 Immigrant ability and the relative flexibility of societies

In contrast to the work of sociologists, economists have been interested in immigrant ability, nurtured in particular by the Roy model. An intriguing development has been the use of individual data to measure where immigrants are in the source-country's totem pole before emigrating with the finding that persons who emigrate did poorly relative to their compatriots who did not emigrate. Yet the conclusion that their relative source-country placement represents lower ability is at odds with the high earnings growth of immigrants measured in assumption-free studies that follow cohorts or individuals.

An interesting idea to pursue that would explain individuals' lower placement in the source country and their subsequent high earnings growth in the host country is that individuals who migrate are constrained in their original countries. Constraints can occur in terms of not being able to acquire schooling, as suggested in the work of Jensen et al. (2006). More generally, one would expect that in migrations from less flexible societies to more flexible societies, those who don't do well in their constrained source-country roles would be the most likely to migrate to more flexible societies, whereupon they would start at relatively low earnings, invest in human capital, and experience high

---

[61] For instance, estimated returns to schooling revealed lower returns to schooling for various Euroethnic groups than for the comparison group even though the Euroethnic groups out-earned the comparison group at every educational level (Duleep and Sider, 1986).

[62] Refer to DiNardo et al. (1996) for an elegant presentation and extension of this method and to Duleep (1988), Duleep and Regets (1997a), and Duleep and Dowhan (2002a, b) for examples of applications. Although there are early examples of sociologists using weighting of observations to compare groups, as in the work of Kitagawa and Hauser, more generally economists can think of the concept of weighting to compare groups as akin to the oft-used practice (of both sociologists and economists) of weighting observations in surveys to make them representative of the general population.

earnings growth. A distinguishing characteristic of the US is that people are less tracked educationally and career wise than in many other economically developed countries, and people can and do change careers even late in adulthood. The fact that newcomers start at low earnings does not mean that they are of low ability.

The Miller/Neo effort (Section 5.2) exploring the relationship between an economic system's suppleness and immigrant labor market outcomes could be expanded to a wide range of immigrant host countries using longitudinal data in each.[63] Such comparisons would be most illuminating if year-of-immigration cohorts were analyzed separately, allowing earnings growth to vary with entry earnings. Given the complex interactions between entry earnings, earnings growth, schooling, and level of economic development of source countries, the best analytical approach would be to estimate earnings trajectories within categories as opposed to trying to control for variables by including them in a regression. Ideally, more than one cohort per country would be studied to help capture the impact of state-of-the-labor market differences (Section 3.3). The OECD index (Section 5.2) could be used as a country-specific measure of labor market rigidity; societal levels of openness towards adult training and career shifts could be measured by the extent to which the native adults in each country pursue schooling and career changes.

Finally, note that flexible societies and economies would be most likely to attract immigrants who wanted to pursue new paths. The selection of these individuals would contribute to low initial earnings, high human capital investment, and high earnings growth.

6.5 Skill acquisition

Perhaps because of the emphasis on immigrant ability (which often conveys a fixed effect) and the accompanying greater emphasis on entry earnings instead of earnings growth (as epitomized in the assumption of stationary earnings growth across immigrant cohorts), there have been relatively few statistical studies of the acquisition of host-country skills, other than the extensive study of immigrant language acquisition, discussed in Chiswick and Miller's chapter of this book.

US immigrants invest in schooling at higher rates than natives (Duleep and Regets, 2002), a phenomenon that is especially pronounced for immigrants lacking initially transferable skills (Duleep et al., 1999; Cortes, 2004a). This occurs even while immigrants work full time or close to full time (Akresh, 2007). Earnings analyses that control for educational achievement thus hide immigrant relative earnings growth. This is especially true for immigrant cohorts with low initial adjusted earnings.

A clear area for further research is the development of models and statistical analyses that illuminate the human-capital-investment strategies immigrants pursue. As a potential

---

[63] Refer to the introduction of this chapter for a synopsis of ongoing longitudinal data efforts in immigrant host countries.

starting point, it is easy to extend the IHCI model to the issue of what type of human capital investment immigrants will choose by considering the transferability of source-country skills to the labor market (τ_M) versus transferability of source-country skills to the production of human capital in the host country (τ_P). Given τ_M, immigrants should pursue the type of human capital investment for which $\tau_P - \tau_M$ is largest. For immigrants who, for instance, do not speak the host-country language, τ_P would be very small for pursuing schooling other than schooling to learn the host-country language! If not pursuing language training, these immigrants would be more likely to pursue training in a linguistic enclave.

A richer understanding of how immigrants acquire skills would be nurtured by a synthesis of the case study—detailed studies of specific groups in specific localities[64]—and nationwide statistical approaches.

Economists generally use nationwide statistical studies over the case-study approach. Yet nationwide surveys, which have the virtue of generalization, are by their very nature less likely to provide detailed information on processes, group identities, and contexts. Nationwide statistical studies often fail to illuminate processes that underlie important correlations and group identities associated with meaningful economic activities.

In nationwide surveys, such as the census or the Current Population Survey, individuals are generally categorized by their occupation and industry. A person could be categorized as a manual worker in the construction industry or a laborer in the restaurant industry. Yet the case-study research of Gallo and Bailey (1996) showed that immigrants and the native born with the same census occupation/industry category are distinguished by the nature of their work and the process by which they become employed, trained, and promoted. Case-study research of this kind has profoundly affected economic research in, for instance, the realization that poorly educated immigrants are not necessarily substitutes for poorly educated natives (Duleep and Wunnava, 1996).[65]

Nationwide statistical studies would benefit by using case-study insights to illuminate the processes of skill acquisition underlying estimated correlations. Case studies could also help delineate "effective groups" via language and ancestry variables and encourage more imaginative uses of existing data in nationwide statistical studies.

The overwhelming problem with case studies is that by focusing on a microcosm, we do not know whether and how case-study results may be generalized. Without

[64] See, for instance, Hagan et al. (2011), who drew on the migration and work histories of 200 Mexican migrants and return migrants, to give detailed information on various types of skill acquisition including English, formal education, on-the-job technical skills, off-the-job technical skills, non-technical skills/qualities, and even outside-of-work-and-school acquisition of human capital.

[65] With respect to group identities, the identities of "effective groups" may not match group definitions available in nationwide surveys. Without appropriate or sufficiently detailed group definitions, important immigrant strategies may remain hidden from the analyst's eye. For further discussion of this point, see Duleep and Wunnava's (1996) introduction.

replicating similar case studies in a variety of different locations, there is no way of knowing which features are peculiar to the situation and which are general. In many, perhaps all case studies, we do not even know whether the results are specific to immigrants.

Case-study research would be enhanced by a careful consideration of variables that may affect the results, including the characteristics of individuals, the characteristics of the area, and the characteristics of the time period in which the study is being conducted. Greater generalization of case-study results could be achieved by utilizing insights from national statistical studies in the selection of observations and in the replication of case studies across areas and time periods.

6.6 Beyond the individual

The analysis of immigrant labor market adjustment has broadened to encompass a variety of contexts beyond the individual traits of immigrants. This development has occurred via a conscious or unconscious interaction between sociologists and economists.

The enclave economy, social networks, and the potential importance of intergenerational persistence, all foci of sociological research, have entered economic models of immigrant assimilation, with a stunning proliferation in recent years (interesting examples include Patel and Vella, 2007; and Postepska and Vella, 2013). A potentially productive path would be to superimpose the sociological concepts on the individualistic models such as Chiswick's IAM and Occupational Mobility Model, and Duleep and Regets' IHIC model.

Dual labor market theory, developed by economists, nourished the sociological concept of segmented assimilation—that different groups of immigrants who have the same level of schooling and age may nevertheless occupy very different worlds. In the literature a picture of segmented assimilation arises in which some immigrant groups economically assimilate while others remain locked in secondary-sector labor market jobs. A more nuanced view to further explore is that skill transferability and permanence (both of the individual and the group) determines what world immigrants are in, and that immigrants who become more permanent can go from one sector to another.

The state of the labor market is another context that affects immigrant labor market adjustment. Social scientists frequently use the identifying assumption that "period effects," often driven by the impact of macroeconomic conditions on labor market outcomes, are identical between immigrants and natives. The statistical literature of the last 15 years makes it clear that this assumption is wrong (Section 3.3). At the same time, the overall macroeconomic effect may reflect a variety of responses that are not, at this point, well understood. Research hints that there are important interactions between labor market conditions, how immigrants earn and their propensity to learn, and that these interactions vary across immigrant groups (Section 3.3).

Beyond the ups and downs of the business cycle, many scholars believe that industrial changes in the US and other economically developed countries have narrowed job opportunities for the poorly educated, with particularly devastating effects for poorly educated immigrants. Yet some research suggests that poorly educated immigrants are less affected than natives by long-term structural changes and economic downturns (see, for instance, Peterson and Vroman, 1992; Powers and Seltzer, 1998; Duleep and Dowhan, 2002a, b; and Hall and Farkas, 2008; and the discussion in Section 3.4). If this conclusion holds up to further research, then why is this so? This is an area where case-study research may continue to nurture a deeper understanding, with implications beyond the study of immigration, to mobility strategies for the poorly educated.

The existence of period effects and over time structural changes underscores the importance of developing longitudinal data that follow multiple year-of-entry immigrant cohorts. Analyses of immigrant earnings and employment based on the experiences of a few cohorts may yield poorly conceived policy prescriptions.

6.7 Immigrant women

An evolving picture of the role women play in the labor market adjustment of immigrants continues to unfurl. Earlier evidence consistently supported a Family Investment Hypothesis. More recent work that follows cohorts and individuals continues to find cross-group patterns of initial labor force participation consonant with the Family Investment Hypothesis yet reveals earnings profiles of immigrant women that resemble those of immigrant men. The higher propensity to work of immigrant women who have initially low earnings challenges traditional labor market models of the decision to work of women; their high earnings growth challenges the Family Investment Hypothesis.

The contradictory findings surrounding the FIH prompted Blau et al. (2003) to sensibly recommend that "Similar studies of other countries need to be done in order to determine whether Canada or the United States is an exceptional case." For such comparisons to be meaningful, however, analysts should allow entry earnings and earnings growth to vary across year-of-entry cohorts as opposed to only letting entry earnings vary (Section 4). Most informative would be non-parametric comparisons.

In thinking about the potential usefulness of the FIH, it is important to remember that although it was developed to explain intergroup differences in the labor force behavior of married immigrant women, and has often focused on women supporting human capital investment by immigrant men, there is nothing uniquely "immigrant" about the FIH. Moreover, the family calculus can go to men supporting women's human capital investment, and over time switching. Consider for instance spouse 1 taking a job to finance spouse 2 attending medical school, and then spouse 1 returning to school when spouse 2 is a doctor. It may be that although the FIH does not explain immigrant–native or intergroup differences in the labor market adjustment of immigrant women, it may still be useful as a theoretical construct guiding analysis of individual family decision making.

More consistent empirical support has rallied around the notion of persistence. Both sociological and economic work reveal that the fact of working by immigrant women may have a persistent and transformative effect. Women who work after migrating, even if they did not work in their countries of origin, continue to work (Duleep and Sanders, 1993, 1994), a finding that resonates with work on native-born women (Nakamura and Nakamura, 1985, 1992a). Sociological research suggests that the experience of working affects power relationships within families, including decisions about whether to stay in the host country. The burgeoning movement from common preference models to bargaining models to depict family decision making (Lundberg and Pollak, 1996) could find new fodder for empirical and theoretical analyses in the labor market transformations of immigrant husbands and wives.

Following immigrant entry cohorts, Duleep et al. (1999) found that women were more likely to work and had high earnings growth in groups in which men had low initial adjusted earnings and high earnings growth. This finding, if confirmed, further cautions against using entry earnings as a predictor of immigrant economic success. It also suggests that assessments of how well immigrants do may want to look beyond individual earnings, and encompass a family perspective. Are the conclusions about over-time trends in immigrant earnings profiles altered when families are brought into the picture? A key research agenda should be to provide insight on labor market adjustment from a family perspective.

6.8 Permanence

Finally, there is the importance of permanence. The extent to which immigrants invest in human capital, what type of human capital investment, whether women work, the extent to which an immigrant's community provides opportunities for growth—indeed all aspects of immigrant labor market adjustment—are likely affected by the degree to which individuals and the communities they are part of are permanently attached to their host country.

Understanding the effect of permanence has strong policy ramifications—should immigration that is temporary be encouraged? One would expect that the longer the duration of guest-worker status of groups, the slower their intergenerational progress relative to other groups. European countries, with their varying histories of guest-worker programs, provide a rich natural-experiments' basis to test the impact of guest-worker programs on subsequent intergenerational progress.

Another area for further research is what determines permanence? Long-run opportunities in the source versus host country (which increase permanence) and the ease of going back and forth (which decreases permanence) appear to be crucial. Both are a function of factors that could change. For instance, proximity is one current determinant of the ease of going back and forth and likely contributes to the lower permanence of both Canadians and Mexicans in the US. Lack of proximity also contributes to the permanence of Chinese illegal aliens, discussed in Section 2.4. Legal issues of course constrain or facilitate the ease of going back and forth. The effect of proximity per se, however, may change with technological developments that would reduce the effect of proximity in much the same way that air travel reduced proximity's effect for internal migration in years past.

6.9 A concluding caveat

From 1990 to 2013, 54% of the growth in the number of international migrants was attributable to growth in migration from economically developing to economically developed countries, while 31% was due to an increase in intra-economically developing country migration (United Nations, 2013). This chapter has focused on the labor market adjustment of immigrants in economically developed countries. Expanding that range is a topic for further research.

ACKNOWLEDGMENTS

This chapter owes a heavy debt to my long-term collaborations with Mark Regets, Seth Sanders, and Phanindra Wunnava. It has also benefitted from conversations and correspondence over the years with Bob LaLonde, Mike Leonesio, Christopher Worswick, and David Green. I would also like to thank an anonymous reviewer for helpful comments.

REFERENCES

Ahmed, B., Robinson, G., 1994. Estimates of Emigration of the Foreign-Born Population: 1980–1990, Population Estimates and Projections Technical Working Paper Series No. 9, US Bureau of the Census.

Akresh, I.R., 2006. Occupational mobility among legal immigrants to the United States. Int. Migrat. Rev. 40 (4), 854–884.

Akresh, I.R., 2007. U.S. immigrants' labor market adjustment: Additional human capital investment and earnings growth. Demography 44 (4), 865–881.

Akresh, I.R., 2008. Occupational trajectories of legal U.S. immigrants: Downgrading and recovery. Popul. Dev. Rev. 34 (3), 435–456.

Antecol, H., Cobb-Clark, D., Trejo, S., 2003. Immigration policy and the skills of immigrants to Australia, Canada, and the United States. J. Hum. Resour. 38 (1), 192–218.

Antecol, H., Kuhn, P., Trejo, S.J., 2006. Assimilation via prices or quantities? Sources of immigrant earnings growth in Australia, Canada, and the United States. J. Hum. Resour. 41, 821–840.

Averitt, R., 1968. The Dual Economy: The Dynamics of American Industry Structure. W.W. Norton, New York.

Aydemir, A., Skuterud, M., 2005. Explaining the deteriorating entry arnigns of Canada's immigrant cohorts, 1966–2000. (2, May), Canadian Journal of Economics 38, 641–671.

Bailey, T.R., 1987. Immigrant and Native Workers: Contrasts and Competition. Westview Press, Boulder and London, Conservation of Human Resources.

Bailey, T.R., Waldinger, R., 1991. Primary, secondary, and enclave labor markets: A training systems approach. Am. Sociol. Rev. 56, 432–445 (August).

Baker, M., Benjamin, D., 1997. The role of the family in immigrants' labor-market activity: An evaluation of alternative explanations. Am. Econ. Rev. 87 (4), 705–727.

Barrett, A., Duffy, D., 2008. Are Ireland's immigrants integrating into its labour market? Int. Migrat. Rev. 42 (3), 597–619.

Barrett, A., Mosca, I., 2013. The psychic costs of migration: Evidence from Irish return migrants. J. Popul. Econ. 26 (2), 483–506.

Barrett, A., McGuinness, S., O'Brien, M., O'Connell, P.J., 2013. Immigrants and employer-provided training. J. Labor Res. 34 (1), 52–78.

Bauer, T., Pereira, P.T., Vogler, M., Zimmermann, K.F., 2002. Portuguese migrants in the German labor market: Performance and self-selection. Int. Migrat. Rev. 36 (2), 467–491.

Bauer, T., Epstein, G.S., Gang, I.N., 2005. Enclaves, language and the location choice of migrants. J. Popul. Econ. 18 (4), 649–662.

Beach, C.M., Worswick, C., 1993. Is there a double-negative effect on the earnings of immigrant women? Can. Publ. Pol. 19, 36–53.

Bean, F., Stevens, G., 2003. America's Newcomers and The Dynamics of Diversity. Russell Sage Foundation, New York.

Bean, F.D., Tienda, M., 1987. The Hispanic Population of the United States. Russell Sage, New York.

Bean, F., Swicegood, C.G., King, A.G., 1985. Role incompatibility and the relationships between fertility and labor supply among Hispanic women. In: Borjas, G.J., Tienda, M. (Eds.), Hispanics and the U.S. Economy. Academic Press, New York.

Beenstock, M., Chiswick, B., Paltiel, A., 2010. Testing the immigrant assimilation hypothesis with longitudinal data. Review of the Economics of the Household 8, 7–27.

Blau, F., 1980. Immigration and labor earnings in early twentieth century America. In: Simon, J., DaVanzo, J. (Eds.), Research in Population Economics. In: JAI Press, 2. Greenwich, CT, pp. 21–41.

Blau, F., Kahn, L., Moriarty, J., Souza, A., 2003. The role of the family in immigrants' labor-market activity: An evaluation of alternative explanations: Comment. (1, March), Am. Econ. Rev. 93, 429–447.

Bonacich, E., Modell, J., 1980. The Economic Basis of Ethnic Solidarity: Small Business in the Japanese-American Community. University of California Press, Berkeley, CA.

Borjas, G., 1985. Assimilation, changes in cohort quality, and the earnings of immigrants. J. Labor Econ. 3, 463–489 (October).

Borjas, G., 1987. Self selection and immigrants. Am. Econ. Rev. 77, 531–553.

Borjas, G., 1992a. National origin and the skills of immigrants. In: Borjas, G.J., Freeman, R.B. (Eds.), Immigration and the Work Force. University of Chicago Press, Chicago.

Borjas, G., 1992b. Immigration research in the 1980s: A turbulent decade. In: Mitchell, O., Sherer, P. (Eds.), Lewin, D. Research Frontiers in Industrial Relations and Human Resources, Industrial Relations Research Association, pp. 417–446.

Borjas, G., 1992c. National origin and the skills of immigrants. In: Borjas, G.J., Freeman, R.B. (Eds.), Immigration and the Work Force. National Bureau of Economic Research. University of Chicago Press, Chicago, pp. 17–48.

Borjas, G., 1994. The economics of immigration. J. Econ. Lit. 1667–1717 (December).

Borjas, G., Bratsberg, B., 1996. Who leaves? The outmigration of the foreign-born. Rev. Econ. Stat. 165–176 (February).

Bound, J., Johnson, G., 1992. Changes in the structure of wages during the 1980s: An evaluation of alternative explanations. (3, June), Am. Econ. Rev. 82, 371–392.

Boyd, M., 1984. At a disadvantage: The occupational attainments of foreign born women in Canada. Int. Migrat. Rev. 18 (4), 1091–1119.

Boyd, M., 1989. Family and personal networks in international migration: Recent developments and new agendas. Int. Migrat. Rev. 23 (3), 638–670.

Bratsberg, B., Ragan, J.F., 2002. The impact of host country schooling on earnings: A study of male immigrants in the United States. J. Hum. Resour. 37 (1), 63–105.

Brettell, C.B., Hollifield, J.F. (Eds.), 2000. Migration Theory. Routledge, New York.

Büchel, F., Frick, J.R., 2004. Immigrants in the UK and in West Germany - Relative income position, income portfolio, and redistribution effects. J. Popul. Econ. 17 (3), 553–581.

Chiswick, B.R., 1978a. The effect of Americanization on the earnings of foreign-born men. J. Polit. Econ. 897–922 (October).

Chiswick, B.R., 1978b. A longitudinal analysis of occupational mobility of immigrants. In: Dennis, B. (Ed.), Proceedings of the 30th Annual Winter Meeting, Industrial Relations Research Association, December 1977. Madison, WI, pp. 20–27.

Chiswick, B.R., 1979. The economic progress of immigrants: Some apparently universal patterns. In: Fellner, W. (Ed.), Contemporary Economic Problems. American Enterprise Institute, Washington, DC, pp. 359–399.

Chiswick, B.R., 1980. An Analysis of the Economic Progress and Impact of Immigrants. Department of Labor monograph, N.T.I.S. No. PB80-200454. National Technical Information Service, Washington, DC.

Chiswick, B.R., 1991. Review of international differences in the labor market performance of immigrants. (April), Ind. Labor Relat. Rev. 570–571.

Chiswick, B.R., Hurst, M.E., 2000. The employment, unemployment and unemployment compensation benefits of immigrants. In: Bassi, L., Woodbury, S. (Eds.), Long-Term Unemployment and Reemployment Policies (Research in Employment Policy, vol. 2). JAI Press, Stamford, CT, pp. 87–115.

Chiswick, B.R., Miller, P.W., 1992. Language in the immigrant labor market. In: Chiswick, B. (Ed.), Immigration, Language, and Ethnicity: Canada and the United States. American Enterprise Institute, Washington, DC, pp. 229–296.

Chiswick, B.R., Miller, P.W., 1994. The determinants of post-immigration investments in education. Econ. Educ. Rev. 13, 163–177.

Chiswick, B.R., Miller, P.W., 2002. Do enclaves matter in immigrant adjustment? City and Community 4 (1), 5–35, 2005.

Chiswick, B.R., Miller, P.W., 2008. Occupational attainment and immigrant economic progress in Australia. Econ. Rec. 84, S45–S56.

Chiswick, B.R., Miller, P.W., 2009. Earnings and occupational attainment among immigrants. Ind. Relat. 48 (3), 454–465.

Chiswick, B.R., Cohen, B., Zach, T., 1997. The labor market status of immigrants: Effects of unemployment rate at arrival and duration of residence. Ind. Labor Relat. Rev. 50 (2), 289–303.

Chiswick, B.R., Lee, Y.L., Miller, P.W., 2005a. Longitudinal analysis of immigrant occupational mobility: A test of the immigrant assimilation hypothesis. Int. Migrat. Rev. 39 (2), 332–353.

Chiswick, B.R., Lee, Y.L., Miller, P.W., 2005b. Immigrant earnings: A longitudinal analysis. (4, December), Review of Income and Wealth 51, 485–503.

Chiswick, B.R., Le, A.T., Miller, P.W., 2008. How immigrants fare across the earnings distribution: International analyses. Ind. Labor Relat. Rev. 61 (3), 353–373.

Chunyu, M.D., 2011. Earnings Growth Patterns of Chinese Labor Immigrants in the United States. Paper presented at the 2011 Annual Meeting of the Population Association of America, Washington, DC. www.paa2011.princeton.edu/download.aspx?submissionId=110457.

Cobb-Clark, D., Kossoudji, S., 1999. Did legalization matter for women? Amnesty and the wage determinants of formerly unauthorized Latina workers. Gend. Issues. 3–14 (Fall).

Cobb-Clark, D., Shiells, C., Lindsay Lowell, B., 1995. Immigration reform: The effects of employer sanctions and legalization on wages. (3, July), J. Labor Econ. 13, 472–498.

Cobb-Clark, D., Connolly, M., Worswick, C., 2005. The job search and education investments of immigrant families. J. Pop. Econ. 18 (4), 663–690.

Cobb-Clark, D., Hanel, B., McVicar, D., 2012a. Are Repeated Cross Section or Longitudinal Estimates of Migrant Assimilation Better? Working Paper, University of Melbourne, A Tale of Two Biases.

Cobb-Clark, D., Hanel, B., McVicar, D., 2012b. Immigrant Wage and Employment Assimilation: A Comparison of Methods. IZA Discussion Paper Institute for the Study of Labor, Bonn, Germany, December.

Cohen-Goldner, S., Gotlibovski, C., Kahana, N., 2009. A Reevaluation of the Role of Family in Immigrants' Labor Market Activity: Evidence from a Comparison of Single and Married Immigrants, IZA Discussion Paper No. 4185.

Constant, A., Massey, D.S., 2003. Self-selection, earnings, and out-migration: A longitudinal study of immigrants to Germany. J. Popul. Econ. 16 (4), 631–653.

Constant, A., Zimmermann, K.F., 2004. Self-Employment Dynamics Across the Business Cycle: Migrants Versus Natives. IZA Discussion Paper No. 1386, Institute for the Study of Labor, Bonn, Germany, November.

Cornelius, W., Marcelli, E., 2000. The changing profile of Mexican migrants to the United States: New evidence from California and Mexico. Lat. Am. Res. Rev. 36 (3), 105–131, 2001.

Cornelius, W.A., Tsuda, T., Valdez, Z., 2003. Human Capital versus Social Capital: A Comparative Analysis of Immigrant Wages and Labor Market Incorporation in Japan and the United States. IZA Discussion Paper No. 476, Institute for the Study of Labor, Bonn, Germany.

Cortes, K.E., 2004a. Are refugees different from economic immigrants? Some empirical evidence on the heterogeneity of immigrant groups in the United States. Rev. Econ. Stat. 86 (2), 465–480.

Cortes, K.E., 2004b. Wage Effects on Immigrants from an Increase in the Minimum Wage Rate: An Analysis by Immigrant Industry Concentration. IZA Discussion Paper No. 1064, Institute for the Study of Labor, Bonn, Germany.

Crossley, T.F., McDonald, J.T., Worswick, C., 2001. Immigrant benefit receipt revisited: Sensitivity to the choice of survey years and model specification. J. Hum. Resour. 36 (2), 379–397.

DaVanzo, J., 1976. Differences between return and nonreturn migration: An econometric analysis. (Spring), Int. Migrat. Rev. 13–27.

DaVanzo, J., 1983. Repeat migration in the United States: Who moves back and who moves on? Rev. Econ. Stat. 65, 552–559 (4, November).

DaVanzo, J., Morrison, P.A., 1981. Return and other sequences of migration in the U.S. Demography 18, 85–101 (February).

DeFreitas, G., 1991. Inequality at Work: Hispanics in the U.S. Labor Force. Oxford University Press, Oxford and New York.

DeFreitas, G., 1993. Unionization among racial and ethnic minorities. (2, January), Ind. Labor Relat. Rev. 46, 284–301.

Demombynes, G.M., 2002. Three ways of looking at immigrant wage growth: Analysis with the 1993–1998 Current Population Survey, Prepared for the Institute for Labor and Employment Conference, 18–19 January.

DeSilva, A., 1996. Earnings of Immigrant Classes in the Early 1980s in Canada: A Re-examination. Working Paper, Human Resource Development Canada.

Dickens, W.T., Lang, K., 1985. A test of dual labor market theory. Am. Econ. Rev. 75, 792–805.

Dickens, W.T., Lang, K., 1988. The reemergence of segmented labor market theory. (2, May), Am. Econ. Rev. 78, 129–134.

DiNardo, F., Fortin, N., Lemieux, 1996. Labor market institutions and the distribution of wages, 1973–1992: A semiparametric approach. (5, September), Econometrica 64, 1001–1044.

Doeringer, P., Piore, M., 1971. Internal Labor Markets and Manpower Analysis. D.C. Heath, Lexington, MA.

Donato, K.P., 1993. Current trends and patterns of female migration: Evidence from Mexico. International Migration Research 27 (4), 748–771.

Donato, K., Durand, J., Massey, D., 1992. Changing conditions in the U.S. labor market: Effects of the Immigrant Reform and Control Act of 1986. Popul. Res. Pol. Rev. 11 (2), 93–115.

Duleep, H., 1988. The Economic Status of Americans of Asian Descent: An Exploratory Investigation. US Commission on Civil Rights, GPO.

Duleep, H., 1994. Social security and the emigration of immigrants. Soc. Secur. Bull. 57, 37–52.

Duleep, H., 1998. The Family Investment Model: A formalization and review of evidence from across immigrant groups. (4, Fall), Gend. Issues 16, 84–104.

Duleep, H., 2007. Immigrant skill transferability and the propensity to invest in human capital. Res. Labor Econ. vol. 27, 43–73 Immigration.

Duleep, H., Dowhan, D., 2002a. Insights from longitudinal data on the earnings growth of U.S. foreign-born men. Demography 39 (3), 485–506.

Duleep, H., Dowhan, D., 2002b. Revisiting the Family Investment Model with Longitudinal Data: The Earnings Growth of Immigrant and U.S.-Born Women. IZA Discussion Paper No. 568, Institute for the Study of Labor, Bonn, Germany.

Duleep, H., Dowhan, D., 2008. Adding immigrants to microsimulation models. Soc. Secur. Bull. 68 (1), 51–65.

Duleep, H., Regets, M., 1992. Some evidence on the effect of admission criteria on immigrant assimilation: The earnings profiles of Asian immigrants in Canada and the U.S. In: Chiswick, B. (Ed.), Immigration, Language and Ethnic Issues: Canada and the United States. American Enterprise Institute, Washington, DC, pp. 410–437.

Duleep, H., Regets, M., 1994a. The Elusive Concept of Immigrant Quality: Evidence from 1960–1980 (1992 American Economic Association version). Working Paper PRIP-UI-28, Urban Institute, Washington, DC.

Duleep, H., Regets, M., 1994b. Country of Origin and Immigrant Earnings. Working Paper PRIP-UI-31 Urban Institute, Washington, DC.

Duleep, H., Regets, M., 1996c. Admission criteria and immigrant earnings profiles. (2, Summer), Int. Migrat. Rev. 30, 571–590.

Duleep, H., Regets, M., 1996a. Family unification, siblings, and skills. In: Duleep, H., Wunnava, P.V. (Eds.), Immigrants and Immigration Policy: Individual Skills, Family Ties, and Group Identities. JAI Press, Greenwich, CT, pp. 219–244.

Duleep, H., Regets, M., 1996b. Earnings convergence: Does it matter where immigrants come from or why? Canadian Journal of Economics 29, S130–S134 (April).

Duleep, H., Regets, M., 1997a. Measuring immigrant wage growth using matched CPS files. Demography 34, 239–249 (May).

Duleep, H., Regets, M., 1997c. The decline in immigrant entry earnings: Less transferable skills or lower ability? Q. Rev. Econ. Finance vol. 37, 189–208 Special Issue on Immigration.

Duleep, H., Regets, M., 1997b. Immigrant entry earnings and human capital growth. Res. Labor Econ. 16, 297–317.

Duleep, H., Regets, M., 1999. Immigrants and human capital investment Am. Econ. Rev. 186–191 (May).

Duleep, H., Regets, M., 2002. The Elusive Concept of Immigrant Quality: Evidence from 1970–1990. IZA Discussion Paper No. 631, Institute for the Study of Labor, Bonn, Germany.

Duleep, H., Sanders, S., 1993. The decision to work by married immigrant women. Ind. Labor Relat. Rev. 677–690 (July).

Duleep, H., Sanders, S., 1994. Empirical regularities across cultures: The effect of children on women's work. J. Hum. Resour. 328–347 (Spring).

Duleep, H., Sider, H., 1986. The Economic Status of Americans of Southern and Eastern European Ancestry. US Commission on Civil Rights. www.law.umaryland.edu/marshall/usccr/documents/cr11089z.pdf.

Duleep, H., Wunnava, P.V., 1996. Immigrants and Immigration Policy: Individual Skills, Family Ties, and Group Identities JAI Press, Greenwich, CT,

Duleep, H., Regets, M., Sanders, S., 1999. A New Look at Human Capital Investment:A Study of Asian Immigrants and Their Family Ties. Upjohn Institute for Employment Research. Kalamazoo, MI.

Duleep, H., Liu, X., Regets, M., 2013. Country of Origin and Immigrant Earnings: 1960–2010. IZA Discussion Paper. Institute for the Study of Labor, Bonn, Germany.

Dustmann, C., 2000. Temporary migration and economic assimilation. Swed. Econ. Pol. Rev. 7 (2), 213–244.

Dustmann, C., 2008. Return migration, investment in children, and intergenerational mobility: Comparing sons of foreign and native born fathers. J. Hum. Resour. 43 (2), 299–324.

Dustmann, C., Frattini, T., 2011. Immigration: The European Experience. IZA Discussion Paper No. 6261, Institute for the Study of Labor, Bonn, Germany.

Dustmann, C., Glitz, A., Vogel, T., 2010. Employment, wages, and the economic cycle: Differences between immigrants and natives. Eur. Econ. Rev. 54 (1), 1–17.

Eckstein, Z., Weiss, Y., 2004. On the wage growth of immigrants: Israel, 1990–2000. J. Eur. Econ. Assoc. 2 (4), 665–695.

Espiritu, Y.L., 1997. Asian American Women and Men. Sage, Thousand Oaks, CA.

Farley, R., 1996. The New American Reality: Who We Are, How We Got Here, Where We Are Going. Russell Sage, New York.

Foner, N., 1997. The immigrant family: Cultural legacies and cultural changes. Int. Migrat. Rev. 31 (4), 961–974.

Foner, N., 1998. Benefits and burdens: Immigrant women and work in New York City. (4, Fall), Gend. Issues 16, 5–24.

Friedberg, R., 1992. The Labor Market Assimilation of Immigrants in the U.S.: The Role of Age at Arrival. Brown University.

Friedberg, R., 1993. The Success of Young Immigrants in the U.S. An Evaluation of Competing Explanations. Brown University, Labor Market.

Friedberg, R., 2000. You can't take it with you: Immigrant assimilation and the portability of human capital. J. Labor Econ. 18 (2), 221–251.

Frijters, P., Shields, M.A., Price, S.W., 2005. Immigrant job search in the UK: Evidence from panel data. Econ. J. 115 (507), F359–F376.

Gallo, C., Bailey, T.R., 1996. Social networks and skills-based immigration policy. In: Duleep, H.O., Wunnava, P.V. (Eds.), Immigrants and Immigration Policy: Individual Skills, Family Ties, and Group Identities. JAI Press, Greenwich, CT.

Gang, I.N., Rivera-Batiz, F.L., 1994b. Labor market effects of immigration in the United States and Europe: Substitution vs complementarity. (2, June), J. Popul. Econ. 7, 157–175.

Gang, I.N., Rivera-Batiz, F.L., 1994a. Unemployment and attitudes toward foreigners in Germany. In: Steinmann, G., Ulrich, R. (Eds.), Economic Consequences of Immigration to Germany. Springer.

Gilbertson, G.A., Gurak, D.T., 1993. Broadening the enclave debate: The labor market experiences of Dominican and Colombian men in New York City. Socio. Forum 8 (2), 205–220.

Grasmuck, S., Pessar, P., 1991. Two Islands: Dominican International Migration. University of California Press, Berkeley, CA.

Green, D.A., 1999. Immigrant occupational attainment: Assimilation and mobility over time. (1, January), J. Labor Econ. 17, 49–79.

Green, D.A., Worswick, C., 2012. Immigrant earnings profiles in the presence of human capital investment: Measuring cohort and macro effects. (2, April), Lab. Econ. 19, 241–259.

Gurak, D., Kritz, M.M., 1992. Social context, household composition and employment among Dominican and Columbian women in New York. Revision of paper published in the Proceedings of the Peopling of the Americas. Conference, May.

Hagan, J., Lowe, N., Quingla, C., 2011. Skills on the move: Rethinking the relationship between human capital and immigrant economic mobility (2, May) Work and Occupations: An International Sociological Journal 38, 149–178.

Hall, M., Farkas, G., 2008. Does human capital raise earnings for immigrants in the low-skill labor market? Demography 45 (3, August), 619–639.

Hansen, J., Lofstrom, M., 2009. The dynamics of immigrant welfare and labor market behavior. J. Popul. Econ. 22 (4), 941–970.

Hatton, T.J., Price, S.W., 2005. Migration, migrants and policy in the United Kingdom. In: Zimmermann, K.F. (Ed.), European Migration-What Do We Know? Oxford University Press, Oxford.

Heckman, J., 1979. Sample selection bias as a specification error. Econometrica 47 (1), 153–161.

Heckman, J., Hotz, J., 1986. An investigation of the labor market earnings of Panamanian males: Evaluating the sources of inequality. J. Hum. Resour. 21, 507–542.

Heston, A., Summers, R., 1991. The Penn World Table (Mark 5): An expanded set of international comparisons, 1950–1988. (May), Q. J. Econ. 327–368.

Hirschman, C., Kasinitz, P., DeWind, J. (Eds.), 1999. The Handbook of International Migration. Russell Sage Foundation, New York.

Hondagneu-Sotelo, P., 1992. Overcoming patriarchal constraints: The reconstruction of gender relations among Mexican immigrant women and men. Gender and Society 6, 393–415.

Hondagneu-Sotelo, P., 1994. Gendered Transitions: Mexican Experiences of Immigration. University of California Press, Berkeley, CA.

Hu, W.-Y., 2000. Immigrant earnings assimilation: Estimates from longitudinal data. (May). Am. Econ. Rev. 368–372, Papers and Proceedings (May).

Hudson, K., 2007. The new labor market segmentation: Labor market dualism in the new economy. Soc. Sci. Res. 36, 286–312.

Husted, L., Nielsen, H.S., Rosholm, M., Smith, N., 2001. Employment and wage assimilation of male first generation immigrants in Denmark. Int. J. Manpow. 22 (1/2), 39–68.

Jasso, G., Rosenzweig, M.R., 1986. What's in a name? Country-of-origin influences on the earnings of immigrants in the United States. Research in Human Capital and Development 2 (4), 75–106.

Jasso, G., Rosenzweig, M.R., 1989. Sponsors, sponsorship rates, and the immigration multiplier. Int. Migrat. Rev. 23 (4), 856–888.

Jasso, G., Rosenzweig, M.R., 1990. The New Chosen People: Immigrants in the United States. Russell Sage Foundation, New York.

Jasso, G., Rosenzweig, M.R., 1995. Do immigrants screened for skills do better than family-reunification immigrants? Int. Migrat. Rev. 29, 85–111.

Jasso, G., Massey, D.S., Rosenzweig, M.R., Smith, J.P., 2000. The New Immigrant Survey Pilot (NIS-P): Overview and new findings about U.S. legal immigrants at admission. (1, February), Demography 37, 127–136.

Jensen, E., Gale, S., Charpentier, P., 2006. On Migrant Selectivity, Working Paper #32, College of William and Mary, Department of Economics, July.

Jensen, L., 1991. Secondary earner strategies and family poverty: Immigrant-native differentials, 1960–1980. Int. Migrat. Rev. 25 (1), 113–140.

Jiobu, R.M., 1996. Explaining the ethnic effect. In: Duleep, H.O., Wunnava, P.V. (Eds.), Immigrants and Immigration Policy: Individual Skills, Family Ties, and Group Identities. JAI Press, Greenwich, CT.

Kahn, J.R., Whittington, L.A., 1996. The impact of ethnicity, immigration, and family structure on the labor supply of Latinas in the U.S. Popul. Res. Pol. Rev. 15, 45–73.

Kanas, A., Chiswick, B.R., van der Lippe, T., van Tubergen, F., 2012. Social contacts and the economic performance of immigrants: A panel study of immigrants in Germany. Int. Migrat. Rev. 46 (3), 680–709.

Kaplan, D.H., 1997. The creation of an ethnic economy: Indochinese business expansion in Saint Paul. Econ. Geogr. 73 (2), 214–233.

Keely, C.B., Kraly, E.P., 1978. Recent net alien immigration to the United States: Its impact on population growth and native fertility. Demography 15, 267–283.

Kim, K.C., Hurh, W.M., 1996. Ethnic resources utilization of Korean immigrant entrepreneurs in the Chicago minority area. In: Duleep, H.O., Wunnava, P.V. (Eds.), Immigrants and Immigration Policy: Individual Skills, Family Ties, and Group Identities. JAI Press, Greenwich, CT.

Kossoudji, S.A., 1989. Immigrant worker assimilation: Is it a labor market phenomenon? J. Hum. Resour. 24, 494–527 (3, Summer).

Kossoudji, S., Cobb-Clark, D., 2000. IRCA's impact on the occupational concentration and mobility of newly-legalized Mexican men. J. Popul. Econ. 13, 81–98.

Kossoudji, S., Cobb-Clark, D., 2002. Coming out of the shadows: Learning about the legal status and wages from the legalized population. (3, July), J. Labor Econ. 20, 598–628.

LaLonde, R.J., Topel, R.H., 1991. Immigrants in the American labor market: Quality, assimilation, and distributional effects. (2, May), Am. Econ. Rev. 81, 297–302.

LaLonde, R.J., Topel, R.H., 1992. The assimilation of immigrants in the US labor market. In: Borjas, G.J., Freeman, R.B. (Eds.), Immigration and the Work Force: Economic Consequences for the United States and Source Areas. University of Chicago Press, Chicago and London, pp. 67–92.

LaLonde, R.J., Topel, R.H., 1997. Economic impact of international migration and the economic performance of migrants. In: Rosenzweig, M.R., Stark, O. (Eds.), Handbook of Population and Family Economics. Elsevier, Amsterdam, pp. 800–850.

Landsdale, N., Ogena, N., 1995. Migration and union dissolution among Puerto Rican women. Int. Migrat. Rev. 29 (3), 671–692.

Launov, A., 2004. An Alternative Approach to Testing Dual Labour Market Theory. IZA Discussion Paper No. 1289, Institute for the Study of Labor, Bonn, Germany, September.

Light, I., 1972. Ethnic Enterprises in America: Business and Welfare Among Chinese, Japanese, and Blacks. University of California Press, Berkeley, CA.

Light, I., 1984. Immigrant and ethnic enterprise in North America. Ethnic and Racial Studies 7, 195–216.

Light, I., Sabagh, G., Bozorgmehr, M., Der-Martirosian, C., 1994. Beyond the ethnic enclave economy. Soc. Probl. 41 (1), 65–80, Special Issue on Immigration, Race, and Ethnicity in America (February).

Lin, C., 2013. Earnings gap, cohort effect and economic assimilation of immigrants from mainland China, Hong Kong, and Taiwan in the United States. Rev. Int. Econ. 21 (2), 249–265.

Lindstrom, D.P., Massey, D.S., 1994. Selective emigration, cohort quality, and models of immigrant assimilation. (4, December), Soc. Sci. Res. 23, 315–349.

Livingston, G., Kahn, J.R., 2002. An American dream unfulfilled: The limited mobility of Mexican Americans. Soc. Sci. Q. 83 (4), 1003–1012.

Lofstrom, M., 2000. Self-employment and earnings among high-skilled immigrants in the United States. In: Cornelius, W.A., Espenshade, T.J. (Eds.), The International Migration of the Highly Skilled: Demand, Supply and Development Consequences. La Jolla, CA, pp. 163–195.

Lofstrom, M., 2002. Labor market assimilation and the self-employment decision of immigrant entrepreneur. J. Popul. Econ. 15 (1), 83–114.

Lofstrom, M., 2011. Low-skilled immigrant entrepreneurship. Review of Economics of the Household 9 (1), 25–44.

Logan, J.R., Zhang, Wenquan, Alba, R.D., 2002. Immigrant enclaves and ethnic communities in New York and Los Angeles. (2, April), Am. Sociol. Rev. 67, 299–322.

Long, J., 1980. The effect of Americanization on earnings: Some evidence for women. J. Polit. Econ. 88, 620–629.

Lowell, B.L., 1996. Skilled and family-based immigration: Principles and labor markets. In: Immigrants and Immigration Policy: Individual Skills, Family Ties, and Group Identities. JAI Press, Greenwich, CT.

Lubotsky, D., 2007. Chutes or ladders? A longitudinal analysis of immigrant earnings. (5, October), J. Polit. Econ. 115, 820–867.

Lubotsky, D., 2011. The effect of changes in the U.S. wage structure on recent immigrants' earnings. (1, February), Rev. Econ. Stat. 93, 59–71.

Lundberg, S., Pollak, R.A., 1996. Bargaining and distribution in marriage. (4, Fall), J. Econ. Perspect. 10, 139–158.

MacPherson, D., Stewart, J., 1989. The labor force participation and earnings profiles of married female immigrants. Quarterly Review of Economics and Business 29, 57–72 (Autumn).

Massey, D.S., 1986. The settlement process among Mexican migrants to the United States. Am. Sociol. Rev. 51 (5), 670–684.

Massey, D.S., 1987. Do undocumented migrants earn lower wages than legal immigrants? New evidence from Mexico. Int. Migrat. Rev. 21 (2), 236–274.

Massey, D.S., 2011. Chain Reaction: The Causes and Consequences of America's War on Immigrants. Paper presented at Annual Migration Meeting, IZA, May, Julian Simon Lecture Series. Institute for the Study of Labor, Bonn, Germany.

Massey, D.S., Singer, A., 1995. New estimates of undocumented Mexican migration and the probability of apprehension. Demography 32 (2), 203–213.

Massey, D.S., Zenteno, R.M., 1999. The dynamics of mass migration. Proc. Natl. Acad. Sci. 96 (6), 5328–5335.

McAllister, I., 1995. Occupational mobility among immigrants: The impact of migration on economic success in Australia. Int. Migrat. Rev. 29 (2), 441–468.

McDonald, J.T., Worswick, C., 1997. Unemployment incidence of immigrant men in Canada. Can. Publ. Pol. 23 (4), 353–373.

McDonald, J.T., Worswick, C., 1998. The earnings of immigrant men in Canada: Job tenure, cohort and macroeconomic conditions. Ind. Labor Relat. Rev. 51 (3), 465–482.

McDonald, J.T., Worswick, C., 1999a. Wages, implicit contracts and the business cycle: Evidence from Canadian micro data. J. Polit. Econ. 107 (4), 884–892.

McDonald, J.T., Worswick, C., 1999b. The earnings of immigrant men in Australia: Assimilation, cohort effects and macroeconomic conditions. Econ. Rec. 75 (228), 49–62.

McManus, W.S., 1990. Labor market effects of language enclaves: Hispanic men in the United States. J. Hum. Resour. 25 (2), 228–252.

Miller, P.W., Neo, L.M., 2003. Labour market flexibility and immigrant adjustment. (246, September), Econ. Rec. 79, 336–356.

Mincer, J., 1978. Family migration decisions. J. Pol. Econ. 86 (5), 749–773.

Mincer, J., Ofek, H., 1982. Interrupted work careers: Depreciation and restoration of human capital. J. Hum. Resour. 17, 1–23.

Morokvasic, M., 1984. Birds of passage are also women. Int. Migrat. Rev. 18 (4), 886–907.

Morrison, D.R., Lichter, D.T., 1988. Family migration and female employment: The problem of under-employment among migrant married women. J. Marriage Fam. 50, 161–172.

Morrissey, M., Mitchell, C., Rutherford, A., 1991. The Family in the Settlement Process. Australian Government Publishing Service, Bureau of Immigration Research, Canberra.

Nakamura, A., Nakamura, M., 1985. The Second Paycheck: A Socioeconomic Analysis of Earnings. Academic Press, Orlando.

Nakamura, A., Nakamura, M., 1992a. The econometrics of female labor supply and children. Economet. Rev. 11 (1), 1–71.

Nakamura, A., Nakamura, M., 1992b. Wage rages of immigrant and native men in Canada and the United States. In: Chiswick, B. (Ed.), Immigration, Language and Ethnic Issues: Canada and the United States. American Enterprise Institute, Washington, DC.

Ngo, H.-y, 1994. The economic role of immigrant wives in Hong Kong. Int. Migrat. 32 (3), 403–423.

Nielsen, H.S., Rosholm, M., Smith, N., Husted, L., 2004. Qualifications, discrimination, or assimilation? An extended framework for analysing immigrant wage gaps. Empir. Econ. 29 (4), 855–885.

North, D., Houston, M., 1976. The Characteristics and Role of Illegal Aliens in the U.S. Labor Market: An Exploratory Study United States, Employment and Training Administration, New TransCentury Foundation.

O'Neill, J.A., 1970. The Effect of Income and Education on Inter-Regional Migration. Department of Economics, Columbia University, Ph.D. dissertation.

Orrenius, P., Zavodny, M., 2005. Self-selection among undocumented immigrants from Mexico. (1, October), J. Dev. Econ. 78, 215–240.

Park, R.E., 1950. Race and Culture. Collected articles of Park published posthumously, edited by Everett C. Hughes, The Free Press, Glencoe, IL.

Park, R.E., Miller, H.A., Thompson, K., 1921. Old World Traits Transplanted: The Early Sociology of Culture. Harper & Brothers, New York.

Passel, J.S., 1999. Undocumented immigration to the United States: Numbers, trends, and characteristics. In: Rosenblum, K.E. (Ed.), Haines, D.W. Illegal Immigration in America. JAI Press, Greenwood, CT, pp. 27–111.

Passel, J.S., Luther, N.Y., 1990. Preliminary Application of the Consistent Correction Procedure to the Mexican-Born Population of the United States: 1960–1980, Discussion Paper Series, The Urban Institute, January.

Patel, K., Vella, F., 2007. Immigrant Networks and Their Implications for Occupational Choice and Wages. IZA Discussion Paper No. 3217, Institute for the Study of Labor, Bonn, Germany.

Pedace, R., Rohn, S., 2008. A Warm Embrace or the Cold Shoulder: Wage and Employment Outcomes in Ethnic Enclaves, US Census Bureau Center for Economic Studies Paper No. CES-WP-08-09.

Perez, L., 1986. Immigrants economic adjustment and family organization: The Cuban successes re-examined. Int. Migrat. Rev. 20, 4–20.

Pesquera, B., 1993. In the beginning he wouldn't even lift a spoon: The division of household labor. In: De La Torre, A., Pesquera, B.M. (Eds.), Building With Our Hands: New Directions in Chicana Studies. University of California Press, Berkeley, CA, pp. 181–195.

Pessar, P., 1987. The Dominicans: Women in the household and the garment industry. In: Foner, N. (Ed.), New Immigrants in New York. Columbia University Press, New York.

Peterson, G., Vroman, W., 1992. Urban labor markets and economic opportunity. In: Peterson, G., Vroman, W. (Eds.), Urban Labor Markets and Job Opportunity. The Urban Institute, Washington, DC, pp. 1–30.

Phillips, J., Massey, D., 1999. The New Labor Market: Immigrants and wages after IRCA. Demography 36 (2), 233–246.

Piore, M.J., 1979. Birds of Passage: Migrant Labor and Industrial Societies. Cambridge University Press, New York.

Piracha, M., Tani, M., Vadean, F., 2012. Immigrant over- and under-education: The role of home country labour market experience, IZA Journal of Migration 1.

Polachek, S.W., Horvath, F.W., 1977. A life cycle approach to migration: Analysis of the perspicacious peregrinator. In: Ehrenberg, R.G. (Ed.), Research in Labor Economics. In: JAI Press, 1. Greenwich, CT, pp. 103–150.

Portes, A., 1995a. Economic sociology and the sociology of immigration: A conceptual overview. In: Portes, A. (Ed.), The Economic Sociology of Immigration: Essays on Networks, Ethnicity, and Entrepreneurship. Russell Sage Foundation, New York.

Portes, A., 1995b. Children of immigrants: Segmented assimilation and its determinants. In: Portes, A. (Ed.), The Economic Sociology of Immigration: Essays on Networks, Ethnicity, and Entrepreneurship. Russell Sage Foundation, New York.

Portes, A., Bach, R., 1985. Latin Journey: Cuban and Mexican Immigrants in the United States. University of California Press, Berkeley, CA.

Portes, A., Mozo, R., 1985. The political adaptation process of Cubans and other ethnic minorities in the United States: A preliminary analysis. (1, Spring), Int. Migrat. Rev. 19, 35–61.

Portes, A., Rumbaut, R.G., 1996. Immigrant America: A Portrait, second ed. University of California Press, Berkeley, CA.

Portes, A., Stepick, A., 1985. Unwelcome immigrants: The labor market experiences of 1980 (Mariel) Cuban and Haitian refugees in South Florida. Am. Sociol. Rev. 50 (4), 493–514.

Portes, A., Truelove, C., 1987. Making sense of diversity: Recent research on Hispanic minorities in the United States. Annu. Rev. Sociol. 13, 359–385.

Portes, A., Zhou, M., 1993. The new second generation: Segmented assimilation and its variants. Annals of the American Academy of Political and Social Sciences 530, 74–96.

Postepska, A., Vella, F., 2013. Determinants and Persistence of Immigrant Ranking across Occupational Groups in the US. Georgetown University, Working Paper.

Powers, M.G., Seltzer, W., 1998. Occupational status and mobility among undocumented immigrants by gender. Int. Migrat. Rev. 32 (1), 21–56.

Powers, M.G., Seltzer, W., Shi, Jing, 1998. Gender differences in the occupational status of undocumented immigrants in the United States: Experience before and after legalization. Int. Migrat. Rev. 32 (4), 1015–1041.

Rashid, S., 2004. Married immigrant women and employment. The role of family investments. Umeå Economic Studies, No. 623. www.usbe.umu.se/enheter/econ/ues/ues623/.

Reimers, C., 1985. Cultural differences in labor force participation among married women. Am. Econ. Rev. 251–255 Papers and Proceedings (May).

Reimers, D.M., 1996. Third World immigration to the United States. In: Duleep, H., Wunnava, P.V. (Eds.), Immigrants and Immigration Policy: Individual Skills, Family Ties, and Group Identities. JAI Press, Greenwich, CT.

Reitz, J.G., 2001. Immigrant success in the knowledge economy: Institutional change and the immigrant experience in Canada, 1970–1995. J. Soc. Issues 57 (3), 579–613.

Rivera-Batiz, F., 1992. English language proficiency and the earnings of young immigrants in US labor markets. Policy Studies Rev. 11 (2), 165–175.

Rivera-Batiz, F., 1996. English language proficiency, quantitative skills and the economic progress of immigrants. In: Duleep, H., Wunnava, P.V. (Eds.), Immigrants and Immigration Policy: Individual Skills, Family Ties, and Group Identities. JAI Press, Greenwich, CT.

Rivera-Batiz, F., 1999. Earnings of undocumented workers in the United States. J. Popul. Econ. 12 (1), 91–116.

Rivera-Batiz, F.L., Sechzer, S.L., 1991. Substitution and complementarity between immigrant and native labor in the United States. In: Rivera-Batiz, F.L., Sechzer, S.L., Gang, I.N. (Eds.), U.S. Immigration Policy Reform in the 1980s. Praeger, New York, pp. 89–116.

Rosholm, M., Scott, K., Husted, L., 2006. The times they are a-changin'. Int. Migrat. Rev. 40 (2), 318–347.

Roy, A.D., 1951. Some thoughts on the distribution of earnings. New Series, Oxf. Econ. Paper 3, 135–146 (2, June).

Rumbaut, R.G., 1994. Origins and destinies: Immigration to the United States since World War II. Socio. Forum 9 (4), 583–621.

Sanders, J.M., Nee, V., 1987. Limits of ethnic solidarity in the enclave economy. Am. Sociol. Rev. 52, 745–767 (December).

Sanders, J.M., Nee, V., 1996. Immigrant self-employment: The family as social capital and the value of human capital. Am. Sociol. Rev. 61 (2), 231–249.

Schoeni, R., 1997. New evidence on the economic progress of foreign-born men in the 1970s and 1980s. J. Hum. Resour. 32, 683–740 (Fall).

Schulte, M.M., Wolf, D.A., 1994. Family Networks of the Foreign-Born Population. Program for Research on Immigration Policy, Discussion Paper PRIP-UI-35, The Urban Institute, Washington, DC.

Schultz, T.W., 1975. The value of the ability to deal with disequilibria. J. Econ. Lit. 827–846 (September).

Schwartz, A., 1976. Migration, age and education. J. Polit. Econ. 701–719 (August).

Shapiro, D., Mott, F.L., 1994. Long-term employment and earnings of women in relation to employment behavior surrounding the first birth. (2, Spring), J. Hum. Resour. 29, 248–276.

Shaw, K., 1994. The persistence of female labor supply: Empirical evidence and implications. (2, Spring), J. Hum. Resour. 29, 348–378.

Simon, J.L., 1989. The Economic Consequences of Immigration. Basil Blackwell, Oxford.

Singer, A., Massey, D.S., 1998. The social process of undocumented border crossing among Mexican migrants. Int. Migrat. Rev. 32 (3), 561–593.

Sjaastad, L., 1962. The costs and returns of human migration. J. Polit. Econ. 70, 80–93.

Stepick, A., 1996. Pride, prejudice, and poverty: Economic, social, political, and cultural capital among Hiatians in Miami. In: Duleep, H., Wunnava, P.V. (Eds.), Immigrants and Immigration Policy: Individual Skills, Family Ties, and Group Identities. JAI Press, Greenwich, CT, pp. 133–146.

Stier, H., 1991. Immigrant women go to work: Analysis of immigrant wives' labor supply for six Asian groups. (1, March), Soc. Sci. Q. 72, 67–82.

Stier, H., Tienda, M., 1992. Family work and women: The labor supply of Hispanic immigrant wives. Int. Migrat. Rev. 26 (4), 1291–1313.

Straubhaar, T., Golder, S.M., 2005. Empirical findings on the Swiss migration experience. In: Zimmermann, K.F. (Ed.), European Migration-What Do We Know? Oxford University Press, Oxford.

United Nations, 2013. International Migration 2013: Migrants by Origin and Destination, United Nations No. 2013/3, Department of Economic and Social Affairs, Population Division, September.

Vanderkamp, J., 1972. Return migration: Its significance and behavior. (4, December), West. Econ. J. 10, 460–465.

Van Tubergen, F., Van de Werfhorst, H., 2007. Post-immigration investments in education: A study of immigrants in the Netherlands. (4, November), Demography 44, 883–898.

Venturini, A., Villosio, C., 2002. Are immigrants competing with natives in the Italian labour market? The employment effect. Int. Labour Rev. 145 (1–2), 91–118, 2006.

Waldinger, R., 1986. Through the Eye of the Needle: Immigrant Enterprise in New York's Garment Trades. New York University Press, New York.

Waldinger, R., 1989. Structural opportunity or ethnic advantage? Immigrant Business Development in New York. Int. Migrat. Rev. 23, 48–72.

Waldinger, R., 1996. Who makes the beds? Who washes the dishes? Black/immigrant competition reassessed. In: Duleep, H., Wunnava, P.V. (Eds.), Immigrants and Immigration Policy: Individual Skills, Family Ties, and Group Identities. JAI Press, Greenwich, CT, pp. 265–288.

Warren, R., Kraly, E.P., 1985. The Elusive Exodus: Emigration from the United States, ccasional Paper No. 8, Population Reference Bureau.

Warren, R., Passel, J., 1987. A count of the uncountable: Estimates of undocumented aliens counted in the 1980 United States Census. Demography 24, 375–393 (August).

Warren, R., Peck, J.M., 1980. Foreign-born emigration from the United States, 1960–1970. Demography 17, 71–84.

White, M.J., Bean, F., Espenshade, T., 1990. The U.S. IRCA and undocumented migration to the United States. Popul. Res. Pol. Rev. 9, 93–116.

Wilson, K.L., Portes, A., 1980. Immigrant enclaves: An analysis of the labor market experiences of Cubans in Miami. (2, September), Am. J. Sociol. 86, 295–319.

Winkelmann, R., 2005. Immigration: The New Zealand experience. In: Zimmermann, K.F. (Ed.), European Migration-What Do We Know? Oxford University Press, Oxford.

Woodrow-Lafield, K.A., 1994. Immediate Relatives of Natives and Immigrants to the United States. Unpublished manuscript, State University of New York at Albany, Center for Social and Demographic Analysis.

Worswick, C., 1996. Immigrant Families in Canadian Labour Market. Department of Economics, Working Papers Series 504, The University of Melbourne.

Xie, Y., Gough, M., 2011. Ethnic enclaves and the earnings of immigrants. (4, November), Demography 48, 1293–1315.

Xie, Y., Greenman, E., 2011. Social context of assimilation: Testing implications of segmented assimilation theory. Soc. Sci. Res. 40 (3), 965–984.

Yezer, A.M.J., Thurston, L., 1976. Migration patterns and income change. South. Econ. J. 693–702 (April).

Zhou, M., 1997. Segmented assimilation: Issues, controversies, and recent research on the new second generation. Int. Migrat. Rev. 31 (4), 975–1008.

Zorlu, A., 2013. Occupational adjustment of immigrants. J. Int. Migrat. Integrat. 14 (4), 711–731.

CHAPTER 4

The Human Capital (Schooling) of Immigrants in America

James P. Smith
Senior Economist, RAND Corporation

Contents

1. Introduction	183
2. Schooling of Migrants and the Native-Born	184
3. The Changing Education Gap of Immigrants	188
4. The Educational Diversity of Migrants	196
5. Foreign Students at American Schools	202
6. Immigrant Education and Generational Assimilation	206
7. Conclusions	208
Acknowledgments	209
References	209

1. INTRODUCTION

Education and immigration have always been tightly linked in American history. Many immigrants came to the United States, at least temporarily, to attend American schools or because they believed that American schools offered the best opportunity for economic advancement for their children. In the economics literature, schooling of immigrants has served as the primary index of immigrant skill in the labor market so that trends in the labor market "quality" of different waves of immigrants largely amounted to comparing trends in immigrant education with that of the native-born. As the price of skill (the income returns to schooling) varied over time and between the US and the main sending countries, the incentives of people with different amounts of education to come to the US would change.[1]

This influence of immigrants on the average skill of the American workforce has always been both direct and indirect. Immigrants are once again a growing fraction of today's workforce, but they will also be parents and grandparents of a significant part of the American labor market in the future. Thus, the issue of the size of intergenerational

---

[1] This paper is in many ways an extension and update of Smith (2006a).

Handbook of the Economics of International Migration, Volume 1A
ISSN 2212-0092, http://dx.doi.org/10.1016/B978-0-444-53764-5.00004-9

transmission of schooling across immigrant generations is a basic determinant in shaping what the country will look like in the decades ahead.

This chapter deals with several salient issues about immigrants to the US and their education. These issues include a comparison of the schooling accomplishments of immigrants and the native-born that emphasizes the considerable diversity in the schooling accomplishments among different immigrant subgroups and between legal and undocumented migrants. I also examine the role of the foreign-born who come to the United States for post-secondary schooling. Finally, I show that the educational generational progress among all groups of immigrants to the US has been quite impressive during the nineteenth and twentieth centuries.

This chaper is divided into six sections. Section 2 documents the most salient recent comparative patterns in the schooling of the foreign-born population in the US, while also providing education data that separate immigrants into three broad groups—Asian, European, and Hispanics. The next section then examines how nativity differences in education for all immigrants, as well as Asian, European, and Hispanic immigrants separately, have changed over time since 1940.

To provide a more detailed perspective about the heterogeneity of immigrants to the US, Section 4 highlights the considerable education diversity that exists in schooling accomplishments within the immigrant population. This diversity spans time of arrival, ethnic background, legal status, and reasons for admission to the US. The perspective of the chapter then shifts in Section 5, which addresses the issue of the impact of foreign students on American schools, especially at the university level. Especially in science, math, and engineering, foreign students now receive a very large fraction of the doctoral degrees awarded in the US. The next section focuses on the intergenerational transmission of schooling to the children and grandchildren of immigrants. This education transmission across immigrant generations turns out to be an important source of social mobility and economic improvement. The final section highlights my main conclusions.

2. SCHOOLING OF MIGRANTS AND THE NATIVE-BORN

Throughout this chapter, education is defined as the number of years of schooling completed. The native-born population was born in the US, while the foreign-born were born in a foreign country. Using data obtained from the 2010 and 2002 Current Population Surveys (CPS), Table 4.1 highlights differences in education distributions between three groups—the foreign-born, the native-born, and the recent foreign-born (those arriving in the US within the last five years). This table also illustrates how those education distributions changed over the first decade of the twenty-first century. I will highlight long-term changes below. Table 4.2 presents the same three-way division from the 2010 and 2002 CPS for the principal ethnic origin classifications of people currently

Table 4.1 Schooling distributions of native-born and foreign-born populations—2010 and 2002 CPS

Schooling	All Foreign-born	Native-born	Recent foreign-born
2010 CPS*			
Less than 5 years	5.6	0.4	6.2
5–8 years	11.9	2.3	10.2
9–11 years	8.9	6.0	7.6
12 years	27.4	33.8	26.3
13–16 years	35.1	47.3	37.0
17–18 years	7.6	7.6	10.1
19+ years	3.5	2.8	2.6
Mean years	12.27	13.59	12.53
All men	12.32	13.59	12.64
All women	12.21	13.59	12.42
2002 CPS†			
Less than 5 years	6.4	0.7	7.4
5–8 years	14.1	3.5	12.8
9–11 years	7.9	7.4	6.9
12 years	26.9	34.4	23.9
13–16 years	34.9	45.2	34.9
17–18 years	6.4	6.3	10.0
19+ years	3.6	2.6	4.3
Mean years	12.00	13.31	12.31
All men	12.15	13.39	12.24
All women	11.85	13.23	12.32

*Calculations by author using the 2010 March CPS for all persons 25 and over. The recent foreign-born are those who migrated within the last five years.
†Calculations by author using the 2002 March CPS for all persons 25 and over. The recent foreign-born are those who migrated within the last five years.

living in the US—Asians, Europeans, and Hispanics.[2] Combined, these two tables reveal the principal salient facts about the comparative education attributes of migrants in the recent past.

On average, immigrants to the US have less schooling than the native-born American population does—in 2010, for example, the mean migrant deficit in education was 1.3 years of schooling. Among recent migrants, the education deficit was even

---

[2] These ethnic classifications are based on country of birth (first generation) and country of parents' birth (second generation). For the third-plus generations (neither they nor their parents were foreign-born), Asians are those who claimed Asian race, Hispanics were defined by Hispanic ethnicity, and Europeans were those who were neither one of those and who also were not Black or Native-American using the race variable.

Table 4.2 Schooling distributions of native-born and foreign-born populations—2010 (A) and 2002 CPS (B)

Schooling	Asian			European			Hispanic		
	Foreign-born	Native-born	Recent foreign-born	Foreign-born	Native-born	Recent foreign-born	Foreign-born	Native-born	Recent foreign-born
A. 2010 CPS*									
Less than 5 years	3.4	0.5	6.2	1.8	0.2	1.7	8.9	1.8	8.6
5–8 years	3.5	2.2	3.3	4.5	1.9	1.3	20.7	5.1	21.1
9–11 years	3.7	2.1	3.8	3.4	4.9	4.9	14.2	11.2	13.6
12 years	21.3	20.7	17.7	26.7	33.1	29.5	30.5	36.2	32.0
13–16 years	47.3	59.0	47.5	47.3	48.4	46.2	22.2	40.6	21.7
17–18 years	14.7	9.2	17.8	10.4	8.4	11.8	2.5	3.6	2.2
19+ years	6.2	6.3	3.7	6.0	3.1	4.7	1.0	1.5	0.8
Mean years	14.22	14.54	14.07	13.89	13.77	14.05	10.39	12.60	10.33
All men	14.70	14.51	14.33	14.22	13.80	14.48	10.33	12.62	10.41
All women	13.82	14.57	13.89	13.60	13.76	13.61	10.46	12.57	10.24
B. 2002 CPS†									
Less than 5 years	2.8	0.2	2.4	1.9	0.4	1.9	11.6	3.8	13.3
5–8 years	5.0	2.1	3.2	6.9	2.9	5.1	24.9	8.9	23.3
9–11 years	4.0	2.6	3.4	4.2	6.2	1.7	12.7	12.8	11.6
12 years	22.4	23.2	16.1	29.5	33.8	22.0	27.5	34.5	25.4
13–16 years	48.4	59.4	50.3	41.7	46.8	41.1	21.4	36.1	22.7
17–18 years	11.7	6.8	18.0	10.4	7.0	19.6	1.3	3.0	2.4
19+ years	5.7	5.6	6.5	5.5	2.9	8.9	1.1	0.9	1.4
Mean years	13.96	14.36	14.73	13.58	13.52	14.61	9.81	11.93	9.84
All men	14.51	14.58	15.11	13.90	13.62	14.70	9.82	12.01	9.39
All women	13.48	14.12	14.39	13.30	13.44	14.51	9.80	11.87	10.31

*Calculations by author using the 2010 March CPS for all persons 25 and over. The recent foreign-born are those who migrated within the last five years.
†Calculations by author using the 2002 March CPS for all persons 25 and over. The recent foreign-born are those who migrated within the last five years.

smaller—about one year less education. This migrant education deficit is slightly higher among women compared to men. American-born men and women have precisely the same amount of schooling, while female migrants trail male migrants by about one-tenth of a year of schooling.

Far more dramatic than these average education differences by nativity, however, are differences within the lower and upper parts of the education distribution. Consider first those at the bottom tail of the education distribution. About 18% of the foreign-born (16% among recent immigrants) had only an elementary school education or less, more than six times the comparable proportion among the native-born. Among recent immigrants in particular, however, the relative ranking actually shifts within the top part of the education distribution, where 14% of recent migrants had more than a college degree compared to 10% of those born in the US.

When we compare the education distributions in the 2010 and 2002 CPS in Table 4.1A and B, we see small steady increases in education accomplishments for all three of our groups—the native-born, the foreign-born, and the recent foreign-born. On average, all three groups experienced about three-tenths of a year increase in mean years of education, with almost no change at all in the comparisons between the groups based on their native or foreign-born status.

These education differences between native and foreign-born populations pale next to the heterogeneity that exists within the migrant population to the US. That diversity already is hinted at by the comparatively fat tails of the foreign-born education distribution in Table 4.1. But the heterogeneity becomes even starker in Table 4.2, which offers comparison among the three principal types of immigrants who come to the US based on their region of origin (Asians, Europeans, and Hispanics) using the 2010 (Table 4.2A) and 2002 (Table 4.2B) CPS to classify their place of birth.

Not surprisingly, differences amongst these broadly defined ethnic groups are very large. On one end are recent European and Asian migrants who actually are more educated than native-born Americans by half a year of schooling on average (14.07 years for recent Asian immigrants and 14.05 years for recent European immigrants, compared to 13.59 years for all native-born Americans in calendar year 2010). Very few recent European migrants to the US are low skilled and 16% claim some post-baccalaureate schooling (compared to 10% among all native-born Americans).

Using schooling as the skill index, Asian migrants score even better. On average, they too are relatively high skilled, albeit with more within-group diversity than the Europeans. While 22% of recent Asian migrants have schooling beyond a college degree, 9.5% have an eighth grade education or less. Both proportions are higher than those for native-born Americans. On the other end of the education skill index lie Hispanic migrants. On average, Latino migrants are much less skilled than the native-born or than either European or Asian migrants. To provide a dramatic illustration, among recent migrants Europeans and Asians have almost four years of schooling more than Latino migrants. The reason is simple—about 30% of recent Latino migrants have only eight years of schooling or less.

If we compare the distributions in Table 4.2A and B, we see that over the last decade the education accomplishments of the average recent Hispanic immigrant have been rising while those of both Asian and European recent immigrants have been declining. The overall increase in the education of recent immigrants during the last decade was also due to the rising fraction of migrants who came from European or Asian countries where the average education of migrants was higher. These recent trends indicate that the differences among recent migrants have been narrowing somewhat. During the last decade, the education gap of new Hispanic migrants compared to Asian and European recent migrants fell by about a year of schooling.

This simple summary highlights salient differences in schooling achievements of the native and foreign-born. On average, new migrants are about a year or so less educated than the typical native-born American. However, the real differences emerge in the tails. Migrants are simultaneously more likely to be considerably more educated (post-baccalaureate schooling) and less educated (without a high school diploma) than are native-born Americans. A good deal of those differences are differentiated in the three major ethnic groups—compared to native-born Americans, European and Asian migrants are far more likely to have training beyond college while Latino migrants are far more likely not to have gone beyond elementary school.

Before examining whether these schooling differences between native- and foreign-born can be explained by a few crucial theoretical and/or institutional factors, I next examine a closely related question—what has happened to these educational disparities by nativity over time?

3. THE CHANGING EDUCATION GAP OF IMMIGRANTS

A primary concern in the economics literature is the changing labor market quality of foreign immigrants to the US (see Borjas, 1994, 1995; Jasso et al., 2000b; Smith, 2006b). Education continues to be the most basic index of skill so it should come as no surprise that this topic has focused on education gaps of migrants compared to the native-born. The discussion often begins with a rapidly changing ethnic composition of migrants to the US.

Before the Immigration and Nationality Act amendments of 1965 repealed the national-origin quotas, Europe and Canada were the dominant sources of immigrants to the US. Even as late as 1950, 90% of the foreign-born population was of either European or Canadian heritage. But with the passage of the 1965 amendments, country-of-origin composition changed dramatically. In 2010, those born in Europe represented only 12% of the foreign-born in the US.

The two principal changes subsequent to the 1965 Act involved increasing flows of migrants from Asia and Latin America. Especially for Latinos, these numbers were augmented by considerable influxes of unauthorized migrants. Foreigners from the Caribbean and Latin America were one-in-five of the foreign-born in 1970 and 53% by 2010. Finally, Asians went from only 3% of the foreign-born in 1950 to a quarter by 2010.[3]

While the 1965 amendments represented the most substantial change in immigration policy in the last 50 years, other subsequent legislation had significant impacts on attributes of migrant flows. Among the two most important were the 1986 Immigration Reform and Control Act (IRCA) and a series of laws that encouraged entry of more-skilled immigrants.[4]

Besides attempting to limit future illegal immigration by adding more resources for border control and by establishing employer sanctions, the IRCA created a program for legalizing illegal aliens already residing in the US. Almost three million unauthorized migrants were legalized through this program (see Smith and Edmonston, 1997). The most important of the recent changes in legal admission policy was the Immigration Act of 1990, which simultaneously reduced the number of visas for unskilled migrants while increasing them for skilled immigrants.

Table 4.3 documents trends by listing for each of the decennial Censuses between 1940 and 1990 and for the 1996, 2002, and 2010 CPS mean education levels of native- and foreign-born populations over age 24. To capture changing flows, means are also presented for the foreign-born population who arrived during the last five years in each data source. Once again, separate data are presented for the three principal broad ethnic groups—Asians, Europeans, and Hispanics—and, given their importance, separately for Mexican migrants.[5]

Education levels have moved steadily higher over time for all groups in Table 4.3. Each decade witnessed another increase in schooling accomplishments for our reference group—the US native-born—although the pace of change has slowed in recent decades. The cumulative change was eventually large—essentially moving the typical adult native-born American from an elementary school graduate in 1940 (8.8 years) to going beyond high school in 2010 (13.6 years). In the last 20 years, mean schooling advanced by about a year among the American native-born compared to 1.8 years during the previous 20-year period between 1970 and 1990.

While starting at a lower base (a deficit of two years in 1940), the foreign-born population has not only moved lockstep with the native-born, but eventually their cumulative change was even greater, reducing their education deficit with the native-born to one and a third years by 2010. No doubt reflecting secular improvements in education in the sending countries and increasing selectivity of migrants, recent immigrants tend to

---

[3] See Smith and Edmonston (1997), and Pew Hispanic Center (2012) for details.

[4] For a summary of the major legislative changes, see Chapter 2 in Smith and Edmonston (1997).

[5] In this and other tables, Hispanics include Mexicans.

Table 4.3 Years of schooling completed, by nativity

	2010	2002	1996	1990	1980	1970	1960	1950	1940
All									
US-born	13.59	13.31	12.99	12.61	11.78	10.84	10.01	9.43	8.77
Foreign-born	12.27	12.00	11.51	11.31	10.59	8.97	7.74	7.46	6.68
1–5 years in US	12.53	12.32	11.73	11.65	11.25	10.36	9.95	n.a.	8.90
Asian									
US-born	14.54	14.36	14.00	13.60	13.01	11.84	10.66	10.43	9.66
Foreign-born	14.22	13.96	13.28	12.94	13.17	11.32	8.37	7.24	7.76
1–5 years in US	14.07	14.73	13.13	12.90	12.50	13.46	12.08	n.a.	10.44
"Europeans"									
US-born	13.77	13.52	13.18	12.82	12.02	11.11	10.34	9.79	9.18
Foreign-born	13.89	13.58	12.89	11.94	10.29	8.99	7.83	7.39	6.74
1–5 years in US	14.05	14.61	14.65	13.63	12.11	10.35	10.32	n.a.	8.95
Hispanics									
US-born	12.60	11.93	11.52	11.58	9.80	9.47	7.39	7.22	5.79
Foreign-born	10.39	9.81	9.27	9.23	8.91	7.91	5.99	5.79	4.71
1–5 years in US	10.33	9.84	8.41	9.14	8.26	8.40	7.23	n.a.	7.25
Mexican									
US-born	n.a.	n.a.	n.a.	11.15	9.50	8.33	6.80	5.81	4.28
Foreign-born	9.51	8.66	7.93	7.71	6.74	5.59	4.39	4.53	3.97
1–5 years in US	9.56	8.53	7.52	7.83	6.33	5.93	4.58	n.a.	6.06

Calculations by author from 1940–1990 decennial Censuses, 1996 and 2010 March CPS. Sample those 25 and above.

have more schooling than the complete resident foreign-born population. However, the education gap between them has narrowed considerably so that time series gains in education among the recent foreign-born are smaller than that of all migrants.

Differences in education by region of origin are large, with Latino and especially Mexican migrants lagging behind the others by a significant margin. Given the better educational opportunities available in the US compared to many of the sending countries, it is not a surprise that within each ethnic group the native-born tend to have more schooling than their foreign-born counterparts. In fact, differences among ethnic groups are far smaller in the native-born population than the foreign-born, an indication of convergence across descendants of immigrants.

To make trends in disparities with the native-born population more transparent, Figure 4.1 plots the extent to which schooling of the native-born population exceeds that of the total and recent foreign-born population. Using the same reference group

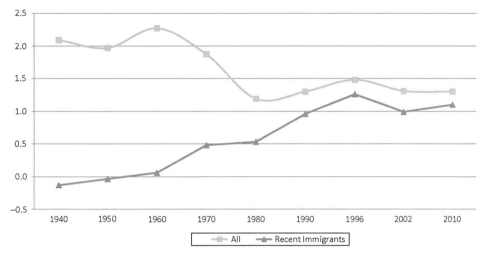

Figure 4.1 *Schooling disparity of all foreign-born (comparison group: all native-born).*

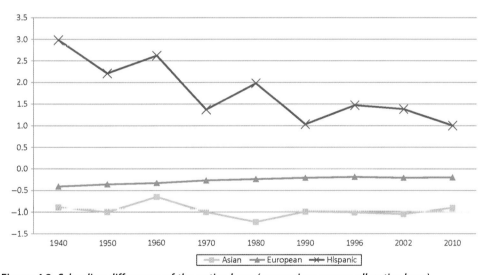

Figure 4.2 *Schooling differences of the native-born (comparison group: all native-born).*

of total native-born population, Figure 4.2 displays disparities in mean schooling of the different US native-born ethnic subpopulations, Figure 4.3 the differentials for ethnic-specific foreign-born subpopulations, and Figure 4.4 education gaps for recent immigrants.

Putting aside within-ethnic-group trends for a moment, two things are particularly striking concerning schooling deficits of the foreign-born in Figure 4.1. First, up to

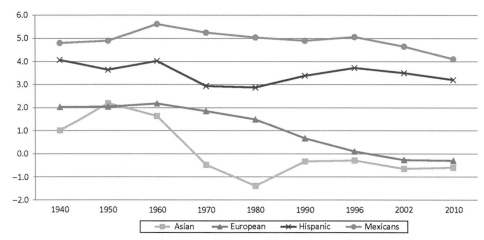

Figure 4.3 *Schooling disparity of all foreign-born (comparison group: all native-born).*

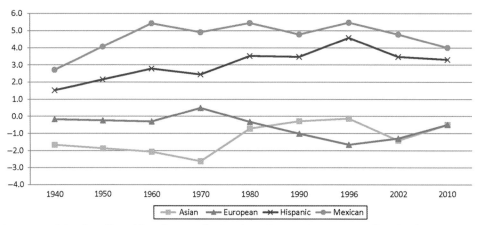

Figure 4.4 *Schooling disparities of recent foreign-born (comparison group: all native-born).*

1980 the schooling disadvantage of the total foreign–born population was declining while it was simultaneously increasing for new recent immigrants. Since the total foreign–born represents the stock of immigrants at a point in time while recent immigrants capture recent flows, these opposing stock-flow trends are not a contradiction. The stock of migrants is weighted heavily by history toward trends for past European migrants. Education increases between censuses are largely due to older, less–educated immigrants dying off. The labor force skill of migrants is much better represented by the stock (all) in Figure 4.1 and over the 70-year period the skill of migrants has actually been improving.

Figure 4.2 summarizes trends for various native-born populations. Compared to the overall average, the native-born of European descent have slightly less than a half-year[6] advantage, while those of Asian background hover around with a year of schooling advantage. What is remarkable about both Europeans and Asians is how little trend exists in this ethnic gap of the native-born. There is a more detectable steady decline in the schooling gap of native-born Latinos until it is about a third as large now as it was in 1940, so that the differences between Latinos and their European and Asian immigrant counterparts have been declining steadily over time.

Figure 4.3 plots education gaps for the full foreign-born populations for each ethnic grouping. In 1940, all groups start out with a schooling disadvantage—about two years for Europeans and Asians and twice that for Hispanics, and almost five years for Mexican immigrants. Subsequently, first for Asians and then for Europeans, these schooling deficits narrowed until currently the total adult foreign-born populations of both groups hold a narrow advantage of the US native-born. In comparison, there is very little change between Hispanics and Mexicans, where the education gap among the foreign-born at best drifts slightly downward, especially in the last decade and a half. Thus, the overall downward trend in the foreign-born education gap results from a narrowing gap between Asians and Europeans, and a slightly falling gap among Latinos, which combined offset any effect of a shift in relative representation toward Hispanics. Figure 4.4 presents the same type of data for recent immigrants. Typically, new Asian and European migrants have had more education than the native-born, an advantage that in 2010 is about the same for both groups. After 1996, the education gap for new Latino migrants experienced a slight closing.

Since they directly capture flows, data on recent immigrants in Figures 4.1 and 4.4 are more sensitive to period changes in legislative and economic incentives in the propensity of foreigners to migrate to the US. A comparison of the more stable within-ethnic group trends in Figure 4.4 compared to the slightly widening gap of recent migrants in Figure 4.1 suggests that the principal impact of the 1965 legislative change was on the composition of migrants—increasingly the representation of less-schooled Latino migrants, since there is little within-ethnic group trend. Two largely offsetting forces dominated the recent period. On one hand were the legalization of mainly Hispanic migrants through the IRCA and the increased flows of unauthorized (again mainly Hispanic) migrants who have less schooling than the average native-born American. On the other hand, there were increased numbers of European and Asian migrants who have education above that of the typical native-born American.

An attempt to highlight trends during the 1990s is provided in Table 4.4, which lists mean schooling of migrants by year of entry into the US using the 1996, 2002, and 2010 CPSs. Among all migrants in 2010, there is a U-shaped pattern across years of entry with

---

[6] The small differences for Europeans are not surprising since they comprise such a large fraction of the total.

Table 4.4 Recent trends in immigrant schooling

Time since immigration	All	Asians	Europeans	Hispanics	Mexicans
2010 CPS					
2006–10	12.53	14.07	14.05	10.33	9.56
2000–05	12.07	14.64	14.66	10.15	9.37
1996–99	12.15	14.83	14.81	10.28	9.61
1990–95	12.09	14.19	14.59	10.33	9.60
<1990	12.38	14.01	13.46	10.56	9.50
2002 CPS					
2000–02	12.51	14.70	14.77	9.87	8.37
1996–2000	12.18	14.51	14.47	9.70	8.75
1990–96	11.71	13.63	14.41	9.55	8.74
1980–90	11.79	13.60	14.11	9.88	8.73
<1980	12.15	14.07	13.01	9.95	8.56
1996 CPS					
1990–1996	11.56	12.80	14.21	8.69	7.89
1980–1990	11.33	13.27	13.68	9.26	7.99
<1980	11.61	13.63	12.49	9.47	7.90

Source: Calculations by author. Sample those 25 and above.

higher schooling levels among pre-1990 migrants compared to those who came between 1990 and 2005, and then after that a subsequent half a year rise to those arriving between 2006 and 2010. Within ethnic groups, the education of Asian and European migrants has been falling since the mid-1990s. There is little evidence of much of an education trend at all among Mexican migrants.

Since data are provided in earlier CPSs for the immigrant cohorts who entered during the 1990s, Table 4.4 allows one to examine the same entry cohort of immigrants six to eight years apart. Within ethnic groups, mean schooling is higher in the more recent 2010 CPS. For example, consider Asian migrants who arrived between 1990 and 1996 using the 1996 CPS. They reported 12.8 years of schooling in the 1996 CPS but by 2010 this had risen to 14.6, an increment of almost two years. While increases for other ethnic groups also exist, they often run about half a year of schooling.

There are several possible reasons for this upward drift in mean schooling within entry cohorts. It may simply reflect "grade" inflation, a well-documented trend in census data even for the native-born. Second, it may be produced by the aging of young, more-educated immigrants who were 19–24 years old in 1996 but who now qualify for the 25-year-old age restriction by 2002, and the exit of older immigrants with low schooling levels who died between 1996 and 2002. Third, it could reflect emigration selection effects if less-educated migrants are more likely to return even temporarily to the sending countries. Circulatory migration of the less educated would produce this pattern since the less educated would be less likely to remain within any specific time since migration interval in successive CPS surveys. Finally, some part of this upward drift may be the consequence of additional post-migration school attendance.

To obtain some notion of the importance of the second and at least a component of the fourth reason, schooling differences with the native-born were calculated for a sample restricted to those aged 31–55 in 1996 and 37–61 in 2002. The younger age threshold of older migrants mitigates against any significant mortality effect while the older age cutoff among the young should reduce the impact of school completion among younger migrants. Finally, the upward adjustment in the age cutoff of the young eliminates the impact of the new entry by 2002 of younger migrants who failed to meet the age threshold in 1996. Schooling increments within time since immigration intervals were only marginally different in this sample, suggesting that these demographic factors of mortality and "aging in" are not the major part of the story.

The exclusion of those factors leaves grade inflation, post-migration education selectivity, and post-migration education accumulation as the major options. Some insights into the latter are provided by Table 4.5, which lists the fraction of new legal immigrants in 2003 who received some type of education during the year after the receipt of their green cards. The second column lists the fraction of respondents who received some form of training during this period, while the next five columns describe the type of training that took place.

The extent of post-green card training and schooling is impressive. A fifth of all new legal immigrants attended school after receiving their green cards. This schooling consisted largely of attending regular schools (especially for those in their twenties), and taking language classes (especially among older new-green-card recipients). Thus, it seems quite likely that some significant part of this rise in schooling between successive surveys is real—new immigrants do add to their schooling after receipt of their green card. But this also seems unlikely to offer a complete explanation. The data in Table 4.4 show that

Table 4.5 New legal immigrants who attended school in the United States after receiving their green cards—2003

Age	% Attended	Type of schooling				
		Regular	Language	GED	Computer	Other
21–30	0.25	0.433	0.478	0.002	0.010	0.078
31–40	0.18	0.264	0.613	0.007	0.016	0.099
41–60	0.16	0.157	0.716	0.009	0.022	0.096
61–80	0.05	0.059	0.791	0.000	0.041	0.109
All	0.18	0.305	0.585	0.005	0.016	0.090

Source: 2003 New Immigrant Survey. Attending is defined as any attendance at the time of the survey. For attendees, a single type of schooling was selected, prioritized by regular, vocational, language and finally other.

this increase in mean education takes place even among immigrants who arrived much earlier. By this time, one would have thought that the incremental schooling behavior would have run its course.

This suggests mostly by default that differential out-migration (temporary or permanent) of less-educated migrants may be an important and underappreciated phenomenon. Greater circular migration alone of less-educated migrants (which seems likely to have taken place) would produce across-year increases of schooling of migrants arrayed by their year of migration. If so, this also implies that the use of the analytical procedure of comparing immigrants stratified by reported time since arrival across surveys taken in different calendar years may be a perilous exercise in spite of how widespread this practice is in the literature. This view is supported by research by Lubotsky (2007), who demonstrated using administrative records that out-migration of previous immigrants was more likely to be low-wage immigrants from their immigrant cohort, which would tend to exaggerate the wage convergence with native-born over their stays in the US. Similarly, Dustmann and Weiss (2007) document that 10 years after arrival to the UK about half of the original immigrant cohort had left the UK. In contrast to the American experience documented by Lubotsky, high-skilled immigrants appear to have been more likely to emigrate.

Several things are clear from this analysis. First, cross-sectional patterns associated with time since immigration may be a poor way of assembling evidence for either assimilation or immigrant quality. It is well recognized to be inappropriate when assessing the amount of assimilation since they are obviously members of different cohorts. It may also be problematic for assessing cohort quality as there may be significant post-immigration changes in the composition of entry cohorts as well as their schooling.

Second, periodic changes in immigration legislation have had important effects on the skill composition of subsequent immigrant cohorts. The most well-documented example concerns the impact of the 1965 National Origin Quota Act, which resulted in a large shift in the ethnic composition of immigrants with fewer Europeans and relatively more Asians and Latinos coming to the US. During the 1970s and 1980s, this shift toward increasing numbers of Latino immigrants in particular led to an increasing gap between the average education of new immigrants compared to that of the native-born.

4. THE EDUCATIONAL DIVERSITY OF MIGRANTS

The foreign-born population represents a combination of very different types of people—legal immigrants, legal non-immigrants (those with visas that authorize stays for limited periods of time), and unauthorized or illegal immigrants. These populations have been historically distinct in many ways, not the least of which is their education. For example, many student visa non-immigrants come to the US attracted by its reputation for superior post-secondary schools. That trend has accelerated in recent decades. In contrast, many illegal immigrants typically worked in jobs within the bottom tail of the skill distribution, especially in the service and agricultural sectors. Not surprisingly, their schooling is often far below that of most American workers. Finally, while legal immigrants come to America for many diverse reasons reflecting the heterogeneous visa categories that allow them to come to the US, especially in recent years some qualify for permanent residence only because they are highly skilled and highly educated. Data on average education of the foreign-born population may be quite sensitive to the relative proportions of these diverse groups of immigrants, and aggregate data may poorly describe each of them.

There were 306 million people living in the US in 2010. Of these, 40.2 million or one in eight were born in another country (Passel and Cohn, 2011). While making distinctions is difficult and measurement is far from perfect, current estimates indicate that roughly 27 million of the foreign-born (or about 68%) were prior legal permanent immigrants to the US.

Who are the rest? About 1.7 million were legal non-immigrants. The remainder of the foreign-born are obviously the most difficult to count, but recent estimates indicate that there are 11.2 million unauthorized residents (Passel and Cohn, 2011). Moreover, the relative proportions of these groups vary significantly across ethnic groups. For example, recent estimates claim that among all foreign-born in the 2010 Census, 29% were unauthorized. The corresponding fraction unauthorized for the Mexico-born population was 58% while for those from India or China the fraction unauthorized was 13%.

Hard data documenting the distinct education attributes of these different subgroups of the foreign-born are almost nonexistent, especially if we strive for nationally representative statistics. The reason is simple—there has been no complete attempt to directly identify in surveys to which of the three groups a foreign-born respondent belongs. Indirect estimates are possible since at least one of the three main subpopulations can be separately identified. The New Immigrant Survey (NIS) was a stratified random sample of new immigrants admitted to legal permanent residence in the US, i.e., granted green cards during 2003. Since the NIS samples legal immigrants only, any discrepancy between, say, the CPS and NIS schooling distributions among recent immigrants would reflect the presence of illegal migrants and legal non-immigrants in the CPS.

Table 4.6 depicts the distribution of schooling of the entire adult 2003 NIS cohort, along with corresponding data based on the 2003 CPS for the foreign-born who entered the US between 1998 and 2003 ("recent foreign-born"). The 2003 CPS is used because it is the same calendar year as the 2003 NIS. These data are also presented for three subgroups—Europeans, Asian, and Hispanics. The Hispanic subgroup is also divided into "recent" non-Mexican Hispanics and "recent" Mexican-born migrants to the US.

Compared to the CPS recent foreign-born population, which includes all three broad categories of immigrants (legal, temporary, and undocumented), while mean education is

Table 4.6 Schooling distributions and average years of legal immigrants and the recent foreign-born—2003

| | All | | | Asian | |
| | | | | | |
Schooling characteristic	*New legal foreign-born*	*Recent foreign-born*		*New legal foreign-born*	*Recent foreign-born*
Less than 5	9.5	5.9		5.4	2.6
5–8 years	13.0	13.9		9.6	5.0
9–11 years	14.4	8.5		14.0	1.6
12 years	14.9	25.4		13.0	18.8
13–16 years	29.1	34.9		35.3	50.7
17–18 years	11.9	8.4		14.7	16.6
19+ years	7.3	3.0		8.1	4.8
Mean years	12.1	12.2		13.2	14.5

| | European | | | Hispanics | |
| | | | | | |
Schooling	*New legal foreign-born*	*Recent foreign-born*		*New legal foreign-born*	*Recent foreign-born*
Less than 5	1.5	2.0		16.1	9.5
5–8 years	2.7	3.8		20.8	23.7
9–11 years	11.7	1.5		17.5	15.2
12 years	13.3	25.9		15.9	28.0
13–16 years	39.4	49.6		19.9	20.2
17–18 years	18.0	13.4		6.2	2.4
19+ years	13.4	4.5		3.6	0.9
Mean years	14.8	14.3		10.0	10.0

| | Non-Mexican Hispanics | | | Mexicans | |
| | | | | | |
Schooling	*New legal foreign-born*	*Recent foreign-born*		*New legal foreign-born*	*Recent foreign-born*
Less than 5	12.2	6.4		22.2	11.6
5–8 years	18.1	13.8		25.0	30.7
9–11 years	15.5	10.0		20.5	18.8
12 years	17.8	35.6		12.9	22.7
13–16 years	24.3	28.6		13.3	14.3
17–18 years	7.7	4.2		4.0	1.3
19+ years	4.5	1.4		2.1	0.5
Mean years	10.9	11.5		8.5	9.0

Recent immigrants are from the 2003 NIS and the recent foreign-born are from the 2003 CPS. The recent foreign-born entered between 1998 and 2003.

very similar there are far more legal immigrants at the top and bottom of the educational hierarchy. Thus, there is much more heterogeneity within the legal immigrant population compared to all recent foreign-born population in the CPS. The pro-skill component of the new legal immigrant population appears as 19% of new legal immigrants have more than a college degree in 2003 compared to a CPS recent foreign-born population almost half as large (11.4%). At the same time, legal immigrant rules for admission into the US also draws 10% of its new flows from those with less than five years of schooling compared to 6% in the CPS.

This comparison varies a good deal across the main immigrant ethnic groups. Not surprisingly, there are large differences in average schooling between our main ethnic groups. Among new legal immigrants, Mexicans trail Asians by four and a half years of schooling and new European legal migrants by more than six years of schooling on average. Even within the Latino new legal immigrant group, Mexicans have two and a half fewer years of schooling than non-Mexican Hispanics. Similar education disparities by region of origin exist in the 2003 CPS. Education diversity within our immigrant ethnic groups is impressive. Forty-two percent of new Mexican legal migrants have only elementary schooling or less compared to 6% of Europeans, 8% of Asians, and about 20% of non-Mexican Latinos. Similar ethnic differences exist at the top of the education distribution. Now new legal Asian immigrants lead the way with 21% of them having more than a college degree. The comparable fractions for European, non-Mexican Hispanics, and Mexicans are 18%, 6%, and 2% respectively.

From where does this heterogeneity in education accomplishments of new legal immigrants derive? Legal immigrants come into the US because they qualify in at least one of a very complex set of rules governing legal admission. Table 4.7A illustrates the source of this diversity by presenting for the 2003 New Immigrant Survey average education by the type of visa that qualified one for legal immigrant status. Alongside these visa-specific mean education levels are placed the percentage of people who qualified for legal admission in each of the visa categories listed in the first column. In order to track recent trends in admissions, data for the 1996 Legal Immigrant Sample are contained in Table 4.7B using the same format as in Table 4.7A.

Variation in education by type of visa is enormous, with a range of nine years of schooling from the highest to the lowest visa category in Table 4.7A for the full sample of new legal immigrants. The most fundamental distinction involves those who were admitted on employment visas compared to those who arrived on family visas, with the former type of immigrant typically being much more educated. Compared to family-based visa categories, there is a distinct pro-skill bias to those admitted on employment visas (Jasso et al., 2000a). The least-educated category are parents who typically did not complete elementary school, while the best educated are those new immigrants who came on employment visas who on average were college graduates. The influence of positive assortative mating in the marriage market is also evident in the ranking of schooling of those admitted through spousal visas: at the top employment (15.7), followed by spouses of US citizens (13.4), and finally spouses of permanent residents (8.0). This variation by visa type is important because over time legislation has loosened or tightened the numerical limits on different types of visas. The most important of these changes in the

Table 4.7A Years of schooling completed among immigrants aged 25 years and over at admission, by visa class and adjustee status, NIS—2003

Percent by region of origin visa class	All NA		Asian 31.0		European 13.7	
	Mean	Percent	Mean	Percent	Mean	Percent
Spouse of US citizen	13.4	32.4	13.9	26.1	15.6	34.4
Spouse of permanent resident	8.0	2.8	11.5	1.2	11.0	0.1
Parent of (adult) US citizen	7.6	13.6	9.6	16.1	12.1	7.1
Sibling, principal and spouse	11.7	7.3	11.7	17.2	11.0	1.8
Family–other	12.1	10.1	13.0	10.2	14.3	3.1
Employment, principal	16.5	6.8	16.7	13.8	16.7	7.4
Employment spouse and child	15.7	4.1	16.1	8.9	16.4	3.3
Refugee/asylee, principal and spouse	12.5	6.9	10.2	2.9	13.1	17.9
Diversity, principal and spouse	14.8	7.8	14.4	3.4	15.1	25.4
Other legalization	8.5	8.3	13.6	0.3	15.3	0.4
Adjustee status						
Adjustees	12.5	57.8	14.7	42.3	14.8	59.6
New arrivals	11.6	42.2	12.1	57.7	14.8	40.4
All	12.1		13.2		14.8	

Percent by region of origin visa class	Hispanic 43.5		Non-Hispanic Mexican 26.4		Mexican 17.1	
	Mean	Percent	Mean	Percent	Mean	Percent
Spouse of US citizen	12.0	35.3	10.7	29.3	13.2	44.5
Spouse of Permanent Resident	7.2	5.3	9.9	2.1	6.3	10.2
Parent of (adult) US citizen	5.1	7.1	7.2	11.0	3.5	21.7
Sibling, principal and spouse	10.9	3.5	11.3	4.2	10.2	2.6
Family–other	11.4	13.7	12.0	15.5	10.2	10.8
Employment, principal	13.4	2.1	14.3	2.2	12.0	2.0
Employment spouse and child	11.2	1.1	11.5	1.2	10.5	0.8
Refugee/asylee, principal and spouse	12.7	4.4	12.7	7.2	NA	0.1
Diversity, principal and spouse	14.4	0.8	14.4	1.3	NA	0.0
Other legalization	8.3	18.6	8.2	26.0	8.8	7.1
Adjustee status						
Adjustees	10.4	69.4	11.0	66.5	9.6	73.9
New arrivals	8.9	30.6	10.6	33.5	5.6	26.1
All	10.0		10.9		8.5	

Figures are for all immigrants in the NIS-2003 based on weighted data.

Table 4.7B NIS-Pilot—1996

Percent by region of origin visa class	All NA		Asian 29.7		European 22.4	
	Mean	Percent	Mean	Percent	Mean	Percent
Spouse of US citizen	13.6	28.8	14.6	19.7	15.1	22.8
Spouse of permanent resident	10.0	10.8	14.6	6.1	12.0	4.7
Parent of (adult) US citizen	7.4	10.7	9.7	11.6	9.8	3.4
Sibling, principal and spouse	13.5	6.2	13.6	15.7	12.0	1.3
Family—other	12.2	11.3	12.3	12.2	13.7	8.7
Employment, principal	16.5	9.0	17.2	12.2	16.9	12.3
Employment spouse and child	15.4	5.3	15.4	9.4	15.3	7.3
Refugee/asylee, principal and spouse	12.7	10.4	11.8	11.1	13.3	24.1
Diversity, principal and spouse	14.7	6.3	15.3	1.5	14.9	12.7
Adjustee status						
Adjustees	13.3	57.7	14.7	45.8	14.5	67.9
New arrivals	11.7	42.3	12.8	54.2	14.4	32.1
All	12.6		13.7		14.4	

Percent by region of origin visa class	Hispanic 32.4		Non-Mexican Hispanic 19.7		Mexican 12.7	
	Mean	Percent	Mean	Percent	Mean	Percent
Spouse of US citizen	12.2	38.0	11.8	41.1	12.8	33.1
Spouse of permanent resident	8.2	21.8	10.8	10.7	7.1	39.0
Parent of (adult) US citizen	5.4	14.8	6.6	12.2	4.2	18.9
Sibling, principal and spouse	8.8	2.3	9.7	2.3	7.5	2.4
Family—other	10.6	13.0	10.6	19.0	11.0	3.6
Employment, principal	13.0	4.5	12.3	6.1	16.3	2.0
Employment spouse and child	14.9	1.5	15.4	1.7	13.5	1.0
Refugee/asylee, principal and spouse	12.8	2.8	12.7	4.6	NA	NA
Diversity, principal and spouse	NA	NA	NA	NA	NA	NA
Adjustee status						
Adjustees	11.2	63.9	12.1	58.5	10.0	72.1
New arrivals	8.3	36.1	9.3	41.5	6.0	27.9
All	10.1		10.9		8.8	

Figures are for all immigrants in the NIS-P based on weighted data.

last two decades is the increase in numerical limits on employment visas, which resulted not only in increased entry of those with employment visas, but also in an increase in the average skill of education of legal immigrants (see Jasso et al., 2000a).

The diversity in visa class of admission varies greatly by ethnic group. On one extreme, almost three-quarters of new legal Mexican immigrants consist either of spouses (55%) or parents (22%), while only 3% qualified using employment visas. In contrast, 33% of new Asian immigrants in 2003 had employment-based visas and 28% qualified on marriage visas. Asians are also unique in that they are the only ethnic group in Table 4.7A in which there were more new arrivals compared to adjustment legalizations of those already residing in the US. This most likely reflects the distances involved, and the more recent increases in flows of Asian immigrants into the US.

If we compare Tables 4.7A and B, the visa categories that had the largest decline in average education between 1996 and 2003 were in the two family categories—parents of US citizens (10 to 8 years of schooling) and siblings (from 13.5 to 11.7). The parents of Mexican immigrants in particular were poorly educated in the 2003 class of legal immigrants—3.5 years of schooling on average. The other factor that appears to have played a role in lowering the mean education of new legal immigrants between 1996 and 2003 was the expansion in the "other legalization" category, a category that eases immigration largely of those in Central and South America (for example, El Salvador and Nicaragua) and cancellation of previous deportation status. As the data in 2003 demonstrate, on average this category has an elementary school education.

5. FOREIGN STUDENTS AT AMERICAN SCHOOLS

Education plays several roles in influencing who comes to the US. Education affects earnings opportunities in the host and sending countries, and therefore alters the incentives about which types of people want to migrate to the US. In addition, higher education in particular is a product in which the US has had historically a distinct comparative advantage. The growing worldwide desire to attend American universities represents a strong draw to foreign nationals to live in the US for at least some period of time. Attendance at US colleges and universities is thought by some to be a way station to subsequently obtaining legal permanent residence in the US. Foreign students attending schools in the US must obtain temporary visas for the duration of their status as students and are legally classified as non-immigrants.[7]

Figure 4.5 plots time series trends in total number of non-immigrants admitted to the US along with total numbers on temporary tourist or business visas and those on student visas. Globalization has a human dimension, as mirrored in the accelerating numbers

---

[7] Other non-immigrants include temporary visitors for pleasure (tourists) or business, foreign diplomats and officials and their families, as well as a number of other smaller categories.

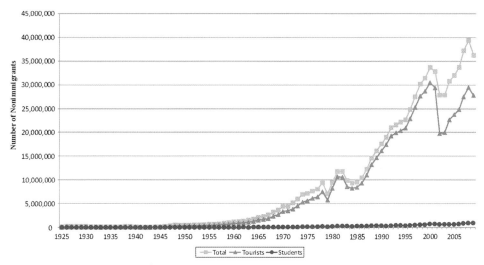

Figure 4.5 *Non-immigrants admitted, 1925–2009.*

of non-immigrants admitted to the US in recent decades. Since 1960, the numbers of non-immigrants to the US have grown from about 1.1 million in 1960 to almost 40 million by 2009. Figure 4.5 indicates that most of this overall surge is accounted for by a single group, those on temporary visas for tourism or business—who comprised 90% of all non-immigrants.[8] There was not much of a recent slowdown as numbers of non-immigrants basically doubled during the 1990s—that is, until September 11. In that calendar year and for a few years thereafter, the number of non-immigrant visas fell by almost 5 million. In the years subsequent to 9/11, numbers of non-immigrant flows have recovered and exceeded their pre-9/11 levels and seem to be back on trend.

When placed on the same scale as all non-immigrants in Figure 4.5, secular trends for foreign students are barely detectable as they only comprise about 2% of the total. However, when plotted in Figure 4.6 on a scale more appropriate to their numbers, we see that the same rapid secular expansion occurred with foreign student visas. Student visas reached three-quarters of a million in 2001, more than double the number in 1990 and more than seven times that in 1970.[9] Once again the events of 9/11 had a detectable negative impact on these trends, but that impact now appears to have been completely temporary.

Another way of gauging the importance of foreign students is to compare them to the size of the total student population in the US. Table 4.8A does that by listing the

[8] Tourist visas made up 84% of all temporary visas for business or pleasure in 2001.

[9] Student visas in Figure 4.6 include visas for academic students (F1), vocational students (M1), and F2 and M2 visas for spouses and children. However, in 2001 for example, spouses and children make up only 6% of the total.

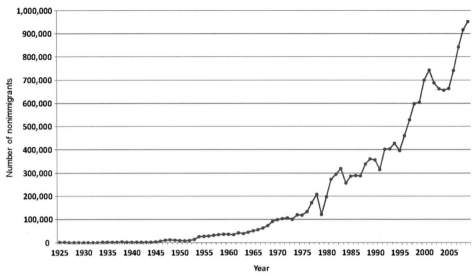

Figure 4.6 Non-immigrant students, 1925–2009.

percentage of all enrolled students who are foreign nationals. In spite of the growth in student visas, the overall numbers remain modest—about 3.4% of students at American colleges and universities are foreign nationals. Foreign student representation varies a great deal by level of schooling and field of study. As Table 4.8A demonstrates, less than 5% of undergraduates are foreign students, while about one in nine of those attending American graduate schools are foreign students.

While the overall impact of foreign students may seem modest, their influence on doctoral programs in general, and particularly in some subfields in the hard sciences, is anything but. Table 4.8B lists the fraction of doctorates awarded to foreign students between 1998 and 2008. Foreign students now earn more than 30% of all doctorates, and more than half of all Ph.D.s in math and engineering now go to foreign students.

There is a tremendous amount of variance across fields, with much lower foreign representation in the non-science and engineering fields (16.5%). Mathematical ability and language issues appear to play some role in the choice of degree. Foreign students receive almost half of all US doctorates in physics, but much less in the biological sciences (28.7%). Psychology, a very large degree-awarding program in the US and a science with both natural and social science arms, awarded only 7.3% of its degrees to foreign students.[10]

Table 4.9 provides another perspective by listing the percentage of American foreign students by region and country of birth for academic years 1980–81, 2000–01, and

[10] An important issue that has received little rigorous analytical attention is the extent to which these foreign students have displaced American students. Such a question is not answered by just the raw numbers alone. For a thoughtful attempt to address this question, see Borjas (2007).

Table 4.8A Enrollment of international students by level of degree

| Academic level | International students (% of US enrollment) | | | | | |
	2001		2006		2009	
Associate	67,667	(1.5)	68,170	(1.4)	77,220	(1.3)
Undergraduate	193,412	(4.7)	187,910	(4.5)	214,240	(4.5)
Graduate	264,749	(11.2)	269,380	(10.7)	294,080	(10.7)
Total	525,828	(3.5)	525,460	(3.4)	585,540	(3.4)

Source: Foreign Science and Engineering Students in the United States, National Science Foundation, NSF 10-234, Table 2, July 2010.

Table 4.8B Enrollment of international students: Percent of doctorates awarded to foreign students holding temporary visas, by field

	1998	2001	2003	2006	2008
All science and engineering	0.284	0.311	0.332	0.386	0.384
Engineering	0.436	0.506	0.552	0.594	0.571
Science	0.242	0.258	0.274	0.320	0.326
Mathematics	0.377	0.431	0.443	0.503	0.467
Physics	0.353	0.402	0.456	0.518	0.496
Biological sciences	0.226	0.218	0.245	0.278	0.295
Psychology	0.046	0.045	0.060	0.074	0.073
Other social sciences	0.254	0.281	0.294	0.313	0.321
Non-science and engineering	0.112	0.123	0.143	0.165	0.165
All	0.222	0.241	0.260	0.310	0.312

Source: Science and Engineering Doctorate Awards: 2007–08, National Center for Science and Engineering Statistics (NCSES), Table 4, National Science Foundation, NSF 11-321, August 2010.

Table 4.9 Foreign students enrolled in institutions of higher education in the United States by region, and selected countries of origin

| | 1980–81 | | 2000–01 | | 2008–09 | |
	Number	Percent	Number	Percent	Number	Percent
Asia	94,640	30.3	302,058	55.1	415,000	61.8
China	2770	0.9	59,939	10.9	98,235	14.6
South Korea	6150	2.0	45,685	8.3	75,065	11.2
Taiwan	19,460	6.2	28,566	5.2	28,065	4.2
India	9250	3.0	54,664	10.0	103,260	15.4
Europe	28,650	9.2	93,784	17.1	87,648	13.1
Africa	38,180	12.2	34,217	6.2	36,937	5.5
Latin America	49,810	16.0	63,634	11.6	67,731	10.1
Middle East	81,390	26.1	23,658	4.3	29,140	4.3
North America	14,790	4.7	25,888	4.7	30,107	4.5

Source: Digest of Education Statistics, Table 234, National Center for Education Statistics, 2010.

2008–09. The most dramatic trend involved Asian students who have been increasing by about 100,000 per decade during that time frame, doubling their proportionate representation from 30% to over 60%. Not surprisingly, two countries stand out above all others—China and India. In 1980, there were fewer than 3000 Chinese students studying in the US—today there are almost 100,000. Similarly, the numbers of Indian students increased over this period from 9000 to over 100,000. South Korea experienced a 10-fold increase in students studying in the US. In the rest of the world, total numbers of European and African students stabilized during the last decade. The main area of decline was the Middle East, and within the Middle East in particular Iran.

The growing numbers of foreign students receiving doctoral degrees from American universities should be viewed in the larger context of a worldwide surge in the demand for degrees beyond the baccalaureate and increasing competition among a relatively few but a growing set of countries (the UK, US, France, Germany, Japan, Australia) for these students. The surge in demand for science and engineering degrees reflects the strong economic growth in Asia and Europe, with only a relatively small part of this demand filled by American institutions. In large part, internal supply in Asia and Europe has responded to meet this demand. For example, in 1999 there were 190,000 doctoral degrees awarded worldwide in science and engineering, and only 45,000 of them were earned in the US. Nor is the US unique in the presence of foreign students in its advance degree programs. To cite just one example, 44% of doctoral engineering degrees in the UK were earned by foreign students—the comparable numbers in the US and France were 49% and 30% respectively.

In most science fields, American top universities continue to rank among the world's elite, especially in their research function. These elite American universities produce a disproportionate number of the best of the next generation of scientists. Many of these trained scientists are now not Americans, and this may prove to be the principal legacy of the penetration of foreign students into American universities. The exact contours of that legacy are not yet clear, but the era of dominance of American-born scholars in research in many fields is most likely on the wane. It is less certain what will happen to the dominance of American universities in research. In certain fields at least, the best of the foreign students remain to teach and to do research at American universities, in part because universities in their home countries still do not offer the same opportunities for merit-based advancement and research.

6. IMMIGRANT EDUCATION AND GENERATIONAL ASSIMILATION

Economic mobility for yourself and your children is deeply tied to our immigration history. Until recently, the conventional view was that in terms of generational assimilation the waves of European immigrants who arrived at the end of the nineteenth century and the beginning of the twentieth century were an enormous success. The success of more

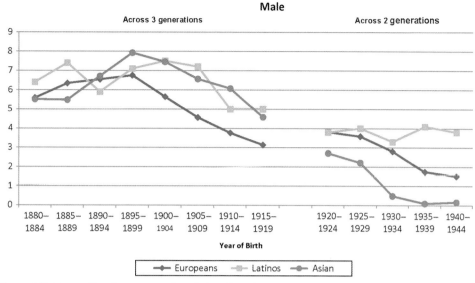

Figure 4.7 *Generational progress of male immigrants.*

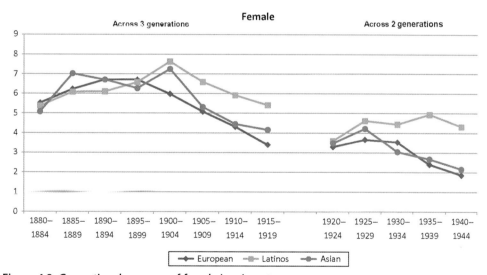

Figure 4.8 *Generational progress of female immigrants.*

recent immigrant waves, especially for Latino immigrants, was viewed as far more problematic.[11]

To generalize across all birth cohorts, Figure 4.7 (for men) and Figure 4.8 (for women) highlight the relative educational progress across generations of the three ethnic

---

[11] This section is based in part on Smith (2003). For a very good earlier contribution, see Card et al. (2000).

groups. In these graphs, the vertical axis represents the number of years of additional schooling between the generations while the horizontal axis indexes the year of birth of immigrants. In these figures, these educational advances can sometimes be measured across all three generations and sometimes only across two generations because the story of the third generation is not yet complete. However, whether measured across all three or just two generations and for men and women alike, the education advances made by Latinos are actually greater than those achieved by either Europeans or Asian migrants. There is certainly no evidence from these data that Latinos have lagged behind these other large immigrant groups in their ability to transmit education accomplishments to their children and grandchildren. For all three broad ethnic groups (Europeans, Asian, and Hispanics) educational progress from the immigrant generation to their sons and daughters, and then on to their grandchildren, is very impressive indeed.

Education transmission across immigrant generations is only one relevant form of immigrant generational transmission. Blau et al. (2013) reported that for education there is a larger transmission from immigrants to their children for father's education than for mother's education. They also showed that this intergenerational transmission extends to other important aspects of behavior including fertility and hours of work for women. That is, the second-generation descendants of immigrants from countries with higher fertility and lower levels of market work among women also exhibit higher fertility and lower levels of market work. This may suggest a strong but decaying transmission of cultural values.

This sharp rise in foreign-born students raises several points that have recently been receiving attention in the academic literature. Stuen et al. (2012) argued that both foreign and domestic students in S and E departments contribute significantly to innovation and the advancement of science, particularly when these foreign students are selected on their student quality rather than their ability to pay. In a series of papers, Borjas (2007, 2009) investigated issues surrounding possible negative effects on domestic students in enrollments and wages from the influx of foreign students. Borjas reported a significant crowd-out of white men by foreign students as well as a significant wage loss for native-born doctorates. The large influx of foreign students could have had a positive impact on rates of innovation, yielding benefits to the American economy in the future (Acemoglu, 2002). Of all the topics discussed in this chapter, the issue of the benefits and costs of the large flows of foreign students is perhaps most in need of additional research in the future.

7. CONCLUSIONS

This chapter deals with a number of issues about immigrants to the US and their education. In part reflecting the reasons why they come to America, immigrants are more highly represented in both the lowest and highest rungs of the education ladder. On average, immigrants have less schooling than the native-born, a schooling deficit that reached 1.3 years in 2002. Perhaps as important as the average difference between immigrants and the native-born population, there is considerable diversity in the schooling accomplishments among different immigrant subgroups. The education of new European and Asian immigrants is higher than that of native-born Americans, while the typical Latino immigrant continues to trail the native-born by about four years of schooling on average.

The education gap of new recent immigrants did rise but only modestly over the last 60 years. This increase was higher among men than among women and appears to be entirely accounted for by the increasing fraction of immigrants who are illegal. Legal immigrants appear to have about the same amount of schooling as native-born Americans, and at the top of the schooling hierarchy have a good deal more.

Education is a key part of immigration policy for other reasons as well, as many immigrants come to the US to obtain advanced schooling degrees, particularly at the doctoral level in the hard sciences and engineering. There has been a large and continuing surge in recent decades in student visas that is particularly focused on China and India in mathematics, the hard sciences, and engineering.

The final issue I deal with is a frequently expressed concern that educational generational progress among Latino immigrants has lagged behind other immigrant groups such as Europeans and Asian immigrants to the US. This concern is largely unfounded, as for both men and women the education advances across generations were in fact larger for Latinos than either Europeans or Asians.

ACKNOWLEDGMENTS

The research was supported by grants from NIH. The expert programming assistance of David Rumpel and Iva Maclennan is gratefully appreciated. Support from NICHD and the RAND Corporation is gratefully acknowledged.

REFERENCES

Acemoglu, D., 2002. Technical change, inequality, and the labor market. J. Econ. Lit. 40 (1), 7–72.
Blau, F., Kahn, L., Yung-Hsu Liu, A., Papps, K., 2013. The transmission of women's fertility, human capital and work orientation across immigrant generations. J. Popul. Econ. 26 (2), 405–435.
Borjas, G., 1994. The economics of immigration. J. Econ. Lit. 32 (4), 1667–1717.
Borjas, G., 1995. Assimilation and changes in cohort quality revisited: What happened to immigrant earnings in the 1980s? J. Labor. Econ. 13 (2), 201–245.
Borjas, G., 2007. Do foreign students crowd out native students from graduate programs? In: Ehrenberg, R.G., Stephan, P.E. (Eds.), Science and the University. University of Wisconsin Press, Madison, WI.
Borjas, G., 2009. Immigration in high skill labor markets. The implications of foreign students on the Eearnings of Doctorates. In: Freeman, R., Goroff, D. (Eds.), Science and Engineering Careers in the United States: An Analysis of Markets and Employment. University of Chicago Press, Chicago, pp. 131–161.

Card, D., Di Nardo, J., Estes, E., 2000. The more things change: Immigrants and the children of immigrants in the 1940s, the 1970s, and the 1990s. In: Borjas, G. (Ed.), Issues in the Economics of Immigration. University of Chicago Press, Chicago, pp. 227–269, Chapter 6.

Dustmann, C., Weiss, Y., 2007. Return migration: Theory and empirical evidence from the UK. Br. J. Ind. Relat. 45 (2), 236–256.

Jasso, G., Rosenzweig, M., Smith, J.P., 2000a. The changing skill of new immigrants to the United States: Recent trends and their determinants. In: Borjas, G. (Ed.), Issues in the Economics of Immigration. University of Chicago Press, Chicago.

Jasso, G., Massey, D., Rosenzweig, M., Smith, J.P., 2000b. The New Immigrant Pilot Survey (NIS): Overview and findings about U.S. immigrants at admission. Demography 37 (1), 127–138.

Lubotsky, D., 2007. Chutes or ladders? A longitudinal analysis of immigrant earnings. J. Polit. Econ. 115 (5), 820–867.

National Center for Education Statistics, 2010. Digest of Education Statistics. US Department of Education, Washington, DC.

Passel, J.S., Cohn, D., 2011. Unauthorized Immigrant Population: National and State Trends, 2010. Pew Research Center, Washington, DC.

Pew Hispanic Center, 2012. Statistical Portrait of the Foreign-Born in the United States, 2010, Washington, DC.

Smith, J.P., 2003. Assimilation across the generations. Am. Econ. Rev. 93 (2), 315–319.

Smith, J.P., 2006a. Immigrants and their education. In: Hanushek, E., Welch, F. (Eds.), Handbook of the Economics of Education, vol. 1. Elsevier, Amsterdam, pp. 156–187.

Smith, J.P., 2006b. Immigrants and the labor market. J. Labor. Econ. 24 (2), 203–233.

Smith, J.P., Edmonston, B., 1997. The New Americans: Economic, Demographic, and Fiscal Effects of Immigration. National Academy Press, Washington, DC.

Stuen, E., Mobarak, A.M., Maskus, K., 2012. Skilled immigration and innovation: Evidence from enrollment fluctuations in US doctoral programmes. Econ. J. 122, 1143–1176.

CHAPTER 5

International Migration and the Economics of Language

Barry R. Chiswick*, Paul W. Miller**

*George Washington University and IZA—Institute for the Study of Labor
**Curtin University

Contents

1. Introduction	212
2. Research Issues and Methodology	214
3. Choice of Destination	216
3.1 Choice of initial destination country	217
3.2 Location choice within a country	225
4. Determinants of Language Proficiency	228
4.1 Exposure	229
4.2 Efficiency	233
4.3 Economic incentives	237
5. Effects of Language on Earnings	240
5.1 Background considerations	240
5.2 Around the globe: different countries, different languages, similar results	244
5.2.1 Australia	244
5.2.2 Canada	246
5.2.3 Germany	248
5.2.4 Israel	250
5.2.5 Spain	251
5.2.6 United Kingdom	253
5.2.7 United States	254
5.3 An overview of the effects of dominant language proficiency on earnings	257
5.4 Ethnic enclaves effects on earnings	257
6. Summary and Conclusions	264
Acknowledgments	265
References	265

Handbook of the Economics of International Migration, Volume 1A
ISSN 2212-0092, http://dx.doi.org/10.1016/B978-0-444-53764-5.00005-0

1. INTRODUCTION

This chapter provides an overview of research on the economics of language, as applied to international migration.[1] The "economics of language" is the study of the determinants and consequences of language proficiency using the methodology and tools of economics.

The beginning of interest by economists in language is usually attributed to Jacob Marschak (1965), who was concerned with the efficiency of communication. Using an evolutionary approach, those aspects of language that were beneficial in facilitating communication would survive, and those aspects (and languages) that were not efficient or effective would tend to disappear. In this framework languages tend to evolve over time. And just as mutations lead to the evolution of different species of plants and animals, isolation and language drift tend to promote the development of new dialects and languages. This approach did not generate much of a literature in economics on the evolution of languages.

It did, however, stimulate interest in language usage in bilingual and multilingual countries (e.g., Canada, Switzerland). Which language or languages become dominant, especially for economic activity, and who learns which language? In some countries, regional or indigenous minority group languages have disappeared or appear to be on the verge of vanishing (e.g., consider Celtic in Ireland and Scotland, the Sami language in Sweden, and indigenous peoples' languages in countries of overseas settlement such as the US, Canada, Australia, and Brazil). In others, attempts have been made in recent decades with various degrees of success to reinvigorate traditional languages (e.g., Catalonian in Spain and Welsh in Wales).

Following several decades of low rates of international migration due to two world wars, the Great Depression, and severe immigration restrictions in many major destinations, international migration started increasing in the 1950s, and it has continued to increase in each decade since. This migration led to an influx of people in various destinations who were not familiar with the primary or dominant language of the destination. This led to interest by economists in the nexus between language and immigration. In addition to advances in economic theory and the development of testable models, economists now had better (not perfect, but better) microdata to estimate their models and test their hypotheses regarding language and international migration.

Most of the research in the economics of language focuses on what can be described as microeconomics—that is, the behavior of individuals. The approach taken has been to view language skills as a form of "human capital". The concept of human capital became important in the 1960s, with the emphasis on schooling, on-the-job training, health and information, all of which transform the person, and migration, which transforms the person's location (Schultz, 1962). It was only since the 1980s, however, that economists have viewed immigrant language skills as a form of human capital and analyzed it in this

---

[1] This chapter is a development of Chiswick, B.R., 2009. The economics of language learning for immigrants: An introduction and overview. In: Wiley, T.G., Lee, J.S., Rumberger, R.W. (Eds.), The Education of Language Minority Immigrants in the United States. Multilingual Matters, Bristol, UK, pp. 72–91.

context (Carliner, 1981; McManus et al., 1983; Tainer, 1988). This interest arose as a result of the rapid growth of the non-English-speaking portion of the increasing immigrant flows into the US and Canada, the emerging interest among economists in the determinants of the adjustment of immigrants to the host society, and the growing interest in the application of human capital theory (Becker, 1964).

Language skills satisfy the three requirements for human capital in that they are productive, costly to produce, and embodied in the person. First, a person's proficiency in the language of the area in which he or she lives is productive in the labor market. Those who speak/read the local language will find it easier to obtain a job and will generally be more productive on the job. In addition, language skills are productive in consumption activities. Those proficient in the local language will be more efficient in the search for higher quality goods and services and at lower prices. Any monolingual English speaker in the Chinese countryside quickly learns this proposition. Immigrants who do not speak the language of the broader society also find that their social and information networks are confined to their immigrant/linguistic enclave, rather than having a wider range. These benefits from proficiency provide economic and social incentives for immigrants to learn the host country's language.

Second, acquiring language proficiency is not without costs. Immigrants spend a considerable amount of their own time and money (for language training schools, books, etc.) to become proficient in their new country's language. Acquiring language skills is not costless even for infants. Even if their own time has no economic value, the time of their parents or other caregivers in speaking and reading to the child is not costless. The costs involved in an immigrant learning a new language would be influenced by several factors, including the person's value of time (wage rate), the person's age, exposure to the destination language (as distinct from being able to avoid its use by living and working in a linguistic enclave), and the "distance" between the person's mother tongue and the language of the destination, among other factors.

Finally, language skills are embodied in the person. Unlike owning physical capital (such as a truck), but like learning to play a piano, language skills cannot be separated from the person.

The idea that language skills are both productive and costly to acquire is not new, but rather at least thousands of years old. See Box 5.1, which relates the story of the Tower of Babel from the Biblical book of Genesis (Chapter 11, verses 1–9). The Tower of Babel provided a biblical explanation for the diversity of languages and the scattering of people: "If, as one people with one language . . . then nothing that they may propose to do will be out of their reach." When their speech was "confounded" and they were scattered, they could no longer cooperate and they became less productive (Tanakh, 1985).[2]

---

[2] An important issue currently facing the US, and most of the highly developed economies, is the inverse of the Tower of Babel story. Immigration is resulting in the coming together of diverse peoples originally speaking a variety of languages who then merge over time into a common culture and a common language, even if they may also retain the languages of their origins.

> ## BOX 5.1 Tower of Babel
>
> Everyone on earth had the same language and the same words. And as they migrated from the east, they came upon a valley in the land of Shinar and settled there.
>
> They said to one another, "Come, let us make bricks and burn them hard." Brick served them as stone, and bitumen served them as mortar. And they said, "Come let us build a city, and a tower with its top in the sky, to make a name for ourselves; else we shall be scattered all over the world."
>
> The LORD came down to look at the city and tower that man had built, and the LORD said, "If, as one people with one language for all, this is how they have begun to act, then nothing that they may propose to do will be out of their reach. Let us, then, go down and confound their speech there, so that they shall not understand one another's speech." Thus the LORD scattered them from there over the face of the whole earth; and they stopped building the city. This is why it was called Babel, because there the LORD confounded the speech of the whole earth; and from there the LORD scattered them over the face of the whole earth.
>
> (Genesis, 11, 1–9)
>
> Source: *Tanakh: The Holy Scriptures, 1986. Jewish Publication Society, Philadelphia, pp. 16–17.*

The structure of this chapter is as follows. In the next section the three major aspects of the relation between language and international migration are outlined, and a broad overview of the methodology adopted in the empirical research is provided. This is followed by separate sections on each of the three major research themes, where the conceptual frameworks followed in the literature are presented, and empirical evidence discussed. The chapter ends with a summary of the findings and a discussion of gaps in the literature that warrant further research.

2. RESEARCH ISSUES AND METHODOLOGY

Much of the research on the economics of language as applied to international migration has focused on three main issues. The first matter addressed is the links between language background and the decision to migrate and the choice of destination by migrants. The language factors that are important include knowledge of a language that is used in the destination country, as well as knowledge of a language which, because it is linguistically close to a language used in the destination, makes learning the destination country language easier. The second issue concerns the determinants of proficiency in the primary or dominant language of the country of destination, including in the labor market, although the model and the methodology can be, and have been, applied to non-migrants who are linguistic minorities and native-born bilingual speakers. The third major concern covers the consequences for immigrants of obtaining proficiency in the dominant language. The consequences of language proficiency that have received the most attention have been in the labor market, particularly earnings. There are, however, other consequences that have not received much attention from economists or other social scientists. The primary focus on earnings has arisen in part because of interest in economic well-being and in part because of the greater availability of data on earnings.

Knowing the dominant language makes a person more efficient in the consumption of goods and services (higher quality and lower prices for goods and services). Investments in other forms of human capital, such as schooling and job training, are likely to be more productive if one can communicate in the dominant language in school and in the labor market. Knowing the dominant language of the destination can also increase the efficiency of parenting. Parents who are proficient in the dominant language can be more effective in teaching the language and culture of the destination to their children, which would be a benefit to them in school and later in the job market. Language skills also have social benefits as they can expand the range of friendship networks beyond one's ethnic/linguistic enclave. Finally, civic involvement is enhanced with knowledge of the host country's language. Indeed, for the US and many other countries, at least a basic knowledge of the destination language is required for immigrants to become citizens and acquire full political and economic rights. This brings about increased political empowerment. There is no doubt that these non-labor market consequences of dominant language proficiency are important. However, to have a manageable review we focus on the labor market consequences.

The particular models advanced by economists in relation to each of these research questions are discussed in Sections 3, 4, and 5. The testing of the models, or the estimation of the equations, relies on multivariate statistical (econometric) techniques.

In general, many economists believe in the importance of testing for the robustness of findings. One set of estimates from one dataset may be insightful, but cannot determine whether the results are unique to that data, group, country or time period, or whether they are generalizable across these dimensions. A hypothesis or model that is not robust, but is valid for only a unique group, time and place, is clearly of very limited value. On the other hand, one has much greater confidence in a hypothesis or model that is robust—that is, supported by analyses of diverse datasets.

The analyses reported below represent a synthesis of the findings on immigrants for different types of data, censuses and surveys, both cross-sectional and longitudinal. They are for immigrants who have legal status, as well as those with an illegal or unauthorized status. Although the data analyses reported below are for the late twentieth and early twenty-first centuries, they are for different datasets across several countries, primarily the US, Australia, Canada, Germany, and Israel, where the destination language is English in the first two, English and French in Canada, German in Germany, and Hebrew in Israel. The particular value of research on Israel and Germany in this context is that whereas English, and to a lesser extent French, is an international language of culture, business and science, which is often learned in school in the country of origin as a second language, this is less so for Hebrew for immigrants to Israel, or for German among the groups of immigrants covered in the empirical research for Germany. That the findings for Israel and Germany parallel those of the other countries is a test of the robustness of the model across destination languages (Chiswick, 1998; Chiswick and Repetto, 2001; Dustmann, 1994). In the case of the links between language background and destination language choice, many destination countries, most countries of origin in the world, and a wide range of languages, are covered.

There are several dimensions of language skills—oral (speaking and hearing) and literacy (reading and writing). Survey and census data on the language skills of immigrants almost always rely on self-reported responses or responses provided by an adult household member. Although some datasets report responses to questions for immigrants on reading and writing, most of the data are regarding speaking skills, focusing on either the self-reported level of competency or identifying the languages spoken on a regular basis. Analyses using literacy skills show the same patterns as those using speaking skills, in part because the two are so highly correlated (Chiswick, 1991; Chiswick and Repetto 2001; Dustmann, 1994). The discussion here will be expressed in terms of speaking proficiency, unless noted otherwise.

3. CHOICE OF DESTINATION

Migration, whether internal to a country or international, is an investment in human capital. Unlike other forms of human capital, such as schooling, health and information, which transform the person, migration transforms where the person lives or works. It is a form of human capital because migration is costly, is beneficial in either consumption or production (e.g., labor market work), and the migration per se cannot be separated from the person.

The costs of migration include out-of-pocket costs (sometimes referred to as direct costs) and foregone earnings (sometimes referred to as opportunity costs). The costs are far greater than merely the costs of moving oneself, family members, and household goods from one point (the origin) to another (the destination). The costs incurred in the origin include the separation from family, friends, and a familiar environment. The set of skills acquired in the origin, including language skills, and which are useful in consumption and production activities, may not be equally useful in the destination. The transferability from the origin to the destination may be limited by geographic differences in technology, by custom, by occupational licensing, etc. The transferability may also be limited by language differences, where language can be considered a technology for communication. A Chinese speaker in a monolingual English country would find that being a consumer who looks for higher quality goods and services at lower prices is more difficult than it was in China, or that the job search process is more difficult. Wages would be lower and employment conditions less desirable if linguistic disadvantages lower the workers' productivity on the job or increase workplace costs (e.g., accidents). Relevant language skills may be important for communicating with supervisors, peers, and subordinates, as well as suppliers and customers or clients.

As a result, part of the cost of migration is the lower earnings during the period of adjusting one's language skills, as well as the cost of direct investment in improving destination language skills (e.g., the opportunity cost and out-of-pocket cost of a language training program). The latter cost may be incurred prior to the migration, in anticipation of the move, or after migration.

The costs of language adjustment depend on many factors, which will be discussed in greater detail below. These costs will include the importance and the ease or difficulty of learning the language of the destination. Potential migrants need not consider just one destination, but may consider the range of potential or available destinations. Therefore, part of the calculation as to which destination is most preferred is the cost of destination language acquisition. The language acquisition costs are lower the "closer" is the language of the origin to that of the destination. Thus, for an Australian, the linguistic cost of adjusting to a destination is cheaper if it is the UK rather than France, or for a Spaniard if the destination is Argentina, rather than Canada. The implication is that language differences are among the factors that influence the choice of destination.

Much of the research on the links between language background and the choice of destination has used aggregate-level data. Two decisions have been studied: the choice of initial destination country; and internal migration in the years following arrival in the host country. Evidence from both streams of literature is reviewed.

3.1 Choice of initial destination country

The research on the links between language background and choice of the initial destination can be illustrated through detailed coverage of the study by Clark et al. (2007), and then covering other studies more briefly.

Clark et al. (2007) try to account for the determinants of migration rates to the US by place of birth for 81 source countries from 1971 to 1998. They based their analysis around the following model:[3]

$$mig_j/pop_j = f(y_j/y_{US})(syr_j/syr_{US}, inq_j/inq_{US}, age_j, pov_j, dist_j, land_j, eng_j, \\ stock_j/pop_j, policy\ variables)$$

(5.1)

where mig_j/pop_j is the flow of migrants from source country j to the US in a particular year, normalized by the population of the source country, y_j/y_{US} is the average (purchasing power parity adjusted) income in the source country j relative to that in the US, the

[3] Time subscripts are suppressed to simplify the notation.

terms in *syr* and *inq* capture respectively differences in average years of schooling and inequality in source country *j* and the US, *age* is the share of the population in the sending country aged 15–29, *pov* is the poverty rate in the origin country, *dist* is the geographic distance of the source country from the US, *land* denotes cases where the origin country is land-locked, *eng* is for where the source country is predominantly English speaking, and the *stock* variable captures the number of previous immigrants from the source country. The Clark et al. (2007) model also contained policy variables, for the number of visas available in the different visa classes, and institutional factors, such as the US 1986 Immigration Reform and Control Act (IRCA) legalization program. Hence, it is seen that the model of equation (5.1) captures economic and demographic drivers of migration in the first five terms, with the remaining terms representing costs and policy parameters. In particular, it was argued that the cost of migration to the US would be higher if the sending country was not predominantly English speaking.

Clark et al.'s (2007) results show that the English-speaking sending countries were associated with a statistically significant higher migration rate to the US in the models that did not include the immigrant stock variables. In other words, having an English language background matters when it comes to understanding rates of migration to an English-speaking country. This effect, however, was not statistically significant where the stock of previous migrants from the sending country was included in the estimating equation. As noted by Clark et al. (2007. p. 267) "Since the immigrant stock reflects past immigration, it captures much of the effect of slow moving fundamentals over the longer term". Included in these fundamentals would be the country-specific cost factors that the English-speaking background variable is used to represent.

Approaches similar to the model that Clark et al. (2007) applied to English-speaking countries have been adopted by other researchers when considering migration flows into countries characterized by a number of official languages. For example, Karemera et al. (2000) examined migration flows to the US, using a common language (English) variable along the lines of Clark et al. (2007), and to Canada, where they use a variable for the language of the origin country being either English or French. Karemera et al. (2000) reported, however, that language commonality was not a significant determinant of migration rates to either the US or Canada over the decade 1976–1986. One of the main differences between the models of Karemera et al. (2000) and Clark et al. (2007) is that the former includes a set of dichotomous variables for region of origin.[4]

The coverage of common languages has been extended further by Pedersen et al. (2008). They examined gross migration flows from 129 countries into 22 OECD

---

[4] The studies in this field are characterized by differences in the choice of dependent variable (whether the immigrant flow is normalized by the source country population, and whether flows or stocks are used), the selection of independent variables, as well as the lag structure of variables. We do not discuss these specification issues in detail here.

destination countries over 1990–2000. The 22 OECD countries have a number of official languages (English, German, Spanish, Italian, etc.), and so the English language variable in the model of Clark et al. (2007) was replaced by a common language variable in the Pedersen et al. (2008) study. This variable was set equal to one where there is a common language between the origin and destination, and it is set equal to zero where there is no common language, with the *Ethnologue: Languages of the World* (2009) being used to classify pairs of countries (see Box 5.2). An additional feature of this study is that it also includes a dummy variable for countries that were ever in a colonial relationship. Presumably this variable is correlated with the common language variable, though this was not examined in the study. Nevertheless, Pedersen et al. (2008) report that the common language variable was an important influence on migration flows, being significant in five of the eight models presented in their main set of results.

Mayda (2010) and Ortega and Giovanni (2009) also examined the determinants of immigration flows to OECD countries. Mayda (2010) covered 14 OECD countries, 79 sending countries, and the time period 1980–1995, whereas Ortega and Giovanni (2009) covered 14 OECD countries, 73 countries of origin, and the longer time period of 1980–2005. Neither study found language background to be of importance to the explanation of migration flows. Ortega and Giovanni (2009, p. 14) argued that "This is hardly surprising as most of the large migratory flows to the OECD (except for Mexico–US) take place between countries that do not share a land border or a common language." Moreover, Mayda (2010, p. 1263) noted that "The impact of a common language, though of the right sign, is not statistically significant and, surprisingly, past colonial relationships do not appear to affect migration rates (this is true whether common language and colony are entered in the regression together or one at a time)."

A more recent study that reports that a common language is important to understanding international migration is Grogger and Hanson (2011). They studied the stock of immigrants in 15 high-income OECD countries in 2000, and employed both common language and an English-speaking destination country variables. Their model has separate equations for the scale of international migration flows of low-skilled (primary educated) and high-skilled (tertiary educated) workers, for the selection on the basis of the skills of immigrants (primary or tertiary educated from a particular origin country in the destination, compared to those who remained in the origin), and for sorting across destinations (the mix of immigrants across the destination countries). The preferred set of results for the scale equation shows that immigrants are more likely to be from a country that has a language in common with the destination country. The results for the selection equation indicate that immigrants that move to a country with a language in common with the origin country are positively selected in terms of education levels, while the findings for the sorting equation suggest that destinations that have a language in common with the origin country attract more highly skilled immigrants. Similar findings are reported for the English-speaking destination country variable.

BOX 5.2 Ethnologue: Languages of the World (16th edition of 2009)

This is a comprehensive reference volume that catalogs 7413 languages, including details on the 6909 known living languages in the world at the time of writing. Each language is part of a language family (that is, its linguistic lineage is provided). For example, the linguistic lineage for English is, from largest grouping to smallest, Indo-European–Germanic–Germanic West–English. This type of connectivity between languages has been used in various ways by researchers to construct a measure of linguistic distance or proximity. It can be illustrated using the algorithm proposed by Adsera and Pytlikova (2012). Thus, they construct their variable as follows:

> First we defined weights: the first equal to 0.1 if two languages are related at the most aggregated linguistic tree level, e.g., Indo-European versus Uralic (Finnish, Estonian, Hungarian); the second equal to 0.15 if two languages belong to the same second-linguistic tree level, e.g., Germanic versus Slavic languages; the third equal to 0.20 if two languages belong to the same third-linguistic tree level, e.g., Germanic West vs. Germanic North languages; and the fourth equal to 0.25 if both languages belong to the same fourth level of a linguistic tree family, e.g., Scandinavian West (Icelandic) vs. Scandinavian East (Danish, Norwegian, and Swedish), German vs. English, or Italo-Western (Italian, French, Spanish, Catalan, and Portuguese) vs. Romance Eastern (Romanian). Then, we constructed the linguistic proximity index as a sum of those four weights, and we set the index equal to 0 if two languages did not belong to any common language family, and equal to 1 if the two countries had a common language. Thus the linguistic proximity index equals 0.1 if two languages are only related at the most aggregated linguistic tree level, e.g., Indo-European languages; 0.25 if two languages belong to the same first- and second-linguistic tree level, e.g., Germanic languages; 0.45 if two languages share the same first- up to third-linguistic tree level, e.g., Germanic North languages; and 0.7 if both languages share all four levels of a linguistic tree family, e.g., Scandinavian East (Danish, Norwegian, and Swedish).
>
> **(Adsera and Pytlikova, 2012, p. 12)**

Obviously, other scales can be derived using this information—see, for example, Belot and Hatton (2012)—and this has been argued by Isphording and Otten (2012) to be a weakness of the approach. They argue, for example, "This linguistic-tree approach has to deal with strong cardinality assumptions, and arbitrarily chosen parameters. Additionally, the approach offers only low variability between different language pairs and is difficult to implement for isolated languages such as Korean" (Isphording and Otten, 2012, p. 5). Both Adsera and Pytlikova (2012) and Belot and Hatton (2012) have used these data for measures of linguistic distance in immigration research. Other researchers, for example Pedersen et al. (2008), have used this source to compile a common language dummy variable.

Source: Lewis, M.P. (Ed.), 2009. Ethnologue: Languages of the World, sixteenth edition. SIL International, Dallas, TX. Online version: http://www.ethnologue.com/.

Beine et al. (2011) examined matters similar to Grogger and Hanson (2011), but from the perspective of changes in immigrant stocks between 1990 and 2000, using data on 195 source countries and 30 OECD countries. Their common language variable was a highly significant determinant of both low-skill and high-skill migration flows. A common language was also associated with a statistically significant positive effect on the skill ratio of these migration flows.

Hence, while the results from the research that has been based on the importance of a common language to understanding international immigration are somewhat mixed, the findings predominantly suggest that a common language is an important determinant of the scale and mix of the migration flows.

There have been a number of developments in the analyses of the effect of language on the choice of destination. Of greatest relevance to this review are the studies that use a measure of "linguistic distance" in place of the common language variable. This development reflects the fact that migration costs are lower where the migrant can easily learn the language of the destination country, for example for migrants with a mother tongue that is linguistically close to the dominant language of the destination (see the next section).

Belot and Hatton (2012) examined the characteristics of migration for 70 source countries and 21 OECD destination countries for 2000/2001. While this study continues the theme of the research by Grogger and Hanson (2011) and Beine et al. (2011) by focusing on educational selectivity, the key feature from our perspective is their linguistic proximity variable. They derive this measure from the language family information presented in the *Ethnologue: Languages of the World* (see Box 5.2). As constructed by these authors, the linguistic proximity variable has values from 1 to 5, according to the number of common nodes in the linguistic tree between the closest official languages of pairs of countries.

The Ethnologue common node measure of Belot and Hatton (2012) was statistically significant and positive in their skill selection equation, a finding that the authors argue shows that the transferability of human capital might be easier when the linguistic gap is less, and hence immigrants can readily learn the dominant language of the destination.[5]

There might be a suspicion that the stronger results obtained with the seemingly superior measure of linguistic distance in Belot and Hatton (2012) are linked to their focus on stocks of immigrants. After all, Grogger and Hanson (2011) found that the conventional common language variable was highly significant in their model that has a focus on stocks, rather than annual flows. This matter can be addressed by reviewing the research of Belot and Ederveen (2012). They examined a panel of 22 OECD countries for the period 1990–2003. The measure of linguistic distance used in their study was based on the work of Dyen et al. (1992): Dyen et al. (1992) constructed a measure of the distance between Indo-European languages based on the proximity of 200 words from each language (see Box 5.3). This variable was included in the estimating equations along with a common language variable. Unlike the research of Belot and Hatton (2012), both the common language and linguistic distance variables were statistically significant,

---

[5] Belot and Hatton (2012) noted that they also estimated equations that included a dichotomous common language variable, and that this common language variable was insignificant in the presence of the linguistic proximity variable.

although the impact of sharing a common language dropped by over one-quarter when the measure of linguistic distance was included in the estimating equation.

An idea of the relative importance of the Belot and Ederveen (2012) measure of linguistic distance for migrant flows can be found from the effects that these authors computed for one standard deviation increases in the various explanatory variables. They report that "Our regression results imply that an increase in linguistic distance with one standard deviation lowers the migration flow with 56% ... This effect is about 50% higher than the effect of raising GDP per capita in the destination country by

---

BOX 5.3 The Dyen Lexicostatistical Percentage Approach

Comparative lexicostatistics is the study of historical relations among speech varieties belonging to the same language family through a quantitative study of cognation among their vocabularies. The lexicostatistical percentage approach is the oldest and most widely used lexicostatistical approach. As explained by Dyen et al. (1992), their application of this approach has four phases. First, they worked with the 200 meanings that had been proposed by Swadesh, and developed phonetic representations (forms) of the words with these particular meanings for the chosen languages (see Swadesh (1952) for an earlier compilation). Then the cognation among the forms in two languages was established through expert judgment. Cognation requires that the forms have descended in unbroken lines from a common ancestor in the same language family. Consideration of the number of cognate forms from the list of 200 meanings gives rise to the so-called lexicostatistical percentage. For example, the value when German and English are compared is 57.8%. The value for the French–English comparison is 23.6%. In other words, German and English are more similar than French and English. The final phase of work by Dyen et al. (1992) involved the categorization of the languages into various groups. It is to be noted that the Dyen et al. work covers only Indo-European languages. An example of Dyen et al.'s (1992) numbers is given below.

Dyen matrix of linguistic distances (higher values mean smaller distance)

Languages	Italian	French	Spanish	German	Dutch	Danish	English	Greek
Italian	1.000	0.803	0.788	0.265	0.260	0.263	0.247	0.178
French	0.803	1.000	0.734	0.244	0.244	0.241	0.236	0.157
Spanish	0.788	0.734	1.000	0.253	0.258	0.250	0.240	0.167
German	0.265	0.244	0.253	1.000	0.838	0.707	0.578	0.188
Dutch	0.260	0.244	0.258	0.838	1.000	0.663	0.608	0.188
Danish	0.263	0.241	0.250	0.707	0.663	1.000	0.593	0.183
English	0.247	0.236	0.240	0.578	0.608	0.593	1.000	0.162
Greek	0.178	0.157	0.167	0.188	0.188	0.83	0.162	1.000

Examples of economics studies using these data are Ginsburgh et al. (2005), Belot and Ederveen (2012), and Adresa and Pytlikova (2012).

Source: Dyen, I., Kruskal, J.B., Black, P., 1992. An IndoEuropean classification: A lexicostatistical experiment. Transactions of the American Philosophical Society, New Series 82 (5).

one standard deviation and much more than a change of one standard deviation in unemployment rates" (Belot and Ederveen, 2012, p. 1096). The importance of the linguistic distance measure in the analysis of migration flows was found in the many tests of robustness these authors conducted.

The final study in our review is by Adsera and Pytlikova (2012). They covered immigration flows in 30 OECD countries from 233 source countries, for the years 1980–2009. Their research is important in the study of the links between linguistic distance and the destination choice of immigrants because they used many measures of linguistic distance or linguistic proximity. Their preferred measure was based on the *Ethnologue: Language of the World*, and ranges from 0 to 1 according to the number of levels of the language family tree shared by the destination and source country languages (see Box 5.2). Belot and Hatton (2012) also used this type of measure. In addition, in tests of robustness, Adsera and Pytlikova (2012) used both a measure based on Dyen et al. (1992) (see also Belot and Ederveen, 2012) and a measure based on the Levenshtein linguistic distance approach produced by the Max Planck Institute for Evolutionary Anthropology (see Box 5.4).

Adsera and Pytlikova (2012) reported that their preferred measure of linguistic proximity is a statistically significant determinant of migration flows.[6] This holds in both bivariate and various multivariate models, including those that take account of both the stock of migrants in the destination and the flow of migrants between countries in the previous period, as well as in models that include destination and origin country fixed effects. Moreover, the finding that linguistic proximity is an important determinant of migration flows was robust with respect to the use of the two alternative measures of linguistic proximity (based on Dyen et al. (1992)—see Box 5.3; and the Max Planck Institute for Evolutionary Anthropology—see Box 5.4). It was also robust with respect to the choice of language to use in the construction of the proximity measure (main official language, any official language, and the major language, where major was defined as that which was used most extensively). It was also robust with respect to when the effects are estimated separately for English-speaking countries and for non-English-speaking destination countries. The estimated impacts were, however, stronger for non-English-speaking destination countries. Adsera and Pytlikova (2012, p. 25) argued that "The likely higher proficiency of the average migrant in English rather than in other languages may diminish the relevance of the linguistic proximity indicators to English-speaking destinations." This greater proficiency in English is likely due to English having become the international language of science, technology, and business.

Table 5.1 summarizes the evidence on the links between language background and the choice of destination among immigrants. It shows that language background matters to destination choice, and that stronger empirical results emerge in studies

---

[6] Adsera and Pytlikova (2012) also used measures of the diversity of languages in both the country of origin and the country of destination.

BOX 5.4 The Max Planck Institute for Evolutionary Anthropology Measure of Levenshtein Linguistic Distance

The Max Planck Institute for Evolutionary Anthropology in Germany has used a "lexicostatistical" approach to develop a measure of linguistic distance, or more precisely the Levenshtein distance, using an algorithm that compares pronunciation and vocabulary of language pairs. This procedure is based on the Automatic Similarity Judgment Program (ASJP). The starting point for this approach is a small Swadesh list (see Box 5.3) of 40 words that describes common things and environments. These words are then expressed in a special phonetic transcription known as the ASJP code. This code uses 41 characters on a standard QWERTY keyboard to represent the common sounds in human communication. Then the number of additions or subtractions of characters (or sounds) required to transform a word in one language into the same word in another language is computed, using the ASJP. Isphording and Otten (2012, p. 7) offer the following illustration:

> . . . to transfer the phonetic transcription of the English word you, transcribed as yu, into the transcription of the respective German word du, one simply has to substitute the first consonant. But to transfer manunt3n, which is the transcription of mountain, into bErk, which is the transcription of the German Berg, one has to remove or substitute each eight consonants and vowels, respectively.

This evaluation is then adjusted to account for differences in world length and the potential similarities in phonetic inventories that might lead to similarity by chance to give the Levenshtein distance measure. Larger values thus indicate languages that are further apart. Some examples of this measure of linguistic distance are provided below.

Examples of closest and furthest language pairs with respect of the Levenshtein distance measure

Closest		Furthest	
Language	**Distance**	**Language**	**Distance**
Distance to English			
Afrikaans	62.08	Vietnamese	104.06
Dutch	63.22	Turkmen	103.84
Norwegian	64.12	Hakka (China)	103.10
Distance to Spanish			
Galician	54.82	Wolof (Senegal)	103.02
Italian	56.51	Igbo Onitsha (Nigeria)	102.84
Portuguese	64.21	Ewondo (Cameroon)	101.87

Source: *Extracted from Table 1 in Isphording and Otten (2012).*

This data source has been used in economic research by Isphording and Otten (2011, 2012) and Adsera and Pytlikova (2012).

that use measures of linguistic distance than in studies that employ simple dichotomous variables to reflect a common language between pairs of countries. In other words, it is not just the knowledge of a destination dominant language that matters, but the ease with which an immigrant can learn the destination dominant language is also very important.

Table 5.1 Overview of studies into the links between language background and destination choice of immigrants

Authors	Countries studied and time period	Language variable	Does language matter to destination choice?
Clark et al. (2007)	Flows to the US from 81 source countries, 1971–1998	English dummy	Yes
Karemera et al. (2000)	Flows to US and Canada, 1976–1986	English/English or French dummy	No
Pedersen et al. (2008)	Flows to 22 OECD countries from 129 source countries, 1990–2000	Common language dummy	Yes
Mayda (2010)	Flows to 14 OECD countries from 79 sending countries, 1980–1995	Common language dummy	No
Ortega and Giovanni (2009)	Flows to 14 OECD countries from 73 source countries, 1980–2005	Common language dummy	No
Grogger and Hanson (2011)	Stock of immigrants in 15 high-income OECD countries in 2000	Common language dummy	Yes
Beine et al. (2011)	Change in stocks between 1990 and 2000, for 30 OECD countries, with 195 source countries	Common language dummy	Yes
Belot and Hatton (2012)	Stock of immigrants from 70 source countries in 21 OECD countries, 2000–2001	Based on the Ethnologue (see Box 5.2)	Yes
Belot and Ederveen (2012)	Flow of immigrants to 22 OECD countries, 1990–2003	Based on Dyen et al. (1992) (see Box 5.3)	Yes
Adsera and Pytlikova (2012)	Flows of immigrants to 30 OECD countries from 233 source countries, 1980–2009	Based on the Ethnologue (see Box 5.2), Dyen et al. (1992) (see Box 5.3) and the Levenshtein distance approach (see Box 5.4)	Yes

3.2 Location choice within a country

The seminal study on the location choice of immigrants within a country is Bartel (1989), which used 1980 Census data.[7] This covered the US. The main set of results in this paper

---

[7] There is no difference in the theory of migration between internal and international migration. Institutional factors, such as regulations, may differ.

was from a conditional logit model, estimated separately for Asians, Hispanics, and Europeans. The explanatory variables used in Bartel's (1989) model included characteristics of the areas within which the immigrants lived, such as the unemployment rate, average wage, and the distance of the location from the immigrant's country of origin. The main such variable, however, was the ethnic concentration measure, defined as the percentage of a specific ethnic group that resided in the particular location. The ethnic concentration variable was a highly significant determinant of location choice for each ethnic group, and within each ethnic group, for the three arrival groups considered. This effect tended to be weaker among the more educated immigrants. Using the Census information on place of residence five years ago, Bartel (1989) examined internal migration patterns. Immigrants were reported to be more likely to change locations than the native-born, and much of this movement was associated with an increase in the geographical concentration of the ethnic group. While this pioneering study did not examine the role of language background per se, the apparent links between ethnic concentrations and language backgrounds were developed in subsequent research.[8]

The approach of Bartel (1989) has been developed by Jaeger (2000), among others. Jaeger (2000) used data from the Immigration and Naturalization Service on immigrants admitted to the US during the 1990–1991 fiscal year, combined with data from the 1980 and 1990 censuses. Bartel's (1989) ethnic concentration variable was expanded to consider the immigrant's region of birth, and the share of immigrants who speak a language other than English that is spoken in the immigrant's country of birth. These location characteristics were considered in conjunction with the share of the population in the location that was born abroad. Jaeger (2000, p. 15) reported that "Region-of-birth concentrations are about three times as important in determining location as language and foreign-born shares." This relative importance held for all visa types other than for the small group of diversity visa immigrants. It also carried over to the analysis of the location choice of the foreign-born in the US who received an adjustment of state to become permanent resident aliens. Nevertheless, this research showed that language background matters for the location choice of immigrants within a country.

The research by Bauer et al. (2005) focused on the links between the location choice of immigrants from Mexico in the US and their English language proficiency. Specifically, they ask whether the choice of the size of enclave community in which to settle is affected by English language proficiency. The analyses were based on data from the Mexican Migration Project, which collected information on migrants to the US from their communities of

----

[8] Zavodny (1999) reported that the fraction of the state population that is foreign born was a highly significant determinant of recent immigrants' location choice for all admission categories considered in her study (family, employment, Immigration Reform and Control Act of 1986 (IRCA) conversions to legal status, and refugee/asylee conversions to legal status), and for all country groups examined (Chinese, Dominican Republic, Mexico, Philippines, Vietnam).

origin in Mexico. The main variables of interest in this study are the proportion of the total population in a particular US location that was from Mexico, and the English-speaking proficiency of the immigrants (can speak and understand English; can understand but not speak English; can neither speak nor understand English). The authors report that ethnic enclave effects are strongest among those who can neither speak nor understand English, and are weakest among those who can both speak and understand English. These results were broadly the same for both first-time movers and for repeat movers. Chiswick and Miller (2005b) showed that residence in an enclave community reduces an immigrant's own destination language proficiency. Combining these results, Bauer et al. (2005, p. 660) concluded ". . . enclaves are a potential source for a 'language trap'; they attract poor proficiency English speakers and sustain their poor abilities." The findings of Bauer et al. (2005) were robust with respect to alternative definitions of an ethnic enclave.

Turning to the Canadian literature, which is of interest due to the language divide between Quebec and the rest of Canada, there are several relevant studies. Hou (2005) contains a detailed analysis of Census of Canada data over the period 1981–2001. The tabulations in this study revealed that as many as 90% of immigrants from Haiti, where French is an official language and Haitian creole is close to French, settle in Montreal. The disproportionate representation (only about 11% of all immigrants in Canada live in Montreal) was maintained when the location of immigrants was examined after 11–15 years of residence in Canada.

McDonald (2003, 2004) used data from the Statistics Canada Censuses for 1986, 1991, and 1996 to estimate conditional logit models of the initial location decision of immigrants in Canada. He estimated models with an aggregate-level ethnic concentration measure, and with measures based on the age, educational attainment, and official language skills of the immigrant population. The impacts of these ethnic concentration measures were allowed to vary between those who usually spoke English or French at home and those who did not. It was shown that immigrants who usually spoke a language other than English or French at home were more likely to settle in a linguistic enclave community than those who spoke English or French at home. The ethnic enclave variable (based on those who speak neither of the official languages at home) was also a statistically significant determinant of initial location choice. The effect of this enclave influence also differed between those who usually spoke English or French at home and those who did not. Hence, both the relative concentration of immigrants from the same ethnic group, as well as the characteristics of these ethnic enclaves, affect the location decisions of recent immigrants. The importance of language background was made clear in the simulation that McDonald (2004) presented for immigrants from the non-Arab countries of Africa. Where the immigrants spoke English at home, the distribution across regions was heavily concentrated in English-Canada. But where the immigrants spoke French at home the distribution across regions was heavily concentrated in Montreal and the rest of Quebec.

Table 5.2 Overview of studies into the links between language background and choice of location within a country

Authors	Country studied and time period	Language variable	Does language matter to location choice?
Jaeger (2000)	US, Immigration and Naturalization Service on immigrants admitted during 1990–1991	Origin language concentration	Yes, for almost all visa types
Bauer et al. (2005)	US, Mexican Migration Project, annual data collection that commenced in 1987	Immigrants from Mexico concentration	Yes, for first-time movers and repeat movers
Hou (2005)	Canada, Census of Canada, 1981–2001	Distribution of immigrants by origin countries which differ in language background	Yes
McDonald (2003, 2004)	Canada, Census of Canada, 1986–1996	Ethnic concentration, with focus on official language skills	Yes

Thus, although the literature on the importance of language background to immigrants' location decisions within a country is sparser than that relating to the choice of destination country, the evidence suggests that language skills matter to the way migrants distribute themselves across regions within a country. This evidence is summarized in Table 5.2.

4. DETERMINANTS OF LANGUAGE PROFICIENCY

Research on the determinants of dominant language proficiency among immigrants from a different linguistic background than the destination has focused on three concepts represented by the three "Es": Exposure to the host country language, Efficiency in learning a new language, and Economic incentives for learning the new language (Chiswick, 1991; Chiswick and Miller, 1995, 2007a). These are conceptual variables, but empirical research requires finding measurable dimensions. Here we review the empirical literature on dominant language proficiency among immigrants using this three "Es" framework. From humble beginnings in the 1980s, this empirical literature has grown enormously. Thus, given the volume of studies, the review that follows is illustrative rather than exhaustive.

An important methodological matter that needs clarification is the measure for the language variable. Two broad measures have been used in the literature. The first is dominant language usage, typically termed "language shift" from origin language to destination dominant language. For example, see Veltman (1983), Grenier (1984), and McAllister (1986). An alternative terminology is "mother tongue retention" (Chiswick and Miller, 2008b). Dominant language usage in preference to the language of the country of origin is generally viewed as a measure of cultural assimilation. The second measure is dominant language proficiency—that is, how well the person can speak (or, in some studies, understand, write or read) the main language of the destination country. This is the human capital skill that researchers focus on when studying labor market outcomes. Dominant language proficiency is focused on in this review, although several key findings from studies of dominant language use are mentioned.

4.1 Exposure

Much of destination language learning among immigrants comes from exposure to the destination language. Exposure can be thought of as having two dimensions—that is, exposure in the origin and exposure after migration.

The datasets used to study the determinants of immigrant's destination language skills generally indicate the country of origin, but provide no direct information on pre-immigration language learning.[9] When conducting research on English-speaking destinations for immigrants from non-English-speaking origins, a proxy measure for pre-migration exposure to English is whether the origin was a former colony or dependency of either the UK or the US. Immigrants in the UK or the US from former colonies (e.g., Nigeria, India, or the Philippines) are found to be more proficient in English than are immigrants from other (non-English-speaking) countries that were not dependencies of the UK or the US (e.g., Thailand or Algeria), other variables being the same (Chiswick and Miller, 2001, 2007a). Similarly, immigrants in Spain from former colonies were reported by Isphording and Otten (2012) to be more proficient in Spanish than immigrants from other countries.

Another way of capturing pre-immigration exposure is to categorize countries according to whether the dominant language of the destination country is an official language or the dominant language of the country of origin, using sources such as the *Ethnologue: Languages of the World* (see Box 5.2). Espenshade and Fu (1997), for example, reported that the language spoken in the country of origin is an important determinant of English language skills among non-native English-speaking immigrants in the US. In analyses based on a binational source of data on Mexico–US migrants, Espinosa and Massey (1997) reported that the English proficiency is higher among migrants from communities (in Mexico) with greater proportions of adult men with US migrant experience,

---

[9] In analysis of the determinants of German language skills among immigrants in Germany with Italian, Spanish, Yugoslavian, Turkish, or Greek nationality, Dustmann (1994) assumed that knowledge of the German language was non-existent at the time of migration.

a variable which is argued to capture the "degree of contact with US culture within the respondent's community" (Espinosa and Massey, 1997, p. 37).

Thus, both the broad indicators provided by country of origin groupings, and the detailed information on origin country exposure where available, present a consistent set of evidence that pre-immigration exposure matters. Pre-immigration exposure has also been found to be an important determinant of proficiency in the dominant language of the destination country in the few studies that have been able to include direct measures. Raijman (2013), for example, studied the proficiency in Hebrew among Jewish South African immigrants in Israel, and reported that the level of Hebrew proficiency before arrival (typically acquired through attendance at Jewish schools and participation in synagogue activities and youth movements) was a highly significant and quantitatively important determinant of post-arrival proficiency.

The most important aspect of exposure to the destination language occurs after migration. Exposure in the destination can be decomposed into time units of exposure and the intensity of exposure per unit of time. Most data that identify the foreign-born members of the population ask the respondents when they came to the destination. From this, a variable for duration or "years since migration" can be computed. Duration has a very large positive and a highly statistically significant impact on destination language proficiency, but the effect is not linear. Rather, proficiency increases rapidly in the early years, but it increases at a decreasing rate; hence after a period of time a longer duration in the destination has a much smaller positive impact (Chiswick and Miller, 2001, 2007a, 2008b; Espenshade and Fu, 1997; Isphording and Otten, 2011, 2012). Grenier (1984) reported a similar pattern in his study of shifts from Spanish to English as the usual language among Hispanics in the US.

This time pattern for destination language proficiency is likely to be due to incentives for investment in language skills. For the following three reasons, an immigrant has the incentive to make greater investments shortly after arrival rather than delaying investments: to take advantage sooner of the benefits of increased proficiency, to make the investments when the value of the immigrants' time (destination wage rate) is lower, and to have a longer expected future duration in the destination.

Duration may affect language proficiency because a longer actual duration increases the amount of exposure to and practice using the destination language. It is found that interrupted stays—that is, when immigrants move back and forth (sojourners)—reduce their language proficiency (Chiswick and Miller, 2001, 2007a, 2008b; Isphording and Otten, 2012). The expectation of an interrupted stay reduces the incentive to invest, implicitly if not explicitly, in language learning, and the destination language skills tend to depreciate during long periods of absence from the destination.

Moreover, those in the destination who report that they expect to return to their origin are also less proficient, other variables being the same (Chiswick and Miller, 2006). This might arise from negative selectivity in return migration, that those having a more difficult adjustment to the new country are more inclined to leave to return to the origin or to go to a third country. Or it might reflect the reduced incentive to invest in destination language skills if the expected future duration (i.e., the payoff period) is short.[10]

Espinosa and Massey (1997) were able to include very detailed information on individuals' migration history in their study of Mexico–US migrants. Included are variables for the period of first entry, the period of last entry, the total time the individual had spent in the US since the first entry, the proportion of time spent in the US since the first entry, the average number of trips taken per year between the first and most recent visits, and the duration of the most recent trip. They report that English language skills increase with each of the latter four variables.

The intensity of exposure per unit of time in the destination is usually more difficult to measure. A few studies have included information on whether immigrants enrolled in formal classes of instruction in the destination language. Raijman (2013), for instance, related Hebrew proficiency of South African immigrants in Israel to whether they studied Hebrew in Israel for more than six months (i.e., through attending an uplan, which is an institute or school designed to teach adult immigrants basic Hebrew skills via an intensive course of instruction). Immigrants in this situation had higher levels of Hebrew proficiency than immigrants who studied for shorter periods or who did not enroll in a formal program of instruction in Hebrew. More often in the research, however, the focus is on the environment in which one lives, comprising both the area and the family. In terms of the area, it is useful to have a proxy measure of the ability to avoid using the destination language. Various measures have been used in the different studies, though the construct used most often is a "minority language concentration" measure. This is typically constructed as the percentage of the population, including the native-born and the foreign-born, in the area (defined by the state/province, region or metropolitan area) where the respondent lives, who speak the same non-destination language as the respondent. For example, the concentration measure for an Italian speaker living in Chicago would be the proportion of the population of Chicago who speak Italian. In other instances, newspapers (Australia) or radio broadcasting (US) in the language of origin have been used either as a substitute for, or in addition to, the minority language concentration measure.[11] The effects on language proficiency of these area-based minority language concentration measures are quite strong. Destination language proficiency is significantly lower among individuals who have greater ease in avoiding

---

[10] Selective emigration could be associated with biased cross-sectional estimates of the coefficients in the models of dominant language proficiency. Espinosa and Massey (1997), however, on the basis of analysis of data on Mexico–US migrants collected in both Mexico and the US, conclude (p. 44) "Our analysis reaffirms most of the findings established by prior studies of linguistic assimilation, lending some confidence to the belief that they are not simply artefacts of sample selection or omitted variable bias."

[11] To mitigate the problem of endogeneity, the instrumental variables technique was used to obtain predicted values for the newspapers and broadcasts (Chiswick and Miller, 1995).

using the destination language by living in a linguistic enclave area (Chiswick, 1998; Chiswick and Miller, 2007a, 2008b; Espenshade and Fu, 1997; Isphording and Otten, 2012; Lazear, 1999; Warman, 2007). Similarly, destination language use is less likely in areas with a geographical environment that favors interactions in the origin country language (Grenier, 1984). Where direct measures of social contact have been available (McAllister, 1986), such as the presence of "close friends from the country of origin", the finding that such contacts reduce dominant language proficiency reinforces those based on the more general characteristics of the area of residence. Similarly, Espinosa and Massey (1997) report that English proficiency is higher among immigrants from Mexico in the US who have more extensive contacts with members of US racial and ethnic groups.

A key role in language learning is played by the family or household in the destination in which the immigrant lives. Both the spouse, if married, and the children matter. Those who married their current spouse before immigrating are likely to be married to someone with the same language background. They are more likely to speak that language to each other at home, thereby limiting opportunities for practicing the destination language at home.[12] On the other hand, those who marry after immigration are more likely to marry someone proficient in the destination language, perhaps because of their own proficiency, and are more likely to practice the destination language. Where the data permit a study of this issue, it is found that, other measured variables being the same, the most proficient are those who married after migration, followed by those who are not married, with those who married their current spouse before migration being the least proficient (Chiswick and Miller, 2005b, 2007a, 2008b; Chiswick et al., 2005a, b; Dustmann, 1994). Grenier (1984) reported that, compared to the non-married, English language use at home was more likely among married Hispanics whose spouse was non-Hispanic, and less likely among Hispanics who were married to a Hispanic. The more direct evidence reported by Dustmann (1994) adds to this: based on analysis of immigrants in Germany, he reported that proficiency in German was higher where the partner has good German-speaking skills. Similarly, Espenshade and Fu (1997) showed that English skills are lowest where the spouse is from the same non-English language dominant country, and highest when the spouse is from any English language dominant country.

Children can have offsetting effects on their parents' proficiency (Chiswick, 1998; Chiswick and Miller, 2007a, 2008b; Chiswick et al., 2005a, b). For example, children can serve wittingly, or unwittingly, as "teachers". Whether they themselves are immigrants or not, children learn the destination language quickly because of their youth and because of their exposure to the destination language in school. They can, therefore, bring it home to their parents.

---

[12] Akresh (2007) reported that, among those immigrants for whom English was not a native language, English was most likely to be used at work and least likely to be used with one's spouse.

Yet, the presence of children can also have negative effects on their parents' proficiency. Parents may speak the language of the origin at home to transmit the origin culture to their children, in part so that their children are able to communicate with the grandparents and other relatives who did not migrate or who migrated but lack proficiency in the destination language. Children may also serve as translators for immigrant parents. The translator role may be more effective in consumption activities and in dealings with the government bureaucracy and the educational and health care systems than in the workplace. Finally, children tend to reduce the labor supply of their mothers who stay at home to provide childcare. To the extent that adults invest in improving their language skills in anticipation of labor market activities, and benefit from doing so, and to the extent that practice using the destination language at work enhances proficiency, children would tend to be associated with lower proficiency among their mothers.

Taken as a whole, the four hypotheses regarding children suggest an ambiguous effect on their parents' proficiency, but due to the latter two, their effect would be less positive or more negative for their mothers than their fathers. Empirically, this is in fact what is found. Where there is no clear effect of children on their father's proficiency, in the same data, it is less positive or more negative for their mothers (Chiswick and Miller, 2007a; Chiswick and Repetto, 2001; Chiswick, et al., 2005a, b; Grenier, 1984). Where there is a positive, albeit small, effect of children on their father's proficiency, the effect for mothers is statistically insignificant (Dustmann, 1994).

There is language learning in the home. Research has shown that the proficiency of one family member is positively associated with that of other family members (Chiswick et al., 2005b). The children's proficiency is more highly correlated with that of their mothers than with that of their fathers. This makes sense since mothers are generally more directly involved in the raising of their children than are the fathers. Similarly, Espinosa and Massey (1997) reported that the English proficiency of migrants from Mexico in the US was higher where they had siblings who were US migrants, and where they had children in US schools.

As a result, particularly due to a weaker attachment to the labor force, immigrant women with children have a lower level of destination language proficiency than do men and than do women without children (Chiswick et al., 2005a, b; Stevens, 1986).

4.2 Efficiency

The second "E", efficiency, refers to the ability to convert exposure into language learning. Age at migration is an important efficiency variable. Because of the greater plasticity of the brain, which decreases with age, language learning decreases significantly with a greater age at migration (Long, 1990). There is a debate in the linguistics literature regarding the "critical period hypothesis", whether there is an age beyond which an immigrant's learning a second language—that is, the destination language—becomes much more difficult. The chart in Figure 5.1, based on data on self-reported speaking proficiency at home from the US 2000 Census of Population for foreign-born males and females, shows the negative relation between proficiency and age at migration. Note that the path for this measure of proficiency is remarkably similar for men and women, a pattern that has also been reported by Dustmann (1994).

The Figure 5.1 data do not suggest any particular critical age at migration for speaking proficiency (Chiswick and Miller, 2008a). This does not rule out a critical period for other dimensions of proficiency, such as retaining an accent. This chart does, however, convey a main finding from the empirical research on the dominant language skills among immigrants, that age at migration is an important determinant (Chiswick and Miller, 2008a; Espenshade and Fu, 1997; Grenier, 1984; Isphording and Otten, 2012).

Education is considered to be another efficiency variable. Other variables being the same, empirically immigrants with more schooling are more proficient in the destination language. This could arise because those with higher levels of schooling are more efficient learners, either inherently (higher ability people get more schooling) or because they acquire learning skills in school. To some extent, this effect for immigrants in the US, Canada, and Australia might be due to being exposed to English as the future immigrants advance up the educational system in the origin (Chiswick and Miller, 1995, 2007a, 2008b; Espenshade and Fu, 1997). It should be noted, however, that this is not likely to be a dominant factor since there is a similar relationship between schooling and Hebrew language skills among immigrants in Israel and most immigrants to Israel arrive without proficiency in Hebrew (Chiswick, 1998; Chiswick and Repetto, 2001). Similarly, Dustmann's (1994) study of immigrants in Germany, where it was noted that German was not the first foreign language learned at school in the origin countries, shows that years of schooling was a significant determinant of German-speaking skills. Isphording and Otten's (2011, 2012)

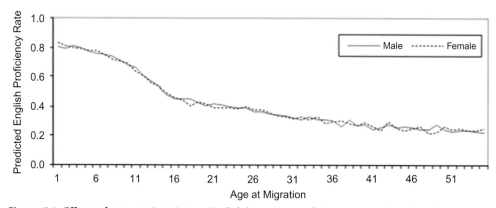

Figure 5.1 *Effects of age at migration on English language proficiency among immigrants from non-English speaking countries, by gender (United States, 2000).* Source: US Census of Population, 2000, Census Public Use Microdata Sample—Sample of the Population.

analyses for Germany also exhibit a strong influence of years of schooling on dominant language proficiency. Notably, where attempts are made to distinguish years of schooling undertaken in the country of origin, and years of schooling undertaken after arrival in the destination country, the latter variable has been shown to have the more important impact on destination language skills (see Evans (1986) for Australia, Espenshade and Fu (1997) and McManus et al. (1983) for the US, and Dustmann (1994) for Germany).

The efficiency with which an immigrant can learn the dominant language of the destination country could also vary with their origin country language skills. Dustmann (1994) and Isphording and Otten (2011) both reported that, in Germany, immigrants with very good ability in writing the home country language were more likely to be fluent in German, whereas those who were classified as illiterate in the home country language were less likely to be fluent in German.

Some languages share many similarities with English (e.g., Dutch), while others are very different (e.g., Korean) and hence make it more difficult to learn English. Language trees have been used by linguists to map out the evolution or historic relations among languages (Crystal, 1987; Lewis, 2009). But what is needed for a statistical analysis of the determinants of the effect of "linguistic distance" on English language proficiency is a quantitative measure of the difficulties that non-English speakers have in learning English.[13] One such measure has been developed and tested using an index of the difficulty that Americans have learning other languages and the assumption of symmetry (i.e., if the Americans have difficulty learning Korean, then the Korean speakers would have difficulty learning English) (Chiswick and Miller, 2005a)—see Box 5.5. This measure of linguistic distance has been shown to be important for understanding the English language proficiency of immigrants in the US, Canada, and Australia (Chiswick and Miller, 2005a). In principle, the methodology could be applied to develop measures of linguistic distance from other languages.

Recently, Isphording and Otten (2011, 2012) have proposed the use of a measure derived using a Levenshtein distance approach (see Box 5.4). They noted that, compared to the measure of Chiswick and Miller (2005a), which has been developed for only one destination country language, English, the Levenshtein distance measure can be readily computed as a continuous variable for any pair of host and home country languages, and does not rely on a symmetry assumption.[14] These authors have applied this measure of linguistic distance in analyses of the dominant language acquisition of immigrants in the US, Germany, and Spain. The results indicate a strong, significantly negative, effect of

---

[13] See McCloskey (1998, pp. 104–106) for an interesting perspective. The heading of McCloskey's discussion is "In Like Fashion, Rhetorical Standards Are Necessary in Linguistics to Measure the Similarity of Languages".

[14] Isphording and Otten (2012) argued that the linguistic distance measure of Chiswick and Miller (2005a) could be biased by incentives for learning a foreign language, while the measure based on Levenshtein distance should be devoid of any such bias.

BOX 5.5 The Chiswick and Miller Measure of Linguistic Distance

Chiswick and Miller (2005a) construct a scalar measure of the distance between English and a myriad of other (non-native American) languages. It is computed using a set of language scores, reported by Hart-Gonzalez and Lindermann (1993), which measure the achievements in speaking proficiency by English-speaking Americans at the US Department of State, School of Language Studies. Specifically, Hart-Gonzalez and Lindermann (1993) report the level of proficiency in a language, using the average exam score after 24 weeks of lessons. These measures are an index of the difficulty native English speakers have learning the language. It is assumed that there is linguistic symmetry: The more distant a language is from English, the more difficult it is for speakers of that language to learn English. These scores range from 1.00 (hardest to learn) to 3.00 (easiest to learn). Examples are provided below.

Linguistic score	Illustrative languages
1.0	Korean, Japanese
1.5	Vietnamese, Arabic
2.0	Polish, Indonesian
2.5	Portuguese, Italian
3.0	Norwegian, Swedish

This linguistic distance score has been criticized by Isphording and Otten (2012, p. 6) because "It has to be assumed that the difficulty of US citizens to learn a particular foreign language is symmetric to the difficulty of foreigners to learn English. Further, it has to be assumed that the average test score is not influenced by other language-specific sources."

This measure of linguistic distance has been applied in analyses of earnings and English fluency by Chiswick and Miller (2005a) and Isphording and Otten (2102), and in analyses of the determinants of bilateral trade by Hutchinson (2005).

Source: Chiswick, B.R., Miller, P.W., 2005. Linguistic distance: A quantitative measure of the distance between English and other languages. Journal of Multilingual and Multicultural Development 26 (1), 1–16.

linguistic distance on immigrant language skills. For the analyses undertaken for the US, the authors also compared the findings obtained using the Levenshtein distance measure with the test–score–based measure of linguistic distance of Chiswick and Miller (2005a). It is shown that these two linguistic measures render qualitatively comparable outcomes.

Another efficiency variable is the motive for migrating. Three broad categories can be distinguished: employment migrants, refugees, and family migrants. The employment migrants are most favorably selected for labor market success in the destination since this is their primary motivation. The refugees, on the other hand, include many who would not have moved except for the political, ethnic, or religious problems they confronted in their origin. As a result, they tend to have the lowest degree of selectivity for success in the destination, and would be expected to have the least transferability of their skills (Chiswick and Miller, 2007a, 2008b). Lawyers and judges, for example, are very rare among employment-motivated migrants because their skills are not readily transferable across countries, but they are not uncommon among refugees. Family migrants fall in between employment migrants and refugees as they are attracted by economic opportunities in the destination as well as family ties, but are not responding to the same forces as refugees.

In some data, the motive for migration or the visa used to gain entry can be identified. When this has been possible, it is found that the employment-motivated immigrants have the highest level of destination language proficiency, followed by the family-based immigrants, with the refugees showing the lowest proficiency (Chiswick and Miller, 2006, 2007a). Espinosa and Massey (1997) examined the independent effect of legal US residence in their study of immigrants from Mexico in the US. They reported (Espinosa and Massey, 1997, p. 44) that "Migrants who lack documents actually spoke and understood significantly more English at the time of their most recent trip than did those who already had received legal US residence." This finding is counter-intuitive, and it is possible that it is attributable to the porous nature of the Mexico–US border.

Immigration policy can also affect the destination language proficiency of immigrants. Some countries (e.g., Canada and Australia) give explicit preference to applicants for immigration who can demonstrate proficiency in the destination language. When Australia increased the language proficiency requirements for employment-based independent immigrant visas, but not for other visas, the English language proficiency of the skills-tested migrants increased, with no significant change for the other groups (Chiswick and Miller, 2006).

4.3 Economic incentives

The economic incentives for acquiring destination language proficiency also play an important role. The returns to becoming proficient are greater when the expected duration in the destination is longer, whether as a worker or as a consumer. Various proxy measures of the expected future length of stay in the destination have been employed, depending on the data available. These include self-reported expectations of the duration of stay (Australia, Germany), re-migration rates of immigrants from the respondent's country of origin (US and Israel), and the distance from the origin (US, Australia, and Canada), since return migration propensities decline with distance. Regardless of the measure, the longer the expected duration of stay, the greater is the investment in destination language proficiency (Chiswick and Miller, 2006, 2007a, b, 2008b; Dustmann, 1999; Isphording and Otten, 2011).

The most problematic aspect of the research on the determinants of destination language skills is estimating the impact on proficiency of the expected increase in earnings from becoming more proficient—that is, using the individual's expected increase in earnings as an explanatory variable. Data are not available for this on an individual basis. Those with higher levels of skills, for example professionals as distinct from laborers, tend to gain relatively more in earnings from proficiency (Chiswick and Miller, 2003, 2007a). If so, the education variable would reflect some of this effect. Dustmann (1994) addressed the incentive to learn issue through the inclusion of a variable for whether the immigrant had ever worked in an analysis of German-speaking fluency estimated for females. This variable had a sizeable effect, which Dustmann (1994, p. 141) argued could "... indicate that those who do not intend to ever participate in the labor market have lower incentives to learn the German language."

The findings reported here for the determinants of destination language proficiency among immigrants are remarkably robust across types of data (census or survey, cross-sectional or longitudinal), countries of destination (US, Canada, Australia, Germany, and Israel), and countries of origin (Chiswick and Miller, 2007a).[15] Findings in relation to writing skills are, however, distinguished from those for speaking skills by the fact that variables that represent contacts with the host country population are not statistically significant (see Dustmann, 1994).

The evidence reviewed above is important in terms of showing that the patterns in most datasets analyzed are highly consistent with the three "Es" model of the development of destination country dominant language skills among immigrants. Table 5.3 provides an overview of the empirical support for the model.

The evidence in Table 5.3 is important for the development of policy on immigrant selection and settlement. This will be discussed in Section 6. But it is also important in terms of enhancing the understanding of many real-world phenomena. Consider, for example, the very low level of English language proficiency among Mexican immigrants in the US. The Mexican immigrants:

1. have a very low level of schooling (an average of about eight years for adult men);
2. have a high propensity to be sojourners, with substantial to and fro migration and often a short expected duration of stay;
3. have low costs of migration because they come from an origin adjacent to the US;
4. are relatively recent immigrants as compared to the Europeans immigrants;
5. tend to live in large Hispanic enclaves where they can live and even work in a Spanish language environment; and
6. finally, are not skill tested for an immigration visa as they tend to be in the US under a visa for family reunification, under a formal or an informal amnesty for former undocumented migrants, or are in an illegal or unauthorized status.

These characteristics of immigrants from Mexico are all associated with lower destination language proficiency among immigrants in general.

---

[15] Charette and Meng (1994) reported that the findings for the determination of language proficiency may not be robust to whether a self-assessed or objective measure is used. This issue has not attracted much attention, most likely because it does not appear to be empirically relevant in research into labor market outcomes (Charette and Meng, 1994). Chiswick et al. (2003), however, argued that both sets of measures contain useful information.

Table 5.3 Overview of empirical support for the three "Es" model of destination language proficiency

Concept, empirical counterparts and expected sign	Selected studies reporting supportive evidence
A. Exposure (+)	
A.1 Pre-immigration exposure	
• Former colony or dependency (+) • Official language/dominant language status of origin country (+)	Chiswick and Miller (2001, 2007a), Isphording and Otten (2012) Espenshade and Fu (1997)
• Pre-immigration contact with dominant language culture (+)	Espinosa and Massey (1997)
A.2. Post-immigration exposure (+)	
A.2.a. Time units of exposure (+)	
• Duration of residence in destination country (+)	Chiswick and Miller (2001, 2007a), Espenshade and Fu (1997), Isphording and Otten (2011, 2012)
• Interrupted stay (−)	Chiswick and Miller (2001, 2007a, 2008b), Isphording and Otten (2012)
A.2.b. Intensity of exposure (+)	
• Minority language concentration (−)	Chiswick and Miller (2001, 2007a), Espenshade and Fu (1997), Lazear (1999), Isphording and Otten (2012)
• Direct measures of contact with members of the destination (+) or origin countries (−)	McAllister (1986), Espenshade and Fu (1997)
• Children (?)	Chiswick and Repetto (2001), Dustmann (1994)
B. Efficiency (+)	
• Age at migration (−)	Chiswick and Miller (1995, 2007a), Espenshade and Fu (1997), Grenier (1984), Isphording and Otten (2011, 2012)
• Education (+)	Chiswick and Miller (1995, 2007a), Dustmann (1994), Espenshade and Fu (1997), Isphording and Otten (2011, 2012)
• Origin country language skills (+) • Linguistic distance (−) • Economic motive for migration (+)	Dustmann (1994), Isphording and Otten (2011) Chiswick and Miller (2005a), Isphording and Otten (2011, 2012) Chiswick and Miller (2007a, 2008b)
C. Economic incentives (+)	
• Expected duration of stay (+) • Expected gain in earnings (+)	Chiswick and Miller (2006, 2008b), Isphording and Otten (2011) Dustmann (1994)

5. EFFECTS OF LANGUAGE ON EARNINGS

The analyses of the consequences for immigrants of destination language proficiency have focused on labor market earnings (Carliner, 1981; Chiswick, 1991, 1998; Chiswick and Miller, 2001, 2005b, 2007a; Dustmann, 1994; Dustmann and van Soest, 2001; Grenier, 1987; Kossoudji, 1988; McManus et al., 1983; Tainer, 1988).[16] This focus has arisen for two reasons. One is the interest in earnings per se, as it is a key determinant of economic status and poverty. The other is the general availability of data on earnings in censuses and surveys that include information on immigrants' destination language proficiency, but not for many other outcome measures.[17]

5.1 Background considerations

The analyses of earnings are generally performed primarily for adult (but non-aged) men because of the technical difficulties in estimating earnings equations for groups, such as women and aged men, who have relatively low labor force participation rates. The equations are usually estimated using the "human capital earnings function", where the natural logarithm of earnings is regressed on a set of explanatory variables, typically including years of schooling, years of labor market experience (and its square), and variables for marital status and racial/ethnic origin. In analyses for the study of the impact of immigrant language proficiency, additional variables include duration in the destination, destination language proficiency and, sometimes, residence in a linguistic concentration (enclave) area (Chiswick and Miller, 1995, 2005b).

Various destination language proficiency variables have been considered for inclusion in such a specification. These usually follow the way the data are collected in the majority of the datasets that are useful for study of labor market outcomes. The standard "census" type question used in the US and Australia is outlined in Box 5.6.

Based on Box 5.6, it is apparent that self-reported English proficiency could be categorized using a five-interval scale. It is assumed that the highest level of proficiency on this scale would be 5 = Speaks only English at home, although there is no information on the proficiency of those who speak only English at home. All other levels relate to

---

[16] While it would be desirable to have data on the language used in the immigrant's workplace, these data are generally not available. Moreover, immigrants may choose (or be chosen for) jobs that match their language skills, rather than the workplace causing language proficiency. One exception is the 2001 and 2006 Census of Canada datasets. These contain information on: (i) knowledge of the official languages (English and French) of Canada; (ii) other languages spoken; (iii) the language spoken most often at home; (iii) mother tongue (the language first learned at home in childhood that is still understood); (iv) the language used most often in the worker's job, as well as any other language used on a regular basis in the job. See Christofides and Swidinsky (2010) for an analysis of the links between language use and earnings among the native-born in Canada based on these data obtained from the 2001 Census.

[17] For an analysis of the effects of dominant language proficiency (in this case Spanish) on the earnings of indigenous people in Bolivia, see Chiswick et al. (2000).

individuals who speak a language other than English at home, and self-report speaking English: 4 = Very well; 3 = Well; 2 = Not well; 1 = Not at all. Evans (1987), who converted the categorical information to a "continuous" measure, proposes the score: 0 = Speaks no English at all; 33 = Speaks English "not well"; 67 = Speaks English "well"; 100 = Speaks English "very well" or speaks only English at home. This is based on Evans's findings that the effects of English proficiency variables on occupational attainment were approximately linear, with little difference in earnings between the "English only" and the "English very well" speakers. The combining of the two most fluent categories has support in the literature—see, for example, Kominski (1989), Espenshade and Fu (1997), and Bleakley and Chin (2004). Thus, Espenshade and Fu (1997, p. 293) argued that "… there is not much difference in English proficiency between immigrants who use a language other than English at home but who say they speak English 'Very Well' and those who use only English at home."

It can also be argued that as the information on dominant language skills is self-reported, and hence possibly subject to reporting errors, the categories specified in the census questionnaire should be further grouped. Hence, in many analyses a dichotomous variable for dominant language proficiency is defined, where, for example, workers who speak English only, or if a language other than English is spoken at home report speaking English "very well" or "well", are distinguished from other workers, with the first group being viewed as proficient in English and the latter group ("not well" and "not at all") viewed as being deficient. Within this framework, some researchers move the group who speak only "well" into the deficient category.

There is a difficult methodological consideration in the estimation of the dominant language-augmented human capital earnings equation outlined above. As discussed in Section 4, one of the influences on dominant language proficiency is the increases in

---

BOX 5.6 Typical Census Language Questions

11.**a** Does this person speak a language other than English at home?

   □ Yes

   □ No → *Skip to 12*

   b What is this language?

   (For example: Korean, Italian, Spanish, Vietnamese)

   c How well does this person speak English?

   □ Very well

   □ Well

   □ Not well

   □ Not at all

Source: *US Department of Commerce, Bureau of the Census, Census 2000 Long Form Questionnaire.*

earnings expected to be associated with improvement in language skills. In other words, in the study of earnings, earnings are held to depend on the immigrant's proficiency in the dominant language. Yet proficiency itself is determined (in part) by the expected earnings payoff from becoming more proficient. Thus, earnings and proficiency are jointly determined.

Related to this, Dustmann and van Soest (2001) drew attention to the potential role of unobserved heterogeneity, where a factor that is important to both the development of dominant language skills and earnings determination is not observed by the researcher. The classic example is ability. This unobserved heterogeneity could be associated with either upward or downward bias in the OLS estimate of the effect of language skills on earnings (Dustmann and van Soest, 2001).

A further problem that has consequences for the correlation of the language variable and the error term in the earnings equation is the possibility that the self-reported language proficiency data suffer from misclassification errors, a factor that has motivated the use of binary indicators of dominant language proficiency in preference to the use of the more detailed information that is often available. The use of dichotomous indicators of proficiency may reduce the gravity of the errors in variables problem, but it will not eliminate it entirely. The misclassification errors that arise with self-reported language data could be either purely random or they could persist over time. Time persistent errors will arise where each individual has an inherent tendency to consistently over-report or under-report their language ability.[18] Random misclassification errors will be associated with a bias toward zero in the estimated impact of language proficiency on earnings. Empirically, unobserved heterogeneity was shown by Dustmann and van Soest (2001) to be associated with an upward bias, which was approximately offset by the negative bias due to misclassification errors. General measurement errors, which were modeled through examination of the correlation of the disturbance terms in the language proficiency and earnings models, were associated with a pronounced negative bias. Dustmann and van Soest's (2001) research suggested that the OLS estimates should thus be considered as lower bounds of the true effects of language skills on earnings.

This finding from the detailed study by Dustmann and van Soest (2001) has been echoed by various studies that adopted a conventional instrumental variables approach to the endogeneity problem. Under this approach a predicted language proficiency variable, rather than the observed proficiency, is entered into the earnings equation. When the dominant language-augmented human capital earnings equation has been estimated using an instrumental variables (IV) approach, the coefficient on the instrumented language variable is extremely large, far too large to be believed (see Box 5.7). This

---

[18] Berman et al. (2003) noted that the relative importance of time persistent errors means that the language variable in their differenced model may have a lower noise-to-signal ratio than the standard language variable in a cross-sectional equation: in their study for Israel, these authors collected at the same time the information on current Hebrew proficiency and proficiency at the commencement of the current job.

econometric problem arises when the instrumented (predicted) variable is dichotomous and the residuals in the auxiliary equation and the main equation are positively correlated because some of the same omitted variables (for example, ability or childhood home environment) are in both equations. The problem of disentangling the endogeneity of earnings and language proficiency has not been resolved (Chiswick and Miller, 1995; Dustmann and van Soest, 2001).

With these considerations in mind, we turn to the empirical evidence. The volume of research precludes an exhaustive review. Rather, we travel the globe, examining a selection of studies from different destination and origin countries (and languages) as well as different time periods, along with different measures of language proficiency. Despite these differences, there seems to be a striking common finding in the mainstream studies: dominant language proficiency among immigrants is rewarded rather handsomely around the globe.

BOX 5.7 Results Using Instrumental Variables

A number of researchers have attempted to accommodate the endogeneity between earnings and destination language proficiency using an instrumental variables (IV) approach. Shields and Wheatley Price (2002, p. 158) offer a concise summary of the results, which we repeat here. Please refer to the original for the relevant references.

Chiswick and Miller (1992), for example, found an increase in the partial effect of language fluency on earnings (t-ratios in parentheses) from 0.169 (12.52, OLS) to 0.571 (5.43, IV) using 1980 United States data and veteran status, foreign marriage, children and minority language concentration measures as identifying instruments. They also noted a change from 0.122 (2.43, OLS) to 0.414 (1.34, IV) amongst immigrants in 1981 Canadian data with foreign marriage and minority language concentration measures as identifying instruments. In Australia the results changed from 0.052 (2.52, OLS) in 1981 and 0.083 (4.75, OLS) in 1986 to −0.243 (1.20, IV) and 0.043 (0.52, IV) respectively, with foreign marriage, number and age of children, and minority language concentration as identifying instruments. Chiswick (1998) found an increase from 0.111 (12.66, OLS) to 0.351 (4.25, IV) using 1983 data from Israel using Tel Aviv, Jerusalem, foreign marriage, number of children, and minority language concentration measures as identifying instruments. Finally, Dustmann and van Soest (1998a), using German socio-economic panel data between 1994 and 1993 found a language effect on earnings increase from 0.0538 (7.08, OLS) to 0.155 (2.28, IV) with father's education measures as identifying instruments.

Using UK data, Shields and Wheatley Price (2002) reported increases in the effects of fluency on earnings from 0.0887 (3.62, OLS) to 0.1651 (3.96, IV) using the languages in which the interview was conducted as instruments, and from 0.0887 (3.62, OLS) to 0.1142 (0.99, IV) using married to a UK-born spouse and the number of dependent children in the household as instruments.

Source: *Shields and Wheatley Price (2002).*

5.2 Around the globe: different countries, different languages, similar results

5.2.1 Australia

The study of the determinants and consequences of the English language proficiency of migrants is of particular interest for Australia. In various formats, throughout the twentieth century, English language tests have played an important role in the admission of immigrants. Under the Skilled Independent Visa category, points are currently awarded on the basis of proficiency in English, among other personal characteristics.[19] A recent increase in the English language requirements for the skill-based independent immigrants, but not for other applicants, provided an opportunity to demonstrate the effect of immigration policy on the skills of immigrants (Chiswick and Miller, 2006). The English proficiency of the skill tested immigrants increased with no change for the others.

The early research on the links between English language skills and labor market outcomes in Australia was based largely on census data, with the 1981 Census marking the first release of unit record Census data. Later research has been based largely on the Longitudinal Survey of Immigrants to Australia.

Two of the early studies for Australia based on census data were by Evans (1987) and Chiswick and Miller (1985). Both used data from the 1981 Census. In Evans's research the focus was on the determinants, including language skills, of occupational status among male immigrants from Mediterranean, Northwest European, Third World, and Eastern European countries. The English language proficiency information was collected using the same format as in Box 5.6, though as tests showed that the effects of the various levels of proficiency were approximately linear, a continuous measure was used, ranging from 0 where the immigrant did not speak English, to 100 where the immigrant either spoke English only or, where a language other than English was spoken at home, English was spoken very well. The dependent variable was an occupational status score. In each instance better language skills were associated with statistically significant increases in occupational status scores. The increases in occupational status associated with improved English language proficiency differed across the four birthplace groups, however, being stronger for those from Third World and Eastern European countries than they were for Mediterranean and Northwest European countries. Evans (1987) noted that Third World and Eastern European countries were, at the time of data collection, not associated with immigrant enclaves in Australia, and thus argued that this pattern across birthplace regions showed that enclave economies can shelter immigrants with poor language skills from adverse labor market consequences. We return to this theme in Section 5.4.

---

[19] See Appendix 1 of Kan (1991) for information on changes in Australia's immigration policy leading up to 1989. As noted by Kan (1991), numerical scoring was used as an administrative arrangement as early as 1979. The importance of the change in 1989 was that the points system was recognized in law.

The study by Chiswick and Miller (1985) was more conventional in terms of its focus on earnings, and its use of dichotomous variables for whether the immigrant spoke a language other than English at home, and for whether an immigrant who spoke a language other than English at home spoke English either not well or not at all. Separate analyses were undertaken for male immigrants from English-speaking countries and for male immigrants from non-English-speaking countries. It was reported that among immigrants from English-speaking countries, language skills did not influence earnings, most likely because nearly all were proficient. However, among immigrants from non-English-speaking countries, those who spoke a language other than English at home but spoke English very well or well had earnings 4.8% lower than monolingual English speakers, while those with poor English skills had a further 6.7% earnings disadvantage. In other words, there was an earnings differential of around 12% between those with poor English skills and monolingual English speakers.

In the 1990s and 2000s the Australian government department responsible for immigration undertook three longitudinal surveys of immigrants. These, respectively, followed immigrants who arrived in Australia between September 1993 and August 1995, arrived between September 1999 and August 2000, and either arrived in Australia or were granted a permanent visa in Australia, between December 2004 and March 2005. The surveys collected very detailed data on the respondents' immigration and settlement experiences, including data on language skills, and they have provided the basis for numerous studies, including those in the research volume edited by Cobb–Clark and Khoo (2006). Chiswick et al. (2005c) use data from the first of these surveys to study the impact of language skills on recent immigrants' earnings. The three waves of this data collection, conducted six, 18, and 42 months after arrival, were used in the analysis. The English Language Proficiency variable was dichotomous, having a value of one for those who speak only English, speak English best, or speak English very well. Various sets of estimates were presented (OLS, selection bias corrected, inertia panel data models), though the set that is most comparable with the literature is the OLS estimation undertaken for each wave of data collection. These results revealed that proficiency in English was associated with between 19% and 24% higher earnings.[20]

Thus, the research for Australia, using census and other datasets, and covering several decades, consistently reports that proficiency in English is associated with a considerable earnings premium, of at least 10% when all immigrants are considered, and possibly as high as 20% when the focus is upon recent immigrants.

---

[20] These results are of further interest as the estimating equations employed in this study took account of visa class, a variable that is generally not available in the censuses and surveys used to study immigrant labor market adjustment.

5.2.2 Canada

Canada is a bilingual country, with English and French being the official languages, though French is predominantly spoken in Quebec and English is spoken by the overwhelming majority in the rest of Canada. This official bilingual status, and the tensions between French-speaking Quebec and English-speaking "Rest of Canada", have provided the background for the development of a rich body of literature examining language issues. Much of this has focused on the native-born, though a somewhat separate literature on immigrants has developed, written mainly by scholars interested in immigrant adjustment. Reflecting the availability of data, the basis of this research in Canada has been similar to that in Australia, with the early research relying on census data, and recent research using a number of more specialized datasets. The analyses for Canada are of special interest due to the findings that emerge in a dual-language labor market, and when some of the specialized datasets are used.

Census of Canada datasets have considerable depth of information on language use and proficiency (see footnote 16), and the studies using these data have differed appreciably in the way the language variables are constructed. Most studies have focused on either the official language information, or on this information in conjunction with home language use or region of residence. The rationale for this approach is described by Carliner (1981, p. 388) as: "Since the purpose of this paper is to analyze wage premiums for language skills rather than shifts in language use, it seemed preferable to classify workers by language currently used rather than by language first used."

Carliner's (1981) analyses, based on 1971 census data, covered observations pooled across the native-born and foreign-born, and incorporated intercept shift terms for a number of immigrant arrival cohorts. The census information on language spoken at home (which Carliner (1981) terms mother tongue for convenience of expression) was combined with that on ability to conduct a conversation in English and French to construct eight language groups, such as monolingual English speaker, native English speaker who also speaks French, and monolingual speakers of other languages who spoke neither English nor French. The latter group who could speak neither English nor French had the lowest earnings (compared to being able to speak an official language) in both Quebec and the rest of Canada, though the disadvantage was three times larger in Quebec (coefficient of −0.281) than in English Canada (coefficient of −0.107). The increments in earnings associated with the acquisition of official language skills differed between French and English, and for Quebec and English Canada. For example, in Quebec the earnings differential between the group who could speak neither English nor French and non-native French speakers was 10 percentage points greater than that between those without official language skills and non-native English speakers. In English Canada, the difference in the earnings outcomes for these comparisons was only 3 percentage points. It is not clear, however, whether these patterns would apply if the foreign-born component of the sample was analyzed separately.

This issue is addressed in Chiswick and Miller (1988). They interact the official language knowledge information with region of residence (Quebec versus the rest of Canada), using data from the 1981 Census of Canada. Separate analyses were conducted for the foreign-born. The results showed that the foreign-born who could not speak English or French had earnings almost 20% below the earnings of English–French bilinguals.[21] Monolingual English speakers earned less than English–French bilinguals in both Quebec and English Canada, whereas monolingual French speakers earned less than English–French bilinguals only in Quebec.

A more recent census data-based study that has a structure similar to Chiswick and Miller (1988) is by Nadeau and Seckin (2010). Thus their study of adult male immigrants was based around earnings equations estimated separately for Quebec and the rest of Canada. They used data from the 1981, 1991, and 2001 censuses. These datasets were examined separately. Information on both the language spoken at home and on the ability to conduct a conversation in an official language was incorporated into the estimating equation, with separate sets of variables used to record each of these language attributes. As around 40% of immigrants in 2000 spoke a language other than English or French at home, and only around 2% could not speak either English or French, it is apparent that these variables will contain different information.

Within the rest of Canada, those who could not speak either English or French earned around 12% less than monolingual English speakers in 2000, and 17% less than bilinguals. This disadvantage had increased slightly since 1980. There was a further disadvantage associated with speaking neither English nor French at home, of 11%, which also was greater than the comparable disadvantage in 1980. It can be inferred that the disadvantage in the labor market associated with a lack of official (English or French) language skills is over 20% in English Canada.

In Quebec, the only official language category that was distinguished on the basis of earnings among the foreign-born adult males was the English–French bilinguals, who had earnings around 12% more than the other official language groups in 2000. However, the use of both English and French in the home, along with the use of a language other than English or French, was associated with significantly lower earnings in 2000. The estimated effects, however, did not exhibit any pattern, in terms of magnitude or statistical significance, across the three datasets analyzed. Nevertheless, the point estimates suggest that those who could not speak English or French, and hence used neither of these languages at home, have earnings 6–14% less than English monolinguals in Quebec.

Turning to studies that use specialized datasets, Ferrer et al. (2006) focused on the role of objective measures of document and quantitative literacy, using the Ontario Immigrant Literacy Survey of 1998 and the Canadian 1994 International Adult Literacy

---

[21] The variable for the absence of official language skills was not interacted with region of residence.

survey. Document literacy refers to the individual's capabilities in locating and using information. Quantitative literacy refers to problem solving in real-world contexts. Given the collinearity between these measures, the emphasis in the study was on an average of these variables. In addition, the authors use a self-reported measure of language skills, and construct a dichotomous variable that is set equal to one where the individual could only express himself poorly or not at all in English or French. This subjective measure of language skills was associated with around a 30% earnings disadvantage, but this earnings disadvantage was reduced by around one-third when the objective measure of literacy was included in the estimating equation.

The objective measure of literacy, given by the average of the document and quantitative scores, was associated with significantly higher earnings. The effect for immigrants educated abroad was approximately the same as that for the native-born, and the effect for immigrants educated in Canada was higher than that for the native-born. A 100-point increase in the literacy score (which corresponds to a 1.5 standard deviation increase in the score that is measured on a 0–500 scale) was associated with 30% higher earnings among immigrants educated abroad and 50% higher earnings among immigrants educated in Canada.

The research for Canada thus shows that proficiency in English or French is associated with an earnings premium of at least 20% and perhaps as high as 30%. English–French bilingualism is not necessarily associated with economic rewards in these studies, even in this dual-language country.

5.2.3 Germany

Germany, as with Israel, has a dominant language that is not an international language. For this reason it is of considerable interest to examine the links between knowledge of German and labor market outcomes among immigrants in that country.

Dustmann (1994) used data from the 1984 German Socio-Economic Panel. Interesting features of this study are the statistical controls for both writing and speaking proficiency as separate variables. In each case good and very good skills were distinguished from intermediate skills, and from the benchmark group of those who spoke (or wrote as the case may be) German badly or not at all. Among males, migrants with good or very good speaking skills were associated with almost 7% higher earnings than those with poor German language skills, and those with intermediate speaking skills had an earnings advantage of around one-half of that amount. Among females, only those in the highest speaking proficiency category were distinguished by having significantly higher earnings. Their earnings advantage (7.1%) over migrants with limited or no German speaking skills was similar to that for males.

Writing abilities were also associated with statistically significant earnings effects among migrants in Germany. However, only those with good or very good writing skills were characterized by statistically significant earnings effects, of 7% in the case of males and 15% in the case of females.

Dustmann (1994) also included variables for both writing and speaking skills in an encompassing model. For males the result was slightly smaller estimated earnings effects associated with each skill. Among females, the effect was that the writing skill variable was statistically significant whereas the speaking skill variable was not. These variables, however, will be highly correlated. Dustmann (1994, p. 151) noted "Since a migrant who is fluent or very fluent in German writing should also be quite fluent in spoken German . . ."

While Dustmann (1994) used only the 1984 wave of the German Socio-Economic Panel, multiple waves of this data collection over 1984–1993 were employed by Dustmann and van Soest (2001, 2002). Both studies have a focus on addressing endogeneity bias, and use only the information on speaking fluency. The 2001 study examines the impact of German-speaking skills on earnings for males only, whereas the 2002 study contains separate sets of estimations for males and females. The studies also differ in their approaches. In Dustmann and van Soest (2001) the five categories in the speaking skills data were collapsed to three: (i) good and very good; (ii) intermediate; and (iii) bad and very bad, to ensure each group was numerically important. This follows Dustmann (1994). The probability of being in these German-speaking skills groups was examined using an ordered probit model, and the latent index from this probability model was used as the language variable in the earnings equation. In Dustmann and van Soest (2002), only a dichotomous German-speaking skills variable was used, where those with good or very good German speaking skills were distinguished from the other proficiency categories. This approach was taken to provide a specification that was similar to that used in studies for other countries.

The patterns of results in the two studies of Germany are similar, and can be described using the more conventional 2002 study. In a standard earnings equation estimated using OLS, German-speaking fluency was associated with about 5% higher earnings for males.[22] Taking account of unobserved heterogeneity resulted in a slightly lower estimate of the earnings premium to speaking skills. Taking account of time-varying measurement errors was associated with a pronounced increase in the estimated effects of speaking proficiency on earnings, to around 14% in one model. However, time-persistent measurement errors did not appear to be overly important.[23]

---

[22] Dustmann and van Soest (2002, p. 484) noted that the OLS estimate of a 5% increase in earnings associated with dominant language proficiency is lower than that reported in other countries, and suggest that this could be associated with their inclusion of the "intermediate" speaking skills group in with those who have poor speaking skills. The evidence reported in Dustmann (1994), based on a more general specification that contained variables for (i) good and very good; (ii) intermediate; and (iii) bad and very bad German-speaking skills, indicates that the Dustmann–van Soest procedure would tend to decrease the estimated effect of dominant language proficiency.

[23] The results reported for women were similar to those discussed for men.

Hence, the research for Germany indicates an earnings premium to German-speaking proficiency of at least 5%. The more rigorous research undertaken by Dustmann and van Soest (2001, 2002) to address the endogeneity issue suggested that the earnings premium could be three times higher than this, at around 15%.

5.2.4 Israel

Analysis of the role of language skills in Israel is of interest for three main reasons. First, unlike English, which is the dominant language in the majority of the immigrant-receiving countries covered in the literature, although Hebrew is the language of religious practice among Jews worldwide, it is not otherwise an international language. Second, Israel is not as developed as countries such as Australia, Canada, Germany, the United Kingdom, and the US that are typically studied in this field of research. Third, the more recent studies of immigrants in the Israeli labor market cover the period following the large inflow of immigrants from the Former Soviet Union (FSU).[24] Very few arrivals knew any Hebrew because the study of Hebrew had been prohibited in the Soviet Union.

Chiswick and Repetto (2001) examined the returns to Hebrew writing and speaking skills using data from the 20% microdata file of the 1972 Census of Israel.[25] They have a focus on foreign-born adult Jewish males. The main language variables were a dichotomous variable for the ability to write a simple letter in Hebrew, and a four-category speaking variable that distinguished among (i) Hebrew only; (ii) Hebrew was the primary language and the individual speaks other languages; (iii) Hebrew was a second language; and (iv) does not speak Hebrew. The results revealed that the earnings of those who speak only Hebrew and those bilinguals for whom Hebrew was the primary language were not significantly different. Compared to these men, however, earnings were 8% lower among bilinguals who reported Hebrew as their second language, and 21% lower among those who could not speak Hebrew.[26]

Similarly, workers who could write a simple letter in Hebrew had earnings around 12% higher than those who could not perform this task. An interesting feature of the results was that when both Hebrew writing and speaking skills were entered into the

---

[24] In 1989 there was a policy shift in the Soviet Union, and restrictions on the movement of Jews to Israel were removed, and rapidly resulted in a more than 15% increase in the Israeli population and labor force.

[25] The 1972 Census of Israel had the richest set of questions on language proficiency in the Israeli Censuses. The 1983 Census had only one question, and the subsequent Censuses had none. Analysis of the 1983 Census question on language provided similar findings as the 1972 Census analysis (Chiswick, 1998; Chiswick and Repetto, 2001).

[26] Other variables being the same, among adult male immigrants in Israel, having been born in an English-speaking developed country is associated with lower proficiency in Hebrew and with higher earnings. Even after controlling for country of birth, speaking English on a daily basis is associated with a highly statistically significant 15% earnings advantage (Chiswick and Repetto, 2001). Further research is needed to determine whether this reflects the role of English as an international language, the high earnings potential of English speakers in the advanced English-speaking countries, or some other factor.

estimating equation at the same time, both were statistically significant: Hebrew writing skills were associated with around 9% higher earnings, and Hebrew speaking skills with around 11% higher earnings. In other words, immigrants who could both speak and write in Hebrew had earnings around 20% higher than those who did not possess these skills.

Berman et al. (2003) used a special 1994 survey to examine the earnings among male FSU immigrants in Israel. Their study therefore covers a much later period than the research by Chiswick and Repetto (2001). The survey contained information on Hebrew-speaking skills on a five-point scale (not at all, a little bit, not so well, well, and very well), which the authors used as a continuous, cardinal measure. Information was collected (simultaneously) on wages and language skills at the time of interview and at the time they started their current job. Also, data were collected for workers in both high-skilled and low-skilled occupations.

Four main findings were reported. First, the continuous variable recording proficiency in Hebrew indicated a 26% difference in wages between the extremes of the proficiency scale (not at all and very well). Second, when separate dichotomous variables were used for each of the language proficiency groups, there was a clear hierarchy of earnings effects in comparison to the reference group of not being able to speak Hebrew, from 31.4% in the top, very well, proficiency category, 19.5% for the second highest, well, category, 14.8% for the not so well category, and 8.6% for the second lowest category of being able to speak Hebrew a little bit. Hence, while these earnings increments are not quite on a linear scale, the linear scale provides a reasonable approximation. Third, this wage effect was diminished only slightly in a differenced model that allowed for ability bias. Fourth, the payoff to Hebrew fluency was higher in the skilled occupations than in the unskilled occupations: indeed, proficiency in Hebrew had little effect in unskilled occupations. This suggests a complementarity between language and occupational skill in the generation of earnings (Chiswick and Miller, 2003).

The findings of Chiswick and Repetto (2001) and Berman et al. (2003) therefore indicate an earnings gap of at least 20% between workers who are proficient in Hebrew and those who lack this skill. There is also evidence of a complementarity between Hebrew language skills and the other human capital needed for entry into skilled occupations. It is noted, however, that these results are based on data collected in 1972 and 1994, reflecting the surprising absence of information on Hebrew language skills in more recent censuses. Further comment on data collection issues is provided in Section 6.

5.2.5 Spain

Research into the effects of dominant language proficiency among immigrants in Spain can offer evidence that complements studies for other countries. This is because of the different dominant language (Spanish), and the fact that the large flows of immigrants into Spain are of relatively recent origin. Budría and Swedberg (2012) noted that the number of foreign workers present in Spain increased by 2.25 million during 2001–2008. However, until the Spanish National Immigrant Survey undertaken during November 2006 to February 2007, there were no nationwide data that would facilitate study of the effects of proficiency in Spanish on the earnings of immigrants. Budría and Swedberg (2012) used these data in OLS and IV estimations. The data on proficiency in Spanish wcre derived from a question which asked respondents to rate their speaking proficiency in the context of the skills needed for communicating at work, at the bank, and with the public authorities/administration. Four response categories were provided, ranging from "very well" to "need to improve". Budría and Swedberg (2012) used these data to construct a dichotomous Spanish language proficiency variable, where immigrants who could speak Spanish very well were distinguished from other immigrants. The Spanish proficiency rate was around two-thirds.

The OLS estimates indicated that adult male immigrants who were proficient in Spanish had 4.8% higher earnings than those who lacked this skill.[27] This language premium is much lower than those generally reported in studies for other countries. It is noted, however, that the partial effect of schooling on earnings was only 1.1%, which is also much lower than the return typically found for other countries. This suggests very low payoffs to skill in the Spanish labor market.

The IV estimates were identified using information on age at arrival in Spain, the presence of a child who is proficient in Spanish, and by plans to stay in Spain for the next five years. Proficiency in Spanish was typically associated with around 25% higher earnings in the IV estimations. This marked change between the earnings premium to dominant language proficiency obtained under OLS and IV estimations is similar to that found for other countries (see Box 5.7).

In IV estimations undertaken for separate samples of better educated and less well educated workers, proficiency in Spanish was associated with almost 50% higher earnings among the better educated, whereas it was associated with around 20% higher earnings among the less well educated. The OLS estimates indicated 6% higher earnings among the better educated and a statistically insignificant 3% higher earnings among the less well educated. This evidence supports the complementarity of human capital skills reported by Chiswick and Miller (2003).

It is apparent from this overview of the first nationwide study of the impact of dominant language proficiency and schooling on the earnings of immigrants in Spain that the returns to human capital in Spain are very low. The large difference between the OLS and IV estimates for the effects of Spanish proficiency is similar to that reported in studies for other countries, and suggests that the OLS findings could be a considerable underestimate of the true impact. Further research, using alternative datasets, is needed on this topic.

---

[27] One aspect of the estimating equation that needs to be noted is that account was not taken of duration of the immigrant's stay in Spain. The inclusion of a years since migration variable in the model was reported to result in little change to the findings.

5.2.6 United Kingdom

In 2000, around 9% of the working age population of Britain was born overseas (Dustmann and Fabbri, 2003). Many of these immigrants are classified as belonging to racial and ethnic minorities (Black Caribbeans, African Asians, Indians, Pakistanis, Bangladeshis, and Chinese). Despite this importance, there has been comparatively little research on the effects of English language proficiency on earnings in the UK. As Dustmann and Fabbri (2003, p. 697) explain in their fairly recent study, "The data sources we use for this analysis are to our knowledge the only datasets for the UK that contain information about immigrants' language proficiency, as well as information on employment status and earnings." The often cited earlier study by Shields and Wheatley Price (2002) was based on an occupational status score, specifically the mean wage of the occupation of employment. Shields and Wheatley Price (2002) captured only the across-occupation gains in earnings associated with proficiency in English and not the within-occupation gains. They found that English proficiency was associated with around 9% higher earnings.

Dustmann and Fabbri (2003) examined data from two surveys, which were collected in the early to mid 1990s. One of these surveys contained self-assessed information on speaking, reading and writing skills, and the other contained interviewers' evaluations of the respondents' spoken language proficiency. Both employment and earnings outcomes were examined. The authors accommodate the bias associated with unobserved heterogeneity using a matching estimator, and the bias associated with measurement error using an IV type approach. Binary indicators of English proficiency were used. Workers with an English mother tongue, and those with a non-English mother tongue who reported speaking English well or very well were defined as proficient when the self-assessed data were used, and those assessed by the interviewer as being fairly fluent or speaking English fluently were defined as proficient under the alternative measure.

They report that dominant language speaking skills were significantly and positively related to the employment probability in an OLS estimation, and writing skills were also related to this labor market outcome, though the partial effects were stronger. When both sets of skills were included in a single equation writing skills were statistically significant whereas speaking skills were not. The estimated effects associated with the language proficiency variables were smaller under the matching approach, though they remained statistically significant, whereas they were larger, though statistically insignificant, under the IV approach. In general, being proficient in English was associated with an increase in the employment probability of between 10 and 20 percentage points.

The estimation of a standard human capital earnings equation using OLS showed that speaking proficiency was associated with around 20% higher earnings and writing proficiency with around 15% higher earnings. Taking account of unobserved heterogeneity resulted in a higher (significant) estimate in one sample and a smaller (insignificant) estimate in the other sample. The estimated effect on earnings of proficiency in English was much higher under the IV type approach (partial effect of 0.356 for the total sample, 0.460 for males, and 0.844 for females), though each of these estimates was statistically insignificant.

Thus, according to the Dustmann–Fabbri (2003) study, dominant language proficiency among immigrants in the UK is associated with substantial improvements in labor market outcomes. The standard OLS estimates of these, of 10–20 percentage points improvement in the employment probability, and up to 20% increase in earnings, are comparable to findings in other highly developed countries.

Miranda and Zhu (2013) based their analyses on the UK Household Longitudinal Survey 2009–2011, and focused on adult males. Their language variable is a measure of deficiency in English, and is termed "English as Additional Language". This was defined from the responses to the question "Is English your first language?" There was a 16% wage differential between those with good and deficient English when estimated using OLS. When IV was used, with language of the country of origin and interactions of this with age-at-arrival as instruments (see Bleakley and Chin, 2004) the estimated wage differential increased to 25%. This estimate was robust to the tests undertaken, which involved the choice of instruments (relying only upon the interaction terms with age-at-arrival) and sample (immigrants only rather than a pooled sample of immigrants and the native-born).

Thus, while there has been limited research in the UK compared to other major immigrant-receiving countries, the studies available reveal that English language proficiency is associated with 15–20% higher earnings. Miranda and Zhu's (2013) IV estimates, which appear to be robust, indicate that the earnings differential could be as high as 25%.

5.2.7 United States

Immigrant flows into the US exceed those into any other country. During the 2000s, for example, more than one million people achieved immigrant status each year. Much of the research on the labor market rewards for dominant language proficiency has been undertaken on immigrants to the US. Initially, this research was concentrated on understanding labor market outcomes among Hispanics. However, as the mix of immigrant arrivals became more diversified following the 1965 Amendments to the Immigration and Nationality Act that removed the severe restrictions on Asian immigration, the coverage of the research broadened. Among what may be termed the milestone studies, the early research was based on the 1976 Survey of Income and Education, whereas the later research has made use of census data.

McManus et al. (1983) used the 1976 Survey of Income and Education in an analysis of the earnings of Hispanic men. They attempted to use much of the information on language use and proficiency in the eight separate questions in the survey. They discarded many of the variables as redundant and created an index of English language deficiency.

Deficiency in English was shown to have negative effects on earnings, where the negative effects increased with higher levels of schooling and experience. When their index of English language deficiency was included in the equation, other variables for immigrant characteristics became statistically insignificant, most likely because of problems created by the construction of the language index.

Kossoudji (1988) also based her analysis on the 1976 Survey of Income and Education. The focus was on foreign-born men of Hispanic and East Asian origin. Unlike McManus et al. (1983), however, and perhaps setting the standard for subsequent analyses, Kossoudji (1988) adopted a simple categorization of the language information, defining only three English proficiency groups: (i) fluent English speakers; (ii) those able to communicate in English; and (iii) those who speak little or no English. Kossoudji looked at the effects of English proficiency on occupational states and on earnings within broad occupational levels. She showed that those with the poorest English skills tend to be employed in lower-level jobs, and that this decrease in occupational status is more pronounced for Hispanics than it is for Asians. Differences in occupational attainment accounted for a negligible part of the overall earnings disadvantage of Asian immigrants with limited English skills, and around one-third of the disadvantage of Hispanic immigrants with limited English skills. English language skills were not statistically significant in the most skilled occupations. Within the low-skilled occupations, only those with the poorest skills tended to be disadvantaged, and this disadvantage was greater for Hispanics than for Asians. The within-occupation wage effects of limited English proficiency at the lowest skill levels were around 20% for Hispanics and 10% for Asians.

Tainer (1988) also used the 1976 Survey of Income and Education for her analysis of the effect of English language proficiency on earnings. She found the effects to be positive and significant for foreign-born men, but there were variations in magnitude by ethnicity. In order to study these effects, Tainer created two language proficiency variables. The first variable, *SPEAK*, was based on the question, "How well do you speak English?", where proficiency was self-ranked on a scale of 1 to 5. The second variable, *INDEX*, was a continuous index (0 to 1) of three variables: proficiency (*SPEAK*), usage at home, and ability to understand English. Since these measures were not directly comparable, Tainer compared their elasticities and found that for foreign-born men, a 1% improvement in *SPEAK* increased annual earnings by 0.08%, and a 1% improvement in *INDEX* increased annual earnings by 0.04% (Tainer, 1988, p. 117). Tainer also compared results for Europeans, Asians, and Hispanics in an effort to distinguish between the effects of language proficiency for different groups. However, for both proficiency variables, only the coefficients for Hispanics were statistically significant at a 5% level (coefficients of 0.17 for *SPEAK* and 0.69 for *INDEX*). Tainer concluded that the earnings of Hispanic and Asian men were more sensitive to English language proficiency than those of European men.

Among the many studies using census data are Chiswick and Miller (2002) and Bleakley and Chin (2004). Chiswick and Miller used 1990 census data in a detailed study of the earnings of male immigrants. Several specifications of the earnings equation were considered, including models with a single dichotomous variable recording fluency in English, which was set equal to 1 if the immigrant speaks only English at home or speaks English "very well" or "well", and with separate variables for each of the census English proficiency groups (see Box 5.6). The models also examined the role of linguistic enclaves, and these results are discussed in Section 5.4.

The results revealed that male immigrants who could not speak English, or who spoke it "not well", had earnings around 19% lower than monolingual English speakers. Workers who spoke English only "well" were at a 9% earnings disadvantage compared to mono-lingual English speakers, whereas those who spoke English "very well" were at a modest 2% earnings advantage compared with monolingual English speakers. When the single dichotomous variable was used to record proficiency in English, the results showed that workers who were proficient in English earned 14% more than those who were not pro-ficient. This premium was of the same order of magnitude as was reported when a similar model was applied to the 1980 US census data (Chiswick and Miller, 1995). The increase in earnings associated with proficiency in English was shown to vary across countries of origin, and ranged from statistically insignificant effects for South Asia and sub-Saharan Africa, to values of about 20% for immigrants from China and Japan. The increase in earn-ings associated with a greater proficiency in English comes about largely from shifting jobs to occupations requiring greater English language proficiency, with a minor role played by higher earnings in the same occupation (Chiswick and Miller, 2012).

A further indication of the heterogeneity of the earnings effect associated with pro-ficiency in English in the 1990 census data is found in the study by Bleakley and Chin (2004). They focused on childhood immigrants, defined as those who were under the age of 18 at the time of arrival in the US. Their further restrictions, in order to get a more homogeneous group, led to a focus on 25- to 38-year-olds. Thus, the shortest duration in the US in their sample would have been seven years. They used a cardinal representation of the census English proficiency information (see Box 5.6), with the value rising with greater proficiency. Much of their analysis was based on models that did not control for educational attainment: in these the English proficiency variable had an extremely large effect on earnings. Once educational attainment was taken into account, however, the effects of English-speaking proficiency were much more modest, with one representative set of results indicating a difference in earnings of only around 6% between those who could not speak English at all and those who could speak English very well.[28] Bleakley and Chin (2004) addressed the problem of the potential

---

[28] Bleakley and Chin (2004) argued that this showed that much of the effect of English language proficiency on earnings is mediated through higher educational attainment, and this has specific policy implications. This is not as great a concern among immigrants who arrive as adults, which is around two-thirds of the foreign-born population in the US.

endogeneity of English-speaking proficiency using an IV estimator, with age at arrival interacted with birthplace region as the identifying instrument. Consistent with results for the US and UK discussed above, the IV estimates were typically 50%, or more, greater than the OLS estimates.

Earnings effects of the magnitude reported in studies of datasets covering the twentieth century also characterize the contemporary US labor market. This is revealed from analysis of data from the American Community Survey (2005–2009). Thus, Table 5.4 presents results from a regression analysis by nativity for the earnings of adult men. Among the foreign-born, those who speak another language at home but who speak English "very well" earn about 1% less than those who speak only English, while those who speak English only "well" earn nearly 24% less. Earnings are even lower for immigrants who are even less proficient. These earnings differentials associated with English-speaking skills for 2005–2009 are much larger, by the order of 50%, than the earnings effects reported by Chiswick and Miller (2002), based on analyses of data for 1990. However, over the same time period the payoff to years of schooling for the foreign-born increased from 4.3% to 6.0%, a 40% increase, and the return from schooling for the native-born also increased. Hence, this change appears to be part of a pattern of a general increase in the effects on earnings of human capital among immigrants and the native-born in the US.

5.3 An overview of the effects of dominant language proficiency on earnings

Table 5.5 presents a summary of the findings described above on the effects of dominant language proficiency on the earnings of immigrants.

Clearly, from the Table 5.5 evidence, the acquisition of dominant language proficiency estimated from OLS analyses is associated with higher earnings. But is investment in destination language proficiency profitable for immigrants? Considering only the labor market earnings impacts, a 15% increase in earnings per year from going from "not proficient" to "proficient" would imply a 30% rate of return on the investment if the cost of the language training involved the equivalent of a half of a year of full-time earnings, a 15% rate of return if it required a full year and a 7.5% rate of return if it required two full years. Even if it required two full years, this is a high rate of return on the investment. Yet this computation does not take into account the consumption, social and civic benefits, or the lowering of the costs of other investments in human capital. Thus, it appears that the investment in destination language proficiency is a profitable investment for immigrants and for society.

5.4 Ethnic enclaves effects on earnings

The earnings of immigrants who live in an ethnic/linguistic enclave may differ from the earnings of immigrants who live outside enclave areas. Such an enclaves earnings effect

Table 5.4 Analysis of earnings by nativity for adult males, United States, 2005–2009

Variable	Native-born	Foreign-born
English very well	−0.009	−0.013
	(2.94)	(4.23)
English well	−0.033	−0.236
	(5.23)	(66.24)
English not well/not at all	−0.003	−0.331
	(0.36)	(82.4)
Years of schooling	0.122	0.060
	(622.29)	(195.88)
Labor market experience	0.044	0.015
	(220.4)	(37.78)
Labor market experience squared/100	−0.075	−0.022
	(195.76)	(29.24)
Log weeks worked	1.145	1.017
	(993.26)	(384.38)
South	−0.046	−0.065
	(47.34)	(29.9)
Married (spouse present)	0.272	0.217
	(260.64)	(95.26)
Years since migration (YSM)	*	0.014
		(50.03)
YSM squared/100	*	−0.019
		(35.73)
Minority language concentration	−0.168	−0.484
(fraction of state population)/100	(8.99)	(38.18)
Constant	3.850	5.476
	(710.10)	453.99
Number of observations	2,763,924	529,773
R-squared	0.3969	0.3959

Dependent variable = Natural logarithm of annual earnings; t-ratios in parentheses.
*Variables not entered. Speaks Only English is the language benchmark.
Source: American Community Survey, United States, 2005–09, microdata file.

may arises because immigrants are willing to sacrifice some of their earnings to live among others who speak their mother tongue and share their cultural characteristics (ethnic goods). Indeed, for many ethnic goods (e.g., ethnic church, friendship networks, marriage markets, as well as ethnic-specific market goods and services), the cost is lower if one lives in a larger ethnic/linguistic enclave (Chiswick and Miller, 1995, 2005b). Thus, only a high wage offer from outside the enclave would induce the immigrant who has a high demand for ethnic goods to live outside the enclave. This gives the appearance of higher nominal wages outside the enclave, although perhaps the same real wages when adjusted for the higher cost of ethnic goods. Other channels of negative influence on earnings of residence in an ethnic enclave include a reduction in job opportunities (Borjas, 2000).

Table 5.5 The effects of dominant language proficiency on the earnings of adult male immigrants*

Country	Typical increases in earnings associated with dominant language proficiency (%)	Illustrative studies
Australia	10–20	Chiswick and Miller (1985), Chiswick et al. (2005c), Evans (1987)
Canada	20–30	Carliner (1981), Chiswick and Miller (1988), Ferrer et al. (2006)
Germany	5–15	Dustmann (1994), Dustmann and van Soest (2001, 2002)
Israel	10–25	Chiswick and Repetto (2001), Berman et al. (2003)
Spain	5	Budría and Swedberg (2012)
UK	15–20	Shields and Wheatley Price (2002), Dustmann and Fabbri (2003), Miranda and Zhu (2013)
US	10–20	McManus et al. (1983), Koussoudji (1988), Tainer (1988), Chiswick and Miller (2002, 2012)

*Based on OLS analyses.

Ethnic enclaves can also provide what Borjas (2000) terms a "warm embrace" that "gives immigrants information about labour market opportunities, provides many job contacts, and allows immigrants to escape the discrimination that they may have otherwise encountered in the labour market outside the enclave" (Borjas, 2000, p. 93). These latter effects would tend to provide immigrants with higher earnings inside the enclave.

Studies of the impact that living in an ethnic enclave may have on immigrants' labor market outcomes have adopted two approaches. Both approaches are based on the expectation that the effect of dominant language proficiency of the individual immigrant on labor market outcomes will vary across birthplace groups that differ in the intensity of the enclave. Under one approach, equations for the determinants of labor market outcomes that include a variable for dominant language proficiency are estimated for various birthplace groups, and the estimated effects of dominant language proficiency are then related to characteristics of the birthplace groups. Under the second approach, an ethnic enclave variable, such as the percentage of the population in the immigrant's area of residence that is from the same country of birth, or that shares the same ethnic or linguistic background, is added to the model of labor market outcomes, and the coefficient on this variable is used in the assessment of the role of ethnic enclaves in the labor market.

Evans's (1987) study for adult male immigrants in Australia in 1981 is an example of the first approach. According to Evans (1987, p. 265), "The ethnic enclaves hypothesis suggests that the effect of English skills on occupational attainment should be much weaker in groups that have developed ethnic enclaves." In Australia, immigration from Mediterranean countries has been a consistent feature of post-WWII migration flows, whereas immigration from Eastern European and Third World countries, for the 1981 dataset analyzed, was of more recent origin. Consistent with the ethnic enclave hypothesis, English language proficiency had a significantly larger effect on the occupational status of immigrants from Eastern Europe and Third World countries than it had on the occupational status of immigrants from Mediterranean countries.

Veltman (1983) presented comprehensive analyses of the determinants of occupational status and earnings among adults belonging to a minority language (defined using mother tongue) group in the US, using the 1976 Survey of Income and Education. Separate analyses were undertaken for the Spanish language group and for non-Spanish minority language groups. The language variables included in the estimating equation distinguished four categories: (i) English monolinguals; (ii) workers whose usual language was English and who often speak another language; (iii) minority language speakers who reported that they spoke English either well or very well; and (iv) minority language speakers who reported that they spoke English either not well or not at all. Among the many findings, Veltman reported that among males with a Spanish mother tongue, those whose usual language was Spanish were at an earnings disadvantage, while among those whose usual language was English, the English–Spanish bilinguals were associated with lower earnings. In other words, the labor market "rewards the most complete type of integration possible, the effective abandonment of the Spanish language as a daily language" (Veltman, 1983, p. 241).

In discussing the findings, Veltman (1983, pp. 390–391) argues "As long as Spanish speaking Americans continue to speak Spanish as their usual language, they are relatively well insulated from direct job competition with members of the White English speaking group ... As Anglicization produces increasingly large numbers of English speaking persons of Hispanic ancestry, members of this group are increasingly drawn into competition for jobs with members of the White English language group. It is at this point that the data suggest that Hispanic Americans are experiencing particular difficulties." This interpretation is consistent with Evans's ethnic enclaves hypothesis.

Studies that adopt the second, more direct, approach have used two main methodologies. Some studies have augmented a conventional human capital earnings equation with an ethnic concentration variable. In these studies the unit of observation is the individual. Hence, a model of the following type is estimated:

$$\ln Y_i = \alpha_0 + \alpha_1 X_i + \alpha_2 Lang_i + \alpha_3 Conc_i + \varepsilon_i$$

where the vector X contains variables for schooling, labor market experience, and other factors typically included in studies of the determinants of earnings, $Lang$ is a measure of the immigrant's proficiency in the dominant language, and $Conc$ is the ethnic concentration variable. This ethnic concentration variable has been defined with reference to the immigrant's ethnic, birthplace, or mother tongue group. For example, Shields and Wheatley Price's (2002) analyses in the UK were based on the percentage of the census ward from the same ethnic group as the respondent. In some analyses the dominant language proficiency and ethnic concentration variables are interacted, to enable the effect of the ethnic concentration measure to differ between immigrants who are, and who are not, proficient in the dominant language.

The second method followed in some studies is based around comparisons of the growth in average earnings of groups of immigrants sharing a small number of characteristics. In these studies the unit of observation is the change in a group average, and the estimating equation is of the form:

$$\Delta \ln_{jkl} = \alpha_0 + \alpha_1 \ln Y_{jkl}(t_0) + \alpha_2 X_{jkl} + \alpha_3 I_j + \alpha_4 I_k + \alpha_5 I_l + \alpha_6 Conc_{jk} + \varepsilon_{jkl}$$

where $\Delta \ln_{jkl}$ is the growth rate in the mean earnings of immigrant workers from country j who live in region k and who arrived in the country in year l. The initial earnings term, $\ln Y_{jkl}(t_0)$, is used to control for convergence in earnings: the immigrants with the lowest earnings in the first year after arrival experience the most rapid growth in earnings in the destination country (Duleep and Regets, 1997). The vector X comprises the proportions of the immigrants in various age and education categories, while I_j, I_k, and I_l are vectors of dummy variables that record the *ceteris paribus* earnings differentials across the birthplace, location, and year of arrival groups distinguished in the analysis. The *Conc* variable has a construction analogous to that used in the studies that have the individual as the unit of observation. For example, in Borjas (2000) the *Conc* variable is defined as the proportion of the population of metropolitan area k (N_k) who were born in country j, namely N_{jk}/N_k.

Examples of studies adopting the first of these approaches are Shields and Wheatley Price (2002) for the UK, Chiswick and Miller (2002) for the US, and Kanas et al. (2012) for Germany.

Chiswick and Miller (2002) based their analysis on the earnings of adult immigrant men in the 1990 US Census. Their concentration variable was defined with respect to languages other than English spoken at home, and was the fraction of the population in the state that speaks the same non-English language at home as the respondent. In the benchmark model, the coefficient of this linguistic concentration variable was negative (−0.006) and highly significant. The coefficient of −0.006 indicates that a 1 percentage point increase in the linguistic concentration measure would be associated with slightly more than a 0.5% decrease in an immigrant's earnings. When a variable for whether the immigrant was proficient in English was added to the model, the coefficient on the linguistic concentration variable changed from −0.006 to −0.005.[29] Further,

---

[29] The estimated impact of residence in a linguistic enclave in the analyses based on the American Community Survey (2005–09) reported in Table 5.4 is also −0.005.

when the linguistic concentration variable was interacted with the English proficiency variable, the effect of residence in a linguistic concentration for those who were not proficient in English was a statistically significant -0.002, whereas it was -0.006 for those who were proficient in English. Chiswick and Miller also explored the implications of this interaction term from the perspective of how the impact on earnings of proficiency in English varied across regions according to the concentration of speakers of the immigrant's home language. They report (p. 43), "This is estimated to be close to 19% for an individual who lives in an area where his origin language is not spoken. Where 20% of the population speaks the immigrant's origin language, the return to English-speaking skills would be 11%." In other words, the economic penalty from not speaking English is smaller among those who live in a linguistic concentration area, which supports Evans's ethnic enclaves hypothesis.

Shields and Wheatley Price (2002) examined the determinants of the mean wage in the immigrant's occupation in the UK. Hence, as noted earlier, they capture occupational wage effects but not any intra-occupational wage effects. Their ethnic concentration measure was incorporated into a model of occupational success in the form of three dummy variables, for living in a census ward with 5–15%, 15–33%, or greater than 33% own ethnic density (the benchmark group was 0–5% own ethnic density). It was reported that these ethnic concentration variables were only marginally statistically significant, "and are indicative of a 4.5% occupational success penalty to living in a high ethnic, minority density (15–33%) census ward" (p. 149).

Kanas et al. (2012) examined the role of ethnic concentration among adult male immigrants in Germany using the German Socio-Economic Panel, 1984–2004. They include in their model a number of social capital variables other than the ethnic concentration. The main social capital variable was the frequency of contacts with friends, relatives, and neighbors. The models were corrected for sample selection. The results showed that ethnic concentration was not a significant determinant of earnings. Nor was there any evidence that the role of ethnic concentration varied according to the language skills of the immigrant. The authors argue (p. 703), "It is possible that Germany simply lacks substantial ethnic concentrations, like the Cubans in Miami or the Chinese in San Francisco, that significantly influence immigrants' economic outcomes." Determining whether there are threshold effects in this regard is an area for future research.

There are two main studies that have used the group-average wage-growth approach: Borjas's (2000) analyses for the US and Warman's (2007) more recent study for Canada. Borjas's (2000) analyses were based on the 1980 and 1990 US censuses. His main ethnic concentration measure was the proportion of the population of metropolitan area k who were born in country j (N_{jk}/N_k). An alternative, relative clustering measure, was also used, where the ethnic concentration measure was normalized by the fraction of the US population that belongs to the particular country of birth group

(N_j/N). Borjas reported that the ethnic concentration variable was a negative and statistically significant determinant of earnings growth between 1980 and 1990, and while the results were weaker when the relative clustering measure was used, they were still indicative of a negative relationship between residential concentration and earnings growth. Borjas reported that the wage growth for a typical Mexican immigrant who moves from Los Angeles (which had an exposure index of 0.11) to New York (exposure index of 0.001) would increase by 4 percentage points, an effect that was described as sizeable. It was also shown that the adverse impact of residence in an ethnic enclave was stronger for the least educated, and it was also usually stronger for the groups of most recent arrivals, compared to longer-term settlers. In other words, in this study the most disadvantaged in the labor market incurred further penalties from residing in an ethnic enclave.

Warman (2007) examined the impact of residence in an ethnic enclave in the context of earnings growth regressions based on data from the Canadian Censuses of 1981, 1986, 1991, 1996, and 2001. The dependent variable in the estimating equation was the earnings growth over either 5-, 10-, 15-, or 20-year periods, for the average foreign-born worker from a particular country who resided in a specific Census Metropolitan Area and who belonged to a particular arrival cohort. Along with country of birth, location of residence, arrival cohort and base year fixed effects, the estimating equation also controlled for initial earnings. It was shown that residence in an ethnic enclave has a negative impact on weekly earnings growth, and this negative effect was more important among immigrants who migrated as adults than it was among immigrants who migrated as children, and it was also more important among high-skilled male workers than it was among their low-skilled counterparts. Warman (2007) illustrated the potential impact of the estimates: it was shown that by living in Montreal (low ethnic concentration) rather than in Vancouver (high concentration), an immigrant from Hong Kong would have 4% higher earnings growth over a five-year period. In other words, similar to Borjas's (2000) finding for the US labor market, the enclave effect is quantitatively important in the Canadian labor market. However, contrary to what Borjas found for the US, Warman's (2007) results indicate that ethnic enclaves afford relative protection to less-skilled workers.[30]

Hence, while the research into the earnings effects of residence in an ethnic enclave is underdeveloped compared to the other areas of research reviewed in this chapter, the evidence strongly suggests that, even controlling statistically for the respondent's own destination language proficiency, other variables held constant, men who live in an ethnic/linguistic enclave receive, on average, lower earnings than men who live outside of their enclave area.

---

[30] This difference could be due to the different definitions of skilled workers in the studies. Borjas (2000) defined a group as skilled if the mean educational attainment is at least 12 years, whereas Warman (2007) separated the immigrants by highest degree obtained, and defined the skilled group as possessing a university degree.

6. SUMMARY AND CONCLUSIONS

This chapter reports on the "economics of language" for immigrants—that is, the influence of language on the choice of destination among international migrants, the determinants of the acquisition among immigrants of destination language proficiency, and the labor market consequences of that proficiency as expressed in their earnings.

There is a tendency among international migrants (and among internal migrants in bilingual countries, such as Canada) to take language issues into account when deciding whether to migrate and the choice of destination. The costs of migration are lower if the migration is to a destination with the same dominant language as that known to the potential migrant. More generally, the smaller the linguistic distance between the dominant languages of the origin and a particular destination, the lower are the adjustment costs in the destination and the higher the migration rate.

The determinants of the destination language proficiency among immigrants have been performed primarily for both males and females on census and large surveys for major immigrant receiving countries such as the US, Canada, Australia, Israel, and Germany. Language proficiency among immigrants is most efficiently modeled according to the three "Es": Exposure to the destination language in the origin and in the destination, Efficiency in acquiring destination language skills, and the Economic incentives for investing in proficiency. Proficiency in the destination language among immigrants increases with the level of their schooling and the duration of their residence in the destination. Proficiency is lower with an older age at migration, if the immigrant was married to the current spouse before migration, and if the migrant lives in a linguistic concentration (enclave) area. Proficiency is also greater the closer are the origin and destination languages (smaller linguistic distance). Among women, but not men, proficiency is lower when there is a larger number of children in the family. There appears to be language learning in the home. The proficiency of a family member is greater if other members of the family are more proficient. In particular, the mother's proficiency is more important than that of the father for the destination language proficiency of their children.

Among immigrants, other variables being the same, earnings are greater for those more proficient in English. The implied payoff to proficiency in terms of labor market earnings for adult males suggests it is a profitable investment. Yet this underestimates the benefits of acquiring proficiency as it does not include the gains from consumption, social and civic activities, and other human capital investments. The computation of benefits also does not take into account the gains from the enhanced English language proficiency of other family members (language learning in the home) when one family member makes investments in destination language training.

An important implication of this analysis for immigration policy is that immigrants either proficient in the destination language, or with characteristics that enhance proficiency, will be more successful in adjusting to the new labor market. Some countries (such as Australia, Canada, the United Kingdom, and New Zealand), but not the US, have skill-based immigration policies that give significant explicit emphasis to these characteristics, including English language skills (plus French in Canada), educational attainment, occupational skills, and age at migration, when issuing permanent resident visas.

Another important policy implication derives from the high rate of return from investments in language proficiency to the individual and to society. This suggests the encouragement of immigrants to invest in language training, through subsidies, access to training programs and other mechanisms as is done explicitly in some countries, with Israel being a primary example. Encouraging immigrants to become proficient in the destination language does not imply a denigration of their culture or language of origin. It does imply a welcoming of them to the full range of opportunities in the educational, economic, social, and civic (political) life of their new home.

The research reviewed in this chapter that has yielded a rich array of findings requires access to quality data. The relative abundance of studies of the determinants of dominant language proficiency, and of the effects of dominant language proficiency on labor market outcomes in Australia, Canada and the US, is a clear reflection of the relative availability in these countries of quality datasets containing information on relevant variables. Conversely, the limited research for the UK and Spain, until recent years, reflects the absence of the required data in earlier years. The limited amount of recent research into language issues in Israel is a result of the unavailability of data.

The research has revealed the importance of dominant language proficiency to immigrants' labor market outcomes, the differences in these labor market outcomes across groups, the potential differences in labor market outcomes depending on the context in which the destination and origin languages are used, and the changes over time in the economic returns to language usage. More research is needed, however, on the effects of language usage on aspects of the consumer, social, family structure, and civic life of immigrants. The inclusion of questions on dominant language proficiency, along with questions on immigrant status and labor market outcomes, demographic and social characteristics, consumption behavior and civic activities in censuses and other large-scale data collections, should be viewed as a priority.

ACKNOWLEDGMENTS

We appreciate the research assistance of Marina Gindelsky and Derby Voon.

REFERENCES

Adsera, A., Pytlikova, M., 2012. The Role of Language in Shaping International Migration, Institute for the Study of Labor Discussion Paper Number 6333, Bonn, Germany.
Akresh, I.R., 2007. Context of English language use among immigrants to the United States. Int. Migrat. Rev. 41 (4), 930–955.

Bartel, A.P., 1989. Where do the new U.S. immigrants live? J. Labor Econ. 7 (4), 371–391.

Bauer, T., Epstein, G.S., Gang, I.N., 2005. Enclaves, language, and the location choice of migrants. J. Popul. Econ. 18 (4), 649–662.

Becker, G.S., 1964. Human Capital: A Theoretical and Empirical Analysis with Special Reference to Education, first ed. National Bureau of Economic Research, New York.

Beine, M., Docquier, F., Özden, Ç., 2011. Diasporas. J. Dev. Econ. 95 (1), 30–41.

Belot, M., Ederveen, S., 2012. Cultural barriers in migration between OECD countries. J. Popul. Econ. 25 (3), 1077–1105.

Belot, M.V.K., Hatton, T.J., 2012. Immigrant selection in the OECD. Scand. J. Econ. 114 (4), 1105–1128.

Berman, E., Lang, K., Siniver, E., 2003. Language-skill complementarity: Returns to immigrant language acquisition. Lab. Econ. 10 (3), 265–290.

Bleakley, H., Chin, A., 2004. Language skills and earnings: Evidence from childhood immigrants. Rev. Econ. Stat. 86 (2), 481–496.

Borjas, G.J., 2000. Ethnic enclaves and assimilation. Swed. Econ. Pol. Rev. 7, 89–122.

Budría, S., Swedberg, P., 2012. The Impact of Language Proficiency on Immigrants' Earnings in Spain, Institute for the Study of Labor Discussion Paper No. 6957, Bonn, Germany.

Carliner, G., 1981. Wage differences by language group and the market for language skills in Canada. J. Hum. Resour. 16 (3), 384–399.

Charette, M., Meng, R., 1994. Explaining language proficiency: Objective versus self-assessed measures of literacy. Econ. Lett. 44, 313–321.

Chiswick, B.R., 1991. Speaking, reading and earnings among low-skilled immigrants. J. Labor Econ. 9 (2), 149–170.

Chiswick, B.R., 1998. Hebrew language usage: Determinants and effects on earnings in Israel. J. Popul. Econ. 11 (2), 253–271.

Chiswick, B.R., 2009. The economics of language learning for immigrants: An introduction and overview. In: Wiley, T.G., Lee, J.S., Rumberger, R.W. (Eds.), The Education of Language Minority Immigrants in the United States. Multilingual Matters, Bristol, UK, pp. 72–91.

Chiswick, B.R., Miller, P.W., 1985. Immigrant generation and income in Australia. Econ. Rec. 61 (173), 540–553.

Chiswick, B.R., Miller, P.W., 1988. Earnings in Canada: The roles of immigrant generation, French ethnicity and language. In: Schultz, T.P. (Ed.), Research in Population Economics. vol. 6. JAI Press, pp. 183–228.

Chiswick, B.R., Miller, P.W., 1995. The endogeneity between language and earnings: International analyses. J. Labor Econ. 13 (2), 245–287.

Chiswick, B.R., Miller, P.W., 2001. A model of destination language acquisition: Application to male immigrants in Canada. Demography 38 (3), 391–409.

Chiswick, B.R., Miller, P.W., 2002. Immigrant earnings: Language skills, linguistic concentrations and the business cycle. J. Popul. Econ. 15 (1), 31–57.

Chiswick, B.R., Miller, P.W., 2003. The complementarity of language and other human capital: Immigrant earnings in Canada. Econ. Educ. Rev. 22 (5), 469–480.

Chiswick, B.R., Miller, P.W., 2005a. Linguistic distance: A quantitative measure of the distance between English and other languages. Journal of Multilingual and Multicultural Development 26 (1), 1–16.

Chiswick, B.R., Miller, P.W., 2005b. Do enclaves matter in immigrant adjustment? City and Community 4 (1), 5–35.

Chiswick, B.R., Miller, P.W., 2006. Language skills and immigrant adjustment: The role of immigration policy. In: Cobb-Clark, D.A., Khoo, S. (Eds.), Public Policy and Immigrant Settlement. Edward Elgar, Cheltenham, UK, pp. 121–148.

Chiswick, B.R., Miller, P.W., 2007a. The Economics of Language: International Analyses. Routledge, London.

Chiswick, B.R., Miller, P.W., 2007b. Computer usage, destination language proficiency and the earnings of natives and immigrants. Review of Economics of the Household 5 (2), 129–157.

Chiswick, B.R., Miller, P.W., 2008a. A test of the critical period hypothesis for language learning. Journal of Multilingual and Multicultural Development 29 (1), 16–29.

Chiswick, B.R., Miller, P.W., 2008b. Modeling immigrants' language proficiency. In: Chiswick, B.R. (Ed.), Immigration: Trends, Consequences, and Prospects for the United States. Elsevier, Amsterdam, pp. 75–128.

Chiswick, B.R., Miller, P.W., 2012. The Impact of Surplus Skills on Earnings: Extending the Over-Education Model to Language Proficiency, Xerox.

Chiswick, B.R., Repetto, G., 2001. Immigrant adjustment in Israel: The determinants of literacy and fluency in Hebrew and their effects on earnings. In: Djajic, S. (Ed.), International Migration: Trends, Policies, and Economic Impact. Routledge, London, pp. 204–228.

Chiswick, B.R., Patrinos, H.A., Hurst, M.E., 2000. Indigenous language skills and the labor market in a developing economy. Econ. Dev. Cult. Change 48 (2), 349–367.

Chiswick, B.R., Lee, Y.L., Miller, P.W., 2003. Schooling, literacy, numeracy and labour market success. Econ. Rec. 79 (245), 165–181.

Chiswick, B.R., Lee, Y.L., Miller, P.W., 2005a. Family matters: The role of the family in immigrant's destination language skills. J. Popul. Econ. 18 (4), 631–647.

Chiswick, B.R., Lee, Y.L., Miller, P.W., 2005b. Parents and children talk: English language proficiency within immigrant families. Review of Economics of the Household 3 (3), 243–268.

Chiswick, B.R., Lee, Y.L., Miller, P.W., 2005c. Immigrant earnings: A longitudinal analysis. Review of Income and Wealth 51 (4), 485–503.

Christofides, L., Swidinsky, R., 2010. The economic returns to the knowledge and use of a second official language: English in Quebec and French in the Rest-of-Canada. Can. Publ. Pol. 36 (2), 137–158.

Clark, X., Hatton, T.J., Williamson, J.G., 2007. Explaining U.S. immigration, 1971–1998. Rev. Econ. Stat. 89 (2), 359–373.

Cobb-Clark, D.A., Khoo, S., 2006. Public Policy and Immigrant Settlement, edited volume. Edward Elgar, Cheltenham, UK.

Crystal, D., 1987. The Cambridge Encyclopedia of Language. Cambridge University Press, Cambridge.

Duleep, H.O., Regets, M.C., 1997. Immigrant entry earnings and human capital growth: Evidence from the 1960–1980 censuses. Res. Labor Econ. 16, 297–317.

Dustmann, C., 1994. Speaking fluency, writing fluency and earnings of migrants. J. Popul. Econ. 7 (2), 133–156.

Dustmann, C., 1999. Temporary migration, human capital, and language fluency of migrants. Scand. J. Econ. 101 (2), 297–314.

Dustmann, C., Fabbri, F., 2003. Language proficiency and labour market performance of immigrants in the UK. Econ. J. 113 (489), 695–717.

Dustmann, C., van Soest, A.V., 2001. Language fluency and earnings estimation with misclassified language indicators. Rev. Econ. Stat. 83 (4), 663–674.

Dustmann, C., van Soest, A.V., 2002. Language and the earnings of immigrants. Ind. Labor Relat. Rev. 55 (3), 473–492.

Dyen, I., Kruskal, J.B., Black, P., 1992. An IndoEuropean classification: A lexicostatistical experiment. Transactions of the American Philosophical Society. New Series 82 (5).

Espenshade, T., Fu, H., 1997. An analysis of English language proficiency among U.S. immigrants. Am. Sociol. Rev. 62 (2), 288–305.

Espinosa, K.E., Massey, D.S., 1997. Determinants of English proficiency among Mexican migrants to the United States. Int. Migrat. Rev. 31 (1), 28–50.

Evans, M.D.R., 1986. Sources of immigrants' language proficiency: Australian results with comparisons to the Federal Republic of Germany and the United States of America. Eur. Socio. Rev. 2 (3), 1–10.

Evans, M.D.R., 1987. Language skill, language usage and opportunity: Immigrants in the Australian labour market. Sociology 21 (2), 253–274.

Ferrer, A., Green, D.A., Riddell, W.C., 2006. The effect of literacy on immigrant earnings. J. Hum. Resour. 41 (2), 380–410.

Ginsburgh, V., Ortuño-Ortín, I., Weber, S., 2005. Disenfranchisement in Linguistically Diverse Societies. The Case of the European Union. Mimeo, Department of Economics, University of Alicante, Spain.

Grenier, G., 1984. Shifts to English as usual language by Americans of Spanish mother tongue. Soc. Sci. Q. 65 (2), 537–550.

Grenier, G., 1987. Earnings by language group in Quebec in 1980 and emigration from Quebec between 1976 and 1981. Can. J. Econ. 20 (4), 774–791.

Grogger, J., Hanson, G.H., 2011. Income maximization and the selection and sorting of international immigrants. J. Dev. Econ. 95 (1), 42–57.

Hart-Gonzalez, L., Lindermann, S., 1993. Expected Achievement in Speaking Proficiency, 1993. School of Language Studies, Foreign Service Institute, US Department of State, Mimeographed.

Hou, F., 2005. The Initial Destinations and Redistribution of Canada's Major Immigrant Groups: Changes over the Past Two Decades. Statistics Canada Research, Catalogue No. 11F0019MIE—No. 254.

Hutchinson, W.K., 2005. "Linguistic distance" as a determinant of bilateral trade. South. Econ. J. 72 (1), 1–15.

Isphording, I.E., Otten, S., 2011. RUHR Economic Papers #274. Linguistic Distance and the Language Fluency of Immigrants. Germany, Bochum.

Isphording, I.E., Otten, S., 2012. The Costs of Babylon—Linguistic Distance in Applied Economics, RUHR Economic Papers #337, Bochum, Germany.

Jaeger, D.A., 2000. Local Labor Markets, Admission Categories, and Immigrant Location Choice. Unpublished manuscript, Department of Economics, College of William and Mary, USA.

Kan, A., 1991. The Australian Experience of Skilled Migration: The Employer Nomination Scheme in the Manufacturing and the Finance, Property and Business Services Sectors. Bureau of Immigration Research, Australian Government Publishing Service, Canberra, Australia.

Kanas, A., Chiswick, B.R., van der Lippe, T., van Tubergen, F., 2012. Social contacts and the economic performance of immigrants: A panel study of immigrants in Germany. Int. Migrat. Rev. 46 (3), 680–709.

Karemera, D., Oguledo, V.I., Davis, B., 2000. A gravity model analysis of international migration to North America. Appl. Econ. 32 (13), 1745–1755.

Kominski, R., 1989. How good is "how well"? An examination of the census English-speaking ability question. American Statistical Association 1989 Proceedings of the Social Statistics Section. pp. 333–338.

Kossoudji, S.A., 1988. English language ability and the labor market opportunities of Hispanic and East Asian immigrant men. J. Labor Econ. 6 (2), 205–228.

Lazear, E., 1999. Culture and language. J. Polit. Econ. 107 (6), 595–612.

Lewis, M.P., 2009. Ethnologue: Languages of the World, sixteenth ed. SIL International, Dallas, TX.

Long, M.H., 1990. Maturational constraints on language development. Stud. Sec. Lang. Acquis. 12, 251–285.

Marschak, J., 1965. Economics of language. Behav. Sci. 10, 135–140.

Mayda, A.M., 2010. International migration: A panel data analysis of the determinants of bilateral flows. J. Popul. Econ. 23 (4), 1249–1274.

McAllister, I., 1986. Speaking the language: Language maintenance and English proficiency among immigrant youth in Australia. Ethnic and Racial Studies 9 (1), 24–42.

McCloskey, D.N., 1998. The Rhetoric of Economics, second ed. University of Wisconsin Press, Madison, WI.

McDonald, J.T., 2003. Location choice of new immigrants to Canada: The role of ethnic networks. In: Beach, C.M., Greene, A.G., Reitz, J.G. (Eds.), Canadian Immigration Policy for the 21st Century. John Deutsch Institute for the Study of Economic Policy. Queen's University, Canada.

McDonald, J.T., 2004. Toronto and Vancouver bound: The location choice of new Canadian immigrants. Can. J. Urban. Res. 13 (1), 85–101.

McManus, W., Gould, W., Welch, F., 1983. Earnings of Hispanic men: The role of English language proficiency. J. Labor Econ. 1 (2), 101–130.

Miranda, A., Zhu, Y., 2013. English deficiency and the native-immigrant wage gap. Econ. Lett. 118 (1), 38–41.

Nadeau, S., Seckin, A., 2010. The immigrant wage gap in Canada: Quebec and the Rest of Canada. Can. Publ. Pol. 36 (3), 265–285.

Ortega, F., Giovanni, P., 2009. The Causes and Effects of International Migrations: Evidence from OECD Countries 1980–2005. Working Paper No. 09.6, Department of Economics, University of California.

Pedersen, P.J., Pytlikova, M., Smith, N., 2008. Selection and network effects-Migration flows into OECD countries 1990–2000. Eur. Econ. Rev. 52 (7), 1160–1186.

Raijman, R., 2013. Linguistic assimilation of first-generation Jewish South African immigrants in Israel. J. Int. Migrat. Integrat. 14, 615–636.

Schultz, T.W., 1962. Investment in human beings. Special Supplement to Journal of Political Economy 70 (5), 1–157.

Shields, M.A., Wheatley Price, S., 2002. The English language fluency and occupational success of ethnic minority immigrant men living in English metropolitan areas. J. Popul. Econ. 15 (1), 137–160.

Stevens, G., 1986. Sex differences in language shift in the United States. Soc. Sci. Res. 71 (1), 31–36.

Swadesh, M., 1952. Lexico-statistic dating of prehistoric ethnic contacts: With special reference to North American Indians and Eskimos. Proc. Am. Philos. Soc. 96, 452–463.

Tainer, E., 1988. English language proficiency and earnings among foreign-born men. J. Hum. Resour. 23 (1), 108–122.

Tanakh, 1985. The Holy Scriptures. Jewish Publication Society, Philadelphia.

Veltman, C.J., 1983. Language Shift in the United States. Mouton, New York.

Warman, C., 2007. Ethnic enclaves and immigrant earnings growth. Can. J. Econ. 40 (3), 401–422.

Zavodny, M., 1999. Determinants of recent immigrants' location choices. Int. Migrat. Rev. 33 (4), 1014–1030.

CHAPTER 6

Immigrants and Immigrant Health

Heather Antecol*, Kelly Bedard**
*Claremont McKenna College
**University of California, Santa Barbara

Contents

1. Introduction	271
2. Determinants of the HIE	273
2.1 Selective immigration	273
2.2 Health care access	274
2.3 Income assimilation	275
2.4 Acculturation	275
2.5 Recent empirical evidence of weight assimilation	276
3. The National Health Interview Survey	277
4. Measuring Immigrant Health and Assimilation	284
5. Analyzing Cohort and Assimilation Effects	290
6. The Healthy Immigrant Effect	291
6.1 Weight patterns by nativity	297
6.2 Immigrant assimilation and cohort differentials	299
7. Conclusions	310
References	311

1. INTRODUCTION

Understanding the determinants of immigrant health is increasingly important in light of their large and increasing presence in the United States: The foreign-born population reached an all-time high of 40 million people in 2010, an increase of 9 million since 2000. The proportion of immigrants in the US population has also grown, from 8% in 1990 to 13% in 2010.[1] The continued immigrant influx has led to a flurry of research on the health differences between immigrants and their native-born counterparts across a wide array of disciplines.[2] A key stylized fact that is generally supported in the literature is the "Healthy Immigrant Effect," henceforth referred to as the HIE. In particular, immigrants arrive in their destination country healthier than their native counterparts, but over

---

[1] http://www.census.gov/how/infographics/foreign_born.html.

[2] For a nice review of the literature on foreign-born health in the US across a variety of health measures (mortality, perinatal health, mental health, overweight and obesity, health and circulatory disease, diabetes, cancers, infectious diseases, injuries, and self-assess health).

Handbook of the Economics of International Migration, Volume 1A
ISSN 2212-0092, http://dx.doi.org/10.1016/B978-0-444-53764-5.00006-2
271

time this health advantage declines. The HIE has been documented in most major immigrant receiving countries, including the US, Canada, Australia, the UK, and Germany.[3]

A number of studies have attempted to identify the contributing factors of the HIE, including selective immigration, access to health care, income assimilation, and acculturation.[4] Of these potential explanations, acculturation appears to play the largest role. One form of acculturation that has received particular attention in the US literature in recent years is weight assimilation: There is generally a positive association between the length of US residence and weight of immigrants (Antecol and Bedard, 2006; Dey and Lucas, 2006; Koya and Egede, 2007; Bates et al., 2008; Roshania et al., 2008; Park et al., 2009; Kaushal, 2009; Hao and Kim, 2009; Oza-Frank and Narayan, 2009; Singh et al., 2011), although there are some important differences by demographic characteristics (gender, race/ethnicity, age of arrival, level of education), sample (year of analysis, comparison group), and methodological approach (cohort effects).[5]

There is one difference that is particularly noteworthy. Specifically, Antecol and Bedard (2006) found evidence that Hispanic immigrants(particularly females) enter the US lighter than their native counterparts but then converge toward native levels using NHIS data from 1989 to 1996. In contrast, Park et al. (2009) found no evidence of unhealthy weight assimilation for Hispanic immigrants comparing NHIS data between 1994–96 and 2004–06.[6] One potential reason for the conflicting results may be due to a break in the rates at which natives and immigrants are gaining weight across the time periods. For instance, if the rates of weight gain for natives and immigrants are similar prior to 1997 but the rate of weight gain for natives is faster than their immigrant counterparts post-1996, then one could mistakenly conclude there is no assimilation toward native weights.

[3] For US evidence see House et al. (1990), Stephen et al. (1994), Kennedy et al. (2006), Hamilton and Hummer (2011), and Huang et al. (2011); for Canadian evidence see Chen et al. (1996), Perez (2002), Deri (2003), McDonald (2003), and Kennedy et al. (2006); for Australian evidence see Donovan et al. (1992), Kennedy et al. (2006), and Chiswick et al. (2008); for UK evidence see Kennedy et al. (2006) and Averett et al. (2012); and for German evidence see Ronellenfitsch and Razum (2004).

[4] For selective immigration evidence see, for example, Marmot et al. (1984), McDonald (2004), Jasso et al. (2004), Kennedy et al. (2006), Sander (2007), Chiswick et al. (2008), Ceballos and Palloni (2010), Ceballos (2011), and Van Hook and Zhang (2011). For access to health care evidence see, for example, Leclere et al. (1994), Laroche (2000), Jasso et al. (2004), McDonald and Kennedy (2004), Breen et al. (2010), Akresh (2009), Pylypchuk and Hudson (2009), Kao (2009), Gorman et al. (2010), and Su and Wang (2012). For income assimilation evidence see, for example, Borjas (1985, 1995), Chiswick (1986), LaLonde and Topel (1992), Duleep and Regets (1994, 1999, 2002), Funkhouser and Trejo (1995), Schoeni (1997, 1998), Hu (2000), and Antecol et al. (2006). For acculturation evidence see, for example, Marmot and Syme (1976), Kasl and Berkman (1983), Stephen et al. (1994), McDonald (2004, 2005), Akresh (2007), Kaushal (2007), Kaestner et al. (2009), Kimbro (2009), and Peek et al. (2010).

[5] For Canadian evidence see McDonald (2004) and Setia et al. (2009), and for Australian evidence see Hauck et al. (2011).

[6] With the exception of Park et al. (2009), the remaining existing literature supports the Hispanic weight assimilation patterns found in Antecol and Bedard (2006).

The purpose of this chapter is to first provide evidence of the HIE using more recent waves of the National Health Interview Survey (1989–2011). We then present a comprehensive survey of the literature that seeks to explain this effect. Finally, we provide further evidence of the role acculturation (as measured by weight measures) plays in explaining the HIE based on more recent data. Given the evidence in the existing literature, we pay particular attention to controlling for arrival cohort, stratifying our analysis by race/ethnicity and gender, and exploring the possibility that the rate at which natives and immigrants are becoming unhealthy may differ from each other and change across time periods.

The remainder of the chapter is as follows. Section 2 reviews the literature on the potential components of the HIE and recent evidence of the HIE. Sections 3 and 4 describe the data and measurement of immigrant health and assimilation respectively. Our empirical framework is presented in Section 5. Section 6 presents updated results on weight assimilation. Section 7 concludes.

2. DETERMINANTS OF THE HIE

Why might immigrants become less healthy the longer they reside in the US? The existence of the HIE has spawned a growing literature that seeks to explain this effect. The usual hypothesized contributing/mitigating factors include: selective immigration, health care access, income assimilation, and acculturation. We discuss the existing evidence on each of these in turn, as well as provide additional evidence for the acculturation hypothesis as measured by weight measures.

2.1 Selective immigration

There are several countervailing selection effects at work with regards to the HIE. First, immigrants are positively selected (on both observable and unobservable characteristics) and are hence in better health either by choice or due to the immigration screening process of the host country (Marmot et al., 1984; McDonald, 2004; Jasso et al., 2004; Kennedy et al., 2006; Chiswick et al., 2008).[7] Second, *unhealthy* immigrants may be more likely to return to their home country (Palloni and Arias, 2003; Turra and Elo, 2008; Van Hook and Zhang, 2011).[8] The evidence on return migration is

---

[7] Mehta and Elo (2012) found that immigrants from the former Soviet Union (FSU) were healthier (less healthy) depending on whether they emigrated from the FSU when it was harder (easier) to obtain permission to emigrate.

[8] Ceballos and Palloni (2010) and Ceballos (2011) suggested that selective return migration may in fact be *positive* for young female immigrants of childbearing age as the reasons for return migration likely differ by the age of the immigrant. They found evidence, however, of selective return migration on poor health in the short run and a negative acculturation effect in the long run.

mixed. Sander (2007) found that *healthier* male immigrants in Germany are more likely to return to their home country while the reverse is true for female immigrants (although the effect for female immigrants is imprecisely estimated). Van Hook and Zhang (2011), on the other hand, found that health is not a key determinant of selective return migration from the US. Or, third, more economically successful immigrants may be more likely to remain in the US (see Van Hook and Zhang (2011) for evidence of this), and to the extent that higher income individuals are healthier this biases the immigrant sample towards being healthier. Finally, less healthy immigrants may be more likely to die prematurely, making it important to consider the sample age range carefully. While positive selection into the US upwardly biases the estimated immigrant health premium upon entry (i.e., the cohort effects, according to Marmot et al., 1984; Jasso et al., 2004; McDonald, 2004), the remaining selection mechanisms downwardly bias the estimates of immigrant health convergence towards lower US health levels. As such, all of the assimilation estimates reported in this chapter should be interpreted as lower bounds.

2.2 Health care access

Improved access to health care for immigrants with time in residence might reduce reported health status by increasing the diagnosis of pre-existing conditions (Jasso et al., 2004; McDonald and Kennedy, 2004).[9] On the other hand, it has also been suggested that increased access to health care may improve reported health status by reducing immigrant/native gaps in preventative health care screening, diagnosis, and treatment of health care problems (Leclere et al., 1994; Laroche, 2000; McDonald and Kennedy, 2004; Read and Reynolds, 2012).[10] Thus, it is difficult to predict the direction of the change in immigrant self-reported health status over time that results from changes in health care access.

However, we do know that immigrant health status is initially higher than that of natives and then falls towards American levels. Two things are therefore necessary for health care access to play a role in immigrant assimilation towards American health levels. First, immigrant health care access must change with the length of time that cohorts remain in the US. Secondly, health care access must either fall the longer immigrants

---

[9] A number of studies have examined the other determinants of immigrant access to health care besides length of US residency including, but not limited to, social networks (Gresenz et al., 2007; Ralston and Escandell, 2012); age at arrival (Kao, 2009); English fluency (Breen et al., 2010); host-country differences in insurance coverage (Lasser et al., 2006; Lebrun and Dubay, 2010); and class of immigration (Pandey and Kagotho, 2010).

[10] Lee et al. (2012) found that insured immigrants are more likely to engage in preventative health care relative to their uninsured counterparts and the negative association between self-reported health and length of US residence is weaker for insured immigrants relative to uninsured immigrants.

remain in the country, which seems incredibly unlikely and contradicts recent evidence (see, for example, Akresh, 2009; Kao, 2009; Pylypchuk and Hudson, 2009; Breen et al., 2010; Su and Wang, 2012), or must lead to the detection of previously unknown health problems that cause immigrants to report worse health.

2.3 Income assimilation

It is well known that most immigrant groups enter the US with lower incomes and employment rates and subsequently converge toward native levels the longer they remain in the country (see, e.g., Antecol et al., 2006; Borjas, 1985, 1995; Chiswick, 1986; LaLonde and Topel, 1992; Duleep and Regets, 1994, 1999, 2002; Funkhouser and Trejo, 1995; Schoeni, 1997, 1998; Hu, 2000).[11] Given immigrant income assimilation and the general finding that health is positively related to income (Sorlie et al., 1993), immigrants should become healthier the longer they remain in the country (Jasso et al., 2004).[12] This is exactly the opposite of the HIE: Immigrants arrive healthier and then become less healthy, not the reverse.

2.4 Acculturation

Exposure to the US environment causes immigrants to adopt native-born behaviors (such as diet and exercise) that have important health implications (Marmot and Syme, 1976; Kasl and Berkman, 1983; Stephen et al., 1994; McDonald, 2004, 2005; Akresh, 2007; Kaushal, 2007; Kimbro, 2009).[13] One of the most important types of acculturation is the role that weight assimilation plays in explaining the HIE. The growing rate of obesity is well documented for the American population (Costa and Steckel, 1995; Philipson and Posner, 1999; Himes, 2000; Philipson, 2001; Chou et al., 2002; Lakdawalla and Philipson, 2002; Cutler et al., 2003; Ogden et al., 2006) and is of great concern to policymakers because of its associated health risks and hence costs. To put it in context,

---

[11] A number of recent studies (see, for example, Orrenius and Zavodny, 2009; Hersch and Viscusi, 2010; and Marvasti, 2010) have investigated and have found some evidence to support the notion that immigrants are more likely to work in riskier jobs than their native counterparts, and therefore are subject to a higher incidence of injury, which may adversely affect their health.

[12] Cawley et al. (2009) explicitly examined the effect of obesity on the labor market outcomes (i.e., the probability of employment, wages, the sector of employment, and work limitations) of immigrants to the US. Their results suggest that obesity does not appear to influence labor market outcomes with the exception of female immigrants who have resided in the US for less than five years who exhibit a lower probability of employment.

[13] Alternatively, the act of migration may lead to worse health due to either the stress associated with the immigration process (Kasl and Berkman, 1983; Kaestner et al., 2009; Dean and Wilson, 2010; Peek et al., 2010) or exposure to discrimination in the host country (Vega and Amaro, 1994; Read and Emerson, 2005; Elo et al., 2008; Johnston and Lordan, 2012). Hamilton and Hummer (2011) found little support that exposure to discrimination prior to immigration influences health outcomes after immigration for black immigrants in the US.

only tobacco use leads to higher rates of premature death than obesity (Chou et al., 2002). In particular, obesity increases the risk of heart disease, stroke, some types of cancer and diabetes, and hence the financial burden due to greater health care consumption and/or productivity loss (Wolf and Colditz, 1998; Sturm, 2002).[14] Of course, these elevated costs are not borne entirely by the obese themselves; half of all health care is paid for by federal, state, and local governments (Chou et al., 2002).

2.5 Recent empirical evidence of weight assimilation

There is a large literature examining the association between weight assimilation and the HIE since our earlier paper (Antecol and Bedard, 2006).[15] While these studies generally find a positive association between length of US residence and weight for immigrants (Antecol and Bedard, 2006; Dey and Lucas, 2006; Koya and Egede, 2007; Bates et al., 2008; Roshania et al., 2008; Park et al., 2009; Kaushal, 2009; Hao and Kim, 2009; Oza-Frank and Narayan, 2009; Singh et al., 2011), there are some important differences by demographic characteristics (gender, race/ethnicity, age of arrival, level of education), sample (year of analysis, comparison group), and methodological approach (cohort effects).[16]

Specifically, some studies focus solely on a single cross-section of data (Koya and Egede, 2007; Bates et al., 2008; Roshania et al., 2008; Hao and Kim, 2009), while others use repeated cross-sections (Antecol and Bedard, 2006; Dey and Lucas, 2006; Park et al., 2009; Kaushal, 2009; Oza-Frank and Narayan, 2009; Singh et al., 2011). Moreover, the majority of the literature uses the NHIS to conduct their analysis; the main exceptions are Bates et al. (2008) (National Latino and Asian American Survey) and Roshania et al. (2008) (New Immigrant Survey). The time periods considered in the existing literature predate 1997 (Antecol and Bedard, 2006), focus on post-1996 (Dey and Lucas, 2006; Oza-Frank and Narayan, 2009), or bridge the two time periods (Kaushal, 2009; Park et al., 2009; Singh et al., 2011). Most studies do not examine the post-2005 time period; the main exception is Singh et al. (2011), who compare 1992–95 to 2003–08. Immigrants are sometimes looked at in isolation (Koya and Egede, 2007; Roshania et al., 2008; Oza-Frank and Narayan, 2009) or compared to their native counterparts (Antecol and Bedard, 2006; Dey and Lucas, 2006; Hao and Kim, 2009; Park et al., 2009; Kaushal, 2009; Singh et al., 2011). In addition, cohort effects are generally not examined in this literature; the main exceptions are Antecol and Bedard (2006), Dey and Lucas (2006), Kaushal (2009), and Park et al. (2009).

---

[14] A related literature has also found that a wage penalty is associated with obesity (Register and Williams, 1990; Hamermesh and Biddle, 1994; Averett and Korenman, 1996; Pagan and Davila, 1997; Cawley, 2000).

[15] For an earlier review of the weight assimilation literature see Oza-Frank and Cunningham (2010).

[16] For Canadian evidence see McDonald (2004) and Setia et al. (2009), and for Australian evidence see Hauck et al. (2011).

There is a general consensus in the literature that Hispanic immigrants are more likely to be obese the longer they live in the US, irrespective of sample or methodological approach. However, two studies—both of which use NHIS data, control for cohort of arrival, and examine immigrants relative to their native counterparts—found conflicting results. Specifically, Antecol and Bedard (2006) found evidence that Hispanic immigrants (particularly females) enter the US lighter than their native counterparts but then converge toward native levels using NHIS data from 1989 to 1996. In contrast, Park et al. (2009) found no evidence of unhealthy weight assimilation for Hispanic immigrants comparing NHIS data between 1994–96 and 2004–06. As previously noted, one potential reason for the conflicting results may be due to a break in the rates at which natives and immigrants are gaining weight across the time periods. Specifically, if the rates of weight gain for natives and immigrants are similar prior to 1997 but the rate of weight gain for natives is faster than their immigrant counterparts post-1996, then one could mistakenly conclude there is no assimilation toward native weights.

The evidence for white and Asian immigrants is mixed; while some studies found evidence of convergence (Bates et al., 2008; Singh et al., 2011) others did not (Antecol and Bedard, 2006; Dey and Lucas, 2006; Kaushal, 2009; Oza-Frank and Narayan, 2009). In addition, weight assimilation is generally found to be weaker for men than women (Antecol and Bedard, 2006; Koya and Egede, 2007; Hao and Kim, 2009). There is also some evidence to suggest that the weight assimilation effect is larger among immigrants with lower levels of education (Kaushal, 2009). Finally, there is evidence to suggest that those who arrive younger are more likely to be obese (Roshania et al., 2008; Kaushal, 2009; Oza-Frank and Narayan, 2009).

3. THE NATIONAL HEALTH INTERVIEW SURVEY

We use data from the National Health Interview Surveys (NHIS) from 1989 to 2011.[17] The NHIS is an annual cross-section survey intended to obtain information about the distribution of illness and the health services that people receive. These data are ideal for our purposes because they include detailed information on health measures (e.g., self-reported health status, activity limitations, weight, and height), as well as detailed information regarding basic socio-economic characteristics (e.g., race, immigration status, years of US residence, education).[18] We restrict our analysis to respondents between

[17] Years of US residence only began to be reported in 1989; as such we do not examine years prior to 1989. The NHIS data included all persons in a household in 1989–96, while the NHIS data in 1997–2011 included detailed information (particularly with respect to our preferred health outcomes) for one adult per household and one child per household. Thus, the sample size in the latter years is substantially smaller than the former years. Throughout our analysis we use annual population weights.

[18] Prior to 1997, measures of weight and height were only collected for individuals aged 18 and older.

the ages of 20 and 64 to account for the possibility that overweight individuals may be less healthy and therefore have higher premature mortality rates.

We focus on four racial/ethnic origin groups: non-Hispanic whites, non-Hispanic blacks, Hispanics, and Asians, henceforth referred to as whites, blacks, Hispanics, and Asians. Respondents reporting other, multiple, or unknown race are excluded from the analysis. A respondent is considered Hispanic if they reported they were of specified (e.g., Mexican, Cuban, Dominican) or non-specified Hispanic origins (e.g., other Spanish, other Latin American), including multiple Hispanic origins. A respondent is considered Asian if they reported Chinese, Filipino, or other Asian Pacific Islander (e.g., Hawaiian, Korean, and Vietnamese).[19]

We focus on two nativity groups: natives and immigrants. We construct nativity status based on the length of US residence question in the NHIS data. This question was asked solely of respondents born outside of the US.[20] A respondent is coded as an immigrant if they reported a value for their length of US residence while a respondent is coded as a native if the length of US residence question was not applicable. Respondents with unknown years of US residence were excluded from the analysis. We also construct four indicator variables for length of US residence: 0–4 years, 5–9 years, 10–14 years, and more than 14 years.

Further, we construct indicator variables for immigrant arrival cohorts based on respondent's reported length of US residence. We assign respondents to five-year cohorts (pre-1980, 1981–85, 1986–90, 1991–95, 1996–2000, 2001–05, 2006–10) using the mid-point of the respondent's length of US residence group to maximize the number of immigrants placed in the correct arrival cohort. In order to make these assignments for respondents who indicated they have resided in the US for more than 14 years, we assume this group's length of US residence is between 15 and 30 years so that we can calculate a mid-point.[21] Also note that natives are assigned a zero value for the year of arrival and cohort indicator variables.

---

[19] The Hispanic origin and race questions changed between the 1989–96 survey years and the 1997–2011 survey years; however, we are generally able to consistently define the four racial/ethnic origin groups across the NHIS survey years.

[20] While alternative definitions could have been employed (such as place of birth), this was not reported for all years in the NHIS. Thus, for consistency we used the same measure across years.

[21] Based on these criteria, immigrants reporting more than 14 years of US residence in 1989–2002 and those reporting 10–14 years in 1989–92 are designated as arriving in 1980 or earlier. Immigrants reporting more than 14 years of US residence in 2003–07, those reporting 10–14 years in 1993–97, and those reporting 5–9 years in 1989–92 are designated as arriving in 1981–85. Immigrants reporting more than 14 years of US residence in 2008–11, those reporting 10–14 years in 1998–2002, those reporting 5–9 years in 1993–97, and those reporting 0–4 in 1989–92 are designated as arriving in 1986–90. Immigrants reporting 10–14 years of US residence in 2003–07, those reporting 5–9 years in 1998–2002, and those reporting 0–4 years in 1993–97 are designated as arriving in 1991–95. Immigrants reporting 10–14 years of US residence in 2008–11, those reporting 5–9 years in 2003–07, and those reporting 0–4 in 1998–2002 are designated as arriving in 1996–2000. Immigrants reporting 5–9 years of US residence in 2008–11 and those reporting 0–4 years in 2003–07 are designated as arriving in 2001–05. Finally, immigrants reporting 0–4 years of US residence in 2008–11 are designated as arriving in 2006–10.

The analysis includes controls for a number of socio-economic characteristics: age, education, marital status, employment status, and region of residence. Age is included in five-year age bins (20–24, 25–29, 30–34, 35–39, 40–44, 45–49, 50–54, 55–59, and 60–64). Education is included as completed years of schooling. While this is how education is reported in 1989–96, education is reported as the highest grade completed in 1997–2011. In order to ensure we have roughly the same years of schooling across time we convert the variables as follows. In 1989–96, those reporting 0–12 years of education and 16–17 years of schooling continue to be assigned their respective years of schooling, those reporting 13–15 years of education are assigned 14 years of schooling, and those reporting 18 years of education are assigned 21 years of schooling. In 1997–2011, those reporting never attended school/kindergarten only through 11th grade are assigned 0–11 years of schooling, those reporting 12th grade (no diploma) are assigned 11.5 years of schooling, those reporting GED or equivalent or high school graduate are assigned 12 years of schooling, those reporting some college (no degree), associate degree (occupational), and associate degree (academic) are assigned 14 years of schooling, those reporting a bachelor's degree are assigned 16 years of schooling, those reporting a master's degree are assigned 17 years of schooling, those reporting a professional degree are assigned 19 years of schooling, and those reporting a doctoral degree are assigned 21 years of schooling. We exclude respondents who did not report their level of education.

Marital status is included as an indicator variable equal to 1 if the respondent is married (spouse in household) and 0 otherwise (including non-reporters). Employment status is included as an indicator variable equal to 1 if the respondent worked last year and 0 otherwise (including non-reporters).[22] In 1989–96 a respondent is considered employed if they reported working in the past two weeks or they reported not working in the past two weeks but had a job in the past 12 months. In 1997–2000 a respondent is considered employed if they reported working in the past week or they reported not working in the past week but had a job in the past 12 months. Finally, in 2001–11 a respondent is considered employed if they reported working in the past 12 months.

Region of residence is included as four indicator variables: northeast, midwest, south, and west. The sample is comprised of 281,786 (12,497), 64,078 (4911), 27,636 (36,367), and 2529 (11,982) white, black, Hispanic, and Asian native (immigrant) women respectively, and 257,234 (11,049), 41,803 (4003), 21,720 (32,275), and 2400 (10,580) white, black, Hispanic, and Asian native (immigrant) men respectively.[23] See Appendix Tables 1 and 2 for summary statistics by nativity and race/ethnic origin for women and men respectively.

---

[22] Results are similar if we exclude non-reporters for marital status and employment status.

[23] Due to a small amount of non-reporting for some health measures, the exact sample sizes vary slightly across our health outcomes.

Appendix Table 1 Summary statistics for women by nativity and race/ethnic origin

	White		Black		Hispanic		Asian	
	Native	Immigrant	Native	Immigrant	Native	Immigrant	Native	Immigrant
Age								
20–24	0.106	0.080	0.138	0.114	0.201	0.119	0.212	0.100
	(0.308)	(0.272)	(0.345)	(0.317)	(0.401)	(0.324)	(0.409)	(0.301)
25–29	0.110	0.106	0.130	0.130	0.168	0.142	0.168	0.134
	(0.313)	(0.308)	(0.336)	(0.336)	(0.374)	(0.349)	(0.374)	(0.340)
30–34	0.118	0.122	0.133	0.150	0.145	0.158	0.115	0.153
	(0.322)	(0.328)	(0.340)	(0.358)	(0.352)	(0.365)	(0.320)	(0.360)
35–39	0.125	0.129	0.130	0.145	0.126	0.145	0.122	0.140
	(0.330)	(0.336)	(0.336)	(0.352)	(0.332)	(0.352)	(0.328)	(0.347)
40–44	0.128	0.134	0.126	0.134	0.110	0.131	0.090	0.136
	(0.334)	(0.341)	(0.331)	(0.340)	(0.312)	(0.337)	(0.286)	(0.343)
45–49	0.123	0.124	0.109	0.127	0.084	0.108	0.101	0.115
	(0.329)	(0.329)	(0.311)	(0.333)	(0.277)	(0.310)	(0.301)	(0.319)
50–54	0.111	0.111	0.094	0.107	0.069	0.083	0.075	0.093
	(0.314)	(0.314)	(0.292)	(0.310)	(0.253)	(0.275)	(0.263)	(0.290)
55–59	0.095	0.099	0.078	0.056	0.054	0.066	0.062	0.071
	(0.293)	(0.298)	(0.268)	(0.229)	(0.226)	(0.249)	(0.241)	(0.257)
60–64	0.084	0.095	0.063	0.038	0.045	0.049	0.055	0.059
	(0.278)	(0.293)	(0.242)	(0.192)	(0.206)	(0.216)	(0.228)	(0.235)
Married	0.658	0.713	0.331	0.427	0.513	0.632	0.500	0.703
	(0.474)	(0.453)	(0.471)	(0.495)	(0.500)	(0.482)	(0.500)	(0.457)
Years of education	13.731	13.888	12.977	13.137	12.683	10.247	14.814	13.958
	(2.451)	(3.164)	(2.429)	(2.996)	(2.662)	(4.158)	(2.382)	(3.678)
Working/employed	0.752	0.668	0.722	0.779	0.718	0.568	0.793	0.675
	(0.432)	(0.471)	(0.448)	(0.415)	(0.450)	(0.495)	(0.406)	(0.468)

Immigrant arrival cohorts

Pre–1980	0.373 (0.484)	0.236 (0.425)	0.246 (0.431)	0.215 (0.411)
1981–85	0.162 (0.368)	0.196 (0.397)	0.184 (0.388)	0.192 (0.394)
1986–90	0.203 (0.402)	0.232 (0.422)	0.225 (0.418)	0.227 (0.419)
1991–95	0.085 (0.279)	0.102 (0.302)	0.108 (0.310)	0.128 (0.334)
1996–2000	0.098 (0.297)	0.126 (0.332)	0.136 (0.343)	0.118 (0.322)
2001–05	0.055 (0.227)	0.076 (0.265)	0.081 (0.272)	0.081 (0.273)
2006–10	0.025 (0.155)	0.032 (0.176)	0.019 (0.137)	0.039 (0.195)
Sample size	281,786	64,078	27,636	2529

Time in destination country

0–4 years	0.143 (0.350)	0.139 (0.346)	0.139 (0.346)	0.204 (0.403)
5–9 years	0.126 (0.332)	0.190 (0.392)	0.187 (0.390)	0.180 (0.384)
10–14 years	0.108 (0.311)	0.177 (0.382)	0.168 (0.373)	0.166 (0.372)
More than 14 years	0.623 (0.485)	0.494 (0.500)	0.507 (0.500)	0.450 (0.498)
Sample size	12,497	4911	36,367	11,982

NHIS data from 1989 to 2011 for individuals aged 20–64. All statistics use NHIS annual weights. Standard deviations are given in parentheses. The sample size is based on activity limitation reports since activity limitation has the highest reporting rate.

Appendix Table 2 Summary statistics for men by nativity and race/ethnic origin

	White		Black		Hispanic		Asian	
	Native	Immigrant	Native	Immigrant	Native	Immigrant	Native	Immigrant
Age								
20–24	0.109	0.080	0.139	0.120	0.210	0.124	0.208	0.106
	(0.311)	(0.271)	(0.345)	(0.324)	(0.407)	(0.330)	(0.406)	(0.308)
25–29	0.111	0.109	0.128	0.126	0.172	0.159	0.160	0.134
	(0.314)	(0.312)	(0.334)	(0.332)	(0.377)	(0.365)	(0.367)	(0.340)
30–34	0.118	0.136	0.138	0.163	0.151	0.166	0.123	0.152
	(0.323)	(0.343)	(0.345)	(0.370)	(0.358)	(0.372)	(0.329)	(0.359)
35–39	0.126	0.139	0.125	0.151	0.124	0.151	0.102	0.143
	(0.332)	(0.346)	(0.331)	(0.358)	(0.329)	(0.358)	(0.303)	(0.350)
40–44	0.130	0.136	0.129	0.138	0.105	0.129	0.088	0.128
	(0.337)	(0.343)	(0.335)	(0.345)	(0.307)	(0.336)	(0.283)	(0.334)
45–49	0.124	0.120	0.110	0.116	0.084	0.099	0.109	0.117
	(0.329)	(0.325)	(0.312)	(0.320)	(0.277)	(0.299)	(0.312)	(0.322)
50–54	0.109	0.113	0.096	0.094	0.067	0.075	0.082	0.094
	(0.312)	(0.317)	(0.295)	(0.291)	(0.250)	(0.264)	(0.275)	(0.291)
55–59	0.091	0.089	0.075	0.053	0.047	0.057	0.067	0.075
	(0.288)	(0.285)	(0.263)	(0.224)	(0.213)	(0.232)	(0.250)	(0.263)
60–64	0.082	0.077	0.062	0.040	0.040	0.040	0.060	0.052
	(0.275)	(0.267)	(0.241)	(0.196)	(0.197)	(0.195)	(0.237)	(0.221)
Married	0.643	0.679	0.456	0.540	0.520	0.627	0.471	0.672
	(0.479)	(0.467)	(0.498)	(0.498)	(0.500)	(0.484)	(0.499)	(0.470)
Years of education	13.780	14.466	12.759	13.670	12.790	10.055	14.866	14.838
	(2.703)	(3.315)	(2.523)	(2.959)	(2.598)	(4.195)	(2.454)	(3.398)
Working/employed	0.881	0.880	0.781	0.870	0.850	0.891	0.839	0.853
	(0.324)	(0.325)	(0.414)	(0.337)	(0.357)	(0.312)	(0.367)	(0.354)

Immigrant arrival cohorts

Immigrant arrival cohorts				
Pre-1980	0.360	0.237	0.224	0.219
	(0.480)	(0.426)	(0.417)	(0.414)
1981–85	0.176	0.196	0.187	0.202
	(0.381)	(0.397)	(0.390)	(0.402)
1986–90	0.201	0.208	0.250	0.235
	(0.401)	(0.406)	(0.421)	(0.424)
1991–95	0.087	0.103	0.104	0.114
	(0.282)	(0.304)	(0.306)	(0.318)
1996–2000	0.106	0.144	0.141	0.117
	(0.308)	(0.352)	(0.348)	(0.322)
2001–05	0.047	0.079	0.090	0.072
	(0.211)	(0.269)	(0.286)	(0.258)
2006–10	0.024	0.032	0.025	0.041
	(0.153)	(0.177)	(0.156)	(0.198)
Sample size	257,234	41,803	21,720	10,580
Time in destination country				
0–4 years	0.146	0.147	0.148	0.190
	(0.353)	(0.354)	(0.356)	(0.392)
5–9 years	0.130	0.191	0.187	0.174
	(0.336)	(0.393)	(0.390)	(0.379)
10–14 years	0.119	0.190	0.177	0.173
	(0.324)	(0.392)	(0.381)	(0.378)
More than 14 years	0.605	0.472	0.488	0.463
	(0.489)	(0.499)	(0.500)	(0.499)
Sample size	11,049	4003	32,275	2400

NHIS data from 1989 to 2011 for individuals aged 20–64. All statistics use NHIS annual weights. Standard deviations are given in parentheses. The sample size is based on activity limitation reports since activity limitation has the highest reporting rate.

4. MEASURING IMMIGRANT HEALTH AND ASSIMILATION

We use the following self-reported health measures: poor health, the existence of at least one activity limitation, and weight. Poor health is an indicator variable equal to 1 if the respondent reported their health was fair or poor and 0 if the respondent reported their health was good, very good, or excellent. Those with unknown health status are assigned a missing value. Panel A of Tables 6.1 and 6.2 reveals that while white and black natives are more likely to suffer from poor health than their immigrant counterparts (irrespective of gender), the same is generally not true for Hispanics and Asians. For example, 8.4% (9.2%) of white male (female) natives report they are in poor health compared to 6.7% (8.7%) of white male (female) immigrants.

Activity limitation is an indicator variable equal to 1 if the respondent reported being limited in any way and 0 otherwise (including unknowns).[24] For all racial/ethnic origin groups and for men and women, natives are more likely to suffer from activity limitations than their immigrant counterparts. For example, 16.2% of black male natives suffer from activity limitations relative to 5.1% of black male immigrants (see panel A of Table 6.2).

We construct three self-reported weight measures. The first is body mass index (BMI), defined as kilograms/meters^2, which adjusts weight for height differences.[25] While BMI is provided directly in the 1997–2011 data the same is not true for the data prior to 1997, so we construct it analogously in the 1989–96 data.[26] Ideally one would instead use measured height and weight as self-reported height and weight are subject to reporting errors that could lead to biased coefficient estimates. While the NHIS does not include measured height and weight, one could correct self-reported height and weight using the methodology outlined in Cawley (2000) and followed in Antecol and Bedard (2006). We show in our earlier work that the results using the corrected or uncorrected measures are similar; therefore we do not apply the correction in this paper.

We construct two additional indicator variables for (height-adjusted) weight: overweight and obese. Overweight equals 1 if the respondent's BMI is greater than or equal to 25, and 0 otherwise (excluding non-reporters). Obese equals 1 if the respondent's BMI is greater than or equal to 30, and 0 otherwise (excluding non-reporters). For both men and women, irrespective of the weight measure used or racial/ethnic origin group,

---

[24] Prior to 1997, limited in any way was further broken down into the following categories: unable to perform major activity, limited in kind/amount of major activity, and limited in other activities.

[25] Self-reported weight and height were reported only for respondents greater than 18 years of age in the 1989–96 NHIS data, while in the 1997–2011 NHIS data this information was collected for the sample adult and the sample child.

[26] In the 1989–96 data height and weight are converted from inches and pounds into meters and kilograms respectively by multiplying height by 0.0254 and weight by 0.453592. In the 1989–96 data, respondents who are less than 1.22 (48) and greater than 2.13 (84) meters (inches) tall are excluded from the analysis, as are respondents who are over 226.8 (500) kilograms (pounds). We also manually constructed BMI in the 1997–2011 data and confirmed the provided measure was calculated correctly.

Table 6.1 Health outcomes for women by nativity, race/ethnic origin, and time period

	White		Black		Hispanic		Asian	
	Native	Immigrant	Native	Immigrant	Native	Immigrant	Native	Immigrant
Panel A: 1989–2011								
Poor health	0.092	0.087	0.182	0.094	0.133	0.143	0.063	0.074
	(0.289)	(0.282)	(0.386)	(0.292)	(0.339)	(0.350)	(0.243)	(0.263)
Activity limitations	0.132	0.099	0.163	0.065	0.116	0.082	0.067	0.049
	(0.338)	(0.299)	(0.369)	(0.247)	(0.321)	(0.274)	(0.249)	(0.216)
BMI	25.767	24.742	28.900	27.008	27.538	26.872	23.870	22.820
	(6.136)	(5.083)	(7.210)	(5.536)	(6.632)	(5.596)	(4.970)	(3.949)
Overweight (BMI 25 +)	0.442	0.391	0.666	0.590	0.579	0.577	0.293	0.236
	(0.497)	(0.488)	(0.472)	(0.492)	(0.494)	(0.494)	(0.455)	(0.424)
Obese (BMI 30+)	0.198	0.136	0.364	0.246	0.294	0.236	0.103	0.052
	(0.398)	(0.343)	(0.481)	(0.431)	(0.455)	(0.425)	(0.304)	(0.221)
Sample size	281,786	12,497	64,078	4911	27,636	36,367	2529	11,982
Panel B: 1989–96								
Poor health	0.088	0.097	0.191	0.086	0.144	0.158	0.079	0.096
	(0.283)	(0.296)	(0.393)	(0.280)	(0.351)	(0.365)	(0.271)	(0.295)
Activity limitations	0.145	0.129	0.175	0.074	0.138	0.119	0.099	0.073
	(0.352)	(0.335)	(0.380)	(0.261)	(0.345)	(0.324)	(0.299)	(0.260)
BMI	24.427	23.975	27.249	25.669	25.727	25.583	23.221	22.058
	(5.268)	(4.539)	(6.370)	(4.859)	(5.691)	(4.857)	(4.833)	(3.509)
Overweight (BMI 25 +)	0.347	0.321	0.580	0.499	0.462	0.473	0.251	0.162
	(0.476)	(0.467)	(0.494)	(0.500)	(0.499)	(0.499)	(0.434)	(0.369)
Obese (BMI 30+)	0.134	0.100	0.274	0.158	0.198	0.166	0.078	0.028
	(0.340)	(0.300)	(0.446)	(0.365)	(0.398)	(0.372)	(0.268)	(0.166)
Sample size	174,572	7546	35,425	2233	12,942	15,552	1163	6201

Continued

Table 6.1 Health ouctomes for women by nativity, race/ethnic origin, and time period—cont'd

	White		Black		Hispanic		Asian	
	Native	Immigrant	Native	Immigrant	Native	Immigrant	Native	Immigrant
Panel C: 1997–2011								
Poor health	0.094	0.082	0.177	0.097	0.129	0.139	0.058	0.066
	(0.292)	(0.275)	(0.382)	(0.296)	(0.335)	(0.346)	(0.233)	(0.249)
Activity limitations	0.125	0.085	0.158	0.063	0.108	0.070	0.055	0.040
	(0.331)	(0.279)	(0.364)	(0.242)	(0.310)	(0.256)	(0.228)	(0.196)
BMI	26.455	25.110	29.677	27.412	28.246	27.270	24.102	23.108
	(6.429)	(5.285)	(7.448)	(5.663)	(6.836)	(5.747)	(4.999)	(4.067)
Overweight (BMI 25+)	0.491	0.425	0.707	0.617	0.624	0.609	0.308	0.263
	(0.500)	(0.494)	(0.455)	(0.486)	(0.484)	(0.488)	(0.462)	(0.441)
Obese (BMI 30+)	0.231	0.153	0.407	0.273	0.331	0.257	0.112	0.061
	(0.421)	(0.360)	(0.491)	(0.446)	(0.471)	(0.437)	(0.316)	(0.239)
Sample size	107,214	4951	28,653	2678	14,694	20,815	1366	5781

NHIS data from 1989 to 2011 for individuals aged 20–64. All statistics use NHIS annual weights. Standard deviations are given in parentheses. The sample size is based on activity limitation reports since activity limitation has the highest reporting rate.

Table 6.2 Health ouctomes for men by nativity, race/ethnic origin, and time period

	White		Black		Hispanic		Asian	
	Native	Immigrant	Native	Immigrant	Native	Immigrant	Native	Immigrant
Panel A: 1989–2011								
Poor health	0.084	0.067	0.148	0.061	0.107	0.100	0.062	0.060
	(0.277)	(0.250)	(0.355)	(0.239)	(0.310)	(0.300)	(0.241)	(0.238)
Activity limitations	0.126	0.084	0.162	0.051	0.110	0.063	0.084	0.042
	(0.331)	(0.277)	(0.368)	(0.220)	(0.313)	(0.243)	(0.278)	(0.200)
BMI	27.209	26.437	27.843	26.074	28.401	27.154	26.147	24.367
	(4.905)	(4.253)	(5.542)	(4.010)	(5.528)	(–.390)	(4.672)	(3.572)
Overweight (BMI 25+)	0.660	0.614	0.681	0.590	0.733	0.685	0.562	0.389
	(0.474)	(0.487)	(0.466)	(0.492)	(0.443)	(0.464)	(0.496)	(0.487)
Obese (BMI 30+)	0.224	0.158	0.279	0.136	0.309	0.205	0.156	0.059
	(0.417)	(0.365)	(0.449)	(0.343)	(0.462)	(0.404)	(0.363)	(0.235)
Sample size	257,234	11,049	41,803	4003	21,720	32,275	2400	10,580
Panel B: 1989–96								
Poor health	0.080	0.074	0.149	0.039	0.103	0.108	0.053	0.070
	(0.271)	(0.262)	(0.356)	(0.194)	(0.304)	(0.310)	(0.223)	(0.255)
Activity limitations	0.140	0.109	0.174	0.063	0.128	0.095	0.096	0.063
	(0.347)	(0.312)	(0.379)	(0.243)	(0.334)	(0.293)	(0.294)	(0.243)
BMI	26.211	25.656	26.598	25.254	26.811	25.070	25.166	23.574
	(4.211)	(3.707)	(4.633)	(3.392)	(4.544)	(3.901)	(4.089)	(3.183)
Overweight (BMI 25+)	0.589	0.551	0.609	0.526	0.638	0.586	0.462	0.293
	(0.492)	(0.497)	(0.488)	(0.499)	(0.481)	(0.492)	(0.499)	(0.455)
Obese (BMI 30+)	0.153	0.105	0.191	0.079	0.195	0.132	0.112	0.032
	(0.360)	(0.306)	(0.393)	(0.270)	(0.396)	(0.339)	(0.316)	(0.175)
Sample size	164,033	6748	24,418	1829	11,084	14,536	1117	5429

Continued

Table 6.2 Health ouctomes for men by nativity, race/ethnic origin, and time period—cont'd

	White		Black		Hispanic		Asian	
	Native	Immigrant	Native	Immigrant	Native	Immigrant	Native	Immigrant
Panel C: 1997–2011								
Poor health	0.086	0.064	0.148	0.067	0.109	0.098	0.065	0.057
	(0.280)	(0.245)	(0.355)	(0.249)	(0.312)	(0.297)	(0.246)	(0.232)
Activity limitations	0.118	0.072	0.157	0.048	0.104	0.054	0.080	0.034
	(0.323)	(0.258)	(0.363)	(0.213)	(0.305)	(0.227)	(0.272)	(0.182)
BMI	27.709	26.797	28.424	26.309	28.976	27.448	26.493	24.650
	(5.146)	(4.438)	(5.828)	(4.142)	(5.736)	(4.468)	(4.815)	(3.660)
Overweight (BMI 25 +)	0.695	0.643	0.715	0.608	0.767	0.712	0.597	0.423
	(0.460)	(0.479)	(0.452)	(0.488)	(0.423)	(0.453)	(0.491)	(0.494)
Obese (BMI 30+)	0.260	0.183	0.321	0.152	0.351	0.225	0.171	0.068
	(0.438)	(0.386)	(0.467)	(0.360)	(0.477)	(0.418)	(0.377)	(0.252)
Sample size	93,201	4301	17,385	2174	10,636	17,739	1283	5151

NHIS data from 1989 to 2011 for individuals aged 20–64. All statistics use NHIS annual weights. Standard deviations are in parentheses. The sample size is based on activity limitation reports since activity limitation has the highest reporting rate.

natives are heavier than their immigrant counterparts (see panel A of Tables 6.1 and 6.2, for men and women, respectively). Perhaps not surprisingly, Asians have the lowest weight measures relative to the other racial/ethnic origin groups by nativity and gender while blacks (Hispanics) have the highest weight measures relative to the other racial/ethnic origin groups by nativity for women (men). For example, 10.3% (5.2%), 36.4% (24.6%), 29.4% (23.6%), and 19.8% (13.6%) of Asian, black, Hispanic, white native (immigrant) women are obese (see panel A of Table 6.1) and 15.6% (5.9%), 30.9% (20.5%), 27.9% (13.6%), and 22.4% (15.8%) of Asian, Hispanic, black, white native (immigrant) men are obese (see panel A of Table 6.2).

Overall, our self-reported health measures generally suggest that immigrants are healthier than natives. Do immigrants converge towards their native counterparts' unhealthy outcomes, i.e., do immigrants experience unhealthy assimilation? In earlier work, Antecol and Bedard (2006) found evidence of unhealthy assimilation (based on a number of health outcomes including obesity) for Hispanic immigrants (particularly females) from the 1989–96 NHIS data. In contrast, Park et al. (2009) found no evidence of unhealthy assimilation for Hispanics (based on obesity) comparing NHIS data from 1994–96 to 2004–06. One potential reason for the discrepancy in the results is that the rate at which natives and immigrants are becoming unhealthy may differ from each other and change across time periods. For instance, if the rate of growth in obesity is similar for immigrants and natives prior to 1997 yet the rate of growth in obesity for natives is faster than that of immigrants post-1996, then one could mistakenly conclude there is no assimilation toward native weights.

In an attempt to ascertain if this is indeed the case we examine the overall self-reported health measures in the two time periods: 1989–96 (panel B of Tables 6.1 and 6.2 for men and women respectively) and 1997–2011 (panel C of Tables 6.1 and 6.2 for men and women respectively). We focus most of our discussion here on our self-reported weight measures because this is the measure Park et al. (2009) employed in their analysis. Moreover, there are no clear differences in the two times periods with respect to reports of poor health while reports of activity limitations in 1997–2011 relative to 1989–96 declined for both men and women irrespective of nativity.[27]

Panels B and C of Table 6.1 reveal that for all weight measures female native average weight increased by more than female immigrant average weight for all racial/ethnic origin groups except Asians between these two time periods. For example, the probability of obesity increased 9.7 (5.4), 13.3 (11.5), and 13.4 (9.1) percentage points for white, black, and Hispanic female natives (immigrants) respectively. While the probability of obesity increased by roughly the same amount for Asian female natives and immigrants over this time period, the probability of being overweight increased more for Asian female

---

[27] This may be an artifact of how the activity limitation question changed between the two time periods (see footnote 13) as opposed to a real decline in the activity limitation over these two time periods.

immigrants (10.1 percentage points) than Asian female natives (5.7 percentage points) over this time period.

The patterns are somewhat different for men (see panels B and C of Table 6.2). For all weight measures, male native average weight generally increased by more than male immigrant average weight for all racial/ethnic origin groups.[28] For example, the probability of obesity increased 10.7 (7.8), 13.0 (7.3), 15.6 (9.3), and 5.9 (3.7) percentage points for white, black, Hispanic, and Asian male natives (immigrants) respectively.

Overall, these patterns point to an important difference between the 1989–96 data and the 1997–2011 data: natives seem to be gaining weight at a faster rate than immigrants in the latter time period but not in the former time period. If one does not account for this in their analysis, one could mistakenly conclude that there is no assimilation toward native weights. The remainder of the chapter formally investigates the assimilation patterns of immigrants, paying particular attention to the differences between the two time periods.

5. ANALYZING COHORT AND ASSIMILATION EFFECTS

We examine immigrant assimilation for all of our self-reported health outcomes following the methodology developed by Borjas (1985, 1995). Specifically, we estimate equations of the following form:

$$Y_i = X_i\beta + A_i\delta + C_i\gamma + T_i\pi + \varepsilon_i \qquad (6.1)$$

where Y is one of our self-reported health outcomes (poor health, activity limitation, BMI, overweight, obese), X is a vector of control variables (age, marital status, education, employment status, region), A is a vector of indicator variables identifying length of US residence (0–4 years (omitted category), 5–9 years, 10–14 years, more than 14 years), which is set equal to 0 for natives, C is a vector of indicator variables identifying immigrant arrival cohorts (pre-1980, 1981–85, 1986–90, 1991–95, 1996–2000, 2001–05, 2006–10), which are set equal to 0 for natives, T is a vector of indicator variables identifying the survey year, i denotes individuals, and ε is a random error term.

This specification (henceforth referred to as Specification 1) gives each immigrant arrival cohort its own intercept and each intercept can be interpreted as the difference between immigrants who have recently arrived (those with 0–4 years of residency) from a specific cohort and natives. Thus, differences in these intercepts represent permanent outcome differences between cohorts. The coefficients for the length of US residence indicator variables (A) measure the effects of immigrant assimilation with respect to the self-reported health outcomes under consideration.

---

[28] Although the probability of being overweight did increase more for Hispanic male natives than Hispanic male immigrants, the difference is extremely small (12.9 percentage points vs. 12.6 percentage points).

In order to identify the cohort and assimilation effects, we restrict the period effect, π, to be the same for both immigrants and natives. However, as previously noted the period effects are clearly different for natives and immigrants between the 1989–96 and 1997–2011 time periods (particularly for our self-reported weight measures). Thus, this may not be a reasonable identifying restriction as it may lead to biased results for our assimilation and cohort indicator variables. As such, we re-estimate equation (6.1) allowing for differential cohort and assimilation effects between the two time periods (henceforth referred to as Specification 2). In other words, we interact C and A with an indicator variable for post-1996, which equals 1 if the survey year is between 1997 and 2011, and equals 0 if the survey year is between 1989 and 1996.

For both Specifications 1 and 2 we also allow for differential aging patterns between natives and immigrants. The remaining control variables (X) are restricted to be the same for immigrants and natives and across survey years. We then estimate Specifications 1 and 2 within racial/ethnic origin group. In other words, we focus on the assimilation patterns of white immigrants to white natives, black immigrants to black natives, Hispanic immigrants to Hispanic natives, and Asian immigrants to Asian natives. Alternatively we could have chosen to use white natives as the base group (a convention typically adopted in the labor market assimilation literature); however, we wanted to avoid confounding possible racial/ethnic origin differences with assimilation.

We estimate all self-reported health equations using a probit model with the exception of BMI, which is estimated using a log-linear regression framework. For interpretative ease, we report probit marginal effects for continuous variables and average treatment effects for discrete variables, evaluated at means, as well as standard errors calculated using the delta method.

6. THE HEALTHY IMMIGRANT EFFECT

In order to determine if there is evidence of the Healthy Immigrant Effect (HIE), we begin by estimating Specifications 1 and 2 for our two measures of self-reported health: poor health and activity limitations. Tables 6.3 and 6.4 present the results for the immigrant cohort and assimilation effects by gender and race/ethnicity for our two measures of self-reported health respectively.[29] For these tables (and all future tables) column 1 represents Specification 1 while column 2 represents Specification 2.

We first focus our discussion on Specification 1. In terms of our poor health measure, the period effects are generally positive (although sometimes imprecisely estimated), which suggests that Americans are reporting poorer health over time. This is generally true for both males and females and for all race/ethnic origin groups, although the effects are more pronounced for whites. The same is not true for our activity limitation variable.

---

[29] We do not report period effects to avoid overly cluttered tables; these effects are available upon request.

Table 6.3 Immigrant arrival cohort and assimilation effects of the probability of poor health by race/ethnic origin and gender (probit marginal effects and standard errors)

	Women							
	White		Black		Hispanic		Asian	
	(1)	(2)	(1)	(2)	(1)	(2)	(1)	(2)
Immigrant arrival cohorts								
Pre-1980	−0.011	−0.042★★	−0.011	−0.067	−0.027★★	−0.041★★	0.045	0.003
	(0.017)	(0.016)	(0.046)	(0.054)	(0.013)	(0.022)	(0.035)	(0.032)
1981–85	−0.017	−0.045★	0.000	−0.060	−0.024★★	−0.037★★	0.030	0.008
	(0.016)	(0.011)	(0.048)	(0.048)	(0.012)	(0.017)	(0.028)	(0.027)
1986–90	−0.006	−0.027	−0.002	−0.061	−0.028★	−0.024★★	0.027	0.012
	(0.017)	(0.014)	(0.043)	(0.035)	(0.011)	(0.013)	(0.024)	(0.021)
1991–95	-0.022	−0.019	−0.075★	−0.070★★	−0.025★	−0.006	0.019	0.032
	(0.014)	(0.015)	(0.026)	(0.030)	(0.011)	(0.014)	(0.023)	(0.027)
1996–2000	−0.031★★		−0.072★★		−0.035★		0.017	
	(0.013)		(0.033)		(0.011)		(0.024)	
2001–05	−0.039★		−0.030		−0.045★		−0.020	
	(0.011)		(0.056)		(0.011)		(0.015)	
2006–10	−0.040★★		−0.019		−0.004		0.019	
	(0.014)		(0.057)		(0.024)		(0.034)	
Time in destination country								
5–9 years	−0.009	0.045★★	0.017	0.083	0.015	0.029★★	0.011	0.033★
	(0.013)	(0.029)	(0.042)	(0.069)	(0.010)	(0.017)	(0.010)	(0.019)
10–14 years	−0.021	0.052	−0.013	0.097	0.027★	0.051★	0.001	0.026
	(0.011)	(0.046)	(0.034)	(0.098)	(0.012)	(0.027)	(0.012)	(0.028)
More than 14 years	−0.034★	0.008	0.025	0.098	0.052★	0.066★	−0.012	0.019
	(0.009)	(0.037)	(0.044)	(0.111)		(0.030)	(0.013)	(0.030)
Immigrant arrival cohort interactions								
Pre-1980•Post-1996		0.054		0.232		−0.028		0.062
		(0.075)		(0.182)		(0.030)		(0.091)
1981–85•Post-1996		0.059		0.217★★		−0.030		0.019
		(0.069)		(0.157)		(0.025)		(0.052)
1986–90•Post-1996		0.034		0.221★		−0.043★		0.018
		(0.048)		(0.125)		(0.018)		(0.040)
1991–95•Post-1996		0.006		0.039		−0.042★		−0.015
		(0.030)		(0.084)		(0.015)		(0.021)
1996–2000•Post-1996		−0.026		−0.052		−0.047★		0.016
		(0.016)		(0.042)		(0.012)		(0.029)
2001–05•Post-1996		−0.037★		−0.017		−0.049★		−0.021
		(0.012)		(0.061)		(0.011)		(0.016)
2006–10•Post-1996		−0.040★★		−0.017		−0.001		0.020
		(0.014)		(0.058)		(0.025)		(0.034)
Time in destination country interactions								
5–9 years•Post-1996		−0.041★★		-0.062		0.000		−0.015
		(0.014)		(0.049)		(0.020)		(0.017)
10–14 years•Post-1996		−0.048★		−0.106★★		0.006		−0.016
		(0.013)		(0.031)		(0.028)		(0.025)
More than 14 years•Post-1996		−0.038		−0.099		0.036		−0.030
		(0.024)		(0.045)		(0.038)		(0.037)
Sample size	293,616		68,790		63,813		14,470	

All models also include age dummies, age dummies interacted with immigrant status, years of education, and indicators for married, employed, region, and survey year. NHIS annual weights are used.
Asterisks: statistically significant at the 5% (★) or 10% (★★) level.

	Men						
	White		Black		Hispanic		Asian	
(1)	(2)	(1)	(2)	(1)	(2)	(1)	(2)
−0.013	−0.040★★	−0.093★	−0.059	0.008	−0.026	0.056★★	0.055
(0.016)	(0.011)	(0.009)	(0.040)	(0.016)	(0.019)	(0.040)	(0.052)
−0.008	−0.039★	−0.079★	−0.054	0.008	−0.028★★	0.055★★	0.038
(0.018)	(0.010)	(0.017)	(0.036)	(0.015)	(0.015)	(0.035)	(0.038)
−0.009	−0.029★	−0.086★	−0.058★★	−0.012	−0.029★	0.037	0.056★
(0.015)	(0.010)	(0.012)	(0.023)	(0.011)	(0.010)	(0.029)	(0.033)
−0.017	−0.009	−0.073★	−0.070★★	−0.015	−0.018	0.025	0.048★★
(0.014)	(0.017)	(0.018)	(0.021)	(0.011)	(0.012)	(0.026)	(0.031)
−0.036★		−0.078★		−0.019		0.024	
(0.008)		(0.018)		(0.011)		(0.027)	
−0.034★		−0.062		−0.036★		−0.012	
(0.011)		(0.026)		(0.009)		(0.017)	
−0.048★		−0.074★		0.015		−0.003	
(0.004)		(0.017)		(0.026)		(0.020)	
0.013	0.085★	0.057	−0.031	0.005	0.046★	−0.003	0.011
(0.015)	(0.038)	(0.047)	(0.037)	(0.010)	(0.017)	(0.009)	(0.017)
0.006	0.095★	0.135★	−0.015	0.000	0.054★	−0.004	0.006
(0.016)	(0.063)	(0.063)	(0.058)	(0.011)	(0.026)	(0.012)	(0.024)
−0.009	0.054	0.166★	−0.013	0.010	0.052	−0.011	−0.003
(0.012)	(0.055)	(0.069)	(0.069)	(0.012)	(0.027)	(0.014)	(0.027)
	0.124★★		−0.071		0.040		−0.044
	(0.108)		(0.038)		(0.044)		(0.014)
	0.130★		−0.048		0.046		−0.033
	(0.097)		(0.054)		(0.037)		(0.020)
	0.076★★		−0.068		0.023		−0.046★
	(0.061)		(0.030)		(0.025)		(0.013)
	0.000		−0.035		0.014		−0.034★
	(0.026)		(0.054)		(0.022)		(0.010)
	−0.032★★		−0.085★		−0.014		−0.002
	(0.011)		(0.016)		(0.014)		(0.022)
	−0.030★★		−0.071		0.034★		−0.016
	(0.012)		(0.024)		(0.010)		(0.016)
	−0.048★		−0.073★		0.015		−0.001
	(0.004)		(0.018)		(0.026)		(0.021)
	−0.037★		0.170★★		−0.036★		0.002
	(0.010)		(0.134)		(0.013)		(0.023)
	−0.041★★		0.238★★		−0.043★		0.034
	(0.011)		(0.182)		(0.016)		(0.047)
	−0.042		0.215		−0.035		0.066
	(0.013)		(0.202)		(0.026)		(0.065)
267,728		45,621		53,857		12,960	

Table 6.4 Immigrant arrival cohort and assimilation effects of the probability of activity limitation by race/ethnic origin and gender (probit marginal effects and standard errors)

	Women							
	White		Black		Hispanic		Asian	
	(1)	(2)	(1)	(2)	(1)	(2)	(1)	(2)
Immigrant arrival cohorts								
Pre-1980	−0.058★	−0.078★	−0.052	−0.070	−0.030★	−0.054★	−0.012	−0.006
	(0.014)	(0.016)	(0.027)	(0.033)	(0.009)	(0.010)	(0.013)	(0.020)
1981–85	−0.067★	−0.065★	−0.054	−0.087★	−0.032★	−0.047★	−0.014	−0.010
	(0.012)	(0.017)	(0.025)	(0.017)	(0.008)	(0.008)	(0.012)	(0.015)
1986–90	−0.055★	−0.064★	−0.057★★	−0.082★	−0.037★	−0.042★	−0.012	−0.014
	(0.013)	(0.012)	(0.024)	(0.015)	(0.007)	(0.007)	(0.011)	(0.011)
1991–95	−0.074★	−0.063★	−0.065★	−0.077★	−0.042★	−0.036★	−0.020★★	−0.021★
	(0.009)	(0.012)	(0.018)	(0.015)	(0.005)	(0.006)	(0.007)	(0.007)
1996–2000	−0.081★		−0.095★		−0.049★		−0.022	
	(0.009)		(0.008)		(0.005)		(0.009)	
2001–05	−0.076★		−0.081★		−0.056★		−0.022★★	
	(0.011)		(0.016)		(0.004)		(0.007)	
2006–10	−0.089★		−0.086★		−0.054★		−0.024★	
	(0.009)		(0.014)		(0.005)		(0.006)	
Time in destination country								
5–9 years	0.023	0.039	0.007	0.097	0.014★★	0.038★	0.007	0.005
	(0.022)	(0.032)	(0.031)	(0.072)	(0.008)	(0.015)	(0.008)	(0.013)
10–14 years	0.002	0.061	0.032	0.107	0.009	0.059★	0.015	0.011
	(0.019)	(0.052)	(0.038)	(0.099)	(0.009)	(0.025)	(0.010)	(0.020)
More than 14 years	0.026	0.086	0.031	0.084	0.028★	0.086★	0.016	0.001
	(0.022)	(0.063)	(0.038)	(0.104)	(0.010)	(0.027)	(0.011)	(0.020)
Immigrant arrival cohort interactions								
Pre-1980•Post–1996		0.001		0.153		0.033		−0.019
		(0.061)		(0.172)		(0.036)		(0.020)
1981–85•Post–1996		−0.044		0.267★		0.019		−0.020
		(0.035)		(0.177)		(0.028)		(0.017)
1986–90•Post–1996		−0.017		0.206★		0.002		−0.010
		(0.038)		(0.136)		(0.019)		(0.019)
1991–95•Post–1996		−0.042		0.117		-0.014		0.000
		(0.026)		(0.099)		(0.013)		(0.019)
1996–2000•Post–1996		−0.082★		−0.087★		−0.050★		−0.022
		(0.009)		(0.012)		(0.006)		(0.011)
2001–05•Post–1996		−0.077★		−0.070★★		−0.056★		−0.021★★
		(0.011)		(0.023)		(0.004)		(0.008)
2006–10•Post–1996		−0.089★		−0.086★		−0.054★		−0.022★★
		(0.009)		(0.014)		(0.005)		(0.007)
Time in destination country interactions								
5–9 years•Post–1996		−0.005		−0.077★★		−0.018		0.003
		(0.039)		(0.023)		(0.013)		(0.019)
10–14 years•Post–1996		−0.037		−0.076		−0.030★★		0.007
		(0.036)		(0.031)		(0.014)		(0.028)
More than 14 years•Post–1996		−0.003		−0.080		−0.034		0.042
		(0.059)		(0.036)		(0.020)		(0.048)
Sample size	294,283		68,989		64,003		14,511	

All models also include age dummies, age dummies interacted with immigrant status, years of education, and indicators for married, employed, region, and survey year. NHIS annual weights are used.
Asterisks: statistically significant at the 5% (★) or 10% (★★) level.

	Men							
	White		Black		Hispanic		Asian	
	(1)	(2)	(1)	(2)	(1)	(2)	(1)	(2)
	−0.045★	−0.069★	−0.061★★	−0.083	−0.018★★	−0.039★	−0.005	−0.009
	(0.015)	(0.016)	(0.023)	(0.023)	(0.009)	(0.009)	(0.014)	(0.018)
	−0.054★	−0.065★	−0.058	−0.074	−0.023★	−0.034★	−0.010	−0.013
	(0.013)	(0.015)	(0.028)	(0.028)	(0.008)	(0.008)	(0.010)	(0.013)
	−0.052★	−0.060★	−0.067★	−0.071★★	−0.025★	−0.032★	−0.010	−0.010
	(0.012)	(0.011)	(0.019)	(0.024)	(0.007)	(0.006)	(0.010)	(0.011)
	−0.063★	−0.071★	−0.087★	−0.085★	−0.028★	−0.023★	−0.014	−0.012
	(0.010)	(0.008)	(0.009)	(0.012)	(0.005)	(0.007)	(0.008)	(0.008)
	−0.067★		−0.075★		−0.035★		−0.027★	
	(0.010)		(0.016)		(0.006)		(0.005)	
	−0.0698		−0.063		−0.041★		−0.025★	
	(0.013)		(0.026)		(0.004)		(0.004)	
	−0.090★		−0.087★		−0.039★		−0.020★★	
	(0.003)		(0.008)		(0.005)		(0.006)	
	0.015	0.031	0.043	0.043	0.005	0.027★	0.010	0.020
	(0.023)	(0.034)	(0.047)	(0.078)	(0.009)	(0.014)	(0.008)	(0.016)
	0.005	0.088★★	0.041	0.140	0.011	0.052★	0.005	0.017
	(0.020)	(0.061)	(0.043)	(0.136)	(0.011)	(0.024)	(0.009)	(0.023)
	0.040★★	0.111★	0.079★★	0.194	0.016	0.065★	0.007	0.020
	(0.025)	(0.071)	(0.057)	(0.167)	(0.011)	(0.025)	(0.011)	(0.023)
		0.120		0.097		0.037		−0.010
		(0.105)		(0.170)		(0.040)		(0.026)
		0.071		0.074		0.016		−0.004
		(0.081)		(0.140)		(0.029)		(0.026)
		0.071		0.035		0.012		−0.003
		(0.066)		(0.097)		(0.023)		(0.021)
		0.088★★		-0.007		-0.010		0.002
		(0.059)		(0.073)		(0.015)		(0.018)
		−0.059★		−0.074★		−0.034★		−0.026★
		(0.015)		(0.017)		(0.007)		(0.005)
		−0.065★		−0.067		−0.040★		−0.025★
		(0.014)		(0.025)		(0.004)		(0.004)
		−0.089★		−0.087★		−0.038★		−0.020★★
		(0.004)		(0.008)		(0.005)		(0.006)
		−0.030		0.011		−0.018		−0.013
		(0.031)		(0.084)		(0.013)		(0.010)
		−0.072★		−0.063		−0.025		−0.012
		(0.016)		(0.040)		(0.014)		(0.016)
		−0.059		−0.065		−0.031		−0.006
		(0.028)		(0.049)		(0.019)		(0.029)
	268,283		45,806		53,995		12,980	

Prior to 1997, Americans appear to be reporting somewhat more activity limitations relative to 1989; after 1997, however, the reverse appears to be true (i.e., reports of activity limitations are declining relative to 1989).[30] We think this is largely an artifact of a change in the survey between the two time periods (see footnote 13) as opposed to a real decline in the activity limitation over these two time periods.

The cohort marginal effects are generally uniformly negative (although sometimes imprecisely estimated) irrespective of gender and race/ethnicity.[31] This implies that immigrants who have recently arrived in the US (those within 0–4 years of residency) are generally less likely to report they are in poor health or suffer from an activity limitation than natives. Moreover, we find some evidence that more recent cohorts are healthier (based on our activity limitation measure) than their earlier counterparts given the magnitude (in absolute value) of the cohort effects appears to be increasing across cohorts (see column 1 of Table 6.4). For example, relative to white natives, white female (male) immigrants who recently arrived in the US are 5.8 (4.5) percentage points less likely to report they suffer from an activity limitation in the pre-1980 arrival cohort while white female (male) immigrants who recently arrived in the US are 8.9 (9.0) percentage points less likely to report they suffer from an activity limitation in the 2001–06 arrival cohort. These differences in health across cohorts are less apparent for our poor health measures, although there is some evidence to suggest a similar pattern for white immigrants irrespective of gender.

Turning to assimilation, we find very little evidence of assimilation for immigrants in terms of self-reported health except for Hispanic female immigrants and black male immigrants. Specifically, the probability of being in poor health increases by 1.5 percentage points as female Hispanic immigrants pass from 0–4 to 5–9 years in the US, but thereafter increases only by 3.7 percentage points. The percentage of male black immigrants reporting poor health conditions, relative to their level during the initial four years of US residence, rises by 5.7 percentage points after 5–9 years, by 13.5 percentage points after 10–14 years, and 16.6 percentage points after more than 14 years. Thus, assimilation towards US levels eventually erases all or most of the initial health advantage (as evidenced by the cohort marginal effects) for female Hispanic immigrants and black male immigrants. Similar patterns are found for our activity limitation measure for Hispanic female immigrants and black male immigrants, although they are less pronounced and tend to be more imprecisely estimated.

As previously discussed, however, our assimilation indicator variables may be biased if we do not appropriately account for the potential differences in the period effects between the 1989–96 and 1997–2011 time periods for natives and immigrants. As such, we allow for differential cohort and assimilation effects by the post-1996 time period (see column 2 of Tables 6.3 and 6.4).

---

[30] These patterns tend to be more pronounced for whites than for the other racial/ethnic groups.

[31] The main exceptions are Asians (irrespective of gender) and Hispanic males for our poor health measure.

There are several noteworthy patterns. First, the cohort effects are generally indistinguishable across the two time periods and continue to largely be negative irrespective of health measure, gender, and race/ethnicity (see previous discussion for notable exceptions). Second, while there is little evidence to support the notion that accounting for differential period effects changes the overall patterns found for our activity limitation measure (the main exception is Hispanic male immigrants), the same is not true for our poor health measure. Specifically, white male immigrants appear to assimilate towards their native counterparts in terms of their reports of poor health, although there is faster assimilation in the period prior to 1997 relative to the post-1996 period. The pattern is quite different for white female immigrants. While there is evidence of assimilation prior to 1997 (although some of the effects tend to be imprecisely estimated), the same is not true post-1996. Turning to Hispanic immigrants, we find evidence that male and female immigrants assimilate toward their native counterparts, although the rate of assimilation is faster (similar) in the period prior to 1997 relative to the post-1996 period for males (females). The pattern for black male immigrants differs from the other immigrant groups; we find no evidence of assimilation prior to 1997, yet there is considerable evidence of assimilation post-1996. Finally, we continue to find no evidence of assimilation for Asian immigrants (irrespective of gender) and black female immigrants. Thus, we find some evidence (depending on racial/ethnic group and health measure) to support the notion that accounting for differential period effects changes the overall assimilation patterns.

Taken together, these results provide suggestive evidence of the HIE. Specifically, we find that recent immigrants do generally arrive in the US healthier than their native counterparts irrespective of gender and race/ethnicity. Moreover, this health advantage appears to decline (and/or is erased) with time in the US (depending on specification and health measure) for white immigrants (irrespective of gender), Hispanic immigrants (irrespective of gender), and black male immigrants, but not for black female immigrants or Asian immigrants (irrespective of gender).

The remainder of the chapter examines the weight patterns of immigrants relative to their native counterparts between 1989 and 2011 using NHIS data. Given the differences in weight assimilation by demographic characteristics documented in the existing literature, we stratify our analysis by race/ethnicity and gender. In addition, we examine assimilation controlling for cohort effects and we explore the possibility that the rate at which natives and immigrants are becoming unhealthy may differ from each other and change across time periods.

6.1 Weight patterns by nativity

In order to determine if immigrants converge to unhealthy American weights, we begin by simply graphing our BMI measure by race/ethnicity from 1989 to 2011 for women (Figure 6.1a) and men (Figure 6.1b). To allow for easy visual analysis of immigrant

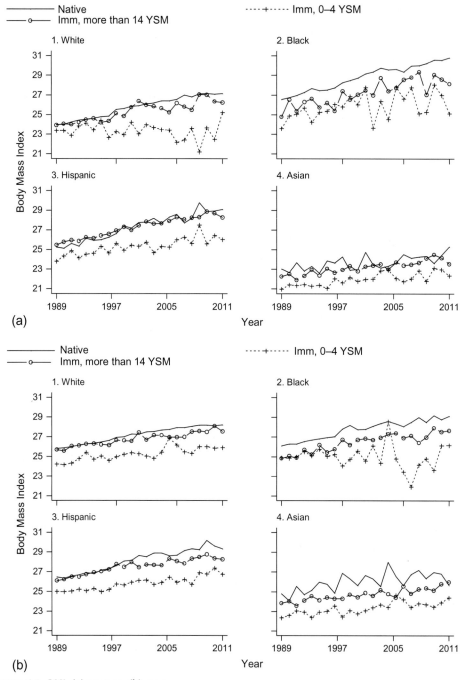

Figure 6.1 *BMI: (a) women; (b) men.*

assimilation patterns, each graph includes a line for natives, immigrants arriving 0–4 years ago, and immigrants arriving more than 14 years ago.

Average BMI rose for both native men and women between 1989 and 2011 for all racial/ethnic groups, although the average BMI level does differ across racial/ethnic groups. Specifically, in 1989 the average native white woman had a BMI of 23.99. Over the next 22 years this rose by 13.2% to 27.15. While the BMIs for the average native black and Hispanic woman in 1989 were 26.56 and 25.23 respectively, the growth rates for both groups were roughly 16%. Asian women had lower BMIs (i.e., 23.04 in 1989) and their growth rate was slower at 10%. The average upward trend for men was slower, with a growth rate of approximately 11% (4%) for whites, blacks, and Hispanics (Asians).

We now examine the immigrant patterns. While we observe the same upward trend in BMI over time for immigrants, holding years since arrival constant, the overall growth rate was generally slower for immigrants relative to natives irrespective of gender or race/ethnicity. Not surprisingly, we find that the longer immigrants reside in the US the higher their BMIs become irrespective of gender or race/ethnicity. Finally, while there is evidence that immigrants are converging towards their native counterparts in terms of BMI, the patterns differ by gender and race/ethnicity. In particular, Hispanic immigrant women who have lived in the US for 0–4 years have lower BMIs than native Hispanics, while Hispanic immigrant women who have lived in the US for more than 14 years have higher BMIs than native Hispanics up until the late 1990s and thereafter have similar BMIs to their native counterparts. In contrast, Hispanic immigrant men who have lived in the US for more than 14 years have similar BMIs relative to native Hispanics up until the mid to late 1990s and thereafter have lower BMIs than their native counterparts. The patterns for white immigrants (irrespective of gender) are similar to those exhibited by Hispanic males. For black and Asian male immigrants, BMIs do not converge to the comparable native level even for the more than 14 years of US residency group. While the same is true for black female immigrants, Asian female immigrants appear to converge towards their native counterparts (although the native series is noisier due to small sample sizes of Asian natives).

Figures 6.2 and 6.3 replicate Figure 6.1 for the percentage of people classified as overweight and obese respectively. In both cases the patterns are very similar. The one noticeable difference is that there appears to be somewhat more immigrant convergence in the overweight designation relative to the BMI and the obese designation. The remainder of the chapter provides a more formal analysis of this immigrant convergence.

6.2 Immigrant assimilation and cohort differentials

In order to determine if there is evidence of immigrant convergence towards American unhealthy weights, we estimate Specifications 1 and 2 for our three measures of weight: BMI, overweight, and obese. Tables 6.5–6.7 present the results for the immigrant cohort

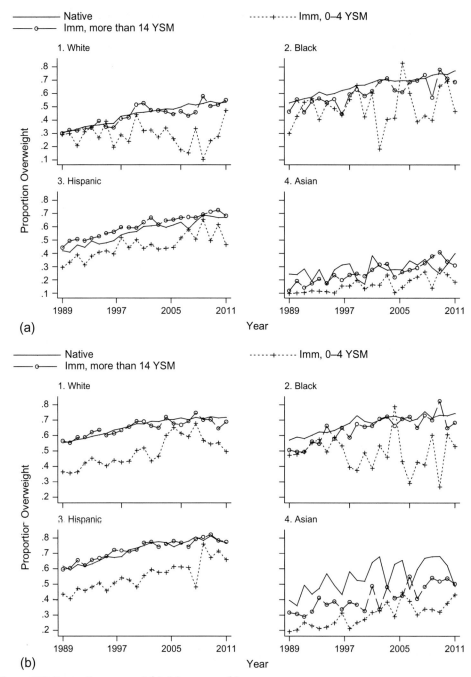

Figure 6.2 *Proportion overweight: (a) women; (b) men.*

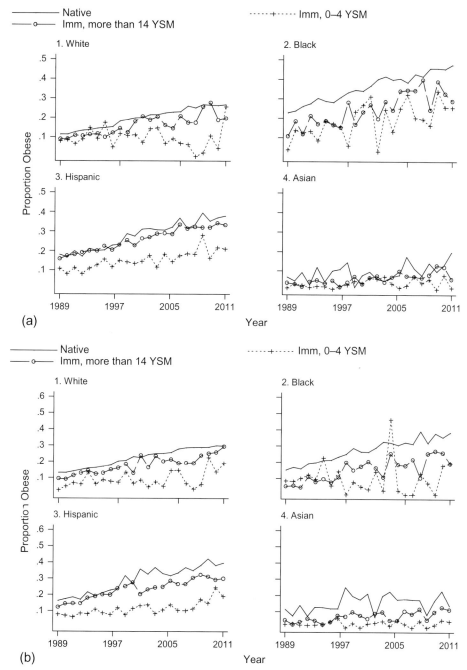

Figure 6.3 *Proportion obese: (a) women; (b) men.*

Table 6.5 Immigrant arrival cohort and assimilation effects of Ln BMI by race/ethnic origin and gender (OLS coefficients and standard errors)

	Women							
	White		Black		Hispanic		Asian	
	(1)	(2)	(1)	(2)	(1)	(2)	(1)	(2)
Immigrant arrival cohorts								
Pre-1980	−0.008	−0.007	−0.032★★	−0.009	−0.007	−0.031★	−0.048★	−0.061★
	(0.012)	(0.021)	(0.019)	(0.031)	(0.009)	(0.014)	(0.018)	(0.024)
1981–85	−0.027★	−0.034★	−0.040★	−0.044★★	−0.021★	−0.040★	−0.048★	−0.053★
	(0.012)	(0.017)	(0.019)	(0.024)	(0.008)	(0.011)	(0.016)	(0.018)
1986–90	−0.016	−0.010	−0.068★	−0.063★	−0.034★	−0.033★	−0.042★	−0.051★
	(0.010)	(0.011)	(0.017)	(0.015)	(0.007)	(0.007)	(0.014)	(0.014)
1991–95	−0.041★	−0.017	−0.088★	−0.089★	−0.051★	−0.044★	−0.064★	−0.062★
	(0.010)	(0.011)	(0.017)	(0.018)	(0.007)	(0.008)	(0.014)	(0.014)
1996–2000	−0.067★		−0.101★		−0.068★		−0.067★	
	(0.011)		(0.018)		(0.007)		(0.014)	
2001–05	−0.083★		−0.136★		−0.088★		−0.057★	
	(0.013)		(0.024)		(0.008)		(0.015)	
2006–10	−0.102★		−0.141★		−0.090★		−0.060★	
	(0.020)		(0.027)		(0.015)		(0.020)	
Time in destination country								
5–9 years	−0.014★★	-0.001	−0.004	0.001	0.003	0.015★	0.001	0.016
	(0.008)	(0.013)	(0.015)	(0.018)	(0.005)	(0.007)	(0.007)	(0.011)
10–14 years	−0.019★	-0.007	−0.005	−0.030	0.000	0.022★★	0.016★★	0.017
	(0.009)	(0.018)	(0.015)	(0.027)	(0.006)	(0.012)	(0.009)	(0.017)
More than 14 years	−0.019★★	-0.021	−0.039★	−0.055★★	−0.006	0.028★	0.018	0.033
	(0.010)	(0.020)	(0.017)	(0.030)	(0.007)	(0.014)	(0.012)	(0.021)
Immigrant arrival cohort interactions								
Pre-1980•Post–1996		−0.050★★		−0.024		0.014		0.043
		(0.029)		(0.043)		(0.021)		(0.042)
1981–85•Post–1996		−0.044★★		0.013		0.018		0.027
		(0.025)		(0.038)		(0.017)		(0.033)
1986–90•Post–1996		−0.054★		−0.005		−0.004		0.030
		(0.019)		(0.029)		(0.012)		(0.026)
1991–95•Post–1996		−0.050★		−0.002		−0.011		0.009
		(0.016)		(0.028)		(0.011)		(0.020)
1996–2000•Post–1996		−0.079★		−0.104★		−0.071★		−0.060★
		(0.013)		(0.022)		(0.008)		(0.016)
2001–05•Post–1996		−0.087★		−0.136★		−0.089▵		0.053★
		(0.013)		(0.026)		(0.008)		(0.016)
2006–10•Post–1996		−0.101★		−0.142★		−0.091★		−0.063★
		(0.020)		(0.027)		(0.015)		(0.020)
Time in destination country interactions								
5–9 years•Post–1996		−0.001		−0.005		−0.012		−0.024
		(0.017)		(0.028)		(0.010)		(0.016)
10–14 years•Post–1996		0.013		0.032		−0.018		−0.009
		(0.023)		(0.036)		(0.015)		(0.024)
More than 14 years•Post–1996		0.053		0.011		−0.033★★		−0.038
		(0.028)		(0.042)		(0.020)		(0.035)
Sample size	282,857		66,383		61,346		14,105	

All models also include age dummies, age dummies interacted with immigrant status, years of education, and indicators for married, employed, region, and survey year. NHIS annual weights are used.

Asterisks: statistically significant at the 5% (★) or 10% (★★) level.

Men

	White		Black		Hispanic		Asian	
	(1)	(2)	(1)	(2)	(1)	(2)	(1)	(2)
	−0.025★ (0.011)	−0.033★★ (0.018)	−0.045★ (0.017)	−0.001 (0.025)	−0.013 (0.008)	−0.010 (0.012)	−0.080★ (0.018)	−0.048★ (0.023)
	−0.038★ (0.011)	−0.032★ (0.014)	−0.053★ (0.016)	−0.008 (0.021)	−0.028★ (0.008)	−0.017★★ (0.009)	−0.086★ (0.016)	−0.058★ (0.018)
	−0.030★ (0.010)	−0.027★ (0.010)	−0.046★ (0.015)	−0.030★ (0.015)	−0.039★ (0.007)	−0.027★ (0.007)	−0.078★ (0.015)	−0.066★ (0.014)
	−0.034★ (0.010)	−0.023★ (0.011)	−0.070★ (0.015)	−0.040 (0.019)	−0.048★ (0.007)	−0.046★ (0.007)	−0.082★ (0.015)	−0.072★ (0.015)
	−0.046★ (0.012)		−0.088★ (0.014)		−0.058★ (0.007)		−0.087★ (0.015)	
	−0.032★ (0.014)		−0.123★ (0.020)		−0.076★ (0.007)		−0.075★ (0.016)	
	−0.036★★ (0.019)		−0.119★ (0.024)		−0.070★ (0.011)		−0.087★ (0.017)	
	0.015★★ (0.008)	0.011 (0.009)	−0.009 (0.011)	−0.039★ (0.015)	−0.002 (0.004)	−0.012★ (0.006)	0.017★ (0.007)	0.006 (0.010)
	0.025★ (0.009)	0.025★★ (0.014)	−0.005 (0.012)	−0.043★ (0.021)	0.000 (0.005)	−0.006 (0.010)	0.032★ (0.009)	0.011 (0.016)
	0.027★ (0.009)	0.039★ (0.016)	−0.005 (0.013)	−0.047★ (0.024)	0.001 (0.007)	0.009 (0.012)	0.017★ (0.011)	0.025 (0.020)
		−0.006 (0.025)		−0.079★ (0.034)		−0.023 (0.019)		−0.082★★ (0.043)
		−0.016 (0.022)		−0.080★ (0.030)		−0.021 (0.015)		−0.069★ (0.034)
		−0.014 (0.018)		−0.043★★ (0.025)		−0.023★ (0.011)		−0.044 (0.027)
		−0.023 (0.016)		−0.050★ (0.023)		−0.009 (0.010)		−0.034★★ (0.020)
		−0.051★ (0.012)		−0.099★ (0.015)		−0.064★ (0.008)		−0.100★ (0.018)
		−0.035★ (0.014)		−0.130★ (0.021)		−0.079★ (0.008)		−0.079★ (0.017)
		−0.036★★ (0.019)		−0.118★ (0.025)		−0.070★ (0.012)		−0.082★ (0.017)
		0.011 (0.015)		0.043★ (0.021)		0.014 (0.009)		0.022 (0.015)
		0.010 (0.021)		0.056★ (0.026)		0.012 (0.013)		0.042★★ (0.023)
		−0.002 (0.024)		0.075★ (0.033)		0.002 (0.017)		0.059★★ (0.035)
	264,851		44,774		52,358		12,695	

Table 6.6 Immigrant arrival cohort and assimilation effects of the probability of being overweight by race/ethnic origin and gender (probit marginal effects and standard errors)

	White		Black		Hispanic		Asian	
	(1)	(2)	(1)	(2)	(1)	(2)	(1)	(2)
Immigrant arrival cohorts								
Pre-1980	−0.066**	−0.059	−0.066	−0.048	−0.071*	−0.169*	−0.105*	−0.134*
	(0.038)	(0.070)	(0.050)	(0.084)	(0.024)	(0.042)	(0.041)	(0.053)
1981–85	−0.099*	−0.112*	−0.078	−0.098	−0.085*	−0.174*	−0.096*	−0.124*
	(0.037)	(0.051)	(0.050)	(0.069)	(0.022)	(0.032)	(0.037)	(0.042)
1986–90	−0.058**	−0.045	−0.105*	−0.081**	−0.090*	−0.138*	−0.064**	−0.092*
	(0.035)	(0.035)	(0.046)	(0.046)	(0.019)	(0.021)	(0.036)	(0.036)
1991–95	−0.114*	−0.068**	−0.170*	−0.146*	−0.130*	−0.124*	−0.096*	−0.107*
	(0.033)	(0.035)	(0.049)	(0.055)	(0.019)	(0.021)	(0.032)	(0.032)
1996–2000	−0.134*		−0.199*		−0.155*		−0.089*	
	(0.035)		(0.051)		(0.020)		(0.032)	
2001–05	−0.169*		−0.221*		−0.181*		−0.064	
	(0.036)		(0.059)		(0.022)		(0.037)	
2006–10	−0.184*		−0.204*		−0.146*		−0.056	
	(0.047)		(0.074)		(0.037)		(0.051)	
Time in destination country								
5–9 years	−0.027	−0.005	0.006	0.006	0.004	0.085*	0.030	0.084*
	(0.027)	(0.040)	(0.034)	(0.048)	(0.014)	(0.021)	(0.021)	(0.037)
10–14 years	−0.027	−0.015	0.012	−0.035	0.038*	0.122*	0.077*	0.088
	(0.030)	(0.061)	(0.037)	(0.071)	(0.015)	(0.031)	(0.028)	(0.059)
More than 14 years	−0.035	−0.057	−0.056	−0.079	0.025	0.131*	0.092*	0.112**
	(0.029)	(0.066)	(0.041)	(0.084)	(0.019)	(0.038)	(0.033)	(0.067)
Immigrant arrival cohort interactions								
Pre-1980•Post–1996		−0.067		0.006		0.117*		0.097
		(0.089)		(0.109)		(0.052)		(0.122)
1981–85•Post–1996		−0.066		0.046		0.116*		0.070
		(0.077)		(0.090)		(0.043)		(0.093)
1986–90•Post–1996		−0.091		−0.026		0.075*		0.060
		(0.059)		(0.078)		(0.033)		(0.070)
1991–95•Post–1996		−0.096**		−0.051		0.014		0.044
		(0.048)		(0.074)		(0.029)		(0.056)
1996–2000•Post–1996		−0.154*		−0.217*		−0.141*		−0.074**
		(0.039)		(0.059)		(0.023)		(0.038)
2001–05•Post–1996		−0.177*		−0.232*		−0.173*		−0.052
		(0.037)		(0.063)		(0.023)		(0.040)
2006–10•Post–1996		-0.183*		−0.206*		−0.149*		−0.058
		(0.047)		(0.074)		(0.037)		(0.050)
Time in destination country interactions								
5–9 years•Post–1996		0.002		0.013		−0.105*		−0.069**
		(0.056)		(0.068)		(0.030)		(0.038)
10–14 years•Post–1996		0.036		0.073		−0.112*		−0.022
		(0.078)		(0.080)		(0.043)		(0.064)
More than 14 years•Post–1996		0.105		0.005		−0.144*		−0.046
		(0.092)		(0.106)		(0.054)		(0.087)
Sample size	282,857		66,383		61,346		14,105	

All models also include age dummies, age dummies interacted with immigrant status, years of education, and indicators for married, employed, region, and survey year. NHIS annual weights are used.
Asterisks: statistically significant at the 5% (*) or 10% (**) level.

	Men						
White		**Black**		**Hispanic**		**Asian**	
(1)	(2)	(1)	(2)	(1)	(2)	(1)	(2)
−0.049 (0.036)	−0.154★ (0.066)	−0.173★ (0.056)	−0.085 (0.096)	−0.084★ (0.025)	−0.075★ (0.040)	−0.234★ (0.048)	−0.154★★ (0.075)
−0.060★★ (0.037)	−0.129★ (0.052)	−0.163★ (0.055)	−0.055 (0.077)	−0.099★ (0.022)	−0.077★ (0.030)	−0.218★ (0.042)	−0.168★ (0.057)
−0.076★ (0.033)	−0.103★ (0.034)	−0.163★ (0.052)	−0.066 (0.055)	−0.111★ (0.019)	−0.095★ (0.020)	−0.207★ (0.039)	−0.175★ (0.042)
−0.091★ (0.034)	−0.094★ (0.037)	−0.176★ (0.053)	−0.072 (0.062)	−0.114★ (0.020)	−0.110★ (0.021)	−0.204★ (0.036)	−0.185★ (0.039)
−0.115★ (0.039)		−0.219★ (0.052)		−0.138★ (0.021)		−0.206★ (0.037)	
−0.081★★ (0.046)		−0.227★ (0.061)		−0.162★ (0.023)		−0.168★ (0.041)	
−0.074 (0.062)		−0.249★ (0.074)		−0.067★★ (0.036)		−0.203★ (0.040)	
0.045★★ (0.024)	0.089★ (0.029)	−0.041 (0.037)	−0.130★ (0.061)	0.009 (0.013)	−0.008 (0.020)	0.012 (0.024)	0.006 (0.040)
0.071★ (0.025)	0.119★ (0.041)	0.013 (0.037)	−0.051 (0.080)	0.042★ (0.015)	0.036 (0.029)	0.072★ (0.031)	0.003 (0.062)
0.056★ (0.025)	0.147★ (0.043)	0.041 (0.040)	−0.034 (0.089)	0.054★ (0.018)	0.061★★ (0.034)	0.113★ (0.038)	0.064 (0.076)
	0.134★★ (0.063)		−0.257★ (0.127)		−0.037 (0.057)		−0.191 (0.112)
	0.114★★ (0.059)		−0.278★ (0.109)		−0.036 (0.046)		−0.124 (0.099)
	0.071 (0.052)		−0.249★ (0.086)		−0.026 (0.034)		−0.103 (0.078)
	0.017 (0.048)		−0.190★ (0.082)		−0.014 (0.029)		−0.069 (0.062)
	−0.105★ (0.042)		−0.271★ (0.055)		−0.146★ (0.024)		−0.229★ (0.012)
	−0.073 (0.047)		−0.261★ (0.063)		−0.166★ (0.024)		−0.172★ (0.042)
	−0.074 (0.062)		−0.244★ (0.074)		−0.066★★ (0.036)		−0.200★ (0.041)
	−0.066 (0.054)		0.124★★ (0.057)		0.024 (0.026)		0.019 (0.055)
	−0.072 (0.072)		0.129 (0.071)		0.012 (0.038)		0.119 (0.084)
	−0.177★ (0.087)		0.190★ (0.072)		0.005 (0.050)		0.121 (0.119)
264,851		44,774		52,358		12,695	

Table 6.7 Immigrant arrival cohort and assimilation effects of the probability of being obese by race/ethnic origin and gender (probit marginal effects and standard errors)

	Women							
	White		Black		Hispanic		Asian	
	(1)	(2)	(1)	(2)	(1)	(2)	(1)	(2)
Immigrant arrival cohorts								
Pre-1980	−0.039	−0.045	−0.162★	−0.066	−0.094★	−0.140★	−0.033★★	−0.039
	(0.031)	(0.056)	(0.042)	(0.096)	(0.019)	(0.030)	(0.016)	(0.023)
1981–85	−0.057★★	−0.086★	−0.136★	−0.139★★	−0.097★	−0.146★	−0.028	−0.044★
	(0.029)	(0.034)	(0.045)	(0.066)	(0.017)	(0.022)	(0.015)	(0.015)
1986–90	−0.037	−0.043	−0.187★	−0.179★	−0.113★	−0.127★	−0.024	−0.035★
	(0.029)	(0.029)	(0.038)	(0.042)	(0.015)	(0.016)	(0.016)	(0.014)
1991–95	−0.057★★	−0.025	−0.179★	−0.186★	−0.130★	−0.111★	−0.036★	−0.047★
	(0.026)	(0.030)	(0.038)	(0.047)	(0.013)	(0.016)	(0.010)	(0.008)
1996–2000	−0.089★		−0.182★		−0.147★		−0.033★	
	(0.024)		(0.038)		(0.012)		(0.012)	
2001–05	−0.106★		−0.216★		−0.140★		−0.033★	
	(0.022)		(0.039)		(0.013)		(0.011)	
2006–10	−0.097★		−0.190★		−0.132★		−0.040★	
	(0.034)		(0.052)		(0.023)		(0.007)	
Time in destination country								
5–9 years	−0.039★★	−0.005	0.022	0.012	0.023★★	0.068★	−0.009	0.009
	(0.021)	(0.035)	(0.042)	(0.062)	(0.014)	(0.025)	(0.010)	(0.021)
10–14 years	−0.057★	−0.005	0.049	−0.018	0.027★★	0.105★	0.009	0.011
	(0.021)	(0.056)	(0.045)	(0.087)	(0.016)	(0.039)	(0.015)	(0.034)
More than 14 years	−0.021	−0.023	−0.006	−0.115	0.042★	0.121★	0.018	0.025
	(0.024)	(0.057)	(0.046)	(0.083)	(0.018)	(0.043)	(0.017)	(0.040)
Immigrant arrival cohort interactions								
Pre-1980•Post-1996		−0.045		−0.103		0.048		0.104
		(0.069)		(0.108)		(0.057)		(0.112)
1981–85•Post-1996		−0.023		0.027		0.073		0.136★
		(0.065)		(0.112)		(0.049)		(0.097)
1986–90•Post-1996		−0.049		−0.004		0.017		0.084★★
		(0.045)		(0.084)		(0.033)		(0.061)
1991–95•Post-1996		−0.060		0.011		−0.032		0.085★
		(0.034)		(0.086)		(0.026)		(0.050)
1996–2000•Post-1996		−0.096★		−0.182★		−0.149★		−0.021
		(0.024)		(0.042)		(0.013)		(0.016)
2001–05•Post-1996		−0.109★		−0.217★		−0.141★		−0.028
		(0.022)		(0.041)		(0.013)		(0.014)
2006–10•Post-1996		−0.096★		−0.191★		−0.132★		−0.041★
		(0.034)		(0.052)		(0.022)		(0.007)
Time in destination country interactions								
5–9 years•Post-1996		−0.023		0.011		−0.039		−0.029
		(0.046)		(0.083)		(0.027)		(0.015)
10–14 years•Post-1996		−0.033		0.069		−0.066★★		−0.023
		(0.062)		(0.114)		(0.035)		(0.025)
More than 14 years•Post-1996		0.074		0.109		−0.072		−0.048
		(0.099)		(0.134)		(0.045)		(0.035)
Sample size	282,857		66,383		61,346		14,105	

All models also include age dummies, age dummies interacted with immigrant status, years of education, and indicators for married, employed, region, and survey year. NHIS annual weights are used.

Asterisks: statistically significant at the 5% (★) or 10% (★★) level.

	Men						
White		**Black**		**Hispanic**		**Asian**	
(1)	(2)	(1)	(2)	(1)	(2)	(1)	(2)
−0.113★ (0.025)	−0.059 (0.059)	−0.100★★ (0.047)	0.189 (0.136)	−0.104★ (0.019)	−0.057 (0.038)	−0.081★ (0.011)	−0.060★★ (0.023)
−0.125★ (0.023)	−0.081 (0.045)	−0.117★ (0.042)	0.116 (0.107)	−0.110★ (0.017)	−0.072★ (0.029)	−0.078★ (0.009)	−0.061★ (0.017)
−0.108★ (0.025)	−0.097★ (0.028)	−0.072 (0.047)	−0.047 (0.055)	−0.137★ (0.014)	−0.104★ (0.018)	−0.075★ (0.010)	−0.061★ (0.012)
−0.106★ (0.025)	−0.060 (0.033)	−0.125★ (0.037)	−0.027 (0.060)	−0.133★ (0.014)	−0.118★ (0.016)	−0.060★ (0.008)	−0.046★ (0.011)
−0.130★ (0.024)		−0.156★ (0.029)		−0.134★ (0.013)		−0.059★ (0.008)	
−0.080★ (0.034)		−0.179★ (0.031)		−0.161★ (0.011)		−0.053★ (0.008)	
−0.069 (0.053)		−0.176★ (0.039)		−0.138★ (0.019)		−0.056★ (0.006)	

White (1)	White (2)	Black (1)	Black (2)	Hispanic (1)	Hispanic (2)	Asian (1)	Asian (2)
0.069★ (0.033)	0.009 (0.042)	−0.032 (0.038)	−0.151★ (0.041)	0.027★★ (0.015)	−0.016 (0.023)	0.041★ (0.019)	−0.004 (0.023)
0.078★ (0.039)	0.012 (0.062)	−0.030 (0.039)	−0.204★ (0.034)	0.037★ (0.018)	0.000 (0.036)	0.077★ (0.026)	0.034 (0.047)
0.124★ (0.039)	0.032 (0.071)	0.003 (0.046)	0.209★ (0.043)	0.075★ (0.021)	0.037 (0.043)	0.116★ (0.027)	0.050 (0.050)

White (1)	White (2)	Black (1)	Black (2)	Hispanic (1)	Hispanic (2)	Asian (1)	Asian (2)
	−0.100 (0.060)		−0.204★ (0.047)		−0.105★ (0.041)		−0.065★★ (0.017)
	−0.095 (0.056)		−0.197★ (0.045)		−0.085★ (0.037)		−0.065★ (0.017)
	−0.052 (0.055)		−0.056 (0.078)		−0.079★ (0.028)		−0.058★ (0.018)
	−0.099★ (0.036)		−0.152★ (0.047)		−0.048★★ (0.027)		−0.053★ (0.011)
	−0.144★ (0.023)		−0.175★ (0.029)		−0.146★ (0.014)		−0.067★ (0.007)
	−0.096★ (0.031)		−0.191★ (0.030)		−0.165★ (0.012)		−0.057★ (0.007)
	−0.070 (0.053)		−0.174★ (0.040)		−0.137★ (0.019)		−0.054★ (0.007)

White (1)	White (2)	Black (1)	Black (2)	Hispanic (1)	Hispanic (2)	Asian (1)	Asian (2)
	0.103 (0.071)		0.244★ (0.113)		0.064★ (0.034)		0.103★ (0.059)
	0.108 (0.097)		0.385★ (0.131)		0.063 (0.047)		0.100 (0.082)
	0.138 (0.115)		0.406★ (0.154)		0.084 (0.058)		0.154★ (0.100)
	264,851		44,774		52,358		12,695

and assimilation effects by race/ethnicity and gender for our three measures of weight respectively.[32] We first focus our discussion on Specification 1 (column 1) followed by a discussion on Specification 2 (column 2).

Consistent with the graphical analysis, the period effects indicate that American BMIs are rising. Between 1989 and 2011, holding all else constant, the average white female's (male's) BMI, probability of being overweight, and probability of being obese increased by 11.6 (8.3), 24.3 (15.4), and 20.5 (21.2) percentage points respectively. Moreover, this pattern holds irrespective of race/ethnicity. However, the magnitudes are substantially smaller for Asians irrespective of the weight measure and are generally larger for blacks and Hispanics, particularly for obesity.

As with the health outcomes, the uniformly negative cohort marginal effects imply that both male and female immigrants irrespective of race/ethnicity with 0–4 years of US residency from every arrival cohort have lower BMIs, a lower proportion of overweight individuals, and a lower proportion of obese individuals than natives (although some of the effects are imprecisely estimated). Moreover, we find suggestive evidence that more recent cohorts appear to be thinner than their earlier counterparts given the magnitude (in absolute value) of the cohort effects appears to be increasing across cohorts. This pattern holds true for all three measures of weight irrespective of gender and race/ethnicity except in the following cases. We find very little evidence of differences across cohorts for Asian recent immigrants (irrespective of gender) in terms of our weight measures, and if we do find cohort differences, they tend to move in the opposite direction (i.e., more recent cohorts are heavier than their earlier counterparts). White male recent immigrants have similar BMIs across cohorts and are more likely to be obese than their earlier counterparts. Finally, black female recent immigrants have similar propensities to be obese across cohorts.

Turning to assimilation, we find very little evidence of assimilation for immigrants in terms of weight except for white and Asian male immigrants, and depending on the weight measure for Asian female immigrants and Hispanic immigrants (irrespective of gender). For those groups that we find evidence of assimilation for, it appears to be gradual. For example, the percentage of Hispanic male immigrants designated overweight (obese), relative to their level during the initial four years of US residence, rises by 0.9 (2.7) percentage points after 5–9 years, by 4.2 (3.7) percentage points after 10–14 years, and 5.4 (7.5) percentage points after more than 14 years. Finally, assimilation substantially reduces, and in some cases eliminates, the initial weight advantage for all immigrant arrival cohorts irrespective of the weight measure (conditional on experiencing assimilation). For example, during their first four years in the US the 1981–85 Asian male cohort had an incidence of being overweight (obese) that was 21.8 (7.8) percentage points below that of Asian natives. But after more than 14 years of US residence,

---

[32] Once again, we do not report period effects to avoid overly cluttered tables; these effects are available upon request.

assimilation had reduced the overweight gap by 11.3 percentage points and more than completely narrowed the obesity gap.

As previously discussed in the self-reported health outcome section, our assimilation indicator variables may be biased if we do not appropriately account for the potential differences in the period effects between the 1989–96 and 1997–2011 time periods for natives and immigrants. Column 2 of Tables 6.5–6.7 presents the results accounting for this potential difference for our three weight measures respectively.

While we often find that cohort effects are indistinguishable across the two time periods and continue to largely be negative irrespective of weight measure, gender, and race/ethnicity, there are several notable exceptions. Specifically, recently arrived white female immigrants from all the pre-1995 cohorts (i.e., 1991–95, 1986–90, 1981–85 and pre-1980) in the post-1996 time period have lower BMIs relative to their counterparts prior to 1997. We find a similar pattern for recently arrived black immigrant men for all three weight measures, for recently arrived Asian immigrant men for BMI and obesity, and for recently arrived Hispanic immigrant men for obesity. In contrast, the probability of being overweight (obese) for recently arrived Hispanic (Asian) female immigrants from all the pre-1995 cohorts in the post-1996 period is lower compared to their counterparts in the earlier time period.

We find suggestive evidence to support the notion that accounting for differential period effects changes the overall assimilation patterns found for our weight measures. We find that Hispanic female immigrants appear to assimilate toward the weights (irrespective of weight measure) of their native counterparts, but this assimilation appears to be faster in the period prior to 1997 relative to the post-1996 period (although some of the interaction effects tend to be imprecisely estimated). Interestingly we did not find evidence of assimilation for Hispanic female immigrants for BMI in Specification 1. We also continue to find that Asian female immigrants appear to assimilate towards the propensities to be overweight of their native counterparts; however, this assimilation appears to be faster in the period prior to 1997 relative to the post-1996 period (although some of the interaction effects tend to be imprecisely estimated). Finally, we continue to find no evidence of weight assimilation irrespective of weight measure for white and black female immigrants or for Asian female immigrants in terms of BMI and obesity.

The patterns are quite different for male immigrants. We continue to find evidence of assimilation for white immigrant males in terms of weight; however, the patterns differ depending on the weight measure. In terms of BMI, white immigrant males appear to have similar assimilation patterns across the two time periods while in terms of overweight and obesity assimilation the assimilation appears to be faster in the post-1996 period (however, some of the effects are imprecisely estimated). While we continue to find no evidence of assimilation for Hispanic immigrant men in terms of BMI, there is some evidence of assimilation in terms of their propensity to be overweight and obese. The patterns, however, again differ for the two weight measures: Overweight assimilation appears to be similar across the two time periods while obesity assimilation appears to be faster in the post-1996 period (although some of the effects are imprecisely estimated). We also continue to find evidence of BMI assimilation for Asian immigrant men but only in the post-1996 period and evidence of overweight/obesity assimilation but the assimilation appears to be substantially faster in the post-1996 period (although some of the effects are imprecisely estimated). Finally, we now find evidence of weight assimilation for black immigrant men, irrespective of weight measure, but only in the post-1996 period. In fact, immigrant black men are actually moving further away from their native counterparts prior to 1997 in terms of their weight (although some of the level effects are imprecisely estimated in the overweight specification).

The results from Specification 2 are more in line with the results we found in our earlier work (Antecol and Bedard, 2006); that is, there is evidence of unhealthy assimilation (based on a number of health outcomes including obesity) between 1989 and 1996. It also sheds light on why our results differed from the results presented in Park et al. (2009), who found no evidence of unhealthy assimilation (based on obesity) between 1994–96 and 2004–06 for Hispanic immigrants. Specifically, one needs to account for the fact that the rate at which natives are becoming heavier differs from the rate at which immigrants are becoming heavier between the two time periods.

Overall, the general patterns found in terms of weight (irrespective of the measure) mirror the patterns found for general health measures. Recent immigrants have lower weights and are healthier than natives, but (depending on gender and race/ethnicity) become heavier and less healthy with time in residence. This suggests that weight, which is largely determined by diet and exercise, is an important contributing factor for explaining the HIE.

7. CONCLUSIONS

It is well documented that immigrants are in better health upon arrival in the US than their American counterparts, but that this health advantage erodes over time: the Healthy Immigrant Effect (HIE). We find support for the HIE in the National Health Interview Survey (1989–2011) using two measures of health (self-reported health status and activity limitations) for all racial/ethnic groups (irrespective of gender) except black female immigrants and Asian immigrants (irrespective of gender).

Further, we find evidence that the weight assimilation patterns of immigrants closely mirror self-reported health assimilation depending on race/ethnicity and gender. Specifically, while white female immigrants are indistinguishable from their native counterparts upon arrival, Hispanic and Asian female immigrants enter the US *lighter* than their native counterparts and then converge towards native levels irrespective of the weight measure for Hispanics and for the overweight measure for Asians. Although black female immigrants enter the US *lighter* than their native counterparts for all three measures of weight, they do not converge towards native weight levels. On the other hand, male immigrants of all racial/ethnic origin groups generally enter the US *lighter* than their native counterparts, and depending on the weight measure we find some evidence of convergence towards native levels for all racial/ethnic origin groups except black male immigrants. Finally, we show that constraining the period effects to be the same for natives and immigrants may lead one to conclude there is no evidence of unhealthy assimilation, particularly if the rates at which natives and immigrants are becoming unhealthy differ from each other and change across time periods.

Understanding the intricacies of the immigrant weight assimilation path may give us some insight into the causes of elevated American weight levels. The fact that most immigrant groups arrive *lighter* than Americans and then converge towards natives suggests that the new cultural or environmental factors that immigrants are exposed to alter their behavior. Unfortunately, their newly acquired eating habits and weight gain increase the probability of health problems and premature death as well as raise health care costs.

REFERENCES

Akresh, I., 2007. Dietary assimilation and health among Hispanic immigrants to the United States. J. Health Soc. Behav. 48 (4), 404–417.

Akresh, I., 2009. Health service utilization among immigrants to the United States. Popul. Res. Pol. Rev. 28 (6), 795–815.

Antecol, H., Bedard, K., 2006. Unhealthy assimilation:Why do immigrants converge to American health status levels? Demography 43 (2), 337–360.

Antecol, H., Kuhn, P., Trejo, S., 2006. Assimilation via prices or quantities? Labor market institutions and immigrant earnings growth in Australia, Canada, and the United States. J. Hum. Resour. 41 (4), 821–840.

Averett, S.L., Korenman, S., 1996. The economic reality of the beauty myth. J. Hum. Resour. 31, 304–330.

Averett, S.L., Argys, L.M., Kohn, J.L., 2012. Immigration, obesity and labor market outcomes in the UK. IZA Journal of Migration, 1 (1), 1–19.

Bates, L.M., Acevedo-Garcia, D., Alegría, M., Krieger, N., 2008. Immigration and generational trends in body mass index and obesity in the United States: Results of the National Latino and Asian American Survey, 2002–2003. Am. J. Public Health 98 (1), 70–77.

Borjas, G.J., 1985. Assimilation, changes in cohort quality, and the earnings of immigrants. J. Labor Econ. 3, 463–489.

Borjas, G.J., 1995. Assimilation and changes in cohort quality revisited: What happened to immigrant earnings in the 1980s? J. Labor Econ. 13, 201–245.

Breen, N., Rao, S., Meissner, H., 2010. Immigration, health care access, and recent cancer tests among Mexican-Americans in California. J. Immigr. Minor. Health 12 (4), 433–444.

Cawley, J., 2000. Body Weight and Women's Labor Market Outcomes, NBER Working Paper No. 7841, National Bureau of Economic Research, Cambridge, MA.

Cawley, J., Han, E., Norton, E.C., 2009. Obesity and labor market outcomes among legal immigrants to the United States from developing countries. Econ. Hum. Biol. 7 (2), 153–164.

Ceballos, M., 2011. Simulating the effects of acculturation and return migration on the maternal and infant health of Mexican immigrants in the United States: A research note. Demography 48 (2), 425–436.

Ceballos, M., Palloni, A., 2010. Maternal and infant health of Mexican immigrants in the USA: The effect of acculturation, duration, and selection return migration. Ethn. Health 15, 377–396.

Chen, J., Ng, E., Wilkins, R., 1996. The health of Canada's immigrants in 1994–95. Health Rep. 7 (4), 33–45.

Chiswick, B.R., 1986. Is the new immigration less skilled than the old? J. Labor Econ. 4, 168–192.

Chiswick, B.R., Lee, Y., Miller, P.W., 2008. Immigrant selection systems and immigrant health. Contemp. Econ. Pol. 26 (4), 555–578.

Chou, S.Y., Grossman, M., Saffer, H., 2002. An Economic Analysis of Adult Obesity: Results From the Behavioral Risk Factor Surveillance System, NBER Working Paper No. 9247, National Bureau of Economic Research, Cambridge, MA.

Costa, D.L., Steckel, R.H., 1995. Long-Term Trends in Health, Welfare, and Economic Growth in the United States, NBER Historical Working Paper No. 76, National Bureau of Economic Research, Cambridge, MA.

Cutler, D.M., Glaeser, E.L., Shapiro, J.M., 2003. Why have Americans become more obese? J. Econ. Perspect. 17 (3), 93–118.

Dean, J.A., Wilson, K., 2010. "My health has improved because I always have everything I need here…": a qualitative exploration of health improvement and decline among immigrants. Soc. Sci. Med. 70 (8), 1219–1228.

Deri, C., 2003. Understanding the 'Healthy Immigrant Effect' in Canada. Working Paper 0502E, Department of Economics, University of Ottawa, Ontario, Canada. Available online at <http://www.socialsciences.uottawa.ca/eco/pdf/cahiers/0502E.pdf>.

Dey, A.N., Lucas, J.W., 2006. Physical and mental health characteristics of U.S.- and foreign-born adults: United States 1998–2003. Adv. Data 369, 1–19.

Donovan, J., d'Espaignet, E., Metron, C., van Ommeren, M., 1992. Immigrants in Australia: A health profile. Australian Institute of Health and Welfare Ethnic Health Series. No. 1.AGPS, Canberra

Duleep, H.O., Regets, M.C., 1994. The Elusive Concept of Immigrant Quality, Working Paper No. PRIP-UI-28, Urban Institute, Washington, DC.

Duleep, H.O., Regets, M.C., 1999. Immigrants and human capital investment? Am. Econ. Rev. 89, 186–191.

Duleep, H.O., Regets, M.C., 2002. The Elusive Concept of Immigrant Quality: Evidence From 1970–1990. IZA Discussion Paper No. 631, Institute for the Study of Labor, Bonn, Germany.

Elo, I., Mehta, N., Huang, C., 2008. Health of Native-born and Foreign-born Black Residents in the United States: Evidence from the 2000 Census of Population and the National Health Interview Survey. PARC Working Paper Series.

Funkhouser, E., Trejo, S.J., 1995. The labor market skills of recent male immigrants: Evidence from the current population survey. Ind. Labor Relat. Rev. 48, 792–811.

Gorman, B.K., Read, J.G., Krueger, P.M., 2010. Gender, acculturation, and health among Mexican Americans, J. Health Soc. Behav. 51 (4), 440–457.

Gresenz, C.R., Rogowski, J., Escarce, J.J., 2007. Social networks and access to health care among Mexican Americans. NBER Working Paper 13460.

Hamermesh, D.S., Biddle, J.E., 1994. Beauty and the labor market. Am. Econ. Rev. 84, 1174–1194.

Hamilton, T.G., Hummer, R.A., 2011. Immigration and the health of U.S. black adults: Does country of origin matter? Soc. Sci. Med. 73 (10), 1551–1560.

Hao, L., Kim, J.H., 2009. Immigration and the American obesity epidemic. Int. Migrat. Rev. 43 (2), 237–262.

Hauck, K., Hollingsworth, B., Morgan, L., 2011. BMI differences in 1st and 2nd generation immigrants of Asian and European origin to Australia. Health and Place 17 (1), 78–85.

Hersch, J., Viscusi, W.K., 2010. Immigrant status and the value of statistical life. J. Hum. Resour. 45 (3), 749–771.

Himes, C., 2000. Obesity, disease, and functional limitation in later life. Demography 37, 73–82.

House, J.S., Kessler, R.C., Herzog, A.R., Mero, R.P., Kinney, A.M., Breslow, M.J., 1990. Age, socioeconomic status and health. Milbank Q. 68, 383–411.

Hu, W.Y., 2000. Immigrant earning assimilation: Estimates from longitudinal data. Am. Econ. Rev. 90, 368–372.

Huang, C., Mehta, N.K., Elo, I.T., et al., 2011. Region of birth and disability among recent U.S. immigrants: Evidence from the 2000 census. Pop. Res. Policy Rev. 30 (3), 399–418.

Jasso, G., Massey, D.S., Rosenzweig, M.R., Smith, J.P., 2004. Immigrant Health-Selectivity and Acculturation. Unpublished manuscript, RAND. Available online at <http://econwpa.wustl.edu/eps/lab/papers/0412/0412002.pdf>.

Johnston, D.W., Lordan, G., 2012. Discrimination makes me sick! An examination of the discrimination–health relationship. J. Health Econ. 31 (1), 99–111.

Kaestner, R., Pearson, J.A., Keene, D., Geronimus, A.T., 2009. Stress, allostatic load, and health of Mexican immigrants. Soc. Sci. Q. 90 (5), 1089–1111.

Kao, D.T., 2009. Generational cohorts, age at arrival, and access to health services among Asian and Latino immigrant adults. J. Health Care Poor Underserved 20 (2), 395–414.

Kasl, S.V., Berkman, L., 1983. Health consequences of the experiences of migration. Annu. Rev. Public Health 4, 69–90.

Kaushal, N., 2007. Do food stamps cause obesity? Evidence from immigrant experience. J. Health Econ. 26, 968–991.

Kaushal, N., 2009. Adversities of acculturation? Prevalence of obesity among immigrants. Health Econ. 18 (3), 291–303.

Kennedy, S., McDonald, J., Biddle, N., 2006. The Healthy Immigrant Effect and Immigrant Selection: Evidence from Four Countries, SEDAP Research Paper No. 164.

Kimbro, R.T., 2009. Acculturation in context: Gender, age at migration, neighborhood ethnicity, and health behaviors. Soc. Sci. Q. 90 (5), 1145–1166.

Koya, D.L., Egede, L.E., 2007. Association between length of residence and cardiovascular disease risk factor among an ethnically diverse group of United States immigrants. J. Gen. Intern. Med. 22, 841–846.

Lakdawalla, D., Philipson, T., 2002. The Growth of Obesity and Technological Change: A Theoretical and Empirical Examination. NBER Working Paper No. 8946, National Bureau of Economic Research, Cambridge, MA.

LaLonde, R.J., Topel, R.H., 1992. The assimilation of immigrants in the U.S. labor market. In: Borjas, G.J., Freeman, R.B. (Eds.), Immigration and the Work Force: Economic Consequences for the United States and Source Areas. University of Chicago Press, Chicago, pp. 67–92.

Laroche, M., 2000. Health status and health services utilization of Canada's immigrant and non-immigrant populations. Can. Publ. Pol. 26 (2), 51–75.

Lasser, K.E., Himmelstein, D.U., Woolhandler, S., 2006. Access to care, health status, and health disparities in the United States and Canada: Results of a cross-national population-based survey. Am. J. Public Health 96 (7), 1300–1307.

Lebrun, L.A., Dubay, L.C., 2010. Access to primary and preventive care among foreign-born adults in Canada and the United States. Health Serv. Res. 45 (6), 1693–1719.

Leclere, F.B., Jensen, L., Biddlecom, A.E., 1994. Health care utilization, family context, and adaptation among immigrants to the United States. J. Health Soc. Behav. 35, 370–384.

Lee, S., O'Neill, A., Park, J., 2012. Health insurance moderates the association between immigrant length of stay and health status. J. Immigr. Minor. Health 14 (2), 345–349.

Marmot, M.G., Syme, S.L., 1976. Acculturation and coronary heart disease in Japanese-Americans. Am. J. Epidemiol. 104, 225–247.

Marmot, M.G., Adelstein, A.M., Bulusu, L., 1984. Lessons from the study of immigrant mortality. Lancet 30, 1455–1457.

Marvanti, A., 2010. Occupational safety and English language proficiency. J. Labor Res. 31 (4), 332–347.

McDonald, J.T., 2003. The Health of Immigrants to Canada. Unpublished manuscript, Department of Economics, University of New Brunswick, Fredericton.

McDonald, J.T., 2004. BMI and the Incidence of Being Overweight and Obese Among Canadian Immigrants: Is Acculturation Associated with Unhealthy Weight Gain? Unpublished manuscript, Department of Economics, University of New Brunswick, Fredericton.

McDonald, J.T., 2005. The Health Behaviors of Immigrants and Native-born People in Canada, SEDAP Research Paper No. 144.

McDonald, J.T., Kennedy, S., 2004. Insights into the 'Healthy Immigrant Effect': Health status and health service use of immigrants to Canada. Soc. Sci. Med. 59, 1613–1627.

Mehta, N.K., Elo, I.T., 2012. Migrant selection and the health of U.S. immigrants from the former Soviet Union. Demography 49 (2), 425–447.

Ogden, C.L., Carroll, M.D., Curtin, L.R., McDowell, M.A., Tabak, C.J., Flegal, K.M., 2006. Prevalence of overweight and obesity in the United States, 1999–2004. JAMA 295 (13), 1549–1555.

Orrenius, P.M., Zavodny, M., 2009. Do immigrants work in riskier jobs? Demography 46 (3), 535–551.

Oza-Frank, R., Cunningham, S.A., 2010. The weight of US residence among immigrants: A systematic review. Obesity Review 11 (4), 271–280.

Oza-Frank, R., Narayan, K.M.V., 2009. Effect of length of residence on overweight by region of birth and age at arrival among US immigrants. Public Health Nutr. 13 (6), 868–875.

Pagan, J.A., Davila, A., 1997. Obesity, occupational attainment, and earnings. Soc. Sci. Q. 78, 756–770.

Palloni, A., Arias, E., 2003. A Re-Examination of the Hispanic Mortality Paradox. CDE Working Paper No. 2003-01, Center for Demography and Ecology, University of Wisconsin—Madison.

Pandey, S., Kagotho, N., 2010. Health insurance disparities among immigrants: Are some legal immigrants more vulnerable than others? Health and Social Work 35 (4), 267–279.

Park, J., Myers, D., Kao, D., Min, S., 2009. Immigrant obesity and unhealthy assimilation: Alternative estimates of convergence or divergence, 1995–2005. Soc. Sci. Med. 69 (11), 1625–1633.

Peek, M.K., Cutchin, M.P., Salinas, J.J., Sheffield, K.M., Eschbach, K., Stowe, R., Goodwin, J.S., 2010. Allostatic load among non-Hispanic whites, non-Hispanic blacks, and people of Mexican origin: Effects of ethnicity, nativity, and acculturation. Am. J. Public Health 100 (5), 940–946.

Perez, C.E., 2002. Health status and health behaviour among immigrants. Health Rep. 13 (Suppl), 1–12.

Philipson, T., 2001. The world-wide growth in obesity: An economic research agenda. Health Econ. 10 (1), 1–7.

Philipson, T., Posner, R.A., 1999. The Long-Run Growth in Obesity as a Function of Technological Change. NBER Working Paper No. 7423, National Bureau of Economic Research, Cambridge, MA.

Pylypchuk, Y., Hudson, J., 2009. Immigrants and the use of preventive care in the United States. Health Econ. 18 (7), 783–806.

Ralston, M.L., Escandell, X., 2012. Networks matter: Male Mexican migrants' use of hospitals. Popul. Res. Pol. Rev. 31 (3), 321–337.

Read, J.N.G., Emerson, M.O., 2005. Racial context, black immigration and the U.S. black/white health disparity. Soc. Forces 84 (1), 181–199.

Read, J., Reynolds, M., 2012. Gender differences in immigrant health: the case of Mexican and Middle Eastern immigrants. J. Health Social Behav. 53, 99–123.

Register, C.A., Williams, D.R., 1990. Wage effects of obesity among young workers. Soc. Sci. Q. 71, 130–141.

Ronellenfitsch, U., Razum, O., 2004. Deteriorating health satisfaction among immigrants from Eastern Europe in Germany. International Journal for Equity in Health 3 (1), 4.

Roshania, R., Narayan, K.M.V., Oza-Frank, R., 2008. Age at arrival and risk of obesity among US immigrants. Obesity 16 (12), 2669–2675.

Sander, M., 2007. Return Migration and the Healthy Immigrant Effect, SOEP Paper 60.

Schoeni, R.F., 1997. New evidence on the economic progress of foreign-born men in the 1970s and 1980s. J. Hum. Resour. 32, 683–740.

Schoeni, R.F., 1998. Labor market assimilation of immigrant women. Ind. Labor Relat. Rev. 51, 483–504.

Setia, M.S., Quesnel-Vallee, A., Abrahamowicz, M., Tousignant, P., Lynch, J., 2009. Convergence of body mass index of immigrants to the Canadian-born population: Evidence from the National Population Health Survey (1994–2006). Eur. J. Epidemiol. 24 (10), 611–623.

Singh, G., Siahpush, M., Hiatt, R., Timsina, L., 2011. Dramatic increases in obesity and overweight prevalence and body mass index among ethnic-immigrant and social class groups in the United States, 1976–2008. J. Community Health 36 (1), 94–110.

Sorlie, P.D., Backlund, E., Johnson, N.J., Rogot, E., 1993. Mortality by Hispanic status in the United States. J. Am. Med. Assoc. 270 (20), 2464–2468.

Stephen, E.H., Foote, K., Hendershot, G.E., Schoenborn, C.A., 1994. Health of the foreign-born population. Advance Data From Vital and Health Statistics 241, 1–10.

Sturm, R., 2002. The effects of obesity, smoking and drinking on medical problems and costs. Health Aff. 21, 245–253.

Su, D., Wang, D., 2012. Acculturation and cross-border utilization of health services. J. Immigr. Minor. Health 14 (4), 563–569.

Turra, C., Elo, I.T., 2008. The impact of salmon bias on the Hispanic mortality advantage: New evidence from social security data. Pop. Res. Policy Rev. 27 (5), 515–530.

Van Hook, J., Zhang, W., 2011. Who stays? Who goes? Selective emigration among the foreign-born. Popul. Res. Pol. Rev. 30 (1), 1–24.

Vega, W., Amaro, H., 1994. Latino outlook: Good health, uncertain prognosis. Annu. Rev. Public Health 15, 39–67.

Wolf, A., Colditz, G., 1998. Current estimates of the economic cost of obesity in the United States. Obes. Res. 6, 97–106.

CHAPTER 7

Immigrants and Demography: Marriage, Divorce, and Fertility

Alícia Adserà*, Ana Ferrer**
*Princeton University, CREAM, and IZA
**University of Waterloo and CLSRN

Contents

1. Motivation: Why Study Immigrant Marriage and Fertility?	315
2. Methodological Challenges to the Study of Immigrant Marriage and Fertility	319
2.1 Immigrant selection and individual heterogeneity	319
2.2 Data limitations to measuring family formation	321
3. Marriage and Divorce Among Immigrants	324
3.1 Microeconomic models of marriage formation	325
3.2 The determinants of intermarriage	331
3.3 Intermarriage as assimilation	335
3.4 Assortative matching in education and language	337
3.5 The timing of family formation	340
3.6 Cohabitation	341
3.7 Stability of marriage	342
3.8 Family reunification policies and their impact on marriage formation	344
4. Fertility	345
4.1 Microeconomic models of fertility	345
4.2 Immigrant differential fertility: mechanisms	346
4.2.1 Selection	*347*
4.2.2 Disruption	*348*
4.2.3 Adaptation	*351*
4.3 Duration in destination and age at arrival	351
4.3.1 Age at arrival, language proficiency, and critical period hypothesis	*355*
4.4 The role of culture: heterogeneity across source countries and adaptation	358
4.5 Son preference	361
4.6 The fertility of the second generation	362
5. Conclusion	366
References	367

1. MOTIVATION: WHY STUDY IMMIGRANT MARRIAGE AND FERTILITY?

In recent years, developed countries have seen the number and diversity of their foreign-born populations increase at a rapid pace. As shown in Table 7.1, foreign-born individuals represented by 2010 over 10% of the population in the major receiving developed

Handbook of the Economics of International Migration, Volume 1A
ISSN 2212-0092, http://dx.doi.org/10.1016/B978-0-444-53764-5.00007-4

countries and this share stood at over 20% for Australia and Canada. With many of these countries facing increasing old-age-dependency ratios and demographic pressures on social services, particularly as baby-boomers retire, the contribution that immigrants can make to the sustainability of population levels and the current structure of welfare states has attracted the interest of both academics and policymakers (United Nations, 2001; Coleman, 2006; Sobotka, 2008). More importantly, immigrants' social outcomes such as their rates of household formation and fertility are ultimately markers of the extent of their assimilation (or adaptation) to the country of reception. In addition, these outcomes affect the role of migrant women in the labor market and the investments made in their children. Motivated by these concerns, a substantial body of research has developed to examine family formation and fertility among immigrants and their children, and the extent to which the fertility of migrant populations differs from or converges to that of the native-born population.

The speed at which this adaptation occurs both in terms of fertility and intermarriage, among other outcomes, has been found to hinge on immigrant characteristics, such as age (or birth cohort), age at migration, education or cultural proximity to the host country (such as social attitudes toward contraceptive measures, gender preferences, and out-of-wedlock childbearing, among many others). In particular, cultural proximity seems to ultimately influence the perception of constraints shaping family formation and hence the integration process.[1] As a result, the variety of cultural backgrounds that immigrants bring with them introduces an extraordinary heterogeneity in empirical analyses that many studies reviewed in this chapter exploit. Finally, the cultural distance between host and sending country and immigration policies at destination will likely influence the perception of constraints and the integration process of immigrants.

A large majority of the studies of family formation reviewed in this chapter aim at measuring the extent of migrant integration in their countries of reception by comparing their patterns of behavior with those of the native-born in outcomes such as the number of children and the timing of childbearing, or the age and prevalence of marriage, among others. Decreases in the immigrant–native differentials are viewed as evidence of a reduction in the influence of the norms of the country of origin and adaptation (or acculturation) to their new environment. The degree of adaptation is also defined by the convergence of immigrants' preferences (in issues such as the desired number or gender of children) to those of natives or by immigrants' propensity to intermarry with native-born.

In particular, as it will become clear when we survey the literature on union formation in Section 3, research on the prevalence and determinants of intermarriage is the focus of most of those papers. This is not surprising given the large and increasing numbers of mixed marriages in the main destination countries. The last two columns in Table 7.1 present the share of native-born individuals married to immigrants, among those married,

---

[1] Given the relative infrequency of these decisions, some researchers argue that acculturation is likely to be a long-term process and complete assimilation may only be reached after several generations (Fernandez and Fogli, 2009).

Table 7.1 Immigration and intermarriage in main host countries in 2010 (in thousands)

Country	Total population	Total foreign-born	%	Mixed marriages (2008–10)*	
				% native-born	*% foreign-born*
EU 27	501,098	47,348	9.4	—	—
Germany	81,802	9812	12.0	6.8	28.5
France	64,716	7196	11.1	7.0	37.0
UK	62,008	7012	11.3	5.1	31.1
Spain	45,989	6422	14.0	3.1	21.0
Netherlands	16,575	1832	11.1	5.1	39.6
Greece	11,305	1256	11.1	1.6	17.1
Sweden	9340	1337	14.3	5.4	34.4
Austria	8367	1276	15.2	6.6	27.1
Belgium[†]	10,666	1380	12.9	6.5	36.2
US	269,394	39,956	12.9	4.4	27.9
Canada[†]	34,484	7472	21.7	—	—
Australia	22,183	6000	27.0	31.3	

*Lanzieri (2012) for European countries; Marriages and Divorces, Australia, 2010 in Australian Bureau of Statistics (2011); American Community Survey (ACS) 2011 for US.
[†]Data on immigrants for Belgium is for 2007 and for Canada for 2011.
Source: Statistics Canada; US Census Bureau; Australian Census Bureau. European data comes from Vasileva (2011). Total population and foreign-born population are expressed in thousands of individuals.

and also the share of married immigrants whose spouse is a native-born. In Europe around 5–7% of natives have formed a mixed marriage and among foreign-born, not surprisingly, the proportion that has intermarried is larger and stands between a minimum of 17% in Greece and over one-third in France, the Netherlands, Belgium, and Sweden. In the US numbers stand at 4.4% for natives and 27.9% for foreign-born. In Australia around 31% of all marriages include both a native- and a foreign-born. In addition to understanding the process of formation of those unions, the literature analyzes their stability and whether their prevalence is similar among individuals of different source countries.

The large immigrant flows to developed countries, particularly to European countries, portrayed in Table 7.1 have also caught the attention of researchers for their potential impact on childbearing trends in countries where fertility was at or below replacement levels (around the 2.1 children per women needed to sustain the population at a constant level). To highlight the growing relevance of births to immigrants in major European destinations, the first two columns in Table 7.2 present the shares of total births from either immigrant women, in the first column, or foreign nationals, in the second column. The data comes from Sobotka (2008), who compiled it from different sources, as indicated in the table, to show the growing share of children born to foreign-born mothers across European countries.[2] In the

---

[2] Finding homogeneous and comparable measures of births to immigrants both across time and across countries is a difficult task. The definitions of immigrants used by research and official statistics vary widely, particularly when it comes to looking at citizenship.

Table 7.2 Share of births and total fertility rates (TFRs) of natives and immigrants

Country	Period	% Births		TFR*		Source
		Migrants	Foreign nationals	Native	Immigrant	
Austria	2000		13.5	1.29	2.03	Kytir (2006)
	2005		11.7			Kytir (2006)
Belgium (Flanders)	2003–04	16.81	12.4			VAZG (2007)
	2001–05			1.50	3.00	
Denmark	1999–03	13.5	11.1	1.69	2.43	Statistics Denmark (2004)
England–Wales	1980	13.3				Schoorl (1995)
	1995	12.6				ONS (2006)
	2001			1.6	2.2	ONS (2006)
	2005	20.8				ONS (2006)
	2006	21.9				ONS (2007)
France	1991–98	12.4		1.65	2.5	Toulemon (2004)
	2004	15	12.4	1.8	3.29	Prioux (2005); Heran and Pison (2007)
Germany	1980		15			Schoorl (1995)
	1985		11.2			Schoorl (1995)
	1995		16.2			Statistisches Bundesamt (2006)
	2004		17.6			Statistisches Bundesamt (2006)
Italy	1999		5.4			ISTAT (2007)
	2004		11.3	1.26	2.61	ISTAT (2006, 2007)
	2005		12.2			ISTAT (2007)
Netherlands	1996	15.5				CBS Statline (2006)
	2005	17.8		1.65	1.97	CBS Statline (2006)
Spain	1996		3.3			INE (2006, 2007)
	2000		6.2	1.19	2.12	
	2004		13.7			
	2006		16.5	1.32	1.64	Roig Vila and Castro Martin (2007)
Sweden	2005	19.5	11.8	1.72	2.01	Statistics Sweden (2006)
Switzerland	1980		15.3			Coleman (2003)
	1997			1.34	1.86	Wanner (2002)
	2000		22.3			Coleman (2003)
	2005		26.3			SFSO (2006)

*TFR data is for native nationals (instead of natives) and foreign nationals (instead of immigrants) in Austria, Flanders, France in 2004, Italy, Spain, and Switzerland.
Source: Data compiled from Tables 1 and 2a, b in Sobotka (2008).

majority of countries the shares are well above 10% and in some cases above 15% of new births. Of course, since immigrant women are likely to arrive at childbearing ages, their shares of births are not surprisingly larger than their own share in the total of the population. In addition, if a large share of these migrant women arrives from relatively high-fertility countries, they may bring with them norms from their countries of birth regarding fertility that exceed the local expectations. The next two columns in Table 7.2 present the total fertility rates (TFR) for natives (or native nationals) and for immigrants (or foreign nationals) across Europe. The immigrant–native gaps are noticeably large in most countries. However, Sobotka (2008) showed in his paper that, given their share in the overall population, the net effect of these migrants coming from high-fertility countries is still relatively small on the period total fertility of most reception countries, ranging between 0.05 and 0.10 increases of the TFR in absolute terms. Moreover, a substantial fraction of papers reviewed in Section 4 show a remarkable either partial or full convergence of the fertility of immigrants, and second-generation individuals, to the levels of native-born in many of the countries analyzed.

In Section 2 we highlight some important methodological challenges that concern all the literature reviewed in this chapter. Section 3 focuses on union formation and dissolution, and Section 4 surveys the mechanisms that drive immigrant fertility in reception countries. We close the chapter with a general overview of findings.

2. METHODOLOGICAL CHALLENGES TO THE STUDY OF IMMIGRANT MARRIAGE AND FERTILITY

Researchers studying immigrant household formation and fertility face two important methodological problems: first, the fact that the sample of immigrants observed in the destination country is a selected group from the country of origin; and, second, the lack of good datasets to appropriately answer some of the common research questions on the field.

2.1 Immigrant selection and individual heterogeneity

When researchers interpret convergence in immigrant family formation patterns to those of reception countries strictly as evidence of adaptation or integration, they may rely on the assumption that immigrants are a random sample of the population of origin. However, some immigration analyses often overlook the process of *immigrant selection* in the source country, which is likely to influence immigrant family formation and fertility. When ignoring likely dissimilarities between the behavior of the non-immigrant and the immigrant populations in the country of origin, differences in observed outcomes or characteristics between immigrants and natives are attributed to the culture of origin or, alternatively, to the process of migration itself (for example, its impact on delaying or accelerating marriage or childbearing), while they may primarily reflect distinctive characteristics of the immigrant population. If immigrant women, for example, are more driven to economic activity than their non-migrant compatriots, we could observe relatively low rates of partnership formation or low fertility in the host country, not because of "assimilation" to norms in destination countries but because of the immigrants' own attitude towards work.

The fact that immigrants are not a random sample of the population of origin has long been incorporated into theoretical models of immigration (Borjas, 1987, 1991, 1999). However, accounting for this fact in empirical models is complicated because the degree of selectivity varies substantially depending on the country of origin and timing of migration, and it is sometimes influenced by non-observable characteristics such as ambition or motivation (Feliciano, 2005). This implies that proper handling of the immigrant selection issue calls for large enough samples of immigrants in the destination country to enable the researcher to account for differences in cultural background, religion, or timing of entry, among other things. Alternatively (or better, additionally), addressing selection adequately may require large amounts of information on the population in the country of origin. Unfortunately both types of data may not be readily available in most cases.

In addition, studies on family formation have to deal with problems of endogeneity: Family formation decisions are so intertwined with educational and labor market choices that it may be unrealistic to regard them as exogenous to one another. Hence, *individual heterogeneity* is likely to drive the association between things such as education and family formation or fertility. Individuals with a strong focus on their careers may also have low preferences for committed partnerships and/or fertility, and this introduces(a different type of) selection bias in the analysis. We may then observe high levels of labor force participation together with low prevalence of marriage and low numbers of children. The direction of the bias is not straightforward. For instance, if children are normal goods, one would expect the effect of income on fertility to be positive, and individuals with more income to have more children since they can afford to pay for the additional services involved in raising them. However, this effect could be underestimated whenever some families have higher incomes precisely because they have postponed or reduced fertility and are exerting more effort in the labor market. Similarly, the effect of education on marriage and fertility can be overestimated if individuals with low preferences for education are more likely to marry early and form families. Again, fully accounting for joint labor market, education and family formation decisions require highly specialized data that it is not typically available to researchers. As a result, few studies can provide causal effects for estimates of intermarriage or immigrant fertility adaptation, among other topics.

A few papers exploit relatively exogenous variations that attenuate some of these biases. For instance, some researchers focus on the behavior of migrant children (those who arrived to the reception country before adulthood), for whom the link between migration decisions and subsequent behavior is more tenuous. Their findings shed more light on integration because individuals in their samples are not so affected by selection into migration as the general migrant population (Bleakley and Chin, 2010; Adserà et al., 2012; Beck et al., 2012; Adserà and Ferrer, 2014). Similarly, others have employed information of countries of ancestry to understand the behavior of the second generation of individuals who were not born on those countries (Fernandez and Fogli, 2006).

Addressing the restrictions that these types of selection issues impose on the data has forced researchers to look for alternative sources of information. In general we identify three main approaches in the literature surveyed in this chapter. A first common shortcut is to proxy for immigrant selection using broad measures (in general aggregate at the country level) such as country-of-origin gross domestic product or income inequality (Borjas, 1987; Cobb-Clark, 1993), distance to the host country (Jasso and Rosenzweig, 1990), pre-migration occupational status (at individual level if available) (Lobo and Salvo, 1998b), or education (Rumbaut, 1997; Feliciano, 2005). A second alternative involves the use of individual panel (longitudinal) data that might help to remove some of the unobserved heterogeneity leading to selection bias through the inclusion of individual fixed effects. However, the high cost involved in collecting panel data information typically means a reduction in sample size or information detail in those types of datasets compared to repeated cross-sections. This greatly handicaps immigration studies, which, as mentioned, require large samples of immigrants. Some widely used longitudinal surveys by migration researchers, such as the German Socio-Economic Panel (G-SOEP), have resorted to oversampling migrant populations. As a third alternative, in the absence of long panel data with sufficiently large samples of immigrants, researchers prefer the use of *synthetic cohorts* of immigrants from pooled cross-section surveys, such as the census. This methodology, introduced by Borjas (1985), allows researchers to follow groups of immigrants with similar characteristics across time, thereby eliminating some of the *cohort*, rather than individual, heterogenenity.[3]

2.2 Data limitations to measuring family formation

Research into family dynamics among immigrants is hindered by the lack of nationally representative data with detailed enough information on important dimensions such as the context of migration (i.e., type of entry visa, national origins, generation status, age at migration, linguistic origins), the migration and assimilation processes (i.e., timing and order of migration among spouses, the presence of children, parents or connections to family members in sending areas or in countries of reception), along with detailed measures of family interactions (i.e., fertility intentions of both spouses, complete fertility and

---

[3] This methodology has been broadly applied to the study of immigrant labour markets (Chiswick, 1978; Ferrer and Riddell, 2008; Clark and Lindley, 2009).

marriage histories) or pre-migration information (i.e., labor force participation, years of schooling or family structure prior to migration).

Incomplete information on fertility and marriage histories may lead researchers to associate the observed behavior of migrants to convergence of marital and fertility propensities to those of the native-born, because of their inability to control for past events (such as previous unions, or children left behind in the country of origin) that affect current propensities. The number of children an immigrant may choose to have in the host country, for example, will depend on the number (and plausibly the gender) of children they had previous to migration, which might be unknown or underestimated if some children did not move with their parents. Lack of detail in the age at arrival is another good example where data limitations restrict the ability to properly test some theoretical models or understand whether some mechanisms put forward by researchers to explain demographic behavior are at work. Even though many datasets lack complete information on age at arrival, others, typically publicly accessible census data, provide five-year intervals. Some models reviewed later in the chapter are concerned with testing whether there are discontinuities in some socio-economic outcomes for specific ages of arrival (particularly during childhood) and in those cases obtaining the exact year of migration is of essence.

The most common sources of data for the studies reviewed here are the census or related surveys, such as the Labour Force Survey (Canada, UK) or the Current Population Survey (US). The main advantage of these datasets lies in affording large samples of all immigrant groups, which allows detailed examination of racial and ethnic patterns of marriage and fertility. However, their lack of detailed family or union formation histories typically confines the analysis that researchers can conduct with these data sources in important ways that introduce selection bias in the estimates. A good example of those limitations is found in most studies of marriage that employ census data. They are confined to currently married couples, as the census typically lacks marital histories. This is prone to bias the observed sample towards endogamous marriages, which have higher stability, and the most recently married, which still have not had time to dissolve (Jacobs and Furstenberg, 1986). One common approach to minimizing potential selection biases is to restrict the sample to younger couples, more likely to be in first marriages.

Cohabitation or any other mode of informal union is particularly difficult to trace because in many surveys it is not specifically reported or counted as such. This is clearly the case for census data, but it can be also a difficulty in otherwise rich datasets such as some population registrars in Europe. Researchers have to make assumptions about unrelated individuals living in the same household for a certain period of time to decide whether they can plausibly be classified as cohabitants. In addition, lack of proper measures of these informal unions may be particularly relevant when studying immigrants since the experience and meaning of cohabitation varies considerably across origin countries. This is one instance in which having information about country of origin becomes important as consensual unions may be very similar to marriage for immigrants from countries with a long tradition in cohabitation.[4]

Another case in which the tradeoffs involved in the use of census data become apparent relates to the use of the *own-children-method* to measure individual fertility. Census data typically reports the number of children living in the household rather than the number of children born. The own–children-method exploits the fact that the vast majority of young children live with their mother at the time of the census to reconstruct women's fertility histories by linking children and mothers living in the same household (Cho, 1973).[5] This estimation strategy presents some challenges when applied to studying the fertility of immigrants (Dubuc, 2009). First, some children may not live with their mothers, because they were left behind in the country of origin under the care of relatives. Second, it may be difficult to properly capture the early childbearing of older women as some of their children may have already left home. To the extent that these effects are important, the own children method will underreport fertility and introduce error in the measurement of the dependent variable. This should be of particular concern if the mismeasurement occurs at different rates for immigrant and the native-born, for instance if departure of children from the household in their late teens or early adulthood is far more common among the native-born population than among migrants (or vice versa) (Adserà and Ferrer, 2014).

There are other challenges to measuring fertility. An important one concerns the choice of the proper aggregate fertility measure to describe the fertility trends in the country. A broadly used measure of fertility is the total fertility rate (TFR), which is a hypothetical measure estimating the number of children a woman would have if she were to give birth according to the prevailing age-specific fertility rates (ASFRs).[6] This is the measure displayed in Table 7.2. An actual measure of the fertility experience of women is the completed fertility rate (CFR), which measures the average number of births that women of a given birth cohort actually have over the reproductive lives. While CFR has the advantage of truly reflecting fertility patterns, it does not reflect current fertility behavior and it needs to collect all the data for a particular cohort until the end of their fertile years to come up with a final estimate. The current fertility patterns are better captured by TFR, which in turn has the disadvantage of being a composite measure that may confound changes in the timing of births (tempo effect) with changes in the quantity of births. Thus, TFR can be an accurate estimate of CFR only when both the timing and quantum of births are not changing much across generations. Hence, during periods in which the timing of births

---

[4] This is the case with cohabitation in some Latin American countries (Castro, 2002; Qian et al., 2012).

[5] For Canada, Bélanger and Gilbert (2003) showed that estimated fertility differentials for immigrants and domestic-born individuals for the period 1996–2001 using both methods are not very sizeable—with a downward bias of the census for women younger than 30 and an upward bias for those aged beyond 30.

[6] ASFRs are obtained by dividing the number of births to women of a given age range (typically five years) by the total population of women of that age that year. The TFR is constructed by aggregating ASFRs.

accelerates and concentrates in the first part of the fertile years, the TFR overestimates the CFR. This is an important consideration as TFRs are typically used to predict population growth and to calculate the demand for public services. When calculating the TFR for immigrant populations, further consideration have to be taken into account. For instance, the age and marital composition of immigrant groups and the disruption effects of migration on fertility all play a role in increasing the volatility of TFRs, leading to even higher distortions in predicted population growth for immigrant groups (Parrado, 2011).

Finally, before opening the discussion of the two central themes of the chapter, it is important to note that comparisons between immigration studies are not straightforward. Different studies use unique samples, diverse definitions of intermarriage and measures of fertility, and include varying sets of control variables. For instance, although the term immigrant commonly designates the foreign-born, in some cases nationality determines immigrant status in some datasets. This problem was already highlighted when discussing Table 7.2, where some studies measure the fertility of the foreign-born and others that of the foreign nationals. Further studies may use different definitions of ancestry to define an endogamous marriage. In some cases they are defined on nativity (whether foreign- or native-born) and in others they also incorporate race/ethnicity to the measure. Finally, limited availability of fertility histories might impose the need touse fertility measures based on the "own child method" rather than on actual births. Despite the different samples and variable definitions employed, several findings appear very robust across the studies in each topic, and we focus on them.

3. MARRIAGE AND DIVORCE AMONG IMMIGRANTS

Family formation has been one of the more prolific areas of research in immigration.[7] Marriage propensities are part of a country's cultural background and hence potentially indicative of cultural differences between the immigrant and native-born populations. Further, the capacity to form and maintain exogamous unions (between a foreign- and a native-born) can be interpreted as the quintessence of successful integration. Duncan and Trejo's (2007) research reveals that selectivity into intermarriage influences ethnic identification, which in itself has important consequences to measure the intergenerational integration of those with immigrant ancestry. Hence, it is not surprising that most studies in this area focus on intermarriage, with marriage propensities receiving only passing attention. Similarly, union dissolution among immigrants has been the object of great interest both among researchers and policymakers because of the special vulnerability of children and women in immigrant families, who could be less established in the labor force and more at risk of poverty than men, who are traditionally the breadwinners in those families (Qian, 2013).

---

[7] Through the chapter we use marriage to refer indistinctly to any form of formal unions, including common law, because these are usually indistinguishable.

We have summarized the main features of the samples and methods used in the most relevant papers in the marriage literature in Table 7.3 to guide the reader through the diversity of results reviewed in this section of the chapter.

3.1 Microeconomic models of marriage formation

The development of the modern economics of the family has its roots in Becker's work.[8] His path-breaking model of household formation underlies current theories of marriage, divorce, fertility and intra-family division of labor. The basic marriage model outlined in Becker's (1974) seminal paper *A Theory of Marriage* assumes that individuals weight the potential contribution of likely partners to household produced goods (companionship, children, quality of meals, among others) to determine the gains of marriage over remaining single. Both options should equal each other in equilibrium. This conceptualization gives rise to a market relationship between the output received in the marriage market and the number of participants in that given market. In a competitive equilibrium (as assumed by Becker), couples are formed in a manner that maximizes aggregate surplus in the marriage market.[9] Hence, the model predicts how changes in the relative availability of men and women might affect the distribution of marriages. The model also has implications in terms of sorting: Individuals with similarities in traits that are complementary to each other will tend to marry (positive assortative matching), whereas individuals with differences in traits that are substitutes will also tend to marry (negative assortative matching). For instance, individuals of similar religious preferences will likely share preferences regarding the manner of raising their children, and this in turn will enhance their gains from marriage. Similarly, two potential partners with comparative advantage in the labor market and in household production respectively (and hence different expected market wages) will benefit from increased household production through division of labor.

The scant empirical support for Becker's prediction of negative assortative matching (on observed wages) prompted Lam's (1988) model of marriage, which extends Becker's framework to include a public good produced within the household. Since many of the commodities produced within families are also jointly consumed within families, it is optimal for marriages to form between people with similar demands for these goods.

Keeley (1977) formulates Becker's model of marriage as a search model, where potential spouses have incentives to seek "suitable" mates. Suitability in this model is measured by a "marital wage" that is not observed, but that can be proxied by a marital offer. In a world with search costs, optimal matches do not always occur, forcing marriage market participants to make decisions about the characteristics of spouses they value most. One of

---

[8] The economics of the family emerged as a distinct field with the publication of Schultz's volume in 1974.

[9] Alternatively, one can assume that gains from marriage are the result of a bargaining process between spouses (Lundberg and Pollak, 1993).

Table 7.3 Summary of main references on marriage

	Year/country	Sample	Intermarriage	Marriage market	Assimilation	Characteristics	Results
Determinants of intermarriage							
Dribe and Lundh (2011)	2003 Sweden	Immigrants 20–59, married in Sweden after 1968	Two types of exogamy, relative to marrying immigrant in same ethnic group	Size of the opposite sex group at settlement level	Age at immigration, time between immigration and marriage, CO	Education, age, race, gender	Exogamy associated with being younger, more time btw migration and marriage, education (except for Asian women) and older age at immigration. Indirect evidence of assortative matching on education
Chiswick and Houseworth (2011)	1980 US	Immigrants married after migration and currently married	Exogamous = married to a different ethnicity (by ancestry or country of birth)	Individuals of marriageable age in the SMSAs (or State), number of opp. sex in the ethnicity group and *MMkt*, total population by region and age group	Years since migration, age at immigration and linguistic distance	veteran, race, gender, times married, education, deviations from mode education of the group, multiple ancestry	Exogamy associated with being younger, time btw immigration and marriage, education (except for Asian women) and older age at immigration (but more likely to marry within ancestry). Linguistic distance has a strong effect on intermarriage (except for Korean and Japanese-speaking women) Evidence of assortative matching

			State level, linguistic similarity of other groups in the state, religious similarity to other groups in the state, group size in the state, group sex ratio	Early marriage customs, Christian background, non-English CO	Generational status, race, education, age, cohabitation, education deviations from group, ethnic diversity index	Strong cultural backgrounds (non-Christian religion, non-English CO, early marriage in country of origin) increase endogamy. No effect of sex ratios Positive assortative matching
Kalmijn and Van Tubergen (2010)	1994–2006 US	Children of immigrants or immigrating <16	Married to NB, married to a 1st or 2nd gen. of the same CO, married a 1st or 2nd gen. of other CO (by mother or father ancestry)			
Georgiadis and Manning (2010)	2000–08 UK	Married immigrants and NB, White, Indian, Pakistani, Bangladesh, Black Caribbean, Black African, Chinese	Married to someone from the CO who came as an adult	None	Generational status	Age, education	Higher intermarriage among second generation. Chinese immigrant women and Black immigrants more likely to intermarry.
Lee and Boyd (2008)	2000 US and Canada	Reported single Asian origin and their spouses	Endogamous = married to same race or intermarried to other race	None	Generational status	Residence, age, education, income, ethnic group,	In both countries, Asian women more likely to intermarry. Among these, the younger and more educated are more likely to intermarry. Overall intermarriage rates higher in US

Continued

Table 7.3 Summary of main references on marriage—cont'd

	Year/country	Sample	Intermarriage	Marriage market	Assimilation	Characteristics	Results
Van Tubergen and Maas (2007)	1971 Netherlands	Married immigrants 18–65	Endogamy = immigrant married to FB spouse of the same CO	Municipality. Group size and sex ratio; dissimilarity index (relative size of the group)	Linguistic proximity	Age at marriage, marriage order; ethnic group religious diversity; education and education relative to the ethnic group	Endogamy depends on the size of the group, favorable sex ratios, and spatial segregation. Linguistic ability, education and religious diversity reduce endogamy
Lievens (1998)	1991 Belgium	Recently married (<5 years) with Turk or Moroccan spouse, arriving 2 years before marriage	Same ethnic; Western European partner	Census district. Group size; ethnic diversity index; socio-economic diversity	Age at immigration, generational status, age at marriage; language	Education, region of origin	Higher intermarriage for older immigrants, those arriving younger, and with high education levels

Assortative matching

	Year/country	Sample	Intermarriage	Marriage market	Assimilation	Characteristics	Results
Furtado (2012)	1970 USA	NB married males, 18–65, with 2 FB parents in 13 ethnic groups	Married to a person with one parent born in same CO as male's fathers CO	County	English ability	Age	Evidence of assortative matching on education. Some specifications evidence of cultural adaptability
Furtado and Theodoropoulos (2011)	2000 USA	Married males 25–65. Asian, Hispanic or White ancestry. FB arriving <18	Both spouses have the same first ancestry	MSA, size of ethnic group	Language	Age, rural, area of residence, veteran status, race	Assortative matching stronger for the NB relative to FB and for immigrants arriving as young children rather than older

Celikaksoy et al. (2006)	1999 Denmark	Married first generation immigrants from Pakistan, Turkey and Yugoslavia. Arrived <13 (20 years in Denmark aged 25–37)	Married to equally educated spouse (above or below the median for the group)	None	Split sample between those culturally assimilated and at conflict with parents	Imported spouse	Assortative matching stronger for Turks and Yugoslavian experiencing conflict with parents and for the sample of not culturally assimilated

Intermarriage as assimilation

Meng and Meurs (2009)	1992 France	Married (CL) immigrants arriving single from Spain, Portugal, Morocco, Algeria, Turkey, Asia and Sub-Saharan Africa	Immigrant married to an NB	Age–ethnic–religious group. Include relative size and sex ratio within MMkt?	Years since migration, French fluency	Age, schooling, religion, CO, residence	
Meng and Gregory (2005)	1981, 1986, 1991, 1996 Australia	All	Marriage between NB (includes New Zealand, UK, USA, Canada) and immigrant from non-English-speaking country	Age-Ethnic–religious group. Include relative size and sex ratio within MMkt	Years since migration, English-speaking ability	Age, schooling, religion, CO	The young, educated, no religious and longer in Australia more likely to intermarry. The intermarriage premium seems to be a reward for assimilation rather than due to unobserved heterogeneity

Continued

Table 7.3 Summary of main references on marriage—cont'd

	Year/country	Sample	Intermarriage	Marriage market	Assimilation	Characteristics	Results
Kantarevic (2004)	1970, 1980 US	FB married (first marriage) males arrived single with no English mother tongue	Married to NB	Ethnic group and State. Use the fraction of potential spouses in the group	Years since migration, entry cohort	Education, age	Intermarriage more likely for younger, better educated and longer in the US. No evidence of causal relationship of intermarriage on earnings

Timing of first union

	Year/country	Sample	Intermarriage	Marriage market	Assimilation	Characteristics	Results
Huschek et al. (2010)	2007 13 European cities	2nd gen. Turks, Moroccan, and Yugoslavians	Timing of first union	Parental education, family size, co-ethnic contact, age, education, CO			
Milewski and Hamel (2010)	2007 France	2nd gen Turkish and NB reference group	Timing of first union and endogamous union. Also marriage to older Turkish	Residence, age, religion education, family size parental education. Also, attended school in Turk and language raised in (for endogamy)			Faster marriage rates among low-educated Turk women. Low-educated Turk women more likely to marry a Turkish immigrant

NB = native-born; FB = foreign-born; CO = country of origin.

the largest and most common search costs involves the spatial distribution of potential partners, which tends to make marriage markets local. As discussed below, the definition of what constitutes a marriage market is central to the empirical analysis of multi-ethnic marriages. Chiswick and Lehrer (1991) and Lehrer (2003) similarly model intermarriage using a search model where, in equilibrium, the marginal cost of finding a more suitable partner equals its marginal benefits.

3.2 The determinants of intermarriage

The marriage models discussed above have distinct implications for marriage markets with significant ethnic diversity. Since similar ethnic backgrounds are likely to be complements in the production of ethnicity-related household public goods (such as compliance with ethnic celebrations, or types of food), these models predict positive assortative matching based on ethnic background. The empirical study of racial intermarriage has a long tradition in the US (Sandefur and McKinnell, 1986; Shoen and Wooldrege, 1989; Bratter and King, 2008), where it was perceived as a measure of the persistence of racial (particularly black–white) divisions. With the increase in migrant population flows towards Western economies, the intermarriage among immigrants has taken center-stage as a separate case to consider. The intermarriage models in this specific case imply that immigrants are more likely to marry other immigrants, preferably those of the same ethnic or religious background. In a study on the causes of exogamous marriages, Kalmijn (1998) grouped the determinants of partner choice in the following three categories: (1) individuals' preferences for certain characteristics in a spouse, (2) influence of the social group of which they are members, and (3) the potential constraints imposed by the structure of the marriage market where they are searching for a spouse.

Applying these categories to the study of homogamy among immigrants, a model of intermarriage could be estimated by the following stylized equation:

$$M_{iki} = X'_{ikj}\beta_0 + Assim'_{ikj}\beta_1 + MMkt'_{kj}\beta_2 + e'_{ikj} \tag{7.1}$$

where M_{ikj} is an indicator of endogamous marriage for individual i of ethnicity k in marriage market j. The independent variables include a vector of individual socio-economic characteristics, denoted as X_{ikj}, a vector of indicators measuring immigrant assimilation ($Assim_{ikj}$), such as immigrant generational status, age at immigration or language skills, and a vector including the characteristics of the individual's marriage market ($MMkt_{kj}$), such as the probability of meeting a potential partner of the same ethnicity within the marriage market, or the sex ratio in the individual's own marriage market.[10] The odds ratio of an endogamous marriage as specified in equation (7.1) is typically

---

[10] Sex ratios, defined as the ratio of male to female individuals within the group/area considered, account for spousal competition in the marriage market. A predominance of men, other things being equal, will increase exogamous marriages for men and reduce them for women.

estimated with linear probability or logit models.[11] Alternatively, the use of log-linear models is not unusual within the sociology literature studying ethnic intermarriage (Rosenfeld, 2002; Qian and Lichter, 2007).[12]

The hypothesis of assortative matching (across immigrant or nativity status) predicts lower rates of endogamous marriage among assimilated immigrants—such as child immigrants who migrated before adulthood or the children of immigrants.[13] Since preferences for partners are more likely to conform to the environment where the individual grew up, the younger the immigrant arrived and the looser the ties to the home country, the more likely he or she intermarries. Hence, the estimated coefficients for the parameters in β_1 associated to assimilation, driven by the hypothesis of assortative matching, are expected to be negative.

The structure of the marriage market (summarized in the term $MMkt_{ikj}$), on the other hand, accounts for the constraints to individuals' preferences resulting from the size of their own group and the gender imbalances within groups. The smaller the group size and the higher the sex imbalance, the higher the predicted rates of intermarriage.[14] Researchers' definitions of appropriate marriage markets are strongly determined by data availability. Among others, Furtado (2012), Furtado and Theodoropoulos (2011), Kalmijn and Van Tubergen (2010), and Chiswick and Houseworth (2011) discussed the effect of gender imbalances within ethnic groups on intermarriage propensities among immigrants to the US, but each analysis used a slightly different definition of the relevant marriage market. We have summarized the sample characteristics and the main control variables included in the analysis in Table 7.3.

Overall, there is strong empirical support for both the "assimilation" of the marriage market and "structuralist" determinants of mixed marriages among immigrants discussed above. Recent immigrants and those arriving at older ages are more likely to form endogamous marriages than those who migrate as young children or have already lived in the country for some time because their cultural barriers with the host population are greater. Similarly, softer ties to ancestry increase the likelihood of mixed marriage among the children of immigrants relative to that of the foreign-born. Adherence to religion (and religiosity) and increased probability of contact with co-ethnics among more recent arrivals

---

[11] The model calculates the odds of endogamous marriages out of the total population married. Alternatively, a model with three marital states (endogamous, exogamous to a native-born, or exogamous to an immigrant from other ethnicity) could be estimated using a multinomial logit model.

[12] Log-linear models are more accurate in that they take the marriage, rather than the individual, as the unit of analysis, but are less flexible in accommodating continuous variables, which are important in understanding the determinants of intermarriage among immigrants.

[13] A recent series of studies assessing the cultural integration of European immigrants (Algan et al., 2012) confirmed the idea that endogamous marriage is more prevalent among first-generation immigrants, but less prevalent among the second generation than among the third.

[14] See Niedomysl et al. (2010) for an exploration on the globalization of marriage.

are all significant predictors of endogamous marriages. Several papers that examine the determinants of intermarriage for different ethnic groups and across generation levels (Lievens, 1998; Gonzalez-Ferrrer, 2006; van Tubergen and Maas, 2007; Kalmijn and van Tubergen, 2010; Dribe and Lundh, 2011) found consistent evidence for the assimilationist approach (see Furtado and Trejo (2013) for an excellent survey of this literature). In this regard, the most comprehensive review of the assimilationist determinants of immigrant marriage is found in Chiswick and Houseworth (2011), whose analysis includes years in the USA, age at arrival, age at first marriage, and linguistic distance from English. After controlling for a wide range of marriage market and individual characteristics, they found that the probability of intermarriage is higher for younger, more educated immigrants whose linguistic distance is closer to English.

With regard to marriage market characteristics, most studies found that it is important to control for marriage market effects, particularly size of the ethnic group, and that these variables usually have the expected sign (Celikaksoy et al., 2006; van Tubergen and Maas, 2007; Dribe and Lundh, 2011; Chiswick and Houseworth, 2011; Furtado and Theodoropolous, 2011). However, the evidence on gender imbalance within ethnic group as a positive determinant of exogamous marriages is more mixed. Some studies did not find significant positive associations between sex ratios and endogamous marriages (Kalmijn and van Tubergen, 2010).

In North America, the analysis of the marriage determinants of particular ethnicities has been greatly dominated by a focus on the marriage patterns of Hispanics and Asians, which constitute the majority of recent immigrants. Data from the American Community Survey 2008 indicates that among "newlyweds" (those who married in the 12 months prior to the survey), 39.4% of native-born Hispanics and 11.7% of foreign-born Hispanics were married to a spouse of a different race/ethnicity. The same percentages among Asians stood at 46.0% and 25.9% respectively (Passel et al., 2010). In many studies and official statistics, particularly those employing US and Canadian data, nativity (place of birth) and race/ethnicity are often intertwined and it becomes difficult to separate those categories to examine them separately.[15] Qian et al. (2012) is a good example of this strand of work. The paper studied the spousal or partner racial/ethnic background among married or cohabiting individuals aged 20–34 in the US 2000 census and it differentiated among US-born and migrants (by age at arrival). Table 7.4 provides some data from this paper on the distribution of partners among major migrant groups (Chinese, Filipino, and Mexican) depending on whether they are co-ethnic (from the same ethnicity), inter-ethnic (other Asian or Hispanic), white or a member of other racial

---

[15] Canadian statistics, for example, often report the rate of intermarriage among *visible minorities* (defined as persons, other than Aboriginal peoples, who are non-Caucasian in race or non-white in color). Data from the 2006 Canadian census indicated that 55.6% of native-born visible minorities and 12.1% of foreign-born visible minorities were in mixed unions (Milan et al., 2010).

Table 7.4 Spousal or partner racial/ethnic composition by gender, ethnicity, and age at arrival, ages 20–34, 2000 PUMS, USA

Ethnicity/ age	% males married or cohabiting with				% females married or cohabiting with			
	Co-ethnic	Inter-ethnic	White	Other	Co-ethnic	Inter-ethnic	White	Other
Chinese								
Arriving at ages 14–19	86.2	8.2	3.6	2.1	76.2	7.2	13.5	3.2
Arriving at ages 6–13	68.4	15	14	2.6	59.2	15.1	20.4	5.3
Arriving at ages 0–5	48.9	9	33.1	9	46.1	8.9	39.4	5.6
US-born	41.5	16.9	34.8	6.9	28.6	11.8	51.4	8.3
Filipino								
Arriving at ages 14–19	75.7	3.3	14.5	6.5	51.7	4.8	30.5	13
Arriving at ages 6–13	57.2	5.9	26.1	10.8	42.7	7.1	33	17.2
Arriving at ages 0–5	37	6.3	42.2	14.6	23.2	4.1	56.4	16.4
US-born	29	8.7	48.7	13.6	20.8	8	53.6	17.6
Mexican								
Arriving at ages 14–19	90.2	4.2	5	0.6	94.5	3.3	1.8	0.4
Arriving at ages 6–13	88.2	4.6	6.1	1.1	90.1	4.2	4.5	1.3
Arriving at ages 0–5	81.1	5.4	12	1.5	82.4	5.2	10	2.4
US-born	64.4	3.6	29.2	2.8	67.1	3.6	25.4	3.9

Source: Excerpts from Table 2 in Qian et al. (2012).

minority groups. Some stylized facts that accord with the theories just described are apparent in Table 7.4. Among groups, co-ethnicity is positively associated with the size of the ethnic group in the US, with Mexicans being the largest of all. Second, the likelihood of intermarriage (or cohabitation outside the ethnic group) decreases monotonically with age at arrival and it is the highest among those born in the US.

To keep the focus of the chapter, below we restrict our attention only to those studies that explicitly consider the role of immigration (nativity), even if it is combined with race/ethnicity, in the analysis. Liang and Ito (1999) offered a descriptive study of the intermarriage patterns of the population of Asian ancestry in the New York city district that are consistent with those found in subsequent studies. Rosenfeld (2002) studied the intermarriage patterns of individuals of Mexican descent in the US. More recently, Lee and Boyd (2008) compared intermarriage among individuals of Asian ancestry in US and Canada, identifying similar roles for different determinants of intermarriage in the two countries. They found a higher intermarriage probability of Asian women relative to Asian men in both countries, and higher overall intermarriage probability in the US.

Finally, an important dimension to consider in the analysis of endogamous marriage is *generational status*. It is commonly believed that a desire to assimilate in the host country should lead immigrants to marry similarly (or more) integrated immigrants within the same generational status, rather than recently arrived immigrants (Pagnini and Morgan, 1990). This would be observed in the data particularly if no new large waves of co-ethnic immigrants are expected to arrive in the host country in the coming years. However, in some cases, strong preferences for co-ethnic marriages and thin local marriage markets might also give rise to the practice of importing partners from the country of origin. This phenomenon may appear in the data as favoring ethnic homogamous marriages to recent immigrants, while in fact those partners are, as the literature traditionally labels them, *imported brides* (since the majority of them tend to be women). This practice seems to prevail among some Turkish and Moroccan minorities in Western Europe (Lievens, 1999). Gonzalez-Ferrer (2006) also found an association between low education and importing a partner among immigrant men to Germany, but not among women.[16]

3.3 Intermarriage as assimilation

The empirical literature has tried to determine to what extent intermarriage is an indicator or a cause of assimilation.[17] It is true that intermarried immigrants in Australia, France, the US, and Canada have more schooling and earn significantly more than immigrants marrying other immigrants, even after controlling for human capital endowments unrelated to marriage (Worswick, 1996; Baker and Benjamin, 1997; Qian and Litcher, 2001, 2007; Kantarevic, 2004; Meng and Gregory, 2005; Meng and Meurs, 2009). There are two possible explanations for this stylized fact. One is that the relationship is spurious, driven by unobserved abilities or preferences of individuals who marry outside their ethnic group. The second option is that the relationship is causal because marrying a native-born spouse speeds up assimilation of the immigrant partner (or, alternatively, marrying endogamously reduces assimilation opportunities for immigrants).

---

[16] Lievens (1999) proposed the hypothesis that women immigrants might import partners to achieve modern goals. Gonzalez-Ferrer (2006), Hooghiemstra (2001), and Celikaksoy et al. (2006), however, found no support for this hypothesis.

[17] In the extreme, selective intermarriage may influence ethnic identification. This may dilute assimilation outcomes if some assimilated individuals no longer identify with the original ethnic category (Duncan and Trejo, 2007).

A model to estimate such effect follows quite easily from equation (7.1). In addition to modeling the odds of intermarriage, researchers introduced a second equation with an outcome y (either education or wages) specified as a function of different assimilation variables, such as years since migration or English ability (*Assim*), a vector of socio-demographic characteristics, including human capital variables (X), and an indicator for endogamous marriage (M_1):

$$y_{ij} = X'_{ij}\beta_0 + Assim'_{ij}\beta_1 + uM_{ij}$$
$$M_{ij} = X'_{ij}\beta_0 + Assim'_{ij}\beta_1 + MMkt'_{ij}\beta_2 + e'_{ij} \tag{7.2}$$

where the sub-indexes i and j refer to the individual and the marriage market respectively. As before, *MMkt* includes variables defining the marriage market of the individual, such as the probability of meeting a potential partner of the same ethnicity within the marriage market, or the sex ratio in the individual's marriage market. These variables are assumed to be exogenous and not to affect earnings other than through their influence on the probability of intermarriage. The system of equations can then be estimated by two-step linear square methods.[18]

In their study on intermarriage and assimilation, Meng and Gregory (2005) compared the earnings of different types of couples in Australia and found a substantial intermarriage premium for immigrants of approximately 20% for men and 46% for women.[19] Natives, on the other hand, have much smaller intermarriage premiums, which suggests that higher earnings are the result of faster assimilation among intermarried immigrants, rather than the result of unobserved characteristics for immigrants who intermarry. A similar result is observed for French immigrants (Meng and Meurs, 2009). Kantarevic (2004), however, reached the opposite conclusion for US immigrants. The difference in results is likely driven by differences in the composition of the immigrant population in the two countries.

Nielsen et al. (2009) used a reform of the Danish immigration policy restricting "migration marriage." The law effectively bans family reunification for unions in which one of the partners is below 24 years of age. Because the policy reform affected marriage behavior of immigrants from different countries differently, it generates exogenous variation in marriage behavior that can be used for identification of the causal effect of immigrant marriage on education outcomes of the children of immigrants, in particular on their dropout rate before the end of compulsory schooling. The authors found that the dropout rate of males increases by 25 percentage points as a

---

[18] This specification corresponds to a model estimated over married individuals. Alternatively, it could be applied to a full sample of individuals, where M_{ij} is a two-dimensional vector of endogamous and exogamous marriage indicators and single is the omitted category. The model can be further disaggregated by ethnic group.

[19] These numbers are the result of the two-step estimation. Estimating an equation similar to (7.1), assuming marriage to be exogenous, results in estimates of the intermarriage premium for immigrants of 5% for immigrant males and 10% for immigrant women.

consequence of marriage to a marriage migrant (or imported bride), whereas the effect for females is small and mostly insignificant.

3.4 Assortative matching in education and language

Educational attainment and language proficiency among immigrants have received special attention within the literature as determinants of intermarriage. This is probably due to the importance that these variables have as predictors of successful economic integration for immigrants. To the extent that endogamy reinforces the traits of the ethnic community, the understanding of how language and education affect intermarriage decisions could explain the speed of intergenerational assimilation. Hence, the role of assortative matching in these two dimensions in explaining the marriage decisions of the second generation has been the subject of much interest. In an early study using the New Immigrant Survey Pilot, Jasso et al. (2000) found positive assortative matching in education among mixed marriages (US citizens and immigrant spouse), with similar levels of schooling within couples. However, the levels of education across mixed couples vary depending on the gender of the US partner. US husband–immigrant wife couples have over two years more of schooling than US wife–immigrant husband couples (that have around 12.5 years on average). Among immigrant couples, the educational attainment of both spouses is very similar when the wife is the principal applicant. When the male is the principal applicant he has on average two more years of education than his wife.

Furtado and Theodoropoulos (2011) distinguished three main channels through which education can affect intermarriage. The *cultural adaptability* effect suggests that education might increase intermarriage because it makes immigrants more likely to accept the social norms in the host country and accept a native partner.[20] The *enclave effect* proposes that as more education is associated with more disperse labor markets and mobility outside the ethnic enclave (Wozniak, 2010), it lowers endogamy by potentially reducing the size of the co-ethnic marriage market. Finally, the possibility of *assortative matching* indicates that the level of educational attainment of an individual will affect the size of the pertinent marriage market. According to the assortative matching theory, similar levels of characteristics increase surplus within marriages. Therefore, potential partners with similar levels of education may be willing to substitute similarities in ethnicity for similarities in education. Through this channel, education might or might not increase the probability of intermarriage depending on the distribution of education within the population. For instance, for a relatively highly educated individual, it would decrease the probability of endogamy among those belonging to immigrant groups with average low education and increase it in highly educated immigrant groups.

---

[20] Grossbard-Shechtman (1993) and Reinharz and DellaPergola (2009), however, suggested that certain types of ethnic or religious education may reduce intermarriage.

The significance of these three mechanisms can be estimated employing a variation of the previous model that explicitly considers the education levels of the ethnic group and of the marriage market:

$$M_{ijk} = X'_{ijk}\beta_0 + \gamma_0 S_{ijk} + \gamma_1 S_{ijk}(S_{jk} - S_k) + Assim'_{ijk}\beta_1 + MMkt'_{jk}\beta_2 + e'_{ijk} \qquad (7.3)$$

where M_{ijk} is an indicator of endogamous marriage for person i of ethnicity j in marriage market k. The education indicators include S_{ijk} that denotes an individual's years of schooling, S_{jk} that refers to the average schooling of the ethnic group j in marriage market k, and S_k that measures the average schooling of the general population in marriage market k. $Assim_{ijk}$ measures individual characteristics that account for immigrant assimilation such as generational status, age at immigration, or language ability. $MMkt_{jk}$ measures other characteristics of the marriage market k for ethnicity j, such as the relative size or sex ratio for the group, and controls for enclave effects. Finally, X_{ijk} is a vector of other individual characteristics that measure the taste for marrying within the same ethnicity, such as age (birth cohort) or ancestry. The effect of individual educational attainment is given by γ_0. If cultural adaptability plays a role, this parameter will be (or tend to) zero as education is supposed to reduce endogamy through this mechanism. The effect of assortative matching is captured by the interaction of an individual's education and the difference between the average education of the ethnic group in the marriage market and the average education of the marriage market. The corresponding estimated parameter, γ_1, is expected to be positive. If the ethnic group is more educated than the average in the marriage market, individual education will increase endogamy; however, if the ethnic group has lower education than the average, high individual levels of education should reduce endogamy.

Most papers find empirical support for the hypothesis that education is positively associated with intermarriage (Card et al., 2000; Meng and Gregory 2005; Qian and Lichter, 2007).[21] However, not all of them distinguish between the different mechanisms. Furtado and Theodoropolous (2011), using the US census 2000, found evidence that the three mechanisms are at work. When there is no assortative matching effect—the average education of the group is similar to the average education in the marriage market—one year increase in the education of an individual leads to 1 percentage point decrease in endogamy. On the other hand, when the education of the group falls below that of the general population by one year, endogamy decreases by 1.6 percentage points. The education of the ethnic group has to be one and a half years greater than that of the general population for a one year increase in individual education to lead to an

---

[21] Curiously, marriage decisions among Asian females do not appear to be sensitive to education but seem driven by strong preference for ethnic endogamy (Dribe and Lundh, 2011; Furtado and Theodoropolous, 2011). Chiswick and Houseworth (2011) found a similar result for female immigrants speaking Japanese or Korean and attributed this to the prevalence of war brides from these origins.

increase in endogamy. The assortative matching effect is stronger for the native-born than for immigrants, and stronger for immigrants arriving as young children than for older immigrants. Using an identical model on data from US census 1970, Furtado (2012) found less support for the cultural adaptability effect of education after controlling for the other mechanisms through which education may affect the probability of inter-marriage. She found, however, robust evidence for the assortative matching mechanism among the second generation of immigrants in the US: Within ethnicities with lower than average education levels (Mexican), the highly educated are more likely to inter-marry than the less educated. The opposite is true for ethnicities with higher than average education levels (Russian), where endogamy is more prevalent among the higher educated.[22]

Celikaksoy et al. (2006) also found support for positive assortative matching in edu-cation. They specifically tested the probability of marrying a spouse with similar levels of education among a sample of Turk, Pakistani, and Yugoslavian immigrants to Denmark, hence their model does not distinguish among different mechanisms. However, they make use of a rich set of cultural and family-related variables to distinguish between indi-viduals who are more culturally assimilated in the country of reception or who are in conflict with their parents and those who are not. Assortative matching seems to be stron-ger for Turks and Yugoslavs who are more culturally assimilated in Denmark but expe-rienced conflict with parents and for the sample of not culturally assimilated individuals of any of the three countries of origin.

Most of the studies reviewed above include language ability as a control in the regres-sions of intermarriage and find that higher proficiency in the language of the country of destination reduces the probability of endogamous marriages. One problem with the use of this variable in the econometric models is its potential endogeneity. Individuals with better language skills may have other unobservable characteristics that favor intermarriage. In an interesting study, Bleakley and Chin (2010) looked at the effect of language ability on several immigrant outcomes, including the probability of marrying, the probability of mar-rying a native-born, and the probability of marrying someone of the same ancestry. They were able to account for the potential endogeneity of language ability by using variation in age at immigration between immigrants from English-speaking and non-English-speaking countries to instrument language ability. We go over this strategy more in detail in Section 4. Their results on language ability are similar to those reported elsewhere in the literature, which suggests that the effect of language on intermarriage is robust to endo-geneity considerations.

---

[22] Additional evidence of both mechanisms is found in Chiswick and Houseworth (2011) using the 1980 US census. They report that education increases exogamy among immigrants (cultural adaptability) and that differences with respect to the modal education of the ethnic group increase exogamy (assortative match-ing). They do not account, however, for the relative education level of the ethnic group.

The assortative matching model can be easily extended to account for the possibility of *status exchange* between immigrants and native-born if intrinsic traits, such as citizenship, are part of the preferred set of characteristics immigrants look for in a spouse. Status exchange refers to the practice of exchanging acquired traits (wealth or education) for ascribed traits (citizenship or belonging to a chaste/social class). In many countries, due to the long periods of residence required before individuals can naturalize, citizenship is easier to achieve through marriage, and in some cases it might be the only way to gain entrance into the country. Choi et al. (2012) in a US–Australia comparative study, found evidence of status exchange, particularly among less-educated spouses and to a greater degree in the US than in Australia. Conversely, Liang and Ito (1999) found no evidence of status exchange among five Asian–American groups.

3.5 The timing of family formation

A different dimension along which immigrants and native-born may differ is their timing of family formation. Studying the timing of marriage among adult immigrants is complicated. On the one hand, as noted above, immigration and marriage could be jointly determined if marriage markets are thin or spousal visas facilitate immigration, encouraging migration as an established couple.[23] Alternatively, if immigration completely disrupts the marriage market of the immigrant, it could be the case that recent immigrants take longer to marry than similar native-born individuals. In addition to these difficulties, information about the timing of marriages outside the country of destination, or even at the time of migration, might not be readily available. Researchers may lack information on the date of the marriage, as typically occurs when employing census data. Nevertheless, some studies show that most immigrant groups in Europe are likely to marry earlier than the natives. In contrast, the study of the timing of marriage decisions of the children of immigrants typically reveals a later age of first marriage than first-generation immigrants, although still earlier than that of the native-born (Algan et al., 2010; Constant et al., 2010; De la Rica and Ortega; 2010; Georgiadis and Manning, 2011; Bisin and Patacchini, 2012).

In Europe, particular attention has been given to the marriage patterns of those of Turkish ancestry. In a cross-country study of second-generation Turks in Europe, Huschek et al. (2010) uncovered a higher rate of first marriages among second-generation Turks in the Netherlands, Belgium, Sweden, and Austria relative to those in France, Germany, and Switzerland. The authors established parental and peer influences as important determinants of first union's rates, but more interestingly the cross-country nature of the data allowed them to assess the influence of the institutional framework in which marriage decisions take place. The results suggest that welfare policies directed

---

[23] The proponents of the *family formation hypothesis* highlight that marriage occurs in many instances in synchronization with migration and some put forward methods to measure the interrelatedness of those events (Mulder and Wagner, 1993).

at helping youth to set up their own households (such as affordable housing) affect the transmission of cultural practices regarding marriage among the second generation, by easing out the material dependence on parents and may speed up union formation. Milewski and Hamel (2010) used the same data source restricted to France, and found significant differences in marital behavior between women of Turkish descent in France and natives. In particular, French-Turkish second-generation women tend to marry earlier and are more likely to enter marriage directly without previous cohabitation than women without immigrant background. They are also more likely to marry a Turkish immigrant, rather than a second-generation Turk or French native-born.

3.6 Cohabitation

The increase in cohabitation and the delay in marriage in most immigrant recipient countries, both part of the *second demographic transition* (Lesthaeghe and Neidert, 2006), have changed the "reference" native-born family to which immigrants may adapt and hence influence the extent of immigrant "assimilation" to the host country's marriage or divorce patterns. Studies examining the prevalence of cohabitation among immigrant couples are far less abundant than those that analyze intermarriage as a form of immigrant assimilation in mainstream society of the host country (see Bernhardt et al. (2007) for Swedish patterns and Trilla et al. (2008) for Spanish patterns). Standard models of cohabitation attribute the increase in the share of cohabitating unions to a change of individual (and societal) preferences that favors a trial period preceding marriage. As a result these models consider the influence of variables that account for uncertainty in future marriage, such as age, education level, partner's place of birth, financial security, or previous living arrangements on cohabitating unions (Bumpass and Lu, 2000). For immigrants, additional variables (such as generational status, cultural background, age at migration, or years since migration) are brought into play to account for assimilation and are expected to play a role similar to that in intermarriage models.

Given the wide dispersion of rates of cohabitation across countries, the importance of taking into account an individual's cultural background when explaining cohabitation stems from the fact that the extent to which observed cohabitation may reflect assimilation to the norms of the destination country should be understood with this cultural context in mind. For instance, as cohabitation is far more common in Latin American than in Asian countries, immigrant cohabitation is expected to be more common among Latin American immigrants, even amongst those from the first generation. Further, cohabitation among the children of Hispanic immigrants to the US, for instance, may indicate affinity with cultural ancestry rather than with US society and hence cannot be readily interpreted as a sign of assimilation.

Brown et al. (2008) compare cohabitation by generation status and race/ethnicity and suggest that levels of cohabitation increase (linearly) across generations for all racial and ethnic groups. Across origins, they are the lowest among Asians (2.4% for first-generation Asians) and highest amongst Puerto Ricans (12% amongst first generation).[24] Generational differences in cohabitation are significant and they typically increase for all immigrant groups. However, these changes are particularly striking for Asians, for whom consensual unions more than double by the third generation. Mexican cohabitation rates increase almost 50% by the third generation, whereas for other Hispanic groups their cohabitation rates double. Patterns of cohabitation uncovered in this study are consistent with the idea that the second generation increasingly enters in cohabitation as a way of delaying marriage while, among other things, they invest in human capital. In Spain, the major foreign-born groups (Moroccans, Ecuadorians, Colombians, and British) are more likely to cohabitate than the native-born, but the large differences are accounted for by demographic characteristics of the immigrant population such as age, citizenship and education level, as well as the couple characteristics, such as being in an endogamous relationship. This is, however, not the case when considering the determinants of endogamous unions among immigrants. The likelihood of Colombians or Ecuadorians being in an endogamous relationship remains high even after accounting for individual and union characteristics (Trilla et al., 2008).

3.7 Stability of marriage

The Becker et al. (1977) model emphasizes the role of uncertaintyandimperfect information in accounting for divorce.While gains from marriage are expected to be positive *ex-ante*, they might be negative *ex-post* when new information about the spouse characteristics or the outside offers to the marriage becomes available. Changes in social norms have increased the market value of women's time and prompted an increasing role of the state in regulating and enforcing monetary compensation following divorce. These factors contribute to reduce the costs of divorce, and possibly account for part of the increase in the rate of divorce in the US in the 1960s and 1970s (before slowly decreasing to a relatively high level) (Stevenson and Wolfers, 2007). To the extent that immigrants might have different norms regarding marital dissolution, or might lack information about divorce regulation in the host country, divorce rates are bound to be lower among them. Lower educational attainment among some immigrant groups, on the other hand, may push marital instability upward (Lehrer, 2003).

The characteristics commonly associated with an increase in the risk of marital disruption are (a) age/cohort-specific influences, (b) premarital experiences, (c) socioeconomic resources, and (d) couple-level characteristics. Higher tensions due to cultural

---

[24] Interestingly the generational patterns of cohabitation diverge from those of marriage, which follow a U-shaped curve, being high for the first generation, low for the second, and high again for the third generation. This is attributed to the importance that legal marital status may have for family reunification or joint migration.

differences and lower socio-economic resources due to social disapproval of intermarriage are potential threats to the stability of heterogamous marriages that may increase their rates of divorce. On the other hand, individuals who have formed a mixed marriage may be particularly endowed to succeed at relationships.

To assess the effect that these factors have on the likelihood of observing a divorce among mixed unions, researchers could estimate the following simple model:

$$D_{ikj} = X'_{ikj}\beta_0 + Spouse'_{ikj}\beta_1 + k\beta_2 + e'_{ikj} \qquad (7.4)$$

where D_{ikj} is an indicator variable for whether individual i, in area k, of cultural origin j reports being divorced. The vector X_{ikj} contains controls for gender, education, premarital experience, and other individual characteristics that may affect divorce rates, including socio-economic characteristics. *Spouse* is a vector that controls for individual i spouse's characteristics, including whether or not they belong to the same cultural group. Fixed area effects, k, such as state, provinces or metropolitan areas, are included to control for different laws or attitudes regarding divorce. The sub-index j can designate different cultural manifestations, such as race, immigrant status, or religious beliefs.

The empirical evidence universally agrees on the idea that heterogamous marriages experience lower stability and higher risk of divorce than co-ethnic marriages (McPherson et al., 2001). There is, however, wide diversity by specific racial groups (Bratter and King, 2008) and the type of inter-faith unions (Lehrer and Chiswick, 1993; Kalmijn et al., 2005). In their study of the stability of racial intermarriage in the US, Bratter and King (2008) documented that the percentage of couples divorcing after 10 years of marriage was elevated among interracial marriages compared to marriages in which couples are of the same race, particularly among more recent marriage cohorts. Although these numbers refer to the overall population, controlling for immigration status does not seem to change the probability of divorce. Interracial couples and mixed-status couples (foreign-born/native-born spouses) had similar risk of divorce than native-born couples. Nevertheless, couples where both spouses are foreign-born have a lower risk of divorce than those formed by two native-born spouses (Zhang and Van Hook, 2009). Jones (1996) observed that the risk of divorce among mixed groups falls in between the divorce patterns of the involved groups if individuals more likely to succeed in marriage are the ones who intermarry. Kalmijn et al. (2007) studied the effect of household income and the relative weight of wives' and husband's income on the probability of union dissolution and concluded that while higher levels of income reduce the risk of dissolution, marriages where females are the main earners in the household are at higher risk of dissolution.

A way of gaining a better understanding of how different factors affect union dissolution between groups is to use decomposition techniques to isolate the impact of *compositional effects* (effects due to differences in the mean values of the risk factors among groups) from other "unexplained" effects. This decomposition technique allows researchers to perform counterfactual exercises such as calculating dissolution probabilities for one group, conditional on having the compositional characteristics of the other. In an interesting study, Phillips and Sweeney (2006) undertook such a decomposition method when looking at a wide range of risk factors affecting marital dissolution for Mexican women. They decomposed the difference in marital dissolution probabilities between US-born and foreign-born Mexican women into a component due to differences in means of the risk factors (US-born Mexican women have more education, are more likely to work, to have cohabitated, or to have had a child before marriage than foreign-born Mexican women) and other unexplained factors. They found that the probability of disruption among US-born Mexican women would diminish by 25% if they had the same compositional characteristics as Mexican-born women.

Immigration has been used to disentangle the effect of cultural norms and institutions on divorce rates. Furtado et al. (2013) studied divorce rate among European immigrant children to the US. They exploited the fact that child immigrants grew up with the host country institutions, but were likely still exposed to the cultural norms of their home country through their family to study the effect of culture on divorce. A simple modification of equation (7.4) can be used to estimate the effect of culture on a sample of child immigrants:

$$D_{ikj} = X'_{ikj}\beta_0 + Spouse'_{ikj}\beta_1 + k\beta_2 + \beta_3 DR_j + e'_{ikj} \tag{7.5}$$

where DR_j is a measure of culture, such as the divorce rate in country of origin j. Although Furtado et al. (2013) could not control for spouse characteristics, they found that culture has a strong impact on divorce rates and that these effects differ by gender. Similarly, Mieke et al. (2011) exploited different types of endogamous marriages to separate the effect of cultural differences and social support on the probability of divorce. They looked at endogamous marriages in which one of the partners migrated through marriage to a more established immigrant. This could, arguably, bring tensions due to cultural differences within endogamous marriages. Since marriage to a partner from the country of origin is usually supported by family and minority group, higher rates of divorce among this type of endogamous union (versus other endogamous unions) could be interpreted as evidence of the isolated importance of cultural differences on divorce rate. The study found that these marriages generally display a higher risk of divorce than other endogamous marriages and this seems to be driven by increased cultural differences between the spouses.

3.8 Family reunification policies and their impact on marriage formation

Immigration policy shapes many aspects of family life for immigrants, such as whether a spouse can legally migrate, the order in which family members arrive, or the size of the marriage market available. Employed-sponsored immigrants or refugees are likely to have distinct family formation patterns from other immigrants. Overall, studies accounting for immigration policies are scant because few surveys contain detailed information on categories of admission or on the timing of migration for all members of the same family that will be necessary to study these effects (Jasso et al., 2000).

Immigration policies also shape the size of the marriage market for immigrants. In the early twentieth century, the US, UK, and Canada restricted family reunification and often restricted female migration, hence hindering family formation and/or forcing intermarriage (see Ralston (1999) for more information on the Canadian case). Sometimes, sudden changes in immigration policies provide exogenous variation in the flow of immigrants and give the opportunity to study marriage or other immigrant behaviour. That is the case of Denmark, where a recent change in immigration policy tightened family reunification policies, in response to the increase in "marriage migration." Nielsen et al. (2009) used this policy change to study the causal effect of marriage on education, as already discussed in this section.

4. FERTILITY

The analysis of immigrant fertility differentials helps to understand the socio-economic integration of immigrant women, and the changing shape of family structure in immigrant recipient countries. Fertility decisions influence and are influenced by educational and labor market participation decisions, which makes them a key indicator of immigrant social integration, particularly for women immigrants. In addition, fertility estimates by ethnic group and generational status have the potential to improve, providing more accurate scenarios for population projections in immigrant recipient countries.

4.1 Microeconomic models of fertility

In 1960, Becker suggested in his article on "An Economic Analysis of Fertility" that fertility could be understood as parental demand for children and hence treated using standard consumer theory. Women make fertility choices under a set of constraints (e.g., economic, educational, and/or institutional) and with a given set of social attitudes towards fertility, contraceptives, gender preferences, out-of-wedlock childbearing related to social norms, and expectations of both destination and origin societies. One of the most important insights of Becker's paper was the hypothesis that the cost of children is partly endogenous because utility arises from both the quality and quantity of children. Therefore, an increase in family income might be devoted largely to increase the expenditure per child (quality) rather than to increases in the number of children. Later, Willis (1974) presented a model of fertility that integrated Becker's quality–quantity tradeoff with a model of household production and human capital investment (based on Becker's (1965) and Mincer's (1963) earlier work). The model predicts a negative relationship between income and fertility due to assumptions on the value of women's time and the quantity–quality interaction (Becker and Lewis, 1973; Willis, 1974).

In the context of immigration, Becker's model has distinct implications. If immigrants are generally perceived to have different preferences for fertility than the norm in the host country, their fertility rates are likely to differ. However, the change in economic environment brought about by migration and the cost of migration itself will have an effect on fertility that might reinforce or offset trends implied by different preferences. All these forces will determine the extent of assimilation or adaptation of migrants. The direction of the fertility change after arrival will of course depend on whether immigrants are originating from high-fertility or low-fertility countries. Since most international migrants move from relatively less developed countries to richer countries and total fertility rates are generally higher in relatively poorer countries, the general expectation has been that migrant's fertility initially exceeds that of the native-born at destination (Ben-Porath, 1973). However, as more recent literature has pointed out, the fast decrease of overall fertility everywhere in the world and the possible selectivity of immigrants within source countries may imply the reverse relation. Next we review the main theories developed to understand the different factors that affect the fertility of migrants.

4.2 Immigrant differential fertility: mechanisms

Goldstein and Goldstein (1981, 1983) and Hervitz (1985) were the first works that analyzed the impact of migration on fertility in a more systematic way and explicitly identified three important mechanisms to explain the differential fertility behavior of migrants: selection, disruption, and adaptation (see Figure 7.1). All three mechanisms

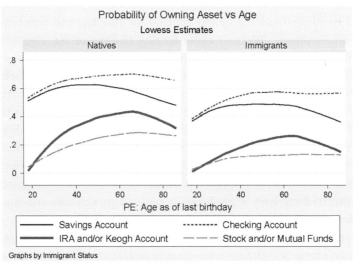

Figure 7.1 *Mechanism of immigrant fertility.*

are likely to shape the fertility of women who migrate as adults, and the independent role of each can be difficult to isolate and assess. Some of these mechanisms can happen together: It may be possible to observe an initial drop in fertility because of disruption at the time of immigration, followed by a subsequent rise in fertility, but also a gradual adaptation towards the fertility levels of the host country.[25] These hypotheses have been tested in the literature, with none of them being conclusively accepted or rejected.

4.2.1 Selection

The *selection hypothesis* posits that individuals who migrate differ systematically from non-migrants in their countries of origin, and this selectivity may explain their subsequent fertility patterns (Kahn, 1988; Forste and Tienda, 1996; Sobotka, 2008). Their fertility preferences may more closely resemble those of the destination country than the source country even before they arrive or they may have some traits that boost their labor market performance. Further, migration policies may reinforce the selection process. For instance, Canada has had long in place policies that target educated immigrants and reward knowledge in local languages, producing an average immigrant profile relatively more educated and closer to the native-born than is typical in other destinations. These policy differences are prone to have important consequences for assimilation issues, including fertility adaptation. In addition, if immigration is considered as a form of human capital investment (Chiswick, 1978), individuals with more expected net benefits from migration and who are more forward looking may be the most likely to move and invest in other forms of their human capital at arrival. Those same individuals may be more prone to trading-off child quantity for child quality.

Although the majority of the migration literature recognizes the importance of taking into account selectivity when making inferences about migrants' behavior, few studies have been able to address this issue properly due to data constraints on pre-migration information of migrants and non-migrants in origin.[26] Even if studies on international migration are constrained by the lack of appropriate information, some researchers have found ways to operationalize measures of selectivity to adequately analyze the data. Kahn (1988) was the first most complete attempt to do this by using both aggregate information on fertility levels about the sending countries and characteristics of the immigrants themselves. To understand whether immigrants are positively or negatively selected into the

---

[25] Some studies note this interaction of mechanisms and warn that immigrant fertility can be overestimated in TFR calculations when women's migration is linked to marriage and family formation (Kulu, 2005; Toulemon et al., 2008; Milewski, 2010; Dubuc, 2012).

[26] A few longitudinal studies on rural to urban migration were able to use information on pre-migration characteristics relative to the pool of potential migrants at origin, which is in general lacking in studies of international migration (Rindfuss, 1976; Courgeau, 1989; White et al., 1995; Jensen and Ahlburg, 2004; Kulu, 2005).

US she constructed a selectivity indicator by comparing the educational attainment of an immigrant cohort with that of the same birth cohort in the sending country. In particular, for each immigrant group the selectivity measure consists of the ratio of the proportion of female immigrants aged 40–44 in 1980 with at least one year of college, to the proportion of the sending country population aged 20–24 in 1960 that was enrolled in higher education at that time. Second, models include an interaction of origin-country fertility levels with individual educational attainment (as a proxy for individual selectivity) to understand whether the relevance of country values varies with education. In addition to standard demographic characteristics, her models include controls for three traditional measures to proxy assimilation, namely years since migration, language fluency, and intermarriage. She noted that when thinking about convergence of fertility behaviors of migrants toward native levels, those who are positively selected relative to their sending-country populations are to some extent already assimilated before moving since they already resemble more the population at destination. In that regard, any norms from their countries of origin should play a lesser role in their choices than among those who are not selected. Her results showed that immigrants are more assimilated in any of the measures (duration, intermarriage, or language), and they move away from the norms of their sending countries. Additionally, positively selected immigrants are the least influenced by those norms.

Blau (1992) analyzed migrant fertility with the 1970 and 1980 censuses. She calculated for each combination of country and years since migration in her data what proportion of women in the source country have the same or higher educational attainment as the respondent. She found that, in general, even if migrants have lower educational attainment than natives, they originate from the top third of the educational distribution in their country of origin. In a more recent paper Choi (2014) employed a similar method to show that Mexican migration to the US is selective of individuals with high fertility and high—relative to Mexican non-migrants—educational attainment.

4.2.2 Disruption

The second mechanism draws attention to the (actual and anticipated) short-term *disruption* of fertility at the time of migration (Goldstein and Goldstein, 1981; Stephen and Bean, 1992). Migration may separate spouses at least temporarily, and individuals who are planning to move may postpone childbearing until after they are settled in their new home. This anticipatory behavior may cause a temporary drop in fertility prior to the move (that may be heightened by moving costs), followed by a rapid resumption (rebound) of fertility afterward (Goldstein and Goldstein, 1981; Andersson, 2004). This anticipation or reverse causality explanation suggests that childbirth reduces individual propensity to migrate, thereby making it more likely that migrants are childless on arrival (Toulemon, 2004). The anticipation of benefits of having births in the country of destination may also be an additional mechanism that leads to a slowdown even before migration. In countries with *jus solis* regimes, being born in the destination country will carry automatically all the benefits of citizenship.[27]

In addition there may be some economic disruption (as defined by Blau, 1992) when the income of both wife and husband is temporarily depressed at the time of migration. A lower husband's income has a clear depressing effect on fertility, whereas lower women's wages have both an income and a substitution effect (lower opportunity cost of childbearing). Sufficiently large income effect will lead to a temporary slowdown in fertility until skills are upgraded or experience is acquired in the new labor market. Both mechanisms, the demographic and the economic, imply a slowdown of childbearing patterns around the time of migration (Hervitz, 1985; Stephen and. Bean, 1992). Nonetheless it is difficult to measure the extent of the disruption before migration since lack of pre-migration information and measures of selectivity interfere with this task. Evidence of short-lived fertility disruption has been shown in Kahn (1994) and Blau (1992) for the US, Toulemon (2004) and Toulemon et al. (2008) for France, Garssen and Nicolaas (2008) in the Netherlands, and Adserà and Ferrer (2013), Ng and Nault (1997), and Ram and George (1990) in Canada, and Jensen and Ahlburg (2004) for internal migrants in the Philippines. Conversely, Mayer and Riphahn (2000) did not find evidence of disruption in Germany.

With regard to the fertility dynamics at the time of migration, the proponents of the *family formation hypothesis*, which is closely related to the *disruption hypothesis*, point to the potential interrelatedness between migration and family formation that boosts fertility immediately after arrival (Alders, 2000; Andersson, 2004; Milewski, 2007; Sobotka, 2008). They suggest that the elevated fertility after migration may not be entirely incompatible with the disruption hypothesis. Disruption may be occurring prior to migration, with the observed elevated fertility caused by the resumption of fertility after disruption. Lindstrom (2003) observed some short-term elevated risk to first births among women who move around the time of marriage in Guatemala, even though adaptation occurs for higher-parity births. Kulu (2005, 2006) presented similar results for internal migrants in Austrian, Estonian, and Polish postwar birth cohorts, and Singley and Landale (1998) for Puerto Rican-born women moving mainland.

Andersson (2004) applied event history techniques to the Swedish population registrar from the 1960 to the 1990s to analyze the childbearing behavior of close to half a million foreign-born women. He found a boost in the risk of childbearing, not only for first but also for higher parities, during the first years after migration to Sweden.

---

[27] Another dimension of the relation between nationality laws and fertility concerns the investment parents undertake on children eligible for citizenship. Avitabile et al. (2014) showed how, after the change in the rules that regulate child legal status at birth in Germany in 1990, birthright citizenship lead to a reduction in immigrant fertility and to an improvement in health and socio-emotional outcomes for the children affected by the reform.

However, after residing in Sweden for at least five years, fertility levels converge toward those of Swedish-born women. He argued that Swedish data do not support disruption at arrival, but that the immediate increase in fertility at arrival hints to a previous postponement or short-term disruption of childbearing in anticipation of the move. Given the interrelatedness of migration and family-building processes, Andersson stresses the importance of controlling for time since migration in models of fertility.

With a similar methodological approach, Kulu (2005) allowed the intensity models of conception to first birth to vary since time of arrival to destination to analyze whether there is some disruption around the time of migration within Estonia for postwar cohorts and also to better understand selectivity. In the same vein, Ford (1990) noted that studies of immigrant fertility that do not consider duration of residence are likely to be misleading. With data from the 1970 and 1980 US censuses, she found that the immigrant fertility in the US rises after arrival perhaps to make up for births (and marriages) postponed before the move. Conversely, with the same data and tracking the same arrival cohort over time for migrants coming from high-fertility countries, Blau (1992) found evidence of some short-lived disruption followed by an increase in the immigrant fertility towards the natives' level. Carter (2000) overcame some of the limitations of cross-section data in the previous papers by using event history analysis with birth history data to better track childbearing patterns of Mexican migrants during the years around migration to the US. She found that it converges toward native levels after increasing immediately after immigration.

Two other methodological approaches have been employed to analyze the existence of disruption. First, instead of just considering duration in destination or years since arrival, Mayer and Riphahn (2000) used the 1996 wave of the German Socio-Economic Panel (GSOEP) to estimate a Poisson model of fertility that includes a measure of the fertile years spent in Germany. By creating a spline function of fertility years in destination it introduced a flexible specification to estimate differences in fertility around the time of arrival. Finally, researchers who used large registrar or census data, and as a result lack longitudinal data or complete birth histories, tend to compare the ratio of infants or of children aged under 5 in migrant households (for different years since migration) to comparable native households (Ng and Nault, 1997; Adserà and Ferrer, 2013).

In general, since the actual disruption, if it occurs, is likely to be short-lived and only impact the timing or spacing of births, it is not expected to explain large aggregate differences in the cumulative number of children ever born, though research remains inconclusive (Goldstein and Goldstein, 1981; Carlson, 1985; Ram and George, 1990; Ng and Nault, 1997; Sobotka, 2008). In a recent paper, however, Choi (2014) found that initial disruption in the fertility of Mexican migrants to the US has a lasting impact on the quantum of fertility. The innovation of her paper is to analyze characteristics of the population pre-migration and compare those who migrate with those who do not in the same birth cohort.

4.2.3 Adaptation

The *adaptation hypothesis* (or assimilation hypothesis, as referred to by many economists) posits that as migrants settle in their new environment their fertility norms and expectations begin to resemble those of the native population (Goldstein and Goldstein, 1981; Stephen and Bean, 1992; Alba and Nee, 1997; Lindstrom, 2003). Ben-Porath (1973) was one of the first to show this with Israeli data. This is at odds with those who propose the *socialization hypothesis* that notes that fertility preferences are determined by the country where migrants spent their childhood (Hervitz, 1985). Thus, for those researchers, adaptation only happens among the second generation.

The speed at which newcomers adapt to the fertility of the destination country may be endogenous to opportunities offered to migrants (e.g., labor market, education, political participation and social integration); to the host country's cultural expectations and policies toward immigrants (e.g., multiculturalism) (Abbasi-Shavazi and McDonald, 2000); and to demographic policies in the country of origin either pro-natalistic (e.g., Ceceascu's regime in Romania) or restrictive (e.g., one child policy in China) that have shaped fertility of migrants, among other things. The interaction of migrants with host-country economic and social environment, both in terms of opportunities and costs, mediates their ultimate fertility decisions. Immigrant women facing better labor market prospects in the host country may decide to reduce/postpone fertility in order to work in the same way as natives have already done as their opportunity costs of childbearing have risen—with technological change and relative gains to women's relatively abundant skills (Galor and Weil, 1996). Absence of informal child care provided by relatives and the need to resort to more expensive forms of formal daycare increases the incentives to trade off children for work (see Carter (2000) for Mexicans in the US) and to devote more resources to the rearing of each child rather than increase their offspring (Becker, 1981).

The fertility adaptation mechanism has received more attention in this literature than other mechanisms not only because it can be interpreted as a sign of immigrants' social integration, but also because it has strong and far-reaching implications for immigrant well-being, that extend to the second generation. As a matter of fact, a large share of the most recent research that explores the adaptation hypothesis has focused on the outcomes of individuals who migrated as children (Bleakley and Chin, 2010; Adserà et al., 2012; Adserà and Ferrer, 2014) and the second generation of immigrants (Parrado and Morgan, 2008; Dubuc, 2012). The next subsections of the chapter review in detail research on the pathways and heterogeneity of the adaptation process across destinations and source countries.

4.3 Duration in destination and age at arrival

The economics of migration literature has long recognized age at immigration as a decisive factor to explain the differential process of adaptation of immigrants in many socio-economic dimensions (Chiswick, 1991; Picot et al., 2005, 2007; Ferrer et al., 2006). From Chiswick's (1978) groundbreaking article in this field, the age at arrival has been used mainly to calculate *duration* in destination. Linear and nonlinear specifications of variables indicating years since migration have been regularly included in models aiming at measuring assimilation, particularly in labor market outcomes. The age at arrival may also be important on its own since it determines the moment in the lifetime at which immigrants are exposed to different spheres and social interactions in the country of destination (e.g., attending or taking children to school, participating in training programs or in different segments of the labor market) as well as the intensity of those interactions. Further there may be some *critical* ages by which socialization occurs for some outcomes (e.g., puberty) or by which some particular skills are learnt (e.g., language).

Most early research on the role of duration has focused the adaptation of the fertility of Mexican migrants to the US level. Part of this literature notes that the relative high fertility of Mexicans at arrival is explained by pronatalistic norms in their country of origin but that with duration in destination the relevance of those norms decreases and migrants assimilate to US levels (Rindfuss and Sweet, 1977; Ford, 1990). Ford (1990), controlling for duration in the US, found progressive adaptation after initial disruption and catch-up at the time of the move. Still, other researchers argued that barriers that result in limited social mobility by Mexican immigrants made their adaptation process difficult. Thus, lower opportunities in the destination local markets explain stubbornly high fertility (Forste and Tienda, 1996; Frank and Heuveline, 2005, among others). Frank and Heuveline (2005) did not find evidence of adaptation among Mexican migrants who have lived in the US for 12 years or more. They added to their models information on Mexican fertility at origin to understand the direction of adaptation, but, given common data restrictions in this literature, they measured it for the whole population instead of limiting the sample to those who eventually migrate or are more likely to do so in the future to account for selectivity. Unfortunately their lack of longitudinal information restricted their ability to obtain proper inferences of changes in the degree of adaptation across migration cohorts. Carter (2000) overcame some of these limitations by using event history analysis with birth history data to better track childbearing patterns of migrants during the years around migration. She found that, after increasing immediately after immigration, the fertility of Mexican migrants decreases over time, but remains above Mexican American levels.

Most of this earlier work has analyzed the assimilation of immigrants employing a unique cross-section of data and comparing the fertility by years since migration. However, with a unique cross-section results may be confounded by migration cohort effects. It is not possible to distinguish between the effect of duration in the country of destination and cohort effects; that is, migrants who arrive at the same destination at different points in time may have differential fertility behavior. These differences may arise from changes in migration policies and the composition of migrants, as well as economic and political circumstances both in origin and destination. To overcome this constraint, Blau (1992) applied the *synthetic cohorts' method*, based on Borjas (1987), to the analysis of fertility assimilation of migrants. Still the synthetic cohort method is subject to problems of selective return migration.

Blau (1992) examined first-generation immigrant women in the 1970 and 1980 censuses, most of whom arrived in the preceding decade (65% and 58% in each census). She estimated a reduced-form model of the individual level fertility in each of the census years separately for immigrants and natives by ordinary least squares.[28] Combining the results of the two regressions she was able to investigate the impact of years of residence in the US on the fertility of migrants by tracking a particular synthetic cohort over time while comparing it to similar natives at each time to determine the period effects. The adaptation or assimilation hypothesis implies a gradual convergence of immigrant fertility to that of natives over time. Still it is important to remember that short-lived disruption may depress fertility of migrants at arrival. Thus, with data that spans only to a very short time frame the estimated direction of migrant–native fertility differentials may be misleading of long-term trends in completed fertility differentials. Comparing the number of children ever born among older migrant and native women would circumvent this possible bias since these women would have already completed their childbearing years. However, as noted, it is not possible to extrapolate directly from the behavior of older migrant cohorts to predict that of recent cohorts because of potential changes in the ethnic composition and period conditions faced by new cohorts.

Looking at migrants coming from high-fertility source countries, Blau (1992) found they have relatively similar unadjusted fertility to US-born women. In 1970, migrants have 0.07 fewer children than natives and only 0.18 more than them by 1980. This is explained by some fertility disruption at arrival in the 1970 data and to immigrant women being positively selected in terms of education when comparing them to their source country. Those unadjusted differentials, as well as their increase between the two censuses, are important data on their own from a policy perspective regardless of whether they arise from differences in characteristics of migrants and natives or from their differential response to them. Adjusting for socio-economic characteristics, immigrant women had fewer children in both census years and seemed more responsive to labor market opportunity tradeoffs than natives. Tracking the relative fertility of synthetic cohorts throughout this period, Blau found that fertility increases from 1970 to 1980, an indication of some

---

[28] Blau (1992) also ran her analysis of synthetic cohorts separately for married women with spouse present and estimated both a reduced-form and a structural model of individual fertility for each year by nativity. The first model included age, age squared, and education of the woman (and husband when present), years since migration and general demographic characteristics. In the structural model, predicted husband's income and woman's wages were included instead of education.

initial disruption. For the cohort of immigrants who arrived in the period 1965–70 the immigrant–native differential in fertility closes by 0.53 children from a gap of −0.63 children in 1970 to −0.1 in 1980. For the cohort who arrived immediately before in 1960–64 the difference increases by 0.38 over the same period. Blau noted that with lack of further data it is difficult to ascertain the completed fertility of those cohorts and, as a result, the final immigrant–native differential. If trends continued though the average migrant of the first cohort would end up bearing over half a child more than a similar native.

A few studies have focused on the fertility of immigrant women who arrived to their destination country before the age of 19. The reasoning behind this sample choice is that the disruption mechanism is unlikely to play any role in child migrants and even the selection mechanism is likely to be greatly attenuated, as migration decisions are mostly made by their parents and are plausibly independent of other variables affecting the child migrant's fertility.[29] Thus, by studying child migrants researchers have been able to focus on understanding the adaptation process in the receiving country and the role that age at migration plays on it. Looking at child migrants has the additional advantage of exploring the existence of *critical ages* at which behaviors can be learnt (Schaafsma and Sweetman, 2001; Bleakley and Chin, 2010). In the case of fertility, an additional effect of the age at arrival could arise if cultural norms regarding reproductive behavior formed at a particular age (for instance, the onset of puberty) are difficult to modify later on (Ryder, 1973).

Among those who focus on migrants who arrived before adulthood, Adserà and Ferrer (2014) use the Canadian Census of Population (20% sample) for the period 1991–2006 to estimate a Poisson model on the number of children that includes a set of indicator variables for age at immigration, from under age 1 to age 18. They found that the fertility rate of individuals migrating up to age 6 is either somewhat lower or indistinguishable from that of natives while that of immigrants who arrived into Canada in their late teens shows a sharp increase relative to immigrants who arrived at earlier ages. The same age at arrival profile is present in England and France (Adserà et al., 2012). Overall, once researchers allow estimates of fertility to vary by age at immigration, they find patterns broadly consistent with the adaptation hypothesis. With few exceptions, women who immigrated at the youngest ages have fertility rates that are most similar to native-born women. Predicted fertility of migrants relative to natives in each destination calculated from basic Poisson estimates in Adserà et al. (2012) is shown in Figure 7.2.[30] It is interesting to observe such similar patterns of relative fertility rising with age at migration in countries with differences in both the extent of selectivity of migration

---

[29] Although Jasso (2004) pointed out that parental immigration to the US among Mexicans is partly influenced by the expectation of better prospects for their children.

[30] The relatively small sample size in the French data compared to the large samples available in both the Canadian and English census explains the fact that the French predictions in Figure 7.2 are less smooth than those for the other two countries.

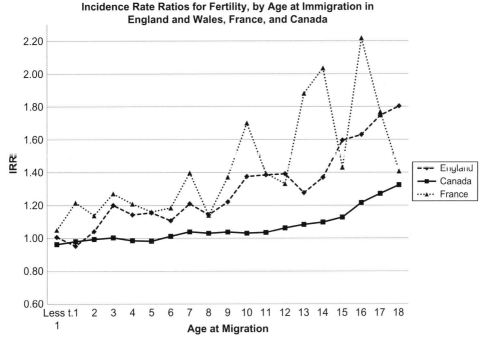

Figure 7.2 *Incidence rate ratios (IRRs) from a Poisson regression of the number of children in the household of women who migrated as children by age at immigration relative to native-born women, in England and Wales, France and Canada.* All models include controls for age, location of residence, and census year. Source: *Estimates from Adserà et al. (2012). Data from Canada comes from the Canadian Census 1991, 1996, 2001, and 2006.The data for England are a subsample of the Office for National Statistics Longitudinal Study (ONSLS), a complete set of linked census records (1971–2001), and that for France come from "Enquête sur Trajectoires et Origines" (TeO) 2008.*

policies and the geographic composition of incoming migration cohorts. Although in all three countries, at least since the 1980s, the fertility of immigrant populations has exceeded that of the native-born (Bélanger and Gilbert, 2003; Adserà and Ferrer, 2010), their contribution to overall fertility, while increasing, remains fairly small (Coleman et al., 2002; Heran and Pison, 2007; Sigle-Rushton, 2008). Nonetheless, the extent to which immigrants will sustain fertility over the longer term is less clear; as we discuss later in the section, evidence from Canada suggests that the fertility of second-generation immigrants may, in fact, fall below that of other native-born groups (Adserà and Ferrer, 2010).

4.3.1 Age at arrival, language proficiency, and critical period hypothesis

As noted, another reason to focus on women who migrated as children and their age at immigration is that there might be critical ages at which individuals learn a particular behavior or skill, such as the local language, that are crucial for future social and economic outcomes. It is well documented that fluency in the language of the destination country decreases with age at immigration, among other things (Chiswick, 1991; Stevens, 1992,

1999; Espenshade and Fu, 1997; Espinosa and Massey, 1997; Akresh, 2007) and should be greater for those migrants who arrive as children. Fluency in the language of the destination country has long been recognized to play a key role in immigrant's outcomes and degree of adaptation (see, e.g., Kossoudji, 1988; Dustmann, 1994; Chiswick and Miller, 1995, 2001; Schaafsma and Sweetman, 2001; Dustmann and van Soest, 2002; Bleakley and Chin, 2004). Studies by Leslie and Lindley (2001) and Dustmann and Fabbri (2003), for example, found that lack of fluency in English has a detrimental impact on the employment and earnings of ethnic minority men and women in Britain. In the case of fertility, a non-official mother tongue may impact the ability of the child-migrant to access local cultural cues through school and peers to form her fertility preferences. Existing analyses have found greater English fluency to be associated with lower fertility in the US (Sorenson, 1988; Swicegood et al., 1988; Bleakley and Chin, 2010) and Canada (Adserà and Ferrer, 2014).

Two works originally analyzed the role of language focus on the fertility of all Mexican immigrants in the US. Sorensen (1988) took advantage of new questions on language use and English proficiency introduced on the 1980 US Census. Her analysis focused on endogamous Mexican American and non-Hispanic white couples living in Texas, New Mexico, and Arizona in which the wife is between 40 and 44 years of age rather than on women's characteristics alone. She found English use at home by both the wife and the husband decreases the likelihood of having an additional child at all parities even after controlling for educational attainment and English proficiency. Among non-Hispanic couples the likelihood to transit to parity five or more is also higher among those with low English proficiency who do not speak English at home, even after controlling for educational attainment and nativity. Swicegood et al. (1988) also employed the 5% Public Use Microdata Sample (PUMS) from 1980 US Census to find a negative effect of English proficiency on the total number of children ever born and in the presence of children under 3 in the household among ever-married Mexican American women aged 15–44. The relevance of English proficiency increases with education, particularly among the younger age groups. The authors argued that opportunity cost calculations rather than cultural factors play a more central role in shaping childbearing behavior of women in their sample.

A problem with estimating the impact of language proficiency on socio-economic outcomes is that proficiency is an endogenous variable and may be correlated with other variables that explain those outcomes such as ability or attitudes towards preserving the ancestral culture. As a result, ordinary least squares (OLS) estimates of the effect of proficiency of the destination language are likely unable to estimate the causal relationship. Bleakley and Chin (2010) used an instrumental variables strategy to circumvent the problem of the endogeneity of language fluency and showed that the outcomes of immigrants from non-English-speaking countries systematically differ from those of other migrants only among those arriving after the *critical period* for language acquisition of 8–9 years of age. They employed microdata form the US Census 2000 to study how marriage and fertility, among other socio-economic outcomes, of childhood immigrants (who arrived before age 15) currently between ages 25 and 55 are related to their age at arrival in US. Consistent with the existence of a "critical period" of language acquisition, there are no significant differences in adult English proficiency among immigrants from English- and non-English-speaking countries who migrated to the US very early in life. Moreover, while the relation between age at migration and English proficiency remains flat for those from English-speaking countries, proficiency decreases almost linearly with age at arrival for those from non-English-speaking countries who arrived after age nine. Bleakley and Chin (2004, 2008, 2010) used these differences between younger and older arrivers on English language skills to construct an instrumental variable for English proficiency. Since age at migration is likely to affect socio-economic outcomes of migrants through channels other than language (e.g., better knowledge of US cultural norms) and, as a result, it may fail the exclusion restriction as an IV, they use immigrants from English-speaking countries to control for the impact of age at migration that is not related to language fluency.

In a first-stage equation, they instrumented language proficiency with an interaction between migrant's age at migration (beyond the critical age of nine) and an indicator for a non-Anglophone country of origin. Results showed that the ordinal measure of English proficiency (0 to 3) decreases by 0.1 for each year that the immigrant arrives after age 9 among those arriving from a non-English-speaking country—a sizeable effect. They used fitted values for English proficiency to estimate a second-stage relationship for fertility outcomes of migrants first for all individuals in the sample and then separately by gender. The number of children present in the household of immigrants with higher English fluency is smaller than for the rest, even though English-proficient women are not significantly less likely to have a child. Among more English-proficient men the reduction in the number of children is also explained by differences at the extensive margin. However, there are not significant differences in the extensive margin when the sample is restricted to married men. Single parenthood or out-of-wedlock births are not significantly related to English proficiency. These findings are robust to controlling in the models for the interaction between age at arrival with either the fertility rate or the GDP per capita in their country of origin as well as to dropping either Canada or Mexico from the sample of migrants.

Adserà and Ferrer (2014) estimated the fertility of migrants who arrived before age 19 to Canada relative to that of natives by age at migration separately for those who have a mother tongue that is an official language in Canada and for those who do not. They did not employ an instrumental variable strategy but instead included in their models interactions of dummy variables for each age at arrival before adulthood with an indicator of whether the mother tongue of the individual is official in their province of residence. Unlike Bleakley and Chin (2010), they did not find a sharp discontinuity in immigrant fertility behavior relative to natives among migrants arriving before or after the age of entry into middle school and whose mother tongue is not official in Canada. Moreover, fertility of both immigrants with and without an official mother tongue increasingly differs from that of natives by age of migration. However, fertility remains lower among immigrants with an official mother tongue than among those without it for any age at arrival.

4.4 The role of culture: heterogeneity across source countries and adaptation

The role of culture in explaining immigrant assimilation is pervasive. The extent of adaptation may hinge on the distance between the norms governing fertility in both the destination and source countries. Those norms or attitudes are part of an individual's cultural background. Even if immigrants leave behind the laws and institutions of their home countries, they do bring a set of beliefs and traditions that may be slow to change and often get passed to their children. Across countries of origin there may be different norms and expectations regarding fertility such as age at first birth or acceptability of out-of-wedlock births. Unfortunately lack of pre-migration information generally limits the ability to study the direction of adaptation in the destination country. Further there may be differential selection across origins and employing country-of-origin averages as references might be misleading. Regardless of these limitations, accounting for heterogeneity of origins in the migrant population has proven to be relevant in explaining variation in fertility outcomes in different contexts (Kahn, 1994; Andersson, 2004; Coleman, 2006; Guinnane et al., 2006; Parrado and Morgan, 2008; Georgiadis and Manning, 2011, among others).

The simplest way fertility models account for cultural background differences is by introducing country-of-origin fixed effects.[31] The majority of such studies report substantial differences in fertility by ethnicity, with some groups adjusting their fertility faster than others. In Britain, Georgiadis and Manning (2011) and Coleman and Dubuc (2010) highlighted the relatively slow fertility assimilation of Pakistanis and Bangladeshis as compared to that of other groups such as Chinese, Indians, and Black Caribbean whose fertility is at or below the UK national average. In Germany, multiple studies mostly employing the German socio-economic panel have shown foreign-born fertility to slowly converge toward native levels since the 1970s (Mayer and Riphahn, 2000; Milewski, 2007), particularly among Polish and Italians. Turkish migrants (and Muslim migrants in general) have always exhibited higher fertility than natives, but there is some evidence of adaptation as their fertility is lower than in Turkey (Kane, 1986; Schoorl, 1995). Schoorl (1990) showed similar patterns in the Netherlands. Sobotka (2008) compiled data on TFR of immigrants from Somalia, Pakistan, Turkey, and Iran from different sources and compared it to western European levels. The fertility of these groups is relatively high compared to that of their country of destination, with the exception of Iranians. In Canada, research shows that up to 1980 Canadian immigrants had lower fertility rates than the Canadian-born

---

[31] Religion is an important determinant of fertility as it typically embodies a broad set of cultural rules surrounding childbearing. However, many surveys do not include questions on religion and many researchers proxy these differences using country of origin instead. A few papers analyzed fertility across religious groups in developed countries (Westoff and Frejka 2007, 2008; Adserà, 2013). Westoff and Frejka (2007) provide an excellent survey of the wide heterogeneity in the fertility of European Muslims depending on their ancestry and country of birth.

(Kalbach, 1970), but the trend has since reversed. A study by Bélanger and Gilbert (2003) suggested that the increase in the share of Canadian immigrants from areas with traditionally high-fertility rates such as the Middle East, Southern Asia, and Latin America is likely responsible for this change in fertility patterns. The literature findings underscore the importance of taking into account the heterogeneity of the foreign-born population and analyzing whether, once controls for origin are included in the empirical analysis, adaptation occurs in a similar way for individuals moving from different places.

In that regard, to study whether child immigrants arriving from certain regions adapt to the rules that guide fertility behavior in the host country faster than others with the same years of exposure, Adserà et al. (2012) estimated a Poisson model that included interactions of a set of age-at-immigration dummies with indicators for each world region of birth. Results showed patterns broadly consistent with the adaptation hypotheses with fertility rising with age at arrival in all three countries they analyzed, Canada, France, and England and Wales, and across all origin groups in each country. However, estimates suggest that the estimated effect of exposure to the host country varies by origin and it is particularly important to explain fertility outcomes of immigrants who come from Africa and Asia to France and from South Asia to England and Wales.

To understand cultural norms that migrants bring with them when they move, some studies compare fertility patterns at origin and destination. Thanks to available census data, this has been done extensively for migrants to the US during the late nineteenth and early twentieth centuries. Guinnane et al. (2006) studied Irish fertility in the US using the 1910 IPUMS and fertility in Ireland with the 1911 Irish Census. They found that the fertility of Irish migrants is higher than that of comparable natives, but relatively lower than that of similar Irish couples in Ireland where marital fertility remained high throughout these years. To understand whether the persistence of source-country norms was specific to Irish migrants, they analyzed the fertility patterns of German migrants. While they found that the fertility of first generation German immigrants was also higher than that of native-born whites, the difference was vastly accounted for by the socio-economic characteristics of that population. Further, the fertility of the second generation of German immigrants was similar to that of the native-born population. Rosenwaike (1973) studied first-generation Italian migrants with the 1910 and 1960 US Censuses and second-generation migrants of Italian ancestry with the 1960 Census. He argued that Italians brought with them patterns of very high fertility from their country, but those who migrated as children (and the second generation) assimilated successfully to the lower fertility of natives. Gjerde and McCants (1995) analyzed how, on the one hand, better economic opportunities at destination than in origin that encouraged high fertility and, on the other hand, cultural norms brought from the source country affected the marital and fertility decisions of Norwegian immigrants to the US. Data from the 1900 PUMS of the US Census show that women of northern European countries in the upper Middle West US frontier had around one and a half more children over a marriage span than native-born. In their historical analysis of Norwegian migrants, they argued that fewer constraints to land access than those faced in their homeland allowed young couples to marry relatively early and have more children than in Norway. Those patterns changed for the second generation and later arrivals when faced with more economic and population pressures that brought ancestral cultural norms (of late marriage and restraint fertility) back into the spotlight.

Finally, to better proxy cultural norms and expectations in origin, some researchers introduced direct and substantive information from source countries in their models with the understanding that dominant behaviors in a country are reflected in those norms. Kahn (1988) used a measure of the net reproduction rate (NRR) dating from the late 1960s to proxy for fertility norms faced by the migrant women she studied in the 1980 US Census and found it accounts for part of the cross-country differentials. Frank and Heuveline (2005) undertook a similar exercise when studying Mexican migrant adaptation.

Blau (1992) examined first-generation immigrant women in the US 1970 and 1980 Censuses and found that, among other things, their home country total fertility rate (TFR) is a significant covariate when explaining their childbearing behavior. Instead of just introducing country-level variables as additional covariates in a model of individual fertility, she employed a two-stage estimate to analyze the migrant–native fertility differentials by place of birth among immigrants once other observable characteristics are taken into account. In particular she estimated the following two equations:

$$F_i = X_i'B + D_iC + \varepsilon_i \tag{7.6}$$

$$C_{nt} = Z_{nt}B_z + Y_{1970} + \varepsilon_{nt} \tag{7.7}$$

Equation (7.6) is a reduced-form analysis of individual fertility F_i that includes individual i demographic characteristics X, a vector of country dummy variables D, and ε_i a stochastic error term. In equation (7.7), the dependent variable C_{nt} is the vector of dummy variables for each country n in the year t estimated in equation (7.6). The model includes Z, a vector of country source variables, a dummy for year 1970, and ε_{nt} a stochastic error term. The source-country variables include total fertility rate (TFR), per-capita GCP, the proportion of women in the source country with the same or higher educational level as the migrants, infant mortality, the proportion of refugees among migrants, and the distance in kilometers between the US and the country of origin. Variables are constructed by weighting the country levels in each country and years since migration group by the distribution of immigrants in each of those cells. Not surprisingly, overall predicted levels of migrant fertility are lower than the total fertility rate at origin. Nonetheless, characteristics from source countries matter and explain fertility differences across nationality groups in the US. TFR in particular and to some extent relative low educational attainment exert a positive force on migrant fertility. As expected the relevance of origin variables increases with the age at arrival and for individuals who married in origin and married within their own ancestry.

As Fernandez and Fogli (2009) note, works that study the first-generation immigrants face problems of selection into migration as well as the possibility of delay, disruption, and catch-up in fertility around the time of migration that can contaminate the inferences one makes about the strength of cultural continuities.

4.5 Son preference

A controversial issue regarding immigrant fertility refers to the persistence of gender preference among some immigrant groups even after migration. Gender preference for children, in particular son preference, is deeply rooted in some cultures and usually associated with the economic environment. Developing rural economies might demand more sons who can better help with physical labor in the fields, and poor households might deem daughters too expensive in cultures where dowries are expected in order to marry them off. Traditional economies where males are the main provider of resources and with few social programs for old age will attach more value to male than female offspring. It is expected that in more developed societies with more equal gender roles in the labor market and where children are not as essential for old-age insurance, son preference should be less important and reflect only gender tastes. It is plausible, however, that immigrants arriving from areas with strong son preference should show some evidence of differential treatment of the offspring if their cultural preferences for a given gender persist well after migration. Pabilonia and Ward-Batts (2007) and Lhila and Kosali (2008) showed evidence of differences in parental labor supply and prenatal health behavior conditional on the gender of the child in developed countries by immigrants from countries with marked son preference, like China, India, South Korea, and Taiwan.

Models of gender preference consider both tastes over offspring gender and the economic value attached to each gender as determinants of gender preference and their potential impact on fertility. In general, gender preference might increase fertility if births continue until the desired gender balance is achieved. However, economic conditions might limit the desired number of children and contribute to limit fertility, particularly if there is room for gender selection (Ben-Porath and Welch, 1976). Work by Klasen and Wink (2003) presented recent evidence of dramatic sex ratio imbalances across different countries, particularly in South East Asia, that can only be accounted for in part by selective abortion. Since incentives for sex selection are stronger at later births, high male to female birth ratios at higher parities can be interpreted as evidence of son preference and typically denote the existence of gender selection.

Using data from different sources (US Federal birth data 1971–2005, California birth data 1970–2005 and the 1980, 1990, and 2000 US Censuses), Abrevaya (2009) looked into the probability of the birth of a boy, conditioning on the gender of the previous child, for different ethnic groups in the US and found substantially higher male to female ratios among Chinese and Indian women for the third and fourth children (and even for the second among Indian). These higher ratios of male births are associated with the use of gender-selective procedures in pregnancies. The imbalance is larger for older women, for the third child and among less educated Chinese, but similar across educational levels among Indian women. The main findings in sex ratio imbalances in the US were confirmed by Almond and Edlund (2008). Indian immigrants to England and Wales also portray abnormal rations, and Dubuc and Coleman (2007) tied this finding to a reduction in fertility of Indian immigrants to Britain not observed among other Asian-origin populations (like Pakistani and Bangladeshi), who in turn maintain normal male to female birth ratios. Almond et al. (2013) used a similar methodology to determine the extent of gender selection among South East Asian immigrants to Canada. They found that religion is a strong determinant of high male to female birth ratios, with Christian or Muslim Asian immigrants (mainly from Pakistan, Bangladesh, Philippines, and Hong Kong) exhibiting normal sex ratios, and other religions such as Hindus and Sikhs showing abnormally high sex ratios and that this persists to a lesser degree among second-generation immigrants. The Canadian case is interesting because of the large size of the immigrant population arriving from countries with high sex birth ratios. With similar data, Adserà and Ferrer (2011) found that Sikhs and Hindus speed fertility up after the birth of two girls, but transit more slowly to third births after two boys are born. Those asymmetries do not appear across other religious groups. They also found significantly altered sex ratios: The likelihood of having a boy either after one or two girls are born increases among those born in South East Asia and among Sikhs. For both groups the bias in the ratios is large for births that occur very close to the previous birth.

4.6 The fertility of the second generation

Because changes in fertility preferences might take more than one generation, research into the adaptation hypothesis also looks at second-generation immigrants to investigate the extent of fertility convergence. Further, the policy relevance of understanding the assimilation of the second generation is evident. In countries with substantial immigration inflows, a large share of the next generation will consist of individuals whose parents were born abroad. Even if the first generation only assimilates partially to native patterns, their children may converge to native levels of education, labor supply or fertility as they adopt cultural cues in their country of birth and respond to local labor market opportunities.[32] In this regard, even persistent native–immigrant fertility gaps would not bring about long-term changes of fertility patterns in the destination country.

---

[32] The assimilation of the second generation has been extensively studied in many dimensions; see the chapter on second-generation outcomes in this handbook by Sweetman and Van Ours (2014).

Empirical studies overwhelmingly find that fertility differences present among immigrants tend to shrink (or disappear) among the second generation of migrants. The fertility patterns of second-generation immigrants to West Germany (Milewski and Hamel, 2010) and second-generation Turkish and Moroccan women in the Netherlands (Garssen and Nicolaas, 2008) are closer to those of the native-born than those of first-generation immigrants. The fertility of second-generation immigrants to the UK tends to converge to the average fertility, with second-generation Pakistani and Bangladeshi women in particular having fewer children and at later ages, compared to the first generation (Dubuc, 2012). Adserà and Ferrer (2010) found that the fertility of second-generation Canadians resembles that of the native-born more closely than that of their parents. Similar results are found in Australia (Abbasi-Shavazi and McDonald, 2000).

In the US, fertility patterns of some groups of immigrants seem to remain high even among the second and third generations (Bean et al., 2000). Blau and Kahn (2007) studied the intergenerational assimilation of Mexican migrants and found very large differentials compared to native non-Hispanic whites in education, labor supply, and fertility during the years 1994–2004. Even though the second generation closes many of those gaps, particularly in education and work, their fertility differentials with natives are still substantial. These findings are confirmed in Blau et al. (2013), who found positive but limited intergenerational transmission of labor force and educational outcomes of all immigrants to their US-born children. However, the fertility assimilation of second-generation US immigrants seems to be slower than in other countries, as it remains 40–65% in excess of that of the native-born.

In the same vein as some studies of the first generation just reviewed, one way the literature analyzes the culture and intergenerational transmission of norms is by looking at the outcomes of variables of interest in the countries of origin of parents or in general of people of the same ancestry as the individuals under analysis. Antecol (2000) used the 1990 US Census to analyze whether female labor force participation (LFP) in the country of ancestry (measured in 1990) explains the gaps in women's LFP among the second generation and beyond. She found a weakly positive correlation. The fact that ancestry is self-reported is a limitation of the study. Instead of directly using data from the country of origin, recent work matches second-generation migrants to information on the characteristics of first-generation migrants from the same ancestry as their parents. These researchers generally employ the large samples of earlier censuses to construct these measures. Among them, using the 1970 US Census that collected data on foreign parentage, Borjas (1993) found significant intergenerational transmission in wages and Card et al. (2000) also in educational attainment and marital assimilation in addition to earnings. Both papers used matched data from 1940 on immigrants from the father's ancestry.

Within this general methodological framework, Fernandez and Fogli (2006, 2009) and Blau et al. (2013) are the most distinctive papers that analyzed the intergenerational transmission of fertility behavior. To understand the role culture plays in the fertility outcomes of the second generation they estimated some variation of the following general model:

$$F_{isjt} = \beta_0 + \beta_1' X_i + \beta_2 \tilde{Y}_i + \beta_3 \tilde{F}_j + f_s + \gamma_t + \varepsilon_{isjt} \tag{7.8}$$

where F_{ijst} is the measure of fertility for a woman i living in the standard metropolitan statistical area (SMSA) or in a region s at time t and of ancestry j; X_i is a vector of individual controls, $\tilde{F}_j$ includes the variables employed to proxy the cultural norms in the country of ancestry, γ_t is a set of year-of-survey fixed effects (if more than one year survey is employed), f_s a set of dummies for SMAS or region of residence, and ε_{isjt} a stochastic error term. In some papers the model also includes $\tilde{Y}_j$, fertility characteristics of the individual's family (e.g., number of siblings a woman has in Fernandez and Fogli, 2006).

Fernandez and Fogli (2009) used data from the 1970 US Census that includes information of parental origin. Their models included both the female labor force participation and the total fertility from the country of origin of the father of the respondent in 1950 as covariates to account for cultural norms. They found that TFR among migrants from the father's ancestry is significantly associated with fertility patterns of the second generation. A one standard deviation increase in the TFR in 1950 is associated with approximately 0.4 extra children, a 14% increase in the number of children in 1970 (Fernandez and Fogli, 2009, p. 149). Additionally they ran the same two-stage model as in Blau, given by equations (7.6) and (7.7), to find that TFR and LFP in 1950 explain variation across estimated country dummies. Results are robust to the inclusion of measures of the average human capital and of quality of education of migrants from the same ancestry. They employed the 1940 US Census to track average parental education of migrants from the father's ancestry. To understand whose culture matters most within a couple, Fernandez and Fogli (2009) created an indicator for whether the husband's father is of the same ancestry as the woman's father and generated two separate interactions of that indicator with the level of total fertility rates (TFR s) and labor force participation (LFP) in the countries of the father of both the wife and the husband. In addition to the indicator for those couples sharing the same ancestry, these cultural proxies are positive and significant when included alone or simultaneously in all models and the size of the coefficients is similar for the wife's and the husband's ancestry covariate. In addition, to see whether the ethnic density in their neighborhood, measured as the proportion of respondents' neighborhood of the same ethnicity, affects fertility separately from the cultural indicator, they included the cultural covariates, the density, and the interaction of both in the models. They found that ethnic density only matters when the fertility in the country of origin is included. The number of children increases by 0.19 with a one standard increase in the TFR of the country of origin in1950.

As Card et al. (2000) noted, a constraint of employing measures of the characteristics of older generations of the same ancestry is the proper interpretation of the findings. Those covariates are bound to capture the impact of both the personal experience of the individual in his home while growing up, as well as the ethnic capital or cultural referents associated with the outcomes measured by the covariate at the group level. The estimated coefficients in these models capture the combined effect of both mechanisms. In an attempt to separately estimate these two mechanisms, Fernandez and Fogli (2006) estimated a model as in (7.6) that included both the total fertility rate in the country of ancestry in 1950 as well as individual characteristics directly related to fertility socialization, namely the number of siblings the woman has. They employed the General Social Survey (GSS) for the years 1977, 1978, 1980, and 1982–87. They found that the effect of culture, measured by the fertility in the country of origin, is quantitative important even after controlling for the number of siblings of the individual. A standard deviation increase in the 1950 TFR is associated with an increase of 0.14 children (half of the variation in the number of children observed across different origins in the US).

Instead of limiting the cultural controls for individuals of the same ancestry to the same year as previous analyses did, Blau et al. (2013) allowed this variable to vary with the birth cohort of the second-generation migrant. They used the 1995–2006 CPS March file, which contains information on the country of birth of each respondent as well as each of her parents, to estimate:

$$F_{it} = \beta' Z_{it} + \sum_c a_c X_{cit} + \varepsilon_{it} \tag{7.9}$$

where F_{it} is the fertility measure of an individual in year t with a mother or father born in country c, Z is a vector of controls, X is the vector of age-adjusted immigrant parent characteristics (father and/or mother), and ε_{it} is the error term. Among other individual covariates, the vector Z includes dummy indicators for whether the father and/or the mother are immigrants, as well as race and ethnicity indicators. However, no controls for the respondent's marital status, education, or location were included. Blau et al. (2013) combined information from the 1970, 1980, 1990, and 2000 US Censuses to construct a vector X of parental characteristics that includes a set of controls on the fertility, labor supply, and schooling of immigrants who were likely of the same age cohort as their parents. Thus, respondents from the same ancestry have different variables attached depending on their age. Since the data expands to recent years, it is able to track compositional changes in the latest waves of immigrants, with a substantial increase of immigrants from Latin America and Asia coupled with a decrease in the weight of second-generation immigrants of European descent that constituted the majority in the previous papers in the literature. Considering for the first time maternal ancestry, it is important since for 28% of their sample only the mother is foreign-born. The inclusion of information from both the father and the mother allowed the authors to study the relative importance of the cultural norms from each parent. Results were robust to pooling all families together or separating them by foreign birth of the father or of the mother and also by marital status. In general, cultural continuities from the mother's ancestry are significant and stronger for fertility than the father's, though the latter are also positive. The sum of the impact of both effects, around 0.5, is comparable across specifications and implies that a one standard deviation increase in immigrant's ancestry fertility increases the second generation's fertility by approximately 0.6 children. If stable for the next generation, at this rate of transmission, after two generations only around 25% of the excess fertility would remain.

5. CONCLUSION

Developed countries have seen the number and diversity of their foreign-born populations increase substantially, and with them the interest in the contribution immigrants make to social and demographic trends. To a large extent, this interest originates from the fact that family formation is often used to measure immigrant assimilation and as such is an indicator of social cohesion. Furthermore, family formation and many other key household decisions are intertwined and have crucial implications for the role of migrant women in the labor market and the investments made in their children, the second generation.

This chapter discusses some of the challenges in estimating trends in family formation and union dissolution among immigrants with incomplete data, and reports the evidence collected from the main studies in the area. The literature on immigrant family formation is diverse but perhaps the two most firm resultshighlighted in this chapter are that outcomes depend greatly on the life-cycle timing of migration and on the cultural norms immigrants bring with them and on the cultural distance to the host country. This underscores the importance of accounting for some measure of cultural origin to distinguish the complex path that each immigrant group follows to demographic integration in single-country studies. In some cases adaptation is relatively quick, but in many instances it may take more than one generation for individuals with immigrant backgrounds to conform to the host-country patterns in marriage or fertility.

Similarly, despite the scarcity of cross-country studies, the evidence suggests that the environment at destination also exerts a great influence on the demographic trends followed by different groups of immigrants. More research is called for in this area, as it remains difficult to distinguish between the effect of the host country on a particular group of immigrants and the selection mechanism that encourages different types of immigrants from a given source country to move to different destinations. Exploiting variation in immigration flows to different countries that share similar environments could help disentangling these effects.

Finally, our review highlights the importance of improving data availability on key variables related to the migration process and lifetime events such as detailed age at migration, complete union and birth stories, and measures of language proficiency and mother tongue, among others. Ample support should be given to some efforts already underway to construct datasets that include information of households at origin as well as destination to better compare migrants, non-migrants and returnees, and address research challenges stemming from migrant selectivity.

REFERENCES

Abbasi-Shavazi, M.J., McDonald, P., 2000. Fertilityand multiculturalism: immigrant fertility in Australia, 1977–1991. Int. Migrat. Rev. 35 (1), 215–242.

Abrevaya, J., 2009. Are there missing girls in the United States? Evidence from birth data. Am. Econ. J. Appl. Econ. 1 (2), 1–34.

Adserà, A., 2013. Fertility, feminism and faith: How are secularism and economic conditions influencing fertility in the West? In: Kaufman, E., Wilcox, B. (Eds.), Whither the Child?. Causes and Consequences of Low Fertility. Paradigm Publishers, Colorado, pp. 1–28.

Adserà, A., Ferrer, A., 2010. The fertility decisions of Canadian immigrants. In: Sweetman, A., McDonald, E., Ruddick, E. (Eds.), Canadian Research on Immigration. McGill-Queen's Press, John Deutchs Institute of Economic Policy, Queen's University.

Adserà, A., Ferrer, A., 2011. Speeding up for a Son? Fertility Transitions among First and Second Generation Migrants to Canada. Princeton University, Mimeo.

Adserà, A., Ferrer, A., 2013. The Fertility of Recent Immigrants to Canada. IZA Working Paper #7289.

Adserà, A., Ferrer, A., 2014. Fertility adaptation of child migrants to Canada. Pop. Stud. 68 (1), 65–79.

Adserà, A., Ferrer, A., Sigle-Rushton, W., Wilson, B., 2012. Fertility patterns of child immigrants: Age at immigration and ancestry in comparative perspective. Ann. Am. Acad. Polit. Soc. Sci. 643 (1, September), 134–159.

Akresh, I.R., 2007. Contexts of language use among immigrants in the United States. Int. Migrat. Rev. 41 (4), 930–955.

Alba, R., Nee, V., 1997. Rethinking assimilation theory for a new era of immigration. Int. Migrat. Rev. 31 (4), 826–874.

Alders, M. 2000. Cohort fertility of migrant women in the Netherlands: developments in fertility of women born in Turkey, Morocco, Suriname, and the Netherlands Antilles and Aruba. Paper presented at the BSPS-NVD-URU Conference, Utrecht/Netherlands, August 31–September 1, 2000.

Algan, Y., Landais, C., Senik, C., 2010. Cultural integration in France. In: Algan, Y., Bisin, A., Manning, A., Verdier, T. (Eds.), Cultural Integration of Immigrants in Europe. Oxford University Press, pp. 49–68.

Algan, Y., Bisin, A., Manning, A., Verdier, T., 2012. Studies of policy reform. In: Algan, Y., Bisin, A., Manning, A., Verdier, T. (Eds.), Cultural Integration of Immigrants in Europe. Oxford University Press.

Almond, D., Edlund, L., 2008. Son-biased sex ratios in the 2000 United States Census. Proc. Natl. Acad. Sci. U. S. A. 105 (15), 5681–5682.

Almond, D., Edlund, L., Milligan, K., 2013. Son preference and the persistence of culture: evidence from South and East Asian immigrants to Canada. Popul. Dev. Rev. 39 (1), 75–95.

Andersson, G., 2004. Childbearing after migration: Fertility patterns of foreign-born women in Sweden. Int. Migrat. Rev. 38 (2), 747–774.

Antecol, H., 2000. An examination of cross-country differences in the gender gap in labor force participation rates. Lab. Econ. 7, 409–426.

Avitabile, C., Clots-Figueras, I., Masella, P., 2014. Citizenship, fertility, and parental investment. American Economic Journal: Applied Economics, (forthcoming).

Baker, M., Benjamin, D., 1997. The role of the family in immigrants' labour market activity: An evaluation of alternative explanations. Am. Econ. Rev. 87 (4), 705–727.

Beck, A., Corak, M., Tienda, M., 2012. Age at immigration and the adult attainments of child migrants to the United States. Ann. Am. Acad. Polit. Soc. Sci. 643 (1, September), 134–159.

Becker, G., 1960. An economic analysis of fertility. Demographic and Economic Change in Developed Countries. Princeton, pp. 209–231, NBER Conference Series 11.

Becker, G.S., 1965. A theory of the allocation of time. Econ. J. 70, 493–517.

Becker, G., 1981. A Treatise on the Family. Harvard University Press, Cambridge, MA.

Becker, G.S., Lewis, H.G., 1973. On the interaction between the quantity and quality of children. J. Polit. Econ. 81 (2), S279–S288, Part 2: New Economic Approaches to Fertility (Mar.–Apr., 1973).

Becker, G.S., Landes, E.M., Michael, R.T., 1977. An economic analysis of marital instability. J. Polit. Econ. 85 (6), 1141–1187.

Bean, F., Swicegood, C., Berger, R., 2000. Mexican-origin fertility: New patterns and interpretations. Soc. Sci. Q. 811, 404–420.

Bélanger, A., Gilbert, S., 2003. The fertility of immigrant women and their Canadian-born daughters. Report on the Demographic Situation in Canada 2002, 91–209.

Ben-Porath, Y., 1973. Labor-force participation rates and the supply of labor. J. Polit. Econ. 81, 697–704.

Ben-Porath, Y., Welch, F., 1976. Do sex preferences really matter? Q. J. Econ. 90, 285–307.

Bernhardt, E., Goldscheider, C., Goldscheider, F., Gunilla, B. (Eds.), 2007. Immigration, Gender and Family Transitions to Adulthood in Sweden. University Press of America, Lanham, MD.

Bisin, A., Patacchini, E., 2012. Cultural integration in Italy. In: Algan, Y., Bisin, A., Manning, A., Verdier, T. (Eds.), Cultural Integration of Immigrants in Europe. Oxford University Press, pp. 125–147.

Blau, F.D., 1992. The fertility of immigrant women: Evidence from high fertility source countries. In: Borjas, G.J., Freeman, R.B. (Eds.), Immigration and the Work Force: Economic Consequences for the United States and Source Areas. University of Chicago Press, Chicago, pp. 93–133.

Blau, F.D., Kahn, L.M., 2007. Gender and assimilation among Mexican Americans. In: Borjas, G.J. (Ed.), Mexican Immigration to the United States. University of Chicago Press, Chicago, pp. 57–106.

Blau, F.D., Kahn, L., Yung-Hsu Liu, A., Papps, K.L., 2013. The Transmission of Women's Fertility, Human Capital and Work Orientation Across Immigrant Generations. J. Pop. Econ. 26 (2), 405–435.

Bleakley, H., Chin, A., 2004. Language skills and earnings: evidence from childhood immigrants. Rev. Econ. Stat. 86 (2), 481–496.

Bleakley, H., Chin, A., 2008. What holds back the second generation? The intergenerational transmission of language human capital among immigrants. J. Hum. Resour. 43 (Spring), 267–298.

Bleakley, H., Chin, A., 2010. Age at arrival, English proficiency, and social assimilation among US immigrants. Am. Econ. J. Appl. Econ. 2 (1), 165–192.

Borjas, G.J., 1985. Assimilation, changes in cohort quality, and the earnings of immigrants. J. Labor Econ. 3 (4), 463–489.

Borjas, G.J., 1987. Self-selection and the earnings of immigrants. Am. Econ. Rev. 77, 531–553.

Borjas, G.J., 1991. Immigration and self-selection. In: Abowd, J.M. (Ed.), Immigration, Trade, and the Labor Market. University of Chicago Press, Chicago, pp. 29–76.

Borjas, G.J., 1993. The intergenerational mobility of immigrants. J. Labor Econ. 11 (1), 113–135.

Borjas, G.J., 1999. Heaven's Door: Immigration Policy and the American Economy. Princeton University Press, Princeton, NJ.

Bratter, J., King, R., 2008. But will it last?: marital instability among interracial and same-race couples. Fam. Relat. 57, 160–171.

Brown, S.L., Van Hook, J., Glick, J.E., 2008. Generational differences in cohabitation and marriage in the U.S. Popul. Res. Pol. Rev. 27 (5), 531–550.

Bumpass, L., Lu, H.-H., 2000. Trends in cohabitation and implications for children's family contexts in the US. Popul. Stud. 54 (1), 29–41.

Card, D., DiNardo, J., Estes, E., 2000. The more things change: Immigrants and the children of immigrants in the 1940s, the 1970s, and the 1990s. In: Borjas, G.J. (Ed.), Issues in the Economics of Immigration. University of Chicago Press, Chicago, pp. 227–269.

Carlson, E., 1985. Increased nonmarital births among foreign women in Germany. Sociol. Soc. Res. 70 (1), 110–111.

Carter, M., 2000. Fertility of Mexican immigrant women in the U.S.: A closer look. Soc. Sci. Q. 81 (1), 404–420.

Castro, M.T., 2002. Consensual unions in Latin America: Persistence of a dual nuptiality system. J. Comp. Fam. Stud. 33, 35–55.

CBS, 2006. CBS Statline. Internet database of the Centraal Bureau voor de Statistiek (Statistics Netherlands), Voorburg.

Celikaksoy, A., Nielsen, H., Verner, M., 2006. Marriage migration: just another case of positive assortative matching? Review of Economics of the Household 4, 253–275.

Chiswick, B.R., 1978. The effect of Americanization on the earnings of foreign-born men. J. Polit. Econ. 86 (5), 897–922.

Chiswick, B.R., 1991. Speaking, reading, and earnings among low-skilled immigrants. J. Labor Econ. 9 (2), 149–170.

Chiswick, B., Houseworth, C., 2011. Ethnic intermarriage among immigrants: human capital and assortative mating. Rev. Econ. Household 9 (2), 149–180.

Chiswick, C.U., Lehrer, E., 1991. Religious intermarriage: an economic perspective. Contemporary Jewry 12 (1), 21–34.

Chiswick, B.R., Miller, P., 1995. The endogeneity between language and earnings: International analyses. J. Labor Econ. 13 (2), 246–288.

Chiswick, B.R., Miller, P., 2001. A model of destination-language acquisition: application to male immigrants in Canada. Demography 38 (3), 391–409.

Cho, L.J., 1973. The own-children approach to fertility estimation: an elaboration. In: International Population Conference, Liège, International Union for the Scientific Study of Population. Ordina, Liège.

Choi, K., 2014. Fertility in the context of Mexican migration to the United States. Demographic Research 30 (24), 703–738.

Choi, K.H., Tienda, M., Cobb-Clark, D., Sinning, M., 2012. Immigration and status exchange in Australia and the United States. Research in Social Stratification and Mobility 30 (1), 49–62.

Clark, K., Lindley, J., 2009. Immigrant assimilation pre and post labour market entry: evidence from the UK labour force survey. J. Popul. Econ. 22 (1), 175–198.

Cobb-Clark, D.A., 1993. Immigrant selectivity and wages: the evidence for women. Am. Econ. Rev. 83 (4), 986–993.

Coleman, D., 2003. Mass migration and population change. Zeitschrift für Bevölkerungswissenschaft 28 (2–4), 183–215.

Coleman, D., 2006. Immigration and ethnic change in low-fertility countries, a third demographic transition. Popul. Dev. Rev. 32 (3), 401–446.

Coleman, D., Dubuc, S., 2010. The fertility of ethnic minority populations in the United Kingdom, 1960s-2006. Popul. Stud. 64 (1), 19–41.

Coleman, D., Compton, P., Salt, J., 2002. Demography of migrant populations: the case of the United Kingdom. In: Haug, W., Compton, P., Courbage, Y. (Eds.), The Demographic Characteristics of Immigrant Populations (Population Studies No. 38). Council of Europe, Strasbourg, pp. 497–552.

Constant, A., Nottmeyer, O., Zimmermann, K., 2010. Cultural integration in Germany. In: Algan, Y., Bisin, A., Manning, A., Verdier, T. (Eds.), Cultural Integration of Immigrants in Europe. Oxford University Press, pp. 69–124.

Courgeau, D., 1989. Family formation and urbanization. Popul. Engl. Sel. 44 (1), 123–146.

De la Rica, S., Ortega, F., 2010. Cultural integration in Spain. In: Algan, Y., Bisin, A., Manning, A., Verdier, T. (Eds.), Cultural Integration of Immigrants in Europe. Oxford University Press, pp. 148–171.

Dribe, M., Lundh, C., 2011. Cultural dissimilarity and intermarriage: a longitudinal study of immigrants in Sweden 1990–2005. Int. Migrat. Rev. 45 (2), 297–324.

Dubuc, S., 2009. Application of the own-children method for estimating fertility by ethnic and religious groups in the UK. J. Popul. Res. 26 (3), 207–225.

Dubuc, S., 2012. Immigration to the UK from high-fertility countries: Intergenerational adaptation and fertility convergence. Popul. Dev. Rev. 38, 353–368.

Dubuc, S., Coleman, D., 2007. An increase in the sex ratio of births to India-born mothers in England and Wales: evidence for sex-selective abortion. Popul. Dev. Rev. 33 (2, June), 383–400.

Duncan, B., Trejo, S., 2007. Ethnic identification, intermarriage and unmeasured progress by Mexican Americans. In: Borjas, G.J. (Ed.), Mexican Immigration to the United States. National Bureau of Economic Research and the University of Chicago Press, Chicago, pp. 229–267.

Dustmann, C., 1994. Speaking fluency, writing fluency and earnings of migrants. J. Popul. Econ. 7, 133–156.

Dustmann, C., Fabbri, F., 2003. Language proficiency and labour market performance of immigrants in the UK. Econ. J. 113, 695–717.

Dustmann, C., van Soest, A., 2002. Language and the earnings of immigrants. Indust. Labor Rel. Rev. 55 (3), 473–492.

Espenshade, T.J., Fu, H., 1997. An analysis of language proficiency among immigrants. Am. Sociol. Rev. 62 (2), 288–305.

Espinosa, K.E., Massey, D.S., 1997. Determinants of English proficiency among Mexican migrants to the United States. Int. Migrat. Rev. 31 (1), 28–50.

Feliciano, C., 2005. Educational selectivity in U.S. immigration: how do immigrants compare to those left behind? Demography 42, 131–152.

Fernandez, R., Fogli, A., 2006. Fertility: the role of culture and family experience. J. Eur. Econ. Assoc. 4 (2–3), 552–561.

Fernandez, R., Fogli, A., 2009. Culture: an empirical investigation of beliefs, work, and fertility. Am. Econ. J. Macroecon. 1 (1, January), 146–177.

Ferrer, A., Riddell, W.C., 2008. Education, credentials, and immigrant earnings. Can. J. Econ. 41 (1), 186–216.

Ferrer, A., Green, D., Riddell, C., 2006. The effect of literacy on immigrant earnings. J. Human Res. 41 (2), 380–410.

Ford, K., 1990. Duration of residence in the United States and the fertility of U.S. immigrants. Int. Migrat. Rev. 24 (1), 34–68.

Forste, R., Tienda, M., 1996. What's behind racial and ethnic fertility differentials. Popul. Dev. Rev. 22 (S), 109–133.

Frank, R., Heuveline, P., 2005. A crossover in Mexican and Mexican-American fertility rates: Evidence and explanations for an emerging paradox. Demographic Research 12, 77–104.

Furtado, D., 2012. Human capital and interethnic marriage decisions. Econ. Inq. 50 (1), 82–93.

Furtado, D., Theodoropoulos, N., 2011. Interethnic marriage: a choice between ethnic and educational similarities. J. Popul. Econ. 24, 1257–1279.

Furtado, D., Trejo, S., 2013. Interethnic marriages and their economic effects. In: Constant, A.F., Zimmermann, K.F. (Eds.), International Handbook on the Economics of Migration, Chapter 15. Edward Elgar, Cheltenham, UK, and Northampton, USA, pp. 276–292.

Furtado, D., Marcén, M., Sevilla, A., 2013. Does culture affect divorce decisions? Evidence from European immigrants in the US. Demography 50 (3), 1013–1038.

Galor, O., Weil, D., 1996. The gender gap, fertility and growth. Am. Econ. Rev. 86, 374–387.

Garssen, J., Nicolaas, H., 2008. Trends in cohort fertility of second generation Turkish and Moroccan women in the Netherlands: strong adjustment to native levels. Dem. Res. 19 (33), 1249–1280.

Georgiadis, A., Manning, A., 2010. Cultural integration in the United Kingdom. In: Algan, Y., Bisin, A., Manning, A., Verdier, T. (Eds.), Cultural Integration of Immigrants in Europe. Oxford University Press, pp. 260–284.

Georgiadis, A., Manning, A., 2011. Change and continuity among minority communities in Britain. J. Popul. Econ. 24, 541–568.

Gjerde, J., McCants, A., 1995. Fertility, marriage and culture: Demographic processes among Norwegian immigrants to the rural Middle West. J. Econ. Hist. 55 (4), 860–888.

Goldstein, S., Goldstein, A., 1981. The impact of migration on fertility: an 'own children' analysis for Thailand. Popul. Stud. 35, 265–284.

Goldstein, S., Goldstein, A., 1983. Migration and Fertility in Peninsular Malaysia: An Analysis Using Life History Data. RAND Corporation, Santa Monica, CA.

Gonzalez-Ferrer, A., 2006. Who do immigrants marry? Partner choice among single immigrants in Germany. Eur. Socio. Rev. 22 (2), 171–185.

Guinnane, T.W., Moehling, C.M., O Grada, C., 2006. The fertility of the Irish in America in 1910. Explor. Econ. Hist. 43 (3), 465–485.

Heran, F., Pison, G., 2007. Two children per women in France in 2006: are immigrants to blame? Fertility among immigrant women: new data, a new approach. Population and Societies no 432, 2004.

Hervitz, H.M., 1985. Selectivity, adaptation, or disruption? A comparison of alternative hypotheses on the effects of migration on fertility: The case of Brazil. Int. Migrat. Rev. 19, 293–317.

Hooghiemstra, E., 2001. Migrants, partner selection and integration: crossing borders? J. Comp. Fam. Stud. 32, 609–626.

Huschek, D., Liefbroer, A., de Valk, H., 2010. Timing of first union among second-generation Turks in Europe: The role of parents, peers and institutional context. Demographic Research 22, article 16.

INE, 2006. Vital Statistics 2005. Definitive Data. Instituto National de Estadística, Madrid.

INE, 2007. Movimiento natural de la población. Resultados provisionales 2006. Instituto National de Estadística, Madrid.

ISTAT, 2006, 2007. Natalità e fecondità della popolazione residente: caratteristiche e tendenze recenti. Anno 2004 [2005].

Jacobs, J.A., Furstenberg Jr., F.F., 1986. Changing places: conjugal careers and women's marital mobility. Soc. Forces 64, 714–732.

Jasso, G., 2004. Have the occupational skills of new legal immigrants to the United States changed over time? Evidence from the immigrant cohorts of 1977, 1982, and 1994. In: Massey, D.S., Taylor, J.E. (Eds.), International Migration: Prospects and Policies in a Global Market. Oxford University Press, Oxford, pp. 261–285.

Jasso, G., Rosenzweig, M.R., 1990. The immigrant's legacy: investing in the next generation. In: Jasso, G., Rosenzweig, M.R. (Eds.), The New Chosen People: Immigrants in the United States. Russell Sage Foundation, New York, pp. 382–410.

Jasso, G., Massey, D.S., Rosenzweig, M.R., Smith, J.P., 2000. Assortative mating among married new legal immigrants to the United States: Evidence from the New Immigrant Survey Pilot. Int. Migrat. Rev. 34 (2), 443–459.

Jensen, E., Ahlburg, D., 2004. Why does migration decrease fertility? Evidence from the Philippines? Popul. Stud. 58 (2), 219–231.

Jones, F.L., 1996. Convergence and divergence in ethnic divorce patterns: a research note. J. Marr. Fam. 58, 213–218.

Kahn, J., 1988. Immigrant selectivity and fertility adaptation in the United States. Soc. Forces. 67.

Kahn, J., 1994. Immigrant and native fertility during the 1980s: adaptation and expectations for the future. Int. Migrat. Rev. 28 (2), 501–519.

Kalbach, W., 1970. The Impact of Immigration on Canada's Population. Queen's Printer, Ottawa.

Kalmijn, M., 1998. Intermarriage and Homogamy: causes, patterns and trends. Annu. Rev. Sociol. 24, 395–421.

Kalmijn, M., van Tubergen, F., 2010. A comparative perspective on intermarriage: explaining differences in marriage choices among national origin groups in the United States. Demography 47 (2), 459–479.

Kalmijn, M., de Graaf, P.M., Janssen, J., 2005. Intermarriage and the risk of divorce in the Netherlands. Popul. Stud. 59, 71–85.

Kalmijn, M., Loeve, A., Manting, D., 2007. Income dynamics in couples and the dissolution of marriage and cohabitation. Demography 44 (1), 159–179.

Kane, T.T., 1986. The fertility and assimilation of guestworker populations in the Federal Republic of Germany: 1961–1981. Zeitschrift für Bevölkerungswissenschaft 12 (1), 99–131.

Kantarevic, J., 2004. Interethnic Marriages and Economic Assimilation of Immigrants. IZA Discussion Paper No. 1142, May.

Keeley, M., 1977. The economics of family formation. Econ. Inq. 15 (2), 238–250.

Klasen, S., Wink, C., 2003. Missing women: revisiting the debate. Fem. Econ. 9 (2–3), 263–299.

Kossoudji, S.A., 1988. The impact of English language ability on the labor market opportunities of Asian and Hispanic immigrant men. J. Labor Econ. 6 (3), 205–228.

Kulu, H., 2005. Migration and fertility, competing hypotheses re-examined. Eur. J. Popul. 21, 51–87.

Kulu, H., 2006. Fertility of internal migrants: comparison between Austria and Poland. Popul. Space. Place. 12 (3), 147–170.

Kytir, J., 2006. Demographische Strukturen und Trends 2005. Statistische Nachrichten 2006 (9), 777–790.

Lam, D., 1988. Marriage markets and assortative mating with household public goods: theoretical results and empirical implications. J. Human Res. 23 (3), 462–487.

Lanzieri, G., 2012. Merging populations: a look at marriages with foreign-born persons in European countries. Statistics in Focus 29/2012.Eurostat, Luxembourg

Lee, S.M., Boyd, M., 2008. Marrying out: comparing the marital and social integration of Asians in the US and Canada. Soc. Sci. Res. 37 (1), 311–329.

Lehrer, E., 2003. The economics of divorce. In: Shoshana, Shechtman (Ed.), Marriage and the Economy: Theory and Evidence from Industrialized Societies. Cambridge University Press, Cambridge, pp. 55–74.

Lehrer, E.L., Chiswick, C.U., 1993. Religion as a determinant of marital stability. Demography 30 (3), 385–404.

Lesthaeghe, R.J., Neidert, L., 2006. The second demographic transition in the United States: exception or textbook example? Popul. Dev. Rev. 32, 669–687.

Leslie, D., Lindley, J., 2001. The impact of language ability on employment and earnings of Britain's ethnic communities. Economica 68 (272), 587–606.

Lhila, A., Kosali, S., 2008. Prenatal health investment decisions: does the child's sex matter? Demography 45 (4), 885–905.

Liang, Z., Ito, N., 1999. Intermarriage of Asian-Americans in the New York City region: Contemporary patterns and future prospects. Int. Migrat. Rev. 33 (4), 876–900.

Lievens, J., 1998. Interethnic marriage: bringing in the context through multilevel modelling. Eur. J. Popul. 14, 117–155.

Lievens, J., 1999. Family-formation migration from Turkey and Morocco to Belgium: The demand for marriage partners from the countries of origin. Int. Migrat. Rev. 33, 717–744.

Lindstrom, D.P., 2003. Rural-urban migration and reproductive behaviour in Guatemala. Popul. Res. Pol. Rev. 22 (4), 351–372.

Lobo, A.P., Salvo, J.J., 1998. Resurgent Irish immigration to the US in the 1980s and early 1990s: a socio-demographic profile. Int. Migrat. 36 (2), 257–280.

Lundberg, S., Pollak, R.A., 1993. Separate spheres bargaining and the marriage market. J. Polit. Econ. 101 (6), 988–1010.

Mayer, J., Riphahn, R., 2000. Fertility assimilation of immigrants: evidence from count data models. J. Popul. Econ. 13 (2), 241–261.

McPherson, M., Smith-Lovin, L., Cook, J.M., 2001. Birds of a feather: homophily in social networks. Annu. Rev. Sociol. 27, 415–444.

Meng, X., Gregory, R., 2005. Intermarriage and the economic assimilation of immigrants. J. Labor Econ. 23 (1), 135–175.

Meng, X., Meurs, D., 2009. Intermarriage, language, and economic assimilation process: a case study of France. Int. J. Manpow. 30 (1/2), 127–144.

Mieke, C.W., Lievens, J., Van de Putte, B., Lusyne, P., 2011. Partner selection and divorce in ethnic minorities: distinguishing between two types of ethnic homogamous marriages. Int. Migrat. Rev. 45 (2), 269–296.

Milan, A., Maheux, H., Chui, T., 2010. A Portrait of Couples in Mixed Unions. Canadian Social Trends, Catalogue No. 11-008, Statistics Canada.

Milewski, N., 2007. First child of immigrant workers and their descendants in West Germany: Interrelation of events, disruption, or adaptation? Demographic Research 17 (29), 859–896.

Milewski, N., Hamel, C., 2010. Union formation and partner choice in a transnational context: The case of descendants of Turkish migrants in France. Int. Migrat. Rev. 44 (3), 615–658.

Mincer, J., 1963. Opportunity costs and income effects. In: Christ, C., et al. (Ed.), Measurement in Economics. Stanford University Press, Stanford, CA.

Mulder, C.H., Wagner, M., 1993. Migration and marriage in the life course: a method for studying synchronized events. Eur. J. Popul. 9 (1), 55–76.

Ng, E., Nault, F., 1997. Fertility among recent immigrant women to Canada, 1991: an examination of the disruption hypothesis. Int. Migrat. 35 (4), 559–580.

Niedomysl, T., Östh, J., van Ham, M., 2010. The globalisation of marriage fields: the Swedish case. J. Ethnic. Migrat. Stud. 36 (7), 1119–1138.

Nielsen, H., Smith, N., Celikaksoy, A., 2009. The effect of marriage on education of immigrants: evidence from a policy reform restricting marriage migration. Scand. J. Econ. 111 (3), 457–486.

ONS, 2006. Birth Statistics. Review of the Registrar General on Births and Patterns of Family Building England and Wales, 2005. Series FM1, No. 34, London Office of National Statistics.

ONS, 2007. Fertility Rate is Highest for 26 Years. News Release, 7 June 2007. Office of National Statistics, London.

Pabilonia, S., Ward-Batts, J., 2007. The effect of child gender on parents' labor supply: an examination of natives, immigrants, and their children. Am. Econ. Rev. 97 (2), 402–406.

Pagnini, D.L., Morgan, P., 1990. Intermarriage and social distance among US immigrants at the turn of the century. Am. J. Sociol. 96, 405–432.

Parrado, E.A., 2011. How high is Hispanic/Mexican fertility in the United States? Immigration and tempo considerations. Demography 48 (3), 1059–1080.

Parrado, E.A., Morgan, S.P., 2008. Intergenerational fertility among Hispanic women: new evidence of immigrant assimilation. Demography 45 (3), 651–671.

Passel, J.S., Wang, W., Taylor, P., 2010. Marrying Out: One-in-Seven New U.S. Marriages is Interracial or Interethnic. Social and Demographic Trends Report, Pew Research Center.

Phillips, J., Sweeney, M.M., 2006. Can differential exposure to risk factors explain recent racial and ethnic variation in marital disruption? Soc. Sci. Res. 35, 409–434.

Picot, G., Hou, F., Coulombe, S., 2007. Chronic Low Income and Low-Income Dynamics Among Recent Immigrants. Analytical Studies Branch Research Paper Series No. 294, Statistics Canada.

Prioux, F., 2005. Recent demographic developments in France. Population-E 60 (4), 371–414.

Qian, Z., 2013. Divergent Paths of American Families, US 2010 Project. Report sponsored by Russell Sage Foundation and American Communities Project of Brown University.

Qian, Z., Lichter, D., 2001. Measuring marital assimilation: intermarriage among natives and immigrants. Soc. Sci. Res. 30 (2), 289–312.

Qian, Z., Lichter, D.T., 2007. Social boundaries and marital assimilation: interpreting trends in racial and ethnic intermarriage. Am. Sociol. Rev. 72, 68–94.

Qian, Z., Glick, J., Batson, C., 2012. Crossing boundaries: Nativity, ethnicity, and mate selection. Demography 49 (2), 651–675.

Ralston, H., 1999. Canadian immigration policy in the twentieth century: its impact on South Asian women. Canadian Women Studies 19 (35), 33–37.

Ram, B., George, M.V., 1990. Immigrant fertility patterns in Canada, 1961–1986. Int. Migrat. 28 (4), 413–426.

Rindfuss, R.R., 1976. Fertility and migration: the case of Puerto Rico. Int. Migrat. Rev. 10, 191–203.

Rindfuss, R.R., Sweet, J.A., 1977. Postwar Fertility Trends and Differentials in the United States. Academic Press, New York.

Roig Vila, M., Castro Martín, T., 2007. Childbearing patterns of foreign women in a new immigration country: the case of Spain. Population-E 62 (3), 351–380.

Rosenfeld, M., 2002. Measures of assimilation in the marriage market: Mexican Americans 1970–1990. J. Marriage Fam. 64, 152–162.

Rosenwaike, I., 1973. Two generations of Italians in America: their fertility experience. Int. Migrat. Rev. 7 (3, Autumn), 271–280.

Rumbaut, R., 1997. Ties that bind immigration and immigrant families. Immigration and the Family: Research and Policy on US Immigrants 3–46.

Ryder, N.B., 1973. A critique of the National Fertility Study. Demography 10, 495–506.

Sandefur, G.D., McKinnell, T., 1986. American Indian intermarriage. Soc. Sci. Res. 15, 347–371.

Schaafsma, J., Sweetman, A., 2001. Immigrant earnings: Age at immigration matters. Can. J. Econ. 34 (4), 1066–1099.

Schoen, R., Wooldredge, J., 1989. Marriage choices in North Carolina and Virginia, 1969–71 and 1979–81. J. Mar. Fam. 51, 465–481.

Schoorl, J.J., 1990. Fertility adaptation of Turkish and Moroccan women in the Netherlands. Int. Migrat. 28 (4), 477–495.

Schoorl, J.J., 1995. Fertility trends of immigrant population. In: Voets, S., Schoorl, J., de Bruijn, B. (Eds.), Demographic Consequences of International Migration, Rapport no. 44. NIDI, The Hague, pp. 97–121.

Schultz, T.W., 1974. Economics of the Family: Marriage, Children, and Human Capital. National Bureau of Economic Research, Inc.

SFSO, 2006. Statistique du mouvement naturel de la population. Résultats définitifs 2005. Swiss Federal Statistical Office, Neuchâtel.

Sigle-Rushton, W., 2008. England and Wales: stable fertility and pronounced social status differences. Demographic Research 19, 459–502.

Singley, S., Landale, N., 1998. Incorporating origin and process in migration-fertility frameworks: the case of Puerto Rican women. Soc. Forces 76 (4), 1437–1464.

Sobotka, T., 2008. The rising importance of migrants for childbearing in Europe. Demographic Research 19 (9), 225–248.

Sorenson, A.M., 1988. The fertility and language characteristics of Mexican-American and non-Hispanic husbands and wives. Socio. Q. 29 (1), 111–130.

Statistics Denmark, 2004. Befolkningens bevægelser 2003. Vital statistics 2003. Danmarks Statistik, Copenhagen.

Statistisches Bundesamt, 2006. Statistisches Jahrbuch 2006. Statistisches Bundesamt, Wiesbaden.

Statistics Sweden, 2006. Tabeller över Sveriges befolkning. Statistics Sweden, Statistiska centralbyrån Stockholm.

Stephen, E.H., Bean, F.D., 1992. Assimilation, disruption and fertility of Mexican-origin women in the United States. Int. Migrat. Rev. 26 (1), 67–88.

Stevens, G., 1992. The social and demographic context of language use in the United States. Am. Sociol. Rev. 57 (2), 171–785.

Stevens, G., 1999. Age at immigration and second language proficiency among foreign-born adults. Lang. Soc. 28 (4), 555–578.

Stevenson, B., Wolfers, J., 2007. Marriage and divorce: changes and their driving forces. J. Econ. Perspect. 21 (2, Spring), 27–52.

Sweetman, A., Van Ours, J.C., 2014. Immigration: What about the children and grandchildren? In: Chiswick, B.R., Miller, P.W. (Eds.), Handbook of the Economics of International Migration, vol. 1. Elsevier, Amsterdam.

Swicegood, G., Bean, F.D., Hervey, E.S., Opitz, W., 1988. Language usage and fertility in the Mexican origin population of the United States. Demography 25 (1), 17–34.

Toulemon, L., 2004. Fertility among immigrant women, new data, a new approach. Population and Societies 400 (April), 1–4.

Toulemon, L., Paihle, A., Rossier, C., 2008. France: High and stable fertility. Demographic Research 19, article 16, pp. 503–556.

Trilla, C., Esteve, A., Domingo, A., 2008. Marriage patterns of the foreign-born population in a new country of immigration: The case of Spain. Int. Migrat. Rev. 42 (4), 877–902.

United Nations, 2001. Replacement Migration, Is It a Solution to Declining and Ageing Population? United Nations Population Division, New York, Sales No. E01.XIII.19.

Van Tubergen, F., Maas, I., 2007. Ethnic intermarriage among immigrants in the Netherlands: an analysis of population data. Soc. Sci. Res. 36, 1065–1086.

Vasileva, K., 2011. Population and social conditions. Statistics in Focus, 34/2011, Eurostat.

VAZG, 2007. Tables on births in Flanders provided by the Flemish Healthcare Agency. Vlaams Agentschap Zorg en Gezondheid.

Wanner, P., 2002. The demographic characteristics of immigrant populations in Switzerland. In: Haug, W., Compton, P., Courbage, Y. (Eds.), The Demographic Characteristics of Immigrant Populations. Council of Europe Publishing, Strasbourg, pp. 419–496, Population Studies, No. 38.

Westoff, C.F., Frejka, T., 2007. Religiousness and fertility among European Muslims. Popul. Dev. Rev. 33.

Westoff, C.F., Frejka, T., 2008. Religion, religiousness and fertility in the United States and in Europe. Eur. J. Popul. 24.

White, M., Moreno, L., Guo, S., 1995. The interrelationship of fertility and geographic mobility in Peru: A hazard model analysis. Int. Migrat. Rev. 29 (2), 492–515.

Willis, R., 1974. Economic theory of fertility behavior. In: Schultz, (Ed.), Economics of the Family: Marriage, Children and Human Capital.pp. 25–80, UMI, NBER.

Worswick, C., 1996. Immigrant families in the Canadian labor market. Can. Publ. Pol. 22 (4), 378–396.

Zhang, Y., Van Hook, J., 2009. Marital dissolution among interracial couples. J. Marriage Fam. 71 (1), 95–107.

CAMEO 2

Immigrants and Religion

Carmel U. Chiswick
George Washington University

Contents

1. Introduction	375
2. Economics of Religion	376
2.1 Transferability of religious human capital	377
2.2 Religious groups as quasi-enclaves	378
2.3 Religious free-riders	379
3. Immigrant Religiosity	380
3.1 Self-selection for religiosity	380
3.2 Religiosity and assimilation	380
4. Immigrant Churches	381
5. Religious Observance, Institutions, and Beliefs	383
References	384

1. INTRODUCTION

Each immigrant embodies a portfolio of human capital, a stock that includes both labor market skills and religious human capital. For the sake of simplicity, we shall assume that when an adult immigrant arrives in the destination he or she already identifies with a specific religion, embodies human capital specific to that religion, and does not intend to convert to another religion. By definition, religious human capital raises a consumer's productivity directly only in religious activities, but complementarities between different kinds of human capital can have indirect effects on productivity in non-religious activities, and vice versa. One consequence of this is that an immigrant's religion not only affects his or her perspective on the new country, but is also affected by the major changes comprising the assimilation process.

Although religion affects an immigrant's consumption choices and labor market activities, the very personal nature of spirituality and religious beliefs makes them difficult to measure on an individual level. This cameo looks mainly at religious behaviors that respond to the usual economic incentives—prices, incomes, and institutions—focusing on adaptations of religious practices among immigrants as they adjust to their destination

Handbook of the Economics of International Migration, Volume 1A
ISSN 2212-0092, http://dx.doi.org/10.1016/B978-0-444-53764-5.09982-5

country.[1] Section 2 begins with a concise overview of the definitions and theory of the economics of religion. Section 3 considers how assimilation into the labor market changes full prices and incomes in ways that induce changes in religiosity. Section 4 looks at the effects of economic or labor market assimilation on religious affiliation, especially the phenomenon of the "immigrant church."[2] Section 5 concludes with a brief discussion of the impact of immigrants' labor market assimilation on endogenous religious institutions in the destination.

2. ECONOMICS OF RELIGION

Religion is best thought of as a bundle of three interrelated goods: a self-produced spiritual good, a club good associated with a particular religion, and an investment good associated with belief in an afterlife (Azzi and Ehrenberg, 1975). These distinctions are useful for economic analysis since each of these goods has different economic properties that generate incentives for acquiring different forms of human capital. Affiliating with a specific religion is analogous to joining a club, where the productivity of each consumer's resource inputs depends in part on the resource inputs and productivity of other consumers in the same club (Buchanan, 1965; Iannaccone, 1992). A spiritual experience, the essential quality that distinguishes religion from all other goods, is self-produced with the consumer's own time and purchased inputs within the context of that club. The technology that a consumer uses for this purpose depends on the set of rules, rituals, and beliefs that effectively define the religion with which he or she affiliates. The so-called "afterlife" good is an investment whose benefits are reaped beyond the lifetime of the investor, the nature of which depends on beliefs associated with the religious technology. This may take the literal form of a life beyond the grave, but it may also take more earthly forms like furthering dynastic ambitions, building a legacy for the future, or strengthening the religious community.

Religious affiliation identifies the group to which one belongs, which one can join or leave, and in which one can participate with varying degrees of intensity. This is different from religiosity, the importance of religion in the consumer's market basket (Lehrer, 2009; Chiswick, 2013). Religiosity is independent of any specific religion, each of which

---

[1] Although the economics of religion is a relatively new branch of economics, its literature has grown rapidly in recent decades. It now has its own professional association, the Association for the Study of Religion, Economics and Culture (ASREC; see URL http://www.thearda.com/asrec) and JEL classification code Z12. For reviews of earlier literature in this field, see Iannaccone (1998) and McCleary and Barro (2006). Chiswick (2010a) presented a concise theoretical overview of the economics of religious behavior.

[2] The term "church" is used here generically, as is common in the literature on the economics of religion, to refer to any religious group or establishment. An immigrant church can thus be a synagogue, mosque, temple, or meeting house where immigrants gather for prayer or religious ritual. The term can also refer to their respective religious groups.

provides a technology for achieving spiritual goals. Affiliating with a specific religion involves adopting one of these technologies, and the technology in turn affects the incentives to invest in various forms of religious human capital. Measures of religiosity proxy for spirituality, a self-produced good that typically involves joining a club whose members share the same religious technology.

2.1 Transferability of religious human capital

Religion must be learned, whether formally or informally, a process that results in the formation of religious human capital (Azzi and Ehrenberg, 1975; Neuman, 1986; Iannaccone, 1990; Chiswick, 2006, 2010a; Hollander et al., 2007). Religious human capital can include—but need not be limited to—religious beliefs, knowledge, familiarity with ritual, or convictions about morality. Whether acquired by training or experience, skills or memories, religious human capital augments a person's ability to satisfy basic spiritual needs and/or increase a sense of belonging to a community of spiritual seekers. Religious human capital can be specific to a particular religious technology or transferable between religions, with transferability being greatest among religions with similar technologies for producing the religious good.

For empirical analysis, religions are aggregated into groups that reflect the transferability of religious human capital among their various congregations. The traditional classifications for the United States are Protestant, Catholic, Jewish, and Other, the latter being a catch-all category of small groups that have little else in common (Kosmin and Keysar, 2006). For many purposes, however, these groups are too broad to be useful (Steensland et al., 2000). Recent surveys subdivide the "Protestant" category into Evangelical Protestant, Mainline Protestant, and African-American Protestant (Smith, 1990). Similarly, "Other" is sometimes subdivided to specify Mormon, Orthodox Christian, Moslem, Buddhist, Atheist/Agnostic, or "None" (i.e., people who say they have no religion).[3] Although these distinctions require larger surveys in order to obtain meaningful sample sizes, they increase within-group homogeneity (i.e., transferability of human capital) and improve the analytical power of variables used to study religious affiliation (Lehrer and Chiswick, 1993; Hofrenning and Chiswick, 1999; Beyerlein, 2004; Lehrer, 2004, 2009; Adsera, 2006).

For given spiritual and social (including networking) benefits, the benefit from religious observance, or from switching religions, is affected by complementarities between religious and general human capital (Chiswick, 2006, 2010a; Hollander et al., 2007). For example, religious human capital that develops literary and analytical skills complements a high secular education and would be less attractive to people with low levels of schooling

---

[3] People who self-report "no religion" may nevertheless seek spiritual experience and have a belief system that guides morality. Whether this is considered to be "secularism," "humanism," or simply "no religion," for analytical purposes it is best viewed as a religion in its own right.

(Botticini and Eckstein, 2012). Similarly, a religion that emphasizes the spiritual value of physical labor would be more attractive to people favoring manual occupations. By altering the complementarity properties of secular and religious human capital, the process of secular assimilation affects an immigrant's religious experience and hence the incentive to invest in destination-specific religious skills.

2.2 Religious groups as quasi-enclaves

Considering religion as a sector of the economy, each religious technology is an industry composed of congregations that are firms supplying their members with a religious (i.e., spiritual) experience. The economic good that a religious firm provides is a club good in that the productivity of one's own resources (money and time) depends in part on resources provided by other members of the group. For example, the religious experience obtained by singing hymns is greater when performed in a group where everyone participates eagerly than when sung alone or with people unfamiliar with the words or tune. Similarly, the emotional impact of religious ritual is greater when shared with fellow believers than when performed among skeptics.

Club-good attributes are an incentive to join a community of people who share the same religion; the experience obtained through that affiliation differs according to whether the group is a small minority in the community or a religious majority, especially if the majority religion is favored (explicitly or implicitly) by law and custom. In a pluralistic country, every religious community may be thought of as a quasi-enclave embedded in the larger society, a market for religion-specific goods and services but without the secular characteristics of a conventional ethnic enclave (Chiswick and Miller, 2005). In a country that is less pluralistic, people may face incentives to adopt the religion practiced by their neighbors or by a majority in the community where they work.

Switching religions involves moving (literally or virtually) from one quasi-enclave to another, and thus is analogous to a migration decision. The cost of such a move is lowest between religions with highly transferable human capital and for people with low levels of religiosity. It is greater for people with high levels of origin-specific religious human capital and for destination religions that require more religion-specific investments. If labor market success in the destination involves adopting a new religion, assimilation requires a greater investment than if destination-specific secular human capital complements the human capital of an immigrant's religion (Chiswick, 2009).

The benefits or profitability of immigration can also be affected by religious considerations. For example, consider an origin-country religion that is disadvantaged, perhaps by outright persecution but also perhaps by economic or social handicap or even just by being too small to benefit from economies of scale. Members of such a group face incentives to switch to a less costly religion, but they can also immigrate to a destination country where their old religion can be practiced in a friendlier environment. Religiously motivated immigrants are often thought of as refugees persecuted in the origin country and forming a tight enclave in the destination. Yet religion also may be a factor for economic migrants if the gain from moving is greater in destinations where their religious group is larger, more favored, or less costly to practice for some other reason.

2.3 Religious free-riders

Like any club, religious groups are susceptible to the problem of free-riders, people who allocate few resources of their own but seek to benefit from the inputs of others. High membership fees are a way of discouraging these marginal participants, but religious groups typically place a high value on attracting new members and many are ideologically opposed to charging membership fees. Religions are more likely to require some sort of sacrifice (a sort of non-monetary membership fee) as a means of discouraging free-riders and to stigmatize outsiders and defectors from the group (Iannaccone, 1992). Stigmatizing non-believers merely serves to strengthen the internal coherence of a small group, but for a large religious group it has the potential to influence society and/or exert political power regardless of the degree of official government support.

Countries with an officially sanctioned state religion effectively award monopoly power to one religious producer, privileging it above all others. Enforcement of that monopoly varies from country to country and time to time, the treatment of dissenting religions running the gamut from vigorous persecution to benign neglect. In contrast, separation of church and state results in a *laissez-faire* regime characterized by free entry and exit of religious firms. These firms produce a variety of religious products, compete with each other for members, and devise various combinations of "sacrifice and stigma" to strengthen the commitment of members to the group (Kelley, 1972; Iannaccone, 1992).

Many countries choose an official state religion in the belief that doing so will increase religiosity within the general population. In any industry, however, a monopolist sells less product and at a higher price than would result from competition among producers. In a competitive religious market, consumers choose the product that suits them best and thus have a greater incentive to devote more resources to religious observance (Smith, 1776, Book V, Chapter I, Article 3). In contrast, granting a monopoly to a single religious group has the opposite effect and increases the incidence of free-ridership (Iannaccone, 1991).[4]

---

[4] Some countries recognize more than one official religion, creating a religious oligopoly or something analogous to monopolistic competition. This case is fairly common in parts of Europe and the former Ottoman Empire, but it has yet to attract the attention of economists. Although the literature has many studies comparing monopoly and competition for various religions, the case of multiple state religions has received little attention.

3. IMMIGRANT RELIGIOSITY

An economic migrant arrives in the destination country with the intention of seeking a higher hourly wage rate than he or she could earn in the country of origin, and the immigrant generally remains in the destination if this intention is realized. Even if the money wage is low during the early phases of an immigrant's adjustment, investing in destination-specific human capital raises the value of time and generally makes all other time-intensive activities more costly. Religiosity, and the search for spiritual experiences, becomes more expensive than in the origin country. Spirituality is also a normal good, however, the demand for which increases with the consumer's income *ceteris paribus*. Thus, income and price effects work in opposite directions. An immigrant moving from a low-wage origin to a high-wage destination experiences an increase in the cost of spirituality, and hence a reduction in quantity demanded, but also a rise in income that at least partially offsets this.

3.1 Self-selection for religiosity

Religious discrimination or stigmatization can be a significant motivation to switch religious affiliations. It can also be a motivation to emigrate from a country where religious stigma has a negative effect on economic opportunities. Immigrants may thus be self-selected for religious dissenters, especially minority groups seeking a destination where their religion is preferred or tolerated (or at least practiced by a large group). Other religiously motivated immigrants may have low levels of religiosity, free-riders with minimal attachment to the origin's dominant religion, seeking a destination where secularism is welcomed or where economic opportunity is independent of religious affiliation.

Most immigrants seek a place where they can prosper without giving up their religious beliefs. If their religion was dominant in the origin and a minority in the destination, adjusting to this change in status increases the cost of both migration and religious observance, perhaps even leading to a decline in religiosity. In some cases, however, religious dissenters migrate as a group to practice their religion freely even if it requires forgoing economic opportunities in the destination. If their religion was a dissenting minority in the origin and a dominant group in the destination, incentives associated with economic adjustment may tempt them for the first time to become free-riders in their religious group. Thus, even people whose religious beliefs were a primary motive for migrating may find their religious attachments weakening as they assimilate in the destination.

3.2 Religiosity and assimilation

Each religious technology includes a range of production techniques for combining resources (time and money) to reach spiritual goals. Adherents of a given religion in a high-wage country will find time-intensive religious practices more expensive, and hence less appealing, than adherents of that same religion in a low-wage country. Immigrants from a low-wage origin, arriving in a high-wage destination with religious human capital appropriate for time-intensive observances, will be at a disadvantage in congregations that follow less time-intensive (more goods-intensive) practices with the religious human capital appropriate for that choice. Thus, we can think of immigrants from low- to high-wage countries as having some religious human capital readily transferable to their co-religionists in the destination and some that is specific to their origin country.

If countries differ in their returns to secular human capital, the complementarity properties of religious human capital may also differ (Chiswick, 2006). An immigrant's religious human capital that complements non-transferable origin-country skills loses this benefit in the destination. Other forms of that same religion's human capital may complement the destination-specific secular skills in which the immigrant is investing. Although an immigrant's religiosity may seem to decline with assimilation into the destination labor market, it may just be that his or her religious behavior is changing in response to an altered set of incentives. As the immigrant adjusts to the destination by investing in country-specific secular skills, he or she faces concurrent incentives to invest in new religious human capital, whether in the same religion or a different one. The urgency of investing in destination-specific religious human capital may be mitigated by joining a congregation of immigrants with similar origins, but this merely delays the adjustment process since it does not alter the fundamental price incentive associated with a higher value of time.

4. IMMIGRANT CHURCHES

People who belong to a dominant religious group in their origin country, whether their attachment to that religion is deep or marginal, are motivated to migrate primarily in search of economic opportunity. If their religion is not dominant in the destination, however, they must adjust to their new status as members of a minority religious group. For example, immigrants from Moslem countries, where Islam is not only practiced by nearly everyone but also privileged by the government, can be disoriented by the non-Moslem environment in their European or American destination. European Catholics immigrating to the US at the turn of the twentieth century typically faced a similar situation, their minority status in the US a strong contrast to the deeply rooted church governance in their home countries. Immigrants with high levels of religiosity may turn to each other for reinforcement in this unfamiliar environment. Immigrants with low levels of religiosity in the origin country are now in a smaller religious community where free-riding is observed and discouraged. Thus, even people whose primary motive for migrating was economic may face incentives to alter their religious attachment in the destination.

Few new immigrants arrive in their destination expecting to change their religious affiliation, and they typically focus their time and energy on investments in destination-specific secular human capital. To the extent that their religious human capital does not transfer well to the destination, the practices of their co-religionists in the destination may seem strange or perhaps even irreligious.[5] In such cases, newcomers often form an "immigrant church," a congregation whose members share a similar origin-specific secular culture (including language and social status) as well as a common religion (Warner, 1998).

Immigrants are attracted to such a church not only for religious expression but also because it is a special kind of enclave where some otherwise non-transferable human capital still has value, a "safe haven" in an otherwise confusing world. New arrivals are welcomed by congregants who have recently experienced similar adjustment problems, who offer sympathy, advice, and (sometimes) material assistance. Clergy in the immigrant churches smooth the adjustment process by helping new congregants find housing and friends who speak their language. They also help immigrants acquire useful information about jobs, transportation, shopping, health care or child rearing and destination-specific skills, the most important of which is the new language. Although enclaves can undermine incentives to adapt rapidly to a new country, these kinds of parareligious church activities attract new immigrants precisely because they facilitate the adjustment process (Warner and Wittner, 1998; Chiswick and Miller, 2005). By way of corollary, however, even an active affiliation with an immigrant church need not imply an increase in religiosity on the part of congregants.

As immigrants assimilate into the destination labor force and experience rising wage rates, their optimal religious practices become less time-intensive and they have an incentive to invest in destination-specific religious human capital. Sometimes this means switching to (joining) a destination-country congregation with religious practices compatible with a higher value of time. In other cases the "immigrant church" evolves with its members, moving with them to a new neighborhood and reducing the time-intensity of religious observance (perhaps described as "assimilation" or even "Americanization") but preserving the language and social life of its members' origin culture.

Immigrant churches are thus a transitional phenomenon that rarely outlasts the immigrants themselves. If assimilating immigrants switch to a destination-specific congregation, the immigrant church atrophies from dwindling membership unless it is replenished with new immigrants from the same origin. If the immigrant congregation assimilates along with its members, its distinction rests increasingly on nostalgia rather than differences in religious substance. The children of immigrants find this less compelling and typically join a destination-country congregation when they leave the immigrant

---

[5] This impression is often reinforced by the origin-country religious community and its leaders, with rhetoric complaining of "godlessness" in the destination. This is presumably intended to discourage emigration, but it also serves to make assimilation more difficult (costly) for new immigrants.

neighborhood and establish families of their own. Even those who stay in the immigrant church rarely continue after their parents retire or die.

5. RELIGIOUS OBSERVANCE, INSTITUTIONS, AND BELIEFS

The adherents of any religion are seekers of spiritual satisfaction, a self-produced good that receives benefits from membership in a group of similar producers. People respond to a change in the cost of inputs into this self-production process by moving along an isoquant determined by the technology associated with their particular religion. They respond to a change in income by moving to a new isoquant of the relevant production function. That is, they respond to new economic incentives by modifying their religious production techniques (observances and practices) rather than their religious technology (theology and beliefs).

For most immigrants, the act of immigration *ipso facto* involves an increase in wage rates, if not immediately then after a brief period of adjustment to conditions in the destination. Time-intensive self-produced goods, including religious observance, are thus more costly in the destination than they were in the origin, and their cost continues to rise over time as the immigrant assimilates into the destination labor force. This induces changes in religious observance towards less time-intensive practices. It also raises the returns to destination-specific religious human capital, partly in response to changes in religious observance and partly because of complementarity with the immigrant's new destination-specific non-religious human capital. Even if income effects raise an immigrant's demand for the religious good, price changes transform the way in which this is achieved.

The institutional context of religious life in the destination country affects the immigrant's religious experience. Some immigrants belonged to a minority religion in the origin country, perhaps even a dissenting religion, and move to a country that is more hospitable to its practice. Those whose religion was practiced by a majority in the origin country, perhaps even sanctioned as an official state religion, may find themselves in a destination where they constitute a minority. This raises the cost—both economic and emotional—of adjustment to the destination, even more so if they also experience host-country discrimination. Joining an immigrant church can offset some of these costs and speed up the adjustment process, but it does not change its basic nature.

The shift towards less time-intensive religious practices does not *ipso facto* affect the basic technology associated with an immigrant's religion even though he or she may appear "less religious" by origin-country standards. Sometimes, however, it can lead to more profound changes. Nobody practices their religion to perfection; people tend to distinguish between "basic" strictures that must be followed and peripheral rules that can be downplayed or even ignored. People tend not to question religious teachings that are inexpensive to follow, but they are more likely to downgrade the importance of teachings that are expensive. A time-intensive practice that is central in a low-wage origin country may be viewed as optional in a high-wage destination. As members distance themselves from these teachings, whether by non-observance or by switching religions, the church itself faces an incentive to modify its position. Such economically induced changes are often the essential difference between the immigrant church and its destination counterpart.

Nowhere is this process more evident than in changing ideas about sex, marriage, and gender roles—changes in "family values" that are often contested by religious traditionalists. In the twentieth century, for example, Catholic immigrants to the US found the religious ruling against contraception increasingly costly as they assimilated into the high-wage American labor market and by the third generation had largely stopped viewing this belief as a core religious value. Similarly, the combination of small family size and similar educational attainment for men and women, persisting over several generations among the children and grandchildren of immigrants to the US, provide experiences that undermine the doctrines of some religions regarding male–female differences in spiritual capabilities and gender-based religious roles (Chiswick, 2010b). Religious theologies that impose barriers based on gender or sexual preference are increasingly costly for adherents to follow. Immigrant churches that insist on the importance of such old-country "family values" invariably lose members to their co-religionist congregations as the immigrants assimilate into the destination country's economic mainstream.

REFERENCES

Adsera, A., 2006. Marital fertility and religion in Spain, 1985 and 1999. Population Studies: A Journal of Demograhy 60 (2), 205–221.

Association for the Study of Religion, Economics and Culture (ASREC). URL: <http://www.thearda.com/asrec>.

Azzi, C., Ehrenberg, R., 1975. Household allocation of time and church attendance. J. Polit. Econ. 83 (1), 27–56.

Beyerlein, K., 2004. Specifying the impact of conservative protestantism on educational attainment. J. Sci. Stud. Relig. 43, 505–518.

Botticini, M., Eckstein, Z., 2012. The Chosen Few: How Education Shaped Jewish History, 70–1492. Princeton University Press, Princeton, NJ.

Buchanan, J.M., 1965. An economic theory of clubs. Economica 32 (125), 1–14.

Chiswick, B.R., Miller, P.W., 2005. Do enclaves matter in immigrant adjustment? City and Community 4 (1), 5–35.

Chiswick, C.U., 2006. An economic perspective on religious education: Complements and substitutes in a human-capital portfolio. Res. Labor Econ. 24, 429–467.

Chiswick, C.U., 2009. The economic determinants of ethnic assimilation. J. Popul. Econ. 22, 859–880.

Chiswick, C.U., 2010a. Economics and religion. In: Free, R. (Ed.), 21st Century Economics: A Reference Handbook. Sage, New York, pp. 777–783, Chapter 76.

Chiswick, C.U., 2010b. Egalitarian religion and economics. The Lighthouse Economic Review 1:1. URL: http://egalitarianreligionandeconomics.blogspot.com>.

Chiswick, C.U., 2013. Economics of Religion: Lessons Learned. Keynote Address to the Association for the Study of Religion, Economics and Culture (ASREC) 12th Annual Conference, Washington, DC.

Hofrenning, S.K., Chiswick, B.R., 1999. A method for proxying a respondent's religious background: An application to school choice decisions. J. Hum. Resour. 34 (1), 193–207.

Hollander, G., Kahana, N., Lecker, T., 2007. Human capital and the economics of religion. In: Chiswick, C., Lecker, T., Kahana, N. (Eds.), Jewish Society and Culture: An Economic Perspective. Bar-Ilan University Press, Ramat Gan, pp. 87–102.

Iannaccone, L.R., 1990. Religious participation: A human capital approach. J. Sci. Stud. Relig. 29 (3), 297–314.

Iannaccone, L.R., 1991. The consequences of religious market regulation: Adam Smith and the economics of religion. Rationality and Society 3, 156–177.

Iannaccone, L.R., 1992. Sacrifice and stigma: Reducing free-riding in cults, communes, and other collectives. J. Polit. Econ. 100 (2), 271–292.

Iannaccone, L.R., 1998. Introduction to the economics of religion. J. Econ. Lit. 36, 1465–1496.

Kelley, D.M., 1972. Why Conservative Churches Are Growing: A Study in Sociology of Religion. Harper & Row, New York.

Kosmin, B.R., Keysar, A., 2006. Religion in a Free Market: Religious and Non-Religious Americans, Who/What/Why/Where. Paramount Market Publishing, Ithaca, NY.

Lehrer, E.L., 2004. Religion as a determinant of economic and demographic behavior in the United States. Popul. Dev. Rev. 30, 707–726.

Lehrer, E.L., 2009. Religion, Economics, and Demography: The Effects of Religion on Education, Work, and the Family. Routledge, New York.

Lehrer, E.L., Chiswick, C.U., 1993. Religion as a determinant of marital stability. Demography 30 (3), 385–404.

McCleary, R.M., Barro, R.J., 2006. Religion and economy. J. Econ. Perspect. 20, 49–72.

Neuman, S., 1986. Religious observance within a human capital framework: Theory and application. Appl. Econ. 18 (11), 1193–1202.

Smith, A., 1776. The Wealth of Nations. Modern Library, New York, 1937.

Smith, T.W., 1990. Classifying Protestant denominations. Rev. Relig. Res. 31, 225–245.

Steensland, B., Park, J.Z., Regnerus, M.D., Robinson, L.D., Wilcox, W.B., Woodberry, R.D., 2000. The measure of American religion: Toward improving the state of the art. Soc. Forces 79 (1), 1–28.

Warner, R.S., 1998. Immigration and religious communities in the United States. In: Warner, R.S., Wittner, J.G. (Eds.), Gatherings in Diaspora: Religious Communities and the New Immigration. Temple University Press, Philadelphia, pp. 3–34.

Warner, R.S., Wittner, J.G. (Eds.), 1998. Gatherings in Diaspora: Religious Communities and the New Immigration. Temple University Press, Philadelphia.

CHAPTER 8

Immigrants' Access to Financial Services and Asset Accumulation*

Nour Abdul-Razzak**, Una Okonkwo Osili[†], Anna L. Paulson[‡]
**University of Chicago
[†]Indiana University-Purdue University at Indianapolis
[‡]Federal Reserve Bank of Chicago

Contents

1. Introduction	387
2. Conceptual Framework	391
3. Data, Summary Statistics, and Empirical Specification	394
3.1 Data	394
3.2 Summary statistics: wealth and financial market participation	395
3.3 Summary statistics: differences in characteristics	400
3.4 Estimating financial market participation	402
4. Characteristics, Immigrant Status, and Financial Market Participation	404
4.1 Estimates of the impact of characteristics on financial market participation and durable goods acquisition	404
4.2 Estimates of the impact of being an immigrant on financial market participation	409
5. Immigrant Adaptation	412
5.1 Legal status	418
6. Potential Explanations	419
6.1 Housing and financial market participation	420
6.2 Country-of-origin characteristics	421
6.3 Ethnic concentration	422
6.4 Remittances, return migration intentions, wealth held abroad	424
6.5 Supply-side factors: location and design of financial institution and products	426
7. Cross-Country Comparisons	427
8. Summary of Findings and Policy Priorities	434
8.1 Key findings	434
8.2 Policy priorities	435
Appendix	436
References	439

---

* The views presented here are our own and not necessarily those of the Federal Reserve Bank of Chicago. Correspondence to: Anna Paulson, Federal Reserve Bank of Chicago, 230 S. LaSalle Street, Chicago, IL 60604, USA (anna.paulson@chi.frb.org).

Handbook of the Economics of International Migration, Volume 1A
ISSN 2212-0092, http://dx.doi.org/10.1016/B978-0-444-53764-5.00008-6

1. INTRODUCTION

A central question facing researchers and policymakers is the extent to which immigrants will adapt to economic and social life in their destination communities. Given that more than 215 million people around the world live outside their country of birth, international migration is increasingly shaping global economic and demographic trends.

Economists and other social scientists have studied the economic progress of immigrants, but their focus has largely been on wages and occupational mobility. However, recent studies of immigrant socio-economic progress in a number of host countries have expanded to include financial market participation and home ownership as key yardsticks of economic and social mobility, along with wages and income (Amuedo-Dorantes and Pozo, 2002; Borjas, 2002; Cobb-Clark and Hildebrand, 2006; Wang, 2012).

Although much of the existing research remains focused on traditional immigrant destination countries such as the United States, Russia, Germany, Saudi Arabia, and Canada, newer destination countries, including Italy, Spain, and Portugal, provide rich sources of cross-country variation (Matha et al., 2001; Shamsuddin and DeVoretz, 1998).

An important contribution of this new body of research is that it draws on the role of immigrants' tastes, preferences, return migration plans, and cultural and economic backgrounds, as well as on the role destination communities of immigrants play in patterns of financial market behavior. Moreover, much of this literature takes into account that immigrants are not randomly drawn from their countries of origin, but instead may selectively choose to migrate to a specific host country environment (Borjas, 1987; McKenzie and Yang, 2012).

In this chapter, we establish stylized facts about immigrant financial participation and asset accumulation, a critical and largely understudied dimension of economic progress. Financial market participation is an important component of socio-economic status, and has implications for households' ability to self-insure against shocks, self-employment, retirement, and intergenerational mobility (Chiteji and Stafford, 1999; Edin, 2001; Shamsuddin and DeVortez, 1998). Importantly, accumulation of financial assets along with, housing, and other durable goods has the potential to influence the pace of social adaptation.

By studying financial market participation, along with housing and durable goods accumulation, we gain important insights into how immigrants adapt to host societies. Do immigrants participate in mainstream financial institutions in numbers that reflect their demographic presence or do they rely on alternative financial services such as payday loans, check cashing, and pawn shops? Are there immigrant–native gaps in the acquisition of durable goods? Do immigrants accumulate housing, financial assets, and other durable goods in their home country? The goal of our analysis in this chapter is to provide a foundation for future research into issues of immigrant financial adaptation.

In previous research, we have found that immigrants are less likely to be connected to the financial mainstream compared to the native-born (Osili and Paulson, 2008,

2010). The empirical work in this chapter focuses on key indicators of financial market participation: ownership of savings and interest-bearing checking accounts.[1] We emphasize savings and checking account ownership because these represent entry-level financial assets with relatively low barriers to participation. However, we also examine forward-looking assets such as stock ownership and individual retirement accounts (IRA) or Keogh and mutual fund ownership, although mean ownership rates tend to be lower for these indicators of financial market participation. For example, in the US, while 68% of native-born household heads had a checking account in 2008 SIPP, only 55% of immigrant household heads had a checking account. This pattern is repeated for stock ownership, and individual retirement account ownership, with the gap between immigrant and native-born increasing with the sophistication of the financial product. In particular, while 23% of the native-born owned stock outside a retirement account, only 11% of immigrants owned stock.

We compare gaps in financial market participation, with immigrant–native gaps in home ownership and ownership of durable goods, which have received some attention in the literature. In general, for the majority of durable goods, immigrant–native gaps in ownership tend to be relatively small as the majority of both native and immigrant households own a vehicle and a computer. However, for home ownership, we find that only 53% of immigrants owned a home in 2008 compared with 69% of native-born.

An important question is how immigrant–native gaps in financial market participation differ across destination countries. A handful of recent studies have examined gaps in financial market participation in Italy, Germany, Luxembourg, France, the UK, Australia, and Europe as a whole (Algan et al., 2010; Bauer et al., 2011; Cobb-Clark and Hildebrand, 2009; Dustmann and Frattini, 2011; Matha et al., 2011; Shamsuddin and DeVoretz, 1998).

In this chapter, we highlight the gaps in immigrant financial behavior using recently available data from the US, which accounts for nearly 20% of all international migrants, and Italy, which has only recently become an important destination for immigrants. We examine three classes of variables that influence immigrants' financial market behavior and their accumulation of durable goods.

First, immigrants' decisions to participate in various financial markets may be explained by characteristics like education, marital status, and the presence of children that influence the behavior of both immigrants and the native-born, as well as by characteristics that are unique to immigrants, such as legal status and time in the host country, language proficiency, and the tendency to cluster in neighborhoods with immigrants from the same home country.

---

[1] We focus our attention on interest-bearing checking accounts because information on ownership of non-interest-bearing checking accounts is available less frequently in the SIPP (approximately once a year). We obtain similar results when we combine both interest- and non-interest-bearing checking accounts (see Figure 8.1).

Second, country-of-origin factors are likely to be important in understanding financial market decisions. Immigrants bring experiences and perspectives acquired in their home country and maintain a wide range of economic and social ties to their home country. For example, immigrants may send remittances to their families at home, affecting the rate and pace of their financial market participation in the host country. Research suggests that immigrants may accumulate assets in the country of origin for portfolio diversification motives, because they intend to return home at some point, or because they are more familiar with investment options in the home country (Coval and Moskowitz, 1999; Dustmann and Kirchkamp, 2002; Dustmann and Mestres, 2010; Mesnard, 2004; Osili and Paulson, 2012; Woodruff and Zenteno, 2001). Researchers have also exploited variation in host country and home country environments. Dustmann and Mestres (2010) showed that that nearly half (46%) of all immigrants in Germany send remittances to family members in the country of origin. However, permanent and temporary migrants behave differently—more than half of the temporary migrants send remittances, while only about one-quarter of permanent migrants do—implying that return migration plans may influence financial behavior.

There are relatively few data sources that allow researchers to study the extent to which migrants maintain economic ties and accumulate assets in both their host and home countries. In this chapter, we rely on US data from the New Immigrant Survey (NIS-2003-1), a nationally representative multi-cohort longitudinal study of new legal immigrants and their children to the US. The data indicate that approximately 17% of immigrants send remittances to family members in their country of origin. We also find that a small portion of these immigrants participate in financial markets in their home countries, with about 17% of the immigrants holding some wealth abroad. In addition, we find that about 45% of these immigrants own a checking or savings account in the US. In general, we do not find any evidence for the hypothesis that owning financial assets in an immigrant's country of origin substitutes for host country financial participation. Instead, we find that similar factors influence financial participation in both origin and host countries.

Taken together we find that country-of-origin experiences prior to migration can also help explain differences in financial market participation for immigrants relative to the native-born. Exposure to a weak institutional environment and banking crises in the country of origin is associated with lower financial market participation in the US (Carroll et al., 1994). This factor is reinforced for immigrants who live in neighborhoods with many other immigrants from the same country. It is likely that ethnic networks can play a role in providing alternatives to mainstream financial products. Data limitations prevent us from examining this hypothesis directly.

The third broad class of variables that we examine is the role of destination communities and host country institutions in shaping immigrant financial market participation and asset accumulation. To study the role of institutional settings, we compare immigrants in the US and Italy. While the US is a traditional destination country, Italy has only recently received large inflows of immigrants after a long tradition as a sending country.

It is important to recognize that immigrants' financial choices, as well as their patterns of housing and durable goods acquisition, are likely destination community attributes such as the relative attractiveness of mainstream financial institutions and the alternative financial services sector, based on criteria such as cost, anonymity, documentation requirements, minimum balance requirements, and convenience.

Consistent with models of savings behavior, we find that socio-economic and demographic characteristics like age, education, family structure, ethnicity, and income play an important role in immigrant and native-born choices of financial services. However, these characteristics are only part of the story.

While there is some evidence that immigrants are as likely as otherwise similar native-born individuals to own a checking account or a home if they have spent enough time in the US, adaptation is less complete for forward-looking financial products, such as savings accounts, IRA/Keogh accounts, and stock and mutual funds. We also find that gaps in ownership between native-born and foreign-born persist in durable asset ownership for goods like household appliances and computers, even with time in destination communities.

The rest of the chapter is organized as follows. In the next section, we present the conceptual framework. We then discuss the data sources used in this chapter, while also comparing wealth and financial market participation of immigrants and the native-born across various racial and ethnic groups, and describe our estimation procedures. In Section 4, we discuss regression estimates of the probability of owning assets of varying complexity, including checking accounts, savings accounts, IRA/Keogh accounts, stock or mutual funds, housing, cars, household durable goods, and computers. This analysis allows us to quantify the effect of characteristics on financial market participation and durable good acquisition, and estimate the gap in participation between immigrants and the native-born after characteristics are controlled for. In Section 5, we examine how various measures of adaptation to the US impact the financial behavior of immigrants relative to the native-born. In Section 6, we consider potential explanations for the persistence of the gap in financial market participation and durable good acquisition, including household characteristics, country-of-origin factors, ethnic concentration, remittances, and wealth held abroad, return migration intentions, and supply-side factors. Section 7 presents a cross-country comparison with Italy. Finally, Section 8 offers conclusions and a discussion of policy priorities based on our findings.

2. CONCEPTUAL FRAMEWORK

Households, whether immigrant or native-born, generally plan their financial strategies over a lifetime rather than over a single short period. The seminal work of Merton (1971) introduced a conceptual framework for considering financial decisions given time-varying investment opportunities. Households may select a portfolio from a wide range of assets by comparing returns, transaction costs, risk profiles, and liquidity in order to smooth consumption over time.[2] This approach suggests that differences in financial market participation between immigrants and the native-born may be driven (at least in part) by differences in household income, education, age, and family structure. The decision to hold a particular asset will also depend on information, tastes, and preferences, which may differ across otherwise similar immigrants and natives.

The literature on portfolio choice emphasizes the importance of fixed transaction costs and risk aversion in explaining financial choices. We recognize that it may be important to account for additional sources of immigrant–native differences, including household characteristics such as race and ethnicity, legal status, language skills, years of experience in the host country, and patterns of residential settlement, which are likely to affect financial decisions (Amuedo-Dorantes and Bansak, 2006; Cobb-Clark and Hildebrand, 2006).

Finally, research suggests that immigrants, largely due to their economic and social ties to the home country, face different incentives than the native-born population (Dustmann, 1994, 1996; Galor and Stark, 1990). In Galor and Stark's (1990) model, migrants work in the host country in the first period and face an uncertain wage regime in the second period. If they return home in the second period, they earn a lower wage in the home country. They find that immigrants have a greater incentive to save than the native-born population, in order to smooth consumption across these high- and low-wage regimes. Thus, it is likely that the level and composition of immigrants' wealth is linked to the probability of return migration to the country of origin, holding other variables constant. The expected returns and costs of asset ownership may also differ across locations.

An important starting point in understanding immigrant–native differences in financial market behavior is to examine differences in wealth and income. In the US and other host countries a growing number of studies find significant immigrant–native gaps in wealth that exceed income differences (Amuedo-Dorantes and Pozo, 2002; Borjas, 1985; Cobb-Clark and Hildebrand, 2006). In a study of wealth of Mexican Americans, Cobb-Clark and Hildebrand (2006) found that racial and ethnic differences in wealth levels are much larger than the corresponding differences in income levels. Their results suggest that much of the wealth gaps for Mexican American households can be attributed to differences in household characteristics, including age of household head and household size. Recent studies have focused on immigrant–native wealth gaps in European countries. Bauer et al. (2011) found significant immigrant–native wealth gaps using evidence from the US, Germany, and Australia. Matha et al. (2011) examined immigrant–native gaps in Italy, Germany, and Luxembourg using comparable data on household wealth holdings and asset ownership. Their findings suggest that immigrant households

---

[2] There are additional motives for savings and wealth accumulation, which include precautionary motives and the desire to leave bequests.

have lower home ownership rates than native-born households. They find considerable cross-country variation in financial asset participation rates, with relatively low immigrant–native gaps in financial asset ownership in Italy, compared with Germany and Luxembourg.

Thus, the gap between immigrants and the native-born in financial market participation can be explained, at least in part, by differences in wealth. Some research on low rates of financial market participation highlights the role of market frictions, mostly in the form of high fixed-entry and/or transaction costs (Bertaut and Starr-McCluer, 2000; Vissing-Jorgensen, 2002), and the role of information networks (Hong et al., 2004). These factors may help explain the large gap in financial market participation that we observe between immigrants and the native-born.

This analysis focuses on financial market participation and asset accumulation. By emphasizing financial market participation and ownership patterns rather than on levels of wealth, we exploit some empirical advantages. Researchers have noted concerns with measurement error and non-response in reported wealth holdings (see Smith, 1995, for example). Survey respondents are more likely to refuse to answer questions about levels of financial wealth than questions about financial market participation. Estimates of financial market participation rely much less on imputed responses relative to information on levels of financial asset holdings.[3]

We also extend our analysis to examine the gaps in ownership of housing and other durable goods. Relatively few studies have investigated immigrant–native differences in housing and the ownership of durable goods. In addition to contributing to net wealth, durable goods such as cars or computers, for example, can improve employment opportunities (Blumenberg and Smart, 2011). Immigrants may use their vehicles as a means of generating income directly as well, particularly where they are self-employed (Fairlie and Meyer, 1996; Newberger, 2007). Many immigrants incorporate vehicles in self employment activity by driving food trucks or cabs as these occupations have low barriers to entry (Blumenberg and Smart, 2011). It has been shown that foreign-born adults with cars are more likely to be employed compared to their counterparts without cars, even in cities with public transportation options. Studies in the Netherlands and Germany show similar patterns, although vehicle ownership rates and use often vary by ethnic background (Harms, 2007; Kasper et al., 2007).

Aside from the direct benefits of home and car ownership, the accumulation of household durable goods can have welfare implications. Specifically, household durable goods, such as washing machines and dishwashers, can provide increased efficiency in the home and free up more time for work and/or leisure (Edin, 2001).

---

[3] Smith (1995) documents item non-response rates for financial market participation of less than 2% in the SIPP. Non-response rates for levels of financial asset holdings are much higher, ranging from 13.3% for checking accounts to 41.5% for stock.

A home computer provides easy access to information that may increase the rate and pace of immigrants' social and economic adaptation.[4] Among the handful of studies that have looked at the direct impact of computers on immigrant adaptation, Chiswick and Miller (2007) found some positive potential impact. Using data from the 2001 Census of Population and Housing in Australia, they found that using a computer at home is associated with 7% and 13% higher earnings for native-born and foreign-born men respectively. For the immigrants, the effects of schooling and English language proficiency on earnings are greater among those that use a computer at home. These results suggest that using a computer can increase the transferability of immigrants' skills to their host country.

3. DATA, SUMMARY STATISTICS, AND EMPIRICAL SPECIFICATION

3.1 Data

The empirical analysis draws on US data, given the importance of the US as a destination country. The analysis mainly relies on recent data from the 2008 Survey on Income and Program Participation (SIPP). The 2001 SIPP panel is also used to provide information on trends over time. The 2008 SIPP is a nationally representative random sample of US households, which is unique in providing detailed information about both the immigration experience and wealth and financial market holdings. Data were collected in 12 quarterly waves from 2008 to 2012. We use immigration information that was collected in wave 2, together with socio-economic and demographic information from the core module in wave 7, and wealth and financial market participation information from the first assets and liabilities module in wave 7 to create a single cross-section of the data for analysis. Further variables relating to durable asset ownership were collected from wave 6. We restrict the sample to households with a reference person who is at least 18 years old and lives in a metropolitan statistical area (MSA) for a total sample of 24,056, of whom about 15% or 3612 households were born abroad. A reference person is considered an immigrant if his or her country of birth is outside the US. All of the analysis makes use of sampling weights to ensure that the data are representative of the US population.

The SIPP data include an unknown number of undocumented immigrants. While the survey procedures themselves do not deliberately screen out undocumented immigrants, it is likely that these individuals are less likely to be willing to participate in the survey. As a potentially useful benchmark, the Department of Homeland Security estimates that about 11.5 million unauthorized immigrants were living in the US in January 2011 (Baker et al., 2012).

---

[4] Malamud and Pop-Eleches (2011) found that the effects of computer home ownership on children were mixed by looking at a government program in Romania that allocated vouchers for the purchase of a computer for low-income families. Although having a computer led to lower school grades in math, English and Romanian, students had higher scores in a test of computer skills and computer fluency.

3.2 Summary statistics: wealth and financial market participation

We begin with an overview of some stylized facts and focus on ownership of the following assets: checking accounts, savings accounts, and IRA/Keogh, stocks/mutual funds. We compare financial asset ownership with the ownership of a home, a car (either one or multiple cars or either direct ownership or through a car loan), durable goods, and computers. The median family with a US-born head has more than five times the total wealth and nearly nine times the financial wealth of the median family with a foreign-born head (see Table 8.1). When we examine the components of financial wealth separately, however, a different picture of the immigrant–native wealth gap emerges. If we restrict our attention to immigrants and natives who own a particular asset, the difference in the amount of wealth held in that asset is much smaller than the difference in total wealth. For example, among households who own an interest-bearing account at a bank, immigrants have a median balance of $580, roughly 44% of that of the median native-born family (see Table 8.1). The value of the median non-interest-bearing account for immigrants is 60% that of the native-born. For stocks, mutual funds, homes, and cars, the immigrant values are 70% or more of that of native-born households. These findings are consistent with recent studies that document that immigrants have substantially lower wealth levels than the native-born, but conditional on holding a given asset, immigrant–native wealth differences are relatively small (Amuendo-Dorantes and Pozo, 2002; Cobb-Clark and Hildebrand, 2006; Hao, 2004; Krivo and Kauffman, 2004; Matha et al., 2011).

Why is the gap between immigrants and the native-born so much larger when we look at total wealth versus its components? One important answer seems to lie in financial market participation. Figure 8.1 presents non-parametric regressions of the likelihood of owning various financial assets for immigrants and the native-born as a function of age.[5] These estimates show that immigrants of all ages are less likely to participate in a wide range of financial markets than the native-born. This pattern is reinforced by the data on financial market participation presented in Table 8.1. While 60% of native-born households have a savings account, only 47% of immigrant households do. Sixty-eight percent of native-born households have a checking account, compared with 55% of immigrant households. Overall, 80% of native-born households have either a savings or a checking account, compared with just 69% of immigrant households.[6] When we

---

[5] For each observation in Figure 8.1, a weighted regression is performed using 80% (bandwidth = 0.8) of the data around that point. The data are weighted using a tri-cube weighting procedure that puts more weight on the points close to the observation in question. The weighted regression results are used to produce a predicted value for each observation.

[6] These figures are lower than similar figures from the 2001 Survey of Consumer Finances (SCF), which reports that 91% of all households have a transaction account. There are two main differences between the SCF and the SIPP data that are likely to account for this discrepancy. First, the SCF over-samples wealthy households and, second, the SCF includes accounts that are likely to be held by wealthy individuals in its definition of transaction accounts (money market mutual funds and call accounts at brokerage firms, for example). In addition, even when sampling weights are used the SIPP under-represents high-income families. See Social Security Bulletin 65 (1), May 2004 for more details.

Table 8.1 Income and wealth of immigrant and native-born households

	All		<40% of income		Whites		Blacks		Hispanics		Asians	
	Native	Imm.	Native	Imm.	Native	Imm.	Native	Imm.	Native	Imm.	Native	Imm.
Income and wealth (in thousands of $)												
Median monthly HH income	1.91	1.30	0.96	0.67	2.08	1.77	1.27	1.35	1.27	0.90	2.10	1.76
Median HH wealth	43.96	8.65	11.41	1.73	64.22	40.78	4.50	5.10	6.50	2.62	69.26	34.20
Median financial wealth	1.75	0.20	0.10	0.00	4.00	1.40	0.03	0.10	0.17	0.01	6.47	1.50
Mean monthly HH income	2.55	2.02	1.06	0.80	2.76	2.71	1.84	1.93	1.76	1.28	3.54	2.68
Mean HH wealth	124.29	71.51	81.84	41.65	147.46	131.09	43.36	35.42	47.08	29.23	154.29	97.37
% who own												
Interest earning assets at banks	72%	58%	55%	43%	78%	69%	51%	58%	57%	43%	81%	72%
Non-interest-bearing checking	25%	26%	24%	23%	25%	25%	21%	21%	27%	27%	23%	30%
IRA or KEOGH accounts	36%	19%	20%	7%	43%	31%	14%	15%	18%	7%	44%	30%
Stock and/or mutual funds	23%	11%	11%	3%	28%	17%	7%	9%	8%	2%	27%	22%
Home	69%	53%	50%	37%	75%	64%	46%	45%	50%	46%	64%	59%
Savings and/or checking	80%	69%	66%	56%	84%	79%	61%	67%	69%	56%	85%	82%
Savings account only	60%	47%	42%	32%	64%	55%	44%	48%	49%	34%	68%	61%
Interest-bearing checking	48%	33%	33%	21%	53%	46%	29%	33%	32%	19%	52%	45%
Any checking account	68%	55%	54%	42%	73%	65%	48%	52%	55%	43%	69%	68%
Have a car	85%	76%	72%	64%	88%	77%	69%	71%	75%	75%	80%	81%
Have multiple cars	49%	41%	23%	22%	53%	41%	30%	29%	43%	41%	44%	48%
Own a car	81%	82%	84%	85%	83%	83%	76%	72%	75%	83%	91%	84%
Own multiple cars	55%	57%	68%	71%	57%	59%	49%	61%	42%	55%	58%	59%
Have a loan on car	37%	35%	24%	24%	36%	32%	39%	36%	47%	36%	27%	33%
Have multiple car loans	13%	12%	6%	3%	12%	11%	14%	19%	20%	11%	9%	11%
Household durable goods	68%	51%	49%	35%	74%	65%	47%	42%	48%	39%	69%	63%
Computer	79%	70%	61%	53%	82%	78%	65%	70%	70%	58%	91%	82%
Any asset	95%	91%	89%	84%	98%	94%	84%	89%	89%	88%	97%	96%

Median wealth, conditional on ownership (in thousands of $)

Interest earning assets at banks	1.30	0.58	0.50	0.20	1.80	1.20	0.31	0.45	0.33	0.19	2.00	1.49
Non-interest-bearing checking	0.33	0.20	0.20	0.10	0.42	0.50	0.17	0.25	0.7	0.12	0.50	0.38
IRA or KEOGH accounts	12.13	7.00	10.00	6.85	13.33	12.30	4.00	5.40	5.50	2.40	20.00	7.00
Stock and/or mutual funds	8.90	6.57	8.50	5.00	9.50	10.17	3.71	9.27	5.00	0.60	20.00	5.00
Home	40.00	29.20	50.00	24.00	43.75	45.00	25.00	15.00	17.50	12.50	60.00	40.75
First car value	3.28	2.31	2.59	1.80	3.43	2.84	2.34	2.66	2.31	1.71	3.40	2.93
All assets	32.51	8.76	14.04	3.02	43.78	31.99	7.46	5.40	6.03	3.43	44.84	22.10
Number of observations	20,444	3512	8026	1603	15,647	1109	2910	360	1728	1300	200	762

Sample is restricted to wave 7 of the 2008–present Survey of Income and Program Participation households with a reference person who is at least 18 years old, lives in an MSA, and has a non-missing value for immigrant status. Data are weighted to reflect the US population. All income and wealth figures are household per capita figures and reported in thousands of dollars.

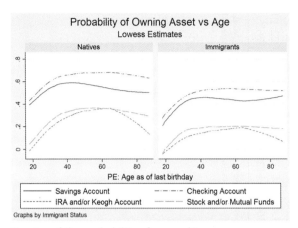

Figure 8.1 *Lowess estimates of the probability of ownership.*

look at riskier assets that tend to be associated with higher returns, the difference between immigrants and the native-born is larger. For example, twice as many (36%) native-born households have an IRA or Keogh account than do immigrant households. Similarly, while 23% of native-born households own stock or a mutual fund, the figure for immigrant households is just 11%.[7]

We note relatively high rates of home ownership for US households, although the households were surveyed after the 2008 housing crisis. Sixty-nine percent of native-born households own a home, compared with 53% of immigrants. Borjas (2002) found that there are two variables that play a key role in determining differences in home ownership rates between immigrants and natives: the national origin of immigrants and the residential location choices made by immigrant households. He also noted that the gap between home ownership rates of immigrants and natives had widened between 1980 and 2000 from 12 to 20 percentage points. Looking at 2008 SIPP data, we see that this gap is similar to patterns observed in 1990 (Borjas, 2002). One potential explanation presented in Borjas (2002) is that the growth of ethnic enclaves in major American cities impacted home ownership patterns.

Based on the rich data on patterns of durable good ownership in the SIPP, we find larger immigrant–native gaps in ownership of household durable goods than for cars and computers. We find that 68% of natives, compared with 51% of immigrants, own the basic household appliances: a washing machine, clothing dryer, a dishwasher, a refrigerator, a stove, and a microwave. When we focus on households that own their homes, we

---

[7] Another way for households to manage risk is through life insurance. We looked at this briefly and found largely the same patterns of ownership among natives and immigrants relative to other financial assets. Among natives, about 56% have life insurance (either through an employer or another means), while 30% of immigrants have life insurance.

find that 70% of immigrants who own homes also own these household appliances compared to 79% of their native-born counterparts who own homes.

When we examine car ownership patterns, we find some interesting results. About 76% of immigrants own a car, compared with 85% of natives. When we take into account the role of financing of vehicles, some striking patterns emerge. Specifically, immigrants who own a car are slightly more likely to own their car outright than natives. Immigrants are also less likely to have a car loan than natives. One possible explanation is that immigrants may face some barriers in access to loans and other forms of credit. As a result, immigrants tend to be an important consumer group for used cars (Newberger et al., 2004). In our sample, we do find that the median car for immigrants is slightly older, 2004, than for natives, 2005. Furthermore, immigrants tend to live in larger households than natives, and have fewer cars per household—1.76 cars for immigrant households versus 1.82 for natives, on average.

The 2008 SIPP data show that 77% of US households own a computer at home— 79% of natives have a computer, compared with 70% of immigrants. Owning a computer with Internet access is important for the pace of immigrant adaptation. However, we are not able to determine Internet access through SIPP. Based on 2010 Census figures, 75.9% of US adults live in a household with Internet access (Census 2010 Tables). Among those who have Internet access, 11.4% use it to take a course online, 35.5% use it for health care information, 33.2% use it to search for government services, and 24.8% use it to search for a job.

To examine trends over time and establish the robustness of the findings above, we have also analyzed the SIPP 2004 panel using most of the variables from wave 6 (2005). In general, the main findings are fairly similar over time, especially regarding financial asset ownership. However, rates of ownership for durable goods (computer ownership and household durables) have generally been increasing over time for US households. We also found a slight decrease in home ownership rates for both immigrant and native households between 2004 and 2008, which is likely due to the impact of the 2008 financial crisis.

In general, comparing immigrants with their native-born counterparts may obscure important differences by racial, ethnic, and income subgroups. When we divide the sample into groups based on income and ethnicity (Table 8.1), we observe that financial market participation varies substantially depending on the subgroup examined. Table 8.1 presents results for households below the 40th percentile of income, for whites, blacks, Hispanics, and Asians. In general, white and Asian immigrants and natives have relatively high rates of asset ownership and Hispanic immigrants and natives have low rates of ownership. However, the gap in financial market participation between the native-born and immigrant households is generally fairly similar across subgroups, with immigrants having lower rates of participation compared to their native-born counterparts.

One notable exception to this pattern is found among black households. Black immigrant households are *slightly more* likely to participate in many financial markets compared to their native-born counterparts. Sixty-seven percent of black immigrant households have a savings or checking account, compared with 61% of black native-born households. However, the reduced gap appears primarily to reflect low financial market participation among native-born black households rather than particularly high asset ownership among black immigrants. We note that black immigrants also differ significantly from native-born blacks in characteristics such as educational attainment, labor market experience, and family structure (see Table 8.2).[8]

3.3 Summary statistics: differences in characteristics

Disparities in wealth and financial market participation between immigrant and native-born households are likely to be driven (at least in part) by differences in household income, age, education, and family structure, as well as other characteristics. Monthly per-capita income is significantly lower for immigrants than for the native-born—$1300 for immigrant households versus $1910 for native-born households (see Table 8.1).

In our analysis, we note that the immigrant–native income gap, while substantial, is much smaller than the wealth gap: The median income of immigrant households is 68% that of native-born households, while the median wealth of immigrant households is just 20% that of the native-born. The large body of empirical work on wealth gaps (e.g., Altonji and Doraszelski, 2005; Blau and Graham, 1990; Dustmann and Fabbri, 2005; Hurst et al., 1998; Menchik and Jianakopolos, 1997; Wolff, 1998, 2000) shows that white households have at least five times the wealth of non-white households yet earn, on average, just twice as much as non-white households.

Like other studies, we find that the gap, both in income and in wealth, depends very much on the comparison group. For example, the median black immigrant household income is higher than the median black native-born household. However, the median income of native-born black households is about 61% that of the median native-born white household.

Table 8.2 provides a detailed comparison of other characteristics of immigrants and the native-born. Compared to the native-born, immigrants are more likely to be married, to have children, and more likely to have a male household head. Immigrants also tend to have significantly less education than the native-born. About 24% of immigrants in the sample have not completed high school, compared with only 7% of the native-born sample. White and Asian immigrants are more likely to have completed education beyond high school, as are white and Asian natives. Hispanic immigrants have

---

[8] Several authors find higher employment rates and income levels for some black immigrants relative to their native-born counterparts (see Butcher, 1994; Foner, 2001; and Waters, 1999, for example).

Table 8.2 Summary statistics, immigrants vs. natives

	All		<40% of income		Whites		Blacks		Hispanics		Asians	
	Native	Imm.	Native	Imm.	Native	Imm.	Native	Imm.	Native	Imm.	Native	Imm.
% Married	49.66%	57.34%	24.68%	44.63%	53.50%	53.33%	29.40%	38.88%	49.06%	60.08%	51.59%	67.76%
% Male	46.94%	53.25%	39.50%	45.84%	48.47%	50.47%	36.60%	50.95%	48.70%	55.41%	60.51%	54.89%
HH size	2.40	3.01	1.92	2.65	2.34	2.51	2.41	2.56	3.01	3.53	2.53	2.80
Education												
Less than high school	7.26%	24.35%	13.84%	33.58%	5.11%	11.18%	13.33%	14.05%	18.04%	42.59%	3.78%	10.14%
High school graduate	22.19%	21.24%	29.59%	25.24%	21.53%	18.03%	24.98%	20.57%	26.16%	26.27%	9.42%	15.07%
More than high school	70.55%	54.41%	56.57%	41.19%	73.36%	70.79%	61.69%	65.38%	55.80%	31.15%	86.79%	74.79%
Number of observations	20,444	3612	8026	1603	15,647	1109	2910	360	1128	1300	200	762

Sample is restricted to wave 7 of the 2008–present Survey of Income and Program Participation households with a reference person who is at least 18 years old, lives in an MSA, and has a non-missing value for immigrant status. Data are weighted to reflect the US population.

relatively low levels of education, with nearly 43% never having completed high school. Hispanic natives are also relatively less educated, with almost one-fifth not having completed high school.

Table 8.3 summarizes some important characteristics of the SIPP immigrant population. More than one-half of the SIPP immigrant population has become naturalized US citizens. Furthermore, English language proficiency appears to be a significant barrier for US immigrants, with only 72% of the immigrant sample reporting they speak English well or very well. Most immigrants arrived in the US as adults (about 86%), and almost half have lived in the US for 17 or more years. Within the SIPP, the Americas (Central, North, and South America, along with the Caribbean) account for nearly 60% of the immigrant sample.

3.4 Estimating financial market participation

The empirical analysis in this chapter accounts for the various factors that are likely to affect the decision to participate in various financial markets. To control for the effect of characteristics on the financial market participation of immigrants and the native-born

Table 8.3 Immigrant characteristics

	All	<40% income	Race/ethnicity White	Race/ethnicity Black	Race/ethnicity Hisp.	Race/ethnicity Asian
% citizen	58.65%	52.81%	71.27%	60.47%	45.90%	65.28%
% speaks English well	72.29%	61.75%	83.99%	88.82%	56.59%	80.07%
% arrived < age 18	13.73%	11.53%	11.66%	12.20%	16.86%	9.91%
% arrived age 18 +	86.27%	88.47%	88.34%	87.80%	83.14%	90.09%
% in US for ≤5 years	19.70%	22.18%	16.45%	29.21%	19.49%	20.79%
% in US 6–16 years	36.95%	38.10%	35.29%	39.20%	37.97%	35.79%
% in US for 17 + years	43.35%	39.72%	48.26%	31.59%	42.54%	43.42%
Region of origin (%)						
The Americas	59.40%	66.59%	35.84%	64.17%	98.75%	4.35%
Asia and Australia	21.61%	16.04%	12.18%	2.70%	0.09%	94.33%
Europe	14.14%	12.53%	47.42%	2.68%	0.17%	0.51%
Africa	3.99%	4.35%	3.44%	29.07%	0.12%	0.57%
Other	0.86%	0.49%	1.12%	1.39%	0.87%	0.23%
Observations	3612	1603	1109	360	1300	762

Sample is restricted to wave 7 of the 2008–present Survey of Income and Program Participation households with a reference person who is at least 18 years old, lives in an MSA, and has a non-missing value for immigrant status. Data are weighted to represent the US population. The Americas includes Central, North and South America, as well as the Caribbean.

more generally, we estimate the decision to participate in a particular financial market using the following linear probability model:

$$S_{isj} = \alpha + \beta_1 I_i + \beta_2 X_i + \delta_s + \varepsilon_{isj}$$

where S_{isj} is the decision to own asset j for household i, who lives in metropolitan statistical area s. Individual controls are incorporated in X_i and include education (high school, some college, bachelor, or advanced degree), income quintiles, wealth quintiles, marital status, sex, age, age squared, and whether the household is headed by a single parent, along with controls for the number of adult males, adult females, and children of various ages living in the household. The estimates also include controls for Black, Hispanic, Asian and "Other" (except when we look only at households belonging to a specific racial or ethnic group). A full set of state controls are included in δ_s. Finally, the regression includes the key variable of interest: I or "immigrant," which is equal to 1 if the household reference person was born abroad. The estimate of the coefficient β_1 indicates the remaining gap in financial market participation between immigrants and the native-born, holding characteristics fixed. For summary statistics of all the controls included in the regression, please see Appendix 8.1.

All of the reported standard errors are corrected to account for the heteroscedasticity that is implicit in the linear probability model.[9] One additional econometric concern is the potential endogeneity of wealth and income. In particular, a household's decision on owning stocks may lead to higher wealth rather than the other way around. We follow the literature in this area and include wealth and income controls and take a number of steps to address this issue. First, the nature of the dependent variable and the way we measure the independent variables minimizes the potential for reverse causality. By focusing on financial market participation, a zero/one variable, and by including wealth and income as quintiles rather than levels, we mitigate the concern that may emerge if we had included the wealth levels (including stock holdings) in a regression where the dependent variable was equal to the level of stock holdings, for example.

The literature on portfolio choice emphasizes the importance of fixed transaction costs and risk aversion in explaining financial choices, and our preferred specification includes income and wealth quintiles. However, to account for endogeneity concerns, we have also estimated all of our models without these variables and the general patterns remain consistent, although the estimated size of the coefficient on being an immigrant is, as one would expect, larger when income and wealth are not included in the analysis.

---

[9] We use a linear probability model because it is computationally attractive given the large number of fixed effects, is consistent under weak assumptions, and because the coefficient estimates are easy to interpret. In particular, the coefficients on interaction terms are straightforward to interpret (see Ai and Norton, 2003). Non-linear estimation methods, such as probit or logit, generate similar results.

4. CHARACTERISTICS, IMMIGRANT STATUS, AND FINANCIAL MARKET PARTICIPATION

Our regression estimates of whether or not a household owns various financial assets or durable goods for the whole sample and various subgroups are shown in Table 8.4. Table 8.4 reports the estimates of the coefficient on the immigrant variable (β_1) for ownership of checking account, savings account, IRA/Keogh account, stock/mutual fund, home, car (loan and outright), household durable goods, and computer for the whole sample, those with income below the 40th percentile, whites, blacks, Hispanics, and Asians. In addition to controlling for immigrant status, the regressions include controls for the complete set of individual and geographic characteristics described above. To conserve space, we have not included the full regression output with all demographic variables for each specification. However, the detailed results are presented in Appendix 8.2.

4.1 Estimates of the impact of characteristics on financial market participation and durable goods acquisition

Before turning our attention to the effect of being an immigrant, we highlight some of the key relationships between education, income, wealth, race and ethnicity, and financial assimilation that are shared by immigrants and the native-born.[10] In general, the estimated impact of education, wealth, and income is similar for checking accounts, savings accounts, IRA/Keogh account ownership, stock and mutual fund ownership, home ownership, household appliance ownership, and computer ownership, so we focus our discussion on checking accounts, the most commonly held financial asset.

Income has a strong positive association with checking account ownership. For the whole sample, relative to the lowest income quintile, households with per-capita monthly income in the second quintile are 7.9 percentage points more likely to have a checking account. Households with incomes in the third, fourth, and fifth quintiles are 11.1–17.1 percentage points more likely to have a checking account than households in the lowest income quintile.

Wealthier households are also more likely to have checking accounts, holding other variables constant. Households in the second wealth quintile are 11.3 percentage points more likely to have a checking account than households in the lowest wealth quintile. The effect of higher quintiles of wealth on the ownership of IRA/Keogh accounts, stock and mutual funds, and homes is even stronger than the impact on checking account ownership.

---

[10] These estimated coefficients are not reported in the tables to conserve space. They are available upon request from the authors.

Table 8.4 Estimates of account ownership for socio-economic and demographic groups

	All (1)	<40% of Income (2)	Whites (3)	Blacks (4)	Hispanics (5)	Asians (6)
Checking account ownership						
Immigrant	−0.0298***	−0.0289*	−0.0404***	0.0563*	−0.0634***	0.0170
	(0.0109)	(0.0173)	(0.0148)	(0.0303)	(0.0237)	(0.0386)
Native ownership rate	67.70%	54.29%	72.60%	47.61%	55.11%	69.23%
Immigrant ownership rate	54.92%	42.50%	65.39%	51.79%	42.61%	67.50%
Adjusted R-squared	0.164	0.145	0.112	0.187	0.137	0.146
Savings account ownership						
Immigrant	−0.0528***	−0.0265	−0.0652***	0.0288	−0.0785***	−0.0328
	(0.0111)	(0.0169)	(0.0157)	(0.0302)	(0.0228)	(0.0408)
Native ownership rate	60.30%	41.64%	64.37%	43.61%	49.21%	68.05%
Immigrant ownership rate	46.70%	32.01%	55.14%	47.83%	34.12%	61.02%
Adjusted R-squared	0.189	0.124	0.154	0.227	0.157	0.148
IRA/Keogh ownership						
Immigrant	−0.0641***	−0.0546***	−0.0803***	−0.0231	−0.0734***	−0.0971**
	(0.00871)	(0.0101)	(0.0138)	(0.0214)	(0.0145)	(0.0384)
Native ownership rate	36.44%	19.85%	42.52%	14.03%	17.91%	44.12%
Immigrant ownership rate	19.20%	6.86%	30.77%	14.63%	7.41%	29.64%
Adjusted R-squared	0.313	0.255	0.284	0.220	0.203	0.253
Stock/mutual fund ownership						
Immigrant	−0.0467***	−0.0359***	−0.0821***	0.0167	−0.0327***	0.000301
	(0.00711)	(0.00707)	(0.0116)	(0.0168)	(0.0101)	(0.0341)
Native ownership rate	23.23%	11.18%	27.97%	6.62%	8.14%	26.89%
Immigrant ownership rate	10.81%	3.14%	17.26%	8.51%	2.04%	21.92%
Adjusted R-squared	0.264	0.206	0.246	0.156	0.130	0.240

Continued

Table 8.4 Estimates of account ownership for socio-economic and demographic groups—cont'd

	All (1)	<40% of Income (2)	Whites (3)	Blacks (4)	Hispanics (5)	Asians (6)
Home ownership						
Immigrant	−0.0205**	0.00262	−0.0361***	0.0396	−0.00783	−0.0124
	(0.00900)	(0.0128)	(0.0124)	(0.0258)	(0.0185)	(0.0330)
Native ownership rate	68.58%	50.39%	74.89%	45.67%	50.18%	63.93%
Immigrant ownership rate	53.31%	36.60%	63.95%	45.28%	45.81%	59.06%
Adjusted R-squared	0.471	0.525	0.421	0.507	0.447	0.508
Observations	24,056	9629	16,756	3270	2428	962
Have a car						
Immigrant	−0.0149*	−0.00609	−0.0680***	0.0451*	−0.00495	0.01000
	(0.00882)	(0.0147)	(0.0119)	(0.0249)	(0.0179)	(0.0301)
Native ownership rate	84.61%	72.31%	88.33%	69.35%	75.25%	80.01%
Immigrant ownership rate	76.16%	64.17%	76.55%	70.91%	74.92%	80.83%
Adjusted R-squared	0.241	0.273	0.173	0.328	0.307	0.321
Observations	24,056	9629	16,756	3270	2428	962
Have multiple cars						
Immigrant	−0.0600***	−0.0452***	−0.0811***	−0.0311	−0.0355*	0.0101
	(0.00943)	(0.0122)	(0.0133)	(0.0242)	(0.0195)	(0.0391)
Native ownership rate	48.77%	22.70%	52.89%	29.63%	42.77%	44.27%
Immigrant ownership rate	41.04%	22.01%	40.90%	28.69%	41.04%	47.91%
Adjusted R-squared	0.396	0.286	0.402	0.392	0.331	0.325
Observations	24,056	9629	16,756	3270	2428	962
Loan on at least one car						
Immigrant	−0.0555***	−0.0475**	−0.0441**	−0.0357	−0.0704***	0.0439
	(0.0126)	(0.0199)	(0.0173)	(0.0393)	(0.0262)	(0.0440)
Native ownership rate	37.11%	23.87%	36.02%	39.42%	46.90%	27.27%
Immigrant ownership rate	34.64%	23.81%	32.43%	36.21%	36.00%	33.48%
Adjusted R-squared	0.125	0.076	0.131	0.105	0.132	0.111
Observations	20,010	6752	14,656	2210	1844	779

Loan on multiple cars

Immigrant	−0.0353★★★	−0.0481★★	−0.0203	0.00726	−0.0743★★★	0.00914
	(0.0126)	(0.0187)	(0.0166)	(0.0459)	(0.0263)	(0.0423)
Native ownership rate	13.00%	6.18%	12.38%	14.18%	9.58%	9.38%
Immigrant ownership rate	11.67%	3.27%	11.45%	19.24%	10.72%	11.39%
Adjusted R-squared	0.067	0.043	0.054	0.073	0.136	0.106
Observations	11,525	2189	8781	969	1024	462

Own at least one car

Immigrant	0.0163	0.0195	0.0120	−0.0407	0.0608★★★	−0.0552★
	(0.0109)	(0.0177)	(0.0144)	(0.0369)	(0.0230)	(0.0319)
Native ownership rate	81.38%	84.15%	82.55%	76.28%	75.05%	91.02%
Immigrant ownership rate	82.12%	85.17%	83.24%	71.75%	73.05%	83.82%
Adjusted R-squared	0.073	0.067	0.069	0.085	0.095	0.078
Observations	20,010	6752	14,656	2210	844	779

Own multiple cars

Immigrant	0.0726★★★	0.0815★★	0.0441★	0.144★★	0.0603★	0.0241
	(0.0175)	(0.0374)	(0.0244)	(0.0616)	(0.0360)	(0.0658)
Native ownership rate	54.92%	68.31%	56.62%	49.06%	41.79%	57.56%
Immigrant ownership rate	57.22%	70.56%	59.22%	61.09%	54.52%	59.42%
Adjusted R-squared	0.115	0.088	0.120	0.065	0.115	0.123
Observations	11,525	2189	8781	969	1024	462

Durable goods (housing appliances)

Immigrant	−0.0389★★★	−0.0168	−0.0395★★★	−0.0535★	−0.0495★★	−0.0561
	(0.0106)	(0.0167)	(0.0145)	(0.0310)	(0.0218)	(0.0376)
Native ownership rate	67.90%	49.10%	73.81%	46.82%	47.74%	68.72%
Immigrant ownership rate	50.92%	35.39%	64.67%	42.43%	38.63%	62.65%
Adjusted R-squared	0.266	0.196	0.211	0.238	0.219	0.334
Observations	22,922	9144	15,976	3105	2327	916

Continued

Table 8.4 Estimates of account ownership for socio-economic and demographic groups—cont'd

	All (1)	<40% of Income (2)	Whites (3)	Blacks (4)	Hispanics (5)	Asians (6)
Own a computer						
Immigrant	−0.0324***	−0.0501***	−0.0244**	0.000625	−0.0571***	−0.0185
	(0.00939)	(0.0170)	(0.0115)	(0.0257)	(0.0216)	(0.0269)
Native ownership rate	78.76%	60.67%	82.00%	64.62%	70.21%	90.85%
Immigrant ownership rate	69.55%	52.76%	78.45%	70.36%	57.62%	82.41%
Adjusted R-squared	0.271	0.215	0.255	0.292	0.203	0.332
Observations	22,922	9144	15,976	3105	2327	916

The sample consists of all 2008–present Survey of Income and Program Participation wave 7 households with a reference person at least 18 years of age with a populated immigrant status who reside in an MSA. The dependent variable is equal to 1 if the household reference person and/or his or her spouse owned the relevant asset and 0 otherwise. Linear models with state fixed effects are used and the results are adjusted to take into account sampling weights. Standard errors, in parentheses, are corrected for heteroskedasticity. In addition to the immigrant status, each regression controls for: income and wealth quintiles, education categories, age, age-squared, marital status, sex, the number of adult males, adult females, children aged 0–5, children aged 6–12, and children aged 13–17 in the household. Columns 1 and 2 also include controls for black, Hispanic, Asian, and "other". *** indicates significance at at least the 1% level, ** at the 5% level, * at at least the 10% level. Data are weighted to represent the US population.

Some studies have focused on the importance of education in lowering the information costs of participating in various financial markets (see Bernheim et al., 2001, for example). Our results are consistent with these theories. We find that checking account ownership increases significantly with education, holding other variables constant. Households headed by someone with a high school diploma are 9.8 percentage points more likely to have a checking account than households headed by someone who has not completed high school. Additional years of schooling raises the likelihood of having a checking account: Households whose head has completed some college are 15.9 percentage points more likely to have a checking account and those with a bachelor's or an advanced degree are more than 20 percentage points more likely to have a checking account than households whose head has not completed high school. The impact of education is similar across the different types of financial assets and durable goods.

There are important differences by race and ethnicity. We note that households headed by Hispanic or black individuals are less likely to own various financial products and durable goods. In contrast, households headed by Asians are as likely to have a savings account, checking account, and computer as households headed by whites. However, Asian-headed households are less likely to have IRA/Keogh accounts. This is consistent with recent empirical studies of household financial behavior that document significant differences in the use of financial services by race, even after controlling for income and education (Altonji and Doraszelski, 2005; Blau and Graham, 1990; Chiteji and Stafford, 1999; Smith, 1995).

4.2 Estimates of the impact of being an immigrant on financial market participation

Even after controlling for characteristics, we find that immigrants are generally significantly less likely to have a checking account. We also find that immigrants are significantly less likely to have a savings account, an IRA or Keogh account, stock or mutual funds. When we examine durable good ownership including a home, standard household appliances, and a computer (Table 8.4), we also find lower rates of ownership for immigrant households compared to their native-born counterparts. The gap in financial market participation and durable good acquisition ranges from 1.5 percentage points (for having a car) to 6.4 percentage points (for an IRA/Keogh account) controlling for wealth, income, education, age, marital status, being a single parent, family structure, and state fixed effects.[11] One category of durable goods that immigrants are either as likely as or more likely than their native counterparts to own is vehicles. We find that immigrants are equally likely to own at least one car, conditional on having a car, than natives.

---

[11] Similarly, we find that immigrants are almost 11.8 percentage points less likely to have life insurance after controlling for various characteristics.

Table 8.5a compares the differences in checking account ownership between immigrants and natives before and after characteristics are controlled for. For the whole sample, the raw gap in checking account ownership is 12.8 percentage points (see Table 8.1). After controlling for characteristics, the gap is predicted to be 2.98 percentage points

Table 8.5 Differences in checking account ownership (a), computer ownership (b), and home ownership (c) before and after controlling for characteristics*

	Difference before controlling for characteristics (1)	Difference after controlling for characteristics (2)	% of difference accounted for by characteristics (3)
(a) Checking account ownership			
All	12.8%	2.98%	76.7%
<40th percentile of income	11.8%	2.89%	75.5%
Whites	7.2%	4.04%	44.0%
Blacks	−4.2%	5.63%	234.5%
Hispanics	12.5%	6.34%	49.3%
Asians	1.7%	1.70%	1.5%
(b) Computer ownership			
All	9.2%	3.24%	64.8%
<40th percentile of income	7.9%	5.01%	36.7%
Whites	3.5%	2.44%	31.3%
Blacks	−5.7%	0.06%	101.1%
Hispanics	12.6%	5.71%	54.7%
Asians	8.4%	1.85%	78.1%
(c) Home ownership			
All	15.3%	2.05%	86.6%
<40th percentile of income	13.8%	0.26%	98.1%
Whites	10.9%	3.61%	67.0%
Blacks	0.4%	3.96%	−900.2%
Hispanics	4.4%	0.78%	82.1%
Asians	4.9%	1.24%	74.5%

*Column 1 is equal to the difference in the percentage of native-born and immigrant headed households who own any type of checking account from Table 8.1. Column 2 is equal to the absolute value of the estimated coefficient, β_1, on the immigrant variable for the checking account ownership regressions displayed in Table 8.4. Column 3 is equal to (column 1 − column 2)/column 1.

(the estimated coefficient β_1 from Table 8.4). This implies that differences in characteristics account for about 10 percentage points or 77% of the difference in checking account ownership between immigrants and the native-born. The remaining 23% is not explained by differences in observed characteristics and may be associated with immigrant-specific attributes.

When we adopt the same specification by race and ethnicity, we find some interesting results. In particular, when we restrict the sample to whites and Hispanics, by comparing white immigrants with native-born whites and Hispanic immigrants with native-born Hispanics, we find that more of the difference in checking account ownership is related to being an immigrant. For example, among whites, 44% of the difference in checking account ownership can be explained by differences in characteristics and 56% has to do with being an immigrant. Among Hispanics, 51% of the gap in checking account ownership between native-born Hispanics and Hispanics who were born abroad may be attributable to their immigrant status (Table 8.5a).

Table 8.5b shows a similar comparison for housing and durable good ownership. We focus on results from computer ownership. We find that for white households below the 40th percentile in income, a majority of the computer ownership differences between natives and immigrants are not accounted for by differences in observed characteristics. This result implies that some unobservable aspects of being an immigrant explain the majority of the difference in computer ownership between native-born and foreign-born households, especially for households below the 40th percentile in income.

When we restrict the sample to households headed by blacks, we find no statistically significant difference in savings account ownership, IRA/Keogh account ownership, or stock and mutual fund ownership. We also do not find significant differences in home and computer ownership between immigrants and the native-born for blacks, once we have controlled for differences in characteristics (Table 8.4). There is a small difference between native and immigrant blacks in checking account ownership and household appliance ownership, but the estimated coefficient is only at the 10% significance level. Recall that black immigrants have similar ownership rates of the various financial assets as native-born blacks (Table 8.1).

The main source of this pattern appears to be that blacks born in the US have lower than expected (given their characteristics) financial market participation and durable goods ownership rates, not that black immigrants have particularly high rates. This is generally consistent with Blau and Graham (1990), who analyzed data from the National Longitudinal Study of Youth (NLSY) and found that almost three-quarters of the black–white wealth gap cannot be explained by measured characteristics.

In addition, we find no significant difference in checking, savings account, or stock and mutual fund ownership, for immigrant and native-born Asians, once characteristics are controlled for. Similarly, we do not find significant differences in home, car, and computer ownership for immigrant and native-born Asians, once characteristics are controlled for. However, Asian immigrants are less likely to have an IRA/Keogh account than otherwise similar Asians who were born in the US.

An important component of our analysis is to confirm the robustness of the findings over time. When we compare these results with the 2004 SIPP results, we find similar trends over time. However, there are slight differences in the impact of race and ethnicity over both waves of the SIPP. Based on the 2004 SIPP results, immigrants are less likely to own a car and computer across ethnic and racial groups compared to their native-born counterparts. We note some important trends over time by race and ethnicity. In 2004, we find that black immigrants are less likely to own a home, have a car, and have a loan on a car, once characteristics are controlled for, compared to native-born blacks. We also find stark differences between Asian immigrants and natives when examining savings account ownership, IRA/Keogh account ownership, and having a car. There is some evidence that Hispanic immigrants experienced smaller gaps in financial market participation in 2004, when Hispanic immigrants are compared to native-born Hispanics. In particular, we did not find any significant difference between Hispanic immigrants and natives in checking account ownership and stock/mutual fund ownership in 2004.

5. IMMIGRANT ADAPTATION

The previous section shows that household characteristics are only part of the story and that just being an immigrant appears to be associated with lower financial market participation and durable goods acquisition. In this section, we discuss the effects of various aspects of the immigrant experience that may impact the likelihood of owning financial assets.

Table 8.6 repeats the regressions presented in Table 8.4 for different subsamples of immigrants that vary in level of adaptation to the US. Specifically, we investigate financial market participation regressions for various financial products with groups of immigrants that vary along the characteristics described earlier. For example, in one regression we restrict the sample to immigrants who have become naturalized citizens. In another, we examine only immigrants who have *not* become naturalized citizens. By comparing the coefficients in these two regressions, we gain insights into how legal status may affect the likelihood that immigrants participate in various financial markets, holding other characteristics fixed. The native-born sample remains the same for each of the regressions.

For comparison purposes, the first column of Table 8.6 presents the estimates for the whole sample from Table 8.4. In columns 4–6, we examine the effect of time in the US by dividing the immigrant sample into three groups: those who have been in the US for less than 5 years, 6–16 years, and 17 or more years. These estimates also restrict

Table 8.6 Estimates of account ownership for immigrant groups compared to the native-born

	All (1)	Citizens (2)	Non-citizens (3)	In US ≥17 years, adult at arrival (4)	In US 6–16 years, adult at arrival (5)	In US ≤5 years, adult at arrival (6)
Checking account ownership						
Immigrant	−0.0298***	−0.0166	−0.0492***	−0.00655	−0.0417**	−0.0596***
	(0.0109)	(0.0128)	(0.0163)	(0.0175)	(0.0168)	(0.0214)
Native ownership rate	67.70%	67.70%	67.70%	67.70%	67.70%	67.70%
Immigrant ownership rate	54.92%	59.80%	48.00%	61.26%	52.79%	49.38%
Adjusted R-squared	0.164	0.154	0.165	0.152	0.159	0.159
Savings account ownership						
Immigrant	−0.0528***	−0.0426***	−0.0636***	−0.0310*	−0.0736***	−0.0662***
	(0.0111)	(0.0129)	(0.0164)	(0.0178)	(0.0166)	(0.0216)
Native ownership rate	60.30%	60.30%	60.30%	60.30%	60.30%	60.30%
Immigrant ownership rate	46.70%	51.34%	40.13%	50.83%	43.88%	42.94%
Adjusted R-squared	0.189	0.184	0.191	0.183	0.190	0.188
IRA/Keogh ownership						
Immigrant	−0.0641***	−0.0551***	−0.0756***	−0.0469***	−0.0698***	−0.0777***
	(0.00871)	(0.0108)	(0.0111)	(0.0143)	(0.0125)	(0.0150)
Native ownership rate	36.44%	36.44%	36.44%	36.44%	36.44%	36.44%
Immigrant ownership rate	19.20%	25.10%	9.40%	26.62%	17.21%	12.61%
Adjusted R-squared	0.313	0.304	0.318	0.308	0.312	0.311

Continued

Table 8.6 Estimates of account ownership for immigrant groups compared to the native-born—cont'd

	All (1)	Citizens (2)	Non-citizens (3)	In US ≥17 years, adult at arrival (4)	In US 6–16 years, adult at arrival (5)	In US ≤5 years, adult at arrival (6)
Stock/mutual fund ownership						
Immigrant	−0.0467***	−0.0573***	−0.0182**	−0.0710***	−0.0251**	−0.0281**
	(0.00711)	(0.00870)	(0.00926)	(0.0117)	(0.0100)	(0.0117)
Native ownership rate	23.23%	23.23%	23.23%	23.23%	23.23%	23.23%
Immigrant ownership rate	10.81%	13.81%	6.57%	12.43%	10.87%	7.95%
Adjusted R-squared	0.264	0.259	0.267	0.261	0.265	0.264
Observations	24,056	22,621	21,879	21,532	21,625	21,104
Home ownership						
Immigrant	−0.0205**	0.00433	−0.0650***	0.00196	−0.0470***	−0.0775***
	(0.00900)	(0.0102)	(0.0141)	(0.0133)	(0.0142)	(0.0181)
Native ownership rate	68.58%	68.58%	68.58%	68.58%	68.58%	68.58%
Immigrant ownership rate	53.31%	63.33%	39.09%	66.60%	49.42%	38.43%
Adjusted R-squared	0.471	0.469	0.472	0.467	0.469	0.473
Observations	24,056	22,621	21,879	21,532	21,625	21,104
Have a car						
Immigrant	−0.0149*	−0.0238**	0.00837	0.0144	−0.0342**	−0.00316
	(0.00882)	(0.0105)	(0.0130)	(0.0134)	(0.0137)	(0.0187)
Native ownership rate	84.61%	84.61%	84.61%	84.61%	84.61%	84.61%
Immigrant ownership rate	76.16%	75.73%	76.78%	80.09%	74.53%	74.35%
Adjusted R-squared	0.241	0.236	0.232	0.226	0.232	0.228
Observations	24,056	22,621	21,879	21,532	21,625	21,104

Have multiple cars

	(1)	(2)	(3)	(4)	(5)	(6)
Immigrant	−0.0600***	−0.0497***	−0.0757***	−0.0450***	−0.0723***	−0.111***
	(0.00943)	(0.0110)	(0.0146)	(0.0151)	(0.0152)	(0.0188)
Native ownership rate	48.77%	48.77%	48.77%	48.77%	48.77%	48.77%
Immigrant ownership rate	41.04%	42.32%	39.24%	47.08%	41.26%	31.99%
Adjusted R-squared	0.396	0.405	0.400	0.408	0.402	0.407
Observations	24,056	22,621	21,879	21,532	21,625	21,104

Loan on at least one car

	(1)	(2)	(3)	(4)	(5)	(6)
Immigrant	−0.0555***	−0.0478***	−0.0681***	−0.0306	−0.0925***	−0.0702***
	(0.0126)	(0.0146)	(0.0191)	(0.0195)	(0.0197)	(0.0252)
Native ownership rate	37.11%	37.11%	37.11%	37.11%	37.11%	37.11%
Immigrant ownership rate	34.64%	33.74%	35.90%	32.16%	34.15%	35.85%
Adjusted R-squared	0.125	0.128	0.127	0.128	0.128	0.129
Observations	20,010	18,914	18,364	18,129	18,142	17,756

Loan on multiple cars

	(1)	(2)	(3)	(4)	(5)	(6)
Immigrant	−0.0353***	−0.0143	−0.0794***	−0.0338*	−0.0454**	−0.0725**
	(0.0126)	(0.0149)	(0.0179)	(0.0174)	(0.0189)	(0.0282)
Native ownership rate	13.00%	13.00%	13.00%	13.00%	13.00%	13.00%
Immigrant ownership rate	11.67%	12.76%	10.01%	9.00%	12.43%	10.96%
Adjusted R-squared	0.067	0.068	0.071	0.070	0.070	0.071
Observations	11,525	10,957	10,575	10,523	10,498	10,228

Continued

Table 8.6 Estimates of account ownership for immigrant groups compared to the native-born—cont'd

	All (1)	Citizens (2)	Non-citizens (3)	In US ≥17 years, adult at arrival (4)	In US 6–16 years, adult at arrival (5)	In US ≤5 years, adult at arrival (6)
Own at least one car						
Immigrant	0.0163	0.00975	0.0274★	0.00425	0.0365★★	0.00731
	(0.0109)	(0.0124)	(0.0166)	(0.0159)	(0.0167)	(0.0226)
Native ownership rate	81.38%	81.38%	81.38%	81.38%	81.38%	81.38%
Immigrant ownership rate	82.12%	82.79%	81.20%	85.46%	82.51%	78.13%
Adjusted R-squared	0.073	0.074	0.073	0.074	0.072	0.075
Observations	20,010	18,914	18,364	18,129	18,142	17,756
Own multiple cars						
Immigrant	0.0726★★★	0.0574★★★	0.102★★★	0.0506★	0.112★★★	0.111★★★
	(0.0175)	(0.0204)	(0.0266)	(0.0269)	(0.0264)	(0.0392)
Native ownership rate	54.92%	54.92%	54.92%	54.92%	54.92%	54.92%
Immigrant ownership rate	57.22%	57.68%	56.53%	61.01%	57.48%	56.54%
Adjusted R-squared	0.115	0.117	0.119	0.118	0.121	0.120
Observations	11,525	10,957	10,575	10,523	10,498	10,228
Durable goods (housing appliances)						
Immigrant	−0.0389★★★	−0.00837	−0.0846★★★	−0.0311★	−0.0559★★★	−0.0592★★★
	(0.0106)	(0.0122)	(0.0162)	(0.0163)	(0.0161)	(0.0219)
Native ownership rate	67.90%	67.90%	67.90%	67.90%	67.90%	67.90%
Immigrant ownership rate	50.92%	58.17%	40.79%	53.80%	50.39%	45.80%
Adjusted R-squared	0.266	0.257	0.263	0.256	0.258	0.253
Observations	22,922	21,548	20,847	20,519	20,599	20,099

Own a computer

Immigrant	−0.0324***	−0.00920	−0.0732***	−0.0306**	−0.0585***	−0.0604***
	(0.00939)	(0.0108)	(0.0149)	(0.0153)	(0.0153)	(0.0194)
Native ownership rate	78.76%	73.76%	78.76%	78.76%	78.76%	78.76%
Immigrant ownership rate	69.55%	74.19%	63.07%	68.45%	69.22%	68.01%
Adjusted R-squared	0.271	0.269	0.268	0.270	0.265	0.268
Observations	22,922	21,548	20,847	20,519	20,599	20,099

The sample consists of all 2008–present Survey of Income and Program Participation wave 7 households with a reference person at least 18 years of age with a populated immigrant status who reside in an MSA. The dependent variable is equal to 1 if the household reference person and/or his or her spouse owned the relevant asset and 0 otherwise. Linear models with state fixed effects are used and the results are adjusted to take into account sampling weights. Standard errors, in parentheses, are corrected for heteroskedasticity. In addition to the immigrant status, each regression controls for: income and wealth quintiles, education categories, age, age-squared, marital status, sex, the number of adult males, adult females, children aged 0–5, children 6–12, and children aged 13–17 in the household, black, Hispanic, Asian, and "other". *** indicates significance at at least the 1% level, ** at the 5% level, * at at least the 10% level. Data are weighted to represent the US population.

the sample to immigrants who arrived in the US as adults.[12] For checking account ownership, home ownership, having a car, and having a loan on at least one car, the negative effect of being an immigrant appears to diminish with time in the US. However, for financial assets that are more forward looking—a savings account, IRA/Keogh account, or stock—even immigrants who have been in the US for 17 or more years and arrived as adults are less likely than otherwise similar native-born households to participate.[13] The effect of being an immigrant on the ownership of a computer and household appliances does not appear to disappear entirely over time, although the significance and magnitude of the coefficient does decrease with more time in the US.

When we compare results on immigrant adaptation in the 2004 SIPP data, we find overall similar trends in financial asset ownership, but differences emerge when we look at asset accumulation and home ownership. For computer ownership, home ownership, and household durable goods ownership, the negative effects of being an immigrant do not diminish with more time in the US.

5.1 Legal status

A number of studies emphasize the effect of legal status on wages and occupation choice. For example, Cobb-Clark and Kossoudji (2002) found that the 1986 Immigration Reform and Control Act (IRCA), which granted amnesty to previously undocumented workers, significantly improved wages and labor market opportunities for this group of workers. Legal status can be a barrier to financial market participation both in perception and in reality.[14] Many US banks now accept identification issued by foreign governments to comply with the USA Patriot Act "Know Your Customer" provisions, and the US Internal Revenue Service issues Individual Taxpayer Identification Numbers (ITINs) to individuals who do not qualify for Social Security Numbers (SSNs) but have taxable income. However, financial institutions have received some scrutiny for extending account ownership to undocumented immigrants, and anecdotal accounts suggest that many immigrants remain concerned that

---

[12] In estimates that are not reported on here, we have also examined the role of age at migration directly. Consistent with other studies that show that immigrants who arrive at younger ages have higher levels of language proficiency and higher earnings compared to immigrants who migrate as adults (see Bleakley and Chin, 2004, for example), we find relatively complete financial adaptation for immigrants who arrive in the US as children, for all of the financial assets that we consider.

[13] The same pattern holds for life insurance. The immigration effect decreases as they spend more time in the US; however, immigrants that arrived before 1993 are still less likely than their counterpart natives to hold life insurance (10.3 percentage points less likely).

[14] Amuedo-Dorantes and Bansak (2006) found that only 9% of the Mexican migrants surveyed by the Mexican Migration Project had a bank account in the US. Approximately 60% of that sample is undocumented.

financial institutions will share their identity and financial information with immigration authorities.[15]

The SIPP data contain information on whether immigrants have become naturalized US citizens. When we compare households headed by naturalized citizen immigrants and native-born households, we continue to find significant differences in financial asset ownership and durable goods accumulation between immigrants and the native-born, once other characteristics have been controlled for (columns 2 and 3). For example, immigrants who are naturalized citizens are 4.3 percentage points less likely to have a savings account, while immigrants who are not citizens are nearly 6.4 percentage points less likely to have a savings account. We find a similar pattern for stock and mutual funds and IRA and Keogh account ownership. Interestingly, there is no statistically significant difference in checking account ownership between citizen immigrants and the native-born, holding characteristics fixed. A similar effect is found for durable goods accumulation, as we no longer see any significant difference between naturalized immigrants who own a computer and standard household appliances and their native counterparts. However, naturalized immigrants are still less likely to possess a vehicle, as well as to have a car loan. These findings (and others) are broadly consistent with Amuedo-Dorantes and Bansak (2006), who found that undocumented immigrants are significantly less likely to have a bank account, while immigrants who speak English fluently, stay for longer periods in the US, and bring their spouses with them are significantly more likely to have bank accounts.

6. POTENTIAL EXPLANATIONS

In this section, we examine a number of potential explanations for the persistent gap in financial market participation between immigrants and the native-born. There are a number of explanations that have received some attention in recent debates. We consider the possibility that prioritizing the accumulation of real assets, specifically housing, slows down the accumulation of financial assets like retirement accounts and stock and mutual funds for immigrants relative to the native-born. We also consider how country-of-origin characteristics and the tendency of immigrants to cluster in neighborhoods with other immigrants from the same country shape financial choices, drawing on our previous work (Osili and Paulson, 2004, 2006, 2008). We supplement this analysis

---

[15] For some immigrants, concerns about proper documentation contribute to a more general distrust of banks. Many people fear that the failure to produce valid immigration papers at a bank will jeopardize their ability to stay in the US (Suro et al., 2002). A nationwide survey of Latin American immigrants living in the US found that 25% believe that to open an account they need a social security number or a driver's license. Other common misconceptions held by immigrants are that they will lose access to the funds in their account when the documentation they used to open an account expires, or that the funds in their accounts will be liquidated if they are deported (Hogarth et al., 2005).

with information from the 2003 New Immigrant Survey (NIS) to examine the role of return migration intentions, remittances, and the possibility of owning assets abroad. In addition, we draw on the existing literature to consider the role of supply-side factors like the location of financial institutions and the characteristics of the products and services they offer.

6.1 Housing and financial market participation

We note that for many households, whether immigrant or native-born, housing is an important component of their asset holdings. In fact, 69% of native-born households and 53% of immigrant households own a home (Table 8.1). Among home owners, median home equity is $40,000 for native-born households and $29,200 for immigrant households. These figures are roughly consistent with previous research. For example, Borjas (2002) and Kossoudji and Sedo (2004) found that while immigrants are less likely to own homes than similar native-born individuals, conditional on home ownership, the difference in home equity between immigrants and the native-born is less significant.

This comparison of home ownership rates and home equity accumulation among immigrants follows the same pattern we have seen for financial market participation: large gaps in the percentage of families who own the asset and smaller gaps in the value of the asset conditional on ownership. However, along other dimensions, home ownership diverges from the patterns we see for financial asset holdings.

Table 8.4 includes regression estimates of the probability of home ownership for various groups of immigrants and natives, controlling for the set of characteristics we discussed earlier. Overall, immigrants are 2 percentage points less likely to own a home than otherwise similar natives. There is no significant difference in home ownership between households headed by naturalized citizens and native-born households. The gap is larger for immigrants who are non-citizens (column 3) and for immigrants who have lived in the US fewer than 16 years (columns 5 and 6). In contrast to the patterns for financial asset ownership, adaptation appears to be complete for immigrants who have lived in the US for 17 years or more, despite their having arrived in the US as adults. There is no statistically significant gap in home ownership between this group of immigrants and otherwise similar natives. Changes in the effects of being an immigrant on home ownership with time in the US most closely resemble those for checking accounts. As for home ownership differences between immigrants and natives in the various subgroups discussed earlier, we only find significant differences for immigrants overall and for whites. Immigrants below the 40th percentile of income, blacks, Hispanics, and Asians have no significant difference in home ownership compared with similar native households. Table 8.5c shows the differences in home ownership before and after controlling for characteristics. We see that characteristics account for 86% of the difference. For whites and Asians, there are more unaccounted for differences in home ownership due to being an immigrant. Overall, these results provide some suggestive evidence that the goal of buying a home in the US may take precedence over accumulating other financial assets.

When we compare these results with the 2004 SIPP results, we find that there are more significant differences between immigrants and natives. In 2004, we find that for immigrants overall, for those below the 40th percentile of income, and for whites and blacks, there are significant differences in home ownership compared with natives in similar situations. In addition, we do not find that the difference in home ownership decreases with time in the US (Table 8.6). Although the magnitude and significance of the difference decrease with time in the US, immigrants who have been in the US more than 17 years are still less likely to own a home than natives (by 2.2 percentage points).

6.2 Country-of-origin characteristics

Immigrant's experience with banks prior to migration is likely to impact their financial choices in the US as well. Even among developed countries, there is significant variation in the fraction of individuals who use financial services. In Sweden, Germany, and Canada, the fraction of people without a bank account is much lower than in the US, around 3%, whereas in some developing countries most people lack a bank account. For example, approximately 75% of households in Mexico lack an account, as do 90% of Kenyans (Beck et al., 2007). Recent survey evidence from the US suggests that a significant fraction of households choose not to hold bank accounts because they "often are imbued with a cultural distrust of banks, and they may be concerned with privacy".

In some countries, banks are not considered a safe place to put money, especially for low-income households. Immigrants who have grown up in origin countries where financial crises, lack of transparency, fraud, inflation, or theft erode account values are likely to distrust banks. For example, the banking crisis that crippled Mexico in the mid-1990s heightened suspicions among Mexicans that banks were unreliable (Hernandez-Coss, 2005).

Not surprisingly, immigrants who come from countries that do a better job of protecting private property and providing incentives for investment are more likely to participate in US financial markets (Osili and Paulson, 2006, 2008). Holding income, education, and wealth (and other factors) constant, we find immigrants from countries with more effective institutions are more likely to have a relationship with a bank and also to use formal financial markets more extensively. These findings are summarized in Figure 8.2 using data from the 2001 SIPP,[16] which shows the predicted relationship between institutional quality and having a bank account for immigrants from various countries. These results are robust to different ways of measuring country of origin institutional quality, adding

---

[16] 2001 SIPP data was used instead of 2008 because during this panel SIPP gathered detailed information on the country of birth for each immigrant. In the subsequent panels, fewer or no countries were reported (only general regions such as Central America).

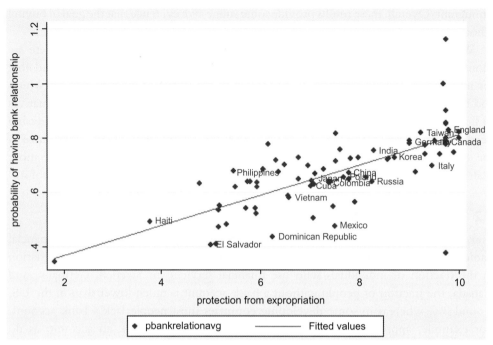

Figure 8.2 Financial market participation and institutional quality using 2001 SIPP data.

additional country-of-origin controls, and various methods of addressing potential bias due to unobserved individual characteristics, including specifications with country fixed effects. The quality of country-of-origin institutions affects the financial market participation of recent immigrants, as well as those with up to 27 years of experience in the US. Country-of-origin institutions also influence the behavior of immigrants who arrive in the US as children, as well as those who migrate as adults. Institutional quality appears to shape preferences and beliefs in a way that influences financial behavior.[17]

6.3 Ethnic concentration

The geographic concentration of immigrants has been shown to have important consequences for the pace of economic and social adaptation. For example, several studies have found that immigrant networks impact employment probabilities (Boeri et al., 2011;

[17] In addition to general country-of-origin characteristics like institutional quality, experiencing adverse financial outcomes may have an important impact on future behavior. In ongoing work (Osili and Paulson, 2007), we find that living through a bank crisis before migrating to the US significantly lowers the likelihood of having a bank account in the US, even controlling for institutional quality in the country of origin.

Munshi, 2003), wage growth, and human capital accumulation (Borjas, 1985, 2000), as well as language proficiency (Chiswick and Miller, 1996).

Residential settlement may have a *direct* impact on financial market decisions if immigrants who reside in ethnically concentrated communities are isolated from mainstream society and lack information and knowledge about US financial institutions.

Social interactions and peer effects have been shown to affect portfolio selection and financial market decisions in other contexts (see, for example, Duflo and Saez, 2003; Hong et al., 2004).[18] Ethnic concentration may also have an *indirect* effect on financial market outcomes if immigrants who reside in ethnically concentrated communities also face less favorable labor market prospects. One study based on German data found a negative effect of ethnic concentration on immigrants' language ability (Danzer and Yaman, 2010).

Not all immigrants settle in the same way. In addition to variation by country of origin, there is also variation in the tendency to cluster for immigrants by metro area: For example, the median Cuban immigrant lives in an area where 17% of the population is also from Cuba, and the median Mexican immigrant lives in an area where 9% of the population is also from Mexico. By contrast, immigrants from Vietnam and India are much less likely to cluster: the former account for only 0.7% of their typical neighborhood, the latter just 0.3%. Ethnic concentration varies by metro area. For example, Mexican immigrants in Chicago account for 4.2% of the population, but in Milwaukee they account for just 0.5% of the population.[19]

In Osili and Paulson (2004), we showed that immigrants who live in ethnically concentrated metropolitan areas are less likely to participate in US financial markets. Our results imply, for example, that if a Mexican immigrant were to move from Chicago (higher ethnic concentration) to Milwaukee (lower ethnic concentration), the likelihood that they would have a checking account would increase by 5 percentage points, and the likelihood that they would have a savings account would go up by 2 percentage points.[20]

Ethnic concentration may also reinforce the effect of country-of-origin characteristics. We find that the effect of home country institutions is stronger for immigrants who live in neighborhoods with other immigrants from the same country (Osili and Paulson, 2006, 2008), likely because their attitudes are reinforced through interactions with others who have had similar experiences.

---

[18] Duflo and Saez (2003) found that an employee's decision to enroll in a 401(K) plan and contribution amounts to a retirement plan in a large university is influenced by the decisions of other employees. Similarly, Hong et al. (2004) argued that social interactions matter for stock market participation because individuals may learn about the benefits and costs from their friends and neighbors.

[19] Calculations from 1990 Census data.

[20] These findings rely on estimates that include MSA fixed effects to address the concern that immigrants choose where to live.

Ethnic concentration can also affect an immigrant's means of commuting to work. While 76% of immigrant households in our sample own a car, they tend to have fewer cars per household than natives. As a result, many immigrants need alternative means of transport, such as carpooling and public transportation. Closer social networks in ethnic enclaves may facilitate carpooling. Research has shown that immigrants living in such enclaves are more likely either to carpool or to use public transit (Kim, 2009; Liu, 2009; Liu and Painter, 2012).

6.4 Remittances, return migration intentions, wealth held abroad

Remittances from immigrants to family members in the home country may also play a role in explaining why immigrant financial market participation lags that of otherwise similar native-born households. However, the relationship between financial market participation and remittances may be complex. Sending remittances may be lower for households with bank accounts, for example, which would tend to increase immigrants' financial market participation. To explore this issue, we examine the New Immigrant Survey (NIS) on financial market participation and remittances (see Tables 8.7 and 8.8). At first glance, these data suggest that immigrants who send remittances are in fact more likely to have a savings, checking, or money market account and to own stock in the US than non-remitters.[21]

Another potential influence on immigrant participation in US financial markets is return migration intentions. Dustmann (1997), Dustmann and Weiss (2007), and Galor and Stark (1990) argued that immigrants who have a higher probability of returning to a lower wage country should save more while they are in the US. High fixed costs may also discourage immigrants who plan to leave the US from participating in US financial

Table 8.7 Financial market participation, remittances, return migration intentions, and wealth held abroad

	% who have savings, checking or money market account	% who own stock
Remit	73.20%	17.25%
Don't remit	50.50%	11.05%
Plan to stay in US	50.19%	8.16%
Plan to leave US	56.41%	20.66%
Own wealth abroad	73.40%	21.16%
Don't own wealth abroad	47.46%	8.51%

Source: Authors' calculations from 2003 New Immigrant Survey data.

---

[21] Of course, one reason to open a bank account is to lower the cost of remitting and to increase access to savings vehicles. Interestingly, Amuedo-Dorantes and Bansak (2006) found that Mexican immigrants who have a bank account bring larger amounts back to Mexico with them when they return.

Table 8.8 Financial market participation for immigrants in country of origin and host country

Variable (mean)	Overall	Africa	Middle East	Asia	Latin America	Europe, Canada, and Oceania	Eastern Europe, Russia and Central Asia
Remittances	16.9%	22.8%	15.4%	19.6%	16.1%	8.4%	12.5%
Financial assets in country of origin							
Check or saving account	4.2%	6.2%	6.1%	6.3%	1.3%	16.1%	4.8%
Own wealth abroad	17.4%	16.0%	17.8%	22.7%	9.8%	47.8 %	21.4%
Financial assets in host country							
Certificate of deposit	2.4%	0.6%	1.2%	4.0%	1.0%	3.9%	2.2%
Checking or saving account	44.9%	43.7%	49.9%	55.5%	33.2%	82.1%	53.1%
Own any stock	11.8%	5.3%	6.9%	17.9%	3.3%	50.0%	12.6%

Source: Authors' calculations from 2003 New Immigrant Survey data.

markets. NIS tabulations of financial market participation as a function of return migration intentions are consistent with the Dustmann (1997) and Galor and Stark (1990) view—those who plan to return to their origin countries appear to have higher rates of account ownership than those who plan to stay in the US (Table 8.7).

Data from the NIS also allow us to examine the role of wealth held abroad. Our tabulations (see Table 8.7) suggest that holding wealth in other countries is not a likely explanation for the lower financial market participation of immigrants in the US, as immigrants who own assets abroad are also more likely to own financial assets in the US.

While these results are suggestive, they are based on data from recent immigrants who are legal, permanent residents and may not apply to all immigrants. In addition, the figures in Table 8.7 do not account for any differences in characteristics that might be correlated with both financial market participation and remittances, wealth held abroad, or return migration intentions.

We also examine the factors that affect immigrants' decisions to send remittances and to own assets in their home country. We find some interesting differences by region of origin in the patterns of remittances and assets held abroad. About 20% of immigrants from Africa and Asia report sending remittances to their home countries. In contrast, immigrants from Europe and Canada have much lower remittance rates—8.4%. However, immigrants from Europe and Canada are more likely to own assets in their country of origin. In the NIS data, on average about 17% of immigrants hold some wealth abroad, while a much smaller percentage (about 4%) maintain a checking or savings account in their home country.

We also investigated the impact of various immigrant characteristics on the likelihood of sending remittances, although we do not report these results in detail here. We find that family ties and family background are important factors in sending remittances. Controlling for age, number of children, education, income, gender, and year of immigration, we find that remittances mostly flow to lower-income families in the home country, consistent with the results of other studies (Dustmann and Mestres, 2010; Osili and Paulson, 2008). The presence of the immigrant's mother in the home country is associated with the likelihood that the immigrant will send remittances, holding other variables constant.

An important insight from the NIS results is that key observable factors (such as education, income, age, marital status) that tend to influence asset ownership in the US (host country) are the same variables that affect financial participation in the country of origin. Educational attainment is associated with financial participation in the US, as well as in the home country. Similarly, married immigrants and those with higher income are more likely to hold assets in both the US and the country of origin, holding other variables constant. These results indicate that it is unlikely that financial participation in the home country crowds out financial participation in the host country.

6.5 Supply-side factors: location and design of financial institution and products

Our analysis emphasizes demand-side explanations for financial market participation.[22] To some extent, the regression analysis controls for many supply-side factors as well. For example, the inclusion of US state fixed effects controls for variation in the supply of financial services at the state level. Of course, much of the meaningful variation in the location and distance to financial service providers may occur at the city level within a state. The 2008 SIPP panel only reported whether an individual resided in an MSA, not which MSA. To the extent that financial institutions   both mainstream institutions like banks and credit unions and alternative financial services providers like check-cashers and currency exchanges—rely on customer characteristics in making decisions about where to open branches, these supply-side factors will be controlled for by the inclusion of household characteristics like income, wealth, education, and immigrant status in the analysis. The potential correlation between the availability of financial services and products and household characteristics should be taken into account in interpreting the estimated coefficients on these characteristics.

In addition to decisions about where to locate, financial institutions may have other practices that make them more or less attractive to immigrant clients. One important

---

[22] For a more complete discussion of financial institution practices as they relate to immigrants, see Paulson et al. (2006), especially Chapter 3.

source of competition is the alternative financial services sector. As of 2008, there were over 48,000 non-bank check-cashing and short-term loan providers, as well as over 10,000 pawn shops, in the US. The number of payday lenders grew nationwide from virtually none in 1994 to more than 22,000 establishments in 2008 (Fellowes and Mabanta, 2008; Temkin and Sawyer, 2004).

In terms of cost per service, banks often charge less. However, to gain access to these services, immigrants need to maintain a bank account, which can be relatively expensive for those with low incomes. Higher-income customers can often avoid paying additional charges, such as overdraft fees, by meeting minimum balance or other requirements (Dunham, 2001).

Minimum balance requirements are one of the most significant barriers to opening a bank account. For every increase of $100 in the initial minimum balance, the probability of owning an account (among lower-income households) decreases by as much as 2.5 percentage points, depending on the type of account (Washington, 2006). Survey responses among Latin American immigrants show that negative views about banks are related to perceptions of high minimum balances requirements (Suro et al., 2002).

The procedures that banks use to screen potential clients may represent an additional barrier. Conventional methods to measure income and credit worthiness may not accurately reflect an immigrant's economic status.[23] Immigrants may not have pay stubs or other standard documentation required in the (increasingly automated) screening processes. For example, the ChexSystems database, which is used by approximately 80% of US bank branches, requires a Social Security Number.

7. CROSS-COUNTRY COMPARISONS

In this section, we compare our findings for the US with findings from Italy, an emerging destination country for immigrants. One advantage of this approach is that data from Italy provide comprehensive information on wealth and immigrant characteristics, allowing us to directly compare results from both countries.

Italy only recently became a destination country for large numbers of immigrants. In the 1990s, the percentage of foreign-born in Italy was less than 1% (Mocetti and Porello, 2010). By 2008, the immigrant share of population had grown to about 6%, with the majority coming from countries of the former Eastern European countries (especially Romania and Albania) and North Africa (Morocco).

---

[23] In fact, a natural extension of this research would be to evaluate how immigrants differ in credit access and propensity to default. Although this is beyond the scope of this chapter, other papers such as Deng and Gabriel (2006) and Wang (2012) do explore part of this question.

By comparing our US findings with the Italian experience, we can assess the extent to which the financial participation and durable good accumulation patterns we have observed in the US may be generalized to other destination countries, particularly countries that have only recently become destination countries for significant numbers of immigrants.

Cross-country comparisons have the potential to yield important insights because regulatory environments and the density of financial institutions differ across countries. We note that Italy has one of the highest numbers of bank branches per land area and bank branches per capita, even ranking above the US (Beck et al., 2007). In addition, the barriers to financial market participation may be lower in some countries compared to the US. Opening a bank account in Italy and other European countries may associate with lower barriers depending on where an individual or household chooses to open an account. For households in Italy, in order to open a bank account at a bank, individuals may be asked to provide one or more of the following: passport or valid ID, tax identification code, recent utility bill, a residence certificate (or valid permit of stay), and or proof of employment in Italy ("Banking Services," 2012). In general, the documentation and fees required will depend on the bank and type of account. However, we note that in Italy and other European countries, households have the ability to open a bank, savings or current account at the post office. At the post office, households are not required to provide proof of employment in Italy (BancoPosta Click, 2012). Furthermore, key services are offered for free including withdrawals and deposits, online statements, and checks. This method may be easier for immigrants as the post office is also able to send money online for a fee.

To understand the impact of host country environments of financial market decisions for immigrants, we examine household data from Italy. We rely on the 2008 Survey on Household Income and Wealth (SHIW), a nationally representative longitudinal study that has information on financial market access and household assets. The 2008 SHIW covers 7997 households and over 19,000 individuals. The 2008 SHIW data is cross-sectional in nature. However, about 4345 interviewed households in 2008 were also interviewed in previous surveys. Our analysis makes use of sampling weights to ensure that estimates are representative. The SHIW data provide three ways of determining immigration status. First, heads of households who are not Italian nationals provide their year of arrival in Italy. Second, heads of households who were born abroad are asked if they have children abroad. Third, if the head of household was born abroad, the interviewer rates his/her ability to speak Italian. We define an immigrant as anyone who has responded to at least one of these three questions. In total, 521 households of the 7977 households surveyed (about 6.5%) were immigrant households. This is consistent with known statistics about the percentage of immigrants in Italy. The SHIW does not include geographical information to allow us to study patterns of settlement among immigrants. So for comparison purposes, we have replicated the SIPP results including immigrants who live in non-MSAs in the US.[24]

Table 8.9 reports a comparison of US and Italian households (updated to reflect any SHIW differences) with SHIW summary statistics. One stark difference between the US and Italian data lies in median household wealth. Italian native households have more than two times the median household wealth of US native households. Italian households also have higher median financial wealth per capita.

When we turn to financial participation and durable asset accumulation rates, we find that both immigrants and natives in Italy have higher rates of checking account ownership than their US counterparts. In addition, we do not find any significant difference between immigrants and native-born households in checking account ownership in Italy. These results are consistent with studies that have found comparable financial asset participation rates among immigrants and natives in Italy (Matha et al., 2011). As noted earlier, households in Italy—both immigrants and native-born households have several options for opening bank accounts, including post office locations. Potential reasons for higher rate of checking account ownership in Italy could include the fact that there are more branches per land and capita, as well as more options for banking services in Italy. Furthermore, the European Commission has promoted having access to a basic bank account for all consumers across Europe, encouraging European banks to offer banking services at lower rates.

In contrast to checking accounts, rates of savings account ownership and stock ownership are significantly lower for Italian households than for their US counterparts. Only 12% of natives and 4% of immigrant Italians own stock, compared with 22% of American natives and 10% of American immigrants. Some studies have pointed to a lack of trust as important factors in explaining the low levels of stock market participation in Italy (Guiso et al., 2004, 2008).

Home ownership rates are comparable for Italian and US native households, but are significantly lower for Italian immigrant households than for their US counterparts. Only 25% of immigrants in Italy own a home, compared with 53% of US immigrants. Car ownership rates in Italy are similar for both natives and immigrants. Approximately

---

[24] Other differences between the Italian data include: Household wealth and financial wealth are generated variables from the survey data, defined as total assets minus total liabilities or total financial assets minus total financial liabilities respectively. Wealth and income data are converted into dollars by the average 2008 exchange rate, and then converted to 2010 dollars. Educational attainment categories are defined somewhat differently. We assume that a vocational secondary school or upper secondary school diploma is equivalent to a high school diploma in the US. We assume three-year university degree/higher education or a five-year university degree is equivalent to a bachelor's degree in the US. We do not have an equivalent for the "some college" category in the Italy data. Stock and mutual fund ownership includes investment funds or indexed funds (i.e., ETFs) in Italy, shares in any public or private Italian company, managed portfolios, and foreign securities in the form of shares. The data include a subjective assessment of the head of household's ability to speak Italian (rated on a 10-point scale) given by the interviewer. We define the category "Speaks Italian Well" to be a score of 8 or higher.

Table 8.9 Summary statistics comparison between US SIPP data and Italian SHIW data

	United States				Italy			
	All		**<40% of income**		**All**		**<40% of income**	
	Native	*Imm.*	*Native*	*Imm.*	*Native*	*Imm.*	*Native*	*Imm.*
Income and wealth (in thousands of $)								
Median monthly HH income	1.83	1.26	0.91	0.64	1.53	1.11	1.16	1.04
Median HH wealth	42.74	8.19	11.35	1.72	101.66	3.84	14.49	1.87
Median financial wealth	1.50	0.19	0.08	0.00	3.17	0.29	1.01	0.00
Mean monthly HH income	2.45	1.96	1.02	0.76	1.82	1.29	1.28	1.12
Mean HH wealth	120.27	68.84	79.91	40.40	177.36	54.19	34.98	9.27
% who own								
Stock and/or mutual funds	22%	10%	10%	3%	12%	4%	3%	1%
Home	69%	53%	51%	37%	73%	25%	41%	12%
Savings and/or checking	79%	68%	65%	55%	89%	84%	80%	82%
Savings account only	59%	46%	40%	31%	21%	10%	20%	9%
Any checking account	66%	54%	53%	41%	84%	80%	71%	77%
Have a car	85%	77%	73%	64%	83%	78%	74%	74%
Have a loan on car	37%	35%	23%	25%	9%	13%	10%	15%
Computer	77%	69%	57%	51%	94%	87%	93%	82%
Any assets	96%	91%	90%	85%	98%	93%	95%	92%
Number of observations	27,532	4143	10,877	1793	7454	521	2958	414

Sample is restricted to wave 7 of the 2008–present Survey of Income and Program Participation households with a reference person who is at least 18 years old and has a non-missing value for immigrant status. Data are weighted to reflect the US population. Italian Survey on Household Income and Wealth data for 2008 is restricted to households with a reference person who is at least 18 years old and has a non-missing value for immigrant status. Data are weighted to reflect Italian population. All income and wealth figures are household per capita figures and reported in thousands of dollars.

83% of Italian nationals have a car, while 78% of immigrants own cars. And, regardless of immigrant status, Italian households have higher rates of computer ownership than their US counterparts.

Tables 8.10 and 8.11 report other important characteristics of Italian households compared to their US counterparts. Taken together, the data show that Italians are more likely to be married and have male heads of households than their US counterparts. Seventy percent of Italian immigrant households have male heads, compared with 53% of US immigrant households. However, Italians (both immigrants and natives) have lower mean levels of educational attainment than US households. A large fraction of the Italian sample has an incomplete high school education (58% of the native sample and 48% of the immigrant sample). Mocetti and Porello (2010) confirmed that Italian immigrants tend to have lower mean levels of educational attainment and are more likely to be employed in unskilled jobs.

Table 8.10 Summary statistics, immigrants vs. natives for US and Italy

| | United States | | | | Italy | | | |
| | All | | <40% of income | | All | | <40% of income | |
	Native	Imm.	Native	Imm.	Native	Imm.	Native	Imm.
% married	49.94%	57.31%	25.13%	44.66%	61.67%	61.89%	52.31%	58.58%
% male	46.73%	53.24%	39.24%	45.83%	62.13%	70.36%	53.90%	68.82%
HH size	2.39	3.03	1.90	2.66	2.51	2.39	2.37	2.32
Education								
Less than high school	8.29%	25.42%	15.62%	34.92%	57.91%	48.21%	70.35%	52.45%
High school graduate	24.03%	21.66%	31.09%	25.74%	32.43%	39.98%	25.03%	38.23%
More than high school	67.68%	52.93%	53.28%	39.34%	9.66%	11.81%	4.62%	9.32%
Number of observations	27,532	4143	10,877	1793	7454	521	2958	414

US Sample is restricted to wave 7 of the 2008–present Survey of Income and Program Participation households with a reference person who is at least 18 years old and has a non-missing value for immigrant status. Data are weighted to reflect the US population. Italian Survey on Household Income and Wealth data for 2008 is restricted to households with a reference person who is at least 18 years old and has a non-missing value for immigrant status. Data are weighted to reflect Italian population.

Table 8.11 Immigrant characteristics for United States and Italy

| | United States | | Italy | |
	All	<40% income	All	<40% income
% citizen	57.90%	51.87%	39.43%	30.50%
% speaks English well	71.17%	60.25%	73.79%	70.86%
% arrived < age 18	14.32%	12.65%	2.70%	3.18%
% arrived age 18+	85.68%	87.35%	97.30%	96.82%
% in country for < 5 years	19.50%	22.22%	52.13%	45.19%
% in country 6–16 years	37.37%	37.76%	40.27%	46.04%
% in country for 17 + years	43.13%	40.02%	7.60%	8.77%
Observations	4143	1793	521	414

US Sample is restricted to wave 7 of the 2008–present Survey of Income and Program Participation households with a reference person who is at least 18 years old and has a non-missing value for immigrant status. Data are weighted to represent the US. population. Italian Survey on Household Income and Wealth data for 2008 is restricted to households with a reference person who is at least 18 years old and has a non-missing value for immigrant status. Data are weighted to reflect Italian population and only report years in country for non-Italian nationals.

Turning to regression results on financial market participation, we report the estimates of the coefficient on the immigrant variable for having a checking account, savings account, stock/mutual fund, home, car, loan on a car, and computer for the whole sample and for those with income below the 40th percentile (Table 8.12). These regressions include the full set of controls used earlier, except for race, as this information is not available in the Italian data.

Table 8.12 Estimates of account ownership for socio-economic and demographic groups in US and Italy

	United States		Italy	
	All	*<40% of income*	*All*	*<40% of income*
Checking account ownership				
Immigrant	−0.0712★★★	−0.0652★★★	0.0323	0.0152
	(0.00876)	(0.0137)	−0.0253	−0.0314
Native ownership rate	66.26%	52.50%	83.72%	70.84%
Immigrant ownership rate	53.50%	41.14%	80.29%	77.44%
Adjusted *R*-squared	0.132	0.105	0.24	0.192
Savings account ownership				
Immigrant	−0.0667★★★	−0.0383★★★	−0.0668★★★	−0.0600★★★
	(0.00872)	(0.0133)	−0.0196	−0.0225
Native ownership rate	58.60%	39.94%	21.35%	20.34%
Immigrant ownership rate	45.93%	31.25%	9.77%	9.02%
Adjusted R-Squared	0.167	0.092	0.026	0.032
Stock/mutual fund ownership				
Immigrant	−0.0608★★★	−0.0419★★★	−0.0278★★	−0.0274★★★
	(0.00529)	(0.00521)	−0.013	−0.00821
Native ownership rate	21.89%	10.44%	11.63%	3.36%
Immigrant ownership rate	10.35%	3.07%	3.92%	0.78%
Adjusted *R*-squared	0.256	0.192	0.167	0.052
Home ownership				
Immigrant	−0.0609★★★	−0.0412★★★	−0.0538★★★	−0.0402★
	(0.00722)	(0.0106)	−0.02	−0.023
Native ownership rate	68.98%	51.37%	72.76%	40.76%
Immigrant ownership rate	53.11%	37.38%	24.95%	12.31%
Adjusted *R*-squared	0.459	0.511	0.665	0.542
Observations	31,675	12,670	7975	3372
Have a car				
Immigrant	−0.0618★★★	−0.0687★★★	−0.0760★★★	−0.130★★★
	(0.00714)	(0.0123)	−0.0239	−0.0285
Native ownership rate	85.10%	72.80%	83.08%	73.87%
Immigrant ownership rate	76.51%	64.48%	77.63%	74.46%
Adjusted *R*-squared	0.196	0.201	0.377	0.396
Observations	31,675	12,670	7975	3372
Loan on at least one car				
Immigrant	−0.0662★★★	−0.0451★★★	0.0187	0.0332
	(0.00981)	(0.0155)	−0.0236	−0.0302
Native ownership rate	36.77%	23.25%	9.36%	10.42%
Immigrant ownership rate	34.60%	24.68%	12.96%	15.26%
Adjusted *R*-squared	0.117	0.069	0.027	0.039
Observations	26,554	9002	6594	2490

Table 8.12 Estimates of account ownership for socio-economic and demographic groups in US and Italy—cont'd

	United States		Italy	
	All	*<40% of income*	*All*	*<40% of income*
Own a computer				
Immigrant	−0.0746★★★	−0.0937★★★	−0.0484	−0.0907★
	(0.00794)	(0.0143)	−0.0339	−0.0478
Native ownership rate	76.61%	57.44%	94.29%	93.49%
Immigrant ownership rate	68.75%	51.08%	86.84%	82.32%
Adjusted *R*-squared	0.242	0.170	0.056	0.078
Observations	30,097	11,971	3775	1163

US Sample is restricted to wave 7 of the 2008–present Survey of Income and Program Participation households with a reference person who is at least 18 years old, and has a non-missing value for immigrant status. Data are weighted to reflect the US population. Italian Survey on Household Income and Wealth data for 2008 is restricted to households with a reference person who is at least 18 years old and has a non-missing value for immigrant status. Data are weighted to reflect Italian population.

We find that our estimates on being an immigrant generally increase in magnitude for the US when we do not control for race and ethnicity. Unlike the US, Italy shows no significant difference between natives and immigrants in checking account ownership. Similarly, Italian immigrants overall are just as likely to own a computer as are Italian natives.

However, we do find some interesting differences when we compare immigrants and their native-born counterparts below the 40th percentile of income. Immigrants in Italy below the 40th percentile in income are 13 percentage points less likely to have a car than native-born households in this income group. Immigrants (both overall and in the 40th income percentile) do not differ from other native-born Italians in the likelihood of having a loan on a car (conditional on having a car). This may suggest that Italian households face lower barriers than US households in accessing credit to purchase a vehicle. For home ownership, we find generally similar trends as in the US, in both the magnitude of the coefficient and significance. Overall, Italian immigrants are 5.4 percentage points less likely than natives to own a home; in the US, the gap is 6.1 percentage points. Both Italian and US households in the 40th percentile income groups have a slightly smaller gap; they are 4 percentage points less likely to own a home than their native-born counterparts.

We now focus on immigrant adaptation and its impact on financial market decisions. The results suggest that the adaptation process for immigrants differs across the US and Italy.[25] For immigrants in Italy, not only do more years in the host country decrease most

---

[25] These results are not reported to conserve space. They are available upon request.

differences in participation rates, but also immigrants are *more* likely to own certain assets than their native counterparts. We find this is the case for checking accounts and computers.

Although there are important differences between the findings for the US and Italy, we do find some noteworthy similarities. In particular, when we examine more forward-looking assets, such as stocks and mutual funds, we find significant and persistent immigrant–native gaps in ownership rates in Italy. Specifically, after spending more than 17 years in Italy, immigrants are still 3.5 percentage points less likely than their native counterparts to own a stock or mutual fund.

Although some aspects of immigrant financial assimilation are comparable across institutional settings, we note that financial behavior may depend on the immigrants' characteristics, as well as their selection process into various destination communities. In Italy, the average immigrant tends to be less educated and more likely to be male than the average US immigrant. There may also be important differences in their motives for migration and plans for the future. Mocetti and Porello (2010) found that recent immigrants to Italy tend to work in unskilled occupations, including industrial and construction sectors.

One key finding from the analysis for the US and Italy is that we do not observe significant differences in checking account ownership rates between immigrants and natives in Italy. We also note that the selection process can also explain higher financial participation by Italian immigrants than US immigrants. Although we cannot test this directly, immigrants in Italy may originate from countries where the majority of people participate in and trust financial institutions. In addition, some European countries require checking accounts to obtain government assistance. These results provide further evidence that immigrant characteristics, host country environments, and origin country experiences jointly shape immigrants' financial participation and durable goods acquisition in host countries.

8. SUMMARY OF FINDINGS AND POLICY PRIORITIES

8.1 Key findings

Based on analysis from the US and Italy, we find significant differences in financial participation and asset accumulation rates between immigrants and the native-born. In the US, we find that immigrant households are less likely than otherwise similar native-born households to own a wide variety of financial assets and durable goods: checking accounts, savings accounts, IRA/Keogh accounts, stock and mutual funds, home, vehicle, basic household appliances, and a computer.

For checking accounts, US immigrants tend to catch up with native-born households over time. We note some similarities in the impact of host country experience on the rate and pace of financial assimilation. Interestingly, Italian immigrants are more likely than natives to own a checking account and a computer over time. This adaptation occurs at a fairly measured pace during the first 16 years that Italian immigrants are in the host country.

When we turn our attention to financial assets that are linked with the future, including stock ownership, we find strikingly different results. Only a small minority of immigrants who arrive after the age of 18 catch up with their native-born counterparts in ownership of stocks, retirement accounts, or mutual funds. The vast majority of immigrants who arrived in the US as adults are less likely than the native-born to have savings accounts, IRA/Keogh accounts, and stock and mutual funds even after 17 years or more in the US. In Italy, a similar pattern emerges—immigrants who have lived in Italy more than 17 years are still less likely than their native counterparts to own a stock or mutual fund or a vehicle. The immigrant–native gap in the ownership of a computer is present for immigrants who have been in the US for more than 17 years. These results suggest that wealth differences between immigrants and the native-born may persist across generations.

In Italy, similar gaps in financial participation and asset accumulation patterns persist with respect to savings account ownership and home ownership. However, we do not find significant immigrant–native gaps for checking accounts or computers in Italy. These patterns reinforce our conclusion that both host country settings and country-of-origin experiences impact immigrants' financial participation rates.

Potential explanations for the lower financial market participation of immigrants include a desire to prioritize the accumulation of real assets, particularly housing, over financial assets, the tendency to locate in ethnic enclaves, and country-of-origin characteristics, including institutional quality. Supply-side explanations are likely to be important as well. Much of the existing literature focuses on understanding supply-side issues related to savings and checking accounts. Supply-side issues may also influence IRA and Keogh account ownership and stock and mutual fund ownership.

8.2 Policy priorities

In addition to policy interventions that focus specifically on home ownership and country of origin experiences, our analysis and recent demographic trends suggest that an important policy priority is to reach the children of immigrants. Persistently lower ownership of savings accounts, IRA/Keogh accounts, and stock and mutual funds among immigrant families puts the children of immigrants at a financial disadvantage relative to children of native-born parents. The children of immigrants comprise a large and growing population segment in many countries, including the US, Canada, Germany, UK, Italy, and Spain. By 2020, second-generation immigrants are projected to outnumber their parents in the US and many European countries (Suro and Passel, 2003).

For children and youth, early exposure to financial literacy either in the home or at school can have an important impact on their financial decisions as adults. Using data from the US, Chiteji and Stafford (1999) found that financial asset ownership among parents influences the portfolio decisions of their adult children. Parents and schools can play important roles in lowering the information costs associated with learning about financial markets. Bernheim et al. (2001) found that adults who took a high school course in money management had significantly higher savings rates than those who were not exposed to these courses in their youth.

Immigrant enclaves are another area where connections to the financial mainstream are fragile and support is needed to connect immigrants (and other low-income residents) to financial service providers and options. In areas of high ethnic concentration, each new account is likely to lead to others, as information about the process and the benefits of account ownership is shared across the community.

A key measure of adaptation for immigrants who come to the US, Italy, and other traditional and non-traditional destination countries is the extent to which they participate in the financial mainstream. By analyzing the wealth and financial decisions of immigrants relative to the native-born, we shed light on both their current economic position and their prospects. This analysis reveals important gaps in financial market participation that are likely to persist across generations. Policy interventions that help immigrants achieve their financial goals have the potential to provide benefits to society as a whole.

APPENDIX

Appendix 8.1 Summary statistics of regressors

	Mean	Standard deviation	Minimum	Maximum
Immigrant	0.158	0.365	0	1
Married	0.509	0.500	0	1
Household head single parent	0.120	0.325	0	1
Male	0.479	0.500	0	1
Age	50.760	16.560	18	86
Age squared	2850.75	1779.894	324	7396
High school	0.220	0.415	0	1
Some college	0.349	0.477	0	1
Bachelors	0.210	0.407	0	1
Advanced degree	0.121	0.326	0	1
Hispanic	0.125	0.331	0	1
Black	0.130	0.337	0	1
Asian	0.036	0.187	0	1
Other	0.023	0.151	0	1
No. of adult males	0.889	0.643	0	8
No. of adult females	0.980	0.590	0	6
No. of children age 0–5	0.203	0.535	0	5
No. of children age 6–12	0.251	0.611	0	8
No. of children age 13–17	0.173	0.474	0	5
No. of observations	24,056			

Sample is restricted to wave 7 of the 2008–present Survey of Income and Program Participation households with a reference person who is at least 18 years old, lives in an MSA, and has a non-missing value for immigrant status. Data are weighted to reflect the US population.

Appendix 8.2 Estimates of checking account ownership for socio-economic and demographic groups

Variables	All (1)	<40% income (2)	Whites (3)	Blacks (4)	Hispanics (5)	Asians (6)
Immigrant	0.0298★★★	−0.0289★	0.0404★★★	0.0563★	0.0634★★★	0.0170
	(0.0109)	(0.0173)	(0.0148)	(0.0303)	(0.0237)	(0.0386)
Married	0.0873★★★	0.0683★★★	0.0805★★★	0.121★★★	0.0611★★	0.119★★
	(0.00894)	(0.0158)	(0.0106)	(0.0277)	(0.0287)	(0.0475)
Household head single parent	0.0350★★★	−0.0410★★	0.0444★★★	0.0156	−0.0595	−0.120★
	(0.0119)	(0.0177)	(0.0154)	(0.0273)	(0.0363)	(0.0693)
Male	−0.00800	−0.0306★★	−0.00163	−0.0214	−0.00443	−0.0427
	(0.00707)	(0.0152)	(0.00794)	(0.0240)	(0.0241)	(0.0333)
Age	−0.000488	−0.000281	0.000356	−0.00702★	0.00546	−0.00374
	(0.00125)	(0.00183)	(0.00146)	(0.00365)	(0.00442)	(0.00660)
Age squared	1.22e−05	1.18e−05	1.54e−06	7.52e−05★★	−3.20e−05	2.92e−05
	(1.13e−05)	(1.63e−05)	(1.30e−05)	(3.36e−05)	(4.34e−05)	(6.17e−05)
High school	0.0979★★★	0.0711★★★	0.0550★★★	0.0894★★★	0.135★★★	0.00806
	(0.0126)	(0.0158)	(0.0178)	(0.0265)	(0.0285)	(0.0735)
Some college	0.159★★★	0.152★★★	0.108★★★	0.194★★★	0.184★★★	0.147★★
	(0.0124)	(0.0159)	(0.0174)	(0.0264)	(0.0307)	(0.0711)
Bachelors	0.207★★★	0.222★★★	0.153★★★	0.239★★★	0.250★★★	0.162★★
	(0.0137)	(0.0210)	(0.0183)	(0.0366)	(0.0428)	(0.0701)
Advanced degree	0.218★★★	0.227★★★	0.159★★★	0.322★★★	0.267★★★	0.111
	(0.0145)	(0.0272)	(0.0191)	(0.0396)	(0.0600)	(0.0738)
Hispanic	0.0662★★★	−0.0728★★★				
	(0.0134)	(0.0208)				
Black	−0.104★★★	−0.129★★★				
	(0.0107)	(0.0150)				
Asian	−0.0328★	−0.0367				
	(0.0176)	(0.0335)				
Other	−0.00881	−0.00662				
	(0.0201)	(0.0303)				
Income quartile 2	0.0786★★★	0.0766★★★	0.0519★★★	0.133★★★	0.108★★★	0.111★
	(0.0107)	(0.0110)	(0.0132)	(0.0248)	(0.0315)	(0.0638)
Income quartile 3	0.111★★★		0.0752★★★	0.189★★★	0.159★★★	0.132★★
	(0.0111)		(0.0133)	(0.0300)	(0.0340)	(0.0591)
Income quartile 4	0.156★★★		0.126★★★	0.217★★★	0.208★★★	0.166★★★
	(0.0116)		(0.0135)	(0.0344)	(0.0393)	(0.0605)

Continued

Appendix 8.2 Estimates of checking account ownership for socio-economic and demographic groups—cont'd

Variables	All (1)	<40% income (2)	Whites (3)	Blacks (4)	Hispanics (5)	Asians (6)
Income quartile 5	0.171***		0.131***	0.274***	0.267***	0.244***
	(0.0126)		(0.0145)	(0.0411)	(0.0471)	(0.0597)
Wealth quartile 2	0.113***	0.119***	0.104***	0.113***	0.119***	0.0970*
	(0.0110)	(0.0144)	(0.0145)	(0.0256)	(0.0276)	(0.0541)
Wealth quartile 3	0.137***	0.148***	0.144***	0.125***	0.0808**	0.0655
	(0.0113)	(0.0166)	(0.0143)	(0.0286)	(0.0335)	(0.0592)
Wealth quartile 4	0.160***	0.189***	0.170***	0.192***	0.0852**	0.0760
	(0.0118)	(0.0185)	(0.0145)	(0.0332)	(0.0406)	(0.0568)
Wealth quartile 5	0.197***	0.242***	0.216***	0.205***	0.0128	0.169***
	(0.0124)	(0.0209)	(0.0150)	(0.0432)	(0.0498)	(0.0561)
No. of adult males	0.0430***	−0.0294**	0.0408***	0.0627***	−0.0252	0.0641***
	(0.00602)	(0.0120)	(0.00756)	(0.0167)	(0.0161)	(0.0231)
No. of adult females	0.0342***	−0.0361***	0.0285***	0.0473***	−0.0347**	−0.0628**
	(0.00635)	(0.0125)	(0.00789)	(0.0164)	(0.0176)	(0.0275)
No. of children age 0–5	0.0270***	−0.0473***	−0.0150*	0.0504***	−0.0383**	−0.0574*
	(0.00645)	(0.0115)	(0.00803)	(0.0177)	(0.0166)	(0.0311)
No. of children age 6–12	−0.00683	−0.00885	−0.00647	0.00669	−0.00760	−0.00311
	(0.00531)	(0.00987)	(0.00652)	(0.0143)	(0.0139)	(0.0250)
No. of children age 13–17	−0.00202	−0.0155	−0.0107	−0.000557	0.0178	0.0143
	(0.00672)	(0.0132)	(0.00806)	(0.0189)	(0.0182)	(0.0344)
Constant	0.346***	0.351***	0.399***	0.317***	0.0890	0.529***
	(0.0347)	(0.0518)	(0.0424)	(0.0983)	(0.107)	(0.171)
Observations	24,056	9629	16,756	3270	2428	962
Adjusted R-squared	0.164	0.145	0.112	0.187	0.137	0.146

Robust standard errors are given in parentheses. ***$p < 0.01$, **$p < 0.05$, *$p < 0.1$.

REFERENCES

Ai, C., Norton, E.C., 2003. Interaction terms in legit and probit models. Economic Letters 80 (1), 123–129.

Algan, Y., Dustmann, C., Glitz, A., Manning, A., 2010. The economic situation of first- and second-generation immigrants in France, Germany and the United Kingdom. Econ. J. 120 (542), F4–F30.

Altonji, J.A., Doraszelski, U., 2005. The role of permanent income and demographics in black/white differences in wealth. J. Hum. Resour. 40 (1), 1–30.

Amuedo-Dorantes, C., Bansak, C., 2006. Money transfers among banked and unbanked Mexican immigrants. South. Econ. J. 73 (2), 374–401.

Amuedo-Dorantes, C., Pozo, S., 2002. Precautionary saving by young immigrants and young natives. South. Econ. J. 69 (1), 48–71.

Baker, B., Hoefer, M., Rytina, N., 2012. Estimates of the unauthorized immigrant population residing in the United States: January 2011, Population Estimates. Department of Homeland Security, March.

BancoPosta Click. <http://www.bancopostaclick.it/cos_c/cos_c.shtml> (accessed 29 August 2012).

"Banking Services." Welcome Office, Friuli Venezia Giulia. <http://www.welcomeoffice.fvg.it/trieste/dailylife/banking-services.aspx> (accessed 29 August 2012).

Bauer, T.K., Cobb-Clark, D.A., Hildebrand, V.A., Sinning, M.G., 2011. A comparative analysis of the nativity wealth gap. Econ. Inq. 49 (4), 989–1007.

Beck, T., Demirguc-Kunt, A., Martinez Peria, M.S., 2007. Reaching out: Access to and use of banking services across countries. J. Financ. Econ. 85 (1), 234–266.

Bernheim, B.D., Garrett, D.M., Maki, D.M., 2001. Education and saving: The long-term effects of high school financial curriculum mandates. J. Publ. Econ. 80 (3), 435–465.

Bertaut, C., Starr-McCluer, M., 2000. Household Portfolios in the United States. Finance and Economics Discussion Series Working Paper 2000-26, Board of Governors of the Federal Reserve System, Washington, DC.

Bleakley, H., Chin, A., 2004. Language skills and earnings: Evidence from childhood migrants. Rev. Econ. Stat. 86 (2), 481–496.

Blumenberg, E., Smart, M.J., 2011. Migrating to driving: Exploring the multiple dimensions of immigrants' automobile use. In: Lucas, K., Blumenberg, E., Weinberger, R. (Eds.), Auto Motives: Understanding Car Use Behaviors. Emerald Group Publishing Limited, UK, pp. 225–252.

Blau, F.D., Graham, J., 1990. Black-white differences in wealth and asset composition. Q. J. Econ. 105 (2), 321–339.

Boeri, T., De Philippis, M., Patacchini, E., Pellizzari, M., 2011. Moving to Segregation: Evidence from 8 Italian Cities, Innocenzo Gasparini Institute for Economic Research, Bocconi University Working Papers 390.

Borjas, G.J., 1985. Assimilation, changes in cohort quality, and the earnings of immigrants. J. Labor Econ. 3 (4), 463–489.

Borjas, G.J., 1987. Self-selection and the earnings of immigrants. Am. Econ. Rev. 77 (4), 531–553.

Borjas, G.J., 2000. Ethnic enclaves and assimilation. Swed. Econ. Pol. Rev. 7, 89–122.

Borjas, G.J., 2002. Home ownership in the immigrant population. J. Urban Econ. 52 (3), 448–476.

Butcher, K.F., 1994. Immigrants in the United States: A comparison with native blacks and other immigrants. Ind. Labor Relat. Rev. 47 (2), 265–284.

Carroll, C.D., Rhee, B.K., Rhee, C., 1994. Are there cultural effects on saving? Some cross-sectional evidence. Q. J. Econ. 109 (3), 685–699.

Chiswick, B.R., Miller, P.W., 2007. Computer usage, destination language proficiency and the earnings of natives and immigrants. Review of Economics of the Household 5 (2), 129–157.

Chiswick, B.R., Miller, P.W., 1996. Ethnic networks and language proficiency among immigrants in the United States. J. Popul. Econ. 9 (1), 19–35.

Chiteji, N.S., Stafford, F.P., 1999. Portfolio choices of parents and their children as young adults: Asset accumulation by African-American families. Am. Econ. Rev. 89 (2), 377–380.

Cobb-Clark, D., Hildebrand, V., 2006. The wealth and asset holdings of U.S. and foreign born households: Evidence from SIPP data. Review of Income and Wealth 52 (1), 17–42.

Cobb-Clark, D., Hildebrand, V., 2009. The asset portfolios of native-born and foreign-born Australian households. Econ. Rec. 85 (268), 45–59.

Cobb-Clark, D., Kossoudji, S., 2002. Coming out of the shadows: Learning about legal status and wages from the legalized population. J. Labor Econ. 20 (3), 598–628.

Coval, J., Moskowitz, T., 1999. Home bias at home: Local equity preference in domestic portfolios. Journal of Finance 54, 2045–2074.

Danzer, A.M., Firat, Y., 2010. Ethnic Concentration and Language Fluency of Immigrants in Germany. IZA Discussion Papers 4742, Institute for the Study of Labor (IZA).

Deng, Y., Gabriel, S.A., 2006. Risk-based pricing and the enhancement of mortgage credit availability among underserved and higher credit-risk populations. J. Money Credit Bank 38 (6), 1431–1460, The Ohio State University Press. Retrieved 21 August 2013 from Project MUSE database.

Duflo, E., Saez, E., 2003. The role of information and social interactions in retirement plan decisions: Evidence from a randomized experiment. Q. J. Econ. 118 (3), 815–842.

Dunham, C., 2001. The role of banks and nonbanks in serving low- and moderate-income communities. Paper presented to the Federal Reserve System Community Affairs Research Conference, Changing Financial Markets and Community Development, 5–6 April, Washington, DC.

Dustmann, C., 1997. Return migration, savings, and uncertainty. J. Dev. Econ. 52 (2), 295–316.

Dustmann, C., 1994. Speaking fluency, writing fluency and earnings of migrants. J. Popul. Econ. 7, 133–156.

Dustmann, C., 1996. The social assimilation of migrants. J. Popul. Econ. 9, 79–103.

Dustmann, C., Fabbri, F., 2005. Gender and ethnicity: Married immigrants in Britain. Oxf. Rev. Econ. Pol. 21, 462–484.

Dustmann, C., Frattini, T., 2011. Immigration: The European Experience. CReAM Discussion Paper No 22/11.

Dustmann, C., Kirchkamp, O., 2002. The optimal migration duration and economic activities after re-migration. J. Dev. Econ. 67, 351–372.

Dustmann, C., Mestres, J., 2010. Remittances and temporary migration. J. Dev. Econ. 92, 62–70.

Dustmann, C., Weiss, Y., 2007. Return migration: Theory and empirical evidence for the UK. British Journal of Industrial Economics 45 (2), 236–256.

Edin, K., 2001. More than money: The role of assets in the survival strategies and material well-being of the poor. In: Shapiro, T.M., Wolff, E.N. (Eds.), Assets for the Poor. Russell Sage Foundation, New York, pp. 206–231.

Fairlie, R., Meyer, B.D., 1996. Ethnic and racial self-employment differences and possible explanations. J. Hum. Resour. 31 (Fall), 757–793.

Fellowes, M., Mabanta, M., 2008. Banking on Wealth: American's New Retail Banking Infrastructure and Its Wealth-Building Potential. Research Brief for Metropolitan Policy Program at Brookings.

Foner, N., 2001. Islands in the City: West Indian Migration to New York. Columbia University Press, New York.

Galor, O., Stark, O., 1990. Migrants' savings, the probability of return migration and migrants' performance. Int. Econ. Rev. 31 (2), 463–467.

Guiso, L., Sapienza, P., Zingales, L., 2004. The role of social capital in financial development. Am. Econ. Rev. 94 (3), 526–556.

Guiso, L., Sapienza, P., Zingales, L., 2008. Trusting the stock market. Journal of Finance 63 (6), 2557–2600.

Hao, L., 2004. Wealth of immigrant and native-born Americans. Int. Migrat. Rev. 38 (2), 518–546.

Harms, L., 2007. Mobility among ethnic minorities in the urban Netherlands. Ger. J. Urban Stud. 46(2).

Hernandez-Coss, R., 2005. The U.S.–Mexico Remittance Corridor: Lessons on Shifting From Informal to Formal Transfer Systems. World Bank Working Paper 47, International Bank for Reconstruction and Development/World Bank, Washington, DC.

Hogarth, J.M., Anguelov, C.E., Lee, J., 2005. Who has a bank account? Exploring changes over time, 1989–2001. J. Fam. Econ. Issues 26 (1), 7–30.

Hong, H., Kubik, J.D., Stein, J.C., 2004. Social interaction and stock-market participation. Journal of Finance 59 (1), 137–163.

Hurst, E., Luoh, M.C., Stafford, F.P., 1998. The wealth dynamics of American families, 1984–94. In: Perry, G.L., Brainard, W.C. (Eds.), Brookings Papers on Economic Activity 1998:1, Macroeconomics. Brookings Institution Press, Washington, DC.

Kasper, B., Reutter, U., Schubert, S., 2007. Transport behavior among immigrants - An equation with many unknowns. Ger. J. Urban Stud. 46 (2), 62–68.

Kim, S., 2009. Immigrants and transportation: An analysis of immigrant workers' work trips. Cityscape: A Journal of Policy Development and Research 11 (3), 155–169.

Kossoudji, S., Sedo, S.A., 2004. Rooms of one's own: Gender, race and home ownership as wealth accumulation in the United States. IZA Discussion Paper 1397, Institute for the Study of Labor, Bonn, Germany.

Krivo, L., Kauffman, R.L., 2004. Housing and wealth inequality: Racial-ethnic differences in home equity in the United States. Demography 41 (3), 585–605.

Liu, C.Y., 2009. Ethnic enclave residence, employment, and commuting of Latino workers. J. Policy Anal. Manage. 28 (4), 600–625.

Liu, C.Y., Painter, G., 2012. Travel behavior among Latino immigrants: The role of ethnic concentration and ethnic employment. J. Plann. Educ. Res. 32 (1), 62–80.

Malamud, O., Pop-Eleches, C., 2011. Home computer use and the development of human capital. Q. J. Econ. 126 (2), 987–1027.

Matha, T., Porpiglia, A., Sierminska, E., 2011. The immigrant/native wealth gap in Germany, Italy, and Luxembourg. Working Paper Series of European Central Bank No. 1302, Conference on Household Finance and Consumption.

McKenzie, D., Yang, D., 2012. Experimental approaches in migration studies. In: Vargas-Silva, C. (Ed.), Handbook of Research Methods in Migration. Edward Elgar.

Menchik, P.L., Jianakoplos, N.A., 1997. Black-white wealth inequality: Is inheritance the reason? Econ. Inq. 35 (2), 428–442.

Merton, R.C., 1971. Optimum consumption and portfolio rules in a continuous-time model. J. Econ. Theor. 3 (4), 373–413.

Mesnard, A., 2004. Temporary migration and capital market imperfections. Oxf. Econ. Paper 56 (2), 242–262.

Mocetti, S., Porello, C., 2010. How does immigration affect native internal mobility? New evidence from Italy. Reg. Sci. Urban. Econ. 40, 427–439.

Munshi, K., 2003. Networks in the modern economy: Mexican migrants in the U.S. labor market. Q. J. Econ. 118 (2), 549–599.

Newberger, R., 2007. Financial access and insurance: A preliminary description of factors that affect immigrants. Profitwise News and Views, Federal Reserve Bank, Chicago, May.

Newberger, R., Rhine, S.L.W., Chiu, S., 2004. Immigrant financial market participation: Defining research questions. Chicago Fed Letter 199, Federal Reserve Bank, Chicago.

Osili, U.O., Paulson, A., 2004. Immigrant–Native Differences in Financial Market Participation. Federal Reserve Bank of Chicago Working Paper WP-04-18.

Osili, U.O., Paulson, A., 2006. What Can We Learn about Financial Access from U.S. Immigrants? Federal Reserve Bank of Chicago Working Paper WP-06-25.

Osili, U.O., Paulson, A., 2007. Bank Crises and Investor Confidence: Learning from the Experience of U.S. Immigrants. Manuscript, Federal Reserve Bank of Chicago.

Osili, U.O., Paulson, A., 2008. Institutions and Financial Development: Evidence from International Migrants in the U.S. Rev. Econ. Stat. 90 (3), 498–517.

Paulson, A., Singer, A., Newberger, R., Smith, J., 2006. Financial access for immigrants: Lessons from diverse perspectives. Federal Reserve Bank of Chicago and The Brookings Institution.

Shamsuddin, A.F., DeVoretz, D.J., 1998. Wealth accumulation of Canadian and foreign born households in Canada. Review of Income and Wealth 44 (4), 515–533.

Smith, J.P., 1995. Racial and ethnic differences in wealth. Journal of Human Resources 30 (Suppl), S158–S183.

Suro, R., Passel, J., 2003. The Rise of the Second Generation: Changing Patterns of Hispanic Population Growth. Pew Hispanic Center, Washington, DC.

Suro, R., Bendixen, S., Lowell, B.L., Benavides, D.C., 2002. Billions in Motion: Latino Immigrants, Remittances and Banking, The Pew Hispanic Center and Multilateral Investment Fund.

Survey of Consumer Finances, 2001. US Board of Governors of the Federal Reserve System, Washington, DC.

Temkin, K., Sawyer, N., 2004. Alternative Financial Service Providers. Fannie Mae Foundation and Urban Institute, Research Area: Immigration. <http://www.urban.org/immigrants/index.cfm> (accessed 9 August 2012).

Vissing-Jorgensen, A., 2002. Towards an Explanation of Household Portfolio Choice Heterogeneity: Non-financial Income and Participation Cost Structures. NBER Working Paper 8884, National Bureau of Economic Research, Cambridge, MA.

Wang, Q., 2012. The Financial Assimilation of Immigrant Families: Intergeneration and Legal Differences. Electronic Dissertation, Ohio State University, <https://etd.ohiolink.edu/>.

Washington, E., 2006. The impact of banking and fringe banking regulation on the number of unbanked Americans. J. Hum. Resour. 41 (1), 106–137.

Waters, M., 1999. Black Identities: West Indian Immigrant Dreams and American Realities. Harvard University Press, Cambridge, MA.

Wolff, E.N., 2000. Recent Trends in Wealth Ownership, 1983–1989. Working Paper 300, Levy Economics Institute of Bard College, New York.

Wolff, E.N., 1998. Recent trends in the size distribution of household wealth. J. Econ. Perspect. 12 (3), 131–150.

Woodruff, C., Zenteno, R., 2001. Remittances and Microenterprises in Mexico. Graduate School of International Relations and Pacific Studies, Working Paper, University of California, San Diego.

CHAPTER 9

From Aliens to Citizens: The Political Incorporation of Immigrants

Pieter Bevelander, Mikael Spång
Malmö University

Contents

1. Introduction	443
2. Contemporary Policies of Immigrant Political Incorporation	445
2.1 Legal status and access to rights for long-term residents	446
2.2 Access to rights for other non-citizens	451
2.3 Naturalization	452
2.4 Citizenship for second-generation immigrants	457
2.4.1 Multiple citizenships	*460*
3. Explaining Differences in Incorporation Policies	464
3.1 Democracy	464
3.2 Human rights	466
3.3 Nationhood	467
3.4 Colonial background and other historical ties	469
3.5 State- and nation-building	470
3.6 Regional integration	471
4. Political Inclusion: Voting and Other Forms of Participation	471
4.1 Citizenship and economic integration	476
4.1.1 Who is naturalizing?	*476*
4.1.2 Economic effects of citizenship ascension	*478*
5. Conclusions	481
References	482

1. INTRODUCTION

Participating in politics and, more generally, in social, economic, and cultural life is central to modern democracy, which has emerged out of struggles for inclusion of the poor, women, the working class, minorities, indigenous peoples and, more recently, immigrants. The overall trend in democratic immigration states since the Second World War is towards increasing equality between citizens and non–citizens and towards easier access to citizenship.

Access to legal status, rights, and opportunities for immigrants has followed a democratizing logic, but it also differs from several of the earlier inclusion processes.

Handbook of the Economics of International Migration, Volume 1A
ISSN 2212-0092, http://dx.doi.org/10.1016/B978-0-444-53764-5.00009-8

Recognition of immigrants' rights has followed less upon claims made by social movements than through decisions made "behind the closed doors of courtrooms and state bureaucracy" (Joppke, 1999, p. 3). When rights have become more established in laws and institutional practices, however, immigrants have made use of their opportunities to take part in politics and have been active in defending and expanding rights and opportunities, albeit in varying degrees (Guiraudon, 1998; Koopmans et al., 2005).

Over the past decade, there have been signs that the inclusion and expansion processes are coming to a halt, even though the signs are at times conflicting. Right-wing populist mobilization against immigration has led to debates about restricting access to rights and making naturalization more difficult. Criteria for residence have become more restrictive, and new conditions have been imposed on the acquisition of citizenship in several countries (Joppke, 2010). The multicultural approach to integration has been criticized over recent decades, with established politicians increasingly voicing this criticism (Joppke, 2010; Kastoryano, 2010; Kymlicka, 2012). In the wake of the September 11 attacks, the protection of civil rights has been curtailed in several states, and it has had obvious effects on immigrants, for instance regarding detention and expulsion (Costello, 2012; Fraga, 2009). Furthermore, states have increasingly introduced the possibility of depriving persons of citizenship, both those who have citizenship from birth and by naturalization. In Denmark, for instance, persons convicted of certain crimes against the state may be deprived of citizenship unless this would make the person stateless (Ersböll, 2010, p. 20).

To what extent this shows the beginning of a reversal of the inclusionary logic is difficult to tell. The political situation today is very different from that of a couple of decades ago, but more extensive reversals of the process of extending rights and opportunities are perhaps less likely. Aside from the entrenchment of legal status, rights, and opportunities in democracies, immigration being likely to increase rather than decrease globally may also be a factor (Hollifield, 2004). Furthermore, as Cornelius et al. (1994) noted in the early 1990s, there is a gap between restrictions and continued acceptance of immigrants. Whereas research has shown the gap between policy and practice in immigration policy is not wider than in most other policy fields, there are clear differences between restrictionist rhetoric and adopted policies and laws, as well as between what is legislated and how this is interpreted by courts and implemented by bureaucracies (Bonjour, 2011; Freeman, 1994; Joppke, 1998a).

In this article, we focus on the political incorporation of immigrants. Political incorporation is a subset of societal integration as it also involves labor market participation and access to housing, education, social security, public services, and cultural life (Bommes and Geddes, 2000; Freeman, 2004; Hochschild and Mollenkopf, 2009; Kivisto and Faist, 2007). These fields are related as opportunities for participating in politics depend on, for instance, socio-economic inclusion. Resources like income, time, knowledge, and networks affect opportunities for people to take part in politics.

Differences with regard to integration policy, such as assimilation and multicultural-ism, also affect the opportunities for political participation as well as the mode of par-ticipating (Bloemraad, 2006; Freeman, 2004; Koopmans et al., 2005; Kymlicka and Norman, 2000). Even though access to such things as jobs and schools often matters most to individuals, political incorporation also has a special importance. By taking part in politics, it is possible both to change the distribution of resources and oppor-tunities in society and to challenge power relations, norms, and attitudes. Being excluded from politics is to lack an important tool to change one's situation as well as that of others (Bohman, 1996; Dahl, 1989). The interrelationship between political incorporation and other forms of inclusion suggests we take a broader look at political incorporation. However, it is beyond the scope of this chapter to deal with socio-economic and cultural inclusion in detail. Nevertheless, in the following, we will highlight some important dimensions in this regard relating both to the impact of resources and mode of participation as well as to the consequences of different inte-gration regimes.

We begin the article by discussing access to legal status (residence), rights, opportu-nities, and the acquisition of citizenship. Access to rights depends partly on entry conditions; immigration policy matters for incorporation policies (Freeman, 2006). We address these dimensions by describing the regulation of access to legal status and rights between different groups of immigrants, the regulation of citizenship acquisition, and the recognition of dual citizenship (multiple citizenships). Factors of relevance in explaining differences in incorporation policies will be discussed in the second section. We then focus, in the third section, on the political participation of immigrants concerning voting and other forms of participation and claim-making in the public sphere. Citizenship is important to social and economic integration, and we address debates and research on the citizenship premium in the fourth section.

2. CONTEMPORARY POLICIES OF IMMIGRANT POLITICAL INCORPORATION

This section deals with the legal and political regulations of the status of immigrants, access to rights, eligibility for acquiring citizenship, and conditions tied to naturalization as well as the regulation of multiple (dual) citizenships. These are all important dimensions of the political incorporation of immigrants. We start by discussing the situation for long-term residents; we then address the regulation of access to rights for other categories of immi-grants, such as seasonal workers, persons with temporary protection, and undocumented migrants. After this, naturalization rules, acquisition of citizenship by socialization for second-generation immigrants, and the question of multiple nationalities are considered before we explain similarities and differences between incorporation regimes.

2.1 Legal status and access to rights for long-term residents

Access to legal status and rights for non-citizens have, since the Second World War, become increasingly equal to that of citizens in Western democratic immigration states. This becomes particularly clear when long-term (permanent) residents and citizens are compared. The major differences between non-citizens and citizens concern the rights for citizens to vote (in national elections) and to stand for office as well as the unconditional right to enter and reside in the state (Castles and Davidson, 2000, Chapter 5; Kivisto and Faist, 2007).

The introduction of the category "permanent resident" is itself an example of the strengthened status for immigrants. This category is, in several democratic immigration states, of rather recent origin; in many countries in Europe it was established as part of the response to postwar labor immigration, when guest workers were not returning home (Hammar, 1990, p. 18f). The development towards strengthening the status of non-citizens and their access to rights has made several scholars emphasize the importance of *jus domicilii* in democratic immigration states. Tomas Hammar (1990) used the notion of denizen to characterize this situation: a strong protection of rights but not a full inclusion in the political community. Examples of this process towards a strengthening of legal status and access to civil and political rights have occurred in several immigration states in Europe. Prior to the Second World War, it was commonly argued that non-citizens should not have rights to participate in politics, and the right to form associations was denied to foreigners, as was, in many cases, the right to engage in political speech. The political participation of foreigners was thought to constitute security problems, problems of foreign policy, and risks regarding the import of political conflicts. However, these views gradually changed in many democratic immigration states after the Second World War, and it was more generally recognized that non-citizens should enjoy the same political rights (except the right to vote) as citizens (Groenendijk et al., 1998; Guiraudon, 1998; Hammar, 1990).

In the Nordic states, non-citizens were afforded the same civil and political rights (except for voting) as citizens in the 1950s and the 1960s. Similar developments are found in other west European states. In 1953, foreigners were given the right to take part in demonstrations and associations in the Federal Republic of Germany, and in 1964 they were afforded the right to form their own associations. A couple of years later, non-citizens got the right to become members of political parties. In some European states, this process was drawn out; it was only in 1981 that non-citizens were granted the right to form their own associations without permission by the state in France. Prior to 1981, the expulsion of persons active in unions and human rights associations was possible, and many immigrants were expelled for their political engagement, which was seen as disrespecting the political neutrality of foreigners in the country (Guiraudon, 1998; Hammar, 1990, Chapter 8).

Voting rights for non-citizens have remained much more controversial than other political rights. In most states, only citizens have the right to vote in national elections.[1] However, steps towards recognizing voting rights were taken in some countries during the 1970s (cf. Hammar, 1990, Chapter 8). Local and regional voting rights were recognized in Sweden in 1975. In Norway, voting rights were granted in local elections for other Nordic citizens in 1978 and extended to all permanent residents in 1983. The same pattern is found in Denmark, where voting rights in local and county elections were granted for Nordic citizens in 1977 and extended to all permanently residing non-citizens in 1981. Similar processes are found in several other countries in Europe; in the Netherlands, local voting rights were recognized for non-citizens in Rotterdam in 1979, and this was expanded to the whole country in 1985. More recent examples of introducing local voting rights include Finland (1991), Iceland (2002), Slovenia (2002), and Luxembourg (2003) (Groenendijk, 2008; Hammar, 1990, Chapter 8).

Most European states today recognize the right to the status of permanent resident (Groenendijk et al., 1998; MIPEX, 2010). The criteria for permanent residence vary between states stipulating few requirements, such as in Sweden, and states in which acquiring permanent residence is almost as difficult as becoming a citizen, such as Denmark and Germany (MIPEX, 2010).

In most states, some period of legal stay in the country is required, ranging from three years in France and five years in several states (such as Denmark, Italy, Germany, Netherlands, Poland, and UK) to states that require longer stay, for instance, eight years in Portugal. Several states, such as Sweden, grant permanent residence for certain groups, such as refugees, from the beginning of their stay. Most European states apply additional criteria, such as ensuring persons are able to support themselves; some states apply extensive criteria in this respect. In Denmark, persons need to be working or studying at the time of application, show they have studied or have had full-time employment for three out of five years prior to application, and demonstrate they have not received certain types of public benefits three years prior to applying (Ersbøll, 2010; Groenendijk et al., 1998; MIPEX, 2010). Another set of requirements that varies between states concerns public order. Denmark is among states with restrictive regulation in this respect: Persons who have been in jail or have been sentenced to jail for more than 18 months are disqualified from being able to apply for permanent residence in Denmark. When sentenced to less than 18 months in jail, persons are temporarily ineligible for applying according to a waiting list. Such waiting lists are used in several European states. Some states require knowledge of language and society; for instance, in Germany, persons need to have command of the German language and to have knowledge of German society.

---

[1] An interesting exception to the common pattern of tying the right to vote to citizenship was the practice in the US of allowing the right to vote for several non-citizens, something that ended only in 1926, when the last state (Arkansas) that had kept alien franchise changed the rules (Coll, 2011).

Similarly, in Denmark, persons need to pass a Danish language test (Ersböll, 2010; Groenendijk et al., 1998; Hailbronner, 2010). Newer regulations in the UK require that persons have command of English (Sawyer, 2010).

The situation in the UK has been different from most states on the European continent because of the Commonwealth association, particularly since the status of British subject, with the right to live in the UK, was applied until the 1981 nationality law. The equivalent to permanent residence in the UK is the so-called indefinite leave to enter or remain (ILR). The somewhat peculiar dimension to this status is that persons who require a leave to enter permit acquire it. Formally, the status is lost when leaving the UK and must be re-established when re-entering the country. For shorter periods of time abroad, this is a formality, but the status of ILR is usually lost when staying abroad for a longer time (e.g., two years) (Groenendijk et al., 1998, p. 59f).

In some European states, such as France and Germany, the development towards recognizing permanent residence for immigrants has been a process in which courts have played an important role. Even though political parties in Germany were less prone to follow the steps towards recognizing rights for aliens in the 1970s, rights for aliens were recognized due to interpretations of the Constitutional Court, which recognized that aliens enjoy rights of free movement and choice of profession similar to citizens on the basis of the Basic Law's article (2(1)) on the free development of personality. The Court argued also that non-citizens, after some time and when return has become less likely, have a legitimate expectation that the German state protect their rights. In the so-called Indian case in 1978, the Court ruled that when authorities renew residence permits, this gives rise to an interest on the part of aliens to continue to be granted residence after some time. Later, the Court ruled also that residents could not be deprived of enjoyment of pension payments when residing in the state. In line with the constitutional principle of Germany being a social state (*Sozialstaat*), the Court ruled that this applies to all—irrespective of nationality (Joppke, 1998b, Chapter 6; Guiraudon, 1998, p. 299f). Local voting rights have also been discussed in Germany: Schleswig-Holstein granted local voting rights to Danish, Irish, Norwegian, Dutch, Swedish, and Swiss citizens in 1989, and Hamburg approved local voting rights for residents who had resided for eight years. However, the Constitutional Court struck down on both decisions, arguing they were contrary to the Basic Law, which entails only German citizens (Joppke, 1998b, p. 194ff).

Courts played an important role also in France. Before the late 1970s and early 1980s, courts had little say vis-à-vis the manifold decisions, decrees, and other instructions issued by government. However, from the late 1970s and onwards, the Council of State declared many of the previous regulations invalid, and it—together with the Constitutional Council—has played an important role in strengthening and upholding the status and rights of non-citizens, for instance through its decision in 1989 that non-citizens could not be excluded from non-contributory benefits (Guiraudon, 1998, p. 298f).

The current residence permit was introduced in 1984; additional requirements restricting the number of immigrants who could enjoy this permit were made by center-right governments and then revoked by socialist governments in the 1980s and 1990s (Groenendijk et al., 1998, p. 31ff). Rights for non-citizens in local elections have been discussed since the early 1980s, and the socialists at the time included it in their party platform but chose not to push for the issue because it would likely not have been approved by the senate. This is what happened to a bill introduced in 2000: after being accepted in the national assembly, it was later defeated in the senate (Bertossi and Hajjat, 2012).

In other states, such as Sweden and the Netherlands, the process towards recognizing permanent residence has been political in nature. Courts play a less important role in both countries; instead, political parties and state administrations have been important actors. In Sweden, avoiding a guest-worker system by stressing equal opportunities and equal living standards for citizens and immigrants in the 1960s provided an impetus for a politically driven process towards *jus domicilii* (Hammar, 1990).

Another example of a politically driven process, although relying to a large degree on the jurisprudence of the EC court, is the recent changes in several European states—e.g., Belgium, Italy, Portugal, and Spain—because of the EC directive 2003/109 on the status of long-term residents. The special residence permit for long-term residents in Spain was first introduced in 1996 (Groenendijk et al., 1998, p. 53f). In Italy, it dates back to 1998; prior to this, only a spouse of an Italian citizen could be granted permanent residence (Groenendijk et al., 1998, p. 77f). In 2007, the EC residence permit for long-term residents was introduced in Italy, and legal regulation of permanent residence was changed in Portugal that year through a new immigration law (MIPEX, 2010). In Belgium, the 1980 Aliens Act introduced the establishment permit, intended to give a secure status for long-term residents or persons having close ties with persons living in Belgium. This regulation entailed a significant shift vis-à-vis earlier practice; lawful use of freedom of speech and association was no longer grounds for expulsion (Groenendijk et al., 1998, p. 20ff). Belgium has also changed the legal regulation of permanent residence in line with the EC directive (MIPEX, 2010).

The changes in residence regulation and access to rights for non-citizens in several European states after the Second World War show the development of *jus domicilii*, which entails that citizens and non-citizens should be treated equally when there are no legitimate reasons for differential treatment. This type of reasoning has for a long time been the basis for inclusion of aliens in the US (Joppke, 1999, p. 22).

US incorporation laws and policies are constitutionally based on two principles: the principle of plenary power and the principle of personhood. Plenary powers entail federal bodies having the right to enact laws and make decisions that are not subject to judicial review. This has been the basis for Congress adopting laws relating to regulating immigration and access to rights. The principle of personhood entails non-citizens being equal to citizens in most respects. This principle has influenced the treatment of non-citizens over the past couple of decades, with the civil rights movement being important in bringing out this idea with regard to immigrants. The Supreme Court argued in the early 1970s (*Graham v Richardson*, 1971) that aliens, like citizens, pay taxes and work, meaning that they should be treated like citizens. This recognition of non-citizens led to courts striking down several laws that restricted their rights in the 1970s. However, the principle of plenary power was not repealed and was ground for restricting rights for non-citizens through the Welfare Reform Act in 1996. Through this legislation, access to social rights and federal welfare programs was restricted for non-citizens (Schuck, 1998, p. 202ff).

Permanent residence in the US is less beneficial and secure than in most other democratic immigration states, and it may be revoked for several reasons, including for minor crimes, for tax evasion, and for stays outside of the country longer than six months. Decisions concerning deportation do not need to be balanced with regard to personal circumstances tying persons to the US (MIPEX, 2010, p. 210). In Australia, persons may apply for a permanent residence visa according to the different routes of entry for work, business, and the like. Visas are valid for five years, allow persons to leave and return, and give access to several social rights (Castles and Vasta, 2004). Canada also utilizes several routes for entry, such as for study, work, and business; beside the basic rules for eligibility, a points system is applied where such factors as language, age, and work experience count. This system was introduced in 1976, replacing previous legislation based on source countries and regional criteria (Reitz, 2004). Access to residence status is relatively easy in Canada, and it is often given from early on in the settlement process. Further, family members and refugees are automatically eligible for permanent residence (MIPEX, 2010, p. 48).

The situation of permanently residing immigrants has been strengthened in some countries in Africa, Asia, and Latin America, but it remains precarious in several states. Most Latin American states allow for permanent residence. In Chile, persons can apply for permanent residence after one year (two years when on a work visa), and it is necessary to show that persons can support themselves; similar rules apply in Uruguay. Some states require a longer stay, for instance three years in the case of Argentina and five years in Mexico. In Argentina, persons are required to have knowledge in Spanish and about society (US Government, 2001).

In most East and Southeast Asian states, permanent residence is primarily offered to high-skilled and professional immigrants, whereas the vast majority of low-skilled migrants do not have access to permanent residence status. In addition, many persons live and work as irregulars (Piper, 2004). Access to secure legal status and rights remains a problem for migrant workers; the guest-worker system and lack of family reunification policies in several East and Southeast Asian states show the conception of transition from alien to citizen is not envisioned and does not provide the basis for policy and legislation (Piper, 2004, p.79f). Japan is also partly an example of this kind of reasoning. The unresolved status of Koreans, who had enjoyed Japanese nationality during the empire but were defined as non-citizens after the Second World War, led to the creation of the status of special permanent resident in the 1980s. The return migration of Japanese from China, labor immigration, and the acceptance of refugees (even though limited in number) were important in establishing the category of long-term resident. As will be touched upon below, the introduction of the status of legal resident has been explicitly tied to deterring immigrants from becoming citizens (Surak, 2008).

2.2 Access to rights for other non-citizens

The equalization of non-citizens and citizens is far less evident in other cases than long-term residents. Seasonal workers and persons having work permits for limited periods of time lack several rights enjoyed by permanent residents. Several European states have wanted to avoid the consequences of postwar labor immigration when setting up new programs for labor immigration; as a result, they have restricted access to resident status. A maximum period of residence and a preclusion of the possibility for family reunification are examples of measures adopted for this purpose (Menz and Caviedes, 2010).

With regard to asylum, granting short-term protection has become more common. The civil wars in former Yugoslavia during the early 1990s were important in the European context for the development towards temporary protection. The introduction of short-term protection caused intense public debate in several European countries, and there were fears that this would be used in many more cases than "mass flight situations," for which the category was originally devised (Fitzpatrick, 2000; Koser and Black, 1999).

In general, asylum seekers enjoy fewer rights than other immigrants (Gibney, 2004). Administrative detention, often in the case of extradition but also during the asylum determination process, includes severe limitations of civil rights (cf. Costello, 2012). Deportation is, on the one hand, a form of extended border control in which states deport persons who have entered the state without proper documentation, visa over-stayers, and asylum seekers whose application has been denied. On the other hand, deportation is used also for expelling persons who have committed crimes, which, according to some scholars, make non-citizens "eternal guests" in the state (Anderson et al., 2011).

Another problem is the legal status of persons in so-called transit zones, which are within geographical borders of the state but are not acknowledged by authorities to be on their territory. One example is the zone at the Paris Charles de Gaulle airport, where persons, including children, are held in custody by French authorities but where French law does not apply (Human Rights Watch, 2009). The UN Rapporteur on the rights of non-citizens criticized international zones in the early 2000s for being "legal fiction," emphasizing that states cannot disregard their obligations in this manner (United Nations, 2003).

The situation for undocumented migrants is also difficult in many countries, and their access to rights is limited (Sager, 2011). Several states in Europe—such as Belgium,

Ireland, Italy, Poland, Portugal, Spain, and the UK—grant the right to education for children in an irregular situation, whereas others, such as Sweden, do not. The Swedish government has declared its intention to implement this right, but it has not yet put forward a bill to parliament. In several countries, such as Germany and France, the right to education is implicitly guaranteed; however, in practice, there are several obstacles to this right. In Germany, schools are required to report irregular status to authorities. The right to health care for irregular migrants is also recognized in several European countries, but it is most often limited to urgent medical treatment. In some states, health care includes preventive care, such as prenatal and maternity care, care for children, and vaccinations; this is the case in Germany and Italy. In a few states, such as Portugal, children are afforded the same rights to health care as regular residents and citizens (Fundamental Rights Agency, 2011).

2.3 Naturalization

The effects of naturalization legislation and policy differ from being an easy and inexpensive procedure with rather few conditions in some states to a difficult, costly, and cumbersome process to become a citizen in other states. Acquisition of citizenship has traditionally been easier in Australia, Canada, and the US than in Europe, but some of the most liberal countries today are found in Europe. For a long time, rules regarding naturalization were made less restrictive in several immigration states, but this liberalization process has partly been reversed over the past decade (Joppke, 2010).

There are several routes for becoming a citizen, and the focus in this section is on the general naturalization rules. Spouses and partners can commonly acquire citizenship more quickly and easily than several other types of immigrants. The acquisition of citizenship for refugees is also easier in several states, and several states outline preferential treatment of persons on the basis of origin. What is often called socialization-based acquisition of citizenship by second-generation immigrants is discussed in the section below.

Common criteria for naturalization are length of stay and good character; the latter is determined through, among other things, criminal records and an adequate livelihood. Several states also require immigrants take language tests or show adequate knowledge of language in other ways, as well as tests regarding knowledge of society. Some states require a declaration of allegiance and loyalty to the state (Castles and Davidson, 2000, p. 86ff; Goodman, 2010).

Among the most liberal rules regarding the length of stay today are found in Australia and Canada, where four years of legal residence is required. In Australia, the required length of stay was changed with the 2007 Citizenship Act from two to four years, and in Canada it was changed in 2009 from three to four years. In both countries, 12 months of absence is allowed. In Australia, persons must have resided in the country for at least

12 months immediately before applying. Both countries have good character requirements and both require knowledge concerning language and society. In Canada, knowledge of the country—especially the rights and obligations of citizenship—is required, as well as proficiency in English or French. This criterion does not apply to persons who are above 50 years old. Persons who have been convicted of crimes in the most recent years before applying are not eligible to apply. In Australia, persons must provide an overseas police clearance certificate when applying for citizenship; moreover, applicants need to pass a citizenship test (MIPEX, 2010). Becoming a US citizen requires five years of legal residence when a green card holder; 30 months of physical presence in the country immediately before applying; being able to read, write, and speak English; passing a test on knowledge regarding society and government; and showing good moral character (Schuck, 1998, p. 201f).

The most liberal naturalization regulation in Europe is found in Belgium, where the residence requirement was lowered in 2000 from five to three years and where earlier requirements regarding language skills (called willingness to integrate) were abolished. Some other states also have rather liberal naturalization laws; according to Marc Howard's citizenship policy index (CPI), states like France, Sweden, and the UK have liberal policies, whereas Austria, Denmark, Greece, and Spain belong to states with restrictive rules (Howard, 2009). In the Migrant Integration Policy Index (MIPEX, 2010), Portugal, Belgium, Sweden, the Netherlands, and Italy are placed before France and the UK. In the case of the UK, it has significantly dropped in ranking from the previous MIPEX report due to legal changes in 2009 (MIPEX, 2010, pp. 22f and 205).

Several European states require five years of residence before naturalizing, but some states require a longer stay, for instance up to 12 years in Switzerland. Among states requiring only five years of residence are Bulgaria, the Czech Republic, France, the Netherlands, Poland, Sweden, and the UK. Among those requiring a longer stay are Austria, Denmark, Greece, Norway, Germany, Hungary, Italy, and Spain. The length of residence is in several states further qualified by requirements of uninterrupted stay prior to application. Some states, such as Bulgaria, the Czech Republic, Greece, Latvia, and Poland, only count years as a permanent resident when determining whether a person is eligible for applying and, in some other states, some of the years of required residence need to be on the basis of a permanent residence permit. One example of this is Austria, which requires five out of ten years as a permanent resident (Goodman, 2010, p. 6ff).

All states in Europe have requirements that relate to one's criminal record, and most states include requirements concerning one's financial situation as well as "good character" or similar. Some states have very strict requirements in this respect. In Austria, persons convicted of any crime will not be granted citizenship. In Denmark, it is not possible to become a citizen when a person has served more than 18 months in prison (or only two months of imprisonment if the crime related to national security). Other states include one's criminal record among the parameters of decision but do not rule out becoming a citizen if convicted of crimes. Instead, persons most often need to wait before being able to apply, with the severity of the crime determining the waiting period. Several states require persons to support themselves, and some states require persons not being dependent on welfare. Some, albeit few, states in Europe have health requirements for becoming a citizen (Goodman, 2010, p. 11ff)

Today, knowledge of language is required in several European countries, as is knowledge of society (Goodman, 2010; Joppke, 2010). Whereas Belgium, Ireland, Italy, and Sweden do not require knowledge of language, many other states do, testing it through interviews and/or written tests. Some states require a language certificate to be provided when applying for citizenship. Denmark, France, Germany, the Netherlands, and the UK also require knowledge of society. In Denmark and the Netherlands, tests of language and knowledge have recently been made more restrictive; tests are now formalized whereas they were previously done through interviews with civil servants (Goodman, 2010, p. 13ff; de Hart and van Oers, 2006).

In most European states, administrative authorities handle applications for citizenship, but there are some exceptions to this. In Denmark, each application for citizenship is addressed by the parliament naturalization committee and accepted or not through parliamentary decision. The right-wing populist Progress Party and, later, the Danish People's Party used this avenue as a way to oppose individuals whom they thought would not be suitable citizens. They thereby made the criteria for becoming a citizen a central political issue (Ersböll, 2010, p. 15ff). In Switzerland, the process is partially political; in some cantons, decisions regarding citizenship are taken by a local vote (D'Amato, 2009; Hofhansel, 2008, p. 181ff).

The more restrictive rules introduced in several European countries reflect a debate concerning a failure of integration and an increasing emphasis on belonging. The introduction of new conditions for citizenship shows a change from perceiving citizenship as a means for integration to viewing it as the culmination of successful integration. Citizenship is looked upon more as a privilege, as a political good that must be earned rather than granted as a matter of right (Joppke, 2010, p. 54ff). Besides increasing the required length of stay, new language and knowledge tests are primarily discussed in this context. Most of the tests of knowledge regarding society focus on politics, economy, and the provision of public goods and services. Only minor parts of the tests relate to traditions and public morality. Among countries including knowledge of public morals, the Netherlands is an example where these types of questions play an important role (16% of the questions concern public morality); conversely, it is not as central in Austria and Germany (Michalowski, 2011).

In the debate regarding language and knowledge tests, it has been common to associate such tests with nationhood and the overall characteristics of the citizenship regime but, as shown in comparative studies, this does not hold true. In her research on citizenship tests, Ines Michalowski concludes that the common assumption—that knowledge tests in countries with restrictive citizenship regimes focus on cultural assimilation—does not hold (Michalowski, 2011). This confirms Joppke's interpretation of citizenship tests, in which he stresses that, rather than to see tests as attempts of re-ethnicization of citizenship, they are better viewed as a form of repressive liberalism or "particular universalism" (Joppke, 2010, p. 137ff). Language and knowledge tests are not primarily focused on particular traditions and values but on universal values: equality, freedom, gender equity, and tolerance. In citizenship tests, these values are rendered national (e.g., Dutch) values, specifying what it entails to be a citizen in a specific state. Consequently, it is not appropriate to see the trend towards making it more difficult to naturalize as another attempt to stress the ethnic, cultural, and linguistic particularities of the nation, Joppke has argued. Instead, it is a form of exclusion built on universal values that not all persons share and/or understand (Joppke, 2010, pp. 123–144).

Despite this trend towards increasing restrictions being evident in Europe over the past decade, there is, using a somewhat longer time perspective, a trend towards liberalization. Joppke estimates that, since the 1980s, naturalization rules have been liberalized in most European countries. Furthermore, the discretionary component to naturalization has decreased, although, in Europe,naturalization is a matter of right only in the Netherlands, Luxembourg, and Germany (Joppke, 2010, p. 45f). The shift in Germany is a case in point; until the early 1990s, when legislation was changed as an outcome of the compromise on asylum between Social Democrats and Christian Democrats, it was strongly emphasized that naturalization was a discretionary decision (Joppke, 1998b, p. 202f). In other countries, there is either more or less discretionary power to deny citizenship, even when conditions are fulfilled. Very wide discretionary powers are found in the case of Greece, where there is also no limitation to the time it may take to process a naturalization application (de Hart and van Oers, 2006, p. 328ff).

In Latin America, some states allow for quick processes of naturalization. In Argentina and Bolivia, two years of stay are required. Most states require a longer stay; in Chile, Colombia, and Mexico persons may apply after five years of residence. In some states, persons from Latin America and Spain can naturalize after a shorter period of stay. This is the case in Costa Rica, where persons from Central and South America and Spain may apply for citizenship after five years whereas other nationals have to wait seven years before being eligible. In Honduras, Central Americans may apply for citizenship after one year, Spaniards and Spanish-Americans may do so after two years, and others after three years. Some states, such as Mexico, require persons to have acquired knowledge of Spanish; Mexico also requires knowledge of history and society as well as a degree of integration in the national culture (US Government, 2001).

Several African countries allow for naturalization after five years of legal residence; this is the case in Gabon, Guinea, Madagascar, Mali, Morocco, Rwanda, South Africa, and Sudan. The lowest requirement regarding residence is Benin, where citizenship may be granted after only three years of residence. Several states require between seven and eight years of residence, for instance the Democratic Republic of Congo, Kenya, Malawi, and Tanzania.

However, a longer stay is required in several states: 10 years is necessary in Angola, Burundi, Egypt, Mozambique, Namibia, Senegal, and Zambia. Some states require an even longer stay, such as 15 years in Nigeria and Chad, 20 years in Uganda, and 35 years in the Central African Republic (Manby, 2010, pp. 64–72). The naturalization of spouses is facilitated in most states in Africa, and reforms undertaken over the last few decades have reduced the gender discrimination in this respect; nevertheless, several states still do not allow women to pass on citizenship to their non-citizen spouses (Manby, 2010, p. 45ff).

Most states in Africa include behavior and character requirements among the criteria for being granted citizenship; lack of criminal record as well as good conduct and morals are common formulations in legislation. Several states require persons to show sufficient income or other means of subsistence. Health requirements are also very common. Several states require prospective citizens to show they are assimilated or integrated into society, they have attachments to it, or that the new country is at the "center of his/her principal interests," as it is expressed in Cameroon's legislation (Manby, 2010, p. 68). Among states that include criteria of assimilation and attachment are Algeria, Angola, Benin, Burundi, Cameroon, Ghana, Madagascar, Mali, Nigeria, and Togo (Manby, 2010, p. 68ff).

Closely related to criteria of integration are language requirements; knowledge of the language of the former colonial state or local languages is required in, for instance, Benin, Kenya, Mozambique, and Tanzania. South African legislation requires persons to communicate in one of its eleven official languages. Most of the countries in North Africa, such as Egypt and Tunisia, require proficiency in Arabic. Some states have far-reaching language requirements; for example, Botswana and Ethiopia require persons to have knowledge in some of the local or national languages. Several states, such as Sudan, had requirements regarding language but removed these criteria in changes to citizenship legislation during recent decades (Manby, 2010, p. 64ff). Some states have racial, ethnic, or religious criteria for becoming a citizen. Liberia is at one end of the spectrum; "non-Negroes" cannot become citizens in Liberia at all. Sierra Leone has far more restrictive rules for naturalization of people who are not "Negroes". In several countries in North Africa, such as Egypt, it is difficult to become a citizen if not of Arab origin or if not Muslim (Manby, 2010, p. 42ff). Aside from legal regulations, administrative and political processes in acquiring citizenship must be taken into account. In most states in Africa, the procedure for becoming a citizen is cumbersome and, in several states, involves decisions by government or parliament (Manby, 2010, p. 64ff).

The situation in states in Asia differs widely between states where there are several criteria for becoming a citizen to those where there are relatively few criteria. In Indonesia, South Korea, Thailand, and Vietnam, persons can naturalize after five years of lawful residence. Some states require a longer stay, for example 10 years in the Philippines. Several states—such as Cambodia, Indonesia, the Philippines, South Korea, and Thailand—require an applicant to know the respective language and history. It is also a common criterion that persons must have means for their own subsistence. Some states require prospective citizens to make investments; this is the case in Bangladesh (US Government, 2001). In Japan, the status of permanent residence was created as an explicit alternative to immigrants becoming citizens (Surak, 2008); in the postwar construction of citizenship legislation, the model of transition from residence to citizenship had been implied but never implemented. With new legislation in 1990, this link was severed with the specific intention of avoiding a situation where immigrants would eventually become citizens. The citizenship legislation is itself not demanding, requiring five years of residence and "upright conduct." The latter is, however, interpreted in terms of assimilation, and authorities—besides demanding an extensive documentation of the applicant's home, family, and workplace—may also interview neighbors and co-workers to determine the moral character of the applicant. This process leads to a very limited number of naturalizations, and the status of permanent residence is considered by many to be more desirable than nationality (Surak, 2008, p. 562ff).

2.4 Citizenship for second-generation immigrants

Citizenship is acquired by birth on the basis of either the *jus soli* or the *jus sanguinis* principle. The latter principle creates problems for children of immigrants, but part of the liberalization of rules for immigrant incorporation over the past half-century has been to facilitate acquisition of citizenship for second-generation immigrants, either by incorporating *jus soli* in citizenship legislation or by having the right to choose the nationality of the state in which the persons are born (Goodman, 2010, p. 26ff; Joppke, 2010, Chapter 2).

Germany is an example of a state that recently has included *jus soli*; as a result, Germany is a much-discussed case since this entailed a fundamental shift in its citizenship legislation. Several democratic immigration states include the possibility of opting for citizenship; when this is an uncomplicated process and not associated with conditions, it makes citizenship an entitlement for second-generation immigrants. However, there are some democratic immigration states that do not follow this pattern. For instance, Denmark recently abolished the optional acquisition of citizenship, and Japan has devised its citizenship legislation in ways that hinder the transition from permanent residence to citizenship (Ersböll, 2010; Surak, 2008).

Citizenship in Australia, Canada, and the US is based on *jus soli*. Australian citizenship was created through the Nationality and Citizenship Act in 1948 (entering into force in 1949); prior to this, UK laws applied and persons were British subjects. The *jus soli* principle was changed in 1986 so that only children with at least one parent being either a citizen or a permanent resident can acquire citizenship upon birth. However, children automatically acquire Australian nationality on their tenth birthday, irrespective of the legal status of their parents (Castles and Vasta, 2004). Canadian citizenship also developed from UK nationality status; prior to the Canadian Citizenship Act of 1946, persons were British subjects (Bloemraad, 2006). The US has applied the *jus soli* principle for a long period of time. However, issues regarding immigration were not central to the establishment of this principle; instead, it was the confirmation after the end of slavery that every person born in the US is a citizen. This is specified in the Fourteenth Amendment of the Federal Constitution. In 1898, the US Supreme Court further specified the birthright citizenship principle by stipulating that it applies to persons born in the US when persons are either permanent residents or in the US on business (not diplomats). The question of whether the *jus soli* principle also applies to children born to undocumented migrants has been raised and, even though the Supreme Court has not ruled on the issue, *jus soli* applies to this category of persons as well (Schuck, 1998, p. 201).

British and French citizenship is based on the *jus soli* principle. The earlier regulation of British subjects was changed after the Second World War; the 1948 British Nationality Act set out who was a British citizen: persons living in the United Kingdom and persons living in countries that were still colonies at the time. In the late 1960s, changes were undertaken regarding the immigration of former colonial subjects to reduce the number of persons immigrating to the UK. The current citizenship legislation was established in 1981, and it includes several categories: British citizen, British Overseas Territories' citizens, British Overseas citizens, British Nationals (Overseas), British subjects, and British protected persons. British citizenship is acquired at birth by children born to parents who are citizens or are settled in the UK (Groenendijk et al., 1998, p. 66; Layton-Henry, 2004).

The *jus soli* principle has been applied in France since the late nineteenth century; for a long time, it was seen as embodying the republican ideal of citizenship. The core principle was the double *jus soli* rule, introduced in 1851, which stipulated that persons born in France to an alien father were to become citizens when reaching the age of maturity (Bertossi and Hajjat, 2012, p. 4f). In the 1980s, however, anti-immigration agitation by Front National made the question of citizenship a major issue of conflict. The new center-right government, which came into power in 1986, introduced several restrictive measures regarding immigration and moved ahead with changes to citizenship regulation; stressing the value of citizenship was among the arguments for change. The proposed reforms met with many protests from left-leaning parties and several associations, and the government backed down from them. A commission was appointed to discuss the issues; it proposed several changes that were taken up by the center-right government in 1993. Even though protests were voiced, they were not as focused as in the debates during 1986 (Hansen and Koehler, 2005).

Revisions of central components of French citizenship legislation were undertaken in 1993, ending the automatic acquisition of citizenship at the age of maturity, modifying the double *jus soli* somewhat, and abolishing the extension of double *jus soli* to former French colonies (enacted in 1973). The new law entailed second-generation immigrants having to express their willingness to become citizens between the ages of 16 and 23, and third-generation immigrants were granted citizenship by birth only when parents had been living in France for at least five years (Bertossi and Hajjat, 2012, p. 11ff; Hansen and Koehler,

2005). When the left returned to office in 1997, it initiated changes to the 1993 law, reinstating persons born to foreign parents being citizens if they still lived in France at the age of maturity and had lived in France during their adolescence. In addition, the double *jus soli* rule was reintroduced for children of Algerian parents. The reform kept the part of the earlier law that focused on willingness to be a citizen by declaring this interest, but parents now can make this declaration with the child's consent between 13 and 16 years of age if the child has lived in France since the age of eight (Bertossi and Hajjat, 2012, p. 13).

Most other states in Europe base citizenship primarily on the *jus sanguinis* principle, although some states have more recently introduced *jus soli* elements into citizenship legislation. The most discussed example is Germany, which included the *jus soli* component by a legal reform in effect from 2000. The new citizenship law followed almost 20 years of debate on the need for reform, and some amendments in the early 1990s, to facilitate naturalization of non-citizens born in the country (cf. Green, 2012; Joppke, 1998b, Chapter 6). Under the *jus soli* component, children of non-citizens are granted German citizenship when at least one parent is a permanent resident and has been residing in the country for eight years. *Jus soli* also gave the right for children born after 1990 to register for citizenship. In order to avoid multiple citizenships, persons are required to choose citizenship at the age of 23. The inclusion of the *jus soli* component entailed a major shift in German policy, but the requirement that at least one parent is a permanent resident also created obstacles. Only about half of the children of non-citizens born in Germany get German citizenship at birth (Green, 2012; Hailbronner, 2010).

Other European states facilitate naturalization by giving a right to opt for citizenship. The Swedish Citizenship Act gives this option to children born to persons being permanent residents for five years (three years in cases of statelessness). Similar rules are found in several European countries, such as Belgium and the Netherlands (Groenendijk et al., 1998, pp. 26, 52). These rules were liberalized in the 1970s and 1980s, but there are several examples of restricting this access to citizenship over the last decade; for example, in Denmark, the option was made dependent on a lack of criminal record in 2000 and abolished altogether (except for other Nordic citizens) in 2003 (de Hart and van Oers, 2006, p. 320ff). There are also some states in Europe where acquisition of citizenship by option has not been available, such as Austria (Groenendijk et al., 1998, p. 69).

In Latin America, most states apply the *jus soli* principle, for example Argentina, Chile, Brazil, Costa Rica, Ecuador, Honduras, Nicaragua, and Uruguay. Some states do not, such as Colombia, where children born to foreign nationals become citizens from birth if at least one of the parents has legal residence in the state (US Government, 2001).

Few states in Africa provide an explicit right to citizenship, and the status of stateless persons remains a problem. As Bronwen Manby put it in a study on citizenship laws in African states, "almost half of the African countries have citizenship laws that practically guarantee that some children born on their territory will be stateless" (Manby, 2010, p. 37). Only 16 states have laws that follow the 1961 Convention on the Reduction of Statelessness. The South African constitution recognizes a constitutional right to citizenship for children, and the Ethiopian constitution does likewise; however, the Ethiopian nationality legislation does not follow this constitutional regulation. Kenya recently adopted new legislation concerning the rights of the child that both follows the Convention on the Rights of the Child and recognizes a right to nationality. Countries following the *jus soli* principle have the strongest protection against statelessness, but few states in Africa (Chad, Lesotho, and Tanzania) base their citizenship legislation primarily on *jus soli*. Several states either allow for children to claim nationality from birth if they are still residing in the country when becoming adults or allow children to have nationality from birth if at least one of their parents is a citizen. The latter kind of regulations is found in Benin, Cameroon, Chad, Ghana, Guinea, Mozambique, Rwanda, Senegal, Tunisia, Uganda, and Zambia. Namibia and South Africa grant citizenship to children born by persons having long-term residence (Manby, 2010, p. 34ff).

Japan is an example of a democratic state where transition from residency to citizenship, common in democratic immigration states, does not apply. This also entails that, besides the naturalization process, there is no special option for citizenship among second-generation immigrants (Surak, 2008).

2.4.1 Multiple citizenships

Multiple citizenships, or dual citizenship,[2] were, for a long time, seen as a problem by states; security risks, dual voting rights, consular issues, and lack of loyalty were among the issues discussed. It was generally argued that dual citizenship might compromise one's allegiance to the state. International and regional conventions on citizenship reflected this concern. However, the stance towards multiple citizenships has, at least partly, shifted during recent decades, and the Council of Europe convention concerning nationality from 1997 is neutral on the issue. Today, an increasing number of states recognize multiple citizenships in principle (Blatter et al., 2012; Faist, 2007; Faist and Kivisto, 2008; Howard, 2005; Sejersen, 2008).

In a study from 2008, Tanja Sejersen showed that of the 115 countries examined, about half of them allow for multiple citizenships. Asian states do so to a lower degree than states in the Americas, Europe, and Africa. The number of states that de facto tolerate multiple citizenships is significantly higher than those that legally recognize a right to multiple citizenships (Sejersen, 2008). When the latter category is included, about 60% of states in the world allow for dual citizenship in some form. Joachim Blatter et al. classify states into several categories: 73 states in the world fully acknowledge dual citizenship, 14 states do so de facto or on the basis of treaties, 24 states show very limited acceptance

---

[2] We will use the terms multiple citizenships and dual citizenship interchangeably. It is rather common to use the term dual citizenship, but it is perhaps more proper to use the term multiple citizenships because states cannot restrict it to citizenship in only two states.

of dual citizenship, and 53 states do not allow for dual citizenship. For another 25 countries, studies have not produced any consistent results (Blatter et al., 2012, p. 9f).

When taking into account the different ways in which persons may become de facto dual or multiple citizens, avoiding dual citizenship is not the overriding concern it once was. International norms, in particular avoiding statelessness, take precedence over avoiding dual citizenship. Fairness and democratic considerations also play a role. The latter is shown in cases where some persons do not have to revoke their previous citizenship because it is either impossible or very costly and difficult. There are thus several reasons for the trend towards increasing acceptance of multiple citizenships. De facto tolerance, the importance of considerations—such as fairness, democracy, and inclusion—in immigration states, and the importance of norms like that of avoiding statelessness are important factors (Faist and Kivisto, 2008). However, facilitating immigration and retaining connections to citizens who settle and naturalize in other countries are also very important reasons for recognizing dual citizenship. The attempt to retain ties with citizens is a particularly prominent objective; states that traditionally have not been very keen on developing a diaspora, such as countries in northwestern Europe, now engage in these practices by allowing for multiple citizenships (de Hart, 2007).

Australia, Canada, and the US allow for multiple citizenships. Becoming a US citizen requires citizens to take an oath of allegiance that entails renouncing other citizenships, and the non-acceptance of dual nationality was upheld for a long time. President Theodore Roosevelt declared, in the early twentieth century, that dual citizenship is a "self-evident absurdity" (cited in Spiro, 1997, p. 1430). Even though dual citizenship has not been fully embraced as an idea of special value, multiple nationalities have become tolerated, as upheld by the US Supreme Court (Jones-Correa, 2001, p. 1012f). Well into the 1960s, US citizens could lose their citizenship either when marrying a foreigner or when voting in elections in another country, but this practice ended when the Supreme Court declared it unconstitutional. The Court ruled that Congress had no power to take away citizenship unless a person voluntarily relinquishes it (Schuck, 1998, p. 167ff). Australia and Canada also allow dual citizenship (Blatter et al., 2012).

In Europe, British nationality laws allowed for multiple citizenships of immigrants and emigrants. The same has applied in France since 1973. Sweden has recognized dual citizenship since 2001; aside from de facto toleration, two types of arguments were important in the Swedish debate. One argument focused on how dual nationality may contribute to immigrant integration. This was the dominant argument in the 1980s, when center-right parties argued against dual nationality. The other argument focused on the possibilities for emigrants from Sweden to retain connections to Sweden when naturalizing in another country. This kind of argument became prominent in the 1990s and was important in changing several center-right parties' views regarding dual citizenship (Gustafsson, 2002; Spång, 2007).

In several other European countries, dual citizenship is not acknowledged. Examples include Austria, Denmark, Germany, Poland, the Czech Republic, and the Baltic states (Howard, 2005). In several states, discussions on dual citizenship have been heated. Allowing for dual citizenship was part of the citizenship reform proposed by the Social Democrats and the Greens in Germany during the late 1990s; however, due to opposition, especially by the CDU/CSU (which organized a petition campaign in the regional election of Hesse in 1999), the governing red–green coalition lost the majority in the Bundesrat and had to enter into negotiations with the Liberals. The government agreed with the Liberals on the *jus soli* reform but not on allowing dual citizenship (Gerdes et al., 2007). The principle of avoiding dual citizenship does not mean, however, that it is not de facto tolerated. European states increasingly came to tolerate dual citizenship from the 1970s onwards. Between 40% and 50% of immigrants naturalizing in Germany since 2000 are de facto dual citizens, and the percentage is approximately the same in Denmark (Ersböll, 2010; Green, 2012).

Some European states allow for dual citizenship only for those who are citizens from birth. Traditionally, this has been a common policy in emigration states in order to retain ties with persons emigrating and settling in other countries (Gorny et al., 2007). A somewhat new trend is that this focus is found also in immigration states. In the Netherlands, the requirement of renouncing citizenship when naturalizing was abolished in 1992 and then reinstated in 1997. With the new citizenship law coming into force in 2003, the possibility of dual citizenship was opened up—but for Dutch-born citizens only. The 1992 decision allowing for dual citizenship can be seen as an outcome of the process of facilitating naturalization that had been a central part of Dutch policy for some time. The reinstating of the principle was largely an outcome of a shift in the public debate on citizenship; instead of looking at citizenship as part of the integration process, it was increasingly seen as the end-point or crowning of successful integration (de Hart, 2007). Some scholars, like Joppke, view the distinction between citizens and non-citizens as well as the recognition of dual citizenship for native-born citizens only as an example of the re-ethnicizing of citizenship laws (Joppke, 2010, p. 63ff).

Several Latin American and Caribbean countries recognize multiple nationalities. Uruguay has done so since 1919, and several of the states in the Caribbean have acknowledged multiple nationalities since independence. However, in most Latin American countries, recognition of multiple citizenships is of more recent origin, for example in Colombia (1991), the Dominican Republic (1994), Costa Rica (1995), Ecuador (1995), Brazil (1996), and Mexico (1998). Some states—such as Argentina, Chile, Guatemala, Nicaragua and Paraguay—only recognize dual nationality on the basis of treaties (Jones-Correa, 2001, p. 999). In most of these states, dual nationals retain their voting rights in the home country, and several states allow for voting at consulates abroad, whereas others do not (for instance, Mexico and the Dominican Republic) (Jones-Correa, 2001, p. 1010f).

Emigrant groups have been important in this trend towards recognizing dual nationality. Emigrant groups, especially in the US, were a driving force in Colombia, Ecuador, the Dominican Republic, and Mexico. In particular, the success of Colombian groups in pressing for dual nationality and voting rights were important for Ecuadorian and Dominican groups to engage in similar attempts to convince their respective parliaments and presidential candidates of their case. In Mexico, competition for support between parties played an important role; the opposition rallied in western and southern US for support, promising dual nationality, and the then governing *Partido Revolucionario Instiucional* (PRI) also joined in. It is clear that campaign fund raising—and, more generally, remittances—are important reasons for politicians in Latin American countries to favor dual nationality (Jones-Correa, 2001, p. 1001ff)

An increasing number of African countries also recognize multiple citizenships: 30 states now allow for multiple citizenships (Manby, 2010, p. 58ff; Whitaker, 2011). Among them are states like Senegal, which has recognized dual citizenship since independence, and states like Ghana and Kenya, which have begun to recognize it more recently. Senegal allows for multiple citizenships and recognizes voting rights as well as the right to hold office for dual citizens. The issue has not become politicized to the degree it has in several other countries (Whitaker, 2011, p. 765ff), such as in Ghana, where dual nationality was recognized during the mid-1990s through amendments of the 1992 constitution, but provisions of how to implement dual nationality were not given until the adoption of a new citizenship law (entering into effect in 2002). The issue has been politicized, with the question of emigrants' right to vote being particularly controversial. The traditional ruling party, the National Democratic Congress (currently in government), has opposed allowing emigrants the right to vote, whereas the opposition New Patriotic Party (in government between 2000 and 2008) has been in favor of it (Whitaker, 2011, p. 769ff).

Kenya belongs to the states that have very recently recognized dual nationality, by a change of the constitution in 2010. Unlike in Senegal, security issues have been important in Kenya, where, due to the large Somali population residing in the country, there are widespread worries regarding allowing dual nationality for immigrants. Kenyan legislation, therefore, allows dual nationality only among Kenyan emigrants (Whitaker, 2011, p. 773). Several countries in Africa do not allow multiple citizenships, for example Algeria, Botswana, Cameroon, Ethiopia, Liberia, Malawi, Tanzania, and Tunisia. Some allow dual citizenship only in some cases, for instance when women acquire the citizenship of their spouse when marrying a foreigner; this is the case in the Ivory Coast and in Zambia, among others (Manby, 2010, p. 63).

In Asia, some states, such as Bangladesh, allow dual citizenship in some form, whereas several states—such as China, Indonesia, and Japan—do not allow or tolerate multiple citizenships. Some states, like Pakistan, allow for dual citizenship only on the basis of treaties with other states. For several states, existing studies give conflicting answers to the extent to which dual nationality is allowed or tolerated; this is the case with India, South Korea, Thailand, and Vietnam (Blatter et al., 2012).

3. EXPLAINING DIFFERENCES IN INCORPORATION POLICIES

The differences between states regarding laws and policies of immigrant incorporation depend on several factors, such as the type of political system, commitment to human rights, nationhood conceptions, regional integration, colonialism, and other historical ties. When considering the incorporation regime, it is important to understand not only that the policies may be explained by several factors but also that access to rights and citizenship for immigrants may have little to do with migration. As noted above, the *jus soli* principle in US citizenship legislation does not stem from considerations regarding immigration but from an attempt to uphold equal treatment of African Americans after the abolition of slavery (Joppke, 2010, p. 37f).

3.1 Democracy

Democratic immigration states with strong commitments to human rights usually grant easier access to a secure legal status and to rights due to the inbuilt inclusion logic of democracies; the claim to political inclusion arises from persons being de facto citizens, by the needs to, for example, abide by the law and pay taxes. The democratic presumption is that the addresses of law need also to be authors of law (cf. Benhabib, 2004; Habermas, 1992). Several scholars have stressed the importance of principles and values central in constitutional democracies when explaining both the extension of rights to non-citizens and the creation of a more secure legal status for immigrants (Freeman, 1994, 1998; Joppke, 2010). Patrick Weil (2001) has stressed the entrenchment of constitutional democratic values as an important factor—together with a high number of permanent residents and the absence of unresolved border issues—in explaining liberalization of citizenship legislation in democratic immigration states.

Several scholars have investigated more specific dimensions to the connection between democracy and expansion of immigrants' rights. Gary Freeman (1994) has stressed the role of client politics; whereas benefits of immigration are specific (for instance, benefits for employers and for immigrants organizing in associations to influence politics), the potential costs are diffuse. Client politics seems particularly suitable to explain developments in the US, but less so in Europe. Joppke (1998a), for instance, has argued that in European states courts and, partly, state administrations explain why there has been a development towards increasing equality between long-term residents and citizens. However, other scholars have emphasized that Joppke's focus on courts is exaggerated as regards several countries in Europe. Much of the expansion of access to rights for non-citizens is better explained by the praxis setting of bureaucracies in several European states. Moreover, in some states, the expansion of rights is the outcome of politically driven processes in which, for instance, social democratic parties played an important role. The expansion of rights has been an outcome of a politically driven process together with praxis setting by bureaucracies operating in an area of little political conflict, as seen through the endorsement of integration policies and citizenship laws in states like the Netherlands and Sweden from the 1960s to the 1980s (Bonjour, 2011; Hammar, 1990). Besides immigration being a low rather than high political issue, what Freeman called "the anti-populist norm" also played a role in explaining liberalization in several democracies. The latter norm may be less strong today; the increasing strength of right-wing populist parties in Europe, and the difficulties established parties face in handling right-wing populist parties, make it more tempting for established political parties and other actors to also play the immigrant card (Freeman, 1994; Guiraudon, 1998).

Much of the discussion concerning both the connection between principles and values in constitutional democracy and the extension of status and rights to immigrants has focused on classical immigration states and states in Europe. When looking at other democratic states, however, this connection is not as obvious; the creation of obstacles to naturalization in Japan demonstrates this. Furthermore, in the Japanese case, the steps taken to create a more secure legal position for immigrants do not stem from constitutional democracy as much as from the impact of international human rights and from problem-solving perspectives (Surak, 2008).

Democracy matters also when trying to explain the acceptance of dual nationality, even though the situation in this regard is far from clear-cut (as shown by several examples in Europe). Beth Whitaker argues that democratization has been very important in explaining the turn towards acceptance of multiple citizenships in Africa, as the process towards democracy both makes questions of voting rights central and allows for diaspora groups to engage in politics. The agitation of diaspora groups in pressing for changes that allow for dual nationality and voting rights for emigrants are important factors in some states, such as Ghana, where diaspora groups in Canada and the UK played an important role. Furthermore, there is also a narrower self-interest among politicians to allow for voting rights since diaspora groups are important for raising funds to participate in elections (Whitaker, 2011, p. 777ff). As discussed above, the same pattern is found in several Latin American states.

The connection between democracy and protection of rights for immigrants is not straightforward. The risks of majority tyranny have been part of debates on democracy for a long time, and immigration and citizenship policies are examples in which this risk is pertinent. Several categories of immigrants lack access to political rights and often have an insecure legal status. Those who have a more secure status and enjoy similar political rights as citizens may lack the necessary resources to be able to participate in politics. Furthermore, there are conceptual reasons for majority tyranny being a particular risk for immigrants. This is because of the conceptual connection between democracy and *demos* circumscribed in place and time, which often leads to restricting immigration for reasons including the realization of a democratic order and a welfare state as well as several other public goods (Benhabib, 2004; Gibney, 2004).

Another reason for the less than obvious connection between democracy and extending immigrants' rights concerns the role of populist argumentation in democracies (Guiraudon, 1998). The mobilization against immigrants in several democratic immigration states over recent decades is clearly important for explaining more restrictive immigration and citizenship policies. For example, in Denmark, the Danish People's Party has played a central role, first by making immigration one of the most important political questions and then by influencing legislation because of its key position in support of center-right governments (Ersböll, 2010). Virgine Guiraudon has emphasized the interrelation between the electoral calculus of politicians, media, and public opinion in this regard. Media coverage of problems relating to immigration makes it potentially electorally beneficial to play on and/or exploit xenophobic and anti-immigrant feelings (Guiraudon, 1998).

Democracy, then, plays an ambivalent role with regard to immigrants' rights and opportunities. On the one hand, the democratic presumption of being able to participate politically when being a de facto citizen point to the importance of facilitating both political participation of non-citizens and easy access to citizenship. This in-built presumption in democracy also explains, several scholars argue, the trend towards liberalization seen in many immigration states since the Second World War. However, on the other side of the relation between democracy and immigrants' rights, xenophobic and anti-immigration sentiments are not only easily articulated in democracies, but they also have a bearing on the electoral calculus.

3.2 Human rights

In the general discussion of democracy and immigrants' rights, several scholars have argued that it is not so much political participation but the rights component of modern democracy that matters. Scholars have stressed that the emerging regional and global human rights regimes after the Second World War have led to an increasing emphasis of rights being based on residence (*jus domicilii*) rather than on citizenship, especially in Europe and Latin America. A cornerstone of the international human rights regime is that enjoying rights, with some exceptions like the right to vote, should not be based on citizenship; several scholars have argued that the impact of this norm is important in explaining the untying of access to legal status and rights from access to citizenship (Benhabib, 2004; Jacobson, 1996; Soysal, 1994).

The importance of human rights in explaining changes to citizenship legislation led, during the 1990s, to a debate regarding post-national citizenship. Yasemin Soysal argued in her book *Limits of Citizenship* (1994) that, when analyzing the incorporation of immigrants, one needs to take social rights as the starting point (as opposed to civil and political rights in T.H. Marshall's scheme); furthermore, Soysal argued one should consider the impact of international and regional human rights conventions. Soysal (1994) claimed that the status and rights of immigrants are increasingly determined by what human rights stipulate. Soysal's and others' arguments on post-national citizenship (cf. Bauböck, 1994) led to much debate, with several scholars criticizing this interpretation. These scholars argued it is not so much the impact of human rights that matters but the democratic traditions and the integration regimes of specific states. With regard to Germany, Joppke (1998b, Chapter 6) has argued that immigration does not render national citizenship obsolete but shows its continued importance. The introduction of *jus soli* elements matters significantly for immigrant incorporation, but this is not understandable from a post-national perspective (Joppke, 1998b, p. 274). Moreover, in spite of the increasing importance of human rights, citizenship still matters for access to several types of rights, and some scholars argue the importance of citizenship has increased over the past decade (Goldston, 2006). Koopmans et al. (2012) have recently shown that liberalization in access to rights continued in several European states until 2002, after when it has stagnated and, to some extent, reversed. It has also been suggested by scholars that we are currently witnessing an increasing importance placed on citizenship when regulating access to rights. States increasingly use citizenship to carve out important exceptions to the enjoyment of human rights (Goldston, 2006).

3.3 Nationhood

Another factor often said to explain differences between incorporation regimes is the conception of nationhood that underlies citizenship legislation. It has been common to differentiate between ethno-cultural and civic-republican conceptions of nationhood. The latter are based on citizens sharing political values and ideas, such as equality and freedom, whereas the former depend on shared belonging in terms of, for example, ethnicity, language, and religion. A minor classic is Rogers Brubaker's (1992) study on the conception of nationhood and citizenship in Germany and France.

Brubaker argued that the more restrictive approach to citizenship in Germany could be explained by the country's stronger emphasis on ethno-cultural conception when compared to France. Brubaker (1992) explained the more open approach in France in terms of the civic-republican conception of the nation. Brubaker's study generated several similar studies of different states, and conceptions of nationhood have figured prominently in studies of naturalization rules (cf. Weil, 2001), citizenship by socialization (cf. Koopmans et al., 2005), and dual citizenship (cf. Faist, 2007). However, in several of these studies, the initial assumption of the importance of nationhood conceptions was revised. In studies on dual citizenship in several European countries, nationhood conceptions were shown to be not important in explaining acceptance of dual nationality. Instead, other factors, including a focus on societal integration, proved to be more important in explaining outcomes in different states (cf. Faist, 2007). Accordingly, several scholars have argued that the connection between nationhood and citizenship is overstated; for instance, they claim it is difficult to understand how the introduction of *jus soli* in German citizenship legislation in 2000 could be explained. It has been claimed that the division of Germany was more important in explaining why West Germany retained citizenship legislation from 1913. The old legislation served as an instrument both to undermine the legitimacy of East German citizenship legislation and to hold the door open for reunification. After unification, Germany embarked also on a substantial overhaul of its citizenship legislation (Gerdes et al., 2007, p. 49f; Joppke, 1998b, Chapter 6).

Comparing France and the US also calls into question the underlying rationale of Brubaker's study (cf. Joppke, 1998b). Both France and the US are traditionally considered examples of states having a civic-republican conception of the nation; however, while the state has played a central role for immigrant integration in France, this has not been the case in the US. This means also that the understanding of what constitutes the republican dimension of citizenship differs; state institutions are responsible for fostering the assimilation of immigrants into the French republican model in ways that they are not in the US, where voluntary associations and markets are more important. The differences in understanding the division between church and state also demonstrate substantial differences to civic-republican conceptions in the two states. In the US, this has largely entailed neutrality of the state, but in France it has, in the tradition of laïcité, entailed the combating of religion in the public sphere. With regard to religion, in Germany—with its ethno-cultural model of the nation, according to Brubaker—there has been more tolerance than in France. The controversy over headscarves in Germany resembles that in France when looking at some aspects of public debate, but the positions of political institutions and courts are quite different (cf. Benhabib, 2002).

The assumption that civic-republican conceptions of nationhood are less ensnared in exclusion has also been questioned. Scholars have pointed to the exclusionary logic implied in civic-republican conceptions of nationhood, for instance when immigrants are seen as not sharing the values of equality, freedom, democracy, and the like that are embodied in the civic conception of the nation (cf. Davidson, 1999). The same claim lies behind Joppke's argument that the major form of exclusion in democratic immigration states today is to be understood in terms of a particular universalism. The new demands being placed on immigrants reflect less the reassertion of specific ethnic and cultural traditions than the suspicion that immigrants do not endorse values central to liberal democracy (Joppke, 2010, p. 137ff).

The character of the integration policy is partly connected to those nationhood understandings. Several democratic immigration states, such as Canada and Australia, adopted multicultural integration policies during the 1970s. It has been commonly argued that multicultural integration policies are conducive for immigrant incorporation because such policies facilitate the formation of associations, inclusion in politics, and easier access to rights and citizenship. In her study of immigrants in Boston and Toronto, Irene Bloemraad (2006) argued that the more successful political inclusion of immigrants in Toronto was largely due to Canadian multicultural policy; however, the conclusions that multiculturalism facilitates political inclusion and participation have, to some extent, been revised over the past decade. Koopmans et al. (2005) noted that immigrant political participation was higher than expected in France and lower than expected in the Netherlands, arguing that access to rights that allow for claims-making in the public, when also tied to assimilation and civic-republican ideals (France), fostered participation in politics. Similarly, multicultural integration policies foster such engagement, but the relation between participation and multiculturalism seems to be curvilinear. Multiculturalism tends to give rise to an inward orientation of groups, discouraging participation in the broader public sphere (Koopmans et al., 2005, Chapters 3 and 4).

Questions concerning the openness of a national citizenship regime to the international community are related both to nationhood understanding and to integration policies. Behind several studies both of transnationalism and of cosmopolitanism lies an assumption that ties that transcend national borders are more encouraged in some states than in others. Traditionally, several emigration states have been interested in developing and sustaining ties to citizens in other countries. Recent studies have shown states with a more internationally oriented state identity are more likely to acknowledge dual citizenship than other states, whereas states with a largely national orientation and that adopt assimilationist policies are less likely to adopt dual nationality (Dahlin and Hironaka, 2008).

3.4 Colonial background and other historical ties

The colonial background is important when wanting to explain citizenship legislation. Aside from the impact manifested in several post-colonial states adopting citizenship legislation similar to that of their respective colonial power, the long- and short-term effects of colonial policy are evident in aspects such as access to rights and naturalization. The colonial background is important in creating special ties between states, such as between Spain and several countries in Latin America, and in the British Commonwealth. Several states in Latin America have treaties with Spain allowing for dual nationality (Rubio Marin and Sobrino, 2010). In the British Commonwealth, the abolition of the status as British subject in the late 1940s and the adoption of citizenship laws in countries becoming independent led to a change in access to rights in Great Britain. The Commonwealth status still has some importance, but the main impact on citizenship issues in former British colonies lies in British legislation shaping the laws and policies of former colonies (Manby, 2010).

The impact of racial and ethnic categories introduced by colonial powers is shown in several states in Africa and Asia. In some African states, access to citizenship by descent is limited to members of groups whose ancestral origins are within the specific state or of African origin (Manby, 2010, p. 42ff). To some extent, this is a reversal of policies adopted during colonial times, when indigenous peoples were subjects of the colonial power, did not have access to rights, and were governed by customary law. This not only led to substantial problems for the post-colonial state in Africa in terms of overcoming the differences between civil law and customary law (Mamdani, 1996), but it also had consequences with regard to persons who were not seen as belonging to the nation that had gained independence. Following independence, creating citizenship laws that confirmed the people becoming independent also created problems for groups seen as non-indigenous. Even in cases where these groups had been settled for a long time, they were excluded from citizenship (Akyeampong, 2006). In some Asian states, such as Malaysia and Indonesia, the British fostered the attitude that the Chinese population was non-indigenous, and the Dutch pursued a similar policy in Indonesia. Despite an ambition to include all Indonesians after independence, the impact of the colonial differentiation was also obvious, for instance, in privileging "natives" over Chinese in economic policies. Under Suharto's rule, there were explicit attempts both to obliterate Chinese-ness, for instance by banning Chinese publications and schools, and to promote assimilation, which encouraged conversion to Islam. To some extent, the distinctions between "native" and Chinese populations, important in the early decades after independence, have—in Indonesia and, in particular, in Malaysia—been replaced with increasing differentiation vis-à-vis new immigrant groups coming as labor immigrants from neighboring countries (Aguilar, 1999).

3.5 State- and nation-building

Citizenship legislation figures prominently in state- and nation-building projects, in which defining who is a citizen and who belongs to the nation is very important. However, the process of defining citizens may entail excluding people belonging to minorities, as evidenced in the previous discussion on persons of Chinese descent in some South Asian countries.

Another example is the exclusion of Russians at the time of independence (around 1990) of the Baltic states. New citizenship laws were set up on the basis of rules and regulations stemming from the inter-war period. Upon independence in the Baltic states, many Russians were not granted citizenship (Groenendijk et al., 1998, p. 72f). Soviet rule entailed attempts of russification, and, in order to mark the newly won independence, Estonia and Latvia based their new citizenship legislation on their respective situations before being annexed by the Soviet Union. Those who could not show their relation to persons being citizens before 1940 were not granted citizenship; instead, they were required to naturalize. As a result, almost half a million persons in Estonia became aliens (Groenendijk et al., 1998, p. 72). The naturalization requirements included knowledge both of the Estonian language and on the Estonian constitution. This excluded several parts of the Russian-speaking population, leading to many debates concerning the problems with such legislation from a democratic perspective. Later, citizenship legislation was amended in order to try to ameliorate the situation, but many Russian descendents in Estonia and Latvia remain non-citizens (Ziemele, 2005).

3.6 Regional integration

Regional integration is also a factor in explaining incorporation regimes. Besides the common practices of states imitating others when constructing citizenship legislation, several states cooperate on a more or less stable basis in developing citizenship laws. Until the last decade, when they parted company on several issues of citizenship, the Nordic states developed common citizenship laws by joint committees (cf. Sandesjö and Björk, 2005).

More recent examples of the impact of regional integration are found in the EU, in which the EC court has significantly extended the rights that accompany persons moving and settling in another member state. Scholars point to the court's importance in relation to protecting rights for member states' citizens when migrating to another member state (cf. Weiler and Wind, 2003). The question of third-country nationals was, for a long time, a matter of debate, but recent EU directives have strengthened their access to rights. As seen in previous sections about reforms regarding long-term residents, EU legislation has played an important role in national reforms (Niessen and Huddleston, 2009).

4. POLITICAL INCLUSION: VOTING AND OTHER FORMS OF PARTICIPATION

Political participation involves several forms of engaging in politics, such as voting and engagement in political parties and associations, taking part in public debate, and civil disobedience. Regarding forms of participation, it has been common to distinguish between conventional and non-conventional forms: Conventional (institutional) forms of participation include voting and participation in political parties and organizations, whereas non-conventional (non-institutional) methods include engaging in boycotts and civil disobedience acts. It is also common to distinguish between low and high costs of participation: Voting is a low-cost activity as is contact with politicians, whereas working in a party or organization are high-cost activities (Rooij, 2012).

Studies of political participation have directed attention to several factors that determine the extent to which individuals participate. Verba et al. (1995, Part 3) argued that resources, engagement, and recruitment affect the level of participation. Among resources are time, money, and civic skills, such as communication and organizational abilities. When addressing immigrant participation, citizenship may be an important resource to complement those more traditionally focused upon in studies of voting and in other forms of political participation (Just and Anderson, 2012). Engagement includes such things as political interest and sense of civic duty, and recruitment refers to people often needing to be asked to participate (Verba et al., 1995, Part 3); these factors are important when looking at immigrant participation. Studies have shown that, in particular, recruitment matters when wanting to explain levels of participation and modes and interlinking of different forms of participation (Rooij, 2012).

Another important issue in studies of political participation concerns how the political system affects levels of participation, as well as the kind of participation persons engage in. Studies have shown, depending on the degree of openness of a political system, that participation will take different forms. In relatively closed political systems, more unconventional methods are likely to be used, whereas the opposite will be the case in relatively more open political systems. These dimensions are important when looking at immigrant participation (Ireland, 1989). However, the characteristics of the citizenship and integration regimes are even more important with regard to immigrants. Koopmans et al. (2005) compared immigrant participation in several west European states, showing there are significant differences in this respect.

Restrictions of immigrants' opportunities to take part in politics have been removed in several democratic states, even though most states reserve the right to vote for citizens. Nevertheless, changes undertaken over recent decades have given access to voting rights on local and regional levels to non-citizens in several countries, as discussed above (Martiniello, 2006). We begin this section by considering voting among non-citizens and voting among naturalized citizens, before moving on to consider other types of participation. Whereas most of those who participate as naturalized citizens or as long-term residents have access to political rights and a secure legal status, this is not the case with irregular migrants. Nonetheless, even irregular migrants engage in some political action, which we consider at the end of this section.

Studies of participation among citizens and non-citizens show that non-citizens participate in politics less than citizens, both citizens from birth and by naturalization (Just and Anderson, 2012; Maxwell, 2010). In the first election (1976) when non-citizens had the right to vote in local and regional elections in Sweden, about 60% took part. At the time, it was thought that the participation rate would most likely increase when more people got accustomed to having the right to vote. However, the turnout has decreased over time and is today below 40% (Bäck and Soininen, 1998; Bevelander and Pendakur, 2011b; Hammar, 1990, Chapter 9). Similar differences between voting turnout of non-citizens and citizens are found in other countries that recognize voting rights for non-citizens at the local level, but the decline in some countries, such as Denmark, has been less pronounced than in other countries, such as Sweden (Togeby, 1999).

The differences between citizens and non-citizens are to be expected for two main reasons: Because citizenship gives access to rights—in particular, the right to vote—and because acquiring citizenship is possible only after staying a number of years in a state, which generally affects one's propensity to participate. In discussions on the socialization effect, some scholars emphasize the more traditional view, namely that political socialization is a long process whereby persons acquire adequate knowledge and an interest to take part in politics during adolescence and as young adults; others argue there is also a significant shaping of the propensity to participate that stems from exposure to the political system. The latter is greater, *ceteris paribus*, where persons have resided for a long period in the state (Just and Anderson, 2012; White et al., 2008).

Regarding those who are citizens, there are fewer differences between persons with or without immigrant background. Studies show there are differences only with respect to voting—not in other respects. In a US study, naturalized citizens vote to a lesser extent than US-born citizens (Bass and Casper, 1999). In a study using data from the European Social Survey (2002/03), with regard to contacting politicians, working in political parties, signing petitions, and civil disobedience, there were no differences between ethnic minorities and majorities (Sandovici and Listhaug, 2010). Studies of participation in Australia show similar patterns between immigrants and citizens from birth; in most cases of participation, there are no major differences between those born in Australia and those born overseas. There are some differences regarding voting between those born overseas in English-speaking countries and those from non-English-speaking countries but, with respect to other forms of participation, persons from non-English-speaking countries do not take part in politics less than others (Bean, 2012).

Standing for office is also a central dimension of electoral politics. In general, proportionally fewer immigrants are elected to political office than who take part in voting. In Germany, the proportion of Turkish immigrants elected to city councils and state parliaments is between 0.5% and 1%. In the Netherlands, immigrant representation is higher in some municipalities, such as Amsterdam and Rotterdam. The same applies in the UK and the US, whereas in France there are fewer immigrants elected to the local levels in big immigration cities (Alba and Foner, 2009).

Regarding which parties immigrants vote for, several studies show that persons with an immigrant background tend to vote to the left. In the UK, close to 90% of Asians and Afro-Caribbeans voted for Labour in 1979, but this declined to about 60% by the end of the 1980s (Anwar, 2001).

Among factors that determine voter turnout rates, money, education, civic status, age, time, civic skills, and access to networks (recruitment) matter in explaining differences between groups. This goes for immigrants as well, but there are also specific factors that affect immigrant turnout besides these factors, such as length of residence, length of citizenship, and geographical location. Studies of voting in France in the early 2000s showed there was a significant neighborhood effect in the propensity to vote

(Maxwell, 2010). Mobilization also matters in explaining differences between groups as well as between cities and regions within the same state. In a study of the 1997 municipality election in Denmark, Lise Togeby (1999) argued that the higher participation rate in the city of Århus compared to Copenhagen could be explained by higher levels of mobilization in Århus.

Besides voting, there are several other important forms of participation. One type of participation connected closely to elections is membership and participation in parties, associations, and interest organizations. Several studies point to lower levels of participation in these associations and organizations among immigrants in most democratic immigration states, but these levels differ both between countries and between different immigrant groups. Togeby (2004) has shown that, in Denmark, Turks participate in unions and in ethnic organizations to a significantly higher degree than persons from the former Yugoslavia; for the Turks, this participation leads to more extensive participation in elections. These differences suggest there are differences between associations and organizations: some contribute to building capabilities that further participation, whereas others do not (Togeby, 2004). Studies in other countries confirm this, for example the study on participation in ethnic associations in the Netherlands (van Londen et al., 2007). Findings from research on immigrant associations in Sweden suggest that the idea of ethnic associations contributing to higher levels of involvement in political processes may be overstated. Research has shown that membership in ethnic associations does not contribute to political participation in the same manner that being a member of associations in general does. However, the reason for this may be less the inward orientation of ethnic and religious associations and more that the civic skills acquired by members in ethnic associations are not translated to other forms of political participation due to a lack of recruitment networks (Strömblad and Adman, 2009).

Participation in public debate is yet another form of participation. Koopmans et al. (2005, p. 78ff) showed, in their comparison of five European states, that migrants and minorities are more visible in the public debate and discourse in the UK than in Germany or Switzerland, with France and the Netherlands being in between. Anti-racist and pro-minority groups are more visible in public discourse in France than in the other countries. In the same study, it was also shown that there are significant differences in the issues raised in the public debate concerning immigration. The dominant theme in Switzerland concerns immigration and asylum policy, whereas non-institutionalized racism and xenophobia are major issues in France and Germany. Discrimination and unequal treatment are major topics in the UK. Homeland-oriented politics are very important in Germany and Switzerland, but they play a marginal role in France and the UK (Koopmans et al., 2005, pp. 88ff and 127ff).

Participation in demonstrations and in other non-institutionalized and, especially, non-conventional forms of politics, such as civil disobedience, are also important. There are several examples of civil disobedience acts involving immigrants but, overall, this remains a rather marginal phenomenon. Koopmans et al. (2005, p. 135ff) showed that demonstrations and violent protests play a more important role in Germany and Switzerland than in the Netherlands and the UK, where public statements make up the bulk of actions taken. Demonstrations are an important action repertoire in France, but violent protests are not.

Institutionalized consultation with associations has been common in several democratic immigration states. Immigrant associations and ethnic and religious associations have been included in policy processes (Entzinger, 1999). The extent to which such consultations take place varies between states: They have been less common in France, which lacks this tradition, than in Canada, Germany, the Netherlands, the Scandinavian countries, the UK, and the US. There has also been a change over time; many consultative bodies involving immigrant associations were set up in the 1970s and the 1980s, but their importance has declined over time. In most cases, the consultative bodies were modeled on the basis of how other associations and organizations had been included in politics. In Sweden, for instance, the corporatist arrangements in other policy sectors became the explicit model (cf. Ålund and Schierup, 1991). Examples from other European states include the commission of racial equality in the UK, set up in relation to the Race Relations Act in the mid-1970s; the commission was an important consultative body for the government. In the Netherlands, a system of consultation was set up in the mid-1980s; in some cases, the Dutch government was obliged to consult with the national body representing immigrants. In several states, like the Netherlands and Sweden, ethnic associations have received funding and other types of support from the state (Odmalm, 2004; van Londen et al., 2007). In some states, there are few examples of consultation at the national level, but consultation exists at regional and local levels. Some associations and researchers have been rather critical of the consultation systems, arguing that they have not provided avenues for immigrants to voice concerns and influence politics (Martiniello, 1999).

When looking at the forms of participation, it is also important to address how the mode of participation depends on the political system and other factors of relevance, such as incorporation policies and nationhood understandings. Koopmans et al. (2005) analyzed the characteristics of political claims-making by, against, and on behalf of immigrants in Britain, France, Germany, the Netherlands, and Switzerland. They showed that there were significant effects in how claims-making was shaped depending on the citizenship and nationhood conception. They argued that this impact is shown with regard to what kind of issues are central to claims; for instance, entry and exit questions were very important in Germany and Switzerland, whereas discrimination and unfair treatment were central in Britain. It is also reflected in the status to which people refer when making claims, for instance as ethnic groups or as immigrants. The action repertoires are affected by the openness of the political system; in systems where immigrants have better access to political participation and arenas for putting forward claims, the action repertoire is more moderate, whereas non-institutional, unconventional, and even violent forms of action are more common in more closed systems (Koopmans et al., 2005).

Contrary to what is common in debates concerning immigrant incorporation, Koopmans et al. found rather low levels of group-based claims made by immigrants, with the exception of Islamic groups (Koopmans et al., 2005, Chapter 4). The shaping of actions and claims through the citizenship regime and nationhood understanding is less evident in relation to religious claims. The latter has attracted much attention over the past decade; some of the most discussed cases of conflicts around immigrant incorporation, such as the French headscarf debate, has centered on the place of Islam in European societies (cf. Benhabib, 2002; Joppke, 2010).

Immigrants who lack access to political institutions and who have an insecure legal and political status may also engage in political acts. One example of this is the immigrant mobilization taking place in Italy over recent years (Oliveri, 2012). In responding to a drive-by shooting that injured two immigrant workers, several hundreds of migrants from Africa, working as orange-pickers, rioted in the city of Rosarno in southern Italy in early 2010. This was the starting point for several other events (such as the strike "day without immigrants" in March 2010) and for mobilizations involving political parties and civil society organizations. Examples like these show that immigrants can act as citizens even when lacking several citizens' rights and resources, thereby also challenging images of migrants as passive victims (Oliveri, 2012).

4.1 Citizenship and economic integration

The first part of this section deals with factors affecting the individual's decision to naturalize. We will provide an update on studies that have tried to explain citizenship ascension in a number of countries. In general, the factors explaining naturalization can be traced from the individual level, the family or group level, and the country level. The second part of this section gives an account of the economic effects of citizenship ascension by the individual in a number of countries.

4.1.1 Who is naturalizing?

In his seminal paper, Yang (1994) argued that most studies explaining citizenship ascension have a starting point in immigrant integration that is seen as a determinant of naturalization. He distinguished between two scholarly traditions. The first stresses the role of socio-economic achievements in the naturalization process; the second emphasizes the importance of the immigrants' cultural adaption to the host society as well as their demographic characteristics. Yang noted that both traditions use immigrants' characteristics as predictors of the probability of naturalization, and both view naturalization as an outcome of the immigrant's successful integration into the receiving country. Another view to predict naturalization is a cost–benefit analysis, which is more in line with an economic view on the ascension of citizenship (Bevelander and DeVoretz, 2008; Yang, 1994). Costs of naturalization could include the loss of citizenship status in the country of origin, implying, in turn, the possible loss of other rights, such as claiming inheritance or real estate in the country of origin. Other incurred costs connected to acquiring citizenship are the time and money invested in different kinds of courses and attached tests before and during the naturalization procedure. When it comes to the benefits of naturalization, the loss of one passport can be offset by the ability to obtain a new passport from the host country. If this country is a member of the EU, this also implies larger possibilities to travel and work in the EU. Naturalization also implies larger political rights to the individual, such as having voting rights in general elections. Finally, naturalization allows for employment opportunities in the civil service, the police, the justice system, and the military—areas normally reserved for nationals of a country. In other words, naturalization expands the pool of potential jobs for immigrants.

A number of studies have assessed the effects of individual characteristics on the propensity to naturalize. In the US (Kelley and McAllister, 1982; Portes and Mozo, 1985), socio-economic variables such as education, occupation, and income are suggested as important factors. Others see cultural and demographic factors as important determinants for naturalization (Barkan and Khokhlov, 1980; Portes and Curtis, 1987). Evans (1988) found for Australia that language proficiency and home ownership are affecting the propensity to naturalize. For Germany (Hochman, 2011), language proficiency is not significant but there are positive effects on naturalization for political interest, period of stay, intention of stay, education and inter-ethnic relations like connections to other Germans. Yunju and Wooksoo (2012) showed that also changing institutional arrangements like welfare reforms can have an effect on the propensity to naturalize. Yang (1994) found that cultural integration is more important than economic integration in the naturalization process in the US. Chiswick and Miller (2009) assessed four factors affecting citizenship ascension: personal characteristics, visa category, country of origin features, and ethnicity of the neighborhood where immigrants live in the destination country. Their results indicate effects connected to personal characteristics like higher level of schooling, proficiency in English, and service in the US Army. In relation to country of origin, they found a higher propensity of citizenship ascension for countries where it is relatively less attractive to be living, both economically and politically, as well as for countries that allow dual citizenship. Controlling for individual characteristics, Dronkers and Vink (2012) tried to assess the effect of citizenship policies on the propensity to naturalize for a number of European countries. Using multilevel analysis, they found that favorable citizenship policies positively affect the propensity to naturalize. However, immigrants from developing countries with unstable political regimes have a higher probability to naturalize than immigrants from other European countries. Individual characteristics like age, language proficiency, and years of residence are important indicators of citizenship uptake by immigrants. By and large, they reiterate the results in Chiswick and Miller's (2009) US study. Also, controlling for individual characteristics and using longitudinal data, Cort (2012) showed that the context of reception, the societal situation towards an ethnic group upon arrival to the country, in this case Latinos in

Los Angeles, has an impact on the naturalization propensity. Finally, most of the studies on the ascension to citizenship are based on cross-sectional data and in principal measuring associations between dependent variables, the uptake of a new citizenship or not, and various independent variables. Few studies used longitudinal data in which the causality between the variables can be measured and by this diminishing the positive selection into citizenship (cf. Bevelander and Helgertz, 2012; Scott, 2008).

4.1.2 Economic effects of citizenship ascension

Over recent decades, a number of studies for different countries in the OECD have tried to measure the effect of citizenship ascension on the employment and earnings of immigrants. The following section will both discuss the outcomes of these studies in relation to the different settings and cover methodological issues in relation to how to measure the effect of citizenship.

Recently, several countries have changed their citizenship legislation with the intention of increasing the economic integration of immigrants. Several studies have been conducted on the effect that a change of citizenship has on the employment and incomes of immigrants over the same period (Bevelander and DeVoretz, 2008; OECD, 2011). In more political terms, as discussed earlier, the granting of citizenship can be seen as an instrument in a socio-economic integration process or as the end reward of such a process. Seen as a reward, a change of citizenship is dependent on a country's specific conditions for the actual change, for example that the individual has acquired a basic proficiency in the new country's language and certain knowledge of laws and customs. This view of citizenship is closely associated with "assimilation"—the idea that immigrants have adapted to the new society to an acceptable degree. In contrast, in a more "multicultural" socio-political setting, a change of citizenship is emphasized as an instrument in the socio-economic integration process (Corluy et al., 2011). Here, the actual naturalization process is seen as an integration tool, in which the individual finds his or her place in the new society by acquiring all the rights and obligations associated with the new citizenship.

The relation between naturalization and labor market integration of immigrants is complex and, to some extent, linked to other factors that affect integration. Some studies suggest there is a "naturalization premium" (i.e., that immigrants who change their citizenship status have higher employment and income levels than the non-naturalized). The following literature review summarizes these studies according to country, methodology, and the factors that could give rise to "the naturalization premium." In general, studies on the relation in the US and Canada show a so-called "naturalization premium," while studies for a number of European countries shows more mixed results (see Table 9.1).

Several factors have been suggested as explanations for the "premium." Some studies claim the premium is linked to potential employers' behavior and attitudes; employers are more inclined to recruit naturalized individuals because the transaction costs are lower for

Table 9.1 Review of studies on the effects of naturalization on labor market integration

Data		Employment	Earned income
Cross-sectional	**No control for selection effect**		
	Chiswick (1978): USA		0
	Bratsberg et al. (2002): USA		+
	Kogan (2003): Austria and Sweden	+ and 0	
	Bevelander and Veenman (2006, 2008): The Netherlands	0 and +	+
	DeVoretz and Pivnenko (2006, 2008): Canada		+
	Akbari (2008)		+
	Euwals et al. (2010): The Netherlands and Germany	0 and +	
	Corluy et al. (2011): Belgium	+	
	Steinhardt and Wedemeier (2011): Switzerland	+	
Cross-sectional	**Control for selection effect**		
	Bevelander and Pendakur (2011a, b): Sweden	+	
	Bevelander and Pendakur (2012): Canada and Sweden	+	+
	Rallu (2011): France and the USA	+	
	Kayaoglu and Kaya (2011): Germany and France	+ and ᵾ	
Longitudinal	Bratsberg et al. (2002): USA		+
	Scott (2008): Sweden		0
	Fougère and Safi (2009): France	+	
	Hayfron (2008): Norway	+	
	Steinhardt (2008): Germany	+	
	Engdahl (2011): Sweden		0
	Bratsberg and Raaum (2011): Norway		0
	Bevelander and Helgertz (2012)		0

+ = positive significant effect; 0 = no significant effect.

naturalized labor than for individuals who have only temporary work and/or residence permits. Citizenship is seen as a signal to employers that the person in search of work intends to stay and settle permanently in the country and is prepared to invest in both human and social capital. In other words, employing someone who is naturalized is regarded as less risky relative to an individual that is a non-citizen (Mazzolari, 2009). Mazzolari (2009) also found that individuals who come from countries that allow dual citizenship have an increase in employment and income.

Other factors considered as important in explaining the positive effect of citizenship on labor market integration are related to an individual profitability calculation. In some countries, only citizens of that country have the right to certain jobs. For example, some jobs in the public sector—such as in the police, in law, and in the military—are open only to those who are citizens of that country. Naturalization means the individual is eligible for this kind of work and is thereby able to improve her or his chances of obtaining work (Bratsberg et al., 2002; Yang, 1994). Having access to different occupations and sectors can also lead to greater professional mobility and a higher earned income (DeVoretz and Pivnenko, 2006). In some countries, naturalization leads to other entitlements, such as unemployment benefits and social allowances.

Individuals who choose to change citizenship can also differ in other respects from those who do not naturalize. The effect of naturalization can also be intertwined with other factors that cannot be controlled for in the analysis (DeVoretz and Pivnenko, 2008). More specifically, the change of citizenship can be regarded as a sign of a drawn-out integration process that is cultural, social, and linguistic. Related to this, Bevelander and Veenman (2006) found no effect of integration courses taken by immigrants on the probability to become Dutch or the probability to be employed in the Dutch labor market. Furthermore, the effect of a change of citizenship will exist before the actual change takes place. In addition to naturalization having a causal and positive selection effect on employment and incomes, Euwals et al. (2010) claimed that a negative selection effect can also occur, meaning immigrants with weak socio-economic profiles have a greater tendency to naturalize in order to be included in different welfare services.

Summarizing the studies that have examined the effect of citizenship on labor market outcomes, the analysis of immigration and naturalization has played a minor role in the field of economics for a long time. One exception is the early work by Chiswick (1978), in which he compared wages of foreign-born men with and without US citizenship, using cross-sectional data from the 1970 US Census. He concluded that naturalized foreign-born men have higher average earnings than non-naturalized foreign-born men. However, controlling for the length of stay, the effect of naturalization on earnings becomes insignificant.

Contemporary studies of the impacts of citizenship acquisition by Bratsberg et al. (2002), Hayfron (2008), Scott (2008), Steinhardt (2008), Engdahl (2011), and Bevelander and Helgertz (2012) used longitudinal data to apply individual fixed effects models that control for self-selection and both observable and non-observable characteristics. Contrary to Chiswick's (1978) seminal study, these studies found a positive impact of naturalization on wages even after controlling for time in the host country. Factors that could explain such an outcome include an individual's decision to invest in human capital or an employer's decision to view citizenship acquisition as an indicator of long-term commitment. Of course, in the short run this investment may affect wages, but in the long run the accumulation of human capital could result in higher wage levels. For the US, the results of Bratsberg et al. (2002) suggest that citizenship acquisition reduces institutional labor market barriers, thereby increasing job opportunities for immigrants.

In particular, they demonstrate an increase in the likelihood of public sector employment as a product of naturalization. Using cross-sectional data, DeVoretz and Pivnenko (2006, 2008) showed that naturalized immigrants in Canada had higher earnings and, consequently, made larger contributions to the Canadian federal treasury than their non-naturalized counterparts. Similarly, Akbari (2008) found naturalized immigrants in the US in 2000 had increased treasury payments as well as higher rates of welfare participation. However, tax payments exceed transfer payments for naturalized immigrants after 10 years of residence. Mazzolari (2009) found employment and earnings increased for naturalized Latin American immigrants in the US when their home countries passed dual citizenship laws and granted expatriates the right to naturalize in the receiving country.

Turning to Europe, recent research on Sweden by Bevelander and Pendakur (2012) point in the same direction. They assert that naturalization helps to improve the employment situation of refugees, particularly for those from lower income countries. Overall, empirical evidence indicates naturalization increases the labor market opportunities of immigrants and helps to facilitate the process of employment integration (see, for example, Bevelander and Veenman (2008) for the Netherlands; Kogan (2003) comparing Austria and Sweden; Steinhardt (2008) for Germany; Steinhardt and Wedemeier (2011) for Switzerland; and Kayaoglu and Kaya (2011) comparing Germany and France). Corluy et al. (2011), examining immigrant outcomes in Belgium, found improved labor market outcomes for non-Western immigrants in general.

Finally, in Table 9.1, we give an overview of studies that have analyzed the effect of citizenship on the economic integration of immigrants. We structure this table according to the data that have determined the choice of analysis method; hence, the studies have been divided into cross-sectional and longitudinal data. Although all the studies have shown an awareness of the selection problem, they have not always taken this into account in the empirical analysis. In studies with cross-sectional data, different kinds of instruments have been included in order to reduce the effects of endogeneity. The same goes for longitudinal studies where it has been possible to control for differences in observed and unobserved individual characteristics.

5. CONCLUSIONS

In this chapter, we have dealt with several dimensions to immigration incorporation, discussing the regulation of access to legal status, rights, and citizenship as well as what may explain differences between states in this regard. We have also dealt with the factors that explain the propensity to naturalize and to what extent becoming a citizen has effects on employment and income. Whereas immigration is a phenomenon that affects almost all states in the world, there are significant differences between states when it comes to access to legal status, rights, and citizenship. In several democratic immigration states in Europe,

North America, and Oceania, access to secure legal status, rights, and citizenship has been made easier after the Second World War. The political incorporation of immigrants was facilitated by changes of legislation and policies. However, during the last decade, several changes have been undertaken to make incorporation more difficult. Legal status has been made less secure and dependent on discretionary decisions in some states, and several states have introduced new criteria for becoming citizens, such as knowledge of language, politics, and history. At the same time, we see the continued liberalization of policies regarding dual nationality. As a result, it is difficult to ascertain where we are heading; there are signs both of increasing restrictions on incorporation and of making incorporation easier.

What incorporation policies make clear, however, is that although the more inclusive approach to incorporation, which characterized the 1950s to the 1990s, showed the increasing importance of *jus domicilii* in contrast to citizenship, this has not led to a post-national situation. We continue to live in a world in which residence and citizenship has major effects on persons' lives. States retain substantial power with respect to allowing entry to the territory, granting or denying access to status and rights, and—by implication of this—to opportunities and possibilities in society.

REFERENCES

Agency, Fundamental Rights, 2011. Fundamental rights of migrants in an irregular situation in the European Union. European Union Agency for Fundamental. Rights, Vienna.

Aguilar, F., 1999. The triumph of instrumental citizenship? Migrations, identities, and the nation-state in Southeast Asia. Asian Stud. Rev. 23 (3), 307–336.

Akbari, A.H., 2008. Immigrant naturalization and its impacts on immigrant labor market performance and treasury. In: Bevelander, P., DeVoretz, D.J. (Eds.), The Economics of Citizenship. Holmbergs, MIM/Malmö University, Malmö.

Akyeampong, E., 2006. Race, identity and citizenship in Black Africa: The case of the Lebanese in Ghana. Africa 76 (3), 297–323.

Alba, R., Foner, N., 2009. Entering the precincts of power. Do national differences matter for immigrant minority political representation. In: Hochschild, J., Mollenkopf, J. (Eds.), Bringing Outsiders In: Transatlantic Perspectives on Immigrant Political Incorporation. Cornell University Press, Ithaca, NY, pp. 277–293.

Ålund, A., Schierup, C.-U., 1991. Paradoxes of Multiculturalism. Avebury, Aldershot.

Anderson, B., Gibney, M., Paoletti, E., 2011. Citizenship, deportation, and the boundaries of belonging. Citizen Stud. 15 (5), 547–563.

Anwar, M., 2001. The participation of ethnic minorities in British politics. J. Ethnic. Migrat. Stud. 27 (3), 533–549.

Barkan, E.R., Khokhlov, N., 1980. Socioeconomic data as indices of naturalization patterns in the United States: A theory revisited. Ethnicity 7, 159–190.

Bass, L., Casper, L., 1999. Are There Differences in Registration and Voting Behavior Between Naturalized and Native-born Americans? Population Division Working Paper 28, US Bureau of the Census, Washington, DC.

Bauböck, R., 1994. Transnational Citizenship: Membership and Rights in International Migration. Edward Elgar, Aldershot.

Bäck, H., Soininen, M., 1998. Immigrants in the political process. Scand. Polit. Stud. 21 (1), 29–50.

Bean, C., 2012. Democratic participation in a globalised world: Immigrants in Australia in the early 21st century. Aust. J. Polit. Sci. 47 (1), 115–131.

Benhabib, S., 2002. Claims of Culture: Equality and Diversity in the Global Era. Princeton University Press, Princeton, NJ.

Benhabib, S., 2004. The Rights of Others: Aliens, Residents, and Citizens. Cambridge University Press, Cambridge.

Bertossi, C., Hajjat, A., 2012. Country Report: France. European University Institute, Florence.

Bevelander, P., DeVoretz, D. (Eds.), 2008. The Economics of Citizenship. Holmbergs, MIM/Malmö University, Malmö.

Bevelander, P., Helgertz, J., 2012. Är det lönsamt att bli medborgare? Malmö University, Mimeo.

Bevelander, P., Pendakur, R., 2011a. Citizenship, co-ethnic populations, and employment probabilities of immigrants in Sweden. Online Journal of International Migration and Integration I-First.

Bevelander, P., Pendakur, R., 2011b. Voting and social inclusion in Sweden. Int. Migrat. 49 (4, August), 67–92.

Bevelander, P., Pendakur, R., 2012. Citizenship Acquisition, Employment Prospects and Earnings: Comparing Two Cool Countries. Working Paper, Robert Schuman Centre, Florence.

Bevelander, P., Veenman, J., 2006. Naturalization and immigrants' employment integration in the Netherlands. J. Int. Migrat. Integ. 7 (3), 327–349.

Bevelander, P., Veenman, J., 2008. Naturalisation and socioeconomic integration: The case of the Netherlands. In: Bevelander, P., DeVoretz, D.J. (Eds.), The Economics of Citizenship, RIIM and IZA Discussion Paper. Holmbergs MIM/Malmö University, Malmö.

Blatter, J., Erdmann, S., Schwanke, K., 2012. Acceptance of Dual Citizenship: Empirical Data and Political Contexts. Institute of Political Science, Universität Luzern, Luzern.

Bloemraad, I., 2006. Becoming a Citizen: Incorporating Immigrants and Refugees in the United States and Canada. University of California Press, Berkeley.

Bohman, J., 1996. Public Deliberation: Pluralism, Complexity, and Democracy. MIT Press, Cambridge, MA.

Bommes, M., Geddes, A. (Eds.), 2000. Immigration and Welfare: Challenging the Borders of the Welfare State. Routledge, New York.

Bonjour, S., 2011. The power and morals of policy makers: Reassessing the control gap debate. Int. Migrat. Rev. 45 (1), 89–122.

Bratsberg, B., Raaum, O., 2011. The labor market outcomes of naturalized citizens in Norway. In: OECD (2011), Naturalisation: A Passport for the Better Integration of Immigrants?. OECD Publications.

Bratsberg, B., Ragan, J.F., Nasir, Z.M., 2002. The effect of naturalization on wage growth: A panel study of young male immigrants. J. Labor Econ. 20, 568–597.

Brubaker, R., 1992. Citizenship and Nationhood in France and Germany. Harvard University Press, Cambridge, MA.

Castles, S., Davidson, A., 2000. Citizenship and Migration: Globalization and the Politics of Belonging. Routledge, New York.

Castles, S., Vasta, E., 2004. Australia: New conflicts around old dilemmas. In: Cornelius, W., Tsuda, T., Martin, P., Hollifield, J. (Eds.), Controlling Immigration: A Global Perspective. second ed. Stanford University Press, Stanford, pp. 141–173.

Chiswick, B., Miller, P., 2009. Citizenship in the United States: The roles of immigrant characteristics and country of origin. Res. Labor. Econ 29, 91–130.

Chiswick, B., 1978. The effect of Americanization on the earnings of foreign-born men. J. Polit. Econ. 86, 897–921.

Coll, K., 2011. Citizenship acts and immigrant voting rights movements in the US. Citizen Stud. 15 (8), 993–1009.

Corluy, V., Marx, I., Verbist, G., 2011. Employment chances and changes of immigrants in Belgium: The impact of citizenship. Int. J. Comp. Sociol. 52 (4), 350–368.

Cornelius, W., Martin, P., Hollifield, J. (Eds.), 1994. Controlling Immigration. Stanford University Press, Stanford, CA.

Cort, D., 2012. Spurred to action or retreat? The effects of reception contexts on naturalization decisions in Los Angeles. Int. Migr. Rev. 46 (2), 483–516.

Costello, C., 2012. Human rights and the elusive universal subject: Immigration detention under international human rights and EU law. Indiana J. Global Leg. Stud. 19 (1), 257–303.

Dahl, R., 1989. Democracy and Its Critics. Yale University Press, New Haven, CT.

Dahlin, E., Hironaka, A., 2008. Citizenship beyond borders: A cross-national study of dual citizenship. Socio. Inq. 78 (1), 54–73.

D'Amato, G., 2009. Swiss citizenship: A municipal approach to participation? In: Hochschild, J., Mollenkopf, J. (Eds.), Bringing Outsiders In: Transatlantic Perspectives on Immigrant Political Incorporation. Cornell University Press, Ithaca, NY, pp. 63–73.

Davidson, A., 1999. Open republic, multiculturalism and citizenship: The French debate. Theory and Event 3 (2), 49–71.

de Hart, B., 2007. The end of multiculturalism: The end of citizenship? Political and public debates on dual citizenship in the Netherlands (1980–2004). In: Faist, T. (Ed.), Dual Citizenship in Europe: From Nationhood to Societal Integration. Ashgate, Aldershot, pp. 77–102.

de Hart, B., van Oers, R., 2006. European trends in nationality law. In: Bauböck, R., Ersböll, E., Groenendijk, K., Waldrauch, H. (Eds.), Acquisition and Loss of Nationality. In: Comparative Analyses, 1. Amsterdam University Press, Amsterdam, pp. 317–358.

DeVoretz, D.J., Pivnenko, S., 2006. The economic causes and consequences of Canadian citizenship. J. Int. Migrat. Inte. 6, 435–468.

DeVoretz, D.J., Pivnenko, S., 2008. The economic determinants and consequences of Canadian citizenship ascension. In: Bevelander, P., DeVoretz, D.J. (Eds.), The Economics of Citizenship. Holmbergs MIM/Malmö University, Malmö.

Dronkers, J., Vink, M.P., 2012. Explaining access to citizenship in Europe: How policies affect naturalisation rates. Eur. Union. Polit. 13 (3), 390–412.

Engdahl, M., 2011. The impact of naturalisation on labor market outcomes in Sweden. In: OECD (2011). In: Naturalisation: A Passport for the Better Integartion of Immigrants? OECD Publications.

Entzinger, J., 1999. Political and Social Participation of Immigrants through Consultative Bodies. Council of Europe, Strasbourg.

Ersböll, E., 2010. Country Report: Denmark. European University Institute, Florence.

Euwals, R., Dagevos, J., Gijsberts, M., 2010. Citizenship and labor market position: Turkish immigrants in Germany and the Netherlands. Int. Migrat. Rev. 44 (3), 513–538.

Evans, M.D.R., 1988. Choosing to be a citizen. The time-path of citizenship in Australia. Int. Migrat. Rev. 22 (2), 243–264.

Faist, T., Kivisto, P., 2008. Dual Citizenship in Global Perspective: From Unitary to Multiple Citizenship. Palgrave Macmillan, Houndmills.

Faist, T. (Ed.), 2007. Dual Citizenship in Europe: From Nationhood to Societal Integration. Ashgate, Aldershot.

Fitzpatrick, J., 2000, Temporary protection of refugees: Elements of a formalized regime. Am. J. Int. Law 94 (2), 279–306.

Fougère, D., Safi, M., 2009. Naturalization and employment of immigrants in France (1968–1999). Int. J. Manpow. 30 (1/2), 83–96.

Fraga, L.R., 2009. Building through exclusion: Anti-immigrant politics in the United States. In: Hochschild, J., Mollenkopf, J. (Eds.), Bringing Outsiders In: Transatlantic Perspectives on Immigrant Political Incorporation. Cornell University Press, Ithaca, NY, pp. 176–192.

Freeman, G., 1994. Can liberal states control unwanted migration? Ann. Am. Acad. Polit. Soc. Sci. 534, 17–30.

Freeman, G., 1998. The decline of sovereignty? Politics and immigration restriction in liberal states. In: Joppke, C. (Ed.), Challenges to the Nation-State: Immigration in Western Europe and the United States. Oxford University Press, Oxford, pp. 86–108.

Freeman, G., 2004. Immigrant incorporation in western democracies. Int. Migrat. Rev. 38 (3), 945–969.

Freeman, G., 2006. National models, policy types, and the politics of immigration in liberal democracies. W. Eur. Polit. 29 (2), 227–247.

Gerdes, J., Faist, T., Rieple, B., 2007. We are all republican now: The politics of dual nationality in Germany. In: Faist, T. (Ed.), Dual Citizenship in Europe: From Nationhood to Societal Integration. Ashgate, Aldershot, pp. 45–76.

Gibney, M., 2004. The Ethics and Politics of Asylum: Liberal Democracy and the Response to Refugees. Cambridge University Press, Cambridge.

Goldston, J., 2006. Holes in the rights framework: Racial discrimination, citizenship, and the rights of noncitizens. Ethics. Int. Aff. 20 (3), 321–347.

Goodman, S.W., 2010. Naturalisation Policies in Europe: Exploring Patterns of Inclusion and Exclusion. European University Institute, Florence.

Gorny, A., Grzymala-Kazlowska, A., Korys, P., Weinar, A., 2007. Selective tolerance? Regulations, practice and discussions regarding dual citizenship in Poland. In: Faist, T. (Ed.), Dual Citizenship in Europe: From Nationhood to Societal Integration. Ashgate, Aldershot, pp. 147–170.

Government, U.S., 2001. Citizenship Laws of the World. In: United States Office of Personnel Management Investigations Service, Washington, DC.

Green, S., 2012. Much ado about not-very-much? Assessing ten years of German citizenship reform. Citizen Stud. 16 (2), 173–188.

Groenendijk, K., Guild, E., Dogan, H., 1998. Security of Residence of Long-Term Migrants. A Comparative Study of Law and Practice in European Countries. Council of Europe, Strasbourg.

Groenendijk, K., 2008. Local Voting Rights for Non-Nationals in Europe: What We Know and What We Need to Learn. Migration Policy Institute, Washington, DC.

Guiraudon, V., 1998. Citizenship rights for non-citizens: France, Germany, and the Netherlands. In: Joppke, C. (Ed.), Challenges to the Nation-State: Immigration in Western Europe and the United States. Oxford University Press, Oxford, pp. 272–318.

Gustafsson, P., 2002. Globalisation, multiculturalism and individualism: The Swedish debate on dual citizenship. J. Ethnic. Migrat. Stud. 28 (3), 463–481.

Habermas, J., 1992. Faktizität und Geltung: Beiträge zur Diskurstheorie des Rechts und des demokratischen Rechtsstaats. Suhrkamp, Frankfurt.

Hailbronner, K., 2010. Country Report: Germany. European University Institute, Florence.

Hammar, T., 1990. Democracy and the Nation State: Aliens, Denizens, and Citizens in a World of International Migration. Avebury, Aldershot.

Hansen, R., Koehler, J., 2005. Issue definition, political discourse and the politics of nationality reform in France and Germany. Eur. J. Polit. Res. 44, 623–644.

Hayfron, J.E., 2008. The economics of Norwegian citizenship. In: Bevelander, P., DeVoretz, D.J. (Eds.), The Economics of Citizenship. Holmbergs MIM/Malmö University, Malmö.

Hochman, O., 2011. Determinants of positive naturalisation intentions among Germany's labour migrants. J. Ethnic Migr. Stud. 37 (9), 1403–1421.

Hochschild, J., Mollenkopf, J., 2009. Modeling immigrant political incorporation. In: Hochschild, J., Mollenkopf, J. (Eds.), Bringing Outsiders In: Transatlantic Perspectives on Immigrant Political Incorporation. Cornell University Press, Ithaca, NY, pp. 15–30.

Hofhansel, C., 2008. Citizenship in Austria, Germany, and Switzerland: Courts, legislatures, and administrators. Int. Migrat. Rev. 42 (1), 163–192.

Hollifield, J., 2004. The emerging migration state. Int Migrat Rev 38 (3), 885–912.

Howard, M., 2005. Variation in dual citizenship policies in the countries of the EU. Int Migrat Rev 39 (3), 697–720.

Howard, M., 2009. The Politics of Citizenship in Europe. Cambridge University Press, Cambridge.

Human Rights Watch, 2009. Lost in Transit: Insufficient Protection for Unaccompanied Migrant Children at Roissy Charles de Gaulle Airport. Human Rights Watch, New York.

Ireland, P., 1989. The state and the political participation of the 'new' immigrants in France and the United States. Revue Francaise d'Etudes Américaines no. 41, 315–328.

Jacobson, D., 1996. Rights across Borders: Immigration and the Decline of Citizenship. Johns Hopkins University Press, Baltimore.

Jones-Correa, M., 2001. Under two flags: Dual nationality in Latin America and its consequences for naturalization in the United States. Int. Migrat. Rev. 35 (4), 997–1029.

Joppke, C., 1998a. Why liberal states accept unwanted immigration. World Polit. 50 (2), 266–293.

Joppke, C., 1998b. Immigration and the Nation-State: The United States, Germany, and Great Britain. Oxford University Press, Oxford.

Joppke, C., 1999. The Domestic Legal Sources of Immigrant Rights: The United States, Germany, and the European Union. EUI Working Paper No. 99/3, European University Institute, Florence.

Joppke, C., 2010. Citizenship and Immigration. Polity, Cambridge.

Just, A., Anderson, C., 2012. Immigrants, citizenship and political action in Europe. Br. J. Polit. Sci. 42 (3), 481–509.

Kastoryano, R., 2010. Negotiations beyond borders: States and immigrants in postcolonial Europe. J. Interdiscipl. Hist. 41 (1), 79–95.

Kayaoglu, A., Kaya, A., 2011. Is National Citizenship Withering Away? Social Affiliations and Labor Market Integration of Turkish Origin Immigrants in Germany and France. University of Louvain, Discussion Paper 2011:33.

Kelley, J., McAllister, I., 1982. The decision to become an Australian citizen. Australian and New Zealand Journal of Sociology 18, 428–439.

Kivisto, P., Faist, T., 2007. Citizenship: Discourse, Theory, and Transnational Prospects. Blackwell, Oxford.

Kogan, I., 2003. Ex-Yugoslavs in the Austrian and Swedish labor markets: The significance of period of migration and the effect of citizenship acquisition. J. Ethnic. Migrat. Stud. 29, 595–622.

Koopmans, R., Statham, P., Giugni, M., Passy, F., 2005. Contested Citizenship. Immigration and Cultural Diversity in Europe. University of Minnesota Press, Minneapolis.

Koopmans, R., Michalowski, I., Waibel, S., 2012. Citizenship rights for immigrants: National processes and cross-national convergence in Western Europe, 1980–2008. Am. J. Sociol. 117 (4), 1202–1245.

Koser, K., Black, R., 1999. Limits to harmonization: The "temporary protection" of refugees in the European Union. Int. Migrat. 37 (3), 521–543.

Kymlicka, W., Norman, W. (Eds.), 2000. Citizenship in Diverse Societies. Oxford University Press, Oxford.

Kymlicka, W., 2012. Multiculturalism: Success, Failure, and the Future. Migration Policy Institute, Washington, DC.

Layton-Henry, Z., 2004. Britain: From immigration control to migration management. In: Cornelius, W., Tsuda, T., Martin, P., Hollfield, J. (Eds.), Controlling Immigration: A Global Perspective, second ed. Stanford University Press, Stanford, CA, pp. 297–333.

Mamdani, M., 1996. Citizen and Subject: Contemporary Africa and the Legacy of Late Colonialism. Princeton University Press, Princeton, NJ.

Manby, B., 2010. Citizenship Law in Africa: A Comparative Study. Open Society Foundation, New York.

Martiniello, M., 1999. The limits of consultative politics for immigrants and ethnic immigrant minorities. In: Entzinger, H. (Ed.), Political and Social Participation of Immigrants through Consultative Bodies. Council of Europe, Strasbourg.

Martiniello, M., 2006. Political participation, mobilisation and representation of immigrants and their offspring in Europe. In: Bauböck, R. (Ed.), Migration and Citizenship: Legal Status, Rights and Political Participation. Amsterdam University Press, Amsterdam, pp. 83–105.

Maxwell, R., 2010. Political participation in France among non-European-origin migrants: Segregation or integration? J. Ethnic. Migrat. Stud. 36 (3), 425–443.

Mazzolari, F., 2009. Dual citizenship rights: Do they make more and better citizens? Demography 46, 169–191.

Menz, G., Caviedes, A. (Eds.), 2010. Labor Migration in Europe. Palgrave, Houndmills.

Michalowski, I., 2011. Required to assimilate? The content of citizenship tests in five countries. Citizen. Stud. 15 (6–7), 749–768.

MIPEX, 2010. Migration Integration Policy Index. British Council and Migration Policy. Group, Brussels.

Niessen, J., Huddleston, T. (Eds.), 2009. Legal Frameworks for the Integration of Third-Country Nationals. Martinus Nijhoff, Leiden.

Odmalm, P., 2004. Civil society, migrant organisations and political parties; theoretical linkages and applications to the Swedish context. J. Ethnic. Migrat. Stud. 30 (3), 471–489.

OECD, 2011. Naturalisation: A Passport for the Better Integration of Immigrants? OECD Publications.

Oliveri, F., 2012. Migrants as activist citizens in Italy: Understanding the new cycle of struggles. Citizen. Studies 16 (5), 793–806.

Piper, N., 2004. Rights of foreign workers and the politics of migration in South-East and East Asia. Int. Migrat. 42 (5), 71–97.

Portes, A., Curtis, J.W., 1987. Changing flags: Naturalization and its determinants among Mexican immigrants. Int. Migrat. Rev. 21, 352–371.

Portes, A., Mozo, R., 1985. The political adaptation process of Cubans and other ethnic minorities in the United States: A preliminary analysis. Int. Migrat. Rev. 16, 35–63.

Rallu, J.L., 2011. Naturalization policies in France and the USA and their impact on migrants' characteristics and strategies. Popul. Rev. 50 (1), 40–61.

Reitz, J., 2004. Canada: Immigration and nation-building in the transition to a knowledge economy. In: Cornelius, W., Tsuda, T., Martin, P., Hollfield, J. (Eds.), Controlling Immigration: A Global Perspective, second ed. Stanford University Press, Stanford, CA, pp. 97–133.

Rooij, E., 2012. Patterns of immigrant political participation: Explaining differences in types of political participation between immigrants and the majority population in Western Europe. Eur. Sociol. Rev. 28 (4), 455–481.

Rubio Marin, R., Sobrino, I., 2010. Country Report: Spain. European University Institute, Florence.

Sager, M., 2011. Everyday Clandestinity: Experiences on the Margins of Citizenship and Migration Policies. Lund University, Lund.

Sandesjö, H., Björk, K., 2005. Nya medborgarskapslagen. Norstedts, Stockholm.

Sandovici, M.E., Listhaug, O., 2010. Ethnic and lingustic minorities and political particpation in Europe. Int. J. Comp. Sociol. 51 (1–2), 111–136.

Sawyer, C., 2010. Country Report: United Kingdom. European University Institute, Florence.

Schuck, P., 1998. The re-evaluation of American citizenship. In: Joppke, C. (Ed.), Challenges to the Nation-State: Immigration in Western Europe and the United States. Oxford University Press, Oxford, pp. 191–230.

Scott, K., 2008. The economics of citizenship: Is there a naturalization effect? In: Bevelander, P., DeVoretz, D.J. (Eds.), The Economics of Citizenship. Holmbergs MIM/Malmö University, Malmö.

Sejersen, T., 2008. 'I vow to thee my countries' – The expansion of dual citizenship in the 21st century. Int. Migrat. Rev. 42 (3), 523–549.

Soysal, Y., 1994. Limits of Citizenship: Migrants and Postnational Membership in Europe. University of Chicago Press, Chicago.

Spiro, P., 1997. Dual nationality and the meaning of citizenship. Emory Law Rev. 46 (4), 1411–1485.

Spång, M., 2007. Pragmatism all the way down? The politics of dual citizenship in Sweden. In: Faist, T. (Ed.), Dual Citizenship in Europe: From Nationhood to Societal Integration. Ashgate, Aldershot, pp. 103–126.

Steinhardt, M.F., Wedemeier, J., 2011. The labor market performance of naturalized immigrants in Switzerland—New findings from the Swiss Labor Force Survey. J. Int. Migrat. Integrat, I-First.

Steinhardt, M.F., 2008. Does Citizenship Matter? The Economic Impact of Naturalizations in Germany. Centro Studi Luca D'Agliano Development Studies, Working Paper.

Strömblad, P., Adman, P., 2009. Political integration through ethnic or nonethnic voluntary associations? Polit. Res. Q. 63 (4), 721–730.

Surak, K., 2008. Convergence in foreigner's rights and citizenship policies? A look at Japan. Int. Migrat. Rev. 42 (3), 550–575.

Togeby, L., 1999. Migrants at the polls: An analysis of immigrant and refugee participation in Danish local elections. J. Ethnic. Migrat. Stud. 25 (4), 665–684.

Togeby, L., 2004. It depends . . . How organisational participation affects political participation and social trust among second-generation immigrants in Denmark. J. Ethnic. Migrat. Stud. 30 (3), 509–528.

United Nations, 2003. Prevention of discrimination. The rights of non-citizens. Final Report of the Special Rapporteur, Mr David Weissbrodt. Economic and Social Council, E/CN.4/Sub2/2003/23.

van Londen, M., Phalet, K., Hagendoorn, L., 2007. Civic engagement and voter participation among Turkish and Moroccan minorities in Rotterdam. J. Ethnic. Migrat. Stud. 33 (8), 1201–1226.

Verba, S., Lehman Schlozman, K., Brady, H., 1995. Voice and Equality: Civic Voluntarism in American Politics. Harvard University Press, Cambridge, MA.

Weil, P., 2001. Access to citizenship - A comparison of twenty-five nationality laws. In: Aleinikoff, A., Klusmeyer, D. (Eds.), Citizenship Today: Global Perspectives and Practices. Carnegie Endowment for International Peace, Washington, DC.

Weiler, J.H.H., Wind, M. (Eds.), 2003. European Constitutionalism Beyond the State. Cambridge University Press, Cambridge.

Whitaker, B.E., 2011. The politics of home: Dual citizenship and the African diaspora. Int. Migrat. Rev. 45 (4), 755–783.

White, S., Nevitte, N., Blais, A., Gidengil, E., Fournier, P., 2008. The political resocialization of immigrants. Resistance or lifelong learning? Polit. Res. Q. 61 (2), 268–281.

Yang, P.Q., 1994. Explaining immigrant naturalization. Int. Migrat. Rev. 28, 449–477.

Yunju, N., Wooksoo, K., 2012. Welfare reform and elderly immigrants' naturalization: access to public benefits as an incentive for naturalization in the United States. Int. Migr. Rev. 46 (3), 656–679.

Ziemele, I., 2005. State Continuity and Nationality: The Baltic States and Russia. Brill, Leiden.

CHAPTER 10

Selective Out-Migration and the Estimation of Immigrants' Earnings Profiles

Christian Dustmann, Joseph-Simon Görlach
Centre for Research and Analysis of Migration (CReAM) and Department of Economics, University College London, Drayton House, 30 Gordon Street, London WC1H 0AX, UK

Contents

1. Introduction	489
2. Evidence on Temporary Migration and Selective Out-Migration	491
2.1 Selective out-migration by country of origin	492
2.2 Selection on education	496
2.3 Selection on earnings	498
2.4 Other characteristics and out-migration	500
3. Estimating Immigrants' Career Profiles	501
3.1 Key research questions and immigrants' career profiles	502
3.2 Estimation and identification of immigrant career profiles	504
3.2.1 Stock sampled data	506
3.2.2 Complete longitudinal data	510
3.3 Numerical example	513
3.4 Interpretation: A simple model of return migration	518
4. Existent Studies on the Estimation of Earnings Equations when Out-Migration is Nonrandom	522
4.1 Studies using stock sampled longitudinal data	523
4.2 Studies using longitudinal data	524
5. Conclusions	528
Acknowledgments	529
References	529

1. INTRODUCTION

A major analytical focus in migration research, itself a widely studied area in modern applied economics, is the career paths of immigrants after their arrival in the destination country (see the seminal work by Chiswick, 1978; and papers by Carliner, 1980; Long, 1980; Borjas, 1985; LaLonde and Topel, 1992; Dustmann, 1993; Hu, 2000; Cortes, 2004; Eckstein and Weiss, 2004; Lubotsky, 2007; and Abramitzky et al., 2013). This focus is hardly surprising given its importance for understanding how immigrants contribute to the labor market, fiscal system, and the economy at large. Yet empirically identifying immigrants' career profiles and their evolution over time presents serious challenges. For example, as pointed out by Borjas (1985), not only may failing to account for changes in the quality of immigrant inflows lead to biased estimates of earnings profiles but the temporariness of many migrations poses its own serious problems for assessing how immigrants' economic outcomes evolve over time.

One primary reason that migration temporariness engenders serious identification issues in estimates of immigrant earnings profiles is that the non-randomness of out-migration may lead to endogenous selection of the resident immigrant population, so that if earnings profile estimations ignore the possibly selective character of out-migration, this omission may lead to biased estimates of the immigrants' career progressions in the destination country. In fact, migration temporariness may itself transform the dynamic optimization problem of the individual immigrant, leading to human capital investment and job search behavior that is set in conjunction with out-migration decisions and determined by—usually unobserved—expectations about future economic conditions in the immigrants' home countries.

In this chapter, we focus on the first issue, the identification of immigrants' career profiles in the destination countries in the presence of out-migration that is selective.[1]

We can illustrate the problem as follows. Suppose that the log earnings of a particular entry cohort of immigrants c are given by $w_{it}^c = \mu_t^c + \varepsilon_{it}^c$, where i and t are index individuals and time respectively, μ_t^c is the mean earnings of entry cohort c at time t, and ε is the deviation of individual earnings from the cohort mean, which collects individual characteristics and follows a certain distribution. The identification problem in estimating the career profile of a particular immigrant entry cohort is then as shown in Figure 10.1, in which the distribution of earnings in period t_1 of all immigrants who arrived in period c has the mean μ_1^c. Assuming a random sample of immigrants interviewed in t_1 and again in period t_2, a simple (linear) earnings regression can be used to identify the wage progression of immigrants in the host country as $\left(\mu_2^c - \mu_1^c / t_2 - t_1\right)$, where μ_t^c is the mean of the log earnings of the immigrants still residing in the country at time t.

This outcome, however, although an unbiased estimate of the growth in the mean earnings of the migrant populations who arrived in period c and residing in the destination country in each of the periods t_1 and t_2, it is not an estimate of the wage growth of individuals from the original arrival cohort, $(\mu_2^c - \mu_1^c)/(t_2 - t_1)$, had out-migration not occurred. That is, an OLS estimator using the two waves of cross-sectional data only produces an unbiased estimate of $(\mu_2^c - \mu_1^c)/(t_2 - t_1)$ if the entire cohort of immigrants that entered in period c still resides in the country in periods t_1 and t_2 or out-migration is random. In the case of non-randomness—for example, only the least successful leaving the country—the distribution of immigrants residing in the host country would be truncated

---

[1] We furthermore focus on selection on earnings levels rather than selection on earnings growth, as does the vast majority of the literature.

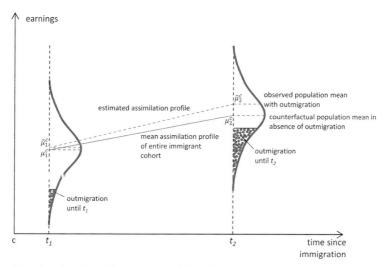

Figure 10.1 *Biased estimation of earnings profiles when out-migration is selective.*

from below, as in the figure. Hence, a simple OLS estimator that ignores this selective out-migration would indicate a steeper wage progression for this cohort.

This chapter, after first providing evidence on the scale of temporary migrations and their possibly selective character (Section 2), explains in more detail the methodological problems involved in estimating immigrant outcome profiles in the presence of selective out-migration (Section 3). We also outline the various ways in which to address these issues. We finally provide an example of how a simple model of endogenous return migration may lead to selection, and how this impacts on empirical estimates. Section 4 then provides an overview of the literature that estimates immigrant earnings profiles while accounting for the temporariness of many migrations, and discusses these papers within the framework we set out in Section 3. Finally, Section 5 summarizes the chapter contents and presents our final thoughts.

2. EVIDENCE ON TEMPORARY MIGRATION AND SELECTIVE OUT-MIGRATION

As shown in Figure 10.2 for a number of major OECD countries, immigration over the last decade has been accompanied by very sizeable out-migration (see OECD (2013) for the country-specific variable definitions). Not only are the profiles for other immigrant-receiving countries similar (OECD, 2013), but increasing evidence is emerging that permanent migrations are—and possibly always have been—the exception rather than the rule. Indeed, the temporariness of migration was stressed even in the early migration literature; for example, Piore (1979) estimated that over 30% of immigrants admitted

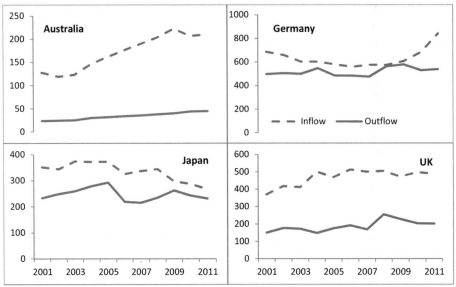

Source: OECD International Migration Outlook 2013

Figure 10.2 *Immigrant in- and outflows in thousands for selected OECD countries.* Source: *OECD International Migration Outlook (2013).*

into the US in the early 1900s subsequently emigrated back to their countries of origin, a figure that actually may have been over twice as large (Bandiera et al., 2013). Such temporariness continues today: During the 2000–2010 period, almost 2.1 million foreign-born residents out-migrated from the US (Bhaskar et al., 2013), a pattern also characteristic of many other countries. A recent report by the OECD (2008), for instance, estimates out-migration rates after five years of residence of 60.4% for immigrants entering Ireland in 1993–98, 50.4% for immigrants entering Belgium in 1993–99, 39.9% for immigrants entering the UK in 1992–98, 39.6% for immigrants entering Norway in 1996–99, and 28.2% for immigrants entering the Netherlands in 1994–98.

Assessing out-migrations, however, is subject to a notable measurement problem: Although many countries carefully register the arrival of new immigrants, most keep no records of immigrants who leave, which greatly complicates the estimation of immigrants' career profiles. Nevertheless, the emergence of better data sources over recent decades has improved the documentation of foreign-born emigration.

2.1 Selective out-migration by country of origin

The most important question in estimating immigrant career profiles in destination countries is not the pure scale of out-migration but whether it is in any way selective and who the out-migrants are. A study by Dustmann and Weiss (2007), for example, used British

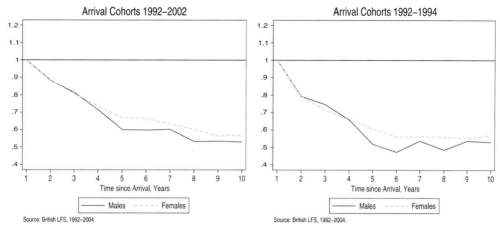

Figure 10.3 *Immigrant survival rates by gender, from Dustmann and Weiss (2007).* Source: *British LFS, 1992–2004.*

Labour Force Survey (BLFS) data on the year of first entry for different arrival cohorts to compute the fraction of each such cohort c that is still in the sample in year $c+j$ and thus estimated the extent of out-migration from the UK. Because the BLFS is not reliable for immigrants who are in the UK for less than a year, however, their base population is all immigrants who have been in the UK for at least one year (i.e., their analysis ignores the many migrations terminated within a year), so their figures underestimate the degree of out-migration.

Figure 10.3 (see also Dustman and Weiss, 2007, Figure 2) shows the survival rate of immigrants in Britain who stayed at least for one year from the first year after arrival until up to 10 years after arrival, with a distinction made between males (solid line) and females (dashed line). The right-hand panel also breaks out the cohorts that arrived between 1992 and 1994. In particular, the graph shows a large reduction in survival rates over the first five years, which, if interpreted as emigration, indicates that among those who stayed for at least one year, only about 60% of the male and 68% of the female foreign-born immigrants remained in Britain five years later.

Figure 10.4 (see also Dustmann and Weiss, 2007, Figure 3) pools male and female immigrants but distinguishes between origin (left panel) and ethnicity (right panel).[2] Overall, it shows a large variation in the emigration propensities across immigrants from different origin countries: The out-migration for immigrants from Europe, the Americas, Australasia, and the Middle East is highest (over 45% of those who are in the UK for at least one year left within five years of arrival), while out-migration for individuals from the Indian subcontinent and Africa is far less pronounced. In fact, there seems to be little

---

[2] Fractions larger than 1 in the left panel are due to sampling error.

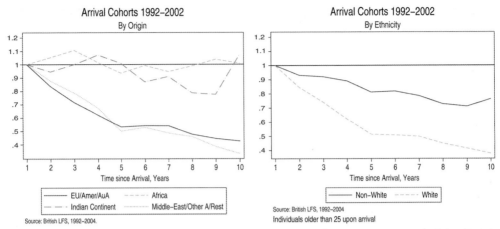

Figure 10.4 *Immigrant survival rates by origin and ethnicity, from Dustmann and Weiss (2007).* Source: *British LFS, 1992–2004.*

indication of any emigration for immigrants from Africa and the Indian subcontinent. Rather, instead of being equally distributed across origin countries, out-migrants seem to come predominantly from English-speaking countries that are economically similar to the UK. Rendall and Ball (2004) reported a very similar picture: Whereas about 65% of immigrants from Canada and the US emigrate within five years, only about 15% of immigrants from the Indian subcontinent do so.

Borjas and Bratsberg (1996), using US data, found similar large variation in out-migration rates across origin countries, with the lowest out-migration rates reported for immigrants from Asia (cf. Dustmann and Weiss, 2007). Specifically, they estimated that only 3.5% of Asian immigrants who arrived in the US after 1975 had left the country by 1980, as compared to 18.4% of European immigrants, 24.8% of South American immigrants, and 34.5% of North American immigrants. Likewise, Jasso and Rosenzweig (1990), using alien registration data for the 20 years between 1961 and 1980, found that Europeans have the highest propensity to leave the US and immigrants from Asia the lowest, with western hemisphere immigrants taking an intermediate place. In an earlier paper analyzing out-migration rates for the 1971 entry cohort, these same authors reported that immigrants from China, Korea, Cuba, the Philippines, and India had the lowest emigration rates, ranging from 14.5% to 41.6%, with emigration rates for Koreans and Chinese not exceeding 22% (Jasso and Rosenzweig, 1982). Canadian emigration, in contrast, was between 51% and 55%, and emigration rates for legal immigrants from Central America, the Caribbean (excluding Cuba), and South America were at least as high as 50% and possibly as high as 70%.

Patterns reported for Canada are not dissimilar. Beaujot and Rappak (1989) reported that out-migration for those arriving in the 1951–70 period was highest for individuals born in the US (50–62%) and lowest for those from Asia (only 1–17%). A similar profile emerges for immigrants to Australia: Based on data from the 1973 Social Sciences Survey of Australian male residents aged 30–64 and the 1/100 census tapes from 1981, Beggs and Chapman (1991) reported that only 3–6% of immigrants from non-English-speaking countries are likely to leave as compared with 20–30% of immigrants from English-speaking countries (see also Lukomskyj and Richards, 1986).

Research for Scandinavian countries indicates that emigration rates for immigrants from industrialized—and in particular, Nordic countries—are far higher than those for immigrants from other regions. For Norway, Bratsberg et al. (2007), using data from the Norwegian population register, estimated that as many as 84% of immigrants from the US leave compared with only 9% from Vietnam. They interpreted this finding to mean stark differences in out-migration behavior based on the home country's economic development and distance from Norway. In addition, their administrative data included information on where foreign-born emigrants travel subsequently. They reported that of those who left Norway, at least 30% of the immigrants from Somalia, 40% from Iran, and two-thirds from Vietnam migrated to a third country rather than returning, while the great majority of out-migrants from neighboring Nordic countries returned home. Like Bratsberg et al. (2007), based on 1991–2000 emigrant data from *Statistics Sweden*, Nekby (2006) found that 28% of working-age emigrants are onward migrants emigrating to a third country. Moreover, whereas emigrants from Asia are as likely to be onward as return migrants, emigrants from Africa are more likely to move to third-country destinations, which suggests that many of the out-migrations observed are not return migrations but migrations that continue to other destination countries. Overall, she found that out-migration probabilities are highest for immigrants from North America and from Western European countries of origin.

The large out-migration propensity of Nordic migrants in comparison to other groups was confirmed by Jensen and Pedersen (2007) for Denmark, who found that although 80% of Turkish immigrants remained in Denmark for 10 years or more, only 20% of the Nordic immigrants did so. Edin et al. (2000) showed similar patterns for Sweden: About 44% of Nordic immigrants had left that country within five years of their arrival, a number that is significantly lower for immigrants from non-OECD countries. Klinthäll (2003) reported similarly large differences among the 1980 and 1990 arrival cohorts of non-Nordic European immigrants to Sweden, whose emigration rates are about twice as high as those of African and Asian immigrants.

The general picture that emerges from these studies is that migrants from developed countries are more likely to leave the host country than migrants from less developed countries, in particular those in Africa and Asia. This pattern is illustrated in Figure 10.5, which combines the estimates—drawn from a large number of empirical studies—on the fractions of postwar immigrants that out-migrated after a certain period. More specifically, it plots the estimated fraction of immigrants who left the host country within a given time since

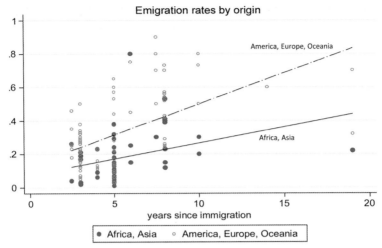

Figure 10.5 *Foreign-born emigration by origin region.*

arrival against the number of years since immigration.[3] This pattern suggests higher emigration rates for migrants from the Americas, Europe, and the Pacific region than for migrants from Africa and Asia. Using this collection of estimates as observation points in a regression of the fraction of out-migrated immigrants on the years since immigration (ysm), we find that the out-migration rate of immigrants from the Americas, Europe, and the Pacific region increases on average by almost twice as many percentage points per year as that of immigrants from Africa and Asia (see Table 10.1). The estimated coefficients and the differences across immigrant groups are illustrated by the fitted lines in Figure 10.5.

2.2 Selection on education

Although a number of papers have examined the relation between educational attainment and out-migration, there is no clear pattern across the literature.[4] For returnees

---

[3] For Figure 10.5, we exclude annual emigration rate estimates that do not refer to a certain number of years spent in the host country, such as Van Hook et al.'s (2006) estimates of annual out-migration. If estimates refer to the fraction of migrants who entered in a certain time interval and left by the end of that interval (as in Bratsberg et al., 2007), the average year of immigration is approximated by the interval midpoint, a choice likely to overestimate emigration rates given that remigration propensities are generally higher during the early post-immigration years. The estimates are taken from Ahmed and Robinson (1994), Alders and Nicolaas (2003), Aydemir and Robinson (2008), Beaujot and Rappak (1989), Beenstock (1996), Bijwaard et al. (2011), Böhning (1984), Borjas and Bratsberg (1996), Bratsberg et al. (2007), Edin et al. (2000), Jasso and Rosenzweig (1982), Jensen and Pedersen (2007), Kirwan and Harrigan (1986), Klinthäll (2003, 2006), Lukomskyj and Richards (1986), Michalowski (1991), Rendall and Ball (2004), Reyes (1997, 2004), and Shorland (2006). The exact numbers used are available upon request.

[4] See Dustmann and Glitz (2011) for a survey on the role played by skill accumulation and education not only in the selection of remigrants from a destination country's population of immigrants, but also on the selection of emigrants from their countries of origin.

Table 10.1 OLS coefficients of time since immigration for foreign-born emigration by origin region

	Fraction that has emigrated by region of origin	
	Africa/Asia	*Americas/Europe/Oceania*
ysm	0.019	0.037
cons	0.075	0.129
N	52	97

from the US among the Puerto Rican immigrant population, Ramos (1992) reported a positive selection on education, and Zakharenko (2008), working with CPS data, estimated the probability of emigration for immigrants to the US from any destination to be lower for highly educated immigrants. He also showed, however, that this result is largely driven by the strong association between higher education and emigration probabilities among longer-term migrants, a linkage that is statistically insignificant for short-term migrants. Lam (1994), on the other hand, using 1971 and 1981 Canadian census data, reported that younger and less educated immigrants to Canada are more likely to stay.

The literature reports similarly mixed results across European countries on the relation between educational attainment and the propensity to out-migrate. For example, Jensen and Pedersen (2007) found a positive relation between out-migration probabilities and educational attainment among immigrants in Denmark, while Dustmann (1996) found that intended migration durations are longer among less educated immigrants in Germany. Nevertheless, he also reported that the probability that immigration is intended to be permanent increases with years of schooling. Also for Germany, Constant and Zimmermann (2011), using information on multiple migration spells, showed that repeat migration is more likely among male and less educated individuals, whereas Beenstock (1996), using data for Israel, showed that the stays of more highly educated immigrants who arrived in the 1970s are more likely to be temporary. For Italy, Coniglio et al. (2009) confirmed that schooling increases the probability of out-migration even among undocumented immigrants. However, Carrión-Flores (2006), using data from the Mexican Migration Project 1982–1999, reported the opposite for Mexican immigrants in the US: They found a positive effect of high educational attainment on the likelihood of returning to Mexico. Maré et al. (2007), on the other hand, found for New Zealand that out-migration is highly likely for both unskilled and highly skilled immigrants.

These contradictory findings again raise the question of the direction of the selection of migrants from their societies of origin and out-migrants from the immigrant population in the respective destination countries, as well as how these two are related. We discuss theoretical models on this issue in Section 3. One insight is provided by Borjas and Bratsberg (1996), who hypothesized that in a context of negative selection of immigrants from their origin societies, emigration by these migrants from the destination country should be positively selected. This was confirmed for linked Finnish and Swedish data by Rooth and Saarela (2007), who found significant selection on educational attainment but no evidence of selection on earnings conditional on education. From a sending country's perspective, Pinger (2010) reported that among temporary emigrants from Moldova, a lower fraction has tertiary education than is the case among emigrants considered to have left permanently. Thus, overall, these studies suggest that the selection pattern of out-migration with respect to educational attainment is context-dependent.

2.3 Selection on earnings

A number of studies investigate the relation between out-migration and immigrant earnings,[5] an association that is far from straightforward. Dustmann (2003), for instance, pointed out that changes in earnings may affect the optimal migration duration through either an income or substitution effect. Whereas the former increases the time a migrant may want to spend in the home country, the latter makes a return more costly. Empirical evidence is mixed, however, on which effect dominates: Most studies on the out-migration of US immigrants found that those earning high wages are less likely to leave, but findings differ for other immigration countries. Early work by Massey (1987) and Borjas (1989), for instance, identified a negative effect of wages on the probability that immigrants to the US will out-migrate, and Abramitzky et al. (2013) reached a similar conclusion for US immigrants even in the so-called age of mass migration. Using US census data from 1900, 1910, and 1920, together with the Integrated Public Use Micro-data Series (IPUMS) for 1900, they constructed a panel of US natives and immigrants from a number of major sending countries who arrived between 1880 and 1900, and found that out-migrants were negatively selected on earnings. In Abramitzky et al. (2012), on the other hand, the same authors noted that for Norwegian immigrants who arrived around the same time there are no significant occupational differences between those who return to Norway and those who stay.

In more recent work, Cohen and Haberfeld (2001) assumed that in the absence of selective out-migration, period effects in earnings regressions for Israeli- and native-born workers in the US should be the same. Using a sample of such individuals from pooled 1980 and 1990 census data, they performed separate earnings regressions for the two groups. If out-migration were random, once years spent in the US and other individual human capital characteristics are controlled for, the coefficient on an indicator variable for being drawn from the 1990 sample should be the same in both regressions. In fact, the estimated coefficient is significantly lower for US-born workers, a finding that the authors interpret as evidence that Israelis who return from the US are negatively selected

---

[5] See also Reyes (1997, 2001), Constant and Massey (2002, 2003), Gundel and Peters (2008), Bijwaard (2009), Kirdar (2009), Yahirun (2009), Van Hook and Zhang (2011), and Bijwaard et al. (2011) for their results on the effect of unemployment spells on the probability of out-migration.

among all Israeli immigrants. For the US, Reagan and Olsen (2000) also found that immigrants' potential wage as predicted by a number of observable characteristics of foreign-born workers included in the NLSY79 is negatively associated with the probability of emigrating. Reyes (1997) identified a negative relation between wages and the probability of return migration by Mexican immigrants in the US, but only during the first year of residence: This effect turns positive for immigrants who have remained in the US for longer. Interestingly, her data, taken from the Mexican Migration Project, suggest similarly sized wage effects for both male and female immigrants. The finding that foreign-born emigrants are negatively selected from the immigrant population is also supported by Lubotsky (2007), a study detailed in Section 4.

Evidence does exist, however, of considerable differences in the relation between earnings and out-migration dependent on both origin and destination countries. Longva (2001), for instance, after dividing the immigrant population residing in Norway in 1980 and 1993 into those from OECD and those from non-OECD countries, found that OECD immigrants who left Norway between 1980 and 1992 or between 1993 and 1997 had higher earnings at the beginning of these periods than those who stayed. For non-OECD immigrants, however, he found the opposite. According to Edin et al. (2000), even though immigrants to Sweden who are economically more successful tend to stay for a shorter time, this dynamic is driven by the fact that these immigrants originate mostly from other Nordic countries. These authors established a negative association, conditional on the source country, between immigrants' incomes and the likelihood of leaving Sweden within five or 10 years after arrival.

Also for Sweden, Nekby (2006), by allowing out-migration rates to change non-linearly along the earnings distribution, showed that for both return and onward migrants, emigration rates are U-shaped with respect to earnings, with high probabilities of emigration for individuals in both low- and high-income groups. This finding is in line with Dustmann's (2003) results for Germany. In that study, using a simple theoretical framework to analyze immigrants' migration durations, he showed that for very low wages, durations increase with wages, while for intermediate- and high-income groups, the effect of wages on the time immigrants spend in Germany is negative. Bijwaard and Wahba (2014) also identified a U-shaped relation between incomes and out-migration probabilities by applying a competing risks model to register data on the entire population of labor immigrants from developing countries to the Netherlands during 1999–2007. Specifically, after modeling transitions between labor market states in the host country and the absorbing state of being in the country of origin, they computed out-migration probabilities for different income groups. They found that such probabilities are U-shaped with respect to income, with the highest probability of leaving among migrants in the lowest income group. They interpreted this finding as an indication that some immigrants leave because of disappointing economic outcomes in the host country, while the migration durations of others are governed by target saving behavior. Yet for immigrants to Israel who were at least age 18 at the time of immigration, Beenstock et al. (2010) found no association whatsoever between immigrant earnings in 1983 and the individual still residing in the country in 1995.

2.4 Other characteristics and out-migration

Several studies investigated the relation between out-migration and individual characteristics other than earnings and education, including the possibility that out-migration probabilities increase around retirement age. Waldorf (1995), for instance, reported that among immigrants to Germany, the intention to return within the next four years increases close to retirement age, while Cobb-Clark and Stillman (2008) found among immigrants to Australia that actual out-migration rates are highest at retirement age. For the US, on the other hand, by computing annual emigration rates for various subgroups of immigrants (based on repeated CPS interviews with the same households), Van Hook et al. (2006) revealed that out-migration rates are higher for younger immigrants. A positive effect of age on the probability of remaining in the host country was also reported by Bijwaard (2010) for immigrants to the Netherlands, although Edin et al. (2000) found no such significant relation for immigrants to Sweden.

In a study of the relation between probability of leaving and age at immigration, Aydemir and Robinson (2008) found that immigrants who arrived in Canada at age 25–29 are slightly less likely to emigrate than immigrants who arrived at older ages (see also Michalowski (1991) for earlier work on the scale and composition of emigrant flows from Canada). Jensen and Pedersen (2007) also provided evidence for Denmark that the relation between age at immigration and out-migration differs by immigrant country of origin. That is, like Aydemir and Robinson (2008), they found that for immigrants from industrialized countries, age at immigration is negatively correlated with the probability of out-migration. They also showed, however, that the correlation is positive for men but insignificant for women from developing countries.

Other factors linked in the literature to emigration decisions include negative health shocks and economic prospects in the migrant's region of origin. As regards the former, Sander (2007), in an analysis of the effect of health shocks on emigration decisions among immigrants in Germany, revealed that negative health shocks do indeed affect the probability of out-migration, although the effect appears to depend on whether these shocks are transitory or permanent. That is, although the likelihood of out-migration increases when shocks to health are transitory, it decreases when they are more permanent. In terms of the relation between return migration and the economic prospects in migrants' region of origin, Lindstrom (1996) reported lower conditional return probabilities for Mexican immigrants in the US who are from economically more active regions in Mexico, an outcome he explained by the higher value that savings accumulated in the US have for these migrants on their return. Reyes and

Mameesh (2002) also found that economically more active and urban regions in the US attract more permanent migrants.

Naturally, out-migration rates vary by immigrant status: Refugees are considerably less likely to leave the host country than economic migrants, and part of the variations in out-migration across immigrants from different countries of origin can be explained by this (e.g., Duleep, 1994; Lundh and Ohlsson, 1994; Klinthäll, 2007; Aydemir and Robinson, 2008). The way in which emigration rates vary among different immigrant groups in the Netherlands is the subject of a study by Bijwaard (2010), who demonstrated that emigration hazards are higher for labor migrants than for individuals who immigrated for family reasons. Out-migration probabilities for various immigrant groups computed by Van Hook and Zhang (2011) from their CPS repeated household survey data also suggest that economic integration and social ties within the US play a major role in determining emigration probabilities, although the direction of causality is unclear.

Obviously, because of space constraints this list of studies is far from exhaustive; rather, this overview of research on the dimensions of foreign-born emigration and selection is a mere indication of the wide range of aspects investigated. In general, the papers reviewed suggest not only that migrants who leave are unlikely to be randomly drawn from the population of entry cohorts but that the direction of out-migration selection is far from homogeneous across either immigration countries or across different immigrant groups to the same country. This observation in turn suggests that any conclusions drawn for one country about the character of out-migration are unlikely to carry over to another country, and perhaps not even to another group of immigrants in the same country.

3. ESTIMATING IMMIGRANTS' CAREER PROFILES

Because immigrants' performance in the destination country has implications for many economic questions, its assessment is a key area of economic research. At the same time, however, it presents a challenging task, particularly given the nonpermanent nature of migration. One particularly problematic aspect is that individual immigrants make their economic decisions in conjunction with their migration plans while considering expected economic conditions in the country of origin (or countries to which they wish to migrate in the future), which adds substantial complexity to otherwise well-understood decisions like investment in human capital or labor supply issues. A second is that individual migrants out-migrate from and remigrate back to the host country in a way that leads to selective out-migration and remigration over the migration cycle. These two issues are inherently connected in that the nature of the selection through return and repeat migration is determined by the immigrants' dynamic life-cycle decisions.

In this chapter, we focus on the second problem, the estimation of immigrants' outcome profiles in the presence of selective out-migration. In doing so, we assume that immigrants' decisions on human capital investment, labor supply, and job choice are not determined by their migration and out-migration plans, a strong assumption but one made in almost all the literature.

Before discussing the issues more formally, however, we need to outline the major questions of interest to the researcher in estimating immigrants' earnings profiles. These questions can then serve as a point of reference in our subsequent discussion of different estimators and data sources, which also outlines the assumptions under which the questions can be answered.

3.1 Key research questions and immigrants' career profiles

As already emphasized, the economic performance of immigrants is of key interest to destination countries and often provides important information for migration policies. Here, to simplify the discussion, we focus on one particular aspect of economic performance: immigrants' earnings over their migration cycle. One key question in the debate over immigration is how much immigrants contribute to the tax and welfare system relative to what they receive in terms of benefits; in other words, what are immigrants' net fiscal contributions.[6] Those at the lower end of the earnings distribution are typically net receivers of transfers, while those further up are net contributors. A typical query on immigrant earnings, therefore, refers to immigrants arriving in a particular year and those who remain in subsequent years:

Q1: What is the growth in mean earnings of the populations of immigrants who arrived in the host country in a particular year and who are observed there in subsequent years?

Because this question refers explicitly to migrants who live and work in the host country in subsequent years net of those who have left the host country, it concerns the selected populations of stayers, not the entire population defined by the arrival cohort. In Figure 10.1, the earnings growth that responds to this question is given by the steeper of the two lines depicted, which refers to the increase in the mean earnings of the two truncated distributions. This parameter can be obtained from repeated cross-sectional data by simply computing the change in the mean earnings of a particular arrival cohort over time using individuals who are in the country at different points in time after the arrival year. The answer to Q1 is thus a combination of the earnings growth of immigrants who arrived in a particular year and stayed in the destination country in subsequent years and that of the population of surviving immigrants, which is an outcome of the compositional changes caused by (possibly selective) out-migration.

---

[6] See, for example, Dustmann and Frattini (2013). See Kerr and Kerr (2011) for a recent survey and Preston (2013) for a discussion of the methodological challenges this literature faces.

Answering Q1 based on repeated cross-sectional data, however, reveals little about whether out-migration is selective because it does not allow compositional effects to be disentangled from individual wage growth. Nevertheless, in many instances, it may be valuable to better understand whether, and in which direction, out-migration is selective and how the earnings of an entry cohort of immigrants would have evolved over time in the host country had nobody left the country. For instance, if one study objective is to help design migration policies that regulate entry, then we need to understand the hypothetical career paths of immigrants in a particular arrival cohort had nobody left the country in subsequent years. If a further objective is to design policies ensuring that the highest performing immigrants remain in the country, then we want to understand the direction, and possibly the drivers, of selective out-migration. Thus, in many instances we may want to answer the following question:

Q2: *What would the growth in mean earnings of the population of immigrants who arrived in a particular year be if there was no subsequent out-migration?*

Unlike Q1, which can be answered based on data moments obtained from repeated cross-sectional data, Q2 requires the construction of a counterfactual scenario (designated in Figure 10.1 by the flatter solid line) in which no migrants have left the destination country after arrival and the mean earnings of immigrants who arrived in a particular year can be observed for all immigrants in subsequent years. As discussed in more detail below, however, constructing this counterfactual situation under plausible assumptions requires more information than is available in repeated cross-sectional data.

A third question of possible interest refers to the mean earnings of a population of immigrants who all belong to the same entry cohort and all stayed in the destination country until T years later; for example, immigrants from Hong Kong living in Canada in 2010 who arrived in 1997, the year Hong Kong's sovereignty was transferred. This question therefore addresses the earnings growth of a cohort of immigrants who survive in the destination country until a certain date:

Q3: *What is the growth in mean earnings of the populations of immigrants who arrived in the host country in a particular year and who all stayed there until at least T years after arrival?*

Two scenarios exist under which the answers to all these questions are identical. The first, in which all migrations are permanent, is trivial. Yet such permanency is assumed in much of the literature on estimating immigrants' earnings profiles even though the studies reviewed in Section 2 suggest that this assumption is implausible for almost all migration situations. Under the second scenario, the process that affects out-migration is exogenous to the process that affects immigrant earnings; in other words, out-migration is independent of earnings. This assumption, although it seems generally implausible, may be less restrictive for particular situations when conditioning on observables and when data on many individual characteristics of immigrants is available to the researcher.

In the next section, we will discuss the conditions under which we can identify the parameters that answer questions Q2 and Q3 above, and what information is needed over and above that contained in repeated cross-sectional data.

3.2 Estimation and identification of immigrant career profiles

In estimating immigrant career profiles, we first consider the following equation:

$$w_{it}^c = \mu_t^c + \varepsilon_{it}^c \qquad (10.1)$$

where w_{it}^c is the log earnings of individual i of entry cohort c in year t, $t \geq c$, which can be decomposed into μ_t^c, the mean log earnings of individual i's arrival cohort in period t if the entire immigrant cohort would stay in the host country, and ε_{it}^c the individual specific deviation of i's earnings from the cohort mean, which depends on unobservable characteristics that affect earnings. We assume that the latter consist of an individual-specific and time-constant component plus a time-variant component, $\varepsilon_{it}^c = \alpha_i + e_{it}^c$. This model can easily be generalized by writing μ_t^c as a function of observable characteristics, so that, for example, $\mu_{it}^c = \overline{\mu}_t^c + x_{it}'b$.

We further assume that out-migration is an absorbing state; that is, once a migrant has left the country, he or she will never return. Out-migration in any year after arrival is then characterized by the following selection equation:

$$s_{it}^c = \prod_{c < \tau \leq t} 1\left[z_{i\tau}^c{}'\beta + u_{i\tau}^c > 0\right]$$

where $1[A]$ is an indicator function that takes the value 1 if A is true, and z_{it}^c and u_{it}^c are observed and unobserved characteristics respectively, that affect the migrant's decision to remain in the host country beyond year t. We also assume that $s_{it}^c = 1$ for $t = c$ (meaning that the population of interest is all immigrants who arrive in year c) and that $E(\varepsilon_{it}^c | s_{ic}^c = 1) = 0$ for all t. The latter means that the expectation of the unobserved term in the outcome equation is equal to zero for the population of all immigrants who arrive at time c. This normalization not only defines the arrival cohort as the base population but implies that the conditional expectation will be zero for all subsequent periods t in the case that all migrations are permanent.

To focus on selection in out-migration, we also assume that conditional on s_{it}^c, ε_{it}^c is independent of μ_{it}^c, and that u_{it}^c is mean independent of z_{it}^c. Selection in this model is thus determined by the assumptions about the correlation between u_{it}^c and ε_{it}^c. This also implies that selection in this model is on earnings *levels*. In abstracting from selection on earnings *growth* we follow the vast majority of the literature. We will show, however, that even in this simpler case, the identification of the direction of selective out-migration requires considerably more model restrictions than generally acknowledged in the literature on the earnings assimilation of immigrants.

The assumption that out-migration is an absorbing state implies that $s_{it}^c = 1$ will always mean that $s_{it-1}^c = 1$; that is, a migrant observed in period t is also observed in period $t-1$. To allow for more complex out-migration and remigration patterns (e.g., repeat migration) would require us to model not only the out-migration process but also the remigration process, which would add considerable complexity and additional identification issues. Hence, although such a model would certainly be interesting, it is beyond the scope of this chapter.

We first consider what could be identified in terms of the earnings growth of a cohort of immigrants that arrived in year c and were observed in two consecutive cross-sectional datasets, years $t_1 \geq c$ and $t_2 > t_1 \geq c$, if only cross-sectional data were available. In this case, the earnings growth of entry cohort c between t_1 and t_2 is given by

$$E\left(w_{it_2}^c | \mu_{t_2}^c, s_{it_2}^c = 1\right) - E\left(w_{it_1}^c |, \mu_{t_1}^c s_{it_1}^c = 1\right) = \left[\mu_{t_2}^c - \mu_{t_1}^c\right] + \left[E\left(\varepsilon_{it_2}^c | \mu_{t_2}^c, s_{it_2}^c = 1\right)\right.$$
$$\left. - E\left(\varepsilon_{it_1}^c | \mu_{t_1}^c, s_{it_1}^c = 1\right)\right]$$
(10.2)

The first difference, $\mu_{t_2}^c - \mu_{t_1}^c = \Delta\mu_{t_1 t_2}^c$, is the earnings growth of the arrival cohort c from year t_1 to year t_2 had nobody out-migrated. Although this parameter answers Q2, it is identified only if the second difference, the expectation of the individual-specific deviations from the cohort means *conditional* on individuals residing in the host country in periods t_1 or t_2, is equal to zero, which will trivially be the case if all migrations are permanent.

If migrations are nonpermanent, however, the last term in brackets will not be equal to zero, except for the special case in which ε is mean independent of both mean earnings and the selection rule: $E(\varepsilon | \mu, u, z) = 0$. In that case, conditional on any observables, the process that determines immigrants' earnings is unaffected by the process that determines out-migration. When out-migration is "exogenous" and the last two last terms in (10.2) equal zero, a simple OLS estimation of equation (10.1) identifies μ_t^c and yields answers to Q1, Q2, and Q3.

While this may be implausible in most applications, it may in some cases be justifiable to assume that selection is independent of ε *conditional* on a set of observable exogenous variables. For instance, if emigration is random *within* country-of-origin education cells $(E \cdot O)$ but not *between* them, then conditioning on country of origin and education in a flexible way will eliminate the selection bias, as now $E(\varepsilon | u, z, E \cdot O) = 0$. Thus, conditional on $E \cdot O$, out-migration is independent of ε (see Cameron and Trivedi (2005, p. 863ff), or Wooldridge (2010, p. 908ff) for general discussions of such estimators).

In most cases, however, selection is a function of both observables and unobservables that are correlated with determinants of earnings. To illustrate, assume $var(u_{it}^c) = 1$, and that $E(e_{it}^c | u_{ic}^c, \ldots, u_{it}^c) = \sigma_{eu}(t) u_{it}^c$—as is the case if, for example, contemporaneous unobservables in the earnings and selection equations are jointly normally distributed, while being uncorrelated across time—and consider the conditional expectation $E(\varepsilon_{it}^c | \mu_t^c, s_{it}^c = 1)$: it follows from our assumptions that

$$
\begin{aligned}
E\left(\varepsilon_{it}^c | \mu_t^c, s_{it}^c = 1\right) &= E\left(\varepsilon_{it}^c | s_{it}^c = 1\right) \\
&= E\left(e_{it}^c | u_{ic}^c > -z_{ic}^{c\prime}\beta, \ldots, u_{it}^c > -z_{it}^{c\prime}\beta\right) \\
&\quad + E\left(\alpha_i | u_{ic}^c > -z_{ic}^{c\prime}\beta, \ldots, u_{it}^c > -z_{it}^{c\prime}\beta\right) \\
&= \sigma_{eu}(t) E\left(u_{it}^c | u_{ic}^c > -z_{ic}^{c\prime}\beta, \ldots, u_{it}^c > -z_{it}^{c\prime}\beta\right) \\
&\quad + E\left(\alpha_i | u_{ic}^c > -z_{ic}^{c\prime}\beta, \ldots, u_{it}^c > -z_{it}^{c\prime}\beta\right)
\end{aligned}
\tag{10.3}
$$

where $\sigma_{eu}(t)$ is the covariance between u_{it}^c and e_{it}^c.[7] Thus, the bias we obtain in estimating $\Delta\mu_{t_1 t_2}^c$ depends on the assumptions made about the correlation between unobservables in the earnings and selection equations. In the above case, the first conditional expectation on the right-hand side reflects selective out-migration determined through time-variant unobservables in the selection equation that are correlated with those in the outcome equation, while the second conditional expectation reflects a situation in which selection depends on time-constant individual-specific fixed effects. Whereas the latter corresponds to selection being systematically related to the immigrants' unobserved and time-invariant productivity, the former reflects selective out-migration that is determined by time-variant shocks to earnings being correlated with time-variant unobservables in the selection equation. Thus, when only repeated cross-sectional data are available, we cannot identify $\Delta\mu_{t_1 t_2}^c$ without assuming that both α_i and e_{it}^c are uncorrelated with selection. Nor will much information emerge about the direction of selection. Repeated cross-sectional analysis, therefore, provides no answer to Q2.

3.2.1 Stock sampled data
One way to move forward in the estimation of $\Delta\mu_{t_1 t_2}^c$ is to use stock sampled data, which is becoming increasingly available either from surveys or administrative sources. One particular design links data on immigrants surveyed at a particular point in time to administrative data that allows the reconstruction of their past employment and earnings histories. Such data are likely to become more available as more efforts are made to link survey information with administrative data sources. In these datasets, the base population is all immigrants of a particular arrival cohort who remain in the host country until at least period T (determined by the year of the survey) and for whom longitudinal data are available for several years between c and T. Whereas the administrative data tend to contain no information on, for example, year of arrival or precise immigrant status, such information can be added from the survey data to produce an informative data source on migrant behavior. Nonetheless, these datasets do not typically provide longitudinal information on the entire entry cohort; rather, the migrant sample is determined by

---

[7] We maintain the assumption of a unit variance for the residual in the selection equation throughout.

the migrants of any entry cohort that have remained in the host country at least until the survey year. Given the restriction that only those immigrants who stay until period T are observed, the advantage of stock sampled over repeated cross-sections for the purpose of identifying immigrant earnings profiles is not the longitudinal dimension, but the information that all individuals who are observed in earlier periods are known to stay until at least period T, as will become clear in our discussion below. Nevertheless, most datasets of that format used in the literature are longitudinal. For example, Lubotsky (2007)[8] linked information on immigrants in the CPS sample who are still residing in the US in 1994 to social security earnings records, thereby providing longitudinal information on these migrants back to 1951. By construction, this dataset contains information on immigrants' earnings only for immigrants observed in the 1994 CPS.

What, then, do such data tell us? One key advantage of these combined datasets over (repeated) cross-sectional data is that they provide a sample of individuals who are all known to stay in the host country until at least some period T. Thus, in any period before T, the analyst observes a sample that will survive in the host country until at least T, which leads to the same selection criterion no matter in which period individuals are observed. As we show below, this provides additional identifying information, over and above that available in repeated cross-sectional data, even if individuals cannot be linked across waves. Nevertheless, whether this is sufficient to identify earnings growth of the original entry cohort depends again on the nature of selective out-migration up to year T. Denoting the survey year by T, the growth of immigrants' earnings belonging to entry cohort c between years t_1 and t_2, with $c \leq t_1 < t_2 \leq T$, is

$$
\begin{aligned}
E\left(w_{it_2}^c \,|\, \mu_{t_2}^c, s_{iT}^c = 1\right) - E\left(w_{it_1}^c \,|\, \mu_{t_1}^c, s_{iT}^c = 1\right) = {} & \left[\mu_{t_2}^c - \mu_{t_1}^c\right] + \left[E\left(\varepsilon_{it_2}^c \,|\, \mu_{t_2}^c, s_{iT}^c = 1\right)\right. \\
& \left. - E\left(\varepsilon_{it_1}^c \,|\, \mu_{t_1}^c, s_{iT}^c = 1\right)\right]
\end{aligned}
\tag{10.4}
$$

Note the difference between equations (10.2) and (10.4). Whereas in (10.2) the selection indicator refers to the particular year in which the cross-section was collected, in (10.4) selection for each wave refers to the same year, year T, reflecting that we look at a sample of immigrants who all remained in the destination country at least until period T. Thus, if the dataset is longitudinal, it will be a balanced panel of immigrants. No matter the nature of the selection, the expression in (10.4) always identifies the earnings growth of immigrants belonging to cohort c who remained in the country until period T. Estimations based on these data, therefore, answer Q3 for immigrants from cohort c who stayed in the host country until year T.

Yet do such data tell us anything about $\Delta\mu_{t_1 t_2}^c$; that is, the hypothetical earnings growth of entry cohort c if all individuals who entered in that year were observed in both

---

[8] Earlier studies of immigrant earnings growth that use stock-based longitudinal data include Hu (2000) and Duleep and Dowhan (2002). See also our discussion in Section 4.

periods t_1 and t_2, and thus answer Q2, except for the trivial cases in which all migrations are permanent or $E(\varepsilon|\mu, u, z) = 0$? To examine this, we reconsider the selection term in (10.3) and assume that $E(e_{it}^c | u_{ic}^c, \ldots, u_{iT}^c) = \sigma_{eu}(t) u_{it}^c$, to rewrite $E(\varepsilon_{it}^c | \mu_t^c, s_T^c = 1)$ as

$$
\begin{aligned}
E\big(\varepsilon_{it}^c \big| \mu_t^c, s_T^c = 1\big) &= E\big(e_{it}^c \big| u_{ic}^c > -z_{ic}^c{}'\beta, \ldots, u_{iT}^c > -z_{iT}^c{}'\beta\big) \\
&\quad + E\big(\alpha_i \big| u_{ic}^c > -z_{ic}^c{}'\beta, \ldots, u_{iT}^c > -z_{iT}^c{}'\beta\big) \\
&= \sigma_{eu}(t) E\big(u_{it}^c \big| u_{ic}^c > -z_{ic}^c{}'\beta, \ldots, u_{iT}^c > -z_{iT}^c{}'\beta\big) \\
&\quad + E\big(\alpha_i \big| u_{ic}^c > -z_{ic}^c{}'\beta, \ldots, u_{iT}^c > -z_{iT}^c{}'\beta\big)
\end{aligned}
\tag{10.3$'$}
$$

where, because of the nature of the data, we condition on the same selection rule for each period. Suppose first that selection depends only on time-constant unobservables in the outcome equation, α_i, so that $\sigma_{eu}(t) = 0$. In this case, the selection term will be constant over time for the same individual, and an OLS estimation of equation (10.1) on the pooled t_1 to T cross-sections with years since migration indicators included would yield the following estimation equation:

$$
w_{it}^c = \mu_{t_1}^c + \Delta\mu_{t_1(t_1+1)}^c \mathbf{1}[t = t_1 + 1] + \ldots + \Delta\mu_{t_1 T}^c \mathbf{1}[t = T] + \varepsilon_{it}^c
\tag{10.1$'$}
$$

where $\mathbf{1}[\,]$ is an indicator function, equal to 1 if its argument is true and zero otherwise. An OLS regression can then be run on (10.1$'$) to identify wage growth $\Delta\mu_{t_1 t_2}^c$ (thereby also answering Q2), although doing so will not identify the entry-level earnings for the original cohort that arrived in period c. Rather, because the last term in (10.3$'$) is unequal to zero for $corr(\alpha_i, u_{it}^c) \neq 0$, it will identify only the mean wage of those individuals of arrival cohort c that remained in the country until period T for the first period in which they were observed.

Assume now that the selection of out-migrants is related not only to the unobservable time-constant variables α_i but also to contemporaneous time-variant unobservables in the earnings equation,[9] a quite plausible assumption for many applications. For instance, negative shocks to wages in a particular period may be correlated with unobservables in the selection equation and trigger an out-migration. In that case, an OLS estimator using stock-based data will not identify $\Delta\mu_{t_1 t_2}^c$ (neither will a difference (or fixed effects) estimator in case the dataset is longitudinal; see below). To illustrate, we consider the conditional expectation of earnings growth between periods t_1 and t_2:

$$
\begin{aligned}
E\Big(w_{it_2}^c - w_{it_1}^c \Big| \Delta\mu_{t_1 t_2}^c, s_T^c = 1\Big) &= \Delta\mu_{t_1 t_2}^c + \Big[\sigma_{eu}(t_2) E\Big(u_{it_2}^c \Big| u_{ic}^c > -z_{ic}^c{}'\beta, \ldots, u_{iT}^c > -z_{iT}^c{}'\beta\Big) \\
&\quad - \sigma_{eu}(t_1) E\Big(u_{it_1}^c \Big| u_{ic}^c > -z_{ic}^c{}'\beta, \ldots, u_{iT}^c > -z_{iT}^c{}'\beta\Big)\Big]
\end{aligned}
$$

The bias term in brackets will only vanish if $\Delta\sigma_{eu}(t) = \sigma_{eu}(t_2) - \sigma_{eu}(t_1) = 0$ and $E\Big(u_{it_2}^c - u_{it_1}^c \Big| u_{ic}^c > -z_{ic}^c{}'\beta, \ldots, u_{iT}^c > -z_{iT}^c{}'\beta\Big) = 0$, meaning that both the covariance σ_{eu} and (whenever $\sigma_{eu} \neq 0$) the selection threshold $-z_{it}^c{}'\beta$ are constant over time. In

---

[9] Restricting the correlation in time-variant unobservables to contemporaneous realizations between e_{it}^c and u_{it}^c simplifies the exposition, but this correlation could be generalized.

particular, the latter will be violated in most scenarios, as selection will depend on non-constant individual characteristics such as age or time already spent in a host country, so that these variables should be included in z_{it}^c. Hence, if selective out-migration is related to time-variant unobservables in the earnings equation, stock-based sampled data will in general not allow us to answer Q2. As stock-based samples are increasingly selective sub-samples of the initial immigrant cohort for large T, individuals with on average high realizations of u are more likely to be contained in the sample. For these immigrants, the selection conditions $u_{ic}^c > -z_{ic}^c{}'\beta, \ldots, u_{iT}^c > -z_{iT}^c{}'\beta$ are less binding, so that selection is less affected by changes in z or σ over time, and hence the bias from the correlation in time-variant unobservables decreases with T.

Can we, then, identify the *direction* of selective out-migration by comparing estimates from stock-based data with those for repeated cross-sectional data for a particular entry cohort, as is done for $\Delta\mu_{t_1 t_2}^c$ in a number of empirical studies (see below)? Remember first the bias arising when cross-sectional data are used. Assuming that the earnings residual of stayers is given as in equation (10.3), the bias can be decomposed into two parts: The first part derives from selection on time-constant unobservables, which is equal to

$$E\left(\alpha_i \mid u_{ic}^c > -z_{ic}^c{}'\beta, \ldots, u_{it_2}^c > -z_{it_2}^c{}'\beta\right) - E\left(\alpha_i \mid u_{ic}^c > -z_{ic}^c{}'\beta, \ldots, u_{it_1}^c > -z_{it_1}^c{}'\beta\right)$$

for unrestricted repeated cross-sections, and equals zero if a stock-based sample is available, for which the conditioning set in periods t_2 and t_1 is the same. Thus, if out-migrants are selected on time-constant unobservables only, OLS estimates on pooled cross-sections are likely to be larger (smaller) than those obtained from stock-based longitudinal data whenever out-migrants are negatively (positively) selected. If in addition selection is on time-varying unobserved determinants of immigrant earnings, the bias from cross-sectional data is augmented by

$$\sigma_{eu}(t_2)E\left(u_{it_2}^c \mid u_{ic}^c > -z_{ic}^c{}'\beta, \ldots, u_{it_2}^c > -z_{it_2}^c{}'\beta\right)$$
$$- \sigma_{eu}(t_1)E\left(u_{it_1}^c \mid u_{ic}^c > -z_{ic}^c{}'\beta, \ldots, u_{it_1}^c > -z_{it_1}^c{}'\beta\right)$$

which generally will be non-zero. Taken together, estimates on cross-sectional and stock-based samples, if observed for the same time periods, will differ by

$$E\left(\alpha_i \mid u_{ic}^c > -z_{ic}^c{}'\beta, \ldots, u_{it_2}^c > -z_{it_2}^c{}'\beta\right) - E\left(\alpha_i \mid u_{ic}^c > -z_{ic}^c{}'\beta, \ldots, u_{it_1}^c > -z_{it_1}^c{}'\beta\right)$$
$$+ \sigma_{eu}(t_2)E\left(u_{it_2}^c \mid u_{ic}^c > -z_{ic}^c{}'\beta, \ldots, u_{it_2}^c > -z_{it_2}^c{}'\beta\right) - \sigma_{eu}(t_1)E\left(u_{it_1}^c \mid u_{ic}^c > -z_{ic}^c{}'\beta, \ldots, u_{it_1}^c > -z_{it_1}^c{}'\beta\right)$$
$$- \left[\sigma_{eu}(t_2)E\left(u_{it_2}^c \mid u_{ic}^c > -z_{ic}^c{}'\beta, \ldots, u_{iT}^c > -z_{iT}^c{}'\beta\right) - \sigma_{eu}(t_1)E\left(u_{it_1}^c \mid u_{ic}^c > -z_{ic}^c{}'\beta, \ldots, u_{iT}^c > -z_{iT}^c{}'\beta\right)\right]$$

$$(10.4')$$

the sign of which is informative about the direction of selection only in very special cases. Supposing, for example, that immigrants are target savers and hence are more likely to out-migrate if they experience a positive earnings shock ($\sigma_{eu} < 0$), and that older individuals are more likely to leave ($-z_{it}^{c\prime}\beta$ increases over time). In this quite plausible scenario, the above difference may be negative even if more productive individuals are generally more likely to stay ($corr(\alpha_i, u_{it}^c) > 0$), e.g., because they face lower integration costs. A comparison between estimates obtained from unrestricted cross-sectional and stock-based samples in this case is not informative about the direction of selection.

To address such more general types of selection, we need to model the process that determines selection and obtain an estimate for the selection term. Such modeling, however, is generally not possible with stock-based data, which do not indicate who leaves the country but only who has survived until period T. What is needed, therefore, is information on those individuals who leave the country.

3.2.2 Complete longitudinal data

Administrative datasets, which are now available for many countries, allow immigrant cohorts to be followed from entry onward and throughout their migration history. For example, assuming that complete longitudinal data are available for a cohort of immigrants who entered the country at time c, each individual in that dataset would be observed for a maximum number of years $\overline{T}$ (determined by the last year for which the survey is available) or until the year that individual leaves the country. Contrary to the stock sampled data discussed above, such data provide information on who left the country between $t-1$ and t.[10] Furthermore, if immigrants are observed from the time of arrival, the mean earnings level μ_c^c of the initial immigrant cohort c can be determined. Further, we can always construct a stock-based sample from complete longitudinal data by conditioning on survival until any year T. In other words, we can answer Q1 and Q3 for different survival cohorts and answer Q2 under the same assumptions as made in the previous sections.

Longitudinal data, however, also allow us to give up some of the restrictive assumptions on $\sigma_{eu}(t)$ necessary for identification of $\Delta\mu_{t_1 t_2}^c$. To illustrate, we first remember our assumption that emigration is an absorbing state; that is, immigrants who have left the country will never return. Even if this is not the case, we can construct such a dataset from longitudinal data by discarding all individuals who dropped out of the sample for some periods. As with out-migration, some migrants who were living in the country in period t_1 have disappeared by period t_2. Hence, for these migrants, we observe no time-variant characteristics for period t_2 that are not changing predictably. We do, however, observe all time-invariant characteristics, as well as characteristics that change systematically (e.g., age). We therefore need to assume that the process determining

[10] Of course, there may be other reasons why individuals drop out of the data, such as panel attrition or transitioning into sectors not covered by administrative data. We ignore these problems in the present analysis.

out-migration does not depend on time-variant observables that refer to period t_2 and change unpredictably.[11]

To focus on selection correlated with the time variant unobservables e_{it}^c, consider the earnings equation in (10.1) written in differences:

$$\Delta w_{it}^c = \Delta \mu_{t_1 t_2}^c + \Delta e_{it}^c \qquad (10.1'')$$

This eliminates α_i from the earnings equation and any selection related to it. Given that being in the country in period t implies $s_{it-1}^c = 1$ (i.e., the individual was in the country in the previous period), a selection equation conditional on $s_{it-1}^c = 1$ can be written as

$$s_{it}^c = \mathbf{1}\left[z_{it}^{c\,\prime} b_t + v_{it}^c > 0 \right] \qquad (10.5)$$

Equation (10.5) can thus be seen as a reduced form selection equation in which all explanatory variables from (10.1), and possibly their leads and lags, can be included in z_{it}^c. As explained above, we cannot include in z_{it}^c time-variant variables realized in period t that change unsystematically because these are not observed if the migrant has left the country in t; thus, we need to assume that such variables do not affect out-migration, which may be restrictive in certain applications.

Assuming now that $v_{it}^c | (z_{it}^c, s_{it-1}^c = 1) \sim N(0, 1)$, and $E\left(\Delta e_{it}^c \,|\, \Delta \mu_{t,t-1}^c, z_{it}^c, v_{it}^c, s_{it}^c = 1 \right) = r_{\Delta e_t v_t} v_{it}^c$, where $r_{\Delta e_t v_t}$ is the covariance between Δe_t and v_t, the expectation of wage growth in (10.1'') for individuals for whom $s_{it-1}^c = 1$, conditional on that individual also being observed in period t, can now be written as

$$E\left(\Delta w_{it}^c \,|\, \Delta \mu_{t,t-1}^c, z_{it}^c, s_{it}^c = 1 \right) = \Delta \mu_{t,t-1}^c + E\left(\Delta e_{it}^c \,|\, \Delta \mu_{t,t-1}^c, z_{it}^c, s_{it}^c = 1 \right)$$
$$= \Delta \mu_{t,t-1}^c + r_{\Delta e_t v_t} \lambda\left(z_{it}^{c\,\prime} b_t \right)$$

where the last equality follows from the normality assumption and $\lambda(z_{it}^{c\,\prime} b_t) = \phi(z_{it}^{c\,\prime} b_t) / \Phi(z_{it}^{c\,\prime} b_t)$ is the inverse Mills ratio (Heckman, 1979). Because $s_{it-1}^c = 1$, whenever $s_{it}^c = 1$, there is no need to condition on $s_{it-1}^c = 1$.

Wooldridge (2010, p. 837f) suggested estimating this model by first estimating simple probit models for each time period to obtain estimates of the inverse Mills ratios and then estimating pooled OLS of Δw_{it}^c on $\Delta \mu_{t,t-1}^c$ and $\mathbf{1}[t = c + 1] \hat{\lambda}_{it}, \ldots, \mathbf{1}[t - T] \hat{\lambda}_{it}$, where the $\mathbf{1}[t = \tau]$ are dummy variables, with $\mathbf{1}[t = \tau] = 1$ if $t = \tau$. Doing so yields the following equation, which can be estimated using pooled OLS:

$$\Delta w_{it}^c = \Delta \mu_{t,t-1}^c + \mathbf{1}[t = c + 1] r_{\Delta e_{(c+1)} v_{(c+1)}} \hat{\lambda}_{it} + \ldots + \mathbf{1}[t = T] r_{\Delta e_T v_T} \hat{\lambda}_{it} + \xi_{it}$$

---

[11] It should be noted that this case is different from standard panel data applications in which we usually observe all variables for individuals who have selected or not selected into a particular state in a particular period, as, for example, in the estimation of wage equations when labor force participation is selective (see, e.g., Wooldridge (1995) and Kyriazidou (1997) for estimators of these models, and Dustmann and Rochina-Barrachina (2007) for a comparison and application).

We can now use a simple F-test of the null hypothesis that $r_{\Delta e_t v_t}$ are jointly equal to zero to test whether out-migration depends on time-variant characteristics that affect earnings. If the null hypothesis is rejected, the estimated OLS standard errors must be adjusted for generated regressor bias.

Although the literature continues to be dominated by selection corrections derived from the assumption of jointly normally distributed unobservables, following Newey (2009), the above attrition correction can be extended to semiparametric estimators in which the predicted inverse Mills ratio $\lambda\left(z_{it}'\hat{b}_t\right)$ is replaced in the differenced wage equation by an unspecified function $\varphi\left(z_{it}'\hat{b}_t\right)$ of the linear index of the selection equation. The latter can be estimated using the semiparametric estimator suggested by Klein and Spady (1993), which does not rely on normally distributed residuals. $\varphi\left(z_{it}'\hat{b}_t\right)$ can then be approximated with a polynomial of $z_{it}'\hat{b}_t$ (see, e.g., Melenberg and van Soest (1996) and Martins (2001) for applications). Table 10.2 summarizes the discussion of identification of immigrants' earnings profiles in terms of the simple model above.

It should be noted that in order to focus on the key issues related to selective out-migration, we have abstracted from several problems that may also affect the estimation of earnings equations. First, if fixed effects estimators are to be used, the explanatory variables in the earnings equation must be strictly exogenous.[12] Otherwise, their predetermination would lead to an endogenous regressor bias in the differenced equation. For example, this assumption of strict exogeneity would be violated were tenure introduced into the level earnings equation, as shocks to wages in the last period might induce individuals to change firms, which would reset their tenure clocks (see Dustmann and Meghir (2005) for a discussion). Addressing this problem requires IV–type estimators.

Table 10.2 Identification of immigrant earnings profiles under selective out-migration

	Selection on time-constant unobservables	Selection on both time-constant and time-varying unobservables
Unrestricted repeated cross-sections		
μ_c	Not identified	Not identified
$\Delta\mu_{t_1 t_2}$	Not identified	Not identified
Stock-based samples		
μ_c	Not identified	Not identified
$\Delta\mu_{t_1 t_2}$	Identified	Not identified
Longitudinal data		
μ_c	Identified if panel starts at $t=c$	Identified if panel starts at $t=c$
$\Delta\mu_{t_1 t_2}$	Identified	Identified

[12] The difference estimator maintains its consistency under the slightly weaker condition that $E(\Delta e_{it}^c | \Delta\mu_{it}^c)=0$.

Second, it may be desirable to distinguish between the different factors that affect immigrant wage growth; for example, labor market experience, time in the destination country, and time effects. Yet a level equation focused on one particular entry cohort does not separately identify the effects of time and period of residence in the host country unless further assumptions are made. One common practice is to assume the same time effects for immigrants and natives (Borjas, 1985); however, there is increasing evidence that this assumption may be violated (see, e.g., Borjas and Bratsberg, 1996; Barth et al., 2004; Dustmann et al., 2010). Hence, it is impossible to distinguish between wage growth stemming from time effects and that resulting from period of residence in the host country without additional identifying assumptions.[13] Additional assumptions are also needed when estimating earnings equations for immigrants in differences if the level effects of years of residence and potential experience are to be identified separately.

3.3 Numerical example

We now illustrate the possible biases from selective out-migration given different assumptions about the correlation between unobservables in the earnings and selection equations, when these are not sufficiently accounted for. We use a simple Monte Carlo experiment that considers only one immigrant cohort. Suppose that the log earnings for immigrant i in one particular entry cohort, net of the effect of observable characteristics other than time spent in the host country, evolve as

$$w_{it} = \mu_t + \alpha_i + e_{it} \equiv \mu_o + \gamma ysm_{it} + \alpha_i + e_{it} \tag{10.6}$$

where for simplicity log earnings w_{it} of immigrant i in period t are specified as linear in years since immigration (ysm), so that $\Delta\mu_{t_1 t_2} = \gamma$ for all t. α_i is a time-constant individual-specific component, and e_{it} includes unobserved factors, which are assumed to be independent and identically distributed across individuals and time and independent of anything else on the right-hand side of the equation. Suppose also that the selection rule for an immigrant remaining in the host country is given by

$$s_{it} = \prod_{\tau \leq t} \mathbf{1}[z_{i\tau}'\beta + u_{i\tau} \equiv \beta_0 + \beta_1 ysm_{i\tau} + u_{i\tau} > 0]$$

then out-migration is an absorbing state (i.e., once out-migrated, an individual will not reappear in the dataset at a later point in time).[14]

---

[13] No such problem exists for natives because the quality of new entry cohorts is usually assumed not to change over time.

[14] Throughout this simulation exercise, we specify that $\mu_o = 2$, $\gamma = 0.02$, $\beta_0 = 0.5$, $\beta_1 = 0.05$, $\alpha \sim N(0, 0.2)$, $e \sim N(0, 0.2)$, and $u \sim N(0, 1)$. We generate a sample of 100,000 individuals (100 for Figure 10.6) who, to abstract from other issues, are all assumed to be observed from the date of immigration up to 30 years for those who do not out-migrate.

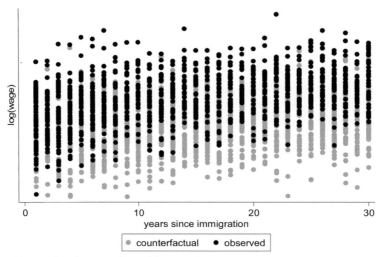

Figure 10.6 *Observed and counterfactual log-earnings.*

Assuming first that u_{it} is correlated only with α_i and not with e_{it}[15] (i.e., selection is on individual-specific time-constant unobservables in the earnings equation), then data generated in our simulation are as shown in Figure 10.6, where the black dots represent the observed log earnings of immigrants still residing in the host country and the gray dots the immigrants from the original arrival cohort who out-migrated. Given our assumptions about the nature of selection (with selection into staying being positively correlated with unobserved productivity α_i), out-migration is negatively selective.

Table 10.3 lists the results of using the OLS estimator for equation (10.6), assuming that the data we have available are either repeated cross-sections (column 2), stock-based data, where immigrants who remain at least 5, 15, or 25 years are observed throughout (columns 3–5), or complete longitudinal data (column 6). The OLS estimates in column 2 show a strong upward bias when applied to the pooled cross-sections. Estimating (10.6) using stock-based data restricted to immigrants that stay for at least a pre-specified number of years and allowing for different cut-off years T yields estimates of the slope parameters that are close to the true parameter values.[16] Hence, if selection occurs on time-constant individual fixed effects in the earnings equation only, OLS on stock-based samples produces parameter estimates that answer both Q2 and Q3.

However, the restriction to individuals remaining for a minimum number of years and the positive correlation between u_{it} and α_i tend to exclude immigrants with the lowest realizations of α_i (and increasingly so when we constrain the sample to survival at

---

[15] We assume that $corr(\alpha, u) = 0.7$.

[16] For small sample sizes, restricting the sample to very short panels may leave too little variation in the explanatory variable and incline estimates to attenuation bias.

Table 10.3 Selection on time-constant unobservables only

	True coefficients	OLS, all observations	OLS, stayed for 5 or more years	OLS, stayed for 15 or more years	OLS, stayed for 25 or more years	FE estimates
cons	2	2.277921 (0.0010001)	2.341263 (0.0028334)	2.438709 (0.0016322)	2.450425 (0.0012547)	—
ysm	0.02	0.0278496 (0.0000591)	0.021146 (0.0008531)	0.0199223 (0.0001797)	0.0200594 (0.0000845)	0.0199664 (0.0000534)

higher *T* values). Hence, the intercept of the earnings equation (reflecting the entry-level earnings of the respective arrival cohort) is overestimated relative to the intercept of the original arrival cohort. Nevertheless, this parameter does provide an estimate for the entry-level earnings of immigrants from a particular arrival cohort that survived until period *T* in the destination country. Finally, the last column of Table 10.3 reports the estimates from a within-group estimation, which, similar to estimation on the stock-based samples, eliminates selection on time-constant fixed effects.

The estimators discussed above, however, although widely used in the literature, produce no consistent estimates if we relax the assumption that selection is correlated with time-constant unobservables only. To illustrate this problem, we assume that in addition to α_i, there is contemporaneous correlation between u_{it} and e_{it},[17] and that only the stock-based sample data are available. In this case, the mean earnings observed in period t, conditional on being observed in $t-1$, are given by

$$
\begin{aligned}
E(w_{it}|\, s_{iT}=1) &= \mu_t + E(\alpha_i|\, s_{iT}=1) + E(e_{it}|\, s_{iT}=1) \\
&= \mu_t + E(\alpha_i|\, u_{ic} > -z_{ic}{}'\beta, \ldots, u_{iT} > -z_{iT}{}'\beta) \\
&\quad + E(e_{it}|\, u_{ic} > -z_{ic}{}'\beta, \ldots, u_{iT} > -z_{iT}{}'\beta)
\end{aligned}
\tag{10.7}
$$

and given our normality assumption, OLS identifies $\Delta\mu_{t_1 t_2} + \sigma_{eu}(t_2) E(u_{it_2}|\, u_{ic} > -z_{ic}{}'\beta, \ldots, u_{iT} > -z_{iT}{}'\beta) - \sigma_{eu}(t_1) E(u_{it_1}|\, u_{ic} > -z_{ic}{}'\beta, \ldots, u_{iT} > -z_{iT}{}'\beta)$.

While, as discussed in Section 3.2.1, the conditional expectation of α_i is constant over time, the conditional expectation of e_{it} may change if (for $\sigma_{eu} \neq 0$) either z_{it} (and thus the attrition probability) or the correlation between out-migration and time-variant unobservables in the earnings equation changes over time. Although either case is sufficient to bias estimates, in fact both apply in our simulated data.

In our simulations we have assumed that the (positive) correlation between e and u, $\sigma_{eu}(t)$, decreases over time, which induces a negative bias. Further, the increase in the probability of a migrant choosing not to leave the host country in a given period implies a reduction of the threshold $-z_{it}{}'\beta$, above which realizations of u_{it} are required for

---

[17] We assume in the simulation that upon immigration, $corr(e_s, u_t) = 0.7$ for $s = t$ but $corr(e_s, u_t) = 0$ for $s \neq t$, with the correlation decreasing over time by 10% per year.

the migrant to stay, so that $E(u_{it_2}|u_{ic} > -z_{ic}'\beta, \ldots, u_{iT} > -z_{iT}'\beta) < E(u_{it_1}|u_{ic} > -z_{ic}'\beta, \ldots, u_{iT} > -z_{iT}'\beta)$, reinforcing the negative bias. Columns 3–5 of Table 10.4 show these downward biased estimates for our illustrative simulation. Because the remaining sample becomes increasingly selected with respect to the initial immigrant cohort when T is larger, the bias in the estimated slope parameter becomes less severe as the time that immigrants must stay to be included in the stock-based sample increases. This is because a subsample with a high T has, on average, high realizations of α_i and u_{it}, so that the selection conditions $u_{ic} > -z_{ic}'\beta, \ldots, u_{iT} > -z_{iT}'\beta$ become increasingly less binding and the bias decreases—which is particularly visible in our estimates in Table 10.4 when we move from $T=5$ to $T=15$. On the other hand, the relatively small bias of the within-group estimator is specific to our simulated population and depends on the model parameters.

Can we learn something about the direction of the selection of immigrants by comparing estimates based on repeated cross-sectional data, and estimates based on stock-based samples? Estimates on the unrestricted repeated cross-sections continue to be above those obtained from stock-based data (column 2). However, other than in the previous case (Table 10.3), the bias consists now of two opposing parts: First, the same upward bias resulting from selection on time-constant unobservables, as in Table 10.3. Second, a downward bias resulting from selection on time-variant unobservables. Thus, the overall repeated cross-sections bias of the OLS estimates in column 2 is smaller in Table 10.4 than in Table 10.3. In this example, the downward bias again arises from both the decrease in σ_{eu} and the decrease in $-z_{it}'\beta$ over time, and its magnitude differs for repeated cross-sections (obtained as the difference in the estimated slope coefficients in Tables 10.2 and 10.3, $0.02785-0.02427=0.00358$) and for stock-based samples (ranging from $0.02-0.008605=0.011395$ for $T=5$ to $0.02-0.018289=0.001711$ for $T=25$), due to the different conditioning rules (see equation (10.4′) above). Hence, when comparing estimates obtained from stock-based samples and from unrestricted repeated cross-sections, this part of the bias does not simply cancel out, and such comparisons are uninformative about the direction of immigrant selection, unless one assumes that selection is on time-constant unobservables only (see also our discussion in Section 3.2.1).

Table 10.4 Selection on time-constant and time-varying unobservables

	True coefficients	OLS, all observations	OLS, stayed for 5 or more years	OLS, stayed for 15 or more years	OLS, stayed for 25 or more years	FE estimates	Corrected estimates
cons	2	2.352842	2.436231	2.485823	2.48313	—	—
		(0.0008919)	(0.0024729)	(0.0015218)	(0.0011942)		
ysm	0.02	0.0242654	0.0086049	0.016204	0.0182887	0.0184484	0.0209794
		(0.000055)	(0.0007664)	(0.0001715)	(0.0000818)	(0.0000528)	(0.001225)

The same holds true for fixed effects estimates (column 6). Like for stock-based samples, the bias here is only due to selection on time-varying unobservables. However, for the same reason as above, a comparison of estimates with those obtained from repeated cross-sections is uninformative about the direction of immigrant selection.

As previously explained, addressing selective out-migration that works through a correlation between time-variant unobservables in the selection and earnings equations requires the specification of a selection rule. Such specification is impossible, however, with stock sampled data because those who leave the country are not observed. Longitudinal data, on the other hand, do allow us to observe those who emigrate in period t in all periods $\tau < t$, which enables specification of a selection equation. We thus continue to assume that data are generated by the process specified above but that the complete (unbalanced) panel is observed, so that an individual is observed until he or she leaves the host country.

Because the assumption that out-migration is an absorbing state means that $s_{it} = 1$ always implies $s_{it-1} = 1$, to identify the slope parameter $\Delta \mu^c_{t_1 t_2}$, we can specify the following selection equation for the differenced earnings equation conditional on $s_{it-1} = 1$:

$$s_{it} = \mathbf{1}[b_0 + b_1 w_{it-2} + v_{it} > 0]$$

where w_{it-2} is chosen as an instrument that satisfies the exclusion restriction $E(\Delta e_{it} | w_{it-2}) = 0$ while being correlated with selection via the individual-specific effect α_i. As we discuss in Section 3.2.2, this reduced form selection equation can contain any variable that is observed for all individuals for whom $s_{it-1} = 1$ and that is informative about selection between periods $t-1$ and t. This also can include realizations of variables in period t if these variables change systematically over time. While in many applications age and other individual characteristics are likely to be determinants of the decision to stay in the host country, our simple simulation example specifies that only years since immigration and the unobserved components in u_{it} affect selection. For expositional purposes, we assumed all immigrants to arrive at the same point in time. Hence, since we estimate a probit model for each year separately, years since migration do not contain additional information for selection. However, since stayers are selected not only on time varying unobservables e_{it}, but also on the time-constant unobservables α_i, earnings lagged by two periods will help identify the selection equation, while being uncorrelated with $\Delta e_{it} = e_{it} - e_{it-1}$.

As explained in Section 3.2.2, for each period t, we use a probit estimator to estimate the selection equations and compute the inverse Mills ratio, which we then insert into the differenced earnings equation as additional regressors:

$$\Delta w_{it} = \gamma \Delta y s m_{it} + r_t \frac{\phi(\hat{b}_0 + \hat{b}_1 w_{it-2})}{\Phi(\hat{b}_0 + \hat{b}_1 w_{it-2})} + \Delta e_{it} \tag{10.8}$$

By estimating this model, we obtain the results given in the last column of Table 10.4. Time-varying coefficients r_t allow for the covariance between the residual of the differenced earnings equation and the selection equation to change with time since immigration. An F-test on the OLS estimates obtained from equation (10.8) rejects joint insignificance of r_t, i.e., that the selection correction terms have no effect on the change in earnings, at the 1% level.[18]

3.4 Interpretation: A simple model of return migration

To interpret the estimated direction of selectivity and to fix ideas about possible sources of selective out-migration driven by skill endowment and accumulation, we extend the work of Borjas and Bratsberg (1996) to produce a simple model of temporary migration.[19] In this model, log earnings in the origin country o and destination country d take the following form:[20]

$$w_l = \mu_l + \varepsilon_l \qquad (10.9)$$

where μ_l, $l = o, d$, denotes the mean log earnings or rental rate of human capital in location l, and ε_l is the deviation in the productive capacity (or human capital) of an individual-working in country l from the mean, which is determined by an individual's (observed and unobserved) human capital. We abstract from variation in ε_l over time, so that it corresponds to the time constant α in the previous subsections. We further assume that the ε_l have a mean of zero and that $\varepsilon_d = \pi \varepsilon_o$, where π is the price of skills in the destination country relative to that in the origin country, implying that all skills are perfectly transferable across countries. It follows that $corr(\varepsilon_d, \varepsilon_o) = 1$. If the price for skills is higher in the destination than in the origin country (i.e., $\pi > 1$), this implies that the variance in earnings is higher in the host country. In this model, skills are *one-dimensional* so that individuals can be ranked on them, and the ranking of individuals on productive capacity is the same in both countries. Individuals know both their skills and the relative skill price π.

According to Borjas and Bratsberg (1996), workers have three options: to stay at home and not migrate at all, to migrate temporarily, or to migrate permanently. Of these, temporary migration may be optimal when having been abroad increases human capital that is valuable at home by a certain amount $\kappa = \tau k$. We extend these authors' model by assuming that this gain in human capital varies with the period of stay in the destination country, in which case earnings when emigrating and returning are given by

---

[18] As would be expected, it does not reject joint insignificance in the differenced earnings equation in the case where selection is on time-constant unobservables only.

[19] See Dustmann et al. (2011) for a generalization of this model to multiple skills and a dynamic setting and Dustmann and Glitz (2011) for a simplified version.

[20] As first discussed in Dustmann (1995), we focus on a human capital accumulation in the host country that has a higher value in the home country as a motive for return. Borjas and Bratsberg (1996) also considered a lower than expected return in the host country as a reason for return migration.

$$w_{do} = \tau(\mu_d + \varepsilon_d) + (1 - \tau)(\mu_o + \varepsilon_o + \tau k) \tag{10.10}$$

where τ denotes the fraction of an individual's working life spent abroad. Assuming that individuals try to maximize income, they will choose to stay in the country of origin if $w_o > w_d$ and $w_o > w_{do}$, choose to migrate permanently if $w_d > w_o$ and $w_d > w_{do}$, and choose to migrate temporarily if $w_{do} > w_o$ and $w_{do} > w_d$. Hence, ignoring the costs of migration, the skill thresholds for which no migration, temporary migration, and permanent migration are optimal can be easily derived by substituting (10.9) and (10.10) into the conditions above.

In Figure 10.7, we illustrate the case in which $\pi > 1$ (i.e., the variance in earnings, as well as the price of skills, is higher in the destination country). Given the skill distribution shown here, those with the lowest skills (with ε_o below the threshold $(\mu_o - \mu_d - k)/(\pi - 1)$) will decide to stay in the country of origin, those with the highest skills (above the threshold $(\mu_o - \mu_d + k)/(\pi - 1)$) will decide to emigrate and remain permanently, and those between the two thresholds will decide to emigrate but will return migrate after spending some time τ abroad. For $\pi > 1$, therefore, selection in this model leads those with higher productive capacity to emigrate, and among those who decide to emigrate, motivates those with the highest productive capacity to stay permanently. It should also be noted that in this simple model, the migration selection depends only on the relative skill price π. The selection of emigrants and remigrants in this model is the exact opposite when the price of skills is higher in the sending country (i.e., $\pi < 1$). Thus, in this model, temporary migrants are always predicted to be drawn from the middle of the skill distribution.

The model further predicts that an increase in the rental rate of human capital in the destination country, μ_d, will cause the two thresholds to shift to the left, whereas an increase in the home country of the value of human capital acquired abroad, κ, will result in a widening of the distance between them. Because in this simple illustrative model gains from a stay abroad can only be realized in the country of origin, a large value for κ makes temporary migration an attractive choice, so that only individuals

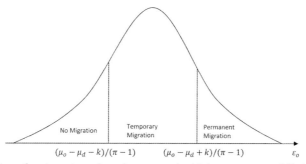

Figure 10.7 *Selection of emigrants and remigrants under higher returns to skills in the host country.*

with very low (very high) ε_0 choose to stay permanently in the country of origin (destination). On the other hand, a high relative return to skills in the host country, π, brings the two thresholds closer together, implying that for most individuals with below (above) average skill endowment, staying permanently in the country of origin (destination) is the preferred option. In this model, therefore, temporary migrants can be hierarchically sorted (Willis, 1986); that is, clearly ranked on skills relative to non-migrants and permanent migrants dependent on the skill prices in the two countries.

In this model, the optimal migration duration for those who decide to emigrate but remain in the host country only temporarily is determined by the first-order condition of w_{do} with respect to τ:

$$\tau = \frac{[\mu_d - \mu_o] + [\pi - 1]\varepsilon_0 + k}{2k}$$

Hence, for $\pi > 1$, the optimal migration duration for temporary migrants increases with initial skill endowment ε_0. Given the opposite case, however (i.e., the price of skills is higher in the country of origin), it will be higher for low-productivity individuals.

As emphasized in other sections, this relation between the time immigrants choose to stay in the host country and their productive capacity has important implications for estimating their earnings profiles. According to our simple model, three dynamics can be predicted: (i) if skill prices are higher abroad, then immigrants will be positively selected from the population of the origin country; (ii) the migration duration for those who emigrate will increase with productivity; and (iii) those with the highest levels of productivity will decide to migrate permanently. This scenario is thus compatible with negatively selective return migration in the sense that of those who emigrate, the lowest productivity individuals will return first. If $\pi < 1$ (i.e., the return to skills is higher in the destination country), those with higher skills will return sooner.

To explicitly relate these observations to the earlier discussion on earnings profile estimation, we assume that skills are normally distributed, with $\varepsilon_o \sim N(0, 1)$ and $\varepsilon_d \sim N(0, \pi^2)$, and $Cov(\varepsilon_d - \varepsilon_0, \varepsilon_0) = (\pi - 1)$. Consider now the mean earnings of those who have emigrated to the destination country and who are observed there in period t:

$$E(w_d | \tau > t) = \mu_d + \pi E(\varepsilon_o | \tau > t) = \begin{cases} \mu_d + \pi E(\varepsilon_o | \varepsilon_o > q(t)) = \mu_d + \pi\lambda(-q(t)) \, if \, \pi > 1 \\ \mu_d + \pi E(\varepsilon_o | \varepsilon_o < q(t)) = \mu_d - \pi\lambda(q(t)) \, if \, \pi < 1 \end{cases}$$

where $q(t) = k(2t - 1) - [\mu_d - \mu_o]/(\pi - 1)$, and λ is the inverse Mills ratio. This calculation raises a number of important issues. First, it is clear that here the entry wage of a particular cohort is composed of the mean wage obtainable by the average individual from the home country who migrates to the destination country, μ_d, and a term that reflects the selection of migrants from the overall population:

$$E(w_d|\tau > 0) = \begin{cases} \mu_d + \pi\lambda(-q(0)) > \mu_d \text{ if } \pi > 1 \\ \mu_d - \pi\lambda(q(0)) < \mu_d \text{ if } \pi < 1. \end{cases}$$

Hence, the mean entry wage of the original arrival cohort (denoted as μ_c^c above) depends on the degree of initial immigrant selection (see de Coulon and Piracha (2005) for a similar model on the selection of emigrants and return migrants from their origin societies). If $\pi > 1$, the entry wage will be larger than that a randomly drawn individual from the home country would earn in the host country, meaning that emigration is positively selective. Also worth noting is that the rule governing return migration depends on the same unobserved productivity term as the earnings equation, ε_o. Thus, not only non-migrants and permanent migrants but also temporary migrants with lower or higher durations of stay can be strictly ordered in terms of their underlying skills to produce an especially simple selection mechanism in which out-migration truncates the skill distribution. This case is the one shown in Figure 10.1, where selective out-migration increasingly eliminates immigrants from the lower part of the earnings distribution. Therefore, the earnings of immigrants in the host country at any period t follow a truncated distribution, one whose truncation is based on the outcome variable, log earnings.

Next, we consider determining wage growth by estimating earnings regressions based on repeated cross-sectional data. Because in this simple model μ_d is constant, the wage growth of the original arrival cohort if all migrations were permanent, $\Delta E(w_d(t))$, equals zero. Hence, when $\pi > 1$ (i.e., out-migration is negatively selective), the wage growth between periods t_1 and $t_2 > t_1$ obtained from repeated cross-sectional data is

$$E(w_d(t_2)|\tau > t_2) - E(w_d(t_1)|\tau > t_1) = \pi[\lambda(-q(t_2)) - \lambda(-q(t_1))]$$

The last term in brackets is always positive for $\pi > 1$: The inverse Mills ratio decreases in its argument, and $q(t)$ increases in t. This leads to an overestimation of the wage growth of the original arrival cohort had nobody return migrated if return is negatively selected. When $\pi < 1$, on the other hand, the term is negative, generating an underestimation if return migration is positively selective.

If we re-examine these same issues using stock sampled data, then

$$E(w_d(t_2)|\tau > T) - E(w_d(t_1)|\tau > T) = \pi[\lambda(-q(T)) - \lambda(-q(T))]$$

where $w_d(\tau)$ is the migrants' earnings in the host country during period τ. Because the last term in brackets equals zero, our stock sampled data produces an unbiased estimate of $\Delta\mu_t^c$ thanks to the special selection type induced in this simple model, in which the time-constant unobservables governing selection are the same as those affecting wages.

4. EXISTENT STUDIES ON THE ESTIMATION OF EARNINGS EQUATIONS WHEN OUT-MIGRATION IS NONRANDOM

Analyzing immigrant assimilation in terms of wages and other native population outcomes has been at the core of economic migration research for many decades (see Dustmann and Glitz (2011) for a survey). Beginning with Chiswick's (1978) analysis of the earnings adjustment of male immigrants to the US and Long's (1980) similar investigation for foreign-born women, a large body of literature has emerged on the estimation of immigrants' earnings profiles. Yet these early studies are often criticized for their reliance on single cross-sectional sample data (e.g., Chiswick, 1978; Long, 1980; and Carliner, 1980, all use 1970 US census data), which do not allow a differentiation to be made between cohort effects and time of residence effects as an individual in 1970 that has been in the US for 10 years must have arrived in 1960, and an individual that has been in the US for 20 years in 1950. Such data thus permit no distinction between wage growth after arrival in the US and differences in immigrants' initial earnings positions after arrival. Moreover, whereas the early literature implicitly assumes that these cohort differences equal zero, Borjas (1985) stressed that, if the quality of successive cohorts deteriorates, this may lead to overestimation of assimilation profiles. Borjas (1985), LaLonde and Topel (1992), Chiswick and Miller (2010), and other researchers addressed this problem by employing repeated cross-sections, which allows addressing of this problem under some assumptions.

As we have already demonstrated, similar issues arise when immigrant out-migration is selective. Even with repeated cross-sectional data, assimilation estimates can still be biased when selective out-migration drives what seem to be changes in cohort quality (see, e.g., Chiswick, 1986). Several early studies took advantage of longitudinal data to address this problem. Borjas (1989), for example, used longitudinal information from the 1972–78 Survey of Natural and Social Scientists and Engineers (which is based on immigrant listings in the 1970 US census) to analyze the earnings paths of a particular immigrant group. He found that among foreign-born scientists and engineers in the sample, attrition—which is assumed to be largely driven by emigration from the US—is more likely for individuals with less favorable economic outcomes. Because this dataset includes earnings information dating back to 1969, it allowed him to perform separate estimations for the 1969–71 earnings of immigrants who stayed until 1978 versus those who left between 1972 and 1978. The results suggest that both initial earnings and earnings growth are lower for immigrants who leave the sample later. In subsequent work, Pischke (1992) addressed the potential bias in the estimation of the earnings assimilation of immigrants in Germany by including fixed effects in his panel estimates, while Lindstrom and Massey (1994) estimated log wage regressions using different samples of Mexicans residing in the US and Mexicans who returned to their native country. Based on their comparison of estimates from single versus repeated cross-sectional data, however, they concluded that selective emigration is unlikely to affect estimates of wage assimilation.

4.1 Studies using stock sampled longitudinal data

A number of more recent studies use stock sampled longitudinal data on immigrants in the US. Hu (2000), for example, compared assimilation profiles from longitudinal social security records matched to the Health and Retirement Survey (HRS) with profiles from the cross-sectional decennial census. The lower immigrant earnings growth suggested by the stock-based longitudinal data (as compared to the repeated cross-sectional data) is consistent with negatively selective out-migration. This interpretation, however, relies on the assumption that the selection of out-migrants occurs on time-constant unobservables only (see our discussion in Section 3.2). Moreover, whereas the census estimates suggest that net of age, education, and time effects, non-Hispanic white immigrants experience an earnings increase, with the 1950–59 and 1965–69 immigrant cohorts catching up with US-born workers within 10 years of arrival, the longitudinal data indicate a decline in earnings residuals by time spent in the US for this population both in levels and relative to the US-born population. For Hispanic immigrants, both data sources indicate an earnings increase, although the HRS data suggest it takes about 35 years to catch up with US-born workers, much longer than the 20 or so years suggested by the census estimates. Nevertheless, because the HRS follows a relatively narrow birth cohort (1931–41), separating the effects of age at immigration or pre-migration experience and changes in average immigrant cohort earnings is difficult.

Lubotsky (2007) addressed this difficulty by using a broader sample, based on 1951–97 social security earnings records matched to the 1990 and 1991 Survey of Income and Program Participation (SIPP) and March supplement to the 1994 CPS, to estimate a log earnings equation with cohort fixed effects, time since immigration indicators, and a number of human capital variables on the right side. He then compared the estimates of the time since immigration effects with those obtained from the 1970–90 cross-sectional census data. Consistent with the hypothesis of negatively selective out-migration, the wage profiles obtained from the longitudinal data are flatter.[21] Like Hu, however, Lubotsky (2007) used stock-based longitudinal data, and—recalling our discussion in Section 3.2.2—this interpretation relies on the assumption that selection occurs only on time-constant unobservables that affect earnings. Under this assumption and given the format of his data, Lubotsky estimated his earnings equation in levels and only included cohort- rather than individual-specific indicators. Consistent with the greater likelihood that it is low-earning immigrants who will leave, the stock-based longitudinal data indicate a less pronounced deterioration in cohort earnings on entry to the

---

[21] A second concern addressed in Lubotsky (2007) is that because of alternative arrival cohort definitions, it cannot be ruled out that migrants, when moving back and forth, have in fact spent time in the US before the stated date of entry. If the incidence of repeat migration increases more over time among low-earnings migrants, then the deterioration in average cohort earnings will be overstated.

US. In an earlier study that used part of the same stock-based longitudinal data as Lubotsky (2007), Duleep and Dowhan (2002) analyzed immigrant assimilation in the US at different quantiles of the earnings distribution and for different years of immigration (cohorts arriving between 1960 and 1983). As estimates are not compared to, e.g., results that would be obtained from repeated cross-sectional data, the direction of selection cannot be determined from their analysis even under the assumption that out-migrants are selected only on time-constant unobservable components of the earnings equation. In their interesting paper using historical data of immigration to the US, Abramitzky et al. (2013) constructed a panel of US residents from 1900–20 census data. Since the panel is restricted to individuals who are still observed in 1920, the data on immigrants amounts to a stock-based sample. Their smaller assimilation estimates obtained from the stock-based panel compared to those from cross-sectional data are consistent with out-migrants being negatively selected, but this conclusion rests on the assumptions regarding the selection process that we discuss above.

For Canada, Picot and Piraino (2012), in large part following Lubotsky (2007), reported that although earnings growth rates based on cross-sectional data are overestimated, the earnings *gap* between Canadian and foreign-born workers appears to evolve similarly whether cross-sectional or stock-based longitudinal data are used, the reason being that at the lower end of the earnings distribution, attrition tends to increase to a similar degree among both immigrants and Canadians, leaving no obvious differences between cross-sectional and longitudinal data in terms of earnings gap evolution.

4.2 Studies using longitudinal data

Whereas the US data used by Lubotsky (2007) and others generally do not follow immigrants from the beginning of their stay in the host country, a number of European studies use datasets that do, thereby enabling analysis of the differences in earnings assimilation between short- and longer-term migrants. In addition, because longitudinal data that are not restricted to migrants residing in the host country until some period T are informative about which migrants leave the host country, in principle they allow selection to be explicitly modeled. Most existing studies, however, in using individual fixed effects to address the potential inconsistency in estimated earnings profiles, maintain the assumption that selection occurs on time-constant unobservables only.

Such an approach was taken in an early paper by Pischke (1992), who estimated the earnings assimilation of immigrants in Germany using data from the German Socio-Economic Panel (GSOEP), which should eliminate any possible bias from selection on individual-specific unobservables. Likewise, Edin et al. (2000) used Swedish register data on immigrants arriving in Sweden between 1970 and 1990 to show that over a quarter of immigrants aged between 18 and 55 on arrival leave the country within five years. In line with the US literature, they also found that emigration is more likely among economically less successful migrants. Then, under the assumption that emigration may vary with earnings levels but not with earnings growth, they demonstrated that if out-migration is not taken into account, earnings assimilation by OECD immigrants is overestimated by about 90%, a figure largely in line with Lubotsky (2007). Arai (2000), however, criticized their results on negatively selective emigration from Sweden on the grounds that much of this finding is driven by the higher mobility of young migrants and the positive correlation of age with earnings, together with a number of sampling issues.

Sarvimäki (2011) analyzed immigrant assimilation in Finland using longitudinal data that follow immigrants from the time of their arrival. To address selective emigration, he compared OLS estimates of immigrant earnings growth based on the whole sample with estimates based only on immigrants that stay for at most five years. Although he does show that short-term migrants experience no earnings growth, he acknowledged that the direction of selection is unclear and his results merely indicate that immigrants who stay are not a random sample of their initial arrival cohort. In terms of the model we use in Section 3, and given that he estimated earnings equations in levels, the differences in earnings growth would be consistent with a variety of scenarios. If, for instance, most of the selection occurs during the first few years and out-migrants are positively selected on time-constant unobservables only, then we expect the OLS estimates of earnings growth to be strongly downwardly biased in any sample that is restricted to short-term migrants. In the presence of negative selection of out-migrants on time-constant unobservables, on the other hand, the differences in the estimates of earnings growth could arise if during the first years after immigration, immigrants tend to leave when facing negative earnings shocks and the effect of time-variant unobservables on selection decreases with the time immigrants have spent in the host country ($\sigma_{eu}(t) > 0$ and $d\sigma_{eu}/dt < 0$). The positive but decreasing covariance between the time-variant components e_{it} and u_{it} induces a negative bias from selection on time-varying unobservables that may dominate the positive bias due to selection on time-constant individual effects, implying lower estimated earnings growth for short-term migrants.

Barth et al. (2012), on the other hand, in their analysis of the role of native–immigrant differences in job mobility, found little difference between short- and long-term migrants in either between- or within-firm wage growth when restricting the sample by dropping immigrants who leave within the first five years after arrival. Nevertheless, their findings permit no conclusion that out-migration is random. Skuterud and Su (2009), using a rotating panel of immigrants and natives in Canada, found little difference between OLS and fixed-effect estimates of immigrant wage assimilation. They reconciled this observation with the contrary findings for stock-based samples from the US (e.g., Hu, 2000; Lubotsky, 2007) in two ways: First, they argued that in the Canadian case, emigrant selection may be less clear because many more able immigrants may move onward to the US. Second, they pointed out that if emigration is correlated with heterogeneity in wage growth rather than wage levels, then it is possible that $E(\alpha_i | u_{ic} > -z_{ic}'\beta, \ldots,$ $u_{it} > -z_{it}'\beta) = 0$, so including fixed effects need not change the estimates of $\mu_t - \mu_{t-1}$ from an unbalanced panel like Skuterud and Su's (2009), which initially also contained migrants who later leave. However, if at least some immigrants can correctly anticipate wage growth and leave when expected wage growth is low, then, in a comparison of estimates based on cross-sectional and stock-based longitudinal data, $E(\mu_t | s_t = 1) - E$-$(\mu_{t-1} | s_{t-1} = 1) > E(\mu_t - \mu_{t-1} | s_T = 1)$, so stock-based longitudinal data will predict flatter wage profiles for immigrants than estimates based on cross-sectional data, which would be an alternative explanation for the difference between repeated cross-sectional and stock-based longitudinal sample estimates reported by Lubotsky and others. Cobb-Clark et al. (2012) analyzed immigrant earnings in Australia; however, their very brief discussion paper did not specify which immigrant cohorts are analyzed or how they change over time. Nevertheless, their results do suggest that compared to longitudinal data, selective emigration tends to bias estimates of employment assimilation upwards when repeated cross-sectional data are used, but that this has less of an effect on wage assimilation profiles.

To analyze earnings assimilation between German-born workers and different immigrant cohorts, Fertig and Schurer (2007) used the German Socio-Economic Panel (GSOEP). As a panel, this dataset enables explicit modeling of out-migration. Specifically, these authors formulated a multiple equations selection model of individual earnings together with the probabilities of employment, survey participation, and staying in the host country under the assumption that unobservables are jointly normally distributed (see our discussion in Section 3.2.2) and include correction terms in the earnings regression. As exclusion restrictions, Fertig and Schurer included family and country-of-origin characteristics as explanatory variables in the selection equation. They only found evidence for assimilation, however, in some of their immigrant groups, possibly because most immigrants in their sample are longer-term migrants who arrived in the early 1970s, whereas the wage observations only begin with the first year of the survey in 1984. In addition, unlike our exposition in Section 3.2.2, these authors assumed that the covariance between unobservables in the earnings and selection equations is constant over time, although they did allow it to be immigrant cohort specific. More important, they included selection correction terms in the levels rather than the differenced earnings equation. This assumes that selective out-migration can be reduced to a static problem where—given observable control variables—selection in each period does not depend on past selection. This ignores that an immigrant being in the country in a given period depends on decisions made in previous periods. If, for instance, out-migration is an absorbing state then such an estimating equation would not appropriately correct for selective out-migration because it ignores whether or not an individual is observed depends on selection in earlier periods. It is important to note that by specifying selection corrections for a differenced earnings equation, as we suggest above, one conditions on past selection, while this is not the case when corrections from static selection equations are simply applied to an earnings equation in levels. This same caveat applies to Venturini and Villosio (2008) and Faini et al. (2009), who used a similar framework for Italy.

Biavaschi (2013), working with US data, challenged the view that emigration is negatively selective. She formulated a selection model and then, using data from the 2000 US and Mexican censuses, semiparametrically estimated the counterfactual density of the wage residuals of Mexican immigrants in the US had there been no out-migration. Biavaschi used an identification at infinity argument to recover this counterfactual distribution if only one cross-section of data is available. She found that emigration is more likely among Mexican-born workers at the upper part of the wage distribution, which implies that in the absence of emigration, the Mexican-born population in the US would have higher wages. Assuming that out-migration is not correlated with unpredictably changing variables that affect wages, an alternative method of accounting for selective out-migration was proposed by Kim (2009). Specifically, he applied a weighting procedure to an overlapping rotating panel constructed from the merged outgoing rotation groups from 1994–2004 CPS data to produce a larger sample size than usually available from true longitudinal datasets. Like Hu (2000), he found that estimates of immigrants' economic assimilation based on repeated cross-sectional data are positive and upwardly biased but that the reverse is likely to be true when selective out-migration is taken into account.

The problem of selective out-migration is recognized well beyond studies of immigrant earnings assimilation. Kaushal's (2011) analysis of the returns to US versus overseas education, for example, showed that, based on longitudinal data from the National Survey of College Graduates, US-educated science and engineering professionals who stay in the country earn more than those who leave, which indicates a bias in cross-sectional estimates of education-dependent earnings trajectories. In this study, however, whether foreign-born individuals acquire their education in the US or abroad does not matter for emigration propensity. Examining the variation in earnings and the change in returns to skills rather than simply the earnings level, Lubotsky (2011) re-emphasized the need to use longitudinal data when emigration is selective. Using a similar longitudinal stock-based sample of immigrants to the US as in Lubotsky (2007), he argued that not only will estimates of wage growth be inconsistent if out-migration is selective, but that estimates of the impact of changes in the wage structure—e.g., due to the increase in the returns to skills since the 1980s—on the earnings gap between native and foreign-born workers will be affected as well. Other studies investigating various effects of selective out-migration on empirical estimates have been conducted by Bratsberg et al. (2010), who analyzed immigrant employment in Norway, by de Matos (2011) for immigrant career paths in Portugal, and Kaushal and Shang (2013) for wage assimilation among US immigrants in different destination areas.

5. CONCLUSIONS

In this chapter, we address selective out-migration—a key problem in estimating immigrant career profiles—by first giving evidence of the temporariness of many migrations and then reviewing the literature that assesses the degree to which emigration is selective along various dimensions. This literature review provides evidence not only that out-migration is heterogeneous with respect to country of origin, immigrant education, and immigrant earnings in the destination country, but that the direction and degree of selective out-migration, far from being uniform, differ across both immigration countries and different groups in the same immigration country.

To outline the potential methodological problems in estimating immigrant earnings profiles, we distinguish three important research questions related to immigrants' economic careers in the destination country. Although two of these are answerable by computing means from observable data, the third requires the construction of a counterfactual scenario. The first question, which is of particular interest to many researchers in the field, explores the evolution of mean earnings of a particular immigrant arrival cohort c that is part of a population that decides to stay in the destination country. Because this question refers to the population of immigrants that remains t years after immigration, it can be answered using repeated cross-sectional data. Researchers may also be interested, however, in such evolution for an entry cohort from among all migrants who survive in the host country until T years after migration. Because answering this second question requires the identification of all immigrants who survived until T in all years between c and T, it is dependent on the availability of stock sampled data of the type we describe above.

A third question concerns the earnings paths in the host country of the original arrival cohort if nobody out-migrates. If selection is correlated with unobservables in the outcome equation, estimates based on repeated cross-sectional data do not answer the question. Under restrictive assumptions about the nature of the selection process, stock-based sampled data will provide an answer to that question, and availability of both stock-based sampled data and repeated cross-sections allows signing the selection of out-migrants. However, given more general assumptions, data are needed that allow modeling of the out-migration selection process; for example, longitudinal data that are not stock sampled. In our discussion, therefore, we suggest selection patterns and various estimators of the parameter underlying this question.

The overall purpose of the chapter is to discuss the different research questions different types of data allow addressing, and under which assumptions. We illustrate how misleading many estimates of immigrant earnings assimilation may be in providing answers to particular questions if the research design does not take into account the possibility of selective out-migration. We also demonstrate the impossibility of making any general statement about the direction of selective out-migration, unless longitudinal data are available that allow modeling out-migration, and that the direction and magnitude of selection may differ both across countries and across immigrant groups within the same country. Unfortunately, the latter implies that we may know far less about immigrant career profiles than the vast literature suggests. On the other hand, the availability of increasingly better data raises hopes that, in the near future, we will be able to more accurately assess immigrant progress in destination countries and the selection on their out-migration.

Overall, because of its strong consequences for all types of policy and such related areas as migration's impact on natives, assessment of immigrants' career profiles is vital to the economics of migration. Even if longitudinal data are available that allow assessment of selective out-migration, the key assumption that we made here is that the process that governs out-migration is independent of decisions that may determine the individual's investments into human capital or other labor market decisions. Hence, one slowly emerging body of literature not covered in this chapter, in estimating immigrant career paths, allows migrants to make their migration plans in conjunction with their economic decisions, including labor supply and human capital investments. Such estimation, however, requires that these decisions be modeled jointly with migration choices (as in Bellemare, 2007), a methodological challenge typical of the many problems that riddle research in this area despite steady progress in recent years. These very challenges, however, open up myriad promising avenues for future study on aspects that still need to be (and can be) addressed.

ACKNOWLEDGMENTS

We thank Albrecht Glitz and Martin Weidner for helpful comments, and Shanka Fernando for excellent research assistance. We acknowledge the support by the Norface programme on Migration. Dustmann acknowledges support by the European Research Council (ERC) Advanced Grant No. 323992.

REFERENCES

Abramitzky, R., Boustan, L.P., Eriksson, K., 2012. Europe's tired, poor, huddled masses: self-selection and economic outcomes in the age of mass migration. Am. Econ. Rev. 102 (5), 1832–1856.

Abramitzky, R., Boustan, L.P., Eriksson, K., 2013. A Nation of Immigrants: Assimilation and Economic Outcomes in the Age of Mass Migration, Working Paper.

Ahmed, B., Robinson, J.G., 1994. Estimates of Emigration of the Foreign-Born Population: 1980–1990, US Census Bureau Population Division Working Paper No. 9.

Alders, M., Nicolaas, H., 2003. One in three immigrants leave within six years. Statistics Netherlands, online, 20 January.

Arai, M., 2000. Comments on Edin, LaLonde and Åslund: emigration of immigrants and measures of immigrant assimilation: evidence from Sweden. Swed. Econ. Pol. Rev. 7, 205–211.

Aydemir, A., Robinson, C., 2008. Global labour markets, return, and onward migration. Can. J. Econ. 41 (4), 1285–1311.

Bandiera, O., Rasul, I., Viarengo, M., 2013. The making of modern America: migratory flows in the age of mass migration. J. Dev. Econ. 102, 23–47.

Barth, E., Bratsberg, B., Raaum, O., 2004. Identifying earnings assimilation of immigrants under changing macroeconomic conditions. Scand. J. Econ. 106 (1), 1–22.

Barth, E., Bratsberg, B., Raaum, O., 2012. Immigrant wage profiles within and between establishments. Lab. Econ. 19 (4), 541–556.

Beaujot, R., Rappak, J.P., 1989. The link between immigration and emigration in Canada, 1945–1986. Can. Stud. Popul. 16 (2), 201–216.

Beenstock, M., 1996. Failure to absorb: remigration by immigrants into Israel. Int. Migrat. Rev. 30 (4), 950–978.

Beenstock, M., Chiswick, B.R., Paltiel, A., 2010. Testing the immigrant assimilation hypothesis with longitudinal data. Review of Economics of the Household 8 (1), 7–27.

Beggs, J.J., Chapman, B., 1991. Male immigrant wage and unemployment experience in Australia. In: Immigration, Trade and the Labor Market. University of Chicago Press, pp. 369–384.

Bellemare, C., 2007. A life-cycle model of outmigration and economic assimilation of immigrants in Germany. Eur. Econ. Rev. 51 (3), 553–576.

Bhaskar, R., Arenas-Germosén, B., Dick, C., 2013. Demographic Analysis 2010: Sensitivity Analysis of the Foreign-Born Migration Component. U.S. Census Bureau Population Division Working Paper No. 98, May 2013.

Biavaschi, C., 2013. Recovering the Counterfactual Wage Distribution with Selective Return Migration, Working Paper.

Bijwaard, G.E., 2009. Labour Market Status and Migration Dynamics, IZA Discussion Paper No. 4530.

Bijwaard, G.E., 2010. Immigrant migration dynamics model for the Netherlands. J. Popul. Econ. 23 (4), 1213–1247.

Bijwaard, G.E., Wahba, J., 2014. Do high-income or low-income immigrants leave faster? J. Dev. Econ. 108, 54–68.

Bijwaard, G.E., Schluter, C., Wahba, J., 2011. The impact of labor market dynamics on the return migration of immigrants. Rev. Econ. Stat.

Böhning, W.-R., 1984. Studies in International Labour Migration. Macmillan, London.

Borjas, G.J., 1985. Assimilation, changes in cohort quality, and the earnings of immigrants. J. Labor Econ. 3 (4), 463–489.

Borjas, G.J., 1989. Immigrant and emigrant earnings: a longitudinal study. Econ. Inq. 27 (1), 21–37.

Borjas, G.J., Bratsberg, B., 1996. Who leaves? The outmigration of the foreign-born. Rev. Econ. Stat. 78 (1), 165–176.

Bratsberg, B., Raaum, O., Sørlie, K., 2007. Foreign-born migration to and from Norway. International Migration, Economic Development and Policy 259–291.

Bratsberg, B., Raaum, O., Røed, K., 2010. When minority labor migrants meet the welfare state. J. Labor Econ. 28 (3), 633–676.

Cameron, A.C., Trivedi, P.K., 2005. Microeconometrics: Methods and Applications. Cambridge University Press.

Carliner, G., 1980. Wages, earnings and hours of first, second, and third generation American males. Econ. Inq. 18 (1), 87–102.

Carrión-Flores, C.E., 2006. What makes you go back home? Determinants of the duration of migration of Mexican immigrants in the United States. In: Society of Labor Economists Annual Meeting, Cambridge, MA.

Chiswick, B., 1978. The effect of Americanization on the earnings of foreign-born men. J. Polit. Econ. 86 (5), 897–921.

Chiswick, B.R., 1986. Is the new immigration less skilled than the old? J. Labor Econ. 4, 168–192.

Chiswick, B.R., Miller, P.W., 2010. Negative assimilation of immigrants: a special case. Indutrial and Labor Relations Review 64 (3), 502–525.

Cobb-Clark, D., Stillman, S., 2008. Emigration and the Age Profile of Retirement among Immigrants. IZA Discussion Paper No. 3874, Institute for the Study of Labor (IZA).

Cobb-Clark, D., Hanel, B., McVicar, D., 2012. Immigrant Wage and Employment Assimilation: A Comparison of Methods. IZA Discussion Paper No. 7062, Institute for the Study of Labor (IZA).

Cohen, Y., Haberfeld, Y., 2001. Self-selection and return migration: Israeli-born Jews returning home from the United States during the 1980s. Popul. Stud. 55 (1), 79–91.

Coniglio, N.D., De Arcangelis, G., Serlenga, L., 2009. Intentions to return of clandestine migrants: the perverse effect of illegality on skills. Rev. Dev. Econ. 13 (4), 641–657.

Constant, A., Massey, D.S., 2002. Return migration by German guestworkers: neoclassical versus new economic theories. Int. Migrat. 40 (4), 5–38.

Constant, A., Massey, D.S., 2003. Self-selection, earnings, and out-migration: a longitudinal study of immigrants to Germany. J. Popul. Econ. 16 (4), 631–653.

Constant, A.F., Zimmermann, K.F., 2011. Circular and repeat migration: counts of exits and years away from the host country. Popul. Res. Pol. Rev. 30 (4), 495–515.

Cortes, K.E., 2004. Are refugees different from economic immigrants? Some empirical evidence on the heterogeneity of immigrant groups in the United States. Rev. Econ. Stat. 86 (2), 465–480.

de Coulon, A., Piracha, M., 2005. Self-selection and the performance of return migrants: the source country perspective. J. Popul. Econ. 18 (4), 779–807.

de Matos, A.D., 2011. The Careers of Immigrants, Working Paper.

Duleep, H.O., 1994. Social security and the emigration of immigrants. Soc. Secur. Bull. 57, 37.

Duleep, H.O., Dowhan, D.J., 2002. Insights from longitudinal data on the earnings growth of US foreign-born men. Demography 39 (3), 485–506.

Dustmann, C., 1993. Earnings adjustment of temporary migrants. J. Popul. Econ. 6 (2), 153–168.

Dustmann, C., 1995. Savings behavior of return migrants. Zeitschrift für Wirtschafts- und Sozialwissenschaften 115, 511–533.

Dustmann, C., 2003. Return migration, wage differentials, and the optimal migration duration. Eur. Econ. Rev. 47 (2), 353–369.

Dustmann, C., (with discussants Bentolila, S., Faini, R.), 1996. Return migration: the European experience. Econ. Pol. 213–250.

Dustmann, C., Frattini, T., 2013. The Fiscal Effects of Immigration to the UK, CReAM DP 22/2013.

Dustmann, C., Glitz, A., 2011. Migration and education. In: Handbook of the Economics of Education, vol. 4, pp. 327–439.

Dustmann, C., Meghir, C., 2005. Wages, experience and seniority. Rev. Econ. Stud. 72 (1), 77–108.

Dustmann, C., Rochina-Barrachina, M.E., 2007. Selection correction in panel data models: An application to the estimation of females' wage equations. Econometrics J. 10 (2), 263–293.

Dustmann, C., Weiss, Y., 2007. Return migration: theory and empirical evidence from the UK. Br. J. Ind. Relat. 45 (2), 236–256.

Dustmann, C., Glitz, A., Vogel, T., 2010. Employment, wages, and the economic cycle: differences between immigrants and natives. Eur. Econ. Rev. 54 (1), 1–17.

Dustmann, C., Fadlon, I., Weiss, Y., 2011. Return migration, human capital accumulation and the brain drain. J. Dev. Econ. 95 (1), 58–67.

Eckstein, Z., Weiss, Y., 2004. On the wage growth of immigrants: Israel, 1990–2000. J. Eur. Econ. Assoc. 2 (4), 665–695.

Edin, P.-A., LaLonde, R.J., Åslund, O., 2000. Emigration of immigrants and measures of immigrant assimilation: evidence from Sweden. Swed. Econ. Pol. Rev. 7 (2), 163–204.

Faini, R., Strøm, S., Venturini, A., Villosio, C., 2009. Are Foreign Migrants More Assimilated than Native Ones? IZA Discussion Paper No. 4639.

Fertig, M., Schurer, S., 2007. Labour Market Outcomes of Immigrants in Germany: The Importance of Heterogeneity and Attrition Bias. IZA Discussion Paper No. 2915, Institute for the Study of Labor (IZA).

Gundel, S., Peters, H., 2008. What determines the duration of stay of immigrants in Germany? Evidence from a longitudinal duration analysis. Int. J. Soc. Econ. 35 (11), 769–782.

Heckman, J.J., 1979. Sample selection bias as a specification error. Econometrica, 153–161.

Hu, W.-Y., 2000. Immigrant earnings assimilation: estimates from longitudinal data. Am. Econ. Rev. 90 (2), 368–372.

Jasso, G., Rosenzweig, M.R., 1982. Estimating the emigration rates of legal immigrants using administrative and survey data: The 1971 cohort of immigrants to the United States. Demography 19 (3), 279–290.

Jasso, G., Rosenzweig, M.R., 1990. The New Chosen People: Immigrants in the United States. National Committee for Research.

Jensen, P., Pedersen, P.J., 2007. To stay or not to stay? Out-migration of immigrants from Denmark. Int. Migrat. 45 (5), 87–113.

Kaushal, N., 2011. Earning trajectories of highly educated immigrants: does place of education matter. Industrial and Labor Relations Review 64, 323.

Kaushal, N., Shang, C., 2013. Earnings Growth of Mexican Immigrants: New versus Traditional Destinations. Working Paper No. 7427, Institute for the Study of Labor (IZA).

Kerr, S.P., Kerr, W.R., 2011. Economic Impacts of Immigration: A Survey. No. w16736, National Bureau of Economic Research.

Kim, S., 2009. Economic Assimilation of Foreign Born Workers in the United States: An Overlapping Rotating Panel Analysis, No. UWEC-2008-19.

Kirdar, M.G., 2009. Labor market outcomes, savings accumulation, and return migration. Lab. Econ. 16 (4), 418–428.

Kirwan, F., Harrigan, F., 1986. Swedish–Finnish return migration, extent, timing, and information flows. Demography 23 (3), 313–327.

Klein, R.W., Spady, R.H., 1993. An efficient semiparametric estimator for binary response models. Econometrica, 387–421.

Klinthäll, M., 2003. Return Migration from Sweden 1968–1996: A Longitudinal Analysis. Almqvist & Wiksell International.

Klinthäll, M., 2006. Immigration, integration and return migration. In: International Symposium on International Migration and Development, Turin, pp. 28–30.

Klinthäll, M., 2007. Refugee return migration: return migration from Sweden to Chile, Iran and Poland 1973–1996. J. Refug. Stud. 20 (4), 579–598.

Kyriazidou, E., 1997. Estimation of a panel data sample selection model. Econometrica, 1335–1364.

LaLonde, R.J., Topel, R.H., 1992. The assimilation of immigrants in the US labor market. In: Immigration and the Workforce: Economic Consequences for the United States and Source Areas. University of Chicago Press, pp. 67–92.

Lam, K.-C., 1994. Outmigration of foreign-born members in Canada. Can. J. Econ. 27 (2), 352–370.

Lindstrom, D.P., 1996. Economic opportunity in Mexico and return migration from the United States. Demography 33 (3), 357–374.

Lindstrom, D.P., Massey, D.S., 1994. Selective emigration, cohort quality, and models of immigrant assimilation. Soc. Sci. Res. 23 (4), 315–349.

Long, J.E., 1980. The effect of Americanization on earnings: some evidence for women. J. Polit. Econ. 88 (3), 620–629.

Longva, P., 2001. Out-Migration of Immigrants: Implications for Assimilation Analysis. Department of Economics, University of Oslo, Memorandum no. 4/2001.

Lubotsky, D., 2007. Chutes or ladders? A longitudinal analysis of immigrant earnings. J. Polit. Econ. 115 (5), 820–867.

Lubotsky, D., 2011. The effect of changes in the US wage structure on recent immigrants' earnings. Rev. Econ. Stat. 93 (1), 59–71.

Lukomskyj, O., Richards, P., 1986. Return migration from Australia: a case study. Int. Migrat. 24 (3), 603–632.

Lundh, C., Ohlsson, R., 1994. Immigration and economic change. In: Population, Economy, and Welfare in Sweden. Springer, Berlin, pp. 87–107.

Maré, D.C., Morten, M., Stillman, S., 2007. Settlement patterns and the geographic mobility of recent migrants to New Zealand. New Zeal. Econ. Paper 41 (2), 163–195.

Martins, M.F.O., 2001. Parametric and semiparametric estimation of sample selection models: an empirical application to the female labour force in Portugal. J. Appl. Econometrics 16 (1), 23–39.

Massey, D., 1987. Understanding Mexican migration to the United States. Am. J. Sociol. 92 (6), 1372–1403.

Melenberg, B., Van Soest, A., 1996. Parametric and semi-parametric modelling of vacation expenditures. J. Appl. Econometrics 11 (1), 59–76.

Michalowski, M., 1991. Foreign-born Canadian emigrants and their characteristics (1981–1986). Int. Migrat. Rev. 25 (1), 28–59.

Nekby, L., 2006. The emigration of immigrants, return vs onward migration: evidence from Sweden. J. Popul. Econ. 19 (2), 197–226.

Newey, W.K., 2009. Two-step series estimation of sample selection models. Econometrics J. 12 (s1), S217–S229.

Organisation for Economic Cooperation and Development, 2008. International Migration Outlook 2008. OECD Publishing.

Organisation for Economic Cooperation and Development, 2013. International Migration Outlook 2013. OECD Publishing.

Picot, G., Piraino, P., 2012. Immigrant Earnings Growth: Selection Bias or Real Progress? Statistics Canada Analytical Studies Branch Research Paper Series 340.

Pinger, P., 2010. Come back or stay? Spend here or there? Return and remittances: the case of Moldova. Int. Migrat. 48 (5), 142–173.

Piore, M., 1979. Birds of Passage: Migrant Labor and Industrial Societies. Cambridge University Press.

Pischke, J.-S., 1992. Assimilation and the Earnings of Guestworkers in Germany, ZEW Discussion Paper No. 92-17.

Preston, I., 2013. The Effect of Immigration on Public Finances, CReAM DP 23/2013.

Ramos, F., 1992. Out-migration and return migration of Puerto Ricans. In: Immigration and the Workforce: Economic Consequences for the United States and Source Areas. University of Chicago Press, pp. 49–66.

Reagan, P.B., Olsen, R.J., 2000. You can go home again: evidence from longitudinal data. Demography 37 (3), 339–350.

Rendall, M.S., Ball, D.J., 2004. Immigration, emigration and the ageing of the overseas-born population in the United Kingdom. Popul. Trends, 18–27.

Reyes, B.I., 1997. Dynamics of Immigration: Return Migration to Western Mexico. Public Policy Institute of California.

Reyes, B.I., 2001. Immigrant trip duration: the case of immigrants from western Mexico. Int. Migrat. Rev. 35 (4), 1185–1204.

Reyes, B.I., 2004. Changes in trip duration for Mexican immigrants to the United States. Popul. Res. Pol. Rev. 23 (3), 235–257.

Reyes, B.I., Mameesh, L., 2002. Why does immigrant trip duration vary across US destinations? Soc. Sci. Q. 83 (2), 580–593.

Rooth, D.-O., Saarela, J., 2007. Selection in migration and return migration: evidence from micro data. Econ. Lett. 94 (1), 90–95.

Sander, M., 2007. Return Migration and the 'Healthy Immigrant Effect', SOEP Papers on Multidisciplinary Panel Data Research No. 60.

Sarvimäki, M., 2011. Assimilation to a welfare state: labor market performance and use of social benefits by immigrants to Finland. Scand. J. Econ. 113 (3), 665–688.

Shorland, P., 2006. People on the Move: A Study of Migrant Movement Patterns To and From New Zealand. New Zealand Department of Labour.

Skuterud, M., Su, M., 2009. Immigrant Wage Assimilation and the Return to Foreign and Host-Country Sources of Human Capital, CLSRN Working Paper No. 30.

Van Hook, J., Zhang, W., 2011. Who stays? Who goes? Selective emigration among the foreign-born. Popul. Res. Pol. Rev. 30 (1), 1–24.

Van Hook, J., Zhang, W., Bean, F.D., Passel, J.S., 2006. Foreign-born emigration: a new approach and estimates based on matched CPS files. Demography 43 (2), 361–382.

Venturini, A., Villosio, C., 2008. Labour-market assimilation of foreign workers in Italy. Oxf. Rev. Econ. Pol. 24 (3), 517–541.

Waldorf, B., 1995. Determinants of international return migration intentions. Prof. Geogr. 47 (2), 125–136.

Willis, R.J., 1986. Wage determinants: a survey and reinterpretation of human capital earnings functions. In: Handbook of Labor Economics. vol. 1, pp. 525–602.

Wooldridge, J.M., 1995. Selection corrections for panel data models under conditional mean independence assumptions. J. Econometrics 68 (1), 115–132.

Wooldridge, J.M., 2010. Econometric Analysis of Cross Section and Panel Data, second ed. MIT Press.

Yahirun, J., 2009. Take Me 'Home': Determinants of Return Migration Among Germany's Elderly Immigrants, California Center for Population Research On-Line Working Paper Series 2009-019.

Zakharenko, R., 2008. Return Migration: An Empirical Investigation, MPRA Paper No. 13755.

Types of Immigrants

CHAPTER 11

High-Skilled Immigration in a Globalized Labor Market

James Ted McDonald*, Christopher Worswick**

*Professor, Department of Economics, University of New Brunswick, Fredericton, N.B., Canada E3B 5A3
**Professor, Department of Economics, Carleton University, Ottawa, Ontario, Canada K1S 5B6

Contents

1. Introduction	538
2. Demographic, Economic, and Policy Context	543
2.1 Modern economies and aging populations	543
2.2 Growth in supply of potential immigrants	543
2.3 Growth in demand for skilled immigration in OECD countries	544
2.4 Gender breakdown in immigration flows	544
3. Theoretical Foundation	545
3.1 Effects of high-skilled immigration on the receiving economy	545
3.2 Public finance implications of high-skilled immigration versus low-skilled immigration	546
3.3 Models of skilled immigration policy	546
3.3.1 Human capital point systems	547
3.3.2 Intended occupation point systems	547
3.3.3 Employer nomination	548
3.3.4 Hybrid selection systems	548
3.4 Temporary foreign worker programs	549
4. High-Skilled Immigration Policy in Practice	550
4.1 Canada	550
4.2 United States	551
4.3 Australia	552
4.4 New Zealand	553
4.5 United Kingdom	554
4.6 Cross-country comparisons	554
4.7 Temporary foreign worker programs and two-step immigration	555
4.7.1 United States	555
4.7.2 Canada	556
4.7.3 Europe	558
5. Research on Labor Market Outcomes of Skilled Immigrants	559
5.1 Earnings and post-migration investments in education	559
5.2 Field of employment, credential recognition, and occupational matching	562
5.3 Immigrant selection and regulated occupations	563
5.4 Boom and bust cycles and occupational targeting	565
5.5 Gender differences in immigrant outcomes and family investment strategies	566

Handbook of the Economics of International Migration, Volume 1A
ISSN 2212-0092, http://dx.doi.org/10.1016/B978-0-444-53764-5.00011-6

6. Effects of Skilled Immigration for both Sending and Receiving Economics   567
  6.1 Evidence of immigration effects on sending economies   568
    6.1.1 Gender and the brain drain   570
  6.2 Evidence of immigration effects on receiving economies   570
    6.2.1 Estimated effects on native earnings   571
    6.2.2 Estimated effects on training of non-immigrants   572
    6.2.3 Effects on research and development, patents, and innovation   573
    6.2.4 Occupational choice   573
    6.2.5 Fiscal impact of immigration   574
    6.2.6 Demographic challenges and immigration   574
7. Summary and Conclusions   575
8. Gaps   576
Acknowledgments   577
References   577

1. INTRODUCTION

In recent decades, a new kind of mass international migration has emerged, driven not so much by a flight from poverty and persecution as by a desire on the part of the migrants to find higher returns on their skills. While some skilled individuals have always sought out the best opportunities for employment internationally, the magnitude of this movement of skilled workers across international borders is unprecedented. This, coupled with active competition among developed (and, increasingly, developing) countries to attract these skilled migrants, creates a new international policy context that is rapidly changing the nature of international migration.

Before proceeding, it is worth considering which developed countries are the main receivers of immigrants in general and skilled immigrants in particular. In the first column of Table 11.1, we present the number of immigrants age 15 and older in 2000 by OECD country. The countries with the largest stock of immigrants are the US (31,389,926), Germany (7,808,149), France (5,600,198), Canada (5,355,210), and Australia (3,475,065). However, given the large variation in population size as indicated in the second column, it is also worth looking at the immigrant percentage of the population in 2000, which is shown in the third column. The top five countries based on this criterion are Luxembourg (31.2%), Australia (22.9%), Canada (21.6%), Switzerland (19.7%), and New Zealand (18.4%). The lack of overlap across the two lists is interesting but perhaps not surprising. The larger countries in terms of population, such as the US, Germany, France, and the UK, have tended to be magnets for immigrants looking for a better life in modern developed countries, whereas newer countries such as Australia, Canada, and New Zealand have embraced open door policies towards immigration in the hope of expanding their relatively small populations given their large and relatively less populated land masses.

Table 11.1 Immigration stocks, population size, and post-secondary education: OECD countries

	All immigrants	Population	Percentage immigrant	Immigrants with PS education	Population, PS education	Percentage immigrant, PS education
Australia	3,475,065	15,187,313	22.8	896,843	2,775,706	25.8
Austria	923,692	6,646,102	13.8	104,742	731,351	11.3
Belgium	831,673	8,446,312	9.8	191,053	1,801,557	23.0
Canada	5,355,210	24,802,222	21.5	2,033,100	7,867,155	38.0
Czech Rep.	432,752	8,587,102	5.0	55,179	861,562	12.8
Denmark	260,132	4,351,857	5.9	62,236	815,554	23.9
Finland	112,430	4,236,542	2.6	21,240	988,530	18.9
France	5,600,198	47,923,796	11.6	1,011,424	8,171,940	18.1
Germany	7,808,149	69,374,372	11.2	1,163,732	11,063,053	14.9
Greece	963,375	9,244,757	10.4	152,882	1,264,939	15.9
Hungary	275,494	8,500,348	3.2	54,465	934,035	19.8
Ireland	313,809	2,977,022	10.5	128,868	713,193	41.1
Italy	2,020,934	48,808,874	4.1	246,925	4,042,259	12.2
Japan	929,100	108,420,000	0.8	278,277	26,573,558	30.0
Luxembourg	110,222	353,697	31.1	23,919	48,809	21.7
Mexico	229,132	64,863,750	0.35	79,651	7,928,524	34.8
Netherlands	1,406,589	12,963,970	10.8	269,836	2,378,935	19.2
New Zealand	549,375	2,979,051	18.4	170,079	691,416	31.0
Norway	218,752	3,592,393	6.0	66,664	823,082	30.5
Poland	728,652	30,811,523	2.3	86,379	3,197,847	11.9
Portugal	585,932	8,604,822	6.8	113,348	741,059	19.3
Slovak Rep.	112,370	4,337,099	2.5	17,587	419,430	15.7
Spain	1,902,040	34,311,474	5.5	401,300	6,303,600	21.1
Sweden	858,025	7,236,860	11.8	208,180	1,461,085	24.3
Switzerland	1,167,440	5,936,047	19.6	276,791	1,000,155	23.7
Turkey	1,064,692	64,252,000	1.6	161,867	3,149,827	15.2
UK	3,944,752	47,682,000	8.2	1,374,408	8,606,517	34.8
US	31,389,926	221,882,560	14.1	8,202,741	59,186,091	26.1

Note: Persons age 15 and older in 2000.

Source: OECD, 2010. International migration database. OECD International Migration Statistics (database), accessed 14 October 2013.

The remaining columns of Table 11.1 present equivalent figures, but for the case of the subpopulation in each country that has some level of post-secondary education. While this is not a perfect measure of skill it is likely to be highly correlated with most notions of skill and this gives an overview of the extent to which the immigrants in a country are relatively skilled or less skilled when compared with the native-born population. The countries with especially large stocks of immigrants with post-secondary education in 2000 were the US (8,202,741), Canada (2,033,100), the UK (1,374,408), Germany (1,162,732), and France (1,011,424). The fact that Canada appears higher on this list than it did in the first column ranking reflects the fact that Canada has historically had a highly educated intake of immigrants, which is also reflected in their sixth column figure of 38.0% of the population with some post-secondary education being immigrants. This figure is high among the more populous countries with large stocks of immigrants such as the US (26.1%), Germany (14.9%), and France (18.1%), but is only 3.1 percentage points larger than the figure for the UK (34.8%). The Canadian figure is also high compared with the other newer and relatively less populated countries with large immigration programs, such as Australia (25.8%) and New Zealand (31.0%). It is also worth noting from the sixth column that many OECD countries with relatively small immigration programs do admit a small but highly skilled group of immigrants, such as Ireland (41.1%), Japan (30.0%), Mexico (34.8%), and Norway (30.5%). One way to interpret this is that countries that do not necessarily want to see large population growth may want to selectively admit highly educated individuals.

In Table 11.2, we present evidence on the rates of post-secondary education among immigrants in each country by source-country region. The eighth column contains the figures of the sixth column of Table 11.1, the fraction of all immigrants in the receiving country with post-secondary education. By comparing each cell of a row to the final cell, we see whether immigrants to that country from a particular source region were relatively more or less educated compared to the overall average for the receiving country. For example, immigrants from Asia to Australia are more likely to have post-secondary education (34.5%) relative to all immigrants to Australia (25.8%), and this is also true for immigrants from Asia to Canada (42.2% for immigrants from Asia and 38.0% for all immigrants). However, this pattern is not present for each of the major immigrant-receiving countries since immigrants from Asia in the UK have a lower rate of post-secondary education (31.7%) than do all immigrants to the UK (34.8%). Once again, we see the high level of heterogeneity across source regions between countries with larger immigration programs and those with smaller ones. For example, immigrants from Europe in the US have a 34.6% probability of having a post-secondary education while the equivalent figures are 20.1% for Australia and 78.7% for Japan.

Tables 11.1 and 11.2 indicate the rich heterogeneity in terms of immigration experience across the OECD countries, driven to varying degrees by geography, history,

Table 11.2 Percentage of immigrants in 2000 with post-secondary education, by OECD country, by region of origin

	Africa	Asia	Europe	North America	Oceania	S/C Amer. Caribbean	Other and unknown	Total
Australia	39.4	34.5	20.1	52.8	21.8	27.5	51.4	25.8
Austria	20.7	18.4	10.2	37.5	20.8	21		11.3
Belgium	26	34.8	19.9	56.9	49.9	36	38.5	23
Canada	51	42.2	32.5	50.4	39.5	34.2	32.3	38
Czech Rep.	45.7	21	12	61.6	35.3	25.5	9.1	12.8
Denmark	20	19.2	25.7	43.4	30.7	30.1		23.9
Finland	14.9	11.9	20.4	22.3	17.9	17.7		18.9
France	17.8	29.6	14.6	58.3	45.3	34.5		18.1
Germany	10.1	17.5	13.1			28.7	19.8	14.9
Greece	27.3	14.5	14.5	29.5	23.9	23.5		15.9
Hungary	37.4	29.4	19.1	32.4	32.1	38.3		19.8
Ireland	51.9	58.3	36.9	58.8	57.6	46.2	38.6	41.1
Italy	8.6	15.3	11.8	22.6	13.4	15.2		12.2
Japan	62	27.8	78.7	79.8	82.1	19.8		30
Luxembourg	20.3	32.6	21	62.2	51.6	28.8	13.4	21.7
Mexico	57	49.1	49.7	25.6	29.6	37.9	23.7	34.8
Netherlands	10.6	25	19.2	47.9	37.4	15.4	39	19.2
New Zealand	48.2	31.6	33.1	51.4	19.3	36.8		31
Norway	23.2	23.1	34.7	45.4	40.7	23.9	47.3	30.5
Poland	49.5	43.6	11.3	12.5	29.9	43.2	7.5	11.9
Portugal	18.4	21.3	21	23	22.7	18.8		19.3
Slovak Rep.	41.7	34.3	15.3	15.5	25	35.1		15.7
Spain	10.5	20.4	24.3	52.6	30.6	22.5		21.1
Sweden	21.7	26.6	22.8	55	49.9	24.4		24.3
Switzerland	30	30.4	21.9	59.6	42.4	29.3	17.3	23.7
Turkey	20.3	27.3	13.6	60.9	37.5		41	15.2
UK	39.2	31.7	32.3	56.4	53.3	28.4	29.6	34.8
US	45.8	45.7	34.6	39.5	29	12	18.5	26.1

Note: Persons 15 and older in 2000.
Source: OECD, 2010. International migration database. OECD International Migration Statistics (database), accessed 14 October 2013.

economics, and public policy. For the purposes of this chapter, it will be important to keep in mind this heterogeneity when considering the different immigration policies under examination.

In this chapter, we review the key features of the new global skilled migration both from a theoretical perspective and from an empirical perspective, drawing on the key findings across the different literatures in the field of the economics of migration. We consider the implications for these flows of skilled workers for: (1) the immigrants themselves in terms of their labor market outcomes, (2) the sending countries whose citizens may benefit or be harmed by this out-migration of skilled workers from countries with relatively low levels of human capital (the so-called brain drain), and (3) the receiving countries whose citizens benefit from the human capital of these new arrivals but may also see the wage returns to skill affected by this new supply. We review the methods of selection of immigrants, ranging from the various types of point systems to employer nomination to selection based on investment of capital or the commitment to start a new business. Cross-country differences in selection are highlighted with linkages drawn to the likely effects of the selection mechanisms on the skills and future labor market outcomes of the immigrants.

In Section 2, we provide an overview of the international context in which this skilled immigration is taking place, with a focus on the demographic changes related to aging societies in OECD countries, the rapid growth in a number of newly industrialized countries, and the expansion of the educated middle class in developing countries in general. We also describe the increased competition for skilled immigrants that has emerged both in terms of increased emphasis on skill by traditional immigrant-receiving countries and the emergence of non-traditional immigrant countries as receivers of skilled immigrants. In Section 3, we present theoretical predictions related to the likely success of skilled immigrants as well as the likely effects that their presence in the receiving country may have. We also detail the types of immigrant selection mechanisms, stressing their advantages and disadvantages. In Section 4, we describe the current and recent immigration policies of a number of major immigrant-receiving countries, such as Canada, the US, and Australia. We review the limited number of cross-country comparison studies in which the effectiveness of different approaches to immigrant selection is the focus. We describe the expanded use of skilled temporary foreign workers and international students and the recent emergence of two-step immigration policies that favor temporary migrants already in the country as sources of permanent immigration. In Section 5, we provide an overview of key results in the literature on the economic performance of skilled immigrants with a particular focus on the wage returns to skill both in terms of regulated and unregulated occupations. In Section 6, we provide an overview of the empirical evidence on the implications of skilled immigration on both the sending countries and the receiving countries. Section 7 contains our conclusions and Section 8 describes the gaps in the literature.

2. DEMOGRAPHIC, ECONOMIC, AND POLICY CONTEXT

2.1 Modern economies and aging populations

The increased longevity of residents of developed economies has raised policy challenges for their governments as the share of the population over the usual retirement age has grown, leading to a greater need for pension and health services to be supported by the declining share of the population in their prime working years. This problem is accentuated in the major immigrant-receiving countries such as Australia, Canada and the US, who underwent a post-World War II baby boom leading to a very large birth cohort whose members are now reaching the age of retirement. Financing public pensions and public health care spending for this very large group of seniors has been used in each country as a motivation for increased immigration so as to expand the labor force over the period in which the baby boomers will be in retirement. However, a large increase in immigration inflows may not have a large impact on the age structure of the receiving country's population, partly because immigration flows large enough to make a change are politically infeasible and partly because, even at arrival, immigrants are typically already in the middle of their working lives.

As noted above, the high earnings of well-integrated skilled immigrants relative to other immigrants mean that they are more likely to be making a positive net contribution to the finances of the receiving country's governments than would other immigrants. In addition, if the immigrants are ready to enter the labor market and relatively young, then their presence in the receiving economy will reduce the dependency ratio, thus alleviating the burden caused by the large baby boom cohort entering retirement. However, if the skilled immigrants are: (1) accompanied by spouses who do not work, (2) accompanied by children who will be enrolled in publicly funded elementary, secondary and/or post-secondary education, and (3) able to sponsor their parents who will eventually draw on public pensions and publicly provided health care, the current or future presence of these family members in the receiving economy will tend to offset the more immediate benefits from an increased intake of skilled immigrants.

2.2 Growth in supply of potential immigrants

With the end of communism in the Soviet Union and the Eastern Bloc countries, a large pool of educated prime age potential immigrants emerged. This, coupled with the removal of barriers from emigration for skilled individuals in the People's Republic of China, meant an unprecedented expansion in the number of highly skilled individuals wishing to emigrate to both traditional immigrant-receiving countries such as the US, Canada, Australia, and New Zealand but also to countries in Europe, where there is an increasing interest in expanding the intake of skilled immigrants. At the same time, the high growth rates in many developing countries have led to an increasingly educated middle class with a growing number of young educated individuals who are attracted to the possibility of a better life in OECD countries. While the effects of the fall of communism in Europe and the opening up of China are unlikely to persist, the general growth effect for both these countries and developing countries (such as India) means that there is likely to be a large and growing pool of skilled workers willing to migrate to OECD countries for decades to come. However, it is also possible that as countries like India and China continue to develop and as growth rates slow in OECD countries, the skilled migration flows could slow or reverse. India and China are increasingly encouraging members of their diasporas in the major immigrant-receiving countries to return and are also increasingly magnets for highly skilled migrants from other areas of the world. Whether the magnitude of these flows will be sufficient to fully offset the large movement of educated workers out of major immigrant source countries such as China and India remains to be seen.

2.3 Growth in demand for skilled immigration in OECD countries

Coinciding with this expansion in the supply of potential skilled immigrants wishing to immigrate to OECD countries has been a substantial increase in demand for skilled immigration from these countries. While traditional immigrant-receiving countries such as Australia and Canada have increased their emphasis on skill in their immigrant selection processes (see Beach et al. (2007) for the case of Canada and Hawthorne (2010) for the case of Australia), other countries such as the UK and Germany have developed an interest in attracting skilled immigrants to their countries for a variety of reasons, which we detail below.

2.4 Gender breakdown in immigration flows

The percentage of total immigrants who are women has risen from 47% in the early 1960s to almost 50% in 2005, with migration flows to developed countries increasing by a similar amount to 52% over the same period (Docquier et al., 2009). In fact, Dumont et al. (2007) showed that, as of 2000, female immigrants outnumbered male immigrants in every OECD country except for Germany, Mexico, Spain and Greece, and the equivalent figures for those countries were each more than 49%. In terms of skilled immigrants, Docquier et al. (2009) showed that the share of women in the highly skilled immigrant population increased significantly in almost all OECD destination countries between 1990 and 2000, and Dumont et al. (2007) showed that by 2000 the share of female immigrants holding a tertiary degree was within 3 percentage points of the figure for immigrant men in the OECD region overall and in the main immigrant-receiving countries: the US, Canada, Australia, and the UK. Also, Pearce (2006) highlighted the fact that 26.8% of skilled worker visas in the US given to women in 2004 involved the woman as the principal visa holder. Similarly, 34.7% of men who received such visas were dependants.

3. THEORETICAL FOUNDATION

Before considering the empirical evidence related to the immigration of skilled workers, we provide an overview of a number of theoretical and methodological issues related to different parts of the immigration literature. Since the review of the empirical research draws from a number of strands of the immigration literature, it is important to review concepts in each of these areas before attempting to draw conclusions from the various analyses.

3.1 Effects of high-skilled immigration on the receiving economy

The impact of immigration on the labor market outcomes of individuals already residing in the country (both the native-born and earlier immigrants) is an important policy question that has proven difficult to fully understand. The basic economic model of supply and demand predicts that an increase in the supply of highly skilled immigrants will reduce the wages of similarly skilled non-immigrants, with the magnitude of the effect depending on the elasticity of substitution between highly skilled immigrant and non-immigrant labor. If highly skilled immigrants are substitutes for natives in the domestic labor market, the reduced wages would then lead to a decreased incentive by non-immigrants to invest in acquiring such skills and so exert a dampening effect on the domestic supply of skilled workers (Fougère et al., 2011). However, these effects may be moderated by other factors. For example, if high-skilled immigrants are complements to both lower skilled workers and to capital then the increase in the supply of high-skilled workers may produce economic changes that increase the demand for their services, mitigating the downward push on wages (Lofstrom, 2000; Regets, 2001). High-skilled workers gain to the extent that they are also owners of capital (Chiswick, 2011). Also, high-skilled immigration can generate positive externalities through increased knowledge flows and collaboration, by, for example, increased ties to foreign research institutions and improved export opportunities for technology (Regets, 2001).

If the assumption of perfect substitutability of high-skilled immigrant and non-immigrant labor within skill levels does not hold, then the impacts on high-skilled native workers will be less pronounced (Cortes, 2008; Ottaviano and Peri, 2008). As Chiswick (2011) noted, some high-skilled occupations require local or destination-specific characteristics, such as linguistic skill or special occupational licensing requirements, reducing the substitutability of high-skilled labor in those fields.

In principle, one could account for all of these effects of immigration within a general equilibrium framework; however, a key methodological issue relates to the endogeneity of the immigration policy itself. This can take a number of different forms. For example, if immigration policy is determined such that the inflow is higher in expansions and lower in recessions,[1] then we would expect a positive correlation between the size of the

---

[1] Such as was the case in Canada prior to the late 1980s.

immigrant intake and the labor market outcomes of the native-born even in the absence of any true impact of immigration on the native-born labor market outcomes. This pro-cyclical immigration policy could make it appear that immigration leads to higher economic growth when in fact it is the immigration policy that is responding to the macroeconomic conditions.

The best practice in the immigration literature for dealing with this question has been to attempt to find either: (1) exogenous variation in the immigrant inflow, or (2) exogenous variation that explains the immigrant inflow but is independent of the labor market conditions (so as to allow for an instrumental variables estimation approach). For example, an unexpected change in the intake of immigrants into the receiving country that is not driven by the state of the economy or other factors that might affect the employment outcomes of workers already in the country could be considered exogenous variation.

3.2 Public finance implications of high-skilled immigration versus low-skilled immigration

Immigration has implications for the public finances of the receiving countries that are closely related to the degree of economic success of the immigrants themselves. The net fiscal impact of an additional immigrant is likely to be increasing in his/her level of human capital as valued in the receiving country. Higher income individuals pay more income tax, more sales tax, and are less likely to receive unemployment and social assistance benefits than are lower income individuals. This can in part explain the growing interest in high-skilled immigration in OECD countries since it is fairly easy to quantify these tax/benefit implications from a high-skilled immigrant.

3.3 Models of skilled immigration policy

A variety of methods has been used by major immigrant-receiving countries to select immigrants based on the likely economic benefits that may occur due to their presence in the receiving country. Below, we review several approaches with an emphasis on the advantages and disadvantages in terms of selecting individuals likely to have economic benefits to the host society. In particular, we focus on: (1) human capital point systems, (2) intended occupation point systems, (3) employer nomination systems, and (4) hybrid point systems with a variety of goals in terms of the type of economic immigrant selected. The last group will include point systems that require employer nomination, two-step processes where temporary residents are favored for permanent residency, and immigrants selected based on being self-employed, entrepreneurs and investors. In addition, we also review the motivations underlying temporary foreign worker programs given the growing linkages between these programs and admission of immigrants through two-step immigrant selection regimes.

3.3.1 Human capital point systems

Traditional immigration point systems are used to select economic immigrants based on predetermined and (primarily) quantifiable criteria. Each criterion is allocated a share of the total points and each applicant is allocated all or part of these points, which are then aggregated to give the applicant a total score. If that score exceeds a minimum threshold then the immigration applicant is accepted and granted permanent residency. If not, then the applicant is rejected. The allocation of points to each criterion and the way that the points are allocated within the levels of each criterion can be thought of as policy levers since they explicitly value the characteristics of the immigration applicant that are seen as desirable—usually in the sense of raising the probability that the applicant will be successful in the receiving economy.

In 1967, Canada was the first country to implement a point system designed to select immigrants in an objective and quantifiable way. Canada was in transition from a pre-ferred country system of immigration (abandoned in 1962), which implicitly discriminated against individuals who were not of European ancestry. Having decided against continuing this policy, the Canadian government was trying to find a fair way to select immigrants who were likely to be successful economically in Canada while at the same time limiting the number of potential immigrants to Canada in a non-discriminatory and objective way.

3.3.2 Intended occupation point systems

While human capital proxy variables such as education, work experience, and language fluency are typically important characteristics in point system designs, intended occupation is also often a key determinant of the allocation of points. If the receiving country's government perceives there to be occupational shortages (or occupations in which employers have difficulty finding qualified applicants for job vacancies at the usual wage rate), they may lobby the government to provide opportunities to bring immigrants into the country to fill these job vacancies (rather than greatly increase the wages offered in order to generate domestic supply of these labor services). To the extent that foreign skills are transferrable in the host country, skilled immigration can address skill shortages more quickly than can an increase in domestic skill levels through education and training. This approach places the onus on the government to balance the need for occupations currently in demand with the longer term implications of an increase in the domestic labor supply in this area.

In the Canadian context, there has been a tension between human capital factors in the point system design and intended occupational factors. For example, after the enactment of the Immigrant and Refugee Protection Act (IRPA) in 2002, the Canadian point system through 2012 has focused on human capital criteria primarily. However, in the later 1960s and 1970s in contrast, the focus was heavily placed on points allocated to preferred occupations. In addition, certain occupations where there was a perception that more immigrants would not be beneficial were also banned from applying under the point system (e.g., physicians without prearranged employment over the period 1975–2001—see McDonald et al., 2012).

3.3.3 Employer nomination

The role of the potential employer in the immigrant selection process has been both influential and controversial. Employers have detailed information on their production processes, and in particular their job requirements and skill at interviewing candidates that could lead to highly reliable selections of potential employees based on the standard human capital proxy variables: education, work experience, and language skills. In addition, employers may be able to incorporate less tangible aspects of productivity such as leadership ability, communication skills, and empathy in their decisions over hiring and sponsoring potential immigrants. Arguably, the employer is in a stronger position to choose a potential immigrant based on these characteristics than would be a visa officer interviewing a potential immigrant under a human-capital-based point system even when the points vary with less concrete factors such as "adaptability" (as is the case in the Canadian point system). Another advantage to employer nomination relates to the incentive that it creates for employers to seek out potential immigrants through investing in advertising and recruitment outside of the receiving country. It is also possible that the process of labor market adjustment in the host country will be facilitated if the immigrant is connected to a job and employer prior to migration. In contrast, a human-capital-based point system is in general more passive in the sense of employers having less of an incentive to invest in the search for potential immigrants except in cases where the immigrants are so clearly skilled that they would have no difficulty passing the point system criteria. The US relies primarily on employer nomination of potential skilled immigrants (who do not have family already in the US) through its temporary visa system (such as the H-1B).

The controversy related to employer nomination primarily relates to the potential for employer discrimination. If employers discriminate against a group based on say race, then one would expect fewer immigrants from the racial groups facing discrimination to be nominated, leading to a smaller share of the intake of immigrants being from those groups. However, eliminating the employers from the immigrant selection process does not eliminate discrimination from the immigrant settlement process since if immigrants from these groups are selected under say a point system but then face the same discriminatory employers in the receiving country's labor market, then the importance of discrimination is not eliminated. The issue of discrimination should be central to discussions of both immigrant selection and immigrant settlement due to its potential importance.

3.3.4 Hybrid selection systems

More recently, we have seen the emergence of new criteria being factored into point systems, revealing their flexibility as ways of selecting immigrants. A growing emphasis has been placed on employer nomination in the selection of skilled immigrants. Points allocated for a prearranged job is one way to incorporate this into a point system. If the point bonus is small, then a person with low human capital might not be admitted under a point system that demonstrates the difference between this type of hybrid point system and a pure employer nomination system.

Another hybrid point system that is growing in popularity is based on a "two-step system" design (Hawthorne, 2010) in which temporary residents of the receiving economy are given a large advantage in the point system for immigrants due to their past work experience and/or education in the receiving country. Prior to this development, countries fully distinguished between immigrants who often had no experience in the receiving economy but were expected to come and settle permanently, and temporary residents who were expected to come and work or study but (at least in theory) not stay permanently. Examples of these two-step systems include the current Australian point system and Canadian point system, which rewards work experience and education in Canada. In the Canadian case, the development of the Canadian Experience Class (CEC) is very much based on this notion of two-step immigration and follows the success of the Australian approach. However, the CEC is not based on a point system but instead imposes minimum thresholds for language fluency before an immigrant can be admitted (see Ferrer et al. (2012) for a review of recent changes to the Canadian immigration system). As will be discussed in a later section, the US in effect has a two-step system as well, since the vast majority of individuals sponsored by employers for permanent residency (green card) were previously granted entry to the US on a skilled worker visa such as the H-1B.

Finally, it is worth noting that many skilled immigrants arrive in OECD countries under a variety of business, investor, and entrepreneurial classes of immigrants. These are often pathways to immigration that bypass the usual point system for the admission of skilled immigrants based on either the capacity to make substantial capital investments in production in the receiving economy or through having unique entrepreneurial skills that are not easily quantified within a point system structure.

3.4 Temporary foreign worker programs

Guest or temporary worker programs exist in both developed and developing countries, and in general share the aim of adding workers to the domestic labor force on a temporary basis to address supply shortages and reduce potential skill bottlenecks. Ruhs (2006) defined temporary worker programs as a right to residence and employment on the basis of a temporary work permit, but without an entitlement to stay permanently in the host country. While it is a general characteristic of temporary worker programs that there is in general no pathway to permanent residency, some countries in some circumstances can allow a limited and regulated transfer into permanent residence based on a set of clear rules and criteria (Ruhs, 2006).

Guest worker programs can target both highly skilled and less skilled workers, and for both types there is an expectation that the employer has been unable to fill the available positions at market wages, and that the temporary workers will not have a negative effect on domestic economic conditions. However, as Martin (2010) pointed out in his survey for Canada, the availability of temporary foreign workers will remove the need for the wage to rise and therefore may create a situation in which the firms employing temporary foreign workers may grow to be dependent on this supply of foreign labor. Also, for highly skilled temporary foreign workers, Green (2003) noted that by filling high-skilled jobs in demand, the presence of guest workers may distort market signals and discourage residents from obtaining the required human capital necessary to be eligible for such occupations.

Luthra (2009) identified advantages that temporary workers provide for employers, including flexible labor, up-to-date skills, and lower expectations regarding working conditions and benefits, which may explain why employers continue to recruit temporary workers even though they are on average paid at the prevailing wage (Udansky and Espenshade, 2001; Luthra, 2009). Also, restrictions on job and geographic mobility for temporary workers can undermine employment opportunities and prevent wage growth (Papademetriou et al., 2009).

4. HIGH-SKILLED IMMIGRATION POLICY IN PRACTICE

Below, we describe the key features of immigration policies in several large immigrant-receiving countries. Our focus is on: (1) the type of immigrants admitted and (2) the method of selection. We begin by describing the immigration policies of selected countries with large immigrant populations or large per-capita immigrant intakes: Canada, the US, Australia, New Zealand, and the UK. We then proceed to consider temporary foreign worker programs and two-step approaches to immigration, drawing from the experiences of a number of countries.

4.1 Canada

As already noted, Canada was the first country to implement a point system for the selection of skilled workers and professionals. The key factors in the allocation of points from the beginning have been education, intended occupation, language fluency (in English and/or French), and age/work experience. As Green and Green (1995) noted, there has been considerable variation in the allocation of points across these factors since 1967. In addition, the importance of intended occupation has also varied considerably.

Natural questions to ask are whether a point system is effective in terms of being able to control: (1) the average characteristics at entry and (2) the labor market performance of the new immigrants in the years after arrival. Beach et al. (2007) addressed the first question for the Canadian case using administrative landing records of all immigrants arriving to stay permanently in Canada between 1981 and 2001 (see also Green and Green, 1995). They found that the larger the inflow rate of immigrants, the lower is the average skill level of the immigrant arrivals and that the basic point system has the effect it is intended to on the skill characteristics of immigrant arrivals. In a later study, Beach et al. (2011) extended this analysis to consider the impact of the point system levers (the points assigned for each characteristic, as well as other policy levers such as the total level of immigration and the economic category share) on the labor market earnings of immigrants shortly after arrival in Canada. The policy levers examined are: the total level of immigrant inflow in a year; the proportion of this total inflow that arrives as economic class immigrants; and the maximum point system weights allocated to education, age at landing, and language fluency in either English or French. They also found strong business-cycle effects on skill levels of immigrants, with higher Canadian unemployment rates reducing the average skill levels of arriving immigrants and higher American unemployment rates having the opposite effect. Raising the total inflow rate of immigration by 100,000 a year is estimated to reduce the average annual earnings of arriving female immigrants by $1098 and that of male immigrants by $1576. Raising the economic class share of total immigration by 10 percentage points (for a given level of inflow) increases entry earnings of landing female immigrants by $2357 and of male immigrants by $3449 per year. Increasing the weight on years of education by 10 points is estimated to raise the average entry earnings levels of female principal applicants (PAs) by $775 and by $1042 for male PAs. A 10-point increase in the weight on language fluency results in a $326 increase per year in average entry earnings for female PAs and a $493 increase per year for male PAs. The effect of increasing points on education is thus quite strong, that on language fluency is more moderate (less than $40).

4.2 United States

In the 1960s, as Canada was moving toward a point system and away from a system based on preferred source country, the US was making a similar transition away from preferred source countries to a non-discriminatory policy. The 1965 amendments to the Immigration and Nationality Act abolished country-of-origin quotas. However, rather than introducing an independent stream of immigration as was done in Canada, the American approach was to base immigration on family reunification. Hatton (2013) noted that this significant policy change led to a large increase in immigration and a major (and perhaps unexpected) change in the distribution of immigrants to the US by source country due to the higher rate of family nomination of immigrants by US citizens whose ethnic origin was not from Europe. Duleep (2013) provided an insightful overview of the US policy history as well as the challenges faced in terms of assessing whether less-skilled immigration has a negative impact on the economic outcomes of less-skilled Americans.

While a number of proposed reforms to US immigration have suggested a dedicated independent entry stream for skilled immigrants (including a current 2013 proposal), the US system has focused on family reunification, with skilled independent immigrants needing to find a way to permanency by transitioning through a temporary visa of some kind. It is important to note, however, that immigration policy is not necessarily the main driver of the size of immigration inflows of particular types of skilled immigrants. For example, Lowell and Khadka (2011) found that procedural changes to visa policies following September 11, 2001 were not the main driver of the downturn in international student numbers to the US observed after 2001. Instead it was the confluence of a number of factors including the business cycle and the increasing globalization of tertiary education.

4.3 Australia

Australian immigration policy development mirrors that of Canada in a number of ways. Their movement away from a preferred country system of immigration occurred roughly a decade later than that of Canada (and the US), but they did adopt a point system of immigration as a way of selecting immigrants based on economic benefit in addition to accepting immigrants based on humanitarian goals or family reunification. Australia moved in the late 1990s to place greater emphasis on factors thought to make an immigrant more likely to find a job shortly after arrival. The Australian approach imposed high standards for English language fluency and implemented rigorous language testing.

Specifically, in 1999, Australia adopted a new point system that shifted the emphasis away from occupational points (formerly 80 out of 165, dropping to 0 out of 150) and an occupation/training-based factor (60) (see Cully (2012) for a description). Other key changes included an emphasis on Australian work experience (from 0 before the change to 10 after) and an elimination of points based on having relatives in Australia (up to 20 before and 0 after the change). In addition, points were introduced for the applicant's spouse's education (up to 5), as well as having arranged employment (up to 5). In addition, the age points were concentrated on younger ages and applicants over the age of 45 could no longer apply. The number of points allocated to English language fluency were not changed; however, mandatory language testing was introduced and the level of language ability required was raised (Boucher, 2013). In addition, applicants under the point system with Australian education were awarded extra points (up to 15) if they had Australian post-secondary education. This allowed the Australian system to tap into the large pool of international students studying at Australian universities, reducing the problems related to educational credential recognition for new immigrants.

However, as Hawthorne (2010) described, this linkage between international student status and access to permanent residency created a perverse incentive on the part of private sector post-secondary education providers to admit academically weak students whose primary goal was not to add to their education to gain human capital but instead to gain permanent residency status in Australia.

Also in 1999, bonus points were allocated for applicants with an occupation on the Migration Occupations in Demand List (MODL). However, Cully (2012) noted that the number of occupations on the list grew rapidly to over 100 by 2008 then to over 400 by 2010. In addition, employers were given the capacity to select migrants through employer sponsorship for permanent residence.[2] By 2010–11, nearly twice as many skilled immigrants were entering Australia under the "demand-driven" selection criteria compared to the "supply-driven" selection criteria. The MODL was revoked in February of 2010, removing the bonus points in the point test in the process. The new model entailed demand-driven skilled migration to be met through temporary skilled migration and the permanent employer-sponsored visa. However, supply-driven immigration was still supported as part of its broader workforce development strategy with a target on specialized skills.

The Australian immigrant selection system has embraced the notion of sponsorship of immigrants, placing even greater emphasis on the role of the potential employer but also the role of the state and territorial governments. Following the New Zealand model, potential immigrants are allowed to make a preliminary "expression of interest" (EOI), which places them in a pool of potential immigrants (Cully, 2012). Employers can see these files and can choose to sponsor individuals for permanent residence, but state and territorial governments are also allowed to sponsor immigrants interested in settling in their state that they see as likely to be successfully economically. This approach has the advantage over a traditional point system in that it is possible to fast-track especially strong applicants since it is no longer the case that formal applications for permanent residence need be processed on a first come, first served basis. An EOI system allows the government to prioritize the processing of applications according to their points test score. Cully (2012) argued that the new system dispenses with the need for a "queue" of applicants, which is equivalent to the sizeable immigrant "backlog" in Canada that reached close to 1 million applications in 2011 and meant that some applicants waited as long as eight years for their applications to be processed.

4.4 New Zealand

New Zealand operates a point system similar to those of Canada and Australia as its method of selecting skilled immigrants (see Government of New Zealand, 2011). Applicants receive points based on their age, education, employability, and qualifications. The point system was first introduced in 1991 and has evolved considerably over time, often moving towards the implementation of the point system in Australia. However, in order

---

[2] Employers also had the option of sponsoring foreign workers for temporary migration with the possibility of sponsoring them as permanent residents in the future.

to be considered, an applicant must be aged 55 or under, speak English, be of "good character," and be healthy. By 2006, international students within New Zealand were awarded extra points and were eligible to immigrate at the end of their programs. In addition, a large number of points were awarded for applicants with a skilled job offer in New Zealand or if the person had a job or qualifications in an area of skills shortage or identified area of future growth.

As already noted, New Zealand was the first country to implement an expression of interest (EOI) application first. This allows for stronger applicants to be invited to submit a full application rather than requiring a full application and processing all applications in order of receipt. Relevant work experience is valued under the point system, especially if it occurred within New Zealand.

4.5 United Kingdom

The UK has a point system determining admission of immigrants from countries outside the European Economic Area and Switzerland.[3] At the time of writing, there were four active Tiers under the point system: (1) highly skilled workers, such as scientists and entrepreneurs; (2) skilled workers with a job offer, such as teachers and nurses; (3) students; and (4) temporary workers, such as musicians coming to play in a concert, and participants in the youth mobility scheme.[4]

Potential immigrants in Tier 1 do not need an employer sponsor while immigrants in the latter three categories require a sponsor. Tier 1 replaced the Highly Skilled Migrant Program (HSMP) that had been introduced in January 2002. Its goal has been to encourage highly skilled people to migrate to the UK to work without having prearranged employment. The HSMP had been a point-based scheme and points were based upon qualifications, past earnings, age, prior UK experience, and successful completion of an MBA program from a specified list. The tier system was introduced in 2008. Tier 1 has four pathways: (1) highly skilled workers; (2) former international students in the UK; (3) entrepreneurs; and (4) investors.

4.6 Cross-country comparisons

While most studies in the literature tend to focus on a single country's immigration experience, there has been growing interest in international comparisons in order to gain insights regarding which country's immigration policies are the most effective in terms of selecting immigrants likely to be successful in the receiving country's economy. Several studies have compared the labor market outcomes of immigrants in Canada relative to those in the US to see whether the existence of the point system in Canada leads to a more highly skilled stream of new immigrants landing in Canada relative to the US.

[3] Exceptions to this rule are Bulgarians and Romanians (until the end of 2013), and Croatians.
[4] Tier 3 was suspended at the time of writing.

Antecol et al. (2003) used Census data for Australia and Canada where point systems have been in place and the US, which has never had a point system but has instead relied primarily on family reunification. They found that the comparatively low skill level of US immigrants is not driven by the absence of a point system but has more to do with geographic and historical ties to Mexico, leading to the entry into the US of relatively low-skilled immigrants. Borjas (1991) analyzed the labor market outcomes of immigrants in Canada and the US, and found that the Canadian point system changes the national origin mix of the incoming immigrants in Canada relative to what it would be in the absence of this skilled immigration program; however, he did not find evidence to indicate that the point system leads to a more highly skilled group of immigrants from a particular country landing in Canada relative to those from the same source country arriving in the US.

4.7 Temporary foreign worker programs and two-step immigration

The last two decades have seen rapid and significant change in temporary worker programs for skilled workers across the main immigrant-receiving countries. This was in part because of a recognition that existing programs were not sufficiently adaptive to labor demand needs in an increasing global competition for skilled workers but also because of a recognition that certain programs had evolved away from their original intent. Canada, Australia, Germany, the UK, and other countries have undergone major reforms to their immigration programs, although the US has not, and it is argued that the US is no longer the magnet for the "best and brightest" as it historically has been (Shachar, 2006; Papademetriou et al., 2009).

Policies aimed at temporary foreign workers are important not just because of their role in addressing skill shortages but also in their potential to provide a gateway to permanent residency for individuals with host-country work experience. It is thus instructive to compare the approach to skilled temporary foreign workers across countries and how their systems have evolved in response to the increasingly competitive world market for highly skilled people.

4.7.1 United States

The US has three major guest-worker programs, for professionals (H-1B), low-skilled farm workers (H-2A), and low-skilled non-farm workers (H-2B), as well as a host of other categories such as student visas and NAFTA visas. The Immigration Reform and Control Act of 1990 set a cap of 65,000 temporary residents who could enter the US under H-1B visas. Individuals were required to hold a bachelor's degree or equivalent, and workers on H-1B visas were given a three-year visa with a possible extension for a total of six years. The original intent was that the H-1B visas would provide employers with easy access to foreign workers and bridge gaps in the labor market until sufficient US science and engineering workers could be trained (Martin, 2010). Takeup grew slowly through the 1990s and the cap was not reached until 1998. However, as demand continued to grow, particularly in the IT sector, the cap was successively raised to a maximum of 195,000 per year by 2003. Also, an additional 20,000 visas were made available for higher degree holders with credentials from US universities and an unlimited number for individuals working at universities and non-profit research institutions. The cap reverted back to 65,000 in 2004, where it remains. Unlike most low-skilled workers, H–1B holders were given a path to permanent residency through employer sponsorship for a green card, and by 2008 90% of employment-based green cards issued were awarded to individuals who had previously held a temporary work permit (Papademetriou et al., 2009). Thus, skilled immigration in effect had become a two-step process to permanent residency.

From the employer perspective, a temporary work visa was the most timely and efficient route to hire highly skilled workers from outside the US, since the alternative was to petition for a green card that could take between four and seven years for approval, and the total number including spouses and children was capped at 160,000 per year (Papademetriou et al., 2009). However, the US skilled immigration system has been criticized on a number of fronts. The process in moving from temporary to permanent status is long, opaque, and uncertain (Martin et al., 2001; Papademetriou et al., 2009), and this has the effect of creating barriers to the recruitment and retention of highly skilled workers. Employer groups argue that the relatively low cap on H–1B visas is far too small to address their needs, especially in the IT sector (Martin et al., 2001; Martin, 2008). Others criticize the program for containing too many loopholes that allow employers to misuse the program by hiring foreign workers at less than market wages for jobs that could easily be filled by American workers (Fulmer, 2009).

4.7.2 Canada

Temporary Foreign Worker (TFW) Programs in Canada have targeted both less-skilled and high-skilled occupations, and both types of workers typically require a job offer as well as a positive Labour Market Opinion issued by Human Resources and Skills Development Canada (HRSDC) before a work permit would be granted. As in other countries, the Labour Market Opinion is intended to protect permanent residents from foreign competition. Normally, the employer must guarantee that a permanent resident cannot be found to do the job and that the occupational standards and wages provided to the TFW correspond to what a permanent resident would obtain for comparable employment (Sweetman and Warman, 2010). Also, temporary work permits are limited in the job and geographic mobility afforded to permit holders.

While the movement of TFWs into Canada has existed throughout Canada's history to varying degrees, the vast majority of the people migrating to Canada over the years have done so as permanent residents. However, the TFW programs have grown in importance over the past 10 years. Sweetman and Warman (2010) illustrated that on December 1st, 1984, there were just over 20,000 TFWs in Canada but by 2008 this number had increased to more than 145,000. The most rapid growth was in the late 2000s, when more workers arrived as TFWs than under the regular Federal Skilled Worker Program. In fact, by 2010, figures from Citizenship and Immigration Canada indicate that the number of TFWs arriving in Canada exceeded that for all new permanent immigrant arrivals together. The bulk of the increase was due to an expansion of the Temporary Foreign Worker Program to include lower-skilled occupations. Foster (2012) described the program as becoming a permanent, large-scale labor pool for many industries, reminiscent of European migrant worker programs. Similarly, Gross and Schmitt (2012) pointed out that the marked expansion in the size of TFW inflows coincided with a persistent pattern of regional disparities in unemployment rates, suggesting that policy constraints for hiring temporary foreign workers are not strong enough to avoid adverse labor market effects.

Martin (2010) argued that Canadian employers have become accustomed to hiring migrant workers, and whose recruitment and training systems evolve to employ them, may make investment decisions that assume migrants will continue to be available. It should come as no surprise that these investors resist policy changes that would reduce their access to migrant workers. Also, Canada has involved employers in the design and administration of many of its guest-worker programs, and gives administering agencies discretion in implementing program rules. In the US and some other countries, by contrast, the goal of employer and worker advocates is often to get as many implementing regulations written into law as possible, which limits the discretion of program administrators and can lead to litigation over violations.

While TFWPs and permanent immigration have been distinct gateways for foreign workers to enter into Canada, the Canadian government introduced the new Canadian Experience Class in 2008 that formalized a pathway through which certain skilled TFWs could obtain permanent residency status. In order to be eligible, TFWs must have acquired 24 months of work experience over a 36-month period immediately prior to submitting their application, and the experience needs to be in managerial, professional, technical, or skilled trade occupations. In addition, former international students who had completed a two-year degree or higher followed by one year of Canadian work experience in a skilled occupation field could also apply for permanent residency. Sweetman and Warman (2010) suggested that with the introduction of this pathway the high-skilled TFW programs took on a substantial nation-building component.[5] Also, Sweetman and Warman (2010) argued that by targeting skilled foreign residents with Canadian labor market experience or education, some of the difficulties in adjusting to the Canadian labor market, experienced previously by skilled immigrants coming

---

[5] There remained no formal pathway for less-skilled workers to obtain permanent residency through the federal system, although some provinces were sponsoring former TFWs for permanent residency through the provincial nominee program.

to Canada through the points system, would be reduced. Sweetman and Warman (2009) found some evidence to support this contention in that male immigrants who had previously worked in Canada as TFWs had significantly better earnings entering the job market as a permanent resident than did immigrants who had no pre-Canadian experience at landing. However, in examining the outcomes of a similar program introduced in Australia in 1999 on which the Canadian Experience Class program was designed, Reitz (2010) concluded that immigrants with prior Australian experience did not have improved labor market outcomes compared to immigrants without prior Australian experience. More generally, Reitz also cautioned that giving private citizens such as employers or persons in educational institutions a formal role in immigrant selection raises the potential for both abuse and fraud. For example, abuse arises if those with power over immigrant selection make unreasonable requests with which prospective immigrants feel obliged to comply in order to maintain their status.

4.7.3 Europe

Around 1974, most Western European countries abandoned policies of migrant labor recruitment and moved towards increasingly restrictive entry rules (Castles, 2006). However, by 2000 the perception about the role of migration began to shift again in response to demographic, economic, and labor market developments (Mahroum, 2001; Doomernik et al., 2009). Demand for labor increased across the spectrum, for unskilled workers willing to perform manual labor and for specialists and skilled workers to meet significant shortages for skilled labor. European policymakers also realized that the competition for high-skilled workers with the traditional immigrant-receiving countries such as the US, Canada, and Australia was becoming increasingly intense, and advocated policy changes to attract the highly skilled that copied elements of both the Canadian-style point system as well as the US temporary H-1B visa for high-skilled workers (Zalatel, 2006; Doomernik et al., 2009).

In the UK, the High Skilled Migrant Programme (HSMP) was introduced in 2002 and was based on a points system similar to the skilled worker programs in Australia and Canada. The program allowed individuals to apply without prior employer nomination or arranged work contract, and while the initial period of residence was one year extendable for an additional three, a right to settle permanently in the UK could then be granted. In this sense, it could be thought of as part of a two-step immigration program. Selection was based on points awarded for education, experience, past earnings, and achievement in the chosen field (Zaletel, 2006).[6] Unlike Canada and Australia, there was no specified quota or target for the number of immigrants accepted through this program.

---

[6] In 2008, the UK also initiated a point system using the same criteria for permanent immigration of high-skilled migrants who apply as individuals or skilled workers with a job offer from employers (Doomernik et al., 2009).

In Germany, the German Green Card (GGC) program was introduced in 2000 as a temporary solution to skilled labor shortages in the German IT sector that arose in the late 1990s. The program was modeled on the US H–1B visa program in that it was employer driven, with the employer being required to demonstrate that no German or EU IT specialist was available. One important difference was that there was no subsequent path to permanent residency: the GGC was valid for five years without the opportunity for any further extension or conversion to permanent status.

In 2009, the European parliament passed legislation creating the Blue Card program that allowed highly skilled non EU citizens to live and work in most countries within the European Union. Applicants were required to have higher education qualifications or at least three years of professional experience, and acceptance was conditional on having a work contract or binding job offer but allowed member states significant autonomy in restricting the number issued or not participating in the program at all. The Blue Card was valid for two years and was renewable, and also allowed for immediate family reunification and access to the labor market for spouses. Just as importantly, after two years Blue Card holders were allowed to move to another member country participating in the Blue Card scheme. This made it easier for Blue Card holders to qualify for long-term residence status by allowing the migrant to accumulate the required five years by working in several member states (Doomernik et al., 2009; Kahanec and Zimmermann, 2011).[7]

5. RESEARCH ON LABOR MARKET OUTCOMES OF SKILLED IMMIGRANTS

5.1 Earnings and post-migration investments in education

There has been a huge volume of research that has sought to analyze the labor market outcomes of immigrants, including unemployment, labor force participation, wealth, occupational attainment, employment stability, and receipt of government transfers, but the principal focus has remained earnings. One of the most notable patterns in immigrant earnings across a number of countries has been the large decline in earnings of immigrants arriving in the 1980s relative to those who arrived previously (see, for example, Borjas (1995) for the US and Baker and Benjamin (1994) for Canada). While Borjas and Friedberg (2009) identified an improvement in the earnings of recent immigrants who arrived in the US in the latter half of the 1990s using Census data, they also found CPS data indicating that the decline in earnings of new immigrants to the US continued after 2000. In Canada, evidence indicates that the decline in entry earnings for immigrants continued into the 1990s (Aydemir and Skuterud, 2005). Schmitt and Wadsworth (2007) found that over the period 1980–2000, relative wage and employment prospects

---

[7] See Kahanec and Zimmermann (2011) for a detailed review of high-skilled immigration policy across European countries, including new EU member states.

for immigrants to the US appear to have deteriorated, particularly among women, but the pattern is less evident for male and female immigrants in the UK.

Declines in earnings across successive cohorts are typically analyzed in the context of the huge changes in source-country composition of immigrant inflows since the middle of the last century, away from the traditional source countries in the UK and Western Europe in the postwar period to Eastern Europe, Asia, Central and South America, and most recently Africa. Numerous authors have considered a variety of possible explanations for variation in worker productivity between immigrants and Canadian-born workers with similar years of schooling and work experience, including differential returns to foreign and host-country experience (Goldman et al., 2011; Green and Worswick, 2012; Lessem and Sanders, 2012), differences in literacy (Ferrer et al., 2006), transitions into and out of high-wage employment (Skuterud and Su, 2012), host-country selection criteria (Clarke and Skuterud, 2012; Abbott and Beach, 2013), differential effects of business-cycle changes (McDonald and Worswick, 1998; Abbott and Beach, 2013), and declining real wages across native-born labor market entry cohorts (Green and Worswick, 2012).

Of particular interest for analysis of high-skilled immigrants are differences in the returns to foreign and host-country education. This is particularly the case since educational attainment is often used to identify high-skilled immigrants, and in fact educational attainment features prominently in point-based immigration selection systems in a host of countries, including Canada, Australia, the UK, Denmark, and Singapore (Papademetriou and Sumption, 2011). A common result in the literature is that the return to foreign education is significantly lower than that of education obtained in the host country (Schoeni, 1997; Friedberg, 2000; Ferrer and Riddell, 2008). Alboim et al. (2005) found that for immigrants in Canada, foreign education is worth only 70% of the value of Canadian education, and foreign university degrees in particular where a foreign degree has a return worth less than one-third that of a degree obtained in Canada by non-immigrants. There also seem to be significant differences in the return to foreign education by source country. Haley and Taengnoi (2011) reported that education and labor market experience received by immigrants from non-English-speaking and less developed countries prior to migration have significantly lower transferability in the US labor market compared to skills obtained in Japan and English-speaking developed countries. Similarly, for Australia, Chan et al. (2012) used data from the Longitudinal Surveys of Immigrants in Australia and estimated substantially higher returns from human capital obtained in Australia and other OECD countries compared with non-OECD countries. Buzdugan and Halli (2009) also found that immigrants to Canada who originate from developing countries experienced the lowest return to education credentials obtained outside of Canada. In contrast, Rodríguez-Pose and Tselios (2010) did not find any evidence of differences in the returns to education between migrants and non-migrants across a range of countries in the European Union, and the results were robust to the inclusion of individual, household, and regional controls.

One reason for differential returns to foreign education relates to the quality of a given level of education. Bratsberg and Terrell (2002) examined the impact of birth country school quality on the returns to education of US immigrants and found that differences in the attributes of educational systems (as measured by teacher–pupil ratios and expenditure per pupil) explain much of the difference in rate of return to foreign education. Sweetman (2004) used international test scores as a proxy for education quality and found a similar result for immigrants to Canada.

A related area of research concerns the returns to education obtained by immigrants in their host countries. This is an issue of particular relevance where immigration programs aim to encourage skilled international students studying in the host country to remain there after the completion of the credential. Bratsberg and Ragan (2002) compared the earnings of immigrants with and without US schooling and found that the returns to education are higher for those with US schooling than for those with foreign education only. They also found that obtaining education in the US is most important for those from less developed, non-English-speaking countries. Kaushal (2011) used longitudinal data to examine science and engineering professionals and estimated that in the first 15 years after arrival, US-educated, foreign-born science and engineering professionals had relatively higher earnings growth than their foreign-educated counterparts. In Canada, Banerjee and Lee (2012) found that the earnings gap between recent immigrants and native-born Canadians was significantly reduced with the attainment of Canadian educational credentials. Kanas and Van Tubergen (2009) observed similar patterns among higher educated immigrants in the Netherlands—specifically, the returns to host-country schooling are much larger than to origin-country schooling. Also, Nordin (2011) showed that immigrants who completed their schooling in Sweden experienced much higher returns to that education than immigrants with only foreign schooling.

Other research has yielded useful insights into the returns to education by comparing the experiences of immigrants across different recipient countries. While confirming a lower return to foreign education among immigrants to the US and Canada, Bonikowska et al. (2011) found that over time, the relative wages of university-educated male and female immigrants in the US showed little change between 1980 and 2005, while those of university-educated male and female immigrants in Canada declined significantly over the same period.

It should be emphasized that many of these studies rely on multiple cross-sections of data, typically consecutive Census files, to infer changes over time or across different arrival cohorts. One potential note of caution relates to the sample attrition through non-random out-migration from the host country over time. Lubotsky (2007) found that relative to such cross-sectional studies, selective out-migration of lower quality immigrants has overstated the wage progress and assimilation of immigrants to the US. Interestingly, Picot and Piraino (2012), using administrative tax file data for Canada, reported that while low-earning immigrants are more likely than their high-earning counterparts to leave the cross-sectional samples over time, the same is true of the Canadian-born population, implying no systematic bias in the trajectory of the immigrant–Canadian-born earnings gap.

5.2 Field of employment, credential recognition, and occupational matching

The matching of suitably qualified workers to jobs with equivalent requirements is a key aspect of a well-functioning labor market. When a worker is unable to find a job with required qualifications that are equal to the worker's qualifications, they may be forced to seek alternative work, resulting in overqualification. A common case is the worker who is unable to find a job that is suitable given his/her education and therefore ends up accepting employment in a job with relatively low educational requirements.

McGuinness (2006) reviewed the different methods used to measure overqualification and evaluated the advantages and disadvantages of each. Measures of overqualification are decomposed into subjective measures, such as self-reported number of years of education needed for the current job, and objective measures, such as defining an individual as overqualified if his/her reported education is at least one standard deviation greater than the mean years of education of the job's occupation.

In an important series of papers, Chiswick and Miller (2008, 2009, 2010a–c) explored the links between education and occupational attainment and their impact on earnings. Of particular interest in a number of these papers is the role of education–occupation mismatches among immigrants: overeducation is the case where an individual's education level is greater than what is usually required for his or her occupation, as might be the case with imperfect skill transferability; undereducation is the case where education level is lower than what is usually required for the occupation, as might arise because of favorable selectivity of immigrants into the host country. In Chiswick and Miller (2008), the authors showed that the lower payoff to schooling for the foreign-born in the US is linked to the labor market outcomes of immigrants in jobs mismatched to their education levels. Specifically they found that two-thirds of the smaller effect of schooling on earnings was attributable to differences by nativity in the payoffs to over/under-education while the rest was to the different distributions of over/under-education between immigrants and the native-born. Similar results were found for immigrants in Australia (Chiswick and Miller, 2010b) and Canada (Chiswick and Miller, 2010c). Chiswick and Miller (2011) provided empirical evidence for the US with a primary focus on the foreign-born. For men, they found greater educational mismatches among the foreign-born than among the native-born. They found that only 26% of all immigrant men were correctly matched compared to 40% for the native-born, while the percentages under-educated and over-educated are 45% and 29% respectively for immigrants, and 26% and 33% respectively for the native-born. Once the focus is placed on immigrants with at least a bachelor's degree, the percentage over-educated rises to 63% for immigrants compared with 50% for the native-born. In addition, they found a return to years of schooling of roughly 11% for both the foreign-born and the native-born. However, when they differentiate between required years of schooling and years of over-education, the former has a return of 13% per year while the latter has a return of only 2% per year and these estimates are roughly the same for the foreign-born and the native-born. Therefore, the return to education needed for the job is high but the return to extra years is low and given the higher rate of being in this situation for immigrants is consistent with lower returns to education on average for immigrants.

5.3 Immigrant selection and regulated occupations

In unregulated occupations, it is reasonable to assume that wages will adjust to absorb the inflow of qualified new immigrant arrivals. However, this is not obvious for the case of regulated occupations since the professional body that controls the regulation for the occupation may be able to prevent access to jobs in this profession to new immigrant arrivals. This could be justified if there are concerns about the equivalency of the foreign training to domestic training. In the absence of these concerns, the domestic workers in the occupations may attempt to limit access to jobs in the occupation by immigrants in order to maintain their wages.

If the immigrants with credentials for a regulated occupation are able to employ their human capital in other occupations with similar wages then this may not be a serious problem since the immigrants' human capital would still be employed and the rate of return on the human capital will be high.[8] However, if this leads the immigrants to work in jobs with much lower wages then the occupational barriers lead to a low return on the immigrants' human capital. This would be a cause for concern for immigrant selection policy since the occupational barriers would lead to a low level of earnings for the new immigrants relative to what one expects based on their human capital proxy variables (such as education). In this case, it would be important to incorporate the existence of these barriers into the immigrant selection process to recognize that immigrants intending to work in these occupations cannot automatically find work in the receiving country's labor market.

Regulated professions in the medical sector are important examples of occupations in which significant barriers exist that immigrants with international credentials must overcome in order to work in their intended occupations. These barriers can relate to whether their credentials are recognized by the source-country professional bodies. They may also relate to the availability of spots in training programs in the host countries (such as medical residency programs) and as such may also relate to the willingness on the part of governments in the receiving country to fund the necessary accreditation programs. In cases

---

[8] This ignores non-pecuniary aspects of working in one's preferred occupation, which are likely also important.

where an influx of immigrants in a particular regulated occupation enter the country, they may not all be given access to the accreditation program if the number of spots in such programs is driven by long-run need for these services rather than by the demand on the part of immigrants for access to these programs.

Lesky (2011) reviewed the processes required for international medical graduates (IMGs) to work as physicians in both Canada and the US.[9] An IMG must be a permanent resident or Canadian citizen in order to apply for a medical residency position in Canada. This can be gained through applying under the point system (of the Skilled Worker and Professionals Program) and, given the high level of education of an IMG, the person is likely to pass the point test and be admitted as a landed immigrant. In the US case, foreign-born IMGs wishing to enter a residency program may be citizens, permanent residents, or have an appropriate temporary visa, which typically requires an employer sponsor.

Relatively little research has been carried out on the certification process of immigrant IMGs and their resulting occupational and earnings outcomes; however, a number of recent studies have shed light on these issues. Kugler and Sauer (2005) analyzed the relicensing decisions of immigrant medical degree holders in Israel. They studied the large influx of IMGs entering Israel from the former Soviet Union between 1989 and 1993. First, the authors developed a model of the decision for these immigrants to relicense and showed that it is possible for there to be both positive and negative selection into relicensing. Next, the authors exploited the fact that these IMGs were assigned to one of two different relicensing tracks depending on past experience and this assignment was used as an instrument in order to separately identify the returns to relicensing as well as the selection into relicensing since a significant fraction of the IMGs chose not to relicense after they arrived in Israel. The fact that the OLS returns are lower than the returns estimated using an IV method indicates that negative selection existed with higher skilled IMGs choosing against relicensing and instead entering the unlicensed sector after arrival. It is important to note that in this historical case, the IMGs had the right to settle in Israel due to their Jewish ancestry. Consequently, this study does not shed light on the possible interaction between immigrant selection models of skilled immigration and the subsequent probabilities of being employed in a regulated profession after arrival in the receiving country.

McDonald et al. (2012) explicitly tackled this issue for the case of IMGs immigrating to Canada and the US. While the certification processes for IMGs are similar in the two countries, their immigration policies, as noted above, differ greatly. Immigration of skilled individuals (without family ties to US citizens) has been dominated by employer

---

[9] See also McMahon (2004) for the US and Boyd and Schellenberg (2007) for Canada. Grignon et al. (2012) provided an international overview of the migration of health professionals and considered relevant economic issues for health professionals trained in both developed and developing countries.

nomination of skilled immigrants (and temporary migrants who eventually gain permanent resident status). For an IMG wishing to immigrate to the US, finding an employer willing to nominate him/her for a job is likely to be difficult, meaning that only the high-ability IMGs with medical credentials that are easily recognized in the US are likely to be sponsored in this way. While employer nomination in Canada is possible, it is a small part of the flow of skilled immigrants into Canada. McDonald et al. (2012) used this difference between the US and Canada, as well as the fact that the Canadian point system has at times included occupational restrictions that in principle banned the admission of IMGs (through an occupation list) to identify the role of the immigrant selection system in the selection of IMGs likely to be able to work as physicians or in other high-skilled occupations in the receiving country. They extended the IMG relicensing model of Kugler and Sauer (2005) to incorporate two different approaches to immigrant selection: employer nomination systems and point systems. Consistent with the predictions of the model, they found that, in Canada, where a point system has been in place, IMGs are less likely to be employed as physicians than are IMGs in the US, where employer nomination is a more important entry path for IMGs (see also McDonald et al. (2011), who employ Census data for the US and Canada to analyze the earnings and post-migration schooling decisions of IMGs).

5.4 Boom and bust cycles and occupational targeting

The existence of regulated occupations with barriers to certification and entry implies that immigrant selection needs to take intended occupation into account to some extent. This naturally raises the question of whether selection (based on characteristics at landing as opposed to employer nomination) should be based on human capital, intended occupation, or something in between. As noted above, the Canadian point system is an example of a skilled immigrant selection system that has swung back and forth between these two competing selection criteria.

While a case can be made that numbers of immigrants entering into the receiving country intending to work in a regulated occupation should be limited, can the same be said for the numbers entering intending to work in unregulated occupations? In a market economy, one would expect wages to adjust to ensure that the new immigrants are absorbed into employment in unregulated occupations. However, this does raise the question of how quickly this adjustment will occur and whether it leads to lower wage rates for the immigrants and the pre-existing population employed in these occupations.

Picot and Hou (2009) shed light on this issue by analyzing the outcomes of immigrants to Canada in the 2000s at the time of the information technology (IT) bust. They found that a large part of the poor performance of immigrants who arrived in the 2000s could be attributed to the decline in the outcomes of immigrants who entered intending to work in IT or engineering occupations. Given the increased emphasis on education under the Canadian point system in the mid-1990s (Beach et al., 2007), there had been a large increase in entry of immigrants with university degrees. There also had been a concentration of these workers in IT and engineering occupations given the strength of the growing IT sector in Canada. They found that when this sector collapsed, this had a large impact on immigrant men with these credentials and can explain a large part of the overall poor performance of immigrants in the 2000s in Canada. Taken together, this reveals the risk of having too large a share of entering immigrants concentrated in particular occupations. Not only can it lead to a decline in wages in that sector, it also raises the risk that if the sector were to decline then the immigrants themselves may have difficulty adapting to employment in new sectors as was the case for IT sector workers in Canada. The Canadian selection policy since 2006 has introduced upper limits on the number of immigrants that can be admitted under each intended occupation, which is a move that in principle should reduce the risk of this happening again.

5.5 Gender differences in immigrant outcomes and family investment strategies

Much of the research on the post-migration labor market outcomes of immigrants has focused only on men. This is likely in large part due to the lower participation rates of women generally and the need to consider econometrically the self-selection of women into work. Another reason, as suggested by Kofman (1999) and Docquier et al. (2009), is because of the popular perception that men move for economic opportunities while women move as part of the family, as wives, mothers, or daughters. Some work simply includes an indicator variable for gender in the regression equation (e.g., Buzdugan and Halli (2009) in their study of the returns to foreign education in Canada, and Rodríguez-Pose and Tselios (2010) in their study of the returns to foreign education in the EU). In research that estimates models separately for men and women, typically the models and discussion of results do not reflect the potentially very different circumstances affecting the labor market outcomes of men and women. Interestingly, results for immigrant men and women tend to be broadly similar. Causa and Jean (2007) considered employment and wage outcomes across 12 OECD countries and found immigrants experience gaps in earnings, employment or both, though the differences narrow with time in the host country. In terms of the returns to foreign education, Ferrer and Riddell (2008) found that in Canada the total returns to foreign education for immigrant men are three-quarters of that of native-born men, while the equivalent figure for immigrant women is two-thirds to three-quarters that of native-born women. Nordin (2011) found that both male and female immigrants to Sweden who have only foreign education experience much lower returns to that education compared to immigrants with some Swedish schooling. For the US, Kaushal (2011) estimated the determinants of earnings of university-educated immigrants and non-immigrants. She showed that the immigrant earnings gap is 9% for men and 3% for women, but both gaps are significantly reduced after controlling for place of education. Aydemir and Skuterud (2005) did not find any evidence of a decline in the returns to foreign education in Canada between 1960 and 2000 for either immigrant men or women, though they found that the return to foreign experience was most pronounced among immigrant men from non-traditional source countries. Abbott and Beach (2013) studied earnings mobility of immigrant and non-immigrant men and women using Canadian administrative tax data. Earnings mobility was only slightly higher for female immigrants than male immigrants, but given that earnings mobility among all male earners was significantly higher than for all female earners, female immigrants displayed higher earnings mobility than their non-immigrant female counterparts.

One paper of note that focuses specifically on gender differences is Adsera and Chiswick (2007), who considered earnings and employment outcomes across a number of European countries. They found that gender differences in earnings are more important among those born outside the European Union, with women doing relatively better than men compared to the native-born of the same gender. They also found that returns to education are larger for immigrant and native-born women than for men.

Adsera and Chiswick (2007) suggested that the fact women are more likely to be "tied movers" as part of a family migration decision means they are relatively more likely to be unemployed or out of the labor force, and to have lower earnings than otherwise comparable immigrant women who are primary movers. Related to this, the notion of family decision-making has given rise to family-based labor market models such as the family investment hypothesis initially proposed by Long (1980) and elaborated upon by Baker and Benjamin (1997), Worswick (1999), and Cobb-Clark and Crossley (2004), among others. This theory proposes that credit constraints faced by recent immigrant families result in females as secondary workers of the family unit finding employment shortly after arrival in jobs that offer few opportunities for wage growth while the males invest in post-migration human capital accumulation. As noted by Purkayastha (2005), female tied movers are seldom the focus in the literature on skilled migration, raising questions about whether such women "change their status from dependent wives to workers, whether or not their jobs actually remain secondary to their primary roles as wives, and under what structural conditions such changes take place" (Purkayastha, 2005, p. 181).

6. EFFECTS OF SKILLED IMMIGRATION FOR BOTH SENDING AND RECEIVING ECONOMICS

The decision to emigrate from one country to another has implications beyond the welfare of the individual and family members. If the person has received public support for his or her education in the sending country, then the decision to emigrate may lead to a loss of earning potential with a coincidental loss of tax revenue. This brain drain may reduce the country's development prospects and this is especially true of developing countries, which may have a shortage of skilled workers relative to developed countries. However, the remittance of income generated in the receiving country may offset some or all of these losses for the sending country.

The decision to leave the sending country also has implications for the receiving country. An increase in skilled immigrants may lead to a reduction in wages of skilled workers in the receiving economy driving down the returns to skill, creating a disincentive for young people in these countries to invest in higher education. However, it may be the case that the arrival of the skilled immigrants stimulates economic activities, perhaps offsetting the effects of skill shortages, and makes positive net contributions to the receiving country's public finances.

6.1 Evidence of immigration effects on sending economies

Between 1960 and 2005 the overall world migration rate increased only modestly from 2.5% to 2.9%, but the share of the foreign-born in the population of high-income countries tripled, and the inflows were increasingly composed of high-skilled migrants from developing countries.[10] Docquier and Rapoport (2012) regard this trend, often referred to as the brain drain, as one of the major aspects of globalization. Reasons for the growth in skilled immigration flows from developing to developed countries include (1) the globalization of the world economy that has facilitated self-selection among international migrants seeking greater economic opportunities and higher returns on their human capital, *making human capital scarcer where it is already scarce and more abundant where it is already abundant* (Docquier and Rapoport, 2012); and (2) the strong focus on immigrant selection systems in high-income host countries such as Canada and Australia that are specifically aimed at attracting highly skilled immigrants (Beine et al., 2011).

There has been much more debate and disagreement about the effects of these migration flows. The traditional view is that the brain drain lowers the development potential of the origin countries of the migrants owing to the loss of highly skilled individuals from countries with relatively low rates of educational attainment. More recently a number of channels have been identified through which out-migration of skilled workers can also generate beneficial effects for the source countries that can partly or totally compensate for the costs of the human capital loss (Beine et al., 2011). One of the most important of those channels is the remittance of money from individuals working abroad. Remittances received by developing countries were estimated at US $338 billion in 2008, an increase of 263% from 2001 (Ratha et al., 2009), and remittances constitute about one-third of total financial flows to the developing world (Lartey et al., 2012). Remittances can have a direct effect on home-country educational attainment by alleviating liquidity constraints that would otherwise prevent households from paying for schooling, especially for small

---

[10] Beine et al. (2011) reported that highly skilled immigrants from developing countries currently represent more than a third of total immigration to OECD countries.

and poor countries in which facilities for further education are limited (Gibson and McKenzie, 2011). Other channels include positive externalities for source-country residents from a larger diaspora through improved business opportunities, knowledge of new markets and related dimensions, as well as positive externalities from "brain circulation and return migration" (Gibson and McKenzie, 2011).

The recent literature has also suggested that opportunities for emigration of skilled workers foster education investments in sending countries more generally by increasing the incentives in the home country to obtain higher education, and this may increase the net stock of human capital in the home country even after accounting for out-migration (Beine et al., 2008, Docquier and Rapoport, 2012). In large part because of the potential benefits of out-migration of skilled workers, various governments have moved formally to integrate the international migration of their skilled workers in its national development plans as a key strategy for national income growth and development. The Philippines in particular has a well-established network of public and private agencies that facilitate worker outflows, as do other countries such as India and Mexico.[11]

In their survey of empirical literature on evidence of a brain gain, Docquier and Rapoport (2012) concluded that high-skilled emigration need not deplete a country's human capital stock and can generate positive network externalities. However, the size and direction of the net effect depend on source-country characteristics such as governance, technological distance, and demographic size. Gibson and McKenzie (2011) also noted that brain gain is more likely when policy barriers limit the number who can migrate. Evidence is also mixed about the effect that high skill levels have on remittance behavior.[12] Using national-level figures on incomes, remittances and stock of migrants, Fain (2007) found that skilled migration is unlikely to boost the flow of remittances to the source country. At the micro level, Bollard et al. (2011) found that the relationship between high skill and the decision to remit is uncertain but that largely because of higher incomes, higher skilled immigrants who do remit are more likely to remit more. Similarly, Funkhouser (1995) found that higher levels of educational attainment among immigrants from Central America are negatively correlated with the incidence of remitting, but among migrants who do remit, those with higher levels of education send more. However, among the most highly skilled from countries with high levels of brain drain, the incidence and amount remitted can be high: Gibson and McKenzie (2012) reported that between 68% and 93% of the developing country high-skilled migrants in their

---

[11] See the 2004 Philippine Development Plan, NEDA; see Khadria (2006) for discussion on India migration trends and policies; see Torres and Kuznetsov (2006) for the Mexican case; Stahl and Appleyard (2007) discussed migration policies in the Pacific Islands.

[12] This issue is one part of a large literature on the net effects of remittances, both direct effects on receiving families through improved education (e.g., Boucher et al., 2005) and reduced poverty (e.g., Adams, 2006; Yang and Martinez, 2006), and on spillover effects through, for example, additional liquidity for small enterprises and investments (Woodruff and Zenteno, 2001).

sample remit, with an average amount remitted of around $5000. Clemens (2011) also found an annual remittance level of about $5000 in his survey of African physicians in the US and Canada. Overall, Gibson and McKenzie (2011) concluded that existing empirical evidence does support the idea that high-skilled migrants remit, particularly back to lower-income countries, and that the level of these remittances can be sizeable relative to per-capita income in their home countries.

6.1.1 Gender and the brain drain

There has been increasing interest in the literature on gender aspects of the out-migration of skilled immigrants. Gender is an important consideration for out-migration from developing countries since, as noted by Docquier et al. (2009), women often face unequal access to tertiary education and highly skilled jobs so that the emigration of educated women is likely to generate higher relative losses of human capital than the emigration of skilled males. This also has implications for home-country development, since higher educational attainment by women is positively associated with investments in children's education (World Bank, 2007). Using a dataset of out-migration from most countries to OECD countries in 1990 and 2000, Docquier et al. (2009) estimated that on average the emigration rate of highly skilled women is 17% above that of highly skilled men, and that the rates of growth in emigration of highly skilled women exceed those for low-skilled women and highly skilled men. Dumont et al. (2007) found that emigration of highly skilled women is higher the poorer is their country of origin. A smaller correlation is found for highly skilled men. The authors also found that emigration of highly skilled women negatively affects home-country infant mortality and secondary school enrolment rates.

Bang and Mitra (2011) were able to explain a significant proportion of the gap between female and male high-skilled emigration rates by accounting for variation in women's access to education and in fertility rates. Specifically, high-skilled women are relatively less likely to emigrate from countries where education opportunities for women are greater and fertility is lower. In a similar vein, Docquier et al. (2011) accounted for interdependencies between women and men's emigration decisions within family units—namely, that women are more likely to follow their spouse than men are—and found that after doing so, skilled women are not otherwise more likely to emigrate than skilled men.

6.2 Evidence of immigration effects on receiving economies

The basic economic model of supply and demand predicts that an increase in the supply of highly skilled immigrants will reduce the wages of similarly skilled non-immigrants, with the magnitude of the effect depending on the elasticity of substitution between highly skilled immigrant and non-immigrant labor. If highly skilled immigrants are substitutes for natives in the domestic labor market, the reduced wages would then lead to a decreased incentive by non-immigrants to invest in acquiring such skills and so exert a dampening effect on the domestic supply of skilled workers (Fougère et al., 2011). However, these effects may be moderated by other factors. For example, if high-skilled immigrants are complements to both lower skilled workers and to capital then the increase in the supply of higher skilled workers may produce economic changes that increase the demand for their services, mitigating the downward push on wages (Lofstrom, 2000, Regets, 2001). High-skilled workers gain to the extent that they are also owners of capital (Chiswick, 2011). Also, high-skilled immigration can generate positive externalities through increased knowledge flows and collaboration by, for example, increased ties to foreign research institutions and improved export opportunities for technology (Regets, 2001).

If the assumption of perfect substitutability of high-skilled immigrant and non-immigrant labor within skill levels does not hold, then the impacts on high-skilled native workers will be less pronounced (Cortes, 2008; Ottaviano and Peri, 2008). As Chiswick (2011) noted, some high-skilled occupations require local or destination-specific characteristics, such as linguistic skills or special occupational licensing requirements, reducing the substitutability of high-skilled labor in those fields.

6.2.1 Estimated effects on native earnings

A large literature exists on these topics that cannot be fully reviewed here due to space constraints. However, given the linkage between skilled migration and its impact on the wage outcomes of prior residents, it is important to touch on a few key studies and summarize their findings. There have been three main approaches to determining the effects of high-skilled immigration on the earnings of high-skilled natives. The first estimates the elasticity of substitution between immigrants and natives and then calculates the wage effect of immigration on different groups of native workers based on the estimated elasticity. Borjas and Katz (2007) estimated that immigration over the 1980–2000 period reduced the wages of native-born workers in each skill group but the effects on higher skilled workers was smaller than for lower skilled workers. Ottaviano and Peri (2008) found that immigrants and natives are not close substitutes and that the estimated negative effects on wages are small. Huang's (2011) analysis found that the hypothesis that immigrants and natives are perfect substitutes within the same skill group cannot be rejected. Borjas et al. (2008) found that foreign-born and native workers are perfect substitutes and that immigrants lower the wages of non-immigrants. Levine (2010) surveyed the limited literature on high-skilled immigrants and concluded that there is no consensus.

A second approach is referred to as "area studies" and typically involves examining the economic outcomes of non-immigrants across a range of areas in relation to growth in the number and concentration of immigrants. Overall, most work in this area has found no significant negative effect of increased immigration on non-immigrants (Altonji and Card, 1991; Butcher and Card, 1991; Card, 1990, 2001,

2005; and Addison and Worswick, 2002, for the case of Australia). Focusing specifically on the highly skilled immigrant population, Graefe and De Jong (2010) found that higher skill immigration has minimal effects on the economic opportunities of high-skilled native workers but negative impacts on low-skilled workers, especially workers in areas with newer or less well established immigrant destinations. Orrenius and Zavodny (2007) analyzed the effects of immigration on non-immigrant earnings separately for professionals, service workers, and manual laborers, and found negative effects of the increase in foreign-born workers on natives in blue collar occupations but not for professionals or higher-skilled workers. Dustmann et al. (2005) found evidence of a small but positive impact of an inflow of immigrants with college degree on wages for college-educated natives in the UK. In a related vein, Grossman and Stadelmann (2012) studied data on international migration flows and found that skilled in-migration triggers productivity effects at the macro level such that the wage rate of skilled workers may rise in host countries (though they are also estimated to decline in source countries).

The third type of research has focused on particular occupations. Huang (2011) found that an increased presence of high-skilled immigrants in science and engineering reduced wages of similarly educated native workers, especially in occupations with lower levels of demand. Borjas (2009) found that an increase in the supply of labor to a particular doctoral field caused by an influx of foreign students reduced the earnings of competing science and engineering Ph.D. students who graduated at about the same time. Borjas noted, however, that the great majority of foreign-born Ph.D.s in science and engineering labor markets entered the US as foreign students and then remained after graduation. Therefore, in many ways the skill sets of migrants and residents in this example may be considered to be fairly similar. Zavodny (2003) found no evidence that immigration to the US of workers with IT skills through H-1B visas depressed the wages of US workers in computer-related occupations (though there might be adverse effects on the group's unemployment rate).

Finally, an important recent paper by Ottaviano et al. (2013) analyzed a model with immigrant workers, native workers, and the potential for offshore production. They found that immigrants and natives in the US do not compete directly since the tasks that they tend to perform are at the opposite ends of the task complexity spectrum, with natives carrying out high-skill tasks and immigrants carrying out low-skill tasks. Offshore workers tend to perform jobs with tasks in the middle of the task complexity spectrum. Higher immigration in this context is associated with higher employment for native workers.

6.2.2 Estimated effects on training of non-immigrants

George et al. (2012) reviewed the theoretical underpinnings of why skilled immigration might affect the provision of training to non-immigrants. They stated that the likely effects of skilled immigration on employer training decisions will vary depending on the extent to which migrants' skills are broadly similar to the kinds of skills that employers could expect to develop through providing training for resident workers.[13] In the case of perfect substitutability between skilled migrants and skilled residents, employers can avoid the costs of general skills training by recruiting skilled migrants, so that skilled immigration is likely to contribute to reduced training provision for existing employees (unless the extra costs of providing firm specific training for migrants are expected to outweigh the costs of providing general skills training for existing employees). However, the impact of skilled immigration on employers' training decisions is uncertain in the case where skilled migrants and skilled residents possess different kinds of skill that are potentially complementary to each other. In commenting on the empirical literature, George et al (2012) reiterated that that there is little systematic empirical evidence that indicates immigration has directly reduced domestic investment in training in the UK.

6.2.3 Effects on research and development, patents, and innovation

Regets (2007) found that that immigrants in science and engineering had positive effects on R&D activity, knowledge collaboration, and increased enrollment in graduate programs, while Hunt and Gauthier-Loiselle (2010) found that a 1 percentage point increase in immigrant university graduates in the US raised patents per capita by about 15%. Also, Peri (2007) showed that, compared to a foreign-born population of 12% in 2000, 26% of US-based Nobel Prize winners between 1990 and 2000 were immigrants. Similarly, Wadhwa et al. (2007) showed that non-citizens account for up to one-quarter of international patent applications from the US. Kerr (2013) provided an overview of research in this area. These findings support the view that skilled immigration adds to both the stock of human capital in the receiving society but also is a key input to innovation activity potentially driving growth in per-capita GDP.

6.2.4 Occupational choice

Peri and Sparber (2011) found that highly educated native- and foreign-born workers are imperfect substitutes. Immigrants holding graduate degrees specialize in occupations requiring quantitative and analytical skills while non-immigrant graduate degree holders specialized more in occupations requiring interactive and communication skills. Peri and Sparber also found that the imperfect substitutability has significant effects on the occupational choices of non-immigrants: when the foreign-born proportion of highly educated employment within an occupation rises, native employees with graduate degrees choose new occupations with less analytical and more communicative content (for a broader review of the effects of immigration, see Kerr and Kerr, 2011).

---

[13] The impacts of skilled immigration are also likely to vary depending on whether the training concerned takes the form of upskilling of existing employees or initial training for newly recruited unskilled workers.

6.2.5 Fiscal impact of immigration

A large literature exists related to the net contribution to a country's public finances from immigrants. Auerbach and Oreopoulos (1999) studied the implications of immigration to the US within a generational accounting framework. They concluded that immigration will reduce the fiscal burden on future generations assuming that it is passed forward to future generations. However, if a policy of "fiscal responsibility" were followed in the US, this would reduce the benefits from immigration. Finally, although they found the net effect of immigration to be positive, it is also "extremely small" relative to the overall fiscal imbalance.

Akbari (1991) found that immigrant households in Canada make a net positive contribution to the public finances (relative to other Canadian households) and this is true even when the immigrant households are broken down by detailed source-country groupings. A recent study by Dustmann et al. (2010) analyzed data from the UK focusing on the fiscal consequences of migration from Central and Eastern Europe after the enlargement of the European Union to include these countries in 2004. They found these immigrants had a positive net contribution to the UK public finances due to the fact that, relative to other UK residents, these immigrants have higher labor force participation rates. They are also found to pay proportionately more in indirect taxes and are much less likely to receive public benefits and services. Schou (2006) looked at the same issue for the case of immigration to Denmark using a computable general equilibrium model. Increased immigration was found to worsen Danish fiscal finances. Collado et al. (2004) analyzed the implications of immigration for Spanish fiscal finances within the context of the challenges faced by significant aging of their population in the near future. Using a general accounting approach, their results suggest that the impact of immigration will be positive. In a related vein, Grossman and Stadelman (2011) found that increasing net high-skilled immigration positively impacted productive public expenditure in areas such as education and infrastructure in the receiving country.

6.2.6 Demographic challenges and immigration

Storesletten (2000) used a computable general equilibrium model to look at the effectiveness of an increase in immigration to the US on the fiscal challenges faced in terms of providing government services and support to the baby boom cohort as it moves into and through retirement years. The analysis suggested that immigration policy can on its own be used to address this policy challenge. One suggested possible approach is to admit 1.6 million 40- to 44-year-old high-skilled immigrants each year. A larger number of skilled immigrants would be needed if this tight age restriction were not politically feasible (which seems likely).

Fougère et al. (2004) also employed a CGE model to consider the implications of immigration within the context of an aging society for the case of Canada. They found that the expected future immigration flows contribute to a 30% reduction in the negative impact of aging on real per-capita GDP. They also concluded that raising the level of immigration would provide further long-run benefits in terms of real GDP.

7. SUMMARY AND CONCLUSIONS

The growth in emphasis on skilled immigration in OECD countries is driven by the perception that skilled immigrants are net contributors to the receiving economy, especially in the context of aging societies and especially for economies faced with large baby boom generations reaching the usual retirement age. The theory and empirical evidence suggest that skilled immigration is likely to lead to greater benefits for the receiving economy than would occur for the same level of immigration but focused on less-skilled immigrants. The implications for the sending country are less clear. There is a loss of human capital but increased remittances will at least partially offset this effect to the extent that remittances continue to be sent back to the home country. A number of other potential benefits to the home country have also been cited, and estimation of these effects is ongoing in the literature.

In terms of immigrant selection policy, the use of point systems is on the rise but the emphasis appears to be shifting away from human capital criteria and towards occupations in demand and prearranged employment. This is partly in response to the mixed track record of human-capital-based point systems in selecting immigrants who will have high earnings in the receiving economies. Employer nomination, especially in occupations where there are skill shortages, is seen as leading to high rates of employment shortly after arrival and high rates of return on human capital. Occupational restrictions on immigrant selection have been found to be important in the case of regulated occupations where entry into the profession or into relicensing programs may be difficult for new immigrants. In this context, simply admitting an immigrant based on general human capital criteria could lead to a marked under-utilization of their human capital (and a loss of valuable human capital for the home country) if their educational credentials do not allow them to work in their intended occupations. However, even in unregulated occupations, concern exists regarding the admission of too many skilled immigrants into specific occupations. Flooding particular occupations with immigrants, even in situations of high demand, can be problematic if the demand suddenly dries up, as was the case in a number of countries after the IT collapse.

The growth of two-step immigration programs where foreigners enter first as temporary residents (workers or students) then are able to convert after around two years to permanent residency is a recent phenomenon that has the potential to grow in coming years. The first step of the process can be thought of as a trial period with limited commitment on the part of the receiving country in which the potential immigrants can gain work experience and/or educational credentials in the receiving country, as well as accumulate host-country language and also possibly gain familiarity with the market and government systems in the host country. The empirical evidence supports the view that these individuals are likely to have high rates of employment and high earnings shortly after arrival relative to other economic immigrants. However, the Australian experience indicates that this type of policy can create perverse incentives. For example, foreigners may enter educational programs in the receiving country not out of an interest in the education per se but as a pathway to permanency. Providers (private but perhaps also public) may respond to this increased demand by creating low-quality educational programs to satisfy the criteria for admission (and earn tuition revenue) but little in the way of human capital development may occur.

Similarly, two-step immigration programs may further the power imbalance between the employer and the temporary foreign worker (TFW). Given the pre-existing concerns about abuse of TFWs by employers, the introduction of a two-step program may further empower abusive employers since the TFW may be even less inclined to report abuse given that the ultimate goal may be gaining permanent residency for themselves and their children rather than just the income from the temporary job. Given these concerns, two-step immigration programs need to be implemented with extensive monitoring of behavior of the industry partners to ensure that they do not lead to bad outcomes for the immigrants themselves as the different agents respond to the new incentives. Related to this is the issue of allowing private sector employers to have a greater degree of control and influence over immigration intakes. If not properly designed and monitored, the resulting immigration program might not be in the country's best interests.

The implications of increased competition for skill are unclear. The increased emphasis on skill by traditional receiving countries coupled with the emergence of new immigrant-receiving countries in Europe may create shortages in highly skilled immigrants wishing to enter the traditional immigrant-receiving countries such as Australia and Canada. This could be compounded should the US embrace higher scale skilled immigration, perhaps through the formal adoption of a point system or through setting much higher targets for both temporary visas and for their conversion to permanent residency.

8. GAPS

While the economics of immigration literature has grown dramatically over the past 20 years, many sub-topics remain relatively under-researched. This, coupled with the quickly evolving policy contexts, means that there are both opportunities to carry out evaluations of these policies but also the need to constantly update past studies to the new policy context.

We have not discussed the issue of the effectiveness of settlement policies such as language training. There does not appear to be much in the way of formal program evaluation in this field for immigrants. This is an important area of research since many immigrant-receiving countries spend vast amounts on post-migration settlement policies that may be especially important for skilled immigrants to allow them to have their skills recognized by employers.

There also does not appear to be empirical research on the implications for immigrant selection and economic outcomes of the increased competition of immigrants across countries. For example, it would be interesting to know the implications of, say, Canadian immigrant performance of an expansion in US immigration.

ACKNOWLEDGMENTS

The authors would like to thank two anonymous referees for helpful suggestions, and Paola Ansieta and John Calhoun for research assistance.

REFERENCES

Abbott, M., Beach, C., 2013. Earnings Mobility of Canadian Immigrants: A Transition Matrix Approach, CLSRN Working Paper 127, October.

Adams Jr., R., 2006. International remittances and the household: Analysis and review of global evidence. Journal of African Economics 15 (S2), 396–425.

Addison, T., Worswick, C., 2002. Impact of immigration on the wages of natives: Evidence from Australian unit record data. Econ. Rec. 78 (240), 68–78.

Adsera, A., Chiswick, B., 2007. Are there gender and country of origin differences in immigrant labor market outcomes across European destinations? J. Popul. Econ. 20, 495–526.

Akbari, A., 1991. The public finance impact of immigrant population on host nations: Some Canadian evidence. Soc. Sci. Q. 72 (2), 334–346.

Alboim, N., Finnie, R., Meng, R., 2005. The discounting of immigrants' skills in Canada: Evidence and policy recommendations. IRPP Choices 11 (2), 2–23.

Altonji, J.G., Card, D., 1991. The effects of immigration on the labor market outcomes of less-skilled natives. In: Immigration, Trade and the Labor Market. University of Chicago Press, pp. 201–234.

Antecol, H., Cobb-Clark, D., Trejo, S., 2003. Immigration policy and the skills of immigrants to Australia, Canada, and the United States. J. Hum. Resour. 38 (1), 192–218.

Auerbach, A., Oreopoulos, P., 1999. Analyzing the fiscal impact of U.S. immigration. Am. Econ. Rev. 89 (2, May), 176–180.

Aydemir, A., Skuterud, M., 2005. Explaining the deteriorating entry earnings of Canada's immigrant cohorts: 1966–2000. Can. J. Econ. 38 (2), 641–671.

Baker, M., Benjamin, D., 1994. The performance of immigrants in the Canadian labour market. J. Labor Econ. 12 (3), 369–405.

Baker, M., Benjamin, D., 1997. The role of the family in immigrants' labor market activity: An evaluation of alternative explanations. Am. Econ. Rev. 87 (4), 705–727.

Banerjee, R., Lee, B., 2012. Decreasing the recent immigrant earnings gap: The impact of Canadian credential attainment, International Migration, published online, 5 September.

Bang, J., Mitra, A., 2011. Gender bias and the female brain drain. Appl. Econ. Lett. 18 (9), 829–833.

Beach, C., Green, A.G., Worswick, C., 2007. Impacts of the point system and immigration policy levers on skill characteristics of Canadian immigrants. Res. Labor Econ. 27, 349–401.

Beach, C., Green, A.G., Worswick, C., 2011. Towards Improving Canada's Skilled Immigration Policy: An Evaluation Approach. CD Howe Institute.

Beine, M., Docquier, F., Rapoport, H., 2008. Brain drain and human capital formation in developing countries: winners and losers. Econ. J. 118 (528), 631–652.

Beine, M., Docquier, F., Oden-Defoort, C., 2011. A panel data analysis of the brain gain. World Dev. 39 (4), 523–532.

Bollard, A., McKenzie, D., Morten, M., Rapoport, H., 2011. Remittances and the brain drain revisited: The microdata show more educated migrants remit more. World Bank Econ. Rev. 25 (1), 132–156.

Bonikowska, A., Hou, F., Picot, G., 2011. Do Highly Educated Immigrants Perform Differently in the Canadian and U.S Labour Markets? Analytical Studies Branch. Statistics Canada Working Paper 329.

Borjas, G., 1991. Immigration Policy, National Origin and Immigrant Skills: A Comparison of Canada and the United States, NBER Working Paper No. 3691.

Borjas, G., 1995. Assimilation and changes in cohort quality revisited: what happened to immigrant earnings in the 1980s? J. Labor Econ. 13 (2), 201–245.

Borjas, G., 2009. Immigration in high-skill labor markets: The impact of foreign students on the earnings of doctorates. In: Freeman, R., Goroff, D. (Eds.), Science and Engineering Careers in the United States: An Analysis of Markets and Employment, NBER Books, National Bureau of Economic Research, May. NBER Chapters Number 11620.

Borjas, G., Katz, L., 2007. The evolution of the Mexican-Born workforce in the United States. NBER Chapters. In: Mexican Immigration to the United States. National Bureau of Economic Research, Inc, pp. 13–56.

Borjas, G., Friedberg, R., 2009. Recent Trends in the Earnings of New Immigrants to the United States. NBER Working Paper 15406; <http://www.nber.org/Papers/w15406>.

Borjas, G., Grogger, J., Hanson, G., 2008. Imperfect substitution between immigrants and natives: A reappraisal, NBER Working Paper No. 13887.

Boucher, A., 2013. Bureaucratic control and policy change: A comparative venue shopping approach to skilled immigration policies in Australia and Canada. Journal of Comparative Policy Analysis: Research and Practice 15 (4), 349–367.

Boucher, S., Stark, O., Taylor, J., 2005. A gain with a drain? Evidence from rural Mexico on the new economics of the brain drain, ARE Working Papers, Paper 05-005, Department of Agricultural and Resource Economics, University of California at Davis.

Boyd, M., Schellenberg, G., 2007. Re-accreditation and the occupations of immigrant doctors and engineers. Canadian Social Trends, Statistics Canada. Catalogue no. 11-008.

Bratsberg, B., Ragan Jr., J., 2002. The impact of host-country schooling on earnings: A study of male immigrants in the United States. J. Hum. Resour. 37 (1), 63–105.

Bratsberg, B., Terrell, D., 2002. School quality and returns to education of US immigrants. Econ. Inq. 40 (2), 177–198.

Butcher, K., Card, D., 1991. Immigration and wages: Evidence from the 1980s. Am. Econ. Rev. 81 (2), 292–296.

Buzdugan, R., Halli, S., 2009. Labor market experiences of Canadian immigrants with focus on foreign education and experience. Int. Migrat. Rev. 43 (2), 366–386.

Card, D., 1990. The impact of the Mariel boatlift on the Miami labor market. Ind. Labor Relat. Rev. 43 (2), 245–257.

Card, D., 2001. Immigrant inflows, native outflows, and the local labor market impacts of higher immigration. J. Labor Econ. 19 (1), 22–64.

Card, D., 2005. Is the new immigration really so bad? Econ. J. 115 (507), F300–F323.

Castles, S., 2006. Back to the Future? Can Europe Meet its Labour Needs Through Temporary Migration? International Migration Institute Working Paper #1.

Causa, O., Jean, S., 2007. Integration of Immigrants in OECD Countries: Do Policies Matter? OECD Economics Department Working Papers No. 564, OECD.

Chan, G., Heaton, C., Tani, M., 2012. The Wage Premium of Foreign Education: New Evidence from Australia. IZA Discussion Paper 6578.

Chiswick, B., 2011. Introduction. In: Chiswick, B. (Ed.), High Skilled Immigration in a Global Labor Market. American Enterprise Institute Press, Washington, DC, pp. 111–154.

Chiswick, B., Miller, P., 2008. Why is the payoff to schooling smaller for immigrants? Lab. Econ. 15 (6), 1317–1340.

Chiswick, B., Miller, P., 2009. Earnings and occupational attainment among immigrants. Industrial Relations: A Journal of Economy and Society 48 (3), 454–465.

Chiswick, B., Miller, P., 2010a. Does the choice of reference levels of education matter in the ORU earnings equation? Econ. Educ. Rev. 29 (6), 1076–1085.

Chiswick, B., Miller, P., 2010b. The effects of educational-occupational mismatch on immigrant earnings in Australia, with international comparisons. Int. Migrat. Rev. 44 (4), 879–898.

Chiswick, B., Miller, P., 2010c. An explanation for the lower payoff to schooling for immigrants in the Canadian labour market. In: McDonald, T., Ruddick, E., Sweetman, A., Worswick, C. (Eds.), Canadian Immigration: Economic Evidence for a Dynamic Policy Environment. McGill-Queen's University Press, Montreal.

Chiswick, B.R., Miller, P.W., 2011. Educational mismatch: Are high skilled immigrants really working on high skilled jobs, and what price do they pay if they are not? In: Chiswick, B.R. (Ed.), High-Skilled Immigration in a Global Labor Market. AEI Press, Washington, DC, pp. 109–154.

Clarke, A., Skuterud, M., 2012. Why Do Immigrant Workers in Australia Perform Better Than in Canada? Is It the Immigrants or Their Labour Markets? University of Waterloo, Mimeo.

Clemens, M., 2011. The financial consequences of high-skill emigration: lessons from African doctors abroad. In: Plaza, S., Ratha, D. (Eds.), Diaspora for Development in Africa. World Bank, Washington, DC, pp. 165–182.

Cobb-Clark, D., Crossley, T., 2004. Revisiting the family investment hypothesis. Lab. Econ. 11 (3), 373–393.

Collado, M., Iturbe-Ormaetxe, I., Valera, G., 2004. Quantifying the impact of immigration on the Spanish welfare state. Int. Tax. Publ. Finance 11 (3), 335–353.

Cortes, P., 2008. The effect of low-skilled immigration on U.S. price: Evidence from CPI data. J. Polit. Econ. 116 (3), 381–422.

Cully, M., 2012. Skilled Migration Selection Policies: Recent Australian Reforms. IZA; <www.iza.org/en/papers/7882_10042012.pdf>.

Docquier, F., Rapoport, H., 2012. Globalization, brain drain, and development. J. Econ. Lit. 50 (3), 681–730.

Docquier, F., Lowell, B.L., Marfouk, A., 2009. A gendered assessment of highly skilled emigration. Popul. Dev. Rev. 35 (2), 297–321.

Docquier, F., Marfouk, A., Salomone, S., Sekkat, K., 2011. Are skilled women more migratory than skilled men? World Dev. 40 (2), 251–265.

Doomernik, J., Koslowski, R., Thraenhardt, D., 2009. The Battle for the Brains: Why Immigration Policy is Not Enough to Attract the Highly Skilled, Brussels Forum Paper Series, March.

Duleep, H.O., 2013. US Immigration Policy at a Crossroads, IZA Discussion Paper 7136, January.

Dumont, J.C., Martin, J.P., Spielvogel, G., 2007. Women on the Move: The Neglected Gender Dimension of the Brain Drain, IZA Discussion Paper No. 2920.

Dustmann, C., Fabbri, F., Preston, I., 2005. The impact of immigration on the British labour market. Econ. J. 115, F324–F341.

Dustmann, C., Frattini, T., Halls, C., 2010. Assessing the fiscal costs and benefits of A8 migration to the UK. Fiscal Studies 31 (1), 1–41.

Fain, R., 2007. Remittances and the brain drain: Do more skilled migrants remit more? World Bank Econ. Rev. 21 (2), 177–191.

Ferrer, A., Riddell, C., 2008. Education, credentials, and immigrant earnings. Can. J. Econ. 41 (1), 186–216.

Ferrer, A., Green, D., Riddell, C., 2006. The effect of literacy on immigrant earnings. J. Hum. Resour. 41 (2), 380–410.

Ferrer, A., Picot, G., Riddell, W.C., 2012. New Directions in Immigration Policy: Canada's Evolving Approach to Immigration Selection, Mimeo, July.

Foster, J., 2012. Making Temporary Permanent: The Silent Transformation of the Temporary Foreign Worker Program. York University Working Paper; <http://www.justlabour.yorku.ca/volume19/pdfs/02_foster_press.pdf>.

Fougère, M., Harvey, S., Mérette, M., Poitras, F., 2004. Ageing population and immigration in Canada: An analysis with a regional CGE overlapping generations model. Can. J. Reg. Sci. 27 (2), 209–236.

Fougère, M., Harvey, S., Rainville, B., 2011. Would an increase in high-skilled immigration in Canada benefit workers? Economics Research International, Article ID 171927.

Friedberg, R., 2000. You can't take it with you? Immigrant assimilation and the portability of human capital. J. Labor Econ. 18 (2), 221–251.

Fulmer, C., 2009. A critical look at the H-1B visa program and its effects on US and foreign workers – a controversial program unhinged from its original intent. Lewis and Clark Law Review 13 (3), 823–860.

Funkhouser, E., 1995. Remittances from international migration: A comparison of El Salvador and Nicaragua. Rev. Econ. Stat. 77 (2), 137–146.

George, A., Lalani, M., Mason, G., Rolfe, H., Bondibene, C., 2012. Skilled immigration and strategically important skills in the UK economy. National Institute of Economic and Social Research Final Report to the Migration Advisory Committee (MAC), 7 February.

Gibson, J., McKenzie, D., 2011. Eight Questions about the Brain Drain. Centre for Research and Analysis of Migration Discussion Paper 1111,University College, London.

Gibson, J., McKenzie, D., 2012. The economic consequences of 'brain drain' of the best and brightest: Microeconomic evidence from five countries. Econ. J. 122 (560), 339–375.

Goldman, G., Sweetman, A., Warman, C., 2011. The Portability of New Immigrants' Human Capital: Language, Education and Occupational Matching, IZA DP No. 5851.

Government of New Zealand, 2011. Competing for Skills: Migration Policies and Trends in New Zealand; <http://www.dol.govt.nz/publications/research/competing-for-skills/report/full-report.pdf>.

Graefe, D., De Jong, G., 2010. Skilled-Immigrant Metropolitan Destinations and Changing Economic Opportunities for Natives, Paper presented at the Annual Meeting of the Population Association of America, Dallas, TX, April.

Green, A., 2003. Introduction. In: Beach, C., Green, A., Reitz, J. (Eds.), Canadian Immigration Policy for the 21st Century. John Deutsch Institute for the Study of Economic Policy. McGill-Queen's University Press, Kingston Chapter 1.

Green, A., Green, D., 1995. Canadian immigration policy: The effectiveness of the point system and other instruments. Can. J. Econ. 28 (4b), 1006–1041.

Green, D., Worswick, C., 2012. Immigrant earnings profiles in the presence of human capital investment: Measuring cohort and macro effects. Lab. Econ. 19 (2, April), 241–259.

Grignon, M., Owusu, Y., Sweetman, A., 2012. The International Migration of Health Professionals, IZA Discussion Paper #6517.

Gross, D., Schmitt, N., 2012. Temporary foreign workers and regional labour market disparities in Canada. Can. Publ. Pol. 38 (2), 233–263.

Grossman, V., Stadelmann, D., 2011. High-skilled immigration: The link to public expenditure and private investments. In: Chiswick, B.R. (Ed.), High-Skilled Immigration in a Global Labor Market. AEI Press, Washington, DC.

Grossman, V., Stadelmann, D., 2012. Wage Effects of High-Skilled Migration: International Evidence. IZA Discussion Paper No. 6611, May.

Haley, M.R., Taengnoi, S., 2011. The skill transferability of high-skilled US immigrants. Appl. Econ. Lett. 18 (7), 633–636.

Hatton, T., 2013. American Immigration Policy: The 1965 Act and its Consequences. Paper presented at the CREAM/NORFACE Conference, Migration: Global Development, New Frontiers, University College, London, April.

Hawthorne, L., 2010. Two-step migration: Australia's experience. Policy Options 39–43, (July–August).

Huang, S., 2011. An Evaluation of Skilled Immigration in the United States. Ph.D. dissertation, University of Kansas.

Hunt, J., Gauthier-Loiselle, M., 2010. How much does immigration boost innovation? Am. Econ. J. Macroecon. 2 (2), 31–56.

Kahanec, M., Zimmermann, K.F., 2011. High-skilled immigration policy in Europe. In: Chiswick, B.R. (Ed.), High-Skilled Immigration in a Global Labor Market. AEI Press, Washington, DC.

Kanas, A., Van Tubergen, F., 2009. The impact of origin and host country schooling on the economic performance of immigrants. Social Forces 88 (2), 893–915.

Kaushal, N., 2011. Earnings trajectories of highly educated immigrants: Does place of education matter? Ind. Labor Relat. Rev. 64 (2), 323–340.

Kerr, S., Kerr, W., 2011. Economic Impacts of Immigration: A Survey, NBER Working Paper No. 16736.

Kerr, W., 2013. U.S. High-Skilled Immigration, Innovation, and Entrepreneurship: Empirical Approaches and Evidence, NBER Working Paper No. 19377, August.

Khadria, B., 2006. Migration between India and the UK. Publ. Pol. Res. 13, 172–184.

Kofman, E., 1999. Female 'birds of passage' a decade later: Gender and immigration in European Union. Int. Migrat. Rev. 33, 269–299.

Kugler, A.D., Sauer, R.M., 2005. Doctors without borders? Relicensing requirements and negative selection in the market for physicians. J. Labor Econ. 23 (3), 437–465.

Lartey, E., Mandelman, F., Acosta, P., 2012. Remittances, exchange rate regimes and the Dutch disease: A panel data analysis. Rev. Int. Econ. 20 (2), 377–395.

Lesky, L., 2011. Physician migration to the United States and Canada. In: Chiswick, B.R. (Ed.), High-Skilled Immigration in a Globalized Labor Market. American Enterprise Institute, Washington, DC, pp. 155–164.

Lessem, R., Sanders, C., 2012. The Immigrant-Native Wage Gap in the United States. Mimeo.

Levine, L., 2010. Immigration: The Effects on Low-Skilled and High-Skilled Native-Born Workers. Congressional Research Service, Washington, DC; <http://digitalcommons.ilr.cornell.edu/key_workplace/690>.

Lofstrom, M., 2000. Self-Employment and Earnings among High-Skilled Immigrants in the United States, IZA DP No. 175.

Long, J., 1980. The effect of Americanization on earnings: Some evidence for women. J. Polit. Econ. 88, 620–629.

Lowell, B.L., Khadka, P., 2011. Trends in foreign-student admissions to the United States: Policy and competitive effects. In: Chiswick, B.R. (Ed.), High-Skilled Immigration in a Globalized Labor Market. American Enterprise Institute, Washington, DC, pp. 83–108.

Lubotsky, D., 2007. Chutes or ladders? A longitudinal analysis of immigrant earnings. J. Polit. Econ. 115 (5), 820–867.

Luthra, R., 2009. Temporary immigrants in a high-skilled labour market: A study of H-1Bs. J. Ethnic. Migrat. Stud. 35 (2), 227–250.

Mahroum, S., 2001. Europe and the immigration of highly skilled labour. Int. Migrat. 39 (5), 27–43.

Martin, P., 2008. Temporary Worker Programs: US and Global Experiences, University of California, Davis Working Paper, March.

Martin, P., 2010. Temporary worker programs: US and global experiences. Can. Issues. 122–128, (Spring).

Martin, S., Lowell, B.L., Martin, P., 2001. US immigration policy: Admission of high skilled workers. Georgetown Immigration Law Journal 16, 619–636.

McDonald, J.T., Worswick, C., 1998. The earnings of immigrant men in Canada: Job tenure, cohort, and macroeconomic conditions. Ind. Labor Relat. Rev. 51 (3), 465–482.

McDonald, J.T., Warman, C., Worswick, C., 2011. Labour Market Outcomes and Occupations of Immigrants with Medical Degrees: Evidence for Canada and the US. In: Chiswick, B.R. (Ed.), High-Skilled Immigration in a Global Labor Market. AEI Press, Washington, DC.

McDonald, J.T., Warman, C., Worswick, C., 2012. Immigrant Selection Systems and Occupational Outcomes of International Medical Graduates in Canada and the United States. McMaster University, Social and Economic Dimensions of an Aging Population Research Papers, Number 293.

McGuinness, S., 2006. Overeducation in the labour market. J. Econ. Surv. 20 (3), 387–418.

McMahon, G., 2004. Coming to America: International medical graduates in the United States. New. Engl. J. Med. 350 (24), 2435–2437.

Nordin, M., 2011. Immigrants' returns to schooling in Sweden. Int. Migrat. 49 (4), 144–166.

Orrenius, P., Zavodny, M., 2007. Does immigration affect wages? A look at occupation-level evidence. Lab. Econ. 14 (5), 757–773.

Ottaviano, G., Peri, G., 2008. Immigration and National Wages: Clarifying the Theory and the Empirics. NBER Working Paper No. 14188.

Ottaviano, G., Peri, G., Wright, G.C., 2013. Immigration, offshoring, and American jobs. Am. Econ. Rev. 103, 1925–1959, (5, August).

Papademetriou, D., Sumption, M., 2011. Rethinking Points Systems and Employer Selected Immigration. Migration Policy Institute Working Paper, June.

Papademetriou, D., Meissner, D., Rosenblum, M., Sumption, M., 2009. Aligning Temporary Immigration Visas with US Labor Market Needs: The Case for a New System of Provisional Visas. Migration Policy Institute Working Paper, July.

Pearce, S.C., 2006. Immigrant Women in the United States: A Demographic Portrait, Special Report, Immigration Policy Center, Summer.

Peri, G., 2007. Higher education, innovation and growth. In: Brunello, G., Garibaldi, P., Wasmer, E. (Eds.), Education and Training in Europe. Oxford University Press, Oxford, UK.

Peri, G., Sparber, C., 2011. Highly educated immigrants and native occupational choice. Industrial Relations: A Journal of Economy and Society 50, 385–411(3, July).

Picot, G., Hou, F., 2009. Immigrant Characteristics, the IT Bust, and their Effect on Entry Earnings of Immigrants, Analytical Studies Branch Research Paper Series, Research Paper No. 315.

Picot, G., Piraino, P., 2012. Immigrant Earnings Growth: Selection Bias or Real Progress? Analytical Studies Branch, Statistics Canada, Paper #340.

Purkayastha, B., 2005. Skilled migration and cumulative disadvantage: The case of highly qualified Asian Indian immigrant women in the US. Geoforum 36, 181–196.

Ratha, D., Mohapatra, S., Silwal, A., 2009. Migration and Remittance Trends 2009: A better-than-expected outcome so far, but significant risks ahead. Migration and Development Brief 11, World Bank, Washington, DC November.

Regets, M., 2001. Research and Policy Issues in High-Skilled International Migration: A Perspective with Data from the United States, IZA DP No. 366.

Regets, M., 2007. Research Issues in the International Migration of Highly Skilled Workers: A Perspective with Data from the United States, Working Paper SRS 07-203, Division of Science Resources Statistics, National Science Foundation Arlington, VA.

Reitz, J., 2010. Selecting immigrants for the short term: Is it smart in the long run? Policy Options, 12–16 (July–August).

Rodríguez-Pose, A., Tselios, V., 2010. Returns to migration, education and externalities in the European Union. Paper. Reg. Sci. 89 (2), 411–434.

Ruhs, M., 2006. The potential of temporary migration programmes in future international migration policy. Int. Labour Rev. 145 (1–2), 7–36.

Schmitt, J., Wadsworth, J., 2007. Changes in the relative economic performance of immigrants to Great Britain and the United States, 1980–2000. Br. J. Ind. Relat. 45 (4), 659–686.

Schoeni, R., 1997. New evidence on the economic progress of foreign-born men in the 1970s and 1980s. J. Hum. Resour. 32 (4), 683–740.

Schou, P., 2006. Immigration, integration and fiscal sustainability. J. Popul. Econ. 19, 671–689.

Shachar, A., 2006. The race for talent: Highly skilled migrants and competitive immigration regimes. New York Univ. Law Rev. 81, 148–206.

Skuterud, M., Su, M., 2012. Immigrants and the dynamics of high-wage jobs. Ind. Labor Relat. Rev. 65 (2), 377–397.

Stahl, C., Appleyard, R., 2007. Migration and Development in the Pacific Islands: Lessons from the New Zealand Experience. Australian Agency for International Development, Canberra.

Storesletten, K., 2000. Sustaining fiscal policy through immigration. J. Polit. Econ. 108 (2), 300–323.

Sweetman, A., 2004. Immigrant Source Country School Quality and Canadian Labour Market Outcomes. Research Paper No. 234, Analytical Studies Branch. Statistics Canada, Ottawa, ON.

Sweetman, A., Warman, C., 2009. Temporary Foreign Workers and Former International Students as a Source of Permanent Immigration, CLSRN Working Paper 25.

Sweetman, A., Warman, C., 2010. Canada's temporary foreign workers programs. Can. Issues. 19–24 (Spring).

Torres, F., Kuznetsov, Y., 2006. Mexico: Leveraging migrants' capital to develop hometown communities. In: Kuznetsov, Y. (Ed.), Diaspora Networks and the International Migration of Skills How Countries

Can Draw on their Talent Abroad. WBI Development Studies, World Bank, Washington, DC, Chapter 5.

Udansky, M., Espenshade, T., 2001. The evolution of U.S. policy toward employment-based immigrants and temporary workers: The H-1B debate in historical perspective. In: Cornelius, W., Espenshade, T., Salehyan, I. (Eds.), The International Migration of the Highly Skilled: Demand, Supply, and Development Consequences in Sending and Receiving Countries. Center for Comparative Immigration Studies, University of California, San Diego, La Jolla, CA.

Wadhwa, V., Saxenian, A., Rissing, B., Gere, G., 2007. America's New Immigrant Entrepreneurs. Duke Science, Technology and Innovation Paper No. 23, Duke University.

Woodruff, C., Zenteno, R., 2001. Remittances and Microenterprises in Mexico. Graduate School of International Relations and Pacific Studies Working Paper, University of California at San Diego.

World Bank, 2007. Confronting the Challenges of Gender Equality and Fragile States. Global Monitoring Report, World Bank, Washington, DC.

Worswick, C., 1999. Credit constraints and the labour supply of immigrant families in Canada. Can. J. Econ. 32 (1), 152–170.

Yang, D., Martinez, C., 2006. Remittances and poverty in migrants' home areas: Evidence from the Philippines. In: Ozden, C., Schiff, M. (Eds.), International Migration, Remittances and the Brain Drain. World Bank, Washington, DC.

Zalatel, P., 2006. Competing for the highly skilled migrants: Implications for the EU common approach on temporary economic migration. Eur. Law J. 12 (5), 613–635.

Zavodny, M., 2003. The H-1B program and its Effects on information technology workers. Federal Reserve Bank of Atlanta Economic Review, Third Quarter.

CHAPTER 12

The Refugee/Asylum Seeker

Aimee Chin*, Kalena E. Cortes**,†

*University of Houston
**Texas A&M University
†To whom correspondence should be addressed. Any errors and omissions are solely the work of the authors.

Contents

1. Introduction	586
1.1 Defining refugees and asylum seekers	586
1.2 Trends in asylum and refugee applications: around the world and in the United States of America	587
1.2.1 World trends	587
1.2.2 Trends in the United States	592
2. Who Migrates? Comparing Refugees to Other Migrants	596
2.1 Conceptual framework: the migration decision	596
2.2 Previous work comparing refugees to other migrants	600
2.3 Refugees in the United States: a snapshot from the New Immigrant Survey	601
2.3.1 Exposure to persecution	601
2.3.2 Demographic, human capital, and labor market characteristics	602
2.3.3 Within-source-country comparisons	610
2.3.4 Discussion	613
3. Economic Assimilation of Refugees in the Host Country	615
3.1 Conceptual framework: the human capital investment decision	615
3.2 Previous research on economic assimilation of refugee immigrants	616
3.3 The economic assimilation of refugees in the United States: evidence from census microdata	619
3.3.1 Characteristics of refugees and non-refugee migrants arriving in the United States 1975–80	621
3.3.2 Long-run labor market assimilation	626
3.3.3 Discussion	634
4. Impacts of Refugees on Sending and Receiving Communities	635
4.1 Impacts in host countries	635
4.1.1 Refugee camps	636
4.1.2 Resettlement	637
4.2 Impacts in sending countries	639
4.2.1 Departure of refugees	639
4.2.2 Return of refugees	640
5. Political Economy Issues	641
5.1 Asylum policies	641
5.1.1 Studies linking asylum policies of nations to economic concerns	642
5.1.2 Studies linking asylum policies of nations to external political concerns	644
5.1.3 The role of the UNHCR's policies in the asylum policies of nations	646

Handbook of the Economics of International Migration, Volume 1A
ISSN 2212-0092, http://dx.doi.org/10.1016/B978-0-444-53764-5.00012-8

    5.2 Modeling host countries' policy choices   647

       5.2.1 The role of other host nations   648

       5.2.2 The role of the UNHCR   649

       5.2.3 The role of the refugees   649

       5.2.4 The role of non-refugee migrants   650

       5.2.5 The role of administrators of the asylum policies of nations   650

6. Concluding Remarks   651

Acknowledgments   655

References   655

1. INTRODUCTION

1.1 Defining refugees and asylum seekers

The United Nations Convention Relating to the Status of Refugees, originating in 1951 and expanded in scope (beyond the post-World War II Cold War context) with the 1967 Protocol, provides the framework for the international regime of refugee protection. The Convention defines a refugee as a person who "owing to a well-founded fear of being persecuted for reasons of race, religion, nationality, membership of a particular social group, or political opinion, is outside the country of his nationality, and is unable to or, owing to such fear, is unwilling to avail himself of the protection of that country."[1] Additionally, international refugee law defines a refugee as someone who seeks refuge in a foreign country because of war and violence, or out of fear of persecution. Regarding the "refugee" and "asylum seeker" distinction, typically until an individual's request for refuge has been formally processed and approved by the host country, he or she is referred to as an asylum seeker. Asylum seekers whose applications are denied lose their legal basis for remaining in the host country and may be deported.

    The United Nations High Commission for Refugees (UNHCR), an agency of the United Nations (UN), protects and supports refugees at the request of a government or the UN, and assists in their return or resettlement. Currently, 145 nations are parties to the Convention, including all OECD countries. Since individual nations set their own asylum policies, there is variation among nations in the asylum application process, including where an asylum application may be filed (only in the host country, or outside it too), the allowable grounds for seeking asylum, and the standard of proof necessary to be recognized as a refugee.

    The United States, for example, recognizes persecution "on account of race, religion, nationality, political opinion, or membership in a particular social group" as grounds for seeking asylum.[2] The asylum and refugee process in the US takes place in two different

---

[1] Article 1.A.2. See United Nations High Commission for Refugees (2012) for the full text of the Convention.

[2] Section 101(a)(42) of the Immigration and Nationality Act.

agencies—the US Citizenship and Immigration Services (USCIS), which is located in the Department of Homeland Security, and the Executive Office for Immigration Review (EOIR), located in the Department of Justice. There are different administrative processes depending on where the application is filed. Asylum seekers located outside of the US typically need a referral to the US Refugee Admissions Program (USRAP), such as from the UNHCR, in order to be considered as a refugee. Individuals with referrals receive help filling out their application for refugee status and are then interviewed abroad by a USCIS officer who determines whether they are eligible for refugee resettlement. Individuals granted refugee status receive assistance traveling to the US, and upon entry in the US receive some training and benefits from the Office of Refugee Resettlement. On the other hand, asylum seekers located inside the US file applications for asylum status, which are handled by the EOIR through one of two distinct channels: affirmative process and defensive process.[3] The main difference between these two processes is that an affirmative process occurs through a USCIS asylum officer, whereas a defensive process occurs with an immigration judge as part of a removal hearing.

There is variation among countries not only in what the asylum application process entails, but also in what rights and benefits refugee status confers. However, two rights spelled out in the Convention—that refugees may not be penalized for entering or being in a country illegally, nor forcibly returned to the country where they face a well-founded fear of being persecuted—are common across signatory nations' asylum policies.

1.2 Trends in asylum and refugee applications: around the world and in the United States of America

In this section we provide a general portrait of the overall trends in applications for refugee and asylum status using data from the UNHCR and Yearbook of Immigration Statistics (YIS) from the US. The UNHCR collects extensive annual data on applications filed in the major industrialized countries of Europe, North America, and Australasia, and in some years such data include applications filed in non-industrialized countries. The YIS data is compiled by the Office of Immigration Statistics in the Department of Homeland Security, and provides annual data on applications filed in the US.

1.2.1 World trends

Figure 12.1 reveals a dramatic shift in asylum applications away from industrialized nations toward non-industrialized nations over the decade 1998–2000 to 2008–10. After declining during the 1990s, total asylum applications increased by 38.8% between the periods of 1998–2000 and 2008–10, to 2.2 million applications in the latter period.

---

[3] The affirmative asylum processing occurs with the USCIS, and the individual must be physically present in the US. If the individual is not granted asylum through the affirmative process then that individual may go through a defensive asylum process with EOIR.

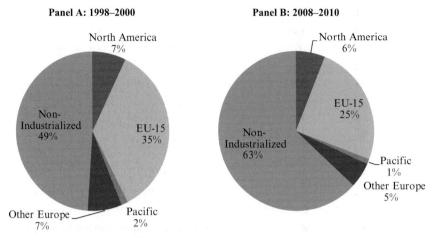

Figure 12.1 *Asylum applications by destination, percentage of world total.* Note: Total number of asylum applications for 1998–2000 and 2008–10 are 1,585,984 and 2,201,114, respectively. Source: *United Nations High Commissioner for Refugees (UNHCR), Statistical Yearbook, several volumes from 1998–2000 and 2008–10.*

The share of asylum applications filed in non-industrialized nations increased by 14 percentage points, from 49% to 63%. South Africa was most heavily impacted—its applications increased by a factor of almost 20 between the two periods, and in 2008–10, South Africa received 48.6% of all applications submitted to non-industrialized nations (after receiving only 4.5% in 1998–2000). Applications also surged in Ecuador by a factor of 45, in Ethiopia by a factor of 397, in Malaysia by a factor of 24, in Sudan by a factor of 17, and in Uganda by a factor of 11. Together, these six nations received 74% of all asylum applications submitted in non-industrialized nations in 2008–10, after receiving just 6.4% in 1998–2000.

The EU-15, the 15 member countries in the European Union (EU) prior to the 2004 enlargement of the EU,[4] experienced the largest declines in asylum applications between 1998–2000 and 2008–10. The number of applications fell by 24.7%, and the share of the world total decreased from 35% to 25%. The shares to other industrialized nations either decreased or remained flat over the decade. Overall, Figure 12.1 depicts a telling story: The median asylum seeker in the world today is seeking refuge in a developing country. This is a great contrast to six decades ago when the Convention was first established; then, western nations accounted for virtually all the refugees and asylum seekers.

Next, Figure 12.2 further illustrates that the variation in asylum applications submitted in industrialized nations from 1982 to 2010 is primarily a function of the variation in

---

[4] The EU-15 consists of Austria, Belgium, Denmark, Finland, France, Germany, Greece, Ireland, Italy, Luxembourg, Netherlands, Portugal, Spain, Sweden, and UK.

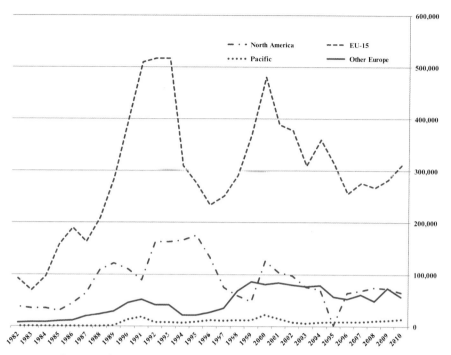

Figure 12.2 *Asylum applications by destination, 1982–2010.* Source: *United Nations High Commissioner for Refugees (UNHCR), Statistical Yearbook, several volumes from 1982 to 2010.*

applications received in the EU-15, which has accounted for more applications over the period than the other three regions—North America, Pacific, and non-EU-15 Europe—combined. An increase in asylum applications from 1988 to 1993 was primarily absorbed by EU-15 nations; North American, Pacific, and non-EU-15 nations all saw minor increases in the period. A second peak in applications from 2000 to 2001 was also mainly felt in the EU-15. Lastly, asylum applications in all four regions fell from 2001 to 2010, and while they fell more sharply in the EU than any other region, the EU continues to receive more applications than the other three regions combined.

In Table 12.1, we examine asylum applications in greater detail by destination country and time. This table shows the average annual asylum applications for 38 destination countries in five periods from 1982–97 to 2006–10. While the UNHCR tracks 38 industrialized nations in its asylum application statistics, 92.8% of all asylum applications submitted in industrialized nations from 1982 to 2010 were submitted in just 15 of those countries. Germany was the most popular destination for asylum seekers, receiving 22.7% of all applications over the period, followed by the US (15.6%) and France (11.1%).

Breaking the data up into four periods of six years each and one five-year period (2006–10) shows a rollercoaster trend, as each period alternates between increasing

Table 12.1 Asylum applications by destination country, 1982–2010

Asylum applications by destination	1982–87	1988–93	% change [(2) − (1)]/(1)	1994–99	% change [(3) − (2)]/(2)	2000–05	% change [(4) − (3)]/(3)	2006–10	% change [(5) − (4)]/(4)
	(1)	(2)		(3)		(4)		(5)	
Australia★	—	90,481	—	163,666	81%	176,407	8%	106,000	−40%
Austria★	86,867	269,711	210%	171,912	−36%	445,269	159%	218,824	−51%
Belgium★	55,363	126,350	128%	167,638	33%	231,677	38%	236,515	2%
Bulgaria	—	204	—	8605	4118%	32,853	282%	10,454	−68%
Canada★	144,866	402,970	178%	392,566	−3%	538,021	37%	342,102	−36%
Cyprus	—	—	—	3461	—	63,357	1731%	108,438	71%
Czech Rep.	—	10,815	—	47,215	337%	168,377	257%	35,249	−79%
Denmark★	61,249	73,845	21%	188,077	155%	111,707	−41%	28,763	−74%
Estonia	—	—	—	97	—	203	109%	295	45%
Finland	239	28,376	11,773%	18,669	−34%	44,884	140%	45,773	2%
France★	461,224	1,161,183	152%	478,146	−59%	1,368,480	186%	713,811	−48%
Germany★	792,463	3,653,494	361%	2,369,030	−35%	1,303,223	−45%	421,687	−68%
Greece★	22,723	44,828	97%	36,899	−18%	98,701	167%	271,086	175%
Hungary	—	16,359	—	54,519	233%	77,322	42%	41,854	−46%
Iceland	3	33	1000%	97	194%	1200	1137%	848	−29%
Ireland	—	213	—	38,080	17,778%	200,572	427%	81,228	−60%
Italy★	58,866	93,154	58%	78,245	−16%	199,872	155%	236,832	18%
Japan	1839	649	−65%	2433	275%	7674	215%	23,172	202%
Latvia	—	—	—	224	—	210	−6%	504	140%
Liechtenstein	—	—	—	1186	—	1518	28%	1404	−8%
Lithuania	—	—	—	1597	—	3248	103%	2865	−12%
Luxembourg	—	114	—	6834	5895%	19,502	185%	11,913	−39%
Malta	—	297	—	2151	624%	9,804	356%	23,643	141%
Netherlands★	73,389	427,873	483%	821,651	92%	571,750	−30%	185,588	−68%
New Zealand	27	8,019	29,600%	23,027	187%	24,746	7%	5,961	−76%

Norway★	23,392	117,574	403%	79,896	−32%	221,535	177%	249,499	13%
Poland	—	9573	—	40,426	322%	107,149	165%	123,880	16%
Portugal	8037	7914	−2%	5977	−24%	2,176	−64%	2,147	−1%
Rep. of Korea	—	—	—	215	—	1,254	483%	6,173	392%
Romania	—	500	—	17,053	—	18,111	6%	11,297	−38%
Slovakia	—	468	—	9251	1877%	126,413	1266%	18,659	−85%
Slovenia	—	—	—	3407	—	45,897	1247%	4182	−91%
Spain	22,539	131,071	482%	101,759	−22%	110,091	8%	58,511	−47%
Sweden★	94,495	542,181	474%	165,652	−69%	574,203	247%	522,212	−9%
Switzerland★	119,213	489,872	311%	513,057	5%	513,026	0%	215,233	−58%
Turkey	15,790	83,464	429%	80,171	−4%	71,642	−11%	140,187	96%
UK★	62,997	432,939	587%	772,155	78%	1,983,469	157%	521,253	−74%
US★	543,044	1,026,424	89%	1,611,312	57%	1,837,044	14%	837,247	−54%
Total	2,648,625	9,250,943	249%	8,476,356	−8%	11,312,587	33%	5,865,289	−48%
Top 15 total	2,600,151	8,952,873	244%	8,009,902	−11%	10,174,384	27%	5,106,652	−49%
Top 15% of all industrialized	**98%**	**97%**		**95%**		**90%**		**87%**	

The 15 industrialized nations receiving the most asylum applications during 1982–2010 ("Top 15") are marked with stars.

Source: United Nations High Commissioner for Refugees (UNHCR), Statistical Yearbook, several volumes from 1982 to 2010.

and decreasing applications. From the period of 1982–87 to the period of 1988–93, applications submitted to the top 15 industrialized destinations increased by 244%, but then decreased by 11% in the following period, 1994–99. The next period, 2000–05, saw a 27% increase among the top 15, but was followed by a steep 49% drop in the most recent period, 2006–10.

Considering the data on a nation-by-nation basis further reveals individual trends that at times go against the general trend. For example, while all nations participated in the significant increase between the first two periods (albeit disproportionately, e.g., Denmark's applications increased 21% while the UK's increased 587%), the overall decrease in applications from 1988–93 to 1994–99 was not seen in every nation. The third period reveals stark differences in trends, even among similar nations. In continental Europe, for example, applications in the third period declined in Austria, France, Germany, Italy, Norway, and Sweden, while rising in Belgium, Denmark, the Netherlands, and Switzerland. The UK and US also bucked the larger trend in the third period, seeing their application rates rise by 78% and 57% respectively.

In contrast, the 27% increase in the fourth period, 2000–05, was more broadly distributed amongst the top 15 nations. Eleven of the 15 countries saw increases, while Switzerland's application rate remained virtually unchanged, and Denmark, Germany and the Netherlands all saw decreases (for Germany, it was the second consecutive period of decline). The final period, 2006–10, was the virtual inverse of the fourth period, with 11 nations seeing decreases in their applications. Only Belgium (2% growth), Greece (175%), Italy (18%), and Norway (13%) received an increase in applications.

Overall, seven of the top 15 nations generally followed the trend of two periods of growth and two periods of decline, though they did not necessarily coincide with the broader, alternating trend of growth and decline. Austria, Canada, Denmark, France, Netherlands, Sweden, and Switzerland fall into this category. Germany was unique as the only nation to report one period of growth and three periods of decline; five nations (Greece, Italy, Norway, UK, and US) reported three periods of growth and one of decline. Belgium was the only nation to report growth in all periods, while Australia did not provide information for the initial period, and reported two periods of growth and one of decline.

1.2.2 Trends in the United States

Having described the overall trend in asylum applications around world, we turn next to the YIS data from the US, which allows us to look further back in time and examine specific source country information. Table 12.2 reveals that, from 1946 to 2000, the distribution of nations that sent the most refugees and asylees to the US shifted in reflection of global trends and regional conflicts. In the post-World War II years, the vast majority of those seeking refuge or asylum in the US came from European nations. Nine of the top 10 nations sending refugees and asylees to the US were from Europe in the periods

Table 12.2 Top ten refugee and asylee sending countries to the United States, 1946–2000

Top 10 countries	1946–50		% Total of all countries	1951–60		% Total of all countries	1961–70		% Total of all countries
1	Poland	78,529	37%	Poland	81,323	17%	Cuba	131,557	62%
2	Germany	36,633	17%	Germany	62,860	13%	Serbia and Montenegro[†]	18,299	9%
3	Latvia	21,422	10%	Italy	60,657	12%	Indonesia	7658	4%
4	Lithuania	18,694	9%	Hungary	55,740	11%	Romania	7158	3%
5	Soviet Union[‡]	14,072	7%	Serbia and Montenegro[†]	44,755	9%	Czechoslovakia*	5709	3%
6	Serbia and Montenegro[†]	9816	5%	Soviet Union[‡]	30,059	6%	Egypt	5396	3%
7	Czechoslovakia*	8449	4%	Greece	28,568	6%	China[§]	5308	2%
8	Estonia	7143	3%	Latvia	16,783	3%	Spain	4114	2%
9	Hungary	6086	3%	Netherlands	14,336	3%	Hungary	4044	2%
10	Austria	4801	2%	Romania	12,057	2%	Poland	3197	2%
Total for all countries		213,347	96%	Total for all countries	492,371	83%	Total for all countries	212,843	90%

Continued

Table 12.2 Top ten refugee and asylee sending countries to the United States, 1946–2000—cont'd

Top 10 countries	1971–80		% Total of all countries	1981–90		% Total of all countries	1991–2000		% Total of all countries
1	Cuba	251,514	47%	Vietnam	324,453	32%	Vietnam	206,857	20%
2	Vietnam	150,266	28%	Laos	142,964	14%	Cuba	144,612	14%
3	Soviet Union‡	31,309	6%	Cambodia	114,064	11%	Ukraine	109,739	11%
4	Laos	21,690	4%	Cuba	113,367	11%	Soviet Union‡	90,533	9%
5	China§	13,760	3%	Soviet Union‡	72,306	7%	Russia	60,404	6%
6	Serbia and Montenegro†	11,297	2%	Iran	46,773	5%	Bosnia-Herzegovina	37,591	4%
7	Cambodia	7739	1%	Poland	33,889	3%	Laos	37,265	4%
8	Iraq	6851	1%	Thailand	30,259	3%	Belarus	24,581	2%
9	Romania	6812	1%	Romania	29,798	3%	Iran	24,313	2%
10	Poland	5882	1%	Afghanistan	22,946	2%	Thailand	22,759	2%
Total for all countries		539,447	94%	Total for all countries	1,013,620	92%	Total for all countries	1,021,266	74%

Prior to 1982 the word asylum is not used in the Yearbook of Immigration Statistics, so no data were reported on asylum cases. Additionally, the method of counting refugees differs prior to 1981. Therefore, in order to construct a consistent data series over time, we use data on pre-1983 years that are reported in post-1983 YIS volumes that provided historical numbers. We do not include more recent years' data because in 2005, the Department of Homeland Security changed the way data on refugees and asylum seekers are reported.
* Prior to 1993, data include independent republics; beginning in 1993 data are for unknown republic only.
† Yugoslavia (unknown republic) prior to February 7, 2003. Prior to 1992, data include independent republics; beginning in 1992, data are for unknown republic only.
‡ Prior to 1992, data include independent republics; beginning in 1992 data are for unknown republic only.
§ Includes People's Republic of China and Taiwan.
Source: Several volumes of the Yearbook of Immigration Statistics (YIS), Immigration and Naturalization Service (INS), 1978–2000, Table 32.

1946–50 and 1951–60, with Poland and Germany ranking first and second respectively in each period. The lone non-European nation in both periods was the Soviet Union, which ranked fifth in 1946–50 and sixth in 1951–60.

The first major shift in incoming refugee and asylee patterns occurred from 1961 to 1970, when Cuba debuted at the top of the list, accounting for almost 62% of all refugees and asylees entering the US. Indonesia (third), Egypt (sixth), and China (seventh) also appeared on the list for the first time, while European nations, led by Serbia and Montenegro (second), held the remaining six spots. The 1970s saw another shift in the pattern. Though Cuba remained the clear number one from 1971 to 1980, accounting for almost 47% of refugees and asylees entering the US, Asia accounted for four nations (Vietnam, Laos, China, and Cambodia), while Iraq appeared on the list, the Soviet Union returned after being absent in the 1960s, and the number of European nations on the top 10 list dwindled to three. The distribution of incoming refugees and asylees continued to shift to Asia in the 1980s, as Vietnam, Laos, and Cambodia accounted for the top three spots respectively and, along with Thailand (eighth), accounted for 60% of incoming refugees and asylees. European nations held just two spots on the list from 1981 to 1990, while Cuba (fourth), the Soviet Union (fifth), Iran (sixth), and Afghanistan (tenth) rounded out the list.

Incoming refugees and asylees in the 1990s were much more diverse. While the top 10 nations of origin accounted for between 83% and 96% of all incoming refugees and asylees in each of the previous periods, from 1991 to 2000 the top 10 only accounted for 74%. Familiar nations Vietnam and Cuba ranked first and second respectively, and Laos (seventh), Iran (ninth), and Thailand (tenth) were also on the list. In the 1991–2000 period there was a big increase in immigration from countries from the former Soviet Union. The Soviet Union, despite being counted as a nation of origin during that time period only in 1991, still ranked fourth on the list. Three nations on the list are former Soviet republics that began being reported as a country of origin only after 1991: Ukraine (third), Russia (fifth), and Belarus (eighth).

Lastly, Figure 12.3 shows the trends in the US of processed refugee and asylum applications (panel A) and percentage of applications denied (panel B).[5] It is apparent from Figure 12.3A that the majority of applications processed in the US primarily come from those individuals seeking refugee status (which, as mentioned in Section 1.1, are filed abroad) and to a lesser extent asylum (filed in the US). From 1980 to 1985, for example, the average number of processed applications for individuals seeking refugee status was over half a million (608,730) applications in this five-year interval, compared with only

---

[5] In order to make the data series in Figure 12.3A consistent across time for both refugees and asylees, we define "processed" applications as those individuals whose applications were either *approved* or *denied* in a given fiscal year; this definition excludes those applications that are pending, or have decisions other than approved or denied (e.g., adjusted, closed). The data series shown in Figure 12.3B for both refugees and asylees is defined as the total number of denied processed applications divided by the total number of processed applications for each subgroup.

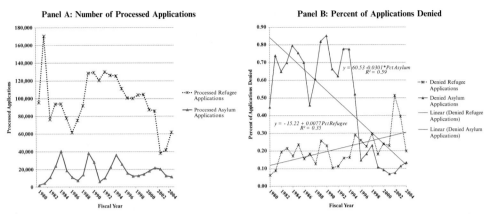

Figure 12.3 *Refugee and asylum applications in the US, 1980–2004.* Source: *Several volumes of the Yearbook of Immigration Statistics (YIS), Immigration and Naturalization Service (INS), 1980–2005, Table 32.*

101,090 processed applications for individual seeking for asylum. The number of processed applications for refugee status hovered around 120,000 per year from 1989 to 1994, but declined slightly to less than 90,000 per year from 2000 to 2004. By contrast, processed applications for those seeking asylee status never exceeded 40,000 applications per year during the entire period from 1980 to 2004.

In Figure 12.3B, we report the percentage of applications denied for each subgroup. Though yearly denial rates of the two groups are highly volatile, refugees seem to have become less likely to be granted entrance while asylees have become more likely over time. In 1980, for example, an asylum application was seven times more likely than a refugee application to be denied; however, by 2004 the positions had reversed. In 1980, only 6.4% of refugee applications to enter the US were denied. Though the number shot up to 21.6% by 1983, the average denial rate for refugees over the five-year period from 1980 to 1984 was only 14.7%. By 2002, a record proportion of 51.5% of refugee applications were denied; though the denial rate fell in 2003 and 2004, the average for the five-year period from 2000 to 2004 was 31.6%—more than double the five-year average from 20 years earlier.

Thus, while refugee application denials were on the rise from 1980 to 2004, the denial rate of asylum applications dropped precipitously in 1996 and remained low in the following years. In 1980, an asylum application had a 44.8% chance of being denied; from 1980 to 1995, the average asylum application denial rate was 68.1%. But in 1996, the denial rate plummeted to 14.8% and remained relatively low from 1996 to 2004.

2. WHO MIGRATES? COMPARING REFUGEES TO OTHER MIGRANTS

2.1 Conceptual framework: the migration decision

In this section we present a simple model to illustrate how refugees might differ from other migrants in quantity and quality. Consider an individual *i* who is in country

0 deciding whether to migrate to country 1. Denote w_{i0}, w_{i1}, and C_{i01} as individual i's wages in country 0, wages in country 1, and direct migration costs between countries, respectively. An income maximizing agent—such as that modeled by Borjas (1987, 1999)—will migrate if the income from migrating net of migration costs exceeds the income from staying, i.e., defining $P^I \equiv I[(w_{i1} - C_{i01}) - w_{i0}]$ where $I()$ is the index function, then an individual will migrate if $P^I > 0$. We obtain the following comparative statics:

$$\frac{\partial P^I}{\partial w_{i1}} > 0 \tag{12.1}$$

$$\frac{\partial P^I}{\partial w_{i0}} < 0 \tag{12.2}$$

$$\frac{\partial P^I}{\partial C_{i01}} < 0 \tag{12.3}$$

That is, when the individual's country 1 wages increase, or country 0 wages decrease, or migration costs decrease, the individual is more likely to migrate.

Of course individuals are motivated by more than economic considerations when deciding whether to migrate. Following Jasso and Rosenzweig (2009), we also include a term capturing the amenities associated with residing in a particular country.[6] Jasso and Rosenzweig gave as examples of amenities the utility gain of living in the same country as one's spouse, or the utility loss of living in a place with a foreign culture. Another example, given our focus on refugees and asylum seekers, is utility loss associated with being persecuted or living under the threat of persecution. Let A_{i0} and A_{i1} denote the amenities for individual i of residing in country 0 and country 1 respectively. A utility maximizing agent will migrate if the utility from migrating net of migration costs exceeds the utility from staying, i.e., defining $P^U \equiv I[V_{i1} - V_{i0}]$ where $I()$ is the index function, $V_{i1} \equiv \beta_1 \cdot A_{i1} + \beta_2 \cdot (w_{i1} - C_{i01})$, $V_{i0} \equiv \beta_1 \cdot A_{i0} + \beta_2 \cdot w_{i0}$, and β_1 and β_2 are non-negative constants, then an individual will migrate if $P^U > 0$.

As with the income-maximizing model, this more general model predicts that the probability of migration is increasing in destination-country wages, and decreasing in source-country wages and migration costs. We also derive the following two additional results with the utility-maximizing model:

$$\frac{\partial P^U}{\partial A_{i1}} > 0 \tag{12.4}$$

[6] We could have stayed with the income maximization framework and encapsulated these amenities into the cost term as in Borjas (1987, 1999), but we wanted to make these non-economic aspects of migration more explicit.

$$\frac{\partial P^U}{\partial A_{i0}} < 0 \tag{12.5}$$

That is, when the individual's country 1 amenities increase or country 0 amenities decrease, then the individual is more likely to migrate.

What does the utility-maximizing model imply for the characteristics of refugees relative to other categories of migrants? It is instructive to look at the variables in turn:

- A_{i0}. The key defining feature of refugees and asylum seekers is that they perceive it to be unsafe to live in country 0—staying there exposes them to serious harm, such as from violent conflict, natural disaster, or persecution. In terms of the model, refugees have an extra disamenity to living in country 0 (i.e., their A_{i0} is lower, and perhaps highly negative), and this may dwarf all other elements entering the migration decision. Thus, individuals in countries with a refugee-producing event will have higher emigration rates. We can also say something about the selectivity of migrants when there is a refugee-producing event relative to when there is only "regular" migration. Imagine a set of individuals who are identical in all ways except in their wage gain from migrating (denoted as $g \equiv w_{i1} - w_{i0}$), then there is some wage gain $\tilde{g}$ above which everyone migrates and below which everyone stays. A decrease in A_{i0} would bring some people with $g < \tilde{g}$ across the threshold to migrate. Thus, comparing refugees, who tend to have lower A_{i0}, to other migrant types, g is less, and it is even possible that it is negative. In other words, because economic gain is less of a factor in the migration decisions of refugees, then refugees will also be less selected along dimensions that are associated with economic gain in country 1. For example, consider a natural disaster, then everyone in the country might be displaced, and there is no selection at all. Or, consider a narrower refugee-producing event, such as persecution of political dissenters, then more emigrants will have attributes that are correlated with being a political dissenter, which are not necessarily the same as attributes that are positively associated with economic gain.

- w_{i0}. Low wages at home are a push factor that sends any migrant, including refugees, to look abroad for better earnings opportunities. We might expect that non-refugees' migration decision would be vastly more sensitive to w_{i0} because they care more about the wage gain from migration, $g \equiv w_{i1} - w_{i0}$. However, a refugee-producing event might itself lead to a decline in w_{i0}, in which case it is refugees who appear more likely to migrate when w_{i0} is low. In the case of a refugee-producing event that decreases wages broadly across the population, we would expect that the marginal migrant to be less selected than in a situation without a refugee-producing event.[7] In the case where

---

[7] If everybody's wages in the country are lowered by some constant, and none of the other variables change, then the emigration rate will rise, with the extra immigrants coming from people previously with an insufficiently small wage gain to justify migrating who now have a sufficiently large wage gain because of the fall in w_{i0}.

wages decrease only for a subset of the population, for example political dissenters losing government jobs, then it is the migration of this subpopulation that would increase.

- A_{i1} and w_{i1}. The pull factors of higher amenities and higher wages in the destination country are expected to play a more pivotal role for non-refugees. For example, family preference migrants might have only one desired destination (e.g., where their spouse is located; for spouse reunifications, A_{i1} is large and positive, and might dwarf other terms in the utility maximization equation). Economic migrants might be especially drawn to the net economic gain, and would choose destinations with higher w_{i1}. Because things like having a common language or culture, or having social connections, increase the economic gain (e.g., Munshi, 2003; Bleakley and Chin, 2004), destination countries most desired by economic migrants might also have a higher A_{i1}. For refugees, even countries offering a low or negative w_{i1} and A_{i1} could be feasible destinations, because the push factor of negative A_{i0} could still make $P^U > 0$, thus there exists a wider set of countries that could serve as feasible destination countries for refugees compared to other types of migrants. There may perhaps be little difference in what are the top choices for destinations across the migrant categories—the US, Canada, Australia, and western European countries are highly desired. However, due to developed countries' restrictive immigration policies, potential migrants often must move down their lists of feasible destinations. For non-refugee migration candidates, the list may consist only of the developed countries, so they may end up staying in country 0 because the best country to which they are able to legally migrate does not satisfy $P^U > 0$. For refugee migration candidates, there is a higher chance of emigration because more countries are feasible. Consistent with this prediction, we saw in Section 1 that many refugees migrate to non-industrialized countries, which often are neighboring countries whose economic opportunities and amenities do not differ much, but which have less immigration restrictions than developed countries and still provide a safer environment.

- C_{i01}. While physical costs of traveling from country 0 and country 1 may be identical among individuals within a country, several notes are worth making. First, as in Borjas (1987), we might also include the time cost of migrating, which would imply higher migration costs for people with higher w_{i0}. If w_{i0} is lower for individuals affected by a refugee-producing event as discussed above, then C_{i01} is also lower, and both w_{i0} and C_{i01} will push these individuals towards higher emigration rates. Second, it may be that there are credit constraints, and some individuals for whom $P^U > 0$ cannot afford the upfront outlay of C_{i01}, because of lack of wealth or ability to borrow money. Then migrants will be positively selected on the basis of wealth and ability to borrow. Candidates for asylum might be less able to afford high migration costs because their assets may have been lost or confiscated, and the social network from whom they could normally borrow might be in a similar plight or be estranged from them, so this might make refugees less able to migrate to destinations entailing higher migration costs. The developed countries are often costlier to enter—not only do they tend to be more distant spatially, but also they tend to have immigration restrictions which require a cumbersome application process or people smugglers to circumvent. Thus, unless humanitarian assistance is used to defray some of the refugees' migration costs, then the refugees who enter developed countries might be positively selected on wealth, and poorer refugee candidates might end up in neighboring countries or the countries to which transportation is provided.

The above discussion highlights that refugees and asylum seekers might be expected to be primarily motivated by push factors, and consequently will tend to be less choosy about the destination country's attributes. For a refugee-producing event that affects country 0's population broadly, resultant migrants will tend to be less selected along dimensions that are associated with wage gain relative to economic migrants. For a refugee-producing event that only affects a subpopulation of country 0, resultant migrants will mirror that subpopulation's characteristics, which may lead to more or less selection along dimensions that are associated with wage gain. All in all, although the model unambiguously predicts an increase in the quantity of refugees originating from country 0 when country 0 experiences a refugee-producing event, it has an ambiguous prediction for the quality of refugees relative to other types of migrants—the relative quality depends on a number of variables, including the nature of the refugee-producing event and the nature of selection in "regular" migration flows from country 0 to country 1.

2.2 Previous work comparing refugees to other migrants

In large, nationally representative individual-level datasets commonly used by social scientists, refugee status is typically not measured, making it difficult to empirically investigate who refugees are, and how they compare to other migrants and natives. For a handful of countries, researchers have been able to link broad socio-economic microdatasets to administrative data on visa type, including Sweden (e.g., Edin et al., 2003), Denmark (e.g., Damm, 2009a), Canada (e.g., Wanner, 2003), and Australia (e.g., Chiswick et al., 2006), enabling the identification of refugees. In the US, the New Immigrant Survey-2003 (NIS) contains socio-economic survey data linked with administrative data on visa type. The NIS provides a representative sample of individuals gaining legal permanent residence in the US in 2003. Akresh (2008) and Connor (2010) used NIS data to compare refugees and other immigrants, and we extend the analysis for a broader set of demographic, health, and labor market characteristics below in Section 2.3.

In the absence of large-scale microdatasets directly measuring refugee status, researchers have pursued one of two approaches for empirical analyses of refugees, either doing original data collection to ensure getting all the desired variables such as refugee status, or using existing large-scale general-purpose datasets but using an indirect measure of refugee status. Studies using the first approach have tended to focus on specific refugee groups and geographic areas in order to make the data collection feasible. For example, a number of studies have focused on the experiences of refugees from Southeast Asia who reside in San Diego County, California (e.g., Rumbaut, 1989; Rumbaut and Ima, 1998), and of refugees from Cuba and the Caribbean who reside in South Florida (e.g., Portes and Stepick, 1985). Studies using the second approach use information about an individual's country of birth and year of arrival in the US to identify a set of individuals who are likely to be refugees in the microdataset (e.g., Cortes, 2004; Bollinger and Hagstrom, 2008, 2011). Even with the arrival of the NIS data, these two approaches will continue to be used because the NIS is limited to a single cohort of migrants receiving their green cards, and thus far follows these migrants up to 6 years afterwards. Thus, in order to learn about other waves of refugees and how refugees adjust over time in the U.S., researchers must turn to other data sources.

2.3 Refugees in the United States: a snapshot from the New Immigrant Survey

To describe refugees in the US, and compare them to other categories of US migrants, we use data from the New Immigrant Survey-2003 (NIS) (Jasso et al., 2006). The NIS is a representative sample of adults who became legal permanent residents of the US between May and November 2003. A total of 8573 adult immigrants were interviewed shortly after permanent residency was granted, between June 2003 and June 2004. To our knowledge the NIS is the only large, broad US microdataset measuring refugee status. In fact, the NIS contains official administrative data (from the US Citizenship and Immigration Service) on each respondent's immigrant class of admission, and we refer to those with "refugees/ asylees/parolees" as their class of admission as refugees.[8] We compare these refugees to immigrants in the other classes of admission.[9] On a weighted basis, refugees account for 6.6% of the sample, family preference immigrants for 67.7%, employment preference immigrants for 9.6%, diversity immigrants for 8.1%, and legalization immigrants for 8.0%.

2.3.1 Exposure to persecution

The most striking difference between refugees and non-refugees is in their exposure to persecution prior to migration to the US. To the question, "Did you or your immediate family ever suffer any harm outside of the US because of your political or religious beliefs, or your race, ethnicity or gender?", 47% of refugees said yes, compared to 4% of non-refugees. Among those refugees responding affirmatively, the frequency of specific types of persecution experienced by the respondent or immediate family was as follows: 39%

---

[8] Parolees are individuals who do not qualify for admission as a refugee or asylee, but gain admission because it is in the public interest, or because of humanitarian reasons.

[9] Because the NIS oversamples less common classes of admission, we always use sampling weights provided by the NIS in order to obtain statistics that are representative of the 2003 cohort of legal permanent residents.

reported incarceration, 46% physical punishment by public officials, 41% physical punishment by others, 31% property confiscation, 48% property damage, 59% loss of job, and 92% verbal or written threats. Refugees who reported any persecution on average experienced 3.5 types out of the aforementioned seven types. The finding of significantly higher pre-migration exposure to persecution for refugees should not be surprising considering persecution and threat of persecution form the basis of admission to the US as a refugee, and supports the premise of our conceptual model described in Section 2.1— that is, refugees face a larger push factor to migrate (i.e., an extra disamenity of residing in their home country).

2.3.2 Demographic, human capital, and labor market characteristics

In Table 12.3, we compare the country of birth composition of refugees and non-refugees. Using the country/region of birth codes provided in the public-use version of the NIS, we list the countries/regions that account for at least 2% of the refugees in the sample. These 12 countries/regions together make up 95% of all refugees in

Table 12.3 Refugees and non-refugees by country of birth, New Immigrant Survey-2003

	Country/Region	% of refugees	% of non-refugees	% of all migrants
1	Europe and Central Asia NEC	20.5	7.7	8.5
2	Cuba	18.3	0.6	1.8
3	Sub-Saharan Africa NEC	10.5	3.3	3.8
4	Middle East and North Africa	8.7	4.2	4.5
5	Ukraine	8.0	0.8	1.3
6	Russia	7.2	0.9	1.3
7	Haiti	6.3	1.7	2.0
8	India	3.7	7.6	7.3
9	East Asia, South Asia and the Pacific NEC	3.6	6.7	6.5
10	Ethiopia	3.3	1.2	1.3
11	Vietnam	2.5	3.1	3.1
12	People's Republic of China	2.3	5.5	5.3
	Total for top 12 refugee-sending countries	**94.9**	**43.2**	**46.6**
	All other countries with ≥1 refugee	5.1	33.7	31.8
	Total for refugee-sending countries	**100.0**	**76.9**	**78.4**
	All other countries with ≥1 non-refugee	0.0	23.1	21.6
	Total for all countries	**100.0**	**100.0**	**100.0**

Data are from the New Immigrant Survey-2003 Adult Sample, and sample weights are used to obtain the statistics reported above. In the public-use version of the data that we use, specific country of origin is provided only for countries with sufficiently many respondents, otherwise only the region of origin is reported. The countries listed out separately are Canada, People's Republic of China, Colombia, Cuba, El Salvador, Ethiopia, Guatemala, Haiti, India, Jamaica, Korea, Mexico, Nigeria, Peru, Philippines, Poland, Russia, Ukraine, UK, and Vietnam, so migrants not from these countries are placed in the residual region groups ("NEC" denotes not classified elsewhere).

the sample, but only 43% of all non-refugees. Refugees in the sample originated from a small set of countries: Cuba, Haiti, Russia, Ukraine, Bosnia-Herzegovina (within the Europe and Central Asia NEC category), Somalia (within the sub-Saharan Africa NEC category), Ethiopia, India, Vietnam, and China. These countries of origin based on the 2003 cohort receiving green cards mirror those shown for refugees arriving in the US in 1991–2000 depicted in Table 12.3, which makes sense because it takes several years of residence in the US before the bureaucratic process for becoming legal permanent resident can be completed. The non-refugees come from a wider array of countries, with one-fifth coming from Mexico (only 0.25% of refugees were born in Mexico). These differences in country of birth distribution by refugee status explain some, but certainly not all, of the differences in socio-economic characteristics by refugee status, as we discuss below.

Table 12.4 displays the results for basic demographic characteristics. On average, refugees are 1.5 years older than non-refugees at the time of the survey. However, the variance in age is lower for refugees, reflecting the fact that non-refugees include many parents admitted under family preference mixed together with economic migrants who have most of their working lives ahead of them. Also, males account for a significantly higher share of refugees relative to all other migrants, but this gender difference ceases to be significant at conventional levels if we remove the immigrants whose class of admission is spouse of a US citizen or legal permanent resident (two-thirds of whom are women). Refugees are also less likely to be married and more likely to have children, with the gap reflecting the higher share of refugees who are either divorced or living together in a marriage-like relationship.

Table 12.5 shows the education and English proficiency measures. Relative to all other migrants, refugees have completed more years of schooling, though the difference is not significant at the 5% level.[10] Underlying this weak positive difference in average years of schooling is a higher high school completion rate (significant at the 1% level) and a lower bachelor's degree completion rate (not significant at conventional levels; p-value is 11%) for refugees relative to non-refugees. Thus, refugees fall in the middle of the distribution of educational attainment among US immigrants, which has grown increasingly bimodal—the US attracts and admits both low-skilled and very highly skilled immigrants. Refugees are clearly more educated than the family preference immigrants, whose characteristics mirror those of immigrants already in the US (who are their sponsors for migration under the family preference classes of admission), and who likely have strong

---

[10] We focus on years of schooling reported at the time of the survey here, but findings are similar when we use years of schooling received in the home country. While schooling received in the home country does technically measure human capital prior to migration to the US, it can be noted that some people with high ability may migrate to the US specifically to further their education, in which case their measured years of schooling in the home country would understate their underlying quality.

Table 12.4 Basic demographic characteristics of new US permanent residents by class of admission, New Immigrant Survey-2003

	Refugees	All non-refugees		Specific category of non-refugee					
				Family		Employment		Diversity	
	Mean (s.d.)	Mean (s.d.)	Difference vs. refugees (p-value)	Mean (s.d.)	Diff (p-val)	Mean (s.d.)	Diff (p-val)	Mean (s.d.)	Diff (p-val)
	(1)	(2)	(3)	(4)	(5)	(6)	(7)	(8)	(9)
Age	40.60	39.09	1.51	40.03	0.57	37.13	3.48	34.03	6.57
	(11.804)	(13.868)	(0.005)	(15.115)	(0.310)	(8.370)	(<0.001)	(9.462)	(<0.001)
Male	0.51	0.43	0.08	0.40	0.12	0.51	0.01	0.56	−0.05
	(0.500)	(0.495)	(<0.001)	(0.489)	(<0.001)	(0.500)	(0.751)	(0.496)	(0.062)
Married	0.65	0.75	−0.10	0.77	−0.11	0.82	−0.17	0.67	−0.02
	(0.477)	(0.435)	(<0.001)	(0.424)	(<0.001)	(0.380)	(<0.001)	(0.469)	(0.359)
Has children	0.77	0.70	0.07	0.71	0.06	0.66	0.10	0.52	0.25
	(0.424)	(0.460)	(<0.001)	(0.454)	(0.004)	(0.473)	(<0.001)	(0.500)	(<0.001)
Adjustee (not new arrival)	1.00	0.54	0.46	0.52	0.48	0.71	0.29	0.08	0.92
	(0.000)	(0.498)	(<0.001)	(0.500)	(<0.001)	(0.452)	(<0.001)	(0.271)	(<0.001)
Years since migrating to US	6.40	5.37	1.02	4.53	1.87	5.89	0.51	1.06	5.34
	(4.355)	(6.564)	(<0.001)	(6.143)	(<0.001)	(4.475)	(0.029)	(2.356)	(<0.001)
Observations	554	8019		4234		1673		1451	

Data are from the New Immigrant Survey-2003 Adult Sample, and sample weights are used to obtain the statistics reported above. The *p*-value reported in the odd-numbered columns in columns (3)–(9) is associated with the null hypothesis that the difference between the group named in the column heading and the refugees is zero; robust standard errors are used. The number of observations reported in the bottom row gives the total individuals in the class of admission interviewed by the NIS, and the actual number of observations used for calculating a given variable's statistics may be slightly less due to missing values for that variable.

Table 12.5 Education and English proficiency characteristics of new US permanent residents by class of admission, New Immigrant Survey-2003

	Refugees	All non-refugees		Specific category of non-refugee					
				Family		Employment		Diversity	
	Mean (s.d.)	Mean (s.d.)	Difference vs. refugees (p-value)	Mean (s.d.)	Diff (p-val)	Mean (s.d.)	Diff (p-val)	Mean (s.d.)	Diff (p-val)
	(1)	(2)	(3)	(4)	(5)	(6)	(7)	(8)	(9)
Years of schooling upon arrival to US	11.66 (4.400)	11.28 (5.057)	0.38 (0.057)	10.85 (4.973)	0.80 (<0.001)	15.08 (3.626)	−3.42 (<0.001)	14.32 (3.141)	−2.66 (<0.001)
Years of schooling completed	12.36 (4.442)	12.11 (4.954)	0.26 (0.207)	11.65 (4.900)	0.71 (0.001)	16.02 (3.675)	−3.65 (<0.001)	14.56 (3.267)	−2.20 (<0.001)
Completed high school degree or higher	0.69 (0.463)	0.64 (0.481)	0.05 (0.009)	0.60 (0.489)	0.09 (<0.001)	0.91 (0.289)	−0.22 (<0.001)	0.89 (0.315)	−0.20 (<0.001)
Completed B.A. or higher	0.25 (0.432)	0.28 (0.449)	−0.03 (0.110)	0.24 (0.425)	0.01 (0.597)	0.66 (0.474)	−0.41 (<0.001)	0.41 (0.492)	−0.16 (<0.001)
Speaks English very well	0.15 (0.357)	0.22 (0.413)	−0.07 (<0.001)	0.19 (0.396)	−0.04 (0.010)	0.49 (0.500)	−0.34 (<0.001)	0.19 (0.396)	−0.04 (0.024)
Speaks English well or very well	0.49 (0.500)	0.48 (0.499)	0.01 (0.596)	0.43 (0.496)	0.05 (0.021)	0.82 (0.381)	−0.34 (<0.001)	0.50 (0.500)	−0.02 (0.534)
Currently enrolled in an English class	0.16 (0.371)	0.13 (0.339)	0.03 (0.058)	0.14 (0.348)	0.02 (0.185)	0.05 (0.214)	0.12 (<0.001)	0.21 (0.404)	−0.04 (0.040)
Currently enrolled in school (besides for English class)	0.14 (0.348)	0.09 (0.286)	0.05 (0.001)	0.10 (0.294)	0.05 (0.004)	0.08 (0.267)	0.06 (<0.001)	0.07 (0.261)	0.07 (<0.001)

Data are from the New Immigrant Survey-2003 Adult Sample, and sample weights are used to obtain the statistics reported above. The *p*-value reported in the odd-numbered columns in columns (3)–(9) is associated with the null hypothesis that the difference between the group named in the column heading and the refugees is zero; robust standard errors are used.

motivations for migration besides just economic gain (e.g., reunification with a spouse or other relatives). However, refugees are clearly less educated than the employment preference and diversity immigrants, two classes of admission that can be plausibly characterized as economic migrants, and that have explicit qualifications in terms of education and skill level. However, some catch-up between refugees and economic migrants can be expected with more time in the US, as Table 12.5 shows refugees are significantly more likely to enroll in school (last row). Refugees in the NIS are primarily enrolling in associate's degree programs (38% of enrolled refugees reporting a specific level of schooling), bachelor's degree programs (23%), and master's programs (12%).

For English proficiency, refugees are less likely to report speaking English very well (as opposed to not at all, not well, or well), though no different in ability to speak English well or very well. This observed difference likely understates the refugees' disadvantage in English proficiency upon arrival in the US, however, because English proficiency at the time of the survey is measured, and refugees have lived in the US about a year longer relative to all other migrants (last row of Table 12.4). Although all immigrants in the NIS are part of the 2003 cohort of legal permanent residents, many of them entered the US prior to 2003. Only 43% of the overall sample are new arrivals to the US, entering the US simultaneously with being granted the green card. The rest are "adjustees" (adjusted from a temporary non-immigrant visa to the green card); all refugees, and 54% of non-refugees, are adjustees (second to last row of Table 12.3). Relative to non-refugee adjustees (who average 8.8 years since arrival in the US) and employment preference immigrants (5.9 years), refugees (6.4 years) have significantly lower English proficiency; for example, refugees are 8.4 percentage points less likely than other adjustees and 33.6 percentage points less likely than employment preference immigrants to speak English well or very well. Based on questions asked to a subsample, we find that refugees' pre-migration exposure to English media (newspapers, magazines, television, videos, movies, radio) is significantly lower. This is consistent with other migrants preparing for life in the US, or being positively selected on English skills, more than refugees. However, considering that refugees are more likely to enroll in English-language classes than other migrants (second to last row of Table 12.5), some catch-up can be expected over time in the US.

For another measure of human capital—health—refugees also look worse than other migrants. In fact, among all the classes of admission, refugees look the worst; they do not lie in the middle of the distribution as for schooling. Table 12.6 (panel A) shows that refugees are significantly more likely to report being in poor or fair health, rather than good, very good, or excellent health, at the time of the survey. They are also significantly more likely to report being diagnosed with a heart problem, high blood pressure, diabetes and psychological problems, among other things, and conditional on the diagnosis the conditions are reported to be more severe in terms of limiting daily activity. Additionally, 18% of refugees report being "troubled with pain" (compared to 9% for other migrants)

Table 12.6 Health and labor market characteristics of new US permanent residents by class of admission, New Immigrant Survey-2003

Panel A. Health characteristics

	Refugees Mean (s.d.) (1)	All non-refugees Mean (s.d.) (2)	All non-refugees Difference vs. refugees (p-value) (3)
In "poor" or "fair" health	0.17 (0.374)	0.09 (0.290)	0.08 (<0.001)
Reports being "troubled with pain"	0.18 (0.388)	0.09 (0.292)	0.09 (<0.001)
Reports having recent depression spell of ≥2 weeks	0.17 (0.375)	0.13 (0.338)	0.04 (0.028)
Diagnosed with high blood pressure	0.14 (0.346)	0.09 (0.291)	0.05 (0.003)
Diagnosed with heart problem	0.04 (0.198)	0.02 (0.123)	0.03 (0.004)
Diagnosed with psychological problem	0.04 (0.190)	0.02 (0.137)	0.02 (0.034)
Diagnosed with asthma	0.04 (0.186)	0.03 (0.163)	0.01 (0.320)
Height (cm)	167.81 (9.306)	165.58 (9.560)	2.24 (<0.001)

Panel B. Labor market characteristics

	Refugees Mean (s.d.) (4)	All non-refugees Mean (s.d.) (5)	All non-refugees Difference vs. refugees (p-value) (6)
Ever worked before migrating to U.S.	0.58 (0.494)	0.57 (0.495)	0.01 (0.646)
Conditional on working before, worked for a government	0.62 (0.487)	0.25 (0.430)	0.37 (<0.001)
Conditional on working before, typical hours worked per week	43.36 (11.665)	43.37 (12.153)	−0.01 (0.989)
Ever worked since migrating to US	0.84 (0.365)	0.59 (0.493)	0.26 (<0.001)
Conditional on working since migrating, first job's typical weekly pay	339 (231)	448 (412)	−109 (<0.001)
Conditional on working since migrating, first job's typical weekly pay, males	344 (171)	496 (457)	−152 (<0.001)
Currently working	0.74 (0.438)	0.54 (0.499)	0.21 (<0.001)
Conditional on currently working, current weekly pay	451 (269)	598 (500)	−147 (<0.001)

Continued

Table 12.6 Health and labor market characteristics of new US permanent residents by class of admission, New Immigrant Survey-2003—cont'd

	Refugees	All non-refugees			Refugees	All non-refugees	
	Mean (s.d.)	Mean (s.d.)	Difference vs. refugees (p-value)		Mean (s.d.)	Mean (s.d.)	Difference vs. refugees (p-value)
	(1)	(2)	(3)		(4)	(5)	(6)
Body mass index (BMI)	25.79 (4.056)	24.87 (4.233)	0.93 (<0.001)	Conditional on currently working, current weekly pay, males	471 (214)	681 (546)	−210 (<0.001)
Overweight (BMI ≥25)	0.55 (0.498)	0.44 (0.497)	0.11 (<0.001)	Conditional on currently working, primary job is a salaried position	0.20 (0.402)	0.30 (0.457)	−0.09 (<0.001)
Obese (BMI ≥30)	0.17 (0.377)	0.11 (0.311)	0.06 (0.001)	Conditional on currently working, primary job is for a government	0.11 (0.310)	0.05 (0.226)	0.05 (0.002)
				Conditional on currently working, primary job's typical weekly hours	40.17 (10.242)	40.65 (10.438)	−0.48 (0.525)

Data are from the New Immigrant Survey–2003 Adult Sample, and sample weights are used to obtain the statistics reported above. The p-value reported in columns (3) and (6) is associated with the null hypothesis that the difference between refugees and non-refugees is zero; robust standard errors are used.

and 17% report a recent spell of depression of at least two weeks (compared to 13% for other migrants). However, there are no significant differences in asthma diagnosis, quality of eyesight and quality of hearing, so it does not appear to be true that refugees' poorer reported health is entirely attributable to refugees systematically interpreting the health questions differently or having more diagnosed conditions because they are more likely to have visited doctors in the US (refugees are temporarily eligible for federally funded health care via the Refugees Medical Assistance program). Besides, measures of health based on weight and height, which can be measured more objectively, also indicate worse health for refugees: refugees have significantly higher body mass index (BMI), overweight rates, and obesity rates. Refugees' worse health status is likely in part an outcome of the refugee-producing event that they faced—the persecution or threat of persecution could have caused physical pain, emotional suffering, and intense stress. Another possible explanation for their worse health relative to other classes of admission is that refugees have worse underlying health irrespective of the refugee-producing event. Refugees appear less positively selected on health relative to other migrants, and especially relative to employment preference and diversity immigrants. This mirrors what we found for education and English proficiency.

Next, Table 12.6 (panel B) compares refugee and non-refugee labor market measures. A summary of the results is that refugees' labor supply is not lower compared to other migrants, but they are observed to have lower pay and lower quality jobs in the US than other migrants, and this is despite refugees holding relatively good jobs in their home countries. The fraction that ever worked prior to migrating to the US is not different between refugees and non-refugees, nor is the typical hours and weeks of work. However, the sector of employment differs considerably, with refugees 37 percentage points more likely to have worked for a government rather than a private company. Government jobs in developing countries are often sought after because they are formal jobs offering steady and relatively high salary and high security of tenure. The fact that a disproportionate share of refugees used to hold government jobs in the home country indicates not only that their livelihoods may have been especially vulnerable in times of political upheaval, but also that it is not the lowest skilled who are entering the US through the refugee admission class.

The fraction that has ever worked since migrating to the US is significantly higher for refugees. This 26 percentage point difference is an overstatement of the difference in ability/willingness to work in the US due to the fact that refugees have lived in the US about a year longer by the time of the survey compared to other migrants, as discussed above for English proficiency. When we restrict attention to adjustees only, the labor force participation gap shrinks considerably, with refugees 7 percentage points more likely to have worked in the US than non-refugees. Conditional on working, refugees' typical hours worked per week are not different from non-refugees; however, their typical weekly pay is significantly lower (these results hold whether or not we restrict sample to adjustees). For the first job in the US, average typical weekly pay is $339 (in year 2003 dollars) for refugees, compared to $448 for non-refugees. The pay gap between refugees and non-refugees widens from a $109 shortfall to a $147 shortfall from the first job to the current job, which is one-third of refugees' mean weekly wages in each job. The pay gap is larger when refugees are compared with employment preference workers—a $530 shortfall in the first job and $713 shortfall in the current job—which is 1.6 times refugees' mean weekly wages in each job. Refugees' jobs differ on dimensions besides wages. Examining the workers' primary job among reported current jobs, we find that refugees are significantly more likely to be in hourly wage rather than salaried positions, and to work for a government (and relatedly, work for an employer covered by a union contract) rather than a private firm, and are significantly less likely to be in managerial positions.

To summarize our analysis using NIS data, we find that refugees are less positively selected on attributes associated with labor market success in the US relative to other migrants who became lawful permanent residents in 2003—refugees are less proficient in English, less likely to have completed college and less healthy, and are observed to earn less in the US. These findings hold not only for the pooled sample of male and female immigrants used in Tables 12.3–12.6, but also separately by gender. In Table 12.7, we present results for a subset of outcomes in which we regression-adjust for both age and sex, and it can be seen that the findings are similar (compare columns (1) and (2)).

2.3.3 Within-source-country comparisons

An interesting question to consider is whether the observed differences in measured characteristics by refugee status arise entirely from the fact that refugees come from different countries, or if differential selectivity in migration within a country could also be playing a role. If countries that tend to experience refugee-producing events also tend to be less developed, then an increase in the quantity of migrants from these countries—with no change in quality—could cause the average refugee to have lower schooling, health, and earnings than the average non-refugee. To assess this, we estimated differences in mean after controlling for country-of-origin fixed effects, which relies on variation in refugee status within a country, and we find similar results (see Table 12.7, column (3)), indicating that they are not solely driven by refugees coming from different countries. However, the fact that the coefficients for the schooling variables decrease (in the case of years of schooling and high school completion, they switch from positive to negative signed) between columns (2) and (3) indicates that migrants from countries that send more refugees to the US have higher average schooling than migrants from other countries (which is why when this between-country variation is eliminated in column (3), the refugee–non-refugee deficit in schooling increases). Likewise, for the various health indicators, the refugee disadvantage increases after controlling for country fixed effects, again indicating that refugee-sending countries tend to send healthier migrants on average. For

Table 12.7 Regression-adjusted mean differences between refugees and non-refugees, New Immigrant Survey-2003

	Unadjusted difference	Control for sex and age	(2)+control for country F.E.	Specification in column 2 restricting sample to migrants from				
				Cuba	Haiti	India	Russia	Ukraine
	(1)	(2)	(3)	(4)	(5)	(6)	(7)	(8)
Exposed to harm prior to migrating to US	0.43	0.42	0.43	0.11	0.33	0.40	0.66	0.59
	(<0.001)	(<0.001)	(<0.001)	(0.021)	(<0.001)	(<0.001)	(<0.001)	(<0.001)
Observations	8437	8437	8437	143	145	732	118	143
Years of schooling	0.24	0.15	−1.26	1.14	−1.25	−4.31	−1.62	−1.32
	(0.237)	(0.471)	(<0.001)	(0.078)	(0.236)	(<0.001)	(0.011)	(0.003)
Observations	8457	8457	8457	143	144	737	119	143
Completed high school degree or higher	0.05	0.06	−0.07	0.07	−0.07	−0.29	−0.11	−0.22
	(0.011)	(0.007)	(0.002)	(0.449)	(0.520)	(0.015)	(0.127)	(0.004)
Observations	8457	8457	8457	143	144	737	119	143
Completed B.A. or higher	−0.03	−0.05	−0.12	0.20	−0.09	−0.39	−0.20	−0.13
	(0.085)	(0.014)	(<0.001)	(0.014)	(0.211)	(<0.001)	(0.052)	(0.029)
Observations	8457	8457	8457	143	144	737	119	143
In "poor" or "fair" health	0.08	0.08	0.10	0.05	0.11	0.19	0.13	0.27
	(<0.001)	(<0.001)	(<0.001)	(0.185)	(0.090)	(0.057)	(0.055)	(0.001)
Observations	8484	8484	8484	143	145	736	119	143
Height (cm)	2.21	1.58	−0.86	−1.19	2.31	5.02	0.32	−1.88
	(<0.001)	(<0.001)	(0.037)	(0.399)	(0.182)	(<0.001)	(0.823)	(0.125)
Observations	7432	7432	7432	132	97	680	109	132
Body mass index (BMI)	0.95	0.60	1.15	0.89	−0.18	0.99	1.05	1.98
	(<0.001)	(0.002)	(<0.001)	(0.274)	(0.864)	(0.054)	(0.179)	(0.011)
Observations	7432	7432	7432	132	97	680	109	132
Overweight	0.11	0.07	0.11	0.00	0.01	0.27	0.11	0.27

Continued

Table 12.7 Regression-adjusted mean differences between refugees and non-refugees, New Immigrant Survey-2003—cont'd

	Unadjusted difference	Control for sex and age	(2)+control for country F.E.	Specification in column 2 restricting sample to migrants from				
				Cuba	Haiti	India	Russia	Ukraine
	(1)	(2)	(3)	(4)	(5)	(6)	(7)	(8)
	(<0.001)	(0.003)	(<0.001)	(0.961)	(0.908)	(0.018)	(0.291)	(0.008)
Observations	7432	7432	7432	132	97	680	109	132
Obese	0.06	0.06	0.08	0.08	0.13	-0.06	0.16	0.12
	(<0.001)	(0.002)	(<0.001)	(0.211)	(0.200)	(<0.001)	(0.027)	(0.099)
Observations	7432	7432	7432	132	97	680	109	132

The sample is comprised of individuals from the New Immigrant Survey–2003 Adult Sample with non-missing age, sex and country of origin, and sample weights are used to obtain the statistics reported above. Each cell is from a separate regression, and reports the difference in mean between refugees and non-refugees, and below in parentheses the p-value associated with the null hypothesis that the difference is zero; robust standard errors are used. The sample is identical in columns (1)–(3), with column (1) having only the dummy for "refugee" as a regressor, column (2) adds sex, age and age squared as controls, and column (3) also adds country of origin dummies as controls. Columns (4)–(8) apply the column (2) specification to samples comprised of migrants from a single country.

example, for height, which is often used as an indicator of health (Steckel, 1995, 2008), we find that refugee-sending countries tend to send taller migrants, but once we restrict comparison to migrants from the same country of origin in column (3), we see that on average refugees are shorter than non-refugees.

To further explore the within-country migrant selectivity by refugee status, we restrict analysis to five sending countries in the NIS that have at least 20 refugees and non-refugees in the sample: Cuba, Haiti, India, Russia, and Ukraine. These five countries collectively account for 43% of the refugees interviewed. The estimation results are reported in columns (4)–(8) of Table 12.7. In each of these countries, refugees were significantly more likely to have been exposed to harm prior to migrating to the US because of their political or religious beliefs, race, ethnicity, or gender. However, there is heterogeneity in terms of selection in education and health. For Haiti, India, Russia, and Ukraine, migrants in the refugee admission class have both lower educational attainment and worse self-reported health than other migrants, though the results for Haiti tend to be less precise. For Cuba, it is actually the refugees who have higher average completed education, and much of this difference is at the margin of college completion. Also, there is no significant difference in self-reported health by refugee status for Cubans, though the point estimate indicates poorer health for refugees.

The within-country comparisons for the five countries suggest the following. First, as already indicated by the country fixed effects models, the average differences by refugee status reported in Tables 12.3–12.6 using migrants from all countries are not entirely driven by differences in country in origin by refugee status—significant within-country-of-origin differences in migrant characteristics by refugee status exist, which is consistent with refugees being selected from the population in a different way than "regular" migration. Second, there is heterogeneity across origin countries in how refugees compare to non-refugees. Potential reasons for the heterogeneity include, among other things, the nature of the refugee-producing event (e.g., the elite in Cuba faced more persecution under the Castro regime, so it may not be surprising that Cuban refugees are significantly more educated than other migrants from Cuba), and the wage structure in the home country (e.g., compressed pay in Russia may motivate the highest ability workers to migrate to the US as economic migrants).

2.3.4 Discussion

Refugees are expected to be more motivated by the push factor of persecution in the source country and less motivated by economic gains in the destination country, thus the model of migration in Section 2.1 predicts that refugees will be less selected on characteristics associated with labor market success in the destination country compared to other migrants. In our analysis using NIS data, we find that refugees are much more likely to report that they or an immediate family member had been persecuted prior to migrating to the US, which is consistent with the premise of a major threat in the home country pushing the individual to migrate. Consistent with the prediction of the model, we find that refugees are less selected on characteristics that are valued in the US labor market. They have lower college completion rates, lower English proficiency, and worse health than other US migrants on average. They are also observed to earn less in the US and hold worse jobs (lower paying and hourly rather than salaried). These differences are more pronounced when refugees are compared to employment preference migrants and diversity migrants, the two classes of admission that are most clearly economic migrants. Relative to the largest category of new legal permanent residents in 2003, the family preference immigrants, the refugees look better; although refugees are still worse in terms of health status, they have more years of completed schooling (especially at the high school degree margin) than family preference immigrants. Refugees are more likely to be currently enrolled in school relative to other migrants, and so with more time spent in the US, we expect refugees' earnings to improve. We turn to the topic of economic assimilation in the host country in Section 3. We note that because only one wave of the NIS is currently available, it is not well suited to explore issues of economic assimilation, therefore we turn to US Census microdata to do this.[11]

We emphasize that the analysis in this section is based on data for a single cohort—the 2003 cohort—of US migrants gaining legal permanent resident status, and as such the findings may not apply in other contexts. First, our findings may not hold for other cohorts. Our country-specific analysis suggested that the specifics of refugee-producing events could affect selectivity of refugees relative to other migrants. Thus, our analysis of this single cohort cannot tell us how the stock of refugees in the US compares to the stock of all other immigrants, as the stocks are the accumulation of all the waves of migration.

A second caveat is that our analysis concerned migrants gaining legal permanent status, and adding undocumented migrants may change the findings. Undocumented migrants tend to be less educated than other foreign-born individuals in the US, so refugees will look better on the dimension of education when compared to them as opposed to green card holders. However, on other dimensions valued by the labor market, it is unclear how refugees compare to undocumented migrants; considering undocumented migrants' high migration costs—often involving people smugglers and physical danger—and US laws restricting their participation in formal sector jobs, we might expect them to be healthier.

Lastly, our findings may not hold for other receiving countries. On the one hand, only a small fraction of refugees in the world end up as legal permanent residents of the US, and it can be expected that it is not random which refugees make successful green card applications to the US. Possibly it is the more wealthy or better connected who manage to

---

[11] The NIS baseline survey contains retrospective questions about some variables, permitting a limited ability to study assimilation. The second wave of the NIS, fielded in 2007–09, was publicly released in April 2014, too late for inclusion in our analysis, but would permit exploration of immigrant assimilation up to 6 years after green card receipt

make it to developed countries, and the other refugees stay in developing countries. On the other hand, different host countries may have different policies toward refugees, which might affect the measured differences between refugees and non-refugees.

3. ECONOMIC ASSIMILATION OF REFUGEES IN THE HOST COUNTRY

3.1 Conceptual framework: the human capital investment decision

Conditional on migrating, individuals entering as refugees may have a different assimilation profile compared to individuals entering as non-refugee migrants. As discussed in Section 2.1, the selection into migration is different, hence their characteristics differ, and this could affect the evolution of wages and other variables in the host country. For a source- and host-country pair that is typically characterized by positive selection in migration (i.e., it is the higher ability workers in the source country who receive the biggest gains from migrating and therefore migrate), a refugee-producing event that affects the source country's population broadly will induce relatively lower ability workers to migrate instead. This new tier of workers may not have the right skills to perform well in the host country's labor market, and some may decide to undertake investments in human capital valued by the host country in order to perform better.

There is another reason why refugees might invest more in host-country-specific human capital besides the initial gap in human capital generated by differential selection into migration. For the very reason that generates differential selection—refugees face persecution or other unsafe environment in their home country—the expected time horizon in the host country will likely differ. There are two cases one should consider. The first case is where refugees have a longer time horizon than non-refugee migrants, and this likely describes refugee migration to developed countries. Refugees may be thought of as migrants intending to stay permanently in the host country, because it is either unsafe to return to the home country or there is nothing to return to. In contrast, non-refugee migrants can return to their home country, either by design (e.g., they enter as temporary workers, once they earn enough income they return to their home country) or by necessity (e.g., they are unsuccessful in finding a job and must return home, or they are deported). Cortes (2004), building on Duleep and Regets (1999), used a two-period model of a migrant maximizing expected utility to illustrate how a difference in the probability of staying in the host country can lead to differences in human capital investments and the wage assimilation profile. Period 1 is for human capital investment or working in the host country, and period 2 is for working (in the host country if the migrant stays, or in the home country if the migrant returns). The key theoretical result is that the optimal choice of investments in human capital valued by the host country is increasing the probability of staying in the host country. Since refugees have higher probability of staying in the host country, the empirical prediction is that refugees will undertake more human capital investments upon their arrival in the host country relative to non-refugee migrants; this result is borne out in US Census data.

A second case is where refugees expect to stay a shorter length of time in the host country than non-refugee migrants. This likely describes migrants who are placed in refugee camps or in neighboring countries due to a refugee-producing event. These living arrangements tend to be temporary, awaiting the abatement of the violent conflict or natural disaster that spurred the refugee migration. Yet the abatement process could be protracted, and this could lead to *ex post* inefficient decisions about human capital investments for refugees. For example, refugees *ex ante* may have thought they would return home quickly but *ex post* they stay much longer in the neighboring host country (perhaps even resettling there); possibly had they known how long they would be in the neighboring country, they would have invested more in skills valued by that host labor market (non-refugee migrants might already possess these skills, or invested in them immediately upon arrival). Even if the migration is of known and limited duration, refugees tend to experience disruptions to human capital investments, as temporary settlements often lack good schools and health care facilities. Thus, in stark contrast to the first case where refugees plan a longer time horizon in the host country, in the second case refugees tend to invest less in host-specific human capital compared to their non-refugee migrant counterparts.

3.2 Previous research on economic assimilation of refugee immigrants

There are many metrics to measure immigrant adaptation in the host country, such as economic, social, or cultural assimilation. The most commonly analyzed metric of assimilation in the economics literature is labor market outcomes (e.g., wages, annual earnings, hours worked, employment, occupational prestige, and self-employment). In general, previous studies have found that refugee immigrants fare worse initially in the host nation's labor market compared to other immigrants, and this pattern has been observed in the US (Akresh, 2008), Canada (Wanner, 2003), Sweden (Edin et al., 2003), and Australia. Over time, however, refugees catch up, and in some cases even surpass other immigrant groups in the host country. Because refugees have a greater degree of certainty about staying in the host country than other immigrant groups (e.g., they cannot return to their mother country because of the persecution they expect to encounter), they are more likely to pursue additional human capital investment, which in turn translates into better labor marker outcomes over time (Cortes, 2004).

Although numerous researchers have examined occupational mobility patterns among immigrants (Stein, 1979; Finnan, 1981; Raijman and Semyonov, 1995; Powers and Seltzer, 1998; Powers et al., 1998), their work faced an important data limitation—available large individual-level datasets typically provide information only on current occupation, yet for the purpose of assessing assimilation it is useful to have information on individuals' occupational history (e.g., job prior to migration, first job in the US, and any subsequent job changes). An additional limitation considering our interest in how refugees perform relative to other migrants is that very few datasets contain information on immigrant class of admission (e.g., refugee, family preference migrant, economic migrant). Akresh (2008) was able to address these limitations by using data from the New Immigrant Survey-2003 (the same dataset we used in Section 2.3), which provides occupation prior to migration to the US, the initial and current occupations held in the US (this is based on retrospective questions asked in the baseline survey), and administrative information on class of admission. She found that refugees and family immigrants experience greater initial downward occupational mobility (vis-à-vis their pre-migration occupation) than economic immigrants, but that over time in the US, refugee immigrants experience more rapid upward occupational mobility than other immigrant groups. Connor (2010) used the same dataset to empirically investigate potential reasons for the refugee gap in earnings and occupational attainment relative to non-refugees, and English proficiency and schooling are found to account for a large share of the gap.

Wanner (2003) examined immigrant earnings assimilation by class of admission in a Canadian setting. He used data from Canada's Citizenship and Immigration Landing Information Data System (LIDS) for the years 1980–95 merged with the 1996 Census of Canada Public Use Microdata File. Wanner (2003) found that while Canada's point system used to screen immigrants for favorable labor market skills does in fact select migrants who have higher earnings upon arrival than those who are not screened (i.e., refugee and family preferences), over time the earnings of these groups converge after controlling for human capital differences. In particular, he found that refugee immigrants had lower earnings upon arriving to Canada, but their earnings growth increased more rapidly than that of the economic visa holders, which resulted in an eventual convergence of earnings levels between these two groups.

Blom (1997) used Swedish register data to study the integration of six refugee cohorts (arriving 1987–92) from the year after arrival to 1993. The study did not compare refugees to other immigrants or to natives, and instead traced their assimilation profiles. With more time in Sweden, the likelihood of being employed increases significantly. Additionally, the likelihood of participating in an educational program also increases over the first few years in Sweden, with about one-quarter of each cohort considered "educationally active" by the third year in Sweden, and this human capital investment may facilitate economic integration later.

Chiswick et al. (2006) used data from the Longitudinal Survey of Immigrants to Australia to analyze the earnings profiles of immigrants by visa type. The data were collected for a sample of immigrants who arrived in Australia September 1993 to August 1995 in three waves, capturing their first 3.5 years in Australia. They found that refugees' initial earnings and wage growth are lower compared to "business skills/employer nominated scheme" and "independent" immigrants, but higher compared to family preference immigrants.

Other studies have looked at the economic adjustment of specific ethnicities of refugee immigrants in the host country (Borjas, 1982; Waxman, 2001; Cohen and Haberfeld, 2007). Since refugees may hail from different socio-economic statuses, which in turn would affect their integration into the host labor market, analyses that only include an indicator variable flagging whether the immigrant is a refugee may be masking the heterogeneous integration of a particular refugee group. Waxman (2001) looked at the economic integration of Bosnian, Afghan, and Iraqi refugees in Sydney, Australia. He found that all three refugee groups are gainfully employed in Sydney, and he attributed the high employment rates of these refugee groups to their high English language competency. The significant positive relationship between English language competency and labor market integration has been observed not just for refugees, but for all immigrant groups as a whole (Chiswick and Miller, 1991, 1999a, b, 2002, 2010; Bleakley and Chin, 2004; Chiswick et al., 2006). Borjas (1982) analyzed the earnings differentials among male Hispanic immigrants in the US and found notable differences in their rate of economic mobility. In particular, the rate of economic progress by Cuban immigrants exceeds that of other Hispanic groups; this result is in part due to the fact that Cuban immigrants have invested more heavily in US country-specific human capital than other Hispanic immigrants. Borjas's findings are consistent with the hypothesis that political refugees face higher costs of return migration than do economic immigrants, and therefore the former have greater incentives to adapt rapidly to the US labor market. However, it was the more educated who tended to leave Cuba and seek asylum, and this positive selection could also be contributing to the faster economic assimilation of Cubans. Cohen and Haberfeld (2007), drawing on microdata from the US Census and on the Israeli Census, compared the educational levels and earnings profile assimilation of Jewish immigrants from the former Soviet Union (FSU) in the US and Israel during 1968–2000. FSU immigrants were entitled to refugee visas in the US. They found that immigrants from the FSU to the US have significantly higher educational attainment, and experience significantly faster rates of earnings assimilation, than their counterparts who immigrated to Israel. They attributed their findings to the self-selection in immigration to Israel and the US, on both measured and unmeasured productivity-related traits. This study supports a point that we made in Section 2.1, that even if a refugee-producing event can be thought to be broad, there may be selection in the ultimate destination country of the refugees.

Other studies have focused on how resettlement policies and community characteristics affect the economic integration of refugee immigrants in the host country (Rogg, 1971, 1974; Taft et al., 1979; Finnan, 1982; Kelly, 1986; Edin et al., 2003). Edin et al. (2003) exploited a refugee placement policy in Sweden that effectively randomly assigned refugees to communities in order to obtain plausibly exogenous variation to exposure to co-ethnics. The authors found evidence of sorting across locations, and when sorting is controlled for (by using initial location assigned by the policy, rather than current location that could be endogenous), living in ethnic enclaves improves labor market outcomes for less skilled refugee immigrants. Specifically, the authors found that the earnings gain associated with a standard deviation increase in ethnic concentration is 13%.

Another popular metric used to measure economic success of refugees is dependence on public assistance. By and large, studies have found that refugees initially do place a larger burden on the public sector than other immigrants, but this difference tends to decline with time spent in the host country (Gustafsson and Osterberg, 2001; Hansen and Lofstrom, 2003, 2009; Edin et al., 2004). For example, Hansen and Lofstrom (2003) analyzed differences in welfare utilization between immigrants and natives in Sweden using a large panel dataset for the years 1990–96. They found that immigrants use welfare to a greater extent than natives and those differences cannot be explained by observable characteristics, but that welfare participation does decrease with time spent in Sweden. They also found that refugees assimilate out of welfare at a faster rate than non-refugee immigrants; however, neither group is predicted to reach parity with natives.

While the aforementioned studies found a decrease in welfare dependence among refugees with time spent in the host country, Åslund and Fredriksson (2009) and Damm (2009b) have findings that suggest that the welfare gap relative to natives or other migrants may not necessarily disappear. Åslund and Fredriksson (2009), exploiting the Swedish refugee placement policy mentioned above that effectively randomly assigned refugees to locations, found evidence of peer effects in welfare use among refugees. Their analyses distinguished between the quantity of contacts (i.e., the number of individuals of the same ethnicity) and the quality of contacts (i.e., welfare use among members of the ethnic group). They found that long-run welfare dependence increases if the refugee is placed in a welfare-dependent community. Damm (2009b) investigated the influence of regional factors on recent refugees' location choices. She found that refugees (whose initial locations are effectively randomly assigned due to Denmark's spatial dispersal policy for refugees) are more likely to relocate when there is lower availability of social housing or a right-wing-dominated government (which might be associated with ease of receiving social assistance) in the initial location.

3.3 The economic assimilation of refugees in the United States: evidence from census microdata

A challenge faced by many researchers studying refugee assimilation is the inability to follow refugee immigrants over an extended period of time. In this subsection we further contribute to the existing literature by comparing the *long-run* economic assimilation of refugees in the US to that of non-refugee migrants. Ideally we would like longitudinal data on the earnings and human capital data for immigrants who are clearly identified by visa status. Though this type of data does not currently exist, it is possible to simulate a panel with census microdata, which offers a large enough number of observations that we can track subgroups of immigrants (e.g., by age, year of immigration, and country of origin) over time and assess the subgroups' assimilation even if we cannot track any individual's assimilation. Thus, we perform our analysis using pooled individual-level data from the 1980, 1990, and 2000 US Census of Population and Housing and the 2005–10 American Community Survey (ACS).[12] Specifically, we analyze a *fixed cohort* of immigrants who entered the US in the years 1975–80.[13,14] We focus on the 1975–80 arrival cohort for various reasons. First, the Census does not include educational attainment in the home country prior to immigrating to the US. Therefore, by focusing on the latest immigrant cohort reported in the 1980 Census, educational attainment in 1980 is a rough proxy for human capital upon arrival. Second, the 1975–80 arrival cohort would have spent 25–35 years by 2010, enabling us to trace out a long-run assimilation profile. Third, focusing on earlier cohorts of migrants, who are much more likely to be of European descent, would provide an analysis of immigrants who are less representative of today's immigrant population in the US. Lastly, the 1975–80 cohort of immigrants allows us to include many other refugee groups not present in the 1970 Census. In fact, the main refugee group in the 1970 Census would be Cubans.

A limitation of both the Census and the ACS is that these datasets do not have a variable measuring refugee status. We follow the methodology used by Cortes (2004), wherein *likely* refugees are defined based on country of origin and year of immigration.[15] Cortes classified immigrants from the following countries as refugees: Afghanistan, Cuba, Soviet Union, Ethiopia, Haiti, Cambodia, Laos, and Vietnam. Individuals from all other

---

[12] We use the 5% samples of the Census data and the ACS samples (which are 1% samples of the US population) from Integrated Public Use Microsample Series (IPUMS) (Ruggles et al., 2010). Since the most recent publicly available census microdata are from 2000, we appended the ACS data, which are also collected by the US Census Bureau, and follow the same questionnaire, in order to follow the immigrants over a longer time period.

[13] More precisely, year of immigration for the 1980 Census is 1975–80, whereas in the 1990 Census, year of immigration is 1975–79. The 1980 arrivals for the 1990 Census are included with the 1981 arrivals and are given a different interval of year of immigration (i.e., 1980–81). Hence, those immigrants included in the 1980 Census, who entered the US before April 1980, are excluded from the sample we analyze from the 1990 Census. To make the sample of immigrants consistent, for the 2000 Census and the 2005–10 ACS samples we also use 1975–79 as the year of immigration.

[14] Our *fixed cohort* is "aged" by 10 years in every census sample. That is, from the 1980 Census we include foreign-born individuals aged 16–45, in the 1990 Census we include ages 26–55, in the 2000 Census we include ages 36–65, and lastly, the 2005–10 concatenated ACS samples we include ages 46–75. Hence, by using a fixed year of immigration and aging each Census year by 10 years, we are creating a synthetic panel of immigrants.

[15] An excellent source cited in Cortes (2004) for data on the timing of refugee inflows is Haines (1996). In addition, Cortes (2004) used the yearly INS volumes of immigration statistics, which includes the total number of refugees, asylum seekers, and immigrants from each country admitted during the fiscal year. After compiling her list of refugee groups from Haines (1996), Cortes then compared them to the INS statistics. She found that the dates and countries correspond very closely.

countries and regions constitute the non-refugee immigrant group in Cortes's taxonomy. It should be noted that in Cortes's study the term "economic immigrants" is used to capture all migrants besides refugees, and the intent of using this terminology was to highlight that refugees are less motivated by economic gains in their migration decision relative to other migrants. However, in practice this residual category includes not only the employment preference and diversity immigrants who we described in Section 2.3 as the most likely to be considered economic migrants, but also every other foreign-born person residing in the US, including family preference immigrants, temporary visa holders, and undocumented migrants. Thus, while we still consider the residual category as being more motivated by economic gains on average, we refer to this group as "non-refugee migrants" instead of "economic immigrants."[16]

3.3.1 Characteristics of refugees and non-refugee migrants arriving in the United States 1975–80

A priori, we would expect that refugees are closer to a random sample from the source country compared to non-refugee immigrants (at least for refugee-producing events that impact the population broadly). Thus, refugees should be more uniformly distributed by age at arrival; in contrast, we would expect non-refugee immigrants to arrive during their prime working ages. Figure 12.4 shows the age at arrival distributions by gender of both refugee and non-refugee immigrants for individuals who entered the US in 1975–80.[17] Consistent with predictions, we observe that non-refugee immigrants are more likely to arrive in the US between the ages of 16 and 30 compared to refugee immigrants. Refugees have fatter tails in their age at arrival distribution, i.e., they are more likely to arrive in the US at younger and older ages compared to non-refugee migrants. Specifically, 47% of the sample is of working age for male non-refugees versus 35% for male refugee immigrants, and 44% of the sample is of working age for female non-refugees versus 32% for female refugee immigrants.

Next, Table 12.8 shows several characteristics from the 1980–2010 Censuses for this fixed cohort of 1975–80 immigrant arrivals.[18] Interestingly, the gender composition of each immigrant group at time of immigration is similar regardless of refugee status. We might have expected that non-refugee immigrants are more likely to be male, if we

---

[16] It is worthy of mention that given the 1975–80 immigrant cohort being analyzed in Section 3, the non-refugee immigrant group may have benefited from the Immigration Reform and Control Act of 1986, which granted legal status to all undocumented immigrants who had arrived in the US prior to 1982. Thus, undocumented immigration may be less of a problem with our fixed cohort of immigrant than with later immigrant cohorts.

[17] Figure 12.4 uses only the 1980 Census data with no age restrictions imposed; later figures and analysis within this section use more census years and impose the age restrictions.

[18] Our analytical sample consist of 201,906 foreign-born individuals (28,348 refugee and 173,558 non-refugee immigrants) pooled over the four census "years" (1980, 1990, 2000, and grouped 2005–10). This is the same analytical sample used in the regression analysis.

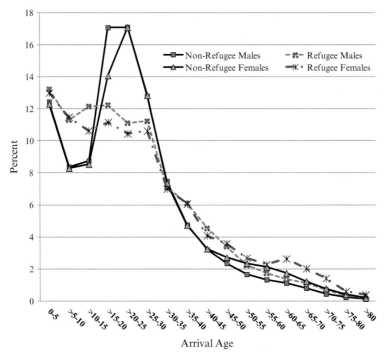

Figure 12.4 *Arrival age distributions of entering immigrants by gender, 1975–80.* Source: *Integrated Public Use Micro Series (IPUMS) 5% samples for 1980.*

assume that men are more likely to come to the US to earn money; however, we observe about 60% of both refugee and non-refugee immigrants are male (column (1) versus column (6)). The share married is also roughly the same for refugee and non-refugees: 72%. Also, both immigrant groups appear to have about the same number of children residing in the household.

While the demographic characteristics of refugee and non-refugees are similar upon arriving in the US in 1980 and do not change much in the subsequent census years, their educational attainment levels, country-specific human capital characteristics, and annual earnings do exhibit differences initially as well as over time. Table 12.8 reveals that non-refugee immigrants were more concentrated in the lower levels of education than refugees in 1980: 47% of non-refugees had less than a high school degree compared to 31% for refugee immigrants.[19] Furthermore, the education distribution for non-refugees

---

[19] In Section 2.3, using NIS data, we found among migrants gaining legal permanent residency in 2003, refugees were weakly less educated. But relative to the NIS sample, the Census sample contains more family reunification migrants and undocumented migrants, who are on average less educated than refugees, hence the result here of refugees being more educated.

Table 12.8 Characteristics of refugees and non-refugee immigrants for the fixed cohort year of immigration 1975–80*

	Panel A: Refugee immigrants					Panel B: Non-refugee immigrants				
	(1)	(2)	(3)	(4)	(5)	(6)	(7)	(8)	(9)	(10)
	All years	1980	1990	2000	2010	All years	1980	1990	2000	2010
Gender										
Male	0.57	0.60	0.57	0.57	0.55	0.58	0.61	0.58	0.57	0.55
Female	0.43	0.40	0.43	0.43	0.45	0.42	0.39	0.42	0.43	0.45
Marital status										
Married	0.72	0.57	0.73	0.77	0.78	0.72	0.58	0.75	0.77	0.76
Number of children										
	1.32	1.03	1.51	1.54	1.17	1.37	0.78	1.67	1.73	1.25
	(1.44)	(1.49)	(1.51)	(1.46)	(1.24)	(1.44)	(1.27)	(1.52)	(1.48)	(1.27)
None	0.39	0.53	0.34	0.31	0.39	0.38	0.62	0.30	0.27	0.37
One to three	0.53	0.39	0.56	0.61	0.57	0.54	0.34	0.59	0.62	0.58
Four to nine	0.08	0.08	0.10	0.08	0.04	0.08	0.04	0.11	0.11	0.05
Educational attainment										
Years of schooling	12.55	11.99	12.68	12.56	12.90	10.77	10.70	10.53	10.51	11.34
	(3.92)	(3.70)	(3.90)	(4.04)	(3.97)	(4.69)	(4.57)	(4.75)	(4.78)	(4.59)
Less than high school	0.20	0.31	0.17	0.17	0.15	0.41	0.47	0.43	0.43	0.35
High school	0.28	0.28	0.25	0.30	0.29	0.23	0.19	0.20	0.25	0.25
1–3 years of college	0.26	0.24	0.31	0.24	0.24	0.15	0.14	0.17	0.13	0.15
4+ years of college	0.26	0.17	0.27	0.28	0.32	0.21	0.19	0.19	0.19	0.25
Other: country specific										
School enrollment	0.12	0.27	0.13	0.06	0.04	0.08	0.15	0.11	0.05	0.03
Low English ability	0.21	0.32	0.17	0.18	0.19	0.32	0.45	0.30	0.29	0.27
Citizenship status	0.65	0.37	0.68	0.84	0.92	0.44	0.09	0.39	0.58	0.69

Continued

Table 12.8 Characteristics of refugees and non-refugee immigrants for the fixed cohort year of immigration 1975–80*—cont'd

	(1)	(2)	(3)	(4)	(5)	(6)	(7)	(8)	(9)	(10)
	Panel A: Refugee immigrants					**Panel B: Non-refugee immigrants**				
	All years	1980	1990	2000	2010	All years	1980	1990	2000	2010
Labor market										
Log annual earnings	10.18	9.44	10.29	10.44	10.46	10.03	9.54	10.05	10.20	10.27
	(1.02)	(1.12)	(0.84)	(0.87)	(0.91)	(0.99)	(1.02)	(0.92)	(0.92)	(0.94)
Observations	28,348	6469	7260	7265	7354	173,558	40,432	44,439	45,134	43,553

*Year of immigration 1975–80 for 1980, 1975–79 for 1990, 2000, and 2010. For the non-binary variables, standard deviations are in parentheses. Sample selection of foreign-born individuals ages 16–45 in 1980, ages 26–55 in 1990, ages 36–65 in 2000, ages 46–75 in 2010. The Census Bureau top-codes annual earnings at $75,000 in the 1980 census; we construct an equivalent top code for annual earnings in the 1990, 2000, and 2010 censuses. For example, in the 1990 census we assign annual earnings of $118,962 (this was calculated as $75,000 × (130.70/82.40); the annual CPIs in 1980 and 1990 were 82.40 and 130.70) to all top-coded observations. Log annual earnings are in 2010 dollars.

Sources: Integrated Public Use Micro Series (IPUMS) 5% samples for 1980, 1990, and 2000; and several pooled annual samples of the American Community Survey (2005, 2006, 2007, 2008, 2009, and 2010) were used to contruct an equivalent 5% sample for 2010 census.

shows little or no improvement from 1980 to 1990, whereas for refugees there is evidence of rising educational attainment. We observe that in 1980, 17% of refugee immigrants had four or more years of college, compared to 19% for non-refugees. By 1990, however, 27% of refugee immigrants had earned a B.A. or better, whereas the share of non-refugees getting a B.A. or better remained flat at 19% in the 1990 and 2000 Censuses. Though they still lag behind refugees in educational attainment, non-refugees showed an increase from 2000 to 2010, when 25% reported having a B.A. or more.

Next, Table 12.8 shows other measures of country-specific human capital accumulation: US school enrollment, ability to speak English, and US citizenship. We observe that refugee immigrants are more likely to be enrolled in school than non-refugees in 1980: 27% versus 15%. We also observe that the English ability of both groups improves over time, with refugees experiencing faster rates of improvement. We observe that in 1980, 32% of refugee immigrants report having low English proficiency compared to 45% for non-refugees. By 1990, however, only 17% of refugee immigrants report having low English proficiency compared to 30% for non-refugees—about a 50% improvement of speaking ability for refugee immigrants. Next, although both groups had similar citizenship status in 1980 (7% of refugees reported being naturalized citizens versus 9% for non-refugees), refugees became considerably more likely to be US citizens by 1990: 68% for refugees versus 39% for non-refugees. The citizenship gap persisted in 2000 and 2010. Overall, it seems that refugee immigrants showed the most improvement from 1980 to 1990 in accumulating more country-specific human capital; in contrast, the improvement for non-refugees occurs later and in smaller magnitude.

Finally, the last row of Table 12.8 presents the unadjusted means of log annual earnings, which is one of our main labor market outcomes of interest.[20,21] This table also allows us to observe the relative gain (or loss) of refugee immigrants over the last three decades. We observe that in 1980 the average refugee immigrant earned 10% less than a non-refugee immigrant. By 1990, however, the annual earnings of refugees were 24% above those of non-refugees. Thus, the relative gain of refugee immigrants from 1980 to 1990 is a striking 34%. Though not reported here, the same pattern is observed if we separate the sample by gender. We also observe that the relative gain in earnings for refugee immigrants continued in 2000 and 2010. It is worth noting that in Cortes (2004), she found that the relative gain of refugees in annual earnings was

---

[20] All dollar amounts are expressed in 2010 dollars in this analysis of Census microdata.

[21] It should be noted that by 2010, the average age is around 60, and potentially selection in labor force participation/retirement can change the composition of the sample of wage earners in 2010 relative to earlier years.

mainly coming from a relative increase in the total annual hours worked and not hourly earnings. Below, we investigate if refugees continued to work these long hours in 2000 and 2010.

3.3.2 Long-run labor market assimilation

In this section, we use regression analysis to further examine reasons why refugees outperformed non-refugee immigrants. We estimate several regression models of the following form:

$$Y_{it} = \alpha_0 + \alpha_1 \cdot D^{1990} + \alpha_2 \cdot D^{2000} + \alpha_3 \cdot D^{2010} + \alpha_4 \cdot D^{\text{Refugee}}$$

$$\alpha_5 \cdot D^{1990} \cdot D^{\text{Refugee}} + \alpha_6 \cdot D^{2000} \cdot D^{\text{Refugee}} + \alpha_7 \cdot D^{2010} \cdot D^{\text{Refugee}} + X_{it} \cdot \gamma + \mu_{it}$$

where Y_{it} is one of our outcome variables of interest (i.e., log annual earnings, log hourly earnings, log annual hours, years completed of schooling, occupation prestige scores, and economic standing scores), D^{1990} is a dummy variable indicating the 1990 census year, D^{2000} is a dummy variable indicating the 2000 census year, D^{2010} is a dummy variable indicating the 2010 census year (designating ACS data from the years 2005–10), D^{Refugee} is a dummy variable indicating a refugee immigrant (measured using the methodology in Cortes (2004) summarized above), and $D^{1990} \cdot D^{\text{Refugee}}$, $D^{2000} \cdot D^{\text{Refugee}}$, and $D^{2010} \cdot D^{\text{Refugee}}$ are interactions of refugee status and the 1990, 2000, and 2010 Census years indicators respectively. The vector X_{it} is a set of control variables, such as age, age^2, age^3, marital status, educational attainment and higher order polynomials, number of own children in the household and higher order polynomials, and regional enclaves indicators (i.e., Midwest, South, and West; Northeast is the omitted category).[22] Lastly, μ_{it} is an error term. Since immigrant outcomes might vary by gender, the above model specification is estimated separately for both male and female immigrants.

The above regression model has several features of interest. For example, if the outcome variable is log annual earnings, the coefficient α_1 gives the growth in earnings of non-refugee immigrants from 1980 to 1990, the sum of the coefficients ($\alpha_1 + \alpha_5$) gives the growth in earnings of refugee immigrants from 1980 to 1990, the coefficient α_5 gives the earnings growth of refugee immigrants relative to non-refugee immigrants from 1980 to 1990, and the sum of the coefficients ($\alpha_4 + \alpha_5$) gives the level of earnings of refugee immigrants relative to non-refugee immigrants in 1990, and analogously for 2000 and 2010.

Table 12.9 presents the results of estimating the above equation with log annual earnings, log hourly earnings, and log annual hours as the dependent variables.[23] As seen in

---

[22] The set of controls changes depending on the outcome variable under study. See the notes of each regression table for the exact set of control variables.

[23] All regression specification reported in Table 12.9 include age, age^2, age^3, marital status indicator, education, and regional enclaves, and state fixed effects as controls.

Table 12.9 Labor market regression results for male and female immigrants

	Panel A: Male sample			Panel B: Female sample		
	(1)	(2)	(3)	(4)	(5)	(6)
	Log annual earnings	Log hourly earnings	Log annual hours	Log annual earnings	Log hourly earnings	Log annual hours
Dummy 1990	0.290	0.167	0.123	0.340	0.201	0.139
	(0.008)	(0.007)	(0.006)	(0.012)	(0.008)	(0.010)
Dummy 2000	0.389	0.260	0.130	0.473	0.309	0.165
	(0.010)	(0.009)	(0.008)	(0.014)	(0.010)	(0.012)
Dummy 2010	0.472	0.287	0.184	0.577	0.355	0.222
	(0.012)	(0.010)	(0.008)	(0.016)	(0.011)	(0.013)
Refugee	−0.228	0.0140	−0.242	−0.059	0.043	−0.102
	(0.018)	(0.012)	(0.015)	(0.023)	(0.015)	(0.019)
Refugee × Dummy 1990	0.301	0.048	0.253	0.265	0.045	0.219
	(0.021)	(0.016)	(0.017)	(0.028)	(0.018)	(0.023)
Refugee × Dummy 2000	0.315	0.056	0.259	0.271	0.077	0.194
	(0.022)	(0.016)	(0.017)	(0.027)	(0.019)	(0.022)
Refugee × Dummy 2010	0.288	0.064	0.224	0.225	0.042	0.183
	(0.022)	(0.016)	(0.017)	(0.028)	(0.019)	(0.022)
Constant	6.981	1.682	5.299	6.862	1.723	5.139
	(0.092)	(0.067)	(0.078)	(0.119)	(0.080)	(0.104)
Controls	Yes	Yes	Yes	Yes	Yes	Yes
State fixed effects	Yes	Yes	Yes	Yes	Yes	Yes
Observations	116,444	116,444	116,444	85,462	85,462	85,462
Adjusted R^2	0.28	0.22	0.09	0.24	0.22	0.07

Sample selection of foreign-born individuals ages 16–45 in 1980, ages 26–55 in 1990, ages 36–65 in 2000, ages 46–75 in 2010. Year of immigration 1975–80 for 1980, 1975–79 for 1990, 2000, and 2010. The Census Bureau top-codes annual earnings at $75,000 in the 1980 census; we construct an equivalent top code for annual earnings in the 1990, 2000, and 2010 censuses. For example, in the 1990 census we assign annual earnings of $118,962 (this was calculated as $75,000 × (130.70/82.40); the annual CPIs in 1980 and 1990 were 82.40 and 130.70) to all top-coded observations. Controls include age, age^2, age^3, married dummy variable, educational attainment and higher order polynomials of education, and regional enclaves (i.e., midwest, south, west, and northeast is the omitted category). Log annual earnings and log hourly earnings are in 2010 dollars. Robust standard errors are given in parentheses.
Sources: Integrated Public Use Micro Series (IPUMS) 5% samples for 1980, 1990, and 2000; and several pooled annual samples of the American Community Survey (2005, 2006, 2007, 2008, 2009, and 2010) were used to construct an equivalent 5% sample for 2010 census.

columns (1) and (4) of panels A and B, controlling for demographic characteristics, human capital accumulation in the US, and state-specific time-invariant effects, refugees significantly outperformed non-refugee immigrants. The annual earnings of both male and female refugees grew by about 60% (the sum of coefficients $\alpha_1 + \alpha_5$). For non-refugees, annual earnings growth was significantly lower; the annual earnings of male and female non-refugee immigrants grew by 29% and 34% (coefficient α_1) between 1980 and 1990, respectively.

Interestingly, both male and female refugees initially start off at a lower earnings level compared to their non-refugee counterparts (note the significant negative coefficients for the refugee indicator). As shown in columns (1) and (4), we observe that male refugees earned 23% less than male non-refugees in 1980, while female refugees earned 6% less than female non-refugees in 1980. However, by the next decennial Census in 1990, both male and female refugees had caught up, and in fact surpassed, the earnings *levels* of both male and female non-refugee immigrants. The estimates in columns (1) and (4) show that the average male and female refugee in 1990 earned 7% and 20% (the sum of coefficients $\alpha_4 + \alpha_5$) respectively more than male and female non-refugees.

Our analysis thus far has shown that despite the fact that refugee immigrants start off in 1980 at a lower earnings level compared to their non-refugee counterparts, by the next Census year in 1990 refugees had caught up and surpassed the earnings levels of non-refugee immigrants. But did this growth in relative earnings continue for refugee immigrants over the next 20 or 30 years? To answer this question, we turn to the rest of the coefficients reported in Table 12.9. In particular, we are interested in coefficients of the last two interactions between the refugee status variable and the 2000 and 2010 Census year indicators. As shown in columns (1) and (4), the earnings growth of male and female refugee immigrants relative to male and female non-refugees continued even after 20 and 30 years upon arriving in the US. The relative earnings gain of male and female refugees from 1980 to 2000 was 32% and 27% respectively, and the relative earnings gain of male and female refugees from 1980 to 2010 was 29% and 22%, respectively. Lastly, Figure 12.5 further illustrates the earnings growth paths for both refugee and non-refugee immigrants by gender. As shown in this graph, though both immigrant groups experience earnings gains with time spent in the US, the earnings gains are far greater for male and female refugees than their male and female non-refugee counterparts.

Since annual earnings are the product of hourly earnings and annual hours, the growth in annual earnings can be decomposed into growth in the hourly wage and growth in annual hours. We further investigate whether refugee immigrants were earning more per hour or simply working more hours.[24] These additional analyses reveal that the relatively faster growth of annual earnings for refugees is primarily due to an increase in annual hours worked.[25] As shown in Table 12.9, for refugee males more than

---

[24] We use the same model specification as in the log annual earnings analysis.

[25] This is consistent with the NIS data analysis in Section 2.3. Although we found among migrants gaining legal permanent residency in 2003 that refugee workers had typical hours worked per week, they had somewhat higher typical weeks worked per year, which yields more annual hours worked. Once we account for the fact that the Census data contain more non-refugees (e.g., family reunification migrants, more recent arrivers) who have lower labor supply, the refugee surplus in annual hours worked would be even larger.

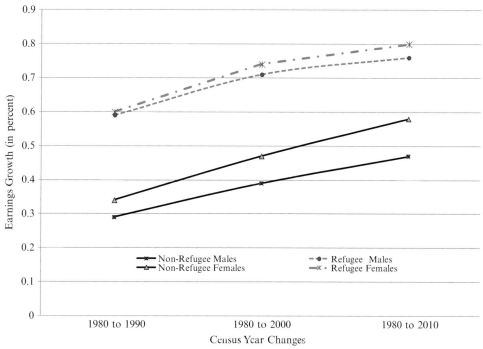

Figure 12.5 *Earnings growth of refugee and non-refugee immigrants.* Source: *Integrated Public Use Micro Series (IPUMS) 5% samples for 1980, 1990, 2000. American Community Survey (ACS) 1% samples for 2005–10.*

80% (0.253/0.301 = 0.84) of the growth in annual earnings is attributable to the increase in annual hours worked, while less than 20% (0.048/0.301 = 0.16) is attributable to hourly earnings growth in 1990. These growth differentials by refugee status observed between 1980 and 1990 persist over the next 20 and 30 years (i.e., comparing 2000 and 2010 to 1980), and the same pattern holds for female refugees.

The coefficients for "Refugee" indicate that upon arrival to the US, refugees work significantly fewer hours than non-refugees but earn hourly wages that are no lower (for women, refugees hourly wages are significantly higher). Thus, the initial disadvantage in log annual earnings that was observed is entirely attributable to the differences in hours worked by refugee status, as refugees actually have higher hourly earnings in 1980.

Next, we explore the occupational attainment of refugees relative to non-refugee immigrants in Table 12.10, which shows the distribution of employed immigrants among seven broad categories of occupations: (1) managerial and professional, (2) technical, sales, and administrative support, (3) service, (4), farming, forestry, and fishing, (5) precision production, craft, and repair, (6) operations, fabricators, and laborers, and (7) military. As seen in panel A, in 1980, the top three occupations for refugee immigrants

Table 12.10 Occupational distribution of refugee and non-refugee immigrants

	Panel A: Refugee immigrant				Panel B: Change for refugees		
Occupational type	1980	1990	2000	2010	$\Delta Ref_{(1990-1980)}$	$\Delta Ref_{(2000-1980)}$	$\Delta Ref_{(2010-1980)}$
Managerial and Professional	0.13	0.23	0.25	0.29	0.10 (0.01)	0.12 (0.01)	0.16 (0.01)
Technical, Sales, and Admin. Support	0.25	0.29	0.26	0.25	0.04 (0.01)	0.01 (0.01)	0.01 (0.01)
Service	0.16	0.14	0.16	0.17	−0.02 (0.01)	0.00 (0.01)	0.01 (0.01)
Farming, Forestry, and Fishing	0.01	0.01	0.01	0.01	0.00 (0.00)	0.00 (0.00)	0.00 (0.00)
Precision Production, Craft, and Repair	0.13	0.12	0.12	0.10	−0.01 (0.01)	−0.01 (0.01)	−0.03 (0.01)
Operations, Fabricators, and Laborers	0.32	0.22	0.20	0.18	−0.10 (0.01)	−0.11 (0.01)	−0.14 (0.01)
Military	0.00	0.00	0.00	0.00	0.00 (0.00)	0.00 (0.00)	0.00 (0.00)

	Panel C: Non-refugee immigrant				Panel D: Change for non-refugees		
	1980	1990	2000	2010	$\Delta NR_{(1990-1980)}$	$\Delta NR_{(2000-1980)}$	$\Delta NR_{(2010-1980)}$
Managerial and Professional	0.14	0.17	0.18	0.23	0.03 (0.00)	0.05 (0.00)	0.09 (0.00)
Technical, Sales, and Admin. Support	0.19	0.20	0.19	0.21	0.01 (0.00)	0.01 (0.00)	0.02 (0.00)
Service	0.19	0.17	0.18	0.20	−0.02 (0.00)	−0.01 (0.00)	0.01 (0.00)
Farming, Forestry, and Fishing	0.06	0.07	0.06	0.05	0.00 (0.00)	0.00 (0.00)	−0.01 (0.00)
Precision Production, Craft, and Repair	0.11	0.13	0.14	0.11	0.02 (0.00)	0.03 (0.00)	0.01 (0.00)
Operations, Fabricators, and Laborers	0.31	0.27	0.24	0.20	−0.04 (0.00)	−0.07 (0.00)	−0.11 (0.00)
Military	0.01	0.01	0.00	0.00	−0.01 (0.00)	−0.01 (0.00)	−0.01 (0.00)

Panel E: Occupational gain/loss of refugees relative to non-refugee immigrants

	$\Delta Ref_{('90-'80)} - \Delta NR_{('90-'80)}$	$\Delta Ref_{('00-'80)} - \Delta NR_{('00-'80)}$	$\Delta Ref_{('10-'80)} - \Delta NR_{('10-'80)}$
Managerial and Professional	0.07 (0.01)	0.07 (0.01)	0.07 (0.01)
Technical, Sales, and Admin. Support	0.02 (0.01)	0.00 (0.01)	−0.02 (0.01)
Service	0.00 (0.01)	0.00 (0.01)	0.00 (0.01)
Farming, Forestry, and Fishing	−0.01 (0.00)	0.00 (0.00)	0.01 (0.00)
Precision Production, Craft, and Repair	−0.03 (0.01)	−0.04 (0.01)	−0.04 (0.01)
Operations, Fabricators, and Laborers	−0.06 (0.01)	−0.04 (0.01)	−0.03 (0.01)
Military	0.00 (0.00)	0.01 (0.00)	0.01 (0.00)

Sample selection of foreign-born individuals ages 16–45 in 1980, ages 26–55 in 1990, ages 36–65 in 2000, ages 46–75 in 2010. Year of immigration 1975–80 for 1980, 1975–79 for 1990, 2000, and 2010. Robust standard errors are given in parentheses.
Sources: Integrated Public Use Micro Series (IPUMS) 5% samples for 1980, 1990, and 2000; and several pooled annual samples of the American Community Survey (2005, 2006, 2007, 2008, 2009, and 2010) were used to contruct an equivalent 5% sample for 2010 census.

were in operations, fabricators, and laborers (32%); technical, sales, and administrative support (25%); and service (16%). For non-refugee immigrants, the top three occupations in 1980 (shown in panel C) were in operations, fabricators, and laborers (31%); technical, sales, and administrative support tied with service (both 19%); and managerial and professional (14%). By 1990, however, the top three occupations for refugee immigrants were in technical, sales, and administrative support (29%); managerial and professional (23%); and in operations, fabricators, and laborers (22%). On the other hand, in 1990, the top three occupations for non-refugees were in operations, fabricators, and laborers (27%); technical, sales, and administrative support (20%); and managerial and professional tied with service (both 17%).

It is apparent in panels B and D that refugees experience greater occupational mobility from 1980 to 1990 than their non-refugee counterparts. As seen in panel B, there was a 10% increase in managerial and professional occupations for refugee immigrants, but only a 3% increase in those same occupations for non-refugees (show in panel D). Panel E shows the occupational gain (or loss) of refugees relative to non-refugees over time. Refugee immigrants over time tend to be employed in more skilled occupations compared to non-refugees. A story consistent with these findings is that refugees are investing more in human capital that is valued in the US. We will investigate whether refugee immigrants indeed obtained more education compared to their non-refugee counterparts.

As mentioned in Section 3.1, an important distinction between refugee and other immigrants is their time horizons in the US. That is, lacking the option of immigrating back to their country of origin, refugee immigrants tend to have a longer time horizon in the host country, and hence may be more likely to invest in country-specific human capital. This may take the form of improving language skills, becoming naturalized citizens, or enrolling in the host nation's schools to raise educational attainment. In Table 12.8, we saw evidence of higher school enrollment rates for refugees in 1980, and more rapid increase in English proficiency and US citizenship rate between 1980 and 1990, which are consistent with refugees investing more in host-country-specific human capital upon their arrival. This could be why, initially, the hours worked for refugees is significantly lower.

Table 12.11 (columns (1) and (4)) shows the results of estimating our regression model with years of completed schooling as the dependent variable. In this analysis we are using the same sample that we used to analyze the earnings assimilation, i.e., the sample of individuals with positive wages. The main results are as follows. First, the coefficient for the "Refugee" dummy is always positive and significant, indicating that in this sample of foreign-born individuals arriving in the US in 1975–80, refugees are more educated than economic immigrants around the time of arrival. As shown in columns (1) and (4), male refugees have 1.33 more years of education compared to male non-refugees in 1980, while female refugees have an additional 0.75 years of education compared to female

Table 12.11 Educational attainment and occupational standing scores (Z-scores) regression results for male and female immigrants

	Panel A: Male sample			Panel B: Female sample		
	(1)	(2)	(3)	(4)	(5)	(6)
	Educational attainment	Hause–Warren Index (HWSEI)	Nakao–Treas Score (PRENT)	Educational attainment	Hause–Warren Index (HWSEI)	Nakao–Treas Score (PRENT)
Dummy 1990	−0.660	−0.399	−0.375	0.196	−0.183	−0.244
	(0.048)	(0.009)	(0.008)	(0.054)	(0.011)	(0.009)
Dummy 2000	−0.873	−0.404	−0.366	0.510	−0.072	−0.158
	(0.059)	(0.010)	(0.009)	(0.066)	(0.013)	(0.011)
Dummy 2010	−0.263	−0.327	−0.281	1.314	0.113	0.0046
	(0.067)	(0.012)	(0.011)	(0.074)	(0.014)	(0.012)
Refugee	1.328	0.108	0.110	0.747	0.077	0.061
	(0.066)	(0.014)	(0.012)	(0.079)	(0.017)	(0.014)
Refugee × Dummy 1990	1.016	0.265	0.202	0.373	0.131	0.146
	(0.094)	(0.021)	(0.018)	(0.110)	(0.024)	(0.020)
Refugee × Dummy 2000	0.972	0.233	0.172	0.172	0.092	0.107
	(0.095)	(0.021)	(0.018)	(0.112)	(0.024)	(0.020)
Refugee × Dummy 2010	0.570	0.190	0.124	−0.191	0.041	0.059
	(0.097)	(0.020)	(0.017)	(0.109)	(0.023)	(0.019)
Constant	−0.567	−1.708	−1.404	−0.947	−0.951	−0.765
	(0.380)	(0.066)	(0.061)	(0.431)	(0.082)	(0.070)
Controls	Yes	Yes	Yes	Yes	Yes	Yes
State fixed effects	Yes	Yes	Yes	Yes	Yes	Yes
Observations	116,444	116,444	116,444	85,462	85,462	85,462
Adjusted R^2	0.13	0.07	0.07	0.11	0.03	0.04

Sample selection of foreign-born individuals ages 15–45 in 1980, ages 26–55 in 1990, ages 36–65 in 2000, ages 46–75 in 2010. Year of immigration 1975–80 for 1980, 1975–79 for 1990, 2000, and 2010. Controls for columns (1) and (4) include age, age^2, age^3, married dummy variable, number of own children in the household and higher order polynomials of this variable, and regional enclaves (i.e., midwest, south, west, and northeast is the omitted category). Controls for columns (2), (3), (5), and (6) include age, age^2, age^3, married dummy variable, and regional enclaves (i.e., midwest, south, west, and northeast is the omitted category). Robust standard errors are given in parentheses. *Sources*: Integrated Public Use Micro Series (IPUMS) 5% samples for 1980, 1990, and 2000; and several pooled annual samples of the American Community Survey (2005, 2006, 2007, 2008, 2009, and 2010) were used to construct an equivalent 5% sample for 2010 census.

non-refugees in 1980. Second, refugees experience a significantly larger increase in educational attainment. The estimated coefficients for "Refugee × Dummy 1990" indicate that among male immigrants, refugees gained one extra year of schooling relative to non-refugees between 1980 and 1990 (panel A, column (1)) and among female immigrants, the relative gain for refugees was 0.37 years (panel B, column (4)). The schooling gap between refugee and non-refugee immigrants does not widen in 1990 and 2000, suggesting that refugees make larger investments in host-country-specific human capital initially upon arrival, and by 1990 appear to be done with such investments.[26] In additional analysis, we find that most of the schooling gains made by refugees bring them over the margin of a B.A. degree completion. In contrast, the schooling gains made by non-refugees, which are already smaller in magnitude to begin with, are over the margin of a high school degree completion. Given the evolution of the US wage structure over the period 1980–2000s (e.g., Autor et al., 2008), which has increasingly favored highly educated workers, these differential education gains by refugee status can be expected to be magnified into large differential earnings gains by refugee status.

Because earnings may not capture economic well-being—for example, they may reflect compensating differentials for unattractive jobs—we analyze two additional measures of economic status available from the IPUMS. The first measure is an updated Duncan socio-economic index, called the Hauser and Warren socio-economic index (HWSEI), which assigns higher scores to occupations with higher earnings and more educated workers.[27] The second measure is the Nakao–Treas Prestige Score (PRENT), an updated version of the Siegel Prestige score, which assigns scores to occupations in accordance with the occupational prestige ratings measured in the 1989 General Social Survey (Nakao and Treas, 1994). Both measures have been transformed into z-scores (variance of 1 and mean of 0). Table 12.11 reports the regression results using HWSEI and PRENT as the dependent variables. In practice, the results for the two indices are quite similar. The coefficient for "Refugee" indicates that, upon arrival, refugees hold more prestigious jobs than non-refugees. This is not surprising, as refugees have significantly higher education even at the outset. This finding is consistent with the Table 12.9 result of (weakly) higher hourly wages, though the significantly lower hours

[26] The coefficients for "Refugee × Dummy 2000" are not materially different from those for the previous decade, but those for "Refugee × Dummy 2010" actually look lower, which is surprising considering we do not think of an individual's educational attainment as capable of declining. This smaller measured refugee–non-refugee gap in educational attainment in 2010 appears to arise from selective exit from employment, as when we use the full sample of immigrants rather than the subset with positive earnings, the interactions with the refugee dummy are basically flat over the three decades 1990, 2000, and 2010.

[27] Specifically, Hauser and Warren regressed occupational prestige ratings measured in the 1989 General Social Survey on occupational earnings and education measured in the census microdata. The resulting statistical model was used to generate socio-economic scores for the entire range of 1990 occupation categories.

worked generate the significantly lower annual earnings in 1980. Next, shifting focus to the interaction terms, we find that the socio-economic standing of refugees increased relative to non-refugees over the decade from 1980 to 1990. This relative socio-economic standing increase was sustained over the next 20 and 30 years, indicating that refugees entered more prestigious occupations by 1990 and stayed in them over the rest of their working lives. These results, taken together with the earlier results, suggest that the refugees' larger earnings gains are accompanied by larger increases in occupational prestige. In other words, following an initial human capital investment stage in the US, refugees are more likely to shift to jobs that not only pay more, but are considered by Americans to be more attractive jobs.

3.3.3 Discussion

Our results are consistent with the human capital investment model described in Section 3.1. Upon arrival in the US, refugees are observed to undertake more investments in human capital that is valued in the US. We observe they are more likely to enroll in school in 1980, and this leads to greater gains in years of completed schooling, B.A. degree completion, and English proficiency relative to economic migrants. It takes time and resources to undertake these investments, hence it is not surprising that in 1980 we observe significantly fewer hours worked for refugees relative to non-refugees. The lower labor supply is responsible for the lower annual earnings observed for refugees relative to non-refugees. But once the investment period is complete, then the model predicts more rapid earnings growth for refugees relative to non-refugee immigrants, and this is exactly what we observed. The higher annual earnings reflect not only more hours worked, but also some returns for the additional human capital investments—hourly wages do increase, there is a shift toward occupations with higher wages and better wage growth, and there is a shift toward occupations considered more prestigious.

These findings on the economic assimilation of refugees relative to non-refugees were obtained using a particular cohort of adult immigrants to the US, namely those immigrating between 1975 and 1980. These patterns may not necessarily apply to earlier or later cohorts of migrants, as the selectivity in migration by refugees and non-refugees could be different over time. It can already be seen that some of the differences in observable characteristics by refugee status found here are different from what we found in Section 2.3 using NIS data, which is a sample of immigrants gaining legal permanent status in 2003; not only is the cohort of arrival different (the NIS contains later cohorts), but the range of migrants covered is different (the NIS contains only new green card holders, the Census contains all types of migrants).[28] Nor would these results necessarily apply to

---

[28] The NIS analysis revealed that refugees were significantly more likely to be enrolled in English classes and college than non-refugees, so their worse labor market outcomes may be attributable to the fact that shortly after migration (which is when the NIS respondents are surveyed), refugees are still in a human capital accumulation phase. Given their investments, it is likely that over time their labor market outcomes will improve relative to non-refugees, as is found here for the 1975–80 arrival cohorts.

other countries, because not only might immigrant selectivity vary by country, but also each country has its own set of asylum and immigrant policies which impact labor market outcomes and the relative incentives to invest in host-country-specific human capital.

4. IMPACTS OF REFUGEES ON SENDING AND RECEIVING COMMUNITIES

Thus far, we have focused discussion on refugees themselves—who they are and how they adjust to life in the host country. Refugees, however, might also be expected to have effects on their sending and receiving communities. There is a large literature in economics examining the effects of immigrants in general on native outcomes in the host country, and to a lesser extent on the people left behind in the source country. In this section, we discuss the subset of papers in this literature that examine the impacts of refugees in particular.

4.1 Impacts in host countries

Countries incur various costs in assisting refugees and operating their refugee regime. For individuals recognized as refugees, host countries might provide or subsidize housing, food, health care, language and job training, schooling, etc., if only initially. In Section 3.2, we discussed some existing studies on the welfare dependence of refugees relative to non-refugees; the general finding is that refugees are more likely than other migrants to receive transfer payments from the government, though with more time spent in the host country the differential decreases. Aside from the direct transfer payments and services to refugees, there are other fiscal costs associated with refugees. For example, countries also expend resources to process asylum applications, provide temporary aid while cases are pending, deport rejected applicants, and maintain border security. It is difficult to assess which costs are incremental costs specific to refugees and which costs would have been incurred anyway regardless of refugees (e.g., a country would have maintained border security operations anyway, though the regular flow of refugees might necessitate more agents; some migrants who apply for asylum may have entered in some other class of admission in a counterfactual world with no refugee regime). It can be noted that even countries that are not generous in the assistance to refugees incur costs for the state apparatus of handling refugees (e.g., keeping tight borders is costly, as is operating temporary detention centers for refugees, though both might reduce the number of refugees and asylum seekers in the country). These fiscal costs associated with refugees might affect others in the host country via government budget constraints and removing resources from other potential uses. Besides through fiscal costs, there are some other ways refugees might affect non-refugees. We discuss some of these spillover effects next.

4.1.1 Refugee camps

Some refugee-producing events generate such massive migration flows into neighboring nations that the only feasible way to address the migrants' immediate humanitarian needs is to set up refugee camps. These camps are intended to be temporary, until the situation improves in the home country enough to permit repatriation, or a permanent solution such as resettlement in willing host nations is implemented. In situations recognized by the UNHCR as refugee crises, the UNHCR leads humanitarian efforts at these camps, and funds them in partnership with other humanitarian aid organizations.

These camps impose various costs on the host country. First, typically the host country's security forces contribute to maintaining order, and preventing instability from spreading to its own population. Salehyan and Gleditsch (2006) argued that refugees contribute to diffusing conflict to neighboring states hosting them. Second, the influx of refugees generates a large increase in demand for food, shelter and other goods and services, which can be disruptive to local markets. Alix-Garcia and Saah (2009), using data on Tanzanian households and variation in refugees provided by the Burundi and Rwandan genocides, found that increased exposure to refugees (closer proximity to the camps) tended to increase the prices of agricultural goods, except for those goods provided by aid. Third, especially for camps operating for longer durations, refugees may increasingly spill into the local communities in order to re-establish their lives, such that locals face increased competition for jobs, schools, health care, etc. Furthermore, there could be public health challenges, since refugees are moving from their homes to new environments with which their immune systems are unfamiliar, they might have been deprived of adequate medical care for considerable time leading up to their flight, and often face crowded and unsanitary conditions in the camps (the camps are hastily put together, and on land that was probably previously uninhabited for a reason). Montalvo and Reynal-Querol (2007), using country panel data and variation in refugees generated by civil wars, found that refugees significantly increase the incidence of malaria in refugee-receiving countries. Baez (2011), using household survey microdata on Tanzania, which received large inflows of refugees due to the genocides in Burundi and Rwanda, found that refugees reduce Tanzanian children's human capital. In particular, child mortality increases, and conditional on survival, child height decreases, rate of infectious diseases increases, and educational attainment decreases.

Jacobsen (2002) argued that states can actually benefit economically from the presence of refugees. Her study focused on Africa in the late 1990s and early 2000s. Jacobsen described how international food and other material aid can make it out into the host community, both incidentally and deliberately so as to assuage the local population who may not be very enthusiastic about hosting refugees. She also mentioned infrastructure improvements that have resulted from refugee inflows and the accompanying foreign aid in Zambia, Tanzania, and Uganda. In Tanzania, refugee-related funding provided the government with the financial flexibility to undertake development projects that it could not afford on its own. Jacobsen also named cases where the entrepreneurial instincts of the refugees themselves brought economic benefits to the host nation, referring to water, communications, and construction initiatives on the part of Liberian refugees in Ghana, for example. Jacobsen did, however, raise the issue that these benefits do not necessarily extend to the entire host population and may not justify the costs associated with hosting refugees. For example, in the aforementioned Alex-Garcia and Saah (2009) study, which found that prices increase in agricultural commodities in Tanzania due to refugees inflows from Burundi and Tanzania, Tanzanian households in rural areas experienced welfare gains due to the price increases (because they are net producers of the goods and benefit from higher prices) while urban households were worse off (because they are net consumers).

4.1.2 Resettlement

When safe repatriation on a timely basis cannot be expected, refugees might seek a new country to settle in. Legal restrictions on immigration form an important constraint in the decision of where to resettle—though developed countries might be sought-after destinations, they also tend to have highly restrictive immigration policies, and the demand for a refugee status visa to enter these countries far exceeds the quotas these countries offer. Thus, refugees may choose less desirable countries that have the virtue of being easier to enter, or they take great risks to enter a desired country illegally and upon entry apply for asylum.

Countries have various motivations to provide assistance to refugees—e.g., for humanitarian reasons, to promote international stability—but face constraints that rein in the actual assistance provided. For example, as discussed above, helping refugees imposes a fiscal burden, and it may be politically unpopular to incur such costs to help non-constituents, especially during economic downturns. Additionally, there may be concerns that generous policies toward refugees might encourage more immigration than otherwise would occur, because genuine refugees change their choice of destination to the more generous one, or individuals whose situations are less dire and who otherwise would not have migrated decide to migrate under a more generous refugee policy regime. Martin et al. (2005) provided an overview of the potential impacts of refugees and the refugee regime on developed countries, and highlighted issues that are unique to refugees versus other categories of migrants.

A large literature examines the impact of immigration on natives in the host countries, and Part IV of this Handbook discusses some of these studies. We therefore focus our discussion here on empirical studies in economics that use data on refugees. These studies are often framed around a broader question about immigrants, rather than about the impacts of refugees per se; however, they use refugees and refugee policy to form an identification strategy. One set of such studies uses the refugee-producing event, such as a natural disaster or violent conflict, to provide variation in natives' exposure to the immigrants. The idea is that while migrant inflows to a particular location are in general endogenous,[29] refugee inflows might be considered exogenous because they are primarily motivated by a major negative shock in the home country (and could not be considered responses to economic opportunities in the destination). For example, Card (1990) used the influx of migrants provided by the Mariel Boatlift to learn about the effect of unskilled immigrants on native labor market outcomes. Angrist and Kugler (2003) used the influx in immigrants from the former Yugoslavia generated by the Bosnian and Kosovo wars to identify the effect of exposure to immigrants on the labor market outcomes of EU natives.

A second set of such studies exploit administrative rules affecting the spatial distribution of refugees within the host country to learn about neighborhood, social network, and peer effects. In the case of large refugee inflows, a common policy has been to disperse the refugees across municipalities upon their arrival in the host country, with the intention that the burden of hosting refugees be shared among communities rather than placed on a small handful of traditional immigrant-receiving communities. The implementation of this policy had led to refugees being effectively randomly assigned to locations in a number of settings, and this has been exploited to deal with problems of endogeneity in an individual's neighborhood, social network, or peer group that typically arises when estimating the effects of those variables using observational data.[30] Note that some refugees do relocate from the neighborhood to which they are first assigned, and what is important for papers using these refugee dispersal policies to get plausibly exogenous variation in neighborhood of residence is: first, to use *initial* neighborhood assignment (that which was intended by the policy; any other observed location, such as current neighborhood, could be endogenous); and second, that many people tend to stay in whatever location they are initially assigned (hence, there is a strong "first stage" impact of initial neighborhood characteristics on current neighborhood characteristics).

The Swedish refugee placement policy has been exploited to answer questions as various as: the effects of living in an ethnic enclave on immigrant labor market outcomes (Edin et al., 2003; Aslund and Fredriksson, 2009) and children's educational outcomes (Åslund et al., 2011); the impact of local labor market conditions (specifically, unemployment rate) on immigrant labor market outcomes (Åslund and Rooth, 2007); the impact of ethnic diversity (specifically, immigrant share) on local government choices of welfare

---

[29] Immigrants choose if, where and when to move, and all these decisions in general depend on conditions in the destination, which complicates measuring the causal impacts of number of immigrants in a location. For example, immigrants may systematically migrate to cities with better work opportunities for them; hence, comparing native labor market outcomes in cities with more and fewer immigrants will not in general give the causal impact of natives' exposure to immigrants.

[30] Usually individuals choose which neighborhood they reside in, which makes it difficult to disentangle the effects of a neighborhood attribute from the effects of individual characteristics correlated with that neighborhood attribute, and by using the neighborhood determined by the refugee dispersal policy then issues about non-random selection into neighborhoods are addressed.

benefit levels (Dahlberg and Edmark, 2008), individual preferences for redistributive policies (Dahlberg et al., 2012) and the size of government (Gerdes, 2011); the impact of and the impact of neighborhood income equality on immigrant health outcomes (Gronqvist et al., 2012). Damm (2009a) used the Danish policy to examine the impacts of living in an ethnic enclave on immigrant labor market outcomes. A large resettlement agency in the US also effectively randomly assigns refugees across US cities, and Beaman (2012) exploits this to learn about the dynamic effects of social network size in labor market outcomes.

A caveat to these studies using refugees and refugee policy to form an identification strategy for a broader research question is that to the extent that refugees differ in material ways from other migrants, the impacts of refugees may well differ from the impacts of immigration in general. Thus, before these estimates can be applied to other migrants, a careful consideration of differences between the refugees studied and other migrants should be undertaken.

4.2 Impacts in sending countries

It is difficult to isolate the impacts of refugees on the refugee-sending country from the impacts of other variables that led to, or that are simultaneous with, the emigration. Also, when refugees who fled are repatriated, it is difficult to separate the effect of the repatriated refugees on local communities from the effects of the conditions that made repatriation possible. In part for these reasons, there has been little research on the effects of refugees on the sending countries. This paucity of research has been noted by Koser and Van Hear (2005), who provided a very useful overview of the potential impacts of refugees on the sending countries.

4.2.1 Departure of refugees

Since refugees are part of the home country's economy, their departure can be expected to have economic consequences for the home country. The impact can be expected to differ depending on the size of the outflow, and the labor market characteristics of the refugees relative to the rest of the population. The smaller the outflow, and the greater the substitutability between refugees and the stayers in production, then the smaller the predicted impact of refugee migration on the home country's economy. To the extent that it is the educated and skilled workers leaving, then the refugee migration is associated with "brain drain". For example, Akbulut-Yuksel and Yuksel (2014) found that the Jewish expulsions in Nazi Germany decreased the educational attainment of Germans who were school-aged at the time of the expulsions; because Jews accounted for a significant share of professors, teachers, and professionals, there were deleterious effects on the human capital formation of other Germans.

Besides the direct impact of the refugees' departure on the host country, refugee migration could also have indirect impacts via remittances and influence on international aid. The plight of the refugees may lead to more international attention to their issues, and generate more funds for the agenda of the refugees. There is a literature on the impacts of remittances (see Chapter 20 in this Handbook), but a couple of points pertaining to refugees can be noted that are also highlighted in Koser and Van Hear (2005). First, because the home country has been devastated by the refugee-producing event, and its economy may still be crippled, remittances may be an important source of funds to help rebuild the country. That is, remittances might be used more productively in refugee-sending places. Second, in the case of political refugees, potentially the remittances and aid can contribute to prolonging violent conflict (e.g., the political refugees are on the losing side of the conflict, flee their home country, and send back funds that are partly used to sustain the opposition). Our statement is not that this is good or bad (i.e., prolonged conflict has to be compared to the alternative, and this varies in different settings), but that remittances can feed the refugee-producing event and potentially generate even more refugees.

4.2.2 Return of refugees

An important principle of the Convention is non-refoulement, i.e., a refugee cannot be returned to his or her persecutor. Thus, if signatories are abiding by the Convention, then repatriation should not occur until the home country becomes safe for the refugee. In practice, there are sometimes strong political pressures to repatriate—on the one hand, it is costly to operate refugee camps indefinitely, and on the other hand, potential host nations might be unwilling to offer permanent resettlement—leading to skepticism about whether a repatriation policy is recommended because conditions have truly improved in the home country or because of political expediency. Toft (2007) discussed some of the issues related to refugee repatriation.

While the more general literature on the impacts of return migration might inform on the impacts of repatriation of refugees on the home country, an important consideration is that refugees tend to have considerably less to return to—the refugee-producing event could have destroyed homes, businesses, and communities. Additionally, refugees might face more problems with reintegration because of the trauma they have been exposed to, or because of the marginalization they may continue to experience. And just as for the impact of refugee outflows on home countries, the impact of refugee repatriation can be expected to depend on the characteristics of the returnees versus stayers. Who returns among those who chose to flee is potentially endogenous; factors that affect the decision to return (rather than stay in camps or be permanently settled) can be correlated with outcomes. Kondylis (2008) found using 2000–01 Rwandan household data that, relative to stayers, refugees returning to Rwanda after 1994 are on average younger, have fewer children, have higher agricultural output (though the difference in output appears to arise from returnees sorting into regions that have higher productivity, and is not observed in within-prefecture comparisons), and higher returns to labor. On the other hand, Kondylis (2010) found that refugees and internally displaced persons returning to Bosnia and

Herzegovina following the 1992–95 war are significantly less likely than stayers to work during the last week using 2001–04 household survey data, despite refugees and stayers having similar educational attainment and skills (as measured by occupation and job types). She argued that the results are consistent with refugees having worse informal social networks for job search.

5. POLITICAL ECONOMY ISSUES

5.1 Asylum policies

Although the nations party to the 1951 United Nations Convention Relating to the Status of Refugees and the 1967 Protocol follow the same set of guiding principles in forming their asylum policies, the asylum policies they implement vary considerably. In this subsection, we describe some of the dimensions along which asylum policies have differed across time and space.

One commonly used measure of the generosity (or toughness) of a country's asylum policy is the asylum recognition rate, which gives the percentage of asylum applications with decisions rendered that successfully resulted in recognition as a refugee (either under the 1951 Convention or some other humanitarian ground). There is a great deal of variation in the recognition rate across time and across countries. While much of the time variation may be due to the composition of the case load—some years may have more severe cases than others, i.e., the applications relate to specific refugee-producing events that are universally regarded as dire and warranting refuge—the regional variation is harder to reconcile completely in this way. For example, in 1997–2002, the North American neighbors US and Canada had recognition rates of 33.5% and 56.4% respectively (Hatton, 2009, Table 4). Also, the Scandinavian countries Denmark, Norway, and Sweden had recognition rates of 54.7%, 37.3%, and 44.4% respectively, though in 2002–06 the ranking of the three countries by recognition rate actually reversed relative to 1997–2002 (Hatton, 2009, Table 4).

In fact, there is considerable variation in recognition rates across regions within the same country. For example, Holzer et al. (2000) found significant differences in recognition rates across Swiss cantons, even after controlling for case composition (e.g., age, sex, year, and country of origin of applicant). Similarly, using data on asylum cases in the US, Ramji-Nogales et al. (2009) found significant differences in recognition rates across individual asylum officers and judges, even for cases brought up within the same region or court involving applicants of the same nationality.

A higher recognition rate might be prima facie evidence of a more generous host country, as it is admitting a higher share of people applying for asylum there. However, it could also be consistent with a host country that makes it difficult for potential asylum candidates to enter the country in the first place (so the total number of applications is low, though conditional on entry to file an application, recognition rates are high).

Conversely, a host country might be stringent on granting refugee status, but offer very generous aid to refugees who have been admitted. Thus, to get a more complete understanding of a country's policy stance toward refugees, it is useful to consider a wider set of policies that relate to refugees besides the recognition rate.

Hatton (2009), in his analysis on the relationship between country's asylum policies and number of asylum applications, classified policies affecting refugees into three broad categories: (1) policies impacting the ability of asylum seekers to gain access to the country's territory; (2) policies related to the processing of asylum applications and the toughness of meeting the country's definition of refugee; and (3) policies affecting individuals gaining refugee status. It is difficult to form an overall measure of policy stance because countries vary considerably in the number of policies as well as the nature of policies even within a narrowly defined topic. Hatton therefore used his indices of policy stance in the three broad categories to reveal time trends in policy stance within countries, and avoided making cross-country comparisons (i.e., he aimed to describe whether a country has become more or less generous toward refugees over time, rather than whether one country is more generous than another country). He found that on average major developed countries toughened their stance toward refugees on an overall basis between 1997 and 2006, as well as in each of the three policy categories. There have been fewer major negative changes in policies pertaining to welfare (which pertain to individuals recognized as refugees), and more negative shifts in the index arising from policies that keep would-be applicants out, or that make it harder for an application to be successful. There is heterogeneity in the trend in policy stance among countries, though; for example, Poland became more generous over the time period, whereas Australia, the UK, and the Netherlands became considerably tougher. Using panel data on asylum applications for source country-receiving country pairs, Hatton found that the shifts toward tougher policies do reduce the number of asylum applications to developed countries.

A number of research papers attempt to explain the fluctuations in policy stance across countries and over time. In the following subsections, we summarize three major sets of variables that have been found to be associated with asylum policies.

5.1.1 Studies linking asylum policies of nations to economic concerns

Numerous studies have found links between the asylum policies of nations and economic influences, such as economic conditions in the host country and the economic attributes of the asylum seekers themselves. These economic influences take at least three different forms: the economic attributes of the asylum seekers, economic conditions in the host country at the time of the refugee inflows, and external economic factors.

Studies that consider the effect of economic characteristics of refugees on their chances of admittance usually take into account the ability of these asylum seekers to integrate into the host country's workforce. Howard (1980), in an examination of Canadian asylum procedures in the 1970s, described how that country sought to admit those applicants with the greatest ability to integrate into Canadian society and avoid becoming drains on the public purse, stressing the importance of employability and entrepreneurial skills in the selection process. She suggested that such highly skilled asylum seekers were at an advantage relative to others who may have been less skilled, even if the threats of political persecution they faced were greater. Zucker (1983) argued a point similar to that of Howard, focusing on the issue of US reluctance to admit asylum seekers from Haiti in the early 1980s, and suggesting that such reluctance stems at least in part from an unwillingness to allow people into the country whose lack of employable skills made them a likely drain on social spending. Lankov (2004) examined the case of refugees from North Korea attempting to enter South Korea via China, and he argued that a major reason that many are turned away is that most North Koreans lack the education and skills to successfully adjust to life in the modern South. To bolster this argument, he pointed out that North Korean refugees in South Korea had only a 50% employment rate, at a time when South Korea's unemployment rate was only 3–4%. He went on to argue that those who do find work earn much less than the national average. Basok (1990) discussed the case of Costa Rica in the 1980s, and she argued that one reason for greater willingness to admit Nicaraguans as refugees relative to Salvadorans was their relative youth, the higher proportion of them that were male, and their greater preponderance of agricultural workers, which may have given them an advantage in finding employment in Costa Rica.

Many articles have looked at how destination countries may be influenced by their own economic conditions in setting asylum policies. Hatton (2009) and Neumayer (2005), using panel data on source–destination country pairs and destination country fixed effects estimation, found significant negative effects of destination unemployment rate on asylum applications and recognition rates respectively. Crisp (1984) discussed the case of Djibouti in the late 1970s, then a newly independent state. At the time, suffering from drought and the destruction of regional trade resulting from a war between Somalia and Ethiopia, the government of Djibouti was eager to repatriate the more than 40,000 refugees of Ethiopian nationality who had arrived in the country. Thus, the desire to repatriate Ethiopian refugees was primarily motivated by Djibouti's economic hardships, and probably not by a change in the safety of living conditions in Ethiopia. In a discussion of efforts by France and Germany to manage foreign labor migration, Bach (1993) briefly discussed how a lack of government funding to help resettle admitted refugees impairs the ability of local organizations to effectively serve their communities and can aggravate hostilities on the part of local populations towards migrants in general and refugees in particular. In a study of changes to asylum policies in the late 1970s, Stein (1983) wondered if increasing economic difficulties in major developed world destination countries, such as the US, Canada, France, and Australia, might weaken the commitment of these countries to accept refugees, particularly those with lower skills. He argued that popular hostility to economic migrants in an environment of economic hardship might spill over to genuine refugees suspected of being economic migrants themselves. In a similar vein, Gibney (1999) suggested that weak labor and housing markets or public austerity in a destination country can stoke animosity among local populations toward refugees and increase pressure to apply tighter restrictions on admittance. In her study of Costa Rica, Basok (1990) suggested that the occurrence of a financial crisis in that nation at the time of the heaviest inflows of asylum seekers from El Salvador contributed to a greater reluctance to grant them refugee status. She compared this situation with that of asylum seekers from Nicaragua who faced an easier task achieving refugee status at a time when the crisis had eased. Finally, consistently violent conflict has been found to be associated with asylum applications and recognition rates (e.g., Neumayer, 2005; Hatton, 2009), and negative economic shocks are a cause of violent conflict (Miguel et al., 2004).

Some studies have also examined how countries adjust their refugee policies so as to maintain good relationships with major trading partners and aid donors. Crisp (1984) argued that the Djibouti government was eager to restart a rail link between the capital, Djibouti City, and Addis Ababa, the capital of Ethiopia, so as to revive the economy somewhat and saw appeasing Ethiopian demands for repatriation of refugees as an avenue for doing so. Lankov (2004) argued that a further reason that South Korea displays such unwillingness to admit refugees from the North who enter via China is a reluctance to complicate relations with China, a trading partner and political power of growing importance. Lankov described how China does not wish to be seen as a transit route for refugees from the North to the South. Also, Basok (1990) argued that Costa Rica took up a refugee policy stance that aligned with US strategic objectives (taking a harder line against refugees from El Salvador, a US ally, and being more lenient with refugees from Nicaragua, a US foe) because, in the midst of its financial crisis, Costa Rica was heavily dependent on US aid.

5.1.2 Studies linking asylum policies of nations to external political concerns

External political concerns have also been cited for country's choices of asylum policies. A number of studies have made arguments that the decision whether or not to admit refugees from a certain country was intimately related to the nature of the relationship between destination country and origin state, while others have made observations on how asylum decisions sometimes take into account the concerns of some third state.

Scheinman (1983, p. 80) asserted that "the granting or withholding of refugee status has become an instrument of the receiving state's diplomacy toward the sending state," a view expounded in several other articles. Howard (1980) detailed suspicions among many refugee advocates in the 1970s that Canadian authorities held a bias in favor of asylum seekers fleeing communist or leftist states such as Hungary, Czechoslovakia, Uganda, and Vietnam, and were far more hostile towards left-wing asylum seekers escaping political persecution in right-wing dictatorial states like Argentina, Chile, and Uruguay.

She suggested that this policy is motivated by a fear of allowing left-wing "subversives" into the country. Zucker (1983) drew a similar conclusion, specifically with regard to Haitian asylum seekers in the US, asserting that a major reason for US reluctance to grant the Haitians refugee status was the presence of a US-friendly right-wing dictator (Jean-Claude Duvalier) in Haiti. She also noted that the US rarely denied refugee status to escapees from communist nations. In a paper on the legal framework of refugee determination procedures in the late 1960s and early 1970s, Evans (1972) discussed how the US Department of State can introduce foreign policy considerations, including US relations with the origin state, as evidence for or against recognition of asylum seekers' claims. In the African context, Jacobsen (2002) drew attention to the case of Tanzania in the late 1990s, where refugees from Rwanda were expelled after allegations that they were pursuing military and political goals from their camps. Refugees from Burundi were not subject to the same treatment despite similar allegations. Jacobsen suggested that this situation emerged because relations between Tanzania and Burundi were much cooler than those between Tanzania and Rwanda, and the Tanzanian government was subsequently less eager to curb the questionable activities of Burundian refugees. Basok (1990) argued that Costa Rican willingness to admit asylum seekers from Nicaragua stemmed from opposition to the Sandinista government in that country. Similar to the argument raised by Howard in the Canadian context, Basok suggested that, while they were admitting Nicaraguan refugees, Costa Rican elites were applying pressure on left-wing asylum seekers from El Salvador on the grounds that they were "subversives" seeking to spread their political ideology among the people.

Basok's article also touched on another avenue through which external political factors may impact asylum policy: the desire to maintain good relations with some third party state. In the case of Costa Rica in the 1980s, as Basok described, this third party state was the US, whose geopolitical objectives in the region the Costa Rican government wanted to further as a way of maintaining closer ties with a major aid donor. To this end, Costa Rica maintained a more welcoming stance towards asylum seekers from Nicaragua than towards those from El Salvador. As mentioned above, Lankov (2004) described how South Korea resisted granting refugee status to many North Koreans to discourage them from using China as an escape route to the South. This was driven in part by a desire to keep up healthy relations with China, who was growing in economic and political importance to the whole region, including South Korea. Lankov did point out, however, that North Korean refugees applying for asylum in South Korea via other Asian nations hardly have better experiences. The South Korean case is also unique for another reason, as Lankov argued that, despite the adversarial nature of relations between North Korea and South Korea, the South does not want to encourage the collapse of the state in the North for fear of an uncontrollable economic, political, and humanitarian catastrophe, and for this reason is sometimes unwilling to accept North Korean asylum seekers.

5.1.3 The role of the UNHCR's policies in the asylum policies of nations

Several studies argue that decisions by the United Nations High Commissioner for Refugees (UNHCR) impact the asylum policies chosen by nations. Crisp (1984), in his analysis of the situation facing Ethiopian refugees in Djibouti in the late 1970s, argued that the UNHCR was too cautious in its attempts to protect the Ethiopians from forcible repatriation. He detailed how the organization was trying not to push the Djibouti authorities too hard on protection issues for fear of provoking a backlash and a mass deportation, but Crisp questioned the usefulness of the Refugee Convention and Protocol under which the UNHCR operates if they are not to be forcefully applied. While Crisp took the UNHCR to task for not preventing repatriation more effectively, Stein and Cuny (1994) argued that the organization is too inflexible about repatriation and should be more willing to assist in the repatriation process when the refugees themselves are pushing to return home. This includes cases in which the conditions that caused the flight in the first place are still present in the origin country. The authors argued that the UNHCR needs to rethink its standards for when it becomes involved in the repatriation process, taking more account of the wishes of the refugees.

Other topics besides repatriation have also stimulated discussion about the UNHCR. In an essay reflecting on the first 50 years of the existence of the UNHCR, Goodwin-Gill (2001) suggested that, especially after 1980, the UNHCR has become increasingly unaccountable, disorganized, incapable of preventing displacement episodes, overly dependent on the financial generosity of donor states, and impotent in holding states up to their commitments. An article with a more specific focus (on the situation of Palestinian refugees in Gaza) is that of Feldman (2007). The thrust of Feldman's argument is that the labeling of displaced Palestinians in the Gaza Strip as "refugees" (as compared to the "natives" of Gaza) after the founding of Israel in 1948 has had long-lasting adverse consequences in Gazan society. This labeling has led to tensions and resentments between the refugees and the natives, not least since only refugees were legally entitled to formal aid, despite the fact that natives were also suffering grievously. It should be noted that Feldman's analysis is concerned not with the UNHCR but with the United Nations Relief and Works Agency for Palestine Refugees in the Near East (UNRWA), the UN's organ for refugee issues in the Palestinian territories. Odhiambo-Abuya (2004) examined the efforts of the UNHCR in Kenya in dealing with refugees from Somalia, Sudan, and Ethiopia in the 1990s. He argued that excessive delays in refugee status determination procedures, caused by a lack of funding, leaves asylum applicants in a state of limbo that enhances their suffering. Odhiambo-Abuya noted also that most asylum seekers are unable to work or otherwise attend to their own needs while awaiting a decision on their claim. He also criticized the wording of the letter rejecting asylum seekers' claims, saying that it is too vague and impairs the applicant's ability to effectively appeal.

5.2 Modeling host countries' policy choices

In this subsection, we discuss potential models of host nation behavior to explain the observed policy differences described in Section 5.1. A simplistic model might have the host nation choosing to allocate its scarce resources over two potential uses: refugee assistance (e.g., number of refugees to admit, quality of services to offer) and all other things. With standard assumptions about preferences, then the usual result is obtained: the optimal allocation is such that the last dollar spent on each good (here, refugee and non-refugee uses) provides the same marginal utility. Even this simplistic model offers explanations for some of the differences in asylum countries observed in Section 5.1. For example, relative to countries that are richer or time periods when its economy is stronger, a country observed at a particular time period may have a lower chosen level of refugee assistance. As another example, encapsulated in the utility function may be ideological alignment with the refugee-sending countries, or national security implications to the host country of a particular refugee-sending stream, and this would produce differences across countries in generosity even if they are responding to the same refugee-producing event.

The simplistic model, though, does not generate the result of under-provision of refugee assistance by all nations collectively, which is a major concern voiced by the UNHCR, human rights advocates, and individuals seeking protection. One way to generate this result is to treat a country's refugee assistance as having a positive externality, or as a public good: if one nation provides more refugee assistance, then other nations benefit too (say, because they derive the positive utility from helping a refugee whether or not they themselves have paid for the help); however, each nation does not fully consider the benefits of its refugee assistance on other nations in choosing the optimal bundle. Thus, each nation chooses a level of refugee assistance that is too low vis-à-vis the social optimum. Though parties to the Convention express a desire to help refugees, any given country has an incentive to free ride and wait for other countries to undertake the costs of helping refugees. When one country toughens its policy stance toward refugees, and takes in a smaller number of these refugees, then it is leaving a larger burden for other countries. If other countries do not shoulder the increase in burden, then there is a cut in overall assistance for refugees. Thus, in general when one country increases its toughness, the remaining countries bear a greater share of the overall burden of assisting refugees or the overall level of assistance decrease. Thielemann (2006) and Suhrke (1998) discussed some potential policies to attain a more equitable distribution of the cost of helping refugees. Countries have not been able to agree upon a burden-sharing scheme, and even among European Union members—a relatively small set of nations with some common regional interests and a stated desire to work together—this has not been possible. As a result, perhaps except in cases where one developed nation has a major stake (e.g., failure to respond adequately could seriously undermine its national security), there tends to be under-provision of assistance to refugees.

Thus far, we have considered the host nation as the sole decision-maker. But there are other agents that are making choices that affect a given host nation's choice of policies toward refugees, and we consider several in the following subsections.

5.2.1 The role of other host nations

In choosing its asylum policies, a host country might consider what other countries' policies are expected to be. After all, if it chooses tougher policies in order to ebb the flow of asylum applicants, but other countries toughen theirs even more, then its objective would not be attained. A simple prisoner's dilemma model can illustrate the inefficiency that can arise when countries behave strategically in setting their asylum policies. Consider two host countries simultaneously deciding whether to provide assistance to refugees (Yes or No). A country incurs cost c per refugee it assists. A country reaps benefit b per refugee assisted, regardless of whether it or the other country paid for the assistance. Figure 12.6 illustrates the payoff matrix expressed on a per-refugee basis (the first value listed in each box is for country 1 and the second value is for country 2) for this static prisoner's dilemma, where α is the share of cost of assistance paid by country 1 (the residual $1 - \alpha$ is paid by country 2). Let $2 \cdot b - c > 0 > b - c$ in order to capture the idea that while it is valuable to aid refugees (e.g., for humanitarian reasons, to promote international stability), unilateral action is very costly. The unique solution to this static game is (No, No): Yes is a strictly dominated strategy, and for any strategy that country 2 can play, country 1 is better off choosing No (if country 2 pursues Yes, country 1 is better off choosing No ($b > b - \alpha \cdot c$) and if country 2 pursues No, country 1 is better off choosing No ($0 > b - c$), and vice versa. Thus, the countries forgo the higher total payoff that comes from providing assistance to refugees.[31] With coordination, such as explicit sharing rules agreed upon before a refugee crisis occurs, efficiency can be improved. Additionally, in a repeated game, there may be more scope for cooperation, as deviating from cooperation might trigger punishments that could make the present discounted value of the payoff stream from always cooperating exceed the payoff stream from reneging today and being punished in all future periods. On the other hand, it is not automatic that improved coordination or cooperation among potential host nations would improve refugees' well-being, as collusive behavior can undermine that objective. For example, all nations might agree to a particular burden-sharing rule, but at a lower level of generosity than would have prevailed in the absence of collective action (see, for example, Facchini et al., 2006).

---

[31] The payoffs displayed in Figure 12.6 indicate the same total payoff whenever refugee assistance is provided. If the marginal cost of refugee assistance is increasing though, then bilateral action (i.e., the (Yes, Yes) strategy) yields a higher total payoff than unilateral action.

		Country 2	
		Yes	No
Country 1	Yes	$b - \alpha \cdot c, \, b - (1 - \alpha) \cdot c$	$b - c, \, b$
	No	$b, \, b - c$	$0,0$

Figure 12.6 *Payoff matrix for host nations.*

5.2.2 The role of the UNHCR

The UNHCR stands to affect individual countries' asylum policies by setting international standards and reducing coordination problems. A more active way the UNHCR might influence individual countries' asylum policies is in its decisions about when to intervene. There are numerous situations that involve individuals fleeing from harm, and the UNHCR exercises some discretion over whether and how to provide assistance. Recognition by the UNHCR of a refugee crisis has major implications, such as access to UN resources for protecting refugees, greater availability of other sources of aid from humanitarian organizations and others parties who work in association with the UN, and clearer grounds for claiming asylum among migrants fleeing the situation. While one perspective is that the UNHCR sets policies first, then potential host nations set theirs holding UNHCR policies fixed, given the discretion UNHCR has about responding to negative shocks producing migrant flows, setting up temporary camps, and condoning repatriation, there is the possibility that the UNHCR's policies are in part responses to decisions made by host nations.

5.2.3 The role of the refugees

Refugees are meant to be the innocent people who are caught in the middle of armed conflict, natural disaster or other negative event, and forced to flee to escape the harm. However, in some cases, refugees may be the combatants (though technically they are not supposed to, as the protection spelled out in the Convention does not apply to combatants; however, combatants can claim to be refugees, and individual claims are difficult to verify, especially during times of mass migration) or may become combatants. More generally, refugees or the refugee regime can be manipulated in order to achieve geopolitical goals. This is argued in Stedman and Tanner (2003). For example, knowing that refugees receive aid from the UNHCR and humanitarian organizations, people on the losing side of a violent conflict might flee across borders, become part of a refugee camp, gather strength by recruiting new members in the camp and devising new strategies, and return to the home country to renew the conflict. Thus, the refugee regime is being exploited to gain access to international aid as well as new recruits for the political cause. Refugees may be manipulated in the sense that, at a vulnerable time, they are being recruited and in some cases coerced to join a political cause. In the general case we might think of host nations and the UNHCR making decisions with geopolitical motives mixed in with the humanitarian one, and the situation highlighted here is that political factions can take advantage of the international aid and attention that comes with being recognized as refugees to further their agenda. This behavior in turn impacts UNHCR and host nation policies. For example, it may extend the duration of a violent conflict, which would generate more refugee flows and make solutions like temporary camps (because the conflict is expected to carry on for years) and repatriation (because the home country is still not safe) infeasible.

5.2.4 The role of non-refugee migrants

While host countries may be interested in helping genuine refugees, they may fear that having a more generous policy stance toward refugees will encourage migrants who do not actually face persecution to use the asylum route to enter the country. Thus, the behavior of potential migrants who do not truly meet the requirements as refugees, but could provide an asylum application that has a chance of meeting the standards for being recognized (verification of individual claims of persecution is difficult, and some mistakes get made), impose constraints on the host country in its choice of asylum policies. Bubb et al. (2011) offered a theoretical model capturing the public good nature of refugee protection, together with the interplay between asylum policies and economic migration. The model has the result that as economic migration increases, host countries may toughen their asylum policies to deter economic migrants from using the asylum route to enter. They argued that lower costs of international travel and rising income inequality has increased the incentives for economic migration over time, and this could be a reason why, although the 1951 Convention was relatively effective at achieving refugee burden–sharing among nations in the past, it fails today.

5.2.5 The role of administrators of the asylum policies of nations

Administrators of a country's asylum policies, such as judges, bureaucrats, and law enforcement officers, affect how generous or tough those policies actually are toward refugees and asylum seekers. For example, a tough law that is never enforced does not de facto reduce refugee assistance. Holzer et al. (2000) and Ramji-Nogales et al. (2009) found significant differences in recognition rates for apparently similar cases across regions within Switzerland and the US respectively. The US study also found significant differences across judges within the same court, and asylum officers in the same regional office. The two studies found that characteristics of the administrator handling the case, such as political leanings and gender, affect the disposition of the case.

Administrator discretion has been found to play a role not only in the disposition of asylum applications, but also in the distribution of international aid to refugees. Aldrich (2010) found considerable variation in the amount of aid received by households among 62 inland fishing villages suffering similar damage from the 2004 Indian Ocean tsunami. For example, villages with more poor and lower caste households received significantly less resources from the large disaster relief fund. Technically these individuals affected by the tsunami are not refugees—they did have to move temporary relief camps, but as there was no crossing of country borders they would be considered internally displaced persons rather than refugees. Nevertheless, this case does illustrate the role of the government bureaucrat in mediating assistance to refugees.

These observed differences in outcomes (i.e., recognition rate, aid) among apparently similar refugees clearly indicate the high degree of discretion that administrators have in enforcing the country's asylum laws. In setting its asylum policies, a country has to consider how a particular policy will be enforced. One issue is simply the cost of enforcement (e.g., more border patrol officers are needed to prevent would-be asylum seekers from entering the country). The other issue relates to how to implement policy changes in areas that have a major discretionary component (e.g., in deciding whether to grant asylum to an applicant, the applicant's claim of persecution in the home country must be assessed).

6. CONCLUDING REMARKS

The 1951 Convention Relating to the Status of Refugees and 1967 Protocol form the basis of the international refugee regime. The early waves of refugees were displaced by World War II and the Cold War that ensued afterwards. By contrast, more recent waves are more heterogeneous not only geographically, but also in terms of the shocks that lead individuals to seek refuge. While many asylum seekers are fleeing civil wars and natural disasters, some originate from settings where there was no single precipitating disaster. Host nations, the UNHCR, and humanitarian organizations are all given the challenging task of assisting large and diverse numbers of migrants requesting recognition as refugees given limited resources.

This chapter offers an economic conceptual framework for considering why the selection in migration and the assimilation process might differ between refugee and non-refugee migrants, and why asylum policies might differ among countries and across time. We discuss studies pertaining to these issues, many of which were descriptive in nature and relied heavily on case studies, and were conducted by researchers besides economists (e.g., anthropologists, sociologists, political scientists, legal scholars, human rights scholars). In addition, we contribute to this literature by performing two complementary empirical analyses to help us better understand the nature of selectivity and assimilation of recent refugees coming to the US. To conclude this chapter, rather than summarize all the findings, we focus on some important takeaways from this chapter:

- First, and foremost, the lack of large-scale individual-level datasets measuring refugee status is a major obstacle in studying selectivity in migration and the longer-term trajectories in socio-economic indicators for refugees in host countries. Indeed, only a few countries have datasets with direct measures of refugee status, and generally these datasets arise from combining administrative data on visa type with some general-purpose socio-economic survey data. For the US, researchers have also used information on country of birth and year of arrival to define likely refugees in general-purpose socio-economic surveys. To better understand who refugees are and what their adjustment process is like, new data collection efforts are needed, which might involve linking existing datasets to administrative data, modifying existing surveys to add questions about refugee status and migration history, or designing new surveys. These data collections endeavors would enable researchers to study refugees with a broader coverage in terms of countries, cohorts of arrival, and outcome variables beyond earnings and unemployment. With more studies, it may be possible to discern general patterns, if any, in the refugee experience, and the factors that contribute to smoother social and economic integration into the host country. Additionally, we might be able to observe how a particular refugee-producing event disperses refugees geographically, both initially and over time across host countries, and to understand the nature of selection into different host countries.

- The existing large-scale empirical studies on the assimilation of refugees have been limited to the richest nations. Given that a majority of recent refugees are hosted by developing countries, the lack of such studies for developing-country host nations is absolutely striking, and this literature gap must be filled. In the above point, we acknowledged that data availability may be an important constraint to conducting these studies, and here we mention data issues that may be more pronounced for poor nations. First, microdatasets that measure migration history if not refugee status are less common for poor nations. Second, even when such microdatasets are available, using the cohort approach to study assimilation—i.e., tracking the same arrival cohort in different cross-sections to piece together their progress in the host country—is unlikely to work because selective out-migration of refugees is likely to be a serious problem in poor nations. While refugees observed in developed nations tend to have the intention of permanently settling there, those observed in developing countries may be more likely to return to their home country or migrate somewhere else offering a better opportunity, which would invalidate the cohort approach for constructing assimilation profiles.[32] Thus, in order to study refugees' experience in developing countries over the longer term, data that are not currently available will be needed, and traditional methods of data collection and analysis will need to be modified to deal with the high mobility of the target population.

- An important difference between refugees and non-refugee migrants is that refugees are significantly more likely to have suffered from harm in the home country. Intertwined with this greater exposure to harm is that refugees tend to be in worse physical and mental health than non-refugees. The so-called healthy immigrant effect, that immigrants have better health upon entry and over time converges to native health (by worsening), has been observed in various developed immigrant-receiving countries including the US and Canada. However, refugees arrive with worse initial health, and it is of great interest to understand if their health status worsens over time or simply converges to that of the native-born population (by improving). To date, the long-term health trajectories of refugees have not been studied using large-scale datasets. Tracing health status changes over time for refugees, and comparing them to other migrants' profiles, would be of great value to policymakers and health professionals. For instance, it might help detect health issues faced by refugees that are hidden when they are aggregated with non-refugees, and lead to better targeted health interventions that may raise the well-being and improve management of chronic health conditions among refugees. Additionally, it might increase our understanding of the refugee's process of economic assimilation—that is, to what extent is initial health disadvantage holding back the economic progress of refugees?

- In the US, various studies have found that the "quality" of immigrants has changed over time, with more recent arrival cohorts looking worse in terms of observed wages and wage growth. Thus, if one were to analyze a single cross-section and infer assimilation profiles by comparing immigrants who recently arrived to those who arrived earlier, then the degree of earnings growth with each additional year in the US would be overstated, because earlier cohorts of immigrants were of higher quality. For refugees, it is likely that cohort quality varies too, because quality is determined by the nature of the refugee-producing event and who it induces to migrate. Refugees who migrate under a refugee-producing event that affects the home country broadly are expected to be less favorably selected on characteristics valued by the destination-country labor markets compared to non-refugee migrants from the same home country. By contrast, a refugee-producing event that only affects a narrower

---

[32] It is not random who decides to stay and who decides to return to the home country or migrate to another country. Given this selective attrition in a particular arrival cohort over time, statistics for a particular arrival cohort in different cross-sections do not reflect the same underlying subpopulation, so the assimilation profile cannot be credibly estimated.

subpopulation would have different implications for differences between refugees and non-refugees. Thus, in predicting the economic, social, and cultural assimilation of refugees in the host country and the impact of an influx of refugees on the native population's labor market outcomes, it would be informative to think first about the nature of the refugee-producing event. In a cross-section, refugees from different cohorts are generated by different events, which would imply that cohort to cohort the quality might fluctuate between positively or negatively selected on labor market characteristics, thus the bias in estimating assimilation rate using a cross-section that exists for non-refugees may not necessarily apply to refugees depending on the particular refugee-producing events included.

• A number of studies do not motivate themselves as studying refugees per se, but rely on natural experiments involving refugees to empirically identify some general economic relationship of interest. An important issue about these studies using such an identification strategy is the external validity of their findings. For example, some have used refugee flows to provide exogenous variation in migration flows in order to identify the causal impact of immigrant population on immigrant and native labor market and other outcomes. Others have relied on refugee dispersal policies to provide exogenous variation in place of residence, in order to identify the causal effects of growing up or living in a "better" neighborhood (e.g., richer, higher school quality). Are the estimated parameters likely to capture the causal effect of immigration or the causal effect of a neighborhood attribute on average, at least for some subpopulation of interest? Are the refugee shocks employed by the studies atypical of the country's other refugees and non-refugee migrants? Are refugee responses to neighborhood attributes likely to be similar to the general population's or other migrant's responses? Assessments of the study's external validity would have to trace the refugees back to the refugee-producing event that led to their arrival, and consider how their characteristics might differ from others, and whether there is likely to be heterogeneity in effect along the characteristics with likely differences.

• Lastly, policy debates have ensued in developed countries about the growing burden of refugees, and the unequal distribution of the responsibility of helping refugees among these nations. However, these discussions tend to forget that a majority of the world's refugees are hosted by developing countries. In fact, the share of asylum applications filed in non-industrialized nations increased from 49% to 63% between the periods of 1998–2000 and 2008–10. Also, developed countries have restrictive immigration policies that make it difficult for individuals seeking refuge to enter, leaving a disproportionate share of the world's refugee burden to be borne by developing countries. More discussion about how to support refugees in host nations that are poor and often have weak institutions, as well as investigation into the interlinkages between a country's "regular" immigration policy and refugee policy, are called for.

ACKNOWLEDGMENTS

The authors are grateful to Michael Baima, Chris Biolsi, Alexander Tengolics, and Jeremy Twitchell for excellent research assistance, and to Barry Chiswick, Paul Miller, Pia Orrenius, and an anonymous reviewer for helpful comments.

REFERENCES

Akbulut-Yuksel, M., Yuksel, M., 2014. The long-term direct and external effects of Jewish expulsions in Nazi Germany. Am. Econ. J.: Econ. Pol. (forthcoming).

Akresh, I., 2008. Occupational trajectories of legal US immigrants: Downgrading and recovery. Popul. Dev. Rev. 34 (3), 435–456.

Aldrich, D.P., 2010. Separate and unequal: post-tsunami aid distribution in southern India. Soc. Sci. Q. 91, 1369–1389.

Alix-Garcia, J., Saah, D., 2009. The effect of refugee inflows on host communities: Evidence from Tanzania. World Bank Econ. Rev. 24 (1), 148–170.

Angrist, J.D., Kugler, A.D., 2003. Protective or counter-productive? Labour market institutions and the effect of immigration on EU natives. Econ. J. 113, F302–F331.

Åslund, O., Fredriksson, P., 2009. Peer effects in welfare dependence: Quasi-experimental evidence. J. Hum. Resour. 44 (3), 798–825.

Åslund, O., Rooth, D.-O., 2007. Do when and where matter? Initial labor market conditions and immigrant earnings. Econ. J. 117 (518), 422–448.

Åslund, O., Edin, P.-A., Fredriksson, P., Grönqvist, H., 2011. Peers, neighborhoods, and immigrant student achievement: Evidence from a placement policy. Am. Econ. J. Appl. Econ. 3 (2), 67–95.

Autor, D.H., Katz, L.F., Kearney, M.S., 2008. Trends in U.S. wage inequality: Revisiting the revisionists. Rev. Econ. Stat. 90 (2), 300–323.

Bach, R.L., 1993. Recrafting the common good: Immigration and community. Ann. Am. Acad. Polit. Soc. Sci. 530, 155–170.

Baez, J., 2011. Civil wars beyond their borders: The human capital and health consequences of hosting refugees. J. Dev. Econ. 96, 391–408.

Basok, T., 1990. Welcome some and reject others: Constraints and interests influencing Costa Rican policies on refugees. Int. Migrat. Rev. 24 (4), 722–747.

Beaman, L., 2012. Social networks and the dynamics of labor market outcomes: Evidence from refugees resettled in the U.S. Rev. Econ. Stud. 79 (1), 128–161.

Bleakley, H., Chin, A., 2004. Language skills and earnings: Evidence from childhood immigrants. Rev. Econ. Stat. 86 (2), 481–196.

Blom, S., 1997. Tracing the integration of refugees in the labour market: A register approach. Statistical Journal 14 (3), 243–265.

Bollinger, C.R., Hagstrom, P., 2008. Food stamp program participation of refugees and immigrants. South. Econ. J. 74 (3), 665–692.

Bollinger, C.R., Hagstrom, P., 2011. The poverty reduction success of public transfers for working age immigrants and refugees in the United States. South. Econ. J. 29 (2), 191–206.

Borjas, G.J., 1982. The earnings of male Hispanic immigrants in the United States. Ind. Labor Relat. Rev. 35 (3), 343–353.

Borjas, G.J., 1987. Self-selection and the earnings of immigrants. Am. Econ. Rev. 77 (4), 531–553.

Borjas, G.J., 1999. The economic analysis of immigration. In: Ashenfelter, O., Card, D. (Eds.), Handbook of Labor Economics, vol. 3A. Elsevier, Amsterdam.

Bubb, R., Kremer, M., Levine, D.I., 2011. The economics of international refugee law. J. Leg. Stud. 40 (2), 367–404.

Card, D., 1990. The impact of the Mariel Boatlift on the Miami labor market. Indust. Labor Rel. Rev. 43 (2), 245–257.

Chiswick, B., Miller, P.W., 1991. Speaking, reading and earnings among low-skilled immigrants. J. Labor Econ. 9 (2), 149–170.

Chiswick, B., Miller, P.W., 1999a. Language practice and the economic well-being of immigrants. Policy Options/Options Politiques, 45–50.

Chiswick, B., Miller, P.W., 1999b. Language skills and earnings among legalized aliens. J. Popul. Econ. 12 (1), 63–91.

Chiswick, B., Miller, P.W., 2002. Immigrant earnings: Language skills, linguistic concentrations and the business cycle. J. Popul. Econ. 15 (1), 31–57.

Chiswick, B., Miller, P.W., 2010. Occupational language requirements and the value of English in the United States labor market. J. Popul. Econ. 23 (1), 353–372.

Chiswick, B., Lee, Y.L., Miller, P.W., 2006. Immigrants' language skills and visa category. Int. Migrat. Rev. 40 (2), 419–450.

Cohen, Y., Haberfeld, Y., 2007. Self-selection and earnings assimilation: Immigrants from the former Soviet Union in Israel and the United States. Demography 44 (3), 649–668.

Connor, P., 2010. Explaining the refugee gap: Economic outcomes of refugees versus other immigrants. J. Refug. Stud. 23 (3), 377–397.

Cortes, K.E., 2004. Are refugees different from economic immigrants? Some empirical evidence on the heterogeneity of immigrant groups in the United States. Rev. Econ. Stat. 86 (2), 465–480.

Crisp, J., 1984. The politics of repatriation: Ethiopian refugees in Djibouti, 1977–1983. Rev. Afr. Polit. Econ. 30, 73–82.

Dahlberg, M., Edmark, K., 2008. Is there a 'race-to-the-bottom' in the setting of welfare benefit levels? Evidence from a policy intervention. J. Publ. Econ. 92, 1193–1209.

Dahlberg, M., Edmark, K., Lundqvist, H., 2012. Ethnic diversity and preferences for redistribution. J. Polit. Econ. 120 (1), 41–76.

Damm, A.P., 2009a. Ethnic enclaves and immigrant labor market outcomes: Quasi-experimental evidence. J. Labor Econ. 27 (2), 281–314.

Damm, A.P., 2009b. Determinants of recent immigrants' location choices: Quasi-experimental evidence. J. Popul. Econ. 22, 145–174.

Duleep, H.O., Regets, M.C., 1999. Immigrants and human-capital investment. Am. Econ. Rev. 89 (2), 186–191.

Edin, P.-A., Fredriksson, P., Åslund, O., 2003. Ethnic enclaves and the economic success of immigrants: Evidence from a natural experiment. Q. J. Econ. 118 (1), 329–357.

Edin, P.-A., Fredriksson, P., Åslund, O., 2004. Settlement policies and the economic success of immigrants. J. Popul. Econ. 17, 133–155.

Evans, A.E., 1972. Political refugees and the United States immigration laws: Further developments. Am. J. Int. Law 66 (3), 571–585.

Facchini, G., Lorz, O., Willmann, G., 2006. Asylum seekers in Europe: The warm glow of a hot potato. J. Popul. Econ. 19 (2), 411–430.

Feldman, I., 2007. Difficult distinctions: Refugee law, humanitarian practice, and political identification in Gaza. Cult. Anthropol. 22 (1), 129–169.

Finnan, C.R., 1981. Occupational assimilation of refugees. Int. Migrat. Rev. 15 (1/2), 292–309.

Finnan, C.R., 1982. Community influences on the occupational adaptation of Vietnamese refugees. Anthropol. Q. 55 (3), 161–169.

Gerdes, C., 2011. The impact of immigration on the size of government: Empirical evidence from Danish municipalities. Scandanavian Journal of Economics 113 (1), 74–92.

Gibney, M.J., 1999. Liberal democratic states and responsibilities to refugees. Am. Polit. Sci. Rev. 93 (1), 169–181.

Goodwin-Gill, G.S., 2001. Refugees: Challenges to protection. Int. Migrat. Rev. 35 (1), 130–142.

Gronqvist, H., Johansson, P., Niknami, S., 2012. Income inequality and health: Lessons from a refugee residential assignment program. J. Health Econ. 31, 617–629.

Gustafsson, B., Osterberg, T., 2001. Immigrants and the public sector budget-Accounting exercises from Sweden. J. Popul. Econ. 14, 689–708.

Haines, D., 1996. Refugees in America in the 1990s: A Reference Handbook. Greenwood Press, Westport, CT.

Hansen, J., Lofstrom, M., 2003. Immigrant assimilation and welfare participation: Do immigrants assimilate into or out of welfare? J. Hum. Resour. 38 (1), 74–98.

Hansen, J., Lofstrom, M., 2009. The dynamics of immigrant welfare and labor market behavior. J. Popul. Econ. 22, 941–970.

Hatton, T.J., 2009. The rise and fall of asylum: What happened and why. Economic Journal 119, F183–F213 (February).

Holzer, T., Schneider, G., Neumayer, E., 2000. Discriminating decentralization: Federalism and the handling of asylum applications in Switzerland, 1988–1996. J. Conflict Resolut. 44 (2), 250–276.

Howard, R., 1980. Contemporary Canadian refugee policy: A critical assessment. Can. Publ. Pol. 6 (2), 361–373.

Jacobsen, K., 2002. Can refugees benefit the state? Refugee resources and African statebuilding. J. Mod. Afr. Stud. 40 (4), 577–596.

Jasso, G., Rosenzweig, M.R., 2009. Selection criteria and the skill composition of immigrants: A comparative analysis of Australian and U.S. employment immigration. In: Bhagwati, J., Hanson, G.H. (Eds.), Skilled Migration Today: Phenomenon, Prospects, Problems, Policies. Oxford University Press, New York.

Jasso, G., Massey, D.S., Rosenzweig, M.R., Smith, J.P., 2006. The New Immigrant Survey 2003 Round 1 (NIS-2003–1) Public Release Data. Retrieved May 3, 2011 from http://nis.princeton.edu.

Kelly, G.P., 1986. Coping with America: Refugees from Vietnam, Cambodia, and Laos in the 1970s and 1980s. Ann. Am. Acad. Polit. Soc. Sci. 487, 138–149 (Immigration and American Public Policy).

Kondylis, F., 2008. Agricultural outputs and conflict displacement: Evidence from a policy intervention in Rwanda. Econ. Dev. Cult. Change 57 (1), 31–66.

Kondylis, F., 2010. Conflict displacement and labor market outcomes in post-war Bosnia and Herzegovina. J. Dev. Econ. 93, 235–248.

Koser, K., Van Hear, N., 2005. Asylum migration. Implications for countries of origin. In: Borjas, G.J., Crisp, J. (Eds.), Poverty, International Migration and Asylum. Palgrave Macmillan, New York.

Lankov, A., 2004. North Korean refugees in Northeast China. Asian Surv. 44 (6), 856–873.

Martin, S., Schoenholz, A.I., Fisher, D., 2005. The impact of asylum on receiving countries. In: Borjas, G.J., Crisp, J. (Eds.), Poverty, International Migration and Asylum. Palgrave Macmillan, New York.

Miguel, E., Satyanath, S., Sergenti, E., 2004. Economic shocks and civil conflict: An instrumental variables approach. J. Polit. Econ. 112 (4), 725–753.

Montalvo, J.G., Reynal-Querol, M., 2007. Fighting against malaria: Prevent wars while waiting for the 'miraculous' vaccine. Rev. Econ. Stat. 89 (1), 165–177.

Munshi, K., 2003. Networks in the modern economy: Mexican migrants in the U.S. labor market. Q. J. Econ. 118 (2), 549–597.

Nakao, K., Treas, J., 1994. Updating occupational prestige and socioeconomic scores: How the new measures measure up. Sociological Methods and Research 24, 1–72.

Neumayer, E., 2005. Asylum recognition rates in Western Europe: Their determinants, variation, and lack of convergence. J. Conflict Resolut. 49 (1), 43–66.

Odhiambo-Abuya, E., 2004. United Nations High Commissioner for Refugees and status determination Imtaxaan in Kenya: An empirical survey. J. Afr. Law 48 (2), 187–206.

Portes, A., Stepick, A., 1985. Unwelcome immigrants: The labor market experiences of 1980 (Mariel) Cuban and Haitian refugees in South Florida. Am. Sociol. Rev. 50, 493–514.

Powers, M., Seltzer, W., 1998. Occupational status and mobility among undocumented immigrants by gender. Int. Migrat. Rev. 32 (1), 21–55.

Powers, M., Seltzer, W., Shi, J., 1998. Gender differences in the occupational status of undocumented immigrants in the United States: Experience before and after legalization. Int. Migrat. Rev. 32 (4), 1015–1046.

Raijman, R., Semyonov, M., 1995. Modes of labor market incorporation and occupational cost among new immigrants to Israel. Int. Migrat. Rev. 29 (2), 375–394.

Ramji-Nogales, J., Schoenholtz, A.I., Schrag, P.G., 2009. Refugee Roulette: Disparities in Asylum Adjudication and Proposals for Reform. NYU Press, New York.

Rogg, E., 1971. The influence of a strong refugee community on the economic adjustment of its members. Int. Migrat. Rev. 5 (4), 474–481, Naturalization and Citizenship: U.S. Policies, Procedures and Problems (Winter).

Rogg, E., 1974. The Assimilation of Cuban Exiles: the Role of Community and Class. Aberdeen Press, New York.

Ruggles, S., Alexander, J.T., Genadek, K., Goeken, R., Schroeder, M.B., Sobek, M., 2010. Integrated Public Use Microdata Series: Version 5.0 (Machine-readable database). University of Minnesota, Minneapolis.

Rumbaut, R.G., 1989. Portraits, patterns, and predictors of the refugee adaptation process: Results and reflections from the IHARP panel study. In: Haines, D.W. (Ed.), Refugees as Immigrants: Cambodians, Laotians and Vietnamese in America. Rowman & Littlefield, New York.

Rumbaut, R.G., Ima, K., 1998. Between Two Worlds: Southeast Asian Refugee Youth in America. Perseus Books Group, Boulder, CO.

Salehyan, I., Gleditsch, K.S., 2006. Refugees and the spread of civil war. Int. Organ. 60 (Spring), 335–366.

Scheinman, R.S., 1983. Refugees: Goodbye to the good old days. Ann. Am. Acad. Polit. Soc. Sci. 467, 78–88.

Steckel, R.H., 1995. Stature and the Standard of Living. Journal of Economic Literature 33 (4), 1903–1940.

Steckel, R.H., 2008. Biological Measures of the Standard of Living. Journal of Economic Perspectives 22 (1), 129–152.

Stedman, S.J., Tanner, F., 2003. Refugee Manipulation: War, Politics, and the Abuse of Human Suffering. Brookings Institution Press, Washington, DC.

Stein, B., 1979. Occupational adjustment of refugees: The Vietnamese in the United States. Int. Migrat. Rev. 13 (1), 25–45.

Stein, B.N., 1983. The commitment to refugee resettlement. Ann. Am. Acad. Polit. Soc. Sci. 467, 187–201.

Stein, B.N., Cuny, F.C., 1994. Refugee repatriation during conflict: Protection and post-return assistance. Dev. Pract. 4 (3), 173–187.

Suhrke, A., 1998. Burden-sharing during refugee emergencies: The logic of collective action versus national action. J. Refug. Stud. 11 (4), 396–415.

Taft, J.V., North, D.S., Ford, D.A., 1979. Refugee Resettlement in the U.S.: Time for a New Focus. New Trans Century Foundation, Washington, DC.

Thielemann, E.R., 2006. Burden Sharing: The International Politics of Refugee Protection, University of California, San Diego Center for Comparative Immigration Studies Working Paper 134.

Toft, M.D., 2007. The myth of the borderless world: Refugees and repatriation policy. Conflict Manag. Peace Sci. 24, 139–157.

United Nations High Commission for Refugees, 2012. Text of "Convention Relation to the Status of Refugees".

Wanner, R.A., 2003. Entry class and the earnings attainment of immigrants to Canada, 1980–1995. Canadian Public Policy/Analyse de Politiques 29 (1), 53–71.

Waxman, P., 2001. The economic adjustment of recently arrived Bosnian, Afghan and Iraqi refugees in Sydney, Australia. Int. Migrat. Rev. 35 (2), 472–505.

Zucker, N.F., 1983. The Haitians versus the United States: The courts as last resort. Ann. Am. Acad. Polit. Soc. Sci. 467, 151–162.

CHAPTER 13

Undocumented Immigration and Human Trafficking*

Pia Orrenius**, Madeline Zavodny[†,‡]

**Federal Reserve Bank of Dallas and IZA, 2200 N. Pearl Street, Dallas, TX 75201, USA
[†]Agnes Scott College and IZA, 141 E. College Ave., Decatur, GA 30030, USA
[‡]To whom correspondence should be addressed.

Contents

1. Introduction	660
2. Theories on Undocumented Migration	662
2.1 The migration decision	663
2.1.1 Models of illegal immigration	663
2.1.2 Empirical evidence on illegal immigration	665
2.2 Migrant self-selection	665
2.3 Immigration and the duration of stay	667
2.4 The role of smugglers	669
3. Enforcement Efficacy and the Political Economy of Undocumented Immigration	671
3.1 Deterrence effects of border enforcement	672
3.2 Deterrence effects of interior enforcement	673
3.3 The political economy of undocumented immigration	675
3.3.1 United States	676
3.3.2 Europe	677
3.3.3 Other countries	679
4. Costs and Benefits of Undocumented Migration	679
4.1 Macroeconomic effects on destination countries	680
4.2 Microeconomic effects on destination countries	682
4.3 Fiscal effects on destination countries	685
4.3.1 Federalist implications	687
4.4 Effects on migrants	687
5. Impacts on Origin Countries	690
5.1 Remittances	692
6. Public Policy and Undocumented Immigration	693
6.1 Legalization programs	693
6.1.1 Impact of legalization on beneficiaries	694
6.1.2 Other economic effects of legalization programs	695
6.1.3 Effects on future flows	696
6.2 Government transfer programs	697
6.3 Schooling	698

* The views expressed here are solely those of the authors and do not reflect those of the Federal Reserve Bank of Dallas or the Federal Reserve System.

Handbook of the Economics of International Migration, Volume 1A
ISSN 2212-0092, http://dx.doi.org/10.1016/B978-0-444-53764-5.00013-X

    6.4 Citizenship and the children of undocumented immigrants   699
7. Human Trafficking   699
    7.1 Models of human trafficking   700
    7.2 Public policy   702
8. Conclusion   703
References   705

1. INTRODUCTION

Undocumented immigration is one of the fastest growing forms of international migration. An estimated 2.5–4 million migrants cross international borders without the proper documents each year (Sunderhaus, 2007). Many more violate the terms of a visa, either by overstaying or working while on a non-work visa. As of 2009, the global stock of undocumented immigrants was estimated at 50 million (United Nations Development Programme, 2009). Given that there are about 214 million international migrants (United Nations Department of Economic and Social Affairs, 2009), undocumented immigrants may comprise almost one-quarter of all immigrants.[1]

Although many of these undocumented immigrants migrate willingly, typically to work or to reunite with family members, some are victims of human trafficking. Human trafficking involves obtaining, transporting, or holding a person, often via deception or coercion, and exploiting them. Many of the victims of human trafficking are trafficked for sexual exploitation, including forced prostitution, but some are trafficked for forced labor or services. Estimates suggest there were over 12 million victims of human trafficking in 2010 (US Department of State, 2010), although not all of them were trafficked across international borders.

The terminology surrounding undocumented immigration and human trafficking is complicated and sometimes value laden. Undocumented immigrants are also referred to as unauthorized, illegal, clandestine, or irregular immigrants or aliens. Some of these terms reflect a particular normative view, while others are relatively neutral. This chapter uses these terms interchangeably without any normative intent. This chapter distinguishes between smuggling and human trafficking, activities that frequently overlap but are differentiated by the immigrant's willingness. The former involves willing migrants who hire smugglers to help them enter a country illegally, while the latter typically involves deception or coercion. Willing migrants can become victims of human trafficking if they are deceived or coerced and then exploited during or after migration.

Unauthorized immigration is a consequence of three main factors: sizeable cross-country disparities in incomes, awareness of these disparities and the means to take

---

[1] Other estimates suggest a smaller fraction of immigrants are undocumented. The International Organization for Migration (2010) estimates that only 10–15% of immigrants are irregular, for example.

advantage of them, and restrictive immigration policies. There are large economic gains to migrants, particularly those who move from developing to developed countries, and globalization and technology have increased awareness of these differences as well as lowered the costs of travel. Destination countries put laws in place restricting immigration in order to protect their citizens from adverse effects attributed to immigration, including labor market competition and negative fiscal impacts. Immigration policies are the most restrictive for low-skilled migrants since their skills are perceived as being less valuable or in ready supply among natives. Restrictive immigration policy can reduce immigrant inflows or change their composition. But, like water flowing downhill, many migrants find ways to circumvent restrictions on immigration—they migrate illegally.

Illegal immigration occurs for many reasons and in myriad ways. Many irregular immigrants move in search of better economic opportunities for themselves or their families. Others migrate to join family members who have already moved. Some cross borders illegally, while others overstay or violate the terms of their visas in order to work, go to school, or remain with family and friends. Visa overstays and violations are the main sources of unauthorized immigration in island nations or countries with relatively secure borders. Migrants who cross international borders without authorization in order to flee civil or political unrest at home are considered refugees, not undocumented immigrants, but failed asylum seekers who remain in the destination country illegally become undocumented immigrants. Many asylum seekers enter in an irregular way, sometimes using a smuggler.

Accurate numbers regarding stocks and flows of undocumented immigrants are difficult to obtain. Few large-scale government surveys ask immigrants about their legal status, and those that do may not receive truthful answers. The complexity of defining undocumented immigration compounds the problem. The stock of undocumented immigrants in a country is often estimated using the residual method, which counts the foreign-born population and then subtracts the estimated number of legal immigrants. In the United States, the change in the legal immigrant count is derived each year from administrative data on lawful inflows (new arrivals, refugees, approved asylum seekers, etc.) and status adjusters (migrants converting from unauthorized to legal status), less estimated emigration and deaths (Passel and Cohn, 2008). Ethnographic studies, apprehensions data, source-country data on return migrants, and surveys of families left behind offer other windows into the undocumented population, but they are likely to capture only select portions of it.

Surveys are likely to undercount the undocumented population even if they do not ask about legal status. Undocumented immigrants may be unwilling to participate in censuses and other surveys for fear of revealing their presence. Their employers and landlords may be unwilling to reveal their presence as well, particularly if hiring or housing them involves penalties. Greater mobility by the undocumented also makes them difficult to count. In the US, large-scale government surveys are estimated to undercount unauthorized immigrants by 10–15% (Hanson, 2006). Undercounts are likely even higher in developing countries.

Undocumented immigrants are present in virtually every country. Like legal immigrants, the undocumented tend to migrate to countries that are more economically developed than their country of origin. No country has more undocumented immigrants than the US, where they account for about 29% of all immigrants, or 3.7% of the total population. In the European Union, undocumented immigrants account for 6–15% of all immigrants, or about 1% of the total population (United Nations Development Programme, 2009). But not all undocumented immigration is to developed countries. Irregular immigration is estimated to account for about one-third of all migration for developing countries (United Nations Development Programme, 2009). In Thailand, for example, estimates suggest 30% of immigrants are irregular, while 45% are in South Africa, and as many as 98% in Kazakhstan (Sabates-Wheeler, 2009; Huguet et al., 2012). Irregular immigrants were estimated to account for almost two-thirds of immigrants living in Southern and Eastern Mediterranean countries in the mid-2000s (Fargues, 2009).[2]

Unauthorized immigration presents both benefits and challenges to host countries. Undocumented immigrants are often a flexible and relatively cheap source of labor, which benefits employers and consumers. Challenges arise, however, if immigrants have adverse labor market effects or impose net fiscal costs. Whether and how to grant legal status, labor protections, or social services to illegal immigrants are conundrums for policymakers.

This chapter discusses research on the theory, practice, and prevalence of undocumented immigration and human trafficking. Until the early 1900s, countries were more likely to impose barriers to emigration than barriers to immigration. The US, for example, imposed few restrictions on immigration, with the notable exception of immigration from Asia, until the 1910s. Today, few countries prohibit or severely restrict exit, but virtually every country has complex restrictions on entry.

2. THEORIES ON UNDOCUMENTED MIGRATION

The decision to migrate is at the core of undocumented migration. However, the illegality of the act implies that models must incorporate border and interior enforcement policy in addition to the usual costs and benefits that affect the decision to migrate. Unauthorized migrants undoubtedly face higher costs and greater uncertainty with respect to both the physical act of migration and the benefits to migration. Migration costs may have fixed and variable components. In addition, costs may be endogenous, further complicating the analysis. In this section, we first review the theory of migration and its implications for migrant self-selection and duration of stay. We then describe models that apply specifically to illegal immigration, namely those that include smugglers and border and interior enforcement.

---

[2] For more country- and region-specific discussion of patterns of irregular immigration, see Castles et al. (2012).

2.1 The migration decision

Early migration models in the classical tradition focus on aggregate labor flows between agricultural and industrial sectors in an effort to explain rural to urban migration and its role in economic development (Lewis, 1954; Ranis and Fei, 1961). Harris and Todaro (1970) added unemployment to the economic development model, with labor flows responding not to the simple wage gap but to the expected income gap, which includes a nonzero probability of unemployment in the destination. In contrast to aggregate analysis, Sjaastad's (1962) neoclassical model focused on the individual's decision to move based on a comparison of the benefits and costs of moving relative to staying. The migrant ultimately chooses the location in which she maximizes net benefits. Benefits are synonymous with earnings in these models, and costs are typically composed of the monetary costs of moving plus foregone earnings and the psychic costs of leaving the origin and living elsewhere. Whether classical or neoclassical, a model with flexible wages, no barriers to mobility, zero moving costs, and income- or utility-maximizing behavior results in an efficient allocation of labor and equalization of wages across regions.

Economists noted early on that labor migration in practice was often inconsistent with the predictions of classical theory. Myrdal (1944) pointed out that there was no significant migration in the US from the South to the North after the Civil War despite enormous wage gaps. Carrington et al. (1996) showed that this puzzle can be resolved by modeling moving costs as a decreasing function of the stock of previous migrants. Sociologists had already made this observation for the case of US–Mexico migration (Piore, 1979). Massey et al. (1987) described US migration as a social process, highlighting the central role of migrant networks in the migration decision. In studying late-nineteenth century mass migration from Europe to the US, Hatton and Williamson (1994) confirmed the roles of wage gaps, industrialization, and the stock of previous migrants as significant explanatory factors in this mass movement. They also noted the importance of demographics in the origin country; the rate of natural population increase in the home country was a significant push factor even after controlling for the wage gap.

Stark's (1991) theoretical work also departed from the neoclassical model of migration by incorporating a number of additional considerations in the migration decision, including the role of risk aversion and consumption smoothing, household decision-making and remittances, asymmetric information, and income inequality.

2.1.1 Models of illegal immigration

Models of unauthorized migration augment the basic migration model by adding enforcement measures, such as border and interior enforcement. The relevant variables depend on the country setting but may include smuggling costs, the probability of apprehension, the probability of deportation, and wage and employment penalties in the destination. Unauthorized crossings, given their illicit and often temporary nature, also entail a bigger role for previous migration experience, migrant networks, and remittances (Taylor, 1987).

The assumptions of perfect mobility and flexible wages are not likely to hold with regard to illegal immigration. Todaro and Maruszko (1987) modeled illegal migration as a function of the income differential across countries and the cost of moving; however, they also took into account the probability of being apprehended at the border, the probability of finding a job, and a wage penalty for illegal immigrant workers. The latter three are functions of unemployment rates in the home and destination countries. A simulation reflecting the US–Mexico case suggests that the employer sanctions imposed as part of the 1986 Immigration Reform and Control Act (IRCA) were too low to significantly reduce undocumented migration. Empirical work appears to be consistent with this finding, although some of the ineffectiveness of employer sanctions in the wake of IRCA was due to their infrequent application and to relatively low fines (Martin and Miller, 2000a).

In his pioneering work on illegal immigration, Ethier (1986a) first assumed that illegal immigrants are unskilled. Then, due to social reasons and because migrants have low incomes and distort the income distribution, the government implements both border and interior enforcement to reduce the influx. Increases in border enforcement raise the unskilled wage, which helps unskilled workers (both legal and illegal); native skilled workers, whose taxes fund enforcement, are hurt. Moreover, the higher unskilled wage may actually attract more migrants in spite of the increased border apprehension rate. Meanwhile, the effectiveness of interior enforcement depends crucially on whether employers can distinguish between authorized and unauthorized workers. In the wake of IRCA, the wages of US-born Hispanics fell, suggesting that employers had difficulty distinguishing among Hispanic workers (Pagán and Dávila, 1996).

Bond and Chen (1987) and Djajić (1987) extended Ethier's model to two countries and introduced capital. In general, they found that enforcement tends to benefit unskilled natives and hurt other factors of production, such as skilled workers and physical capital. Additionally, in the absence of capital flows and if the host country is large enough, enforcement in the host country reduces wages in the origin country. The host country can gain from this strategy as long as the wage effect is large and the marginal cost of enforcement is low, but it represents a welfare loss to the origin country as well as to the world (Bond and Chen, 1987). However, if physical capital is mobile, it will respond to higher enforcement by flowing out of the destination country toward the origin country, which pushes wages back up. In this stylized setting, enforcement can improve global welfare.[3]

---

[3] See Yoshida and Woodland (2005) for a more comprehensive review of theoretical models of illegal immigration.

2.1.2 Empirical evidence on illegal immigration

In line with migration theory, applied work has generally found that wage gaps, employment opportunities, and migrant networks are the main drivers of unauthorized international migration (Massey and Espinosa, 1997; Hanson and Spilimbergo, 1999; Munshi, 2003; Orrenius and Zavodny, 2005). In addition to funding their own consumption and saving, irregular migrants typically remit some income to help their families (Durand et al., 1996; Woodruff and Zenteno, 2006). In Western Europe, where irregular migration is less likely to be motivated by employment and migrants frequently seek asylum upon arrival, the generosity of social programs and the likelihood of a favorable asylum ruling play important roles in the decision to migrate illegally (Boeri and Brücker, 2005; Jandl, 2007).

Relative wages and employment opportunities depend on cyclical and structural trends in the source and destination countries. Labor supply shocks, such as large birth cohorts, drive down wages in the origin country and are an important push factor; they accounted for about 40% of Mexico–US labor flows between 1980 and 2000 (Hanson and McIntosh, 2010). Recessions and other macroeconomic shocks that depress wages or devalue the currency and deplete savings are also important; the 1994 Mexican "tequila crisis" resulted in an emigration spike, as did the collapse of a massive pyramid scheme in 1997 in Albania. Host-country conditions are also important; in the US, the 2007–09 housing bust and ensuing financial crisis led to a dramatic decline in illegal immigration (Massey et al., 2009; Borger and Muse-Orlinoff, 2010). In Europe, the sovereign debt crisis of 2009–12 reversed the massive migrant inflows to Southern Europe that occurred in the 1990s and 2000s (Kasimis, 2012).

Unauthorized migration appears to stem from a lack of legal migration alternatives combined with lax enforcement. It is not generally due to other disqualifying factors, such as migrants being legally inadmissible because they do not meet other requirements, such as not having a criminal background. Irregular migrants to the US tend to be young men. Men and women differ greatly in their likelihood, method, and motives for migrating illegally (Valdez-Suiter et al., 2007). Women are less likely to illegally migrate and, when they do, tend to be tied movers who accompany or join family members; they also tend to overstay visas rather than to undertake perilous border crossings (Donato, 1993). Men who are unauthorized migrants tend to work initially in seasonal jobs, such as construction and agriculture, and their migration is highly correlated with the host-country business cycle (Hanson, 2006). Irregular migration may be more common among females in Asia than in Europe or North America, particularly in occupations seen as "typically female," such as domestic service, low-level health care, and entertainment (Castles et al., 2012).

2.2 Migrant self-selection

The migration literature has long observed that migrants are not randomly selected from the home population. The net gains from immigration and immigration policies affect not only how many people migrate but also which people migrate. Borjas (1987) showed that a simple income-maximizing model of migration has clear implications for migrant self-selection: namely, migrants from countries with wider (narrower) income distributions than the destination country will be negatively (positively) selected. Subsequent work has tried to square this theoretical implication with the empirical evidence, which is often contradictory. In the Mexico–US case, where the majority of migration is unauthorized, many studies find that migrants are from the middle or upper half of the Mexican education or wage distributions (Chiquiar and Hanson, 2005; Orrenius and Zavodny, 2005; Cuecuecha, 2010; Kaestner and Malamud, 2014).[4]

Binding migration costs could be the reason that most studies of Mexico–US migration find evidence of intermediate or positive selection. Less-educated workers, who reap the largest relative gains from migration, may simply be too poor to afford the move. McKenzie and Rapoport (2007) provided evidence that migration costs play a key role in migrant selection; using ENADID data from Mexico, they showed that migrants from migration-intensive communities are negatively selected, while those from low-migration communities are positively selected. Massey et al. (1987) and Massey and Espinosa (1997) noted that migration prevalence is a good proxy for migration costs.

There are studies of migrant self-selection in other countries, although few of them concern undocumented immigrants. In a study of the 1999 Ecuadoran crisis, Bertoli et al. (2009) compared the ensuing emigration to Spain and the US, much of which was unauthorized. The great majority of Ecuadorians went to Spain despite the fact that wages were higher in the US, a result partly explained by imputed migration costs, which were estimated to be five times higher to go to the US due to differences in immigration policies and enforcement levels in the two host countries. The results suggest that US-bound migrants were positively selected both on education and on unobservable characteristics.

Some studies look at selection and return migration, although few consider the case of unauthorized migrants.[5] In theory, return migrants may be negatively selected if "failures" in the host country return migrate, or they may be positively selected if migrants are target earners and hence successful migrants return home (Piore, 1979). Generally, selection of return migrants should reinforce migrant selection so that if it is negative (positive) initially, returns should be positively (negatively) selected among

---

[4] Some studies have found evidence of negative selection in the Mexico–US case (Ibarraran and Lubotsky, 2007; Fernández-Huertas Moraga, 2011). However, those studies use data with missing information on the characteristics of people or entire households that move. Negative selection may be observed if education is endogenous with respect to migration, and individuals who plan to migrate leave school earlier than they would have otherwise (Caponi, 2011).

[5] Studies of self-selection among return migrants include, among others, Borjas and Bratsberg (1996) for the US case, Dustmann and Weiss (2007) for the UK case, Constant and Massey (2003) for the German case, Coulon and Piracha (2005) for the Albanian case, and Akee (2010) for Micronesia.

the pool of migrants (Borjas and Bratsberg, 1996). Coniglio et al. (2009) derived a model in which illegal status is taxed in the destination country. The resultant "skill waste" is an incentive for those with the most skill to return home, which leads to positive selection of return migrants. Lacuesta (2006) found that return migrants to Mexico earn significantly more than non-migrants, but he did not compare them to permanent emigrants.

Accounting for selection is important since it affects estimates of immigrant assimilation and sheds light on migration's consequences for the origin country. Ibarraran and Lubotsky (2007) showed that negative selection in return migration has led researchers to overestimate the wage progress of immigrants who stay. Borjas (1987) pointed out the difficulty of using cross-sectional data to estimate assimilation if cohort quality changes over time; if cohort quality is falling over time, estimates of immigrants' performance relative to natives based on cross-sectional data are biased upward.[6] In general, positive selection in return migration would help mitigate concerns about brain drain and may stimulate economic development at home, reducing future emigration.

Immigration policy, the generosity of government programs, and the macroeconomy also affect migrant selection. Chiswick (1999) noted that, *ceteris paribus*, favorable self-selection is most pronounced among economic migrants, who have higher returns to migration in the labor market than migrants who have other motives for moving (e.g., tied movers and refugees). In a study of migration to France, Gross and Schmitt (2006) found that high-skilled migrants respond almost exclusively to financial incentives, while low-skilled migrants are sensitive to many push and pull factors, including "cultural clustering." Hartwich (2011) argued that Australian immigration has been so successful because immigration policies prioritize skilled migrants who can more easily integrate into Australian labor markets.

Enforcement actions also affect selection. Migrants who face higher migration costs are more positively selected. Orrenius and Zavodny (2005) showed that increased US border enforcement results in higher mean levels of education among unauthorized immigrants from Mexico. Cohen et al. (2009) noted that the generosity of welfare programs not only affects the skill composition of migrants but can be affected by it; a host country may curtail its welfare system if it is absorbing low-skilled migrants.

2.3 Immigration and the duration of stay

Return migration prevails among unauthorized migrants. Until recent decades, most Mexican migrants did not settle in the US. Instead, they spent an average of six months to a year in the US per trip and made four to five such trips over a lifetime (North and Houstoun, 1976; Cornelius, 1978). Among immigrants to Western Europe (admittedly,

---

[6] Carliner (1980) and DeFreitas (1979) also estimated age–earnings profiles of immigrants and compared them to natives.

mostly legal) 20–50% are estimated to eventually return home (Bijwaard, 2010). Factors that explain return and repeat migration and hence duration of stay include migrant characteristics, networks, economic conditions, migration costs, and immigration policy. More subjective factors, such as presence of family members, climate, culture, and lifestyle, also play a role (Cornelius, 1978; Dustmann and Weiss, 2007; Gibson and McKenzie, 2011). Erroneous information about conditions in the destination can also result in return migration (Borjas and Bratsberg, 1996).

Hill (1987) incorporated return and repeat migration into a life-cycle model of migration. Utility is a function of consumption, time at home, and the number of trips. Increases in home wages reduce total time abroad but have an indeterminate effect on frequency of trips; higher travel costs reduce the number of trips but have an indeterminate effect on total time spent working abroad.

The empirical evidence on the determinants of duration of stay among illegal immigrants is, like much of the literature in this area, overwhelmingly focused on Mexico–US migration. Using Mexican Migration Project data, research found that undocumented immigrants have shorter migration spells than documented immigrants (Lindstrom, 1996; Reyes, 2001).[7] Undocumented migrants from households with more assets have longer durations of stay, as do higher-wage migrants and migrants with US-born children (Massey and Espinosa, 1997; Reyes, 2001). More educated migrants return home sooner (Lindstrom, 1996; Reyes, 2004). Agricultural workers also have shorter durations of stay.

The motive for migration also affects duration of stay. For example, some studies found that duration of stay is positively correlated with economic conditions in the home country and negatively correlated with conditions in the destination (Lindstrom, 1996; Massey and Espinosa, 1997). This is consistent with a target saving motive for migration, where migrants with investment motives (target savers) stay longer abroad than migrants with pure consumption motives.[8] According to Hill (1987), target savers should return home sooner if host country wages rise. Counter to the target saving model, Reyes (2001, 2004) found that men who receive wage increases stay in the US longer, and unemployed men return home sooner. The US–Mexico pattern may be similar to return migration among Filipinos; Yang (2006) found that although most Filipino migration is consistent with income maximization (the "life-cycle model"), certain subgroups of migrants are clearly motivated by target-income considerations.

Immigration policy, whether in the form of border enforcement, interior enforcement, or a legalization program, may also affect migrants' duration of stay. However, the direction of the impact is more of an empirical question than a theoretical one

[7] Many studies found that legal status increases duration of stay, but this result is likely driven by endogeneity. After all, the longer migrants stay, the more likely they are to acquire legal status.

[8] It is also possible that this finding is driven by joint causality, where wealth, economic growth, and migration are determined simultaneously.

(Hill, 1987). Among Mexicans, the probability of return migration from the US fell from 54% to 25% between 1987–92 and 1995–2000 (Reyes, 2004). Recent work has shed light on this issue. Angelucci (2012) found that border enforcement as measured by Border Patrol linewatch hours has a significant negative effect on migrant outflows, which implies that tougher enforcement increases the duration of stay among the stock of unauthorized immigrants. Thom (2008) simulated a theoretical model and demonstrated that although trip duration should rise with migration costs and enforcement, total time spent in the destination country should fall. Angelucci (2012) and Reyes (2004) found that tougher border enforcement deters return migration, leading to permanent settlement among illegal immigrants from Mexico. In earlier work, Kossoudji (1992) concluded that migrants apprehended on a preceding trip, but not the current trip, have longer durations of stay than those who were never apprehended.[9]

The availability of visas also affects duration of stay among undocumented migrants. Massey and Espinosa (1997) found that having more visas available reduces return migration to Mexico, perhaps because migrants assess a greater likelihood of being able to adjust their status if they stay in the US. Reyes (2001) found that average spell length among undocumented migrants increased substantially after IRCA legalized 2.3 million Mexicans during 1986–89. Somewhat at odds with these findings, Reyes (2004) found that the number of people granted legal permanent residence is positively related to the probability of return migration among undocumented and documented migrants. Returns may be temporary, however, and may reflect the resumption of some circular migration.

2.4 The role of smugglers

Many unauthorized immigrants never illegally cross borders. In the US case, for example, nearly half of all illegal immigrants enter the country legally through a port of entry and then overstay or violate the terms of their visa (Pew Hispanic Center, 2006). However, among those who illegally cross borders, the demand for smugglers has grown commensurate with rising border controls (Jandl, 2007; Gathmann, 2008). The share of unauthorized US–Mexico border crossers using smugglers has increased from about 80% in 1990 to over 90% in the mid to late 2000s.[10] Although no aggregate data are available for Europe, border statistics from Central and Eastern European countries confirm a similar trend underway there; border apprehensions have been declining since

---

[9] In contrast, Massey and Espinosa (1997) did not find an effect of the probability of apprehension on return migration; rather, the only significant policy variable is the availability of visas, which reduces the probability of return.

[10] Data on smuggling usage are from the Mexican Migration Project website at http://mmp.opr.princeton.edu/results/results-en.aspx (accessed 18 October 2012). Although smuggler usage rates are very high among Mexicans, studies suggest they are even higher among Central Americans (Martin and Miller, 2000b).

2000, while the number of apprehended smugglers has risen (Jandl, 2007).[11] In Hungary, the share of illegal entrants using human smugglers was 20–25% in the mid-1990s but had surpassed 70% by 2003 (Futo and Jandl, 2004).

Several factors in addition to enforcement levels affect migrants' use of smugglers. Arcand and Mbaye (2013) showed that Senegalese migrants' willingness to pay for a smuggler is an increasing function of their subjective discount rate (impatience) and a decreasing function of their degree of risk aversion. Willingness to pay for a smuggler also increases with the expected wage in the destination.

While using a smuggler increases the probability of a successful crossing (Singer and Massey, 1998), it also drives up migration costs, which is a deterrent for unauthorized crossers. Along the US–Mexico border, average smuggler prices have risen in inflation-adjusted terms from about $600–1000 in 1990 to $1500–2000 by the mid-2000s (Roberts et al., 2010).[12] Spener (2009) noted that enforcement operations drive up smuggling prices by requiring migrants to buy a more complex portfolio of smuggling services than in the past and by pushing traffic to remote areas, making it harder to cross a border undetected. Relying on data from the Mexican Migration Project, Gathmann (2008) found that the US border buildup between 1986 and 2004 raised smugglers' fees by 17% and crossing times by two to five additional days. The implied elasticity between Border Patrol hours and smuggling costs is about 0.25, implying that a 10% increase in enforcement hours causes smuggling costs to increase by 2.5%. Roberts et al. (2010) used Department of Homeland Security administrative data to estimate a smuggler cost elasticity of 0.25–0.38.

On the supply side, smuggler prices are also affected by criminal penalties on smugglers and the degree of competitiveness in the smuggling market (Roberts et al., 2010). Most studies suggest that the smuggling market along the US–Mexico border is characterized by many service providers who offer differentiated products (López-Castro et al., 1997; Spener, 2001, 2004). Studies do not generally support the common perceptions that small providers have been squeezed out by organized crime and that drug cartels have come to monopolize human smuggling along the Southwest border (Andreas, 2001; House Committee on Homeland Security, 2006; Goddard, 2012).[13] Väyrynen (2003) made a

---

[11] In Europe, successive EU enlargement has led to a shift from irregular migration stemming from within the region to illegal flows from outside the region, typically from the former Soviet republics, Pakistan, and Iraq (Jandl, 2007).

[12] Mexicans pay very low smugglers' fees compared with illegal immigrants from more distant nations. Chinese migrants on the smuggling ship *Golden Venture* that went aground in New York in 1993 had paid around $30,000 in fees (Martin and Miller, 2000a). Chinese smugglers interviewed by Zhang and Chin (2004) reported a median smuggling fee of $50,000. Studies suggest certain migrants, such as women, pay more than others (Fuentes and García, 2009).

[13] Zhang and Chin (2004) made a similar observation regarding Chinese smugglers (also known as snakeheads).

similar point regarding illegal migration in general; smuggling rings are often run by migrants' relatives or acquaintances. Crime syndicates are more likely to be involved in human trafficking and other criminal activities, such as drugs and prostitution.

Another characteristic of smuggling markets is that they are always changing. Strategies constantly evolve to help smugglers and their clients avoid detection and apprehension (Andreas, 2001). Site-specific surges in enforcement result in a diversion of flows around those areas; increased vigilance and physical barriers along land borders are met with more attempts through designated ports of entry; and increased requirements for documentation result in more falsified paperwork and fraudulent use of visas, identification cards, and passports (Jandl, 2007; Koslowski, 2011). In Guzman et al.'s (2008) model, smugglers divide their time between learning new techniques and arranging crossings (producing smuggling services). The government takes smugglers' response into account when setting border enforcement levels. Efficient smuggling reduces border frictions, and an exogenous improvement in smuggling technology leads to a decline in the optimal level of border enforcement because the increased resources required to enforce the border imply higher taxes, the costs of which exceed the benefits of more enforcement. In practice, the government tends to respond with more, not less, border enforcement when confrontations escalate (Andreas, 2001).

Smugglers also adapt to host-country patterns and practices. In Western Europe and Canada, smugglers transport migrants across borders so that they can apply for asylum upon arrival (Martin and Miller, 2000b; Jandl, 2007). Indeed, the Canadian government uses asylum applications as one indicator of the number of migrants being smuggled into the country (Martin and Miller, 2000b). In Southern Europe and the US migrants are typically smuggled into the country to work, not to claim asylum, although that pattern may be changing in Europe as a result of the recent political unrest in the Middle East and Northern Africa.

3. ENFORCEMENT EFFICACY AND THE POLITICAL ECONOMY OF UNDOCUMENTED IMMIGRATION

Empirical research on unauthorized immigration shows that changes in economic conditions in the destination country play a larger role in migration behavior than do changes in border enforcement. As described in Section 2 above, there is considerable evidence that relatively good labor market prospects in the US, for example, have been the most important pull factor in unauthorized immigration from Mexico (Jenkins, 1977; Blejer et al., 1978; Bean et al., 1990; Espenshade, 1990; Hanson and Spilimbergo, 1999; Dávila et al., 2002). The same is true for many Central Americans (Espenshade, 1995; Massey and Sana, 2003). Illegal immigration to Southern Europe has similarly been driven primarily by economic opportunity (King and Rybaczuk, 1993).

The trend toward rising border enforcement is pervasive. One reason is that illegal immigration is usually viewed as undesirable by destination countries. Cox and Glenn (1994) noted that illegal immigration is politically unacceptable because it suggests that a government cannot control its own borders. The government will therefore always attempt to take back control of its borders (or, at a minimum, will *appear* to be trying to doing so). Typically, governments have chosen to fortify external borders in order to deter unauthorized immigration. However, better technology has improved the cost-effectiveness of interior enforcement, and as a result new programs such as electronic verification of work authorization are on the rise. This section surveys the literature on the effectiveness of border enforcement and gives an overview of recent research that evaluates interior enforcement measures. It concludes with a discussion of studies of the political economy of illegal immigration.

3.1 Deterrence effects of border enforcement

Unauthorized migrants can be deterred by increasing the costs of unauthorized migration or by reducing the benefits. Tougher border enforcement via increased manpower, better technology, and harsher penalties should raise apprehension probabilities and migration costs. Recent years have seen an unprecedented increase in US border enforcement, including a doubling of the number of Border Patrol agents since 2000, the construction of new border fences, federal criminal prosecution of unauthorized crossers, streamlined deportation proceedings, and implementation of new technology (National Research Council, 2011; Rosenblum, 2012). European Union nations have also implemented more controls along the EU's external border, including adding border guards and sea patrols, and creating Frontex in 2004 (Leonard, 2009; Frontex, 2012).[14]

Some studies examined the direct relationship between border enforcement and illegal immigration, while others studied indirect effects and unintended consequences. Most empirical evidence concerns Mexico–US migration. Angelucci (2012) considered Mexico–US migration from 1980 to 2003 and found that the responsiveness of illegal inflows to Border Patrol linewatch hours has increased over time, suggesting that border enforcement has become more effective. Amuedo-Dorantes and Bansak (2011b) found that an increase of one-half million linewatch hours, the average annual increase along the Southwest border between 1990 and 2003, reduced intentions to remigrate among a sample of male return migrants by about 14%. Massey and Riosmena (2010) found that increased linewatch hours reduced the probability of illegal migration among Mexican

---

[14] The full name of Frontex is the European Agency for the Management of Operational Cooperation at the External Borders of the Member States of the European Union. Since individual member nations are responsible for controlling their own external borders, Frontex's mission is to primarily act in a coordinating and advisory capacity.

migrants but had no effect on Central Americans. Borger (2010) also found a negative relationship between linewatch hours and Mexicans' propensity to migrate. Hanson and Spilimbergo (1999) concluded that tougher border enforcement is correlated with lower wages in Mexican border cities, suggesting that enforcement prevents or delays illegal entries into the US and therefore has a deterrent effect. Cornelius and Salehyan (2007) noted that although an individual's perception of the difficulty of crossing the border is not related to whether that person migrates, having been apprehended previously negatively affects a person's probability of migrating.

Higher enforcement increases the demand for smugglers, which should raise the price of hiring a smuggler and act as a deterrent to potential illegal immigrants. Several studies reported evidence of increased demand for smugglers in response to higher enforcement (Singer and Massey, 1998). As discussed above in Section 2.4, research shows that stricter enforcement leads to higher smugglers' fees (Gathmann, 2008; Roberts et al., 2010). Orrenius (1999) found that a 20% increase in the smuggling fee causes a 13–21% decline in the probability of migrating.

Some studies on Mexico–US migration found little direct evidence of deterrence effects of border enforcement on migration but considerable evidence of migrants' adaptive behavior. Dávila et al. (2002) found that although increased linewatch hours reduce apprehensions initially, the effect dissipates as migrants avoid Border Patrol sectors with enhanced enforcement. Orrenius (2004) similarly found that migrants choose border crossing locations strategically in order to circumvent more heavily enforced areas. A pattern of evasion is particularly noticeable in studies that consider the aftermath of Operations Hold the Line in El Paso and Gatekeeper in San Diego, launched in 1993 and 1994 respectively, after which migrants shifted their crossings away from these urban areas toward more remote locations (Massey et al., 2002; Carrión-Flores and Sørensen, 2007). Gathmann (2008) likewise found a high elasticity of "geographic substitution," where migrants circumvent more enforced border regions. One consequence of long, arduous treks through the harsh border terrain has been a rising number of migrant deaths (Eschbach et al., 1999; Cornelius, 2001; US Government Accountability Office, 2006) Fatalities among Africans migrating to Spain by boat have also risen, although the trend is best explained by an increase in the number of migration attempts, not an increase in the risk of dying (Carling, 2007). Research also documents that increased US border enforcement has led to reduced circularity and less return migration among undocumented immigrants (Kossoudji, 1992; Reyes, 2004; Riosmena, 2004).

3.2 Deterrence effects of interior enforcement

Interior enforcement mechanisms targeting irregular migrants have increased along with border enforcement over the last few decades. Technology has greatly increased the efficacy of interior enforcement programs and reduced their cost, contributing to their increased use.[15] As the theory suggests, an important advantage of interior enforcement over border enforcement is the negative effect on unauthorized workers' wages, which reduces the labor market pull factor (Ethier, 1986b). However, one significant drawback of interior enforcement is the possible diversion of illegal immigrant workers into the informal sector, or "black market." Another unintended consequence is a surge in fraudulent and falsified documents. The literature finds evidence of all three effects. What is markedly absent from the literature is estimates of the deterrent effects of interior enforcement with regard to how many potential immigrants are deterred from migrating and how many are spurred into leaving.

In the US, it was not illegal to employ unauthorized immigrants until the passage of the 1986 Immigration Reform and Control Act (IRCA). IRCA mandated employer sanctions, which—despite the fact that they were rarely applied—appear to have adversely affected wages for Hispanic workers (see Section 6.1.2). The inability to discern which workers were unauthorized likely contributed to IRCA's negative wage effect among Hispanic workers as a whole (Bansak and Raphael, 2001; Brownell, 2005). Despite evidence that employer sanctions had an adverse wage impact, it is widely recognized that they did not deter illegal immigration but instead resulted in widespread document and identity fraud (US Government Accountability Office, 2005; Martin, 2007). That said, no rigorous work has attempted to disentangle the migration effects of employer sanctions from the other aspects of IRCA, which likely spurred more illegal immigration (Orrenius and Zavodny, 2012).

In the US, E-Verify, the federal electronic verification system recently mandated by several states, greatly improves employers' ability to screen their workers. Before E-Verify, employers received no-match letters from the Social Security Administration that alerted them to which employees had mismatched or nonexistent Social Security numbers. Orrenius and Zavodny (2009) found that the ramping up of the Social Security no-match program after the 9/11 terror attacks led to a decline in employment, hours worked, and earnings among recent male Latin American immigrants relative to other similar groups more likely to hold legal status.

The implementation of the 2007 Legal Arizona Workers Act, which mandated E-Verify among the state's employers, resulted in a significant shift out of wage and salary employment and into self-employment among non-citizen Hispanic immigrants, a group with a high share of unauthorized workers (Bohn and Löfström, 2013). A study looking more broadly at E-Verify provisions across several states found that mandating electronic verification of work authorization resulted in significant declines in employment rates and wages among men likely to be unauthorized immigrants (Amuedo-Dorantes and Bansak, 2012).

---

[15] It bears noting that while electronic verification of a worker's employment authorization is inexpensive, detaining and deporting immigrants is costly (National Research Council, 2011). Detention and removal may also be controversial among the public, who often do not view irregular migrants as criminals who warrant detention (Martin, 2007). Mass detention and deportations can also create political tensions with countries of origin.

Worsening labor market prospects could, in theory, motivate unauthorized migrants to return home. Arizona's law is associated with a 17% drop in the population of non-citizen Hispanics in Arizona, more than twice the decline in neighboring states during that time (Bohn et al., 2014). There is no direct evidence that these individuals returned to their home countries. However, Mexican household survey data show a significant increase in return migration between 2005 and 2010 compared with a decade earlier (Passel et al., 2012). Not all of these returns were voluntary, however. Removals to Mexico were at record highs during the period 2008–11; the share of deportees among return migrants during this period is estimated to have been between 5% and 35% (Passel et al., 2012).

Several additional interior enforcement programs have been implemented in the US since the mid-2000s, but there is little research yet documenting their effects. Under the Secure Communities program, Immigration and Customs Enforcement (ICE) agents detain and deport unauthorized immigrants who have committed only minor offenses and who previously would never have come to the attention of immigration authorities. Meanwhile, 287(g) agreements allowed local police departments to check suspects' legal status and detain unauthorized immigrants. While these programs may not affect unauthorized immigrants' wages directly, they may impede migrants' mobility and hence their ability to change jobs or move to locations with better opportunities.

3.3 The political economy of undocumented immigration

Illegal immigration creates winners and losers. Employers, complementary workers, and illegal immigrants benefit, while competing workers lose. Taxpayers as a whole are also harmed if the fiscal costs of unauthorized immigrants exceed the tax revenues they generate. Although there are significant gains for some groups and losses for others, the net effect may be minimal. In the US case, Hanson (2009) argued that the net economic effect of illegal immigration is small, perhaps even zero.

In Ethier's (1986a) model, border enforcement is inefficient because it drives up wages of unskilled workers, including existing undocumented workers, conferring gains on the current stock of unauthorized migrants and potentially attracting new ones. Border enforcement is also a drain on taxpayers. Worksite enforcement is less costly than border enforcement and reduces the wages of unauthorized workers, resulting in welfare losses for existing migrants and fewer incentives for others to migrate. Nevertheless, Bond and Chen (1987) noted that domestic enforcement is welfare enhancing for the host country only under special circumstances, such as when the marginal cost of enforcement is low and the host country is large enough that penalties on illegal workers drive down wages in the home country. Under different circumstances, or in the presence of capital mobility, enforcement increases can result in welfare losses.[16]

---

[16] Yoshida and Woodland (2005) extended Bond and Chen's model and discuss implications for global welfare.

The fact that immigration creates winners and losers makes it difficult to formulate an immigration policy that is in the national interest. As Calavita (1994) noted, immigration policy involves a series of tensions, or "paired oppositions." These include workers versus employers, economics versus politics, and liberal democratic principles versus the type of policing necessary to enforce immigration laws. As a result, immigration policy frequently fails to achieve its stated intentions. In addition, politicians are often reluctant to admit there is a need for low-skilled labor and hence to create *legal* pathways for low-skilled foreign workers. The result is illegal immigration.

Immigration policies that would create programs allowing low-skilled workers to enter legally may also fail because, in many cases, illegal workers may be preferred. Berlinschi and Squicciarini (2011) noted that employers can hire illegal migrants for less than the minimum wage and without adhering to labor market regulations, which leads to lower labor costs that translate into cheaper goods and services and higher profits. Moreover, illegal immigrants do not qualify for transfer programs, which benefits taxpayers. Hanson (2009) also noted that, in the US case, illegal immigration is far more responsive to changes in labor demand than is legal immigration, which is encumbered by quotas, regulations, and backlogs.

Labor market concerns drive native sentiment regarding immigration policy. Mayda (2006) looked at natives' sentiments vis-à-vis immigration using cross-country survey data. She found that, consistent with the predictions of factor endowment models, skilled individuals are more likely to be pro-immigration in countries where the skill composition of natives relative to immigrants is high. This result is robust to inclusion of non-economic determinants of feelings toward immigrants, such as how immigration affects crime, cultural and national identity, and whether immigration is illegal or made up of political refugees. Scheve and Slaughter (2001) found a similar result for the US case; less-skilled (more-skilled) people prefer more restrictionist (less restrictionist) immigration policy even when controlling for other, non-economic determinants of preferences. Facchini and Mayda (2009) expanded the cross-country analysis to explore the determinants of immigrant attitudes in welfare states. In countries where immigration is unskilled, they found that natives' skill (income) is positively (negatively) correlated with pro-immigration preferences.

3.3.1 United States

Immigration policy offers many telling insights into the political economy of illegal immigration and into how the government may cater to special interests. In the US, the historical emphasis on border—not interior—enforcement is best understood through a political economy lens. As noted above, interior enforcement is more efficient than border enforcement, yet US authorities have either left employers alone or have effectively helped ensure their access to undocumented workers (Ethier, 1986a; Hanson and Spilimbergo, 2001). Calavita (1992) gave several historical examples of the direct influence of growers on immigration policy, including the increase in the number of Bracero workers after Operation Wetback in 1954, when farmers complained that increased border enforcement resulted in illegal immigrants being unable to readily cross the border. As discussed earlier, it was not illegal to employ unauthorized workers until implementation of the 1986 Immigration Reform and Control Act (IRCA).[17] Martin (1990) noted that the agriculture lobby only agreed to support IRCA after they were promised a legalization program specifically for agricultural workers and a guest-worker program to ensure the future supply of farmworkers.[18] As discussed above, once IRCA was implemented and employer sanctions were finally in place, the government rarely applied them and, when they did, the fines were low (Juffras, 1991; Calavita, 1994).

Hanson and Spilimbergo (2001) showed that enforcement is responsive to economic conditions. They tested whether the correlation between border enforcement and sectoral shocks is consistent with the prediction of a political economy model that the government relaxes enforcement when the demand for undocumented workers is high. They found that a rise in relative commodity prices in the apparel, fruits and vegetables, and livestock industries and an increase in housing starts are negatively associated with border enforcement six to ten months later.

Since 2001, the political debate around illegal immigration has shifted. As described above in Sections 3.1 and 3.2, US border and interior enforcement have intensified at the federal and state levels. In light of the two recessions and lackluster recoveries during the years 2000–2012, economic arguments for more labor migration, particularly from Mexico, have lost traction. Anti-illegal immigrant groups have become increasingly vocal and succeeded in blocking comprehensive immigration reform and even Congressional approval of more limited measures, such as a "DREAM Act" that would allow undocumented immigrants who were brought into the US as children to adjust to legal status.

3.3.2 Europe

Since the 1980s, Europe has emerged as a major destination for global migrants, refugees, and asylum seekers, many of whom are undocumented (Altamirano, 1999). In 2007, the European Commission estimated that there were between 4.5 and 8 million illegal immigrants living in the European Union and net inflows were 350,000–500,000 per year (European Commission, 2007). The majority of illegal immigrants entering by sea comes from North Africa and arrives in Spain or Italy (Tervo et al., 2009). Another route brings migrants from Asia and the Middle East and goes through Turkey and then across the eastern Mediterranean Sea to Greece.

---

[17] From 1952 to 1986, the so-called "Texas Proviso" exempted US employers from criminal penalties for harboring unauthorized immigrants.

[18] The guest-worker program was the H-2A visa, and the "Special Agricultural Worker" provision resulted in about 1 million permanent resident visas granted to individuals who claimed they had worked at least 90 days on a farm in the prior year (Orrenius and Zavodny, 2003).

Irregular labor migrants have not flowed into Northern and Western Europe in large numbers.[19] Employment opportunities in those countries' highly regulated labor markets are limited, and those nations have adopted restrictive policies, particularly with regard to non-European migrants. Boeri and Brücker (2005) asked why European countries resist labor migration despite potential economic gains. They argued that rigid labor markets limit the gains to migration and increase adverse effects on natives, such as unemployment.[20] Generous social transfers and unemployment benefits are additional reasons why those countries try to keep low-skilled foreign workers out.

Southern Europe, in contrast, had unprecedented inflows of irregular migrants in the 1990s and 2000s, marking a striking reversal from earlier decades when nations such as Italy, Greece, and Spain were themselves sending countries (Triandafyllidou, 2010).[21] During the economic boom of the 1990s, illegal immigrants found steady work in the informal economy and, in the case of Italy and Spain, were eventually regularized in a series of amnesties.

The formation of the European Union and the dismantling of internal borders within Europe through the implementation of the Schengen agreement have put tremendous pressure on member states that comprise the external border of the union to prevent illegal immigration. As Altamirano (1999) explained, this is very difficult for three reasons. First, there is the logistical challenge of patrolling long mountainous and maritime borders, such as those in Greece, Italy, and Spain. Second, these economies rely on tourism and, hence, on open borders that facilitate travel. Heavily fortified roads and ports may deter tourists. Third, these nations have large informal sectors that rely on migrant labor, and it may not be in their national interest to prevent the bulk of irregular entries. According to Baldwin-Edwards (1997), the informal sector makes up 15–30% of GDP in Greece and Italy.

The illegal influx into Southern Europe has caused conflict among EU members. Irregular immigration came under EU jurisdiction when the Treaty of Amsterdam went into effect in 1999 (Tervo et al., 2009). Member nations still maintained control over their own borders, however. In April 2011, tens of thousands of Tunisian refugees arrived in Italy, where they were issued temporary permits. In response, France temporarily

---

[19] Heckmann (2004) noted that after steep increases in illegal immigration to Germany in the early 1990s, inflows have trended downward, although the number of migrants smuggled to Germany is steadily increasing. Jandl (2007) noted the same trends hold for irregular migration into East and Central European countries and claimed that improved border controls, better home-country conditions, and passport-free travel for Romanians and Bulgarians have acted together to reduce irregular flows.

[20] Boeri and Brücker noted another motivation for tough migration policies in these nations, namely a race to the top among neighboring countries who fear that migrant flows will be diverted to the nation with the most lax policies.

[21] Migration to Southern Europe was extensive until the global financial crisis in 2008–09 and the European sovereign debt crisis that followed (Sirkeci et al., 2012).

closed its border to trains carrying North African migrants from Italy (Naegelen, 2011). Citing fear of rising refugee inflows, a year later the EU Council approved reforms to the Schengen agreement that included broadening national governments' powers to reintroduce internal border controls (Euronews, 2012). Reducing the European Commission's role in setting border enforcement policy is seen as a setback for the continued formulation of joint migration policies at the EU level.

3.3.3 Other countries

Canada has massive immigration relative to its population. One in five Canadians was born abroad (Statistics Canada, 2009). However, illegal immigrants are few in number, and they are typically visa overstayers, not surreptitious border crossers (Buchignani and Indra, 1999). Their low numbers are partly a result of Canada's geographic remoteness and proximity to the US (a preferred destination for illegal immigrants). But authorities have also made timely policy changes and regularized the status of illegal immigrants or potential illegal immigrants, such as asylum seekers, keeping the undocumented population low (García y Griego, 1994; Buchignani and Indra, 1999).

Other western hemisphere nations with significant populations of irregular migrants include Costa Rica, a destination for Central Americans from Nicaragua and Honduras, and the Dominican Republic, where over 500,000 Haitians live with irregular status (Castles et al., 2012). South Africa and fast-growing nations in West Africa draw large inflows of irregular migrants from poorer African nations. In Asia, Malaysia is estimated to host over 1 million irregular migrants, mainly from Indonesia and the Philippines. Relatively new destinations include Turkey, which continues to experience an influx of irregular migrants from the former Soviet Union, especially Moldova and Ukraine, that began with the end of the Cold War.

4. COSTS AND BENEFITS OF UNDOCUMENTED MIGRATION

Economic theory predicts that immigration creates gains for destination countries and for migrants themselves. Effects on origin countries, discussed in Section 5 below, are more theoretically ambiguous. Although the bulk of the gains accrue to the migrants, destination countries reap the advantages of an increase in population and labor supply. There are distributional consequences, however. Factors that are complementary to immigrants gain, while factors that are substitutable for immigrants, such as competing workers, may lose. Immigrants may impose fiscal costs as well.

The costs and benefits of undocumented immigration differ from the impact of other types of immigration if the characteristics or behaviors of undocumented immigrants systematically differ from those of other immigrants, or if destination countries treat undocumented immigrants differently with regard to access to labor markets, education, or government transfer programs. For example, undocumented immigrants may be less skilled than other immigrants and therefore contribute less to economic growth. Their fiscal impact may differ if they are more likely to work off the books and not pay taxes or if they are barred from transfer programs.

4.1 Macroeconomic effects on destination countries

Immigration increases national income, or gross domestic product (GDP), by increasing the supply of labor—see, for example, Borjas (1995, 1999) and Bodvarsson and Van den Berg (2009) for formal models. Most of the income gains accrue to the immigrants themselves, but natives benefit as well. The productivity of resources that are complementary to immigrant labor increases, and the returns to capital, land, and complementary labor rise. These gains are bigger the more immigrants differ from natives. The macroeconomic effects of illegal immigration thus will differ from those of legal immigration if illegal immigrants are less—or more—similar than legal immigrants to natives. In developed countries, where most natives are skilled and illegal immigrants tend to be less skilled than legal immigrants, illegal immigration therefore may create bigger gains (per immigrant) in the short run than legal immigration.[22]

Few, if any, studies distinguish between the macroeconomic effects of legal and illegal immigration. Studies that model the effects of illegal immigration on the host-country economy typically use a neoclassical production function with capital and labor and must assume that illegal immigrants are either perfect or imperfect substitutes for native workers. Models also assume either that illegal immigrants earn their marginal product in competitive markets or that they earn less than their marginal product because they are exploited, and either that labor markets clear or that there are labor market frictions that can result in unemployment. Some models have only one production good; others have two, typically with one made by skilled native workers and the other made by unskilled natives and illegal immigrants.

Liu (2010) discussed four channels through which illegal immigration may affect natives' welfare. In the displacement effect, illegal immigrants displace natives from their jobs, which reduces their welfare. In the wage-depressing effect, the increase in labor supply due to illegal immigration reduces wages and hence reduces native welfare.

---

[22] However, differences in the responsiveness of the wages of skilled versus unskilled workers to increases in the supply of labor and external effects of skilled immigrants, such as promoting invention and innovation or stimulating trade, may make the income gains from legal immigration bigger than those from illegal immigration if legal immigrants are more skilled. Borjas (1995) provided a discussion. In addition, differences in assimilation—increases in skill—between legal and illegal immigrants and endogenous changes in skill levels among natives in response to immigration may cause the long-run effects to differ. We are not aware of any theoretical work that has thought carefully about these issues with respect to legal versus illegal immigration.

The exploitation effect incorporates the positive effect of lower wages on profits, which boosts natives' welfare. Finally, the capital consumption effect assumes that illegal immigrants do not contribute to capital accumulation but only consume some output that otherwise would be available for natives' consumption and investment; this reduces native welfare.

The predicted effect of illegal immigration on natives' welfare depends critically on the assumptions made and hence on the relative magnitudes of these four channels. In Hazari and Sgro (2003), illegal immigration reduces natives' consumption in the long run if immigrants are perfect substitutes for natives but is likely to boost natives' consumption if they are imperfect substitutes; Moy and Yip (2006) showed that the impact on natives' consumption is ambiguous even if illegal immigrants are perfect substitutes for natives when capital consumption and exploitation effects are included in the model. Pavilos (2009) and Liu (2010) developed models in which illegal immigration can raise natives' consumption and social welfare. Pavilos's calibrations for the US suggest that increasing the illegal immigrant share of the labor force by 1 percentage point boosts consumption by 0.4% each period and native lifetime welfare by 0.84%; Liu's (2010) calibrations likewise indicate that an increase in the illegal immigrant population share from 4% to 5% would boost native consumption by 0.45% each period.[23] However, when Pavilos (2009) added a binding minimum wage for unskilled native workers to his model, illegal immigration caused native consumption to decrease and native unemployment to increase.[24]

Because of the difficulty of distinguishing between legal and illegal immigrants, little empirical work has examined macroeconomic impacts of illegal immigration. Indeed, we are not aware of any empirical work that directly examines the effect of illegal immigration on GDP or on natives' consumption. A few studies examined the effect on unemployment. Bean et al. (1994) studied the effect of Operation Hold the Line, which attempted to seal the border between El Paso, United States, and Juarez, Mexico, in 1993 and thereby reduce illegal immigration. They concluded that the initiative led to a decrease in apprehensions of illicit border crossers in the El Paso region, and hence presumably led to a decrease in undocumented immigrant inflows to El Paso. It did not lead to a noticeable change in the unemployment rate or job postings in El Paso in the short run. However, the unemployment rate they examined includes both US natives and immigrants—legal and illegal—living in El Paso. Winegarden and Khor (1991) reported that undocumented immigration does not have a sizeable effect on unemployment among youth and minorities in the US.

---

[23] A similar model by Sarris and Zografakis (1999) applied to Greece suggested that its 3.2% labor force share of unauthorized immigrants has boosted real GDP by 1.5%, total private investment by 0.9%, and real total private consumption by 0.13%.

[24] Djajić (1987) also incorporated a minimum wage into a model that examined illegal immigration, unemployment in the source and destination countries, and spending on enforcement.

Another potential macroeconomic impact of illegal immigration is on prices. If undocumented immigration causes wages or other employer costs to fall, prices for labor-intensive goods then typically fall as well. Cortés (2008) found that a 10% increase in the share of low-skilled immigrants—legal and illegal combined—in the US labor force causes the price of immigrant-intensive services to fall by 2%. Lower prices for goods and services raise real incomes, particularly for people living in regions with high immigrant shares.

Finally, little research has examined unauthorized immigration's macroeconomic impact through indirect channels, such as labor market flexibility. Unauthorized immigrants are typically more responsive to market forces than legal immigrants (Hanson, 2007). In many countries, legal immigration is governed by complex rules and subject to bureaucratic delays that cause inflows to be only loosely linked to the pace of economic growth. Unauthorized immigrants, in contrast, typically enter in greater numbers when an economy booms, and some leave when an economy weakens. They are more likely than natives and other immigrants to move across employers, sectors, and regions in response to economic opportunities. Such mobility speeds wage and unemployment convergence across regions within a country, helps smooth regional business cycles, and makes the economy more efficient (Borjas, 2001). It also reduces the adverse impact of negative local demand shocks on natives' employment (Cadena and Kovac, 2013). The informal nature of illegal employment, with workers hired and fired at will as economic conditions change, also contributes to labor market flexibility (Hanson, 2007). On the other hand, the availability of low-skilled illegal immigrant workers may slow the pace of structural adjustment and technological progress, reducing economic growth and international competitiveness in the long run (Djajić, 2001).[25]

4.2 Microeconomic effects on destination countries

The economic literature on the microeconomic effects of immigration focuses on labor market outcomes. The canonical model predicts that immigration reduces wages and employment in the short run among competing native workers who are perfect substitutes for immigrants (see, for example, Chiswick, 1982; Grossman, 1984). Complementary factors of production, such as capital and workers with different skills than immigrants, gain from immigration. In the long run, competing native workers can upgrade their skills, reducing immigration's adverse effects. If immigrants are not perfect substitutes for natives, however, immigration may not have a negative effect

---

[25] The Commission of the European Communities (2003, p. 26) claims: "The presence of large numbers of illegal residents has a negative influence—as a source of cheap labor, liable to exploitation and in the long-term preventing necessary structural reform and thereby contributing to the inefficiency of the labour market."

on any native workers even in the short run. The labor market impact of immigration thus depends critically on the elasticity of substitution between immigrants and natives.

There is considerable debate within the economics literature about how substitutable immigrants are for native workers (see, for example, Borjas et al., 2011; Ottaviano and Peri, 2012). Unauthorized immigrants are likely to be less substitutable than legal immigrants for natives for a number of reasons. Fewer employers may be willing to hire unauthorized immigrants, especially in countries that impose sanctions on employers who hire them.[26] Because unauthorized immigrants have limited labor market opportunities, skilled workers are less willing to migrate illegally than unskilled workers (Chiswick, 1988a). The skill set of unauthorized immigrants therefore may not overlap much with that of natives, particularly in developed countries.[27] In addition, unauthorized immigrants may be clustered in areas with large numbers of immigrants because of limited fluency in the destination country's language or a belief that living among other immigrants reduces the risk of being caught. Such geographic concentration may further reduce competition between unauthorized immigrants and native workers.

Little empirical work has directly examined the substitutability of unauthorized immigrants for native workers. Using annual estimates of the number of workers by industry in Italy, Venturini (1999) found that, among workers in the shadow economy, foreigners are less substitutable than natives for workers in the formal sector, and foreign workers are complements to native workers in some industries. The study did not compare irregular and regular foreign workers.

Most studies of the impact of illegal immigration on labor market outcomes in the US found little effect. Hanson et al. (2002) concluded that increased border enforcement along the US–Mexico border has little effect on wages in US border cities, suggesting that undocumented immigration has a minimal impact on wages in those areas. Marcelli (2008) found that the inflow of unauthorized Mexican immigrants during the 1990s is not significantly negatively related to wages among young adult men in California in 2000. Hotchkiss et al. (2012) reported that legal workers—natives and immigrants combined—earn only 0.15% less if they work for a firm that hires workers who appear to be undocumented immigrants than those who work for a firm that does not. Hotchkiss and Quispe-Agnoli (2013) found no evidence that legal workers are displaced when their employers hire workers who appear to be undocumented immigrants. However, Martin (1986) claimed that unauthorized immigrants displace US natives in low-wage, low-skill

---

[26] Hotchkiss and Quispe-Agnoli (2013) found that undocumented immigrants in the US, as proxied by workers who are using an invalid Social Security number, have less elastic labor supply with respect to wages than other workers. This reduced sensitivity to wage changes is consistent with undocumented immigrants having fewer options than other workers.

[27] Consistent with this, Hotchkiss and Quispe-Agnoli (2013) reported that almost three-quarters of the observed 30% wage differential between documented—native and immigrant—workers and undocumented workers is due to differences in productivity.

sectors like agriculture, construction, food processing, and services. He argued that use of network recruitment, ethnic supervisors, and subcontractors has led to natives and even some legal immigrants being excluded from many workplaces in those industries.

If undocumented immigrants have an adverse effect on natives' labor market outcomes, it is likely to be concentrated among natives who are the most substitutable for undocumented immigrants. In developed countries, this is most likely to be low-skilled racial or ethnic minorities. For example, Cobb-Clark and Kossoudji (2000, p. 323) noted that undocumented women in the US, most of whom are unskilled and do not speak English well, "are most likely to be in competition with young inner-city minority women who are also unskilled."

However, empirical work generally does not indicate adverse effects on disadvantaged natives. In a study of the southwestern US, an area with many undocumented immigrants, Müller and Espenshade (1985) concluded that Mexican immigrants do not take jobs away from native-born blacks or reduce their incomes. Using estimates of the undocumented Mexican population in the southwestern US in 1980, Bean et al. (1988) concluded undocumented immigrants have little effect on the earnings of US-born Mexican-American, black, and white males. Some of their results indicate that native women's earnings are actually slightly higher in areas with a greater concentration of undocumented Mexican workers. Bean et al. (1987, p. 685) noted that these findings are "more consistent with the argument that undocumenteds may hold jobs that others disdain than they are with the view that undocumenteds compete with natives and (especially) minorities with jobs and wages." DeFreitas (1988) reported that recent Hispanic immigration, much of it undocumented, does not have a significant negative effect on wages or employment among low-skilled black or Hispanic native men but does appear to have a significant negative effect on low-skilled black female natives' wages. More recent work by Borjas et al. (2006) found a significant negative impact of all immigrants, not just the undocumented, on wages and employment among blacks.[28]

The most adverse labor market effects of undocumented immigration are likely to be on other immigrants. Research on all immigrants, not just the undocumented, suggests this is the case (see, for example, Zorlu and Hartog, 2005; Ottaviano and Peri, 2012). However, Bean et al. (1988) found no evidence that undocumented Mexican immigrants have a significant negative effect on the wages of legal Mexican immigrants in the southwestern US. Kugler and Yuksel (2011) similarly concluded that recent Latino immigrants, many of whom are undocumented, do not have a significant adverse effect on earlier Latino immigrants' labor market outcomes in the US. Hotchkiss and Quispe-Agnoli (2013) reported evidence that having a greater number of undocumented workers boosts separation rates from firms among earlier undocumented workers, but it is not clear whether this effect is due to a rise in voluntary or involuntary separations.

---

[28] A computable general equilibrium (CGE) simulation by Sarris and Zografakis (1999) for Greece suggested that households that are poor or are headed by an unskilled worker are hurt by illegal immigration.

Unauthorized immigration may also affect labor market outcomes among complementary workers. Cortés and Tessada (2011) concluded that low-skilled immigration to the US, much of it unauthorized, increases average hours of paid work and decreases hours of household production among highly educated native women. The ready availability of immigrants as housekeepers, gardeners, and child care providers increases highly educated women's labor supply in the marketplace while decreasing it in the home.

Undocumented immigration may have microeconomic impacts beyond the labor market. Because unauthorized immigrants tend to be concentrated at the bottom of the skill and wage distribution, unauthorized immigration may exacerbate inequality. For example, Pavilos and Yip (2010) showed that, under reasonable assumptions, illegal immigration causes an increase in wealth inequality if illegal immigrants are perfect substitutes for unskilled native workers. Adding endogenous skill acquisition by natives to the model causes the distribution of wealth to become even more unequal. We are not aware of any empirical work on the effect of unauthorized immigration on the distribution of wealth, but one study examined the effect on the distribution of income. Using estimates of the distribution of undocumented immigrants across US states in 1980, Winegarden and Khor (1993) concluded that undocumented immigration increases income inequality among natives, although the effect appears to be small.[29]

Finally, the availability of unauthorized immigrant workers also may affect an economy's industrial composition, product mix, or production techniques. The presence of undocumented immigrants may slow firms' mechanization or offshoring. It also may keep labor costs low enough to reduce the inflow of imported goods. For example, illegal immigrants from Nicaragua working in Costa Rica allegedly reduced labor costs in the export agricultural sector, helping boost international competitiveness (Wiley, 1995). Djajić (1997) noted that the availability of cheap, clandestine foreign labor is essential to the survival of firms in the agricultural sector and the garment industry in the US.

4.3 Fiscal effects on destination countries

The direct net fiscal impact of immigrants is the difference between taxes paid and transfer payments and other immigrant-related costs borne by the government. The indirect fiscal impact includes changes in taxes paid by and transfer payments made to natives as a result of immigration-induced changes in earnings or participation in transfer programs; the indirect effect is harder to estimate than the direct effect. Estimates of the net fiscal impact of immigrants vary dramatically across countries and over time.

The net fiscal impact of unauthorized immigrants can differ from that of legal immigrants for several reasons. Since unauthorized immigrants tend to earn less than legal

---

[29] Kremer and Watt (2006) argued that migration by low-skilled workers serving as private household workers may reduce inequality by boosting labor supply among high-skilled native women, as in Cortés and Tessada (2011), and by increasing the wages of low-skilled natives.

immigrants, they tend to pay less in taxes. Unauthorized immigrants are more likely to work off the books than legal immigrants, further reducing how much they pay in taxes. On the other hand, in most countries unauthorized immigrants are eligible for fewer government transfer programs than legal immigrants. This reduces the adverse fiscal impact of unauthorized immigration. In addition, unauthorized immigrants tend to be younger than other immigrants, making them more likely to work and less likely to incur publicly funded health care costs. Unauthorized immigrants also may be less likely to have dependents in the host country, further reducing their fiscal cost.

Estimates of the net fiscal impact of unauthorized immigrants must decide how to treat two contentious aspects: the children of unauthorized immigrants, and enforcement costs. As discussed in Section 7.4 below, some countries automatically grant citizenship to unauthorized immigrants' children who are born there. Such children typically are eligible for government transfers on the same terms as other citizens. Since their family incomes tend to be low, they have high eligibility rates for means-tested programs. However, takeup rates are likely lower than among other groups because their families fear revealing their presence to authorities or jeopardizing any chance to regularize their status (Watson, 2010; Vargas, 2011). Moving citizen children's publicly funded education and other costs from the unauthorized immigrant to the citizen side of the ledger substantially reduces the fiscal cost of unauthorized immigration.

Some enforcement costs vary with the number of unauthorized immigrants while others are fixed. For example, the total cost of apprehending, detaining, and deporting unauthorized immigrants increases with the number of unauthorized immigrants, although there are likely to be some economies of scale. Physical barriers erected to deter entry are a public good, in contrast, so their costs should not be allocated to unauthorized immigrants.

Other costs of unauthorized immigrants include costs due to congestion, or costs that rise when a country has more people. A country needs more roads, police and fire fighters, parks, sanitation services, and so on when it has more people. Such costs depend little on whether an immigrant is legal or unauthorized, however.

Most attempts to calculate the net fiscal impact of unauthorized immigrants in the US concluded that they pay less in taxes than they receive in services, on average (Congressional Budget Office, 2007). Nonetheless, estimates suggest that over half of unauthorized immigrants in the US pay income and payroll taxes through employers withholding from their paychecks or by filing tax returns (Congressional Budget Office, 2007). Unauthorized immigrants also pay sales taxes and, either themselves or through their landlords, property taxes.

In economies with large informal sectors and high rates of tax avoidance, tax receipts may be small from undocumented immigrants and natives alike. Djajić (1997) noted that high payroll taxes can give employers a significant incentive to hire people "off the books." Off-the-books workers are not necessarily immigrants; in Italy, for example, natives constitute the bulk of such workers (Venturini, 1999). Other benefits of off-the-books workers to employers include the possibility of paying piece rate and avoiding constraints imposed by labor unions and government regulations, such as regulations regarding hiring, firing, minimum wages, and working hours (Djajić, 1997). For models of illegal immigration and the underground economy, see Dell'Aringa and Neri (1987) and Djajić (1997).

4.3.1 Federalist implications

The fiscal impact of undocumented immigrants can differ between national and sub-national levels because of the types of services provided by various levels of government and because of differences in revenue sources. Depending on the federal structure of taxes and transfers, undocumented immigrants may impose net fiscal costs on some levels but create net fiscal gains for others. For example, in the US, the federal government receives income taxes and payroll taxes paid by unauthorized immigrants, and it bears the cost of border and some interior enforcement. Unauthorized immigrants are ineligible for virtually all federally funded government transfer programs. The federal government therefore may well have a net fiscal gain from undocumented immigration (Rothman and Espenshade, 1992). States and localities receive income from sales and property taxes, and bear most education and health care, and local law enforcement costs, such as jailing unauthorized immigrants detained for non-federal crimes. Unauthorized immigrants are a net fiscal drain on state and local governments (Congressional Budget Office, 2007).

Undercounting of undocumented immigrants can compound differences in these fiscal impacts. If transfers are made from the federal government to sub-national governments on a per-capita or need basis, such transfers will be too low if undocumented immigrants are undercounted in surveys. Areas that bear the greatest fiscal burdens from undocumented immigration will be the most underfunded. This may contribute to the fact that immigrants are perceived more negatively in immigrant-intensive areas in the US, particularly in areas with relatively generous transfer programs (Hanson et al., 2007).

4.4 Effects on migrants

The income gains to migration can be substantial. Clemens et al. (2008) reported that the average worker can more than quadruple his or her earnings by migrating to the US. The average gain to a moderately skilled worker migrating from a developing country would be around $10,000 a year, about double the average GDP per capita in such countries. Given such potential gains, the question should perhaps not be why so many people become immigrants but, rather, why so few (Portes and Rumbaut, 2006).

However, the gains are likely to be smaller for undocumented immigrants than for legal immigrants. Sabates-Wheeler (2009), for example, reported that Ghanaian and Malawian irregular immigrants to the UK and Malawian irregular immigrants to South Africa had positive income gains, but they were smaller than among legal migrants. Studies of US agricultural workers, many of whom are unauthorized, found that undocumented immigrants earn 5–33% less per hour than other immigrants (Taylor, 1992; Isé and Perloff, 1995; Pena, 2010). Borjas and Tienda (1993) similarly reported that undocumented immigrants as a whole, not just those working in agriculture, earn 30% less than legal immigrants in the US. Research on the wage gains from obtaining legal status in the US suggests that the undocumented experience a wage penalty of 6–13% (Rivera-Batiz, 1999; Kossoudji and Cobb-Clark, 2002; Amuedo-Dorantes et al., 2007). In Italy, legal immigrants earn about 8% more than irregular immigrants, controlling for other observable characteristics (Baldacci et al., 1999). In Spain, the gap is about 12% (Connor and Massey, 2010).

Wages could be lower among unauthorized immigrants for several reasons. Chiswick (1986, 2001) attributed lower wages among unauthorized immigrants to lower skill levels, which may be partly a consequence of the likelihood of deportation; unauthorized immigrants are reluctant to invest in host-country-specific skills that will lose value if they are deported. Massey (1987) attributed the difference to unauthorized immigrants having less work experience and less employer-specific capital than legal immigrants because unauthorized immigrants are more likely to engage in repeat migration and therefore switch jobs more frequently. He also argued that undocumented immigrants have less social capital—smaller networks with contacts to high-paying employers—than legal immigrants.[30] Rivera-Batiz (1999) reported that differences in observable characteristics, such as education, English ability, and duration of US residence, can partially account for the 40% wage gap he found between legal and illegal Mexican workers in the US. Nonetheless, he found that a significant wage penalty remains after controlling for such factors. Baldacci et al. (1999) similarly showed that differences in socio-economic factors can explain part, but not all, of the difference in wages between legal and illegal immigrants in Italy.

In addition, unauthorized immigrants may earn less because they are trapped in the secondary labor market. In a segmented, or dual, labor market, the secondary market encompasses jobs that pay low wages, lack opportunities for advancement, and have few worker protections or benefits (Doeringer and Piore, 1971; Piore, 1979). Kossoudji and Cobb-Clark (1996, 2000) found that undocumented status appears to restrict

---

[30] However, Granberry and Marcelli (2007) reported that, among Mexican immigrants in the US, the unauthorized do not appear to have less social capital than legal immigrants, at least in terms of reporting that they have helped and have been helped by a family member or friend when in need of help to resolve a crisis.

mobility beyond a narrow set of occupations in the US.[31] Differences between undocumented and legal immigrants can occur even within an occupation. In a sample of garment workers in Los Angeles, California, undocumented immigrants work for smaller firms and are more likely to be paid piece rate than legal immigrants; these job differences can account for the entire 10% wage gap between legal and illegal immigrants in their sample (Gill and Long, 1989).

Some research suggests that undocumented immigrants do not earn less than their legal counterparts, however. Massey (1987) concluded that legal status has no direct effect on wages among male Mexican migrants to the US, nor does it affect the kind of job migrants hold. Kaushal (2006) found that immigrants who had not finished high school do not experience significant earnings gains after gaining legal status in the US. Consistent with this, Löfström et al. (2013) reported that upward mobility and increased wages after obtaining legal status are largely limited to US immigrants who overstayed a visa, a group that tends to be relatively well educated; there are few gains among workers who crossed the border clandestinely, a group that tends to have relatively little education.

Although it may involve gains relative to remaining in the source country, irregular immigration can involve many downsides as well. These include exploitation, extortion, exclusion, insecurity, discrimination, lack of rights, and lack of safety at work (Sabates-Wheeler, 2009). Language barriers, lack of awareness of rights, and fear of being deported often hinder unauthorized immigrants from reporting workplace violations. Deskilling is common, with many unauthorized immigrants holding jobs below their education or skill level because they are unable to obtain necessary credentials or to find employers willing to hire them into "good" jobs. Among US agricultural workers, illegal immigrants are less likely to have employer-sponsored health insurance and to earn a bonus than their legal counterparts (Kandilov and Kandilov, 2010). Unauthorized immigrants in Los Angeles and New York report having worse jobs than legal immigrants along a variety of dimensions, including exposure to unhealthy conditions (Enchautegui, 2008). In many countries with extensive social welfare systems, unauthorized immigrants are ineligible for unemployment insurance, and their employers often successfully pressure them to not apply for workers' compensation if they are injured on the job. Undocumented immigrants may have less access to health care as well. In California, undocumented Latino immigrants reported less use of health care services than otherwise comparable legal Latino immigrants and US-born Latinos (Ortega et al., 2007).[32]

---

[31] However, Chiswick (1988b) argued that illegal aliens in the US experience considerable job mobility, and their earnings improve sharply as they accumulate US experience, particularly with the same employer. Chiswick (1988a) concluded that the occupational attainment among a sample of apprehended unauthorized workers is only slightly lower than among recent legal immigrants from the same origin country.

[32] Better health among undocumented immigrants—the "healthy immigrant" paradox—may partially account for the difference, but the estimates controlled for self-reported health status.

Networks appear to play an important role in determining undocumented immigrants' outcomes. In addition to affecting the number and characteristics of undocumented immigrants, networks influence where undocumented immigrants live and work, thereby affecting how well they do in the destination country. Munshi (2003) found that Mexican immigrants—most of them undocumented—with bigger established networks in the destination county are more likely to work and more likely to hold a higher-paying non-agricultural job.

5. IMPACTS ON ORIGIN COUNTRIES

The overall impact of undocumented immigration on origin countries is unlikely to differ considerably from the impact of legal immigration. Differences are likely to arise primarily because of differences in the characteristics of undocumented versus legal immigrants. In addition, the impact may differ because undocumented immigration tends to be more circular and of shorter duration than legal migration. Remittances also tend to depend on legal status.

Out-migration can lead to a number of changes in origin countries. Because it reduces the population, emigration is likely to reduce the number of workers. This reduction in the labor force is likely to lead to higher wages, all else equal. Labor force participation rates may change among the remaining population, either rising because of higher wages and the need to replace the earnings of out-migrants or falling because migrants send home remittances that enable some family members to stop working. If emigrants disproportionately earn high or low wages or incomes, emigration may cause inequality to change. The returns to human capital may change, motivating the remaining population to acquire more or less education than previously. In addition, expectations to themselves engage in undocumented migration in the future may affect young people's decisions about human capital accumulation.

Differences in the selectivity of undocumented versus legal immigrants may cause the effects of emigration to differ between the two groups. As discussed in Section 2.2, undocumented immigrants are likely to be less positively selected than legal immigrants. "Brain drain" is therefore unlikely to be a major concern regarding illegal immigration. Nonetheless, undocumented immigrants are disproportionately young adults who otherwise would be active in the home-country labor force. Their emigration therefore will tend to boost wages at the lower end of the wage distribution if undocumented emigrants are disproportionately drawn from there, which would also reduce inequality.

Empirical evidence suggests that undocumented emigration has had a significant impact on wages in Mexico. Mishra (2007) concluded that emigration from Mexico, most of it illegal immigration to the US, raised nominal wages in Mexico by 8% between 1970 and 2000. However, the effect is not concentrated at the bottom of the wage distribution. Instead, the upwards wage pressure is concentrated at the middle of the education distribution (Hanson, 2007; Mishra, 2007). This is consistent with findings that Mexican emigration, particularly from rural areas, the major sources of undocumented immigrants, is disproportionately from the middle of the education distribution (Chiquiar and Hanson, 2005; Orrenius and Zavodny, 2005; Kaestner and Malamud, 2014).

Emigration from Mexico has also affected wage inequality there. Since the wage effects have been greatest among the relatively educated, emigration has exacerbated wage inequality in Mexico (Mishra, 2007). The relative wages of low-skilled workers have fallen (Aydemir and Borjas, 2006). However, McKenzie and Rapoport (2007) noted that the relationship between emigration and inequality appears to have an inverse U-shaped pattern in the rural communities in Mexico, where unauthorized immigration predominates. This occurs because initial migration is concentrated at the middle of the distribution, where individuals have the means and incentive to migrate, but then spreads to the bottom of the distribution as remittances and networks enable more people to emigrate. Emigration thus ultimately reduces inequality.

Empirical evidence suggests that emigration from Mexico has affected educational attainment there as well. Because undocumented immigrants have relatively low returns to education and skill, people who anticipate becoming undocumented immigrants have less incentive to accumulate human capital.[33] Research suggests the opposite—"brain gain"—may occur when highly skilled people emigrate from developing countries because of higher returns to skill abroad, emigration that typically occurs through legal channels (Beine et al., 2001; Batista et al., 2012). In rural Mexico, international migration does not appear to have a significant effect on children's educational attainment (Boucher et al., 2009). However, it is difficult for researchers to unpack the various effects on human capital accumulation created by the possibility of migrating illegally in the future. Changes in the wage distribution, changes in family structure, and remittances sent home by undocumented immigrants all affect human capital accumulation.

Finally, the impacts of undocumented and legal immigration may differ since undocumented immigration tends to be more circular and of shorter duration. Greater circularity may boost some effects. For example, if returning migrants bring home new ideas or facilitate technology transfer, undocumented immigration may have a bigger impact than legal immigration since undocumented migrants are more likely to return home. However, Castles et al. (2012) argued that undocumented immigrants are less likely than legal immigrants to bring back positive social remittances, such as technology

---

[33] In addition, emigration has direct effects on human capital accumulation in migrant households. Young people may leave school to work or to provide household services, or simply because an adult influence has left, when a family member migrates. McKenzie and Rapoport (2011) concluded that boys living in a migrant household are more likely to drop out of school to migrate, and girls are more likely to drop out of school to provide household services. Antman (2012), however, concluded that paternal migration from Mexico to the US has a positive effect on girls' education.

or development-friendly attitudes, because they have little exposure to them while working in the informal sector and living underground in the host country. Shorter stays abroad also may cause undocumented immigration to have less impact than legal immigration.

5.1 Remittances

Remittances are an important source of funds for many immigrant-sending countries, and remittances are one of the primary motivations for migration. Cash or in-kind transfers sent home or brought back by international migrants may contribute to economic development in origin countries at the national and regional levels. At the household level, remittances may boost consumption and investment. However, remittances also may lead to decreases in labor force participation and increases in inequality. They also may finance additional out-migration. Although there is a large economics literature on remittances, few studies have explicitly examined the role of migrants' legal status in remittances.

Illegal immigrants may be more likely to remit and may have higher remittances than legal immigrants for several reasons. The undocumented are more likely to have characteristics associated with sending remittances, such as being a recent immigrant, leaving dependents behind in the source country, and moving in search of better economic opportunities (Pena, 2013). Undocumented immigrants' earnings are typically more volatile because of less job stability and ineligibility for government transfer programs; remittances can act as a form of insurance against such uncertainty (Dustmann, 1997). Remittances also may ensure a place back home if an undocumented immigrant is deported. However, undocumented immigrants may also have lower earnings than legal immigrants, as discussed above, which will depress remittances, all else being equal.

Empirical evidence indicates that undocumented immigrants typically send more remittances than legal immigrants. Among Mexican migrants to the US, undocumented immigrants are more likely to send back remittances, and they remit a greater fraction of their earnings than their documented counterparts (Amuedo-Dorantes et al., 2005; Amuedo-Dorantes and Pozo, 2006). Illegal Bulgarian immigrants to Spain likewise remit more than their legal counterparts, controlling for earnings (Markova and Reilly, 2007). However, legal African immigrants are more likely to remit than their illegal counterparts (Bollard et al., 2010). Among Latin American and Caribbean immigrants, undocumented immigrants are more likely to say that increasing their families' consumption is the reason they remit; legal immigrants are more likely to remit to accumulate assets (Amuedo-Dorantes, 2007). Remittances appear to fall after large-scale legalization programs (Cornelius, 1989; Amuedo-Dorantes and Mazzolari, 2010). Consistent with remittances acting as insurance, undocumented immigrants appear to remit more when enforcement increases in the host country (Vaira-Lucero et al., 2012).

6. PUBLIC POLICY AND UNDOCUMENTED IMMIGRATION

Public policy affects undocumented immigration in a number of ways. Most importantly, enforcement programs and legal immigration policies affect the stock and flow of undocumented immigrants and their composition. But other policies and programs matter as well. Many countries have enacted legalization programs that enable irregular immigrants to receive legal status. Receiving legal status typically increases immigrants' eligibility for government transfer programs, but even irregular immigrants are eligible for certain programs in some countries. Perhaps the most common publicly funded program for which irregular immigrants are eligible is primary and secondary schooling. Access to public higher education tends to be more limited. Another important aspect of public policy regarding children is whether the children of undocumented immigrants are also eligible for citizenship if born in the destination country. This section explores public policy in these areas.

6.1 Legalization programs

Many countries have implemented legalization programs that allow irregular immigrants to convert to legal status. Such programs are also referred to as regularizations or amnesties, with the latter term often used pejoratively. Legalization programs occur in a variety of formats, ranging from one-time amnesties to ongoing regularization mechanisms. Most programs grant permission to live and perhaps work in the host country for a specified period; as a result, regularized immigrants frequently lapse back into illegality over time.[34] A few legalization programs grant permanent residence and a pathway to citizenship.

As undocumented immigration has grown, legalization programs have become common. France, Greece, Italy, Portugal, and Spain have implemented multiple legalization programs since the 1980s. The US had a large-scale legalization program in 1986, the Immigration Reform and Control Act (IRCA), and several smaller programs that were limited to specific groups. Argentina, Thailand, and Venezuela are among the developing countries that have had large-scale legalization programs.[35]

The typical legalization program requires applicants to prove that they have resided in the host country since a certain date and that they do not have a criminal record. Applicants

---

[34] Interestingly, not all eligible undocumented immigrants participate in legalization programs. This is particularly true for programs that offer only temporary legal residence. The costs of participating may not outweigh the gains. Applicants typically must pay a fee, and they reveal their presence to the government, putting themselves at greater risk of deportation if their application is denied. In addition, they may become less employable if participating requires that they or their employers must pay taxes on their labor and were not previously doing so (Sarris and Markova, 2001).

[35] For lists of countries that have implemented legalization programs and details, see, among others, Meissner et al. (1987), Sunderhaus (2007), Gang and Yun (2008), and Epstein and Weiss (2011).

usually must pay a fee. Some countries have imposed work or language requirements or limited eligibility to certain origin countries. The average length of the application period was 30 weeks in the amnesty programs surveyed by Sunderhaus (2007).

In addition to full-fledged legalization programs, some countries have ongoing regularization procedures that allow individuals who meet certain conditions to receive legal status. Conditions typically include living and working in the host country for a specified period. Spain implemented such a scheme, the Settlement Program, in 2006 (Sabater and Domingo, 2012). In the US, undocumented immigrants commonly received legal permanent resident status by being sponsored by a relative or an employer until the Illegal Immigration Reform and Immigrant Responsibility Act (IIRIRA) of 1996 imposed three- or ten-year bans on re-entry into the US for such undocumented immigrants. Even so, Jasso (2011) noted that about 40% of people who received US legal permanent resident status in 2003 had previous experience as unauthorized immigrants.

6.1.1 Impact of legalization on beneficiaries

Legalization programs offer a number of benefits to migrants receiving legal status. At a minimum, these benefits include protection under the law, greater ability to travel, and reduced exploitation. Programs that grant permission to work or permanent legal status confer even greater benefits.

The main impact of legalization programs on beneficiaries appears to be an increase in their earnings. In the US, Latin American immigrants who legalized their status under IRCA experienced wage increases in the range of 6–13%, with slightly larger effects among women than men (e.g., Rivera-Batiz, 1999; Kossoudji and Cobb-Clark, 2002; Amuedo-Dorantes et al., 2007).[36] Rivera-Batiz (1999) found that changes in observable characteristics, such as improvements in English, explain less than half of the wage gains among Mexicans who legalized their status under IRCA.

Earnings rise for beneficiaries because legalization helps them to move to better jobs and earn higher returns to education. In the US, the earnings gains after legalization are bigger among well-educated immigrants than among less-educated immigrants (Kaushal, 2006, Pan, 2012). Much of the gains appear to be due to beneficiaries moving to higher-paying occupations (Lozano and Sørensen, 2011). Consistent with this, the benefits of having legal status are larger for workers in skilled occupations (Orozco-Alemán, 2010) and for well-educated immigrants (Kaushal, 2006; Pan, 2012).

Legalization programs do not necessarily increase employment among beneficiaries, however. Some research concludes that employment rates fell among immigrants who legalized their status under IRCA; men became more selective about the jobs they were

---

[36] More recent work by Barcellos (2011) using a regression discontinuity design and data from large-scale surveys found smaller wage gains, 2–3%.

willing to hold, while women exited the labor force, perhaps because they became eligible for more government transfer programs after they became legal (Amuedo-Dorantes et al., 2007; Amuedo-Dorantes and Bansak, 2011a).[37]

Unauthorized immigrants' children benefit from legalization programs in several ways. Families in which everyone has legal status are more likely to take up government benefits for which native-born children are eligible, and families that legalize status may become eligible for such benefits. Increased family income and greater stability lead to better assimilation and greater socio-economic advancement. They also appear to lead to better educational outcomes. Mexican-American young adults complete more years of school if their parents were able to legalize their status in the US (Bean et al., 2006, 2011). Having a father who legalized his status is also associated with better English proficiency and higher earnings among Mexican Americans (Bean et al., 2006), and having a mother who legalized her status is positively associated with reading and math standardized test scores among Hispanic children (Pan, 2011).[38]

6.1.2 Other economic effects of legalization programs

Legalization programs can have fiscal and labor market effects that extend far beyond immediate beneficiaries. On the fiscal side, the impact can be positive or negative. Legalization programs boost tax revenues if newly legalized immigrants switch from working off the books to the formal sector. Tax revenues also increase if immigrants' earnings rise after they legalize. However, these tax gains may be offset by higher transfer program expenditures if newly legalized immigrants become eligible for transfer programs or if their take-up of benefits increases. This may explain why countries with bigger transfer programs, as proxied by unemployment benefits as a share of GDP, are less likely to enact an amnesty (Casarico et al., 2012).

Newly legalized immigrants may become more substitutable for natives and legal immigrants. They may no longer be confined to the informal sector, for example.[39] This may lead to adverse effects on competing workers. However, if unauthorized immigrants were working off the books, they and their employers had an advantage over workers and businesses that followed the law. Legalization programs can level the playing field if this labor is now taxed; reduced competition from the informal sector may offset

---

[37] However, another study concluded that employment rates rose among female immigrants who likely benefited from IRCA (Pan, 2012). Employment fell, albeit insignificantly, among men likely to have legalized under a 1997 US legalization program (Kaushal, 2006).

[38] Consistent with this, young children of undocumented Mexican immigrants have higher odds of having developmental problems than the children of legal Mexican immigrants or of US natives (Ortega et al., 2009).

[39] Casarico et al. (2012) found that countries are more likely to implement an amnesty the greater the mismatch between workers' occupations and their education, a proxy for unauthorized immigrants being trapped in the informal sector.

increased competition in the formal sector. Regularizations in southern Europe, a region characterized by high taxes and large informal sectors, have largely failed in moving newly legalized immigrants to the formal sector, however (Organization for Economic Cooperation and Development, 2000).

Legalization programs can lead to increased discrimination against workers who are suspected of being unauthorized immigrants if they are accompanied by increased enforcement. A legalization program that increases employer penalties for hiring unauthorized workers, like IRCA in the US, can result in lower wages and make it more difficult for workers suspected of being unauthorized to find jobs. By acting as a tax on unauthorized workers, employer sanctions will lower labor demand if employers cannot distinguish between legal and illegal workers. Penalties may also make employers reluctant to hire workers who appear to be foreign and hence may be unauthorized, regardless of their true legal status, or willing to hire such workers only at lower wages. Cobb-Clark et al. (1995) found that wages among manufacturing workers in the US fell in areas where more fines were imposed on employers for IRCA violations, although the effect is small.[40] Wages among Hispanics fell by 6–8% after IRCA (Bansak and Raphael, 2001; Bansak, 2005), and employment rates fell by almost 2% (Lowell et al., 1995).[41] Pagán and Dávila (1996) reported that wages and on-the-job training fell even among US-born Mexican Americans after IRCA.[42]

Legalization programs may have macroeconomic effects as well. A simulation by Eren et al. (2011) suggested that an amnesty in the US would boost GDP, the capital stock, consumption, labor productivity, and overall social welfare, although the effects are small. The results are driven primarily by an increase in savings because newly legalized immigrants remit less and keep more of their savings in the host country after legalizing their status. Amuedo-Dorantes and Mazzolari (2010) found that remittances declined substantially among Mexican immigrants who were able to legalize their status under IRCA. A decrease in remittances has implications for the origin country's economy as well.

6.1.3 Effects on future flows

Legalization programs may encourage additional illegal immigration. Illegal immigration may increase because of hopes for future legalization programs or desire to reunite with newly legalized family members in the host country. Cornelius (1989, p. 698) noted that

---

[40] Fry et al. (1995) noted that the effect of fines depends on whether the fines are based on paperwork requirements, which apply *ex ante* (before workers' legal status is known), or hiring fines, which apply *ex post* only to unauthorized workers.

[41] Gentsch and Massey (2011) similarly found that the labor market deteriorated for both legal and illegal Mexican immigrants after the IIRIRA further increased enforcement in the US in 1996.

[42] However, Donato and Massey (1993) concluded that wages fell only among the undocumented, not among all Mexican immigrants. They argued that this finding is inconsistent with increased discrimination against Mexican migrants per se.

after IRCA in the US, "male family heads who secured amnesty for themselves quickly began sending for their wives and children in Mexico, whether or not these dependents themselves could qualify for legalization, using *coyotes* to guide them across the border."

Another reason why legalization programs may stimulate additional illicit inflows is their labor market impact. Ethier (1986b, p. 262) noted that an amnesty reduces employers' risk of hiring illegal workers, which increases the wage they are willing to pay. This increase in wages induces more illegal immigration: "amnestied workers are at least partly replaced by new illegal immigrants." To avoid this paradox, countries often couple a legalization program with increased enforcement, both along the border to reduce inflows and in the interior to discourage hiring.[43] Despite its increased enforcement provisions, IRCA failed to stem the flow of unauthorized immigrants into the US (Donato et al., 1992; Orrenius and Zavodny, 2003). This may be because employers depended on a continued stream of low-cost undocumented labor. Hanson and Spilimbergo (2001) showed that authorities appear to relax US–Mexico border enforcement when US demand for undocumented labor is high. More generally, the balance between amnesties, border enforcement, and interior enforcement may be affected by rent seeking among politicians or bureaucrats, desire to reduce the fiscal burden of immigration, and employers' concern about profits (Chau, 2003; Karlson and Katz, 2003; Gang and Yun, 2008).

6.2 Government transfer programs

Undocumented immigrants are ineligible for cash social assistance programs in most countries. Klugman and Pereira (2009) reported that over 90% of developed and developing countries alike deny benefits to irregular immigrants. In the US, for example, undocumented immigrants are ineligible for cash means-tested transfer programs, with the exception of the child tax credit for those who file income tax returns.

As a result, unauthorized immigrants are less likely to participate in transfer programs, at least in the US. Among US agricultural workers, for example, unauthorized immigrants and their families are less likely to participate in most means-tested transfer programs than US natives or legal immigrants. The one exception is public medical assistance, which unauthorized immigrants and their families are more likely than other groups to use (Moretti and Perloff, 2000). This is not a surprise since undocumented immigrants are less likely to have employer-sponsored health insurance (Marcelli, 2004; Kandilov and Kandilov, 2010). Unauthorized immigrants also are more likely to receive private charitable assistance, such as a community food bank. Interestingly, these results hold both unconditionally and conditionally on having a US citizen child. Unsurprisingly, having a US citizen child raises

---

[43] Chau (2001) modeled the opposite dynamic inconsistency problem: countries that increase enforcement stimulate more illegal immigration. Countries may have an overly generous amnesty program in order to increase the credibility of their enforcement program.

the likelihood that an unauthorized immigrant farm worker's family participates in at least one government transfer program (Moretti and Perloff, 2000). Unauthorized Mexican immigrants living in Los Angeles County who participate in welfare programs also primarily access it through their US-born children, who are very likely to be eligible given high poverty rates among this population (Marcelli and Heer, 1998).

In some countries, irregular immigrants are eligible for health care services from publicly funded providers, including hospitals. In most countries, some or all irregular immigrants have access to emergency health care. In the US, for example, most hospitals cannot refuse emergency care to undocumented immigrants. Medicaid, the public health insurance program, covers the cost of emergency care for undocumented immigrants who meet the income and other eligibility requirements. Pregnant undocumented immigrants may also be eligible for Medicaid-funded prenatal care in some states. Only 7% of developed countries allow irregular immigrants access to publicly funded preventative care immediately after their arrival; about 30% make access available over time. For example, public hospitals in France provide health care services to irregular immigrants who have lived in the country for at least three months, and other providers after three years. No developing countries give new unauthorized immigrants access to publicly funded preventative care, although some do allow it over time (Klugman and Pereira, 2009).

Even where they do have access to health care, undocumented immigrants may be unable or unwilling to use it. Undocumented immigrants may face language and cultural barriers to care, or they may not be aware that they have access. In places without a right to health care, seeking it can be risky. In Germany, Sweden, and France, health care providers are required to inform authorities if they know they are treating an undocumented immigrant (Sabates-Wheeler, 2009). Networks appear to play an important role in whether undocumented immigrants utilize health care services (Devillanova, 2008).

6.3 Schooling

Undocumented immigrant children's access to education differs across countries. Developed countries are more likely than developing countries to allow undocumented immigrant children access to public schools, but over 40% of developed countries do not allow such children access, including Singapore and Sweden (Klugman and Pereira, 2009). In Belgium, undocumented immigrant children have a right to attend school but, unlike for other children, schooling is not compulsory. In Poland, schooling is compulsory for all children, but undocumented immigrant children do not count for funding purposes, so schools may refuse to enroll them. Developing countries that do not allow undocumented immigrant children access to public education include Egypt, India, and the United Arab Emirates.

In the US, the Supreme Court ruled in 1982 in *Plyler v. Doe* that elementary and secondary public schools must admit unauthorized immigrant children and must receive the same funding for them as for other children. Access to tertiary education is more limited. Unauthorized immigrants are not eligible for any federally subsidized educational loans or grants, and most states require that unauthorized immigrants pay out of state tuition to attend public colleges and universities even if they graduated from high school in the state. Chin and Juhn (2011) found that Mexican-born young men who live in states that allow undocumented immigrants to pay in-state tuition appear to be slightly more likely to attend college, but Hispanics who immigrated as children are not more likely to graduate from high school in such states.

Restricting access to education for undocumented immigrant children is likely short-sighted, particularly in developed countries. Increasing the human capital of people who are likely to remain in a country increases a country's productivity and GDP in the long run. However, little economic research has systematically investigated these issues. Research on the long- and short-run effects of educational access on undocumented immigrant children is needed. Research on the effects on other children is needed as well since there may be peer effects or spillovers because of funding issues.

6.4 Citizenship and the children of undocumented immigrants

Some countries confer citizenship based on place of birth, the *jus soli* ("right of soil") principle, while others confer citizenship based on family heritage, the *jus sanguinis* ("right of blood") principle. Some 30 countries—most of the Western Hemisphere—are *jus soli*. Under *jus soli*, the children of unauthorized immigrants are citizens of the host country by virtue of being born there. No European country automatically grants citizenship to the children of unauthorized immigrants who are born there; Canada and the US are the only advanced economies that do so. Since the 1980s, several countries have stopped automatically granting citizenship based on place of birth, including Australia, the Dominican Republic, India, Ireland, New Zealand, and the UK (Feere, 2010).

Citizenship confers a host of important benefits to the children of unauthorized immigrants. It makes those children eligible for transfer programs and schooling on the same terms as other citizens. As adults, they will be eligible to vote and work. In some countries, including the US, the children may be able to sponsor their parents and siblings for legal residence after reaching a certain age.

Birthright citizenship laws may affect undocumented immigrants' behavior. Critics claim that unauthorized immigrants have children ("anchor babies") to create a toehold in the host country. Having children who are citizens of the host country may make unauthorized immigrants reluctant to return home, particularly if they are from a country that does not allow dual citizenship. Economic research has not examined these possibilities, however.

7. HUMAN TRAFFICKING

Human trafficking is akin to slavery, with men, women, and children forced to work or live in certain places against their will. Examples include Latin Americans and Asians smuggled into the US and not allowed to leave manufacturing jobs until the debt they incurred to migrate is worked off; African and Eastern European women duped by the promise of jobs and then forced into prostitution in Western Europe; and children enslaved in brothels in Southeast Asia.

About one-fifth of the global stock of 12.3 million forced laborers is internationally trafficked (International Labour Office, 2005). The flow of people trafficked across international borders is estimated at 600,000–800,000 annually (US Government Accountability Office, 2006). Globally, almost 2 out of 1000 people are victims of human trafficking; in Asia and the Pacific this ratio is as high as 3 per 1000 people (International Organization for Migration, 2011). Human trafficking is highly lucrative, producing an estimated profit of $31.7 billion a year (International Labour Office, 2005). This makes trafficking the fastest growing source of income for organized crime and its third greatest source of income, behind only drugs and arms (Obuah, 2006).

Human trafficking is linked to smuggling since some victims are smuggled across international borders. Others leave their home country voluntarily and enter destination countries legally, becoming ensnared in forced labor only after arrival. Many victims of trafficking are recruited in their countries of origin by replying to false job advertisements. Relatives also often play an important role, either by encouraging family members to migrate without understanding the attendant risks or by selling family members, particularly children, because of poverty (Frontex, 2011).

Victims of international trafficking are primarily from developing countries, while their destinations vary widely. The main destinations of trafficking victims are Western Europe and Russia, but they also include North America, Asia, and increasingly the Middle East (Omar Mahmoud and Trebesch, 2010). Trafficking typically occurs from poorer to richer countries, but not all destination countries are rich by a global standard; trafficking occurs from Nepal to India and from Burkina Faso to Cameroon, for example (Dessy et al., 2005). Some countries, like Nigeria, are hubs, or both a source and a destination for human trafficking, while others are primarily transit countries rather than sources or destinations (Akee et al., 2010). As with all illicit activities, of course, it is difficult to accurately ascertain the numbers and paths of victims of human trafficking.

7.1 Models of human trafficking

Human trafficking is an industry subject to supply and demand much like any other industry. In some models, the supply side is composed of victims, and traffickers are the intermediaries between supply and demand (e.g., Omar Mahmoud and Trebesch, 2010). In other models, the supply side is composed of traffickers, and victims are the good that is supplied and demanded (e.g., Dessy et al., 2005; Wheaton et al., 2010). In both types of models, the demand side is composed of employers or customers for the labor and services that victims provide.

Economic conditions play an important role in the supply of trafficking victims. People become victims of human trafficking largely because of economic hardship at home, which pushes them to consider migrating, makes them vulnerable to being tricked, or makes their relatives push them into migrating or being trafficked. Consistent with this, international flows of trafficking victims are negatively related to source-country GDP (Akee et al., 2010, 2011). Unemployment among female youth, the prime target for sexual exploitation, is positively related to the number of victims trafficked out of a country for sexual exploitation (Danailova-Trainor and Belser, 2006).

Economic and political turmoil also contribute to trafficking. Trafficking is relatively high from source countries that are transitioning to market-based economies from socialist economies (Akee et al., 2011). Market deregulation and capital inflows have made women vulnerable to trafficking in agriculture-based societies (Clark, 2003). Ethnic, religious, or language fragmentation and external conflict—being involved in a war or other conflict between two countries—appear to increase trafficking (Akee et al., 2010). The presence of internally displaced persons or refugees in a country also appears to increase trafficking since those groups are particularly vulnerable (Akee et al., 2010).

The extent of trafficking is related to the volume of emigration in general from a source country. Omar Mahmoud and Trebesch (2010) found that human trafficking is positively related to emigration flows—particularly illegal flows—from regions in Belarus, Bulgaria, Moldova, Romania, and Ukraine. Their results indicate that a 1 percentage point increase in migration prevalence translates into a 5% increase in the predicted probability of human trafficking at the household level. Larger emigration flows may make it easier for traffickers to ensnare victims simply because there are more people who want to leave. Omar Mahmoud and Trebesch also noted that large migrant flows create a shadow economy of middlemen offering services such as false documents, smuggling across borders, or help procuring work abroad. Traffickers may collaborate with these middlemen or free ride on their reputations.

Traffickers perceive a profitable market created by demand for cheap manual laborers and prostitutes in both developed and developing countries and by a large supply of potential victims. Like smuggling, trafficking is a market that is relatively low cost and easy to enter. Omar Mahmoud and Trebesch (2010) noted that the risks of detection, prosecution, or arrest are much lower for human trafficking than for other illicit activities that involve transporting items across borders, such as the drug and arms trades. This is partly because victims are often unwilling to testify against traffickers for fear of reprisal or deportation.

On the demand side, research indicates that the demand for human trafficking increases with income and openness. International flows of trafficking victims are positively related to destination-country GDP (Akee et al., 2010, 2011). International flows of sex trafficking victims are positively related to the share of international trade in the destination country's GDP and to the proportion of the population involved in prostitution (Danailova-Trainor and Belser, 2006).

7.2 Public policy

As awareness of human trafficking has risen, countries have created international agreements to combat it. The primary international agreement regarding human trafficking is the United Nations Protocol to Prevent, Suppress and Punish Trafficking in Persons, Especially Women and Children, created in 2000 and called the Palermo Protocol. As of 2011, 142 countries had signed the Palermo Protocol (US Department of State, 2011). In 2010, the European Parliament adopted a directive on human trafficking that increased penalties for traffickers and provided stronger protection for victims in EU-member nations.

Research indicates that such agreements and cross-country coordination are needed to reduce trafficking. Well-intended actions by individual countries can backfire. The flow of international trafficking victims can simply shift to other countries when a single country adopts policies aimed at reducing trafficking, such as increasing penalties for traffickers, increasing protection for victims, or increasing border and interior enforcement. As Cho et al. (2011) noted, adopting such policies unilaterally imposes a negative externality on other countries. They found that policies aimed at prosecuting traffickers and preventing trafficking diffuse across contiguous counties and main trading partners. However, they conclude that destination countries do not appear to have successfully pressured source or transit countries to change their policies.

Unilateral anti-trafficking policies also can, paradoxically, increase trafficking or exploitation. For example, an anti-trafficking law that prohibited young women in Burma from visiting border regions unless accompanied by a male relative caused trafficking to flourish by increasing the cost of travel for women and forcing them to rely on middlemen to cross borders (Buckland, 2008). A model by Akee et al. (2011) of the interaction between traffickers and buyers of trafficking victims predicted that, if buyer demand is price inelastic, increases in enforcement in destination countries will increase willingness to pay there and therefore increase the international flow of trafficking victims. Granting legal protections, such as amnesty, to victims also will lead to an increase in trafficking. Increases in enforcement in source countries will increase willingness to pay there and therefore reduce the international flow of victims by keeping them at home to be exploited there. Akee et al.'s test of their model with data on 187 countries indicated that amnesties and laws prohibiting prostitution increase international trafficking for both source and destination countries. In Friebel and Guriev's (2006) model, illegal immigration is financed by debt/labor contracts. Migrants who borrow in order to migrate may become forced laborers until the debt is repaid. Friebel and Guriev showed that increased border controls may increase the use of debt-labor contracts—and thereby may increase forced labor—by increasing the cost of migration. Such research points to the need for international cooperation in order to successfully reduce trafficking.

Children account for a sizeable share of trafficking victims. Dessy and Pallage (2006) argued that child labor and trafficking are linked, sometimes in a paradoxical way. Children who work are more likely to be trafficked, so awareness of this risk reduces parents' willingness to have their children work. Better enforcement against trafficking can increase child labor supply by reducing parental concerns and therefore, paradoxically, can lead to an increase in child trafficking. Dessy et al. (2005) developed a model in which increases in enforcement in one or a subset of countries will tend to raise the price of trafficked children, making it more costly for other countries to protect children and making children elsewhere more vulnerable to trafficking. Reducing child trafficking therefore may require coordinated efforts across countries, much like Akee et al. (2011) and Friebel and Guriev (2006) suggested for human trafficking in general.

Some models, however, predict that unilateral anti-trafficking policies can be successful. For example, in Tamura's (2010) model of the interaction between smuggling and trafficking, a smuggler can decide to try to transform a willing migrant into a trafficking victim if it appears profitable to do so. The model predicts that increases in penalties for trafficking or in the probability of apprehension, either at the border of the destination country or in its interior, will reduce trafficking. In Friebel and Guriev's (2006) debt/labor model, amnesties that offer undocumented immigrants legal protections make debt/labor contracts less profitable for lenders because the contracts are not legally enforceable; only coercion enforces the contracts. Amnesties therefore may reduce the volume of undocumented immigration funded by debt/labor contracts and thereby reduce forced labor. Both of these studies, however, are purely theoretical models, without the empirical tests of Akee et al. (2011) and Cho et al. (2011).

Although research is mixed on whether anti-trafficking policies can reduce human trafficking, economic development in source countries is likely to reduce trafficking. Better economic opportunities at home are likely to reduce international migration and child labor, both of which make people vulnerable to being trafficked. Economic development also can alleviate the desperate circumstances that lead some families to push relatives, especially women and children, into becoming trafficking victims. However, there may be an inverse-U shaped relationship between economic development in source countries and human trafficking. Trafficking may initially increase as countries transition from low to middle stages of development and migration increases (United Nations Development Programme, 2009).

8. CONCLUSION

Unauthorized immigration accounts for an important and rising share of international migration. Every year, millions of people migrate from and to almost every country in the world without the proper documents, while others violate the terms of a visa.

Despite the sizeable magnitude of the flow and stock of undocumented migrants, the illegal status of this population complicates efforts to study it. Economic research to date has largely focused on one particular group of undocumented migrants: Mexicans in the US. There is a smaller literature on undocumented migration in Europe and relatively little work on other areas.

Undocumented migrants differ from other immigrants in several ways. Undocumented migrants typically face higher migration costs, which changes the magnitude and composition of flows. These migration costs are largely a function of the extent of border enforcement. Many undocumented immigrants rely on smugglers, whose prices rise as border enforcement increases. The strength of border and interior enforcement also affects duration of stay and circularity among undocumented immigrants in the destination country. In general, unauthorized immigrants do not stay as long as legal migrants, but this pattern has been changing as immigration policy and economic conditions have changed in origin and destination countries in recent years.

Theory and empirical research often give ambiguous conclusions about the economic impact of unauthorized immigration on both source and destination countries. In addition, theoretical predictions are highly dependent on various models' assumptions, and empirical findings about specific areas at a given point in time are typically not generalizable. There is a need for more research that is specific to unauthorized immigration, as opposed to immigration in general. A number of interesting questions merit further examination, including the unintended consequences of border and interior enforcement, the reasons for the surprisingly small estimated labor market impacts, the effect of rising enforcement on migrant self-selection, and the changing role of developing nations from source to destination countries. Estimates of the deterrent effects of interior enforcement on potential migrants are practically nonexistent.

More models of optimal immigration policy and more empirical research into the effects of immigration policies are needed. Restrictions on legal avenues to migration give rise to unauthorized migration, but our understanding of the tradeoffs between a larger flow of legal migrants or a larger flow of illegal migrants is limited. Immigration usually involves intermediaries, such as destination-country government agencies, smugglers, or traffickers. Little research has examined interactions between these actors.

Trafficking is often linked to unauthorized immigration because of the illegal nature of both. Unlike unauthorized immigration, trafficking involves coercion, although the line can be blurry since some victims of trafficking start out as voluntary migrants. The nascent economic literature on trafficking indicates that economic conditions affect the number, sources, and destinations of trafficking victims. Because of the egregious nature of trafficking, ways in which public policy can best reduce it is an important area for future research.

Above all, more and better data are needed in order for us to better understand the determinants and consequences of unauthorized immigration. Estimates of stocks, flows, and characteristics of undocumented immigrants are highly uncertain even in countries that otherwise have comprehensive and accurate population data. Collecting more and better data risks running afoul of civil liberties, however, and unauthorized immigrants are unlikely to divulge their status to authorities, even when confidentiality is assured. Increased interior enforcement that creates a climate of fear is likely to make it even more difficult for academics and governments to learn about this important population of immigrants.

REFERENCES

Akee, R.K.Q., 2010. Who leaves and who returns? Deciphering immigrant self-selection from a developing country. Econ. Develop. Cultur. Change 58, 323–344.

Akee, R.K.Q., Basu, A.K., Chau, N.H., Khamis, M., 2010. Ethnic fragmentation, conflict, displaced persons and human trafficking: An empirical analysis. In: Epstein, G.S., Gang, I.N. (Eds.), Migration and Culture. Emerald Group, Bingley, UK.

Akee, R.K.Q., Bedi, A., Basu, A.K., Chau, N.H., 2011. Transnational Trafficking, Law Enforcement and Victim Protection: A Middleman Trafficker's Perspective, IZA Discussion Paper No. 6226, IZA, Bonn.

Altamirano, D., 1999. Illegal immigration in Europe: Balancing national and European Union issues. In: Haines, D., Rosenblum, K. (Eds.), Illegal Immigration in America: A Reference Handbook. Greenwood Press, Westport, CT.

Amuedo-Dorantes, C., 2007. Remittance patterns of Latin American immigrants in the United States. In: Pozo, S. (Ed.), Immigrants and Their International Money Flows. W.E. Upjohn Institute for Employment Research, Kalamazoo, MI.

Amuedo-Dorantes, C., Bansak, C., 2011a. The impact of amnesty on labor market outcomes: A panel study using the Legalized Population Survey. Ind. Relat. 50, 443–471.

Amuedo-Dorantes, C., Bansak, C., 2011b. The Effectiveness of Border Enforcement in Deterring Repetitive Illegal Crossing Attempts, Unpublished manuscript, San Diego State University Department of Economics.

Amuedo-Dorantes, C., Bansak, C., 2012. The labor market impact of mandated employment verification systems. American Economic Review Papers and Proceedings 102, 543–548.

Amuedo-Dorantes, C., Mazzolari, F., 2010. Remittances to Latin America from migrants in the United States: Assessing the impact of amnesty programs. J. Dev. Econ. 91, 323–335.

Amuedo-Dorantes, C., Pozo, S., 2006. Remittance as insurance: Evidence from Mexican immigrants. J. Popul. Econ. 19, 227–254.

Amuedo-Dorantes, C., Bansak, C., Pozo, S., 2005. On the remitting patterns of immigrants: Evidence from Mexican survey data. Federal Reserve Bank of Atlanta Economic Review 90, 37–58.

Amuedo-Dorantes, C., Bansak, C., Raphael, S., 2007. Gender differences in the labor market: Impact of IRCA's amnesty provisions. American Economic Review Papers and Proceedings 97, 412–416.

Andreas, P., 2001. The transformation of migrant smuggling across the U.S.–Mexican border. In: Kyle, D., Koslowski, R. (Eds.), Global Human Smuggling: Comparative Perspectives. Johns Hopkins University Press, Baltimore, MD.

Angelucci, M., 2012. U.S. border enforcement and the net inflow of Mexican illegal migration. Econ. Dev. Cult. Change 60, 311–357.

Antman, F.M., 2012. Gender, educational attainment, and the impact of parental migration on children left behind. J. Popul. Econ. 25, 1187–1214.

Arcand, J., Mbaye, L.M., 2013. Braving the Waves: The Role of Time and Risk Preferences in Illegal Migration from Senegal, IZA Discussion Paper No. 7517, IZA, Bonn.

Aydemir, A., Borjas, G.J., 2006. A Comparative Analysis of the Labor Market Impact of International Migration: Canada, Mexico, and the United States, NBER Working Paper No. 12327, NBER, Cambridge, MA.

Baldacci, E., Inglese, L., Strozza, S., 1999. Determinants of foreign workers' wages in two Italian regions with high illegal immigration. Lab. 13, 675–710.

Baldwin-Edwards, M., 1997. Third Country Nationals and Welfare Systems in the European Union, Jean Monnet Working Papers in Comparative and International Politics No. 12.97, University of Catania.

Bansak, C., 2005. The differential wage impact of the Immigration Reform and Control Act on Latino ethnic subgroups. Soc. Sci. Q. 86, 1279–1298.

Bansak, C., Raphael, S., 2001. Immigration reform and the earnings of Latino workers: Do employer sanctions cause discrimination? Ind. Labor Relat. Rev. 54, 275–295.

Barcellos, S.H., 2011. Legalization and the Economic Status of Immigrants. Mimeo, RAND, Santa Monica, CA.

Batista, C., Lacuesta, A., Vicente, P.C., 2012. Testing the 'brain gain' hypothesis: Micro evidence from Cape Verde. J. Dev. Econ. 97, 32–45.

Bean, F.D., Telles, E.E., Lowell, B.L., 1987. Undocumented migration to the United States: Perceptions and evidence. Popul. Dev. Rev. 13, 671–690.

Bean, F.D., Lowell, B.L., Taylor, L.J., 1988. Undocumented Mexican immigrants and the earnings of other workers in the United States. Demography 25, 35–52.

Bean, F.D., Espenshade, T.J., White, M.J., Dymowski, R.F., 1990. Post-IRCA changes in the volume and composition of undocumented migration to the United States: An assessment based on apprehensions data. In: Bean, F.D., Edmonston, B., Passel, J.S. (Eds.), Undocumented Migration to the United States: IRCA and the Experience of the 1980s. RAND, Santa Monica, CA.

Bean, F.D., Chanove, R., Cushing, R.G., de la Garza, R., Freeman, G.P., Haynes, C.W., Spener, D., 1994. Illegal Mexican Migration and the United States/Mexico Border: The Effects of Operation Hold the Line on El Paso/Juarez. Research paper, US Commission on Immigration Reform, Washington, DC.

Bean, F.D., Brown, S.K., Leach, M., Bachmeier, J., Chávez, L.R., DeSipio, L., Rumbaut, R.G., Lee, J., 2006. How Pathways to Legal Status and Citizenship Relate to Economic Attainment Among the Children of Mexican Immigrants. Mimeo, University of California, Irvine.

Bean, F.D., Leach, M.A., Brown, S.K., Bachmeier, J.D., Hipp, J.R., 2011. The educational legacy of unauthorized migration: comparisons across U.S.-immigrant groups in how parents' status affects their offspring. Int. Migrat. Rev. 45, 348–385.

Beine, M., Docquier, F., Rapoport, H., 2001. Brain drain and economic growth: Theory and evidence. J. Dev. Econ. 64, 275–289.

Berlinschi, R., Squicciarini, M., 2011. On the Political Economy of Illegal Immigration. Mimeo, LICOS Centre for Institutions and Economic Performance, K.U. Leuven.

Bertoli, S., Fernández-Huertas Moraga, J., Ortega, F., 2009. The determinants of international migration accounting for self-selection, Paper presented at the Second Conference on Migration and Development, September, Washington, DC.

Bijwaard, G.E., 2010. Immigrant migration dynamics model for The Netherlands. J. Popul. Econ. 23, 1213–1247.

Blejer, M.I., Johnson, H.G., Porzecanski, A.C., 1978. An analysis of the economic determinants of legal and illegal Mexican migration to the United States. Res. Popul. Econ. 1, 217–231.

Bodvarsson, O.B., Van den Berg, H., 2009. The Economics of Immigration: Theory and Policy. Springer, Dordrecht.

Boeri, T., Brücker, H., 2005. Why are Europeans so tough on migrants? Econ. Pol. 20 (629), 631–703.

Bohn, S., Löfström, M., 2013. Employment effects of state legislation. In: Card, D., Raphael, S. (Eds.), Immigration, Poverty, and Socioeconomic Inequality. Russell Sage Foundation, New York.

Bohn, S., Löfström, M., Raphael, S., 2014. Did the 2007 Legal Arizona Workers Act reduce the state's unauthorized immigrant population? Rev. Econ. Stat. 96, 258–269.

Bollard, A., McKenzie, D., Morten, M., 2010. The remitting patterns of African migrants in the OECD. J. Afr. Econ. 19, 605–634.

Bond, E.W., Chen, T.J., 1987. The welfare effects of illegal immigration. J. Int. Econ. 23, 315–328.

Borger, S.C., 2010. Self-Selection and Liquidity Constraints in Different Migration Cost Regimes. Working Paper, Office of Immigration Statistics, Washington, DC.

Borger, S., Muse-Orlinoff, L., 2010. Economic crisis versus border enforcement: What matters most to prospective migrants? In: Cornelius, W., Fitzgerald, D., Lewin-Fischer, P., Muse-Orlinoff, L. (Eds.), Mexican Migration and the U.S. Economic Crisis: A Transnational Perspective. Center for Comparative Immigration Studies, University of California, San Diego.

Borjas, G.J., 1987. Self-selection and the earnings of immigrants. Am. Econ. Rev. 77, 531–553.

Borjas, G.J., 1995. The economic benefits from immigration. J. Econ. Perspect. 9, 3–22.

Borjas, G.J., 1999. The economic analysis of immigration. In: Ashenfelter, O., Card, D. (Eds.), Handbook of Labor Economics, vol 3. Elsevier Science, Amsterdam.

Borjas, G.J., 2001. Does immigration grease the wheels of the labor market? Brookings Paper. Econ. Activ. 2001, 69–119.

Borjas, E.W., Bratsberg, B., 1996. Who leaves? The outmigration of the foreign-born. Rev. Econ. Stat. 78, 165–176.

Borjas, G.J., Tienda, M., 1993. The employment and wages of legalized immigrants. Int. Migrat. Rev. 27, 712–747.

Borjas, G.J., Grogger, J., Hanson, G.H., 2006. Immigration and African-American Employment Opportunities: The Response of Wages, Employment, and Incarceration to Labor Supply Shocks, NBER Working Paper No. 12518, NBER, Cambridge, MA.

Borjas, G.J., Grogger, J., Hanson, G.H., 2011. Substitution Between Immigrants, Natives, and Skill Groups, NBER Working Paper No. 17461, NBER, Cambridge, MA.

Boucher, S., Stark, O., Taylor, J.E., 2009. A gain with a drain? Evidence from rural Mexico on the new economics of the brain drain. In: Kornai, J., Mátyás, L., Roland, G. (Eds.), Corruption, Development and Institutional Design. Palgrave, Basingstoke, Hampshire, UK.

Brownell, P., 2005. Sanctions for Whom? The Immigration Reform and Control Act's Employer Sanctions Provision and the Wages of Mexican Immigrants. SSRC/UCI Summer Migration Institute. (unpublished manuscript).

Buchignani, N., Indra, D., 1999. Vanishing acts: Illegal immigration in Canada as a sometime social issue. In: Haines, D.W., Rosenblum, K.E. (Eds.), Illegal Immigration in America: A Reference Handbook. Greenwood Press, Westport, CT.

Buckland, B.S., 2008. More than just victims: The truth about human trafficking. Publ. Pol. Res. 15, 42–47.

Cadena, B.C., Kovac, B.K., 2013. Immigrants Equilibrate Local Labor Markets: Evidence from the Great Recession, NBER Working Paper No. 19272, NBER, Cambridge, MA.

Calavita, K., 1992. Inside the State: The Bracero Program. Immigration and the INS, Routledge, New York.

Calavita, K., 1994. U.S. immigration policy: Contradictions and projections for the future. Indiana J. Global Leg. Stud. 2, 143–152.

Caponi, V., 2011. Intergenerational transmission of abilities and self-selection of Mexican immigrants. Int. Econ. Rev. 52, 523–547.

Carliner, G., 1980. Wages, earnings and hours of first, second, and third generation American males. Econ. Inq. 18, 87–102.

Carling, J., 2007. Migration control and migrant fatalities at the Spanish-African borders. Int. Migrat. Rev. 41, 316–343.

Carrington, W.J., Detragiache, E., Vishwanath, T., 1996. Migration with endogenous moving costs. Am. Econ. Rev. 86, 909–930.

Carrión-Flores, C., Sørensen, T., 2007. The Effects of Border Enforcement on Migrants' Border Crossing Choices: Diversion, or Deterrence? Unpublished manuscript, University of Arizona Department of Economics.

Casarico, A., Facchini, G., Frattini, T., 2012. Spending More is Spending Less: Policy Dilemmas on Irregular Migration. Centro Studi Luca d'Agliano Development Studies Working Paper No. 330, Centro Studi Luca d'Agliano Development Studies, Milan, Italy.

Castles, S., Cubas, M.A., Kim, C., Ozkul, D., 2012. Irregular migration: Causes, patterns, and strategies. In: Omelaniuk, I. (Ed.), Global Perspectives on Migration and Development: GFMD Puerto Vallarta and Beyond. Springer, New York.

Chau, N.H., 2001. Strategic amnesty and credible immigration reform. J. Labor Econ. 19, 604–634.

Chau, N.H., 2003. Concessional amnesty and the politics of immigration reforms. Economics and Politics 15, 193–224.

Chin, A., Juhn, C., 2011. Does reducing college costs improve educational outcomes for undocumented immigrants? Evidence from state laws permitting undocumented immigrants to pay in-state tuition at state colleges and universities. In: Leal, D.L., Trejo, S.J. (Eds.), Latinos and the Economy: Integration and Impact in Schools, Labor Markets, and Beyond. Springer, New York.

Chiquiar, D., Hanson, G.H., 2005. International migration, self-selection, and the distribution of wages: Evidence from Mexico and the United States. J. Polit. Econ. 113, 239–281.

Chiswick, B.R., 1982. The impact of immigration on the level and distribution of economic well-being. In: Chiswick, B.R. (Ed.), The Gateway: U.S. Immigration Issues and Policies. American Enterprise Institute for Public Policy Research, Washington, DC.

Chiswick, B.R., 1986. The impact of illegal aliens and the enforcement of immigration law. In: Thorton, R.J., Aronson, J.R. (Eds.), Forging New Relationships among Business, Labor and Government. JAI Press, Greenwich, CT.

Chiswick, B.R., 1988a. Illegal Aliens: Their Employment and Employers. W.E. Upjohn Institute for Employment Research, Kalamazoo, MI.

Chiswick, B.R., 1988b. Illegal immigration and immigration control. J. Econ. Perspect. 2, 101–115.

Chiswick, B.R., 1999. Are immigrants favorably self-selected? American Economic Review Papers and Proceedings 89, 181–185.

Chiswick, B.R., 2001. The economics of illegal immigration for the host economy. In: Siddique, M.A.B. (Ed.), International Migration into the 21st Century. Edward Elgar, Cheltenham, UK.

Cho, S., Dreher, A., Neumayer, E., 2011. The Spread of Anti-Trafficking Policies: Evidence from a New Index, IZA Discussion Paper No. 5559, IZA, Bonn.

Clark, M.A., 2003. Trafficking in persons: An issue of human security. J. Hum. Dev. 4, 247–263.

Clemens, M., Montenegro, C., Pritchett, L., 2008. The Place Premium: Wage Differences for Identical Workers Across the U.S. Border. Mimeo, Center for Global Development.

Cobb-Clark, D.A., Kossoudji, S.A., 2000. Mobility in El Norte: The employment and occupational changes of unauthorized Latin American women. Soc. Sci. Q. 81, 311–324.

Cobb-Clark, D.A., Shiells, C.R., Lowell, B.L., 1995. Immigration reform: The effects of employer sanctions and legalization on wages. J. Labor Econ. 13, 472–498.

Cohen, A., Razin, A., Sadka, E., 2009. The Skill Composition of Migration and the Generosity of the Welfare State, NBER Working Paper No. 147384, NBER, Cambridge, MA.

Commission of the European Communities, 2003. Communication from the Commission to the Council, the European Parliament, the European Economic and Social Committee and the Committee of the Regions on immigration, integration and employment.

Congressional Budget Office, 2007. The Impact of Unauthorized Immigrants on the Budgets of State and Local Governments. Congressional Budget Office, Washington, DC.

Coniglio, N.D., De Arcangelis, G., Serlenga, L., 2009. Clandestine Migrants: Do the High-Skilled Return Home First?" Working Papers 1/6. Sapienza University of Rome.

Connor, P., Massey, D.S., 2010. Economic outcomes among Latino migrants to Spain and the United States: differences by source region and legal status. Int. Migrat. Rev. 44, 802–829.

Constant, A.F., Massey, D.S., 2003. Self-selection, earnings and outmigration: A longitudinal study of immigrants to Germany. J. Pop. Econ. 16, 631–653.

Cornelius, W.A., 1978. Mexican Migration to the United States: Causes, Consequences and U.S. Responses. Migration and Development Study Group, Center for International Studies, Massachusetts Institute of Technology, Cambridge, MA.

Cornelius, W.A., 1989. Impacts of the 1986 US immigration law on emigration from rural Mexican sending communities. Popul. Dev. Rev. 15, 689–705.

Cornelius, W.A., 2001. Death at the border: Efficacy and unintended consequences of US immigration control policy. Popul. Dev. Rev. 27, 661–685.

Cornelius, W.A., Salehyan, I., 2007. Does border enforcement deter unauthorized immigration? The case of Mexican migration to the United States of America. Regul. Govern. 1, 139–153.

Cortés, P., 2008. The effect of low-skilled immigration on U.S. prices: Evidence from CPI data. J. Polit. Econ. 116, 381–422.

Cortés, P., Tessada, J., 2011. Low-skilled immigration and the labor supply of highly skilled women. Am. Econ. J. Appl. Econ. 3, 88–123.

Coulon, A., Piracha, M., 2005. Self-selection and the performance of return migrants: The source country perspective. J. Popul. Econ. 18, 779–807.

Cox, D., Glenn, P., 1994. Illegal immigration and refugee claims. In: Adelman, H., Borowski, A., Burnstein, M., Foster, L. (Eds.), Immigration and Refugee Policy: Australia and Canada Compared, vol. 1. University of Toronto Press, Toronto, pp. 283–309.

Cuecuecha, A., 2010. Las características educativas de los emigrantes mexicanos a Estados Unidos. EconoQuantum 7, 9–42.

Danailova-Trainor, G., Belser, P., 2006. Globalization and the Illicit Market for Human Trafficking: An Empirical Analysis of Supply and Demand. ILO Working Paper, International Labour Organization, Geneva.

Dávila, A., Pagán, J.A., Soydemir, G., 2002. The short-term and long-term deterrence effects of INS border and interior enforcement on undocumented immigration. J. Econ. Behav. Organ. 49, 459–472.

DeFreitas, G., 1979. The Earnings of Immigrants in the American Labor Market. Ph.D. dissertation, Columbia University.

DeFreitas, G., 1988. Hispanic immigration and labor market segmentation. Ind. Relat. 27, 195–214.

Dell'Aringa, C., Neri, F., 1987. Illegal immigrants and the informal economy in Italy. Lab. 1, 107–126.

Dessy, S.E., Pallage, S., 2006. Some surprising effects of better law enforcement against child trafficking. J. Afr. Stud. Dev. 1, 115–131.

Dessy, S.E., Mbiekop, F., Pallage, S., 2005. The Economics of Child Trafficking (Part II), CIRPÉE Working Paper 05–09, Centre interuniversitaire sur le risque, les politiques économiques et l'emploi, Montreal.

Devillanova, C., 2008. Social networks, information and health care utilization: Evidence from undocumented immigrants in Milan. J. Health Econ. 27, 265–286.

Djajić, S., 1987. Illegal aliens, unemployment and immigration policy. J. Dev. Econ. 25, 235–249.

Djajić, S., 1997. Illegal immigration and resource allocation. Int. Econ. Rev. 38, 97–117.

Djajić, S., 2001. Illegal immigration trends, policies and economic effects. In: Djajić, S. (Ed.), International Migration: Trends, Policies and Economic Impact. Routledge, London.

Doeringer, P., Piore, M.J., 1971. Internal Labor Markets and Manpower Analysis. D.C. Heath, Lexington, MA.

Donato, K.M., 1993. Current trends and patterns of female migration: Evidence from Mexico. Int. Migrat. Rev. 27, 748–771.

Donato, K.M., Massey, D.S., 1993. Effect of the Immigration Reform and Control Act on the wages of Mexican migrants. Soc. Sci. Q. 74, 523–541.

Donato, K.M., Durand, J., Massey, D.S., 1992. Stemming the tide? Assessing the deterrent effects of the Immigration Reform and Control Act. Demography 29, 139–157.

Durand, J., Parrado, E., Massey, D.S., 1996. Migradollars and development: A reconsideration of the Mexican case. Int. Migrat. Rev. 30, 423–445.

Dustmann, C., 1997. Return migration, uncertainty and precautionary savings. J. Dev. Econ. 52, 295–316.

Dustmann, C., Weiss, Y., 2007. CReAM Discussion Paper Series 0702, Centre for Research and Analysis of Migration. Return Migration: Theory and Empirical Evidence. Department of Economics, University College London.

Enchautegui, M.E., 2008. The job quality of U.S. immigrants. Ind. Relat. 47, 108–113.

Epstein, G.S., Weiss, A., 2011. The why, when, and how of immigration amnesties. J. Popul. Econ. 24, 285–316.

Eren, S., Benítez-Silva, H., Cárceles-Poveda, E., 2011. Effects of Legal and Unauthorized Immigration on the US Social Security System. Levy Economics Institute of Bard College Working Paper No. 689, Levy Economics Institute, Annandale-on-Hudson, NY.

Eschbach, K., Hagan, J., Rodriguez, N., Hernández-León, R., Bailey, S., 1999. Death at the border. Int. Migrat. Rev. 33, 430–454.

Espenshade, T.J., 1990. Undocumented migration to the United States: Evidence from a repeated trials model. In: Bean, F.D., Edmonston, B., Passel, J.S. (Eds.), Undocumented Migration to the United States: IRCA and the Experience of the 1980s. RAND, Santa Monica, CA.

Espenshade, T.J., 1995. Unauthorized immigration to the United States. Annu. Rev. Sociol. 21, 195–216.

Ethier, W.J., 1986a. Illegal immigration: The host-country problem. Am. Econ. Rev. 76, 56–71.

Ethier, W.J., 1986b. Illegal immigration. American Economic Review Papers and Proceedings 76, 258–262.

Euronews, 2012. EU ministers agree Schengen treaty changes. www.euronews.com/2012/06/07/eu-ministers-agree-schengen-treaty-changes (accessed 12 September 2012).

European Commission, 2007. Communication from the Commission to the Council, the European Parliament, the European Parliament, the European Economic and Social Committee and the Committee of the Regions – Third Annual Report on Migration and Integration, Commission of the European Communities.

Facchini, G., Mayda, A.M., 2009. United Nations Development Programme Human Development Reports Research Paper 2009/3. The political economy of immigration policy. United Nations Development Programme, New York.

Fargues, P., 2009. Work, refuge, transit: An emerging pattern of irregular immigration south and east of the Mediterranean. Int. Migrat. Rev. 43, 544–577.

Feere, J., 2010. Birthright Citizenship in the United States: A Global Comparison. Center for Immigration Studies, Washington, DC.

Fernández-Huertas Moraga, J., 2011. New Evidence on Emigrant Selection. Rev. Econ. Stat. 93, 72–96.

Friebel, G., Guriev, S., 2006. Smuggling humans: a theory of debt-financed migration. J. Eur. Econ. Assoc. 4, 1085–1111.

Frontex, 2011. Situational Overview on Trafficking in Human Beings. Frontex, Warsaw.

Frontex, 2012. Annual Risk Analysis. Frontex, Warsaw.

Fry, R., Lowell, B.L., Haghighat, E., 1995. The impact of employer sanctions on metropolitan wage rates. Ind. Relat. 34, 464–484.

Fuentes, J., García, O., 2009. Coyotaje: The structure and functioning of the people-smuggling industry. In: Cornelius, W.A., Fitzgerald, D., Borger, S. (Eds.), Four Generations of Norteños: New Research from the Cradle of Mexican Migration. Center for Comparative Immigration Studies, University of California, San Diego.

Futo, P., Jandl, M., 2004. A Survey and Analysis of Border Apprehension Data from 22 States. 2003 Yearbook on Illegal Migration, Human Smuggling and Trafficking in Central and Eastern Europe. International Centre for Migration Policy Development, Vienna.

Gang, I.N., Yun, M.-S., 2008. Immigration amnesty and immigrant's earnings. In: Chiswick, B.R. (Ed.), Research in Labor Economics. vol. 27. Elsevier, Oxford, UK.

García y Griego, M., 1994. Canada: Flexibility and control in immigration and refugee policy. In: Cornelius, W., Martin, P., Hollifield, J. (Eds.), Controlling Immigration: A Global Perspective. Stanford University Press, Stanford, CA.

Gathmann, C., 2008. Effects of enforcement on illegal markets: evidence from migrant smuggling along the southwestern border. J. Publ. Econ. 92, 1926–1941.

Gentsch, K., Massey, D.S., 2011. Labor market outcomes for legal Mexican immigrants under the new regime of immigration enforcement. Soc. Sci. Q. 92, 875–893.

Gibson, J., McKenzie, D., 2011. The microeconomic determinants of emigration and return migration of the best and brightest: Evidence from the Pacific. J. Dev. Econ. 95, 18–29.

Gill, A., Long, S., 1989. Is there an immigration status wage differential between legal and undocumented workers?: Evidence from the Los Angeles garment industry. Soc. Sci. Q. 70, 164–173.

Goddard, T., 2012. How to Fix a Broken Border: Disrupting Smuggling at its Source. Immigration Policy Center Perspectives on Immigration.

Granberry, P.J., Marcelli, E.A., 2007. 'In the hood and on the job': Social capital accumulation among legal and unauthorized Mexican immigrants. Socio. Perspect. 50, 579–595.

Gross, D.M., Schmitt, N., 2006. Why Do Low- and High-Skill Workers Migrate? Flow Evidence from France, CESifo Working Paper No. 1797, CESifo Group, Munich.

Grossman, J.B., 1984. Illegal immigrants and domestic employment. Ind. Labor Relat. Rev. 37, 240–251.

Guzman, M.G., Haslag, J.H., Orrenius, P.M., 2008. On the determinants of optimal border enforcement. Econ. Theor. 34, 261–296.

Hanson, G.H., 2006. Illegal migration from Mexico to the United States. J. Econ. Lit. 44, 869–924.

Hanson, G.H., 2007. Emigration, labor supply, and earnings in Mexico. In: Borjas, G. (Ed.), Mexican Immigration to the United States. University of Chicago Press, Chicago.

Hanson, G.H., 2009. United Nations Development Programme Human Development Reports Research Paper 2009/2. The Governance of Migration Policy. United Nations Development Programme, New York.

Hanson, G.H., McIntosh, C., 2010. The Great Mexican emigration. Rev. Econ. Stat. 92, 798–810.

Hanson, G.H., Spilimbergo, A., 1999. Illegal immigration, border enforcement, and relative wages: Evidence from apprehensions at the U.S.–Mexico border. Am. Econ. Rev. 89, 1337–1357.

Hanson, G.H., Spilimbergo, A., 2001. Political economy, sectoral shocks, and border enforcement. Can. J. Econ. 34, 612–638.

Hanson, G.H., Robertson, R., Spilimbergo, A., 2002. Does border enforcement protect U.S. workers from illegal immigration? Rev. Econ. Stat. 84, 73–92.

Hanson, G.H., Scheve, K., Slaughter, M.J., 2007. Public finance and individual preferences over globalization strategies. Economics and Politics 19, 1–33.

Harris, J.R., Todaro, M.P., 1970. Migration, unemployment and development: A two-sector analysis. Am. Econ. Rev. 60, 126–142.

Hartwich, O.M., 2011. Selection, Migration and Integration: Why Multiculturalism Works in Australia (and Fails in Europe). Centre for Independent Studies Policy Monographs, Population and Growth Series 4, Sydney, Australia.

Hatton, T.J., Williamson, J.G., 1994. Migration and the International Labor Market 1850–1939. Routledge, London.

Hazari, B.R., Sgro, P.M., 2003. The simple analytics of optimal growth with illegal migrants. J. Econ. Dynam. Contr. 28, 141–151.

Heckmann, F., 2004. Illegal migration: What can we know and what can we explain? The case of Germany. Int. Migrat. Rev. 38, 1103–1125.

Hill, J.K., 1987. Immigrant decisions concerning duration of stay and migratory frequency. J. Dev. Econ. 25, 221–234.

Hotchkiss, J.L., Quispe-Agnoli, M., 2013. The expected impact of state immigration legislation on labor market outcomes. J. Policy Anal. Manage. 32 (1), 34–59.

Hotchkiss, J.L., Quispe-Agnoli, M., Rios-Avila, F., 2012. The Wage Impact of Undocumented Workers. Federal Reserve Bank of Atlanta Working Paper No. 2012–4, Federal Reserve Bank of Atlanta, Atlanta, GA.

House Committee on Homeland Security, 2006. A Line in the Sand: Confronting the Threat at the Southwest Border. US House of Representatives, Washington, DC.

Huguet, J., Chamratrithirong, A., Natali, C., 2012. Thailand at a Crossroads: Challenges and Opportunities in Leveraging Migration for Development. Migration Policy Institute, Washington, DC.

Ibarraran, P., Lubotsky, D., 2007. Mexican immigration and self-selection: New evidence from the 2000 Mexican census. In: Borjas, G.J. (Ed.), Mexican Immigration to the United States. University of Chicago Press (for NBER), Chicago.

International Labour Office, 2005. A Global Alliance Against Forced Labour. International Labour Office, Geneva.

International Organization for Migration, 2011. World Migration Report 2011. International Organization for Migration, Geneva.

Isé, S., Perloff, J.M., 1995. Legal status and earnings of agricultural workers. Am. J. Agr. Econ. 77, 375–386.

Jandl, M., 2007. Irregular migration, human smuggling, and the eastern enlargement of the European Union. Int. Migrat. Rev. 41, 291–315.

Jasso, G., 2011. Migration and stratification. Soc. Sci. Res. 40, 1292–1336.

Jenkins, J.C., 1977. Push/pull in recent Mexican migration to the U.S. Int. Migrat. Rev. 11, 178–189.

Juffras, J., 1991. Impact of the Immigration Reform and Control Act on the Immigration and Naturalization Service. RAND, Santa Monica, CA.

Kaestner, R., Malamud, O., 2014. Self-selection and international migration: New evidence from Mexico. Rev. Econ. Stat. 96, 78–91.

Kandilov, A.M.G., Kandilov, I.T., 2010. The effect of legalization on wages and health insurance: Evidence from the National Agricultural Workers Survey. Appl. Econ. Perspect. Pol. 32, 604–623.

Karlson, S.H., Katz, E., 2003. A positive theory of immigration amnesties. Econ. Lett. 78, 231–239.

Kasimis, C., 2012. Greece: Illegal Immigration in the Midst of Crisis. Migration Information Source, Washington, DC.

Kaushal, N., 2006. Amnesty programs and the labor market outcomes of undocumented workers. J. Hum. Resour. 41, 631–647.

King, R.L., Rybaczuk, K., 1993. Southern Europe and the international division of labour: From emigration to immigration. In: King, R.L. (Ed.), The New Geography of European Migrations. Belhaven, London.

Klugman, J., Pereira, I.M., 2009. Assessment of National Migration Policies: An Emerging Picture on Admissions, Treatment and Enforcement in Developing and Developed Countries. United Nations Development Programme Human Development Reports Research Paper 2009/48. United Nations Development Programme, New York.

Koslowski, R., 2011. The Evolution of Border Controls as a Mechanism to Prevent Illegal Immigration. Migration Policy Institute, Washington, DC.

Kossoudji, S.A., 1992. Playing cat and mouse at the U.S.–Mexican border. Demography 29, 159–180.

Kossoudji, S.A., Cobb-Clark, D.A., 1996. Finding good opportunities within unauthorized markets: U.S. occupational mobility for male Latino workers. Int. Migrat. Rev. 30, 901–924.

Kossoudji, S.A., Cobb-Clark, D.A., 2000. IRCA's impact on the occupational concentration and mobility of newly-legalized Mexican men. J. Popul. Econ. 13, 81–98.

Kossoudji, S.A., Cobb-Clark, D.A., 2002. Coming out of the shadows: Learning about legal status and wages from the legalized population. J. Labor Econ. 20, 598–628.

Kremer, M., Watt, S., 2006. The Globalization of Household Production. Harvard University Department of Economics, Mimeo.

Kugler, A., Yuksel, M., 2011. Do recent Latino immigrants compete for jobs with native Hispanics and earlier Latino immigrants? In: Leal, D.L., Trejo, S.J. (Eds.), Latinos and the Economy: Integration and Impact in Schools, Labor Markets, and Beyond. Springer, New York.

Lacuesta, A., 2006. Emigration and Human Capital: Who Leaves, Who Comes Back and What Difference Does It Make? Documentos de Trabajo No. 0620, Banco de España.

Leonard, S., 2009. The creation of FRONTEX and the politics of institutionalization in the EU external borders policy. J. Contemp. Eur. Res. 5, 371–388.

Lewis, W.A., 1954. Economic development with unlimited supplies of labor. Manchester School of Economics and Social Studies 22, 139–192.

Lindstrom, D.P., 1996. Economic opportunity in Mexico and return migration from the United States. Demography 33 (3), 357–374.

Liu, X., 2010. On the macroeconomic and welfare effects of illegal immigration. J. Econ. Dynam. Contr. 34, 2547–2567.

Löfström, M., Hill, L., Hayes, J., 2013. Wage and mobility effects of legalization: evidence from the New Immigrant Survey. J. Reg. Sci. 53, 171–197.

López-Castro, G., Latapí, E., Augustín, Martin, P., Donato, K., 1997. Factors that Influence Migration, Team Report to Mexico/United States Binational Study on Migration.

Lowell, B.L., Teachman, J., Jing, Z., 1995. Unintended consequences of immigration reform: discrimination and Hispanic employment. Demography 32, 617–628.

Lozano, F., Sørensen, T.A., 2011. The Labor Market Value to Legal Status, IZA Discussion Paper No. 5492, IZA, Bonn.

Marcelli, E.A., 2004. The unauthorized residency status myth: Health insurance coverage and medical case use among Mexican immigrants in California. Migraciones Internacionales 2, 5–35.

Marcelli, E.A., 2008. Unauthorized Mexican immigration and youth labor market outcomes in California in the 1990s. In: DeFreitas, G. (Ed.), Young Workers in the Global Economy: Job Challenges in North America, Europe and Japan. Edward Elgar, Cheltenham, UK.

Marcelli, E.A., Heer, D.M., 1998. The unauthorized Mexican immigrant population and welfare in Los Angeles county: A comparative statistical analysis. Socio. Perspect. 41, 279–302.

Markova, E., Reilly, B., 2007. Bulgarian migrant remittances and legal status: Some micro-level evidence from Madrid. S. E. Eur. J. Econ. 5, 55–69.

Martin, P., 1986. Illegal Immigration and the Colonization of the American Labor Market. Center for Immigration Studies, Washington, DC.

Martin, P., 1990. Harvest of confusion: Immigration reform and California agriculture. Int. Migrat. Rev. 24, 69–95.

Martin, P., Miller, M., 2000a. Smuggling and trafficking: A conference report. Int. Migrat. Rev. 34, 969–975.

Martin, P., Miller, M., 2000b. Employer Sanctions: French, German and U.S. Experiences. International Migration Paper No. 36, International Labour Organization, Geneva.

Martin, S., 2007. Unauthorized Migration: U.S. Policy Responses in Comparative Perspective. Mimeo, Institute for the Study of International Migration, Georgetown University, Washington, DC.

Massey, D.S., 1987. Do undocumented migrants earn lower wages than legal immigrants? New evidence from Mexico. Int. Migrat. Rev. 21, 236–274.

Massey, D.S., Espinosa, K.E., 1997. What's driving Mexico–U.S. migration? A theoretical, empirical, and policy analysis. Am. J. Sociol. 102, 939–999.

Massey, D.S., Riosmena, F., 2010. Undocumented migration from Latin America in an era of rising U.S. enforcement. Ann. Am. Acad. Polit. Soc. Sci. 630, 294–321.

Massey, D.S., Sana, M., 2003. Patterns of U.S. migration from Mexico, the Caribbean, and Central America. Migraciones Internacionales 2, 5–39.

Massey, D., Alcarón, R., Durand, J., Gonzáles, H., 1987. Return to Aztlán: The Social Process of Migration from Western Mexico. University of California Press, Berkeley, CA.

Massey, D.S., Durand, J., Malone, N.J., 2002. Beyond Smoke and Mirrors: Mexican Immigration in an Era of Economic Integration. Russell Sage Foundation, New York.

Massey, D.S., Pren, K.A., Durand, J., 2009. Nuevos escenarios de la migración México–Estados Unidos. Las consecuencias de la Guerra antiinmigrante. Papeles de Población 15, 101–128.

Mayda, A.M., 2006. Who is against immigration? A cross-country investigation of individual attitudes towards immigrants. Rev. Econ. Stat. 88, 510–530.

McKenzie, D., Rapoport, H., 2007. Network effects and the dynamics of migration and inequality: Theory and evidence from Mexico. J. Dev. Econ. 84, 1–24.

McKenzie, D., Rapoport, H., 2011. Can migration reduce educational attainment? Evidence from Mexico. J. Popul. Econ. 24, 1331–1358.

Meissner, D., North, D., Papademetriou, D.G., 1987. Legalization of undocumented aliens: Lessons from other countries. Int. Migrat. Rev. 21, 424–432.

Mishra, P., 2007. Emigration and wages in source countries: Evidence from Mexico. J. Dev. Econ. 82, 180–199.

Moretti, E., Perloff, J.M., 2000. Use of public transfer programs and private aid by farm workers. Ind. Relat. 39, 26–47.

Moy, H.M., Yip, C.K., 2006. The simple analytics of optimal growth with illegal migrants: A clarification. J. Econ. Dynam. Contr. 30, 2469–2475.

Müller, T., Espenshade, T.J., 1985. The Fourth Wave: California's Newest Immigrants. Urban Institute Press, Washington, DC.

Munshi, K., 2003. Networks in the modern economy: Mexican migrants in the U.S. labor market. Q. J. Econ. 118, 549–599.

Myrdal, G., 1944. An American Dilemma: The Negro Problem and Modern Democracy. Harper, New York.

Naegelen, J., 2011. Sorry, we're closed: amid migrant fears, Europe could bring back border controls. Time, May 4. www.time.com/time/world/article/0,8599,2069634,00.html.

National Research Council, 2011. Budgeting for Immigration Enforcement: A Path to Better Performance. National Academies Press, Washington, DC.

North, D.S., Houstoun, M.F., 1976. The Characteristics and Role of Illegal Aliens in the U.S. Labor Market: An Exploratory Study. Linton, Washington, DC.

Obuah, E., 2006. Combating global trafficking in persons: the role of the United States post-September 2001. Int. Polit. 43, 241–265.

Omar Mahmoud, T., Trebesch, C., 2010. The economics of human trafficking and labour migration: Micro-evidence from Eastern Europe. J. Comp. Econ. 38, 173–188.

Organization for Economic Cooperation and Development, 2000. Combating the Illegal Employment of Foreign Workers. Organization for Economic Cooperation and Development, Paris.

Orozco-Alemán, S., 2010. Effect of Legal Status on the Wages of Mexican Immigrants in the United States. Unpublished manuscript, University of Pittsburgh Department of Economics.

Orrenius, P.M., 1999. The Role of Family Networks, Coyote Prices and the Rural Economy in Migration from Western Mexico: 1965–1994, Federal Reserve Bank of Dallas Working Paper 99–10, Dallas, TX.

Orrenius, P.M., 2004. The effect of U.S. border enforcement on the crossing behavior of Mexican migrants. In: Durand, J., Massey, D.S. (Eds.), Crossing the Border: Research from the Mexican Migration Project. Russell Sage Foundation, New York.

Orrenius, P.M., Zavodny, M., 2003. Do amnesty programs reduce undocumented immigration? Evidence from IRCA. Demography 40, 437–450.

Orrenius, P.M., Zavodny, M., 2005. Self-selection among undocumented immigrants from Mexico. J. Dev. Econ. 78, 215–240.

Orrenius, P.M., Zavodny, M., 2009. The effects of tougher enforcement on the job prospects of recent Latin American immigrants. J. Policy Anal. Manage. 28, 239–257.

Orrenius, P.M., Zavodny, M., 2012. The economic consequences of amnesty for unauthorized immigrants. Cato J. 32, 85–106.

Ortega, A.N., Fang, H., Perez, V.H., Rizzo, J.A., Carter-Pokras, O., Wallace, S.P., Gleberg, L., 2007. Health care access, use of services, and experiences among undocumented Mexicans and other Latinos. Arch. Intern. Med. 167, 2354–2360.

Ortega, A.N., Horwitz, S.M., Fang, H., Kuo, A.A., Wallace, S.P., Inkelas, M., 2009. Documentation status and parental concerns about development in young US children of Mexican origin. Acad. Pediatr. 9, 278–282.

Ottaviano, G.I.P., Peri, G., 2012. Rethinking the effects of immigration on wages. J. Eur. Econ. Assoc. 10, 152–195.

Pagán, J.A., Dávila, A., 1996. On-the-job training, immigration reform, and the true wages of native male workers. Ind. Relat. 35, 45–58.

Pan, Y., 2011. Gains from legality: Parents immigration status and children's scholastic achievement. Louisiana State University Department of Economics Working Paper 2011–05, Louisiana State University, Baton Rouge, LA.

Pan, Y., 2012. The impact of legal status on immigrants' earnings and human capital: Evidence from the IRCA 1986. J. Labor Res. 33, 119–142.

Passel, J., Cohn, D., 2008. U.S. Population Projections: 2005–2050. Pew Research Center.

Passel, J., Cohn, D., Gonzalez-Barrera, A., 2012. Net Migration from Mexico Falls to Zero—And Perhaps Less. Pew Research Center, Washingon, DC.

Pavilos, T., 2009. Welfare effects of illegal immigration. J. Popul. Econ. 22, 131–144.

Pavilos, T., Yip, C.K., 2010. Illegal immigration in a heterogeneous labor market. J. Econ. 101, 21–47.

Pena, A.A., 2010. Legalization and immigrants in U.S. agriculture. B.E. Journal of Economic Analysis and Policy 10, 1–24.

Pena, A.A., 2013. Remittances and undocumented migration. In: Ness, I. (Ed.), The Encyclopedia of Global Human Migration. Wiley Blackwell, Oxford.

Pew Hispanic Center, 2006. Modes of entry for the unauthorized migrant population, Fact Sheet.

Piore, M.J., 1979. Birds of Passage: Migrant Labor and Industrial Societies. Cambridge University Press, Cambridge, UK.

Portes, A., Rumbaut, R.G., 2006. Immigrant America: A Portrait, third ed. University of California Press, Berkeley.

Ranis, G., Fei, J.C.H., 1961. A theory of economic development. Am. Econ. Rev. 51, 533–565.

Reyes, B.I., 2001. Immigrant trip duration: The case of immigrants from Western Mexico. Int. Migrat. Rev. 35 (4), 1185–1204.

Reyes, B.I., 2004. Changes in trip duration for Mexican immigrants to the United States. Popul. Res. Pol. Rev. 23, 235–257.

Riosmena, F., 2004. Return versus settlement among undocumented Mexican migrants, 1980 to 1996. In: Durand, J., Massey, D.S. (Eds.), Crossing the Border: Research from the Mexican Migration Project. Russell Sage Foundation, New York.

Rivera-Batiz, F.L., 1999. Undocumented workers in the labor market: An analysis of the earnings of legal and illegal Mexican immigrants in the United States. J. Popul. Econ. 12, 91–116.

Roberts, B., Hanson, G., Cornwell, D., Borger, S., 2010. An Analysis of Migrant Smuggling Costs along the Southwest Border. Office of Immigration Statistics, Department of Homeland Security, Washington, DC.

Rosenblum, M.R., 2012. Border Security: Immigration Enforcement Between Ports of Entry. Congressional Research Service, Washington, DC.

Rothman, E.S., Espenshade, T.J., 1992. Fiscal impacts of immigration to the United States. Popul. Index 58, 381–415.

Sabater, A., Domingo, A., 2012. A new immigration regularization policy: The settlement program in Spain. Int. Migrat. Rev. 46, 191–220.

Sabates-Wheeler, R., 2009. The Impact of Irregular Status on Human Development Outcomes for Migrants. United Nations Development Programme Human Development Reports Research Paper 2009/26,United Nations Development Programme, New York.

Sarris, A., Markova, E., 2001. The decision to legalize by Bulgarian illegal immigrants in Greece. In: Djajić, S. (Ed.), International Migration: Trends, Policies and Economic Impact. Routledge, London.

Sarris, A.H., Zografakis, S., 1999. A computable general equilibrium assessment of the impact of illegal immigration on the Greek economy. J. Popul. Econ. 12, 155–182.

Scheve, K.F., Slaughter, M.J., 2001. What determines individual trade-policy preferences? J. Int. Econ. 54, 267–292.

Singer, A., Massey, D.S., 1998. The social process of undocumented border crossing among Mexican migrants. Int. Migrat. Rev. 32, 561–592.

Sirkeci, I., Cohen, J., Ratha, D., 2012. Migration and Remittances during the Global Financial Crisis and Beyond. World Bank, Washington, DC.

Sjaastad, L.A., 1962. The costs and returns of human migration. J. Polit. Econ. 70, 80–93.

Spener, D., 2001. Smuggling migrants through South Texas: Challenges posed by Operation Rio Grande. In: Kyle, D., Koslowski, R. (Eds.), Global Human Smuggling: Comparative Perspectives. Johns Hopkins University Press, Baltimore, MD.

Spener, D., 2004. Mexican migrant-smuggling: A cross-border cottage industry. J. Int. Migrat. Integrat. 5, 295–320.

Spener, D., 2009. Clandestine Crossings: Migrants and Coyotes on the Texas–Mexico Border. Cornell University Press, Ithaca.

Stark, O., 1991. The Migration of Labor. Basil Blackwell, Cambridge, MA.

Statistics Canada, 2009. Immigration in Canada: a portrait of the foreign-born population, 2006 census. Immigration: Driver of population growth. www12.statcan.ca/census-recensement/2006/as-sa/97-557/p2-eng.cfm (accessed 12 September 2012).

Sunderhaus, S., 2007. Regularization Programs for Undocumented Migrants. Verlag Dr, Müller, Berlin.

Tamura, Y., 2010. Migrant smuggling. J. Publ. Econ. 94, 540–548.

Taylor, J.E., 1987. Undocumented Mexico–U.S. migration and the returns to households in rural Mexico. Am. J. Agr. Econ. 69, 626–638.

Taylor, J.E., 1992. Earnings and mobility of legal and illegal immigrant workers in agriculture. Am. J. Agr. Econ. 74, 889–896.

Tervo, H., Hossain, K., Stepien, A., 2009. Illegal immigration by sea as a challenge to the maritime border security of the European Union with a special focus on maritime surveillance systems. In: Koivurova, T., Chircop, A., Franckx, E., Molenaar, E.J., VanderZwaag, D.L. (Eds.), Understanding and Strengthening European Union–Canada Relations in Law of the Sea and Ocean Governance. The Northern Institute for Environmental and Minority Law. University of Lapland Printing Centre, Rovaniemi.

Thom, K., 2008. Repeated Circular Migration: Theory and Evidence. Johns Hopkins University, Baltimore, MD, Job Market Paper.

Todaro, M.P., Maruszko, L., 1987. Illegal immigration and U.S. immigration reform: A conceptual framework. Popul. Dev. Rev. 13, 101–114.

Triandafyllidou, A., 2010. Irregular Migration in Europe: Myths and Realities. Ashgate Publishing, Aldershot.

United Nations Department of Economic and Social Affairs, 2009. Trends in International Migrant Stock: The 2008 Revision. Population Division, United Nations Department of Economic and Social Affairs, New York.

United Nations Development Programme, 2009. Human Development Report 2009. United Nations Development Programme, New York.

US Department of State, 2010. Trafficking in Persons Report 2010. US Department of State, Washington, DC.

US Department of State, 2011. Trafficking in Persons Report 2011. US Department of State, Washington, DC.

US Government Accountability Office, 2005. Weaknesses Hinder Employment Verification and Worksite Enforcement Efforts. US Government Accountability Office, Washington, DC.

US Government Accountability, 2006. Human Trafficking: Better Data, Strategy, and Reporting Needed to Enhance U.S. Antitrafficking Efforts Abroad, US Government Accountability Office, Washington, DC.

Vaira-Lucero, M., Nahm, D., Tani, M., 2012. The Impact of the 1996 Immigration Policy Reform (IIRIRA) on Mexican Migrants' Remittances, IZA Discussion Paper No. 6546, IZA, Bonn.

Valdez-Suiter, E., Rosas-López, N., Pagaza, N., 2007. Gender differences. In: Cornelius, W., Lewis, J. (Eds.), Impacts of Border Enforcement on Mexican Migration: The View from Sending Communities. Center for Comparative Immigration Studies, University of California, San Diego.

Vargas, E.D., 2011. Mixed-Status Families and Public Assistance: The Impact of Both States and Families, Western Political Science Association 2011 Annual Meeting Paper.

Väyrynen, R., 2003. Illegal Immigration, Human Trafficking and Organized Crime, Discussion Paper No. 2003/72, United Nations University/WIDER.

Venturini, A., 1999. Do immigrants working illegally reduce the natives' legal employment? Evidence from Italy. J. Popul. Econ. 12, 135–154.

Watson, T., 2010. Inside the Refrigerator: Immigration Enforcement and Chilling Effects in Medicaid, NBER Working Paper No. 16278, NBER, Cambridge, MA.

Wheaton, E.M., Schauer, E.J., Galli, T.V., 2010. Economics of human trafficking. Int. Migrat. 48, 114–141.

Wiley, J., 1995. Undocumented aliens and recognized refugees: The right to work in Costa Rica. Int. Migrat. Rev. 29, 423–440.

Winegarden, C.R., Khor, L.B., 1991. Undocumented immigration and unemployment of U.S. youth and minority workers: econometric evidence. Rev. Econ. Stat. 73, 105–112.

Winegarden, C.R., Khor, L.B., 1993. Undocumented immigration and income inequality in the native-born population of the U.S.: Econometric evidence. Appl. Econ. 25, 157–163.

Woodruff, C., Zenteno, R., 2006. Migration Networks and Microenterprises in Mexico. Mimeo, University of California, San Diego.

Yang, D., 2006. Why do migrants return to poor countries? Evidence from Philippine migrants' responses to exchange rate shocks. Rev. Econ. Stat. 88 (4), 715–735.

Yoshida, C., Woodland, A.D., 2005. The Economics of Illegal Immigration. Palgrave Macmillan, New York.

Zhang, S., Chin, K., 2004. Characteristics of Chinese Human Smugglers. Research in Brief, US Department of Justice, Washington, DC.

Zorlu, A., Hartog, J., 2005. The effect of immigration on wages in three European countries. J. Popul. Econ. 18, 113–151.

CHAPTER 14

Guest or Temporary Foreign Worker Programs

Philip Martin
University of California, Davis

Contents

1. Summary	718
2. Introduction	720
2.1 Definitions and data	721
2.2 Why international migration?	722
3. Globalization, Differences, and Migration	724
3.1 Demographic and economic differences	724
3.2 Communications, transportation, and rights	727
4. Guest-Worker Programs	729
4.1 Rationales	729
4.2 Attestation versus certification	731
4.3 Contracts versus free agents	732
4.4 Distortion and dependence	733
5. Regional Migration Systems	736
5.1 Americas	736
5.1.1 Canada	736
5.1.2 Caribbean and Latin America	739
5.1.3 Mexico	741
5.2 Europe	744
5.2.1 From emigration to immigration	745
5.2.2 Freedom of movement	746
5.2.3 Turkey and Germany	747
5.2.4 EU: Europe needs migrants	748
5.2.5 Norway, Switzerland, and Russia	751
5.3 Asia and the Middle East	752
5.3.1 Singapore and Japan	753
5.3.2 GCC countries	754
5.3.3 Migrant-sending countries	755
5.3.4 Israel	757
5.4 Africa: refugees and migrants	757
5.5 Oceania and Pacific islands	758

Handbook of the Economics of International Migration, Volume 1A
ISSN 2212-0092, http://dx.doi.org/10.1016/B978-0-444-53764-5.00014-1

6. Migration and Development   760
       6.1 Recruitment   762
       6.2 Remittances   765
       6.3 Returns   767
7. Conclusions   770
References   771

Man is of all sorts of luggage the most difficult to be transported.

Adam Smith

1. SUMMARY

Guest or temporary foreign worker programs (TFWPs) aim to add workers to the labor force but not permanent residents to the population. This terminology emphasizes the rotation principle at the heart of TFWPs: Migrants are expected to work one or more years abroad before returning to their countries of origin. If employer demand for migrants persists, there may be replacement migrants, but the employment–migrant ratio in the host country should remain near 100%, meaning that most foreigners related to the program are employed.

Most of the world's 110 million migrant workers in 2010 were settled immigrants and often naturalized citizens of the countries in which they were employed. However, a significant share, a third or more, were guest workers, temporary foreign workers admitted for periods ranging from a few weeks to several years. The most typical guest worker is a low-skilled Indian or Filipino employed in a Gulf oil-exporting country for two to three years; migrant workers in the Gulf rotate in and out of the country to fill year-round jobs. There are many other types of TFWPs, from those that admit seasonal farm workers for several months to those that admit IT professionals as probationary immigrants.

Most guest-worker programs are unilateral, in the sense that governments of migrant-receiving countries allow employers to recruit where and how they wish. However, guest workers are sometimes recruited under the terms of bilateral agreements, as with the Mexico–US Bracero program of 1942–64 (CRS, 1980). There were almost 200 bilateral labor agreements in 2002 (OECD, 2004).

Employers are the key actors in guest-worker programs, beginning the process of temporary labor migration by requesting permission from governments to hire foreign workers to fill vacant jobs. Most governments require employers to have their need for foreign workers certified, meaning that the employer tries to recruit local workers at specified wages and working conditions under the supervision of the host-country Ministry of Labor, which certifies that the employer can hire guest workers if the recruitment of local workers is unsuccessful. Certification is the rule, especially for low-skilled workers, but is often routine. For example, over 95% of US employer requests for low-skilled H-2A and H-2B workers are certified.

An alternative to certification is attestation, which involves employers asserting or attesting that they are abiding by specified recruitment conditions, such as offering the prevailing wage for the job and not seeking guest workers to replace workers on strike. Employer attestations effectively open border gates to foreign workers, with enforcement activities usually delayed until after guest workers are in the country and employed.

After deciding whether and how employers receive permission to employ guest workers, governments must make other decisions, including whether to allow guest workers to bring their families, whether family members can work and access education and social services, and how to respond to employer and worker requests for work-permit renewals. Some guest-worker programs, including the US H-1B and several Canadian, Australian, and European programs, are probationary immigrant schemes that allow guest workers to become immigrants. Other TFWPs, such as those in the Gulf oil exporters, discourage work-permit renewals and settlement.

All guest-worker programs fail, in the sense that some of the migrants settle and the migrant–employment ratio usually falls over time, explaining the aphorism that there is nothing more permanent than temporary workers. Migrant settlement does not necessarily prove that guest-worker programs are "bad," since migrants and their employers as well as sending and receiving countries benefit from temporary labor migration.

All models of "optimal migration" urge more labor migration from poorer to richer countries (Benhabib and Jovanovic, 2012). The arrival of migrant workers can generate extra output and benefit employers and complementary workers, and there can also be positive externalities from additional workers, such as dampening inflationary pressures if labor autarky would have prompted widespread wage increases (Kindleberger, 1967). The World Bank (2005, Chapter 2) estimated that increasing the number of low-skilled migrant workers in industrial countries by 50%, from 28 million to 42 million, would raise global economic output by $356 billion in 2005, more than removing all trade restrictions.

The issue is how to design and administer guest-worker programs to minimize settlement due to distortion, the fact that some employers make investment decisions that assume migrants will continue to be available, and dependence, as occurs when migrants and their families come to rely on foreign jobs and wages. Distortion and dependence mean that employer and migrant incentives may not align with the rotation rules and expectations of TFWPs (Ruhs and Anderson, 2010).

Guest workers are normally tied to a single employer; if they lose their job, they lose the right to be in the country. The economic impacts of guest workers in receiving countries are concentrated in sectors and among employers who hire them. Governments may recognize the potential distortion that can occur with employer reliance on guest workers, and sometimes try to offset wage depression or a slower increase in wages due to guest workers by calculating what the US H-2A program calls an adverse effect wage rate (AEWR), the wage that would prevail in the absence of guest workers. Most governments require employers to try to recruit local workers and to pay both local and guest workers the higher of the minimum wage, the prevailing wage, or the calculated AEWR. In the US H-2A program, the AEWR is normally the highest and most debated of the three wages.

Sending workers abroad can speed up development at home, as workers send home remittances and return with skills learned abroad. The effects of out-migration on development are often summarized by the three Rs: recruitment or who goes abroad; remittances or the amount earned abroad that is sent home; and the multiplier effect of remittance spending, and returns, an examination of who returns and do returned migrants rest and retire or do they use skills acquired abroad to speed up development? (Martin et al., 2005).

There are three major lessons of a half-century of guest-worker programs. First, most TFWPs become larger and last longer than anticipated due to distortion and dependence. Second, there is no automatic link between labor migration and development in migrant-sending areas. The three Rs can operate in ways that speed up development, or they make migrant-sending areas more dependent on sending workers abroad over time. Third, managing the movement of workers from one country to another is a difficult political economy challenge, involving migrant-sending governments that aim to protect their nationals abroad while migrant-receiving governments navigate between employers seeking to get work done at low cost and local workers who fear that guest workers will lower wages.

2. INTRODUCTION

Temporary migrants, also known as guest workers, are persons employed temporarily away from "home." Temporary and home are subject to considerable variation in definition, from several months to several years, and "home" can mean a place to which a migrant returns after a few months or a place where someone grew up but intended to leave. The major motivation for temporary labor migration is higher earnings, but there may also be non-economic motivations, including the desire of youth to experience work and culture elsewhere as well as older workers starting over after a personal event such as a divorce.

Most people do not emigrate, even from "emigration areas," and few move without connections to employers, workers, or friends and relatives in the destination area. There has been an enormous expansion of research on labor recruitment networks, as when employers use contractors and other intermediaries to recruit and often supervise migrants as well as informal social networks that link workers in origin and destination areas. This recruitment and network research finds that the socio-economic costs of migrating even long distances are generally falling, helping to explain why internal and international migration flows can rise even if the fundamental demographic and economic differences that motivate migration shrink (Taylor and Martin, 2001; Kuptsch, 2006).

2.1 Definitions and data

The United Nations Population Division defines international migrants as persons outside their country of birth or citizenship for 12 months or more (www.unmigration.org). The UN definition is inclusive, embracing persons born outside the country who are considered to be citizens of a country when they arrive, as with ethnic Germans arriving in Germany, settler immigrants, temporary foreign workers and students, and irregular or unauthorized foreigners. In a world of about 200 sovereign nation states and 7.1 billion people, there were an estimated 214 million migrants in 2010, 3% of world residents, including half who were in the labor force of the country to which they moved.

Three trends are apparent in Table 14.1. First, the number of international migrants has been increasing faster than the global population, so that the migrant share of the global population rose from 2.2% in 1970 to 3.1% in 2010. Second, the share of the world's migrants in more-developed countries[1] has been rising steadily, from just over 40% in 1960 to 60% in 2010. Third, even though the number of international migrants in less-developed countries has been rising, the migrant share of the population of

Table 14.1 International Migrants and Global Population, 1960–2010

	World	More developed	Less developed	More dev.	Less dev.
International migrants, mid-year (thousands)					
1960	75,901	32,085	43,816	42%	58%
1970	81,527	38,283	43,244	47%	53%
1980	99,783	47,727	52,056	48%	52%
1990	154,005	89,656	64,349	58%	42%
2000	174,934	110,291	64,643	63%	37%
2010	213,944	127,711	86,232	60%	40%

				Pop. share		Migrant share		
	World	More developed	Less developed	*More dev.*	*Less dev.*	*Global pop.*	*More dev.*	*Less dev.*
Global population, mid-year (billions)								
1960	3.0	0.9	2.1	31%	69%	2.5%	3.4%	2.1%
1970	3.7	1.1	2.6	29%	71%	2.2%	3.6%	1.6%
1980	4.4	1.1	3.3	26%	74%	2.3%	4.2%	1.6%
1990	5.3	1.2	4.0	23%	77%	2.9%	7.4%	1.6%
2000	6.1	1.3	4.8	21%	79%	2.9%	8.7%	1.3%
2010	6.9	1.2	5.7	18%	83%	3.1%	10.3%	1.5%

More developed is Europe, North America, Australia/New Zealand, Japan, and the ex-USSR.
Source: UN, DESA, Population Division.

---

[1] The UN defines more developed areas as Europe and North America, Australia/New Zealand, Japan, and the ex-USSR, "where it is presented as a separate area."

Table 14.2 International migrants in 2010 (millions)

Origin	Destination Industrial	Destination Developing	Total
Industrial	55	12	68
Developing	73	74	147
Total	128	87	215
Industrial	26%	6%	32%
Developing	34%	34%	68%
Total	60%	40%	100%

Source: UN Population Division (2010). International Migration Report.

less-developed countries has been falling, to 1.4% in 2010. By contrast, over 10% of the residents of more-developed countries in 2010 were international migrants.

International migrants can be divided by their origin and destination. In 2010, the largest stock of migrants involved persons who moved from one developing country to another (Table 14.2). Some 74 million people were south–south migrants, moving from countries such as the Philippines to Saudi Arabia or from Nicaragua to Costa Rica. The second largest stock, involving 73 million migrants, south–north migration, as when Mexicans move to the US or Turks to Germany. The third largest stock was the 55 million north–north migrants who moved from one industrial country to another, as from Canada to the US. Finally, 13 million people moved from north to south, as with Japanese nationals who work or retire in Thailand.

The countries with the most migrants, as measured by the United Nations, include the US, with 43 million migrants in 2010; Russia, 12 million;[2] Germany, 11 million; and Saudi Arabia, Canada, and France, about 7 million each. These six countries included 87 million migrants, or 40% of the global total. Countries with the highest share of migrants in their populations were Gulf oil exporters such as Qatar, where over 85% of residents were migrants, and the UAE and Kuwait, with 70% migrants. The countries with the lowest shares of migrants in their population include China, Indonesia, Vietnam, Peru and Cuba, where less than 0.1% of residents were born outside the country.

2.2 Why international migration?

International migration is the exception, not the rule. The number one form of migration control is inertia: most people do not want to move away from family and friends. Second, governments have significant capacity to regulate migration, and they do, with passports, visas, and border controls. One item considered by many governments when

---

[2] Migrants usually move over national borders, but sometimes borders move over people. Some of the migrants in Russia are citizens of ex-USSR countries who were in Russia when the Soviet Union collapsed in 1991, and were considered nationals of Moldova or Georgia rather than Russians.

deciding whether to recognize a new entity that declares itself a nation state is whether it is able to regulate who crosses and remains within its borders.

International migration is likely to increase in the twenty-first century for reasons that range from persistent demographic and economic inequalities to revolutions in communications and transportation that increase mobility. There are also more borders to cross. There were 193 generally recognized nation states in 2000, four times more than the 43 in 1900 (Lemert, 2005, p. 176).[3] Each nation state distinguishes citizens and foreigners, has border controls to inspect those seeking entry, and determines what foreigners can do while inside the country, whether they are tourists, students, guest workers, or immigrants.

Most countries discourage immigration, meaning that they do not welcome the arrival of foreigners who wish to settle and become naturalized citizens. Some also discourage emigration, such as the efforts of Communist nations to prevent emigration symbolized by the Berlin Wall between 1961 and 1989, and the continuing effort of the North Korean government to prevent its citizens from leaving.

Five countries plan for the arrival of a total of 1.5 million immigrants a year. The US accepts 1.1 million immigrants, Canada 250,000, Australia 125,000, New Zealand 50,000, and Israel 25,000. However, the number of newcomers arriving in industrial countries exceeds 1.5 million a year, as European countries resettle some refugees and often reluctantly accept family members of settled immigrants.

International migration is both a national and an international issue, raising questions about how to combine national and international governance of migration (Betts, 2011). Should migrant-sending countries have a voice in setting the immigration policies of migrant-receiving countries? Should migrant-receiving countries intervene in migrant-sending countries to prevent an outflow of refugees? Some developing country leaders have called for more foreign aid to prevent out-of-control migration to countries that do not want to open their doors. The late President Boumedienne of Algeria warned that if industrial countries did not provide more foreign aid: "No quantity of atomic bombs could stem the tide of billions . . . who will some day leave the poor southern part of the world to erupt into the relatively accessible spaces of the rich northern hemisphere looking for survival" (quoted in Teitelbaum and Teitelbaum, 1980).

The first step to make migration a manageable challenge is to understand why globalization encourages migration. The economic growth associated with globalization can turn emigration nations into destinations for migrants, as in Ireland, Italy, and Korea, or it can entrench the desire to migrate abroad at least temporarily, as in the Philippines and Jamaica. The challenge is to manage migration to reduce the economic differences that encourage people to cross borders, and to understand how investment, remittances and aid can stimulate what has been termed stay-at-home development.

---

[3] Lemert (2005, p. 176) says there were fewer than 50 generally recognized nation states in 1900.

3. GLOBALIZATION, DIFFERENCES, AND MIGRATION

Globalization has increased linkages between countries, as evidenced by sharply rising flows of goods and capital across national borders and the growth of international and regional bodies to set rules for trade and investment. However, controlling the entry and stay of people is a core attribute of national sovereignty, and flows of people are not governed by a comprehensive global migration regime. Most nation states do not welcome newcomers as immigrants, but almost all countries richer than their neighbors have legal and unauthorized or irregular foreign workers.

3.1 Demographic and economic differences

Most of the world's people are in developing countries, where almost all population growth occurs. The world's population, which reached 6 billion in October 1999 and 7 billion in 2011, is growing by 1.2% or 80 million a year, with 97% of the growth in developing countries.

In the past, significant demographic differences between areas prompted large-scale migration. For example, Europe had 21% of the world's almost 1 billion residents in 1800 and the Americas 4% (Table 14.3). When there were five Europeans for every American, millions of Europeans emigrated to North and South America in search of economic opportunity as well as religious and political freedom.

Will history repeat itself? Africa and Europe had roughly equal populations in 2000, but fast-growing Africa is projected to have three times more residents than shrinking Europe in 2050. If Africa remains poorer than Europe, the two continents' diverging demographic trajectories may propel young people from overcrowded cities such as Cairo and Lagos to Berlin and Rome.

The economic differences that encourage international migration have two dimensions, one fostered by inequality between countries and the other by inequality within countries. The world's almost 200 nation states have per-capita incomes that range from less than $250 per person per year to more than $50,000, a difference that provides a

Table 14.3 World population by continent, 1800, 2000, 2050 (percent shares)

	1800	1999	2050*
World (millions)	978	5978	8,909
Africa	11	13	20
Asia	65	61	59
Europe	21	12	7
Latin America and Caribbean	3	9	9
Northern America	1	5	4
Oceania	0	1	1

*Projected.
Source: UN (1999). The World at Six Billion, Table 2.

Table 14.4 Global migrants and per-capita income gaps, 1975–2005

	Migrants (millions)	World pop. (billions)	Migrants world pop.	Annual mig. (millions)	Countries grouped by per-capita GDP ($)			Ratio high–low	Ratio high–mid
					Low	Middle	High		
1975	85	4.1	2.1%	1	150	750	6200	41	8
1985	105	4.8	2.2%	2	270	1290	11,810	44	9
1990	154	5.3	2.9%	10	350	2220	19,590	56	9
1995	164	5.7	2.9%	2	430	2390	24,930	58	10
2000	175	6.1	2.9%	2	420	1970	27,510	66	14
2005	191	6.4	3.0%	3	580	2640	35,131	61	13

The 1990 migrant stock was raised from 120 million to 154 million, largely to reflect the break-up of the USSR. 2005 data are gross national income.
Sources: UN Population Division and World Bank Development Indicators; 1975 income data are 1976.

significant incentive, especially for young people, to migrate for higher wages and more opportunities. Young people are most likely to move within countries and over national borders because they have the least invested in jobs and careers at home and the most time to recoup their "investment in migration" to reach the destination.

The number of migrants doubled between 1985 and 2010, a period in which nominal per-capita incomes in rich countries tripled, from $12,000 to almost $39,000. The 30 high-income countries had 1.1 billion residents in 2010, a sixth of the world's population, and their gross national income was $43 trillion, 80% of the global $62 trillion (World Bank, 2012b, pp. 392–393).[4]

The average per-capita income of $39,000 in high-income countries was almost 12 times the average $3300 in low- and middle-income countries. Despite rapid economic growth in many developing countries, including East Asian "Tigers" such as Korea and Singapore in the 1990s and China and India more recently, the ratio of per-capita incomes between high-income and low-income countries has widened over the past quarter century, from 44 in 1985 to 76 in 2010. The gap has also widened for middle-income countries, from 9 to 10 (Table 14.4).

The fact that an average person can increase his or her income by 10 times or more by crossing a national border is a powerful incentive to migrate, especially for a young person beginning to work. Labor force projections suggest that almost all labor force growth will be in developing countries, while labor forces in high-income countries will shrink. In 2010, for example, the 613 million workers in more developed countries were almost

---

[4] High-income countries had $43 trillion or 69% of the world's $62 trillion gross national income in 2010, while low- and middle-income countries had $19 trillion (at purchasing power parity, high-income countries had $42 trillion or 55% of the $76 trillion in GNI, and low- and middle-income countries had $34 trillion).

Table 14.5 World, DC, LDC economically active population (EAP) 1980–2020 (thousands)

	1980	1985	1990	1995	2000
World EAP	1,929,556	2,160,150	2,405,619	2,604,941	2,818,456
More dev. EAP	522,683	544,271	568,832	573,626	589,151
Less dev. EAP	1,406,873	1,615,879	1,836,787	2,031,315	2,229,305

	2005	2010	2015	2020
World EAP	3,050,420	3,279,373	3,481,270	3,651,283
More dev. EAP	604,521	613,388	611,392	602,977
Less dev. EAP	2,445,899	2,665,986	2,869,878	3,048,307

Change	1980–90	1990–2000	2000–10	2010–20
World EAP	25%	21%	17%	17%
More dev. EAP	9%	5%	4%	5%
Less dev. EAP	31%	26%	21%	20%

Source: ILO Laborsta, <http://laborsta.ilo.org/>.

20% of the global labor force of 3.3 billion. By 2020, the labor force of high-income countries is expected to shrink to 603 million, while the labor force of developing countries is expected to expand by about 400 million to 3 billion (Table 14.5). If employers in rich countries do not adopt labor-saving innovations, as in agriculture, their demand for workers may induce more south–north labor migration.

In lower-income countries, half or more of workers are employed in agriculture, a sector that is often taxed despite the fact that farmers and farm workers usually have below-average incomes (Taylor and Martin, 2001). There are many ways to tax farmers in developing countries with limited banking systems, including selling them needed inputs such as seed and fertilizer via monopoly firms that charge high prices, or having only one buyer for the commodities they produce that pays below-market prices. Taxes are the difference between the higher price that farmers pay for inputs and the lower world price or the difference between the higher world price for the commodities they produce and the lower farm price. Taxes that keep farm incomes below nonfarm incomes encourage rural–urban migration, which is one reason why the urban share of the world's population surpassed 50% for the first time in 2008.

Industrial countries had "Great Migrations" off the land after World War II that provided workers for expanding factories and accelerated urbanization. Similar Great Migrations are underway today in countries from China to Mexico. This rural–urban migration has three implications for international migration. First, many ex-farmers and farm workers accept 3-D (dirty, dangerous, difficult) jobs, whether inside their countries, as with rural–urban migrants in China, or abroad, as with Mexicans who fill jobs ranging from farm worker to gardener to kitchen helper. Second, rural–urban migrants make physical as well as cultural transitions when they move from villages to cities, and some find that this transition from village to city is as easy abroad as at it would be at home, especially if friends and relatives are already abroad. Third, rural–urban migrants within a country usually get closer to the country's exits, since labor recruiters who arrange foreign jobs are usually in the cities with government agencies that issue passports and have airports that can transport workers abroad.

3.2 Communications, transportation, and rights

Differences encourage migration, but it often takes networks or links between areas to encourage people to move. Migration networks are a broad concept, including communication factors that enable people to learn about opportunities abroad, the migration infrastructure of recruiters, travel agents and others who actually move migrants, and the rights regime that allows migrants to remain abroad. Migration networks that bridge borders have been shaped and strengthened by three revolutions of the past half century, in communications, transportation, and rights.

The communications revolution helps potential migrants learn about opportunities abroad. The best information comes from family and friends who are already abroad, since they can provide information in an understandable context. Ever easier communication via cell phones and the Internet permits information about available jobs to quickly cross national borders, as with information on farm jobs that travels faster to rural Mexico than to nearby towns that may have double-digit unemployment rates. Movies and television programs depicting the good life in high-income countries may encourage especially young people to assume that the grass is greener abroad, and that migration is the fastest path to upward mobility. Even if migrants know that movies and television exaggerate life abroad, some of those who move and wind up with low wages and poor conditions say that life is not "too bad."

The transportation revolution highlights the declining cost of travel. British migrants unable to pay one-way passage to North American colonies in the eighteenth century often indentured themselves, which means they signed contracts that obliged them to work for three to six years for whoever met the ship and paid the captain. Transportation costs today are far less, typically less than $2500 to travel anywhere in the world legally and up to $20,000 to be smuggled into another country. Most studies suggest faster payback times for migrants today than two centuries ago, so that even migrants who paid high smuggling fees can usually repay them within two or three years (Kyle and Koslowski, 2011).

The communications and transportation revolutions help migrants to learn about opportunities and to cross national borders, while the rights revolution affects their ability to stay abroad. After World War II, most industrial countries strengthened the constitutional and political rights of individuals within their borders to prevent a recurrence of fascism, and the 1948 Universal Declaration of Human Rights enshrined many fundamental human rights in a document signed by most of the world's governments.

As migration from developing to industrial countries increased in the 1990s, there was pressure to roll back the rights of foreigners in order to manage migration. Germany and most other European governments included liberal asylum provisions in their postwar constitutions to avoid another situation as occurred when those fleeing Nazi Germany were refused refuge abroad and perished in concentration camps. Foreigners seeking a better life soon learned that, if they applied for asylum in Germany and other European countries, they received accommodation and food while their applications and appeals were pending, and sometimes could work on the side. The German government distributed asylum seekers throughout the country, and required local communities to generate the taxes needed to provide them with housing and food (Martin, 2004).

With over 1000 foreigners a day applying for asylum in Germany in the early 1990s, and over 90% found not to be refugees in need of protection, there was a wave of attacks on foreigners that resulted in deaths, no-go zones, and a revival of nationalist groups that asserted that "Germany is for Germans." The German government did not want to modify the constitution, but also needed to do something to deal with the flood of asylum seekers.

There was a three-pronged response to the flood of asylum seekers. First, Germany and other European countries required nationals of the countries sending the most asylum seekers to obtain visas, so that Turks could no longer board a plane, land in Germany, and request asylum. Second, European governments imposed fines on airlines bringing foreigners without proper visas. Third, Germany and other European governments made it difficult for foreigners from "safe" countries or who transited through safe countries on their way to Germany to apply for asylum, so that a Turk who passed through Hungary was returned to Hungary to apply there. Germany maintained a constitutional right to asylum, but quickly reduced the number of applications from over 400,000 a year to less than 100,000 a year.

The US in the mid-1990s went through a similar debate about migrant rights, and once again the issue was the cost of caring for foreigners. The cost of welfare assistance rose sharply in the early 1990s, when President Clinton promised to "end welfare as we know it." The Commission on Immigration Reform (CIR) asked whether the US government should reduce the number of needy immigrants admitted, such as the elderly parents of newly naturalized US citizens, but allow those who arrived to have full access to the welfare system, or whether the US should maintain immigration at high levels but reduce the access of newcomers to welfare assistance.

The CIR and President Clinton urged Congress to choose rights over numbers—that is, to continue to treat immigrants as future Americans and give them full access to most welfare programs, but to reduce admissions of needy immigrants who needed assistance. However, most employer groups and migrant advocates chose numbers over rights. Employers wanted continued access to immigrant workers, while migrant advocates believed (correctly) that new arrivals whose access to welfare was curbed would eventually regain access. Congress in 1996 enacted laws that favored numbers over rights, meaning that immigration levels were kept high while the access of newcomers to welfare was curbed.

Balancing migrant numbers and migrant rights is a major challenge for governments and international organizations (Ruhs and Martin, 2008). Countries with the highest shares of migrants in their labor forces, such as the Gulf oil exporters, extend few rights to migrants, explaining why it is very hard for a guest worker to become a naturalized citizen of Saudi Arabia or the United Arab Emirates. Countries that grant more rights to foreign workers, such as Sweden and other Scandinavian countries, have relatively few, in part because migrant workers with full rights cost more.

The tradeoff between migrant numbers and migrant rights arises in country policies as well as at the World Trade Organization. In negotiations that aim to free up trade in services, some developing countries argue that migrant "service providers" should not be covered by minimum wage laws in a richer destination country because requiring employers to pay minimum wages would make developing country workers more expensive and reduce the number likely to be hired.

4. GUEST-WORKER PROGRAMS

Economies have three major sectors, agriculture, industry, and services. The fact that especially young people leaving the agricultural sector in developing countries are willing to fill jobs in all sectors of industrial country labor markets suggests that labor migration can provide a perfect match between "excess" developing country workers and vacant industrial country jobs.

The major public policy issue is not the fact that migrants *can* fill vacant jobs in industrial country agriculture, industry, and services sectors. Instead, the major issue is whether and how to regulate the movement of workers over national borders. A century ago, settlement migration predominated, which generally meant that a person left one country to begin anew in another (even though many returned). Today, most workers cross national borders as temporary workers.

4.1 Rationales

The major rationales for guest-worker programs are summarized in Table 14.6. There are other arguments, including the assertion that workers should be freer to cross borders to increase trade in services; that multinational firms should be allowed to assemble diverse work forces in any country in which they operate to remain competitive; and that allowing migrants to circulate between developing and developed countries gives the migrant the best of both worlds while benefiting both societies, as the migrant acts as an economic bridge between the two.

Table 14.6 Rationales for guest-worker programs

Rationale	Typical origin/goal	Examples
1. Labor shortages or best and brightest	Migrants fill vacant jobs without wage increases; allow employers to recruit in global labor market	European guest-worker and US Bracero programs One argument for expansion of US H-1B program in 1990s
2. Foreign policy concerns	Facilitate returns of unauthorized, channel inevitable migrants, promote cooperation	German-East European programs in 1990s, Italy–Albania and Spain–Morocco programs
3. Cross-border commuting	Acknowledge that political boundaries can divide natural labor markets	Border commuter programs that enable "trusted travelers" to cross easily
4. Cultural exchange, development assistance	Exchange visitors, working holidaymakers, and trainees	Trainees in Korea and Japan; US J-1 visa, Commonwealth WHMs

There are three broad types of temporary worker programs (Martin et al., 2005):

- *Seasonal Programs, Seasonal Jobs.* These programs usually have temporary foreign workers filling temporary or seasonal jobs. Migrants tend to be temporary in such programs because the jobs they fill are seasonal, which gives them fewer reasons to remain abroad when their jobs and contracts end. Under some programs, such as those involving Polish workers employed seasonally in Germany and Mexican farm workers in Canada, workers who abide by the terms of their seasonal work visas (return when their jobs end) get priority to re-enter next season.

- *Temporary Workers, Permanent Jobs.* These are the most TFWPs, and their aim is to rotate temporary foreign workers through year-round or permanent jobs. In most cases, temporary workers receive one- or multiple-year work permits, but there is wide variation in employer and migrant rights to extend stays and to adjust status. In Italy, temporary workers can slip in and out of legal status as their employers register them for a year but do not re-register them for the next year.

- *Probationary Immigrant Programs.* These migrant worker programs extend more rights to foreign workers as their duration of stay lengthens. During the 1960s, most European temporary worker programs initially issued one-year work and residence permits. If employers requested that a migrant's permits be renewed, the renewal was normally for two years and usually enabled a migrant to unify his/her family in the country of employment (assuming that the migrant could show suitable accommodations). After another two-year renewal (say after five years), the migrant generally had immigrant or settlement rights, meaning that he/she could work in almost all jobs not requiring citizenship. After a total of five to 10 years of lawful residence and employment, the migrant could naturalize.

Workers of all skill levels are found in each type of program, but the general rule is that ease of entry and duration of stay rise with years of education. This means that most seasonal workers are low skilled, the temporary workers who rotate through permanent jobs are primarily low skilled and semi-skilled, and the migrants in probationary immigrant programs are most likely to be professionals with college degrees, such as nurses and computer programmers.

4.2 Attestation versus certification

Programs that admit foreign workers vary from country to country, but they can be compared along two important dimensions: namely, what employers must do to satisfy governments that foreign workers are needed (sometimes called economic needs tests), and the wages and work-related rights of migrants in host-country labor markets. Under most temporary-worker programs, employers must satisfy the government that foreign workers are needed to fill vacant jobs before they arrive, a process called certification in the US and many other countries.

Certification means that the government controls the border gate, which is not opened until the employer convinces the Ministry or Department of Labor (DOL) that local workers are not available. In countries with low unemployment rates and strong employment services, the certification process tends to be quick and straightforward, as in Ireland in the late 1990s, where most employers obtained quick approval of requests for migrants. However, when employers request migrants despite high unemployment rates, certification can be contentious, as in US agriculture, where some farm employers request certification to hire migrants despite unemployment rates above 10% (Martin, 2008).

The US uses certification to protect low-skilled US workers. The H-2A and H-2B programs allow employers to request seasonal foreign workers to fill temporary or seasonal US jobs, generally those lasting less than 12 months. The H-2A program, which has no ceiling on admissions, certified almost 100,000 farm jobs in 2010 as needing to be filled by migrants. The H-2B program, which admits a maximum 66,000 temporary workers a year to fill nonfarm jobs, generally runs out of visas soon after they become available.

One practical difficulty with certification is that, before employers ask the labor department to certify their need for migrant workers, they have generally identified the foreign workers they want to fill the jobs. Thus, the employer does not want its ads or labor department recruitment efforts to identify local workers, since the migrants abroad are already in the process of obtaining passports, health checks, and making other preparations to fill the jobs. Certification can become contentious when local workers who respond to ads are not hired, when local workers promise to appear when needed to fill seasonal jobs but do not, or when, as in the H-2A program, employers are required

Table 14.7 Employer requirements and migrant rights

Employer requirements	Worker rights	
	Contractual worker	*Free agent worker*
Certification	H–2A/B	
Attestation	H–1Bs	Foreign students
No employer tests	Au pairs; exchange visitors	Intra-EU migrants, working holidaymakers

Source: see text.

to continue hiring local workers until the job is at least 50% completed, even if hiring a local worker means that a migrant worker must be sent home early.[5]

The alternative attestation process gives employers practical control over migrant worker entries and employment. Under the US H-1B program, employers can complete a Labor Condition Applications that "attests" that the rate of pay offered to the foreign worker is the higher of the actual wage paid to similar US workers or the prevailing wage for the job in question, that the employment of H-1Bs will not adversely affect the working conditions of similar US workers, and that there is no strike or lock-out at the workplace (Martin, 2012a). DOL does not verify the data submitted by employers and there are few checks on the employer premises unless there are complaints.

The US L-1 intra-company transfer program is even more employer friendly, since it does not have prevailing wage and no-strike requirements and requires only that the employees transferred to the US have been employed by the foreign affiliate at least one year. These employer requirements are summarized in Table 14.7.

4.3 Contracts versus free agents

Foreign workers normally receive work and residence visas that tie them to a particular employer. If the migrant is laid off or fired, she/he usually loses the right to remain in the country after a grace period that ranges from a week to a month. This "indentured servitude" aspect of temporary-worker programs that ties a particular worker to a particular employer makes them unpopular with most unions. They argue that temporary workers who are dependent on employers to remain in the country are unable to effectively assert their rights.

Migrant workers could more effectively protect their rights if they had freedom of movement in the host-country labor market, meaning they could move from one employer to another within a sector or area or throughout the labor market. Regional free labor markets such as the EU allow such freedom of movement, so that EU nationals can move and seek jobs on an equal basis with local workers (except for those requiring

---

[5] Examples of such disputes, and the litigation they spawn in US agriculture, are documented in reports of the Commission on Agricultural Workers (1992).

national citizenship).[6] Unauthorized migrants also have freedom of movement, and some migrant advocates say that this freedom of movement can give the unauthorized more "market protections" than if they were guest workers tied to a particular employer.

Foreign students, working holidaymakers, and other migrants who are primarily in the host country for another purpose, but who are also allowed to work, are generally free agents in the labor market. The employers who hire them satisfy no or minimal requirements, in the sense that there is often no supervised recruitment required and employers must satisfy only minimum wage laws.

Logic and experience suggest that freedom to change jobs in the host-country labor market can be a powerful protection for migrants, allowing them to escape abusive employers. However, most temporary-worker programs aim to fill particular job vacancies, so most temporary workers are required to work for the employer whose "need" for migrants has been certified by a government agency. The cases in which governments do not officially determine that migrants are "needed," such as intra-EU migration, generally involve relatively small numbers of migrants or migrants whose major purpose is something other than work, as with foreign students and working holidaymakers.

4.4 Distortion and dependence

Temporary-worker programs tend to get larger and to last longer than anticipated because of distortion and dependence. Most employers in host countries do not hire temporary workers. Distortion means that the minority of employers who hire migrant workers have a different labor supply than employers who hire only local workers. The employers who hire migrants generally face limited supplies of especially low-skilled workers at home and almost unlimited supplies abroad.

Hiring workers to fill low-skill jobs is not easy (Waldinger and Lichter, 2003). Employers who would face high turnover among local workers hired to fill seasonal jobs in agriculture or year-round jobs in low-wage manufacturing and services can find migrants to be a godsend. If current migrant workers are tapped to recruit their friends and relatives, they bring to the workplace only those who can learn the job and often take responsibility for training the new hire. As a result, the hiring and training that often takes a large share of management time in high-turnover workplaces becomes a function of the migrant network, freeing managers for other tasks (Marshall, 2007).

Some of the employers hiring temporary workers assume that migrants will continue to be available and make investment decisions that reflect this assumption. In this way, farmers who depend on migrants may plant fruit trees in areas with few workers, assert that they will go out of business without migrants to pick their crops, and resist efforts to reduce the availability of temporary workers because doing so would reduce

---

[6] Migrants moving within the EU can have prearranged jobs, as with Portuguese workers who move to the UK, or move as free agents and change jobs.

the value of their orchard investment, as when paying higher wages or buying machinery would raise costs and reduce profits. Having some but not all employers hire migrant workers leads to economic distortion in the sense that some employers face different labor supplies than others. The employers who rely on migrants may not have to raise wages as local workers move up in the labor market because of the availability of foreign workers, while other employers adjust to changing local labor conditions (Martin, 2009).

The other half of the migration equation that helps temporary-worker programs get larger and last longer than expected is dependence, the fact that some migrants and their families as well as regions of labor-sending countries may develop economic structures that assume foreign jobs, earnings, and remittances will continue. If the opportunity to work abroad legally is curbed, and the three Rs of recruitment, remittances, and returns have not set in motion economic development that makes migration self-stopping, migrants may continue to seek jobs abroad outside legal channels in order to avoid reductions in their incomes.

Most researchers conclude that the Bracero programs between 1942 and 1964 sowed the seeds of subsequent unauthorized Mexico–US migration, via distortion in rural America (the expansion of labor-intensive agriculture) and dependence in rural Mexico (population and labor force growth without economic development) (Martin, 2003, Chapter 2). There is growing evidence that migrant-dependent regions are evolving in labor-sending countries around the world, from Albania to Zimbabwe. Residents live better because of remittances (poverty is reduced), but the spending of remittances may not lead to the investment that sets in motion the kind of development that makes migration self-stopping (Martin, 2010).

The realities of distortion and dependence should encourage governments considering new temporary-worker programs to proceed cautiously. The key is to find economic mechanisms that minimize distortion and dependence, including taxes to encourage employers to look for alternatives to migrants and subsidies to encourage temporary workers to return to their countries of origin as their contracts require and provide funds for economic development.

Thinking about distortion requires recognizing that employers always have choices when deciding how to get work done. Migrant workers are in many cases the "easy" path for employers, since they substitute foreign for local workers who have found better jobs.

Once migrant networks take over responsibility for recruiting and training new workers, employers have an incentive to maintain migration. In an analogy with irrigation, farmers flood fields with water if water is cheap, ensuring that all plants receive water, but they may install plastic pipes and drip lesser quantities of water to each plant if water is expensive. Similarly, employers can work collectively to maximize the pool of low-skilled workers available, or invest individually to develop and retain what is likely to be a smaller and more skilled workforce. In many countries, employers seek to maximize the pool of low-skilled migrants available.

One way to minimize distortion and protect migrants is to realize that payroll taxes for social security and unemployment and other insurance add 20–40% to wages (Martin, 1983). These taxes, generally paid mostly by employers, should be collected on wages paid to migrants to level the playing field between migrant and local workers—if employers do not have to pay these taxes on the wages of migrants, migrants are cheaper than local workers. However, migrants are generally not eligible for the benefits financed by employer-paid payroll taxes.

Tax revenues could be used to combat distortion by supporting the restructuring of migrant jobs, such as promoting labor-saving mechanization. For example, in an industry such as agriculture, it is often hard for one farmer to finance or implement mechanization, since packers and processors want hand or mechanically picked crops, but not both (Martin, 2003, Chapter 8). Thus, the employer's share of payroll taxes on migrant wages could reduce distortion, with the amount of money available for such a program contingent on how many migrants are employed and the taxes paid on their wages.[7]

It should be emphasized that mechanization is not the only alternative to migrants. In some cases, local workers may be attracted to "migrant jobs" after they are restructured, as with garbage collection in the US, whose labor force was "renationalized" by having consumers put their trash in large containers that are lifted by a truck operator. In other cases, payroll taxes may accelerate market segmentation in capital-intensive and labor-intensive directions, as when some elderly have in-home caregivers and others have technology such as cameras linked to computers that enable them to live alone with video monitoring that can summon help quickly in emergencies. The universal truism is that wages held down by more migrants will lead to more labor-intensive ways to get work done, and wages bid up by fewer migrants will encourage the development of labor-saving alternatives.

Tax revenues can also be used to encourage migrants to abide by the terms of their contracts and depart after a year or two abroad. One way to encourage departures is to refund the migrant's share of payroll taxes when the migrant surrenders his/her work visa in the country of origin. This is not withholding wages, it is refunding worker contributions to programs from which short-term migrant workers are unlikely to benefit. If the migrant share of payroll taxes were refunded in countries of origin, governments

---

[7] To recognize that each sector is different, boards or committees representing employers, workers, and government could decide how to spend the accumulated payroll tax funds to reduce dependence on temporary workers over time—that is, there would not have to be a one-size-fits-all formula. Involving worker advocates in tripartite boards could promote the development of decent work in particular migrant-dependent sectors.

and development institutions could match the refunds to support projects that create jobs in the migrants' home area.

5. REGIONAL MIGRATION SYSTEMS

5.1 Americas

The North American migration system includes the world's major emigration and immigration destinations, defined by numbers, such as the 300,000–400,000 Mexicans who move each year to the US, or in per-capita terms, as Canada aims to increase its population by 1% a year through immigration. Emigration rates are very high from many Caribbean nations. Jamaica, with 2.7 million residents, has about 27,000 emigrants a year, 1% of its population, and thousands more leave as temporary workers for Canada and the US.

5.1.1 Canada

Canada and the US include about 5% of the world's population but receive over half of the world's anticipated immigrants, about 1.5 million a year. Canada is an exception among industrial countries, with high levels of immigration, generous social welfare programs, and significant public satisfaction with immigration policies (Reitz, 2013). Many analysts trace this satisfaction to Canada's point system, under which foreigners seeking to immigrate are assessed on the basis of their education, youth, work experience, and knowledge of English or French.

Canada admitted a record 280,700 immigrants in 2010 via three major front doors:
- Economic or independent skilled workers and business investors, 187,000 or 66%
- Family unification, 60,200 or 21% and
- Refugees, 24,700 or 9%.[8]

Almost half of Canada's immigrants are from Asian countries. The leading countries of origin included the Philippines, the source of 36,600 immigrants in 2010, India, 30,300, and China, 30,200.

Canadian immigration patterns mirror those of the US, and Canadian policy changes were similar until the 1970s. For example, the US barred Chinese immigrants in 1882; Canada took steps to limit Chinese immigration in 1885. Immigration to Canada peaked between 1895 and 1913 (Figure 14.1), when 2.5 million newcomers arrived in a country that had a 1913 population of 7 million. Canada's "white only" immigration policy, which favored entries from Europe and the US, ended in 1962, while the US opened the door to Asian immigrants in 1965.

Major differences between Canada and the US emerged in 1967, when Canada developed a point selection system to select most of its immigrants. Under this system, foreigners seeking to enter Canada as skilled workers must earn at least 67 points on a

---

[8] Another 8800 foreigners were other immigrants (www.cic.gc.ca/english/resources/statistics/menu-fact.asp).

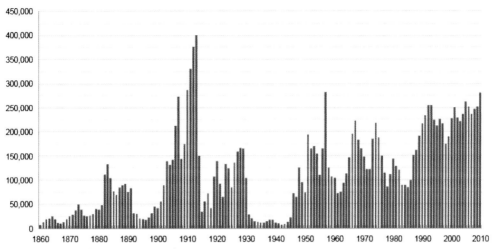

Figure 14.1 *Immigration to Canada 1860–2010.*

100-point scale.[9] Education is worth up to 25 points (for an M.S. or Ph.D.), knowing English and/or French is worth up to 24 points, and up to 21 points are awarded for work experience. Those aged 21–49 get 10 points, those employed legally in Canada with a temporary work visa get 10 points, and up to 10 points are awarded for "adaptability," such as having studied or worked in Canada. This point system and negligible illegal migration allow the Canadian government to "micro-manage" immigration to spur economic growth (Reitz, 2013).[10]

Selecting immigrants on the basis of their education ensures that half of the adult immigrants arriving in Canada have college degrees, twice the share of Canadian-born adults who have college degrees. However, Canada's immigrants are concentrated in three cities, Toronto, Vancouver, and Montreal, where there are many settled immigrants and college-educated Canadians, making it hard for even educated newcomers to find jobs that use their education and training. The result is often "brain waste," as when an immigrant doctor drives a taxi. Worries about declining employment rates and earnings of immigrants in Canada have prompted the Canadian government to expedite the recognition of degrees earned outside Canada.[11]

---

[9] The point test is online (www.cic.gc.ca/english/immigrate/skilled/apply-factors.asp).

[10] The Canadian Experience Class, introduced in 2008, allows temporary foreign workers with at least two years of experience in a "skilled occupation" and foreign students who have graduated in Canada and have one year of work experience in Canada to apply for immigrant status without leaving Canada.

[11] There are 13 jurisdictions, 15 regulated professions, and more than 400 regulatory bodies that deal with worker credentials, prompting Joe Volpe, then minister of citizenship and immigration, to say in 2005 that Canada has "an arcane infrastructure of professional organizations that essentially mitigate against the immediate integration of these highly skilled immigrants." Several business leaders unveiled a website, hireimmigrants.ca, to promote the hiring of qualified immigrants. Private firms, such as World Education Services (www.wes.org/), offer to assess foreigners' credentials for a fee.

Canada is a bilingual and multicultural society. The goal of achieving unity between English and French speakers has been the focus of Canadian politics for much of the past several decades, and many of the policies that make Canada a bilingual and bicultural society also support immigration and immigrant integration.[12] The Canadian government offers language training programs, access to social services, and human rights and equality guarantees to help immigrants to integrate into French-speaking Quebec and the English-speaking provinces.[13]

Canada also admits temporary visitors or non-immigrants, persons expected to leave after a period of work, tourism, or business in Canada. Chapter 16 of the North American Free Trade Agreement permits Canadian, Mexican, or US professionals, including accountants, engineers and lawyers, to work in another NAFTA country by showing an offer of employment, a professional credential and a passport at the border. Most of those who have taken advantage of NAFTA's free-movement provisions are Canadians employed in the US.

Like the US, Canada traditionally favored settler immigration over temporary workers. Canada has had guest-worker programs with Caribbean nations since the mid-1960s, and in the early 1970s added Mexico to what is now the Commonwealth Caribbean and Mexican Seasonal Agricultural Workers Program (SAWP). About 20,000 guest workers are admitted each year under the SAWP, most work on Ontario fruit and vegetable farms, and most return at the end of the season as required.[14]

In 2002, the Canadian government responded to employers complaining of labor shortages with the Pilot Project for Hiring Foreign Workers in Occupations that Require Lower Levels of Formal Training. The relaxed criteria for employers as well as an economic boom in energy-exporting provinces such as Alberta sharply increased the number of temporary foreign workers in Canada, raising annual admissions from 100,000 a year in the 1990s to over 200,000 a year in the twenty-first century. Some 1.5 million temporary foreign workers entered Canada between 1990 and 2010.

Most temporary foreign workers have two-year contracts that can be renewed once. However, the Canadian Experience Class introduced in 2008 that allows up to 10 points for Canadian experience means that some guest workers can become immigrants because of their youth, knowledge of English or French, and Canadian work experience. Employers can and do ask provincial governments to nominate guest workers for

---

[12] When asked what makes Canada unique in a Focus Canada poll, multiculturalism was in the top group with national health care, the flag, and the Charter of Rights and Freedoms, and ahead of hockey, bilingualism and the Royal Canadian Mounted Police (Reitz, 2013).

[13] The Quebec government has, since the early 1960s, had the right to select immigrants to bolster the number of French speakers. However, many of the immigrants selected by Quebec authorities leave soon after their arrival in Quebec for the English-speaking provinces of Ontario and British Columbia.

[14] Initially, only married Mexican men with children could participate, and they had to report to an office in Mexico soon after their contracts ended in order to be assured the right to return the following year.

immigrant visas, raising questions about the "exploitation" of guest workers seeking immigrant visas and the declining "quality" of immigrants.

An example of the promises and pitfalls of work-to-immigrate programs is the Maple Leaf Foods plant in Brandon, Manitoba. About three-fourths of the 2200 workers employed in Brandon by Maple Leaf, Canada's largest meatpacker, are temporary foreign workers. After at least six months of satisfactory work, Maple Leaf can nominate the guest workers, who speak English, Spanish, Ukrainian and Mandarin, to the provincial government for immigrant visas.[15] The guest workers, who are represented by a union, are eager to please Maple Leaf in order to become immigrants. Critics say that if Maple Leaf raised wages, it could attract local workers (Rural Migration News, 2010).

Canada is likely to remain a major country of immigration, attracting mostly skilled immigrants and embracing multiculturalism. However, worries about the declining economic success of immigrants and concerns about discrimination against the growing number of "visible minorities" may threaten Canada's welcoming embrace. If the Canadian Experience Class expands, employers will gain more influence in the immigrant selection process, which could raise union opposition to admitting guest workers who can make the transition to immigrant status.

5.1.2 Caribbean and Latin America

The seven countries of Central America, with over 40 million residents, sent few immigrants to the US until civil wars erupted in the mid-1980s. Fighting displaced tens of thousands of Guatemalans, Nicaraguans, and Salvadorans, many of whom found their way to the US. The US government initially granted asylum to Nicaraguans, who were fleeing a government the US opposed, but not to Guatemalans and Salvadorans, who were fleeing governments the US supported. Resulting lawsuits eventually allowed most Central Americans in the US an opportunity to become immigrants.[16]

In addition to family unification and unauthorized migration, a series of natural disasters including Hurricane Mitch in Honduras and Nicaragua in 1998 and earthquakes in El Salvador in 2001 encouraged migration and settlement. The US government to grant unauthorized Central Americans in the US when these disasters struck "Temporary Protected Status" so they could work legally and send home remittances to help in rebuilding, and renewed this TPS several times.

Similar to Central America, the 15 independent Caribbean nations and dependencies have over 40 million residents and some of the world's highest emigration rates.[17] At least

---

[15] Over 70% of the 11,200 immigrants in Manitoba in 2008 were provincial nominees.

[16] The settlement of the *American Baptist Churches v. Thornburgh* suit in 1991 allowed many Central Americans in the US to remain, and the Nicaraguan Adjustment and Central American Relief Act of 1997 allowed most to become immigrants and sponsor relatives for admission.

[17] During the 1960s and 1970s, many former Caribbean colonies became independent countries. Since 1983, most islands have voted against independence, including Puerto Rico in 1998.

10% of the people born in the Big Four Caribbean countries, Cuba, the Dominican Republic, Haiti and Jamaica, have emigrated, usually to the US. For example, there are a million Cuban-born US residents. The US considers all Cubans who reach the US to be refugees, which sometimes encourages exits in small boats. Under the so-called wet-foot, dry-foot policy, Cubans intercepted at sea are returned to Cuba while those who reach US land can stay as immigrants. Most Cuban immigrants have settled in southern Florida, where their success has helped to turn Miami into a US gateway to Latin America (Portes and Stepick, 1993).

Dominican immigrants are concentrated in New York City, and network ties are so strong that half of the residents of the Dominican Republic have relatives in the US (Levitt, 2001). Haiti shares the island of Hispaniola with the Dominican Republic and, as the poorest country in the Western Hemisphere, Haitians migrate to the neighboring Dominican Republic as well as to the US (Maingot, 1999). To reduce the out-migration of Haitians, the US government threatened military intervention in 1994 to restore to power the elected president, Jean-Bertrand Aristide. Aristide regained the presidency, but the economy continued to flounder, prompting some Haitians to attempt the 720-mile trip by boat to Florida. Haiti suffered a severe earthquake on January 12, 2010 that caused over 300,000 deaths, prompting the US government to suspend deportations to Haiti and to offer TPS to Haitians in the US.

Jamaicans have been migrating to the UK and the US for decades, both as temporary workers and immigrants. As an English-speaking country that trains doctors and nurses to international standards, many Jamaican health-care professionals find it relatively easy to find foreign jobs. The World Bank in March 2010 reported that 75% of the nurses trained in Jamaica have left for Canada, the UK, and the US. Their reasons for emigration range from low pay in Jamaica, about $600 a month for an RN, to better working conditions and more opportunities abroad.

During the nineteenth and early twentieth centuries, Europeans and Japanese migrated to both North and South America. During the 1990s, some of the descendents of these Spanish, Italian, and Japanese emigrants returned to their ancestors' countries of origin. For example, economic turmoil in Argentina prompted a return to Italy and Spain until the 2008–09 global recession. Over 300,000 ethnic Japanese Brazilians and Peruvians known as nikkejin moved to Japan until the 2008–09 recession, and an economic boom in Brazil prompted them to return to Brazil. Migrants from poorer countries continue to move to richer neighbors, as from Bolivia and Paraguay to Argentina.

Colombia and Ecuador send migrants to the US and Spain. In the past, Colombians migrated to richer Venezuela for higher wages and more opportunities, but this migration has largely stopped. Spain signed migration and development agreements with Colombia and Ecuador in May 2001 that allow Spanish employers to recruit workers in these countries who are expected to return with skills acquired in Spain and accelerate development at home. However, few Colombians and Ecuadorians were admitted under these agreements, in part because Spanish employers have to pay their transportation costs. For this reason, most Colombians and Ecuadorians get to Spain on their own and seek Spanish jobs.

5.1.3 Mexico

Mexico and the US have shared a 2000-mile border for the past 150 years, but Mexico became the major source of US immigrants only in the past three decades. In 1800, Mexico and the US had populations of roughly equal size, 6 million, and Mexico's per-capita GDP was about half that of the US. Northern Mexico (now the southwestern US states) was transferred to the US by the Treaty of Guadalupe Hidalgo in 1848, ending a war that began when American settlers moved into Texas, then Mexican territory, and rebelled against Mexican authority. The relatively few Mexican residents of what is now the southwestern US became Americans, and there was relatively little migration and trade between these so-called Distant Neighbors for the next century (Riding, 1989).[18]

The US population grew with immigration and births throughout the nineteenth century, and the economy industrialized in the first half of the twentieth century. Mexico had high birth and death rates and a much slower growing population than the US, and its economy remained largely agricultural. During World War I, when Mexico was undergoing a civil war, the US government approved the recruitment of Mexicans to work on US farms and railroads. These so-called Braceros (arms) were young Mexican men admitted as temporary foreign workers between 1917 and 1921 and again between 1942 and 1964 (Craig, 1971).

Both Bracero programs began as wartime emergencies, when farmers said that labor shortages might reduce food production. Critics, on the other hand, accused farmers of seeking Mexican workers to hold down wages. With a guaranteed supply of labor, US agriculture expanded, and both Bracero programs got larger and lasted longer than expected because of distortion in the US economy and dependence in rural Mexico. Distortion reflected the investments in orchards and vineyards made by US farmers who assumed that Braceros would be available at current wages, so they resisted efforts that would have raised their labor costs, such as an end to the Bracero program.

Dependence reflects how many rural Mexicans and their families became accustomed to US wages in areas that offered little opportunity. As the Bracero program expanded in the 1950s, some Mexicans moved to the Mexico–US border to increase the chance that a US farmer would select them.[19] This means that, when the Bracero program ended in 1964, thousands of Braceros and their families in Mexican border cities had no way to

---

[18] Mexico's desire to avoid closer ties with the US were summarized in the aphorism, "Poor Mexico, so far from God, so close to the US."

[19] Farmers had to pay transportation costs from the place of recruitment in Mexico. By moving to border cities, Mexicans improved their chances of being selected by US farmers.

earn a living. The Mexican and US governments cooperated to try to provide an alternative to illegal migration, modifying their trade laws to promote maquiladoras, factories in Mexican border cities that imported components from the US, hired Mexican workers to assemble goods such as TVs, and re-exported the finished products.[20] The maquiladoras never provided many jobs for ex-Braceros, who were almost all men, because maquiladoras preferred to hire young women who were often getting their first wage job.

Many rural Mexicans had worked in the US as Braceros, but there was relatively little illegal Mexico–US migration between the mid-1960s and mid-1970s, the so-called golden era for US farm workers. The United Farm Workers union won a 40% wage increase for grape pickers and other farm workers in the 1960s, largely because neither Braceros nor unauthorized Mexicans were available. After a boycott of table grapes that became La Causa, most California table grape growers signed contracts with the UFW that raised farm worker wages significantly because they had little access to guest or unauthorized workers.

During the 1970s, farm worker wages rose faster than the earnings of nonfarm workers, and many seasonal farm workers received benefits such as health insurance and pension benefits for the first time. A series of peso devaluations in the late 1970s and early 1980s increased illegal Mexico–US migration and forced the Mexican government to change its economic development strategy. During most of the twentieth century, Mexico had an import-substitution policy, which means that high tariffs protected Mexican producers of autos, appliances and other goods, and created relatively high-wage jobs in Mexican factories. The majority of Mexicans who were subsistence farmers did not get the relatively few high-wage jobs. The discovery of oil in the Gulf of Mexico in 1978 was expected to continue import substitution, but the oil-fired Mexican miracle ended when the price of oil fell in the early 1980s (Martin, 1993).

With illegal Mexico–US migration rising, the US government enacted the Immigration Reform and Control Act (IRCA) of 1986, hoping that sanctions or fines on employers who knowingly hired unauthorized workers would discourage Mexicans from trying to enter the US illegally. The spread of false documents negated IRCA's sanctions, while IRCA's legalization programs made 2.3 million Mexicans legal immigrants who could sponsor their family members for immigrant visas. IRCA legalization helped Mexicans to spread throughout the US and into new industries, as from seasonal farm jobs to year-round jobs in construction, meatpacking and other manufacturing, and services that ranged from restaurants to janitors.

There were 4.3 million Mexican-born US residents in 1990, including over half who were legalized in 1987–88. Two decades later, there were over 12 million Mexican-born

---

[20] In the mid-1960s, Mexico had high tariffs. There were no tariffs on components imported into maquiladoras if the assembled products were exported. Instead, tariffs were paid only on the value added in Mexico, which was often 10–20% of the value of the good reflecting Mexican wages.

US residents, an increase of almost 8 million. How did the number of Mexican-born residents almost triple in two decades? There were three inter-related reasons: Changes in Mexico that propelled more Mexicans to "go north for opportunity," the diffusion of Mexicans throughout the US as a result of legalization, followed by an economic boom in the late 1990s that reduced the US unemployment rate below 5%, and the failure of the US government to develop an effective strategy to enforce immigration laws at the border and inside the US.

The Mexican economy expanded less rapidly than the US economy during the 1980s, prompting the Mexican government to abandon its import substitution development strategy. Mexico confirmed its new economic policy by joining the General Agreement on Tariffs and Trade (now the World Trade Organization) in 1986, hoping that foreign investors would create factories that employed Mexicans to produce goods for export, following in the footsteps of Asian "Tiger economies" such as Korea and Taiwan. The troubled history of Mexico–US relations meant that the Mexican government preferred non-US investors. However, after the Berlin Wall fell in 1989, Mexico realized that Europeans would invest in eastern Europe and Japan in Asia, prompting Mexican President Salinas to propose NAFTA.

A Canada–US Free Trade Agreement (FTA) went into effect in 1989 with little fanfare. Mexico hoped that negotiating a similar Mexico–US FTA would send a signal to US investors that their investments would be safe in Mexico. However, Canada did not want to be left out, and the resulting North American Free Trade Agreement between Canada, Mexico, and the US was negotiated. NAFTA was expected to accelerate economic and job growth in all three countries, but especially in Mexico, with the desired side-effect of reduced Mexico–US migration.

Most of the changes associated with NAFTA occurred in Mexico, and they produced more Mexico–US migration, a migration hump, rather than less. For example, Mexican factories that had been producing for the relatively small Mexican market often closed rather than retooling with modern machinery to produce for the much larger NAFTA markets, and imports of cars and appliances rose. There were also factory closures in the US, but US workers who lost their jobs did not move to Mexico, whereas some of the Mexican workers who were displaced moved to the US.

Small farmers who produced corn to make their own tortillas were expected to buy cheaper corn from the American midwest and grow fruits and vegetables for Canadians and Americans. Instead, many quit farming, and they and their children migrated to the US, especially as the Mexican government made other changes that encouraged rural out-migration. Most rural Mexicans lived on ejidos, the communal farms created by Mexico's 1917 Constitution that ensured peasants had access to some farmland. As part of its market-opening policies, Mexico changed its land policies to allow ejido land to be bought and sold, loosening links between rural Mexicans and their land (Martin, 1993).

The migration hump associated with NAFTA led to frictions between the Mexican and US governments. The Mexican government objected when the US government began to fence the Mexico–US border, and repeatedly asked the US government for new guest-worker programs and legalization for unauthorized Mexicans in the US. There were no major US immigration reforms to accommodate these Mexican requests, but Mexico–US migration fell during the 2008–09 recession and the decreased inflow, combined with more deportations, reduced net Mexico–US migration to zero in 2010. It is not clear whether this apparent stop to mass Mexico–US migration is a temporary lull or an outcome of the economic changes wrought by NAFTA, socio-political changes in Mexico, and enforcement in the US.

5.2 Europe

There were 32.5 million foreigners in the EU-27 nations in 2010, including 31 million in the EU-15 countries. Over 20 million of these foreigners were not citizens of EU member states, while 12 million were EU citizens, such as Poles in the UK. There were an estimated 2–4 million unauthorized foreigners in the EU (Biffl, 2012).

A larger number of EU residents were born outside the country in which they are now living, some 47 million, suggesting 15 million naturalized citizens, 90% in the EU-15 member states (the US has 17 million naturalized citizens). Most foreign-born residents are in four countries: Germany, 9.5 million; France, 7.1 million; UK, 6.8 million; and Spain, 6.3 million.

The leading sources of intra-EU migrants are Romania, 2.2 million; Poland, 1 million; and Italy, almost a million. The leading sources of non-EU migrants are Turkey (there are about 2.5 million Turks in EU countries); Morocco, 2 million; and Albania, 1 million. Each nationality is concentrated in one or two EU countries, Turks in Germany, Moroccans in Spain and France, and Albanians in Greece and Italy.

About half of the workers aged 25–64 in the EU-27 labor force have medium skills, a quarter are university graduates, and a quarter are low-skilled, meaning they have not completed secondary school. Over 40% of non-EU nationals in the EU labor force are low-skilled. Most of these low-skilled workers are guest workers recruited in the 1960s and 1970s to work in factories and their children. During the 1970s and 1980s, these recruitment industries restructured, and many of the guest workers who lost jobs had a hard time finding new ones. Aging low-skilled guest workers, and their children and grandchildren with less-than-average levels of education, find it hard to obtain good jobs in Europe's increasingly knowledge-based economies.

New migration policies and EU enlargement have increased the share of newly arrived non-EU foreigners with higher skills; the harder it is to enter another country, the more likely that those who succeed have high skills. Central Europeans fill low-skilled jobs in EU-15 nations, as with Poles in Germany and Britain, even though southern

European countries such as Portugal have the highest shares of (native) low-skilled workers in their labor forces (70% in Portugal).

Almost all EU countries welcome highly skilled migrants, but many see low-skilled migrants as contributing more to population growth than to productivity growth. With the demand for formal low-skilled workers falling faster than supply, low-skilled non-EU nationals have much higher unemployment rates and lower earnings than natives. Furthermore, many non-EU migrant families have only one earner and a larger than average size, which reduces per-capita income in the families of non-EU migrants.

5.2.1 From emigration to immigration

Europe was shaped by emigration during the nineteenth century, while the Americas were shaped by immigration from Europe. Some 60 million Europeans left for the New World between 1820 and 1914, as industrialization, wars, and the search for economic opportunity encouraged out-migration.

After World War II, there was a reshuffling of people in order to get the "right" people inside the right borders. Many of those who had been brought to Germany to work went home to new countries or old countries with redrawn borders, while millions of Germans returned to Germany. There was also migration between colonial powers and their overseas provinces, as from France to Algeria, and between colonies and mother countries, as from India and the Caribbean to Britain.

By 1960, the major impetus for migration to Europe was economic. Western European nations such as France and Germany became manufacturing powerhouses, producing goods such as VW cars that were often exported because their currencies were undervalued. Since money went further in Europe, local savings stayed home and Americans invested in Europe.[21] The combination of very low unemployment in most European countries, a baby boom that reduced the labor force participation of women, an expanded higher education system that kept some young people out of the labor force, and better pension benefits that supported earlier retirement limited the supply of local workers at a time when there were new construction and factory jobs being created (Martin, 2004).

These unusual economic conditions in France, Germany, and other Western European countries, namely more jobs than workers at a time when nearby countries such as Italy and Spain had more workers than jobs, prompted employers to ask their governments to allow them to recruit foreign workers. The foreign workers were termed guest workers (Gastarbeiter), stressing that they were seen as one- or two-year additions to the French and German workforces rather than as immigrants invited to settle.

---

[21] The German DM was undervalued in the sense that $1 bought 5 or 6 DM rather than the 4 DM it "should" have purchased, which made dollar investments in Germany attractive for US investors and discouraged German investors from investing in the US, since they could buy fewer dollars.

If employers still needed foreign workers after the two-year period was up, the assumption was that guest workers would return to their countries of origin with savings and be replaced by fresh recruits.

Europe's economic boom lasted far longer than anticipated, and both employers and guest workers wanted to prolong their stays. Employers did not want to send experienced workers home, while the young guest workers quickly adapted to life abroad and did not want to return to lower wages and perhaps joblessness in Italy, Greece, and other poorer countries. Guest workers gained the right to change jobs and have their families join them with longer stays, and some settled in the cities near their jobs, so that the population of foreigners rose faster than the number of foreign workers. As excess supplies of workers in Greece, Italy, and Spain diminished, France, Germany and other European countries looked further afield for guest workers, to Turkey, Yugoslavia, and Morocco.

Most European nations stopped the recruitment of guest workers in 1973–74, when oil price hikes induced recessions and the restructuring of manufacturing-based economies. European governments did not force guest workers to leave, even if they lost their jobs and were collecting welfare benefits. France and Germany offered bonuses to settled migrants who left, but most guest workers knew that economic conditions were even more difficult at home and elected to stay. European nations today are struggling to integrate these guest workers and their children, who often have unemployment rates that are two or three times higher than the rates of natives. For example, with the unemployment rate for Turkish youth twice the rate of German youth, there are worries that more Turkish migration could add to joblessness and the underclass rather than employment.

5.2.2 Freedom of movement

The European Union includes 27 of Europe's 50 countries and two-thirds of its 740 million people. A core principle of the EU is "freedom of movement," meaning that a citizen of an EU member state may travel to another EU member state and work there on an equal basis with natives. For example, a French worker who applies for a job at VW in Germany must be treated just like a German applicant, and can complain if a private employer discriminates in favor of local workers (public sector jobs can be restricted to nationals of the country).

Relatively few EU nationals move from one country to another, although an increasing number of northern Europeans retire in southern European countries such as Spain and Portugal and more young people are studying outside their country of citizenship as curricula are standardized and teaching in English spreads. The EU added 10 member states in Central Europe in 2004, and Bulgaria and Romania joined in 2007. However, the so-called "old" EU-15 countries that recruited guest workers and got unanticipated settlers, such as France and Germany, were reluctant to allow Poles, Czechs, and Romanians immediate freedom of movement to seek jobs.

The EU negotiated seven-year waiting periods before Greek, Spanish, and Portuguese workers got freedom of movement rights in the 1980s. EU-15 countries were allowed to restrict migration for up to seven years for the countries that joined the EU in 2004 and 2007. Based in part on projections that few Central Europeans would emigrate, three old EU-15 nations, Ireland, Sweden, and the UK, decided not to restrict migration from the so-called "new accession" countries; the 12 others did. In a major surprise, over a million Eastern Europeans, mostly Poles, moved to the UK and Ireland to work. Even though the British government concluded that the migrants were economically beneficial, the backlash against "too much migration" prompted the UK and other EU governments to deny freedom of movement to Bulgarian and Romanian workers after these countries joined the EU (Parker, 2007).

Immigration was a major issue in May 2010 elections that brought a new coalition Conservative–Liberal Democrat government to power; it pledged to reduce net annual migration from 242,000 in 2010 to less than 100,000 by 2015. Between 1997 and 2009, net migration to the UK was 2.2 million, an average 183,000 a year, reflecting the policy of the Labor government elected in 1997 to expand immigration to bolster economic growth. However, sensing the growing opposition to immigration, the Labor government introduced a five-tier entry system to reduce the influx and rationalize the immigration system in 2007.[22]

The new British system may provide a model for other EU countries. It provides three tiers or entry channels for foreign workers, one for students, and one for working holidaymakers. Non-EU foreigners coming to work in the UK are divided into three groups: Tier 1 is for highly skilled workers who do not need a British job offer, Tier 2 is for skilled workers with a British job offer, and Tier 3 is for low-skilled workers but currently is suspended, meaning there are no admissions). Tier 4 is for students and Tier 5 is for other temporary workers, including working holidaymakers and athletes. The British government also created an independent Migration Advisory Committee to answer three "S" questions posed by the government when employers request permission to employ foreign workers, namely, is the job in question skilled, is there a labor shortage, and is admitting foreign workers the sensible response?

5.2.3 Turkey and Germany

Most foreigners in EU countries are from outside the EU, from countries such as Morocco, the ex-Yugoslavia, and Turkey. Some of these non-EU countries, including Croatia and Turkey, could become EU member states, which would give Croatians and Turks freedom of movement rights throughout an enlarged EU.[23] Turkey applied for EU entry in 1987, was rebuffed in 1989, and has been in accession negotiations since 2005, but fears of too much migration have complicated Turkey's accession negotiations.

---

[22] The new system collapsed 80 entry doors to five, although some of the five have subcategories (www. ukba.homeoffice.gov.uk/visas-immigration/working).

[23] Joining the EU means being accepted as a candidate, fulfilling the so-called Copenhagen criteria of having a democracy and market economy, and accepting or negotiating exceptions and transition periods to the 35-chapter, 80,000-page acquis communitarie, the law of the EU.

Turkey is a growing a country of 77 million. Some 2 million Turks worked in Western European countries in the 1960s and 1970s, and many settled, and at the time of writing there were 3.5 million Turks in Western Europe, two-thirds in Germany. These Turks, and their children and grandchildren, have high unemployment rates, in part because many have not learned German.

Fears that Turkish-speaking ghettos could become a source of poverty and Islamic fundamentalism in the heart of Europe complicate Turkey's bid to join the EU. Ex-banker Theo Sarrazin, whose 2009 best-selling book argued that poorly integrated Turks and other Muslims threaten Germany's viability, argued that a growing underclass will cause increasing problems. Sarrazin's many critics agree that Turks generally, and second- and third-generation Turks in particular, lag behind Germans in school completion rates and employment. However, they say the reasons for slow Turkish integration lie with successive German governments that did not develop effective integration policies and in the failure of many Germans to welcome foreigners.

Germany is a social welfare state, which helps to explain a fundamental difference between US and German attitudes toward low-skilled migrants who do not learn English and German. In the US, lack of education and English are seen primarily as a private problem for the migrant and his/her family, with spillover effects restricted to perhaps additional welfare payments and more crime. In Germany, by contrast, low-skilled foreigners and their children are generally eligible for welfare benefits, so the failure of some foreigners to learn German and find jobs is seen as a burden for German taxpayers and society.

Turkey is negotiating with the European Commission in Brussels, the executive responsible for proposing common migration policies among the EU member nations. The EU divides issues into three groups or pillars, and migration is a third-pillar issue. First-pillar issues are those that are the primary responsibility of the EU Commission and Parliament, such as trade and agricultural policy, second-pillar issues are those that are the responsibility of national governments, such as defense policies, and third-pillar issues are those in which responsibility is shared between the EU and member governments, including immigration. The Commission has made significant progress developing uniform rules for dealing with asylum seekers. Under so-called Dublin rules, foreigners seeking asylum must apply in the first safe country they reach, and the decision made as to whether the foreigner is a refugee is binding on other EU member states.

5.2.4 EU: Europe needs migrants

The European Commission has been less successful in persuading EU member states to open doors to more immigrants. The Commission persuaded national governments to approve a Blue Card program to admit non-EU foreign professionals, such as computer programmers from India and health-care workers from Africa, issuing work and residence permits to those that have university degrees and a job offer that pays at least

1.5 times the average gross salary (1.2 times in labor-short occupations). Blue Card holders can have their permits renewed and, after five years in the EU, can apply for permanent residence status.[24] The EU dimension is that, after 18 months in the EU member state that admitted them, Blue Card holders have the right to move to another EU member state and work there.

The Commission and many EU member states complain that they receive too many low-skilled migrants and too few highly skilled migrants. In a bid to discourage unwanted low-skilled migration, the Commission and several EU member states have signed "mobility partnership agreements" with migrant-sending countries that require a country such as Senegal to police its harbors to discourage migrants from leaving in small boats for Spain's Canary Islands. In return, the Spanish government promised to admit several thousand Senegalese to work legally for a year or two. Spain and Italy have signed mobility partnership agreements with countries from Albania to Senegal, and the EU has funded migrant resource centers in many migrant-sending countries to discourage illegal migration by providing information on jobs available to those who migrate legally.

Europe is aging and shrinking. Today there are four workers for each retiree, a ratio expected to shrink to two workers per retiree in 2050. In order to finance the retirement of baby boomers at current pension and benefit levels, EU countries will have to reduce benefits, encourage more people to work longer, or add workers to the labor force by raising fertility or increasing immigration. Most European countries already have pro-natalist policies, such as making monthly payments to families with children, such as Sweden's program that provides several hundred dollars a month for each child, and raises the allowance for three or more children. Germany in 2007 expanded the payments to new mothers, most of whom get two-thirds of their net or after-tax earnings for a year, with low-income mothers eligible for 100% of their previous net earnings.

In addition to raising fertility, European countries could increase immigration to stave off population decline. However, the number of immigrants would have to be very large. In 1995, the Big Four EU countries, France, Germany, Italy, and the UK, included two-thirds of EU-15 residents (those in the 15 EU countries before enlargement in 2004 and 2007) and received 88% of EU-15 immigrants.

There are three demographic targets that policymakers could aim for:

1. To maintain their 1995 populations at mid-1990s fertility rates, immigration into the Big Four EU countries would have to triple, from 237,000 a year to 677,000 a year (Table 14.8).
2. To maintain their 1995 labor forces, the Big Four would have to increase immigration fourfold to 1.1 million a year.

---

[24] EU member states decide who to admit, and member states decide whether the employer or the foreigner submits the application for the EU Blue Card, which can be valid from one to four years. Blue Card holders can have their families join them within six months, and their spouses can receive work permits.

Table 14.8 Immigration required to avoid population decline in Europe

Average annual number of migrants required: 2000–2050

	Actual immigration in 1995 (thousands)	Immigration required to maintain 1995 pop. (thousands)	Multiple of 1995 immigration	Immigration required to maintain 1995 working-age population (thousands)	Multiple of 1995 immigration	Immigration required to maintain pop. support ratio* (thousands)	Multiple of 1995 immigration
EU (15 countries)	270,000	949,000	4	1,588,000	6	13,480,000	50
Big 4 EU	237,000	677,000	3	1,093,000	5	8,884,000	37
France	7000	29,000	4	109,000	16	1,792,000	256
Germany	204,000	344,000	2	487,000	2	3,630,000	18
Italy	6000	251,000	42	372,000	62	2,268,000	378
United Kingdom	20,000	53,000	3	125,000	6	1,194,000	60
Other EU countries	33,000	272,000	8	495,000	15	4,596,000	139
United States	760,000	128,000	0	359,000	0	11,851,000	16

*Migrants necessary to maintain 1995 population ratio of persons ages 15–64 to those ages 65 or older.
Source: United Nations, Replacement Migration: Is It A Solution to Declining And Aging Population? <www.un.org/esa/population/publications/migration/migration. htm>.

3. To "save social security," which means keeping the ratio of persons 18–64 years old to persons 65 and older at 1995 levels, immigration would have to increase 37-fold, to almost 8.9 million a year.

Most Europeans do not want more immigrants. EU nations currently receive 300,000–500,000 legal newcomers a year, including returning citizens, family members of settled foreigners, guest workers, and asylum applicants; there are also several hundred thousand unauthorized foreigners. In countries that have generous welfare states and strictly regulated labor markers such as Sweden, unemployment rates for foreigners from outside the EU are two or three times the rates for natives and EU nationals. In countries with less regulated labor markets and less generous welfare states such as Spain, unemployment rates for non-EU foreigners are often lower than for natives.

5.2.5 Norway, Switzerland, and Russia

Not all European countries that receive migrants are EU member states, and four non-EU member states have a free-movement agreement with the EU under the European Free Trade Agreement: Iceland, Norway, Switzerland, and Liechtenstein. Norway was the world's richest country in 2010 due to North Sea oil, with a per-capita income of $85,000, compared to $47,000 in the US and $43,000 in Germany. Over 11% of Norway's almost 5 million residents are immigrants, almost half of whom have become naturalized Norwegians. Norway's anti-immigrant Progress Party is the second largest, winning almost a quarter of the vote in September 2009 elections. Norway was also the scene of a massacre by a fundamentalist Christian who opposed multiculturalism and Muslim immigration, Anders Behring Breivik, who killed over 70 people on July 22, 2011.

Switzerland is the world's second richest country, with a per-capita income of $70,000 in 2010, and has one of the world's highest shares of foreign-born residents, over 20%.[25] Most of Switzerland's migrants are from EU countries, including France and Germany, but many are from ex-Yugoslavia and an increasing number are from African countries. Switzerland has one of Europe's strongest anti-migrant political parties, the Swiss Peoples Party (SVP), which won almost a quarter of the vote in October 2011 elections. The SVP drew attention to its anti-migrant message with billboards showing white sheep on a Swiss flag kicking out a black sheep, with the tag line "for security," a reference to the SVP's call to deport foreign criminals.

Russia is the most populous European country, with 143 million residents in 2010, and the country with the most immigrants, estimated by the UN at 12 million.[26] The government's goal is to raise the population to 145 million by 2025, but not via immigration.

---

[25] There were 1.7 million foreigners among the 8.2 million Swiss residents in 2010, including 1.1 million foreigners from EU countries.

[26] The Federal Migration Service estimated 9.7 million legal foreigners in Russia in 2010, including 6 million migrant workers.

Immigrants in Russia, most of whom are nationals of the 11 ex-USSR countries in the Commonwealth of Independent States, can enter Russia without visas, but are supposed to obtain work permits before going to work.[27] Many do not, so that Tajiks, Uzbeks, and other CIS nationals are vulnerable to being underpaid and harassed by authorities.

Wages are much higher in Moscow and St Petersburg than in poor and agricultural CIS countries that range from Armenia to Moldova to Uzbekistan, and migration networks have evolved to help migrants to find jobs in Russian cities that can pay much higher wages than can be earned at home. Russian nationalists use a holiday celebrated to mark the end of foreigners in Russia, November 4, to call for an end to immigration from Muslim nations with slogans such as "Russia for Russians" and "Migrants today, occupiers tomorrow." President Vladimir Putin signed a decree in May 2012 requiring migrant workers to pass a Russian language test to receive work permits, and said that penalties on unauthorized migrants and their employers would increase.

5.3 Asia and the Middle East

Asia is home to 60% of the world's people but less than 30% of the world's international migrants. Asia's 50+ countries represent migration extremes. Japan, China, and Indonesia have very few migrant workers, while Gulf oil-exporting countries rely on migrants to fill over 90% of private sector jobs. There is also significant rural–urban migration within countries, including almost 20% of the 1.4 billion Chinese who live away from the place in which they are registered, typically young rural men and women who move from interior to coastal provinces to work in factories and on construction sites.

Asian nations perceive themselves to be different in managing migration. Unlike traditional immigration countries such as Canada and the US, or reluctant countries of immigration in Europe, almost no Asian nation considers itself a destination for settler immigrants. Instead, Asian nations see themselves as sending and receiving temporary or contractual workers, meaning that most migration is labor or guest-worker migration involving two to three years in destination countries.

Two other factors distinguish international migration in Asia. First, among migrant-receiving countries, there is more diversity in national labor migration policies than in national economic policies, which generally stress high savings and foreign investment to create jobs that employ local and migrant workers to produce goods that are exported. Migration policies form a triangle, marked by Singapore's welcome-the-skilled and rotate the low-skilled at one corner, Japan welcoming skilled foreigners and getting few while resisting low-skilled guest workers, and the Gulf Cooperation Countries depending on migrants to fill over 90% of private-sector jobs. Second, there appears to be convergence in the migration policies of labor-sending governments, with countries from Bangladesh to Vietnam aiming to send more skilled workers abroad and to diversify the destinations of migrants to include more high-wage European and North American destinations.

---

[27] Georgia withdrew from the CIS in 2009, but remains a "participant."

Most international labor migration in Asia involves workers moving from one Asian nation to another for temporary employment. The first significant flows of workers in the Asia-Pacific region began after oil price hikes in 1973–74, when Gulf oil exporters turned to foreign contractors who hired foreign workers to build infrastructure projects such as roads and bridges. As the demand for labor shifted from construction to services, and from men to women, there were predictions that Arab migrants would replace Asians in GCC countries for language and cultural reasons (Birks and Sinclair, 1980). This did not happen and, despite efforts to "nationalize" Gulf workforces by prohibiting foreigners from filling some jobs, mostly Asian migrants continue to fill almost all private sector jobs in the oil-exporting countries.

There is also migration from poorer to richer Asian countries, as Indonesians move to Malaysia and Burmese to Thailand. Many of these intra-ASEAN migrants are unauthorized despite periodic legalizations and efforts to curb the rising share of migrants in the workforces of many sectors, from agriculture and construction to garments and electronics manufacturing.

5.3.1 Singapore and Japan

The migration policies of the major Asian countries receiving migrants can be framed by a triangle. At one corner is Singapore, which welcomes foreign professionals and their families to settle but rotates less-skilled migrant workers in and out of the country. Hong Kong is another city state with a welcome-the-skilled and rotate-the-unskilled migrant worker policy. As the financial and supply chain hub for southeastern China, the Hong Kong government has, since 1999, allowed employers to hire foreigners with professional skills not available locally who are paid market wages (in the first decade, half of such migrants had Ph.D.s). Foreign professionals may arrive with their families and receive permanent residence status after seven years.

Japan and South Korea, by contrast, are homogeneous societies largely closed to foreigners; less than 2% of residents are foreigners. In both countries, foreign professionals and the descendents of past emigrants, ethnic Koreans and ethnic Japanese can stay in the country indefinitely, but there is a contrast in policies toward the low-skilled. In Japan, unauthorized foreigners, trainees, and students fill low-skilled jobs, while Korea since 2004 has hired guest workers paid the minimum wage under the Employment Permit System to fill jobs in manufacturing, construction, and agriculture.

Many Japanese leaders want to open doors wider to migrant workers, but most Japanese in opinion polls oppose especially low-skilled guest workers, in part because foreigners are often associated with crime.[28] Ex-Prime Minister Junichiro Koizumi expressed the feelings of many Japanese toward low-skilled foreigners in 2005 by saying:

---

[28] Most of the 200,000 visa overstayers in 2008 were from the same countries as most of the foreigners living in Japan, Korea, China, and the Philippines. The Chinese seem to arouse the most fear (Onishi, 2008).

"Just because there is a labor shortage does not mean we should readily allow [migrants] to come in" (quoted in Kashiwazaki and Akaha, 2006).

Korea made one of the world's most rapid transitions from sending workers abroad to receiving migrant workers. The number of Korean migrants in GCC oil exporters peaked in 1981; the Korean government had encouraged Korean construction firms to bid on contracts to provide jobs for Korean workers who were laid off as a result of the recession induced by higher oil prices in the mid-1970s. The experience gained by Korean firms and workers in the Middle East was applied to large-scale infrastructure projects in Korea in the 1980s.

South Korea began to run out of entry-level workers in the 1980s, and in 1991 allowed employers to hire foreign trainees who were supposed to learn skills in Korea that could be applied in Korean-owned factories in their countries of origin. The small and mid-sized Korean manufacturers who hired most of the trainees did not have foreign operations, making the trainee program effectively a low-skilled guest-worker system. The Korean government acknowledged that trainees were guest workers with the first European-style guest-worker program in Asia, the Employment Permit System in 2004, which permits foreigners to work up to four years and 10 months in Korea. Citizens of 15 Asian countries, from China to Vietnam, must pass a Korean language test before they are put on lists from which Korean employers select guest workers.

5.3.2 GCC countries

The Middle East, which stretches from Western Asia to North Africa, includes countries at the sending-workers-abroad and importing-workers extremes of the spectrum. After oil prices rose in the 1970s, migrant workers were employed in GCC countries to fill jobs created by the spending of higher oil revenues on infrastructure. Some of these migrants came from countries very dependent on remittances, including Palestine, Jordan, and Lebanon.

The GCC countries of Bahrain, Kuwait, Oman, Qatar, Saudi Arabia, and the United Arab Emirates had 16 million foreigners among 45 million residents in 2012, including 9 million foreigners among the 28 million residents of Saudi Arabia. During the 1970s, most of the migrant workers were Arabs, but GCC governments encouraged often foreign employers with local partners to shift from Egyptians and Palestinians to Indians and Filipinos, especially after the 1990–91 Gulf War, reportedly to avoid security threats that could arise if Arab workers demanded a share of the oil wealth.[29] In 2010, almost three-fourths of the migrant workers in GCC countries were Asian.

Managing migrants in GCC countries relies on the sponsorship or kafala system that requires all foreigners to have a local citizen sponsor who grants permission for foreigners

---

[29] Kapiszewski noted that some Arabs regard borders imposed by colonial powers as artificial and expect the emergence of a pan-Arab state to share oil wealth.

to enter the country, monitors their stay, and approves their exit. Since the sponsor is responsible for all aspects of the foreigner's stay in the country, foreigners without a sponsor cannot legally remain in the country, so disputes over wages, accommodations, working conditions, or other work-related issues can prompt the sponsor to withdraw sponsorship and force the worker to depart.

Many sponsors are only nominally involved with the migrants they sponsor. Instead, GCC citizens sponsor foreigners in exchange for payments from employers, recruiters, and others who charge migrants $1000–2000 for three-year contracts to work in GCC countries for $200 a month. Most low-skilled migrants never meet their sponsor, dealing with sponsors only through intermediaries who may be Indians or Filipinos.

The sponsor system is roundly criticized by UN and human rights groups who allege that it leads to the exploitation of migrants. Many sponsors keep migrants' passports, limiting their mobility. Several GCC countries beginning with Bahrain are considering replacing sponsors with government agencies and ending the requirement that sponsors are liable for violations of local laws committed by migrants away from the workplace. Qatar and Saudi Arabia are considering changes to sponsorship that would allow migrant workers to petition the government agency that acts as a worker's sponsor to change employers.

Saudi Arabia and GCC countries have attempted to "nationalize" their workforces by restricting an ever-lengthening list of private sector jobs to natives. Instead of replacing foreigners with natives, nationalization so far has resulted mostly in ghost employees, natives on the payroll who do not work. Native youth in GCC countries mostly shun the private sector jobs filled by migrants as requiring too much work for too little pay. The Saudi government is building six new "economic cities" with the help of migrant workers that aim to employ Saudis in white-collar private sector jobs.

Thailand and Malaysia are examples of middle-income countries that attract migrants from poorer neighbors, especially Burma and Indonesia. Thailand has about 2 million foreign workers, 5% of the Thai labor force, and they are concentrated by industry, occupation and geography, with most employed as laborers in agriculture and fisheries, construction, manufacturing such as garments, and domestic helpers in Bangkok and the richer southern part of the country. Malaysia has a similar number of migrants in a smaller labor force, and the migrants are similarly concentrated. Governments in Thailand and Malaysia are criticized regularly for their treatment of migrant workers.

5.3.3 Migrant-sending countries

The Philippines sends more workers abroad than any other Asian country. According to the government, there are 96 million Filipinos at home and 9 million abroad. Remittances top $20 billion a year, equivalent to 10% of GDP. The Philippines may be the only large country that has a fully developed "migration economy," with government offices devoted to preparing workers to go abroad and welcoming them home, and an entire migration infrastructure that ranges from educational institutions teaching nursing to Canadian and US standards to recruiters who obtain foreign job offers and train seamen, entertainers, and other types of workers for foreign jobs.

Over 1.5 million Filipinos left for overseas jobs in 2012, an average of over 3800 a day or the equivalent of 10 large airplanes. About three-fourths are land-based and a quarter fill jobs on the world's ships, where Filipinos are the most common nationality. In recent years, two-thirds of those leaving the Philippines to work abroad had been employed overseas before, meaning that many Filipinos work abroad, return home to rest, and then go abroad again.

The Filipino government, which is obliged by Republic Act 8042 to protect Filipinos abroad, has one of the best systems for managing the outflow of workers. Most Filipino migrants leave legally, and the Philippine Overseas Employment Administration reviews worker contracts before departure (Abella et al., 2004). The several thousand Filipino recruiters must be licensed, and the fees they can charge migrants are regulated. One unusual law makes Filipino recruiters jointly liable with foreign employers to fulfill the terms of migrant worker contracts, which means that returning workers can complain to the POEA and, if they have valid complaints, the Filipino recruiter who sent them abroad must cover any unpaid wages or benefits that cannot be collected from the foreign employer.

Indonesia sends about half as many workers abroad as the Philippines, 700,000 a year, via a system that is often condemned for exploiting vulnerable migrants. Both men and women go abroad to work, but the abuse of Indonesian domestic workers in private homes in Malaysia and Saudi Arabia has prompted the Indonesian government several times to halt the departure of Indonesians leaving to be domestic helpers.[30] Indonesian domestic workers are paid less than those from other countries, sometimes only half as much as Filipinos, in part because they are less likely to understand English. The fact that many are from rural areas and not familiar with modern appliances often leads to conflicts, prompting calls for training Indonesian women before they go abroad.

South Asian countries from Bangladesh to Sri Lanka send large numbers of migrant workers abroad. Deployments of Bangladeshis reached almost 900,000 in 2008, but have since fallen because of the 2008–09 recession and recruiting irregularities that have left Bangladeshis who thought they had work permits illegally abroad because they had only tourist visas (Martin, 2012b). The Bangladeshi government tries to protect migrants abroad, but widespread corruption means that most migrants pay far more than the

---

[30] After an Indonesian woman was burned with an iron by her Malaysian employer in 2009, Indonesia banned domestic workers from leaving for Malaysia for over two years until a new MOU was signed that aimed to improve protections for Indonesian domestic workers by giving them the right to retain their passports and limiting the fees that Indonesian recruiters can charge women going abroad. Similarly, after an Indonesian domestic worker was beheaded in Saudi Arabia for killing her employer in 2011 (allegedly in self defense), Indonesia suspended deployments in order to negotiate an agreement to improve protections.

official maximum recruitment charge of 84,000 taka ($1025) for a job in Malaysia or Saudi Arabia. Once abroad, Bangladeshis are often the lowest paid migrant workers, earning $150–200 a month.

5.3.4 Israel

Israel is a special case, welcoming Jews to immigrate under the aliyah or law of return. Immigration to Israel increased rapidly after 1989 with the opening of borders in Eastern Europe and the demise of the Soviet Union. Some 200,000 immigrants arrived in 1990, when Israel had 5 million residents, and eventually a million persons from the ex-USSR migrated to Israel, although some later moved on to Germany and the US.

Israel occupied the West Bank and Gaza after wars in 1976 and 1973. During the 1970s and 1980s, over 100,000 Palestinians commuted daily to jobs in Israel. The infitada that began in the late 1980s prompted the Israeli government to limit the number of commuting Palestinians to reduce terrorist incidents, and migrants from other countries were recruited to fill the jobs once held by Palestinians. Israel today is a country of 8 million that includes about 6 million Jews, a million Israeli Arabs, and almost a million foreigners, including Filipino caregivers, Chinese construction workers, and Thai farm workers.

The Israeli government in summer 2012 was struggling with the 60,000 migrants from Eritrea and Sudan who arrived since 2005; they are often called "infiltrators," and opinion polls suggest that most Israelis would like to see them expelled. However, it is hard to return migrants to Eritrea and Sudan, so the Israeli government has placed primary emphasis on halting the influx by building a fence on its border with Egypt in the Sinai desert and a detention facility for those apprehended. The government in 2012 offered migrants from South Sudan who depart voluntarily $1300.

5.4 Africa: refugees and migrants

Africa during the 1990s was associated with long lines of people fleeing civil wars, such as Hutus and Tutsis fleeing genocide in Rwanda in the mid-1990s. Africa has a seventh of the world's people, a fourth of the world's nation states, and a fourth of the world's 10 million refugees. Many African nations host refugees from each other. There are Mauritanian refugees in Mali, and Malian refugees in Mauritania.

Africa in 1994 witnessed one of the world's largest recent refugee movements, as 2 million Rwandans left their country. Some 500,000 mostly ethnic Tutsi residents were killed in a genocide organized by the Hutu-led government and, after the Tutsi-led rebel army defeated the government's military forces, Hutu leaders encouraged Hutus to flee with them to the Congo to avoid retaliation, helping to destabilize conditions in eastern Congo.

South Africa is the major destination of sub-Saharan migrants. South African mines were used to recruit migrant workers from neighboring countries, but after the end of apartheid in 1994, the government of Nelson Mandela discouraged the recruitment of foreign miners and many of the mines invested in labor-saving machines.

As Africa's richest country, South Africa draws migrants from neighboring countries as well as from further north, and is struggling to develop a migration policy. The African National Congress party, in power since 1994, has been reluctant to deport unauthorized migrants from neighboring countries that sheltered anti-apartheid activists, so that citizens of Zimbabwe and Mozambique often move to South Africa for higher wages and find ways to stay.

Migrants in South Africa are often willing to work for lower wages and are more entrepreneurial, which can fuel resentment and xenophobia. Unemployment among Black South Africans exceeds 25%, and some of the stores in the Black suburbs surrounding major cities are operated by migrants. Resentment against migrants in these Black areas exploded in May 2008 and left over 60 migrants dead, prompting a round of soul-searching on how to better manage migration. The government has made it easier for large employers seeking to bring foreign professionals and skilled workers into the country to replace South Africans who emigrate, but has not fulfilled its promise to create jobs for South Africans (Migration News, 2012).

5.5 Oceania and Pacific islands

Oceania is the world's least populous region, with fewer than 40 million people, including almost two-thirds in Australia. Australia and New Zealand welcome immigrants from around the world and permit freedom of movement between themselves under the Trans-Tasman Travel Agreement, an informal agreement made in 1973 that allows citizens of Australia or New Zealand move freely between the countries and work in most jobs. Most of the movement is from New Zealand to Australia.[31]

Australia was originally the destination for British criminals. Beginning in 1788, some 160,000 convicts were shipped to New South Wales, then a British colony. Free British and European immigrants also arrived, and 50,000 immigrants a year arrived during the gold rushes of 1851–60. Australia encouraged immigration from Europe after World War II and ended its White Australian immigration policy in 1971, which made it easier for Asians to immigrate.

Australia admitted 185,000 immigrants in 2011–12, plus an additional 254,000 temporary visas to foreign students, 223,000 working holiday visas, and 125,000 temporary foreign worker visas (the 457 visa). In recent years, about 20% of immigrants to Australia were born in New Zealand, 14% in the UK, and 10% each born in India and China. Over half of the new arrivals settled in New South Wales, anchored by Sydney, and Victoria, whose capital is Melbourne. Australia, with 23 million residents in 2012, gets half of its annual population increase from immigration. Asians are more than half of the

---

[31] For example, in 2011–12, about 54,000 New Zealanders moved to Australia and 14,000 Australians moved to New Zealand, making net New Zealand migration to Australia 40,000 for the year.

immigrants currently arriving, and Mandarin has become the most popular language other than English spoken at home, displacing Italian.

New Zealand's immigration history is different. As one of the last places to be discovered and settled by Europeans, British settlers made a treaty with indigenous Maoris in 1840. The number of Maoris declined with disease and warfare as the number of European settlers rose, and by 1900 there were 800,000 Europeans and 40,000 Maoris. Fully independent since 1947, New Zealand admits about 35,000 immigrants a year, increasing its population by almost 1% a year with immigration.

Both Australia and New Zealand have Canadian-style point systems so that most immigrant visas go to young foreigners who have education and know English. There are several streams or doors that admit skilled immigrants, and smaller streams that admit immigrants joining family members settled in Australia and New Zealand. Australia planned to admit 168,700 immigrants in 2010–11, about the same as in previous years (another 15,000 foreigners a year arrive as refugees and asylum seekers). Two-thirds of immigrants to Australia arrive via the skill stream, meaning that someone in the household obtained enough points for knowledge of English, education, and work experience in shortage occupations. Would-be immigrants can also obtain points if they promise to settle in regional (rural) Australia.

Australia and New Zealand have traditionally welcomed settlers, not guest workers. However, both countries recently expanded their temporary-worker programs to admit both skilled and seasonal workers. Australia has a 457 visa that allows employers to request the admission of skilled foreign workers, who can remain in Australia for up to four years. The number of 457 visas issued jumped in recent years to over 100,000 a year, as did reports of abuse of foreigners seeking to make the transition from worker to immigrant.

Both Australia and New Zealand have working holidaymaker programs that allow youths aged 18–30 to work seasonally in agriculture for up to a year during a work- and study visit of up to two years. Both countries also have large numbers of foreign and language students, many of whom work part time. Both countries recently began seasonal-worker programs with Pacific islands, many of which have relatively few residents and some of which are threatened by climate change.

New Zealand launched the Recognized Seasonal Employer (RSE) in 2007, and Australia made its Pacific Seasonal Worker Pilot Scheme permanent in 2012. Both programs allow farmers to hire seasonal workers from Pacific island nations such as Tonga. New Zealand farmers first try and fail to recruit New Zealand workers before turning to RSE migrants, and promise to pay half of the migrants' transportation costs. RSE migrants come to New Zealand without their families for up to seven months. Pacific island governments regulate the recruiters who screen their citizens wishing to work in Australia and New Zealand, and can blacklist entire villages if too many migrants do not return home.

Some Pacific island countries are protectorates with unusual migration issues. The Commonwealth of the Northern Mariana Islands (CNMI) is a US territory that was allowed to make its own immigration policies. The CNMI government allowed Chinese and other firms to establish garment factories, import migrant women to sew clothes, and send them to the US with "Made in the US" labels. The number of migrant workers exploded, so that CNMI natives were less than half of residents in 2005. Congress cracked down, and required the CNMI government to follow US wage and migration laws, which is shrinking the number of guest workers.

Rising ocean levels may prompt emigration from some Pacific island countries and territories. Tuvalu is the third smallest country with fewer than 10,000 residents, including almost half in the capital city of Fanafuti, on four reef islands of about 10 square miles. Tuvalu's islands are less than three meters above sea level, making people, housing, and agriculture vulnerable to storm surges. The question for Tuvalu and similar Pacific islands is whether they should make major investments in coastal defenses against storm surges or relocate elsewhere.

6. MIGRATION AND DEVELOPMENT

There are millions of workers in developing countries who would like to move to industrial countries to earn in one hour what they earn in a day or a week at home. Should industrial countries open their doors wider to such low-wage workers?

The World Bank and many economists focused on promoting economic development say yes, pointing to the remittances to argue that migration can reduce poverty and speed development in migrant countries of origin (Bhagwati, 2003; Pritchett, 2006). These organizations and authors often see more migration from lower to higher income countries as inevitable, and call for speeding up the third wave of globalization, migration, so that people can join in the freer movement of goods (trade) and money (finance). Trade and finance are regulated by international organizations, but migration is not. National governments determine who can enter and what foreigners can do inside their borders. Some groups of nations, notably the European Union, have added free movement of labor to free flows of goods and capital within the now 27-nation group of nations, but EU member states continue to determine how many and which non-EU foreigners can enter and stay.

There are many efforts to increase international migration and to improve the governance of the migration that occurs. Pritchett (2006) argued that more migration would increase global economic output in the same way that freer trade creates more wealth by allowing countries to specialize; in the extreme, Pritchett would have some countries producing workers to send to others. Pritchett begins with five forces that promise more international migration, including persisting economic and demographic inequalities, uneven globalization, and the existence of hard-to-trade goods and services. With globalization reducing barriers to the movement of goods and services, and communications and transportation revolutions lowering the cost of information and travel, Pritchett sees liberalizing labor migration as the last frontier in globalization.

There are calls for a World Migration Organization to set rules to pry open more doors in rich countries for migrants from poorer countries. Meanwhile, governments have since 2006 met each year at the Global Forum on Migration and Development to discuss ways to improve protections for migrants and to ensure that migration contributes to development in migrant-sending nations.

It is widely agreed that an ideal world would have few barriers to international migration, and very little unwanted migration. Managing international migration in ways that protect migrants and contribute to development in both countries of origin and destination is an increasingly important global challenge. If employers recruit workers in another country who would otherwise be unemployed, if these guest workers send home remittances, and if returning migrants use skills learned abroad to raise productivity at home, migration can speed up development. However, there is no automatic link between migration and development, meaning that policy can make a difference to ensure that the window of opportunity opened by international migration results in faster development.

International migration moves people or human capital from one country to another. The three Rs summarize the impacts that migrants can have on the development of their countries of origin:

- Recruitment deals with who migrates. Are migrants persons who would have been unemployed or underemployed at home, or key employees of business and government whose departure leads to layoffs and reduced services?
- Remittances to developing countries now exceed $1 billion a day. Can the volume of remittances be increased by increasing migration and reducing the cost of transferring small sums between countries? Once remittances arrive, are they spent to improve the education and health of children in migrant families or do they fuel competition for fixed assets, as when land or dowry prices rise?
- Returns refer to migrants who come back to their countries of origin. Do returning migrants bring back new technologies and ideas and stay, do they circulate between home and abroad, or do they return to rest and retire?

The impact of the three Rs on the differences between areas that prompt migration vary across migrant-sending countries, which is one reason why the link between migration and development is often described as uncertain or unsettled (Papademetriou and Martin, 1991; Skeldon, 1997, 2008). Economically motivated migration can set in motion virtuous circles, as when young workers who would have been unemployed at home find jobs abroad, send home remittances that reduce poverty and are invested to accelerate economic and job growth, and return with new skills and technologies that lead to new industries and jobs. The result is a convergence in economic conditions and

opportunities between sending and receiving areas as predicted by the factor-price equalization theorem.[32]

The alternative vicious circle between more migration and slower development, and
thus even more migration, can unfold if employed nurses, teachers or engineers are
recruited for overseas jobs, so that the quality and accessibility in health and schooling
declines in migrant-sending areas or factories lay off workers for lack of key managers.
In the vicious circle, migrants abroad do not send home significant remittances, or send
home remittances that fuel inflation rather than create new jobs. Migrants abroad do not
return, or return only to rest and retire, so that there is only a limited transfer of new ideas,
energies, and entrepreneurial abilities. If the vicious circle unfolds, more migration can
slow development and increase the pressure for out-migration.

6.1 Recruitment

Migration is not random: Young people are most likely to move over borders because
they have the least "invested" in jobs and careers at home and the longest period to
recoup their "investment in migration" abroad. However, even among young people,
exactly who migrates is heavily shaped by the recruitment efforts of employers in destination areas, recruiting agents in sending areas, and networks that link them. For example, if employers want IT professionals and nurses, networks are likely to evolve to help
young computer specialists and nurses to move abroad. Alternatively, if foreign
employers recruit maids and farm workers, networks are likely to evolve to move
low-skilled migrants over borders.

The recruitment of migrants has been concentrated near the extremes of the education ladder. Employers in destination countries often seek migrants with college educa-
tions and low-skilled migrants. The overseas recruitment of well-educated professional
workers is generally done openly, as employers advertise and brokers or agents recruit
nurses, IT specialists, and teachers to fill foreign jobs. The result can be a virtuous or
vicious circle, with the experiences of India with IT specialists and Africa with doctors
or nurses perhaps framing the extremes.

India had only 7000 IT specialists in the mid-1980s, according to NASSCOM, but
multinationals recognized their skills, and recruited Indian IT specialists for operations outside India. Brokers soon emerged to specialize in the recruitment and deployment of Indian

---

[32] The factor-price equalization theorem assumes that there are two countries, C1 and C2, with two goods,
G1 and G2, produced by two inputs, capital and labor (Mundell, 1957). If G1 is capital intensive and G2 is
labor intensive, and the price of capital relative to labor, R/W, is lower in C1 than in C2, C1 is the capital-
intensive country and C2 is the labor-intensive country. Countries export primarily commodities that
require intensive use of the relatively cheaper factor, so that C1 should export mostly G1 to C2, while
C2 exports G2 to C1, narrowing the costs of capital and labor in the two trading countries. With wage
differences narrowing, there is less economic incentive to migrate from the lower to the higher wage
country—that is, trade is a substitute for migration.

IT workers to foreign jobs. Some Indians returned with contracts to provide computer services to the firms that had employed them abroad, and the Indian government, at the behest of the then nascent IT outsourcing industry, reduced barriers to imports of computers, upgraded the communications infrastructure, and allowed the state-supported Indian Institutes of Technologies to set quality benchmarks for IT education.

Employing Indians in India to do computer work for clients abroad became a growing industry that had important spillover effects in India. The growing outsourcing industry supported efforts to improve India's electricity and telecommunications infrastructure, promoted merit-based selection systems in higher education and employment, and improved the quality of IT services in India as Indians were offered some of the same world-class services offered to clients abroad. The virtuous circle was completed with a sharp jump in enrollment in science and engineering schools, making India a leading provider of low-cost IT specialists and services (Heeks, 1996).

By contrast, the recruitment of African doctors and nurses by hospitals in high-income countries is alleged to have set in motion a vicious circle of poorer health care just when the need for health care is growing because of AIDS and initiatives to improve immunization. Many African countries retained colonial-era education systems, so that doctors and nurses are being trained to colonial-power standards. Financially strained health-care systems in Africa often find it hard to lure doctors and nurses to poorer rural areas, so they often assign new graduates who received government support for their education to rural areas, and enforce these assignments by withholding licenses until a year or two of service is completed. The result is often a bad experience that prompts many newly licensed health-care professionals to emigrate.

Health care is a peculiar sector, with government strongly influencing the demand for health-care professionals via building hospitals and setting charges for patients and drugs and influencing the supply of health-care workers by subsidizing training and by setting salaries. Some African countries, including Ghana, Liberia, and Mozambique, have half or more of the doctors and nurses who trained in these countries abroad (Clemens and Pettersson, 2008). However, governmental efforts to limit the emigration of health-care professionals may not be the proper response to an inadequate wage in underserved rural areas, since barriers to out-migration interfere with personal rights and may be evaded. In many African countries, the number of trained nurses not employed in nursing exceeds estimates of nursing shortages.

The World Health Organization, which estimated a shortage of 4.3 million health-care workers in 40 sub-Saharan African countries in 2008, developed a best-practice code to regulate the recruitment of African health-care professionals modeled on the 2003 Commonwealth Code of Practice for International Recruitment of Health Workers. This Code calls for MOUs between the governments of countries sending and receiving health-care workers and encourages governments in countries that receive African health-care workers to subsidize training in African sending countries (Connell, 2010).

Jamaica is a commonwealth country that has one of the world's highest rates of out-migration of professionals. Three-fourths of Jamaican university graduates have emigrated, and "migration fever" is reportedly very common among university students who assume that they will have higher wages and better working conditions abroad (Thomas-Hope, 1999).[33] Jamaican Minister of Foreign Trade Anthony Hylton called for "bilateral and multilateral arrangements with countries like England and the United States, so that they pay at least a part of the training cost to the government for recruiting people that we have trained and will not necessarily benefit from their service" (quoted in Migration News, 2001).

The Philippines is a country that wants to send more health-care workers abroad. There are several differences between the Philippines and African and Caribbean countries that demand compensation for the recruitment of their health-care workers, including the fact that nursing education in the Philippines is often financed privately, so that individuals rather than governments are investing in education for foreign labor markets. Some 6500–7000 nurses graduate from Filipino nursing schools each year, and many plan to go abroad for better pay, more professional opportunities, and because of ties to relatives abroad.[34] Pay for Filipino nurses abroad was reported to be $3000–4000 a month in 2003, versus $170 a month in urban areas and $75–95 a month in rural areas of the Philippines.[35] Private recruiters compete with each other to match Filipino nurses with foreign jobs on wages and working conditions abroad as well as prospects for becoming an immigrant who can settle abroad.[36]

The government professes little concern about Filipino nurse emigration. Then-Labor Secretary Patricia Sto. Tomas in 2002 said that nurses are "the new growth area for overseas employment," and that Filipinos have a comparative advantage because of their care-giving skills and English. She said: "We won't lose nurses. The older ones, those in their mid-40s, are not likely to leave. Besides, the student population reacts to markets quickly. Enrollment is high. We won't lack nurses" (quoted in Migration News, 2002).

Instead of heath-care professionals emigrating, some developing countries are attracting foreign patients to private hospitals that provide high-quality care at lower-than-home-country prices. Health tourism, a form of Mode 2 provision of services in the GATS, brings patients to health-care workers rather than moving health-care workers over borders to patients (Connell, 2006). India in January 2004 created a task force to

---

[33] Jamaica has replaced some of its emigrant health-care workers with Cubans.

[34] The Philippines Nurses Association Inc. (PNA) estimated in 2002 that 150,885 Filipino nurses were abroad, and noted that experienced nurses with specialty training were most in demand overseas.

[35] Since it is easiest to go abroad as a nurse, some Filipino doctors, who earn $300–800 a month, are reportedly retraining as nurses so they can emigrate.

[36] For example, one agency promises Filipino nurses that their US hospital employers will sponsor them for immigrant visas (www.nursestousa.com/).

"assess the opportunities for promoting India as a health destination and recommend specific types of health facilities which can be made available for this purpose" (Financial Express, 2004), while the Malaysian government calls "health tourism" a growth industry and supports its expansion.[37]

6.2 Remittances

Remittances to developing countries, the portion of migrant incomes that are sent home, were $372 billion in 2001, over $1 billion a day. Remittances to developing countries have risen with number of migrants, and surpassed official development flows in the mid-1990s. Unlike foreign direct investment and private capital flows, remittances were stable during the 2008–09 recession, while FDI and private capital flows fell sharply (Sirkeci et al., 2012).

Remittances have two major components: workers remittances, the wages and salaries that are sent home by migrants abroad 12 months or more, and compensation of employees (called labor income until 1995), the wages and benefits of migrants abroad less than 12 months.[38] Many countries do not know how long the migrants who remit funds have been abroad, so most analyses combine workers remittances and compensation of employees when studying remittances and their effects. For example, Mexico reports most money inflows under worker remittances, while the Philippines reports most under compensation of employees. The volume of remittances depends on the number of migrants, their earnings abroad, and their willingness to remit.

A handful of developing countries receive most remittances (World Bank, 2012a). India received $55 billion in remittances in 2010, China $51 billion, Mexico $23 billion, and the Philippines $21 billion. Remittances are the largest share of the economy in a diverse group of countries, including ex-USSR countries whose Soviet industries collapsed, such as Tajikistan and Moldova, island countries such as Tonga and Samoa, and Central American countries with large diasporas in the US, including Honduras and El Salvador.

Studies demonstrate convincingly that the best way to maximize the volume of remittances is to have an appropriate exchange rate and economic policies that promise growth (Ratha, 2004). Since the September 11, 2001 terrorist attacks, many governments have tried to shift remittances from informal to formal channels—that is, via regulated financial

---

[37] About 60% of foreigners who seek treatment in Malaysia are from Indonesia, and in October 2003 the Health Ministry set fees under three packages priced between RM450 and RM1150, and has recommended floor and ceiling prices for 18 procedures performed for cardiology, orthopedics, and plastic surgery (Business Times, 2004).

[38] A third item not generally included in discussions of remittances are migrants' transfers, which is the net worth of migrants who move from one country to another. For example, if a person with stock migrates from one country to another, the value of the stock owned moves from one country to another in international accounts.

institutions such as banks. Migrants have demonstrated a willingness to transfer money via formal channels, especially if it is easy and cheap to so, but this usually requires banking outlets in migrant communities at home and abroad and competition to lower transfer costs.

The US–Mexico remittance market is unregulated, in the sense that Mexicans in the US decide on their own how and how much to remit. Several Asian countries, by contrast, have tried to specify both the amount of remittances migrants must send and the form in which they are remitted. For example, many Korean migrants in the Middle East in the late 1970s were considered employees of their Korean construction company, and had their wages paid in Korean currency to their families in Korea; they received only a small stipend in local currency while abroad. Korea no longer sends workers abroad, but some of the Chinese and Vietnamese who go abroad to work remain employees of Chinese and Vietnamese firms. Their wages are paid in the same way that Koreans were paid—namely, most go to the migrant's family or bank account in local currency. The Philippines attempted to specify how much should be remitted in the 1980s, but abandoned this forced-remittance policy after protests from migrants.

Forced-remittance programs are unpopular with migrants. Migrants from Jamaica, Barbados, St Lucia, and Dominica have been sent to US farm employers since 1943 under the auspices of the British West Indies Central Labor Organization, which charged migrants 5% of what they earned for liaison and other services. BWI CLO required US employers of Jamaican migrants to deposit 20% of each worker's earnings in a Jamaican savings bank. Returned migrants complained that they had difficulty accessing these savings in Jamaica, and received them with no interest, prompting the bank to begin paying interest.

Similarly, between 1942 and 1946, Mexican Braceros had 10% of their earnings sent from US employers directly to the Bank of Mexico. Many of the wartime Braceros say they never had these forced savings returned to them in Mexico, and the Mexican government says it has no records of what happened to the money. Suits filed in the US against Wells Fargo Bank, the US bank that transmitted the funds to Mexico, and the Mexican government in 2005 created a fund to pay former Braceros and relatives of late Braceros living in Mexico up to $3500 each.[39]

Remittances can reduce poverty and improve the lives of recipients. Most remittances are used for consumption, helping to explain their stability[40] even as exchange rates and

---

[39] The Mexican government, without admitting it lost the 10% of Bracero wages withheld by employers and sent via banks to Mexico, agreed in 2005 to pay $3500 in compensation to Braceros living in Mexico. However, only 49,000 of the 212,000 Mexican applicants could provide the required documentation to receive payments (Rural Migration News, 2009).

[40] Automatic stabilizers in developed countries, such as unemployment insurance, help to stabilize the flow of remittances to developing countries that have the same economic cycles as the countries in which their migrants work.

investment outlooks change. In an apparent paradox, remittances to high-debt and less-transparent countries may be more stable than those to middle-income open economies that attract foreign investment. Presidents of many countries, including Mexico and the Philippines, acknowledge the important contributions that remittances make to financial stability and development. Mexico has a much touted 3×1 program, matching each dollar donated by migrants abroad for government-approved infrastructure projects in migrant areas of origin with another dollar each from the federal, state, and local governments (Orozco and Rouse, 2007).

The spending of remittances can generate jobs. Most studies suggest that each $1 in remittances generates a $2–3 increase in GDP, as recipients buy goods or invest in housing, education, or health care, improving the lives of non-migrants via the multiplier effects of remittance spending (Taylor and Martin, 2001). The exit of men and women in the prime of their working initially reduces output in migrant-sending areas, but the arrival of remittances can lead to adjustments that maintain or even increase output. For example, families who lose workers to migration can shift from crops to livestock, which require less labor, and rent their crop land to other farmers, which may lower input costs with economies of scale and increase crop production.

In addition to remittances, migrants can steer foreigners' investments to their countries of origin and persuade their foreign employers to buy products from their countries of origin. For example, professionals abroad can be important sources of remittances for their countries of origin and can also steer investments from richer countries into their countries of origin. Having migrants abroad increases travel and tourism between countries, as well as trade in ethnic foods and other home-country items. Migrants abroad may undertake many other activities, including organizing themselves to provide funds for political parties and candidates. Many of these activities are informally organized, making it difficult to ascertain their volume and impacts.

6.3 Returns

The third R in the migration and development equation is returns. There is no automatic relationship that ensures more migration will generate faster development. In the virtuous circle linking migration and development, returning migrants provide the energy, ideas, and entrepreneurial vigor to start or expand businesses at home or go to work and, with the skills and discipline acquired abroad, raise productivity at home. Migrants are generally drawn from the ranks of the risk-takers at home, and if their new capital is combined with risk-taking behavior upon their return, the result can be a new push for economic development.

On the other hand, if migrants settle abroad and cut ties to their countries or origin, remittances may decline and their human capital may be "lost" to their country of origin. If migrants return only to rest and retire, they may have limited development impacts.

Finally, migrants could circulate between sending and receiving areas, and their back-and-forth circulation can contribute to economic growth in both countries.

Most cases of migration contributing to development involve countries that experienced rapid development and isolating the contribution of returned migrants. Taiwan provides an example. Taiwan invested most of its educational resources in primary and secondary education in the 1970s, so Taiwanese seeking higher education often went abroad for study, and over 90% were believed to remain overseas despite rapid economic growth in Taiwan.[41] During the 1980s, before the end of martial law, some Taiwanese abroad began to return, while others maintained "homes" in North America and spent so much time commuting that they were called "astronauts."

Taiwan's government developed the Hinschu Science-based Industrial Park in 1980 to create a rival to Silicon Valley and provided financial incentives for high-tech businesses to locate in Hinschu, including subsidized Western-style housing (Luo and Wang, 2002). The park was a major success, employing over 100,000 workers in 300 companies with sales of $28 billion by 2000. About 40% of the park's companies were headed by returned overseas migrants, and 10% of the 4100 returned migrants employed in the park had Ph.D. degrees.

The Taiwanese experience suggests that investing heavily in the type of education appropriate to the stage of economic development, and tapping the "brain reserve overseas" when the country's economy demands more brainpower, can be a very successful development strategy. Then Chinese leader Premier Zhao Ziyang called Chinese abroad "stored brainpower overseas," and encouraged Chinese cities to offer financial subsidies to attract them home, prompting the creation of "Returning Student Entrepreneur Buildings."[42] However, most Chinese who studied abroad remain abroad: 580,000 went abroad since 1979, but only 25% returned by 2002.

The poorest countries that are developing slowest pose the largest challenge to encouraging returns. The International Organization for Migration (IOM) operates a return-of-talent program for professional Africans abroad, providing them with travel and housing assistance and wage subsidies if they sign two-year contracts that require them to work in the public sector of their country of origin. The United Nations Development Program has a similar Transfer of Knowledge Through Expatriate Nationals (TOKTEN) program that subsidizes the return of teachers and researchers.

Many of the professionals involved in such return-of-talent programs have an immigrant or long-term secure status abroad and remain in their country of origin only a year or two. Expanding return-of-talent programs could become very expensive, since it is

---

[41] These students were highly motivated to pursue advanced studies. Before they could do abroad, they had to complete two years of military service and obtain private or overseas financing.

[42] Shanghai reportedly has 30,000 returned professionals, 90% with M.S. or Ph.D. degrees earned abroad, who are employed or starting businesses (Tempest, 2002; Kaufman, 2003).

widely asserted that there are two or three African-born professionals outside Africa for every non-African professional trying to speed development in Africa. Sussex University's Richard Black called subsidized return-of-talent programs "expensive failures," since they bring temporary return, but not the "investment that [return] should bring" (quoted in Beattie, 2002), although in another report the conclusion was softened to "there is much uncertainty about the impacts of migration and return on development (Ammassari and Black, 2001, p. 40).

Even if migrants do not return, they could contribute to development in their countries of origin in other ways. Many analysts point to the potential of "circular migration" to speed development, or diaspora-led development that involves especially skilled emigrants promoting trade links with and investments in their countries of origin. Some recommend that migrant-sending governments maintain links to their citizens abroad by permitting or allowing dual nationality or dual citizenship. In one optimistic scenario, Bhagwati (2003) imagined "a Diaspora model [of development], which integrates past and present citizens into a web of rights and obligations in the extended community defined with the home country as the center." Bhagwati wants migrant-receiving governments to send some of the taxes levied on the migrant incomes in rich countries to their countries of origin.

Migrants abroad can generate social as well as monetary remittances, as when they demand honesty in government or more democracy when they return (Levitt and Levitt, 1998). Migration exposes people to new opportunities as well as new ideas, and most of the research focuses on how migrants moving from poorer to richer countries transmit ideas that increase the emphasis on hard work, the importance of education, and savings and investment. There are many proposals but few concrete examples of migrants and diasporas formally advising or intervening in the governments of their countries of origin to speed development. Some of the Mexicans who migrated to the US were elected to office in Mexico, but their plans to speed up development were not always well received.[43]

It should also be acknowledged that diasporas may slow rather than speed economic development in their countries of origin. Diasporas sometimes support and fund one side in civil wars and conflicts, as in Sri Lanka, prolonging them (Orjuela, 2008). Government fears that the diaspora could favor one side in an internal conflict are the reason why some governments are reluctant to engage their diasporas.

---

[43] Andres Bermudez, California's so-called Tomato King, was elected mayor of his 60,000 resident hometown, Jerez, in the state of Zacatecas. He first won election in 2001, but that victory was set aside because he had not lived in the town for 12 months. The residency requirement was reduced to six months and he was hailed as a binational symbol when he was elected mayor in 2004. He served as mayor for two years before making a failed bid for Mexico's federal congress (Quinones, 2009).

7. CONCLUSIONS

Most industrial countries have several temporary-worker programs. Most are unilateral, meaning that migrant-receiving governments establish rules that employers must follow in order to receive permission to employ foreign workers. After receiving government approval to hire foreign workers, some countries allow employers to recruit migrants anywhere, subject only to sending-country rules, while others require employers to follow recruitment and employment rules that are set out in bilateral agreements. Many bilateral programs have goals beyond filling vacant jobs, including promoting development in areas of migrant origin, training migrants, and facilitating the return of unauthorized foreigners.

Most policies toward these temporary workers in effect welcome skilled workers to settle and aim to rotate low-skilled workers through permanent jobs. If the three Rs of recruitment, remittances, and returns lead to economic convergence between labor-sending and labor-receiving countries, labor migration has a "natural end," and guest-worker programs help to manage declining labor migration flows. In these cases, migration can be a win–win–win proposition for migrants, employers, and sending and receiving governments, but there are enough counter examples to know that there is no automatic mechanism to assure win–win–win outcomes. Determining why some cases produce desirable outcomes for all parties, and others do not, could be accelerated by close examination of the extremes to determine which variables are most important.

There has been a proliferation of sector-specific guest-worker programs aimed at rotating low-skilled migrants through particular types of jobs in higher-wage countries. Some of these, such as Canada's farm worker programs with Mexico, Guatemala, and Caribbean countries, are considered best-practice models because they operate under the terms of government-to-government MOUs, use government agencies in the source countries to handle recruitment, and include features that encourage circulation. The most important factor encouraging circulation in these low-skill programs is seasonality: The migrant has no economic reason to remain after the seasonal (farm) job ends.

ILO conventions and recommendations establish a core set of rights for migrant workers and encourage the development and sharing of best practices worked out in social dialog between unions, employers, and governments. Most best practices stress empowering migrants by providing them with information about their rights in the labor market abroad, giving them the identification and rights needed to access banks and other institutions abroad, and developing incentives to get migrants to report the worst abuses of their rights.

Giving migrants accurate information about foreign jobs, access to institutions and protections abroad, and providing incentives for migrants and employers are an important first step to close the often large gap between migrant rights and realities. As labor migration increases as a result of fast-growing labor forces in developing countries and slow-growing labor forces in industrial countries, mechanisms that align migrant, employer, and intermediary behavior with labor laws and conventions, and provide economic incentives to conform, offer the best hope for narrowing the gaps that prompt labor migration.

REFERENCES

Abella, M., Martin, P., Midgley, E., 2004. Best practices to manage migration: The Philippines. Int. Migrat. Rev. 38 (4), 1544–1559.

Ammassari, S., Black, R., 2001. Harnessing the Potential of Migratoin and Return to Promote Development. IOM Migration Research Series No.5. 5.

Beattie, A., 2002. Seeking consensus on the benefits of immigration. Financ. Times, 9, 22 July.

Benhabib, J., Jovanovic, B., 2012. Optimal migration: a world perspective. Int. Econ. Rev. 53 (2), 321–348.

Betts, A. (Ed.), 2011. Global Migration Governance. In: Oxford University Press, www.oup.com/us/catalog/general/subject/Politics/InternationalStudies/?view=usa&ci=9780199600458.

Bhagwati, J., 2003. Borders beyond control. Foreign Aff. 82 (1, January–February), 98–104.

Biffl, G., 2012. Low-Skilled Migrants in Europe. Mimeo. http://migration.ucdavis.edu/rs/more.php?id=179_0_3_0.

Birks, J.S., Sinclair, C.A., 1980. International Migration and Development in the Arab Region. ILO.

Business Times, 2004. Robust growth in revenue for health tourism sector. 4 February, Business Times (Malaysia).

Commission on Agricultural Workers, 1992. Final Report. US Government Printing Office, Washington, DC.

Connell, J., 2006. Medical tourism: Sea, sun, sand and … surgery. Tour. Manage. 27 (6, December), 1093–1100. www.sciencedirect.com/science/article/pii/S0261517705001871/.

Connell, J., 2010. Migration and the Globalisation of Health Care: The Health Worker Exodus? Edward Elgar.

Craig, R., 1971. The Bracero Program: Interest Groups and Foreign Policy. University of Texas Press, Austin.

CRS, Congressional Research Service, 1980. Temporary Worker Programs. Background and Issues. Prepared for US Senate Committee on the Judiciary, February.

Financial Express, 2004. Govt sets up task force on health tourism. Financial Express. 11(January).

Heeks, R., 1996. India's Software Industry: State Policy, Liberalisation and Industrial Development. Sage Publications, http://dl.acm.org/citation.cfm?id=524286.

Kashiwazaki, C., Akaha, T., 2006. Japanese Immigration Policy: Responding to Conflicting Pressures. Migration Information Source. www.migrationinformation.org/Profiles/display.cfm?ID=487.

Kaufman, J., 2003. China reforms bring back executives schooled in US. Wall. St. J. 6 (March).

Kindleberger, C., 1967. Europe's Postwar Growth - The Role of Labor Supply. Harvard University Press, Cambridge, MA.

Kuptsch, C. (Ed.), 2006. Merchants of Labor. In: ILO, Geneva www.ilo.org/public/english/bureau/inst/publications/books.htm.

Kyle, D., Koslowski, R., 2011. Global Human Smuggling: Comparative Perspectives. Johns Hopkins University Press. http://jhupbooks.press.jhu.edu/ecom/MasterServlet/GetItemDetailsHandler?iN=9781421401980&qty=1&source=2&viewMode=3&loggedIN=false&JavaScript=y.

Lemert, C., 2005. Social Things: An Introduction to the Sociological Life. Rowman & Littlefield.

Levitt, P., 2001. The Transnational Villagers. University of California Press.

Levitt, P., Levitt, P., 1998. Social remittances: Migration driven local-level forms of cultural diffusion. Int. Migrat. Rev. 32 (4, Winter), 926–948. http://www.jstor.org/stable/2547666.

Luo, Y.-L., Wang, W.-J., 2002. High-skill migration and Chinese Taipei's industrial development. In: International Mobility of the Highly Skilled. OECD, Paris, pp. 253–270. www.oecd.org/sti/innovationinsciencetechnologyandindustry/internationalmobilityofthehighlyskilled.htm.

Maingot, A.P., 1999. Emigration dynamics in the Caribbean. The cases of Haiti and the Dominican Republic. In: Appleyard, R. (Ed.), Emigration Dynamics in Developing Countries. 3, Mexico, Central America and the Caribbean, Ashgate, Brookfield, VT, pp. 178–231.

Marshall, R., 2007. Getting Immigration Reform Right. EPI Briefing Paper #186, March, www.sharedprosperity.org/bp186.html.

Martin, P., 1983. Labor-intensive agriculture. Sci. Am. 249 (4 October), 54–59.

Martin, P., 1993. Trade and Migration: NAFTA and Agriculture. October. Institute for International Economics, Washington, DC. http://www.iie.com/.

Martin, P., 2003. Promise Unfulfilled: Unions, Immigration, and Farm Workers. Cornell University Press, Ithaca.

Martin, P., 2004. Germany: Managing migration in the 21st century. A Global Perspective. In: Cornelius, W.A., Tsuda, T., Martin, P.L., Hollifield, J.F. (Eds.), Controlling Immigration. Stanford University Press, pp. 221–252. www.sup.org/book.cgi?id=4189.

Martin, P., 2008. Managing Mexico–United States migration: Economic and labor issues. In: Escobar, A., Martin, S. (Eds.), Mexico–U.S. Migration Management: A Binational Approach. Lexington Books, pp. 61–88. https://rowman.com/ISBN/9780739125779.

Martin, P., 2009. Importing Poverty? Immigration and the Changing Face of Rural America. Yale University Press. http://yalepress.yale.edu/yupbooks/book.asp?isbn=9780300139174.

Martin, P., 2010. Migration and development. In: Denemark, R. (Ed.), The International Studies Encyclopedia. vol. 8. Wiley-Blackwell, pp. 5116–5138. http://isanet.ccit.arizona.edu.

Martin, P., 2012a. High-skilled migrants: S&E workers in the United States. Am. Behav. Sci. 56 (August), 1058–1079. http://abs.sagepub.com/content/56/8/1058.full.pdf+html.

Martin, P., 2012b. Reducing migration costs and maximizing human development. In: Omelaniuk, I. (Ed.), Global Perspectives on Migration and Development. Springer, www.springer.com/social+sciences/population+studies/book/978-94-007-4109-6.

Martin, P., Abella, M., Kuptsch, C., 2005. Managing Labor Migration in the Twenty-First Century. Yale University Press. http://yalepress.yale.edu/yupbooks/book.asp?isbn=0300109040.

Migration News, 2001. Latin America. Migrat. News 8 (10, October). http://migration.ucdavis.edu/mn/more.php?id=2468_0_2_0.

Migration News, 2002. Southeast Asia. Migrat. News 9 (6, June). http://migration.ucdavis.edu/mn/more.php?id=2650_0_3_0.

Migration News, 2012. South Asia, Middle East. Migrat. News 19 (4, October). http://migration.ucdavis.edu/mn/more.php?id=3797_0_3_0.

Mundell, R., 1957. International trade and factor mobility. Am. Econ. Rev. 47, 321–335.

OECD, 2004. Migration for Employment Bilateral Agreements at a Crossroads. OECD, Paris. www.oecdbookshop.org/oecd/display.asp?sf1=identifiers&st1=9789264108684.

Onishi, N., 2008. As its work force ages, Japan needs and fears Chinese labor. New York Times 15 (August).

Orjuela, C., 2008. Distant warriors, distant peace workers? Multiple diaspora roles in Sri Lanka's violent conflict. Global Network. 8 (4, October), 436–452. http://onlinelibrary.wiley.com/doi/10.1111/j.1471-0374.2008.00233.x/abstract.

Orozco, M., Rouse, R., 2007. Migrant Hometown Associations and Opportunities for Development: A Global Perspective. Migration Information Source. www.migrationinformation.org/Feature/display.cfm?id=579.

Papademetriou, D., Martin, P. (Eds.), 1991. Unsettled Relationship: Labor Migration and Economic Development, Contributions in Labor Studies No. 33. Greenwood Publishing Group.

Parker, G., 2007. UK fails to see benefits of migration. Financ. Times 18 (February).

Portes, A., Stepick, A., 1993. City on the Edge: the Transformation of Miami. University of California Press, Berkeley.

Pritchett, L., 2006. Let Their People Come: Breaking the Gridlock on Global Labor Mobility. Center for Global Development. www.cgdev.org/content/publications/detail/10174/.

Quinones, S., 2009. Andres Bermudez dies at 58; 'Tomato King' and Mexican officeholder. Los Ang. Times 8 (February).

Ratha, D., 2004. Understanding the Importance of Remittances. October Migration Information Source. www.migrationinformation.org/Feature/display.cfm?ID=256.

Reitz, J., 2013. New initiatives and approaches to immigration and nation building. In: Hollifield, J., Martin, P., Orrenius, P. (Eds.), Controlling Immigration: A Global Perspective. Stanford University Press.

Riding, A., 1989. Distant Neighbors: A Portrait of the Mexicans. Knopf.

Ruhs, M., Anderson, B. (Eds.), 2010. Who Needs Immigrant Workers? Labour Shortages, Immigration, and Public Policy. Oxford University Press. www.oup.com/us/catalog/general/subject/Economics/Labor/?view=usa&ci=9780199580590.

Ruhs, M., Martin, P., 2008. Numbers vs. rights: Trade offs and guest worker programs. Int. Migrat. Rev. 42 (1), 249–265. www.blackwellpublishing.com/journal.asp?ref=0197-9183&site=1.

Rural Migration News, 2009. H-2A re-engineering, Braceros. Rural Migration News 15 (1, January). http://migration.ucdavis.edu/rmn/more.php?id=1408_0_4_0.

Rural Migration News, 2010. Canada: Ontario, Maple Leaf. Rural Migration News 16 (1, January). http://migration.ucdavis.edu/rmn/more.php?id=1511_0_4_0.

Sirkeci, I., Cohen, J., Ratha, D., 2012. Migration and Remittances during the Global Financial Crisis and Beyond. World Bank. http://publications.worldbank.org/index.php?main_page=product_info&cPath=0&products_id=24219.

Skeldon, R., 1997. Migration and Development: A Global Perspective. Addison-Wesley.

Skeldon, R., 2008. International migration as a tool in development policy: A passing phase? Population and Development Review 34 (1, March), 1–18.

Taylor, E., Martin, P., 2001. Human capital: Migration and rural population change. In: Gardener, B., Rausser, G. (Eds.), Handbook of Agricultural Economics. vol. I. Elsevier Science, Amsterdam, pp. 457–511. http://www.elsevier.nl/.

Teitelbaum, M.S., Teitelbaum, M.S., 1980. Right versus right: Immigration and refugee policy in the United States. Foreign Aff. 59 (1, Fall), 45–46.

Tempest, R., 2002. China tries to woo its tech talent back home. Los Ang. Times. 25 (November).

Thomas-Hope, E., 1999. Emigration dynamics in the Anglophone Carribbean. In: Appleyard, R. (Ed.), Emigration Dynamics in Developing Countries. In: Mexico, III. Central America and the Caribbean. Ashgate, London, pp. 232–284.

Waldinger, R., Lichter, M., 2003. How the Other Half Works: Immigration and the Social Organization of Labor. University of California Press.

World Bank, 2005. Global Economic Prospects: The Economic Implications of Remittances and Migration. www.worldbank.org/prospects/gep2006.

World Bank, 2012a. Remittances Data. www.worldbank.org/prospects/migrationandremittances.

World Bank, 2012b. World Development Report Indicators 2012. Key Indicators of Development 392–393.

INDEX

Note: Page numbers followed by *b* indicate boxes, *f* indicate figures and *t* indicate tables.

A

Acculturation
  family formation, 316
  HIE, 275–276
  permanence, 146
ACS. *See* American Community Survey (ACS)
Adverse Effect Wage Rate (AEWR), 719–720
Africa
  doctors and nurses, recruitment of, 763
  dual citizenship, 463
  emigration, 81
  immigration policy, 78
  naturalization
    behavior and character requirements, 456
    language requirements, 456
    length of stay, 455–456
  refugees and migrants, 757–758
Age-specific fertility rates (ASFRs), 323–324
Aliens Act 1980, 449
American Community Survey (ACS), 257, 619–621
Anti-immigrant Progress Party, 751
Asia
  dual citizenship, 463–464
  guest worker program
    Bangladesh, 756–757
    Indonesia, 756
    the Philippines, 755–756
    Singapore and Japan, 753–754
  healthy immigrant effect (*see* Healthy immigrant
    effect (HIE))
  migration
    credit-ticket system, 63
    indenture, contracts of, 63
    labor market, impact of, 63–64
    restrictive policies, 66
    in southern and eastern Asia, 63
  naturalization, 456–457
  schooling (*see* Schooling)
Asylum seekers. *See also* Refugees
  administrative detention, 451
  definition, 586–587
  deportation, 451

  destination country, 587–592, 588*f*, 589*f*, 590*t*
  migration costs, 599
  political economy (*see* Political economy)
  restrictions, immigration policy, 77
  short-term protection, 451
  United States, trends in, 592–596, 593*t*, 596*f*
Atlantic economy, 94–98
Australia
  dual citizenship, 461
  holidaymaker programs, 759
  immigrant visas, 759
  language proficiency
    dichotomous variables, 245
    Evans's research, 244
    longitudinal surveys, 245
    skill-based independent immigrants, 244
  naturalization, 452–453
  permanent residents, 450
  refugee immigrants, earnings profiles of, 617
  restrictive policies, immigration, 65
  skilled immigration, 552–553

B

Borjas model, 30–31
Bracero program, 69, 734, 741–742
Brain drain
  human capital, 43–44
  immigrant selection, 73–74
British Labour Force Survey (BLFS), 492–493
British Nationality Act of 1948, 458

C

Canada
  dual citizenship, 461
  fertility, 354–355, 355*f*, 358–359
  IT sector, 565–566
  language proficiency
    census data-based study, 246, 247
    document and quantitative literacy, 247–248
    English–French bilinguals, 247
    official bilingual status, 246
    Quebec, 247

Canada (*Continued*)
   permanent residents, 450
   political economy, 679
   refugee immigrants, earnings assimilation, 617
   skilled immigration, 550–551
   temporary foreign workers
      Canadian Experience Class, 738–739
      education, 736–737
      labor shortages, 738
      language training programs, 738
      multiculturalism, 739
Canadian Citizenship Act of 1946, 457–458
Chinese Exclusion Act of 1882, 64
Citizenship
   in African countries, 459–460
   in Australia, Canada, and US, 457–458
   colonial powers, 469–470
   in Denmark, 457, 459
   economic integration, 476–481
   in France, 458–459
   in Germany, 457, 459
   human rights, 466–467
   in Japan, 460
   in Latin America, 459
   multiple/dual citizenship, 460–464
   nationhood conceptions, 467–469
   regional integration, 471
   state- and nation-building projects, 470–471
   Swedish Citizenship Act, 459
   in UK, 458
Citizenship Act, 452–453
Citizenship policy index (CPI), 453
Cohabitation
   cultural context, 341
   data limitations, 322–323
   generation status, 341–342
   Latin American immigrants, 341
   race/ethnicity, 341–342
   second demographic transition, 341
Commission on Immigration Reform (CIR),
      728–729
Commonwealth of the Northern Mariana Islands
      (CNMI), 760
Completed fertility rate (CFR), 323–324
Contract labor, 54–56
Country of origin, 158
   census-based analyses, 135, 135*f*
   cohorts, 123

cultural and linguistic affinity, 57–58
economic outcomes, 60
fertility (*see* Fertility)
financial market participation, 421–422, 422*f*,
      424, 425*t*
GDP per adult *vs.* US median initial earnings,
      135–136, 136*f*
national-origin composition, 134–135
role of, 134
selective out-migration, 492–496
skills of immigrants, 137
source-country variations, 137

D

Denmark
   citizenship acquisition, 457, 459
   naturalization
      criminal record, 453–454
      language and knowledge tests, 454
      parliament naturalization committee, 454
   permanent residents
      period of legal stay, 447–448
      voting rights, 447
Divorce
   immigrant children, cultural norms, 344
   mixed marriage, 343
   monetary compensation, 342
   risks, characteristics, 342–343
   social norms, changes in, 342
   US-born and foreign-born Mexican women,
      343–344
Djibouti, 643–644
Dominican Republic, 740
Dual citizenship
   in African countries, 463
   in Asia, 463–464
   in Australia, Canada, and US, 461
   democracy, 465
   in European countries, 462
   fairness, democracy, and inclusion, 461
   in Latin American and Caribbean countries,
      462, 463
   in Sweden, 461
Durable goods accumulation. *See* Financial market
      participation
Dyen lexicostatistical percentage
      approach, 222*b*

E

Economically active population (EAP),
    725–726, 726t
Economic assimilation, refugees
    Australia, 617
    Canada, 617
    high employment rates, 618
    human capital investment decision, 615–616
    immigrant earnings, 617
    Israel, 618
    Jewish immigrants, 618
    occupational mobility, 616–617
    resettlement policies and community
        characteristics, 618–619
    Sweden, 617
    in United States
        arrival age distributions, gender, 621, 622f
        census microdata, 619–635
        country-specific human capital accumulation,
            623t, 625
        educational attainment, 622–625, 623t
        gender composition, 621–622, 623t
        log annual earnings, 623t, 625–626
    welfare utilization, 619
Education
    earnings and post-migration investments,
        559–562
    fertility, 320
    foreign students, American schools, 202–206, 205t
    intermarriage, 337, 338–339
    non-refugees, 603–606, 605t, 631–633, 632t
    refugees, 603–606, 605t, 622–625, 623t,
        631–633, 632t
    US native and foreign-born populations
        1965 amendments, 188–189
        CPS mean education levels, 189–190, 190t
        disparities within-ethnic group, 190–191, 191f,
            192f, 193
        distribution of, 184–188, 185t, 186t
        entry cohort of immigrants, 193–195, 194t
        generational assimilation, 206–208, 207f
        illegal immigrants, 196–197
        IRCA, 189
        legal admission, visa class, 199–202, 200t, 201t
        legal permanent immigrants, 196–197, 198t,
            199–202
        less-educated migrants, out-migration of, 196
        National Origin Quota Act, 196

new legal immigrants, post-green card training,
    195–196, 195t
non-immigrants, 197, 202–203, 203f
student visa non-immigrants, 196–197
Emigration
    African countries, 81
    European emigration, 81
        cultural and linguistic affinity, 57–58
        Danish emigrants, 59
        demographic transition, 56–57
        farmers and artisans, 58
        friends and relatives effect, 57–58
        immigrant networks, 57
        intercontinental emigration (1846–1939),
            56, 57f
        Irish emigration, 57, 59
        mobility transition, 56–57
        occupational attainment, 59
        return migration, 58
        schooling, 91–93
        seasonal migration, 58
        wage gaps, 56–57
    life cycle
        industrial revolutions and demographic
            transitions, 89–91
        migration hump, 89
        mobility transition, 89
        political transitions, 91
        Third World emigration, 91
    in southern and eastern Asia, 63
    unemployment, 98–99
Enclave economy, 168
    case-study evidence, 143–144
    Cuban and Chinese immigrants, 145
    definition, 143
    earning returns, 144
    ethnic concentration effect, 144
    Korean immigrants, 145
    linguistic concentration, 144
    vs. mainstream economy, 145–146
    non-pecuniary benefits, 145
    self-employed immigrants, 145
Europe
    births, share of, 317–319, 318t
    economic outcomes, immigrants, 60
    emigration
        cultural and linguistic affinity, 57–58
        Danish emigrants, 59

Europe (*Continued*)
 demographic transition, 56–57
 farmers and artisans, 58
 friends and relatives effect, 57–58
 immigrant networks, 57
 intercontinental emigration (1846–1939),
  56, 57*f*
 Irish emigration, 57, 59
 mobility transition, 56–57
 occupational attainment, 59
 return migration, 58
 schooling, 91–93
 seasonal migration, 58
 wage gaps, 56–57
family formation, timing of, 340–341
guest worker program
 Blue Card program, 748–749
 emigration to immigration, 745–746
 freedom of movement, 746–747
 Norway, 751
 population decline, 749, 750*t*
 Russia, 751–752
 Switzerland, 751
 Turkey and Germany, 747–748
indenture system, 54–56
intercontinental migration, 53–54
mixed marriages, 316–317, 317*t*
restrictive policies, immigration, 65–66
short-distance migration, 53–54
slave trade, 54, 55*t*
total fertility rates, 317–319, 318*t*
wage effects of migration
 capital mobility, 61–62
 labor demand elasticity, 60–61, 60*f*
 land prices and rents, 62
 Swedish wages, 61
 unskilled immigration, 62
Exogamous marriages, 331, 334*t*

F
Family formation
 census data and surveys, 322
 cultural proximity, 316
 divorce (*see* Divorce)
 education, effect of, 320
 family reunification policies, 344–345
 immigrant selection, 319–320
 individual panel (longitudinal) data, 321

intermarriage (*see* Intermarriage)
 joint labor market, 320
 microeconomic models, 325–331
 migrant children, behavior of, 320–321
 synthetic cohorts, immigrants, 321
 timing of, 340–341
Family Investment Hypothesis (FIH), 150
 cohort methodology, 155–156, 157
 domestic migration, 152
 earnings growth, 157
 family investment return, 151–152
 host-country language proficiency, 153
 labor force participation, 153
 longitudinal Social Security earnings data,
  156–157, 156*f*
 market wage, 151, 152
 married immigrant women *vs.* native-born
  women earnings, 152–153
 net family gain, 152
 price of wife's non-market activity, 151–152
 reservation wage, 151, 152
Family reunification, 344–345
Fertility
 adaptation, 346*f*, 351
 ASFRs, 323–324
 births, share of, 317–319, 318*t*
 census data and surveys, 322, 323
 CFR, 323–324
 cultural norms, 358–361
 disruption, 346*f*, 348–350
 duration in destination, age at migration
  Canada, Poisson model, 354–355, 355*f*
  immigrant women, 352–354
  language proficiency, 355–357
  Mexican migrants, 352
  synthetic cohort method, 352–354
 education, effect of, 320
 gender preference, 361–362
 immigrant selection, 319–320
 immigrant women, 154
 individual panel (longitudinal) data, 321
 joint labor market, 320
 microeconomic models of, 345–346
 own-children-method, 323
 second-generation immigrants, 362–366
 selection, 346*f*, 347–348
 socialization hypothesis, 351
 TFRs, 317–319, 318*t*, 323–324, 360–361

FIH. *See* Family Investment Hypothesis (FIH)
Financial market participation
    immigrants *vs.* native-born households
        account ownership, 404, 405*t*, 412–419,
            413*t*
        bank account, 421, 427
        characteristics, 400–402, 401*t*, 402*t*, 404–409
        checking account ownership, 404, 409–412,
            410*t*, 437*t*
        children and youth, 435–436
        country of origin and host country,
            424, 425*t*
        country of origin institutional quality,
            421–422, 422*f*
        ethnic concentration, 422–424
        financial decisions, 391–392
        financial institutions, 426–427
        fixed transaction costs and risk aversion,
            392, 403
        high- and low-wage regimes, 392
        housing, 420–421
        legal status, 418–419
        linear probability model, 402–403
        non-response rates, 393
        portfolio choice, 391–392
        regressors, 402–403, 436*t*
        remittances, 424, 424*t*, 426
        return migration intentions, 424–425, 424*t*
        SIPP data, 394
        US and Italian data, 394, 430*t*, 431*t*,
            432*t*
        wealth and income, 392–393, 395–400, 396*t*
        wealth held abroad, 424*t*, 425
    socio-economic status, component of, 388
Finland
    immigrant assimilation, 525
    local voting rights, 447

G

General Agreement on Tariffs and Trade (GATT),
    82–83, 743
German Socio-Economic Panel (GSOEP), 321,
    350, 526–527
Germany
    asylum applications, 589, 590*t*
    citizenship acquisition, 457, 459
    emigration rates, 58
    fertility rates, 358–360

    permanent residents
        Constitutional Court, role of, 448
        local voting rights, 448
        period of legal stay, 447–448
    undocumented migrants, 451–452
Globalization
    economically active population, 725–726, 726*t*
    global migrants and per-capita income gaps,
        725, 725*t*
    migration networks
        communication revolution, 727
        migrant rights, 728–729
        transportation revolution, 727
Golondrinas, 58
Gravity model of migration, 6, 7
Great Depression, 8
Great Recession, 98, 99
Guest worker programs. *See* Temporary foreign
    worker programs (TFWPs)

H

Hauser and Warren socio-economic index
    (HWSEI), 632*t*, 633–634
Healthy immigrant effect (HIE)
    determinants
        acculturation, 275–276
        health care access, 274–275
        income assimilation, 275
        selective immigration, 273–274
        weight assimilation, 276–277
    factors affecting, 272
    Hispanic immigrants, 272, 308–309
    immigrant arrival cohort and assimilation effects,
        290–291
        activity limitation, 291–296, 294*t*
        Asian female, 308–309
        BMI, 302*t*
        differential period effects, 297, 309
        Hispanic female and black male, 296
        male immigrants, 309–310
        marginal effects, 296, 308
        obese, 306*t*
        overweight, 304*t*
        poor health, 292*t*
    immigrant health and assimilation measures
        activity limitation, 284
        men, 287*t*
        poor health, 284

Healthy immigrant effect (HIE) (*Continued*)
    unhealthy assimilation, 289
    weight measures, 284–290
    women, 285*t*
    National Health Interview Surveys (NHIS)
      age and schooling, 279
      employment status, 279
      health measures, 277–278
      immigrant arrival and cohort indicator
        variables, 278
      marital status, 279
      nativity groups, 278, 280*t*, 282*t*
      racial/ethnic origin groups, 278, 280*t*, 282*t*
      region of residence, 279
    weight patterns, nativity
      immigrant patterns, 299
      obese, 301*f*
      overweight, 300*f*
      unhealthy American weights, 297–299, 298*f*
HIE. *See* Healthy immigrant effect (HIE)
Hispanic immigration, 684
Human capital
    brain drain, 43–44
    budget constraints, 27
    Burda's analysis, 21
    circular migration, 42–44
    credit and poverty constraints, 32–33
    immigration policy, 29–30, 40
    income inequality, 32
    international students, 42
    labor supply, 9–10
    migration costs, 28–29, 31–32
    political institutions, 35
    remittance behavior, 40–41
    role of, 41–42
    schooling, US immigrants (*see* Schooling)
    self-selection model, 30–32
    taxes and social insurance, 34–35
    temporary and return migration, 42–43
    unemployment, 33–34
    wages
      individual *vs.* household migration decisions,
        37
      migration rate, 36
      network effects, 37
      skilled wages, 36
      trade and migration, 37–38
      unskilled wages, 36

Human rights, 466–467
Human trafficking
    economic and political turmoil, 701
    market deregulation and capital inflows, 701
    public policy, 702–703
    sex trafficking victims, 701
    sexual exploitation, 701
    supply and demand, 700

I

Illegal immigrants
    in Canada, 679
    education, 196–197
    in Europe, 677–679
    remittances, 692
    smugglers, 669–670, 673
    stock, US, 81
    unemployment rates, 33–34
Immigrant Assimilation Model (IAM), 111–112,
    164–165
Immigrant churches, 381–383
Immigrant Human Capital Investment (IHCI)
    model, 127, 163–164
Immigration Act of 1917, 64, 92
Immigration Commission, 60
Immigration Reform and Control Act (IRCA), 133,
    189, 217–218, 418–419, 742
Indenture system, 54–56
Individual attributes and motives
    admission status
      extended family and community networks,
        138–139
      kinship *vs.* skills, 138
      refugees, 139–141
    constraints, 130–131
    country of origin, 158
      census-based analyses, 135, 135*f*
      GDP per adult *vs.* US median initial earnings,
        135–136, 136*f*
      national-origin composition, 134–135
      role of, 134
      skills of immigrants, 137
      source-country variations, 137
    immigrant ability, 165–166
      country-of-origin characteristics, 129
      decline in, 128, 130
      income–distribution–ability, 129
      Roy's theory of self-selection, 128

immigrant's short-term and long-term goals, 124–125
legal *vs.* illegal immigrants, 141–142
permanence, 159–160, 170–171
  China International Project, 132
  CPS–Social Security data, 132
  legal status, 134
  Mexican Migration Project (MMP), 132, 133
  Mexican undocumented population, 133
  return to investment, 133
  secondary-sector jobs, 131
  vs. temporary immigrants, 131, 132
  wage growth, 133
schooling, 166
  high-education immigrants, 125–126, 126*t*
  higher school attendance, 127
  Indochinese immigrant, 127–128
  low-education immigrants, 125–126, 126*t*
  median entry earnings, 125–126, 125*t*, 126*t*
  skill transferability, 126–127
Individual Taxpayer Identification Numbers (ITINs), 418–419
Intercontinental migration, 53–54
Intermarriage
  as assimilation, 335–337
  divorce, 343
  education, assortative matching in, 337, 338–339
  ethnic identification, 324
  in European countries, 316–317, 317*t*
  language proficiency, 339
  race/ethnicity, 331–335, 334*t*
  references, 326*t*
  status exchange, 340
International medical graduates (IMGs)
International migration
  contract labor, 54–56
  immigrant selection
    and assimilation, 70–72
    and brain drain, 73–74
  immigration policy
    in Asia and Africa, 78
    bilateral agreements, 83
    European guest-worker programs, termination of, 76–77
    family reunification, 77–78
    GATT/WTO, multilateral agreement, 82–83
    government immigration policies, 77, 77*t*
    labor market conditions, 76–77
    labor migrants, 77–78
    open border policies, 82
    points systems, 76–77
    public attitudes, 79–80
    refugees and asylum seekers, 77
  indenture system, 54–56
  international capital flows, 66
  labor market adjustment (*see* Labor market)
  long-distance migration, 53–54
  North Atlantic triangular trade, 54
  in postwar period
    Asia, 68–69
    cultural affinities, 69–70
    friends and relatives effect, 69–70
    geographic distance, migration costs, 69–70
    Latin America and Caribbean, 68
    Middle East, 68–69
    poverty rates, 70
    proximity and policy, 69
    Soviet Union, 68
    US, annual immigration rate, 67–68
    Western Europe, 67–68
    world migrant stock, 66–67, 67*t*
  slave and non-slave migrants, Americas, 54, 55*t*
International Organization for Migration (IOM), 768

J

Jamaica, 740

L

Labor force participation (LFP), 363, 364
Labor market
  Asian migrants, 63–64
  Burda's analysis, 21
  case-study research, 167–168
  convergence, 158–159
  decline in initial earnings, 107–108, 158
    Borjas's empirical methodology, 113, 116–118, 128
    Chiswick's IAM, 114–115
    Western European immigration, 112
  destination-relevant human capital, 148
  dual labor market theory, 168
  earnings assimilation, 147
  earnings growth, 106–107
    actual *vs.* estimated earnings, 119–120, 120*f*
    country-of-origin cohorts, 123

Labor market (*Continued*)
  cross-sectional approach, 111–112, 118, 119*f*
  fixed-cohort-effect methodology, 118–119, 119*f*
  foreign-born men *vs.* US natives, 119–121, 120*f*, 121*t*
  Mexican immigrants, 121–122, 123
  selection bias, 122–123
  stationary, 118
  wage regressions, 123
  year-of-entry immigrant cohorts, 118
  zero earners and self-employed, 123–124
  educational investments, 148
  enclave economy, 168
    case-study evidence, 143–144
    Cuban and Chinese immigrants, 145
    definition, 143
    earning returns, 144
    ethnic concentration effect, 144
    Korean immigrants, 145
    linguistic concentration, 144
    vs. mainstream economy, 145–146
    non-pecuniary benefits, 145
    self-employed immigrants, 145
  fiscal effects, 76
  French labor market, 75
  host-country recessions, 99
  immigrant women, 169–170
    fertility, 154
    FIH (*see* Family Investment Hypothesis (FIH))
    host-country-specific skills, 150
    labor force behavior, 150
    ramifications, 153–154
  individual-level determinants, 148
  individual longitudinal data, 107
  international skill transferability, 166–167
    Chiswick model, 109, 110
    host-country-specific skills, 109–110
    immigrant assimilation, 108–109
    opportunity costs, 109
    source-country human capital, 109–110
  labor market flexibility
    Australian immigrants *vs.* natives, 162
    education and career changes, 160
    immigrant economic adjustment, 162
    immigrant–native wage gaps, 162
    "Overall Strictness of Employment Protection" index, 161, 161*f*
    rigid structures, 160
    supple labor market structure, 160
    unemployment, 161–162
  macroeconomic conditions, 147–148
  marriage and fertility, 320
  non-refugees, 607*t*, 609
  occupational mobility model, 110–111, 163
  OECD countries, 75–76
  period effects, 146–147, 168, 169
  permanent community, 146
  refugees, United States
    characteristics of, 607*t*, 609
    economic assimilation, 626–634, 627*t*, 629*f*, 630*t*, 632*t*
    regression analysis (*see* Regression analysis)
  restrictive immigration laws, 99
  schooling, immigrants, 183
  skilled immigration (*see* Skilled immigration)
  Soviet Union, 75
  structural changes, host economy, 149–150, 158
  structures, 142, 143
  unemployment rates, 147
  US labor market, 75–76
Language proficiency
  in Australia
    dichotomous variables, 245
    Evans's research, 244
    longitudinal surveys, 245
    skill-based independent immigrants, 244
  biblical explanation, 213, 214*b*
  bilingual and multilingual countries, 212
  in Canada
    census data-based study, 246, 247
    document and quantitative literacy, 247–248
    English–French bilinguals, 247
    official bilingual status, 246
    Quebec, 247
  costs involved in, 213
  destination choice of immigrants
    aggregate-level data, 217
    Canada, 227
    conditional logit model, 225–226
    costs of language adjustment, 217
    determinants, 264
    Dyen lexicostatistical percentage approach, 221–222, 222*b*

educational selectivity, 221
English-speaking countries, 218
human capital investments, 216
language background, 223–224, 225*t*
language differences, 216–217
Levenshtein linguistic distance approach,
 223, 224*b*
linguistic distance, 221–223
linguistic proximity, 223
low-skill and high-skill migration flows,
 220–221
microeconomics, 212–213
migration rate determinants, 217
OECD countries, 218–219
source country, 217–218
US location, 226–227
dominant language proficiency, 257, 259*t*
dominant language usage, 228–229
economic incentives, 237–239
 data types, 238
 earnings, 237–238
 empirical support, 238, 239*t*
 expected duration of stay, 237
efficiency
 age at migration, 233–234
 critical period hypothesis, 233–234, 234*f*
 education, 234–235
 employment migrants, 236–237
 family migrants, 236–237
 in Germany, 235
 Levenshtein distance approach, 235–236
 linguistic distance, 235, 236*b*
 refugees, 236–237
empirical evidence, 243
ethnic enclaves effects
 cultural characteristics, 257–259
 earning growth rate, 261
 earnings growth regression, 263
 ethnic concentration variable, 260–261
 in Germany, 262
 group-average wage-growth approach, 262–263
 human capital earnings, 260
 labor market, 259
 linguistic concentration variable, 261–262
 occupational attainment, 259–260
 occupational wage effects, 262
 in UK, 262
 wage effect, 257–259

evolutionary approach, 212
exposure
 empirical support, 239*t*
 English-speaking destinations, 229
 family/household, 232
 Hebrew proficiency, 231–232
 individuals' migration history, 231
 minority language concentration, 231–232
 negative selectivity, 230–231
 parents' proficiency, 232, 233
 pre-immigration exposure, 229–230
 time pattern, 230
in Germany
 speaking skills data, 249
 statistical controls, 248
 time-varying measurement errors, 249
 writing abilities, 248–249
human capital earnings function, 240
instrumental variables approach, 242–243, 243*b*
in Israel
 continuous variable recording proficiency, 251
 dichotomous variables, 251
 Hebrew fluency, 251
 Hebrew writing and speaking skills, 250–251
 male FSU immigrants, 251
 wage effect, 251
language-augmented human capital earnings,
 241–242
local language proficiency, 213
misclassification errors, 242
mother tongue retention, 228–229
research issues and methodology
 civic involvement, 215
 data analyses, 215–216
 dominant language, 214–215
 language factors, 214–215
 oral and literacy skills, 216
 proficiency determinants, 214–215
 robustness testing, 215
self-reported English proficiency, 240–241, 241*b*
in Spain
 dichotomous language proficiency, 251–252
 IV estimations, 252
 OLS estimates, 252
 schooling, 252
in United Kingdom
 Household Longitudinal Survey, 254
 OLS estimation, 253–254

Language proficiency (*Continued*)
    racial and ethnic minorities, 253
    self-assessed information, 253
    in United States
        dichotomous variable recording fluency,
            255–256
        educational attainment, 256–257
        Hispanic and East Asian men, 255
        monolingual English speakers, 256
        regression analysis, 257, 258*t*
        SPEAK and INDEX variables, 255
        Survey of Income and Education,
            254–255
    unobserved heterogeneity, 242
Legalized Population Survey (LPS), 133
Levenshtein linguistic distance approach, 223
Linear probability model, 402–403

M

Malaysia
    asylum applications, 587–588
    bilateral agreements, 78
    health tourism, 764–765
    irregular migrants, 679
Marriage. *See* Family formation
Mexican immigrants
    birth and death rates, 741
    Bracero programs, 741–742
    import-substitution policy, 742
    IRCA, 742
    NAFTA, 743
    in US, 527
Mexican Migration Project (MMP), 132
Migrant Integration Policy Index (MIPEX), 453
Migration Occupations in Demand List (MODL),
    553
Migration theory
    employment conditions, 7–8
    human capital investment model (*see* Human
        capital)
    labor market conditions, 7–8
    role of policy, 8
    Sjaastad's model
        age and migration decisions, 25–26
        consumer model, 15–17
        family migration decisions, 22–24
        kinship and migrant networks, 17–18
        life-cycle stages, 18–19

        migration uncertainty, 13, 19–21
        relative deprivation, 24–25
        remittances, 13
        Smith, Adam, 5–6
Mincer model, 22, 23
Mixed marriage. *See* Intermarriage
Multiple citizenship
    in African countries, 463
    in Asia, 463–464
    in Australia, Canada, and US, 461
    democracy, 465
    in European countries, 462
    fairness, democracy, and inclusion, 461
    in Latin American and Caribbean countries,
        462, 463
    in Sweden, 461

N

Nakao–Treas Prestige Score (PRENT),
    632*t*, 633–634
National Health Interview Surveys (NHIS)
    age and schooling, 279
    employment status, 279
    health measures, 277–278
    immigrant arrival and cohort indicator
        variables, 278
    marital status, 279
    nativity groups, 278, 280*t*, 282*t*
    racial/ethnic origin groups, 278, 280*t*, 282*t*
    region of residence, 279
Nationality and Citizenship Act, 457–458
National Origin Quota Act, 196
Naturalization
    in African countries
        behavior and character requirements, 456
        language requirements, 456
        length of stay, 455–456
    in Asia, 456–457
    in Australia and Canada, 452–453
    costs, 476–477
    employment opportunities, 476–477
    in European states
        applications for citizenship, 454
        criminal record, 453–454
        discretionary decision, 455
        language and knowledge tests, 454–455
        length of stay, 453
    individual characteristics, 477–478

labor market integration, 478–481, 479t
  in Latin America, 455
Net reproduction rate (NRR), 360
New Immigrant Survey (NIS), 197, 600, 601–615
  basic demographics characteristics, 603, 604t
  birth codes, country/region of, 602–603, 602t
  education and English proficiency characteristics, 603–606, 605t
  health characteristics, 606–609, 607t
  labor market characteristics, 607t, 609
New Zealand
  holidaymaker programs, 759
  immigrant visas, 759
  RSE, 759
  skilled immigration, 553–554
NHIS. See National Health Interview Surveys (NHIS)
NIS. See New Immigrant Survey (NIS)
Non-refugees
  higher wages, 599
  in United States
    basic demographics characteristics, 603, 604t
    birth codes, country/region of, 602–603, 602t
    earnings growth of, 628, 629f
    education, 603–606, 605t, 631–633, 632t
    English proficiency, 603–606, 605t
    health characteristics, 606–609, 607t
    1975–80 immigrant arrivals, fixed cohort of, 621–622, 623t
    labor market characteristics, 607t, 609

O
Occupational mobility model, 110–111, 163
OECD countries
  bilateral agreements, 83
  employment protection, 161f
  immigration flows, 219, 223
  out-migration, 491–492, 492f
  post-secondary education, 540, 541t
  skilled immigration, 538, 539t
Out-migration, 6
  characteristics, 500–501
  cross-sectional data, 490–491
  earnings equation estimation
    longitudinal data, 524–527
    stock sampled longitudinal data, 523–524

education
  Canadian census data, 496–497
  in Denmark, 497
  in Germany, 497
  Italy, 497
  longer-term migrants, 496–497
  Mexican Migration Project, 497
  short-term migrants, 496–497
  human capital investment, 490
immigrants' career profiles
  entry wage, 521
  estimation and identification, 504–513
  human capital, 519–520
  longitudinal data, 510–513
  Monte Carlo experiment, 513
  observed and counterfactual log-earnings, 514
  OLS estimator, 514
  one-dimensional skills, 518
  optimal migration duration, 520
  skill distribution, 519
  stock sampled data, 506–510
  tax and welfare system, 502
  temporary migration, 518–519
  time-constant fixed effects, 514, 515t
  time-variant unobservables, 516, 516t
job search behavior, 490
OLS estimator, 490–491
stock sampled longitudinal data, 523–524
in Sweden, 499–500
temporary migration
  alien registration data, 494
  Asian immigrants, 494
  BLFS data, 492–493
  Canadian emigration, 494–495
  documentation, 492
  foreign-born emigration, 495–496, 496f
  gender, immigrant survival rates, 493, 493f
  Nordic migrants, 495
  OECD countries, 491–492
  origin and ethnicity, 493–494, 494f
  Scandinavian countries, 495
  South American immigrants, 494
  Vietnam migration, 495
  US immigrants, 498
"Overall Strictness of Employment Protection" index, 161, 161f
Own-children-method, 323

P

Permanent residents
  in Australia and Canada, 450
  civil and political rights, 446
  courts, role of, 448–449
  in democratic immigration states, 446
  in East and Southeast Asian states, 450–451
  indefinite leave to enter/remain (ILR), UK, 448
  in Latin American states, 450
  local and regional voting rights, 447, 448
  period of legal stay, 447–448
  in US, 449–450
Political economy
  asylum policies
    Canadian asylum procedures, 642–643
    destination countries, 643–644
    external political factors, 644–645
    trading partners and aid donors, 644
    UNHCR's policies, 646
  host countries' policy
    administrators, 650–651
    non-refugee migrants, 650
    payoff matrix, 648, 649f
    refugees, 649–650
    UNHCR, 649
Political incorporation
  citizenship acquisition (*see* Citizenship)
  democracy and immigrants' rights, 464–466
  legal status and rights
    asylum seekers, 451
    permanent residents (*see* Permanent residents)
    persons in transit zones, 451
    seasonal workers, 451
    undocumented migrants, 451–452
  naturalization
    in African countries, 455–456
    in Asia, 456–457
    in Australia and Canada, 452–453
    in European states, 453–454, 455
    in Latin America, 455
  political participation (*see* Political participation)
  societal integration, 444–445
  socio-economic inclusion, 444–445
Political participation
  associations and organizations, 474
  citizenship
    employment opportunities, 476–477
    individual characteristics, 477–478
    labor market integration, 478–481, 479t
  claims-making, 475
  conventional and non-conventional forms, 471
  demonstrations and civil disobedience, 474–475
  engagement, 471–472
  institutionalized consultation, 475
  low and high costs, 471
  public debate, 474
  recruitment, 471–472
  resources, 471–472
  voting rights, 472, 473–474
Principle of personhood, 449–450

R

Recognized Seasonal Employer (RSE), 759
Recruitment, 761
  African doctors and nurses, 763
  health-care workers, 764
  Indian IT specialists, 762–763
  Jamaican university graduates, 764
Refugee Convention, 77
Refugees
  birth codes, country/region of, 602–603, 602t
  definition, 586–587
  Ethiopian refugees, 643–644, 646
  in host countries
    economic assimilation (*see* Economic
      assimilation, refugees)
    refugee camps, 636–637
    resettlement, 637–639
  migration decision
    higher migration costs, 599
    higher wages, 599
    income-maximizing model, 597–598
    low wages, 598
    regular migration, 598
    utility-maximizing model, 597–600
  political economy (*see* Political economy)
  refugee status, 600–601
  in sending countries
    refugee repatriation, 640–641
    refugees' departure, 639–640
  Swedish register data, 617
  United States, 586–587
    basic demographics characteristics, 603, 604t
    earnings growth, 628, 629f
    education, 603–606, 605t
    English proficiency, 603–606, 605t
    exposure to persecution, 601–602
    health characteristics, 606–609, 607t

labor market characteristics, 607t, 609

occupational distribution, 630t

regression-adjusted mean differences, 610–613, 611t

trends in, 592–596, 593t, 596f

welfare dependence, 619

world trends, 587–592

Regression analysis

annual earnings, hourly earnings, annual hours, 626–628, 627t

educational attainment, 631–633, 632t

HWSEI, 632t, 633–634

PRENT, 632t, 633–634

Religion

assimilation, 380–381

beliefs, 383–384

free-riders, 379

immigrant churches, 381–383

institutional context, 383

quasi-enclaves, 378–379

religious human capital, 377–378

religious observance, 383

self-selection, 380

Remittance, 761

components, 765

forced-remittance programs, 766

migration decision, 40

poverty, 766–767

US-Mexico remittance market, 766

Republic Act 8042, 756

Retirement, 34

Return-of-talent programs, 768–769

S

Schooling, 166

European immigrants

earnings inequality and skill premia, 93–94

exogenous schooling revolution, 92, 93

primary schooling, 92

US 1917 Immigration Act, 92

foreign students, American schools

enrollment of, 204, 205t, 206

non-immigrants, 202–203, 203f, 204f

student visas, 203–204

high-education immigrants, 125–126, 126t

higher school attendance, 127

Indochinese immigrant, 127–128

low-education immigrants, 125–126, 126t

median entry earnings, 125–126, 125t, 126t

skill transferability, 126–127

US native and foreign-born populations

1965 amendments, 188–189

CPS mean education levels, 189–190, 190t

disparities within-ethnic group, 190–191, 191f, 192f, 193

distribution of, 184–188, 185t, 186t

entry cohort of immigrants, 193–195, 194t

exogenous and endogenous hypothesis, 94

generational assimilation, 206–208, 207f

illegal immigrants, 196–197

IRCA, 189

legal admission, visa class, 199–202, 200t, 201t

legal permanent immigrants, 196–197, 198t, 199–202

less-educated migrants, out-migration of, 196

National Origin Quota Act, 196

new legal immigrants, post-green card training, 195–196, 195t

non-immigrants, 197, 202–203, 203f

secondary school enrollment, 94

student visa non-immigrants, 196–197

Seasonal Agricultural Workers Program (SAWP), 738

Seasonal migration, 58

Seniority rights, 26

Skilled immigration

in Australia, 552–553

in Canada, 550–551

employer nomination, 548

finance implications, 546

gender breakdown, 544

growth rates, 543–544

human capital point systems, 547

hybrid selection systems, 548–549

implications, 542

intended occupation point systems, 547–548

labor market outcomes

education, 559–562

employment and credential recognition, 562–563

gender differences and family investment strategies, 566–567

immigrant selection, 563–565

IT sector, in Canada, 565–566

regulated occupations, 563–565

modern economies and aging populations, 543

in New Zealand, 553–554

Skilled immigration (*Continued*)
  OECD countries, 538, 539*t*
  post-secondary education, 540, 541*t*
  receiving economy
    demographic challenges, 574–575
    economic changes, 545
    fiscal impact, 574
    native workers, 571–572
    non-immigrants, training of, 572–573
    occupational choice, 573
    patents and innovation, 573
    pro-cyclical immigration policy, 545–546
    research and development, 573
    supply and demand, 545
  sending economy
    in Canada and Australia, 568
    gender and brain drain, 570
    The Philippines, 569
    remittances, 568–569
  TFW program (*see* Temporary foreign worker
    programs (TFWPs))
  in UK, 554
  in United States, 551–552
Slave trade, 54, 55*t*
Smith, Adam, 5–6
Smugglers, 669–671
Social Security Numbers (SSNs), 418–419
Student visas, 196–197, 203–204
Survey on Household Income and Wealth (SHIW),
  428–429
Survey on Income and Program Participation
  (SIPP), 394
Sweden
  dual citizenship, 461
  local and regional voting rights, 447
  naturalization, 453
  permanent residence, 447–448, 449
  refugee immigrants
    educational program, 617
    placement policy, 618–619
    welfare utilization, 619
Swedish Citizenship Act, 459

T

Taiwan, 768
Temporary foreign worker programs (TFWPs), 730*t*
  AEWR, 719–720
  in Africa, 757–758
  in Asia
    Bangladesh, 756–757
    Indonesia, 756
    The Philippines, 755–756
    Singapore and Japan, 753–754
  attestation *vs.* certification, 731–732, 732*t*
  in Canada, 556–558, 736–739
  in Caribbean and Latin America, 739–741
  characteristics, 549
  contracts *vs.* free agents, 732–733
  distortion and dependence, 733–736
  in Europe, 558–559
    Blue Card program, 748–749
    emigration to immigration, 745–746
    freedom of movement, 746–747
    Norway, 751
    population decline, 749, 750*t*
    Russia, 751–752
    Switzerland, 751
    Turkey and Germany, 747–748
  in Mexico, 741–744
  in Middle East
    GCC countries, 754–755
    Israel, 757
  migrant settlement, 719
  migration and development
    recruitment, 762–765
    remittances, 765–767
    returns, 767–769
  Oceania and Pacific islands, 758–760
  probationary immigrant programs, 730
  seasonal programs, seasonal jobs, 730
  temporary workers, permanent jobs, 730
  in United States, 555–556
Temporary migration
  alien registration data, 494
  Asian immigrants, 494
  BLFS data, 492–493
  Canadian emigration, 494–495
  documentation, 492
  foreign-born emigration, 495–496, 496*f*
  gender, immigrant survival rates, 493, 493*f*
  Nordic migrants, 495
  OECD countries, 491–492
  origin and ethnicity, 493–494, 494*f*
  Scandinavian countries, 495
  South American immigrants, 494
  Vietnam migration, 495

A Theory of Marriage, 325
Total fertility rates (TFR), 317–319, 318*t*, 323–324,
    360–361, 364
Transfer of Knowledge Through Expatriate
    Nationals (TOKTEN) program, 768

U

Undocumented immigration
    asylum seekers, 661
    cheap labor, 662
    deterrence effects
        border enforcement, 672–673
        interior enforcement, 673–675
    duration of stay
        agricultural workers, 668
        economic conditions, 668
        empirical evidence, 668
        immigration policy, 668–669
        life-cycle model, 668
        return and repeat migration, 667–668
        visa availability, 669
    economic opportunities, 661
    European Union, 662
    factors, 660–661
    fiscal effects
        children, 686
        federalist implications, 687
        sales taxes, 686
    immigration policy, 660–661
    International Organization for Migration
        estimation, 660*np*
    legalization programs
        on beneficiaries, 694–695
        citizenship and the children, 699
        economic effects, 695–696
        future legalization programs, 696–697
        government transfer programs, 697–698
        schooling, 698–699
    macroeconomic effects
        host-country economy, 680
        labor market flexibility, 682
        low-skilled illegal immigrant workers, 682
        natives' consumption, 681
        wage-depressing effect, 680–681
    microeconomic effects
        geographic concentration, 683
        Hispanic immigration, 684
        income inequality, 685

        in Italy, 683
        Latino immigrants, 684
        undocumented women, US, 684
    migrants effects, 687–690
    migrant self-selection
        accounting, 667
        1999 Ecuadoran crisis, 666
        enforcement actions, 667
        macroeconomy, 667
        US-bound migrants, 666
    migration decision
        border and interior enforcement, 663–664
        border enforcement, 664
        empirical evidence, 665
        Ethier's model, 664
        Immigration Reform and Control Act (IRCA)
            and flexible wages, 664
        interior enforcement, 664
        mobility and flexible wages, 664
        neoclassical model, 663
        unskilled wage, 664
        wage gap, role of, 663
    origin countries, impacts
        brain drain, 690
        out-migration, 690
        remittances, 692
        in rural Mexico, 691
    political economy
        in Asia, 679
        Canada, 679
        Europe, 677–679
        United States, 676–677
    residual method, 661
    sexual exploitation, 660
    smugglers, 669–671
    in Thailand, 662
    US large-scale government surveys, 661
    visa overstays and violations, 661
Unemployment, 98–99, 161–162
Union dissolution. *See* Divorce
United Farm Workers (UFW), 742
United Nations Convention Relating to the Status
    of Refugees, 586
United Nations High Commission for Refugees
    (UNHCR), 586–587
    asylum applications, destination countries,
        589, 589*f*
    role of, 646, 649

United States
    annual immigration rate, 67–68
    asylum applications, 592–596, 593*t*, 596*f*
    education, native and foreign-born populations
      (*see* Education)
    financial market participation (*see* Financial
      market participation)
    Haitian asylum seekers, 644–645
    H-2A program, 731–732, 732*t*
    H-1B program, 732
    H-2B program, 731, 732*t*
    illegal immigrants, stock of, 81
    illegal Mexico–US migration, 742
    indenture system, 54–56
    interwar immigration, 65–66
    language proficiency
      dichotomous variable recording fluency,
        255–256
      educational attainment, 256–257
      Hispanic and East Asian men, 255
      monolingual English speakers, 256
      regression analysis, 257, 258*t*
      SPEAK and INDEX variables, 255
      Survey of Income and Education, 254–255
    refugees, 586–587, 592–596, 593*t*, 596*f*
      basic demographics characteristics,
        603, 604*t*
      economic assimilation (*see* Economic
        assimilation, refugees)
      education, 603–606, 605*t*
      English proficiency, 603–606, 605*t*
      exposure to persecution, 601–602
      health characteristics, 606–609, 607*t*
      labor market characteristics, 607*t*, 609
      occupational mobility, 616–617
      regression-adjusted mean differences,
        610–613, 611*t*
      trends in, 592–596, 593*t*, 596*f*
    restrictive policies, immigration, 64, 65
    skilled immigration, 551–552
    slave trade, 54, 55*t*
    wage effects of migration
      capital mobility, 61–62
      labor demand elasticity, 60–61, 60*f*
      land prices and rents, 62
      Swedish wages, 61
      unskilled immigration, 62
US Citizenship and Immigration Services (USCIS),
    586–587

W

Welfare Reform Act, 449–450
White Australia policy of 1901, 65
Work permit, 78
World Health Organization, 763
World Migration Organization, 761

Y

Yearbook of Immigration Statistics (YIS), 587,
    592–595, 593*t*, 596*f*